Science and Corporate Strategy

STUDIES IN ECONOMIC HISTORY AND POLICY
THE UNITED STATES IN THE TWENTIETH CENTURY

Edited by
Louis Galambos and Robert Gallman

Other books in the series:

Peter D. McClelland and Alan L. Magdovitz: *Crisis in the making: the political economy of New York State since 1945*

Hugh Rockoff: *Drastic measures: a history of wage and price controls in the United States*

William N. Parker: *Europe, America, and the wider world: essays on the economic history of Western capitalism*

Richard H. K. Vietor: *Energy policy in America since 1945: a study of business–government relations*

Christopher L. Tomlins: *The state and the unions: labor relations, law, and the organized labor movement in America, 1880–1960*

Leonard S. Reich: *The making of American industrial research: science and business at GE and Bell, 1876–1926*

Margaret B. W. Graham: *RCA and the VideoDisc: the business of research*

Michael A. Be.._.ein: *The Great Depression: delayed recovery and economic change in America, 1929–1939*

Michael J. Hogan: *The Marshall Plan: America, Britain, and the reconstruction of Western Europe, 1947–1952*

Science and Corporate Strategy

Du Pont R&D, 1902–1980

DAVID A. HOUNSHELL
JOHN KENLY SMITH, JR.

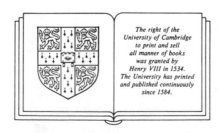

The right of the
University of Cambridge
to print and sell
all manner of books
was granted by
Henry VIII in 1534.
The University has printed
and published continuously
since 1584.

CAMBRIDGE UNIVERSITY PRESS
Cambridge
New York   New Rochelle   Melbourne   Sydney

Published by the Press Syndicate of the University of Cambridge
The Pitt Building, Trumpington Street, Cambridge CB2 1RP
32 East 57th Street, New York, NY 10022, USA
10 Stamford Road, Oakleigh, Melbourne 3166, Australia

First published 1988

Printed in the United States of America

Library of Congress Cataloging-in-Publication Data
Hounshell, David A.
Science and corporate strategy: Du Pont R&D, 1902–1980 / David A.
Hounshell, John Kenly Smith.
p. cm.
Bibliography: p.
Includes index.
1. E. I. du Pont de Nemours & Company – History. 2. Chemical
industry – United States – History. 3. Research, Industrial – United
States – History. I. Smith, John K. (John Kenly), 1951–
II. Title.
HD9651.9.D8H68 1988   388.7'66'00973–dc19   87–31151

British Library Cataloguing in Publication Data
Hounshell, David A.
Science and corporate strategy.
1. United States. Research & development
by E. I. du Pont de Nemours & Company,
1902-1980. Chemical Industries
I. Title II. Smith, John K.

607'.2'73

ISBN 0 521 32767 9

TO THE MEMORY OF TONY DE MOOR

Contents

Illustrations

Figures

Photographs

Tables

Editors' Preface

Scholars, public officials, and businessmen alike have long struggled to understand the sources of technological progress in America's twentieth-century economy. Who could question the significance of their quest? Technological innovations have been making a vital contribution to economic growth in this country since the early years of this century; today they are all the more important as U.S. business attempts to meet the competition of efficient, innovative foreign producers. Unfortunately, our knowledge of the process of technological change – especially in the modern corporation and its extensive research and development facilities – remains only rudimentary. As yet, we know very little about the precise relationships between science and technology and between corporate structure and the ability to innovate. Recently, a number of excellent histories of the early years of corporate R&D have appeared, but heretofore no historian has written a full-length, intensive study of the origins and evolution of the R&D establishment in one of the nation's leading, high-technology firms.

This is one of the reasons that David A. Hounshell and John Kenly Smith's *Science and Corporate Strategy: Du Pont R&D, 1902–1980* is such a valuable addition to the literature on American economic, business, and technological history. Du Pont has long been one of the nation's leading corporations. It has been one of the pioneers in the development of new business strategies and of new forms of corporate organization. It has as well experimented extensively with different approaches to corporate R&D, and this important story is the one that Hounshell and Smith recount in this carefully researched volume. This book gives a remarkably full sense of how complex and difficult the business decision-making process was where it touched upon research and development: Should research be centralized or decentralized? Should it stress fundamental innovations or less glamorous, but economically important, development work closely tied to production? Should the company research its way into new fields or acquire existing firms? Hounshell and Smith show their readers how Du Pont's executives made these vital decisions and what impact they had upon the company, its technology, and the several areas of scientific inquiry with which this very large and successful corporation was involved. We are, then, especially pleased to add this innovative volume to the series Studies in Economic History and Policy: The United States in the Twentieth Century.

Louis Galambos   Robert Gallman
Professor of History   *Kenan Professor of Economics and History*
Johns Hopkins University   *University of North Carolina at Chapel Hill*

Authors' Preface

For more than eighty years, industrial research and development laboratories have been transforming U.S. business, the economy, and indeed our entire material culture. Industrial research and development laboratories have been seen as houses of magic, as university research laboratories in exile, as instruments of big business that manipulate once-pure scientists for corporate ends, or as second-rate research institutions. We regard all these interpretations as far too simplistic. Our investigations indicate that they fail to capture the complex character of these important twentieth-century institutions. In the following study of research and development at the Du Pont Company – one of the nation's R&D pioneers and consistently among the top ten spenders for research – we try to avoid easy generalizations and provide a fuller analysis of modern corporate R&D than has any previously published work. As the book shows, there was a complex interplay between the modern corporation, public policy, developments within scientific disciplines and the scientific community, and international politics and events.

Science and Corporate Strategy is the outgrowth of an idea of Edward G. Jefferson, chairman and chief executive officer of Du Pont from 1981 to 1986 and a former research chemist. He felt that a history of the company's research and development programs would make an important contribution to U.S. historical scholarship and to current issues in public policy. Jefferson's idea resulted in a research project housed at the Hagley Museum and Library in Wilmington, Delaware, an institution devoted to the preservation and interpretation of the history of U.S. business and technology. We were asked to conduct the research and to write a scholarly history, tasks we undertook on two conditions, both stated in the contract between Du Pont and Hagley. The first was that we be given unrestricted access to the corporation's records and its employees. The second was that the authors "shall have the right to determine the scope, content, and details of the book." Since the beginning of the project in September 1982, Du Pont has fulfilled its agreement regarding both access and academic freedom. The statements, interpretations, opinions, and conclusions in the book are solely the responsibility of the authors.

The Du Pont Company supported the research for and writing of this book through a grant to the Hagley Museum and Library, which among other expenses covered part of our salaries throughout the life of the project. *Science and Corporate Strategy* has been published entirely on its own merits. Neither Hagley nor the Du Pont Company provided any kind of subvention to Cambridge University Press. In exchange for unrestricted access to Du Pont's records and employees and complete academic freedom, the authors waived all rights to royalties from the sale of this book. We appreciate the Cambridge University Press's willingness to undertake such a large project and to work closely with us in bringing our manuscript into print.

We have greatly benefited from the criticism offered us by two advisory committees, which usually met jointly. These committees regularly followed our work from its earliest outline in March 1983 to its final draft in February 1987. Alfred D. Chandler, Jr., chaired our Academic Advisory Committee and lent his great understanding of Du Pont and modern business history to our work. We are greatly indebted to him for his criticism and help in negotiating the agreement between Hagley and Du Pont. Other members of the Academic Advisory Committee included John J. Beer, Reese V. Jenkins, Glenn Porter, and Arnold Thackray. Each contributed significantly to this work through often-demanding criticism. We especially thank Glenn Porter, who first as head of Hagley's Regional Economic History Research Center and then as overall director of Hagley offered us a comfortable home for our undertaking.

Howard E. Simmons, Jr., vice president for central research and development, chaired an advisory committee made up of current and former Du Pont research directors and one general manager who began his career in research. Simmons worked with us from the outset and ensured that the corporation aided our research in every way. We sincerely thank him for his contributions. Other members of the Du Pont committee included Charles H. Arrington, Jr., William A. Franta, Norton A. Higgins, Sheldon E. Isakoff, Robert M. Joyce, Klaus A. Saegebarth, Herman E. Schroeder, and Phillip J. Wingate. Both individually and collectively, these men possess a deep understanding of Du Pont's research and development programs, and they shared that understanding while offering us frank criticism, both formal and informal, of our work. As a result, our own understanding was greatly deepened. We are particularly indebted to Robert Joyce for the many, many hours he devoted to making sure our chemistry was correct and to straightening out more than a few backward sentences. He was a constant critic and helpmate, and we sincerely thank him. We also thank Jean Morris, Wallace B. Thompson, and Frederick J. Darnell, each of whom served as our advance person when we began a research campaign in a new part of the company's operations.

Robert P. McCuen played an especially important role in the completion of this project. He served as an intermediary between Hagley and the company from the project's inception to its conclusion. We are much in his debt for his expert handling of the project's sometimes unusual demands on the company. We thank the dozens of scientists, engineers, research managers, and executives in Du Pont, both active and retired, whom we interviewed about their careers and the company. Most of these formal interviews are now part of the permanent collections at the Hagley Museum and Library. Special thanks go to Howard W. Swank, formerly vice president and general manager of Du Pont's Textile Fibers Department and a seasoned veteran of that department's research division, for his extensive criticism of our material on Du Pont and the synthetic fibers revolution.

During our research in Du Pont's records, we were aided by many records managers, librarians, and secretaries. We are especially grateful to Louis R. Wonderly, David J. Hellman, and Catherine D. Malatesta for their help with the records of the board of directors, Executive Committee, Finance Committee, and Special Compensation Committee; Clare F. Gallagher for her help with the main records of the Central Research and Development Department; and Margaret B. Thorne for developing at the Experimental Station an important historical collection, which has now been donated to the Hagley Museum and Library. Felix Spitelle of Du Pont's Records Management Center helped us locate hundreds of boxes of records stored there.

Of course our greatest debt within the Du Pont Company is to Edward Jefferson for conceiving this history and for providing the critical ingredients to make it happen. Without his enthusiasm for the project, this book would not have been written. We can only hope that the value of *Science and Corporate Strategy* to the academic, business, and policymaking communities justifies the extensive financial and human resources that were devoted to its completion.

Most of the pre-1941 records of the Du Pont Company are preserved at the Hagley Museum and Library. We thank Richmond D. Williams, formerly head of the library, for his cooperation with our use of those records. Special thanks go to Michael Nash, curator of manuscripts, for his unwavering support of our project, and to his present and former colleagues, Marjorie McNinch and John Rumm. The Imprints Collection at Hagley was also important to our study, and we are indebted to Heddy A. Richter and her staff for their help. We thank Jon Williams of the Pictorial Collections Department for guidance with the photographic illustrations. Rob Howard lent his talents to this book by drawing several of the figures.

We were singularly fortunate that Mary E. Meyers accepted our invitation to join the project. Her typing of the manuscript through several drafts was excellent, and her outstanding transcription and editing of our extensive oral history interviews lightened our load considerably.

We are grateful that Louis Galambos, coeditor of the Cambridge University Press series in which this book appears – Studies in Economic History and Policy: The United States in the Twentieth Century – was interested in publishing the book. He provided us with outstanding editorial guidance from midway through the project. We also thank Frank Smith at Cambridge for his confidence in our venture and for his successful effort to steer our manuscript through to publication – on schedule. Katharita Lamoza did a splendid job managing the book's production. Susan Greenberg accomplished the herculean task of preparing the index.

This project has been an exciting cooperative endeavor for us. Few scholars can hope for a richer set of historical records from which to draw and better questions on which to write. In these regards, this project has been ideal. *Science and Corporate Strategy* should be looked upon as one of the achievements of the Hagley Program in the History of Industrial America, the joint graduate program of the University of Delaware and the Hagley Museum and Library. Both authors came to this program with technical backgrounds and emerged as historians interested in a broad range of problems in the history of business, technology, and politics. This book reflects not only the focus of Hagley but also the excellent training that its graduate program has offered to students for more than three decades.

Antonio de Moor was also an engineer whose interests in history steered him into the Hagley Program in 1985. We had the pleasure of knowing Tony all too briefly while we were at work on this book. A battle with leukemia took him back home to the Netherlands before he had completed a year of study and, on March 23, 1987, Tony died at the age of thirty-two. He is sorely missed.

Although many people have contributed to our book's makeup, we accept full responsibility for whatever shortcomings may remain.

David A. Hounshell   John Kenly Smith, Jr.
Boston, Massachusetts   Bethlehem, Pennsylvania

ıction

ıd of economics, or ideological com-
played a major role in transforming
Jnited States. Precisely how, when,
e are questions for discussion and
ıat the rise of big business was a
ıtion. Shortly after the turn of the
but still big – businesses made a
by creating an institution new both
ıdustrial research and development
ın the electrical, chemical, photo-
tries, and they possessed one thing
logies that had emerged in one way
developments and were particularly
ement through a scientific approach
search and development laboratory
ıg business. Science became a part

ıd development laboratory did not
.... .xecutives at such firms as General
Electric, Du Pont, Eastman Kodak, and American Telephone and Telegraph.
For one thing, in each of these firms, many of the functions later performed
by R&D laboratories had been and were being carried out elsewhere in the
corporation, albeit to a much smaller degree and in a less formal manner.
Moreover, the role of the R&D laboratory in these corporations and the
relationship between science and corporate strategy were subject to significant change over the course of this century as a result of both external
factors (e.g., federal regulation, antitrust laws, developments in the scientific
community, and competition) and internal factors (e.g., changes in leadership, cash position, and scientific discoveries). There was no single strategy
for science within the corporation across the course of this century. Science
has been a dynamic element, changing and being changed by other elements
of corporate performance.

This study examines the relationship between science and corporate strategy in one U.S. firm, E. I. du Pont de Nemours & Company, from the
inception of its first formal R&D laboratory in 1902 until 1980. The case

of Du Pont is not intended to be representative of other firms within the chemical industry or elsewhere in U.S. business. Nor is it predicated on its uniqueness. Rather, this history of research and development at Du Pont is offered as an important story in and of itself and one that provides a window through which to observe the changing relationships between science and corporate strategy as they were subject to both internal and external pressures.

Du Pont's research and development program stemmed from the company's heritage and, more immediately, larger trends in science-based industries. Within the firm, there had been a tradition of science-based innovation beginning with the founder, Eleuthère Irénée du Pont. In 1802, du Pont established black powder mills along the Brandywine River five miles north of Wilmington, Delaware. His grandson, Lammot, turned out to be particularly innovative. He had been trained in chemistry at the University of Pennsylvania and in 1857 made an important innovation in black powder manufacture by figuring out how to substitute sodium nitrate for potassium nitrate. In 1880 he convinced his highly reluctant family members to diversify Du Pont's business by manufacturing dynamite, a product much more dependent on chemical knowledge than black powder.[2] Indeed, it was in the dynamite end of the explosives business that Du Pont established its first formal research and development facility, the Eastern Laboratory (1902). Within a short period, this laboratory dramatically demonstrated that research paid.

Outside the Du Pont Company, there were important precedents in industrial research from which Du Pont could draw. During the last quarter of the nineteenth century, scientists – many with PhDs – had been making important contributions to several big businesses in the United States. In 1875, the Pennsylvania Railroad hired Dr. Charles Dudley to establish a laboratory, which through rigorous scientific testing subsequently led to the development of standards for the Pennsylvania's major purchases such as rails, lubricating oils, and paints.[3] Herman Frasch's small laboratory played a similar role in John D. Rockefeller's growing oil empire while also contributing significantly to improvements in petroleum refining.[4] In steel manufacture, Andrew Carnegie hired Dr. Ernst Fricke and soon learned that he could not afford to pursue his business without the aid of a scientist. As Carnegie wrote in his autobiography, "Great secrets did the doctor open to us.... Nine-tenths of all the uncertainties of pig-iron making were dispelled under the burning sun of chemical knowledge."[5] Numerous academic scientists also consulted with industrial firms before 1900.[6]

But the work of a lone scientist in a business like the Pennsylvania Railroad, Standard Oil, or Carnegie Steel (or consulting for such companies) was fundamentally different from the sort of institutionalized industrial research and development that arose in the United States after 1900. The "invention factory" of Thomas A. Edison offers perhaps the most important U.S. precedent for the modern R&D laboratory. Treated in many popular accounts of his life as an inspired, lone inventor, Edison was in fact a research and development manager. In 1876, he established a laboratory at Menlo Park, New Jersey, and announced to the world that it would produce "a minor invention every ten days and a big thing every six months or so."[7] With a team of assistants and instrument makers, Edison no doubt increased his productivity, but not until he undertook to develop a commercially viable system of electric lighting in 1878 did his invention factory take on the trappings of the modern R&D laboratory.

Backed by several New York financiers and put in the public limelight by his own boastful claims, Edison turned to science and academically trained scientists (both inside and outside the university) for help. Indeed, a well-known physicist had first encouraged Edison to undertake work on electric lighting. As Edison's work proceeded, he soon had several scientists with advanced degrees working in his laboratory. At its height, the Menlo Park laboratory had a total of some forty employees, ranging from glass-blowers and machinists to physicists and chemists.[8]

The fascinating story of Edison's development of the first commercial electric light and power system has been well told. But two salient points in this history need emphasis. First, while Edison was managing the Menlo Park complex, he built up what was acknowledged to be the best-equipped laboratory in the United States if not the world – a fact that academic scientists greatly bemoaned. Second, with a team of first-rate physicists, chemists, and engineers, Edison took his project from a mere claim made in a newspaper to a commercial success in less than four years.[9] But rather than keeping his Menlo Park invention factory open and fully exploiting the facility, Edison diverted his attention to the immediate commercial exploitation of electric lighting. Only later, in the second half of the 1880s, did Edison return to invention as a primary business when he opened his much larger and better-equipped laboratory at West Orange, New Jersey.[10]

Paradoxically, the years in which Edison's laboratories were most successful were ones in which the U.S. public believed that all technological progress flowed from the minds of individual inventive geniuses rather than from teams of scientists and engineers. Historians have therefore called this the "era of heroic invention." Edison's very success and his unequaled ability to manipulate the press for his own ends did much to perpetuate the growing myth of heroic invention in the United States.

Given the myth, it is perhaps understandable that U.S. corporations such as Du Pont looked elsewhere, particularly to Germany, for precedents and guidance in the establishment of their own research laboratories. Arthur D. Little, a great advocate of formally organized industrial research organizations, acknowledged Germany's leadership in a 1913 presidential address before the American Chemical Society: "Germany has long been recognized as preeminently the country of organized research. The spirit of research is there imminent [sic] throughout the entire social structure."[11] The German coal tar dye industry in particular had led the way through its development of formal R&D laboratories within the corporation – laboratories whose work was a central part of corporate strategy. Indeed, German dye firms had taken over world leadership in chemical manufacture from the early pioneers in Britain and France in part because of the R&D organizations they developed.[12]

Yet the establishment of R&D laboratories by German dyemakers was not a single act of invention. Rather, as George Meyer-Thurow has argued, "industrial research...was an evolutionary development."[13] The synthetic dye industry began in 1856 when William H. Perkin, an English student of the great German organic chemist August Wilhelm Hofmann, discovered how to synthesize a brilliant mauve dye from aniline and subsequently pursued the commercial exploitation of his discovery. In Britain, France, Switzerland, and Germany, a number of firms were founded to manufacture the new synthetic aniline dyes. The discovery by two German chemists of the entirely new class of alizarin dyes in 1868 gave great impetus to the industry, particularly in Germany. Alizarin's replacement of the natural dye called madder raised the question of whether other important natural dyes, such as indigo, could be synthesized. German chemists both inside and outside academia rose to this challenge. Their quest was aided by some important breakthroughs in dye chemistry by Adolph von Baeyer's students, Emil and Otto Fischer of the University of Munich. Von Baeyer finally synthesized indigo after many years of work. Peter Griess and Otto Witt uncovered an enormously important class of dyes — the azo group — in 1876, a discovery that fueled interest in new syntheses by several German dye firms.

The institution in 1876 of much stricter patent laws in Germany essentially stopped the prevalent practice of firms freely copying competitors' dyes and led firms such as Bayer to seek a deliberate means of bringing new, proprietary colors into the market. New colors were an absolute necessity in a world becoming increasingly dominated by consumerism. Bayer's managers tried several different ways to harness academic science to their commercial problems, but success eluded them until the early 1880s when they recalled several PhD chemist-employees, who had been occupying quasi-postdoctoral positions in German universities, to headquarters. There the company focused their work on the discovery of new colors. One of the chemists, Carl Duisberg, soon found three new commercially important azo colors. As a result of these successes, Duisberg began to build for himself and Bayer something of a research empire. By 1890, Bayer's directors approved the construction of a large, modern laboratory fully equipped with instruments, supporting facilities, and a well-stocked library. Duisberg had also secured a charter isolating the lab from Bayer's immediate manufacturing concerns. Subsequently, Duisberg's design of the laboratory was widely copied in Germany and elsewhere.

The opening of Bayer's laboratory represented the end of a long period of experimentation on how best to employ science in the solution of industrial problems and the beginning of the era in which industrial research was fully institutionalized. R&D would become one of the triumvirate of modern business, taking its place beside sales and manufacturing as a major corporate function that had to be properly managed. Bayer's first research laboratory was by no means perfect, and the institution continued to expand in the years that followed.[14] The experience of Badische Anilin- und Soda-Fabrik (BASF) roughly paralleled that of Bayer.

What distinguished these German corporate chemical laboratories and set them apart from other approaches to innovation? Heinrich Caro, the director of BASF's research from 1883 to 1890, put his finger precisely on the answer. He said that modern corporate chemical research, as exemplified by the dye business, called for *wissenschaftliche Massenarbeit* – "massive scientific teamwork" – rather than the efforts of the individual chemist.[15] Moreover, once researchers had uncovered the mechanisms of reactions, such as the diazo reaction, they could then pursue the invention of new dyes in a highly regular, systematic way – what Caro termed "construction bound to scientific rules."[16] This in turn amplified the great rewards of undertaking what John J. Beer would later call a "massed assault" on a commercial objective. As Beer says of *wissenschaftliche Massenarbeit*:

> The number of routine experiments that had to be conducted to find a single promising color was large. When such a color was discovered, it was sent to the dye-testing division, where it was subjected to a battery of tests to indicate whether and under what conditions it would tint any one of the common fibers, or such other items as wood, paper, leather, fur, or straw. Then each item successfully tinted was subjected to several agents of destruction to determine fastness. Of 2,378 colors produced and tested [by Bayer] in the year 1896, only 37 reached the market. This tedious, meticulous experimentation, in which a thousand little facts were wrenched from nature through coordinated massed assault, admirably illustrates the method and spirit introduced into scientific inquiry by the rising industrial laboratory of the late nineteenth century.[17]

The early work of the industrial R&D pioneers in the United States displayed many of these same attributes. This is not surprising because many of the U.S. pioneers, including Du Pont, took their cues from developments in Germany.

Were there alternatives to the establishment of corporate R&D laboratories in the United States? Certainly some existed. Firms could have chosen not to do their own R&D but rather to buy turnkey technology developed by independent inventor-entrepreneurs; indeed, some firms pursued that path. Some continued to hold to the popular view that technological development occurred through the acts of independent, heroic inventors. Still others relied heavily on consultants. Academic scientists; "consulting" chemists, physicists, and engineers; and firms such as Arthur D. Little, Inc., played an important role for companies not having their own R&D organization, as well as for some firms that did. The private research institute and the university research institute were two other alternatives, and indeed some firms chose this path.[18] The turn-of-the-century chemist and popularizer of science, Robert Kennedy Duncan, strongly believed in the research institute approach. His infectious enthusiasm for making science the handmaiden of technology led to the establishment of a program of industrial fellowships and, most important, to the founding of the Mellon Institute in 1915. Mellon was joined by many other important private research institutes, testimony to their obvious utility to U.S. firms seeking R&D help.[19] More recently, university research institutes have become legion. Still another alternative to the individual corporate R&D lab was the trade association research facility. In England, such undertakings were common in the late 19th and early 20th centuries. In the United States, they were less popular, and those that were organized appear to have been less effective than their British counterparts. Many advocates of organized, scientific research and development seriously considered the trade association R&D alternative but ultimately rejected it, believing such an approach was not really possible because of the threat of antitrust violations. English manufacturers had no such concerns; U.S. business leaders increasingly had to worry about the effect of public policy on their firms.[20]

The public response to the rise of big business, manifested in the passage of the Sherman Antitrust Act, provides a critically important context for the rise of R&D laboratories in the United States. Rapid industrialization after the Civil War led to a period characterized by some as chaos – chaos for workers and capitalists alike. Faced with instability, U.S. society began what historian Robert Wiebe has called a "search for order."[21] Capitalists sought to govern competition through trade agreements and, when these failed, through corporate mergers. In turn, the public demanded protection from the abuses that could result from this process and from the growing power of the larger corporate combines. Hence the Sherman Act of 1890. Hence too the regulatory movement in industries that were seen as public utilities. At roughly the same time, the public sought order in other areas of U.S. life, such as the management of the nation's natural resources, the regulation of financial markets, and the production of pure foods and drugs. In spite of the Sherman Act – indeed because of it, some have said – the merger movement reached a feverish pitch after the severe depression of the mid-1890s.[22] In response, the administration of Theodore Roosevelt began in 1902 vigorously to enforce the antitrust laws. The creation of the Antitrust Division of the Justice Department in 1903 allowed Roosevelt to use the Sherman Act as, in Ellis Hawley's words, "a positive policy for maintaining competition."[23]

While these events were unfolding, some corporations sought new ways to maintain leadership in their respective industries. Tapping and nourishing the growing U.S. scientific community provided a handful of corporations with the means of maintaining or establishing a secure competitive position. It is no coincidence that the pioneers of modern industrial research and development in the United States established and bolstered their laboratories during the initial wave of antitrust law enforcement by the Roosevelt and Taft administrations. With older avenues closed to corporations in search of industrial order, firms such as General Electric, Du Pont, Eastman Kodak, and American Telephone and Telegraph turned to formal, in-house, scientifically oriented research programs.[24] At Du Pont, the establishment and early growth of R&D laboratories occurred within this total context of mergers and consolidations, growing antitrust and anti–big business sentiment, heightened attention to Edison's work, increasing awareness of how R&D laboratories were benefiting German chemical firms, and a new sense by industrialists that many of the growing numbers of scientists in the United States might be willing to pursue entirely new careers outside academia.

Founding research laboratories in 1902 and 1903 was probably the easiest decision Du Pont's leaders ever made regarding research and development. What followed were all of the difficult issues regarding the management of industrial research: Should research be organized in a centrally managed unit or along decentralized manufacturing lines of business? Or should both avenues be pursued? If both approaches were pursued simultaneously, how should the central research organization relate to the decentralized research organizations? How much should the company spend on research? (Was less than 1 percent of sales and 3 percent of earnings "enough" in the early years? Was $484 million, or 3.6 percent of sales and 68 percent of earnings, "too much" in 1980?) How should managers allocate these research dollars – toward short-term work in support of established businesses or toward longer-term objectives to develop entirely new products and businesses? What is the ideal program to pursue along this allocation spectrum? How is the productivity of research or its return on investment measured? Should laboratory researchers aim to produce high-caliber scientific work or is some lesser form of science good enough given corporate objectives? Once costly research projects are initiated, how do research managers and corporate executives know when either to abandon or strengthen a particular project? These were the issues Du Pont's managers faced from the beginning of the company's research and development programs; they address the same problems today.

A series of related – and also perennial – questions emerged at the outset relating to the management of scientists and research engineers. How would Du Pont recruit and retain high-caliber scientists? On the one extreme, a career in academic science would always be a siren song for industrial scientists; at the other extreme, a career in management promised far greater pecuniary rewards than were typical in research.[25] Thus, keeping mature scientists in the industrial research laboratory was always a difficult problem. A number of other issues governed the choice scientists would make about working in Du Pont's laboratories. What kind of publication policy would the company follow? How would Du Pont protect expensively won proprietary information yet provide the ambitious researcher an opportunity for recognition by peers in the scientific community through publication? How much latitude would the company give to individual research entrepreneurs within its increasingly bureaucratized structure? How would the company's research program relate to university research, and how would Du Pont use consultants, most of whom were university professors?

Integrating research with the two other major functions of the corporation, manufacturing and marketing, also posed problems. "Success" in industrial research is often ultimately judged by its return on investment, which means that a piece of laboratory research must be scaled up and put into profitable commercial practice – development. The problem of successfully developing a laboratory finding, product, or process has been one of the greatest faced at Du Pont, particularly given the nature of much of its business, which demands large-scale, capital-intensive plants and processes. "Research" functions had to be related to "development" functions, but Du Pont's managers found no simple formula for consistently achieving this goal.

Very early, Du Pont's executives/owners (especially Pierre S. du Pont) recognized that a key ingredient in successful industrial research was continuity. This entailed the provision of adequate research facilities, the sustained support of researchers in spite of cyclical swings in the U.S. economy, and a willingness to pursue particular research and development projects even though their apparent payoff date was either unclear or far out on the horizon. Research became one of the most deeply rooted elements of Du Pont's corporate culture, especially after the discovery and successful development of neoprene and nylon in the 1930s. A particularly virulent attack on Du Pont by the Justice Department's Antitrust Division in the 1940s led executives to conclude that the corporation's growth would have to be based almost exclusively on the fruits of research. Consequently, late in the decade they dramatically expanded the company's research program and directed it more toward the fundamental side, from whence had come neoprene and nylon. As a result, Du Pont's research program took on a life of its own.

Some would later charge that the research operation at Du Pont had become obsessed with its own objectives rather than those of the corporation; research was no longer responsive to the company's manufacturing and marketing functions. Following a long period of decline in Wall Street's confidence in Du Pont, executives in the 1970s seemed intent upon "killing the sacred cow of research."[26] Yet, in spite of these seeming attacks on research and wide swings in executive leadership, Du Pont's strong research tradition persisted and sustained those in the laboratory. The turmoil of the 1970s notwithstanding, researchers executed work the commercial importance of which became clear only in the 1980s. Although shaken, the research tradition remained intact, and in 1979 new corporate leadership reasserted the company's commitment to that tradition. The company that had developed such products as cellophane, neoprene, nylon, Teflon, Orlon, and Dacron turned a significant share of its research attention to the life sciences — to pharmaceuticals, health care products, and crop protection chemicals.

The decision to stake much of Du Pont's future on the life sciences came almost eighty years after the company established its first research laboratory. From a handful of academically trained chemists working in a small laboratory, Du Pont's research ranks had grown to some six thousand research and development personnel, including chemists, biologists, physicists, toxicologists, engineers, and a host of other specialists. Shortly after 1980, Du Pont's research budget would exceed a billion dollars, supported by sales of about $30 billion.[27] These figures differ markedly from the $100,000 to $200,000 spent on research in the first years, an expenditure supported by sales of less than $30 million. A thousand-fold growth in sales and a ten-thousand-fold rise in research expenditures is suggestive of one of the company's major trends in this century.

The executives who founded and nourished Du Pont's early research laboratories could not have foreseen these trends. They could have hoped for the increase in sales, but it is unlikely that they could have imagined the substantial growth in the company's R&D expenditures. These growth figures speak of great change in Du Pont's twentieth-century history, but they mask the history's continuity. In establishing research laboratories after the turn of the century, Du Pont demonstrated its leadership of U.S. corporate R&D, especially in the chemical industry. Throughout the next eight decades, Du Pont maintained its position, at least in terms of expenditures. Doing so was neither easy nor cheap. The founders of Du Pont's formal R&D program could have told a more recent executive that it would be so. They understood this situation because the "experimental era" of Du Pont's R&D program, 1902–21, revealed both the promise and problems of this important twentieth-century institution.

PART I

The Experimental Era:
1902–1921

In 1902 two signal events occurred in the Du Pont Company. First, the hundred-year-old family firm passed into the hands of three younger du Pont cousins, T. Coleman, Pierre S., and Alfred I. The older du Ponts from whom the cousins bought the company were tired, leaderless, and ready to sell out to anyone, including businessmen who were not du Ponts. As the three cousins quickly discovered when they were negotiating the purchase, their elders actually had no idea of the total assets or net worth of the company. With sounder financial and managerial control and aggressive action, the cousins believed they could effectively consolidate the U.S. explosives industry. And they did. By 1905 they had succeeded in bringing three-fourths of the industry under the control of a single management, the Executive Committee of the E. I. du Pont de Nemours Powder Company. They had transformed what historians Alfred D. Chandler, Jr., and Stephen Salsbury have described as a "cartel of many family firms" into a "modern, centrally administered corporation with its own operating, sales, and auxiliary departments," all controlled by the du Pont family.[1]

The new, consolidated Du Pont Company manufactured three types of explosives: black powder, dynamite, and smokeless powder. The black powder business was old, fragmented, and declining in both sales and earnings. The dynamite business was newer, concentrated, growing, and highly profitable. Smokeless powder, a firearms propellant, was still in its infancy. Du Pont's smokeless powder business was aimed primarily at the military market, although some powder was sold in the sporting market. This business had just become profitable when the cousins consolidated the industry. (See Table I.1 for data on the company's sales, earnings, and assets, 1904–21.)

The second major event of 1902 occurred when the Eastern Dynamite Company, a subsidiary of Du Pont, established the Eastern Laboratory, a facility divorced from any immediate manufacturing responsibilities and with a specific mission to improve the company's high explosives products and processes through scientific research and development. Only the General Electric Company had initiated anything comparable in the United States. The new laboratory, headed by Charles L. Reese, a PhD chemist with both academic and industrial experience, quickly demonstrated that corporate research paid – and paid handsomely. Subsequently, Du Pont's Executive

Table I.1. *Financial Summary of the Du Pont Company, 1904–21 (in millions of dollars)*

	1904	1906	1907	1911	1914	1916	1918	1919	1921
Gross receipts	26.1	30.8	31.7	33.4	25.2	318.8	329.1	105.4	55.3
Net earnings	4.4	5.3	3.9	6.5	5.6	82.1	43.1	17.7	7.6
Total assets	57.2	66.6	70.9	83.2	83.4	217.9	303.3	241.0	252.2

Source: All data from Du Pont annual reports.

Committee established a second research facility in 1903, the Experimental Station, located on the banks of the Brandywine River across from Du Pont's first black powder works, dating back to 1802. (See Table I.2 for data on Du Pont's R&D expenditures and staff, 1906–21.)

Unlike the Eastern Laboratory, the Experimental Station's mission became grandiose. Initially, it was to be simply a small laboratory to screen inventions coming to Du Pont from outside, independent inventors. But soon after the laboratory was authorized, the Executive Committee radically altered the Experimental Station's charter in response to changes in public policy. Both the Army and the Navy, major consumers of Du Pont powder, were being pressured from within and from outside to develop their own experimental capabilities as well as to build their own manufacturing capacity. Du Pont's executives saw this as a threat to the company's fledgling smokeless powder business and resolved to make the Experimental Station an instrument with which to stay well in front of the military. Hence, the military would continue to be dependent upon Du Pont for its powder and know-how. The Executive Committee also intended the new Experimental Station to serve as Du Pont's "general" laboratory. It was to carry out research not only on smokeless powder but on black powder and dynamite as well. Moreover, the Station would explore new developments in related fields. So the Experimental Station had a broad, almost all-encompassing mission, which contrasted sharply with the narrower, clear-cut goals of the Eastern Laboratory.

The difference in the focus and, more important, measurable performance of Du Pont's two research facilities soon led to a major conflict within the company about research management. Should research be organized along departmental and product lines such as at Eastern Laboratory or along more general, centralized lines at a central facility such as at the Experimental Station? This debate was to be only the first of many on this crucial issue in the management of research at Du Pont. Other debates quickly followed.

Du Pont predicated its two pioneering laboratories on the basis of being an explosives manufacturer. These laboratories worked within this context for most of the first decade of this century. But by 1909, external events had begun to change their research and development programs. Growing competition from the military as a manufacturer of smokeless powder and increasing chants in Washington against the "powder trust" led executives to seek some means of diversifying their business.

They pursued this goal in the decade from 1911 to 1921, probably the most volatile one in the company's entire history. Four corporate restructurings occurred (one in 1911, two in 1914, and another in 1921); Du Pont was convicted of restraint of trade in violation of the Sherman Antitrust Act and was forced to divest some of its black powder and dynamite assets in 1913; Pierre S. du Pont and a close circle of friends and relatives acquired T. Coleman du Pont's large block of Du Pont Company stock and hence gained tighter control of the company; World War I led the company to

Table I.2. Research and Development Statistics for the Du Pont Company, 1906–21

	1906	1907	1911	1914	1916	1918	1919	1921
Total expenditures (thousands of dollars)	150	219	309	250	639	2,748	3,447	1,734
Expenditures as percentage of sales	0.5	0.7	0.9	1.0	0.2	0.8	3.3	3.1
Expenditures as percentage of earnings[a]	2.8	5.6	4.7	4.5	0.8	6.4	19.5	22.8
Expenditures as percentage of earnings[b]	2.8	5.3	4.5	4.2	0.8	6.0	16.3	18.6
R&D staff (total salaried)	n.a.	n.a.	111	95	200	475	652	135

Note: n.a. = not available. [a]Expenditures/Earnings. [b]Expenditures/(Expenditures + Earnings).

Sources: Pre-1911: Executive committee minutes. 1911–12: Charles L. Reese, "Statement of the Chemical Department Including the Eastern Laboratory and the Experimental Station," May 29, 1913. 1913–14: Charles L. Reese, "Report of Expenditures and Accomplishments of the Chemical Department during the Years, 1912, 1913, 1914, and 1915," April 5, 1916. 1915–18: Charles L. Reese, "Report of Expenditures and Accomplishments of the Chemical Department during the Years 1916, 1917, and 1918," Sept. 19, 1919. 1919: William Coyne to Irénée du Pont, "Chemical Department 1921 Appropriation," Nov. 29, 1920. 1920: William M. Whitten, Jr., to Charles L. Reese, "Semi-Annual Report of the Chemical Department, Jan.–June, 1920, Inclusive," Sept. 28, 1920. William M. Whitten, Jr., to Charles L. Reese, "Semi-Annual Report of the Chemical Department, July–December, 1920, Inclusive," March 31, 1921. 1921: C. M. A. Stine to treasurer, Aug. 10, 1927.

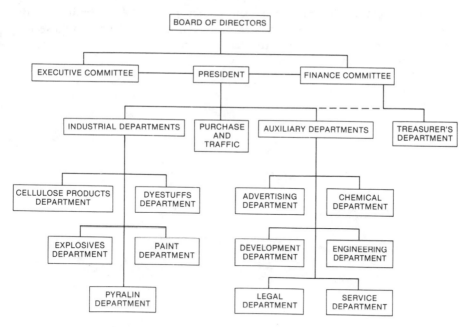

Figure I.1. Organization of the Du Pont Company, December 1921. Source: Du Pont Company Organization Charts, Imprints, Hagley Museum and Library.

expand dramatically its smokeless powder factories and its research and development efforts aimed at finding a use for them after the war; at the same time, the war generated unprecedented profits for the company; Du Pont bought into the paint and celluloid plastics businesses and initiated a long and costly effort to become a profitable manufacturer of synthetic dyestuffs; executives personally and for the corporation acquired large holdings of General Motors stock; and the nation experienced a severe economic recession in 1920–21, an event that prompted a complete reorganization of the company, including its R&D, into autonomous operating divisions whose activities were monitored and coordinated by a central corporate office. (See Figure I.1 for a chart of Du Pont's organization, December 1921.)

By the end of 1921, the die had been cast for Du Pont's research and development programs. The structure – with decentralized, departmental research divisions supported by a central research department – would remain thereafter essentially untouched. Most of the important cast of characters shaping R&D during the next two decades would already be on the scene, making their presence known. Du Pont was well on its way to becoming a diversified chemical manufacturer rather than merely an explosives producer. Volatile change would come to an end, and the company would be poised to take advantage of the subsequent periods of "normalcy" and depression. In the early 1900s, however, that promising future would seem all too distant as the cousins struggled to turn the enterprise into a more profitable, more controlled business.

1

Organizing for Research and Development, 1902–1911

When the three du Pont cousins purchased the Du Pont Company from their elders in 1902, they had no clear idea of how they would manage the company. Certainly they had no master plan to establish the nation's second significant corporate research and development program. Yet within two years they had not only organized an executive committee to manage the new company, but they and their fellow members of the Executive Committee had also set the company on the road to becoming a major research institution in the United States. Du Pont supported not just a single research laboratory but two, the Eastern Laboratory and the Experimental Station. They were remarkably different organizations in their missions and capabilities. By mid-1904, the coexistence of the two laboratories led the Executive Committee to ponder the question of how best to manage research. Some members pushed for a consolidation of research into a single organization while others argued for greater decentralization along manufacturing lines. After much heated debate resulting in a stalemate, the Executive Committee determined not to alter the existing research arrangements but rather to expand the operations of both. The two laboratories would operate independently for the remainder of the decade.

During this period, evidence mounted that the highly structured, mission-oriented research pursued at Eastern Laboratory paid handsome dividends, whereas the results of the less focused general research of the Experimental Station were not clear. The Experimental Station's program offered great promise in the long run because much of it was of a high-risk, high-reward nature. Yet in the short run, it could not show any immediate, measurable return on the company's investment. Nevertheless, the Experimental Station had become a significant institution within Du Pont; its importance to Du Pont became evident only after its first decade. Even then, the contribution could not be calculated easily in a way similar to Eastern Laboratory's. Rather, the Station's benefit to Du Pont was largely intangible.

The years between 1902 and 1911 were ones of organizing for research and development – of establishing two laboratories that represented fundamentally different approaches to research management and of struggling with these approaches. During this period, Du Pont hired research managers and researchers in both laboratories who would become major figures in the company's research program in the coming decades. Because of the size of the company and its organization, executives gained a firsthand view of research and the myriad problems surrounding its management. They continued to nurture research despite the problems they encountered.

Establishing the Executive Committee

On February 4, 1903, T. Coleman du Pont, the president and major stockholder of the Du Pont Company, notified his associates Pierre S. du Pont, Alfred I. du Pont, Francis I. du Pont, J. Amory Haskell, Hamilton M. Barksdale, and Arthur J. Moxham that they would thereafter "constitute an Executive Committee in charge of matters of all kinds pertaining to the powder and high explosives business." The committee would direct the affairs of the many smaller companies that would soon be consolidated into a single, incorporated firm legally known as E. I. du Pont de Nemours Powder Company. Coleman noted that he would serve as the chairman of this important committee. His cousins Pierre and Alfred were to be responsible, respectively, for finance and accounting and for the manufacture of black blasting and black sporting powder. A seasoned veteran of the powder business, Haskell was put in charge of sales of all the company's explosives, and his protégé Barksdale was given responsibility for the manufacture of dynamite and other high explosives. Coleman assigned to his younger cousin, Francis, the duty of managing smokeless powder manufacturing operations. Coleman's and Pierre's mentor in industrial management and finance, Moxham, assumed responsibility for what would be known later as the Development Department. As Coleman wrote, Moxham's department was to be "in charge of competition of all kinds, developements [*sic*], and of experimental work"[1] (see Figure 1.1).

Moxham had earlier urged Coleman and Pierre to organize the Executive Committee for managing the new company, and no doubt the cousins regarded him as the most qualified associate to handle the development of the company's resources. From the outset, the Executive Committee recognized that development was critical to the company's success and that "experimental work" – research and development – would play an important role in this process. Like the other committee members in their respective areas, Moxham moved quickly to centralize managerial control of the Development Department, especially since he was a leading advocate of rationalization. Yet when it came to the experimental work for which he had been given responsibility, Moxham soon learned how difficult the management of research would be.

Barksdale's High Explosives Department had only recently established its own research program, and Barksdale was unwilling to give up control of it to Moxham's Development Department. Thus from the moment the Executive Committee became the steward of the Du Pont Company, the organization and management of research and development were

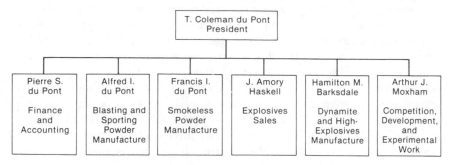

Figure 1.1. Du Pont Company Executive Committee Responsibilities in 1903.

problematical. Moxham soon succeeded in convincing his colleagues to establish under the care of the Development Department a General Experimental Laboratory (soon called the Experimental Station), but Barksdale maintained with complete autonomy his department's research program, housed in the new Eastern Laboratory.

The Founding of Eastern Laboratory

On July 9, 1902 – two months before A. J. Moxham's arrival in Wilmington to help the du Pont cousins manage their new acquisition – chemists finished moving their apparatus into the Eastern Laboratory, recently completed at the site of the Repauno Chemical Company at Gibbstown, New Jersey, across the Delaware River from Chester, Pennsylvania.[2] Named after its and Repauno's parent holding company, Eastern Dynamite Company, the new research laboratory had been given a broad mandate by Hamilton Barksdale, president of the holding company and general manager of the Repauno company. The new laboratory's director, Charles L. Reese, outlined six objectives for Eastern Laboratory in his first annual report:

1. To improve as far as possible the chemical operations now employed.
2. To investigate the explosives now being manufactured, to revise their formulas and to put them on a scientific basis.
3. To devise or discover new explosives for general and specific purposes.
4. To keep in touch with all new and improved processes which have any bearing on operations connected with the explosives industry.
5. To investigate new explosives brought forward by outsiders or suggested by members of the Company.
6. To train young chemists and keep the plants supplied with technical assistants.[3]

These clearly defined objectives could be viewed as a break with the past, but they were not entirely new at Repauno in 1902. From the founding of the Repauno dynamite works in 1880, its managers had realized that "chem-

ical work" was necessary to maintain and improve product yields and quality and to ensure safer manufacturing operations. As consumers of
explosives gained experience in the use of dynamite, they and the federal
government pushed for the development of new high explosives, such as
nonfreezing dynamite and safety explosives, to meet their particular needs
as well as to satisfy new safety standards. The very nature of high-explosives
manufacture demanded that chemical knowledge be brought to bear on
practice. The accidental death of Lammot du Pont, the father of three presidents of the Du Pont Company in the twentieth century (Pierre, Irénée, and
Lammot), in an explosion of the nitrating house at Repauno in 1884 un-
derscored this need for knowledge.

When the Du Pont–backed Repauno works began manufacturing operations, neither the final product nor its manufacturing process had been
perfected. Although in concept the manufacture of nitroglycerin was simple
– the nitration of glycerin by reacting refined glycerin with mixed nitric and
sulfuric acids – in practice there was much room for improvement or error.
Trained in chemistry at the University of Pennsylvania, Lammot worked
full time at Repauno and in 1882 engaged the assistance of Walter N. Hill,
a Yale-educated chemist from the Naval Torpedo Station at Newport,
Rhode Island. Du Pont and Hill initially concentrated their efforts on improving the yield of nitroglycerin in the nitration step and then on getting
better separation of the nitroglycerin from the waste acids. Because of complaints about Repauno's waste acids killing sturgeon and shad in the Delaware River and the obvious monetary loss from this dumping, Lammot
carried out successful laboratory studies to find a means of acid separation
and recovery. He and Hill soon made arrangements to introduce the process
on a manufacturing basis. The full-scale installation was completed for
testing on March 29, 1884. That day, in trying to work out problems with
the process, du Pont and Hill, along with six other men, perished when the
nitroglycerin house exploded.[4]

The accident – a painful blow to the family and the company – led to
the appointment of Oscar R. Jackson as plant superintendent. Son of Charles
T. Jackson, one of the discoverers and pioneers of modern anesthesia, Jackson possessed outstanding training in chemical science. After graduating
from Harvard University in 1876, he spent three years in Munich, Germany,
working with Professor Adolf von Baeyer, the great organic chemist who
gained industrial fame for synthesizing indigo, and with his protégé Emil
Fischer, also a major contributor to organic chemistry and synthetic dyes.
Chemists at Repauno marveled when Jackson would give one of his "pet
demonstrations" by making synthetic indigo "right before their eyes" –
something he had learned from Baeyer and Fischer. Beginning his seventeen-
year tenure as superintendent at the age of twenty-nine, Jackson had a strong
commitment to improving the Repauno product and plant through chemical
science.[5]

In 1889, Jackson hired an assistant, James Lawrence, a Scottish immigrant with a dozen years of technical experience in dynamite production. Together they undertook the problem of acid separation and recovery that had been abandoned with the deadly explosion of 1884. Jackson and Lawrence soon succeeded, and their recovery process, wrote historians Van Gelder and Schlatter in 1927, "has been in practically continuous operation ever since, although it has been rebuilt, improved, and enlarged many times."[6] Two years later, Lawrence developed a new process for separating the nitrated glycerin from the waste acids, raising yields by 6 to 9 percent.[7] Jackson later hired a number of academically trained chemists to continue work on chemical control (i.e., monitoring yields and performing materials balances), improvement of yields and products, analysis of raw materials, and a wide range of work associated with manufacturing operations.[8] Repauno also analyzed the high explosives of competitors.

To the managers of Repauno and Eastern Dynamite, Hamilton Barksdale and J. Amory Haskell, there was no question that chemical work paid. The improvement in acid recovery meant reduced manufacturing costs. Higher yields of nitroglycerin saved increasingly expensive glycerin. Product improvements and standardization – and the careful monitoring of competitors' products – ensured that Repauno would maintain its position as the leading manufacturer of high explosives in America.[9]

The chemical research and development pursued at Repauno had been carried out in a makeshift "works" laboratory. The laboratory was thus an arm of the plant's manufacturing operations. Yet the positive results of bringing chemical knowledge to bear on the problems of dynamite manufacture led Haskell and Barksdale to establish in July 1902 a general chemical laboratory to work on problems associated with high-explosives manufacturing. They took a bolder step when they determined to isolate it from immediate responsibility for day-to-day manufacturing operations at the plant.[10] Moreover, this new facility, the Eastern Laboratory, would do work for the entire Eastern Dynamite Company, which operated other plants besides Repauno. The direction of the new laboratory would be vested in the hands of a chemist with a PhD from the University of Heidelberg, Charles Lee Reese.

Dr. Reese – he never let anyone in the company address him any other way – had come to Barksdale's attention because of his work at Repauno for the New Jersey Zinc Company. In mid-1900, Barksdale decided to integrate backward by building a plant to manufacture fuming sulfuric acid by the new contact process. New Jersey Zinc held the rights to the process adopted by the Repauno management. This soon led Reese to Repauno as a consultant on the installation of the acid plant. Reese had only recently joined New Jersey Zinc as its chief chemist.[11]

Prior to his employment with the firm, Reese had had a checkered career as an academic chemist. He entered Johns Hopkins University as a freshman but after a year transferred to the University of Virginia, from which he was graduated with a degree in chemistry in 1884. From Charlottesville,

he moved to the University of Heidelberg to study under the aging chemist
Robert Wilhelm Bunsen. Reese received the PhD degree from Heidelberg
in 1886. Before he returned to the United States, he briefly studied organic
chemistry at Göttingen with Victor Meyer (who would shortly succeed
Bunsen).[12] But even a German PhD in chemistry was not sufficient to land
Reese a substantial teaching appointment in the United States. From 1886
to 1888, Reese held the dubious position of "assistant in chemistry" at
Johns Hopkins University. (Reese's parents lived in Baltimore, so the position at Hopkins was merely a device to give Reese some official connection
with the chemistry department, which had already achieved distinction as
the leading department in the country.) Reese filled in for one term at Wake
Forest College in 1888 and then moved further south to take a permanent
position in chemistry and physics at the South Carolina Military Academy
– the Citadel – in Charleston. A distinguished chemist at Johns Hopkins,
Ira Remsen, had recommended Reese for this and other positions, saying,
"I consider Dr. Reese well qualified to fill the chair of chemistry in a first
class institution of learning."[13] In 1896, Reese resigned from the Citadel
and returned to his family's home in Baltimore. For almost three years he
held the part-time position of "instructor" at Johns Hopkins, but only during
1897 did he receive aid from the university in the form of a fellowship.
Positions at Ohio University, Sewanee College, and Washington University
eluded him.[14]

Finally in December 1899, after failing to receive the job as superintendent
of the Greenville Fertilizer Company, Reese applied for the position at New
Jersey Zinc Company. As usual, he relied upon the chemistry faculty at
Hopkins for recommendations, and they emphasized Reese's growing
knowledge of and commitment to industrial chemistry. All argued that
Reese's theoretical training and quantitative skills would make him an excellent chemist in a technical laboratory. Reese was hired.[15] The New Jersey
Zinc Company was to be the critical catalyst for Reese's career and rise to
prominence in Du Pont and in the chemical profession.

New Jersey Zinc had only recently purchased a U.S. license for the patented Schroeder-Grillo contact acid process and had constructed its first
such plant in Wisconsin. But impurities in New Jersey Zinc's ore caused
problems. Hired to address these, Reese soon identified arsenic oxide as the
culprit and developed a process to get rid of the impurity. Reese's work for
New Jersey Zinc at the Repauno works impressed J. Amory Haskell and
Hamilton Barksdale and led them early in 1902 to offer Reese the position
of director of the new experimental laboratory at Repauno. Their decision
to hire Reese was also clearly influenced by the deteriorating mental health
of Oscar Jackson, who had long provided critical technical guidance at
Repauno.[16]

Even before he officially joined the Repauno Chemical Company, Reese
began to plan for the staffing and physical arrangements of the Eastern
Laboratory. There is no evidence to suggest that Barksdale and Haskell had

any preconceived notions about the organization and ultimate size of the new laboratory. Reese wrote Barksdale that he wished to hire a chemist soon to be graduated from Johns Hopkins University as an analyst. Barksdale replied that he and Oscar Jackson had intended to transfer one of the chemists from the works lab to the new laboratory as an analyst, but he yielded to Reese. "If you secure this young man," wrote Barksdale, "then he and [the works chemist] would give you a working force to start with, thus giving us more time in which to determine just how much more, and what character of assistance [will be] necessary."[17] In addition to the analytical chemist, Barksdale transferred one other chemist from the plant to the Eastern Laboratory. These two men were initially the only bench chemists at Eastern, but Reese moved quickly to hire additional chemists for the new undertaking. Within six months the laboratory's chemical staff had grown to nine, including Reese, plus a chief clerk and several "lab boys." (See Table 1.1 for a digest of the Eastern Laboratory staff in 1902.)

Reese's arrival and his initial selection of chemists to staff the laboratory provided an important base on which to found an effective industrial research organization. Before he moved on to higher levels of research management, Reese succeeded in hiring several excellent chemists who would contribute to the explosives industry and especially to research management at Du Pont during the next forty years. Equally important, Reese instituted procedures that would become the cornerstone of all Du Pont research policy and that would begin, almost immediately, to yield tangible, economically beneficial results.

Reese recognized that previous experimental work had been "more or less desultory" and usually improperly recorded and reported. When chemists at the new laboratory began work in 1902, Reese demanded that they record their experiments and write periodic reports outlining the results of their work. Having some familiarity with Repauno's chemical operations and its problems, Reese initiated a research program aimed at solving those problems, increasing yields, and improving products. In 1911 Reese argued that the most important early work done at Eastern had been the improvement of yields of nitroglycerin. Research, he noted, "added considerably to our knowledge of the conditions to be considered in the nitrating process." Other important work undertaken in 1902 included the development of a more rapid process of separating nitroglycerin from the waste acids and improved methods of distilling the recovered waste acids for reuse.[18] These were the same problems that had confronted both Lammot du Pont and Oscar Jackson.

The separation project provides a particularly instructive view of the early operations of the Eastern Laboratory. With some mixtures of nitric and sulfuric acids, separating the nitrated glycerin from the waste acids took as much as three hours — far longer than the hour-long nitrating process. Sidney Emery's extensive research at the Eastern Laboratory in 1903 suggested that colloidal silica in the mixture slowed down the separation process, and he

Table 1.1. *The Eastern Laboratory's Research Staff, 1902*

Name	Position	Qualifications	Remarks
Charles L. Reese	Director	PhD, University of Heidelberg, 1886. Two years industrial experience as chief chemist, New Jersey Zinc Co.	By 1900, a Heidelberg PhD was viewed as "a cheap degree" by those in the know because of how relatively simple it was to obtain.
Sidney S. Emery	Analytical chemist	Academic training unknown. Chemist, Harrison Bros. & Co. Employed by Repauno prior to Dec. 1, 1896 and after Aug. 1, 1901.	Took leave from Repauno, Dec. 1, 1896, to Aug. 1, 1901, because of substance abuse (ether and chloroform). Regarded as excellent analytical chemist. Served as Reese's assistant, 1903–4.
Arthur L. La Motte	Chemist	Some work at MIT and University of Pennsylvania, no degrees. Six years as plant chemist, Repauno Works.	From his "Diary of a Dynamiter," La Motte appears to have been a jack-of-all-trades.
Charles F. Lindsay	Chemist	PhD, Johns Hopkins University, 1902.	Became research chemist for General Electric, 1903.
T. J. Wrampelmeier	Chemist	PhD, University of Michigan. Eleven-year veteran of explosives chemistry.	Became founding director of Du Pont's Experimental Station, 1903 and in same year Du Pont's foreign business representative.
John W. McCoy	Chemist	BA, Chemistry, University of Delaware, 1901. One year of postgraduate work at Delaware.	Moved quickly into plant and general management. Member of Executive Committee, 1936–47.
Richard T. Cann, III	Chemist	BA, Chemistry, University of Delaware, 1901.	Became superintendent of Du Pont's Ashburn, Mo., dynamite plant.
Willis O. Heard	Chemist	Unknown.	
J. B. Braunstein	Chemist	Unknown.	

discovered that by adding sodium fluoride the silica could be taken out in the form of silicon tetrafluoride. This discovery quickly became known throughout the trade as "SE Compound," its name derived from Sidney Emery's initials. With the addition of SE Compound, separation time was reduced to as little as fifteen minutes and never more than an hour. As Reese noted in 1911, "it is difficult for those who have not operated Nitroglycerine lines without the use of SE compound to appreciate the troubles which were experienced previous to the introduction of this material. It has been estimated that if this problem had not been solved, it would be necessary at the present time to have our separating equipment two to three times as large as it now is."[19]

As director of the Eastern Laboratory, Reese had patented SE Compound in his own name, "claiming it was customary for the director to take out patents, citing Edison as an example."[20] The attachment of Emery's initials to the compound and Reese's actions relating to another Eastern Laboratory development suggest that more than once Reese patented others' work in his own name. In early 1903 he instructed his research staff that they would have to develop a nonfreezing dynamite within a week. Arthur La Motte had already been at work on such a development. Although the week turned into months, La Motte developed a nonfreezing dynamite that he initially called "XD" and later renamed "Arctic Powder"; it consisted of 6 percent trinitrotoluene, 6 percent tetranitronaphthalene, and 88 percent ammonium nitrate. La Motte demonstrated this new high explosive in mid-May to Reese, Barksdale, Haskell, and Francis du Pont. He received high praise and additional support to conduct extensive tests with his powder. Two weeks later, Reese told La Motte that this powder was "the best non-freezing powder ever invented."

The development and testing of the powder proved more difficult than initially expected, but La Motte persisted and arrived at several commercially viable formulations of Arctic Powder. By January 1904 La Motte's successful work had come to the personal attention of his distant relative Pierre S. du Pont, now treasurer of Du Pont and a major stockholder. Yet Reese soon informed La Motte that he, as the director of the Eastern Laboratory, would take out the patent on Arctic Powder in his own name. La Motte bridled at the idea and discussed the issue with Francis and Pierre du Pont, who advised him "to patent Arctic myself and not let Reese do it!" La Motte's diary entry for June 3, 1904, reads as follows:

> Told Reese I had decided to take out patents in my own name. He said why? I said "two friends of mine in Wilmington advised me to." He said, "All I've got to say is you've got two damn fool friends in Wilmington. Who are they?" When he heard he didn't speak to me.[21]

More than failing to speak to La Motte, Reese quickly managed to terminate La Motte's association with the laboratory. On June 13, Hamilton Barksdale informed La Motte, much to La Motte's regret, that he was being transferred to the Sales Department of Eastern Dynamite Company. As a concession, Barksdale allowed La Motte to patent his own development and to take a vacation before assuming his new duties. La Motte later reported that as soon as he had rejected Reese's offer to patent Arctic Powder, the Eastern Laboratory lost all interest in it. Two years later, however, when Eastern had not succeeded in developing alternatives to Arctic Powder, Reese asked La Motte to return to the laboratory. La Motte declined this offer.[22]

Reese's insistence on patenting his subordinates' work as well as his other actions made La Motte – and probably others – contemptuous of him. Reese's mannerisms and dealings often offended. Du Pont's prominent dye chemist, Herbert A. Lubs, later wrote candidly in his article on Reese in the *Dictionary of American Biography* that "some of [Reese's] younger subordinates during the earlier days of his industrial career felt a certain intolerance and haughtiness in his manner." But Lubs insisted that Reese's "close associates did not share this view." In the early days of the Eastern Laboratory, perhaps only Hamilton Barksdale and J. Amory Haskell would have been considered Reese's close associates.

The Controversy over Laboratories and the Management of Research

Despite personal animosities and grievances that may have been harbored against Reese by his staff, the early work of the Eastern Laboratory was important for the growth of the high-explosives business. Under Reese's direction, Eastern's improvement of nitrating and separation processes, its standardization and revision of powder formulas, its increase in overall yields, and its attention to chemical control in all the plants of Eastern Dynamite Company (a function that commanded the greatest share of Reese's personal attention) demonstrated decisively by 1904 that the venture to establish a research organization had been successful.[23] Yet in mid-1904, Barksdale informed his colleagues on Du Pont's Executive Committee, which now controlled Eastern Dynamite, that Eastern Laboratory was at a critical juncture in its history.[24]

Barksdale had requested an appropriation for the expansion of the Eastern Laboratory. Considering Barksdale's request at a special meeting, the Executive Committee realized that the expansion of Eastern – indeed, its very existence – posed questions about the management of research that had not been foreseen or hammered out when Coleman du Pont placed A. J. Moxham in charge of "experimental work" and when the Executive Committee had authorized the founding of the General Experimental Laboratory in 1903. Barksdale's request thus raised for the first time the "whole question of laboratories" and how research would be managed at Du Pont. Rather than taking immediate action, the committee appointed a subcommittee to review the issues. Hamilton Barksdale, Henry F. Baldwin, Alfred I. du Pont, and Francis I. du Pont served on this special committee.[25]

When the subcommittee first met in late June 1904, it discussed a number of issues, ranging from what the company's policy should be toward its employee-inventors and research personnel to what structure the company should adopt to achieve the greatest efficiency in its research effort. The committee also tried to work out useful definitions and boundaries for various types of company laboratories. All agreed on the definition and function of a "works laboratory" in which routine chemical and physical tests were "made in order to properly direct the carrying on of the work of the plant." Works laboratories could not and should not, the committee concluded, "undertake the development of new processes at all."[26]

The issue lay in the difference between a "departmental laboratory" and a "general experimental laboratory." Although the debate was carried out on a general level, there were strong undercurrents of a growing rivalry between the Eastern Laboratory and the General Experimental Laboratory (soon to be known as the Experimental Station). In discussing the departmental laboratory, Barksdale argued that its object was "the improvement of the art in that branch of the explosive manufacture that comes within the province of its department. This embraces not only the improvement of existing methods and products [and] the development of new processes and explosives, but also the selection and training of competent young men for positions of assistant superintendents of the different plants of the department."[27] The committee was well aware that Eastern Laboratory was the only departmental laboratory of the new Du Pont Company. Every member acknowledged that the Eastern Laboratory had been successful. Yet Alfred I. du Pont, the head of the black powder department, and H. F. Baldwin, his counterpart in smokeless powder,[28] saw no reason to found laboratories comparable to Eastern for their own departments. Rather, they initially supported the views of Francis I. du Pont, who argued that "a General Experimental Laboratory is the proper plan" for conducting research and development in the Du Pont Company. Such a laboratory was defined as one "doing work for all manufacturing plants owned by the Company. This laboratory undertakes the development of new processes and scientific work generally, as may be directed by the heads of the departments or by the Executive Committee. Its organization also handles all patent matters, etc., for all departments of the Company."[29]

Barksdale opposed such a strategy. Pointing to the undisputed record of the Eastern Laboratory, which he had helped to found, Barksdale maintained that "for thoroughly efficient work a laboratory should be situated at a manufacturing plant."[30] Later, he explained that a general experimental laboratory removed from manufacturing plants could not readily obtain raw materials in the amount and of the quality necessary to do meaningful work. Equally important, such a laboratory could not serve as an effective training ground for plant managers. Although not discounting Eastern's success, Francis I. du Pont argued that any laboratory equipped with the best facilities and staffed with creative, well-trained personnel could achieve the same or better results.[31]

This internal debate constitutes one of the most important moments in the history of Du Pont's research and development program. The Executive Committee faced for the first time many of the fundamental issues concerning the structure and management of research in a modern corporation. Barksdale appears to have framed the argument for decentralization. He first enumerated the Eastern Laboratory's achievements. The question, Barksdale pointed out, was not whether research would be done but "how can future expenditures for purposes of research and development be most efficiently and wisely made?" He succinctly raised the questions with which the full subcommittee had been grappling:

1. Shall there be one or more laboratories for purposes of research and development?
2. If only one, shall the [General] Experimental Laboratory or the Eastern Laboratory be taken as the foundation for [the] consolidated experimental and scientific station?
3. If more than one, shall they consist of a general experimental laboratory and . . . departmental laboratories for each department or the latter only?
4. If more than one, shall the work of each be restricted within clearly defined lines, and if not, how shall future duplication of expensive apparatus and useless repetition of experimental work be avoided?[32]

Barksdale, Baldwin, and Alfred du Pont recommended to the Executive Committee "that we should carry out researches and experimentations to the fullest extent" both along departmental or manufacturing lines and in a general laboratory. They believed that Du Pont's "future permanent success" would stem "in large measure" from research and development. The Executive Committee accepted their recommendation and voted unanimously to appropriate $12,000 for an extension to Eastern and $5,000 for the purchase of new equipment.[33] Barksdale, whose High Explosives Operating Department generated the lion's share of the profits of the company, had triumphed in maintaining and expanding Eastern.

That left unanswered the question of how the company could avoid duplication of research effort and inefficient dual management. "We believe," Barksdale, Baldwin, and Alfred du Pont argued, "it would be unwise to endeavor to restrict within defined lines the fields of study of individual men in the two laboratories. The minds of these men should be as untrammeled as possible. We should encourage suggestions from all sources." Equipment duplication, they recognized, was far easier to avoid: "So far as special apparatus goes, one laboratory should supplement the other while each should know what the other has accomplished, and both should cooperate towards the common goal of greatest possible achievement." They recommended that the directors of the two laboratories be instructed to work out a satisfactory division of labor and that they should be directly responsible for avoiding "useless duplication of equipment and experiments."[34] Although this policy was easy to articulate, adherence to it would pose problems when the two research laboratories directly competed in projects.

Du Pont's Executive Committee compromised, deciding that research would be conducted in both departmental and central laboratories. The committee would try to maintain the best of both strategies, decentralization as well as centralization. This approach to research management did not meet with the unquestioning approval of Francis I. du Pont, who was at that time directing the efforts of the General Experimental Laboratory. Francis reminded his peers on the Executive Committee that they had earlier established the General Experimental Laboratory "with a view of saving expense in all departments." He argued that the Du Pont Company should not commit itself "to the policy of continuing two research laboratories – one a general laboratory and the other a departmental laboratory – for no other reason than because the departmental laboratory at Repauno has been a success."[35] But the Executive Committee rejected Francis's advice.

The Founding of the Experimental Station

As the new head of "Competition, Developments, and Experimental Work," [36] Arthur J. Moxham quickly sought clarification about what the president meant by his charge. "I understand developments," wrote Moxham, "to mean such items as improving our strategic position in the matter of raw material ... and a proper consideration of receiving points for such material as may be distributed to all the combined interests...." For his duties under experimental work, Moxham wondered if Coleman meant "cover[ing] new inventions or innovations in the powder business brought to us from exterior sources, but not to include any control of such developments as naturally would find their inspiration in the daily work of our Operative [Manufacturing] Department."[37] Coleman responded by saying that he concurred with Moxham's conception of developments, but he broadened in a most important way Moxham's definition of his responsibilities under the rubric of "experimental." "I think," noted Coleman, "it would be advisable for you to control the developments of any important inspiration or new idea conceived in our manufacturing department,... bringing it to a point where you could either yourself drop it or take up with the Executive Committee, the advisability of adopting it."[38] This gave Moxham a broader mandate.

Although Moxham sought at once to gain in practice the control over experimental work that Coleman had given to him in theory, he found this goal difficult to achieve. He directed his immediate efforts at the establishment of a broad base of support within the company. Although details are sketchy, by April 1903 Moxham was working with an "Experimental Committee."[39] Circumstantial evidence suggests that Moxham, Francis I. du Pont, Alfred I. du Pont, and Hamilton Barksdale constituted the Experimental Committee, although Pierre S. du Pont may have served rather than Barksdale. It took only half a dozen meetings of the Executive Committee before Moxham succeeded in convincing his colleagues to direct the Experimental Committee to consider the establishment of a laboratory for his department.[40]

Moxham had titillated the committee's imagination by proposing a research project that had great significance for the Du Pont Company: to find, through "original research," a method of synthesizing glycerin on a commercial basis. Such a project, of course, was naturally the province of the Eastern Laboratory. Citing the success achieved in Germany and England through formal research institutions, Moxham asked the Executive Committee "to put at our disposal some better arrangement than now exists in the matter of an experimental laboratory, which should be absolutely divorced from any operative tendency." Moxham noted that in his own mind he had not settled on the best location for such a research laboratory. He leaned toward its establishment in New York City, however, because all the necessary chemicals were most readily available there. "On the other hand," Moxham ventured, "as the Repauno Chemical Company has expended a considerable sum of money already in this direction, it might be better to turn over to our committee the control of this laboratory."[41]

Hamilton Barksdale immediately recognized Moxham's proposal as a threat to his own province. He sought — and succeeded, at least temporarily — in restricting the charter for what was to become the Experimental Station. The Executive Committee was reminded that the Experimental Committee had been established "to see that inventions, improvements or suggestions reaching us from outside are not sidetracked or buried without proper consideration." Although it was "necessary to establish an experimental laboratory exclusively under the charge of the Experimental Committee," such a laboratory "need not interfere" with the Eastern Laboratory because it "has its hands full in its regular work." Moxham's ideas of taking over Eastern or setting up a laboratory in New York City were dead.[42] Initially, the Executive Committee envisioned that its General Experimental Laboratory would be devoted merely to screening and improving inventions and developments originating from outside the Du Pont Company.

External events, however, soon brought about a major shift in research policy. While Moxham was planning the new laboratory, Francis du Pont delivered to his colleagues on the Executive Committee a report with a clear warning.[43] The relationship that the Du Pont Company had enjoyed with the navy and the army during the 1890s was under stress. Du Pont and the navy had worked closely together during the 1890s to develop a satisfactory smokeless powder for both cannon and small arms; indeed, the navy had literally pulled Du Pont into the smokeless powder business in 1891.[44] Over the decade, Du Pont and officers and chemists at the Naval Torpedo Station at Newport, Rhode Island, had freely exchanged scientific and technical information. The army's Ordnance Bureau had relocated the headquarters of the inspector of powder to Wilmington in an effort "to further the development . . . of smokeless powder."[45] As part of this relocation, the army had furnished Du Pont big guns, and Du Pont in turn supplied the army with platforms, ranges, targets, and other ballistic paraphernalia.

But by 1898, the military's relationship with Du Pont had begun to cool. That year, Congress appropriated money for the navy to construct a smokeless powder plant at Indian Head, Maryland, thirty miles below Washington on the Potomac River. The Indian Head plant greatly supplemented the output of the navy's experimental smokeless powder production facilities at Newport and also provided the navy with an up-to-date research and development facility for smokeless powder. Ostensibly, Indian Head's production facility was not constructed to compete with private manufacturers such as Du Pont but only to provide a yardstick measure for how much powder should cost. Its research facilities were supposed to aid the navy in establishing specifications and standards for the powder it purchased from private concerns. Both specifications and prices had become sore points between the military and private manufacturers after 1898. With Du Pont actively seeking to consolidate the entire industry into what the *New York Times* called in 1903 the "Smokeless Powder Trust," the military grew increasingly suspicious of the company. It would seek to expand the navy's output of smokeless powder at Indian Head and to build a comparable facility for the army.[46]

In late July 1903, Francis du Pont informed the Executive Committee that the Ordnance Department of the army was planning to build a plant for manufacturing smokeless powder near its Sandy Hook Proving Grounds and that this plant – built in 1906–07 as the Picatinny Arsenal – would include research and development facilities. It appeared to him that "the government's smokeless powder business will be taken more and more out of the hands of private makers." Faced with the government's actions and the growing concern within the military over having to depend on a single private supplier for smokeless powder, Francis argued that it was imperative for Du Pont to establish a laboratory to "conduct original research on powders" and to engage the services of experts in the field. The establishment of such a laboratory, Francis suggested, would "secure greater respect from the government" and would be a sign of Du Pont's "utmost progressiveness." Such a laboratory would also allow Du Pont greater control over the process of establishing specifications for military powders. Francis added an important new wrinkle to prior discussions of research when he pointed out that being "progressive" meant more than doing research and development on powder alone; the company must also be concerned with the guns in which the powder was used. To achieve this capability, he recommended the establishment of a joint research and development venture with the Bethlehem Steel Company, which already had a substantial ballistics

testing facility.[47] It appears that the Executive Committee paid close attention to Francis's stern warning. The committee approved his recommendation to establish a central department to deal with government powder
sales, and it gave him and Moxham permission to open negotiations with
Bethlehem for joint research on ballistics.[48] Soon the committee began to
alter the original charter of the General Experimental Laboratory.

Although Executive Committee activity slowed down during the late summer of 1903, Moxham advised his colleagues on July 29 that they could
expect to spend as much as $75,000 for the experimental laboratory they
had earlier authorized.[49] Francis had issued his warning only the week
before. By September, the committee had shifted completely to Francis's
side and was prepared to spend far more for the new laboratory than
Moxham had initially projected. Moxham reported on the matter of the
experimental laboratory to the Executive Committee on September 8, 1903.
He noted that he and Francis were considering what relationship should
exist between his department's laboratory, as defined and authorized earlier,
and the one approved by the Executive Committee to ensure that the military
would consider Du Pont progressive.[50]

Responding to Moxham's report, the Executive Committee took a firm
stance and established the policy that would serve as the initial charter of
the General Experimental Laboratory. "[Our] policy should be one," agreed
the committee, "of fully developing the Experimental Laboratory, embodying in that such tools and apparatus as may be needed for the smokeless
powder end of things. We believe that in this laboratory should be concentrated everything of a general nature in the way of apparatus and tools for
tests."[51] Moreover, the committee determined that even if the proposed
joint venture with Bethlehem were to fall through (which eventually happened), Du Pont would build a ballistics research and testing facility. In
addition to establishing these major policies about the direction of Du Pont
research, the Executive Committee also concluded that research and development work on safety explosives – what would soon be known as "per-
missibles" – would be done by the new laboratory.

The Executive Committee's decision on permissible explosives research
came in response to growing political pressure for federal regulation of mine
safety. These pressures were part of the same political reform movement –
Progressivism – that led to the enforcement of the Sherman Antitrust Act
by the Theodore Roosevelt administration. In his regular report on "experimental matters," Moxham had argued that Du Pont must take up the
study of safety explosives "along broad lines."[52] Reformers were seeking
legislation that would restrict the types of explosives used in mining to those
that would not, unlike nitroglycerin dynamites, set off "fire-damp," the
dangerous mine gas consisting principally of methane.[53] The Executive Committee clearly recognized the importance of developing such safety explosives. But rather than instructing the High Explosives Operating Department
to set the task before the Eastern Laboratory, the Executive Committee

approved Moxham's recommendation that the development of safety explosives should be the province of the soon-to-be-established experimental
laboratory.[54] This decision, perhaps more than any other factor, headed
Moxham and Barksdale toward the showdown of mid-1904 over what the
proper role of the General Experimental Laboratory should be. Without
question, the relatively new and not completely staffed Eastern Laboratory
was the logical institution to work on safety explosives. But because Moxham had gained no say over the affairs of Eastern (even though Coleman
had theoretically put him in charge of all experimental matters), he was
unwilling to leave to others the filling of this urgent need in which Du Pont
had "to take a proper lead."[55]

Six weeks after the Executive Committee broadened the mission of the
General Experimental Laboratory, Moxham noted that "we are now considering the establishment of a temporary laboratory at [a small textile mill
on the Brandywine River] pending the construction of the permanent laboratory."[56] A month later he had indeed secured space in a mill dating back
to 1756. In addition to hiring researchers, Moxham noted, there were plans
to employ a "patent office draftsman" at the laboratory, a sign that he
envisioned the new facility as being an "invention factory" like the one
Edison had founded a quarter-century earlier at Menlo Park, New Jersey.[57]

By the end of 1903 Moxham had made significant organizational strides.
He had succeeded in convincing Coleman to rename his department simply
the Development Department, and he had brought Coleman to accept a far
broader definition of "development" than had been agreed upon in the
earliest days of the Executive Committee. No longer restricted to raw materials procurement, development now meant strategic planning for economic growth. Moxham believed that the research program was an intimate
part of that process, so the Development Department remained in charge
of experimental matters.[58] He had also recruited the first permanent head
of the new research laboratory: Francis I. du Pont. Dr. T. J. Wrampelmeier,
who had been employed briefly at Eastern Laboratory, had served initially
as the acting director when the temporary laboratory first opened. But in
November 1903 he resigned to become Du Pont's European representative.[59] Soon Moxham reported that the establishment of the laboratory and
the selection of Francis as its head had led the military to applaud the
Du Pont Company's "progressive policy."[60] Francis's strategy had begun to
work even before the new laboratory was fully functioning.

Moxham shared with the Executive Committee his and Francis's musings
about how the company would account for the productivity of the laboratory's work – no small issue in the management of research in a modern
corporation. They believed that the laboratory must "be put entirely upon
its merits as a business department." In other words, the laboratory had to
yield a profit. The difficulty was in determining how to account for the
laboratory's work. Moxham and Francis proposed the following arrangement: the results of the laboratory would be comparable to patents or

inventions acquired outside the company. In other words, a fixed sum or royalty could be assigned to the value of specific laboratory results. Therefore, any work done by the laboratory would be considered as its property, and once sufficiently developed, an invention, process, or product worked out by the laboratory would be for sale to the Operative (or Manufacturing) Department. If the Operative Department wanted to adopt the results of the laboratory, it could purchase them outright or pay a royalty. Moreover, Moxham and Francis argued that should the Operative Department not elect to buy the laboratory's work, the laboratory should be free to sell such work outside the company. "In this way," believed Moxham, "the Experimental Laboratory will be placed upon a commercial basis, and [at] the end of two or three years the records will be proper measure of its utility and value. The experimental work will of necessity call for considerable sums of money per annum if properly conducted, and we will act in the dark unless we have some contra account by which the wisdom of these expenditures can be measured."[61]

Moxham's and Francis's heady optimism that the new laboratory would quickly generate a profit remained undampened when the Executive Committee held a special meeting to consider more precisely how the laboratory, or Experimental Department, would be handled in an accounting sense. Moxham considered such a meeting critical because the Experimental Department was "getting down to a working bearing." The committee heard Moxham outline a procedure for the laboratory to charge other departments for its experimental work. He sought the committee's permission to allow his department "to exact payment for all expenditures on new developments before turning such developments over to [an] operating department." Maintaining that "it might well be that at the end of the year the department would be self-sustaining," Moxham nevertheless requested from the Executive Committee a monthly appropriation to cover the Experimental Department's expenses. The committee accepted Moxham's general guidelines regarding accounting methods, including the notion of property ownership, and granted Moxham $3,000 per month for Experimental Department expenses.[62] The experimental laboratory was "upon its feet as a going concern."[63]

The Operation of the Experimental Station

The new laboratory began to function almost at once. Moxham and Francis were assisted by D. M. McDonald, whose responsibilities included "having charge of the organization and records and the method of work." Under McDonald were the "chemists, assistants, draughtsmen, etc., each receiving instructions from the director and being made responsible for the carrying out of work assigned to him. . . ." Francis noted that "as soon as the laboratory undertakes a piece of work, it is given a card and index number and filed in an index of unfinished work, with the name of the man that has been made responsible for it. Here the card remains until the formal report is made, when the date of the report is marked on the card and it is transferred to a file of finished work." He reported that his research team had been supplied with basic apparatus for chemical and physical investigations, and when the laboratory was completed, it would include "an outfit for the manufacture of instruments and appliances to be used in the development of new processes."[64]

Work at the experimental laboratory was varied. The initial list of projects included the following: routine chemical analyses; moisture analysis of wood and fiber pulp; black powder analysis; study of dynamite; improvement of smokeless powder; investigation of the French explosive "Cheddite"; investigation of the German explosive "Amanol"; trial of a new smokeless powder; development of a method of bleaching and purifying cotton; an effort to purify guncotton without so much steam; the design of a continuously working smokeless powder press; an effort to manufacture colorless smokeless powder; efforts to improve black powder manufacture; work on nonfreezing dynamite; an examination of the explosive "Dreanite"; an attempt to make briquette charcoal; development of a smokeless powder charge for blank cartridges; and construction of a hexagonal die for making smokeless powder for a twelve-inch breech-loading rifle.[65]

Such diversity must have strained the resources of the staff, which was neither large enough nor adequately qualified to manage this array of tasks. The laboratory's director fitted the mold of the lone inventor far better than that of the credentialed chemist directing a scientifically based industrial research laboratory. Francis was the son of Francis Gurney du Pont, who had managed the company's black powder works on the Brandywine for some two decades and who in the 1890s had directed Du Pont's pioneering effort in smokeless powder manufacture at Carney's Point, New Jersey. Francis had graduated from Yale's Sheffield Scientific School in 1895 and returned to the Delaware Valley to work for his father as a plant chemist. Although a major part of his duties included training technicians and other workers to perform routine tests and analyses, Francis also found time to make important improvements in smokeless powder manufacturing processes.[66] Yet for all his technical and scientific talents, Francis I. du Pont would eventually demonstrate that he was not a successful research manager. By 1907, the Executive Committee (from which Francis had resigned in 1904) could not count on regular reports, nor could it find evidence of a well-organized and well-balanced approach to research and development. In 1907, Francis would step down as director of the Experimental Station.[67]

Francis's initial staff was severely lacking in scientific credentials as compared to Reese's staff at Eastern Laboratory. (See Table 1.2 for information on the charter members of the Experimental Station staff.) Of this motley bunch, three individuals need to be highlighted. The first is Fin Sparre, who was by far the best trained and most experienced chemist among the lab-

Table 1.2. *The Experimental Station's Research Staff, 1903*

Name	Position	Qualifications	Remarks
Francis I. du Pont	Director	BS, Sheffield Scientific School, Yale University, 1895. Significant inventions in smokeless powder processes, 1895–1902.	
Daniel M. McDonald	Assistant director and office manager	"Familiar with black powder."[a] No academic degree.	Monthly salary: $100.
Charles E. Arnold	Chemist	Attended Ohio State University. Chief Chemist, Dominion Iron and Steel Co., Sydney, Cape Breton Island, Nova Scotia	Associate of A. J. Moxham at Lorain Steel Company and at Dominion Iron and Steel Co. Monthly salary: $175.
George Gentieu	Assistant chemist	"Plant man from Carney's Point" smokeless powder plant.[b] "A plumber by trade."[c]	Monthly salary: $100.

oratory's charter members. Born in Bergen, Norway, in 1879, Sparre received undergraduate training in chemistry and engineering in Oslo and did some graduate work in Dresden, Germany. He worked in the Norwegian powder and munitions plant before emigrating to the United States in 1903. Thirteen days after arriving in the United States, Sparre accepted a position of chemist at the new Experimental Laboratory. Over the next decade he would demonstrate to the highest levels of management that he possessed outstanding abilities as a chemist and a rare ability to judge areas ripe for development. In 1911 he became director of the Experimental Station and in 1919 director of the Development Department, a position he would hold until his retirement in 1944. Indeed, much of Du Pont's diversification during this period can be attributed to Sparre's work. He was also a member of Du Pont's board of directors from 1930 until his death in 1944.[68]

J. N. Wingett, known to his peers as "the Wizard," is the second individual whose charter membership is noteworthy. As the inventor of a promising system of continuous black powder manufacture, Wingett had been hired by Moxham to perfect this system. Moxham guaranteed Wingett $65,000

Table 1.2. (*cont.*)

Name	Position	Qualifications	Remarks
Fin Sparre	Chemist	Undergraduate degree in chemistry and engineering, Technical College of Oslo, Norway (Kristiania). Graduate study at Technical College of Dresden, Germany. Plant experience: Norwegian government powder and munitions plant.	Monthly salary: $100. Later became chief chemist at Experimental Station and then director. Headed Development Department from 1919 to 1944 and was central figure in Du Pont's diversification. Member, board of directors.
J. N. Wingett ("The Wizard")	Independent inventor	No academic credentials. Held patent application for a continuous process for black powder manufacture.	Monthly salary: $300. Du Pont also paid $65,000 in cash for patent application. Salary was paid while the invention was being perfected.
Hudson Maxim	Independent inventor	Academic study at Kent's Hill, Maine, academy. Coinventor of transversely perforated nitrocellulose powder.	Monthly salary/retainer: $500. Brother of Hiram Maxim, inventor of machine gun and early automobile pioneer.

*a*Charles E. Arnold, Sr., *My Remembrances of the Du Pont Experimental Station* (n.p.: n.p., 1947), p. 8.
*b*Ibid.
*c*Frank P. Gentieu, "The First Fifty Years at Carney's Point," *The Carney's Pointer* (July 1951), B-6.

in cash solely for filing his patent application, as well as a monthly salary of $300 while he worked out the bugs in his system and put his application in order. According to a contemporary, the Wizard "had to have a room garlanded with sweet smelling flowers with canary and mocking birds to entertain him while he communed with the spirits to invent."[69] More impressive was the Wizard's Spook Room, a small room painted jet black and furnished with only a small black table and two black chairs. "If you were troubled for an answer to your problem," wrote another researcher, "just have a seance with the Wizard."[70] Wizard Wingett appears to have been far more the medieval alchemist than the modern industrial chemist. Yet this man drew the second highest salary of any member of the laboratory. Another independent inventor, Hudson Maxim, received the highest salary of $500 a month.[71]

Maxim had been the principal factor in Moxham's campaign to establish a laboratory for the Development Department. As an independent inventor, Maxim provided Du Pont with the means to become a successful manufacturer of smokeless powder. He and Robert Carl Schüpphaus had patented a transversely perforated nitrocellulose powder that won the favor of the U.S. government. In October of 1898, the older group of du Ponts, including Francis Gurney du Pont, purchased the American patent rights to the Maxim-Schüpphaus powder and began manufacturing it for the army at the Carney's Point plant. The du Ponts and Maxim hammered out an amiable relationship whereby, in effect, the company paid Maxim a monthly salary of $500. Working out of both his London home and his laboratory in Landing, New Jersey, Maxim continued to make refinements to his powder and to notify the company of such improvements. But on several occasions Maxim offered Du Pont options on related inventions and developments that, contended A. J. Moxham, needed to be evaluated in a laboratory. When the new experimental lab was established, Maxim's salary was taken directly out of its salary account.[72]

Later, in January 1905, Du Pont and Maxim broadened their agreement whereby any of Maxim's developments in explosives would become the exclusive property (in the United States only) of the Du Pont Company. Once this contract was signed, the Executive Committee began making special appropriations to the Development Department for Maxim's $6000 annual salary. The Du Pont Company agreed to pay Maxim 20 percent of its net profits on sales attributable to his work up to a limit of $200,000. Thereafter, the company would pay him 10 percent of profits up to an amount of $50,000 annually. Maxim's salary accrued as part of the respective $200,000 and $50,000 limits.[73] This agreement came on the heels of Maxim's invention of a new smokeless powder with apparently far better stability than the relatively unstable nitrocellulose powders consumed by the government. For this reason, A. J. Moxham dubbed Maxim's new powder "Stabillite."

Contracts such as those with Maxim and Wingett were common in the years from 1870 to 1900. Even companies possessing noteworthy in-house technical staffs often made far greater expenditures for both the talents and products of independent inventors than for their own research programs.[74] Du Pont was no exception. What Du Pont learned with Maxim and Stabillite, however, was that even a good invention almost always demanded expensive, painstaking, labor-intensive development work to perfect both product and manufacturing process. Maxim could not command such necessary resources. Moreover, such development work required patience and diligence as well – attributes not usually possessed by a compulsive inventor such as Maxim. Hence the nascent industrial research and development laboratory, well-organized and efficiently run, would prove more often than not to be the most effective institution for bringing an idea or invention to the marketplace. Of course, some industrial R&D laboratories would provide safe harbors for a limited number of the more archetypal, compulsive inventors. But the primary attribute of the R&D laboratory in the twentieth century would be its capability of conducting organized assaults on particularly well-defined problems. The independent inventor could make no such concerted campaign; the case of Stabillite clearly demonstrates this while also illustrating the pitfalls of industrial research and development.

The Development of Stabillite

The Executive Committee was quick to push the development of Maxim's new smokeless powder. If successful, the new powder would give Du Pont an important proprietary advantage over its new competitor, the U.S. government.[75] Maxim's powder promised to be a definite improvement over pure nitrocellulose powders, not only because it seemed to be more stable than guncotton but also because its manufacture required neither the addition of a volatile solvent nor the slow drying process typical of nitrocellulose smokeless powders. Moreover, the powder appeared not to suffer from the normal shrinkage defects of nitrocellulose powders, hence the final size of the finished grain could be easily controlled. In the manufacture of Stabillite, nitrocellulose was mixed with what was known to chemists of the day as "the yellow compound" or "the yellow kid," trinitroanisole. Stabillite could then be worked like the early plastic celluloid, which meant that when heated it could be easily rolled into colloidal sheets and then slit and perforated to form grains of powder with suitable burning characteristics. The speed and flexibility with which Stabillite could be manufactured promised to revolutionize the smokeless powder business.[76]

Late in 1903, the Executive Committee granted Francis du Pont $2,000 for experimental work on Maxim's new smokeless powder.[77] Although Francis pursued research at the new experimental laboratory in 1904, most of the work was conducted at Maxim's personal laboratory at Landing, New Jersey, until the end of 1904.[78] Du Pont chemists aided Maxim. At the end of 1904, the Executive Committee instructed Moxham to secure an agreement with Maxim for the U.S. rights to his invention. Soon the committee appropriated $5,000 for more experimental work on the powder.[79] On the basis of Francis's sanguine report on Stabillite's future, the Executive Committee authorized Moxham to broaden the agreement with Maxim whereby he would also surrender his foreign rights to Stabillite for $115,000. The two parties quickly signed such a contract.[80]

Development work in Wilmington increased to a feverish pitch, and Du Pont tried to sell a large order of the experimental powder to Mexico, with whom Maxim had been negotiating prior to Du Pont's purchase of his patent application. Initial tests of Stabillite, however, led the Mexican government to conclude that "the inventor, Mr. Maxim, ha[s] not sufficiently studied the subject to develop an entirely satisfactory powder."[81] Nevertheless, the Development Department poured almost $100,000 into experimental work on Stabillite during 1906. Such intensive work appeared to pay off. After initial tests with small samples of Stabillite, the navy asked Du Pont to prepare estimates of how long it would take and how expensive it would be to erect a plant with a capacity of a million pounds per month. This inquiry and the $200,000 it had spent on Stabillite encouraged the Executive Committee to try to persuade the military to place some large orders for Stabillite for trials. Both the development of Stabillite and the negotiations with the army and the navy proceeded slowly, however. Before the company had reached a purchase agreement with the navy for 10,000 pounds of experimental powder and the army for 1,000 pounds, Du Pont had sunk another $88,000 into the product's development.[82]

Tests by the army and navy proved disappointing. After firing only proof-test rounds at its Indian Head proving ground, the navy abandoned the tests altogether. Ballistics tests by the army also showed little promise.[83] In July 1909 – about six years after the original invention – the Executive Committee issued an ultimatum to the Development Department: the powder's defects had to be remedied or the project would be abandoned. Moreover, the Executive Committee moved that the "experiments with Stabillite should not deter the Experimental Station from efforts to develop other powders."[84] By the end of 1910, all hope for making Stabillite a commercially viable product had been given up. Writing in 1910 for the Development Department, Irénée du Pont called Stabillite a technical success but a commercial failure.[85]

What were the defects of Stabillite and how did the Du Pont research staff attempt to remedy them? One of Stabillite's problems was that it was highly toxic and caused severe skin irritations to those who handled it. Even worse, Stabillite proved to be unstable. The trinitroanisole solvent reverted back to picric acid. The powder sometimes suffered from spontaneous combustion if degradation occurred under certain circumstances.[86] Maxim's haste and Du Pont's enormous respect for Maxim had resulted in serious misjudgment. Du Pont's research organization at the Experimental Station sought to rectify these problems through a variety of approaches. Perhaps the most interesting attack on the stability problem was the Experimental Station's attempts to purify the ingredients. Purifying both the trinitroanisole and the nitrocellulose resulted in "considerably reduce[d] decomposition to picric acid."[87] But because the purification methods used were mechanical refining techniques (grinding, washing, and centrifuging) rather than true chemical purification, such an approach quickly reached its limits.

Stabillite's greatest problem was its erosion – literally, the wearing away through abrasion – of the interior of both big and small guns. From

Du Pont's earliest submission of the powder to the army and navy, erosion with Stabillite far exceeded typical erosion from nitrocellulose powders. Knowing well that granulation and perforation affected not only burning characteristics (rate and pressure) but also erosion, Du Pont researchers tried to find the right granulation to minimize erosion. They also experimented with additives and various glazes in an effort to reduce erosion. A ballistics expert looking back on Stabillite in 1915 argued, as Irénée had in 1910, that by the end of 1910 erosion had been reduced to a level not appreciably higher than that of nitrocellulose powder and stability had been achieved.[88]

The earlier deficiencies detected by both the navy and the army, however, had been fatal to Stabillite. Moreover, the Du Pont Company and the Experimental Station had helped to make Stabillite obsolete through its adoption of nitrocellulose powders stabilized with diphenylamine – one of the most significant developments in the history of the smokeless powder business. The addition of diphenylamine-stabilized service powders and radical improvements in their drying times had, in essence, destroyed the extensive work done by the Experimental Station on Stabillite. This was to be merely the first important episode in which Du Pont's research would prove to be capital-destructive.[89]

The company derived some benefit, however, from its work on Stabillite, which was embodied in more than 150 research reports generated at the Experimental Station between 1904 and 1910. When some members of Congress launched a particularly virulent attack against the "powder trust" during hearings for the army and navy appropriations bills for 1911, Du Pont, the army chief of ordnance, and his counterpart in the navy pointed to these reports and the entire Stabillite project as a sure sign that Du Pont maintained a progressive research and development policy. Francis's political strategy of 1903 had been a success, despite the laboratory's failure to develop a commercially viable product.[90]

The Black Powder Continuous Process

A similar fate was in store for the Station's efforts to develop a continuous process for manufacturing black powder. When the three du Pont cousins took the reins of the Du Pont Company in 1902, two of them – Alfred I. and Pierre S. – knew the business of manufacturing black powder. Following his graduation from Massachusetts Institute of Technology, Pierre returned to the Du Pont powder yards on the Brandywine where he had played as a child. His new position proved to be discouraging to him because it mainly involved routine work (drying powder samples and determining their specific gravity). He was also supposed to suggest improvements on the basis of chemical work but found virtually every practice on the Brandywine hopelessly antiquated. Within three years, Pierre transferred to the Carney's Point smokeless powder plant, where he made a significant improvement in smokeless powder for shotguns.[91] Alfred knew the black powder business even better than Pierre. Although he studied chemistry at MIT in the early 1880s, Alfred dropped out after two years and returned to the Brandywine. He moved quickly up the Du Pont Company ranks; by 1890 he was an assistant superintendent for the Hagley and Lower Yards. He acquired one-tenth ownership of the older company, and by the time the new venture was launched in 1902, Alfred possessed an intimate knowledge of the black powder business.[92]

Soon after Coleman organized the Executive Committee, Alfred requested an appropriation of $3,000 for experimental work on a wet mixing process for black powder.[93] Alfred, who had made a number of improvements in black powder manufacture, sought to develop an idea that had been tried by a number of inventors. Black powder was made by incorporating sulfur, charcoal, and sodium nitrate. The initial process was begun by thoroughly mixing dry batches of powdered sulfur and charcoal. A batch of this mixture was then added to a specified amount of sodium nitrate in an incorporating mill; small amounts of water were added periodically while roll wheels blended the ingredients. The idea of wet mixing was to combine the ingredients in correct proportion into a slurry on a continuous basis and then to dry the slurry. Such an approach offered advantages in speed of production and, more important, in safety. But in practice inventors had been unable to prevent the sodium nitrate from crystallizing on the black powder's surface. Alfred sought a solution to this problem.

Alfred's experiments soon led to a far more ambitious development project. By the time the Executive Committee authorized Moxham to establish an experimental laboratory, the object was not only to perfect the wet mix process but also to develop a fully integrated, continuous process for black powder manufacture, which by reducing unit costs would increase Du Pont's already effective competitive advantage. Moxham probably had a hand in pushing this project, for it was he who worked out the agreement with the "inventor" of the continuous process machinery, "Wizard" J. N. Wingett.[94] While the stories recounting the Wizard's Palm Room, his Spook Room, and his means of "communing with the spirits to invent" might lead one to dismiss the whole black powder continuous process project out of hand, such a view would be mistaken. During the next seven years, the Executive Committee spent almost $200,000 on the project. Moreover, during the early days of the continuous process project, the Executive Committee continued to appropriate money for the separate development of Alfred's wet mix ideas; indeed, they pushed this project beyond the point thought prudent by Alfred himself.

The Executive Committee's actions stemmed from its strong and early commitment to the improvement of manufacturing processes. In spite of Wingett's idiosyncrasies, the committee had reason to believe that the management of the continuous process project was in good hands because it was housed in the Experimental Station.

Yet, between 1903 and 1907, the development of the project moved more slowly and was far more expensive than the Executive Committee anticipated. Numerous times, both Moxham and Francis asked the committee for additional appropriations for the project. Each time the committee approved these additional expenditures after thoroughly questioning the project leaders.[95] But in the fall of 1907, a major personnel change and the financial panic influenced the course and pace of the project. Aware that Francis du Pont had been unable to manage effectively the Station's entire experimental program, Moxham relieved Francis as director of the Station and replaced him with C. Marshall Barton. Moxham charged Barton with making the Station "a real business proposition." Francis became "technical advisor" to the Development Department, and in that capacity he continued to direct the work on the black powder continuous process.[96] Barton at first told Moxham that completion of this project was imminent, but within a month he presented a different case.[97] More – much more – money was needed to complete the design and construction of the continuous process machinery.

Through October 1907, the Executive Committee had authorized a total of $110,000 for the project, not including Wingett's salary.[98] When the treasurer signaled the Executive Committee that the financial panic had begun to affect the company's cash flow in a most serious way, the Executive Committee held a special meeting to consider curtailing the company's expenditures. Cutbacks in personnel were recommended, and the Development Department was instructed to finish the continuous process at a cost of not more than $3,000.[99] Alfred du Pont began to question the advisability of continuing the project, but the Executive Committee was unwilling to abandon it even though Moxham asked for more funds when the $3,000 was exhausted.[100]

After the panic had ended, the Executive Committee granted another large appropriation for completion of the project. But when this sum failed to yield any results, the committee took concerted action to remedy the situation.[101] First, T. Coleman du Pont determined to separate the Experimental Station from the Development Department and to place it under the supervision of the company's treasurer, Pierre du Pont. Coleman took pains to point out that under Pierre the Station would continue to "devote its energy to new processes and original research as heretofore."[102] Once Pierre assumed responsibility for the Experimental Station, he no doubt saw the necessity of a special review of the black powder continuous process. This occurred when the Executive Committee formed a special ad hoc committee consisting of Francis du Pont, Irénée du Pont (Pierre's younger brother), and Frank L. Connable (Alfred du Pont's protégé).[103]

The ad hoc committee found that, despite some problems, the continuous process was almost perfected and recommended that additional funds be granted to make necessary modifications in the machinery.[104] Expressing a different view, Alfred du Pont, who was out of the country, argued that the whole process had been engineered "to make it as lavish and as expensive as possible" and that it probably would not ever work correctly.[105] Nevertheless, for the remainder of 1908 and throughout 1909, with the support of Pierre, the Executive Committee continued to fund experimental work at a level of $2,000 per month (excluding the salaries of Wingett and Francis du Pont).[106]

By mid-1909, however, some profound realities had begun to emerge. Believing that the process had been sufficiently well developed, the Development Department initiated patent work with the aid of Wingett and the company's patent attorneys, Harding and Harding of Philadelphia. To the Development Department's surprise, the attorneys found almost all Wingett's 200 claims to be "worthless and unpatentable." With this revelation, the Development Department, now under the direction of Irénée du Pont and once again responsible for the Experimental Station, terminated the company's contract with Wingett. The results of actual tests were equally disturbing. Caking and other physical problems hindered the operation of the machine, but the major problem was the finished powder itself. It suffered from significantly low specific gravity and inferior ballistics characteristics. Moreover, inspection under a microscope revealed that the sodium nitrate had crystallized on the surface of the grains – the same problem that had taxed inventors for at least a half-century.[107]

These problems notwithstanding, the Development Department continued to support experimental work even after Wingett departed. In February 1910, Irénée du Pont (who had taken over supervision of the Station from his older brother, Pierre) requested another $14,000, which led the Executive Committee to appoint yet another ad hoc committee to assess the merits of the appropriation. Irénée and Alfred comprised this committee.[108] Their report accurately assessed the pros and cons of the matter. There had been some mechanical difficulties, but these appeared to be almost totally eliminated. The character of the product itself posed more serious drawbacks, particularly the crystallization of sodium nitrate. Given these problems, Alfred and Irénée expressed "material doubt as to the possibility" of black powder being made satisfactorily with this process, "but the possibility of overcoming the difficulties is such, and the value of the process if perfected is such that we are warranted in continuing experiments at the rate of not exceeding $1,000.00 per month which seems sufficient in view of the rate of expenditure during the past year when better progress has been made than during the average of previous years."[109]

Alfred's and Irénée's recommendations were accepted, and the full-time staff of the Experimental Station took charge of the project on November 1, 1910, pushing its development through the first quarter of 1911.[110] Their results were largely negative. In his annual report for the Experimental Station for 1911, Barton concluded that there was "considerable doubt as to any net advantage in the continuous process as at present proposed over the regular [batch] process." The Station dropped work on the overall continuous process in the spring of 1911 and devoted its efforts to the perfection of only the first step – the wet mix process – with the object of integrating it with existing batch processes for pressing, graining, glazing, and drying.[111] The continuous black powder process machinery was ordered scrapped in January 1912, and the idea was abandoned after some $200,000 (excluding salaries) had been sunk into the venture. By the end of 1911, the director of the Experimental Station had concluded that the more limited wet mix process did not give "a product in any way superior to the dry incorporation." No economies could be realized by the wet mix process, the report continued, and "there would seem to be no reason to continue the study."[112]

Was the initiation of the project and the long-continued support for it a case of misjudgment on the part of the Development Department and the Executive Committee? Certainly not, at least from the perspective of the participants, including the skeptical Alfred du Pont. The rewards for successfully developing a continuous process for black powder manufacture were enormous. Even if the project took many years and much money, Du Pont's executives believed it should be pursued until the process was proven successful or impossible. While he was responsible for the Experimental Station, Pierre du Pont articulated a policy that encompassed the continuous black powder project and served as the basic guiding philosophy for Du Pont R&D in the twentieth century:

> In our Experimental Laboratory we should at all times endeavor to have in force some investigations in which the reward of success would be very great, but which may have a correspondingly great cost of development, calling for an extended research of possibly several years, and the employment of a considerable force. I outline this policy for two reasons; first, that it will tend to build up a line of well trained men whose continuous employment will be certain. Second; and more important, the value of the Laboratory will eventually be much greater on this account.[113]

If errors of judgment were committed, they occurred in the management of this development. Moxham may have reacted too quickly in offering a contract to an obviously eccentric independent inventor rather than developing the idea completely in house. Once Wingett was employed, however, he was clearly not properly managed by Francis du Pont. The Executive Committee eventually realized this and created a niche in the corporation in which Francis could be "free to exercise his ingenuity."[114] As Alfred wrote in 1908, what the Experimental Station "needs is somebody to handle the development of these new processes and explosives with more vigor...."[115] Francis was clearly not the man Alfred had in mind, though once Francis was relieved of his duties as director of the Station and put primarily on the continuous process, he demonstrated that he could move the project along (even though he could not or would not report on his work in an acceptable manner).

The black powder project raised other issues about the management of research. Perhaps the biggest was determining when to stop. Alfred du Pont articulated this issue most clearly. He believed that the cases of Stabillite and the continuous process demonstrated that the Station had been unable to make a determination of when to stop. Not only did the Experimental Station need someone who could push projects with more vigor, it needed someone who could "decide within a reasonable length of time as to [a project's] respective merits. It takes too long as matters are at present conducted at the Experimental Laboratory to arrive at any conclusion regarding the value of any new process, or the value of any alteration made in any explosives in order to determine its success." If a project has value, Alfred maintained in black-and-white terms, "it should be determined as soon as possible; if not, further expenditures in its so-called development should be discontinued."[116]

A. J. Moxham approached the issue differently. Writing to Francis's successor, C. M. Barton, when he relieved Francis of his duties as director of the Station, Moxham stressed that "the tendency of all experimenters is to continue to work on with an experiment just as long as any improvement seems to them possible. So tempting is this tendency that sooner than give up an experiment at a time when it has already reached the stage of profit they will retain control of it... because of the very love of the study they are making.... Hence it becomes a matter of good business judgement as to when to 'put in the peg' and call an experiment finished."[117]

There was an implicit notion in Moxham's statement that a research manager should not call an experiment finished until it was ripe for commercialization – a rather different view than the one held by Alfred du Pont. And where did the continuous process project fall in this spectrum? It seems as though the Executive Committee pursued a middle ground, not far from Irénée du Pont's position. As long as a project continued to make progress, as long as there promised to be economic rewards, and as long as expenditures were not exorbitant, then it should be funded. The key to good research management was knowing when to continue pursuing the project and when to quit. Successful gamblers have been noted to possess the same sense of judgment.

Projects and Policies: The Experimental Station, 1904-1911

In the Du Pont Company's annual report for 1907, T. Coleman du Pont wrote that "during the past few years, we have been particularly active in research with the result that we are on the eve of launching several new developments of great value."[118] Without doubt, he had in mind Stabillite, the black powder continuous process, and the company's expensive, abortive effort to develop a pulp powder keg.[119] But there were other projects as well, most of which had been initiated soon after the General Experimental Laboratory was founded. Some of these projects turned out to be of great value to the company.

Although the Station's projects ranged widely, common themes are evident. Several projects stemmed from the company's desire to lower manufacturing costs through substitution of materials or chemical synthesis of natural materials. For example, during its first decade, the Station pursued two different methods of producing glycerin, the synthesis of amyl acetate, and fixation of atmospheric nitrogen. Each of these projects had a direct bearing on the company's immediate manufacturing problems.

In justifying the creation of the Experimental Station, Moxham had identified obtaining glycerin from some source other than a by-product of soap manufacture as the best example of how "original research" would yield clear economic benefits for the Du Pont Company. Glycerin was a prime ingredient in high explosives. With the growth in high explosives manufacture, glycerin costs had risen dramatically. Apparently, Eastern Laboratory was already at work on the problem; Moxham nevertheless forged ahead with two glycerin projects at the Station. The first was a synthesis project, just like Eastern Laboratory's, whereas the second was an attempt to obtain glycerin as a by-product of ethanol production by fermentation.[120] Pierre had specifically cited these glycerin explorations as examples of his policy that the Station should always be pursuing a few long-term, expensive, but potentially rewarding projects.[121] The Station supported both approaches until 1909, when the Development Department terminated the fermentation route. Nevertheless, as Irénée du Pont wrote Hamilton Barksdale in 1911, the Station continued to play the "long shots" by funding synthesis work long after Eastern Laboratory abandoned its own project.[122]

The Station found quicker success with the synthesis of amyl acetate, an important solvent for smokeless powder and nitrocellulose lacquer manufacture. Chemists developed a process for synthesizing amyl acetate, but the company did not commercialize it. Rather, the Station's work armed Du Pont's Purchasing Department with "a 'club' to obtain a better price on crude fusel oil" (i.e., unrefined amyl acetate).[123] This was only the first of many subsequent instances in which research would be used as a weapon to keep suppliers' prices in line.

The company's executives saw the Experimental Station's work on nitrogen fixation as a long-term project. Potentially it offered advantages in nitric acid production (a major ingredient in high explosives manufacture) and an opportunity to get into the agricultural fertilizer business. Not until the 1920s would Du Pont enter these areas — and then not directly through any work done by the Station. But funding a comparatively small research project on nitrogen fixation over a long period of time kept Du Pont abreast of worldwide developments in the rapidly evolving technology (see Chapter 9).

Many of the Station's projects centered on the immediate commercial needs of Du Pont's businesses, particularly in smokeless powder. While working on Stabillite, the Station played a critical role in developing tests for long-term powder stability. By 1911, the Station possessed perhaps the most extensive facilities of any organization in the world for conducting constant temperature and constant humidity tests on powders. Without these facilities, understanding and improvement of stability would have been impossible. Du Pont's rapid introduction of diphenylamine as a stabilizer in 1908 resulted from this expertise. Once the Station found its permanent home along the Brandywine opposite its first, temporary location, outstanding ballistics research became one of the hallmarks of Du Pont's research program (just as Francis du Pont had hoped). The Station also made contributions to smokeless powder manufacturing during this period.[124]

The development of the permissible explosive Nyalite was one of the most significant contributions of the Station during this period. Moxham had had research on safety explosives in mind when he advocated establishing the Experimental Station. Like glycerin synthesis, safety explosives were firmly within the scope of Eastern Laboratory's work, but the Station pursued them as well as other areas of high explosives manufacture. On the basis of some European precedents, Station chemists formulated in 1905 the nitrostarch compound named Nyalite. In 1916, the head of Du Pont's Pittsburgh sales office called Nyalite "one of the best [permissible] explosives ever produced... [which] made it easy sailing for Du Pont [sales] representatives."[125]

Although the Station met with success in developing an important permissible explosive, the financial panic of 1907 brought an end to the duplication of research efforts between Eastern Laboratory and the Experimental Station. The panic forced Barton and his superior, Pierre du Pont, to lay off seven of the Station's sixteen chemists and therefore to set priorities for research more carefully.[126] At the same time, the company established an experimental board composed of H. Fletcher Brown (a growing figure in Du Pont's smokeless powder business), Charles L. Reese, Francis I. du Pont, and C. M. Barton.[127] To the experimental board fell the task of more carefully allocating the company's research resources and settling disputes that had arisen between Eastern Laboratory and the Station. Some disputes were minor, such as the different rates charged by the two laboratories for identical analytical work. But the major ones were territorial in nature.

Since 1903, Moxham had advocated that the Station establish a model testing gallery for safety explosives. No doubt Barksdale bitterly opposed this plan, arguing that Eastern Laboratory was the rightful home for such a facility. A stalemate arose over the issue. With increasing outside pressure to develop newer and safer high explosives for mining operations, the experimental board ended the impasse in mid-1908 by giving Eastern Laboratory exclusive responsibility for the construction and operation of the expensive test tunnel. The board also ruled against the Station conducting work in areas related directly to high explosives, such as nonfreezing dynamite, continuous nitration of glycerin, and dinitroglycerin. With the board's guidance, the Station's manager focused research on "subjects connected with the study of smokeless powders and black powders."[128]

The experimental board's role grew in the period between 1908 and 1911. It began to evaluate the merits of undertaking new research projects and terminating existing ones. The board helped Reese and Barton make tough decisions about their research programs. For example, it advised Barton to terminate the glycerin-by-fermentation project in mid-1909 over the objections of his chief chemist, Fin Sparre.[129]

The establishment of the experimental board, coupled with Pierre's and Barton's much sounder management of the Station after 1907, eventually led to the Station's being moved back under the control of the Development Department, now headed by Pierre's younger brother, Irénée. In this and subsequent positions, including the company's presidency, Irénée paid careful attention to the company's research programs; he brought noteworthy chemical knowledge, judiciousness, and energy to his duties. In the brief period he was in charge of the Experimental Station, Irénée left his clear imprint. But good management aside, at the end of 1910, the Executive Committee wanted to know if its large expenditures for research work at the Experimental Station had yielded any profits.[130] After all, almost every member of the committee must have remembered A. J. Moxham's assertion at the founding of the research laboratory that it had to pay its way and his contention that it would quickly generate profits.[131]

When the Executive Committee asked for a profit and loss statement from Irénée, the Station's permanent facilities were less than six years old. Located on a site that Fin Sparre described as "allow[ing] almost unlimited extension of the work and almost unlimited constructions," the Station sported a fireproof laboratory, a rifle range, a fifteen-pound gun testing facility, and a variety of smaller support facilities.[132] Pierre had formulated an aggressive equipment acquisition policy, with funding equal to half the general operating budget.[133] Largely under Sparre's leadership as chief chemist, the Station significantly increased the quality and quantity of its research staff. The panic of 1907 had temporarily reduced the staff to nine chemists, but by 1911 Sparre had thirty-five chemists working under him, many with excellent academic credentials.[134]

Despite this impressive growth in numbers and quality, Irénée still had to decide whether research at the Experimental Station paid. His report left plenty of doubt. Stabillite, the black powder continuous process, the pulp keg, and the glycerin studies had yet to pay a cent. In fact, they had cost a king's ransom. There were a few clear-cut cases of Station projects turning a profit, but the vast majority were indeterminate from a profit and loss standpoint. Part of this, Irénée argued, resulted from an inadequate time horizon.[135] But the fact that there were no convincing concrete data that the Station had generated profits stemmed from the very nature of the Station's mission. It was handmaiden to the Development Department, subject to that department's beck and call for information on all manner of questions; it was also a kind of departmental laboratory for the Black Powder Operating Department, a business that was mature if not dying, and for the Smokeless Powder Operating Department, one that had not yet come fully into its own. Irénée might have added that a big chunk of the money sunk into research at the Station had been spent not with the aim of creating profits but of meeting federal regulations that, if not met, could be potentially catastrophic. In any case, Irénée probably knew very well that the accountant's calculations of profits generated by the Experimental Station would be dwarfed by those reported by Charles L. Reese for the Eastern Laboratory.

The Eastern Laboratory, 1904–1911

When in early 1911 Charles L. Reese submitted his report on the Eastern Laboratory's contribution to profits, he did indeed claim substantial savings through research. Taking four subjects alone – nitroglycerin manufacture, nitric acid production and use, glycerin refinement, and the low-freezing Lydol dynamite (dinitrotoluene) – Reese reported savings of $840,000 for 1908, 1909, and 1910. Total expenses of the chemical division of the High Explosives Operating Department (the Wilmington office and the Eastern Laboratory) amounted to about $338,000. As Reese concluded, "In consideration of the fact that only four of the many subjects worked upon at the Eastern Laboratory are included in the estimate of saving, it is safe to say that the Eastern Laboratory has justified its existence."[136]

The work of the Eastern Laboratory during the period 1904 to 1911 followed very closely along its initial lines. Chemists devoted their attention to process improvement (e.g., achieving higher yields, improving recovery techniques, and speeding up nitrating and separation processes), product improvement, and new product development. As Reese liked to point out, even small process improvements showed up in important ways on the accountant's sheets. For example, when glycerin supplies grew short in 1910, Reese was able to point to a long-established downward trend in the consumption of glycerin per pound of finished dynamite. Between 1905 and 1910, the consumption figure had been lowered by 20 percent.[137]

Process improvements accounted for much of this figure, but the laboratory's success in finding substitutes for glycerin in high explosives was also a factor. The search for glycerin substitutes led to entirely new classes of explosives, such as nitrohydrene powders.[138] In another instance, the laboratory sought to produce a low-freezing dynamite with a nitroglycerin base but developed a dinitrotoluene explosive, introduced commercially in 1907 as Lydol.[139]

The Eastern Laboratory's development of another important explosive, trinitrotoluene (TNT), resulted from an entirely different objective. Not only the product but also the way it was developed had important consequences for Eastern and indeed the entire Du Pont Company. The laboratory undertook the development of European-invented TNT primarily because of its potential as a military explosive for the United States.[140] Eastern's director gave the project to a young PhD chemist who had been employed by the laboratory in 1907, Charles M. A. Stine. In his first two years, Stine had already demonstrated his capability as an industrial chemist. He had helped solve the pressing problem of repeated fires in the manufacture of ammonium nitrate, and he had conducted some rather fundamental research in an effort to eliminate the leakage of nitroglycerin from dynamite cartridges. Borrowing initially from earlier German work on TNT, Stine carried out an extensive series of experiments on the nitration of toluene. These experiments ran across the research spectrum from applied to fundamental. On the fundamental side, Stine took pride in demonstrating that Beilstein's melting point for TNT was incorrect and that his own determination had become the standard. On the applied side, he worked out a three-stage nitration and refining process for TNT. Stine used TNT to demonstrate that similar development work could and should be carried out in a semiworks. Sized somewhere between a laboratory setup and a full-scale commercial plant, a semiworks provides data on the effects of scaling up a chemical process, which are critical for designing a full-scale plant and evaluating the quality of the product. This was a new concept at Eastern. Because Stine's work proved so successful, he firmly believed that a semiworks was "the only way properly to study processes of this type";[141] because he quickly moved up in the ranks of Du Pont research management, the use of semiworks became standard.

The research and development work at the Eastern Laboratory allowed the High Explosives Operating Department to change the mix of high explosives it manufactured. In the period up to 1911, the product line expanded from pure nitroglycerin dynamite to at least ten distinct types of high explosives. Eastern's work made it possible to sell specialty explosives at premium prices – one of the later hallmarks of Du Pont's business philosophy. Reese prided himself that during 1910, more than 30 percent of the dynamite sold "represented special powders which have been developed at the Eastern Laboratory."[142] In the case of what contemporaries called low- and nonfreezing dynamites, research provided the means to overcome the terrible dangers posed in handling frozen dynamite. Moreover, the Eastern Laboratory's work allowed Du Pont to meet federal regulations for permissible explosives.[143]

Though the long stalemate with the Experimental Station over which laboratory would get the mine-testing gallery for safety powders had hampered Eastern's development efforts, once the experimental board advised the Executive Committee that Eastern was the rightful location for the gallery, the laboratory moved quickly. It purchased the equipment for the testing gallery from Germany, where state regulation of explosives had earlier forced explosives manufacturers to study mine safety factors. The testing gallery allowed the laboratory to study the German Carbonite safety powders and the English Monobels. With this knowledge in hand, the laboratory formulated its own versions of both.[144] The testing gallery was the first such facility in the United States and was later copied by the Bureau of Mines, the federal agency that established whether an explosive was permissible or not.

The Eastern Laboratory's success stemmed in large part from the very nature of its mission. It was a departmental laboratory with clearly defined objectives. Yet there is more to the explanation of its unqualified success. The laboratory's research personnel played a critical role as well. Charles Reese may not have gotten along very well with his staff of chemists, but after 1906 this was no longer a problem. Hamilton Barksdale moved Reese into a higher supervisory position that year when he created the chemical division of the High Explosives Operating Department. Reese thus became the chemical director of the department. This promotion freed him from direct supervision of the Eastern Laboratory, although he was ultimately responsible for it. He continued to exercise leadership over the chemical operations of the entire department. Reese chose Arthur M. Comey as the new director of the Eastern Laboratory.[145] Under Comey's learned and meticulous management, Eastern became a spirited, high-quality research organization and a major breeding ground for an important segment of Du Pont's entire research management in the 1920s.

It is interesting that Reese chose his successor from outside rather than inside the Eastern Laboratory. He and Comey had first met in 1884 in Heidelberg, where both studied under Bunsen. Comey had pursued a far more successful academic career than Reese. He served as an instructor of chemistry at Harvard, where he organized the summer school for chemistry, and in 1899 he was appointed professor of chemistry at nearby Tufts College. Yet academic chemistry proved unsatisfactory to Comey. After four years at Tufts, he left to establish himself as a "consulting chemist" in Boston. During his early years as a consultant and analytical chemist, he assembled data for the first edition of what became a standard reference work, *A Dictionary of Chemical Solubilities: Inorganic* (1896).[146] Once he was at Eastern, Comey's reputation and his personal characteristics allowed him to recruit an impressive number of capable chemists. By 1908, he had succeeded in hiring Fletcher B. Holmes (later the first director of the Jackson Laboratory for organic chemistry research); Charles M. A. Stine (later Reese's successor as chemical director, the creator of Du Pont's well-known fundamental research program, and an Executive Committee member); Hamilton Bradshaw (later Stine's assistant chemical director); Clifford A.

Woodbury (Comey's own successor at Eastern); E. K. Gladding (later head of the nylon division of the Rayon Department and successor to Fin Sparre as director of the Development Department); and E. G. Robinson (later assistant director of the Experimental Station and eventually the general manager of the Organic Chemicals Department). These are only some of the more prominent men Comey hired; he also employed exceptionally talented chemists who would remain within the research ranks at the Eastern Laboratory.[147]

By 1911 Comey had become a seasoned manager of research and development at Eastern and an articulate spokesman for how successful research should be managed.[148] His staff included twenty-seven academically trained chemists, many with PhDs from U.S. and German universities, and an overall staff of eighty employees. These employees worked in sixty-six buildings on the fifty-acre grounds of the laboratory.[149] Certainly Comey did not radically alter the research program or philosophy established by Reese. Rather, he seems to have fine-tuned the work of the Eastern Laboratory. Overall, except for one important detail, the objectives of a departmental research laboratory so carefully laid out and forcefully argued by Hamilton Barksdale in 1904 appear to have been fully met.[150]

Barksdale had maintained that a departmental laboratory would be more productive than a central laboratory. The profit and loss reports submitted to the Executive Committee by Charles Reese and Irénée du Pont at the beginning of 1911 clearly bore out Barksdale's views. But Barksdale had also pleaded his case for the Eastern Laboratory on the basis that it would serve as a superb training facility for chemists to enter plant management. Judging from the record of early Eastern chemists entering plant management and moving on to higher responsibilities in manufacturing, Barksdale was correct. But on the debit side of the ledger, this sort of upward mobility played havoc with the research program of the laboratory. Reese had quickly detected this problem. As he later noted, "one of the functions of the [Eastern] Laboratory in the early days was to furnish men to fill positions in the works as works' chemists and Assistant Superintendents, but this plan, with the rapid growth of the Company, resulted in a constant change in the Laboratory organization, so that it was impossible to keep a force of men who were experienced in the principal lines of work for which the Laboratory was established."[151] Reese and Comey had recognized, in much the same way Pierre du Pont had, that continuity was a crucial element in the proper conduct of research. Nevertheless, in the future, many researchers would, in Comey's words, "make the laboratory a stepping stone to other positions to the manifest detriment of the laboratory."[152] This problem would be another of those perennial issues that the company would face in the decades ahead.

In spite of the laboratory being mined by the manufacturing division for its technically trained chemists, the Eastern Laboratory was successful. Its success played the paramount role in radically changing the management of the entire Du Pont Company's research program when acting president Pierre S. du Pont and the Executive Committee decided to reorganize the management of the company early in 1911.

Conclusion: Finding the Du Pont R&D Formula

In the period between 1902 and 1911, the Du Pont Company experimented with two significantly different approaches to industrial research and development. On the one hand, the company pursued a research strategy closely aligned with a manufacturing department and with well-defined, short-range commercial objectives. This decentralized, departmental research as embodied in the Eastern Laboratory quickly proved to be highly profitable for the company. On the other hand, the company supported a "general" or "central" research laboratory – the Experimental Station. Although the initial objectives of the laboratory quickly changed in response to governmental action, the Station increasingly took on long-range, high-risk research and development projects that were not closely coupled to the company's immediate manufacturing processes and problems. Executives such as Pierre du Pont consciously supported this strategy because they believed that the potential rewards for such research warranted the risks. Along with higher risks, research and development at the Station presented substantial problems of management control. Projects such as Stabillite and the continuous black powder project posed the critical question for managers and executives alike of deciding how long they would support such projects and when they should quit. No rule book existed to guide these leaders, nor does such a book exist today.

Despite the problems posed by the kind of research done at the Experimental Station, Du Pont's executives were unwilling to scrap the Station, even in bad financial times. Neither in 1904, when the first great debate over research management occurred within the Executive Committee, nor at any other point during this period did executives question their faith that the Station's research programs would benefit the company. As Francis du Pont had suggested when he called for rechartering the Station in 1903, many of the Station's contributions to the company would be intangible. In the coming years, Francis's views were borne out when the Justice Department allowed Du Pont to retain all of its smokeless powder capacity as part of the antitrust case settlement in 1913. Within the military (mainly because of work at the Station), Du Pont had earned a reputation as a leader in smokeless powder science and technology, and this clearly saved the company's business.

Full realization of these intangible benefits lay in the future, but during the period up to 1911, many of Du Pont's executives – especially Pierre du Pont and his younger brother – demonstrated that they supported long-range, high-risk, high-reward research. This approach would become a hallmark of Du Pont R&D later in the century. In spite of Pierre's faith in the work of the Experimental Station, early in 1911 he and his colleagues on the Executive Committee restructured the company's management. This reorganization, which was not initiated because of R&D management problems, nonetheless had an important bearing on the company's research programs. During the next ten years, Du Pont R&D would move increasingly away from the Eastern Laboratory model of close affiliation with and control by particular business operations and toward the tight, centrally controlled structure sought by Moxham when he first advocated the creation of the Experimental Station.

2

Reorganization and Diversification

In January 1911, acting president Pierre du Pont and the Executive Committee decided to reorganize the management of the Du Pont Company. Effective February 1, 1911, their plan called for greater centralization of the company's high-level management under the direction of a general manager. Pierre and his cousin Coleman charged Hamilton Barksdale with the responsibility for all operations of the company, including its research and development laboratories.[1] Barksdale had not only been the cocreator and defender of the Eastern Laboratory but also a critic of the general approach to research pursued by the Experimental Station. With his new responsibilities, the performance of the Station was now his problem. Given Eastern's outstanding record of return on investment, Barksdale quite naturally turned to the laboratory's founding director, Charles L. Reese, to oversee the Station's operations.[2]

Barksdale's decision set the management of Du Pont research on a course toward greater and greater centralization. Initially, Barksdale wanted Reese merely to supervise both the Eastern Laboratory and the Experimental Station but to keep the operating departments fully in control of the activities of the laboratories. Such an arrangement posed problems for Reese, however. Over the course of the next five or six years, he gradually consolidated the direction of Eastern and the Station while gaining power within the corporation as well. By 1917, Reese controlled a large, highly centralized research department and was elected to the company's board of directors.

Paradoxically, however, the trend toward greater central control over Du Pont's research function ran counter to the most significant development of the decade after 1911, the diversification of the company. As Du Pont moved into new, nonexplosives businesses – mostly through acquisition of firms or technologies – and as the size and power of Reese's Chemical Department grew, managers in the company's businesses charged that research had become less and less responsive to their commercial needs. The lessons of research organized along the lines of the Eastern Laboratory in its first decade were lost as Reese became more and more entrenched in the research model offered by the Experimental Station. Eventually, in 1921 Reese's research empire crumbled when the managers of the newly organized, autonomous industrial departments demanded that they have control over the research for their departments. With this move, the era of tightly controlled, fully centralized research management at Du Pont came to an end.

The role played by R&D in the company's diversification program changed significantly over the course of the decade. Du Pont's initial diversification strategy was based on utilizing the company's plants, know-how, and R&D capabilities in smokeless powder (i.e., nitrocellulose) technology. The goal was to find uses for Du Pont's smokeless powder plants because political developments in Washington after 1907 signaled a significant decline, if not end, to Du Pont's government business. Du Pont's R&D managers, who were extremely confident about the company's technical capabilities, advocated internal generation of these nonpowder, nitrocellulose-based businesses. But as events unfolded, the company's executives found it easier to buy small companies and then to rely on Du Pont's R&D organization to rationalize these businesses and to gain a competitive, proprietary advantage through improved products and processes.

By 1912 anti–Du Pont sentiment in Washington had eased, thus offering executives hope of maintaining a return on their smokeless powder investments. Then suddenly the outbreak of war in Europe in 1914 fueled an unprecedented expansion of Du Pont's smokeless powder plant capacity. This expansion was so great that by 1916 the company's executives concluded there was no way the company could diversify itself strictly on the basis of nitrocellulose powder assets. At roughly the same time, the executives recognized the company's political vulnerability if it did not enter the dyestuffs business. The war had cut the United States off from imported German dyestuffs and other organic chemicals, which had totally dominated U.S. markets. With Du Pont standing as the largest U.S. manufacturer of diphenylamine – a key dyestuffs intermediate – the company's executives found themselves open to charges that Du Pont was using all this diphenylamine for stabilizing the smokeless powder sold to the European belligerents rather than converting it into greatly needed dyestuffs for domestic manufacturers. Some members of the Development Department had already advocated that Du Pont enter the manufacture of organic chemicals (both in dyestuffs and pharmaceuticals), but the company did not move on this recommendation until its executives saw the futility of trying after the war to use all its smokeless powder capacity and the political danger of putting all its diphenylamine into war matériel. With these conclusions, Du Pont undertook a new strategy of diversification.

The new strategy – especially the dyestuffs component of the strategy – significantly affected Du Pont's R&D programs. Du Pont, although flush with cash, could not buy a dyestuffs business. The few small companies that existed in the United States were not for sale. To Reese and his growing staff fell the responsibility of home-growing a business. At the same time, the Development Department implemented other pieces of the new diversification strategy, which added to the Chemical Department's burdens. As the company moved toward greater diversification and as the Chemical

Department grew in size and bureaucratic rigidity, dissatisfaction over the department's abilities and responsiveness also grew. The war-induced change in strategy led eventually to a complete undermining of the top executives' confidence in the Chemical Department's ability to aid Du Pont in becoming a diversified chemicals manufacturer.

Formation of the Chemical Department

The "radical" reorganization of 1911, which resulted in the Experimental Station being placed under Reese's supervision, was not directed toward eliminating particular problems with Du Pont's research and development programs but rather at solving what Chandler and Salsbury have called "the problem of succession."[3] President T. Coleman du Pont and his younger cousin Pierre S. du Pont had grown concerned over the fact that the company's senior executives were still actively managing the manufacturing and auxiliary departments of the company. Coleman sought a way to bring younger managers up to higher levels. He wished to see senior managers focusing their attention on larger issues rather than on day-to-day operations. With Pierre's support and the Executive Committee's approval, Coleman instituted the following reorganization: Members of the Executive Committee occupying posts as department administrators resigned from their departmental positions. In their place, Coleman appointed Hamilton Barksdale as general manager, who in turn was given authority to select men to head the operating units for which he was responsible – Black Powder, High Explosives, and Smokeless Powder.[4]

As Chandler and Salsbury have pointed out, Coleman's reorganization failed completely to solve the problem of executive succession. Coleman and Pierre anticipated that Barksdale would occupy the position of general manager for only two years and that his assistant, Irénée du Pont, whom they had chosen, would succeed him. They were thus grooming Irénée to take charge of the entire company. Irénée du Pont, who had been trained in chemical engineering at the Massachusetts Institute of Technology (BS, 1897; MS, 1898), had left a general contracting business to work for his brother, Pierre, and cousins, Coleman and Alfred, when they bought the company in 1902. He served as acting treasurer in Pierre's stead when his brother took a prolonged trip to Europe in 1905 and remained as assistant treasurer until 1909, when at age thirty-three he took charge of the Development Department. With this change, the Experimental Station – in which Irénée had taken an active interest – was moved back under the direction of the Development Department. He always exhibited a keen sense in technical matters, and he later maintained that his position as Director of Development was "the most interesting job that I had with the Du Pont Company."[5]

Irénée's appointment coincided with the Congressional attack against

Du Pont in 1909. With the company indicted for – but not yet convicted of – violating the Sherman Antitrust Act, the House of Representatives amended the Naval Appropriations Bill in January to prohibit the government from purchasing powder "from any trust or combination in restraint of trade or from any corporation having a monopoly of the manufacture of gunpowder."[6] The Senate passed the House version, thus effectively precluding Du Pont's supplying powder for the Navy. The appropriations bill also provided funds for the expansion of the navy's powder factory at Indian Head, Maryland. Du Pont's Executive Committee moved swiftly to find a means of utilizing idle smokeless powder plants.[7] After considering both Charles Reese and Irénée to lead the Development Department in this task, the committee chose Irénée. As head of the Development Department and supervisor of the Experimental Station, Irénée was in a good position to carry out this complex undertaking. But the major reorganization plan of 1911 left open the question of how the diversification efforts of the Development Department would be carried out and who would be responsible for the Experimental Station.

The Development Department job – including responsibility for diversification – fell to R. R. M. Carpenter. But Carpenter would not have control over the Experimental Station. When it approved Coleman's reorganization plan, the Executive Committee failed to specify to whom the Station would report. A subcommittee consisting of Pierre, Barksdale, and Moxham subsequently determined that it would be placed under the direction of the general manager rather than the head of the Development Department.[8] The subcommittee's decision effectively separated the company's research laboratories from the Development Department's diversification efforts. Once Barksdale placed control of the Eastern Laboratory and the Experimental Station in Charles Reese's hands, diversification became more problematical, largely because Reese paid such great attention to matters of chemical control and process and product development within the context of Du Pont's existing businesses. Here is where he had been so successful at Eastern Lab. Perhaps because Barksdale anticipated some of these later problems, a brief period of uncertainty prevailed before he determined to place both the Eastern Laboratory and the Experimental Station under Reese.[9]

On the surface, it appeared that Barksdale had decided to centralize research under Reese. He confused the matter, however, by insisting that the Eastern Laboratory was still owned and controlled by the High Explosives Operating Department even though it was under the Chemical Department's direction. By implication, the same would be true of the Smokeless Powder Operating Department and the Experimental Station.[10] Reese's position was further complicated by Barksdale's giving Irénée responsibility for almost all matters relating to research. Because of his prior experience as head of the Development Department, with supervision over the Experimental Station, Irénée was by no means a passive observer of

Reese's new department. He played a critical role in maintaining the Chemical Department's involvement with the Development Department's activities (including diversification) in spite of the obvious structural deficiencies in the new organizational scheme.[11]

As chemical director, Reese's immediate concern was to gain control over his new areas of responsibility – monitoring the chemical operations of the other two manufacturing departments (Black Powder and Smokeless Powder) and supervising work at the Experimental Station. This was no mean task. The general budgets of the Eastern Laboratory, the Experimental Station, and the Chemical Department's Wilmington office totaled almost $300,000, roughly 3.7 percent of the company's earnings and 0.75 percent of its total sales (see Tables 2.1 and 2.2). The Eastern Laboratory had twenty-nine chemists on its staff of some eighty employees, and the Experimental Station employed thirty-six chemists among a total staff of about one hundred. The scale of the chemical control work assumed by the department is unclear, but the "downtown" office had nine "chemical assistants" on the salary roll to carry out such work. These assistants were aided by three chemists "in training" for work with the manufacturing departments. Indeed, these "downtown chemists" formed one of three divisions of the Chemical Department. The other two divisions, the Eastern Laboratory and the Experimental Station, also employed chemists to perform routine tests on products made by the manufacturing departments. The salary roll of the entire Chemical Department (including supervisors, chemists, and secretaries) totaled 112 persons at the end of 1911.[12]

In an effort to centralize operations, Reese sought control over information flowing into and out of his department. He instructed all department heads, Executive Committee members, and other officers of the company to submit directly to him rather than to the laboratory directors all communications about new work by or policies of the Eastern Laboratory and the Experimental Station. He also demanded that he receive copies of all routine correspondence addressed to the laboratories.[13] At the same time, Reese initiated a policy whereby research reports would be sent out by his office instead of by the laboratory directors.[14] Reese would add a cover letter to these reports – almost always repeating statements made by the laboratory directors – interpreting the significance of the particular findings.[15] For reasons that are unclear, Reese avoided attempting immediately to centralize reporting for the department as a whole. Rather than issuing monthly or semiannual reports for the whole Chemical Department, which encompassed the work of the downtown office and the research laboratories, Reese merely forwarded to the Executive Committee the individual general reports of the laboratories.[16]

Although the reorganization of 1911 resulted in a nominally centralized Chemical Department, Reese found it difficult to effect any fundamental change in the performances of the two research laboratories for which he was responsible. As for the Eastern Laboratory, he would have only wanted it to continue showing the impressive return on investment that it had previously recorded. As for the Experimental Station, however, Reese wanted it to make an acceptable "profit" by running more like Eastern. At least up to 1915, he failed at the Station. Submitting a two-year profit and loss statement to the Executive Committee in early 1913, Reese reported impressive savings generated by the Eastern Laboratory. With an annual budget of some $100,000 per year, Eastern claimed profits of about a million dollars per year (a figure that was soon hailed nationally by Arthur D. Little as evidence of the benefits of industrial research).[17] The Experimental Station was another matter. Reese could demonstrate only small savings. He found it necessary to explain to the Executive Committee why this was so.

Reese argued as Irénée had two years earlier that "by far the greater part of the work which the Station is called upon to undertake is work from which no direct saving can be expected."[18] Much of the Experimental Station's work was performed at the request of other departments of the company, often resulting in inefficient research. "Requests for experimental work," Reese wrote, "are sometimes made without due consideration being given to the relative importance of the cost of the work, and of the benefits to be expected in case of success. Moreover, it happens at times that work which we feel to be unpromising is undertaken as a concession to the faith of those who are particularly interested or who have originated the suggestion."[19] The Station, Reese maintained, should not be held accountable for poor return-on-investment showings for such research work.

Despite these problems, Reese argued that the Station brought enormous, though intangible, rewards to the Du Pont Company. These were precisely the ones anticipated a decade earlier by Francis I. du Pont. Reese said that he had maintained Francis's policy of undertaking research at the Experimental Station "with the idea of putting the Company in possession of complete and detailed information on the subject of Smokeless Powder, with the expectation that this would tend to increase the confidence of the Army and Navy in the Company and its experts." The Station's work, Reese noted, "has been conducted with marked scientific ability and painstaking accuracy, and this fact is known and fully recognized by the experts in the Army and Navy." As proof, Reese could cite the successful lobbying efforts of army and navy ordnance officers to maintain Du Pont's smokeless powder operations intact rather than to break them up in the consent decree growing out of the federal government's antitrust suit.[20] As the decree recognized, splitting up the smokeless powder business "would tend to destroy the practical and scientific co-operation now pursued between the Government and the defendant company. . . . "[21] Within months of Reese's report, World War I began, and this decision proved to be an enormous boon to the Du Pont Company. The cash generated by Du Pont's smokeless powder sales during the war would create the capital necessary for the company's ventures into other product lines, thus providing the basis for Du Pont's rise as a giant, diversified company.

Table 2.1. *Chemical Department R&D Expenditures, 1911–21 (in thousands of dollars)*

	1911	1912	1913	1914	1915	1916	1917	1918	1919	1920	1921
Total	309	327	322	250	460	639	1,305	2,748	3,447	3,084	1,734
Wilmington office	98	87	86	65	78	107	181	318	570	528	298
Experimental Station	108	135	122	81	270ᵃ	367	627	871	951	741	269
Eastern Laboratory	110	104	114	104	110	164	404	847	575	379	230
Jackson Laboratory							23	594	1,137	1,168	558
Delta Laboratory							70	119	213	174	129
Redpath Laboratory										93	94
Cellulose Products Laboratory										261	144

ᵃMost of this increase resulted from work done for the operating departments. The Experimental Station's appropriation for 1915 was only $105,000.

Sources: 1911–12: Charles L. Reese, "Statement of the Chemical Department including the Eastern Laboratory and the Experimental Station," May 29, 1913. 1913–14: Charles L. Reese, "Report of Expenditures and Accomplishments of the Chemical Department during the Years, 1912, 1913, 1914, and 1915," Apr. 5, 1916. 1915–18: Charles L. Reese, "Report of Expenditures and Accomplishments of the Chemical Department During the Years 1916, 1917, and 1918," Sept. 9, 1919. 1919: William Coyne to Irénée du Pont, "Chemical Department 1921 Appropriation," Nov. 29, 1920. 1920: William M. Whitten, Jr., to Charles L.Reese, "Semi-Annual Report of the Chemical Department, July-December, 1920, Inclusive," March 31, 1921. 1921: C. M. A. Stine to Treasurer, Aug. 10, 1927.

Table 2.2. *R&D Expenditures in Relation to Du Pont's Sales and Earnings, 1911–21*

	1911	1912	1913	1914	1915	1916	1917	1918	1919	1920	1921
Gross receipts ($ millions)	33.4	36.5	26.7	25.2	131.1	318.8	269.8	329.1	105.4	94.0	55.3
Net earnings ($ millions)	6.5	6.9	5.3	5.6	57.8	82.1	49.3	43.1	17.7	14.6	5.8
Surplus carried forward ($ millions)	1.5	2.0	1.4	1.8	1.4	19.6	15.6	24.1	3.4	(1.7)[a]	(3.6)[a]
Accumulated surplus ($ millions)	16.7	18.6	5.7	7.5	9.0	28.6	44.2	68.3	71.4	69.7	66.1
Total research expenditures ($ thousands)	309	327	322	250	460	639	1,305	2,748	3,447	3,048	1,734
Total research expenditures (% of sales)	0.93	0.90	1.2	1.0	0.35	0.20	0.48	0.84	3.3	3.3	3.1
Total research expenditures (% of earnings)	4.8	5.1	6.1	4.5	0.80	0.77	2.8	6.4	19.5	21.2	29.9

[a]Figures in parentheses are negative.

Sources: Financial data from annual reports. Research expenditures from Chemical Department R&D expenditures, 1911–21.

The Eastern Laboratory's million-dollar annual "profit" stemmed from the tightly focused research that had prevailed since 1902. Chemical control work was the centerpiece of Reese's approach to industrial research. As Fin Sparre, director of the Experimental Station, remarked somewhat contemptuously, "It is clear that the quickest way of achieving financial returns in research work are in connection with the study of existing factory problems, particularly such as show inferior yields."[22] Certainly that was the major path pursued by Eastern. It continued to focus on questions relating to chemical control in the manufacture of high explosives and to the improvement of manufacturing processes. But the laboratory also succeeded in product improvement and the development of new high explosives.[23]

The Experimental Station, conversely, could point to few unambiguous instances of financially successful research and development work. Sparre wrote that although the Station was responsible for chemical control work for the Black Powder Operating Department, "there are no problems of chem-yields, the only research work being in connection with the quality of the powder." Smokeless powder manufacture was different, but as Sparre noted, chemical control work resided "with the management of the Smokeless Powder Operating Department or with the Main Office of the Chemical Department," not with the Experimental Station.[24]

Reese and Sparre sought to make the Station the smokeless powder equivalent of the Eastern Laboratory. Product improvement presented few problems, but process research proved difficult, if not impossible. The Station had never been fully equipped to carry out process research in smokeless powder production. In particular, it lacked semiworks apparatus for the nitration of cotton fiber. With Reese's support, the Station sought to rectify this deficiency, but the head of the Smokeless Powder Operating Department thought that handling the mixed acids used in the nitration process posed too many hazards to the Brandywine River, Wilmington's main source of water.[25] Reese and Sparre sought to compromise by building and operating a semiworks at Du Pont's Carney's Point smokeless powder plant – an approach reminiscent of the Eastern Laboratory. But the experimental board (of which Reese and Sparre were members) vetoed the idea, arguing that Station chemists could carry out process improvements based on experimental work conducted by the Smokeless Powder Operating Department at its manufacturing plants. Sparre assigned a Station chemist to assemble plant-generated data.[26] By the time this work was complete, war had broken out in Europe, and Du Pont's task became not radical process improvement but rapid expansion of capacity. As Sparre wrote Reese, "there would be little, if any, opportunity for experimental work for some . . . time to come."[27] Commenting later on the Station's deficiencies in process improvement, another research manager said, "better work could have been done and stronger men developed if this research laboratory had been located at Carney's Point."[28] Hamilton Barksdale's position of 1904 had proven correct. Nevertheless, the Station had been engaged in important work, and this centered on diversifying the company's business.

Early Diversification Efforts

The debate over whether the Experimental Station should have a complete smokeless powder semiworks points up the inherent conflict in the Station's charter. On the one hand, it was to serve for the black and smokeless powder businesses a role comparable to the Eastern Laboratory's for the high explosives business. But on the other hand, it was to serve as the company's center for more radical innovation – innovation not immediately tied to the company's existing businesses. As Sparre recognized when he submitted the Station's two-year profit and loss statement, a return on investment was far easier to achieve with the former approach than with the latter. Innovation – broadening the company's scientific and technological basis – captured the greater part of Sparre's attention both as chief chemist and, after Barton's transfer to another position in Du Pont, as director of the Experimental Station. Du Pont's early diversification efforts – stimulated by attacks on "the Powder Trust" – turned Sparre's attention to this endeavor. Research work aimed at diversification would not necessarily pay immediate dividends. In fact, Sparre later argued, the odds were overwhelmingly against any particular project succeeding.[29]

Du Pont's Executive Committee moved rapidly to initiate a broad-based research program on nitrocellulose after the Naval Appropriations Bill was passed in January 1909. Their aim was to find ways to use the company's smokeless powder plants to manufacture other products. For this reason, the committee selected Irénée du Pont to replace the ailing William B. Dwinnell as manager of the Development Department and put the Station back under his control. Irénée's duties included developing new articles and new processes of manufacture and securing supplies of raw materials. The department, anticipating Congress's hostility, had already begun to gather information on the manufacture of artificial silk, artificial leather, and celluloid when Irénée took the helm. Although these three products were attractive because Du Pont could conceivably use some of its smokeless powder plants for their production, the question remained whether Du Pont could make a profit in these businesses.[30]

In the case of artificial leather, Irénée believed Du Pont should proceed immediately to build a plant. Irénée submitted to the Executive Committee an appropriation request to cover design costs on the same day the committee reviewed the Development Department's progress report on alternative uses for guncotton and other products of the company's smokeless powder plants. Though eager to find ways to guard against owning idle plants, the Executive Committee rejected Irénée's request and asked him to prepare a full report on artificial leather manufacture, including prospects for its development and growth vis-à-vis natural leather.[31]

In subsequent discussions with the committee, Irénée focused attention on one particular point: No one had manufactured a high quality, premium-priced product, which the market seemed ready to accept. Irénée thought that Du Pont's superior know-how and its nitrocellulose capacity would combine to allow the company to produce much-higher quality material with a greatly enhanced profit margin.[32] The Executive Committee, influenced by Irénée's thinking about artificial leather and other such products, worked toward a diversification strategy of developing premium-quality products that would command premium prices. Du Pont's R&D capabilities would make this strategy attainable. Although some members were opposed, the Executive Committee granted the Development Department funds for the further study of artificial leather. Soon it would fund an experimental plant for the manufacture of this new product at one of the smokeless powder plants that the company was closing.[33] The committee also asked Irénée to look further into the manufacture of artificial silk.

The Development Department's intense interest in nitrocellulose for non-powder applications soon began to penetrate the research program of the Experimental Station. In late May 1909, Sparre outlined for Barton an ambitious program of research on nitrocellulose. Although Sparre's program would greatly benefit the company's smokeless powder business, it was also consciously designed to generate the knowledge Du Pont needed to diversify its product line based on nitrocellulose chemistry and technology. As Sparre wrote, "this company should be thoroughly conversant with [nitrocellulose chemistry] . . . so as to be prepared to the greatest extent to enter business[es] other than the present manufacturing of powder. . . . "[34]

Barton sent copies of Sparre's letter to members of the experimental board asking them to review it so as to avoid "undesirable duplication of work on this subject at the various laboratories."[35] The board found no objection to Sparre's plan. Irénée also approved it but encouraged Barton to submit the proposal to J. A. Haskell, head of the Smokeless Powder Operating Department.[36]

Although generally in favor of the Station's proposal, Haskell raised an important question. He wondered if "someone from your laboratory should be sent to the other side [i.e., to Europe] to look into and make a careful report as a starter of the investigations made in England and on the Continent." As Haskell explained, on his trip to Europe in 1908 H. Fletcher Brown had observed "that at each of the large Nobel plants one research laboratory was kept practically exclusively for guncotton [i.e., nitrocellulose] work."[37] Haskell believed that the Station could gain access to this research under the terms of the 1907 agreement between Du Pont and the Nobel–Dynamite Trust Company, Limited (the European explosives cartel with which Du Pont had been contractually aligned since 1897).[38]

Some members of the experimental board were skeptical that Du Pont could obtain broad information on nitrocellulose, but Haskell argued that Du Pont should at least try to secure the European research reports. As Haskell reminded Barton, such reports might "not be absolutely conclusive," but if used by Du Pont chemists in conjunction with a tour of European factories and laboratories and with research at the Station, they could save the company time and money.[39]

The experimental board cautiously attempted to secure information from the British by asking one of Du Pont's representatives touring Nobel facilities to confer with "the Gun Cotton research laboratory at Ardeer, and ascertain what work has been done at Ardeer along these lines, and ask for copies of any reports to their investigations, so that we may not go over the same grounds."[40] The British obliged. Soon Irénée du Pont, C. M. Barton, and Fin Sparre began planning for Sparre to take an extended tour of Nobel facilities to study principally nitrocellulose-related topics, including artificial silk and celluloid.[41]

Sparre spent much of the fall of 1909 in Europe, and his trip played an important role in his rise as one of Du Pont's chief diversification strategists. He codified his findings in twenty-one formal reports and dozens of personal letters to Barton, which soon began to shape the Station's research program and the company's diversification strategy.[42] If there was a common theme to Sparre's findings, it was that the research force at the Experimental Station was capable of carrying out a major diversification program based on nitrocellulose chemistry and technology.

Much of Sparre's attention was focused on artificial silk. He concluded, "My impression is that artificial silk is a good thing and that we could manufacture it easily. However, it would be a pretty bad thing to develop ourselves, because there are so many fine points about the machinery and I presume also about the process itself."[43] Henry de Mosenthal, chief executive of the English Nobel trust and an accomplished chemist, sought to convince Sparre that the business "could not be run in connection with powder factories." The British had tried it and "had found that out too late." But Sparre remained convinced that Du Pont's "knowledge of nitration, acids, ether, alcohol, etc. must be valuable also for this industry, and if we buy rights and experience, we can do it as well as other people." De Mosenthal also argued that in the future viscose silk would be the cheapest process and would undermine the profitability of nitrocellulose silk – a point Sparre found hard to accept.[44]

Sparre had also considered the manufacture of celluloid. His discussions with German experts from the Vereinigte-Köln-Pulver-Fabriken, part of the Nobel group, confirmed his earlier views. He had been advocating that Du Pont should not integrate fully in celluloid but should only sell nitrocellulose to U.S. celluloid factories thus utilizing excess smokeless powder plant capacity. The Germans thought this approach best for Du Pont.[45] The

Experimental Station would still have to do basic studies on the chemical stability of, nitration processes for, and purification of nitrocellulose. These studies would be a major part of the Station's research program for 1910.[46]

Irénée du Pont fully supported the Station's program even though much of the immediate pressure to find alternative uses for Du Pont nitrocellulose was off. The federal government had recently submitted large orders for powder, and there was a "decreased likelihood" of Congress banning the army and navy from ordering Du Pont powder.[47]

Nevertheless, the earlier pressure to find outlets for nitrocellulose had already propelled the company into the artificial leather business. In September 1909, Irénée had received funds from the Executive Committee to build an experimental artificial leather plant at the company's Oakland, New Jersey, smokeless powder plant.[48] Within six months chemists and engineers from the Station had achieved the premium grade product Irénée sought by using an advanced process they thought was unique. The key to this process was solvent recovery, which Du Pont had brought to a fine art in its smokeless powder plants. Irénée believed Du Pont could gain market leadership in artificial leather with this technology.[49]

Irénée's confidence was soon shattered. Word got out that the Fabrikoid Company, the U.S. pioneer in artificial leather, had had a fire in its solvent recovery area. Development Department personnel concluded – quite erroneously – that if Fabrikoid had developed its own solvent recovery process, the rest of its process must have also been as advanced as Du Pont's. Irénée convinced the Executive Committee (with a dissenting vote from Alfred du Pont) to buy Fabrikoid for $1.2 million.[50]

Once the contract to buy Fabrikoid had been signed, the Development Department learned that it had bought a pig in a poke. At Irénée's request, Fin Sparre spent two days in Newburgh, New York, carefully going over Fabrikoid's processes. His report to C. M. Barton was a tale of backward, inefficient, and often dangerous processes and included a long list of areas in which research at the Experimental Station could lead to substantial process and product improvements. Sparre made it clear that science had had no place in the Fabrikoid works.[51]

Sparre pinpointed one major problem with Fabrikoid's operations – the use of inferior solvents. But it took Du Pont executives several months to realize the full extent of this problem. Not long before Du Pont bought the Fabrikoid plant, its owners had substituted cheap "acetone oil" and "P2" solvents for the more expensive amyl acetate. The products made after this substitution were inferior and resulted in "a profound distrust of [Fabrikoid] on the part of its entire clientele," a response that became apparent only after Du Pont's acquisition.[52] Two years passed before Du Pont could straighten out the Newburgh factory and repair the damage done to the Fabrikoid name in the marketplace.

Under Sparre's leadership, first as chief chemist and after 1911 as director, the Experimental Station contributed to making Du Pont Fabrikoid a successful enterprise yielding healthy profits until the post–World War I recession.[53] In February 1911, the Station issued its first formal research report on Fabrikoid topics, and by the end of the decade the number of reports had grown to fifty-eight. The bulk of these reports involved product and process research, but the Station also conducted basic studies of importance to the Fabrikoid business under the rubric of "nitrocellulose research."[54]

Irénée's active interest in Fabrikoid never waned as he moved up the company ranks toward the presidency. His older brother, Pierre, also closely followed the business, primarily because he saw enormous potential for better grades of artificial leather in the automobile industry. Indeed, as the automobile industry grew in the 1910s, so grew Fabrikoid's business.[55] Irénée's and Pierre's close watch over Du Pont's artificial leather business suggests how they viewed research and how Irénée regarded Charles L. Reese as a research director.

Both du Pont brothers recognized that Fabrikoid artificial leather was decidedly inferior to genuine leather – even after Du Pont had straightened things out at Newburgh. They proposed that a research program be undertaken "to produce a grade of Fabrikoid which would measure up with the best quality of leather."[56] The principal defects of artificial leather were unequal stretching (the nitrocellulose coating was laid on a woven cloth backing and hence stretched too much along the diagonal of the cloth), "clothiness" (rapid wear of the coating at folds and corners thus exposing the backing), and poor resistance to the weather (a major drawback, because Du Pont intended artificial leather for automobile tops and upholstery).

After February 1, 1911, all Fabrikoid research came under the direction of Reese and the newly established Chemical Department. Reese proved unenthusiastic about the development of artificial leather.[57] Meanwhile, Irénée (particularly after he became chairman of the Executive Committee in 1915) pushed Reese by providing him with many concrete suggestions on how improvements might be made in artificial leather. These ranged from using a felt backing rather than woven cloth to doing fundamental studies of genuine leather to developing an artificial leather entirely different from the conventional nitrocellulose and castor oil film spread on a cloth backing.[58] Irénée forcefully reminded Reese that the "possibilities for a successful product of this character are so great that we should give the study energetic attention." As chairman of the Executive Committee, Irénée asked Reese, "Won't you please advise me in detail of what you propose to do and who you propose putting on this work[?]"[59] At the same time, Frank Kniffen, head of the Du Pont Fabrikoid Company, the subsidiary in charge of Fabrikoid operations, also prodded Reese and told him that "we are anxious to be the pioneers" in developing nonnitrocellulose artificial leather. Kniffen stressed that ultimately Du Pont should aim for the development of a commercially viable artificial shoe leather.[60]

Reese eventually responded to these pressures. Charles E. Arnold of the Experimental Station was put in charge of Fabrikoid research after the first

chemist, Walter E. Masland, resigned from the company. Arnold first conducted a thorough literature survey of how artificial leather had been made
and how it might be made. This search yielded more than eighty approaches
that put Reese somewhat at a loss on how to proceed. Reese conveyed his
feelings to Irénée when he sent him Arnold's report.[61] Irénée had no such
problem. He wrote Reese that "it would seem that others have worked in
a more or less random way" and that Du Pont would do better if it approached the subject more rationally. He suggested which lines of research
the Experimental Station should pursue and why.[62]

During the next four years, Arnold and his staff of researchers at the
Station pursued the kind of research recommended by Irénée.[63] Although
this research failed to yield an artificial leather that matched the quality of
genuine leather, definite improvements were made. In September 1916,
Pierre du Pont took time to congratulate the Experimental Station on these
improvements, which included embossing the coating to imitate a wide
variety of leathers.[64]

When wartime circumstances led to increased use of rubber soles in boots
and shoes, Du Pont's Fabrikoid executives concluded that the Chemical
Department could develop a satisfactory artificial leather for shoe uppers.[65]
Researchers worked hard to achieve this goal and even went so far as to
do product testing by outfitting some forty mail carriers in Wilmington with
shoes made from the Station's most promising grade of artificial leather.
Encouraged by the results, they arranged for a local shoe store to sell 150
pairs of artificial leather shoes. Their appearance was good, they wore well
for inexpensive shoes, and they were waterproof. But they also lacked ventilation, their coating was too soft, and they cracked from frequent
bending.[66]

Despite Irénée's and Pierre's hopes, Du Pont research and development
failed to produce an artificial leather satisfactory for boots and shoes. Nevertheless, Du Pont know-how clearly aided the development of the Fabrikoid
business. Under Du Pont's management, the Fabrikoid business improved
its return on investment from 0.5 percent in 1911 to 20 percent in 1919 –
the figure that Irénée had projected when, as head of the Development
Department, he purchased the Fabrikoid Company. Profits had averaged
about 15 percent during this period.[67]

Although pressure to diversify abated when the company began receiving
increased government orders for smokeless powder late in 1909, the Development Department and its Experimental Station continued to follow
closely developments in artificial silk and celluloid manufacture.[68] After
making an initial survey of the celluloid business, the Development Department concluded that its best strategy would be to sell its nitrocellulose
to existing celluloid companies rather than getting into the messy business
of celluloid fabrication. Sparre shaped the Experimental Station's research
program to accord with this strategy. At the same time, however, he undertook a program at the Station to see if Du Pont could secure a competitive

advantage in celluloid manufacture. Seeing celluloid's expensive plasticizer, camphor, as a target of opportunity, Sparre proposed looking at camphor substitutes, especially acetaldol, in which he had long been interested. By the time the Station had obtained some initial encouraging results, the Chemical Department had taken control of the Station. Sparre reported these findings to Reese and counseled him to send them to Irénée because of the latter's great interest in the subject.[69]

Reese followed Sparre's advice. Although he suggested that follow-up work would be done, Reese warned that the Germans had recently developed a substitute for camphor that seemed so good that they began marketing the new celluloid immediately. All signs pointed toward success, Reese noted, until winter came and the celluloid "developed a degree of brittleness which made it unfit for use." He feared that Sparre's acetaldol substitute might exhibit the same tendency.[70]

Encouraged by Irénée, Sparre proceeded with a more rigorous study. By 1913, the Station had made significant progress and had succeeded in fabricating good transparent sheets of celluloid with acetaldol as the plasticizer.[71] The Station's work provided Du Pont with the bargaining chip it needed to secure more extensive information about the celluloid business from the Germans. Du Pont had found it impossible to gain the information from U.S. celluloid manufacturers. If Du Pont were to go into the celluloid business, it would need far more information than it currently possessed. Pierre du Pont and the development director, R. R. M. Carpenter, achieved an agreement with the Germans to allow Walter S. Carpenter, R. R. M.'s assistant and younger brother, to make a thorough study of the Germans' celluloid-manufacturing operations and business.[72]

Walter Carpenter had left Cornell University in 1909 during his senior year to help manage Du Pont's nitrate interests in Chile. On his return to the United States in 1911, he became R. R. M.'s assistant when the latter was named director of development. The younger Carpenter took responsibility for the Development Department's celluloid study during the second half of 1913 and throughout 1914. Following his detailed analysis of the German business, in February 1914 Carpenter issued a comprehensive report on Du Pont's options for entering the celluloid business.[73] This report demonstrates Carpenter's penchant for details, clarity of thought, and superior strategic thinking – characteristics that would lead him eventually to the presidency of the company.

Carpenter laid out four means by which Du Pont could enter the celluloid industry. First, repeating Irénée's and Sparre's earlier statements, Du Pont's interests would best be served if it could simply sell nitrocellulose to celluloid manufacturers. But he doubted if this were possible, because celluloid makers already produced their own nitrocellulose. Second, Du Pont could pursue an alternative strategy of trying to get celluloid manufacturers, faced with expanding their business, to buy Du Pont's nitrocellulose rather than add capacity of their own. Carpenter also saw this as unrealistic. Third, Du Pont could enter the business from scratch, relying on its R&D capabilities. Fourth, the acquisition of an existing firm would bring Du Pont into the business, but this option would largely negate the still-perceived need of employing the company's nitrocellulose plants.

Not long after Walter Carpenter submitted his report, his older brother proposed to the Executive Committee that Du Pont purchase the Fiberloid Company's celluloid business for $1.5 million. The committee rejected the proposal. Instead, it suggested that the Development and Chemical departments pursue the internal-generation route.[74]

By the fall of 1914, all factors pointed toward Du Pont's entering the celluloid business through its own research and development efforts. Sparre and the Experimental Station had continued to pursue camphor substitution and had developed an excellent celluloid using a plasticizer of 50 percent camphor and 50 percent acetaldol.[75] The Station also pursued substituting cheap short-staple cotton for the more expensive tissue paper as the basis of celluloid. The company, unable to convince American companies to buy Du Pont's nitrocellulose, had hired an expert in celluloid manufacture who had worked for both the Fiberloid and the Viscoloid companies.[76] Sparre and the Carpenters believed that Du Pont possessed all the necessary resources to penetrate the celluloid business in a big way. In seeking funds from the Executive Committee to build an experimental celluloid plant at the Experimental Station, the Development Department argued that

> a celluloid plant [built and] operated by the du Pont Company will not be without its own advantages.... Among these advantages may be mentioned probably cheaper source of part of the raw materials manufactured by the du Pont Company, such as acids and alcohols, more efficient method of nitro-cellulose manufacture which should result in cheaper cost of production, probably greater knowledge of cellulose, which many result in a cheaper substitute of the expensive tissue paper now nitrated by celluloid companies, and advantage of a large sales force to press a more active campaign than is now customary in the celluloid business.[77]

The Executive Committee concurred and granted the appropriation for the semiworks.[78]

The Experimental Station moved quickly. But before it could issue a single report on the operation of the semiworks, the Executive Committee had done an about-face. This change resulted not from a reversal in thinking among Executive Committee members but rather from a complete reshuffling of the committee's membership following the second reorganization of the company in 1914. As R. R. M. Carpenter pointed out to the new committee, the former committee had rejected a proposition to buy into the celluloid industry, "believing that it was better to build a plant at one of our smokeless powder plants." But the new, younger committee opted to buy into the business, especially after Pierre du Pont, the influential acting president, let it be known that he favored this approach.[79]

Before proceeding to buy a firm, the Executive Committee gave the Experimental Station about nine months to demonstrate that cheap, short-staple cotton could be used to make celluloid.[80] When in September 1915 the Station had failed, the Executive Committee voted to purchase the largest manufacturer of celluloid in the United States, the Arlington Company of Arlington, New Jersey, for $8 million. This sum represented the second most expensive acquisition by Du Pont in the period up to 1924.[81] In reporting the Arlington acquisition to the board of directors, the Executive Committee stated that the company would enlarge Arlington's present profits through Du Pont know-how – the same know-how that the Development Department and the Executive Committee had earlier championed when advocating building rather than buying a business.[82]

But in spite of Du Pont's assumed expertise in nitrocellulose chemistry, the Arlington purchase proved to be a poor investment by the company's own standards. Between 1916 and 1920, the average return on investment was only 4.3 percent – far below the company's goal of 15 percent.[83] Du Pont research failed to contribute markedly to the celluloid business, even though the Chemical Department, seeking to emulate Reese's success with the Eastern Laboratory in high explosives, established a research and development laboratory there in 1917 – the Delta Laboratory – and placed one of its leading organic chemists in charge. The Delta Laboratory was initially devoted exclusively to process and product research, but eventually Reese turned over to the laboratory responsibility for chemical control of the Arlington plant.[84]

The Experimental Station took another major tack to secure a cost advantage for the Arlington works. It tried to develop a commercially viable process for synthesizing camphor. The Station's work, based on a purchased patent, resulted in the erection of a small commercial camphor plant. In the context of World War I, with camphor prices rapidly rising, the plant was successful. But as soon as the war ended, the plant became a commercial disaster. Only later in 1933 did Du Pont build a successful, 4.5-million-pound synthetic camphor plant utilizing entirely different chemistry.[85]

Du Pont's acquisition of the Arlington Company was its last major play in trying to realize the company's initial diversification strategy – a strategy based on using the company's nitrocellulose plants and its R&D capabilities in nitrocellulose chemistry. At the time of the Arlington purchase, the war was already pushing the company toward a major overhaul of its diversification strategy. By 1916, aided greatly by Fin Sparre, the Development Department had formulated an entirely different strategy. This approach would lead Du Pont into new areas of business and would greatly strain Reese's Chemical Department.

The Experimental Station had played a significant role in Du Pont's initial diversification efforts. Particularly in the first years after the reorganization of 1911 when he had not fully consolidated power over Sparre and the Station, Reese had been something of a bystander in the matter of diversification. But two corporate reorganizations of 1914 allowed Reese to centralize fully the management of Du Pont's entire research program and brought him to a more critical position in the diversification of the company.

The Reorganizations of 1914

In January 1914, at Pierre's urging, Coleman du Pont returned to Wilmington to reassume his duties as full-time president of the company (Pierre had been serving as acting president on and off since 1909 while Coleman recovered from a severe stomach ailment and while he managed the construction of New York's famous Equitable Building). Coleman's resumption of the presidency coincided with his and Pierre's full realization that Hamilton Barksdale was not willing to turn over the job of general manager to the young Irénée. This precipitated a short-lived reorganization, effective March 1, 1914, that abolished the general manager's position and created eight vice presidents who reported to the president. As a vice president, Barksdale continued to be in charge of the Manufacturing; Chemical; Engineering; and Light, Heat, and Power departments. Therefore, during this brief period, Reese reported to Barksdale without having to go through Irénée du Pont. Irénée assumed responsibility for the Purchasing, Nitrates, and Development departments.

Barksdale bridled at Coleman's reorganization, and during the next few months he, Arthur J. Moxham, and William du Pont (son of an earlier, powerful Du Pont Company president and a major stockholder living in Orange, Virginia) became sore points between Coleman and Pierre. By August 1914, Coleman offered to sell Pierre all his Du Pont Company stock. After several exchanges between the two cousins, they reached an accord they thought would solve the executive managerial problems of the company, particularly the question of executive succession. Although this new arrangement set off bitter family battles, it prepared the company for the challenge and opportunities presented by the larger, bloody war in Europe.[86]

Effective September 19, 1914, Irénée du Pont became chairman of an entirely new, younger Executive Committee, which was given "full power in the control of the Company's affairs."[87] All the seasoned incumbents gave up their administrative and executive duties. Although Coleman (whose severe stomach problems would soon return) retained the title of president and Pierre assumed the position of acting president, both stepped down from the Executive Committee and gave up their attendant responsibilities. They continued to serve on the Finance Committee, however, which now reported directly to the board of directors.

The reorganization of September 1914 affected the Chemical Department in one important respect: The chemical director now reported directly to the chairman of the Executive Committee.[88] Evidence suggests that Irénée would have liked to replace Reese with Sparre as chemical director. When asked by Coleman to suggest ideas for reorganizing the company a month prior to the second shuffle of 1914, Irénée gave Reese poor marks as a research director. "So far as chemical control of our manufacturing operation is concerned, this Department is satisfactory," wrote Irénée. But, he continued, "I have misgivings for the progress of research work under Reese, as I do not think he is a deep thinker on research matters; his chemical knowledge is not as broad as another available man [Fin Sparre] and his mechanical knowledge is meagre."[89] Irénée evidently lacked the power to replace Reese. The votes were not there. But Irénée never changed his mind about Reese's deficiencies as a research director, even though Pierre arranged Reese's election to the board of directors in 1917.[90]

Irénée nevertheless made the best of the situation, as did Reese. As general manager, Barksdale had continued to advocate preserving as much of the Eastern Laboratory model of organization as possible. But under Irénée, who favored a strong central research organization, Reese was quickly able to consolidate power. Soon he was issuing a single annual report for the Chemical Department rather than passing on the reports of the respective laboratory directors.

Not long after the war in Europe began seriously to affect Du Pont's diversification strategy, Irénée secured the services of Sparre for the Development Department. It would be Sparre who, working under R. R. M. and Walter S. Carpenter, would formulate Du Pont's new strategy of diversification, while Irénée exercised leverage over Reese. Irénée saw research as critical to the company's development strategy. During his tenure as chairman of the Executive Committee and later president of the company, Irénée insisted, as he had said earlier, that "research work should be continued and on even a larger scale."

The situation created in Du Pont by the war would add new meaning to Irénée's words, for within a four-year period, Du Pont's R&D expenditures would grow sevenfold. During this period, however, as research became more tightly centralized, the company's diversification strategy was pushing Du Pont's organizational structure to its limits. Reese would struggle to maintain a powerful Chemical Department, but eventually that centralized structure would give way.

3

World War I and the Venture into Dyestuffs

World War I stands as one of the great watersheds in the Du Pont Company's history. Just at the moment executives were considering consolidating all the company's shrinking smokeless powder production into a single factory, war broke out in Europe. Du Pont's smokeless powder sales had fallen to a mere 8 percent of the company's total sales in mid-1914, a period of economic recession. The recession continued in the United States in 1915, but the European belligerents' demand for military powder quickly brought unprecedented sales and profits for Du Pont. From sales and earnings in 1914 of $25.2 million and $5.6 million, respectively, Du Pont's business soared in 1915 to $131.1 million in sales and $57.4 million in net earnings (a figure that included amortization of new plant capacity). The following year sales reached $318.9 million and earnings $82.1 million. As Chandler and Salsbury point out, "In the single year 1916, the company's gross receipts and net earnings both exceeded the combined totals for all the prewar years since the three cousins had taken control!"[1]

The war allowed Du Pont and its stockholders to amass a fortune. But it also forced the company to rethink its strategy of diversification. Since 1908, the company had sought new businesses but only in areas that could employ Du Pont's nitrocellulose-based technology. Pursuit of this strategy had already proven difficult, and the war greatly multiplied the problems. It took more than two years of dramatic expansion of smokeless powder capacity before executives concluded that in the postwar era, Du Pont would flourish because of its organization (including its research staff), not because of its nitrocellulose plant investments. Freed from the idea of restricting its diversification program to nitrocellulose-based businesses, Du Pont's executives could pursue a new strategy of making it a truly diversified chemical company. A critical element in this was Du Pont's venture into dyestuffs and related organic chemicals.

Germany had totally dominated the U.S. dyestuffs, pharmaceuticals, and organic chemicals markets, but Britain's blockade of Germany cut off the importation of these chemicals into the United States. Du Pont was dependent on the Germans for its supply of diphenylamine, the stabilizer for smokeless powder and an important dye intermediate as well. Forced to build its own diphenylamine plant, Du Pont soon found itself in the uncomfortable position of being the largest U.S. producer of diphenylamine and related organic chemicals but not contributing to the solution of the war-imposed dye crisis. This situation played perfectly into the hands of the Development Department, which was seeking to chart a new diversification strategy. The Executive Committee soon concurred with the Development Department that Du Pont had to venture into dyestuffs – not just because it made strategic sense but because it was politically necessary.

Throughout this period, Fin Sparre loomed large in the formulation of Du Pont's new diversification strategy. When the Development Department sought the help of an "industrial chemist of broad experience" to help formulate the new strategy, it turned to the Experimental Station's director.[2] Sparre initially took a temporary leave of absence from the Station but wound up staying in the Development Department until his retirement in 1944. He worked under the direction of R. R. M. Carpenter until 1917 and then under Walter S. Carpenter, Jr. In May 1919 Sparre assumed the position of director of the Development Department reporting to the younger Carpenter, who was vice president in charge of development until he became treasurer in 1921. Late in 1916, Sparre developed a comprehensive strategy, which he and R. R. M. Carpenter sold to the Executive Committee as encompassing "a practically complete system of excess plant utilization." But, more critically, it promised to create "the nucleus of [a] system of new industries."[3] Early in 1917, the Executive Committee approved the Development Department's plan to diversify Du Pont into the following areas: dyestuffs and allied organic chemicals; vegetable oils, paints, and varnishes; water-soluble chemicals (e.g., formic, oxalic, and tartaric acids); and industries related to celluloid and to cotton purification.[4]

Among these, Du Pont's venture into dyestuffs turned out to be the most taxing and important for the company. Research played a critical role in this venture, and in many respects Du Pont's research program "grew up" with the dyestuffs business. Time would soon demonstrate that Sparre and his superiors in the Development Department had underestimated the many technical problems that stood as hurdles in Du Pont's race to become a successful dyestuffs manufacturer. To Charles L. Reese's Chemical Department fell much of the actual responsibility for getting Du Pont into the business, and the Chemical Department expanded rapidly. As Du Pont's diversification strategy unfolded, the dyestuffs venture pointed up the problems of having a closely managed central research organization working for a business that demanded tight integration of research and development with manufacturing and marketing.

The dyestuffs venture provided an important object lesson for Du Pont's executives. They concluded that the internal generation of new businesses was too demanding. The acquisition of businesses or technologies and their improvement through R&D was a far better way to proceed. The venture into dyestuffs seemed to those who lived through it an endless nightmare of scientific, technical, manufacturing, and marketing problems that could not have been anticipated at the outset. But prideful Du Pont research personnel had convinced executives that the problems would not be insurmountable. For a long time after the dyestuffs venture, executives were more skeptical of the opinions of research men.

The Push toward Organic Chemicals Manufacture

When World War I began, Du Pont was still fundamentally an explosives manufacturer. It depended on Germany for two important organic chemicals, diphenylamine and toluene, used respectively as the stabilizer in smokeless powder manufacture and for making trinitrotoluene (TNT). The company's managers recognized that Du Pont's smokeless powder and TNT businesses were threatened if it did not take swift action to manufacture these two organic compounds. In doing so, Du Pont also took its first significant step toward becoming an organic chemicals manufacturer.

Two years before the Development Department advocated entering the organic chemicals business, Reese had set both the Eastern Laboratory and the Experimental Station to work on the problem of manufacturing diphenylamine. Following an extensive literature search, Reese and his chemists decided that the Germans probably made diphenylamine by heating aniline and aniline hydrochloride in an autoclave at 230 degrees centigrade. The reaction, they figured, split off ammonium chloride and formed diphenylamine. Reese gave the Eastern Laboratory the responsibility of developing processes for the manufacture of aniline starting with the nitration of benzene. He charged the Experimental Station with working out the process for preparing aniline hydrochloride and for optimizing the final reaction that yielded diphenylamine. It is unclear why he divided the labor this way.

Although this process presented unusual equipment difficulties because of the corrosive action of aniline hydrochloride, Du Pont started up a commercial plant at the Repauno plant in December 1914 – only four months after the European war began. The Repauno works was also chosen as the site for the manufacture of the intermediate aniline. Reese informed the Executive Committee that within four months the diphenylamine plant would be capable of turning out 50,000 pounds per month.[5] It was none too soon, because the company's purchasing agents believed that Du Pont's supplies of diphenylamine would be exhausted by March 1915. By mid-1916, this new plant was producing roughly 75,000 pounds of diphenylamine a month and was meeting Du Pont's immediate needs for smokeless powder manufacture.[6]

No sooner had Du Pont's chemists worked out the diphenylamine process than they pursued a different method – one that would present fewer equipment problems and provide higher yields. Experimental Station chemists developed a catalytic process using aniline and a small amount of iodine. By basing their ideas on a footnote in a recently published article in *Journal für praktische chemie*, they succeeded in developing a process with higher yields and less rapid decay of equipment. With world powder orders rapidly mounting, Du Pont's executives immediately authorized the design and construction of a plant to make 150,000 pounds of diphenylamine a month by the new process.[7] Du Pont's R&D organization had made it possible for the company to continue making smokeless powder that met the stringent specifications of the military. The Experimental Station's success was perhaps its most significant to date and probably justified the many years in which the Station had been a drain on the company's resources.

Rapidly declining supplies of toluene posed similar problems – and opportunities – for Du Pont's research organization. By December 1914, the company's purchasing agents were unable to buy enough toluene to keep Du Pont's TNT plants running at full capacity. Reese immediately initiated work to develop a process for synthesizing toluene, as well as to find substitutes for it.[8] According to Reese, "we first bent our efforts to its production by cracking coal and water-gas tar, and also by the Friedel and Crafts reaction from benzene, and the reverse reaction from xylene and the higher homologues. Plants were built and operated [using both approaches]."[9]

The Eastern Laboratory's research on synthesizing toluene soon led its chemists in several directions. One involved the nitration of xylenes to trinitroxylenes (TNX), which could be mixed with TNT and cast into shells. This idea soon proved to be an excellent one that resulted in the navy ordering 30 million pounds of the new explosive, TNX.[10] But more important, Eastern's work on toluene synthesis, combined with research on diphenylamine, enabled the laboratory to develop and manufacture tetryl (trinitrophenylmethylnitramine), a detonating powder previously made only in Germany and a safer substitute for fulminate of mercury.[11]

Chemists in the Chemical and Development departments could begin to see the connectedness of Du Pont's efforts in organic chemicals manufacture. Starting with the same coal tar derivative, Du Pont could make a variety of organic compounds, and these in turn could serve as intermediates for final products, including dyestuffs. As Charles Reese informed the National Research Council in 1921, "Because of the success of our chemists in meeting the requirements for diphenylamine and toluene by synthetic processes, we were encouraged to believe that we had in our organization men who could master, through research, the great problem of producing dyes in this country, which were so much needed when the supply was cut off by the German monopoly. As we are manufacturers of explosives which require the same raw materials and similar processes to those used in the manufacture of dyes, we decided to branch out into the dye industry."[12]

Du Pont's entry into the dye business did not come as swiftly and smoothly as Reese implied, but it certainly flowed out of the company's work with organic chemicals. By March 1915, it had become apparent that the United States faced a serious problem in obtaining dyestuffs. Within four months, the Development Department had put together an internal study arguing for a limited venture into dyestuffs manufacture. The report, written by A. D. Chambers (who would become the first superintendent of Du Pont's dyeworks and after whom Du Pont would name its plant), drew heavily on an earlier one written by the chief organic chemist at the Experimental Station, A. E. Houlehan. Houlehan had identified twelve organic compounds that were used as intermediates in drug and dye manufacture. He argued that, "with the exception of one or two special cases," Du Pont should not "engage at this time in the complete manufacture of dyes." Rather, he concluded, "If this Company could get in touch with a number of the dye manufacturers in this country and find out their needs, it is believed that there are a number of intermediate compounds that it would be of profit to manufacture."[13]

Adopting this suggestion, Chambers enumerated a list of organic chemicals that Du Pont was making – or could easily make – for itself. "For all these products," Chambers argued, "there is a demand in the Country and in fields which we have not, up to this time, entered."[14] Chambers estimated relatively small gross sales for these organic compounds, but after an interview with the newly formed National Aniline and Chemical Company, the possibility of Du Pont's selling intermediates looked promising.[15] After six months of negotiations, the Development Department abandoned the idea of selling dye intermediates to National Aniline and Chemical Company. But it did not abandon the idea of selling intermediates. In mid-December 1915, Morris H. Poucher, the head of the American Badische Company, one of the United States's principal importers of German dyes and a subsidiary of the largest German dyestuffs manufacturer, made a proposal that commanded the Development Department's – and soon the Executive Committee's – attention.[16]

Left isolated by the British blockade and intense anti-German sentiment, Poucher proposed that Du Pont manufacture dye intermediates, not for American consumption but for export to "three or four large dye plants in England." In turn, these British firms would export half their finished dyes to the United States through a company to be half owned by Du Pont. Poucher demanded an immediate response from Du Pont to his proposal.[17]

Ultimately, the Executive Committee rejected Poucher's proposition, but in reaching this decision, Du Pont's executives faced squarely for the first time the risks borne by the company if Du Pont did not undertake dyestuffs manufacture. Walter S. Carpenter articulated Du Pont's options. If Du Pont chose merely to sell dye intermediates, it had two alternatives: (1) Because all Du Pont's plants capable of making intermediates were fully utilized for war matériel, Du Pont could cut back its production of explosives and sell some of the organic compounds as intermediates. (2) It could build new plants for intermediates manufacture. If the latter course were pursued, Du Pont would also have to "develop an entirely new supply of crude material [i.e., feedstock]," because the company had already contracted for as much feedstock as it could buy in the market. Carpenter thought the second option would be expensive and would also overburden the company's already-busy scientific and technical personnel. But he warned about the consequences of not facing this challenge. Should the dye-starved U.S. textile industry be forced to cut back production, Du Pont and other explosives manufacturers would be subject to severe criticism for cornering the market on intermediate feedstocks and enriching themselves by selling explosives in Europe – the United States was still at peace – rather than aiding domestic manufacturers.[18]

Carpenter's warning did not hit home immediately. But within a month Du Pont began to feel the effects of the worsening U.S. dyestuffs situation. By January 1916, Du Pont's Arlington and Fabrikoid divisions had begun to experience difficulties in obtaining dyes used for coloring celluloid lacquers and artificial leather. For example, Du Pont had been forced to substitute a natural dye for the synthetic dye it regularly used, and purchasing agents feared that sellers would repudiate existing dye contracts in an effort to cash in on the steep rise in dye prices.

Because of this situation, the Chemical Department initiated dyestuffs research at both the Experimental Station and the Eastern Laboratory. Initially, Reese directed research at synthesizing only the dyes used by the company, but by mid-1916, Du Pont's chemists had begun "to take up various dye problems in order to become familiar with this character of research and to accumulate information that would be of value if the Company should decide to enter the dye-manufacturing business, giving special attention to such dyes as could be made from products already manufactured by the Company, or in plants which will be available after the war."[19]

The Development Department had held informal discussions with Adolph Liebmann, a chemist from the English dye firm of Levinstein, Ltd., who was formally visiting Du Pont in connection with matters relating to mineral separation. These discussions led to the shift in research emphasis and to a quickened pace for Du Pont's move into dyestuffs manufacture.[20] When Liebmann reported back to his boss, Herbert Levinstein, that Du Pont desired to obtain technical information on dyestuffs, Levinstein immediately sent him back to Wilmington to negotiate formally the sale of information to Du Pont. Liebmann met with Reese, Chambers, and others in the Development Department in late March 1916. Although no formal agreement emerged from this conference, Liebmann arranged for two Du Pont representatives – one of whom was specified to be Chambers – to go to England "to look thoroughly into the dye situation with the Levinsteins." Chambers was to "mak[e] an inspection of their plants and general conditions," while "the other man with the assistance of [Du Pont's] London office, for example, [was] to look into their financial condition and also negotiate some arrangement with them."[21]

Development Department head R. R. M. Carpenter immediately made arrangements for "the other man" by engaging his brother, E. N. Carpenter, to represent Du Pont in London. A resident of Wilkes-Barre, Pennsylvania,

E. N. Carpenter had worked for Du Pont in South America until 1915. Apparently, R. R. M. Carpenter believed he could not spare anyone from his department and called on his brother to proceed to London, as he said, "to carry on certain work which will be explained later."[22]

On April 8, Chambers and E. N. Carpenter departed for England in the company of Adolph Liebmann. Once in London, they immediately took up discussions with Herbert and Edgar Levinstein. Following four days of meetings in London and Manchester, Chambers and Carpenter toured the Levinstein dyeworks at Blackley, outside Manchester. Chambers worked almost four weeks at the plant, while Carpenter spent perhaps five days there during the same period. Together they gained a reasonably clear picture of Levinstein's business and an idea of Herbert Levinstein's position with respect to a possible relationship between Du Pont and Levinstein. Near the end of the discussions, Levinstein expressed his desire for Du Pont and Levinstein to form some sort of combination and to bring British Dyes, Ltd., into it as well.[23] Beyond this accord, there is no evidence of any agreement having been reached, and subsequent events are not entirely clear.

By early June 1916, the Development Department had issued a report to the Executive Committee calling for Du Pont to purchase all 6,000 £10-shares of Levinstein's common stock. After extensive discussion over several days, the Executive Committee authorized the Development Department to purchase Levinstein's common stock at six times book value.[24] The committee also determined to put the Levinstein operation in the High Explosives Operating Department – a logical home given the number of intermediates already manufactured by the department and the recent addition of an organic chemicals research lab at the Eastern Laboratory.[25]

Throughout the summer, as Du Pont chemists worked to learn more about dye synthesis, negotiations between Du Pont and Levinstein proceeded in fits and starts. Du Pont's Executive Committee appropriated funds for a complete appraisal of Levinstein's property and sent A. D. Chambers back to England to close the contract. But on August 2, Chambers cabled Wilmington that the British government, which was then aggressively trying to promote a British dyestuffs industry, had objected to the sale. As an alternative, Herbert Levinstein proposed creating a separate U.S. dye company; for a quarter interest in this company, Levinstein would provide the new company technical information on dyestuffs manufacture.[26]

Chambers's news brought about a protracted series of negotiations in Wilmington and in England with the Levinstein brothers and with the British government. During this period, the Executive Committee showed an increasing inclination to enter dyestuffs manufacture, and its members concurred with the Development Department that Du Pont needed "to secure as soon as possible from the experienced chemists and workers in England, France, Italy or Switzerland, the information now existent in the art."[27] At the same time, the Executive Committee realized the importance of gaining knowledge of the U.S. market for dyestuffs. It achieved this information when it retained Morris R. Poucher as a special consultant and promised him the title of manager of dyestuffs sales if Du Pont entered the business. Though both Poucher and Du Pont clearly recognized that Poucher had "nothing tangible to sell," his knowledge of dye sales in the United States was excellent. Moreover, Poucher offered the company the services of eight of his associates who were skilled in marketing dyestuffs as well as samples of all dyes marketed by Badische.[28] Poucher and his associates developed a list of dyes that Du Pont should manufacture as a first step in building a complete line of dyestuffs.

By the time Poucher was retained as a consultant, the Executive Committee had all but decided to enter the dye business. The committee believed in late September 1916 that the only remaining hurdle was the successful negotiation with the British for technical information on dyestuffs manufacture. To this end, J. Amory Haskell, Chambers, and Poucher departed for England to begin discussions that would culminate on November 30, 1916, in a contract with Levinstein. For an annual payment from Du Pont of £25,000 for ten years, Levinstein agreed to divulge entirely its secret processes for dye manufacture. These included processes for synthetic indigo, which Levinstein had recently obtained when it purchased the indigo plant lately built by Hoechst and confiscated by the British government.[29] The Executive Committee, the Development Department, and the Chemical Department must have been greatly pleased by the Levinstein agreement and by the prospects for a Du Pont dyes business. But during the next half-dozen years, Du Pont's decision to become a dyestuffs manufacturer tested the patience of its executives and tempered the enthusiasm of its scientific and technical staff.

Many of Du Pont's problems stemmed from the company's trying to do in months what had taken the Germans six or seven decades to achieve: (1) the development of a corps of expert dye chemists and technical personnel who had accumulated years of "craft" knowledge of dye synthesis, semiworks operations, testing procedures, and a whole gamut of "tricks" inherent to dye manufacture; (2) the development of a large, diversified line of dyestuffs suitable for different types of fibers; (3) the development of entirely new dyestuffs; and (4) the development of a capable marketing organization in this complex business. Both the Development Department and the Executive Committee believed that in the dye business the most profitable firms were those with the most complete line of dyes.[30] But building a complete line posed particular problems, especially for the Chemical Department. For example, prior to the agreement with Levinstein, the Development Department asked the Chemical Department to become familiar with the manufacture of sulfur black and related dyes in case Du Pont's negotiations with Levinstein failed.[31] At the same time, the Chemical Department undertook development of basic dyes because Levinstein's line was particularly weak. Not assured of an agreement with Levinstein, the department also worked on developing the intermediates necessary for the commercial synthesis of indigo.[32] The Chemical Department's experience with dyestuffs prior to the signing of the Levinstein agreement probably enhanced the company's ability to derive maximum benefit from the Levinstein agreement.

No sooner had the ink of J. A. Haskell's signature on the Levinstein contract dried – and well before the Executive Committee ratified the contract – than a team from Du Pont's Chemical and Engineering departments sailed for England to master Levinstein's dye chemistry and technology. Charles M. A. Stine, C. Chester Ahlum, Elmer K. Bolton, William A. Taylor, and T. Lees Bartleson represented the Chemical Department, and Maurice du Pont Lee, C. F. Maguire, and several draftsmen went from the Engineering Department.[33] Stine had recently been named head of the Organic Division of the Chemical Department and previously had been in charge of organic research at the Eastern Laboratory. Ahlum was also a veteran organic chemist at Eastern whose specialty had become and would continue to be semiworks design and operation. Du Pont had only recently hired Taylor, an instructor at the University of Wisconsin, to work on sulfur colors. Bolton was also relatively new at Du Pont, having turned down a position in organic chemistry at Harvard in 1915 to pursue a career in industrial chemistry. Bartleson had just been hired as a research chemist at the Experimental Station fresh out of an undergraduate chemical engineering program at Swarthmore College.[34]

After two months of intensive work at Levinstein's plant outside Manchester – but before they believed they were finished – the team returned to the United States, their stay cut short by Germany's vow to torpedo any neutral ship entering or departing British harbors after February 3, 1917. The team hurriedly departed for the United States on February 2. As Ahlum recalled, fearing for their lives, "we kept life preservers with us at all times" on the voyage home.[35]

The following months were critical ones, both for the returning chemists and for others in the Chemical and Development departments. The chemists wrote massive reports on the information obtained from Levinstein. These became "the bible" for Du Pont's dye business. For example, Stine and Ahlum submitted a 400-page report, "Intermediate Products and Azo Colors," consisting of recipes for 40 intermediates, general information on azo colors and laboratory control of manufactured dyestuffs, and recipes for 230 azo colors. Bolton and Bartleson wrote extensive reports on naphthalene compounds and their preparation.[36] Even with such extensive though incomplete information, questions remained about how to proceed, which intermediates and dyes to produce first, how to organize for dyestuffs research, and how to put together such technical parts of the business as testing and marketing support.

Rather than formulating a master plan, complete with estimates of costs for each phase of the process, the Development Department elected to pursue development in a piecemeal fashion.[37] Such a strategy posed problems for the company. Much like the unsupervised child that wades progressively further from seashore until suddenly the bottom drops out, Du Pont waded deeper and deeper into dyestuffs. Fortunately, Du Pont's rapidly growing wartime cash surplus kept the dye venture afloat. Few other companies would have possessed that kind of life preserver.

Early in 1917, after President Woodrow Wilson broke off diplomatic relations with Germany, the Executive Committee formally approved construction of an indigo plant, which was to be a virtual copy of the former Hoechst plant now owned by Levinstein.[38] This plant and all the later dye plants would be located at the Deepwater Works, on the Delaware River south of the Repauno site. The committee also established a Miscellaneous Manufacturing Department to serve as the operating department for the dyes business and for Du Pont's recently acquired businesses in celluloid and paint manufacture. The new department was headed by Pierre's and Irénée's youngest brother, Lammot du Pont. Lammot soon brought A. D. Chambers into the new department to head up the dyestuffs venture.[39]

Chambers's and Lammot's initial efforts in the Miscellaneous Manufacturing Department pointed up the problems with Du Pont's piecemeal approach to the venture. After the Executive Committee approved one or two appropriation requests for pieces of the dyeworks, several members of the committee began to question the incoming stream of such requests. A single request for the first $7,000 of an estimated $60,000 nitrotoluol intermediates plant touched off a major debate in the Executive Committee over how the company should proceed. H. Fletcher Brown initiated the debate by questioning the appropriation of funds prior to the submission of complete plans. Enough of the committee agreed with Brown to block the $7,000 appropriation.[40] Lammot then tried a different tactic. He submitted an authorization request for the entire cost of the plant – now $69,790 – rather than the smaller sum. But the committee split five to four against the appropriation. The five who rejected the request wanted a comprehensive report on exactly what developments were contemplated in the dye business, what the estimated costs would be, "what we have spent and what we have obligated ourselves to spend to date."[41]

Lammot had no recourse but to prepare such a report, and the following week he delivered an oral summary of the dyestuffs venture. His report must have appeased some members, for the committee approved his request for funding the nitrotoluol plant as well as several other projects.[42] When Lammot later submitted his written report on the dye venture, however, the Executive Committee again sounded an alarm. Three things had now become apparent. First, the committee recognized that the "extent and scope" of the dye industry seemed almost limitless. Second, it appeared almost certain that the capital required for this venture would exceed the amount estimated in Lammot's report. Third, the committee observed that actual appropriation requests had constantly shown substantial increases over those originally estimated. After an extensive discussion, the committee resolved that Lammot du Pont should update his report every sixty days. Although some members of the committee wanted to put the dye venture on hold until Lammot submitted his first updated report, the committee proceeded to appropriate funds as requested by Lammot. At least one member continued to vote against all dyestuffs appropriations until a satisfactory, comprehensive master plan was approved.[43] Lammot never delivered such a master plan, no doubt because neither he nor anyone else in Du Pont knew with any certainty what the dye business entailed.

In mid-June 1917, Lammot submitted a revised report on the cost of Du Pont's dye venture. His new figures, including construction costs, research, fees to Levinstein and to Poucher, materials, and required working capital amounted to slightly over $7 million.[44] Two months later, when the United States's entry into the war had begun to put upward pressure on prices, Lammot's revised calculations came in at $8.75 million.[45] By the beginning of 1919, Du Pont's investment in dyestuffs manufacture had reached $11 million.[46] Hardly had an Executive Committee meeting gone by that its members did not sink more of the company's cash into the dyeworks. Indeed, the name for the site – Deepwater – well suited the venture.

A good deal of the $11 million had been sunk into research and development facilities and personnel for dyestuffs. As with virtually every aspect of the business, Du Pont's projections had not come close to anticipating the need for and costs of R&D capability in the dye business. Whereas the Germans had long recognized that one of the keys to their success in organic chemicals was *wissenschaftliche Massenarbeit,* it took Du Pont several years to understand this fully.

As noted earlier, the Chemical Department had begun hiring a growing number of organic chemists in 1914 when diphenylamine and toluene shortages threatened the company's business. With a clear need for organic research, the Executive Committee had funded the construction of organic laboratories at both the Experimental Station and at the Eastern Laboratory. Even before the Levinstein agreement was signed and ratified, Charles Reese had pulled together dye and dye intermediates research groups at both these facilities and had encouraged the construction of small semiworks at the sites. Shortly before Du Pont's scientific and technical team departed for England, Reese had selected Charles Stine to head a new organic chemicals division of the Chemical Department, to be operated out of the Wilmington office. In effect, Stine supervised the organic work of both the Experimental Station and the Eastern Laboratory.[47]

By the beginning of 1917, the Station's organic division consisted of twenty-two chemists and nineteen lab assistants and other workers, and Eastern's organic workforce must have been comparable if not larger. The rapid growth of Du Pont's organic chemicals research led Reese to reorganize the Chemical Department in February 1917 and to formalize the work of the organic division, the duties of which Reese described as "work in connection with intermediates, dyes, pharmaceuticals and photographic chemicals."[48] In dyestuffs, Stine's problem was to coordinate effectively the work of the two rival laboratories, each having a different research heritage. It was not long before Stine, Reese, and others realized that such coordination was impossible. Following the model of the Eastern Laboratory, they determined to found a research facility dedicated to dye research at Deepwater Point. The laboratory would still be controlled, however, by Reese's Chemical Department and not by the Miscellaneous Manufacturing Department, which was responsible for the manufacture and sales of dyestuffs.

C. Chester Ahlum, one of the chemists who had gone to England, recalled that the new laboratory was designed after the team returned to the United States and while they were writing their reports on Levinstein's processes. He was also among a small group who determined the laboratory's precise location at Deepwater Point, which was mostly a swamp known as Skunk's Misery. The group settled on Fenton's Beach, a summer resort area complete with an amusement park and numerous cottages, since it was the highest piece of ground owned by Du Pont. Rather than leveling the existing structures, Du Pont used them during the early days of the dye laboratory. The Fenton Beach schoolhouse – a one-story clapboard structure – housed the first semiworks equipment of the laboratory.[49]

In early May 1917, the Executive Committee appropriated the initial funds for construction of the permanent laboratory, projected to house about one hundred chemists, technicians, and clerks.[50] Reese soon announced the chief personnel for the new laboratory, which was named the Jackson Laboratory in honor of chemist Oscar R. Jackson. Revealing his bias for the Eastern Laboratory and its style of research, Reese appointed Fletcher B. Holmes director of the new facility and A. E. Houlehan assistant director. Holmes, who had received a baccalaureate from Harvard in 1902, had served as assistant director of the Eastern Laboratory since 1905. Before joining Du Pont in 1903, he had worked as an analytical chemist for Carnegie Steel Company. Houlehan, who had earned a doctorate from Cornell in 1912, had served as a research chemist at the Experimental Station and was head of the organic section there.[51] Holmes and Houlehan quickly took over direction of the dyestuffs research and selected chemists to head the various divisions of the laboratory.

By the time the Jackson Laboratory opened, it was already inadequate for Du Pont's growing needs in dyestuffs research. Convinced of this by the Chemical Department, the Executive Committee appropriated funds to construct a second, equally large laboratory building at the Jackson Laboratory.[52] Soon the Chemical Department and the Miscellaneous Manufacturing Department were back, asking the Executive Committee for additional authorizations for semiworks buildings, laboratories for each of the dye and intermediates "areas" at the plant, and – the most expensive facility of all – a technical laboratory.[53]

Apparently, no one in the Development or Chemical departments had anticipated the need in dyestuffs manufacture for a technical laboratory, where dyestuffs were tested on all types of media (cotton, silk, wool, fur, paper, leather, etc.) and where the manufacturer in effect conducted research for its customers on the best techniques for achieving specific objectives in dyeing. Du Pont's Experimental Station had done similar work in smokeless powder but for only one customer – the military – and in a far more limited fashion. "Tech lab" work in dyestuffs represented an entirely new R&D function at Du Pont, one that would later be necessary in such other areas of the company's business as plastics and textile fibers. German dye firms, for example Bayer, had long operated these facilities. Now Du Pont's Executive Committee recognized the need for this type of a facility and promptly appropriated the necessary funds in 1918.

Altogether, by mid-1919, Du Pont had invested about $1.2 million in research and development facilities at the Jackson Laboratory.[54] This figure represented roughly 10 percent of the company's total capital investment in dyestuffs manufacture up to that point. The workforce at the laboratory exceeded 550 persons, including administrators, chemists, technicians, and mechanical and service workers – well above the number of staff originally anticipated by Reese and others.[55] Everywhere at the dyeworks, plant, personnel, and costs mushroomed.

Despite such a large investment in research capability, Du Pont's dyestuffs business was in trouble by 1919. The end of the war posed serious questions for Du Pont and other U.S., British, and French manufacturers that had entered the industry. Would the return to peace also bring the return of German dye imports? Would the millions of dollars invested by other U.S. firms in dyestuffs plant lead to overcapacity and hence destructive competition? If not, could Du Pont afford to expand its dye business in order to achieve a position of leadership in the industry? How would Du Pont acquire the knowledge to produce a much broader range of dyes than it currently was capable of manufacturing?

In January 1919, the Executive Committee asked Lammot du Pont to restudy Du Pont's investment in dyestuffs.[56] This question was particularly important at a time when Pierre du Pont and his assistant John J. Raskob had taken advantage of attractive opportunities for investment in the automobile industry.[57] Lammot's report contained both good and bad news. He demonstrated that domestic demand for dyestuffs was well above domestic production. But he could not predict how the U.S. Congress would handle the threat posed by the reentry of German dyestuffs into the U.S. market. Moreover, Lammot's report projected a lower return-on-investment (ROI) figure than the Executive Committee expected. Confounded by this report and the entire dyestuffs situation, the committee looked to the more powerful Finance Committee for answers on how much deeper it was willing to go with dyestuffs. The Executive Committee asked the Finance Committee if it was willing to fund an expansion in dyestuffs investment over the next five years up to a total of $40 million with the promise of an eventual 10 percent minimum ROI.[58] The Finance Committee responded that "we should proceed with the dyestuffs investment on the assumption that it will eventually be successful and that therefore the existing policy [of expansion] should not be changed."[59] However, the Finance Committee made its decision on the eve of a severe postwar recession that brought more than one firm in the United States to its knees. Though possessing an envious cash surplus, Du Pont was not immune to this steep downward swing in the U.S. economy.

The recession of 1920 deeply penetrated the Du Pont Company's dyestuffs research. From a total wage and salary roll of 565 at the Jackson Laboratory in mid-1920, Du Pont cut large numbers of chemists, technicians, and laborers, dropping the roll to 217 six months later. After these layoffs, Chester Ahlum recalled, "no research division [at the Jackson Laboratory] then had any chemists' helpers. Research chemists washed their own dishes, ran their own errands and did all of the experimental work."[60] Personnel cuts adversely affected Du Pont's dyestuffs research team – a team that had already been struggling with the burden of catching up with chemists in the German dye industry.

Much of the Jackson Laboratory's problem – and hence the company's problem – stemmed from the very nature of the industry. The Germans had made an art of developing a new dye, patenting it, and then marketing it anonymously. That is, they sold dyes that could not be linked explicitly with particular patents. They followed this procedure because they wanted to divulge as little information as possible about their dye line. Such dyes were labeled "unclassified," and in the marketplace they commanded significantly higher prices (ca. 40-50%) than "classified" colors. The latter dyes were considered staple dyes; their formulation and sometimes even their processes of manufacture were known. But unclassified dyes were different. Although patent searches sometimes proved useful in identifying such dyes, there was no guarantee that this strategy would work. Dye patents described dyes "either as the result of a process or as a compound of a certain structure." They also sometimes "cover[ed] fifty or more examples, a quarter of which may be described as possessing properties somewhat like" the dye of interest.[61] A further difficulty with using dye patents arose from the *Umgehungs Patente* – evasion patents – taken out by a company deliberately to send competitors down dead ends.[62] Hence, even after Du Pont and other manufacturers gained access to the thousands of German patents confiscated during the war, making sense of them was well-nigh impossible.

U.S. dye consumers wanted Du Pont and other U.S. dye firms to duplicate exactly the line of dyes marketed by the Germans prior to the war, not to develop a new line of dyes. The Germans had sold more than 900 different dye types (and several thousand brand names of dyes) at a time when domestic dye firms marketed only about 120 dyes. Most of those 900 dyes were unclassified. Merely to identify these dyes, to discover what intermediates to use, and to determine what processes to employ entailed an enormous investment of time and money in research. Even when Du Pont managed to obtain samples of popular unclassified German dyes, such as those Poucher brought to Du Pont from Badische, identification was always difficult and sometimes impossible, especially when the dye proved to be a mixture of compounds rather than a pure ingredient. The problem was not unique to Du Pont and other U.S. dye manufacturers; seasoned German firms that employed the world's best dye chemists often found it impossible to identify a competitor's dye. As R. E. Rose, head of Du Pont's technical laboratory wrote, "The truth is that it takes nearly as much effort to decipher the correlation between patent and commercial dye as it does to discover the color originally, and this has been the chief cause of the delay in making the newest dyes."[63] Du Pont chemists E. F. Hitch and I. E. Knapp put the matter more bluntly: "No matter how much we may dislike to be followers and not pioneers, we must, in the first few years, confine our efforts in this field largely to the manufacture of colors that have already been produced by foreign manufacturers."[64]

Although perhaps correct, such a strategy was discouraging, particularly in the face of possible renewed imports by the Germans. In late 1919, U.S. dye companies succeeded in producing only a hundred more dyes than they had made before the war.[65] The process of duplicating what the Germans had done – of learning the entire repertoire – seemed almost hopeless. And all this work would be for naught if German dyes reentered the market.[66] Du Pont had other problems as well. The dyes Du Pont succeeded in manufacturing were often viewed by consumers as inferior. Du Pont's initial runs of indigo, for instance, had turned out green rather than blue. More serious, the company found it difficult to standardize a given dye; Du Pont had not anticipated the whole process of mixing different batches of a given dye, with slightly different shades, to achieve a standard color. In short, the company lacked the know-how that came from years of experience.[67]

Although Du Pont's agreement with Morris Poucher provided the company with expertise in marketing dyestuffs, it lacked comparable expertise in the scientific and technical end of the business. This was true in spite of the Levinstein agreement and Du Pont's swelling ranks of PhD organic chemists. Between 1917 and 1921, Du Pont pursued several means to rectify this situation. The Development Department's Fin Sparre took the first step when he established a rapport with Thomas H. Norton, a commercial agent for dyestuffs in the U.S. Department of Commerce.[68] Norton followed the dyestuffs situation in the United States and had compiled the first U.S. census of dyestuffs, published in 1916. This census covered all synthetic dyestuffs used in the United States, including imported and domestically manufactured dyes. For example, it provided data on the quantity and value of about 5,600 brands – both classified and unclassified – imported from Europe. The census also provided information on formulations of and intermediates for classified dyes. In many respects, Norton's census constituted the most important source of information on dyestuffs published in the United States before 1917.[69]

Sparre managed to get Norton to send Du Pont galleys of his census prior to its publication.[70] He soon convinced Norton to join Du Pont's Chemical Department as a specialist on dyestuffs. But Norton's knowledge of dyestuffs turned out to be too limited to help Du Pont, and he left the company's employ in 1920, perhaps a victim of the recession.

Du Pont tried other measures to gain expertise, including the purchase of other dye manufacturers. In May 1918, the company purchased the United Piece Dye Works's manufacturing plant at Lodi, New Jersey, which specialized in a few dyes not made by other U.S. manufacturers. Within a few years, Du Pont closed this plant and moved its equipment to the Deepwater facility.[71] Later in 1918, the Executive Committee debated whether to purchase the Bayer Company's U.S. plant, property, and patents which had been confiscated in 1917 after Congress created the Alien Property Custodian.

Lammot du Pont argued strenuously for purchasing the Bayer operation, principally because of patents it held for dyestuffs, pharmaceuticals, and rubber chemicals, but also because of Bayer's pharmaceuticals plant and its plant for manufacturing nigrosine and induline dyes, which Du Pont had not developed.[72] Bayer's dyeworks were, as Lammot recognized, "Largely an approximate duplication of our Deepwater plant." Regarding pharmaceuticals, Lammot reminded his colleagues on the Executive Committee that "It has always been our intention at some time to go into the production of pharmaceuticals." Sparre had especially pushed diversifying into pharmaceuticals. By purchasing the American Bayer, whose products included aspirin as well as a number of other drugs, Du Pont could enter the field far easier than by generating a business within the company.

Lammot raised the level of his argument for buying Bayer to a more general – yet more fundamental – level. He suggested that Du Pont could not "be permanently successful in the dye industry or in organic chemical products unless we build up a broad comprehensive business along the lines of the various branches of organic chemistry." Here is where the Germans had succeeded particularly because of their ability to cooperate on an interfirm level. But because of the Sherman Antitrust Act, no such cooperation was possible in the United States. If Du Pont wanted to compete with the Germans in the postwar era, it would have to diversify "to the same extent as the Germans." Lammot continued in a deeper, more prophetic vein:

> Leaving aside the question of German competition, it is obvious that only by a broad comprehensive business can we justify the employment of experts, experimental laboratories and research to the greatest extent. It is a fact that experience gained in one branch of organic chemistry is frequently of great value and importance in the other branches; in

fact many of the processes and materials used in the synthesis of important natural products such as camphor, glycerine, rubber, etc., are the same as those used in the dyestuffs industry.

Despite Lammot's cogent arguments, the Executive Committee ultimately rejected his request to bid roughly $5 million for the Bayer Company's U.S. operation. Instead, the company voted to submit a bid of no more than $3.5 million. Perhaps the committee was too concerned about having duplicate dyestuffs plants.[73] As it turned out, Sterling Products Company bid the highest sum ($5.31 million) and quickly sold off Bayer's dye business for $2.5 million, keeping the pharmaceuticals for itself.[74]

This sale generated a major controversy in Congress and among some chemical manufacturers. They objected to the Alien Property Custodian selling one U.S. manufacturer approximately 1,200 patents on coal-tar chemicals and processes. This smacked of destroying the German dye cartel merely, as Haynes wrote, "to build an American dye trust."[75] At the suggestion of a young lawyer, Francis P. Garvan, the Alien Property Custodian responded in 1919 by creating, through an executive order by U.S. president Woodrow Wilson, a non-profit corporation – the Chemical Foundation, Incorporated – and giving it ownership of all German chemical patents. In turn, the Chemical Foundation was empowered to grant nonexclusive licenses "upon equal terms and a royalty basis, to any bona fide American individual or corporation."[76] Royalty moneys went to defend the organization's rights to these patents and, should surplus funds exist, to support in a broad way the development of chemistry in the United States.

Although the swift creation of the Chemical Foundation eased Du Pont's concerns over patent licensing, it still did not provide the company with the expertise it needed. Until the recession hit, Du Pont continued to recruit chemists that had had practically any experience with dyestuffs. Executives who followed Du Pont's dyestuffs venture most closely concluded that Du Pont needed to recruit experienced dye chemists from Europe, especially from Switzerland and Germany. Early in 1919, Du Pont had tried unsuccessfully to obtain an agreement with a "suitable" European dyestuffs manufacturer to secure "extra assistance . . . in the development of our dyestuffs industry."[77] Perhaps because Morris Poucher had worked for the Badische company and may have believed he still had connections, Du Pont then tried to hire a senior chemist at Badische named René Bohn, who was also one of the directors of the company. Bohn not only declined but issued a severe warning to Du Pont not to proceed further with recruitment plans. When in early 1920 Irénée du Pont discussed recruiting German dye chemists with Eysten Berg, Du Pont's European technical representative, Berg also advised Du Pont to abandon its plans, particularly in light of the Bohn affair. He feared that German reprisals would ultimately do the company more harm than the good obtained by hiring German dye chemists.[78]

Despite these warnings, Du Pont's executives remained convinced that the company needed to secure the services of German dye chemists. The manager of Du Pont's dyestuffs operation developed a specific plan to achieve this goal, and the Executive Committee approved this plan in a special meeting held in July of 1920. But recognizing the importance of the goal, its probable high dollar costs, and its potential for international repercussions, the committee asked the Finance Committee to ratify its action. Two days later, the Finance Committee did so unanimously.[79]

The plan called for empowering A. D. Chambers, the manager in charge of dye manufacture, Cesare Protto, Poucher's long-time associate and manager of the technical section of the dye sales division, and Elmer Bolton, now director of dye research for the Chemical Department, "to contract for the expert services of men . . ., the duration of such contracts, the description of the duties to be performed, the remuneration to be paid by said corporation for the services to be rendered, and all other terms, conditions and provisions of said contracts to be . . . determined" by Chambers, Protto, and Bolton.[80] In short, the Executive Committee had suspended all its employment rules and had written Chambers and the others a blank check to obtain expertise, whatever the cost.

Chambers moved quickly. He detailed his special assistant, Eric C. Kunz, to Europe to begin a concerted, though clandestine, recruitment campaign. Swiss born and educated, Kunz had come to Du Pont when it purchased the Lodi plant of the United Piece Dye Works. He had worked for a Swiss dye firm before being recruited by the chief chemist for United Piece Dye Works.[81] Apparently, Kunz contacted a large number of chemists at several of the German dye firms, including Badische and Bayer. If they were interested in talking seriously to Du Pont, the chemists went to Lucerne, Switzerland, where they were interviewed by Chambers, Protto, and Bolton. Du Pont's recruitment program had all the makings for industrial espionage. All the German chemists had signed contracts containing *Karenz-Verpflichtungen* (clauses barring them from working for another company in the same field for three years). Du Pont offered some of these chemists as much as $25,000 a year for five years to go to Wilmington (perhaps ten to fifteen times as much as they were earning in Germany). Several accepted Du Pont's invitation, but a number of the chemists contacted and interviewed reported Du Pont's solicitations to their supervisors.[82]

When Chambers, Protto, and Bolton closed contracts with four German chemists and one chemical engineer – all with PhDs – from Bayer and proceeded to move them to Wilmington, the intrigue intensified. Two of the chemists, Max Engelmann (a pharmaceuticals expert) and Henry Jordan (an azo dye specialist) were arrested at the Dutch border with a "suitcase filled with papers and drawings" ostensibly belonging to the German Bayer company. (The chemists and Du Pont claimed that these were their personal papers and had been unjustly seized.) The two other chemists, Otto Runge (an intermediates expert) and Joseph Flachslaender (a sulfur color specialist), sailed from Rotterdam on the Dutch steamer *Ryndam* only to be greeted in New York with warrants for their arrest. Exactly what happened to the engineer, G. MacDonald, is unclear. Altogether Du Pont closed contracts with at least ten German chemists.[83]

Du Pont's recruitment of these men caused an uproar in Germany and created a short-lived backlash at home, both in the company and in U.S. chemical circles. The Germans were particularly upset because, despite Germany's arrest warrant, which the Dutch authorities had honored, Elmer Bolton and the head of Du Pont security, aided by the U.S. State Department, succeeded in getting Runge and Flachslaender released in New York by telling the U.S. authorities that these men were critical to the success of the U.S. dye industry.[84] Exactly how Engelmann and Jordan got out of jail in Cologne and to Wilmington is not known, but the State Department must have aided this process, to the dismay of the Germans.[85] Charles Herty, who had become a major proponent of U.S. dyestuffs manufacture, published an editorial in the *Journal of Industrial and Engineering Chemistry* criticizing Du Pont's actions.[86] At the Jackson Laboratory, where the ranks had been depleted by six months of layoffs, the most severe of which had come about the time Du Pont closed the contracts with the Germans, there were rumblings of discontent. Not only had Germany recently been the enemy, but the chemists Du Pont had hired were also being paid huge sums of money – information that had become public knowledge because of the outcry in Germany.[87]

In the face of this criticism, President Irénée du Pont defended the company's decision. Writing the company's representative in Germany, who was taking a good deal of abuse, du Pont stressed,

> After two years work in the development of the dye industry we felt sure that many needless experiments could be avoided if there were available in this country men who had practical experience in the dye industry.... Like you, I have no doubt that American chemists in time can solve the same problems which were solved by the German chemists. Neither Germany nor the United States has a monopoly in brains, but there is a grave economic waste, both in money and time, in slowly and laboriously performing over again experiments which have already been made.[88]

Du Pont's hiring of the German chemists, argued Irénée, was a sound decision intended to save both time and money. As he wrote Charles L. Reese about discontent in the Chemical Department's ranks, "It is also especially necessary that we make more rapid progress in the practical 'know-how' of producing satisfactory dyes at satisfactory costs, and our lack of results, as measured by our losses after a two years' trial, would force even the most stubborn to try the expedient that has been adopted."[89]

Soon after the Germans started work at Deepwater – under the titles of "special assistants" to A. D. Chambers – discontent dissipated. Chester Ahlum recalled that everyone at the dyeworks was "expecting they were going to be stiff-necked, overbearing 'Huns' [but] everyone was agreeably surprised when they turned out to be gentlemen, able in their field, cooperative and not prone to bark commands and take credit for them-selves."[90] Harold Elley, who would eventually direct dyestuffs research, noted that "they knew their processes backwards and forwards.... They were nice people with whom to deal."[91] The Germans contributed to Du Pont in another way, according to research manager William Calcott. Although straightening certain things out at the dyeworks and providing the company with a deeper and wider base of knowledge, the Germans were able "to assure the management that we were, after all, fundamentally on the right track."[92]

The employment of the German chemists did not make Du Pont's dye venture an immediate financial success. In fact, with the recession keeping sales low, the business continued to lose considerable sums of money. Faced with continued losses, in late April 1921 the board of directors of the Du Pont Company instructed the Executive Committee to prepare a com-prehensive report on the dye venture. This report was to summarize the events leading up to Du Pont's entrance into the business, the present status of the venture, and projections of future performance.[93] Although Du Pont, along with all the other American dye manufacturers, had lobbied hard for protection to keep German dyes out of the United States, it was still unclear when the board took this action if Congress, pushed by the textile lobby, would oblige. In many respects, Du Pont's dye venture hung in the balance of the tariff question. In May 1921, Congress passed an emergency tariff that promised temporary protection against German imports. But perma-nent protection was held in abeyance until September 1922, when President Warren G. Harding signed the Fordney-McCumber Tariff, which offered the protection needed by the fledgling U.S. dye and organic chemicals industry.[94]

Du Pont's continued losses in dyestuffs during the remainder of 1921, a very negative forecast of earnings in late 1921, and the perceived lack of a plan to deal with the situation may have led to the resignation in January 1922 of the general manager of Du Pont's dyestuffs business, Charles A. Meade, who had earlier succeeded Lammot du Pont in that role.[95] The Executive Committee immediately appointed one of its members, F. W. Pickard, to succeed Meade.[96] During the next two months, Pickard, Cham-bers, Protto, Bolton, and Willis Harrington, who had served directly under Meade, formulated a plan for dealing with the continued losses in this business. When Pickard submitted his department's plan to the Executive Committee in late February 1922, it received the full support of the com-mittee.[97] But more important, it evoked the considered views of President Irénée du Pont. Pickard had recommended an aggressive but realistic pro-gram for dyestuffs research and expansion. Irénée endorsed Pickard's pro-posal, saying that it was "the very minimum of what is warranted." Lest he be misunderstood, du Pont told his colleagues he would not advocate "going ahead full-speed on everything and repeating errors of the past thereby." Du Pont's dye business would soon succeed, argued Irénée confidently, for a number of reasons. It appeared that the U.S. dye industry would indeed have the tariff protection it needed. But, equally important, du Pont stressed that the company was now as well or better equipped than its competitors to win a large share of the market. Here, he was thinking not only about the plant at Deepwater and the superior sales staff, but also about its newly acquired "foreign chemical talent."[98]

Du Pont's recruitment of German dye chemists definitely aided its quest to become a profitable dyestuffs manufacturer. So did the tariff. The company stopped losing money on the dye venture in 1923 and by 1928 had begun to earn a return approaching the company's ROI standards. Managers and executives who lived through this venture clearly viewed it as a long, difficult struggle – one they were not anxious to repeat. Unquestionably, some of these men thought that Du Pont's huge investment in dyestuffs – reputed by Walter Carpenter to have reached $40 million before Du Pont earned any profits – could have been better deployed elsewhere, such as in the budding automobile industry.[99] But executives such as Irénée, Lammot, and Pierre du Pont, who shared a vision of how scientific research could support modern industry, looked beyond the simple profit and loss statements in evaluating Du Pont's dye business and the research that lay behind it. In choosing to enter the dyestuffs business, executives had taken the critical first steps in putting the company on an entirely different scientific and technical base – that of organic chemistry. Fin Sparre had clearly articulated this strategy and forcefully argued for its adoption. As he said, it would create the "nucleus of the system of new industries." In the ten years after World War I, this is precisely what occurred. Du Pont's successful businesses in tetraethyllead and Freon manufacture would rest firmly on the scientific and technical base in organic chemistry established by the dyestuffs venture. In the 1930s, Du Pont's growing expertise in organic synthesis would lead to even better products and profits.

The Chemical Department's research program had played a critical role in Du Pont's dyestuff venture. The department had responded to the challenges posed by diphenylamine and toluene shortages. It quickly moved beyond these objectives and carried the company closer to the dyestuffs venture. Had the Chemical Department not been able to achieve a successful synthesis of diphenylamine and toluene, it is unlikely that Du Pont would have proceeded any further. Once the Executive Committee determined to sign an agreement with Levinstein, Chemical Department chemists assumed the major responsibility for transferring the knowledge of Levinstein's comparatively limited dye business to Du Pont. The construction of the Jackson Laboratory at the new dyeworks provided the department with an even greater dyestuffs research capability. Yet in undertaking the dye venture, in trying to achieve in a year or two what the Germans had built up over a long period of time, the Chemical Department and the entire company had gotten in over their heads. Du Pont's new dye chemists, aided by a handful of seasoned German scientists, had to learn to swim in short order.

Charles Reese, whose leadership of dyestuffs research at Du Pont brought him national recognition, could well be proud of his department's achievements. But while Reese was receiving the plaudits of the National Research Council, Du Pont executives were debating the best way to organize dyestuffs research and development. Criticism of the Chemical Department had arisen because of its lack of responsiveness to the immediate pressing needs of the "dye business" (i.e., manufacturing and sales). Although the Jackson Laboratory was located at the dyeworks, it was, like the Eastern Laboratory, controlled fully by Reese and his assistants. The enormous losses in the business during the postwar recession brought this issue to the fore. The resulting debate over how best to organize research in a diversifying company was part and parcel of a much larger debate over the entire Du Pont Company's organization.

4

Decentralization

The postwar recession that began in 1919 and continued through 1921 brought to a head an intense debate in the Executive Committee over how best to organize the increasingly diverse businesses of the Du Pont Company. An important part of this debate concerned the company's research and development program, embodied in the Chemical Department. Indeed, Reese and his assistants saw the situation as a crisis and responded by making organizational changes in the Chemical Department that increasingly assumed the appearance of decentralized management of research. The debate in the Executive Committee ended in early September 1921, when the members voted formally to adopt a multidivisional, decentralized management structure. Under this plan, the Executive Committee created departments in explosives, dyestuffs, Pyralin (celluloid plastics), paints, and cellulose products (Fabrikoid and lacquers), each run as a separate business and controlled by a general manager. The crisis for the Chemical Department ended three months later when the newly appointed general managers convinced the Executive Committee to decentralize fully the Chemical Department. In Charles Stine's words, the committee "dismembered" the Chemical Department.[1]

The decentralization of Du Pont's research, as approved by the Executive Committee on December 7, 1921, was not the inevitable outcome of Du Pont's overall decentralization but rather the result of the general managers' perceptions that the Chemical Department had been unresponsive to the manufacturing and sales needs of Du Pont businesses. The general managers of the new product-focused departments had been given full control over manufacturing and sales functions in their areas. They believed that to carry out their jobs satisfactorily they needed better control over the research and development function than they were getting from the Chemical Department. Hence, they advocated having their own R&D divisions. The general managers, it should be emphasized, did not press the Executive Committee to decentralize the company's Engineering Department even though the report on reorganization approved by the Executive Committee called for each department to carry out its own engineering activities. Because of its achievements during the war, the central Engineering Department was viewed as something of a miracle worker, and the general managers were happy to let it remain intact. Research was another matter.

Well before the Executive Committee formally concurred with the general managers, Reese was fully aware of the criticism directed at his department. He tried genuinely to accommodate his critics but in the end failed to maintain control over all of Du Pont's research.

Crisis in the Chemical Department

Du Pont's diversification efforts and the war had greatly strained Reese's Chemical Department. Not only had the ranks of the department swollen in number, but the locations of Du Pont research facilities had grown in number and geographical area. The scope of Du Pont's businesses was far greater in 1918 than in 1911 when Reese assumed control of the new department. Coordination of research now involved five geographically separated laboratories[2] and a product line consisting of black powder, smokeless powder, dynamite, artificial leather, celluloid plastics, celluloid films, lacquers, paints and varnishes, and dyestuffs. Getting into dyestuffs alone strained the capacities of the Chemical Department. It grew so fast and under so much pressure in the period after 1915 that Reese and his assistants had never stopped to consider problems as they developed. (See Table 4.1 on the growth of Reese's staff.) More important, the process of centralizing research, which seemed to Reese and the Executive Committee the best way to deal with the war and diversification efforts, actually worked against fostering a research program that was sensitive to the company's immediate business needs.

After the war, the Chemical Department sought to take stock of itself by holding a two-day convention at the Hotel Traymore in Atlantic City, New Jersey. The purpose of the convention was to build an esprit de corps and "to give the newer employees in the department an opportunity to become acquainted with the older employees in this and other departments and also with the officials who are responsible for the direction and the policies of the Company."[3] Charles Stine organized a program including addresses by Reese, Irénée du Pont, and other major figures from Du Pont's executive and research ranks.[4] But less that two weeks before the convention, Reese fell seriously ill and underwent major surgery, forcing the cancellation of the convention.[5] Had the meeting come off, it might have resulted in increased understanding of the problems of coordinating research with other activities of the company. In any case, the Chemical Department never took another opportunity to engage in self-assessment until 1920, when it was under full siege by the manufacturing units of the company.[6]

In early 1917 the rapidly growing Chemical Department had adopted a divisional scheme corresponding partly with Du Pont's businesses and partly with branches of chemistry. These divisions included Black and Smokeless Powder, Organic Chemicals (i.e., dyestuffs), Acid, Solvent, and High Explosives (see Figure 4.1). Sometime between the end of 1917 and mid-1919,

Table 4.1. *Chemical Department Personnel, 1911–21*

	1911	1912	1913	1914	1915	1916	1917	1918	1919	1920	1921
Total Salaried (includes clerical and stenographers)	111[a]	111[a]	115[a]	95[a]	160[a]	200[a]	395[a]	475 (6/18)[a]	652 (7/19)[b]	639 (1/20)[c] 470 (5/20)[c]	n.a.
Experimental Station											
Salaried	53[d]	53[d]	52[e]	39[f]	76[e]	91[e]	100[g]	166 (4/18)[f]	155 (7/19)[b]	145 (1/20)[c]	99 (1/21)[c]
Chemists	24[d]	24[i]	18[j]	15[k]	43[e]	54[e]	61[g]	n.a.	84 (8/19)[l] 79 (10/19)[o]	51 (7/20)[m]	37 (1/21)[b] 21 (12/21)[p]
Eastern Laboratory											
Salaried	36[d]	33[d]	n.a.	n.a.	n.a.	n.a.	n.a.	n.a.	78 (7/19)[b]	64 (1/20)[c]	n.a.
Technical (including chemists)	29[d]	26[d]	n.a.	n.a.	n.a.	n.a.	115[q]	n.a.	n.a.	53 (5/20)[c]	n.a.
Jackson Laboratory											
Salaried	—	—	—	—	—	—	n.a.	n.a.	229 (7/19)[b]	230 (1/20)[c] 223 (6/20)[r]	180 (1/21)[c] 126 (12/21)[r]
Delta Laboratory											
Salaried	—	—	—	—	—	—	—	n.a.	32 (7/19)[b]	37 (1/20)[c]	20 (1/21)[c]
Redpath Laboratory											
Salaried	—	—	—	—	—	—	—	—	—	24 (12/20)[e]	n.a.
Wilmington office											
Salaried	23[d]	32[d]	n.a.	n.a.	n.a.	n.a.	n.a.	n.a.	158 (7/19)[b]	163 (1/20)[c]	95 (1/21)[c]
Technical	15[d]	19[d]	n.a.	n.a.	n.a.	n.a.	n.a.	n.a.	n.a.	63 (1/20)[c]	45 (1/21)[c]

Note: Numbers in parentheses are date (month/year) of information. n.a. = information not available. — = did not exist.

[a] Charles L. Reese, "Developments in Industrial Research," Delivered at the Meeting of the American Society for Testing Materials, at the Hotel Traymore, Atlantic City, June 26, 1918.

[b] Semi-Annual Report of the Chemical Department, Jan.–June, 1920.

[c] William H. Whitten, "Semi-Annual Report of the Chemical Department, July–December 1920."

[d] "Comparative Statement of the Number of Men and Salaries of the Chemical Departments, December 31, 1911 and December 31, 1912."

[e] Hamilton Bradshaw, "Summary Report of Work Done at the Experimental Station, June to December 1916, Inclusive," Mar. 1917.

[f] A. P. Tanberg to L. O. Bryan, "Station Organization – Present and Past," May 3, 1921.

[g] "Diagram of Organization," Experimental Station, Jan. 1, 1917. Salaried staff is estimated from chart.

[h] Annual Report of the Experimental Station, Jan. 22, 1912.

[i] Estimate from comparison of 1912 and 1913 in "Comparative Statement" (note d).

[j] Annual Report of the Experimental Station for 1913, Dec. 31, 1913.

[k] Annual Report of the Experimental Station for 1914, Dec. 31, 1914.

[l] Hamilton Bradshaw to Assistant Director, Chemical Department, Aug. 4, 1919.

[m] "Organization Chart, Experimental Station, July 15, 1920.

[n] Same chart as used for note m but with new date and chemists' names eliminated, Jan. 1, 1921.

[o] "Organization Chart, Experimental Station, Oct. 1919.

[p] "Development of Chemical Department."

[q] "Dyna-Item," vol. 3, no. 14, Oct. 14, 1920.

[r] C. C. Ahlum, "Thirty Seven Years with Du Pont," May 3, 1947.

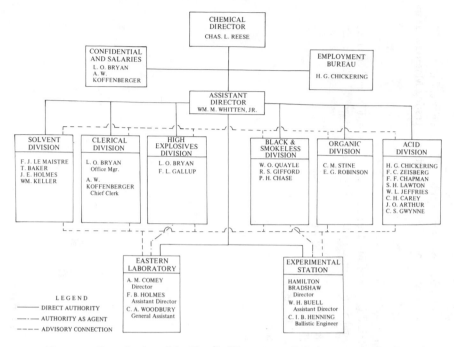

Figure 4.1. Organization of the Chemical Department, February 1, 1917. Source: Redrawn from blueprint in Series II, Part 2, Box 291, Hagley Museum and Library.

Reese changed his department's structure. Now he had two assistant directors, one for "research" and the other for "operative chemical engineering." In addition, Reese created four product-oriented divisions, each run by a manager: Cellulose, Explosives, Miscellaneous Chemicals, and Organic. Three staff divisions were also created: Elementary Processes, Inspection and Standards, and Intelligence. Finally, there were the research laboratories, each headed by a director: Delta (celluloid), Eastern (high explosives), Experimental Station (black and smokeless powder and miscellaneous areas), and Jackson (dyestuffs) (Figure 4.2). This latter reorganization, coupled with the onset of the recession, appears to have precipitated much of the dissatisfaction with the Chemical Department.

Criticism of the Chemical Department began to surface late in 1919. Under pressure, the Chemical Department reached an agreement with the Engineering, Development, and Manufacturing departments "govern[ing] the relations between these Departments in the performance of experimental and technical supervising functions."[7] This agreement, which went into effect January 1, 1920, sought "to provide definite means for placing responsibility for undertaking experimental work and for controlling expenditures within predetermined limits." Six months later, Reese's assistant, William M. Whitten, Jr., argued that "the projected plan has met with

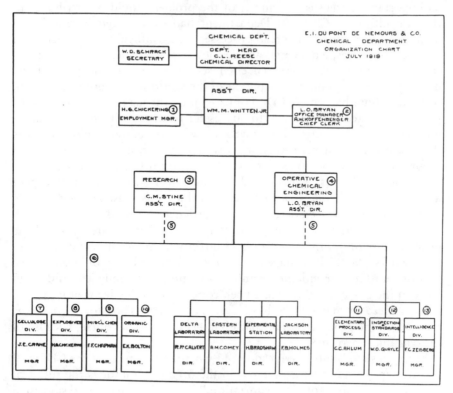

Figure 4.2. Organization of the Chemical Department, July 1919. Source: Series II, Part 2, Box 291, Hagley Museum and Library.

immediate success and has not only accomplished its purpose, but incidentally has been the means of bringing about more thorough advance consideration and more logical planning of experimental work." He believed that the Chemical Department had become "more alert and more responsive to the requirements of the Manufacturing Departments."[8]

Whitten could write these words because be believed them to be true. Earlier in the year he had called a meeting of the Chemical Department's top personnel (assistant research directors and laboratory directors and assistant directors) to discuss the following question: "Wherein does the Chemical Department fail to meet its obligation to serve the chemical and chemical engineering requirements of the manufacturing operations of the Company?"[9] Whitten asked each man to prepare a position paper on this question, which would be distributed to the others. These papers – almost twenty in number – constitute one of the most thoroughgoing self-assessments of research in the Du Pont Company's history.[10] With one or two exceptions, there was strong agreement that criticism of the Chemical Department by the manufacturing units was fully justified.

Although a large number of different diagnoses were offered, there was an important consensus that much of the problem could be attributed to the difficulties the Chemical Department had experienced in translating laboratory work into commercial processes. These difficulties stemmed from technical problems, managerial deficiencies, heavy reliance upon young and relatively inexperienced research chemists, and the crushing pace of the diversification program in the context of the world war. A number of men, many of whom had entered Du Pont's employ through the Eastern Laboratory, suggested that the key to successful relations with manufacturing units lay in devoting more attention to semiworks operations. Nowhere was this more needed than in dyestuffs research, which as noted above, had begun to consume the lion's share of the Chemical Department's budget.

Fletcher B. Holmes, A. E. Houlehan, and Elmer K. Bolton wrote cogent analyses of the Chemical Department's problems as illustrated by the dye venture. Holmes's memorandum in particular stressed that thorough semiworks experiments were "absolutely essential if we are to avoid the great expense of transferring processes directly from the laboratory to a full sized works plant." If managed properly, the procedure would guarantee utmost coordination with the manufacturing units. Certainly it would avoid some of the grave errors that had been committed in the dye venture where "plants were in many cases built even before the laboratory work was finished on the process."[11] This path had been taken, of course, because of the wartime emergency.

In response to Whitten's question of "whether the cause [of the Chemical Department's problems] is inherent in the organization, or is the result of improper functioning of the organization," the position papers all suggested that the latter was the case. No one questioned whether a central research organization was really the best way to organize research. But growing problems in the dyestuffs business and Irénée du Pont's particular attention to this problem soon led to a major debate about how best to organize research.

In November 1920, Irénée (now president of the company) proposed to the Executive Committee that the dyeworks be split off from the Miscellaneous Manufacturing Department, organized as a separate department, and have its own chemical division to do research, development, and chemical control work for dyestuffs manufacture.[12] That Irénée made this proposal to decentralize dyestuffs research is curious because he had steadfastly rejected the idea of decentralizing the company's overall management structure and would continue to reject the idea until September 1921.[13] But Irénée believed that the dyestuffs business was a special case. He observed that dyestuffs manufacture, chemical control, and research "must be far more closely coordinated than in any other of the company's activities." Furthermore, he argued that "under the existing form of company organization it is impossible to secure this necessary close coordination."[14]

Irénée's resolution failed to receive enough votes. Reese had been invited to the meeting to share his views on the matter. Obviously, he argued strenuously against Irénée's plan, but he also compromised by offering the committee a plan of his own to improve the effectiveness of research at the Jackson Laboratory and to achieve better coordination with the manufacturing end of the business. First, Reese's plan called for putting Charles Stine, who at this time was officially assistant chemical director for research, in charge of a new dyestuffs division in the Chemical Department. Under Stine would be Fletcher B. Holmes, director of the Jackson Laboratory; A. E. Houlehan, associate director; C. Chester Ahlum, assistant director for semiworks and plant design; and Elmer K. Bolton, assistant director for intermediates and azo colors. Reese outlined four other divisions within the Jackson Laboratory and specified chemists to head them. To provide closer cooperation with the manufacturing department, Reese proposed that Stine and someone comparable from manufacturing meet weekly to review both research and manufacturing problems, to resolve issues, and to make immediate and binding decisions affecting both the Chemical Department and the Manufacturing Department.[15] The committee endorsed Reese's compromise.

As events turned out, Reese's proposed meetings quickly developed into a small council that met weekly at the dyeworks's technical laboratory. The efficacy of Reese's plan is not entirely clear. But Charles Meade, vice president in charge of dyestuffs, wrote Irénée du Pont that after only a few meetings, it appeared the council had made "considerable progress...in the better harmonizing of chemical and operating work."[16]

Reese carried his compromise even further in December 1920 by organizing comparable research divisions for cellulose and explosives, each headed by an assistant director of the Chemical Department (see Figure 4.3). As Whitten wrote, this "partial reorganization" was for "the purpose of accomplishing a certain degree of decentralization." With three research divisions closely aligned to the company's manufacturing divisions, the Chemical Department would now not be so open to criticism. Each of the assistant directors, Whitten noted, "has the facilities and the authority necessary to allow him to act as a Chemical Director to an industry or a group of industries. It is believed that this change will result in still more alert and responsive service to operations by the Chemical Department."[17]

These changes still did not fully satisfy Reese's critics. In January 1921, R. R. M. Carpenter and Irénée du Pont exchanged letters about the Chemical department's problems. Carpenter suggested that the Development and Chemical departments be merged and put under one manager. Irénée liked the idea but said that with the exception of H. Fletcher Brown, there was no one in the Du Pont Company who had both the "chemical knowledge" and "good financial judgement."[18] He did not even consider Reese. Further consideration of this matter soon led to Brown's election to the Executive Committee with responsibilities for oversight of the Chemical and Development departments. This move required enlarging the Executive Com-

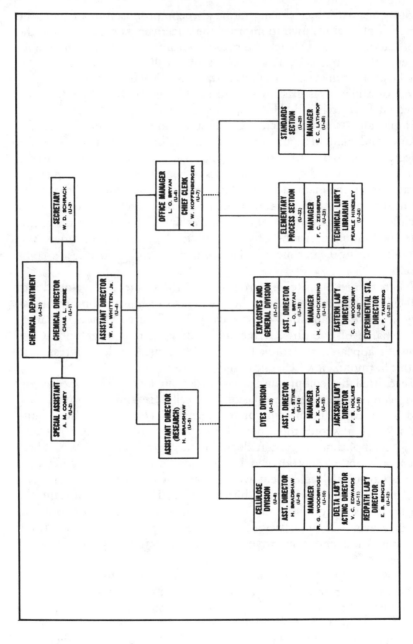

Figure 4.3. Organization of the Chemical Department, February 1921. Source: Du Pont Company Organization Charts, Imprints, Hagley Museum and Library.

mittee. When Irénée proposed Brown's appointment, he justified it by saying, "There has been some lack of satisfaction with the Chemical Department work which many be due to either a lack of representation on the Executive Committee, or the mental make up and habits of the Director of that department. In either case improvement would be expected."[19] As noted earlier, Irénée never respected Reese's abilities very much. Perhaps his earlier proposal that dyestuffs research be turned over to the new dyestuffs department was an attempt to get around Reese in this critical research and manufacturing area.

In any case, the move toward decentralization of the entire company that gathered momentum as Du Pont's profits turned into losses led to the virtually total undermining of Reese as Du Pont's research director. Irénée in particular never imagined that events would unfold in this manner. Du Pont's decision to decentralize its management structure is admirably discussed in Alfred D. Chandler's classic *Strategy and Structure* and need not be described here. But it is important to stress that decentralization did not lead inevitably to the dismemberment of the Chemical Department.

The Decentralization of Research

When the Executive Committee formally adopted the multidivisional, decentralized management structure on September 7, 1921, it did so on the basis of a final report written by three of its members following lengthy discussions, numerous other reports, and a joint meeting of the Executive and Finance committees.[20] The report had recommended that the autonomous, product-focused departments be managed by general managers and that each department be responsible for its own sales, manufacturing, purchasing, engineering, and research activities. The committee debated the question of decentralized purchasing and opted to retain its centralized purchasing office after providing general managers with certain controls over the central office. But it embraced the report's other precepts by approving the plan and, on the same day, selecting a new Executive Committee and appointing general managers of the industrial departments.

Apparently, there were still some executives, including President Irénée du Pont, who remained skeptical about breaking up the Chemical Department. In fact, evidence exists to suggest that some never even considered that adopting the decentralized plan meant breaking up Reese's department.[21] But after the reorganization went into effect, the new general managers and assistant general managers met and pushed hard for the decentralization of the Chemical Department. As Irénée du Pont wrote H. G. Haskell in mid-October, "The proposition has come up to split up the Chemical Dept. and divide it among the industrial divisions, excepting a central nucleus for filing reports and perhaps doing some general research work. The industrial managers are a unit for this and I believe have the best of the argument. I think Reese is of the opinion they are wrong but with them united against him there is no use in his winning his point, as the usefulness of the Chemical Dept. would be seriously injured thereby."[22] Irénée's remarks suggest that he believed he could block the splitting up of the Chemical Department but that the costs would be too high.

The Executive Committee delayed acting upon the general managers' request for a week so that Reese could formulate a response. Reese apparently petitioned his assistants to enumerate reasons why decentralizing the Chemical Department was a bad idea and then incorporated their reasons into his own for presentation to the Executive Committee.[23] The general managers formulated their own position and conveyed it in a cogent memorandum to the committee. Their view prevailed:

> It is the unanimous opinion of the General Managers that the direction of research, bearing upon current problems, and the chemical control of existing manufacturing operations, is one of the most important phases of management. In fact, the improvement of our products through research and the maintenance of high yields through chemical control are so vital to most of our industries as to be the deciding factor in determining success or failure. If, then, the Chemical Department continues to function as it has in the past, responsible only to the Executive Committee (its responsibility cannot be divided between the Executive Committee and the industrial departments) the managements of the industrial departments will thereby be deprived of the effective control of the activities of their departments and can at some future time, with unanswerable logic, escape responsibility in case of unsatisfactory performance.[24]

To assume control and accountability, the general managers wanted their own chemical divisions. They acknowledged the advantages of a centralized research department as argued by Reese: "coordination of research, avoidance of duplication of effort, promulgation of results which are of interest to more than one department, and the maintenance of a staff of consulting experts on special branches of the sciences, such as physical chemistry, bacteriology, colloidal chemistry, etc." But they argued that chemical divisions within the industrial departments "in no wise remove either the necessity for the central Chemical Department continuing to perform such functions, nor would it affect the desirability of continuing them.... Research of an involved scientific nature and all research on products which are not connected with existing manufacturing processes employed by the Company would, under the plan, be carried out by the central Chemical Department."[25]

The general managers then enumerated the advantages of separate chemical divisions within industrial departments. Clarity of mission and responsibility, "avoidance of conflict between the Chemical Department and the management," and the fostering of better relationships between research and plant personnel were foremost among them. For scientists in an industrial department, argued the new general managers, "their relation to the success of the business will be more intimate and less academic than if they remain members" of the Chemical Department. Finally, the general managers stressed that splitting up the Chemical Department would be easy because it was "already organized broadly along industrial lines, and, with the exception of the Experimental Station, maintains laboratories at the manufacturing plants of the industrial departments for the study of problems peculiar to these departments."[26]

Faced with these arguments and the whole spirit of reorganization, the Executive Committee voted on October 19, 1921, to allow an industrial department to establish its "own chemical division for the purpose of plant chemical control and improvement of product but that general chemical research shall remain under the direction of the Central Chemical Department." The committee instructed H. Fletcher Brown, the vice president who was now "advisor on chemical matters," to work out a plan of decentralization in conjunction with Reese and the general managers.[27] This plan was the formal process by which, as Charles Stine said, the Chemical Department was "dismembered."[28] During the next several weeks, Brown, Reese, and the general managers formulated a decentralization process, which the Executive Committee approved on December 7, 1921, after much consideration. Under the plan adopted, personnel from the various divisions of the old Chemical Department were transferred to their respective industrial departments.[29]

The transfers left the Chemical Department gutted. Since May 1920, the recession had been eating away at the department's work force. From a high of about 500 scientific and technical employees, the Chemical Department's staff had dropped to about 300 before the reorganization. But decentralization meant that most of these men went to the industrial departments. In fact, only 21 scientific and technical employees remained in the new central Chemical Department, and the Executive Committee authorized the new department to spend only $322,000 for research in 1922 – a far cry from the $3 million annual budgets Reese presided over in 1919 and 1920.[30] As Vice President F. W. Pickard said to a group of Philadelphia businessmen in early 1920, "during the war the duPont Co. built up the largest organization of trained chemists in America, if not in the world."[31] By the time of decentralization, the recession had undone much of that, although as Elmer Bolton argued, the severe financial losses sustained by Du Pont in dyestuffs and other new ventures in 1920 and 1921 gave the company an opportunity to get rid of all the unqualified research personnel it had hired because of the wartime emergency.[32] But the reorganization of 1921 – at least as it appeared to Reese – devastated his organization even more than had the recession.

Soon after the decentralization of the Chemical Department, the Explosives Department established a laboratory for smokeless powder research at the company's pioneering smokeless powder plant, Carney's Point, New Jersey. When the new laboratory opened, the department moved all its smokeless powder research from the Experimental Station. This move was no doubt long overdue. But it also carried an important message. With all the industrial departments except the Paint Department operating laboratories proximate to their manufacturing sites – research organized along the Eastern Laboratory model – the Experimental Station's role in Du Pont research was left up in the air. Would it become, as Irénée envisioned, merely a "central nucleus for filing reports and perhaps doing some general research work" or, as anticipated by the general managers, Du Pont's center for "[r]esearch of an involved scientific nature"? The latter was the type of research facility that some executives had hoped the Station would become when it was created in 1903.

Looking at the situation in late 1921, both Reese and Stine could have argued – and no doubt did – that Du Pont's executives had gone too far in decentralizing the company's research. The previous decade had proven to be a roller coaster ride for the Chemical Department. Reese had moved from directing the research of an industrial department to controlling the research of the entire company in a single, centralized organization. Diversification of the company's business had clearly pushed the company in this direction. The extreme centralization of research during a period of increasing diversification opened Reese and his department to severe criticism for being unresponsive to the commercial needs of these new businesses. But after the war Reese moved his research organization back toward a more decentralized structure. Indeed, the general managers pointed out that the Chemical Department's late 1920 reorganization was but a single, logical step from the decentralization of research they were advocating.

For Reese, decentralization must have seemed a staggering blow. No longer was the Chemical Department responsible for chemical control work, an area that Reese had developed to a fine art at the Eastern Laboratory. Also, the department would not be responsible for product and process improvement, a second area in which he had achieved handsome rewards through scientific research. Now at fifty-nine years of age, Reese must have felt that the most challenging and successful days of the Chemical Department were over. But for the much younger Charles Stine, the plan offered new vistas and opportunities that he would explore in the coming decade.

Repauno Dynamite Plant Control Laboratory, Gibbstown, New Jersey, 1897. This laboratory was the forerunner of the first Du Pont R&D laboratory, established in 1902 as the Eastern Laboratory.

J. Amory Haskell, cofounder of the Eastern Laboratory.

Hamilton Barksdale, cofounder of the Eastern Laboratory.

Charles L. Reese, founding director, Eastern Laboratory, and Du Pont chemical director, 1911–1924.

The Eastern Laboratory, Repauno dynamite plant site, Gibbstown, New Jersey, 1902.

The Eastern Laboratory Staff, 1902. Standing, left to right: Charles F. Lindsay, Richard T. Cann, John W. McCoy, Willis O. Heard. Seated, left to right: Charles L. Reese (director), Sidney S. Emery, Jesse B. Braunstein. Not pictured: Arthur L. La Motte, T. J. Wrampelmeier.

The Eastern Laboratory Staff, 1908. Top row, left to right: Wheeler, Fletcher B. Holmes, Backus, Charles M. A. Stine, Gallup, W. C. Holmes, Hamilton Bradshaw, Power, Clifford Woodbury, Bowland, Cowgill, Dance. Bottom row, left to right: Gray, Gambel, Le Maistre, Allen, E. G. Robinson, Arthur M. Comey (director), William S. Weedon, Eddy, Dougherty, Fleming, Paul, Sidney S. Emery.

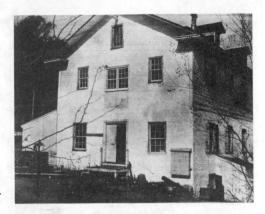

Rokeby Mill, temporary home of
the Experimental Station, 1903–06.

Francis I. du Pont, director of the Experimental Station, 1903–1907.

Pierre S. du Pont, c. 1907. This photograph was taken about the time du Pont had assumed responsibility for the Experimental Station. During this period he enunciated a policy for the Station to engage in high risk, high reward research and development work.

Arthur J. Moxham, founder of the Experimental Station.

Building 1, Experimental Station, 1906.

C. Marshall Barton, director of the Experimental Station, 1907–1911.

Fin Sparre, director of the Experimental Station, 1911–1915, architect of Du Pont's post-World War I diversification strategy, and director of the Development Department, 1919–1944.

The Experimental Station, 1919. The roof of Building 1 is barely visible through the trees in the lower right. The new organic chemistry laboratory (Building 173) is partly obscured by trees in the middle of the photograph. Tennis courts and auxiliary buildings are evident at the left and left center. By 1984, the Experimental Station would occupy the entire area captured in this photograph.

The Jackson Labora-
tory, Dyeworks, Deep-
water, New Jersey,
1917.

Dyeworks, Deepwater, New Jersey, 1935. The Jackson Laboratory complex and the Technical
Laboratory are located in the
lower right hand portion of the
photograph.

Irénée du Pont, president of the Du
Pont Company, 1919–26.

PART II

Creating a Chemical Empire

In the 1920s, the Du Pont Company management built an organizational framework and established a fundamental business strategy that served the company well for nearly a half-century. (See Table II.1 for data on the sales, income, investment, and number of employees of the company, 1921–41.) Through an aggressive policy of diversification, Du Pont became a broad-based chemical company. By 1931, Du Pont had ten industrial departments producing explosives, plastics, finishes, dyestuffs and organic chemicals, pigments, rayon and cellophane, heavy chemicals, ammonia, electrochemicals, and photographic film. The company's management put together this chemicals empire – Du Pont was one of the nation's ten largest firms and by far the biggest chemical producer – primarily through the acquisition of technology and companies. Each move the company made, however, was a strategic one designed to accomplish a particular goal or take advantage of an opportunity. Fin Sparre, head of the Development Department, and others at Du Pont became adept at connecting an emerging technology with a rapidly growing market. And it was the departmental research and development divisions that did the coupling. In this era, commercialization, not science or invention, was the forte of Du Pont R&D. (See Table II.2 for statistics on Du Pont's R&D program, 1921–41.) In the 1920s, chemical technology was advancing so rapidly, especially in Europe, that Du Pont could select technologies for further development in the United States. The company did not have to rely on the unpredictable process of invention to generate new opportunities. They were seemingly everywhere.

What this country provided was an enormous market. Increasingly affluent and consumption-minded Americans spent freely on all kinds of goods. Of course, the twenties was the decade of the automobile. The number of cars on U.S. roads increased from 8 million in 1920 to 27 million in 1929. This enormous growth created markets for all kinds of chemical products from plastics to paints to gasoline additives. Other new technologies had lesser but still important impacts. The motion picture proved to be an effective medium for advertising women's clothing. Fashions began to change rapidly, creating a demand for cheaper dresses. New appliances such as the refrigerator changed people's food-buying habits. To the Du Pont management, these social, economic, and technological changes presented great opportunities to introduce new products for a new era. But such

Table II.1. *Financial Summary of the Du Pont Company, 1921–41*
(in millions of dollars)

	1921	1926	1931	1936	1941
Sales	55.3	90.4	163.5	258.1	480.1
Operating income	7.3	9.4	19.0	44.3	57.5
Average operating investment	84.7	140.8	365.4	449.5	628.4
Average number of employees	n.a.	15,228	31,041	45,938	60,029

Note: All data from annual reports. n.a. = not available.

Table II.2. *Research and Development Statistics for the Du Pont Company, 1921–41 (in thousands of dollars)*

	1921	1926	1931	1936	1941
Total expenditures	1,734[a]	2,224[a]	5,400[b]	7,652[c]	12,400[c]
Expenditures as percentage of sales	3.1	2.5	3.3	3.0	2.6
Expenditures as percentage of earnings	23.8	23.9	28.4	17.3	21.6
R&D professional staff	135[c]	241[c]	755[d]	912[d]	1,341[d]

[a]C. M. A. Stine to J. Simpson Dean, Aug. 10, 1927, CRDD Files.
[b]"Expenditures for Experiment and Research," LMSS 10A/418, Box 11.
[c]Development Department, 1946 Report, Ira T. Ellis to C. H. Greenewalt, Feb. 14, 1955, Acc. 1814, Box 34.
[d]"Research Study – Interim Report [to the Executive Committee]," July 7, 1948, in Official Annual Research and Development Statistics, CRDD Files.

potential for growth could not be realized by merely selling basic chemicals; sophisticated new products had to be developed and integrated into existing fabricating and marketing networks.

To meet this challenge, the Du Pont management articulated an innovation strategy that became the focus of the company's activities: develop technologically advanced materials from basic raw materials and sell these materials to fabricators who will process them into final goods to be sold to consumers. For example, Du Pont made cellophane film and sold it to fabricators who cut and repackaged it, printed on it, or made bags out of it. Du Pont would reap its profits from this middle ground, not by integrating backward into lower-return commodities or forward into high-selling-cost consumer items. In this industry, the maximum profits resulted from the value added through manufacturing, and here Du Pont focused its activities.

A critical aspect of this strategy involved doing extensive technical service work to show fabricators, who were usually small companies, how to use the new materials. Although this work is usually not considered research or development, it was an essential part of Du Pont's innovation strategy. To create demand for its products indirectly, the company frequently advertised to the ultimate users – for example, Du Pont's ads promised consumers fresher and cleaner food if it was wrapped in cellophane. All this technical service and advertising effort depended on Du Pont's having a strong market, or even better a proprietary, position with products, so that the demand that this activity created would ultimately result in increased sales for Du Pont, not for somebody else. Thus in the 1920s, Du Pont R&D encompassed a broad range of activities from invention to technical service, but the great bulk of the effort went into developing nascent technologies into commercial products.

Because of the diverse and unrelated nature of Du Pont's products, the small remnant of the central Chemical Department had a difficult time finding a mission for itself until Charles M. A. Stine, a research director with considerable vision, took over in 1924. The rebuilding of the department into a major research organization is the subject of Chapter 5.

Chapters 6 and 7 show how the fortunes of two of the original departments, Paints and Dyestuffs, were dramatically improved by the commercialization of new products. In paints, Du Pont discovered and developed its first big product that it could claim entirely as its own: Duco finishes. Du Pont's commercialization of the General Motors–discovered tetraethyl-lead gasoline antiknock additive and Freon refrigerants transformed the struggling Dyestuffs Department into the powerful Organic Chemicals Department. At the same time, Du Pont was building new organizations around technology acquired from France: rayon, cellophane, and synthetic ammonia. Chapters 8 and 9 explore these developments.

Chemical technology during this era was an international phenomenon. Du Pont's executives keenly appreciated this fact and sought ways to control its deployment in markets they considered their own. One way to achieve this goal was through international agreements. Chapter 10 discusses the company's Patents and Processes Agreement (1929) with Imperial Chemical Industries (ICI) and its failed attempt to reach a similar agreement with the German chemical giant, I. G. Farben. The ICI agreement multiplied the effectiveness of Du Pont's research because the two companies shared their research findings, thus providing new leads and reducing excursions down dead ends.

By 1930, Du Pont's chemical empire was virtually complete. (See Figure II.1 for a chart of the company's organization in the early 1930s.) Its commercialization capabilities were truly remarkable. Du Pont could – and did – respond swiftly to developments in the industry that threatened its empire. Chapter 11 discusses the great and diverse resources drawn upon by Du Pont

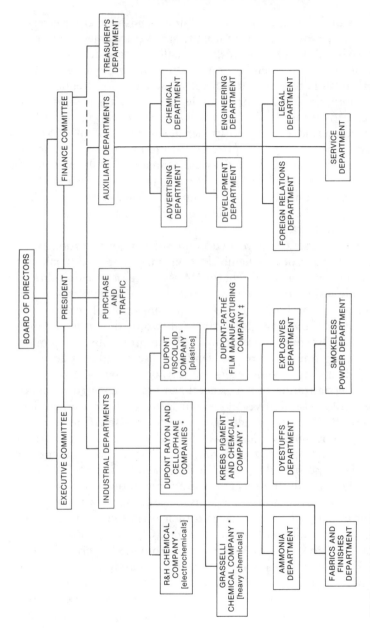

* Wholly owned subsidiaries

‡ DuPont controlled (51%) subsidiary

Figure II.1. Organization of the Du Pont Company, 1931. Source: Adapted from Du Pont Company Organization Charts, Imprints, Hagley Museum and Library.

when its large lithopone pigments business was threatened by a new pigment, titanium dioxide. These resources, including R&D capability, ensured that Du Pont would become a major player in the titanium dioxide business. Overall, Part II portrays Du Pont research in an era when it was concerned more with commercialization than with science or invention.

5

Rebuilding a Central Research Organization

When the Executive Committee voted to accept the general managers' bid to run their own research programs, it would have been relatively easy to abolish the Chemical Department. The department also could have become, as Irénée du Pont initially envisioned, merely the clerk of the Experimental Station. Neither of these scenarios unfolded, however. Two factors led to Du Pont's pursuit of a third alternative, the rebuilding of a central research organization alongside the growing industrial department R&D units. First, Du Pont's leaders realized that some research did not fit neatly into the departmental structure; the company needed a research organization not tied to immediate commercial goals. It needed an organization to carry out general, longer range research, which was both more scientific and entrepreneurial in nature than that pursued in the industrial departments.

Executives did not reach this conclusion overnight. Rather, they had to be educated about these research needs, and Charles M. A. Stine played the role of the Executive Committee's teacher on research. Stine, the research entrepreneur par excellence, was the second factor that led Du Pont to rebuild the remnant of the once large and powerful Chemical Department into a high-caliber central research organization. Stine was at once a visionary and a superb salesman. Yet he also carefully cultivated the support and good will of the industrial departments. In short, he convinced everyone in Du Pont that the company needed a strong, scientifically oriented central research organization. Stine could not achieve his goals until his supervisor, Charles L. Reese, retired in 1924; even then, several more years were required before he had organized the Chemical Department as he had envisaged in 1921.

Charles Stine, Research Entrepreneur

Stine's career at Du Pont prior to decentralization had been successful by any standard. But it had proceeded step-by-step with Reese's. Although Stine considered himself to be an industrial chemist who had demonstrated a keen interest in process and product development, he retained his enthusiasm for scientific studies. In this respect, he was far different than Reese, and this difference proved to be critical after the Chemical Department was decentralized. Stine's enthusiasm for science shaped his philosophy of industrial research. As a research manager in 1919, he complained that Du Pont's chemists attacked problems too empirically – or so it appeared from the way they wrote their reports. Stine requested that in the future, Du Pont's chemists explain the "theoretical consideration" the problem had received before work was initiated.[1] Stine reiterated his views in 1920. In an addendum to his critique of the Chemical Department, he stated that two factors – inadequate literature searches and unwillingness to consult experts – impaired the efficiency of Du Pont's chemists. On the latter issue, Stine noted that chemists were reluctant to discuss their problems with men who could give them a theoretical point of view. He believed that research efficiency meant bringing to bear on a given problem all the available resources, and theory was one way to avoid doing a long and expensive series of experiments in which only one variable was changed at a time. Stine believed that theory had its place in industrial research, just as did pilot plants.[2] Once in charge of the Chemical Department, theory would become his watchword and would lead the company to a whole new conception of industrial research.

Stine had risen rapidly through the hierarchy of the Chemical Department. He had served as a research supervisor at Eastern Laboratory for seven years, and in 1916 Reese transferred him to the Wilmington office to serve as head of the newly created organic division of the Chemical Department. Here Stine became deeply involved with Du Pont's entry into the dyestuffs business. In 1919, he became assistant director for research of the department, and after its breakup two years later, he was de facto chemical director for what was left of it. Even during the debates surrounding the disembodiment of the Chemical Department, Stine's views on research began to make their way into the Executive Committee's discussions. For example, after Stine gave a presentation to the Executive Committee in August 1923, Irénée du Pont told Reese that "it was a most interesting talk and I feel did a great deal of good in awakening interest among the Executive Committee members to the necessity of a chemical concern pushing research and chemical control."[3] Nine months later, Reese retired early, and the committee replaced him with the forty-two-year-old Stine. This move acknowledged what had already taken place unofficially. Reese had become a figurehead for Du Pont research. His value to the company after 1921 came not from what he did within the company but from how he represented it in the world outside Du Pont as president of such organizations as the Manufacturing Chemists Association (1920–23), the American Institute of Chemical Engineers (1923–25), and the American Chemical Society (1934–35).

Stine's Initial Strategy: Research for General Motors

When the Executive Committee decentralized the Chemical Department, Stine's immediate response was to grasp at straws in a desperate attempt to save what was left of it. Worried that the new central Chemical Department would not have enough funding to support a sufficient number of researchers and an aggressive research strategy, Stine initially asked the Executive Committee if the Chemical Department could contract to do research work for noncompeting companies.[4] But the Executive Committee chose to defer action on this unusual request until it had decided at what level to fund the department. To determine this figure, the committee asked the Chemical Department to submit for the 1922 budget three separate proposals, the lowest of which was referred to as the "Rock Bottom."[5] Accompanied by Stine, Reese lobbied heavily for the highest budget when the Executive Committee met to consider the matter. Stine's cogent arguments for the importance of a healthy central research organization carried the day; the committee approved the top budget of $322,000. At the same meeting, the Executive Committee acted on Stine's earlier request by saying that the Chemical Department could undertake work for outside, noncompeting firms provided that Du Pont's legal liability was safeguarded and that the Executive Committee approved each such instance of research for hire.[6] Stine correctly read between the lines of such consent that the Executive Committee would not really welcome such proposals.

Yet Stine and the Chemical Department got far more support in a related matter: doing chemical research for General Motors. When the Executive Committee was determining if and how to decentralize the Chemical Department, Reese and Stine were actively trying to consummate a general research agreement with General Motors that had been discussed during the previous three years. The pending breakup of the Chemical Department added extra incentive for them to tie down this contract.

Du Pont's desire to carry out research and development work for General Motors stemmed initially from its acquisition of extensive shares of General Motors stock. As Chandler and Salsbury explain in detail, Pierre du Pont's long-time assistant and financial wizard, John J. Raskob, had begun purchasing GM stock for himself early in 1914, and Pierre followed soon after. By the end of 1915, more than half of Pierre's non–Du Pont equity holdings was GM stock. With a rapidly growing cash surplus from wartime powder sales, the Du Pont Company itself invested in General Motors stock in late 1917 upon the urging of Raskob and GM president William C. Durant. Du Pont bought $25 million of GM stock, almost 25 percent of GM's outstanding shares and the largest such transaction in U.S. financial history up to that point. Subsequently, Du Pont invested another $22 million in GM before its Finance Committee decided, in mid-1919, that Du Pont owned enough of the automaker's equities (some 33 percent). In advocating these purchases, both Pierre and Raskob argued that Du Pont would benefit in two ways: through rapid growth in the value of the GM stock and through the leverage this would give Du Pont in securing GM's substantial business in such products as artificial leather, celluloid plastics, and paints and varnishes. Raskob also stressed that buying GM stock – and gaining control of GM for the "Du Pont interests" – would "afford many opportunities to keep our important men occupied with big things after the war."[7]

Two days after the Armistice, Irénée du Pont wrote to J. Amory Haskell, the former Du Pont vice president who had been named a member of GM's executive and finance committees. He reminded Haskell that he was to initiate discussions with GM about how the automaker could use the resources of Du Pont's Development, Chemical, and Engineering departments.[8] Irénée's letter began a series of discussions lasting almost four years. Irénée, his brother Lammot, Reese, and especially Stine wanted an agreement whereby Du Pont's Chemical Department would assume responsibility for GM's chemical research, leaving GM to do "mechanical" research. Despite ostensible control of GM by Du Pont, such an accord was never reached. The differently perceived needs of research at Du Pont and GM and especially the strong-mindedness of GM's research director, Charles F. Kettering, precluded such an agreement. Kettering had already become something of a legend through such inventions as the electric cash register and the electric automobile starter.[9]

In responding to Irénée du Pont's letter, Haskell pointed up the differing research needs of GM and Du Pont. He did not believe that Du Pont's Chemical Department could "be of any very great help to the General Motors." Rather, GM needed to have its own "Research Station" in Detroit and encompassing all the activities of GM.[10] Obviously, Haskell did not feel that Kettering's laboratory, located – at Kettering's insistence – in Dayton, Ohio, was fulfilling GM's needs. (Only later, in 1924, was Alfred Sloan able to force Kettering to move his operation to Detroit.)

Although Haskell's letter threw water on Du Pont's burning desire for the Chemical Department to conduct GM's chemical research, the idea was rekindled in 1919 when a growing problem in automobiles – fuels and engine knock – presented Du Pont with an opportunity to demonstrate its research prowess. The Chemical Department hoped the problem would lead to a broad research agreement with GM.

Not surprisingly, Charles Stine first broached this issue. Stine wrote to the president of General Motors, William C. Durant, that engine development had been attacked "almost exclusively along the line of obtaining greater efficiency of motors using a standard grade of gasoline." If the fuel were changed, however, "the problem is ... changed from a fundamentally mechanical one to a fundamentally physical-chemical one, the combustion of fuel in an engine cylinder being essentially a combination of physical-chemical phenomena." Stine pointed to the virtual absence of data and understanding of such phenomena, saying that hitherto engine development had been done "by cut and try, qualitative methods." Du Pont's scientists, Stine argued, would approach the fuel problem from a more fundamental perspective. He outlined eleven ways in which research would provide a better understanding of a "complete cycle of the gas engine operation." Such research would not be cheap. As Stine noted, "It seems fairly certain

... that this problem cannot be solved without the expenditure of a considerable sum of money," perhaps as much as $100,000."[11]

Very quickly it became apparent that Durant and others at General Motors, particularly Kettering, were not interested in undertaking such a fundamental study of fuels and their combustion in engines. Stine nevertheless authorized Eastern Laboratory to initiate a thorough literature search. But before this search could be completed, he gained a better sense of how GM viewed the problem of the internal combustion of fuels.[12] Kettering, who had just been named head of all of GM's "technical and engineering developments and research work," had a different idea in mind. Rather than gaining a fundamental understanding of what took place in an engine cylinder, Kettering sought a quick fix both for using kerosene as a motor fuel and for eliminating engine knock – "something that may be added at slight expense in small quantities, in a convenient form" to the fuel.[13] Stine responded by arguing that the scope of the fuel problem in internal combustion engines was far broader than "merely the discovery of some cure-all which can be added in small quantities" to fuels.[14] Du Pont's go-between Haskell seems to have arranged a meeting in which these differences in approach could be ironed out. Kettering's main research chemist, Thomas Midgley, and Du Pont's research directors met in Wilmington, but no definitive accord was reached on how Du Pont and GM would cooperate in fuel research.[15]

Midgley's visit was nevertheless helpful. Stine learned that GM possessed some resources for fuel research not available at Du Pont. GM was better equipped to handle chemical problems related to the cracking or hydrogenation of petroleum because it operated a semiworks-scale cracker at its Dayton laboratory. Du Pont, conversely, was better fit for "the study of dopes for auto engine fuel." Also, because of the Eastern Laboratory's sophisticated experience with the study of the velocity and nature of explosion propagation, such research "might be logically allocated to the du Pont Research Laboratories." As Stine argued, the "previous experience of the various laboratories and the present facilities should serve as an adequate guide of such decisions." He stressed that "it might be advisable and considerably cheaper to give consideration to the utilization of the chemical research facilities of the Du Pont Company rather than to contemplate the complete duplication of all such facilities, as the occasion may arise, by the General Motors Corporation."[16] As in the earlier discussions, the issue of who should pay for fuel-related research, Du Pont or GM, surfaced and was left unresolved. GM officials believed that Du Pont should fund its own research, whereas Reese and Stine argued that research costs should be allocated on the basis of respective gains to the two corporations.

Stine pressured Kettering and his associates to reach a general research agreement between Du Pont and GM. But Kettering asked for more patience and time to allow GM "to formulate our viewpoints dealing with cooperative work to be carried on by your Laboratories and the 'General Motors'

Laboratories."[17] Stine showed patience, as did other Du Pont officials, but each time he thought progress had been made, a setback occurred.[18]

The Eastern Laboratory's conclusions from its literature search proved to be the first major blow to the cooperative research attempt. The Eastern Laboratory report argued that Kettering's initial statement of the motor fuel problem was invalid. Kettering's goal was to develop a knock suppressant additive to kerosene to make it a usable motor fuel, the idea being that kerosene was much cheaper and more abundant than the better-performing gasoline. Eastern Laboratory researchers argued that even if the known knock suppressors such as aniline and similar aromatic amines could be manufactured economically, their addition to kerosene would drive up demand for kerosene and render Kettering's initial premise invalid. John Marshall, assistant director of the Eastern Laboratory, noted that the fundamental problem of understanding "the mechanisms of the combustion in the engine cylinder" remained untouched. The Eastern Laboratory had, however, recently undertaken this more basic study with the concurrence of Kettering.[19]

Given the Eastern Laboratory's conclusions, Stine believed it important to meet with Kettering and his associates to review the situation and to arrive at some decision regarding cooperative research.[20] Kettering displayed irritation at Stine's impatience and lack of appreciation for what he was trying to do.[21] Not until April 22, 1920, did Du Pont and Kettering have an opportunity to air fully the question of cooperative research. Once again, however, the radically different research styles and objectives of Kettering and Du Pont's Chemical Department spiced the meeting and militated against such a broad research agreement. Initially, some of Du Pont's executives thought otherwise. In the meeting, John J. Raskob, chairman of GM's Finance Committee, negotiated a multipoint proposed agreement on Du Pont–GM cooperative research. Both Lammot du Pont and Charles Stine took careful notes on the agreement. Lammot presented his version to Du Pont's Executive Committee and asked for its approval "in principle," the committee's last step prior to final authorization.[22] Stine and Reese appeared optimistic that the agreement would be signed. But Stine soon had doubts.

In a frank letter to Lammot du Pont, who would henceforth handle research negotiations with GM, Stine argued that the "real object" of Kettering's visit to Wilmington was not to negotiate a cooperative research agreement but "to see if he could interest the du Pont Company in the manufacture of aniline on a large scale for wholesale treatment of motor fuels with a view to suppressing the knock and increasing the efficiency of the motor." Stine, the seasoned research veteran, worried about undertaking such a project, which meant that Du Pont would have to make a substantial new investment in aniline plant. He questioned the validity of GM's patents on the use of aniline and similar aromatic amines as knock suppressors. Patents aside, there was "also the question of whether someone is likely to get something much better than aromatic amines to serve the same purpose in the near future."

Stine's concerns grew out of his basic mistrust of Kettering's research: "There is the question of how thoroughly the General Motors may have canvassed the motor fuel situation and *their conclusions* as a result of their consideration of the problem *and* there is the question of the degree to which we can depend upon the accuracy of their conclusions."[23] On the basis of his belief that Kettering and Midgley had not studied the fundamentals of fuel behavior in an engine cylinder, Stine obviously did not place much stock in their research. Such mistrust flavored the subsequent events in GM–Du Pont research relations. In a carefully muted fashion, Reese and Stine expressed their concerns about the use of comparatively large amounts of aniline as a knock-suppressing additive. These concerns were on the table when Du Pont sent its finally approved contract for cooperative research to Kettering for his signature.[24] Kettering chose to ignore the document, despite Lammot du Pont's intense desire and numerous efforts to secure Kettering's signature.

As a consequence of Stine's doubts about aniline, Du Pont moved slowly and cautiously even though Lammot's official policy was that Du Pont should help GM develop aniline and stand ready to become a manufacturer.[25] Such caution proved to be wise, because within a year Midgley and Kettering found a new antiknock candidate, selenium oxychloride, which they believed was "twenty-four times as strong as aniline."[26] Six months later, Midgley found that if a very small amount of tetraethyllead (TEL) were added to gasoline, the problem of knock in high compression engines was virtually eliminated. Stine's initial fears about the thoroughness of GM's research had been borne out.

Had Du Pont accepted GM's work on aniline as a knock suppressor as definitive, it could have easily committed itself to the construction of a large aniline plant that would have been superfluous by the time it opened. The moment GM discovered that selenium oxychloride was an effective antiknock compound, it moved swiftly to terminate a very small ($2500) research project that the Eastern Laboratory was doing for GM on flame propagation in an engine cylinder. Especially with the TEL fix, Midgley and Kettering regarded such research as "wasting money."[27] Had Du Pont been able to convince GM to pursue a more fundamental approach to the study of fuel in an internal combustion engine, there might have been alternatives to TEL. Finally, the discovery of TEL served to undermine the possibility of consummating a general research agreement between Du Pont and GM. The joint development of TEL was done under a separate, specific contract involving the Organic Chemicals Department rather than a general one, much to Stine's dismay.[28]

The TEL research and development episode came at precisely the time Stine was seeking a means to keep the Chemical Department afloat following the decentralization of research. Lammot doggedly pursued the general agreement, which Stine had put on the table in June 1920, until late 1922 when he committed a memorandum to the file saying such an effort no longer "seem[ed] possible."[29] Later, under a specific contract with GM similar to the TEL agreement, Du Pont developed manufacturing processes for Freon refrigerants, another of Midgley's discoveries.

The Development of a New Strategy

Having failed to consummate the GM agreement and recognizing that it was impolitic to survive by contracting for research with the outside world, Stine was forced to rethink matters and to begin to formulate a new role for the Chemical Department. It took him several years to do so. But once he was officially named director of the department in 1924, he moved to bring the department's research capabilities to new heights.

Stine's success in rebuilding the Chemical Department after 1921 rested on his ability to ride the tide of diversification that had occasioned the breakup of his department. He did so by staying on top of departmental developments and the new technologies being brought in by the company's aggressive acquisitions program. He also fostered good relations with the industrial departments on which his organization depended and was thus able to strengthen his organization. By following the development of all Du Pont's chemical technology, Stine was eventually able to see the common scientific bases underlying these seemingly different technologies. Stine then moved to secure from the Executive Committee larger budgets for general research.[30]

Initially, however, the Chemical Department was entirely dependent on the industrial departments for its survival. (See Table 5.1 for a breakdown of the Chemical Department's source of funds and its research staff in the 1920s.) None of its budget was for "general investigations" pursued alone by the Chemical Department. Rather, all the department's research funds came from the industrial departments and the Development Department. Hence, the Chemical Department initially pursued no long-range or general research strategy – a striking contrast to the earlier Experimental Station. De facto, the Chemical Department was the departmental laboratory for the Paint Department until that department built its Central Technical Laboratory (later called the Marshall Laboratory) for paint research in Philadelphia in 1927. Between 1922 and 1927, 60 percent of the Chemical Department's budget came from the Paint Department and its successors. Stine also depended heavily on the Development Department for funds – more than $100,000 a year between 1922 and 1930. With Development Department funds, the Chemical Department often played the role originally envisioned by A. J. Moxham when he advocated establishing an experimental laboratory: screening or evaluating inventions coming to Du Pont from the outside. Sparre's Development Department also often asked the

Table 5.1. *Chemical Department Expenditures, 1922–30 (in thousands of dollars)*

	1922	1923	1924	1925	1926	1927	1928	1929	1930
Total	265	295	361	449	560	660	825	950	1,188
Percentage of total expenditures accounted for by industrial departments and Development Department	88	87	80	90	92	87	69	54	52
Work for industrial departments	123	151	289ᵃ	253	370	437	469	415	419
Investigation of new industries for Development Department	109	94		152	143	139	97	100	200
General investigations by Chemical Department	0	0	11	4	13	26	101	190	278
Fundamental research	0	0	0	0	0	25	109	180	230
Administrative and miscellaneous	34	51	61	38	33	33	51	65	59
Number of employees on research staff on January 1	21	28	38	42	60	70	79	79	114

ᵃIndustrial department figure includes Development Department expenditures.

Sources: 1922–23: Charles L. Reese to the Executive Committee, March 27, 1924, Acc. 1784. 1924: "Development of the Chemical Department," 1940, Acc. 1784. 1925–30: Annual Chemical Department Budget Appropriations, 1925–30, Acc. 1784.

Chemical Department to pursue ideas that had emerged within the Du Pont Company.

In an attempt to assess the performance of the Chemical Department, the Executive Committee asked Reese, shortly before his resignation as chemical director, to prepare a profit and loss statement on the work of the Chemical Department for the previous two years. They suggested that he classify the projects as those accomplished solely by the Chemical Department, those done jointly with others, and those started by the Chemical Department and finished by others. Reese tried to follow these instructions and put together numbers which showed that the company had gotten a positive return on the money the Chemical Department had spent. Reese's report highlighted the department's hodgepodge of projects. It had, among many other projects, tried to put together and then sell a process for recovering glycerin from fermentation slops (a project not radically different from the one pursued much earlier at the Experimental Station), developed new corrosion-resistant ferrous and nonferrous alloys, improved the durability of lithopone white pigment, initiated testing on the durability of paints, and attempted unsuccessfully to prevent the yellowing of nitrocellulose plastics on exposure to sunlight.[31]

The Executive Committee also asked the Chemical Department to assume responsibility for chemical control in certain company processes. This work, they argued, would not only provide honest data on yields (which they apparently were not getting from the industrial departments), but would also give the Chemical Department the opportunity to provide constructive criticism of these processes. The department did some work along these lines late in Reese's tenure. But five months after Stine was named chemical director, he wrote to the Executive Committee that he had been thinking about "our obligations (if any)" regarding chemical control. He argued that his department should not be saddled with this kind of work and asked the committee if they concurred. With tacit approval from the committee, the Chemical Department soon stopped its chemical control activities.[32]

Stine still had to prove to the Executive Committee what a central research department could do for the Du Pont Company. He knew that executives wanted to see direct monetary returns from his department's work. But in many cases, such as the development of an important ingredient for Duco fast-drying lacquer, Stine considered it impossible to determine the value of the work. Although he tried to assess the savings for the company from some of the larger projects, he made no attempt to calculate a total benefit in his first annual report. This was the last time that he would do any such calculations. Perhaps through extensive private discussions with members of the Executive Committee, he made his point that research cannot be accounted for like other business activities.

In this report, Stine defended his department's research program from potential criticism that it had not come up with anything big. His rebuttal provides evidence about his research strategy in the mid-1920s, when his department was under growing pressure from the industrial departments to come up with "striking advances" in products and processes. Stine said that he was not insensitive to this criticism. Some executives and managers had even suggested that the reason the Chemical Department had not developed "radically new things" was because its research was actually tied too closely to the departments' businesses. The solution, they thought, lay in more completely divorcing the Chemical Department from the commercial concerns of the departments. Such criticism could well have been occasioned by the increasing awareness of the successful central research programs at other companies, such as General Electric. Stine countered this suggestion:

> I do not believe that it would be possible for a central Chemical Department to produce the desired results if the department were actually divorced from the great mass of work which it now carries out for the various industrial departments, set off to one side and, in a manner of speaking, directed to "invent some good, *big*, profitable things." The intimate touch with the various industrial lines of the Company is, to my mind, absolutely indispensable.

Stine then skillfully turned the emerging criticism to his department's gain. He argued that the Chemical Department was "so completely tied up" with work for the industrial departments that it possessed neither the personnel nor the budget "to undertake work along any very *radically new* lines." If more resources were forthcoming, he would gladly reorient the focus of the Chemical Department. Yet he cautioned that his approach, although oriented toward Du Pont's manufacturing lines, might ultimately undermine current practices:

> I have in mind attention to such problems as synthetic resins to serve as substitutes for Pyralin window sheeting. I cite this particular example because I wish to make another point in this connection. Should work of this nature be successful (either within the duPont Company or outside of the Company), immediate consideration of the effect upon Arlington's business is involved. It, therefore, seems logical at the same time to give considerable attention to the question of so altering Arlington's products that wider fields of usefulness may be found for them because of improved properties, and yet confine the alterations to such developments as may not preclude continuation of the manufacture in the present equipment. It should be recognized that the question of the development of any new process or product has many angles.[33]

Stine had thus suggested that the research and development he wanted to pursue might ultimately destroy some of the company's capital. He sought to make it clear that he hoped this would not be the case; he indicated that in the development of new synthetic resins to replace Pyralin window sheeting, his department would try to ensure that Arlington's present equipment could be used. But there were no guarantees. The odds would be better, however, if the Chemical Department maintained its contacts with the industrial departments by continuing its shorter-range research programs while also initiating these longer-range programs aimed at "radical" innovation. Stine's unstated message was clear nevertheless: If the Executive Committee wanted more work done on big new things, then it would have to give him more staff and money.

Over the next few years, Stine got both, principally because the paint and ammonia manufacturing departments increased the amount of work that the Chemical Department did for them. By 1928, his staff had increased to seventy-nine chemists, and his budget was over $800,000.[34] Since 1925 Stine had also succeeded in winning increasing appropriations from the Executive Committee for "general investigations" – or what he often called "pioneering applied" research. A mere $4,300 in 1925, these research funds grew to over $100,000 in 1928, and for 1929, Stine requested $190,000, more than 20 percent of his total budget.[35] By this time, too, as will be discussed in Chapter 12, he had created – with the Executive Committee's approval – a fundamental research program with a budget roughly equal to that of the "general investigation" research budget. Together, these two research programs or budget categories provided Stine's Chemical Department with unprecedented independence. Stine could now formulate a comprehensive research strategy for the Chemical Department, which would provide far greater stability for the department than it had experienced since decentralization in 1921.

Before 1928, Stine had complained that his department lost through transfers to other departments half as many staff as it hired.[36] Usually, Chemical Department researchers would become so involved in their work for an industrial department that they would transfer into that department. This led to constant turnover in personnel – a phenomenon that Charles Reese had first encountered in the early days of the Eastern Laboratory two decades earlier. But the growing independence of the department and Stine's management style led by 1928 and 1929 to the creation of a new climate in the Chemical Department. Now, chemists sought to stay with the department for their whole careers.

By the end of the 1920s, the Chemical Department was no longer the gutted remnant of decentralization. It had become a vital force in Du Pont's research and development program, and the department's director – first Stine and, after mid-1930, Elmer K. Bolton – became the major spokesman for Du Pont R&D. Though not apparent on an organization chart, the director of the Chemical Department was indeed the chemical director for the company. He coordinated Du Pont's entire research program by chairing the meetings of all the company's departmental research directors and by assuming responsibility for knowing how Du Pont's research front was advancing and where it was lagging.[37]

Stine succeeded in revitalizing the Chemical Department for a number of reasons. Foremost was his ability as both salesman for and manager of research. He demonstrated that he could sell the Chemical Department's service to the industrial departments while also selling research to the company's Executive Committee. In 1929, Stine explained his approach to work for the industrial departments:

> I have for the last six or seven years been engaged in the organization of a Central Chemical Department and the building up of suitable personnel for conducting chemical research, with a view to the proper co-ordination of the Central Chemical Department with the existing chemical sections of the various departments of the Parent Company, as well as with those of the du Pont subsidiaries, such as the du Pont Viscoloid, du Pont Rayon, and du Pont Ammonia companies.
>
> Perhaps the most important idea which I have attempted to keep before my assistants in this work is the necessity for continuous intimate contact with the various departments and subsidiaries which we have been attempting to serve. This has been brought about chiefly by frequent exchange of visits and by carrying on work in the Central Chemical Department of immediate current interest to the various departments and subsidiary companies. We have been very much concerned to insure that the personnel of the Central Chemical Department should have a proper acquaintance with the sales and production points of view of the production departments which we serve.[38]

Had Du Pont not become a greatly diversified chemical company by the mid-1920s, Stine would probably have had problems selling his ideas about fundamental research to the Executive Committee. Stine recognized that, in spite of their seeming differences, many of Du Pont's businesses rested upon common scientific bases. He wished to focus the Chemical Department's research program on these bases. For example, Stine argued that pioneering applied work on resins would benefit Du Pont's paint, plastics, and film businesses. More fundamental research on polymerization would provide the key to attacking problems common to these businesses. Thus, in advocating a more general research program for the Chemical Department, including his elite fundamental research program approved by the Executive Committee in 1927, Stine could argue with conviction that his department's research would not, as Francis Bacon wrote centuries earlier, be "barren of works." Rather, it would inevitably contribute to the company because it rested squarely on Du Pont's broad industrial base. With Du Pont being a highly diversified chemicals company, its central Chemical Department's general and fundamental research programs stood a far greater chance of success than would otherwise have been the case. In this sense, as in a purely pecuniary one, Stine owed much of his department's success to the industrial departments, including their research and development organizations.

6

Research to the Rescue:
Du Pont Finishes

At the same time that Stine was reestablishing the credibility of the Chemical Department, the industrial departments were building their own research organizations. The 1921 corporate reorganization and the breakup of the Chemical Department left the company's R&D in disarray. Only the Dyestuffs and Explosives departments, through the Jackson and Eastern laboratories, respectively, maintained large technical organizations. But even their programs suffered considerably from the corporatewide retrenchment of 1920 and 1921. It would take almost a decade for Du Pont to rebuild its research organization to its postwar peak.[1]

The establishment and subsequent growth of the company's industrial R&D divisions was directly connected to the pressing problems of the individual departments. Long-range, highly theoretical or speculative research had no place in these organizations. For the first few years, the departmental research activities focused on the assimilation of newly acquired technology. Much of this work centered on process and product improvement and was frequently done in the plant. Later, with the new technology in place, the emphasis shifted to more innovative research aimed at the development of related new products and processes and important modifications of the old ones. This change in strategy occurred in the mid to late 1920s. Although each department independently developed and ran its research programs, in general, all followed the same path in the two decades after 1921.

Following the precedent it had set earlier with explosives, the Du Pont Company looked for industries that might be consolidated and integrated. The paint business appeared to be a likely candidate. In the World War I era, a large number of small localized companies manufactured finishes consisting of pigments and resins dispersed in linseed or China Wood oil, combined with a mineral oil solvent. In 1917, with the object of creating a large, integrated firm, Du Pont began to purchase paint companies. But it soon abandoned this strategy because the company could not make a satisfactory profit.[2] Between 1918 and 1920, Du Pont's paint business yielded only a 3.5 percent return on investment at the same time that the industry's largest firm, Sherwin-Williams, was earning over 12 percent.[3] Du Pont faced an uphill battle trying to enter this highly conservative industry about which it knew nothing. Eventually, the company established a prominent place for itself not by competing with the traditional products but by commercializing two new kinds of finishes, low-viscosity nitrocellulose lacquers (Duco) and alkyd resin paints (Dulux). Du Pont's research capability proved to be the key to improving the profitability of its paint business.

Success did not come quickly or easily. Improving paints proved to be much more difficult than raising the yield of nitroglycerin in the nitration process. While Du Pont chemists were trying to improve the paints, salespeople had to convince distributors to carry them. Consumers of paint – master painters and the general public – had a difficult time distinguishing a good from a bad product. Only after several years of use would the difference become apparent. In this type of business, consumers favored tried-and-true over new-and-improved products. Sherwin Williams, the industry leader, had a long-established reputation as a producer of quality finishes.[4]

Heavy losses in the paint business were one of the primary reasons Du Pont reorganized in 1921, creating five autonomous operating divisions. Soon, the new Paint Department began to turn a profit on its approximately $10 million in sales. But Du Pont still had less than 4 percent of the market, and management remained dissatisfied with the return on its investment.[5] To create a more favorable public image for its products, the Paint Department management decided in 1923 to put the Du Pont name on its numerous brands of paint and adopted the chemical engineer as the centerpiece of its advertisements.[6] The message the company sought to convey was that Du Pont was using science and engineering to improve its product. At this time, however, the Paint Department did almost no research.[7] The first major breakthrough in finishes came from another company laboratory.

Duco lacquer was invented in the Cellulose Products Department, which had responsibility for applications of nitrocellulose solutions. One advantage of a diversified company is that discoveries made in one department sometimes can be developed by another. The company had acquired a small lacquer business with the purchase of the International Smokeless Powder and Solvents Company in 1904 and the Arlington Company in 1915. Lacquers made by dissolving nitrocellulose in amyl acetate to form a syrupy solution had been used for some time for dip-coating small items such as brush handles and metal toys. Upon evaporation of the solvent, a permanent film formed. Another product that the department wanted to make was nitrocellulose motion picture film. Researchers in the department's Redpath Laboratory in Parlin, New Jersey, had been attempting to develop a commercially acceptable film since 1915.[8]

Duco became Du Pont's first major invention because it initiated a revolution in paint technology. Its discovery at the Redpath Laboratory in the summer of 1920 resulted from experiments that had gone awry. Chemists at Parlin were attempting to remedy a defect in their films. Static electricity on Du Pont's movie film caused streaks on the unexposed film when it rolled through a camera. Experiments under the direction of Earl C. Pitman showed that the addition of small amounts of sodium acetate to nitrocellulose film increased its conductivity, thereby eliminating the buildup of static electricity. The experiments also showed that sodium acetate lowered the viscosity of the solutions, but for many months no one realized the significance of this result. In July 1920, Pitman decided to try a full-scale test and made up a fifty-gallon drum of thick nitrocellulose jelly to be cast into a film. However, a power failure at the plant delayed the test for several days, and when the drum was reopened the researchers were surprised to find a thin, syrupy material. The credit for realizing that this less viscous solution might find application as a lacquer traditionally has gone to Edmund M. Flaherty, who was superintendent of the Parlin plant. Flaherty's name appears on the basic patent even though J. D. Shiels, chief chemist at the Pyroxylin Laboratory, had a stronger case based on the documents that Du Pont gathered in preparation for awarding a bonus for this discovery. Because the invention was an idea, it proved impossible to say who had thought of it first. The "A" bonus committee decided to divide the credit between them.[9] Apparently, Flaherty and Shiels saw in this nitrocellulose solution the answer to a long-standing dilemma of lacquer makers.

Up to this time, lacquer manufacture was a sideline business of chemical manufacturers who made nitrocellulose for other products. In 1919, ten companies sold about 500,000 gallons of lacquer and thinners at about two dollars per gallon. This represented only about 0.25 percent of the nation's output of finishes. Significantly, no paint manufacturer produced nitrocellulose lacquers. Although there were several factors limiting their use, the major obstacle was that all these lacquers contained only about 6 percent nitrocellulose. At higher concentrations, the solution became so thick that a smooth, even coating could not be obtained. Dilute lacquers had to be applied in several coats to form an adequately thick film. Using them was both time-consuming and expensive, since large quantities of amyl acetate solvent were lost through evaporation. It was no secret that the key to broader application was finding a method of producing a satisfactory lacquer with a higher nitrocellulose content. To this end, researchers in the 1910s had used chemical and physical means to degrade nitrocellulose so that the viscosity at any given solid concentration would be much lower than that of standard solutions. They had succeeded in doing this, but the lacquers they produced yielded only brittle films. It soon became widely held that low-viscosity lacquers showed no promise.[10] Flaherty and Shiels shared this belief until Pitman's "failed" experiments led them to reexamine it. As is frequently the case with new materials, the first uses of Duco were not the ones that were ultimately the most successful. In January 1921, after roughly six months of development work, Du Pont began to sell the new lacquer for traditional applications: brush handles, pencils, builders' hardware, and light fixtures. This new product, called Viscolac, contained up to 16 percent nitrocellulose, three times the amount of competitive lacquers.[11]

Viscolac's success came in the automobile industry. In early 1922, Harry C. Mougey of General Motors's Dayton laboratory visited Du Pont to discuss automotive paints.[12] The car manufacturer had recently formed a corporatewide committee to study this problem, because finishes had become a headache for GM. Cars took too long to paint, and the resulting finish soon faded and cracked. The only cheap and durable finish at the time was black baked enamel, but Alfred P. Sloan believed that colors would enhance the appeal of lower-priced cars.[13] At the time, color finishing a car was a long and tedious process stretching over weeks. To make matters worse, all the cars being finished had to be housed and therefore took up enormous space in the plants.[14] General Motors had considerable incentive to explore new finishes.

General Motors's inquiry did not catch Du Pont completely by surprise. In early 1921, Du Pont had refinished several cars with Viscolac.[15] Even earlier, low-concentration nitrocellulose lacquers made by the Arlington Company had been used to refinish some cars on the West Coast, and the finish had held up well upon exposure to desert sun and alkali.[16] In 1922, General Motors decided to test various finishes on exposure panels. Flaherty and R. C. Williams took Viscolac test panels to Dayton for this experiment. There, Flaherty testified later, he talked to Charles F. Kettering, the head of GM's Dayton research organization, who wanted more durable finishes for his air-cooled car. Kettering wanted a car that did not need to be stored in a garage.[17] The first finish experiments were done with Viscolac, which did not adhere well to metal and produced a dull, washed-out finish. In August 1922, Du Pont added more of a finer-ground pigment to the automotive lacquer and changed the name to Duco. This product turned out to be brittle, so Du Pont developed a softener to make a tougher film. By early 1923, William P. Allen, general manager of the Cellulose Products Department, wrote to the Du Pont Executive Committee that no more radical changes in the lacquer would be necessary.[18]

The development of Duco proceeded rapidly because the GM operating divisions, especially Buick and Oakland, did extensive experiments with the new finish. R. C. Williams played the critical role of liaison between the Du Pont chemists and GM's production people. Du Pont's Allen stated that "although normally a problem like this would have been worked out in Dayton, the interests of the individual units has led them to do their own work."[19] At first Buick showed the most interest, but this division was satisfied with its existing finishing operation.[20] Oakland, a struggling division with little to lose, took over the lead. The paint superintendent at Oakland worked hard to improve the new finish and find the best uses for it.[21] Other GM divisions also experimented with Duco but had serious reservations about using it on their cars. Chevrolet, the lowest-priced model, was completely satisfied with its durable and cheap black baked enamel finish. At the next level, Olds was looking for a cheaper finish, but Duco appeared to be too expensive. The top-of-the-line car, Cadillac, approached the new finish with extreme caution because it did not want to take any chances with its luxury image.[22] Cadillac head H. H. Rice expressed his concerns to Kettering:

> I think one of the most dangerous things the corporation could do would be to adopt, generally, the new method of painting before it had been tried in every conceivable fashion. I can conceive of a bad engine or other mechanical fault in a car which would do less damage, from an advertising standpoint, than poor paint.[23]

Cadillac had an expensive and time-consuming painting process that did not give a long-lasting finish, but the customer at least knew and accepted what he or she was getting.

Further tests on Duco showed that it had outstanding durability. In the summer of 1923, Oakland decided to use it on its light blue touring sedan. At this time, Frank O. Clements, Kettering's assistant in Dayton, wrote to President Sloan that "Duco is coming along very rapidly; in fact, it is proving so successful and interesting that it worries us a bit. We are not having the proper quota of troubles."[24] General Motors had, in a relatively short time, learned how to use this new finish effectively.

Not only was Duco more durable than existing color finishes, but it also could be applied in much less time and with less labor than conventional paints and varnishes. Previously, five different kinds of coatings were applied over a period of one to two weeks. First came the primer; then the surface, color, and rubbing coats were applied; then came a finishing coat. The coloring and rubbing coats were the weakest links in the system, and Duco replaced these.[25] It cut the number of process steps by one-third, and it eliminated three twenty-four-hour drying periods. But the labor needed to finish a body declined only by 15 percent.[26]

Duco lacked only one thing: the high luster of traditional varnishes. One solution was to use a standard finishing varnish over the Duco. This added an extra step, however, and the outer coating would last less than a year. As an alternative, Oakland omitted the finishing varnish and instead rubbed the Duco surface to get as high a gloss as possible and often applied a wax finish.[27] Still these cars had less luster than those finished by the standard method. But the enthusiastic public response to the 1924 Oaklands suggested to many at GM, including Sloan, that mirrorlike luster was not an absolute necessity.[28]

Sloan, who always paid close attention to marketing, felt that the time was right for the switch to Duco, although Buick and Cadillac continued to complain about the lack of luster of the Duco finish.[29] In early 1924, Sloan wrote to Du Pont's Allen that "I am very anxious to have them weigh fully and seriously the desirability of using Duco finish in a very large way on our models forthcoming August 1, 1924.... I recognize the desirability of being conservative and all that sort of thing, but that can be overdone as well as everything else."[30] By the following summer, every division offered at least one model finished with Duco.[31] Sloan seems to have played a major role in this conversion. When a Du Pont representative visited the Fisher body plant in mid-1924, Lawrence Fisher referred to Duco as "this damned stuff." Nevertheless, Williams reported back to Du Pont that "Fisher gave the impression of one resigned to his fate and trying to make the best of it."[32] The implication was that Fisher would be using Duco in spite of his reservations.

Sloan's perception of the market proved correct, and Duco soon took over automobile finishing. In 1925, Du Pont sold over a million gallons at a price of about five dollars a gallon. Sales doubled the following year, yielding a profit of nearly $3 million. Three years later, Du Pont sold $14 million worth of Duco lacquers, which accounted for 12 percent of the company's sales and a slightly higher percentage of its profit.[33]

Before Duco had proven successful, it had caused a crisis in Du Pont's one-year-old departmental structure. This was the first, but not the last, time that research discoveries would undermine existing products and cause realignments within the company. Duco was the property of the Cellulose Products Department; but the Paint Department's most profitable division, the Flint Paint and Varnish Company, had a thriving automotive paint business. In 1923, Flint earned 70 percent of the department's earnings on a little more than one-third of its sales.[34] Obviously, the Paint Department and its Flint subsidiary were worried about Duco. The general managers of the two departments requested that the Development Department undertake a study to determine how to handle Duco organizationally. Flint argued the automotive business was its area and "that the exploitation by Parlin of Viscolac products for coating automobiles is an unwarranted invasion of the special province of [Flint], which should in fairness be so curbed and adjusted as to protect the rights of the Flint Division in its own proper and exclusive field.... [N]o branch of the Company should be permitted to destroy the business of another branch and render its plant investment useless."[35] Since Du Pont certainly did not want to suppress this promising development, the real conflict was over control of the new finish.

The Development Department's Norman P. Wescott (later backed by the Executive Committee) ruled in Parlin's favor. This decision is an outstanding example of the Du Pont management's commitment to innovation regardless of the organizational problems it caused or the capital it destroyed. Wescott stated that "the Du Pont Company is fundamentally a manufacturing concern, and under its present plan of organization the provinces of its various divisions are determined on the basis of manufacturing rather than selling activities...." He reminded Flint that the organization of the company was not fixed but is "fairly subject to such re-arrangement from time to time as changing conditions may warrant...." On the issue of the new development destroying existing capital, Wescott concluded "that the damages wrought will be simply another instance of the injury which is frequently attendant upon industrial evolution. In such circumstances the unavoidable misfortune to the individuals concerned may be hard, but can not be said to be unfair." Finally, he recommended that when Duco had proven successful, the Flint organization should be absorbed by Parlin.[36] Two years later, the two departments were merged, and the management of the former Cellulose Products Department assumed command of the new one, the Paint, Lacquer, and Chemicals Department.[37] In 1931, Du Pont changed the name of this department to the Fabrics and Finishes Department.

Earlier, the discovery of Duco by Parlin had awakened the old Paint Department to the need for finishes research. Because Du Pont's paint organization did not build its own laboratory until 1927, it contracted with the Chemical Department to do most of its research, including that usually done at the plant.[38] Aided by the Chemical Department, the Paint Department also sought to develop a slower-drying variety of Duco that could be applied with a brush. Du Pont hoped to capture much of the furniture refinishing market with this product. In 1926, "Brush Duco" caught on, primarily because of public enthusiasm for Duco automotive finishes. Technically, the product had problems; it dried too rapidly, and the pigments settled out into a hard cake on the bottom of the can.[39] Soon, though, Du Pont would replace the nitrocellulose in Brush Duco with a new kind of film-forming material.

In 1926, chemists in Du Pont's Chemical Department began to investigate synthetic resins that could be used to improve Brush Duco. The most promising candidates appeared to be alkyds, condensation polymers of glycerin and phthalic anhydride, produced by the General Electric Company.[40] Du Pont's researchers found that when they modified these resins, they formed excellent films. Alkyd resin finishes, Du Pont discovered, were durable and had high initial gloss, unlike Duco, which had to be rubbed. In drying time, the alkyds were halfway between Duco and standard paints and could be either brushed or sprayed. Du Pont could not establish a patent position for its new modified alkyd resins because GE, in January 1927, had applied for a broad patent on them. In order to commercialize its product, Du Pont was forced to make a patent licensing agreement with GE.[41]

Du Pont named its alkyd resins "Dulux" and developed them initially as undercoats for Duco automotive lacquers. By 1929, Du Pont had developed new uses for its Dulux alkyd resins and sold over 1 million pounds.[42] The hard-drying enamel found extensive use on refrigerators, kitchen cabinets, washing machines, and metal signs.[43]

Du Pont had hoped that the combination of Duco and Dulux would put the company into a position of leadership in the paint industry. However, Sherwin-Williams survived the technological changes of the 1920s and retained its top position in the 1930s. Obviously, being first in finishes required something more than pioneering technology. Unlike Du Pont, Sherwin-Williams had an extensive distribution network, and in 1926 and 1930 Du Pont seriously considered buying its chief competitor principally for its marketing setup.[44] During this period, Du Pont's paint business was probably about half that of Sherwin-Williams, which was a dramatic improvement over the early 1920s.[45]

Lacking Sherwin-Williams's marketing advantages and faced with increased competition after the Depression began in 1929, Du Pont decided to exercise its proprietary advantage – the Duco patents – to gain better control over the industry. Although Duco was clearly a Du Pont innovation, there had been considerable doubt whether there was anything technically new about it. In 1921, the company had filed two patent applications on its discovery. One, in the name of E. C. Pitman, claimed the reduction of viscosity of nitrocellulose by the addition of small amounts of sodium acetate; the other one, in the name of Edmund Flaherty, claimed lacquers made from Pitman's nitrocellulose. Du Pont lawyers struggled without success for several years to convince the patent examiner that Flaherty had invented something new. Finally patent attorney Chester Biesterfield developed an argument that was accepted.[46] In 1927, Flaherty's patent was issued in May and reissued in September. Du Pont had recalled the original patent to correct a calculation error but at the same time made some critical alterations in its wording. The final version claimed all nitrocellulose lacquers below a certain viscosity.[47] In correcting the error in the original patent, Du Pont raised that limit by a factor of three, bringing most of the competitive products under the claims of the patent.[48] By 1930, there were about 250 manufacturers of Duco-type lacquers.[49] These competitors believed that Du Pont's patents were invalid because of the extensive prior art in the field and because Du Pont had initially claimed only the sodium acetate process. In the interim between the application for the patent and its final issue, Hercules had rediscovered a better method for making low-viscosity nitrocellulose by treating it with hot water under pressure, a process that had actually been patented in Germany at the turn of the century.[50] The other lacquer manufacturers ignored the fact that even this product fell within the claims of the reissued and reworded patent.

Although Du Pont had approximately a third of the market, in 1931 it decided to protect its patents and offered to license the other manufacturers for a royalty of four cents per gallon. The license also established a minimum price set by Du Pont. About fifty manufacturers signed up, but others balked because they considered Du Pont's patents to be invalid. Forcing the issue, Du Pont sued two manufacturers, Glidden Paints and Dabney and Jones.[51] In the course of the case, the defendants showed that others had produced low-viscosity nitrocellulose by various methods prior to Du Pont and argued that the Flaherty patent should be restricted only to the sodium acetate method, thereby leaving the other, preferred methods as open art.[52]

Du Pont, conversely, relied primarily on the argument that it had made the first commercially successful low-viscosity nitrocellulose lacquer and therefore deserved the patent. It was true, the company argued, that others had produced low-viscosity nitrocellulose, but no one had been able to make it into a useful lacquer.[53] Du Pont lost the first round in the courts because the judge focused on the technical aspects of the invention. He ruled that "all that Flaherty did was to carry out what was already known, and by trial and error fix the [viscosity] limit which should be observed. If genius was demanded, surely he was no inventor.... "[54] However, in the Appellate Court, the judges dismissed the technical aspects of the case by stating that all the chemistry was confusing anyway. They overturned the lower court's decision and accepted Du Pont's argument of commercial success. The judges felt that since Du Pont had pioneered Duco, then it must have been something new and unanticipated.[55] With this ruling, the opposition collapsed and took licenses.

From 1934 to 1944, when the Flaherty patent expired, Du Pont received a royalty of six cents per gallon and set minimum prices for the industry.[56] In the first year, Sherwin-Williams paid Du Pont $400,000 in royalties,[57] almost repaying the $500,000 that Du Pont had spent to defend the patent.[58] Ultimately, the Duco patent royalties probably amounted to about $10 million.[59] This sum, plus Du Pont's earnings from its own sales of Duco, provided a great return for an R&D project that cost a total of $750,000.[60] Although Duco would receive competition from the alkyd paints, it remained an important product through the 1950s.[61]

The successful commercialization of Duco turned the Du Pont Company's finishes business into a profitable and growing one.[62] In the decade after 1928, the Fabrics and Finishes Department was one of the two largest in the company. Between 1922 and 1940, Du Pont increased its market share from 3 to 10 percent. In industrial and automotive finishes, the company enjoyed a much larger market share.[63] This dramatic improvement, brought about largely by one product, would be repeated in other departments in the 1920s, but the cost would be much higher.

Research Efficiency: The Organic Chemicals Department

In 1931, the Dyestuffs Department changed its name to the Organic Chemicals Department (Orchem, as it became known). The following year its sales surpassed those of all the other departments. Orchem had come a long way since its shaky start a decade earlier. Following a long and expensive struggle, dyestuffs had begun to make a satisfactory profit in the late 1920s.[1] Du Pont was one of the four major U.S. dye producers and controlled about a quarter of the market.[2] Dyes proved to be a good business for Du Pont, but they would not grow as fast as the new products. Nevertheless, Du Pont's dye-manufacturing business provided Orchem with the know-how to develop successfully a wide range of other organic chemicals and products. Among these, tetraethyllead had the most immediate impact on sales and earnings in the 1920s, but Freon and Teflon, which both originated in the 1930s, opened up new areas of chemistry that Du Pont would profitably exploit. Still, dyestuffs accounted for the majority of the department's sales throughout this period.[3]

The successful production of dyestuffs required an extensive infrastructure, which included research laboratories for working out dye-manufacturing processes, a semiworks for scaling up these processes, plant laboratories for testing the purity of raw materials and products, and a technical laboratory for studying the application of dyes. For many years, Orchem's management struggled to get this operation into working order. But once this costly organization had been established, it could be used to produce all kinds of organic chemicals. By the mid-1940s, Orchem would be manufacturing 3,000 compounds, a third of which did not relate directly to dyes.[4]

In the 1920s and 1930s, the chemists in the Orchem laboratories strengthened Du Pont's dye business by improving manufacturing processes and the dyes themselves. First, Du Pont had to learn to make dyes of consistently high quality. As long-time Orchem laboratory director William S. Calcott recalled, "Our difficulties, which appeared legion, were largely due to lack of experience of operators, supervisors, chemists, and everyone else, and as experience was gained the operations slowly improved in yield, quality, and cost."[5] Over time, Orchem continued to improve its standard dyes and at the same time developed additional shades and colors. For example, in 1931, the Orchem laboratory produced Pontamine Diazo Blue 5GL, which was a greener and brighter version of the General Dyestuffs Company's dye.[6] Although no new major types of dyes were pioneered by Du Pont, the company's success in the dye business in large measure could be traced to the competent research organization that the Organic Chemicals Department built up after the reorganization of 1921.

The architect of this successful research organization was Elmer K. Bolton, the chemical director of the Dyestuffs Department from its inception in 1921 until 1929. As director of the Chemical Department in the 1930s, he played a critical role in the discovery and development of nylon.[7] Bolton had received an excellent education in organic chemistry. It is not clear why he decided upon it as a profession. His father had operated a men's furnishing store in Frankford, Pennsylvania, a suburb of Philadelphia. After receiving an undergraduate degree from Bucknell in 1908, Bolton went to Harvard, where he completed a PhD.[8] A fellow graduate student, Roger Adams, who later became an eminent professor of organic chemistry at the University of Illinois, recalled that Bolton – a big, redheaded fellow with a moustache – "was recognized by other students as very ambitious, industrious, and brilliant. At the same time, he was by far the most popular man personally among our group and was always one who could and did lead us to a good time after our long hours of study were over."[9] Upon graduation, Bolton received a Sheldon Travelling Fellowship, the highest award that Harvard bestowed on its doctoral recipients. He went to the Kaiser Wilhelm Institute, where he worked under Richard Willstätter (who would win a Nobel Prize in 1915). Bolton isolated the pigments in geranium, red sage, and dark red chrysanthemum flowers. In his autobiography, Willstätter remembered Bolton as "an adept and steadfast collaborator" who had a weakness for making small arithmetic errors. Willstätter recalled that he once told Bolton he ought to be a bank teller. Bolton replied that he had done just that during his summers in Philadelphia.[10] His return to the United States in 1915 marked the end of a long-standing tradition that U.S. chemists needed to study in Germany to complete their education. After the war, few U.S. chemistry students studied in Germany.

Bolton joined the Du Pont Company in August 1915. E. P. Kohler had offered him a teaching position at Harvard, but Bolton took an industrial job because he had a girlfriend in Philadelphia he wanted to marry and because Du Pont paid more than Harvard.[11] Bolton worked in the laboratory less than a year and a half. He would establish his reputation as a research manager, not as a chemist.

Near the end of his time at the bench, he was put in charge of a small group of chemists studying dye processes. Because of a misunderstanding with a laboratory helper, over a hundred pounds of methyl violet dye was accidentally dumped into the Brandywine River, which flows past Du Pont's Experimental Station. According to Bolton, "[f]or a number of hours the Brandywine was a beautiful violet colored stream as it flowed through the city of Wilmington. There appeared to be no comment expressing appreciation of the improvement in the aesthetic appearance of the stream.... For a short time I was positive that my tenure with du Pont was about to end abruptly, but fortunately this event never transpired."[12] He had just begun his long association with dyes. As noted in Chapter 3, Bolton was a member of the delegation that went to England to bring back information from Levinstein on the manufacture of dyestuffs. Upon his return, he became part of a small group in the Chemical Department headed by Charles M. A. Stine that was concerned with the organization and planning of research work in the field of dye chemistry. After a brief stint as assistant general manager of the division that made dyes for silk, Bolton was promoted to manager of the organic division of the Chemical Department. He served in this capacity until the breakup of the Chemical Department in 1921.

Drawing on his German experience, Bolton put together a research approach tailored to the needs of the Du Pont dyestuffs business. It concentrated on the development of economical manufacturing processes for dyes the Germans had been manufacturing for some time. He felt his strategy was the only one that would "lead to results in the shortest time with the minimum expenditure of money."[13] The first step, Bolton argued, was to do a complete and systematic literature review. (He noted that young chemists frequently did this hastily in order to begin laboratory work.) Experimental work should begin, he believed, at the point where earlier investigations had stopped. His next step was to develop a thorough understanding of the problem. In particular, he meant that standards had to be set for the final product. Otherwise, the chemist would have no way of knowing the quality of the dyes that he made. Next, the chemist had to develop a method of manufacture, using pure materials to minimize the problem of by-products and side reactions. To Bolton, this procedure was the key to the success of the German dye industry. Throughout his career as a research director, Bolton would insist that laboratory experiments be done with pure chemicals. After these experiments had shown the course of the reaction under ideal conditions, methods could be worked out for the manufacture of a dye with less pure plant-grade materials. Frequently, the chemist who had developed the method of manufacturing a dye would follow it to the plant and become the superintendent of its production. Bolton believed that in the pot-and-kettle dye processes, men with research training were also needed in manufacturing.

Until the mid-1920s, Bolton's research organization focused its efforts on developing manufacturing processes for dyes. The department's general manager, Willis F. Harrington, felt that research in new areas should wait until they got the dye business solidly in the black.[14] Harrington later recalled that he answered Bolton's almost daily telephone call with the question, "Well, what have you to show in the way of accomplishment today to justify your existence? Why should you and your organization be continued?"[15] Certainly, this kind of atmosphere was not conducive to broad-based research.

But the severe competition that Du Pont encountered in dyestuffs soon led Harrington to alter his strategy. He asked Bolton to look for new opportunities in organic chemicals that were outside the dyestuffs field. Bolton selected synthetic rubber as a promising research subject and authorized work to begin in the fall of 1925.[16] This work eventually led to the discovery of neoprene by the Chemical Department in 1930. Yet Bolton never allowed research to overwhelm development. In 1929 he wrote, "The conception of an idea is of great value but of equal importance is the translation of the idea into a manufacturing process and plant."[17] Good chemistry might be interesting and fun to do, but Bolton always wanted to know what was going to ring the cash register or what it would "put in the barrel."[18]

There was little room for the heroic inventor in his laboratory because the innovation process required group effort, not just individual performance.[19] He did not turn his staff loose to work on whatever they pleased, for he believed that research should be run as efficiently as any other aspect of Du Pont's business. His ability as a research manager was noted by Harrington:

> He has been most successful in directing research work and keeping the researchers headed directly toward the goal and has definitely prevented these wide digressions which are so upsetting and wasteful of time; but I think that he has had that particular appreciation always of the significance of points which appear wiser for side digression.... For a Director of Research to strike a happy balance in this type of problem is ... one that requires great ingenuity.[20]

Besides coping with the ever-present dyestuffs problems, Bolton and his research organization had to deal with a major challenge soon after the 1921 reorganization.

Tetraethyllead

Orchem capitalized on its hard-won expertise in development when it undertook the manufacture of tetraethyllead (TEL), a gasoline additive that eliminated engine knock. Du Pont did not discover this use for TEL or the process to make it; however, because of TEL's extreme toxicity, no other company proved competent to manufacture it. One other firm tried, with disastrous results. After Orchem developed a controllable process, TEL proved to be a fast-growing and very profitable product. In the depth of the Depression, TEL earned nearly as much money as dyes on less that half the sales volume.[21]

On March 24, 1922, General Motors president Pierre S. du Pont wrote to his brother, Du Pont Company president Irénée du Pont, that after several years of research, Charles F. Kettering's Dayton Laboratory had discovered a highly effective antiknock compound that could probably be manufactured economically. Kettering estimated that the use of gasoline containing a few parts per thousand of TEL would allow a 25 percent increase in horsepower and fuel efficiency because higher compression engines could be used. Engine knocking, a phenomenon associated with the rate of combustion in the cylinder, led to power loss and even engine damage at high compression ratios. Initially, Kettering's researchers prepared TEL from ethyl iodide, a process that was too expensive for commercialization. Although the product looked very good, Pierre warned that the liquid was very toxic if absorbed through the skin and would result in lead poisoning almost immediately.[22] Despite the risks involved in the manufacture of TEL, the potential reward was large because it would take 60 million pounds of it to treat all the gasoline consumed annually in the United States.

Du Pont became actively involved in the development of TEL in the summer of 1922. Irénée visited Dayton with Pierre in July and learned that the uneconomical iodide process probably would be replaced by one that used the much less expensive ethyl bromide.[23] A few days later, the du Pont brothers and Kettering toured the Du Pont Dye Works. Kettering requested that Du Pont build a 100-pound-per-day pilot plant as the first step toward constructing an 8-million-pound-per-year plant. To get a more detailed idea of what GM had accomplished, Du Pont dispatched to Dayton Dyestuffs Department assistant general manager, Willis F. Harrington, Bolton, and one of his assistants, William S. Calcott.[24]

Calcott, a thirty-year-old chemical engineer from the University of Virginia, would play a leading role in the development of TEL at Du Pont. His expertise in the manufacture of organic chemicals would later lead to his promotion to director of the Dyestuffs Department's major research facility, the Jackson Laboratory. Calcott joined Du Pont in 1915 after working a short period for the General Electric Company. A few years later, he became involved in Du Pont's effort to become a dye manufacturer. Though Calcott's education had been in chemical engineering, Bolton regarded him as "a very clever chemist."[25]

When the Du Pont delegation visited GM's experimental plant located in Moraine City, just outside Dayton, they found that the reaction had been carried out only on a small scale. After the visit, Harrington agreed to do two things for Kettering: set up a small unit to manufacture one gallon of TEL a day and begin a study of a full-scale process.[26]

In September, Harrington reported to Kettering that with the bromide process the Du Pont researchers had obtained yields that were 85 percent of the theoretical amount. He also felt that they understood the process sufficiently well to pursue material cost studies and the design of apparatus suitable for the manufacture of substantial quantities of TEL. On the basis of this report, GM authorized Du Pont to go ahead with the construction of a 1,300-pound-per-day plant.[27]

Under great pressure from his superiors to begin production, Calcott tried to start up the plant in September 1923, before ventilation equipment was installed. He encountered serious difficulties in keeping the reaction under control, which led to the exposure of the operators to the highly toxic TEL. In that first month of operation, a plant workman died from TEL poisoning. Calcott later claimed that he was unaware that TEL had cumulative effects on the body, that the symptoms of poisoning were unlike those of inorganic lead, and that it was absorbed through the skin.[28] C. Chester Ahlum, who worked in the semiworks, recalled that TEL was originally handled in open buckets and that operators dipped their fingers in it to test its clarity. This led to dozens of minor cases of poisoning, the symptoms of which were primarily nervous disorders.[29]

What Calcott and Du Pont actually knew about the specific hazards of TEL – it had been discovered in 1852 – is unclear. By the end of 1922, Midgley had been warned about the experience of a German researcher, Dr. E. Krause, who wrote, "The compounds seem to possess, even in very reduced doses, the malicious and creeping poisonous effects which are possessed by inorganic lead compounds.... [However] they do not produce the typical symptoms of lead poisoning, ... but a slow weakening and enfeebling of the whole body, which ultimately results in death. Frequently the effects of poisoning appear only after a long 'latent' period." In his own research, Krause continued, "I have used every possible means of precaution ..., nevertheless, I think that I have severely damaged my health." Several of his co-workers had died of illness that he thought could be directly related to organic lead poisoning.[30] This posed a dilemma for GM and Du Pont. The new material was indeed dangerous to manufacture, but when diluted for use in gasoline was relatively safe.[31] The companies decided to begin marketing the small amounts that could be manufactured.

First introduced to the public at one gas station in Dayton in February 1923, ethyl premium gasoline proved to be very popular and the demand for it grew rapidly. In early 1924, Du Pont agreed to increase its production rate more than five times on what Irénée du Pont called a "war order" priority. By August, Du Pont was producing 700 gallons of TEL a day.[32] While this higher rate of production was achieved, there had been several more deaths. In the spring, two of Kettering's workers died in Dayton. In July, Giuseppe Cianci, a laborer in the Du Pont plant, succumbed. Two weeks later, Frank A. Hanley, a pipefitter from the Engineering Department, died. Sim Jones, another plant employee, died two months later.[33]

After the first three deaths, General Motors president Alfred P. Sloan established an internal committee of experts to study the hazards associated with the manufacture of TEL. Coming from an explosives manufacturing concern, Irénée told Sloan that TEL was not as dangerous to make as nitroglycerine and was less hazardous for the consumer than dynamite. Still, du Pont went along with Sloan's proposal and put a Du Pont Company doctor on the committee.[34] In spite of its efforts, the committee was unable to prevent a serious occurrence of poisoning at an experimental TEL plant in the Bayway, New Jersey, Laboratory of Standard Oil. This event nearly led to the outlawing of TEL.

Standard had entered the TEL picture because it had obtained the rights to a cheaper process that used ethyl chloride instead of bromide. Charles A. Kraus, an authority on organic metallic compounds at Clark University, developed the process for Standard. In retrospect, it appears to be an obvious step to substitute chlorine for bromine, but the Du Pont chemists had for some reason discounted this method for making TEL and missed their opportunity to control this important innovation. With the rights to the chloride process, Standard sought to become a partner with GM in the development of TEL.[35]

Standard's insistence that it be allowed to manufacture TEL threatened Du Pont's position as the sole producer. Of the three companies involved, Du Pont had the weakest position because it held no major TEL patents. Still, Sloan supported Du Pont's objection to Standard becoming a second producer.[36] Although it is never clearly stated in the surviving correspondence, the basis of the Du Pont–GM cooperation on this project appears to have been the financial and managerial connections between the two corporations as well as Du Pont's expertise in the manufacture of organic chemicals.

In spite of Sloan's deference to Du Pont in chemical matters, Standard became a partner in the development of TEL. Kettering pushed hard for a second supplier because he had been unhappy with the rate of expansion of production, even though Du Pont had fulfilled its contractual obligations.[37] By the summer of 1924, everyone agreed that Standard's chloride process would be cheaper than the bromide one. Production of TEL had been limited because of shortages of bromide. Faced with this situation, GM brought Standard on board as half-owner of the Ethyl Gasoline Company. When the company was formed in August, Standard was busy building its 100-gallon-per-day plant for the experimental manufacture of TEL by the chloride process. Sloan had decided that Standard should be allowed to operate at least one small plant for "psychological" reasons.[38]

To thwart Standard's competition, Orchem wanted to get a chloride process plant operating first. Calcott was again put under great pressure to begin production. But because the chloride process was difficult to control, he insisted on building an intermediate-size unit to work out the bugs in the process. The major problem was eliminating sudden pressure increases in the reactor that blew out the safety discs and filled the room with TEL vapors. Orchem did not wait for Calcott to finish his experiments and ordered company engineers to begin designing the full-scale unit.[39] The Engineering Department turned the new plant over to the Dyestuffs Department in December 1924, but by this time the whole future of TEL had become uncertain.[40]

In late October, disaster struck Standard's Bayway TEL plant. Of the forty-five people working in the laboratory, thirty-five had suddenly become ill. Over the next week, five men died, some in a state of delirium. Newspapers across the country, but particularly the *New York World*, detailed the horrible effects of "loony gas." Public health authorities in several states considered banning the use of TEL.[41] Deaths had occurred earlier, but none had received the publicity of the Standard incident. Kettering was in Europe looking for new sources of bromine when the accident happened. His traveling companion, James McEvoy, reported to Sloan that "[Kettering] is very upset and worried and neither he nor I can understand how the Standard allowed this matter to obtain such broad publicity. The situation was just as at Dayton, and I do not see why it could not have been handled in the same way."[42] In reviewing the Bayway situation, Sloan concluded that there was really nothing new to be learned from it. His committee of experts had already laid out the hazards in considerable detail.[43] In other words, Standard appeared to have been negligent in its handling of TEL. A Du Pont delegation had visited Bayway in September and had termed the precautions there to be "grossly inadequate," because there was "more or less constant exposure to fumes and opportunity for direct physical contact."[44] According to Calcott, the Standard plant was little more than large-scale laboratory apparatus.[45] The five deaths at Bayway ended Standard's bid to become a TEL producer. Afterward, Du Pont's role in the Ethyl Corporation increased because Sloan asked Irénée du Pont to become a board member and pledged that Du Pont would always be Ethyl's exclusive manufacturing agent.[46]

Even in the wake of the Standard disaster, Du Pont started up its chloride process plant in early 1925 and experienced the same problems that Calcott had hoped to prevent with his semiworks units. Pressure surges kept bursting the reactor safety discs, sending plumes of TEL into the air. Over a six-week period in early 1925, four Du Pont employees in the chloride plant died of TEL poisoning. A fifth had to be permanently confined to a mental hospital. After these poisonings, Du Pont released thirty-one TEL workers as a precautionary measure.[47]

Although the chloride plant could not be safely operated, the GM–Du Pont contract stipulated that Du Pont would shut down its bromide unit by April 15, 1925. Irénée du Pont informed Midgley that Harrington would not be able to run the chloride plant at full capacity for some time "because he is unwilling to jeopardize his men and the whole success of the undertaking by hurrying the manufacture, thereby increasing the hazard of a repetition of our previous trouble."[48] Increased production was not critical at this time anyway because sales had fallen by 60 percent in the first four months of the year. This situation prompted Ethyl to suspend sales of TEL pending an investigation of the hazards it posed to the health of workers and consumers.[49]

Sales of TEL remained suspended for a year while the U.S. surgeon general conducted an investigation into the impact of TEL on public health. Although the investigation focused on problems with the use of TEL, the surgeon general visited the Du Pont manufacturing plant and was reported to be impressed with what he saw.[50] In his committee's final report, the surgeon general concluded that as a low-concentration additive in gasoline, TEL posed a very small health risk to the public. The amount of lead that it would put into the air was small compared with the amount that came from outdoor white paint. The production and sales of TEL began again in May 1926, and with the process now under control there were no more deaths in the Du Pont chloride plant.[51]

Du Pont was the only producer of TEL until 1948. When the patents expired, Du Pont withdrew from its arrangements with the Ethyl Corporation and began to sell the product itself.[52] Because this company had been the sole supplier, TEL turned out to be a very profitable product even though Du Pont had played no role in its discovery. The close ties between GM and Du Pont, the latter company's expertise in the manufacture of organic chemicals, and the poisonous properties of TEL combined to give Du Pont a monopoly as effective as one produced by patents. Following the TEL precedent, General Motors provided another important product for Du Pont, one that would open up an entirely new area of chemistry for commercial exploitation.

Freon and Fluorocarbon Polymers

In the late 1920s, the Du Pont Company sold more than half the refrigerant gases that went into the increasingly popular small units used in household refrigerators and in numerous commercial applications. Beginning in the mid-1920s, sales of these machines skyrocketed, increasing over tenfold (from 65,000 to 730,000 a year) between 1925 and 1929. The most common refrigerant used in these machines was sulfur dioxide, which the Dyestuffs Department manufactured. When Du Pont purchased the Roessler and Hasslacher Chemical Company in 1930 – largely to obtain a captive supply of sodium metal for the TEL process – it also obtained R&H's methyl chloride refrigerant business. In 1930, Du Pont sold over $600,000 worth of the two products. Sulfur dioxide held 85 percent of the market, primarily because it was cheap. Its major shortcoming was its toxicity, but sulfur dioxide has a pungent odor that usually prevents overexposure to it. Methyl chloride cost nearly ten times as much as sulfur dioxide but was not nearly as corrosive to metals. It was also much less toxic than sulfur dioxide, but it had no odor to warn of its presence.[53] The danger of the existing compounds was dramatically demonstrated in 1929, when more than a hundred people died in a Cleveland hospital from a leak in the refrigeration system.[54] Although safety concerns had not stopped 2.5 million homeowners from installing household refrigerators, fears about poisoning probably had something to do with the fact that 85 percent of U.S. families with electricity had no refrigerators in their homes.[55]

Kettering initiated refrigerant research at GM before the Cleveland disaster because he had become fascinated with the possibilities in refrigeration and air conditioning and because Frigidaire was a GM subsidiary. In 1928, he commissioned Midgley, who had left GM for Cornell, to do the work. Within a few days, Midgley had decided that chlorine- and fluorine-substituted hydrocarbons looked like promising compounds because of their surprisingly nontoxic and nonflammable properties. He had come to this conclusion at least partly on the advice of Albert Henne, who had done his doctoral work on these kinds of compounds. Because of its physical properties and nontoxicity, dichlorodifluoromethane (CCl_2Fl_2), later called Freon 12, soon emerged as the best candidate for commercialization.[56] After having experienced so many problems with TEL, a small plant was as far as GM was willing to go in the manufacture of a chemical. GM called upon Du Pont for subsequent development.[57]

By September 1930, Orchem had a good process for making Freon 12, so Du Pont received permission from the board of directors of the newly formed Kinetic Chemicals Company to build a 3,000-pound-per-day plant. Kinetic Chemicals was a Du Pont–GM joint venture in which Du Pont held 51 percent of the stock. Du Pont also received a $50,000-per-year management fee, and General Motors earned a 5 percent royalty for the use of its patent rights. With the plant completed in December 1930, Kinetic began to offer Freon 12 for sale. In spite of the worsening Depression, the following year was a good one for the new product. The company sold over a million pounds, which yielded a return on investment of 70 percent, but Freon's future appeared uncertain. In 1932, Kinetic signed contracts with only seven of the roughly fifty other refrigerator manufacturers in the United States. Some of the nonlicensed manufacturers apparently attempted to sabotage Freon, charging that the new compound was unsafe.[58]

The controversy centered on the fact that in a flame, Freon 12 decomposed to give some toxic compounds such as chlorine, hydrochloric acid, and phosgene. The opponents of Freon sought to have it classified so that it could not be used in rooms that contained hot metal surfaces or open flames. In effect, they wanted to ban Freon-containing refrigerators from kitchens. Several agencies, including the American Standards Association and the New York City Fire Department, classified the new refrigerant in a category that severely restricted its use.[59] But subsequent tests performed by Du Pont and the National Board of Fire Underwriters showed that the decomposition of Freon really posed a negligible risk under most circumstances.[60] These tests helped allay fears about the compound.

Throughout the 1930s, sales of refrigerators increased, reaching 2 million units per year for household use. By the end of the decade, sales of Freon were nearly $4 million a year, and profits about $1 million.[61] Of course, the growth of Freon took away business from Du Pont's other refrigerants, but the profitability of Freon was much greater. It proved to be a good money-maker in the short term and in the long term led Du Pont into new fields of chemistry.

Teflon

Refrigerant research at the Jackson Laboratory led to the entirely unexpected discovery of a fluorocarbon polymer, polytetrafluoroethylene, that Du Pont later trademarked "Teflon." Roy J. Plunkett, who had received his PhD from Ohio State in 1936, had been using tetrafluoroethylene as an intermediate compound for the preparation of a particular Freon compound. On the morning of April 6, 1938, his assistant, Jack Rebok, attached a small cylinder of the gas to a laboratory reactor. When he opened the valve, nothing came out. They suspected that the cylinder was not empty, and a quick weighing confirmed their suspicions. Plunkett turned the cylinder upside down after removing the valve, and a small amount of white powder poured out. Scraping the bottom of the cylinder with a wire yielded more solid and prompted them to saw it in half. The gas inside had spontaneously polymerized into a solid.[62] Tests on the new material showed that it had remarkable properties. Teflon was unaffected by most acids and corrosive chemicals; it remained solid and stable at temperatures much higher than any other plastic; and it would not melt like other plastics.[63]

Polymers were not a primary interest of Orchem, and little was done with the discovery until early 1941, when the Chemical Department took it up and developed a polymerization process and techniques for fabricating shapes from the intractable polymer. Commercial development of Teflon was carried out by the Plastics Department on a crash basis because the polymer was needed in several areas critical to the war effort. After the war, it would become a highly profitable product for Du Pont. Freon and Teflon initiated an ongoing research effort on fluorocarbons that led to numerous products in subsequent decades. Some of these developments will be discussed in Chapter 21. Teflon was Orchem's great discovery of the 1930s, an era when the department still relied heavily on outside inventions.

Newport Chemical Company

By 1930, six firms had come to share the United States market in dyestuffs and allied organic chemicals. These firms had reached something of a stalemate. Innovation in dyestuffs was incremental, and no one discovery could alter significantly the position of any dye producer. Realizing this fact, a Development Department study argued that these six competitors could expand their individual businesses only in two ways: "by [undertaking] additional lines of chemical manufacture, not dyestuffs or intermediates, or by the purchase of some competitor." Du Pont, the study concluded, could gain market share by acquiring the Newport Chemical Company. What made this proposition appealing was the fact that Newport had secured an outstanding position in vat dyes, an area Du Pont sought to strengthen. Newport had an exclusive U.S. license from Scottish Dyes on one important product that Du Pont particularly wanted – Jade Green, a highly profitable dye that was growing in popularity.[64]

But equally important was Newport's scientific and technical talent. As the Development Department argued,

> Newport has a specially capable technical staff for the production of organic chemicals which, along with their good manufacturing knowledge and ability, is reflected in the high quality of their finished dyestuffs and intermediates. The value of their strong technical and manufacturing organizations is probably one of the principal arguments in favor of du Pont considering acquisition of the Newport interest.[65]

The Development Department maintained – and the Organic Chemicals Department concurred – that unless Du Pont was able to purchase the U.S. IG dye firm, complete with German technical resources, the Newport Chemical Corporation would be the best acquisition in organic chemicals manufacture. Because there was little real hope of successfully negotiating with the IG, Du Pont's executives moved swiftly to buy Newport.

The Development Department's assessment of the Newport company proved to be extremely accurate. Jade Green and other anthraquinone dyes contributed substantially to the dyestuffs business. Sparre reported to the Executive Committee that Jade Green had earned Newport $600,000 in 1929 alone. Du Pont would also gain noteworthy scientific and technical talent. Newport employed forty research chemists when Du Pont purchased the company, and it spent $180,000 annually on research at its Carrollville, Wisconsin, laboratory.[66] Immediately after the acquisition, Orchem transferred several of the Carrollville scientists to the Jackson Laboratory and also shuffled its research management to take advantage of Newport's talent. The most significant change occurred in 1932, when E. G. Robinson, general manager of the department, named Newport's Ivan Gubelmann as director of the chemical division.

A native of Switzerland, Gubelmann had earned his doctorate at the technical institute in Zurich in 1912. Like Du Pont's Elmer K. Bolton, Gubelmann had studied with the great organic chemist, Richard Willstätter. He first worked as a research chemist for Monsanto from 1912 to 1916 and then joined Newport as chief chemist. At Newport, Gubelmann helped the company to become a profitable organic chemicals manufacturer. He quickly moved up the ranks, serving as chemical director (1919–24) and vice president (1924–31). When Du Pont bought Newport, Gubelmann was named manager of the Carrollville works. But soon he was moved to Wilmington.[67] Gubelmann knew not only the dyestuffs business but also a good deal about rubber and photographic chemicals and camphor synthesis. With Gubelmann's leadership, the Organic Chemicals Department designed and built a highly touted synthetic camphor plant at Deepwater, and its dyestuffs division developed a stronger position in anthraquinone dye derivatives and the important new Monastral phthalocyanine dyes.[68] Though called "Ivan the Terrible" behind his back, Gubelmann has been described as "a soft-spoken little man, only an inch or two taller than five feet." His underground nickname perhaps derived from the way he pursued a research idea: "he held onto it as tenaciously as a bulldog and he shook it vigorously and frequently like a terrier with a rat in its mouth."[69] In 1938, Gubelmann was promoted to assistant dyestuffs division manager under A. D. Chambers, and when Chambers retired in 1941, Gubelmann succeeded him until his own retirement in 1950.[70] By all accounts, Gubelmann was an excellent organic chemist, particularly in dyes, and a good judge of talent. Among many of the Newport chemists he hired, two in particular contributed substantially to Du Pont's Organic Chemicals Department: John M. Tinker and Otto Stallman.

Tinker remained at Carrollville until 1934, when he was transferred to the Jackson Laboratory to head the new products division. A graduate of the University of Chicago (BS, 1918), he joined Newport in 1919 and moved up to head the naphthalene division and then the intermediates division. Tinker became assistant director of the Jackson Laboratory in 1938 and director in 1943, thus heading one of the most prestigious research laboratories in the Du Pont Company. He served as director until his retirement in 1962. P. J. Wingate has argued that "when it came to analyzing a complex chemical problem and then putting it into simple language that others could easily understand he was without an equal in Jackson Laboratory."[71]

Otto Stallman had earned his PhD from Giessen after completing a study of triphenylmethane dyes. Largely because he sought the hand of an American woman, Stallman came to the United States in 1922. Gubelmann offered him a job at Newport. Stallman remained at Carrollville until 1938, when Du Pont closed down all operations and moved the remaining researchers to the Jackson Laboratory. Soon after, Gubelmann appointed Stallman head of the miscellaneous dyes division, a unit responsible for many of the older dyes Du Pont manufactured. But Stallman's division was also given charge of the new Monastral dyes, an important new field of synthetic colors. Stallman remained in this position until 1949, when he became John Tinker's special assistant until he retired in 1961.[72]

Although Gubelmann, Tinker, and Stallman were the three most prominent Newport research men, others contributed to Du Pont's organic chemicals business as well. Herman Schroeder noted that when he headed the vat dyes division in the mid-1940s, the former Newport chemists were the best men in the division. Some older staff members of the Jackson Laboratory viewed the Newport chemists as a clique and believed that Gubelmann and Tinker favored former Newporters.[73] That may have been true, but it was equally true (just as the Development Department argued in 1930) that the Newport research organization was deep in talent. When purchased by Du Pont, that talent quickly surfaced and contributed significantly to the already strong Organic Chemicals Department research organization. Few acquisitions by Du Pont have given the company such a boon in research capability.

Conclusion: Research Intensity

By 1940, Orchem had become a chemical colossus, manufacturing thousands of compounds that found uses in diverse markets. Supporting this broad range of manufacturing activities was a large and well-organized research organization. Orchem had come a long way since its early struggle to become a dyestuffs producer. During the 1920s and 1930s, the department put its dyestuffs business on a sound and stable footing while at the same time diversifying into important new products such as TEL and Freon. Much of this success can be attributed to the ability of the research organization to develop effective and economical processes for producing organic compounds. The addition of the Newport Chemical Company personnel strengthened an already strong research organization. The Orchem chemists and engineers became highly skilled in the development of new processes in the laboratory and in scaling up those processes into larger units. Thus Orchem became the low-cost producer of many competitive dyes and other chemicals. Throughout this era, there were not many important inventions made in the Jackson Laboratory. Teflon, the notable exception, was truly a serendipitous discovery. Still, the strategy of Orchem management served the department well, and it became one of the largest, most independent, and most profitable departments in the company. Only the Rayon Department surpassed it.

8

New Fibers and Films for a New Era: The Rayon Department

Starting with relatively undeveloped French technology in the early 1920s, Du Pont within two decades invested $100 million in three products, rayon and cellulose acetate textile fibers and cellophane films. Two of the three were outstanding successes. Rayon experienced rapid growth in the 1920s, whereas cellophane expanded at a tremendous rate in the 1930s. Du Pont entered cellulose acetate later and generated a smaller, less profitable business. But rayon, which first found markets as a silk substitute, soon was used in a wide range of textiles, and cellophane packaging film played a key role in the merchandising revolution the United States experienced in the thirties.

These new products followed the Du Pont "formula": They were technically sophisticated materials made from a cheap raw material, cellulose. They were sold in the form of fibers and rolls of film to fabricators for further processing. Du Pont made significant technical improvements to both products, but could obtain a strong patent position only on its moistureproof cellophane. This encouraged Du Pont to do considerable promotional work with cellophane, and it was one of the company's outstanding products for forty years. Rayon became a large, moderately profitable business that was significant because it positioned the company to lead the synthetic fiber revolution with nylon, Orlon, and Dacron.

Rayon

When the company entered the rayon business in 1920, it had been interested in artificial silk fibers, the precursors to rayon, for more than a decade. As noted in Chapter 2, the Development Department had investigated nitrocellulose fibers as early as 1908. Nitrocellulose textile fibers had been pioneered by Count Chardonnet in France in the 1890s. In the first decade of the twentieth century, his artificial silk became popular for decorative trimming, tassels, and braids, all of which were in great demand for the embellishment of home interiors. At the same time that Chardonnet was developing his product, the Englishmen Charles F. Cross and Edward F. Bevan discovered that if they treated cellulose with aqueous caustic soda and then with carbon disulfide, it could be transformed into a yellow viscous liquid that they called viscose. A solid could be regenerated by immersion of the viscose in an acid bath. They patented this process in 1892, but commercial production of viscose – later called rayon – fibers would not begin in England until 1908.[1]

In 1916 artificial fibers was one of many industries that Du Pont considered entering as part of its diversification plan. Fin Sparre concluded that the artificial silk industry was probably the most profitable industry in the United States and showed "great future possibilities."[2] At that time, the only manufacturer of rayon in this country was the American Viscose Company, a subsidiary of Courtaulds, Limited, the long-established British textile company. The new company, which had been founded in 1910, sold 360,000 pounds of rayon the following year. After that, sales and profits grew rapidly. By 1912 the company was making a 77 percent return on its investment.[3] In part, it was these high profits that brought rayon to Du Pont's attention.

In late 1916, Du Pont attempted to buy the American Viscose Company, but the British firm had high hopes for its American venture and did not want to get out of the business entirely. At the time of Du Pont's offer, it was building a new plant that would increase productive capacity from 7 to 17 million pounds per year. Nevertheless, Courtaulds offered to sell Du Pont 60 percent of its interest in the American Viscose Company for $30 million. Du Pont considered this price much too high because the value of the company's assets was only $10 million.[4]

Stymied with rayon, Du Pont again considered nitrocellulose fibers. As Sparre put it, "this is a very important subject and one that should not be allowed to be lost to the company." He thought that the company should get into the business during the war because "there is a genuine shortage of artificial silk due to elimination of importations from abroad, while no serious future competition is as yet apparent except the Viscose Company...."[5] Du Pont unsuccessfully negotiated with the Tubize Company of Belgium to buy the plant that it was building at Hopewell, Virginia.[6] With this setback, Du Pont began to put together its own process at the Experimental Station. The small technical group that was formed later played a key role in the establishment of the Du Pont rayon business. In January 1920, while a semiworks nitrocellulose spinning unit was being constructed, Sparre requested that the Experimental Station stop all work on nitrocellulose fibers.[7] Du Pont was about to enter the artificial silk business from a different direction.

In late 1919, the French rayon company, Comptoir des Textiles Artificiels, proposed that Du Pont join them in an American artificial silk venture. After several months of negotiations, Du Pont agreed to provide up to $4 million for a 60 percent interest in the new company. The Du Pont Fibersilk Company was established on April 16, 1920.[8] After the word rayon was coined in 1924, the company was renamed the Du Pont Rayon Company; later, in 1936, it became the Rayon Department of the Du Pont Company. Leonard

A. Yerkes, an assistant director of the Development Department, became president of the new company. Before joining Du Pont, Yerkes had been a vice president of Joseph Bancroft and Sons Company, a Wilmington textile dyeing and finishing company. He had received a BS degree from the University of Pennsylvania and had started at Bancroft as a chemist. Yerkes was probably hired by Du Pont because of his experience in the textile business. He had been sent to investigate the French plant before Du Pont signed the agreement.[9] On the basis of his recommendation, Du Pont decided to go ahead with the project and began to transfer French rayon technology to the United States.

The original Du Pont rayon plant, built in Buffalo, New York, was almost an exact copy of the French one. But even with a duplicate plant, production of satisfactory fibers proved difficult because the process was a complicated one that had not been completely standardized. Because so many different variables affected the quality of the rayon produced, Du Pont had to conduct many long and tedious experiments before the plant could manufacture a yarn of uniform quality.[10]

From the beginning, rayon manufacture owed much more to technology than to science. Forming textile fibers from natural cellulose involved dissolving it, extruding the liquid through small holes, "regenerating" the filament to solid cellulose, and treating the final product. Although the word "spinning" has been associated with the production of rayon filaments, it is not the same as traditional textile spinning. Rayon filaments were formed by the extrusion of the viscose solution through numerous very small holes in discs called spinnerets. The liquid filaments were extruded directly into a dilute sulfuric acid bath that converted or "regenerated" the viscose back into solid cellulose. The filaments then went through a long series of post-spinning operations that were critical to the properties of the final yarn. The French employed large glass bobbins to wind up the regenerated filaments. Then the yarn went through ten separate finishing steps. These operations included washing sulfuric acid from the filaments; reeling them on skeins; bleaching, drying, spooling, and twisting the filaments into yarns; and winding the final product on cones.[11]

The Du Pont rayon plant began production in the spring of 1921, and it marketed its first yarns in May. In the following calendar year, Du Pont sold 1.5 million pounds of rayon, which yielded over a 33 percent return on the company's investment of $4 million.[12] Rayon was profitable from the start, partly because fashion trends in the early 1920s favored its use.

Before 1930, rayon found markets primarily as a low-price substitute for silk. American silk consumption had increased two and a half times between 1915 and 1925. Four years later, a record 87 million pounds of silk, a third more than in 1925, were imported into this country. Apparently caught offguard by this rapid increase in demand, Japanese silk producers could not immediately increase production. So prices soared from a little over $3.00 a pound before World War I to a high of $9.50 a pound in 1920.

As supply slowly caught up with demand in the 1920s, the price dropped continuously, but it was still $4.00 a pound in 1929.[13]

The reason for this surge in demand appears to have been changes in women's fashions. After the war, hemlines rose from six inches above the ground in 1919 to twelve inches in 1920 and eighteen inches in 1925. Between 1927 and 1930, hemlines were at the knee. This unveiling of the female leg made sheer hosiery a must for a fashionable appearance. Also, the new generation of young women rejected their Victorian mothers' medieval armamentlike underwear. Instead they favored soft, naturally fitting garments. Contemporary fashions, epitomized by the sleek and slinky flapper, required a material with the properties of silk. In this early period, rayon was simply the middle-class woman's silk.[14] As S. L. Johnston wrote in the *Du Pont Magazine*, "the Colonel's lady and Judy O'Grady are not only sisters 'under the skin,' but they look alike, dress alike, and the average man cannot tell one from another."[15]

These were boom times for the rayon industry. American Viscose, Du Pont, and the other rayon producers averaged a 33 percent return on investment per year between 1921 and 1928. High profits accrued because rayon prices depended on those of silk, not on production costs. In this era, the price of rayon was almost always a third that of silk.

Although buying rayon in large quantities, consumers were far from satisfied with it. The early yarns were weak, harsh, brittle, and irregular. When wet, rayon garments virtually disintegrated.[16] Du Pont's chemists and engineers tried to improve the product and lower its production cost. They made continuous and significant progress in both these areas in the 1920s and 1930s. When one company made an important advance, however, the others usually followed it rather quickly. Patents played little role in this business. By 1920, the original patents had all expired, and the rayon companies realized that process improvement patents frequently gave away more than they protected. For a process patent to be valid, claims had to be very specific. So competitors could either work the process secretly or find ways to avoid infringing the narrow claims.[17] The occasional important rayon patent was usually licensed to all the producers. This lack of possible patent coverage, however, did not impede Du Pont's rayon research activities.

From the beginning, Du Pont spent considerable sums of money on rayon research but was no more successful at it than its competitors. As one early rayon researcher, Ferdinand Schulze, wrote in 1952, Du Pont research "frequently played a leading role, and frequently a pioneering one as well in the industry; in other instances it struggled to meet and keep up with the competition."[18] The initial research, led by George Rocker, centered on the problems in the French process. Rocker had joined Du Pont as a chemist in 1910, had directed the research on nitrocellulose fibers at the Experimental Station, and served as the first chemical director of the Du Pont Fibersilk Company from 1920 to 1924.[19] This work consisted largely of troubleshooting around the plant. Rocker and his assistant, Howard J.

White, soon had pinpointed twenty-five variables that had to be precisely controlled in order to produce a uniform product. One early process difficulty concerned the gathering of the regenerated filaments from the acid bath and stringing them on fragile glass bobbins. If all the air had not been removed from the viscose, the filaments would break whenever an air bubble went through a spinneret hole. And the frequent handling of the yarn in the post-spinning operations often damaged the delicate unfinished fibers.[20] Thus Du Pont's major research efforts focused on simplifying the complicated and uncontrolled French process.

The rayon organization established a technical division in 1924. Before this, the technical employees of the department worked in the corners of the plant. By 1924, the chemical staff consisted of a director and three chemists. Four years later, the department spent half a million dollars to build a laboratory to house the thirty-two technical staff members in the technical division. This division, officially organized in March 1928, had seven sections: chemical, development, engineering, mechanical experimental, patent, purchasing, and service.[21]

Between 1924 and 1928, Ernest B. Benger served as chemical director for the Rayon Department. He held a PhD in chemistry from the University of Wisconsin and had joined Du Pont in 1917. In the next few years, he worked as a research manager for Fabrikoid synthetic leather at the Experimental Station and for photographic film at the company's Redpath Laboratory in Parlin, New Jersey.[22] Benger would be very influential in Du Pont's synthetic fiber activities until his retirement in 1946. After 1928, the general managers of the technical division had backgrounds in engineering and production, not in research.

With the formation of the technical division, Yerkes brought in Ernest K. Gladding to be the head of the new department and kept Benger on as the assistant general manager. Gladding had graduated from the Worcester Polytechnic Institute with a BS degree in chemistry and joined the Du Pont Company's Eastern Laboratory in 1910. During and immediately after World War I, he was a production superintendent in two explosives plants. Following a brief period as chemical superintendent of the dye works, he joined the rayon group in 1920. At the time of his transfer to the technical division, he was the production manager for the Rayon Department.[23]

Two years after Gladding's appointment, Benger left the Rayon Department to become assistant director of Du Pont's Chemical Department. In 1932, Gladding was demoted to assistant general manager to make room at the top for Maurice du Pont Lee, an engineer who had served in several executive positions for the Rayon Department.[24] The surviving records suggest that Lee left the management of the research program to Gladding. With the exception of a severe cutback in 1930, the department's research expenditures grew steadily throughout the period, reaching over a million dollars by 1934.[25]

In the opinion of Schulze, Du Pont's major contribution to the art of viscose was the development of the "cake to cone" process.[26] In this process, each group of fibers taken from the regeneration bath was drawn up over a revolving wheel, then down through a funnel and into a rotating cylindrical box that imparted some twist into the fibers and threw them against the outer wall of the box. Eventually a cylindrical shaped "cake" of rayon was formed.[27] The Du Pont "cake to cone" process modification cut the number of post-spinning operations from twelve to five. Not only did this lower costs, but it also improved the quality of yarn because it greatly reduced the total amount of handling.[28] Overall, this project was typical of rayon research in that it involved a highly empirical approach to problems that were of direct interest to the plant. Not covered very well by patents, the "cake to cone" process was widely imitated by the other companies.[29]

The sources of lower unit costs over time in Du Pont's rayon plants were studied by economist Samuel Hollander in the early 1960s. He concluded that a very high percentage of cost improvements came from incremental engineering – that is, minor and low-cost modifications to existing equipment. In one case, it took only small outlays of cash to make an old plant as efficient as a new one. Overall, rayon research and development activities focused on product improvement and process simplification. Although personnel in formally organized research organizations contributed to these efforts, most of the work was done by plant personnel. Over a long period, there were no radical or rapid changes in rayon fibers or technology. As experience accumulated, better production methods evolved.[30]

Besides the simplification of the production process, the most important technical change in the 1920s and 1930s involved continual increases in the dry and wet strength of rayon fibers. A significant increase in the wet strength of rayon made it a more durable fiber that could survive many washings. The use of improved wood pulp, the elimination of impurities in the wash water, and process simplification all contributed to the production of stronger yarns. The biggest gains resulted from the application of tension to the newly formed filaments in the spinning bath. Du Pont purchased from the Fiberloid Company patents covering a set of floating rollers on glass pins that were an improvement over the glass hooks used by the French. Du Pont researchers improved the new technology, which led to further increases in strength. As the continuous filaments became stronger, rayon producers realized that satisfactory staple fiber could be made. Staple fiber was an important rayon innovation of the late 1920s. Technologically, it complicated the process. The continuous filaments had to be chopped into short fibers that were spun using traditional textile machinery.[31] But rayon staple opened up many new applications, especially in woven goods.

Changing fashions dictated another change in rayon technology. Rayon found markets as artificial silk primarily because the high-luster fibers made attractive stockings. In 1926, the Paris couturiers declared that only dull yarns would be used in their creations. Even though they did not use rayon anyway, they influenced the design of all clothing, not just the most expensive. This change sent the rayon manufacturers scurrying to find ways to deluster rayon.[32]

Several manufacturers arrived at the same answer to this problem at about the same time. Du Pont was one of them, but it soon learned that others had already discovered that the addition of a small amount of titanium dioxide white pigment would deluster the yarn. One of the rayon manufacturers, the Tubize Company, had already taken a license from New Jersey Zinc Company on the controlling Singmaster patent. Du Pont licensed the patent.[33] As in other instances in the rayon industry, when one firm had an advantage over the others it did not exploit it to the maximum extent. Tubize could have refused to license its patent, but cooperation, not conflict, was the general strategy of the rayon manufacturers.

The new delustered yarn changed dramatically the opinion of the fashion designers. The French couturiers succumbed to rayon, and most respected department stores began to carry rayon dresses. Rayon no longer depended on excess demand for silk to establish market niches. About 1930, the synthetic fiber began to take markets away from its former model. By the late 1930s, rayon had almost completely captured the silk dress and underwear trade, leaving to silk only the hosiery field (soon to be taken away by nylon).[34] The widespread adoption of rayon staple, also in the thirties, brought it into direct competition with woolen and cotton woven fabrics. Continuous filament rayon had already made significant inroads in the knitted cotton underwear business. Sales of rayon underwear increased five times between 1925 and 1928, making it the most popular underwear fabric. Rayon next found applications in dresses, suits, blouses, and shirts. This market provided most of the growth of output in the 1930s. Consumption of woven rayon goods increased sixfold between 1927 and 1939. By the mid-1930s, 85 percent of the dresses sold contained some rayon.[35]

The rayon profit bonanza ended permanently with the stock market crash in 1929. For the next nine years, rayon's return fell from 33 to a mere 7 percent a year.[36] This situation did not arise from newcomers – the Depression eliminated five rayon producers – but from competition among the well-established companies.[37] High profits had prompted each major manufacturer to increase its investment until overproduction brought prices tumbling down. The industry's production capacity rose 150 percent in the boom years between 1925 and 1929. Even in the Depression years that followed, the combined capacity increased by another 50 percent. In 1930, total rayon consumed equaled only 62 percent of total plant capacity.[38] These adverse economic conditions led to price cutting by the previously cooperative rayon producers.[39] Manufacturers realized that their business in the 1930s would be dramatically different than it had been in the 1920s. According to Yerkes, rayon's return on investment would be 10 percent under the best conditions, which was still 5 percent below the company's requirement for capital expenditures.[40]

One way to raise profits was to find new, large-volume uses, and the largest potential market at the time appeared to be as a replacement for cotton in tire cords. Du Pont pioneered the use of rayon tire cord but because of the evolutionary nature of the invention was unable to protect the product with strong patents. Research oriented toward higher-strength yarns, begun as early as 1925, produced a satisfactory tire cord in 1934, but widespread adoption did not come until 1943. During this period, the rubber companies also had been working on rayon tire cords and had obtained patents that kept Du Pont from dominating the field.

The work of the Rayon Department chemists had begun in an effort to make stronger rayon filaments. In 1925, Yerkes and his research director Benger had initiated a research program to make rayon threads for such uses as sewing thread.[41] About a year later, rayon researcher William Henry Bradshaw succeeded in making yarns much stronger than the standard production ones. These early promising results convinced Yerkes that more work was worthwhile. He and Bradshaw shared a commitment to make a rayon tire cord in spite of long-standing objections. Because of rayon's weakness when wet, skeptics argued that a small abrasion on the surface of a tire would allow water to enter the tire, attack the rayon cords, and cause blowouts.[42] Despite this criticism, by 1928 Benger felt that the work was at an interesting and important stage of development and that it would do "something really big" for the company.[43] Years of painstaking research would be necessary before Benger's prediction would come true.

In the late twenties, Bradshaw had attempted to make rayon fibers that were as strong as natural cotton, commonly thought to be the theoretical limit to rayon's strength. Sharing this belief, Bradshaw tried to minimize the degradation of the cellulose in the fiber-forming process. He achieved significant improvements in rayon filament strength by using wood pulp with a higher cellulose content, removing all impurities from the processing chemicals, and most important, developing better ways of applying tension to the newly spun fibers in the regenerating bath. In 1930, when Bradshaw made fibers that were as strong as cotton, tire cords became the major focus of this research.[44]

From the production point of view, tire cord fibers looked very appealing to Du Pont. The process could be much simpler than that for textile yarn because the spun filament needed only to be washed, dried, and twisted. The desulfuring and bleaching steps could be eliminated, as could the requirement that the yarns dye uniformly (a need that imposed exacting standards on every step in the production process).[45]

After Du Pont had spun several hundred pounds of yarn, it interested the Goodyear Rubber Company in testing the new material. The two companies worked together on developing rayon tire cords, although no formal agreement satisfactory to both parties could be reached.[46] The first test tires failed because the rayon cords did not adhere to the rubber. Over the next several years, Du Pont and Goodyear independently discovered new adhesives that worked satisfactorily.[47] When tests on 200 trucks and buses in 1934 showed that rayon tire cords increased the life of heavy-duty tires, Du Pont expected to sell large quantities of its fiber in the near future.[48] With the development looking so promising, the company tried to obtain patents for its newly trademarked "Cordura."

Because of the extensive prior art in the field, Cordura could not be protected. In 1932, Gladding learned that a British patent had been issued on the use of rayon in tire cords. He found this patent "rather disconcerting in view of the fact that the inventor has apparently covered the subject quite well and knows what he is talking about. . . . [T]his patent is a disappointment to us and just goes to show that there is very little new under the sun."[49] Perhaps in desperation, Gladding suggested that Du Pont hasten its patent application in hopes of getting an interference declared between Du Pont's and the British patent.

Besides the British threat, Goodyear also had a good chance to obtain patents based on rayon cord. It had discovered the major advantage of using rayon in tires: When hot, it is 50 percent stronger than cotton. Ten years later, this would become the critical factor in the use of rayon cords in synthetic rubber tires that ran hotter than natural rubber. Du Pont's patent advisor, Frederick M. Pralatowski, pointed out that Du Pont had invented the yarn; Goodyear had only discovered its properties. Expressing his frustration, Pralatowski wrote, "There must be something about Cordura yarn which is different from these other yarns and it must have been difficult to put these characteristics into a viscose yarn or someone else would have done it."[50] Yet, he still could not come up with a patent strategy that would keep others from making similar products.

With the patent situation unresolved, Du Pont began to produce tire cord in 1936. Three years later, the company had four customers who bought nearly 9 million pounds of yarn, representing over 3 percent of the tire cord business. The use of rayon tire cords greatly accelerated during the switch from natural to synthetic rubber tires in World War II. In 1944, Du Pont and several other manufacturers produced 119 million pounds of rayon tire cord. Du Pont's weak patent position and the government's intervention in wartime industry made a proprietary position impossible.[51] Still, Cordura was a good product, and in the long run tire cord gave rayon a needed boost just when other new fibers began attacking rayon's traditional markets in the early 1950s.

Originally, Du Pont made good profits on whatever quality rayon it produced. After overexpansion and the Depression turned the business into a highly competitive one, the company relied on product and process improvements to maintain an adequate return on its large investment. Improvements in fiber strength opened up new profitable textile and industrial applications. Cellophane, a chemically similar product, might have followed the same path as rayon except that Du Pont discovered a patentable improvement that gave the company control of this rapidly growing business.

Cellophane

The outstanding success of nylon has overshadowed the excellent performance of cellophane. First manufactured in the United States by Du Pont in 1924, cellophane found limited markets until a moistureproof variety was introduced three years later. Its sales then took off, tripling between 1928 and 1930; in the Depression year of 1931, they increased another 60 percent. Cellophane not only grew rapidly, it was also very profitable.[52] Between 1925 and 1938, its return on investment averaged 36 percent, over twice that of chemically similar rayon. In 1938, cellophane accounted for 10 percent of Du Pont's sales and a quarter of its profits.[53]

The company's entrance into the cellophane business proved timely. The changing structure of retail merchandising, especially in the food industry, led to increasing demand for attractive packaging materials. In 1924, a *Du Pont Magazine* article stated that "the old cracker barrel, the spice box, [and] the candy pail" had been relegated to the cellar, having been "relics of an older day in the art of merchandising.... The unit package now predominates."[54] In a few years, the number of self-service stores greatly increased. Manufacturers soon realized that the appearance of a package, or eye appeal, sold products. Cellophane proved so effective in promoting purchases that it became known as the silent salesman.[55]

Because cellophane was so different from existing packaging materials, Du Pont had to do extensive technical service, marketing, and advertising to support its new film. These kinds of activities are not usually thought of as research and development, but in the case of cellophane they were essential for the rapid growth of sales. While the chemists and engineers were learning to produce cellophane more efficiently, the sales force literally created markets for it.

It was late 1921 when Du Pont began to investigate cellophane.[56] Although films had been manufactured in Great Britain around 1900, success in making and selling transparent viscose sheets awaited the work of Jacques Edwin Brandenberger. After receiving a PhD in chemistry in Berne, Switzerland, Brandenberger worked primarily on dyeing, bleaching, and printing cotton textiles. While employed by the Blanchisserie et Teinturerie de Thaon, he began to experiment with viscose as a textile finishing material. Within a few years, viscose appeared to him to be more interesting than coated textiles. By 1912, he had built a machine to produce cellophane, a word he coined from cellulose and diaphane, which means transparent. The following year, the Comptoir des Textiles Artificiels bought the Thaon firm's interest in cellophane and set up Brandenberger in a new company, La Cellophane, SA.[57] It was through the parent company that Du Pont had licensed rayon and, three years later, the cellophane technology, know-how, and patents.

On January 6, 1923, the two companies reached an option agreement that allowed Du Pont to make an independent assessment of cellophane before executing a full-scale agreement.[58] Du Pont sent a four-man commission led by Executive Committee member William C. Spruance to France for several weeks of study.[59] Upon his return, commission member Howard J. White showed some cellophane samples to Fin Sparre, director of the Development Department. The samples had been subjected to extremes of hot and cold on their transatlantic voyage and had become yellow and brittle. After White had finished telling him what a good product cellophane was, Sparre slammed his hand down on the samples, shattering them.[60]

In spite of this inauspicious introduction, Sparre wrote a highly favorable report based on the commission's findings.[61] White reported that the manufacturing process was "entirely practical and satisfactory for operation in the United States." Even though the French claim that the same viscose solution could be used to make rayon or cellophane had proven false, the same equipment at least could make either type of viscose. The heart of the cellophane process was the hopper from which a thin film of liquid viscose was extruded into a dilute sulfuric acid and sodium sulfate bath. The lips of the hopper had to be adjusted to a fine tolerance to produce a uniform film.[62] The acid bath regenerated the viscose into a solid. The film then passed through sixteen more baths that included several washing steps, one to remove sulfur, one for bleaching, and one to add glycerin, which prevented the film from becoming brittle. (The last was the key step that Brandenberger had added to the earlier films.)[63] In general, White and Sparre saw no major problems in the process.

As part of its assessment, Du Pont sent salesmen into the field to determine the sales prospects for cellophane in the eastern United States. La Cellophane already was exporting 400,000 pounds of cellophane per year to this country. The largest single consumer was the S. F. Whitman Company of Philadelphia, which used it to wrap boxes of candy, including its famous sampler.[64] The overriding factor that limited the use of cellophane appeared to be cost. It was nearly twice as expensive as the most costly wrapping materials, tinfoil and gelatin. But Sparre correctly believed that these alternative wrappings would not compete directly with cellophane because they were so dissimilar. He agreed with Spruance, who had written him that "cellophane has some more or less unique advantages, some of which have not been exploited and the sales possibilities in the U.S. should afford some fields and uses which appeal less strongly to the European market."[65] Sparre concluded that Du Pont could easily sell half a million pounds and an additional half-million without much more effort. He also felt that the product had enormous possibilities if it proved to be sufficiently moisture-proof and could be adapted to automatic wrapping machinery.[66]

Sparre cautioned, however, that Du Pont's entry into the cellophane business would be a risky proposition because the projected high profits were calculated on the basis that Du Pont would be the sole seller of cellophane in this country.[67] Technical and legal experts inside the company and an outside patent attorney all concluded that Brandenberger's patents could not be used to prevent anyone from making cellophane.[68] Sparre stated that "the patent protection at present is exceedingly inadequate not to say worthless."[69] Most of Brandenberger's patents had been issued in 1911 and would expire in 1928. He held no product patent, and those for his process were very weak.

In spite of the patent situation, Du Pont's Executive Committee decided to exercise its option for the purchase of cellophane. On June 23, 1923, Du Pont and the French interests concluded an agreement that formed the Du Pont Cellophane Company. Du Pont contributed five-sixths of the first $1 million and received 52 percent of the 100,000 shares of common stock. For one-sixth of $1 million and its patents, processes, and trade secrets, the French concern got 48 percent of the stock. An additional $1 million would be raised by issuing preferred stock.[70] Organizationally, the new company became part of the Du Pont rayon venture. Leonard Yerkes served as head of both companies, and William Spruance became chairman of the board of the new company. The plant was built at the Buffalo rayon works.[71]

Using French blueprints, designs, and equipment, Du Pont constructed a cellophane manufacturing facility in about nine months. The critical piece of machinery, the viscose extrusion hopper, was imported from France. To expedite the plant start-up, the French sent a Swiss-trained chemical engineer and four trained operators to Buffalo.[72] Du Pont sent three operators to France to gain experience in operating a plant. The hopper operator had to be an especially skilled and experienced workman. Brandenberger himself participated in the start-up on April 1, 1924.[73] Less than a year after signing the contract, Du Pont was selling cellophane. Benger later stated that it would have taken Du Pont five to eight years of research at a cost of about $1 million to enter the business on its own.[74] The purchase of the French technology allowed DuPont to enter the business cheaply and quickly.

In addition to providing technical advisors, the French sent along a sales expert, James Piani, who spent four years working for the Du Pont Cellophane Company. Piani wrote an article about cellophane for the December 1923 edition of *Du Pont Magazine*. He introduced the new Du Pont product with a description of its properties:

> Thin as tissue but hard to tear; like paper but not paper; transparent as glass but not glass – a non-fragile waterproof product with a singularly wide range of uses – that's cellophane.[75]

Despite this list of qualities, cellophane's sales strategy would take several years to develop. To head its sales division, the company hired forty-year-old Oliver F. Benz, a marketing specialist who in the following years masterminded a wide-ranging and intensive campaign that made cellophane a household word, if not a national sensation.[76] Du Pont launched its sales program by opening an office in New York City and exhibiting cellophane at the National Confectioners Association Meeting.[77] But in the first four months, sales proved to be disappointing. In November, board member Frederick Pickard summed up the problem for his colleagues by arguing that Du Pont had been overenthusiastic about cellophane's business prospects. Although Sparre had predicted that the company could sell 1 million pounds a year, the November sales figures were only about 30,000 pounds or 360,000 pounds a year. Pickard dismissed the belief that cellophane's high prices accounted for its small sales, and he predicted that Du Pont could not sell any more cellophane if it cut prices by 33 percent. On the positive side he noted that his company was getting a lot of small accounts, and he hoped that "every new place it is introduced [would be] a new center from which the thing can spread."[78]

Within a few weeks, Yerkes asked the board to approve a price cut "to increase sales and widen distribution." He added that he had no data but based his decision solely on instinct and the reports that his salesmen were bringing from the field.[79] Benz had met with the representatives of the Swift Company, who told him that cellophane was much too expensive to use in the highly competitive meat-packing industry. The cost of the cellophane needed to wrap a one pound package of bacon was more than their profit on that item. Yerkes thought that decreasing the price would at least show how responsive demand would be to price.[80] Although his board opposed the price reduction, Yerkes prevailed, and a 20 percent price cut took effect in February 1925. Sales increased immediately, and by the end of the year the company had attained its expected 1-million-pound sales volume.[81] Although part of the cause of the poor sales was the recession of 1924 and the seasonal demand for cellophane, Yerkes's price-cutting strategy set a lasting precedent.

Such a strategy was crucial because Du Pont lacked a strong patent position on plain cellophane. Yerkes stated this explicitly in his five-year cellophane forecast in 1928:

> The basic thought which we had in mind in the preparation of this forecast was the elimination of competition in this country.... We have laid down, first, the policy of having plant capacity always considerably in excess of sales, and second, a constant and very drastic reduction in price.... What I am trying to make clear is that we have deliberately endeavored to make it unattractive for new capital to go into the cellophane business in this country, thereby safeguarding our future situation.[82]

Ten additional price cuts in the next five years would bring the price down to one-fourth of the original.[83] These drastic price reductions were made possible in large part by the increasing size and productivity of the Du Pont plants. The economies of large-scale production raised further barriers to entry for potential competitors.[84] Despite these price cuts, cellophane was always more expensive than other wrapping materials such as glassine

(a glazed, semitransparent paper) and waxed paper. The high price of cellophane challenged the creativity of the Du Pont sales team to find uses for
it. But by 1925, Benz had begun to put together a sales strategy that would
prove to be extraordinarily successful.

As in other lines of its business, the Du Pont Company did not wish to
integrate too far forward and become involved in a wide range of fabricating
activities. Du Pont would sell mainly cellophane plain sheets and rolls. Printing, embossing, or any further processing would be done by other companies. By contrast, in France, La Cellophane owned a plant that turned
factory seconds into bags, envelopes, and similar goods.[85] For the production
of such goods in America, Benz decided that Du Pont would license a limited
number of manufacturers as converters of cellophane. The company's converter policy became one of the keys to Du Pont's future marketing
strategy.[86]

Between 1925 and 1928, Benz's original group of six salesmen developed
significant markets. He happily reported that there were "no large cookie
bakers not now using cellophane." *Fortune* detailed how the bakers had
been converted:

> Bluff, hearty "Kick" Jorgenson . . . strode into the office of a Cleveland
> cookie maker named Wolf, [who] was a notoriously ill-tempered gentle-
> man, the bane of all salesmen. While Jorgenson was talking away
> Mr. Wolf rudely turned his back and left the room. Taking up some
> cookies lying on Mr. Wolf's desk, he neatly wrapped them in Cello-
> phane, left them in plain view and departed. When he stopped in again
> a month later, Mr. Wolf, considerably more amiable, gave him an order
> — the first in the baking field.

After Wolf started using cellophane, Grennan of Detroit followed. To keep
up with Grennan, the nationwide cookie baker Ward tried it in the Detroit
area. When Ward switched to cellophane for all its cookies, it surpassed
Whitman's as Du Pont's biggest account.[87] The success with cookies led
Benz to try cakes and crackers. But in these applications, cellophane's lack
of moistureproofness precluded its use.

Piani's early statement that cellophane was "waterproof" quickly came
back to haunt Du Pont. The confusion centered on the difference between
waterproof (cellophane will hold water) and moistureproof (cellophane
readily transmits water vapor). The distinction became apparent in the
marketplace. A candy manufacturer complained that his suckers were sticking to the cellophane wrapper; knives wrapped for the Remington Company
rusted, and cellophane-encased cigars dried out. The National Biscuit Company ran tests on Du Pont's material and found it to be only one-fiftieth as
moistureproof as the waxed paper they used.[88] Upon hearing this discouraging result, Chemical Director Benger wrote to Benz that permeation by
moisture "is a characteristic which we at the present time have to admit"
and that moistureproofness "will probably require years to accomplish."[89]

The National Biscuit Company had offered to work with Du Pont on improving cellophane, but Benger concluded that if it was really that bad, it probably was not worth the effort. Still, he proposed putting one man to work on the project.

The moistureproofing problem was the first major research project for the new cellophane company. Its solution gave Du Pont the patent protection it lacked for cellophane and opened up very large markets for the product. In terms of dollars and cents, it was one of the most cost-effective research projects in the history of the company. Benger later recalled that cellophane research in 1924 was practically nonexistent. In August of that year, he received $6,000 for laboratory equipment and research on cellophane problems. He quickly picked out moistureproofing as his laboratory's number one project.[90]

This was the kind of project that Benger liked. He later described his research philosophy:

> Obviously a research man's business is to look at [a product's defects], look at his process, where it is clumsy, where it is expensive, and where it causes trouble to workmen or in the final product. He has to look at it from the customer's point of view, through salesmen's eyes.[91]

The view he was getting in 1924 was not a good one. Benger believed that the moistureproofing situation was of such great importance that it should be investigated immediately in spite of the long list of unsolved process problems. He also stated that his experience as a research manager convinced him that the only way to solve problems of this kind was to assign one good research man to it on a full-time basis. He concluded that if the company were not willing to invest five or ten thousand dollars in the project, then it should not be initiated.[92] Yerkes gave him the go-ahead.

To do the research, Benger hired William Hale Charch, a twenty-seven-year-old PhD chemist. After graduating from Ohio State University, he had gone to work with Thomas Midgley in the General Motors Laboratories. After about two years at GM, he was laid off. Benger was initially unimpressed with Charch's résumé, but his secretary convinced him to give him an interview. Obviously, Benger saw something he liked because he gave Charch the job.[93] Using his own intuitive style of research, Charch set out to make cellophane moistureproof and to score what would be his first major triumph in a long career at Du Pont.

Early in 1925, Charch started by trying numerous waterproofing coatings, such as rubber latex and wax, but none of these proved satisfactory. Soon he began to concentrate on mixtures of nitrocellulose and wax. The French had had some limited success with nitrocellulose as a moistureproofing agent.[94] Charch and his assistant, Karl Prindle, found a new composition that increased the film's resistance to the passage of water vapor a hundredfold. But other problems remained to be solved to make a flexible, nontacky coating that would adhere to the cellophane film. Eventually,

Charch and Prindle developed a four-component system that included a film former (nitrocellulose), a moistureproof barrier (wax), a plasticizer, and a blending agent. The ingredients were chosen so that the wax would dissolve in the coating solution but upon evaporation of the solvent would deposit a layer of wax within the nitrocellulose coating.[95] Charch had moisture-proofed cellophane.[96]

Charch required less than a year to discover a satisfactory coating, and its development took only a year and a half. The research had cost $15,000, and development $50,000.[97] In April 1926, Du Pont sent samples of coated cellophane to the Bureau of Standards for testing, and in June 500 pounds were made for trade sampling. After the patent application was filed on January 3, 1927, Du Pont began to solicit small orders, and the manufacturing process was transferred to production machinery two months later.[98] Moistureproof cellophane became an instant success even though it sold for a third more than the already expensive plain cellophane.[99]

The Du Pont Cellophane Company's management soon began to see that moistureproof cellophane would have a dramatic impact on sales. Benger wrote to Brandenberger that "it is so good that its use will undoubtedly extend and eventually it will appear in a great many fields where cellophane has never been successful before."[100] Also, moisture-proof cellophane was twice as impermeable to water vapor as the best waxed paper. Within a few years, sales of moistureproof film surpassed those of plain cellophane.[101]

By late 1928, the Du Pont Cellophane Company's management concluded that its product was about to enter a period of unprecedented growth. Board member Frederick W. Pickard wrote to Yerkes that if the 1928 growth rate carried into 1930, "we would reach rather astonishing sales figures." In that year, cellophane gained footholds in many industries and total demand grew 63 percent. But even its most sanguine supporters did not realize how rapidly cellophane would expand in the next few years. A five-year forecast prepared at the end of 1928 underestimated the next year's sales by nearly 30 percent, 1930 sales by 100 percent, and 1931 sales by 200 percent.[102] As the United States slid deeper into economic depression, cellophane soared to new heights.

The cellophane bonanza attracted another firm into the business. The new U.S. cellophane manufacturer had gotten its technology from the same source as Du Pont. In 1928, Brandenberger's chief engineer and his secretary quit La Cellophane and started their own company, Sidac, in Belgium.[103] La Cellophane tried to sue Sidac, but the case became bogged down in the Belgian court system. The new company set up a U.S. subsidiary, Sylvania, which produced 440,000 pounds of cellophane in 1930. By 1932, Sylvania had captured more than 17 percent of the plain cellophane market. But Du Pont believed that its patents would preclude competition in the more lucrative moistureproof cellophane business.[104]

Besides protecting its basic patent, Du Pont sought to build a wall of defensive patents around moistureproof cellophane. Du Pont's central Chemical Department director, Elmer Bolton, warned a Union Carbide representative "that any other company that tried to manufacture cellophane would be in difficulty with many patents in view of the long time we have been working on cellophane and the amount of work which has been done not only to strengthen the position with regard to cellophane but to build up a defensive patent situation as well."[105] As part of this program, Du Pont filed for additional patents on the composition of the coatings, the method of applying them, and the apparatus needed to do it. Overall, Du Pont filed thirteen new applications soon after the initial patent was issued. A few years later, Yerkes authorized a $20,000 research project as a "defensive program" to investigate the use of moistureproofing agents other than waxes, which were the only class of materials disclosed in the original cellophane moistureproofing patents.[106] All this effort proved worthwhile when Du Pont successfully enforced its patents against Sylvania.

Early in 1931, Sylvania president Roger N. Wallach showed to Du Pont cellophane manager John E. Hatt a sample of a new moistureproof material that Sylvania was going to sell. Du Pont soon started legal action against the potential competitor.[107] Sylvania indicated that it was willing to negotiate a settlement at an August 1932 meeting between Du Pont's retained counsel, William S. Pritchard, and Sylvania's counsel, Stanwood S. Mencken. The latter pointed out that the case confirmed the old adage that in a patent suit the defendant can never win. Even if Sylvania won the suit, Du Pont's patent would be invalidated and anyone could enter the business. Like Du Pont, Sylvania was not anxious to see new competition enter the field. Mencken suggested that the two parties get together to discuss a settlement.[108]

An agreement was signed in April 1933, by which Sylvania in exchange for a license to use Du Pont's moistureproof patents agreed to pay a royalty of 2 percent on sales up to a quota and 30 percent on sales over the quota. This penalty royalty rate was so high that cellophane made under it probably could not have been sold at a profit. Sylvania's quota started at 20 percent of the market in 1933 and rose 1 percent a year until it reached a maximum of 29 percent in 1942.[109] Sylvania's actual sales fell increasingly below the quota after 1937, so contractual limitations were not in reality the constraining factor on Sylvania's sales. In 1941, when Sylvania could have had 28 percent of the market, it had only 20.7 percent.[110] The smaller company probably did not concern itself with increasing its market share too much because the total market for moistureproof cellophane was growing so fast that both companies enjoyed healthy earnings and growth while maintaining fairly constant market shares.

Du Pont gave Sylvania a generous contract rather than risk losing its patent in a court suit. Over the twelve years of the agreement, only $2 million in royalties was paid by Sylvania. The low rate of royalties did not seriously affect its ability to compete for customers. In fact, Sylvania proved to be a tough competitor in many market areas.[111]

To create markets for cellophane, Du Pont representatives worked very closely with manufacturers to help them wrap their wares in it. The new material would not work with conventional wrapping machines, which had been designed for a stiffer product, such as waxed paper. Although machines were produced to handle plain cellophane, many users could not afford to buy them, so existing machinery often had to be adapted for cellophane. Because moistureproof cellophane would not heat seal, Du Pont developed adhesives to hold packages together. In 1931, the company hired a mechanical engineer, Ralph C. Russell, to work on machinery problems. His job was to assist customers in choosing machinery and help them convert their existing equipment to use cellophane. He also worked with machinery makers. To solve the heat-sealing problem, Du Pont by 1932 had developed a coating containing a thermoplastic material.[112] The use of moistureproof cellophane with a heat-sealing coating, according to *Modern Packaging* magazine, "gave tremendous impetus to high speed wrapping and bagging machines...reducing packaging costs and attracting more and more products into packaging." Later on, Du Pont expanded its engineering technical services to include such things as laying out the entire finishing area of a bakery. To help manufacturers decide what kind of package to use, Du Pont started a package design and development service in 1930. Frequently, Du Pont had to learn the business of its customers as well as or even a little better than they knew it themselves.[113]

Du Pont had to go to extraordinary means to penetrate the bread market. Baker after baker told Du Pont's salesmen that white bread was a highly competitive staple product and that the cost of cellophane wrapping was three times their profit per loaf. Robert R. Smith later recalled that he did extensive work to try to sell cellophane to bakers when he joined the Du Pont Company in 1933. Starting as a salesman in the western Pennsylvania district, three years later Smith moved to Wilmington to do cellophane promotion work, and he became promotion manager in 1940. Ten years later, he became sales director for cellophane.[114]

Later Smith explained how Du Pont had persuaded bakers to use cellophane. He claimed that the "specialty bread end of the bakery business was something that we had to create. There was not any such thing as specialty breads in this country prior to 1934 baked by the wholesale baker. They just did not bake them." This new product gave Du Pont salesmen a new angle from which to approach bakers, since they could convince them that specialty breads wrapped in cellophane would increase profits. White bread was an undifferentiated product; it was the same nearly everywhere, so consumers knew exactly how much to pay for it. But specialty breads, such as rye, raisin, or cracked wheat, would be novel, and the purchaser could be expected to pay a higher price. Smith would tell a baker, "Why don't you put out a raisin loaf? Put that raisin loaf in cellophane and you have something to talk about going around to these stores. Price it at 12 cents instead of 10 cents . . . and let us see what happens."[115] Consumers took the bait while Du Pont and the wholesale bakers split the extra profits made on the bread.

As a cellophane promotion specialist, Smith took on the door-to-door bakery trade, which accounted for a sixth of bread sales. He rode with salesmen, watched them make their calls, and did experiments to isolate the factors that determined whether the housewife bought something. From Smith's research, Du Pont produced a booklet and a salesperson training film entitled "Selling in Seconds." Both stated that a housewife decided if and what to purchase in the first ten seconds after she answered the door. In order to sell effectively in that short time interval, the salesman had to rely on the visual appeal of his goods, not on his sales pitch. To optimize the housewife's exposure to the baked goods, Du Pont recommended that the salesman carry his basket containing cellophane-wrapped items to the door and hold it at an angle so that she could quickly see all the appetizing bread, cakes, and doughnuts.[116] This kind of sales service went far beyond what is usually thought of as advertising or promotion. But Smith did it because he felt that increased sales of baked goods would lead to increased sales of cellophane.

Visual selling became an important part of retailing in the 1930s, in part because of the growth of self-service markets. In the Depression era, drug, hardware, and grocery stores were redesigned so that merchandise was openly displayed.[117] Previously, goods had been stacked on high shelves behind a counter and a sales clerk had retrieved them for the customer. Not being able to see all the available brands or swayed by the influence of the sales clerk, the shopper usually asked for specific name brand items. Open display meant that products frequently had to sell themselves, and manufacturers soon found out that packaging could make a difference between otherwise similar products. Cellophane played an important role in packaging for visual selling.

Du Pont's promotional activities made cellophane part of the popular culture of the Depression decade. Perhaps its bright and sparkling appearance helped give the impression that things were not really all that bad. Children made toys of cellophane wrappers, and women used it to make small ornaments to decorate hats. Cellophane became the object of numerous cartoons. The most famous one, by H. W. Haenigsen, which appeared in the *New Yorker* in 1931, showed a well-dressed gentleman who upon seeing his newborn infant exclaimed, "My word! – No Cellophane."[118] A 1940 nationwide poll indicated that cellophane was considered the third most beautiful word in the English language, behind mother and memory. Cole Porter said it best when he wrote, "You're the top, you're cellophane."[119]

Cellophane proved to be a timely innovation. Du Pont's management perceptively recognized the changing nature of product merchandising and

Table 8.1. *Average Percentage Return on Investment for Du Pont Rayon and Cellophane, 1922–39*

	Rayon		Cellophane	
First five years	(1922–26)	30.1	(1924–29)	51.6
Second five years	(1927–31)	15.2	(1930–34)	26.8
Third five years	(1932–36)	7.8	(1935–39)	28.6

Source: Stocking and Mueller, "The Cellophane Case and the New Competition," *American Economic Review* 45 (Mar. 1955):62.

found a product that benefited from and at the same time accelerated these changes. The only problem facing the company was the patent position. Du Pont did not want to embark on an expensive and extensive promotional program if others were going to benefit from its efforts. Technical service, market development, and advertising are expensive, so Du Pont wanted to ensure a suitable return on its investment.

The moistureproofing patents provided the key to Du Pont's strategy. Once protected by broad patents, Du Pont felt free to carry out its comprehensive plan. The moistureproof patents gave the company much more control over cellophane than it exercised over rayon, and the comparative profit figures show the importance of this difference (see Table 8.1).

Whereas rayon's return fell by about fifty percent in each period, cellophane increased its profitability in the third five-year period.

Pioneering Research

As soon as Du Pont had become firmly established in the rayon business, General Manager Yerkes began to worry about the impact of process or product improvements on Du Pont's rayon business. Because the rayon research staff was so closely tied to short-range problems, Yerkes proposed spending some money on what he called "pioneering research." In November 1927, he reported to the board of directors of the Du Pont Rayon Company that "our position in the industry has so improved and the capital we have invested in it so great, it seems to us to justify some consideration to Pioneering Research on Rayon, which we may attempt to describe as being a search for new compounds which could be used in the manufacture of rayon."[120] Yerkes felt that new developments were inevitable and that his company should spend about $50,000 a year in order to keep in touch with the field. Immediately after this program was authorized, Benger went to Europe to look for a cellulose chemist to head the group. He spent one month in Europe unsuccessfully trying to find a qualified person who would accept the job.[121] Upon his return, he gave the job to Church, who had recently succeeded in developing moistureproof cellophane.

At first, Church saw his new responsibility as "finding alternative means of making rayon as an assurance against future competitive methods which may threaten the present products."[122] He suggested as a starting point studying new solutions for the rayon-spinning process. But he soon felt constrained by this conservative approach and wanted to expand research into synthetic resins.[123] Church received support for his point of view from the viscose process research director, G. Preston Hoff. "In view of extreme activity shown by investigators thruout [sic] the world on problems related to cellulose," Hoff wrote Church, "we are hard pressed to find a line of work which is not covered by someone else who has been actively engaged for several years prior to our interest in the field."[124] Accordingly, Church attempted to have his charter broadened.

But not even the assistant general manager of the technical division, Benger, could initiate research on non-cellulose-based fibers. In the spring of 1930, both Benger and Church asked Gladding to permit more work on synthetic resins.[125] Relations between Benger and his boss had already been strained during the cut-back and reorganization of the division earlier in the year. In July, Benger left the Du Pont Rayon Company to become assistant chemical director of the Chemical Department.[126] His transfer also ended the discussion of synthetic resins. A month after his departure, one of Church's chemists wrote to Benger that "it might be helpful to restate the aim of our pioneering group at Buffalo which is to study the compounds, reactions, and solutions of cellulose which may be used in the production of threads and films."[127]

Yerkes even ignored Irénée du Pont's suggestion that Du Pont broaden its horizons on textile research. At a Finance Committee meeting Irénée, now vice chairman of the board, asked if Du Pont was doing any research on textile fibers made from synthetic resins. Committee chairman Walter Carpenter passed the query on to Yerkes, who did nothing about it.[128]

In the fall of 1933, after several years of arguing for this type of research, Church vented his frustrations in a long letter to Gladding. He complained,

> In our some ten years rayon experience, we have in but two cases bent any part of our research program in a direction other than one relating directly to the most immediate manufacturing and selling problems. . . .
> In only one case have we pioneered in the field of new technical knowledge – otherwise we have been working within the classical technology which is more or less known and generally available to all interested.
> . . . We question whether this policy has not become outgrown. Both rayon and cellophane have for practical purposes grown up. Unless we concede that there will be no radical departures in the synthetic fiber (or film) industry in the next ten years, then it must be concluded that

our technical program falls short in its more radical and forward looking aspects.[129]

Charch felt that the company needed a broad and basic program to keep in touch with developments outside the rayon field. "Our ultimate objective," he suggested, "would be to produce something new and unique in the fiber field which might represent some basic new industry, such as for instance, the development of a wool substitute, a fur substitute, or bristle substitutes, or special fibers for a multitude of industrial uses." He proposed beginning a broad-based, long-term research program on synthetic fibers. Not long after Charch wrote this memorandum, a research group in the central Chemical Department prepared the first polyamide fibers, a precursor of nylon. When fully developed as nylon, the Chemical Department's finding would spell the eventual decline of Du Pont rayon. But fortunately for the company, the next generation of fibers would be a Du Pont development.

Conclusion: Building a Base

By the late 1930s, the Rayon Department was the largest and most profitable one in the company. The rayon and cellophane businesses had grown rapidly, and to support these products, the Rayon Department built an impressive research organization. With rayon, the researchers made significant improvements but none that led to lasting advantages for Du Pont over the competition. The moistureproofing of cellophane, however, gave the company a proprietary product that opened new markets in food packaging. To protect these established businesses, General Manager Yerkes authorized expenditures for pioneering research only on cellulose compounds. But soon the discovery of synthetic fibers in the Chemical Department would transform the pioneering research organization into one of the company's outstanding laboratories. In the 1940s, it would put Du Pont into the leading position in the synthetic fibers industry. Du Pont had initiated that revolution with nylon, of course. The successful commercialization of nylon would require the expertise of the Rayon Department in textiles, as well as that of the Ammonia Department in high-pressure technology.

9

From Nitrates to Nylon: The Ammonia Department

Unlike the other diversification efforts discussed in the previous chapters, Du Pont's move into ammonia production in the mid-1920s began as a backward integration to ensure a supply of cheap nitrogen for the company's explosives. However, the economies of scale of ammonia manufacture drove Du Pont and its competitors to build enormous plants, which resulted in serious overcapacity. This prompted the departmental management to seek out new uses for ammonia and its by-products and to develop new products from them. This effort produced some successes, but it was not until the development of nylon that Du Pont would collect a full return on its major investment in high-pressure technology.

In terms of technical difficulties encountered and the amount of capital sunk into the project, Du Pont's ammonia venture followed the same trying path that the development of dyestuffs had taken earlier.[1] As in the Dyestuffs Department, the ammonia organization built around this emerging technology became one of the best technical organizations in the company. Its creator, Roger Williams, would be rewarded for his efforts with a seat on the Executive Committee in 1945.

When Williams joined Du Pont in 1918, the company had already been investigating methods for utilizing atmospheric nitrogen for over a decade. A nitrogen molecule consists of two tightly bound atoms that are chemically inert under most conditions. At the turn of the twentieth century, the world's supply of fixed or usable nitrogen came from deposits in the Chilean desert. In 1900, there was plenty of natural nitrate to meet the world's needs, but the rapidly growing use of nitrate fertilizers and the strategic military importance of nitrates for explosives raised concerns, especially in Europe, about dependence on the Chilean product. In the first decade of this century, numerous overseas researchers explored ways to make atmospheric nitrogen react with oxygen (to make nitric oxide and thence nitric acid) or hydrogen (to make ammonia). Several processes would be commercialized before the war, and several others were in the development phase.[2]

World War I raised the production of nitrogen-containing explosives to unprecedented levels. The allies alone consumed over 3 billion pounds of explosives, including nitrocellulose smokeless powder and TNT (trinitrotoluene) high explosives.[3] In the United States, the government launched an extensive program to develop a domestic synthetic nitrogen industry, spend-

ing $127 million and building two plants that produced only small amounts
of ammonia or nitric acid. Soon the government withdrew from the business
except for maintaining the Fixed Nitrogen Research Laboratory, which
would play an important role in the establishment of Du Pont's ammonia
business.[4]

After the war ended in November 1918, Du Pont increased its interest in
nitrogen fixation, especially after learning that the Germans had produced
their own nitrates by synthesizing ammonia from nitrogen and hydrogen
in large high-pressure plants. The Haber-Bosch process had been developed
by Badische Anilin und Sodafabrik just prior to the outbreak of the war.
When German stockpiles of Chilean nitrates ran low – the military had
planned for only a short war – synthetic ammonia proved indispensable for
the production of explosives and fertilizer. The Chemical Department studied the available literature on the Haber-Bosch process to keep up with the
situation.[5] The company's continuing interest in this field led to the employment of Roger Williams in the year that the war ended.

After leaving the graduate program in physical chemistry at the Massachusetts Institute of Technology in 1916, Williams joined the Nitrogen
Products Company (Providence, Rhode Island), which was trying to commercialize a nitration fixation process discovered by a professor at Brown
University. Williams had started his education at the University of Nebraska
but had transferred to MIT, where he worked under Arthur A. Noyes.
Completing his BS in chemistry in 1914, he remained at MIT with the goal
of securing a doctorate in physical chemistry. Marriage sidetracked his plans,
however. In 1916, he left the academy and worked as a research chemist
for the Nitrogen Products Company until he joined Du Pont two years later.[6]

Among other duties as assistant head of the general division of the Chemical Department, Williams investigated processes for nitrogen fixation. The
most attractive to him was the Haber-Bosch process. Although the large
investment required seemed to make it unprofitable, Williams was convinced
that Du Pont "by force of circumstances" would have to build a Haber
plant. Development Department director Sparre sharply disagreed with Williams, arguing that the process was of no interest to Du Pont because the
company's real interest was in the oxidation of ammonia to make nitric
acid; Du Pont was not interested in the production of ammonia per se.[7]
Then the debate over nitrogen fixation was postponed for several years as
the company entered into a prolonged financial and organizational crisis.

Sparre's interest in the subject was revived in early 1922 by a report on
recent articles detailing the development of the Claude process in France.
In 1917, Du Pont had first learned of the work of Georges Claude, a French
physicist and engineer whose explorations were supported by L'Air Liquide,
a producer of industrial gases. Because of the extremely high pressure he
employed – 900 to 1,000 atmospheres, compared to 200 atmospheres for
the Haber-Bosch process – Du Pont had considered his process to be a
scientific curiosity. By 1922, however, Claude had a small plant operating

in France, a commercial plant in England, and a very large one projected for Sweden. The principal advantage of the Claude process was its five-times-higher conversion of nitrogen and hydrogen into ammonia. Sparre believed that the increased conversion from a Claude plant would lower the investment required to produce a given amount of ammonia and make the process more economically attractive. He contacted Claude, who said he would not be ready to discuss licensing his process for another year.[8]

In January 1923, Sparre met a representative of L'Air Liquide in New York, who informed him that Claude had completely developed his process and that it was a technical success. He added that it also looked good commercially because the estimated investment was only a third to a quarter that of a Haber plant. Enthusiastic about the prospects of the Claude process, Sparre reported to the Du Pont Executive Committee that Claude's "claims are quite remarkable because if substantiated would make the process not only very much superior to the Haber process on account of the reasonable investment and practicality of relatively small plants, but the process should also be a great commercial success."[9]

Williams, who had been left in the recently dismembered Chemical Department, was skeptical about the French claims. He calculated that in a large-scale plant, the Claude process, at best, would produce ammonia only 5 percent cheaper than the Haber technique. Still, Williams conceded that since Du Pont would eventually have to get into this business, it was better to get in on a small scale "without large capital or experimental expenditures and yet on a modestly profitable basis."[10] This conservative approach did not appeal to Sparre, who had developed more grandiose plans for Du Pont ammonia.

Sparre had abandoned his earlier contention that Du Pont should be interested only in oxidation of ammonia to nitric acid and now saw ammonia as an opportunity for the company to become the leader in developing high-pressure technology. At the time, the only U.S. ammonia plant, owned by the Allied Chemical Company, produced 5,000 tons a year. Because this was a modified Haber-type plant, Sparre believed that the Claude process would make it obsolete. He envisioned that synthetic ammonia was "coming on" and that Du Pont needed to act soon because the company consumed the equivalent of 11,000 tons a year of ammonia (mostly in the form of nitric acid) and needed to assure itself a low-cost supply of this vital raw material. Du Pont did not yet have a process for converting ammonia to nitric acid, but Sparre maintained that until one was developed, ammonia could be marketed externally. The National Ammonia Company sold more than 5,000 tons of ammonia a year for uses such as refrigeration. To obtain these outlets for its products, Sparre recommended purchasing the National Ammonia Company to complement Du Pont's investment in the Claude process.[11]

Du Pont's Executive Committee followed Sparre's advice and by July 1924 had concluded agreements with the Claude interests and National

Ammonia to form a holding company, Lazote, Incorporated. Claude supplied the process and 25 percent of the capital in the new company; Du Pont would manufacture ammonia; National Ammonia would sell it.[12] Sparre was named president of the new company; Frederick Wardenburg, an engineer who had joined Du Pont in 1907, became vice president; and Roger Williams was appointed technical director.[13] Starting with only the few men who could be spared from other projects, Williams would have more than a hundred technical men working for him by the middle of 1930. For experienced personnel, he recruited more than a half-dozen men from the government's Fixed Nitrogen Research Laboratory. Among them was Alfred T. Larson, a Harvard PhD and recognized authority on catalysts. These men formed the nucleus of Williams's research organization.[14]

In May 1925, Du Pont began construction of its first ammonia synthesis unit at Belle, West Virginia. The plant would not operate on a commercial basis for nearly a year and a half, reaching full capacity at the end of 1927. The Claude process never gave Du Pont the technological and commercial advantage that Sparre had promised. (In fact, when Du Pont began to build bigger units, it used the somewhat different Casale process.) From the start, the combination of high temperatures and pressures and corrosive chemicals took a heavy toll on the process equipment. Valves and other minor parts had to be replaced frequently, and there were numerous failures in the major process units.[15] Even with the plant in operation for the last third of 1927, heavy technical expenses consumed all the income and then some. The ammonia venture showed a $750,000 loss for 1927. In the following year, one in which business boomed, Du Pont earned no return on its approximately $8 million investment.[16] A major component of the technical expense resulted from Lazote's diversification into methanol production.

Initially, Lazote did not see methanol as a business opportunity but as a way to improve its ammonia process. Lazote made hydrogen for ammonia synthesis by passing steam over hot coke to get a mixture of hydrogen, carbon monoxide, and carbon dioxide. It was essential to remove the carbon monoxide from the mixture because it would poison the catalyst used for ammonia synthesis, and this removal had been accomplished by using some of the hydrogen to convert carbon monoxide into methane. Williams calculated that if carbon monoxide could be hydrogenated to methanol instead of methane, the hydrogen consumed in this purification step would be reduced by one third. Methanol currently had much more value than methane.[17] Williams put his catalyst man, Larson, to work on the methanol problem, and he developed a catalyst that was free of patent complications. By the end of 1926, Lazote was producing methanol at the modest rate of 60,000 gallons a year, about 1 percent of the total U.S. consumption. A year later, the company decided to begin producing methanol in much larger quantities and as a separate operation.[18] American production of methanol grew rapidly as several other companies also went into this business. Both methanol and ammonia prices fell rapidly as competition increased in the late twenties.[19]

The year 1927 initiated what *Fortune* magazine called the International Nitrogen Rush. The major synthetic ammonia manufacturers in the United States and Europe began to expand their production capacity at a rapid rate by building bigger and more efficient plants. The U.S. producers, principally Allied Chemical Company and Du Pont, multiplied their output by a factor of six between 1928 and 1930.[20] These two companies had about 65 and 25 percent of the market, respectively. In late 1927, Du Pont authorized expansion that would triple its plant capacity; eight months later, the company allocated 7 million dollars to expand its ammonia output to 40,000 tons a year. Further authorizations in 1929 raised the projected output to nearly 70,000 tons a year. Even before the Depression began in the fall of 1929, a worldwide glut of ammonia had developed. Initially, Du Pont was not hurt badly by overcapacity. Compared to previous years, 1929 proved to be fairly good for Du Pont's ammonia venture; it made a small profit on record sales of $7.5 million. During the next two years, however, sales fell more than 40 percent and losses rose to $400,000 a year.[21] In 1931, Du Pont's newly formed Ammonia Department was in a difficult financial position. As it had done with its other joint ventures, the Du Pont Company bought out the minority interest in its ammonia business in 1929 and formed the Du Pont Ammonia Corporation.[22]

The conflicting pressures of expanding production and economic depression played havoc with Williams's research organization. In 1929, research expenditures were over half a million dollars and represented 7 percent of the department's sales. The next year, with a major expansion underway, R&D expense rose to about 10 percent of sales, nearly three times the company average. In the first six months of 1930, Williams's staff grew from 67 to 121 technically trained personnel. In the fall, however, layoffs began, and the plant process section was shifted to the Production Department. Further personnel cuts reduced his organization to less than 50 technically trained men.[23] One of those who kept his job, John C. Woodhouse, recalled that in the spring of 1933, Williams told his research staff that unless they came up with something new before the end of the year, they were going to be out of business.[24] Fortunately for all of them, 1933 turned out to be the best year in the ammonia venture's history; the operation earned nearly a million dollars profit.[25]

Although part of this success can be attributed to the economic upturn, considerable credit belongs to Williams, who had initiated new research strategies when the first signs of overcapacity had appeared several years earlier. Until 1928, his staff had concentrated on the problems of getting the plant into satisfactory working order. Once this had been done, there was plenty of opportunity for process improvement. Of particular note was the development of the contact process for the production of hydrogen, a process which effectively doubled the output of hydrogen and simplified its purification. The Ammonia Department showed its first profits in 1932 because it had sold the rights to this process to the Japanese.[26] The development of the contact hydrogen process represented the kind of research that Williams wanted his staff to undertake.

In this period, the informally organized technical group, facing demanding problems that required immediate solutions, developed the esprit de corps of a military unit that has gone through many campaigns together. When the focus of their work began to shift toward what is more usually thought of as research, Williams successfully managed to keep the original atmosphere intact. He ran an unusually effective research program. The Ammonia Department technical organization worked on three types of problems in addition to plant- and process-related ones. Very early, it became apparent that the capacity for production of ammonia and methanol would exceed demand. So Williams initiated research to find new uses for these products. Similarly, he instructed part of his staff to look for new chemicals that could be made from those that the department already made. Finally, he sought new applications for the high-pressure catalytic technology that Du Pont had developed at such a high cost. Generally, his research strategy centered on broadening and extending the techniques that had been learned in ammonia synthesis.[27]

The most successful project was the development of methanol antifreeze. Hans C. Duus, a Harvard PhD physical chemist, investigated methanol as an antifreeze and as a motor fuel. The former use proved to be successful; the low price of gasoline, however, ended research on the latter. At the time Duus began to experiment with methanol antifreeze, ethanol dominated the market. Traditional wisdom held that methanol boiled at such a low temperature, 149 degrees Fahrenheit, that all of it would soon evaporate out of a radiator. However, upon looking more closely at the data on methanol and ethanol water solutions, Duus discovered that solutions that would give the same freezing protection had about the same boiling point.[28] Also, to achieve the same level of antifreeze protection required less than three-fourths as much methanol as ethanol. After testing methanol in several cars to make sure that it did not boil away, Du Pont began to market it as "Zerone" antifreeze in 1930, and within a few years, the product had become very popular with consumers.

In other similar projects, Williams's staff developed long-chain alcohols, which were by-products of methanol production, for hydraulic brake fluid and combined carbon monoxide and ammonia to produce urea fertilizer. New product research led the department into acrylic resins that formed the basis for Du Pont's Lucite (see Chapter 21). The biggest payoff would come in 1935, when Du Pont faced the challenge of developing an entirely new technology for the production of nylon. Fortunately for the Ammonia Department, the intermediate compounds for nylon – adipic acid and hexamethylenediamine – could be produced by high-pressure catalytic methods.

With these two important products added to the list of eighty that the department already manufactured at Belle, the plant became the biggest in the entire Du Pont Company, representing an investment of over $50 million.[29]

The large investment required for high-pressure plants, probably more than any other factor, shaped Roger Williams's research program. It was necessary to build a large plant in order to achieve significant economies of scale. But once a large, expensive plant had been built, it had to operate at nearly full capacity to be profitable. To keep the plant running, Williams originally tried to find new uses for ammonia and by-product carbon monoxide. These measures proved to be inadequate after the economic collapse in the early 1930s. In this era, a new strategy evolved from the recognition that the Ammonia Department's "capital" included an outstanding technical organization and expertise in high-pressure catalytic technology. These assets could be used to produce new products that would not be commodities like ammonia and methanol but more like the company's other successful products, many of which required high-pressure techniques.

10

Du Pont R&D in the International Sphere

In 1929, the mature, well-diversified Du Pont Company signed an agreement with the recently formed British combine, Imperial Chemical Industries, to exchange scientific and technical information on a routine basis. Du Pont had devised this agreement with ICI as a means of achieving a division of world markets without violating the Sherman Antitrust Act. Du Pont and ICI agreed to grant each other exclusive licenses for patents and secret processes owned by the other, thereby dividing world markets for their diverse products. But to view the 1929 Patents and Processes Agreement merely as a market-sharing arrangement and nothing more would be a grave mistake. Rather, the agreement led to extensive sharing of scientific and technical information through the exchange of various reports and frequent visitations by each other's scientists and engineers. This sharing broadened and deepened Du Pont's research capabilities, and it also led to significant economies in Du Pont's research by reducing the number of dead ends researchers went down in their pursuit of new or improved products and processes. The Du Pont–ICI agreement loomed large in the history of Du Pont's R&D programs between 1929 and 1948. Only under mounting pressure from an antitrust suit brought against it and ICI did Du Pont cancel the agreement in mid-1948.

Before World War II broke out, Du Pont's executives unsuccessfully sought a similar agreement with the German chemical combine, I. G. Farben. Instead of a general scientific and technical exchange, the German and American companies arrived at more limited agreements in a few areas in which the Germans needed Du Pont's technology. In general, the Germans believed they had more to lose than gain by signing an agreement comparable to the one between Du Pont and ICI.

International Agreements before 1929

Though primarily a domestic chemicals manufacturer, the Du Pont Company operated in an international arena in which it had both allies and adversaries. Through often complex international agreements, Du Pont sought to limit adversity in the marketplace or, at the very least, to establish rules for play – to agree on the "ethics of the game," as one Du Pont official wrote in 1923.[1] For Du Pont, the ideal would have been an outright market-sharing agreement whereby Du Pont and its international "competitors" would establish boundaries that defined where particular companies could or could not sell their products. By doing so, competition would be eliminated or at least governed by the competitors themselves. Du Pont had once lived in that ideal world when it was only an explosives manufacturer and the explosives cartel allocated the international markets for black powder, smokeless powder, and dynamite. But as with so much of Du Pont's business, the U.S. government's prosecution of Du Pont for violation of the Sherman Act shattered or at least cracked Du Pont's ideal world. In 1913, Du Pont was forced to abrogate its earlier international agreement that divided world markets for dynamite and smokeless military powder after it lost its antitrust case.[2]

After World War I, Du Pont and its former British ally reached a new accord that provided the basis for the important Patents and Processes Agreement signed by Du Pont and ICI in 1929. The contract of January 1, 1920, was essentially a patents and processes agreement. Du Pont and Explosives Trade Limited granted each other exclusive and nonexclusive licenses for explosives product and process patents held by each other.[3] Such a licensing arrangement was a clever way to achieve a division of world markets between the two companies. As Sir Harry McGowan, head of the British firm, saw it, the new agreement was " 'a camouflage' to cover all relationships between" Du Pont and Explosives Trade Limited.[4] Such a view frightened Du Pont's executives, whose nerves were still raw from Du Pont's day in antitrust court and fear of yet another. They took pains to state that the 1920 agreement "means what it says and not more or less."[5]

Du Pont's 1929 Patents and Processes Agreement with ICI

The 1920 agreement remained in force for almost a decade. The formation in 1926 of Imperial Chemical Industries, Limited, out of Nobel Industries, Limited (formerly Explosives Trade Limited); Brunner, Mond and Company; British Dyestuffs Corporation; United Alkali Company; and several smaller firms, however, raised the question of how the agreement would be handled. Late in 1927 Du Pont sent a delegation to London to discuss this issue with ICI's top executives. Du Pont hoped to extend the 1920 agreement to nonexplosives areas common to both companies. But Du Pont's delegation discerned that ICI's chairman, Sir Alfred Mond, was not anxious to enlarge the agreement's scope.[6] Sir Harry McGowan, former chairman of Nobel Industries, now ICI's president, and a long-time friend of the Du Pont Company and the du Pont family, confirmed this view. In confidence, he told the du Ponts that Mond's reticence stemmed from his desire to reach a broad agreement with Du Pont's major competitor, Allied Chemical and Dye Corporation, a company in which Brunner, Mond and Company was the largest shareholder. Mond believed that Allied, strong in both dyestuffs and high-pressure nitrogen-fixation technology, offered ICI more than Du Pont. In fact, he argued that ICI had nothing to gain technically from a broadened agreement with Du Pont and much to lose (Mond feared incurring the wrath of Germany's enormous chemical combination, I. G. Farben, or at least precluding ICI's reaching a similar agreement with IG).[7] As for Du Pont, its executives were also concerned about entering into a larger agreement with ICI without a similar agreement with I. G. Farben or at least an agreement that kept IG out of the U.S. market.[8]

At subsequent meetings between Du Pont and ICI in March 1928, little progress was made. Mond had shifted his ground slightly. He now sought a tripartite agreement between ICI, Du Pont, and Allied – a goal that Du Pont's executives resented.[9] Six months later, Du Pont and ICI ended their stalemate and agreed to begin earnest negotiations that would lead to a new, broadened patents and processes agreement. Evidently, McGowan had convinced Mond to sell ICI's holdings in Allied in order to facilitate an agreement with Du Pont. At any rate, both ICI's and Du Pont's highest officials agreed "in principle it would be desirable to extend the Patents and Processes Agreement to other products of mutual interest." Both sides recognized that "there [were] many complicating factors," but they decided to let their presidents "appoint representatives to seriously explore this subject."[10] Lammot du Pont appointed Fin Sparre, director of the Development Department and a skilled, hard-line negotiator, as Du Pont's representative; McGowan chose G. W. White of ICI's New York office and Francis Walker of its dyestuffs group.[11] Beginning in March of 1929 and continuing intermittently until an agreement was signed in October, these negotiations laid bare many of the problems and pitfalls of coupling the research organizations of two different companies.

Du Pont's and ICI's chief executives sought an agreement that preserved their respective domestic markets and satisfactorily divided other world markets or at the very least established rules of competition in these other markets. But for Du Pont, because of the Sherman Act, only a patents and processes agreement whereby technical information was exchanged as part of exclusive licensing arrangements could achieve this goal.[12] Both companies felt that there were great risks in sharing their technical knowledge with each other. Would ICI give more to Du Pont than it got in return? Or was Du Pont a technically and scientifically superior organization, and would an extended agreement diminish this superiority?[13]

General managers and research directors especially worried about the matter. E. G. Robinson, general manager of the Organic Chemicals Department and a former research manager, told Fin Sparre, "As far as dyes and intermediates are concerned, we are very definitely of the opinion that the information which we could furnish them would be of much greater value than that which we could expect to receive."[14] ICI's managers had similar doubts. In preparing for the first negotiating session, Francis Walker asked his peers one important question: "In what technical fields can I.C.I. claim to be ahead of DuPont? In other words, where are we likely to have more to give than to get?"[15] Most ICI men believed their company was superior in all realms of the business.

During the first round of negotiations, ICI's representatives accused Fin Sparre of withholding information in areas in which Du Pont's general managers felt Du Pont was technically superior, such as organic chemicals.[16] Harry McGowan addressed this concern in a personal letter to Lammot du Pont. He argued that technical exchanges on explosives and other products had always been made such "that they should be mutually advantageous." When Du Pont chemists visited their British counterparts, McGowan said, "our people have always adopted the attitude that our factories and the experience of our Technical staff are to them an open book." He then made his point: "Now you and I are not going to argue as to which side benefits to the greater extent from these exchanges of visits; we desire to ensure, however, that so far as possible the advantages should balance."[17] Evidently, McGowan's words struck home; Lammot reportedly "issue[d] a directive instructing them to be more forthcoming."[18] Thereafter, McGowan's and Lammot's determination to extend the 1920 agreement to other products greatly expedited the negotiations, although it by no means eliminated the managers' concerns.

Throughout the negotiations, the British never fully appreciated Du Pont's insistence that the final contract had to be a patents and processes agreement and not a territorial or market-sharing arrangement. The idea of antitrust legislation was entirely foreign to them.[19] But by walking the fine line of the law, as interpreted by Du Pont's Legal Department, Sparre was able to make the 1929 agreement far more than a territorial agreement.[20] He insisted that the key to making the agreement legal in the United States was the payment for technical information exchanged between the two parties.

This payment provision proved to be both the critical catalyst in making the agreement truly an information sharing one and a sore point among ICI's representatives during the life of the agreement. Negotiators determined that if payments were to be made on information exchanged, then the two companies should not limit exchanges only to "fully developed processes." They agreed to include "current developments as they occur ... provided such an arrangement would not interfere with the legality of the agreement."[21] This broadened goal greatly complicated the matter of determining credits and debits for information exchanged between the two companies. As White informed McGowan, "the administration of this new agreement will require constant attention."[22] Following a review and slight rewording of the document by Du Pont's Legal Department so that it could "be shown to any enquiring Senator," both companies signed the agreement in October 1929.[23]

Although the contract runs for eight printed pages, its major provisions can be succinctly stated. Du Pont and ICI agreed to "disclose to the other as soon as practicable, or in any event within nine months from the date of this agreement, or from the date of filing application for letters patent covering patented inventions, or from the time any secret invention becomes commercially established, information in respect of all patented or secret inventions now or hereafter during the life of this agreement."[24]

As would soon become apparent, an important provision in the contract that Sparre had earlier advocated was left out for reasons that are unclear. The agreement was very specific about industries and products in which Du Pont and ICI would cooperate. But what about a revolutionary invention leading to the development of an entirely new industry? Sparre had envisioned such an eventuality, and he unsuccessfully sought a special provision stipulating that "such inventions should be offered only for [licensing in] the exclusive territory [i.e., home market] of the other party, the inventor being free to retain exclusive rights for neutral territory."[25] Du Pont's discovery of neoprene synthetic rubber and nylon in the 1930s brought this weakness in the contract to the fore, and when Du Pont and ICI renewed the contract in 1939, they agreed to the insertion of a clause similar to that originally proposed by Sparre.[26]

The 1929 Patents and Processes Agreement partitioned the world into exclusive and neutral or nonexclusive license territories. As with the previous agreement with the Nobel company, Du Pont claimed "the countries of North America and Central America [i.e., from Colombia to Mexico], exclusive of Canada, Newfoundland, and British possessions" as its mandated territories in which ICI would not compete. ICI took the British Empire, except for Canada, as its sphere of exclusive operations. To their jointly owned Canadian Industries, Limited, Du Pont and ICI granted exclusive licenses for Canada. In the other areas of the world or neutral territories, the two companies granted each other nonexclusive licenses when requested. When licenses were granted, Du Pont and ICI pledged the exchange of knowledge and technical support. Such exchanges had to be paid for; this was the only way Du Pont believed it could avoid violating the Sherman Act.[27]

The payment provision would always be a sticky point in the contract. So would the matter of exchanging preliminary research findings. Throughout the negotiations, both parties expressed their desire that scientific or technical information be exchanged "from its inception" at either company. But Du Pont's Legal Department ruled that such a provision would be in violation of the Sherman Act and thus undermine the entire agreement. Despite this setback, Du Pont and ICI agreed verbally to keep the other fully informed on "all development work," even in its most preliminary stages.[28] As with the missing "major inventions" clause, there was much room for differing interpretations of this essentially "gentlemen's agreement" reached between Lammot du Pont and Sir Harry McGowan.

Soon after the agreement was signed, ICI's research managers sensed that their counterparts at Du Pont were not forthcoming in sharing research data. Based on the experience of one ICI delegation, ICI's manager in New York complained that some of Du Pont's departments were withholding research reports. Company president Lammot du Pont immediately issued a memorandum to all general managers of departments ordering that "discussions and exchange of information on research were to be absolutely complete and to take in research at the earliest stages with two exceptions: firstly where disclosure might prevent taking out a patent, and secondly where subjects are expressly excluded by this agreement."[29] Lammot also sought to reassure ICI of Du Pont's good faith and earnest intentions by immediately sending his chief research manager, Charles Stine, to England. ICI's executives and top research managers took Stine's early visit as an encouraging sign. Stine carried with him copies of all the Chemical Department's issued patents, pending applications, and proposals yet to be filed as well as a large number of his department's reports (with sections on military powders and other items excluded from the agreement excised).[30]

Stine had his own agenda in England. Foremost was his desire to reform ICI's opinions about the nature of research at Du Pont. When Pollitt had visited Wilmington before the agreement had been signed, he had determined – for reasons that are unclear – that Du Pont's research was almost exclusively very short-range work and that there was "little real fundamental long-distance research in progress" at Du Pont. Such a view rankled Stine, the architect of Du Pont's two-year-old fundamental research program, which had already yielded the first of two landmark papers on polymerization by Wallace H. Carothers. As Stine told ICI's Smith, he was "very anxious to remove [Pollitt's] impression" about Du Pont research.[31] Stine also wanted to gain a "comprehensive" understanding of ICI's research programs, especially the fundamental research that ICI was sponsoring at several British universities and in Holland.[32]

Stine's long familiarity with ICI's explosives research and his personal friendship with William Rintoul, one of ICI's top two research managers who like Stine had come out of explosives, put him in an excellent position to achieve his objectives. Rintoul and his colleague F. A. Freeth attempted "to show him everything in [their] power" during the month Stine spent in England.[33] Stine was impressed by what he saw, particularly by the new laboratories at Winnington in which ICI's extensive work on high-pressure reactions was done, the semiworks and chemical engineering research facilities at Billingham, ICI's work on synthetic resins, and by its research on titanium dioxide pigments.[34] He was completely taken, however, by the fundamental research sponsored by ICI at several English universities and at Amsterdam. Within two weeks of his return to the United States, Stine arranged for three members of his fundamental research staff to go to England for six weeks to review thoroughly what Professors Frederick G. Donnan (physical chemistry, University of London), William A. Bone (chemical engineering, Imperial College), Eric K. Rideal (physical chemistry, Cambridge), and Antonius M. J. F. Michels (high-pressure reactions, University of Amsterdam) were doing in their university laboratories.[35] Stine also invited Michels to spend three months in the United States in the fall of 1930 consulting at Du Pont and lecturing at U.S. universities at which Du Pont had close ties.[36] Altogether, as Stine noted in his annual report for 1929, his visit to ICI allowed him "to obtain a very useful bird's-eye-view of the research work in progress," thus ensuring "coordination and cooperation in connection with our chemical research."[37]

While in England, Stine took one important, though not entirely satisfactory, step to facilitate the exchange of information between the two companies. He negotiated a gentlemen's agreement with his ICI counterparts whereby the Chemical Department would act as Du Pont's central clearinghouse for the exchange of all research reports, including those produced by the industrial department research divisions. Stine recognized that maintaining control over or at least some accounting of the exchange of information and reports between two such large organizations would be problematic, and he hoped his agreement would minimize difficulties. Upon his return to the United States, Stine met with Du Pont's Foreign Relations Committee and Fin Sparre to review his agreement with ICI. This group endorsed Stine's understanding, and the Executive Committee subsequently adopted it as Du Pont's official policy.[38]

Although soundly conceived, Stine's policy proved difficult to manage, mainly because of Du Pont's decentralized structure. For example, at the very moment departments were informed of Stine's policy, delegations from several different departments were in England conferring with their ICI counterparts and gathering reports of interest to them. Without centralized means of accounting for reports exchanged, their existence and whereabouts sometimes remained unknown to researchers from other departments. Stine and John K. Jenney, secretary of Du Pont's Foreign Relations Committee (soon to be organized as an independent department), thought it would be easy for delegations going to England and departments receiving delegations from ICI to list for the Chemical Department's clearinghouse the reports exchanged directly between Du Pont and ICI research personnel. But this was not as easy as it sounded.

Throughout the lifetime of the agreement, there were always problems in exchanging reports. Depending on the area of research and the laboratory that generated them, some reports seemed relevant to as many as eight different research units in Du Pont or ICI, and each wanted a copy at the moment the report was issued. This problem both stemmed from and was compounded by Du Pont's and ICI's research organizations not being mirror images of each other. Also, the sheer number of reports exchanged posed administrative burdens. For instance, in the area of dyestuffs and organic chemicals research alone, by 1935 Du Pont's Organic Chemicals Department had received almost 5,000 reports from ICI's dyestuffs group, and each unit had sent the other details of some 1,700 processes.[39] Though the Chemical Department continued to act as a clearinghouse until the agreement was canceled, by 1935 it had given up hope that it could maintain an accounting of, much less control over, the exchange of information.[40]

Other problems of coordination in the exchange of technical information also arose. Before and immediately after the Patents and Processes Agreement was signed, Du Pont's Foreign Relations Committee, a three-member subcommittee of the Executive Committee, was responsible for the company's relationship with ICI. The Foreign Relations Committee hoped that its secretary, John Jenney, could serve as the "one point in the organization" which had "at least a general idea of what is taking place under" the agreement.[41] Thus Jenney's office was intended to be Du Pont's central unit in which all policy matters concerning ICI would be handled or at least coordinated – a role that paralleled the Chemical Department's in technical matters. But it soon became apparent that the agreement called for attention far beyond the scope of an executive subcommittee and its secretary.

Du Pont's executives realized this fact only after the agreement had been in force for a year. To achieve more effective coordination, they created the Foreign Relations Department, a move ICI had made much earlier. The new department was given loose, centralized control over the administration of the agreement. That is, it established guidelines for exchanges, often coordinated visits by technical delegations to and from ICI, served as a central archive for correspondence between Du Pont and ICI, and acted as an ultimate arbiter on policy. The goal of the Foreign Relations Department, however, remained precisely the same as the subcommittee's: to maintain an element of control over the agreement without usurping too much authority from the industrial departments and, foremost, "always to preserve a spirit in the two companies which will make possible the most complete and frank disclosure of . . . technical knowledge."[42] As Fin Sparre argued, administration of the agreement had to be structured so that Du Pont's "chemical divisions . . . will maintain the closest and most efficient contact with the technical organization of ICI in order to obtain the fullest benefit of research and development on the other side."[43]

In discussing policies and procedures with Sparre and Jenney, Du Pont's research directors articulated one very important point about ICI's and Du Pont's exchange of scientific and technical information: "Direct contact between the [scientific and] technical men in similar industries is the prime desideratum. The maximum benefit of the agreement can be best obtained by personal contact rather than exchange of correspondence and reports."[44] That Du Pont's research managers firmly believed in this premise is borne out by the extensive number of technical delegations the company sent to and received from ICI and by its appointment of a scientific and industrial specialist in London to do nothing but identify areas, projects, and researchers in ICI that Du Pont should follow. Moreover, to follow areas in which it considered ICI's research of great significance, such as the high-pressure field, Du Pont often stationed research personnel at ICI on an extended basis.[45]

The Patents and Processes Agreement provided Du Pont's research personnel with a legitimate means of exchanging information and comparing notes with their counterparts at ICI in areas that had previously been regarded as strictly confidential and proprietary. In a sense, therefore, the agreement opened up Du Pont research and allowed its researchers greater intellectual freedom – not exactly the idealized world of academic science but far more than the stereotyped picture of tight-lipped, line-toeing industrial researchers. The hundreds of reports written by Du Pont's researchers about their findings and exchanges in England provide abundant testimony that the agreement provided intellectual ferment as well as the more mundane but no less important practical know-how that Sparre knew would be exchanged.[46] Moreover, at the management level, exchanges provided Du Pont's research directors an opportunity to examine their own organizations by studying ICI's or by hearing critiques offered by their ICI counterparts.

Even with the formal contract and the gentlemen's agreement that R&D information would be exchanged from the outset of a development, however, U.S. patent law allowed Du Pont to keep some of its research work out of ICI's view for a long time, much to ICI's dissatisfaction. Three important examples occurred during the life of the agreement: Du Pont's discoveries and development of neoprene synthetic rubber and nylon and its follow-up work on ICI's polyethylene. As will be discussed more fully below, Du Pont's fundamental polymer research group under the leadership of Wallace H. Carothers discovered in April 1930 both neoprene and the first laboratory-synthesized fiber. This latter work led in 1934 to the discovery of nylon polyamide fibers. With both of these discoveries, Du Pont capitalized on provisions in the U.S. patent law that allowed it to delay public disclosure both in the form of patents and publications for about two years after the initial discovery. Although Lammot du Pont and Sir Harry McGowan had agreed that the two companies would exchange research findings very early, ICI simply had no certain way of knowing if Du Pont were upholding its end of the bargain save what Du Pont disclosed in patents. In Britain, however, ICI had to disclose information much earlier because of the British system of provisional patent applications. Hence Du Pont enjoyed a distinct advantage.[47]

In instances of seemingly important discoveries – instances that Fin Sparre had envisioned in 1929 – Du Pont's research managers chose not to inform ICI of its work, contrary to the gentlemen's understanding. With the discovery of neoprene, Du Pont faced for the first time the problem of whether to disclose information to ICI. Correspondence between Jenney and Harold W. Elley, director of research for the Dyestuffs Department (which had been given responsibility for neoprene's development) makes clear that the Dyestuffs Department was not anxious to inform ICI about neoprene. For Elley's benefit, Jenney quoted verbatim Du Pont's obligations and then told him that if his department did not disclose information on neoprene to ICI, Du Pont had two choices: It could simply tell ICI that it was flagrantly violating the agreement in this instance, or it could cancel the agreement entirely.[48]

Fin Sparre, however, offered a middle ground. He argued that he had foreseen such an eventuality when he was negotiating the agreement and, though the final contract lacked such a provision, Du Pont and ICI had agreed that there would be cases of exceptionally important inventions that would call for separate agreements. Neoprene was simply the first such instance. He urged that the head of Dyestuffs, E. G. Robinson, inform his ICI counterpart that Du Pont had made a truly exceptional discovery and that it would be withholding information on this discovery from ICI and handling its own foreign patent work.[49] Robinson followed Sparre's advice and in late August 1930 officially informed ICI that Du Pont had discovered how to polymerize chlorobutadiene "to produce plastic and resinous products" but that it would suspend the agreement in this instance.[50]

Du Pont did indeed withhold information on neoprene's development until October 1931, when Lammot du Pont sent McGowan advance copies of an article on neoprene written by Carothers's group that was to appear in the November issue of the *Journal of the American Chemical Society*. Lammot also informed McGowan that "several patent applications on file in Great Britain" would be "open[ed] for inspection" shortly before the Carothers article appeared.[51] Three years later when nylon was discovered, Du Pont's experience with handling the neoprene case made it far easier to "hide" (ICI's term) this major invention. Unlike the case of neoprene, Du Pont never even gave ICI a hint until nylon's development was well along the way. On January 14, 1937 – more than two and a half years after nylon's discovery – Lammot informed McGowan about Du Pont's nylon project and explained why his company had not furnished ICI with information about it.[52] After the discoveries of neoprene and nylon, Du Pont's Chemical Department adopted an official (but strictly internal) policy of withholding information from ICI "on specific lines of work if it is decided they represent a major development."[53] Despite their tacit approval of Sparre's "exceptional invention" scenario outlined during the original negotiations in 1929, ICI's managers were annoyed by Du Pont's claim that neoprene and nylon constituted such inventions and by their consequent withholding of information.[54]

ICI eventually had its own "exceptional invention" – polyethylene. However, by no means were the tables fully turned on Du Pont. ICI discovered polyethylene (or "polythene," as the English called it) in early 1933 as a result of its high-pressure research. Du Pont received a report of the discovery in September 1933 and subsequent periodic reports on polyethylene throughout the 1930s and early 1940s.[55] Because of Du Pont's handling of neoprene and nylon, ICI notified Du Pont in 1939 of its intention to treat polyethylene as a "major" or "exceptional" invention, outside the Du Pont–ICI agreement.[56] Initially, Du Pont objected because it did not see parallels between polyethylene and neoprene and nylon, and the matter was not settled until the 1940s. ICI assumed that, in the absence of a formal agreement on polyethylene and because it continued to provide Du Pont with research and manufacturing information on polyethylene, Du Pont would continue to reciprocate.[57] Such was not the case.

Much to ICI's ire, Du Pont's Chemical Department withheld from ICI its important research on polyethylene between May 1939 and May 1940. During this time, without ICI's knowledge, Du Pont applied for a patent on "the novel features" of its lower-pressure process and thereby staked an important claim to the product's commercialization. ICI later cited other instances in which Du Pont had willfully withheld from ICI information on polyethylene.[58]

Du Pont's actions on neoprene, nylon, and polyethylene stemmed from its managers' uneasiness about the early exchange of information. Despite Lammot du Pont's executive order that information be exchanged early in a research and development project, it was not always done. Rayon Department general manager Leonard Yerkes perhaps best expressed the concerns of his colleagues at Du Pont: "I think the sending of purely preliminary laboratory information leads to a competitive situation which is undesirable."[59] By this, Yerkes meant that early disclosure made it difficult for a company to fortify sufficiently its proprietary position on a development such as a neoprene or a nylon. Yerkes was probably correct.

Concern over disclosure of scientific and technical information by Du Pont was not the only issue that sometimes separated the two companies. ICI's research managers objected to Du Pont's patent strategy, which they described as "to patent everything, including minute details of manufacturing processes."[60] As with the timing of its disclosure to ICI, Du Pont's patent policy stemmed from the nature of U.S. patent law, which allowed patentees to maintain patents even though such patents were not "worked." Consequently, corporations such as Du Pont with industrial research and development laboratories often pursued a highly defensive patent strategy. That is, they employed their researchers in finding small modifications or variations as well as alternatives to basic patents as a means of protecting a basic patent. Historian Leonard Reich has demonstrated how AT&T effectively followed a comprehensive defensive strategy in protecting its telephone system, and we have noted how Du Pont's industrial departments conducted research work along similar lines.[61]

ICI's managers objected to this strategy because they believed it resulted in disclosing too much information to competitors, "possibly suggest[ing] new ideas to them which might enable them to see a way round the master patent." Moreover, such prodigal patenting cost a great deal in both time and money. Patent experts at ICI argued that both the District of Columbia Court and the Supreme Court had determined that minor patents surrounding a basic one were very weak and essentially nondefensible. "Du Ponts," they concluded, "really therefore cannot safeguard themselves against being hedged in by minor patents filed by competitors, nor can they so hedge in potential competitors."[62]

ICI further disliked Du Pont's strategy because it usually forced ICI to pursue a similar strategy. ICI's own patent strategy was one of relying mainly upon a master patent and then extending its life "by filing at intervals a limited number only of important patents, rather than a great number of minor ones."[63] Far more serious than this, however, was ICI's concern — never expressed openly to Du Pont — that Du Pont's patent strategy had resulted in the Americans patenting information for themselves that ICI had given to Du Pont through the normal channels of exchange. Du Pont's handling of polyethylene greatly irritated ICI's research managers, and they cited four instances in which Du Pont had acknowledged receipt of information relating to ICI's polyethylene research and subsequently patented this information for the Du Pont Company. Du Pont saw the matter very differently. Its research managers believed that Du Pont research had greatly improved ICI's process for making polyethylene and that this work, growing out of Du Pont's special expertise, was entirely original. As one ICI official expressed Du Pont's attitude, "they claim... that they have done much on the process side and that we only invented the product and a half-baked way of making it."[64] This statement was, however, a reasonably accurate assessment of the situation.

Du Pont's policies and actions annoyed ICI managers and greatly strained the alliance. This irritation grew particularly strong when Du Pont's and ICI's representatives met to evaluate the value of patents and processes exchanged and to assign specific monetary value to each on the basis of a true assessment. Fin Sparre, who had negotiated the agreement for Du Pont and who continued to exercise the greatest control over it at Du Pont until his retirement in 1944, was absolutely adamant on this placing a dollar value on the exchange of information.

Conversely, ICI's representatives (many of whom had originally seen the agreement solely as a ruse for a market-sharing agreement) believed that the information exchanged between the two companies probably had about equal monetary value. They saw no reasons to go through an elaborate assessment. Yet Sparre would not hear of a blanket fifty-fifty valuation. Without question, Sparre's insistence on an extensive, detailed assessment of the exchange agreement resulted from Du Pont's interpretation of the antitrust law. But Sparre also sought an accurate assessment because he believed that Du Pont had contributed more to ICI than vice versa. Since his days as chief chemist at the Experimental Station, Sparre had believed Du Pont was a scientifically and technically superior organization. Sparre's attitude prevailed within Du Pont's research ranks. This view embittered ICI managers, in part because of their pride but also because of some lingering doubts that Du Pont's chauvinism might indeed be accurate. As ICI's historian wrote, "What rankled most on the ICI side, amongst those well-qualified to judge, was an uneasy feeling that the achievements of ICI's research, in spite of polyethylene and Perspex [acrylic resin], did not stand up well in comparison with results from du Pont."[65]

During the life of the agreement, Du Pont and ICI conducted their evaluations at five-year intervals. Before the first evaluation, however, the two companies met in October and November of 1930 to evaluate the first year of exchanges. Fin Sparre headed Du Pont's delegation in this and all save the last subsequent evaluations. His hubris and hard bargaining irritated his ICI counterparts.[66] But he almost always got his way.

Soon after the agreement was signed in 1929, Sparre had envisioned making a complete list of all of Du Pont's patents and secret processes available to ICI and then basing the evaluation on the precise processes that ICI chose to examine and adopt, and vice versa.[67] ICI saw no need for such an elaborate plan. If its managers could not persuade Sparre to accept the idea of the simple assessment, then they hoped he would limit the evaluation of the exchange of information "to a few processes of outstanding merit."[68] By April 1930, Sparre had backed off his original idea but had not completely embraced ICI's offer. ICI's managers believed quite correctly that Sparre's compromising posture had arisen because of the findings of a recent delegation from Du Pont's Organic Chemicals Department to its ICI counterpart, the former British Dyestuffs Corporation.[69] A. D. Chambers, the man who had led Du Pont into the dyestuffs business and successfully through its trial by fire, headed the delegation and determined that his department "had gotten very nearly as much out of the exchange of information with I.C.I. as they had given."[70]

After such conclusions from the research organization that had been most skittish about Du Pont's agreement with ICI, Sparre loosened up considerably. He did not fully yield to ICI, however, as evidenced by his tabulation of patents and processes offered by Du Pont to ICI.[71] ICI's negotiators knew Sparre well enough to anticipate that he would argue Du Pont's superiority in all matters, and therefore they sought "to counter the citation of specific things" claimed by Sparre.[72] Thus, the first series of meetings to evaluate the agreement set the tone for subsequent evaluations. ICI's P. C. Allen confided to his diary in 1942 how Du Pont operated in these meetings. Alluding to Wendell Swint, head of Du Pont's Foreign Relations Department and Sparre's co-negotiator, Allen wrote, "his technique is to advance deep into our territory, then retreat a quarter of the way back, yelling that he has been robbed."[73] As ICI's historian wrote, Sparre and his aides "went out of their way to belittle the value of information offered to them by ICI."[74]

At each evaluation session, Du Pont's goal was to arrive at a "considerable differential" in the value of research and process information exchanged between the two companies.[75] By demonstrating that ICI or Du Pont paid the other substantial sums of money for licenses, Du Pont believed it could demonstrate to any critic that its agreement with ICI was truly a patents and processes arrangement, not a market-sharing covenant. Sparre's goal to create a large differential between one company's credits from and debits to the other also perfectly fitted his pride in Du Pont's research and development. No doubt, before the negotiations he envisioned that ICI would pay Du Pont a large sum of money for Du Pont's superior know-how. But ICI was prepared for Sparre and Du Pont; its negotiators could also drive a hard bargain. At the end of the first evaluation, Sparre had won only a small differential of $125,000 – a figure he regarded as "comparatively small" and an outcome he certainly had not expected. As he reported to the Executive Committee, "It was astonishing to find that the work of the two companies has paralleled each other to a remarkable extent."[76]

Subsequent evaluations followed very much in the path cut out during the first one. The dollar differentials arrived at for each five-year period were minuscule compared to the amount of effort, time, and often acrimonious argument that was put into arriving at these figures.[77] Not only the legal maintenance of the agreement but also the scientific and technological prowess of the two companies was at stake in these negotiations.

This stake of pride was perhaps best revealed in an extensive survey that Sparre ordered before the first full five-year evaluation. Through Wendell Swint, Sparre wanted to know what each general manager thought of the agreement, particularly whether Du Pont had given more than it received in the deal.[78] With two minor exceptions, Du Pont's general managers believed that Du Pont had provided more than it had received. The Fabrics and Finishes Department claimed to have furnished five times as much valuable information as it had received and suggested that its research and development organization was far superior to its counterpart at ICI.[79] Several other departments made similar arguments. Admitting that ICI possessed superior or better knowledge was perhaps a sign of weakness, anathema to a Du Pont research director. But ICI's managers felt the same way.

Yet this 1934 survey produced a remarkably accurate qualitative assessment of the agreement's impact on Du Pont's research organizations, particularly on its best research units such as that of the Organic Chemicals Department, the Ammonia Department, and the Chemical Department. The Ammonia Department's F. A. Wardenburg argued that the agreement had given its R&D men an important "point of view":

> At the time nitrogen was included in this Agreement, our work was in the more or less preliminary stage, that is, we had only been in the manufacture of ammonia for a few years and our knowledge of the subject was quite incomplete. We obtained from I.C.I., then, the point of view and experience of ammonia operation which had been carried on considerably longer than our own operation had been. It is true that the process used by them was different from the one that we were proposing to use, but at the same time, the ability to check up on process details, equipment details and manufacturing costs, was of very considerable advantage to us in determining the course we should pursue.[80]

Other departments stressed that often ICI's research had provided "negative results" that had kept its researchers from going down dead-end paths.[81] These tacit and impossible-to-measure benefits accrued to Du Pont's research organizations throughout the life of the agreement.

Du Pont also enjoyed some big and more easily measured R&D results from its relationships with ICI. ICI's development of an excellent manufacturing process for methyl methacrylate in the early 1930s provided Du Pont with the means to market its Lucite clear acrylic sheeting. Du Pont's U.S. competitor, Rohm and Haas Company, had hoped to gain exclusive control of the U.S. market for its Plexiglas but was forced to obtain a process license from ICI.[82] More important was ICI's development of the phthalocyanines, an important new class of dyes that Du Pont dubbed the "Monastral" dyes.[83] ICI continued to provide important information on methyl methacrylates and phthalocyanines to Du Pont until the agreement was canceled in 1948.

The Patents and Processes Agreement was due to expire in 1949. ICI's historian suggests that some of the British company's younger executives had begun to question the wisdom of the agreement in the early 1940s, because of the changing nature of world chemical markets and because they thought Du Pont had been high-handed in its handling of neoprene, nylon, and polyethylene.[84] Before the two chemical giants had an opportunity to assess whether such an agreement continued to be in their best interests, however, the Department of Justice in 1944 brought suit against them for restraint of trade under the Sherman Act. The suit eventually forced Du Pont to cancel the agreement in 1948.[85] It was far easier for ICI's and Du Pont's executives to conceive of going their own ways after World War II than before. With Germany's defeat and the consequent breakup of I. G. Farben beginning with the Nuremberg trials of IG's executives and ending with the actions of the Anglo-American High Commission, both ICI and Du Pont could feel more secure in their respective domestic and international markets.

Sylvester T. Ryan, the judge who tried *U.S. vs. I.C.I., et al.*, refused to accept the argument that ICI's and Du Pont's agreement resulted in the genuine exchange of scientific and technical information. But the overwhelming historical evidence demonstrates that this was indeed the case. By aligning with ICI through the Patents and Processes Agreement, Du Pont gained not just greater market security but also a greatly extended research capability that helped it and ICI to prosper in the interwar years. Du Pont and ICI also achieved a greater parity with I. G. Farben in R&D capability than would have been possible otherwise. It allowed Du Pont's R&D managers the opportunity to avoid costly duplication of research and provided greater breadth and depth in talent.

Perhaps the most tangible evidence of the value of ICI's research capabilities to Du Pont emerged in 1948 when research managers from Du Pont's Organic Chemicals and Rayon departments were in the throes of finding a way to dye two important new synthetic fibers, Orlon acrylic and Dacron polyester. It had not been possible to color these fibers with existing dyes and dyeing techniques. ICI's dyestuffs researchers were also hard at work on dyes for their own polyester fiber, Terylene. The two companies cooperated closely on this difficult dyeing problem. When Orchem's research managers learned that the Du Pont–ICI agreement was to be canceled, they estimated that Du Pont would have to hire thirty first-class research chemists to generate the amount of research that Du Pont was receiving on the single critical problem of dyeing synthetic fibers.[86] President Crawford Greenewalt said Du Pont would have to double its research staff in dyestuffs just to match ICI's research capability.[87]

Relations with I. G. Farben

When Du Pont and ICI originally negotiated their Patents and Processes Agreement, both companies sought to reach a similar agreement, either individually or jointly, with the new, vast German chemical combine, I. G. Farbenindustrie Aktiengesellschaft. Du Pont had hoped that the Fordney-McCumber Tariff and the work of the Chemical Foundation would keep the Germans out of the American dyestuffs market, but this did not occur. By 1923, Du Pont's Executive Committee resolved to explore negotiating an agreement with the German dye industry because "some form of arrangement with the German Dyestuffs interests would be distinctly beneficial to the Du Pont Dyestuffs Department."[88] Du Pont had earlier tried unsuccessfully to interest German dye firms in some sort of joint venture in the United States, but now as a way of gaining much-needed know-how, Du Pont sought only an agreement for the exchange of technical information with the Germans similar to the 1907 agreement.[89] When the general manager of the Dyestuffs Department, F. W. Pickard, went to Germany to open negotiations, however, he learned that "the feeling of the I.G. members against the DuPont Company is actually more strongly hostile than we had suspected."[90] The Germans had not forgotten Du Pont's recruitment of German dye chemists in 1920 and Du Pont's leadership in winning the dye tariff fight. IG's hostility toward Du Pont precluded any agreement. As the 1920s proceeded and as Du Pont entered new areas of chemistry such as high-pressure technology, its managers felt an even greater need for access to German know-how. Yet at the same time, Du Pont's R&D organizations were providing it with improved capability to put up a good fight. As Lammot du Pont told the IG in 1927, "We neither fear your competition in this country nor doubt our own ability to stand up in the fight." Still, he recognized that Du Pont "would be better off in the end without it."[91]

During the late 1920s, Du Pont and the much-enlarged and consolidated I. G. Farben negotiated over a proposed merger of IG's U.S. dyestuffs company, General Dyestuffs, and Du Pont's dyestuffs business as well as a pooling of resources in synthetic ammonia.[92] But the Germans ultimately backed out of any such proposal, largely because they saw no benefit and no little risk in sharing information in organic chemistry and on the Haber-Bosch ammonia process. During the 1930s, however, Du Pont both independently and with ICI continued to seek a general patents and processes agreement with IG because its leaders remained convinced that it could benefit greatly from controlled competition and access to IG's scientific and technical know-how.

IG's attitude toward Du Pont changed considerably as Du Pont's R&D capabilities grew stronger during the decade. Du Pont's invention and development of neoprene and nylon in particular brought about this transformation, but even these important inventions were insufficient to yield a general patents and processes agreement. Despite increasing political risks, Du Pont negotiated with the Germans between 1934 and 1938. These negotiations intensified when IG's Fritz ter Meer came to Wilmington in 1935. Although ter Meer discussed a number of issues with Du Pont, he sought above all a satisfactory licensing agreement on Du Pont's monovinylacetylene (MVA) patents, which would give IG a "short and elegant way" (IG's words) to make butadiene, an important ingredient for its buna synthetic rubber process.[93] Walter Carpenter recorded that ter Meer was "very anxious to bring about an arrangement with the duPont Company, under which we would have cooperation, including exchange of patents and processes between the German IG and du Pont on the broad subject of synthetic rubber."[94] Du Pont's executives were frank in expressing their frustration over how, on so many previous occasions, IG had slammed the door on an agreement with Du Pont:

> Du Pont pointed out to Dr. ter Meer, in some detail, that each time the duPont Company have endeavored to cooperate with I.G. that I.G. had eventually committed themselves elsewhere. This covered dyes, photographic chemicals, pharmaceuticals, hydrogenation of oil and ammonia.[95]

Ter Meer must have gotten a clear picture that Du Pont would not easily be bullied.

IG's desire to get a license on Du Pont's MVA patents and Du Pont's continued hope of reaching a broad information-sharing agreement with IG led in 1936 to another period of intense negotiations. President Lammot du Pont assigned the company's primary negotiator, Fin Sparre, to head its delegation.[96] Several of Du Pont's research directors, led by Chemical Director Elmer K. Bolton, toured IG's research laboratories and conferred with their IG counterparts. Bolton reported that the Germans had been very frank and forthcoming about their work and that "Dr. ter Meer and his associates very greatly welcomed this opportunity of exchanging general research experiences." This feeling led Bolton to conclude that IG respected

Du Pont's R&D capabilities and did indeed have "a desire...for closer relations" with Du Pont.[97]

But negotiations to achieve a broad agreement failed, both because of increasing pressure on IG from the Nazi government to step up synthetic rubber manufacture and because IG's executives continued to believe that the company would give more to Du Pont than it got in return. This view outraged Fin Sparre. When ter Meer began to claim great superiority for IG, Sparre could only "stand it so long." Then he would get up and say, "Well, I'm done, and I mean it; I won't be treated the way you're pretending to treat us. You can go down and check out at the [H]otel [du Pont] and get out. I'll not have another thing to do with this thing. You go make your own bed."[98]

Although these negotiations failed to yield a general technical-information-sharing agreement, IG's need to license Du Pont's patents on MVA and Du Pont's desire to obtain licenses on IG's styrene resins patents resulted in two specific licensing agreements dated September 14 and November 22, 1938.[99] Less than a year later, Du Pont and IG signed another specific licensing agreement, this one on Du Pont's new wonder material, nylon.

Du Pont had hoped to build an impregnable international patent position on nylon. But because nylon's inventor, Wallace H. Carothers, had argued categorically in print that caprolactam could not be polymerized and because IG's research organization found a way to do so, IG built its own patent position on "nylon 6," an alternative to Du Pont's nylon 6-6. Although Du Pont's researchers believed that nylon 6 was inferior to their product because of its lower melting point, IG developed it with such speed and agility that Du Pont soon concluded that IG was going to "beat the pants off us in Europe."[100] To protect its nylon business in the United States, therefore, Du Pont was forced to license nylon to IG. Du Pont gave IG much of its hard-earned nylon-processing technology and exclusive rights to nylon in Germany and other parts of Europe. IG agreed to stay out of Du Pont's domestic market and the remainder of the European and Asian markets. The two firms signed the nylon agreement in May 1939, but before the licensing could be fully implemented, the outbreak of war in Europe led Du Pont to propose the cancellation of this and the MVA and styrene agreements. On May 15, 1941, Du Pont and IG formally canceled the three agreements, and all hopes of exchanging information and know-how with IG were dashed.[101]

Although Du Pont and I. G. Farben never reached a general accord, Du Pont nevertheless benefited from the limited contact its executives and research managers had with their counterparts at IG. If nothing else, IG's extensive research programs served as a spur to the development of Du Pont research. For example, in 1930, Jasper Crane, the member of Du Pont's Executive Committee who was responsible for Du Pont's international activities, formulated a comprehensive statement about IG's research programs and their role in the German company. Crane had inspected several IG research laboratories and had held "frequent discussions about research with some of their leading men."[102] He was, therefore, in a good position to compare IG's research style and capabilities to Du Pont's.

Crane argued that IG's commitment to research could be gauged by the fact that it spent 3 percent of its total sales on research. He considered this figure so impressive that he doubted it. (Du Pont itself spent 2.9 percent of its sales on R&D in 1930, and that figure would go as high as 3.9 percent in 1932.) But he acknowledged that "the number and size of their laboratories, the large number of technical men employed, the elaborate attention paid to patents, are all evidence that research is a major part of the policy of the I.G." Executives at IG, Crane stressed, have "faith that their chemical research will develop every few years a new process of outstanding importance, a big income producer." Moreover, IG had concentrated its efforts on what one IG official called "suppress[ing]" nature – that is, creating chemicals to replace natural products. As Crane concluded, "We cannot help but be impressed . . . by the I.G.'s vision of the possibilities of research."[103]

Crane proposed that Du Pont should share this "vision of the possibilities of research." But he stressed that by no means should Du Pont slavishly imitate IG because he found several faults with its approach to research. He argued that IG was often too lavish in its research expenditures: "Materials, equipment, men, are massed in the attack on the problem in hand. One of their weaknesses in research seems to me to be this very dependence on mass attack to solve their problem." Crane cited several instances in which IG could have achieved far greater research efficiency by a more thoroughgoing study of "the fundamentals of the problem to determine the inherent virtues and defects of the products." He also suggested that IG's "inordinate conceit" would ultimately hurt its research.[104]

When Elmer Bolton visited IG's research organizations in May 1936, he observed many of the same things as Crane. He too was impressed with the scale of IG's research and its excellent facilities for research. Although IG's research staff may have been conceited, Bolton found that they by no means ignored others' research. He detailed the "complete" way in which IG gathered intelligence: "Literature and patent surveys are thoroughly organized covering all countries and languages, so that new developments are brought to the attention of their chemists as soon as possible." Bolton concluded that "a great deal of [IG's] time and money is spent in imitative work."[105] Riding high on the crest of nylon's and neoprene's development – products of fundamental research – Bolton was critical of IG's research. He had apparently forgotten that much of Du Pont's research had been imitative, particularly in the early days of the dyestuffs venture. Within a couple of years, Bolton would be reminded about how valuable such research work could be when IG managed to drive a wedge through Du Pont's nylon patent position by carefully going over every step of Carothers's research and detecting the single misstep that Du Pont had taken on its nylon journey. Imitative research, when done well, could pay handsome rewards.

Bolton himself had helped lead an intense "imitative" research campaign in the late 1920s and early 1930s when the development of titanium dioxide threatened to destroy the company's large pigments business. Du Pont was the largest producer of lithopone pigment in the United States. Titanium dioxide would rapidly displace lithopone, and if Du Pont could not control its development, it stood to lose in a big way. To gain this control, Du Pont drew upon all its resources, including its agreement with ICI, its excellent R&D capability, and its extensive cash reserves. These resources added up to what might be called "development power."

11

Development Power: The Case of Titanium Dioxide Pigments

Du Pont's entry into the manufacture of titanium dioxide (TiO_2) white pigment illustrates the complexity of technological innovation in the mature, decentralized corporation. The numerous methods that the company employed to gain a position in the new technology and the many company departments that concerned themselves with the issue formed a complex matrix of innovation. On the technological side, Du Pont had the options of developing a process in its own research laboratories, obtaining one through its Patents and Processes Agreement with ICI, hiring consultants and experts to build a plant, or purchasing an existing process or firm. To get into titanium dioxide as quickly as possible, Du Pont explored all these avenues to innovation.

Yet there were some organizational problems in this undertaking. Du Pont's numerous acquisitions of the late 1920s had left the company with three departments that made lithopone, the standard indoor white pigment of the time. Thus it was difficult for any of these departments to respond effectively to the TiO_2 threat. Among a number of actors, the Development Department played a leading role in getting the company into the TiO_2 business. To explore alternative processes and to develop one for Du Pont, the Development Department relied heavily upon the Chemical Department rather than the research units of the threatened departments. The Chemical Department had barely begun its work, however, when Du Pont's leaders concluded that TiO_2 was penetrating its lithopone business more rapidly than they had predicted. To resolve this crisis, Du Pont purchased one of the two U.S. firms that manufactured TiO_2. In this era, research was only one of the many approaches to innovation and more often than not played a supporting role in the development of new technology for the company. But as with several other acquisitions, Du Pont's research yielded a significant improvement in the TiO_2 manufacturing process that allowed it to dominate the business.

Du Pont's Lithopone Business

By 1930, Du Pont was the largest U.S. producer of lithopone, a mixture of zinc sulfide and barium sulfate. First prepared in the 1870s, lithopone had grown popular in the twentieth century because of its cost advantage over other white pigments. Production in the United States had grown from 33,000 tons in 1914 to 200,000 tons in 1928, with sales totaling nearly $20 million.[1]

Du Pont had first become a lithopone manufacturer when it purchased the Harrison Brothers Paint Company in 1917. Later, between November 1928 and May 1929, the company tripled its output of lithopone (thereby raising its market share to 37 percent) when it acquired, respectively, the Cleveland-based Grasselli Chemical Company and the Krebs Pigment and Chemical Company of Newport, Delaware. Du Pont purchased Grasselli chiefly to increase its production of sulfuric acid and other heavy chemicals, but along with these products came extensive lithopone capacity.[2] The company supplemented this capacity with the high quality lithopone plant of Krebs. Initially, Du Pont's executives operated both Grasselli and Krebs as subsidiaries and, therefore, did not consolidate Du Pont's lithopone business. This meant that three different units in the company were responsible for lithopone sales, manufacture, and research.

In 1930, the Executive Committee decided to consolidate its lithopone business and research in the Grasselli organization. Until this time, Du Pont had too many actors involved to respond effectively to the growing threat from TiO_2. At one time, as many as four departments of the company were involved in the company's pigment development.[3] Yet the usually rigid bureaucratic lines in the company proved to be far softer than one might expect, owing to the hard work and advocacy of William Richter, general manager of the Fabrics and Finishes Department and member of both the Grasselli and Krebs subsidiaries' boards of directors. With Sparre, Richter effectively coordinated Du Pont's entry into the manufacture of TiO_2.

The Threat of Titanium Dioxide

Titanium dioxide pigments had been produced in the United States since 1918, but their high cost had limited their application. The use of TiO_2 as a pigment had been developed independently in the United States and Norway about 1912. In 1916, the American inventors, A. J. Rossi and L. E. Barton, established the Titanium Pigments Company at Niagara Falls to make TiO_2 by a fusion process. Four years later, they made an agreement with the Norwegian firm that gave them the rights to the European company's superior sulfuric acid process for TiO_2. In that same year, the National Lead Company bought the controlling interest in the U.S. company. Commercial production began the following year.[4]

From the chemical-processing standpoint, the manufacture of TiO_2 was straightforward. It involved dissolving ilmenite, an iron and titanium oxide ore, in concentrated sulfuric acid. After cooling, most of the iron precipitated out as ferrous sulfate. The titanium sulfate liquor was then concentrated and heated to convert the sulfate to the oxide, which precipitated. The product was then dried at a high temperature.[5]

This development had not gone unnoticed by the Du Pont Company. In 1916, even before the company went into the paint business, Sparre had submitted a TiO_2 sample to the Chemical Department for analysis.[6] A few years later, President Irénée du Pont wondered if Du Pont should not enter the business and was told that its high manufacturing costs made it less attractive than lithopone.[7] This ended discussion of the topic until the late 1920s, when TiO_2 of improved quality and lower cost threatened Du Pont's substantial investment in lithopone capacity.

Even before the purchase of Grasselli and Krebs, F&F's Richter had wanted to join up with the Commercial Pigments Corporation (CPC) to make TiO_2 pigments. This newly formed company was owned by the same group that ran the Commercial Solvents Corporation (CSC), a manufacturer of butanol, a solvent for Duco lacquers. Richter knew the CSC people well. He discussed this proposition with Sparre, who stated that CPC's patent picture was very cloudy and that Du Pont should not pursue a deal with CPC. Besides the patent problem, CSC wanted $5 million when the company only had $1.25 million worth of tangible assets.[8]

Richter and Sparre did not see TiO_2 as an immediate threat to lithopone until the declining cost of the new product brought it into direct competition with the older pigment. In December 1929, the National Lead Company announced that it was lowering the price of its Titanox pigments about 10 percent. On a hiding-power basis, this made TiO_2 competitive with lithopone. Du Pont's initial response came from the assistant director of the lithopone research group, who wrote to his superior, James Eliot Booge, that "in less than ten years there will no lithopone manufactured in the United States with possibly the exception of a few thousand tons." He pointed out that lithopone had found markets primarily because it offered the most hiding power for the lowest cost. Now that Titanox could provide equivalent hiding power at the same cost as lithopone, the substitution would begin and accelerate rapidly, especially because the earlier high price of TiO_2 had given it the reputation of being a high-quality pigment.[9]

Booge concurred in this assessment and sounded the alarm. In a letter to the head of Krebs, Zack Phelps, Booge concluded that Du Pont had to enter the titanium pigment business immediately. He recommended building a plant based on the CPC process and then altering it to avoid infringing on CPC's patents. As part of earlier negotiations, Booge had toured the CPC plant in Baltimore and in addition could draw on the experience of Lewis H. Haupt, who had been an engineer for CPC in 1928 and had joined the Krebs Company before its acquisition by Du Pont. What Booge did not consider was that, even if Du Pont could make TiO_2, it could not sell it as a pigment without infringing on patents.[10]

The patents on TiO_2 pigments stood in the way of Du Pont's entering the business. The National Lead Company held patents on the coprecipitation from solution of TiO_2 with either barium or calcium sulfate to produce an extended pigment.[11] CPC, conversely, made only pure TiO_2 but also held the patent on its use as an additive to lithopone. In 1928, Krebs had taken a license under this patent so that it could sell titanated lithopone.[12] While Development and Legal Department personnel explored the patent situation, Krebs, Grasselli, and the Chemical Department, which had in November 1929 initiated exploratory research on TiO_2 manufacturing processes, unsuccessfully attempted to agree upon a single goal for Du Pont's TiO_2 development program.

Krebs's Phelps informed Grasselli and the Chemical and Development departments that he thought that Du Pont should buy TiO_2 from CPC and mechanically mix it with extenders to make "synthetic titanox" to avoid infringing on the National Lead Company's patents. He also informed his Executive Committee liaison and chairman of the board of the Krebs subsidiary, Willis F. Harrington, about the issue.[13] From this time onward, Harrington kept close tabs on the development and interceded in several disputes between departments. He also sat on the board of directors of both Du Pont and Grasselli, just as Richter did. At the end of 1929, Richter wrote to Phelps that he should get together with the Grasselli people on the problem and that he saw no reason why Wilmington had to be involved directly "in keeping this development alive and carried to an early solution."[14]

But an early solution did not come. Despite the jeremiads of Booge, which earned for him Richter's label of "professional crepe hanger," Du Pont made little headway on the TiO_2 problem.[15] One reason was that Booge himself found it impossible to focus his staff's attention on TiO_2. After buying out Krebs, Du Pont learned that the former management had signed a contract to purchase increasingly large quantities of a zinc liquor that was to be used primarily to make a new high-strength lithopone. Du Pont discovered that Krebs did not have a satisfactory process for making any kind of lithopone from the liquor. Booge's lithopone research group was given the task of solving this urgent problem. The work ultimately proved to be unsuccessful.[16]

Du Pont's progress on TiO_2 was also held up by the attitude of Grasselli's management, which was usually represented by its number-three officer, Emmet C. Thompson, who did not share in the growing consensus that TiO_2 pigments would rapidly supersede lithopone. Grasselli pinned its hopes on improving lithopone to the point at which it would once again be a better buy than TiO_2. Booge's group had done considerable work on a new process to make a lithopone with increased hiding power. On a small scale, they had succeeded in raising its hiding power by 20 percent, but Booge thought that almost another 20 percent increase would be necessary to compete with TiO_2. In February 1930, the operating and research divisions of Grasselli met to discuss the prospects of reaching the higher goal in time to head off further inroads by TiO_2 into the lithopone market. Better lithopone was needed, they thought, within six months. The official conference report noted that the prospects for achieving this goal were good, but this opinion appears to have been that of the operating division only.[17] Booge wrote directly to Thompson stating the odds for success were only one in five. He conceded that, although it was a long shot, the new process was the one chance lithopone had to keep pace with TiO_2.[18] Even then, if TiO_2 received as much research attention as had lithopone, TiO_2 would eventually whip lithopone in the marketplace.

Thompson became interested in TiO_2 only after it began to invade Grasselli's lithopone stronghold, the linoleum industry.[19] Upon hearing of Thompson's conversion, Richter informed Charles Stine and Fin Sparre that the "titanium pot has finally boiled over and [Grasselli] now want[s] to throw in the high gear and to do it with all dispatch."[20]

With Thompson on board, Du Pont explored all aspects of the TiO_2 situation in the first quarter of 1930.[21] The president of CPC, William D. Ticknor, told Richter that he still wanted to form a joint venture with Du Pont – and that it had better act soon before all the lithopone business disappeared. Richter responded to this latter assertion with a laugh and told him to "stop romancing." Although Ticknor left the door open for further talks,[22] Sparre was in no hurry to negotiate.

Sparre had accepted the conclusion of a report prepared by his staff member D. W. Jayne that National Lead and CPC did not have sufficiently strong patents to control the manufacture of TiO_2 pigments. Jayne discounted most of Ticknor's arguments about the strength of his TiO_2 patents and pointed out that National Lead's most important ones on composite pigments would expire in a few years. Seeing holes in the patent coverage, Sparre felt "more optimistic all the time about the possibility of developing our own process."[23] He wanted the Chemical Department to put together a process that did not infringe on any patents, a task he thought would be relatively simple. Some manufacturing disadvantages might result from the altered process, but this could be tolerated, Sparre asserted, because Du Pont's highly efficient technical and commercial organization could probably turn the balance to the company's favor. Additionally, if Du Pont decided not to go ahead with commercialization of the process, Sparre believed that the Chemical Department still needed to work out the details so that it would have good data to use in bargaining with CPC or National Lead.[24]

With the Development Department footing the bill, Stine's Chemical Department employed all its resources to assess the TiO_2 situation. Soon after Du Pont signed the Patents and Processes Agreement, Stine visited ICI's Winnington laboratory, where they were working on a TiO_2 process at the semiworks level. ICI's staff proposed – and Stine agreed – to divide the TiO_2 problem in half: ICI would handle "the work of finding the best method for production of crude titanium dioxide," if Du Pont would concentrate its research on "the actual pigment."[25] Following the meeting, Stine requested that John L. Keats, the head of his department's TiO_2 research group, come to England to work with ICI. Stine also wrote to Krebs and Grasselli saying that a joint development with ICI could save time and money.[26]

Despite Stine's enthusiasm for ICI's work, Sparre dismissed the ICI process as being only in the initial stages and based on ideas that had been discarded a decade earlier.[27] Perhaps because of Sparre, Stine's goal for a joint R&D effort with ICI fell by the wayside.

At the same time that Stine was investigating the ICI process, Keats's research group in the Chemical Department had begun to try to duplicate the CPC process in the laboratory.[28] This was not what the Development Department had asked it to do; Jayne expressed surprise when he met with the TiO_2 group and learned that it was not trying to develop a patent-free process.[29] The Chemical Department's program also did not meet with Booge's approval. He wanted the Chemical Department to develop a process for making a salable pigment instead of focusing on determining yields in the various steps and assessing the patent situation.[30] Not being able to keep everyone or even anyone happy, the Chemical Department stuck to its original goal of duplicating the CPC process.

Researchers in Keats's group were under considerable pressure to come up with a process so that a pilot plant could be constructed in the summer of 1930. As the first step in this direction, Bradshaw wanted to talk to the ex-CPC employee, Haupt, about that company's plant. Because the Legal Department had no major objections, Bradshaw went ahead and consulted with him. By the end of March, Bradshaw was beginning to look for a location for the pilot plant even though the process had not been perfected.[31] Pushed to keep the project moving, Bradshaw told Sparre that under normal circumstances he would not consider immediately building a pilot plant because his research team needed six more months to build and run smaller-scale equipment in order to gain the needed process information. The only reason that a pilot plant was feasible at this stage of development was because of the information that he had gotten from Haupt about the CPC plant. With twelve chemists on the project, such intense work would cost the Development Department dearly, especially once construction of the pilot plant got under way.[32]

In addition to the large expenditures anticipated, several problems remained to be solved. Chemists were still trying to optimize the process variables and were paying no attention to patent infringement. Bradshaw felt that at least one important and several minor patents would have to be infringed on by the Du Pont process. At best, he hoped to get the process to the point where only patents of doubtful validity would be infringed on. Bradshaw concluded that they would not be able to develop a patent-free process in time for Du Pont to begin manufacture on schedule (probably sometime in 1931).[33]

But in July 1930, Bradshaw wrote to Grasselli's Thompson that he favored a delay of several months in the construction of the semiworks. He wanted to delay for two reasons. First, he had arranged for Norbert Specht, who had previously been in charge of TiO_2 production at the Auer plant in Germany, to come to the Station as a consultant on the project. Second, Bradshaw wanted to clarify some of the puzzling aspects of the patent situation. His analysis suggested that the National Lead Company had a strong patent position but had not used it to hamper the operations of its competitors. Before going ahead with the semiworks, Bradshaw wanted to confer with CPC about National Lead's patents. So the Chemical Department pursued two paths of development. One was aimed simply at getting the CPC process going and the other at finding ways to avoid infringing on patents.[34] By September, he had spent $75,000 on the project and estimated it would require at least another $300,000 before Du Pont would be ready to build a commercial plant.[35]

In late 1930, while the Chemical and Development departments were continuing to debate the various process and patent problems, National Lead reduced the price of its Titanox pigments by another 10 percent. Richter noted that even before this price reduction, TiO_2 had been quietly creeping into the entire paint field. Lithopone sales were down more than 20 percent in 1930, and profits had fallen by over 40 percent. He pointed out to an Executive Committee member that National Lead's price cut was but "one more spur" to Du Pont's entry into TiO_2 manufacture.[36] Soon, Du Pont would reopen negotiations with Ticknor of CPC.

In February 1931, Sparre reversed his previous position and informed the Executive Committee that Du Pont had no alternative except to buy one of the existing TiO_2 producers. The business was developing too fast for Du Pont to wait for a process to be developed internally. He estimated that it would cost $2.5 million and take at least two more years before Du Pont could have a plant in operation. Once it had been built, Sparre did not think that the plant would be a profitable investment because by that time, he believed, National Lead and CPC would be "firmly in the saddle."[37] At that point, Du Pont's entrance into the business would lead to falling prices and lower profits for everyone.

National Lead showed no interest in negotiating with Du Pont, but CPC was willing, if not eager, to reach an agreement. Ticknor needed money to continue Commercial Solvents Corporation's several patent suits against alleged infringement on his patents for the production of butanol by fermentation.[38] Ticknor wanted such a high price for CPC that Sparre concluded that a cooperative venture would be necessary. He recommended consolidating CPC and the Grasselli lithopone division into a new company 70 percent owned by Du Pont.[39] He arrived at this percentage by comparing the prospective earnings of the two organizations. The Executive Committee authorized Sparre to begin negotiations on this basis on March 4, 1931. Du Pont representatives found the CPC plant in good working order, and Sparre decided that the patent situation was satisfactory but not ideal.[40] On August 1, 1931, Du Pont and CPC concluded an agreement to form a new company, the Krebs Pigment and Color Corporation. It had $10 million in assets and was operated as a subsidiary of the Grasselli Company. This successfully ended Du Pont's desperate eighteen-month effort to get into the TiO_2 business.[41] When the president of Du Pont's new Krebs Company, Carl H. Rupprecht, explained to Ticknor all the research that Du Pont had done on TiO_2, Ticknor was amazed by the rate at which Du Pont had been spending money. He estimated that his company's total development and initial operating costs had been only $370,000, which is about the same figure that Bradshaw had estimated a year earlier for developing Du Pont's process.[42]

Extended TiO_2 pigments soon confronted the new organization. To hold its market position, argued Booge, now the technical director of the new company, Krebs would have to sell more than just titanated lithopone. Anticipating the expiration of National Lead's patents in a few years, he wanted to do research on extended pigments so that Krebs would be prepared to enter the business. Rather than rely upon the Chemical Department for such research, Booge transferred it to his own organization as soon as the CPC agreement was signed.[43] In his own departmental research unit, he moved carefully and cautiously to avoid trouble with National Lead.[44]

Rather than fight each other, Du Pont and National Lead signed a patent and process exchange agreement in 1933. The negotiations had begun a year earlier when National Lead's president, Edward J. Cornish, inquired about an exchange of plant visits before his company went ahead with the construction of a new plant at Perth Amboy, New Jersey.[45] Richter thought it might be a good idea if Du Pont could broaden the agreement to include cross-licensing of patents, particularly those on extended pigments. He found National Lead officials willing to sign such an agreement. Because of National Lead's previous ties to European firms, the Du Pont–National Lead agreement was not implemented until 1933.[46] This agreement finally ended Du Pont's – and especially Sparre's – worries about the complex TiO_2 patent situation. Even before the agreement, the National Lead Company had chosen not to sue CPC for infringing on its patents on the manufacture of TiO_2. The firm wanted to push for rapid growth of TiO_2 pigments and believed that in an expanding business there would be plenty of room for a smaller competitor such as CPC. This attitude did not change when Du Pont bought the majority interest in CPC.[47]

Even with the legal obstacles removed, the Krebs Company did not move aggressively into extended pigments. Its managers may have been reluctant to go into this business because extended TiO_2 directly replaced lithopone, whereas the TiO_2-lithopone mixture used considerable quantities of the older pigment. Also, the shift to TiO_2 had not happened as rapidly as had been expected. For the first few years after the merger, lithopone held its ground fairly well. In 1932, lithopone accounted for over three-quarters of the Krebs company's sales. The Depression had caused the price of zinc to fall dramatically, and labor costs had decreased too. In addition, Du Pont had consolidated its lithopone manufacturing in its most efficient plants.[48] However, Walter Carpenter charged that lithopone had done so well only because Krebs had not expanded its TiO_2 capacity fast enough and that this had actually hurt the company's position in the extended TiO_2 pigments field.[49]

Getting this message, Krebs's president, Rupprecht, submitted a 5-million-dollar appropriation request in July 1934 to build a new plant to produce extended TiO_2 pigments. He stated that lithopone sales had begun to decline dramatically and that Krebs was totally unprepared to meet the situation. Fortunately for Krebs, however, its competitors had not planned large expansions of their extended TiO_2 plants, so Krebs still had an opportunity to capture a good share of the market. Rupprecht concluded that "we face the necessity of a decision to either stand still and see our lithopone business reduced to a loss or proceed aggressively to meet the new order in white pigments...."[50] The Executive Committee granted Krebs the appropriation, and Du Pont became a major producer of all types of TiO_2 pigments.

Several decades later, Du Pont would become the dominant manufacturer of TiO_2 pigments after it began operating its innovative chloride process plant in the 1950s. This process originated in Chemical Department studies going back to 1931. In that year, X-ray examination of TiO_2 pigments revealed that they could be produced in several crystalline forms. One type, "rutile" TiO_2, proved to have about 20 percent more hiding power than the commercially produced "anatase" type.[51] Following a decade of off-and-on work on rutile TiO_2, Du Pont began selling it commercially in 1941.[52] The success of this proprietary product and process was enormous. TiO_2 paralleled Du Pont's experience with other products such as cellophane, in which the company's researchers made significant modifications to products acquired from external sources. The case of titanium dioxide suggests that although the paths of innovation at Du Pont were many, in the decentralized corporation there were sometimes hurdles across those paths.

Nevertheless, the resources that Du Pont commanded in its pursuit of innovation were enormous and ultimately allowed Du Pont to prevail. The TiO_2 pigment episode illustrates the methods that the Du Pont Company used between the wars to establish a strong position for itself in emerging technologies. When faced with the options of developing its own process or buying the technology, Du Pont's management chose the latter as the most effective way of entering the business. Once the new technology had been assimilated within the company, then the research organization could focus on particular aspects of it. This process-and-product-improvement type of research dominated the company's industrial department research program between 1921 and the early 1930s.

But during the next decade, Du Pont's ideas about innovation would change dramatically. Neoprene and nylon, both products that emerged from Charles Stine's elite fundamental research program in the Chemical Department, would bring executives and research managers alike to a new formula for innovation. No longer would acquisition and rationalization be the watchwords. Now the emphasis would be on more basic research. Du Pont's new slogan would be "Better Things for Better Living through Chemistry."

PART III

"Better Things for Better Living through Chemistry"

In the 1930s, Du Pont shifted its strategy from getting into new markets to creating new products for these markets. The basic departmental structure that the company had established in the 1920s would provide a framework for the firm's growth for the next forty years. Earlier, the company had relied on its capital, development skills, and diversified structure to take advantage of new technology that had originated outside the firm. The process of invention, management believed, was too unpredictable to institutionalize within the corporate structure. So Du Pont kept a sharp watch for new developments anywhere in the world but especially in small entrepreneurial companies. Du Pont's opportunistic research strategy of getting in early and obtaining exclusive patent rights was highly successful in the 1920s. The economic constraints caused by the Great Depression and numerous antitrust prosecutions put an end to Du Pont's diversification through acquisition. At the same time, however, two research discoveries led Du Pont management to see research in chemical science as a source of new products.

In 1927, Chemical Director Charles M. A. Stine began an experiment in pure science or fundamental research. One of the fields that he chose, the study of polymers, turned out to be a gold mine for new materials. Du Pont captured the lead in the emerging field of polymer science because of the pioneering work of Wallace H. Carothers, whom Stine had hired for his fundamental research unit in 1928. In the course of work on the nature of long-chain molecules, Carothers's group discovered neoprene synthetic rubber and nylon. Chapter 12 explores the origins and subsequent evolution of Du Pont's fundamental effort and chronicles Carothers's brilliant, though tragic, career.

When neoprene and nylon appeared in the laboratory, Du Pont had expertise in both rubber and textile fiber technology within its diversified organization. The successful development and commercialization of these new materials depended on this knowledge and upon the expertise that the Chemical Department had built up in polymer science. Manufacturing these products required the development of entirely new technologies. It is no exaggeration to state that in the 1930s Du Pont was the only company in America that had the breadth and depth of skills necessary to manufacture neoprene and nylon. Chapter 13 addresses the lesser known but critical half of R&D – development.

The success of new polymer materials depended in no small degree upon Du Pont's excellence in chemical engineering, a discipline that had made major strides in the 1920s. Du Pont research chemical engineers, who originally were part of Stine's fundamental research program, contributed importantly to this developing field and ensured that the company's expertise was state of the art. Chapter 14 explores Du Pont's highly successful chemical engineering research program.

During the 1930s, Du Pont research managers attempted to achieve some degree of uniformity across the company in matters of research administration. Although the industrial departments had developed research organizations suited to their particular needs, each laboratory had to deal with questions about managing research, the use of consultants, recruiting, record keeping, and publications. Chapter 15 looks at the conduct of research at Du Pont between the two world wars.

12

The "Radical Departure": Charles Stine's Fundamental Research Program

On December 18, 1926, Chemical Department Director Charles Stine submitted to the Executive Committee a short memorandum entitled "Pure Science Work," which initiated a sequence of events that led to the discovery of neoprene synthetic rubber and nylon. These revolutionary new products had a profound impact on Du Pont's research strategy even though the program as conceived by Stine did not survive a decade.

This "pure science or fundamental research work" represented "a sufficiently radical departure from previous policy" that Stine decided to make a special presentation to the committee. The research Stine wished to undertake had "the object of establishing or discovering new scientific facts" as contrasted with Du Pont's current research, which "applied previously established scientific facts to practical problems." Stine pointed out that "fundamental or pioneer research work by industrial laboratories was not an untried experiment" but rather had been successful in the German chemical industry and in the General Electric Company. He recognized that universities did a considerable amount of fundamental research but pointed out that there were some important gaps in their programs. To support this argument, he cited Herbert Hoover's article, "The Vital Need for Greater Financial Support to Pure Science Research" in which Hoover maintained that the rapid growth of industrial research was depleting the reserve of scientific knowledge that formed the basis of technological innovation. Or as Stine put it, "applied research is facing a shortage of its principal raw materials."[1]

Stine argued that his vaguely defined research program would yield a real return. He listed four reasons why Du Pont should spend its money on this new kind of industrial chemical research. First was the scientific prestige or "advertising value" to be gained through the presentation and publishing of papers. Second, interesting scientific research would improve morale and make the recruiting of PhD chemists easier. Third, the results of Du Pont's pure science work could be used to barter for information about research in other institutions. Fourth, pure science work might give rise to practical applications. Although Stine personally believed that these would inevitably result, he felt that his proposal was totally justified by the first three reasons.

To make his proposal more attractive to the Executive Committee, who had two years earlier expressed concern that the Chemical Department had not developed anything new, Stine remarked that General Electric's Willis Whitney had said that although his laboratory "had tried from the beginning to confine their activities to fundamental or pure science work, the rapidity with which they find practical applications staring them in the face is so great that for some time not more than 10% of their whole effort had been devoted to pure science work."[2] If Stine inserted this statement as bait, the Executive Committee did not take it. It deferred action until Stine could submit a more detailed proposal.[3] Perhaps the committee turned down Stine's initial request because it lacked a clear statement of what kind of research he was proposing. In various places, he alluded to it as fundamental, pure, and pioneering research. Soon Stine selected fundamental research as the appropriate label.

The term apparently originated from the idea that practical problems could best be solved through the application of fundamental scientific principles. In the 1910s, C. E. K. Mees of Eastman Kodak and Arthur D. Little both endorsed this approach to research.[4] In an era that saw science being touted as a universal panacea, it is not surprising that it should have also been prescribed for the solution to technological problems. By 1920, the term "fundamental research" had become part of a Du Pont research manager's vocabulary.[5] But the pressing needs of business and a shortage of qualified researchers prevented Du Pont from doing much research of this type. Stine hoped to rectify this situation with his program.

After discussing his original proposal with Emmet Reid of Johns Hopkins University, Whitney of General Electric, and Edward B. Craft of the Bell Telephone Laboratories, Stine submitted a more detailed proposal to the Executive Committee in March 1927.[6] In this document, he used the term fundamental research synonymously with pure science, although he made no mention of this latter expression. Perhaps the Executive Committee found the familiar term fundamental research more acceptable than pure science. But Stine really did want to do pure science at Du Pont. He pointed out that the research he was proposing differed from even the most scientific applied research. He distinguished fundamental research from the adjoining type, what he called pioneering applied research in his research spectrum. The difference, he noted, "is based primarily on the scope of the work and the extent to which it is limited by the recognition, from the start, of certain practical goals." To clarify the distinction between "pioneering applied" and "fundamental" research, he stated that the former "might result in something of great value or might come to naught. But the latter is bound to result in the discovery of new highly useful and in some cases indispensable knowledge." At first, this seems like a very curious distinction. What Stine meant was that pioneering applied research is a form of gambling. For example, he pointed out that the Organic Chemicals Department's investigation of synthetic rubber or the Badische company's work on high-pressure reactions of carbon monoxide and hydrogen might not produce anything useful. But the investigation of the scientific foundations of chemical technology – fundamental research – had to yield significant results in the long run. Science would improve upon traditional knowledge.[7]

In his proposal, Stine persistently argued that fundamental research eventually would allow Du Pont to treat materials in a more rational and scientific manner. He proposed the following lines of work: colloid chemistry, catalysis, the generation of physical and chemical data, organic synthesis, and polymerization. Stine discussed each of these topics. For example, on colloids he argued that the "study of colloidal solutions in organic liquids ... is practically a virgin field from a scientific standpoint. ... Our progress in [their] utilization ... has been made slowly and painfully, principally by the 'shotgun method.'" Catalysis, Stine noted, "represents probably the most remarkable and most important development in modern chemistry. ... , [yet] the mechanism of the action of catalysis is unknown. There is consequently no scientific basis for selecting the best catalyst for a given process." On physical-chemical data, Stine cited the value of fundamental work on distillation as one example. "In order to design a full scale plant intelligently," he maintained, "a great deal of data is necessary which is not at present available in engineering reference books." Stine was unable to make any concrete suggestions regarding work on organic synthesis, but regarding polymerization he stressed that almost nothing was "known about the actual mechanism of the change which takes place, so that the methods used are based almost solely on experience." He added that many of the company's present problems in all these areas would have been helped if this kind of work had been started five to ten years earlier but cautioned that it would produce results too slowly to be of help in the immediate future.

From the outset, Stine felt that his program would succeed only if he could hire "men of proven ability and recognized standing in their respective fields."[8] But he realized that it would be difficult, and maybe impossible, to recruit such men, all of whom worked in academia and had developed specific lines of research. Alternatively, Stine proposed to do what General Electric and Bell Laboratories had done successfully, hire "men of exceptional scientific promise but [with] no established reputation. In this case, the nature of their work can largely be determined by us."

The funds required for the project depended on the number of lines of work undertaken. Stine estimated that each group consisting of one first-class man and several assistants would cost about $40,000 a year. A 1928 budget of $250,000 would allow work along five or six lines. He eventually hoped to spend between $300,000 and $500,000 a year on fundamental research. In his closing paragraph, Stine contended that this kind of research program needed to be ensured of continuity even in times of low earnings. He thought that it would take five years to get his program going properly.

At its next meeting, the Executive Committee approved Stine's proposal in principle and asked him to submit a budget.[9] It is impossible to reconstruct the discussion that occurred, so the reason for the positive decision cannot be firmly established. Without Stine's salesmanship, it seems unlikely that any program of this type would have been approved. Two other factors, however, appear to have figured prominently: Irénée du Pont's handing over the presidency to his brother Lammot, and the committee's feeling that Du Pont had emerged from a period of consolidation in good financial condition after its earlier diversification. Irénée's position on fundamental research cannot be positively determined, but at least one episode suggests that he favored leaving this kind of work to the universities.

Scientists at MIT in 1925 had tried to convince the Chemical Department to purchase X-ray equipment that could be used to study the structure of materials. On this issue Irénée wrote to Stine that he "was inclined to think that we would get more per dollar of expenditure by following in that game rather than leading. It is rather far from our experience and pretty advanced in application."[10] Perhaps it is not coincidence that Stine did not put his fundamental research proposal before the committee until Irénée had retired. Traditionally, the story has been told that Stine went to Lammot du Pont's house on weekends and talked to him about fundamental research while Lammot indulged in one of his favorite hobbies, chopping wood. Apparently, Stine convinced the pragmatic Lammot to give it a try. Stine wanted to announce the new undertaking in *Industrial and Engineering Chemistry*, but Lammot du Pont preferred not to start off with a "hurrah." He told Stine first "to saw the wood and let the publicity take care of itself."[11]

In the same meeting that the committee passed Stine's proposal, it also passed another resolution that sheds some light on the fundamental research decision. The committee asked the Chemical, Development, and Engineering departments to prepare a proposal on studies of new chemical industries that the company might enter and that would utilize Du Pont's technical and organizational skills. The committee stated that Du Pont should consider additional diversification because the company's lines of business were all in good shape.[12] This expansive attitude reflected the company's affluence. The year 1926 was a good one in the chemical industry; sales and profits exceeded those of 1925. Also, it was a fantastic year for General Motors. Nearly three-quarters of Du Pont's net income came from dividends on its GM stock. The Du Pont share of GM's profits had risen from nearly $12 million in 1925 to $30 million in 1926. In this latter year, Du Pont paid out 97 percent of its earnings as dividends.[13] Clearly the company had money to spend on new investments, on broader-based research programs, and on Stine's fundamental research project.

In funding fundamental research, the Finance Committee gave Stine even more than he asked for. Beginning in April 1927, $25,000 a month was set aside for fundamental research. This annual rate of $300,000 was much more than Stine could possibly spend for several years. Funding was to be continued at this rate until experience indicated that it should be modified. Although fundamental research would be charged against this reserve, the actual expenditures were subject to annual approval by the appropriate committee.[14] As part of his 1927 budget, Stine received $115,000 to build a new laboratory for fundamental research, which Du Pont chemists quickly dubbed "Purity Hall."[15] With the new building under construction, Stine began to look for twenty-five scientists to fill it.

To head a group to study the properties of dispersions of liquids and suspensions of solids, which form a part of the field of colloid science, Du Pont hired Elmer O. Kraemer, a twenty-nine-year-old assistant professor at the University of Wisconsin, who had been a consultant for Du Pont.[16] Kraemer had entered Wisconsin at age sixteen and became committed to colloid chemistry in his junior year. He graduated in 1918 and three years later went to the University of Uppsala as an American Scandinavian Foundation Fellow. After a year at the University of Berlin, he returned to Wisconsin to finish his dissertation under his Uppsala teacher, Theodor Svedberg, who was a visiting professor. Kraemer then taught at Wisconsin for three years before joining Du Pont.[17] As soon as he accepted the position in May 1927, he began to plan his fundamental research program.[18] Through Kraemer, Du Pont obtained access to the latest work of Svedberg, who received the Nobel Prize in chemistry in 1926.

One of Kraemer's graduate students at Wisconsin, James Burton Nichols, joined Du Pont in late 1927 and began to construct a facsimile of Svedberg's ultracentrifuge. Nichols had done his undergraduate work at Cornell and had done a senior thesis in colloid chemistry under Wilder Bancroft, one of the leading physical chemists in America. Finishing his undergraduate work in three and a half years, Nichols arranged to work with Svedberg at Wisconsin during his semester there in the spring of 1923. According to Nichols, he chose a project that was so speculative that no one else wanted it: to construct a very powerful centrifuge that would cause very small particles to settle from solution and that could be used to determine the distribution of particle sizes. At Wisconsin, Nichols and Svedberg built an ultracentrifuge from a cream separator, but they encountered serious difficulties.[19]

Upon his return to Sweden, Svedberg and his associate Herman Rinde perfected a device that could produce a force 5,000 times that of gravity. Svedberg then began to use the ultracentrifuge to study proteins. His discoveries that hemoglobin was a molecule of singular molecular weight, not a mixture of different-size molecules, and that a protein extracted from a land snail had what seemed an unbelievable molecular weight on the order of 5 million had an important impact on the emerging fields of polymer chemistry and biochemistry. To do this work, Svedberg had built an even more powerful centrifuge that created a centrifugal force nearly 100,000 times that of gravity.[20] This machine was the prototype for the one that Nichols constructed at Du Pont.

Nichols had spent several years working with Svedberg in Uppsala after completing his MS at Wisconsin in 1924. After finishing his work in Sweden, he joined Du Pont in November 1927.[21] After constructing an ultracentrifuge, the critical parts of which had been made by Svedberg's mechanic, Nichols began to study the particle sizes of Du Pont's pigments and the relationship between particle size and pigment properties.[22] This colloid work would be the biggest fundamental research project in 1927 and 1928.

By the end of 1927, Stine had eight men at work on several lines of fundamental research.[23] The colloid group consisted of Kraemer, Nichols, and Robert V. Williamson, a PhD from the University of Wisconsin who had joined Du Pont in 1923. Guy B. Taylor, a veteran Du Pont researcher who had earned his PhD in physical chemistry from Princeton University in 1913, led a second group concentrating on catalysis research. For the summer of 1928, he was joined by Hugh S. Taylor and George B. Kistiakowski, both consultants from Princeton. Another Du Pont employee, Arthur W. Kenney, an MIT PhD, began to use X rays to study the structure and composition of materials.

In the fall of 1927, Stine still did not have anyone for his organic group. Roger Adams later stated that Stine had offered him a job. At this time Adams was already a full professor and chairman of the Chemistry Department at the University of Illinois, so originally Stine might have been hoping to hire a leader in the field.[24] Failing to get Adams, Stine then offered a position to Carl S. Marvel, Adams's colleague at Illinois. Marvel, too, declined the job.[25] Stine turned next to Louis F. Fieser, an associate professor of organic chemistry at Bryn Mawr College. Fieser, who had gotten his PhD from Harvard in 1924, wrote to his mentor, James B. Conant, asking his advice on the Du Pont offer. Fieser's concerns show how tenuous was the relationship between academic and industrial scientists in the late 1920s:

> Of course, every facility for one's work is available and the salary "would probably be twice my present one." It does sound attractive! I never expected to go into industrial work but the thing which makes a decision so difficult in this case is that I don't have to sell my soul at all; they even said that I could bring my quinones along and continue my present work.
>
> They are gambling, I think, that the men selected for this work will turn out to be Langmuirs and Coolidges, men who will make a credible showing before the scientific public and also contribute definitely to the primary business of the concern.... I have never been thrilled by the technical applications of chemical principles; are the chances very great that I will develop such interests? The van't Hoff carbon atom appeals to me a thousand times more than contact acid, the development of synthetic ammonia, or methanol. Am I apt to change?[26]

Apparently, he did not think so because he stayed at Bryn Mawr until 1930, when he went back to Harvard, where he pursued a distinguished career in academic chemistry.

At about the same time, Du Pont attempted to hire Henry Gilman, another Harvard graduate, who was professor of organic chemistry at Iowa State University.[27] Turned down by Gilman, Stine tried to recruit Reynold C.

Fuson, a Minnesota PhD who had been a National Research Fellow at Harvard and had been an instructor there before moving to Illinois. Stine's assistant, Arthur P. Tanberg, wrote to Fuson: "It is our intention that the work of these men shall be published almost without restriction, and we are, of course, in a position to facilitate their work to a much greater extent than is possible in most of the universities." Fuson too refused the offer, citing his preference for the university atmosphere.[28] Stine had hoped to have fifteen men working on fundamental organic chemistry and to spend nearly half his budget on it. But by the beginning of 1928, he had succeeded in hiring only one man, a thirty-one-year-old instructor from Harvard named Wallace Hume Carothers.

During his nine years at Du Pont, the brilliant but mercurial Carothers not only made important contributions to polymer science but also led a research effort that produced neoprene and nylon.[29] He had become interested in chemistry after reading Robert Kennedy Duncan's popular books while he was a high school student in Des Moines, Iowa.[30] After graduating from high school, Carothers spent a year completing the course at Capital City Commercial College, where his father taught. In the fall of 1915, he entered Tarkio College in Missouri as a science major, and simultaneously accepted a position in the Commercial Department. Later he assisted in the English Department. Carothers prided himself on his ability to write clear and forceful prose, a skill evident in his scientific papers. When his chemistry professor, Arthur M. Pardee, left Tarkio for the University of South Dakota, Carothers filled in as the chemistry instructor, though he was still an undergraduate. After graduating in 1920, he studied organic chemistry at the University of Illinois and obtained a masters degree. Then, joining Pardee in South Dakota, Carothers taught courses in analytical and physical chemistry to save enough money to return to Illinois for a PhD.

At South Dakota, Carothers carried out his first original work on the application to organic reactions of G. N. Lewis's theory on the role of electrons in chemical bonding. This work produced a paper, "The Double Bond," which his longtime friend and chemistry professor at Cornell University, John R. Johnson, considered one of Carothers's outstanding publications, a pioneer paper in the field, and one that foreshadowed later developments.[31]

Returning to Illinois in 1922, Carothers worked under Roger Adams on platinum oxides as catalysts for the reduction of organic compounds. But Carothers soon became bored by the drudgery of graduate school. He wrote to a friend that "it contains all the elements of adventure and enterprise which a nut screwer in a Ford factory must feel on setting out for work in the morning." Only his research, which was driven by "the insatiable curiosity of the true scientific spirit" kept him jumping the hurdles toward his PhD. For the 1923–24 year, the college awarded him the department's most prestigious fellowship, the extra income from which Carothers used to support his passion for billiards and coffee. Still, he fantasized about escaping from graduate school by opening his own laboratory in New York, Paris, Vienna, or Berlin, where he could "test some ideas of vast commercial importance."[32] Whatever these ideas were, neoprene and nylon were not among them. Carothers completed his doctorate in 1924 and remained at Illinois as an instructor for two years until he was hired by Harvard University. Although Carothers believed that Harvard was the "academic paradise" for teaching, he really did not like to do it. He preferred research.[33] Soon Du Pont offered him a job that ostensibly entailed nothing but research.

Carothers resisted Stine's recruitment efforts until he was absolutely sure that fundamental research literally meant pure science. It is not clear exactly how he had come to Du Pont's attention; perhaps Roger Adams, a consultant for the company, had recommended him. Unsure about what would be expected of him, Carothers asked if he could continue to work on the thermal decomposition of ethylmetal compounds, looking for evidence of free radicals. "The problem," he explained, "has some . . . explicit bearings on theoretical chemistry, but none so far as I know [will] be of any practical use." Stine replied that at Du Pont Carothers could continue to work on whatever he pleased but the growth of his group would depend on his "capacity for initiating and directing work that we consider worthwhile undertaking." Carothers turned down the job offer without giving any reasons.[34]

A few days later, though, he wrote a long letter detailing his major concerns, which were professional, financial, and personal. Carothers said that his overriding desire was for scientific advancement; therefore, he had to weigh Du Pont's offer against his present position. Harvard was getting a new laboratory and more money for research, and Carothers thought his teaching load might be reduced. He worried that at Du Pont he might have to "suppress the development of an investigation." Conversely, Carothers felt that he would have more and higher-quality assistants at Du Pont than at Harvard. Looking at the financial aspect, he did not feel that the difference in salary, $5,000 versus the $3,200 a year paid by Harvard, was adequate to compensate for the loss of "the real freedom and independence and stability of a university position." Coming from a family of modest means and having had to work his way through college, Carothers took money matters seriously. Initially he had asked for a salary that even he called "fantastic." At the personal level, Carothers wondered how he would fit in at Du Pont, especially since he suffered "from neurotic spells of diminished capacity which might constitute a much more serious handicap there than here." He stressed that he had gone through a difficult period of adjustment in Cambridge and feared something similar if he moved to Wilmington.[35]

Upon receiving this letter, Stine dispatched one of his assistants, Hamilton Bradshaw, to Cambridge to see Carothers. In the intellectual Bradshaw, Carothers found a kindred spirit. They must have talked about the challenges offered by polymer research and the kind of support that Du Pont promised.

Also, Bradshaw raised the salary offer by 20 percent. Ten days later, Carothers decided to join the Du Pont Company.[36] He wrote to a friend, "It is a fairly heavy gamble. I may not like it but it looks alluring."[37]

While finishing the semester at Harvard, Carothers began to contemplate his work at Du Pont and for the first time actively began to consider polymers.[38] Writing to Bradshaw shortly after accepting the Du Pont position, Carothers set down his ideas about polymerization. His discussion contains the basis of the classic research that he did at Du Pont. At this time, German chemists were debating whether polymeric substances were held together by the same forces that operate in smaller molecules or whether some other kind of force peculiar to these substances was involved. This latter view received support from X-ray crystallography, which seemed to show that polymers consisted of loosely bound aggregates of smaller molecules. In the early twenties, Hermann Staudinger began to publish articles asserting that polymeric molecules are practically endless chains held together by ordinary chemical bonds. Carothers espoused this point of view and devised a scheme to prove it. He wrote Bradshaw, "I have been hoping that it might be possible to tackle this problem from the synthetic side. The idea would be to build up some very large molecules by simple and definite reactions in such a way that there could be no doubt about their structures. This idea is no doubt a little fantastic but after all, [Emil] Fischer synthesized an [eighty-unit] peptide."[39]

In the weeks following his move to Wilmington in February 1928, Carothers's correspondence indicates that his new situation pleased him. In a jocular mood, he wrote to his friend and fellow chemist Johnson:

> A week of the industrial slavery has already elapsed without breaking my proud spirit. Already I am so accustomed to the shackles that I scarcely notice them. Like the child laborers in the spinning factories and the coal mines, I arise before dawn and prepare myself a meagre breakfast. Then off to the terrific grind arriving at 8 just as the birds are beginning to wake up. Harvard was never like this. From then on I occupy myself by thinking, smoking, reading, and talking until five o'clock.

More seriously but enthusiastically, he continued:

> Regarding funds, the sky is the limit. I can spend as much as I please. ... Nobody asks any question as to how I am spending my time or what my plans are for the future. Apparently it is all up to me. So even though it was somewhat of a wrench to leave Harvard when the time finally came, the new job looks just as good from this side as it did from the other.[40]

Because Carothers was a well-rounded person with numerous talents and interests, including art, sports, politics, and music, he quickly made many friends in Wilmington. Almost everyone liked and admired him. Carothers appeared to be a stereotypical odd-ball genius only to those who did not know him well.[41]

For the next two years, Carothers seemed to be contented with the overall working conditions at Du Pont.[42] But he still was not sure what was expected from him. In his 1929 mid-year report, he reiterated that "my chief interest is in the purely theoretical aspects of the subject, ... [and] if the future development of this program follows the logical path indicated by our present progress, we shall soon be devoting attention to ... the study of ... materials [that] are more likely to have a bearing on ideas of nutrition and metabolism than any field in which the Company is immediately interested."[43]

Following this declaration of his commitment to pure science, he asked "whether I have properly comprehended what the directors mean by fundamental research." With his characteristic insight, Carothers pointed out the ambiguity that marked Du Pont's fundamental research program: "I have taken it to mean purely theoretical research – my interests lie especially along this line. On the other hand, researches might be fundamental and still have purely practical aims. Such research should, I think, be directed immediately towards those aims." But Carothers did not see his own work fitting this latter definition. He continued his work on the theory of polymerization.

Seeking to resolve the controversy over polymerization, Carothers proposed to build long-chain molecules one step at a time by carrying out well-understood chemical reactions. He chose one of the simplest reactions to test his hypothesis: alcohols reacting with acids to form esters. He added a new twist, though. Carothers reasoned as follows: If each reacting molecule has only one alcohol or acid group, then one reaction is all that can occur. But if the molecules have a group capable of reaction at each end, then the molecules can continue to react, building up a long chain in the process.[44] Carothers thought of using this esterification reaction during his first visit to Du Pont after learning that the company made resinous polymers for paints by a similar process.[45] Reacting compounds with an alcohol group on each end with analogous acids, he made polyesters that contained up to twenty-five alcohol-acid pairs and had molecular weights between 1,500 and 4,000. Carothers called these new molecules "condensation polymers" to distinguish them from those formed from double bonds, which he called "addition polymers."

Studying these and other related types of compounds, Carothers produced a thorough, logical, and massively documented case that polymers were just ordinary molecules, only longer. Many of Carothers's contemporaries agreed with his co-worker Julian Hill, who later recalled, this work "finally laid to rest the ghost ... that polymers were mysterious aggregates of small entities rather than true molecules." Carothers published his findings in a landmark paper on polymerization in *Chemical Reviews*.[46]

By the end of 1929, Stine felt that his fundamental research program had been "marked by excellent progress," since "publication of results has occasioned favorable comment from numerous sources, and several of our men are earning increasing recognition in the scientific world."[47] Also, his group leaders were beginning to act as internal consultants in their special fields. By this time, Carothers had eight men working for him, six of whom had PhDs; Kraemer's colloid group had grown to six; Taylor had three PhDs in his group; and Kenney and his assistant did the X-ray work.[48] In June 1929, Stine established a chemical engineering group under Thomas H. Chilton, a chemical engineer who had joined Du Pont in 1925. With his staff of five men, Chilton began fundamental studies of fluid flow, heat transfer, and distillation.[49] (This important research will be discussed in a subsequent chapter.)

Most of the new men had come straight from graduate school; Stine apparently had given up trying to hire young professors. Of the new hirees, there were PhDs from MIT, Princeton, Harvard, Michigan, Johns Hopkins, Stanford, and Colorado. Samuel Lenher, a PhD physical chemist who had done postdoctoral work with Max Bodenstein in Berlin and G. N. Lewis at Berkeley, possessed the most outstanding scientific credentials.[50]

In spite of Stine's problems in finding first-rate men – in 1929 he spent only half as much money as he was allotted – by all measures his program was a success. In explaining his fundamental research program to his counterpart in Imperial Chemical Industries, Stine stated that "the increased diversification of the company's business [and] the fundamental relationships underlying the various chemical processes involved had led [him] to feel that a certain amount of fundamental research must be carried on, in order that knowledge in certain sections of the chemical and physical sciences might be increased along lines likely to be of future interest to the Du Pont Company." If, Stine asserted, he could foresee the exact course of chemical development for the next ten years, then this work would not be necessary. He concluded that he "hoped that eventually from research work of this nature there shall emerge developments which shall be entirely new and interesting and profitable as ventures for the Du Pont Company."[51] Actually, Stine had to wait only a few months for such important developments to occur.

In the history of the Du Pont Company and industrial research, April 1930 was a *mensis mirabilis*. Within weeks of each other, chemists in Carothers's group produced neoprene synthetic rubber and the first laboratory-synthesized fiber. These results were not the stated or implicit goals of Carothers's research, but in retrospect, the discovery of the fiber was the more predictable outcome of the experiments then in progress.

Neoprene was discovered incidentally during a project initiated to study the chemistry of an unusual compound, a short polymer consisting of three acetylene molecules, divinylacetylene (DVA). Several years earlier, researchers in Du Pont's Dyestuffs Department had tried unsuccessfully to make synthetic rubber from DVA. In early 1930, Carothers was asked to explore its chemistry by the new assistant director of the Chemical Department, Elmer K. Bolton, who had recently come from the Dyestuffs Department where he had directed research on acetylene polymers. He would be a key actor in both the neoprene and nylon dramas.

In the mid-1920s, Bolton had initiated a program to find a rubber substitute because of a personal experience and the rising price of natural rubber. Bolton had become interested in it when he was in Germany doing postdoctoral work ten years earlier. The Germans were then working on methyl rubber, a substitute used during World War I. In 1925, when the British cornered the market for rubber, raising the price from $0.12 to $1.12 a pound, Bolton began to consider synthetic rubber as a possible Du Pont research objective.[52] A few other companies also began synthetic rubber research while prices were high.

These efforts were directed toward making rubberlike substances, not toward reproducing natural rubber. Ever since Greville Williams discovered in 1860 that the basic building block of rubber was a single small molecule, isoprene, chemists had been trying to make natural rubber by laboratory synthesis. They had all failed because no one could duplicate the complex chemical reactions that result in the formation of rubber molecules. Failing to turn isoprene into rubber, chemists experimented with other related chemicals, the simplest of which was butadiene.[53]

When the Du Pont Company's senior management pointed out that not even the Germans had been able to make a satisfactory synthetic rubber, Bolton proposed that his chemists attempt to make butadiene as a preliminary step. Butadiene was not commercially available, but he thought that it could be made from acetylene, an important starting compound for chemical production before natural gas and petroleum were widely used. He obtained a patent for a butadiene process that was never put into practice.[54] This work, however, made Bolton sensitive to the possible links between acetylene, butadiene, and synthetic rubber.

The connections between these three substances were reinforced when Bolton attended an American Chemical Society meeting in late December 1925, where he heard Father Julius A. Nieuwland, chemistry professor at Notre Dame University, describe his experiments with acetylene.[55] Nieuwland briefly mentioned that he had discovered a cuprous chloride catalyst that joined acetylene molecules together in chains of varying length. Bolton hoped that Nieuwland's catalyst would be the key to making butadiene or even synthetic rubber from acetylene.[56] Eventually, it proved to be essential for producing neoprene.

The relationship between Nieuwland and the company began as a gentleman's agreement; Du Pont offered to file and prosecute patent applications for him if he would give the company an option on them. Also, it established a $750-a-year fellowship to support one of Nieuwland's graduate students. Early in 1928, Du Pont decided to formalize all its consulting arrangements and offered Nieuwland an annual fee of $1,000. Presumably because he was a cleric, Nieuwland did not want to receive cash or sign a contract. But one of his ecclesiastical superiors, James A. Burns, convinced him that a legal agreement was in his and Notre Dame's best interest and that the annual payment could be received in the form of journal subscriptions.[57] This seemed to satisfy all the parties involved.

Using Nieuwland's catalyst, researchers at the Jackson Laboratory tried without success to produce butadiene or rubberlike substances. During this work, Du Pont chemists isolated a new compound, monovinylacetylene (MVA), which consists of two acetylene molecules.[58] Although MVA is the key intermediate compound used to make neoprene, reactions of MVA and DVA with themselves created nothing but hard, brittle solids. In the second half of the twenties, the collapse of the British rubber production restrictions caused a dramatic decline in the price of natural rubber. Du Pont's interest in synthesizing rubber declined as well. In 1929, when rubber sold for 20 percent of its peak price four years earlier, Du Pont expended little effort on synthetic rubber.[59]

The research path that led to the discovery of neoprene changed direction twice in the next few years, first toward finishes and then toward fundamental research. In 1928, Du Pont sent Arnold M. Collins, a thirty-one-year-old PhD chemist in the Chemical Department, to the Jackson Laboratory to develop a finish from the hard, inert films that Nieuwland and Du Pont chemists had prepared from liquid DVA. Collins succeeded in producing a protective coating, called Synthetic Drying Oil, eventually used on metals in corrosive environments.[60] After the Jackson Laboratory began to manufacture the coating on a small scale, Collins went back to the Experimental Station, where he continued to work with his new product. At the beginning of 1930, Collins was transferred again, this time into Carothers's group.

During a project initiated, according to Carothers, to "study the chemistry of [DVA] without particular emphasis on immediate commercial possibilities," Collins unexpectedly produced neoprene.[61] Carothers later recalled that Bolton suggested looking at the reaction of DVA with some polymerizing agents.[62] Carothers assigned Collins to do the experiments because he had worked with DVA while developing Synthetic Drying Oil. Over the next several months, Collins performed numerous experiments, but the major thrust of the work seems to have been to prepare and polymerize very pure DVA. When Collins produced clear films instead of the normally yellow ones, Carothers decided to attempt to isolate and identify the impurities in the crude DVA that might cause the yellowing.[63] Upon distilling the crude DVA, Collins recovered a liquid that preliminary analysis suggested was a new compound. On April 17, he recorded in his laboratory notebook that an emulsion of the new liquid, which had been prepared the week before, had solidified "to white, somewhat rubber-like masses. They sprang back to original shape when deformed but tore easily."[64] This was the first sample of neoprene.

Carothers informed Bolton of the discovery in a short memorandum dated April 18, 1930, in which inexplicably he did not mention synthetic rubber.[65] He credited Collins with discovering a new liquid compound that upon sitting reacts with itself to form a flexible and elastic, though not very strong, solid. Most of the memorandum concerns the effects of the new material as an impurity in Synthetic Drying Oil and its potential use as a drying oil. Carothers did not even point out the structural analogy between Collins's liquid and isoprene, the chemical constituent of rubber, even though he correctly identified the new liquid as 2-chloro-1,3-butadiene. (Carothers later named it chloroprene to reinforce the analogy to isoprene and rubber.) Bolton, however, before passing the memorandum to Stine, wrote the formulas for chloroprene and isoprene on his copy.[66]

Everyone immediately realized that Collins had found a new and unique compound formed from the reaction of MVA and cuprous chloride. No one had discovered it before because Nieuwland's catalyst is needed to make it. About the same time as Collins's discovery, researchers at the University of Chicago came very close to discovering it independently. All they lacked was Nieuwland's catalyst.[67] In the next few years, Carothers and his colleagues systematically investigated compounds similar to chloroprene. This work resulted in twenty-three published papers that Carothers described as "abundant in quantity but a little disappointing in quality."[68] Among other things, these papers indicated that no other MVA or DVA derivatives had any commercial potential. The Jackson Laboratory soon took over the development and commercialization of neoprene. By the summer of 1930, part of Carothers's group would be busy exploring the ramifications of the other April 1930 discovery.

Another member of Carothers's research group, Julian W. Hill, discovered a synthetic fiber while attempting to produce chains longer than anyone had ever prepared in the laboratory. Carothers had earlier decided that the way to build long polymer chains was to extend simple chemical reactions by using molecules that could undergo them at both ends. One such reaction was that of a carboxylic acid with an alcohol in the presence of an acid catalyst to give an ester, eliminating water. Carothers figured that such a reaction between a dicarboxylic acid and a dialcohol should build long polyester chains. But by the end of 1929, the polyesters built by Carothers and his group seemed to have hit a size limit at molecular weights of 5,000–6,000. Carothers decided that the water formed as the second product in the ester-forming reaction could hydrolyze ester groups back to acid and alcohol in the presence of the catalyst, and that the molecular weight limit reflected an equilibrium between the forward and back reactions.

The key to building longer molecules was to find a way of removing that water. He remembered that at a conference several years earlier he had heard of what now seemed like the appropriate device – a molecular still. In contrast to the usual laboratory distillation column, the molecular still was in essence a pot equipped with a cold surface that could be placed very close to the polymerization mixture. The idea was to make the equilibrium polymer in the usual way and then to finish the reaction in the molecular still, in which the cold surface trapped water molecules from just above the polymer and removed them from the mixture. Carothers and Hill constructed a modified version of this instrument that allowed them to remove the by-product water. Then Hill began heating an unusual acid-alcohol pair, because he and Carothers had decided that the reaction of a sixteen-carbon-chain acid with a short, three-carbon-chain alcohol would promote the formation of longer molecules. While removing a sample of the resultant product from the still, Hill observed that the molten polymer could be drawn into fibers. He then made an extremely important and unexpected discovery, that after cooling, these pliable filaments could be stretched or "cold drawn" to form very strong fibers. Further tests on the sample showed that it had a molecular weight of over 12,000, far higher than any condensation polymer prepared previously.[69]

Encouraged by this result, new combinations were tried. Enough polymer was made to evaluate the so-called 3-16 polyester and other related ones. These polyesters proved to be unsuitable for textile fibers because they melted below 100 degrees centigrade, were partially soluble in dry-cleaning solvents, and were sensitive to water.[70] By this time the invention of neoprene and promising but impractical synthetic fibers, and several other factors, combined to push fundamental research toward more clearly defined goals.

Although these two discoveries would eventually have a large impact on Du Pont's fundamental research program, the promotion of Elmer Bolton to chemical director in June 1930 brought about an immediate change in research philosophy and style. Stine moved up onto the Executive Committee as one of five men appointed between 1929 and 1930 to replace an earlier generation. Specifically, Stine replaced H. Fletcher Brown as advisor on research.[71] As an Executive Committee member, however, Stine had to keep up to date on all the business of the company, not just on research matters. His role would be that of an advisor, not as a director or overseer. Bolton, then, was free to run the Chemical Department the way he wanted.

Having been a key figure in Du Pont's long and difficult struggle to become a profitable dyestuffs producer, Bolton had become a commercially oriented, pragmatic research director. In a position paper on research written for an internal research director's meeting, Bolton remained true to the principles that he had set down in his 1920 "Research Efficiency" statement. Research could be managed, according to Bolton, like any other part of Du Pont's business. If not properly conducted, research would lead to "a loss of time and expenditure of money out of proportion to the return that might be expected."[72] For Bolton, the timing of research was critical if Du Pont was to take advantage of commercial opportunities. From his long experience in industrial research, he was suspicious of research programs that would not be expected to yield results for five or ten years. In fact, Bolton had opposed the fundamental research program at its inception.[73] Now it became his responsibility.

Bolton's synthetic rubber program, while he was chemical director of the Organic Chemicals Department, exemplified his approach to fundamental research. Like Stine, he believed that chemists should use their chemistry in their work, but Bolton wanted them to use it to solve specific, well-defined problems, not to explore areas of interest, such as catalysis or polymerization. When Bolton's researchers did not create synthetic rubber, he stopped the work.[74] To the contrary, Stine emphasized the need for continuous effort if fundamental research was ever going to generate useful knowledge. In Stine's lexicon, the synthetic rubber project would be pioneering applied research; but Bolton would run the Chemical Department's fundamental research program in the same manner that he had run his earlier ones.

Unlike Stine, Bolton felt that fundamental research should be more closely directed or managed to give Du Pont direct competitive advantages. In his opinion, the company could not afford to allow its elite group of chemists to pursue purely theoretical avenues because he believed that in academia and industry "every field of chemistry is being searched for new ideas that can be harnessed to practical applications."[75] Whereas Stine had maintained that fundamental research was justified by the scientific prestige that it would bring the company, Bolton emphasized the fourth and originally nonessential reason, "practical applications." Stine had envisioned fundamental research as providing a basis for the scientific rationalization of existing chemical technology; Bolton saw it as the necessary first step in the creation of new industries. It appeared to him that Du Pont had already taken the first step with neoprene and synthetic fibers.

Wishing to publish his synthetic-fiber findings, Carothers encountered opposition from Bolton's new assistant, Ernest B. Benger, who had been a rayon research manager. Like Carothers, Benger felt that it was unlikely that anything of practical significance would emerge from the studies of linear polyesters, but Benger felt that "on the basis of the possible great importance of the work, if successful, . . . I have taken the attitude that the work should not be published and that our position should be protected by a well planned patent program." Carothers responded to Benger by suggesting that he had made, unilaterally, a rather important change in policy and remarked that he was now uncertain about the future course of his work on polymerization. To clarify matters, Benger looked up Stine's original documents, which stressed the importance of publication, and sent them to Bolton.[76] Carothers waited another year before publishing his paper; in the meantime, the department filed a broad patent application, which tried to claim all synthetic fibers. Du Pont received the patent but realized that because it was so broad, it probably would be ineffective against synthetic fibers that were not specifically disclosed.[77]

Even though the polyester's melting points were too low for commercial fibers, they had displayed some encouraging aspects. The Rayon Department's Pioneering Research Laboratory director Charch reported that the new fibers "possess[ed] the most remarkable set of physical properties of any artificial or synthetic fiber that has come to our attention, being in fact in a distinct class of its own as compared to viscose yarns."[78] In particular, the polyesters, unlike all other fibers, retained nearly all their strength when wet, and had an elasticity that only silk could match. Encouraged by these results, Carothers and Hill soon decided to try the chemically analogous polyamides. (These compounds are made by combining an acid and an amine.) It was known that simple amides melted at higher temperatures than the corresponding esters. So Carothers and Hill tried to make fibers from a few compounds of this type. Nylon is a polyamide, but in 1930 no satisfactory fibers could be produced with the newly discovered fiber drawing techniques. Only later was it shown that an aminocaproic acid polymer sample prepared in July 1930 would have yielded a nylon fiber.

After this unsuccessful attempt, Carothers and Hill gave up on polyamide fibers. Carothers explained this decision a few years later:

> In retrospect it seems that the decision not to make further immediate attacks on the amides was rather foolish. But there were several factors involved: The aminocaproic acid polymer should have been a relatively favorable case but apparently failed; we suspected that the . . . [viscosity] . . . was so high that [the] reaction stopped prematurely; we had had some previous experience with polyamides . . . and were impressed with the unexpectedly low molecular weight of the products and the difficulty of doing anything with them [because of their insolubility and high melting points].[79]

Hoping to find fibers with melting points between the polyesters and the polyamides, Carothers and his assistants made fibers from mixtures of the two. Of course, there are an infinite number of combinations, and his two men assigned to the project could try only a few of them. They attempted to make fibers from readily accessible starting compounds, but these experiments yielded weak fibers. The work proceeded at a slow pace because results were neither "reproducible [n]or predictable." As Carothers put it, "the molecular still was not a very tractable tool."[80] Eventually, they did learn how to make superpolymers without using this device; however, by this time, Carothers had run out of patience and ideas for fibers. Besides, the work was getting fairly far afield from the kind of scientific exploration that he enjoyed. His concerns and research had moved into other areas. Generally, he was unhappy about his lack of scientific progress and felt frustrated because he was not sure what Bolton expected from him.

As the economic situation deteriorated, Bolton tightened the reins on the fundamental research groups. By this time, they had begun to devote much more time to applied subjects.[81] The elite group of chemists that Stine had set up in Purity Hall was losing its special status. By 1932, the "academic era" had ended. In his annual report for that year, Bolton stated that "our research program as a whole, particularly our fundamental and pioneering applied research, has been materially revamped with the object of effecting a close relationship between the ultimate objectives of our work and the interests of the company."[82] This change had not gone unnoticed, since Carothers had already begun to complain about the new order of things.

Carothers had an opportunity to express his concerns when Experimental Station director Tanberg requested from each group leader a summary of the first five years of the fundamental research program with special reference to its relevance to the commercial interests of the company. After listing the activities and accomplishments of his group, Carothers wrote a thoughtful answer to his own rhetorical question, "What is fundamental research?"[83] He stated that before accepting Du Pont's offer, he had come to the conclusion, "through considerable conversation and correspondence" with Stine and Bradshaw that fundamental research was pure research with its object to increase the body of scientific knowledge and that "any financial profit that might accrue would be so much gravy." In terms of its scientific contributions, his group had been very successful, Carothers asserted, but his "understanding of present policy toward fundamental research is that it is expected to pay its own way." Although his group had not generated any direct profits, he felt that there were some developments that might pay off with returns many times the original investment. In any event, Carothers did not want to work on turning his scientific findings into new products.

Just as he had done three years earlier, Carothers asked Du Pont's research management to define fundamental research. Earlier, he had formulated his program on the assumption that scientific results were the singular goal. Carothers had no confidence in his ability to turn science into technology: "If I had been asked to do research on anything that I pleased with the mutual understanding that the object was to develop something that would bring in a direct profit, I should never have accepted the job," he argued. Furthermore, Carothers stressed, "there are certainly people that do have this ability, but I think that they are rather rare, and I doubt that there are any on the present fundamental research staff."

The "pay your way" signals that Bolton was sending out to the groups in Purity Hall, Carothers contended, were causing a great deal of confusion and anxiety. He wrote:

> The only guide we have for formulating and criticizing our own research
> problems is the rather desperate feeling that they should show a profit
> at the end. As a result, I think that our problems are being undertaken
> in a spirit of uncertainty and skepticism without any faith in a successful
> outcome or even without any clear idea of what would create a successful
> outcome.

In conclusion, Carothers suggested that to put things back on the right course, fundamental research should be guided by scientific, not commercial, considerations. He was skeptical that "pure research in chemistry can be made to pay any direct and sizable returns." In his opinion, pure science researchers should keep the company up to date on the latest analytical techniques and equipment, perform quick evaluations of ideas, and act as internal consultants for problems anywhere in the company. And if changes were necessary, then Du Pont should scale down its effort – but not eliminate it. After all, he argued, the company spent a considerable sum of money each year supporting academic research; similar work in-house should be at least as productive.

Although he was the most eloquent and outspoken critic of Bolton's stewardship of the fundamental research program, Carothers was not the only one who was uncertain about the future course that the research would take. In the summer of 1931, just four years after the beginning of the program, the leaders of fundamental research groups met with Benger and Cole Coolidge, the assistant director of the Experimental Station, to discuss fundamental research in an industrial laboratory. The agenda for the meeting suggests that Stine's earlier assertions were now being questioned, if not revised.[84] It asked for a definition of fundamental research, how it differed from other kinds of research, and what its immediate objectives were. A number of the questions followed. "In what way may fundamental research have a monetary value for an industrial company?" This included two kinds of benefits: direct (technical discoveries and consulting services) and indirect (creating publicity, facilitating education within the company, stimulating ideas, producing valuable contacts with outside individuals and institutions). Would fundamental research be economically justifiable if it did not lead to important discoveries? Stine had argued that the indirect benefits were a sufficient return. Additional items on the agenda inquired whether one "can determine in advance what kinds of fundamental research are apt to be most profitable to a given industrial organization?" And if this could be done, then "what should determine the restrictions that could properly be placed on fundamental researches that do not promise monetary reward?" The message behind this reassessment of fundamental research clearly was that in the 1930s it was going to have to pay its own way in the Du Pont Company.

As part of the reevaluation process, someone in the Chemical Department administration – probably Benger – gave a talk to the fundamental research group leaders, emphasizing the fact that their job was *not* to seek breakthroughs similar to the ones Carothers had made recently. Apparently, a gold-rush mentality had taken over Purity Hall. He cautioned against "the gambling spirit" that was merely interested in unrelated hunches in the hope of making a big find and stated that he preferred the staff to pursue a "thoroughgoing cultivation of a field," which was less "showy but more effective in the long run." Benger stated that it was long-established Du Pont policy to let others do the preliminary ground breaking and testing of new developments to determine the extent of their potential usefulness. Du Pont should let the small companies take chances because a gambling spirit was more suited to entrepreneurs than it was to thoroughgoing scientists. During this latent period, Du Pont should be watchfully waiting, then at the appropriate moment would catch up through intensive activity. It was economically futile, Benger asserted, for Du Pont to be "too far ahead of the general march," and the company should not do anything sooner than necessary. He maintained that the management of the company "had very little interest in basic knowledge. . . . "[85]

Going back to Stine's original concept of fundamental research, Benger stated that it should maintain a high level of scientific knowledge in the company so that new ideas could be quickly recognized and developed ahead of other companies. Additionally, fundamental research should develop basic science as a guide for attacking practical problems, act as an educational resource for the rest of the company, and discover "new generalizations of phenomena." In this latter category, he pointed to the moistureproofing of cellophane. Finally, Benger stated that the major failing of the fundamental research program had been its isolation from the rest of the company. It should have been providing continuous extension courses to the men in the plants, giving applied researchers the newest and most useful information available, and doing more consulting work for the departments.

Benger's ideas about fundamental research were not greatly different from those of Stine. However, Stine did not really worry very much about the mechanism by which the results of fundamental research would be communicated to other parts of the company. In general, he believed that the research director would assume the responsibility.[86] Benger wanted the researchers to do this work themselves. Whereas Stine had built Purity Hall for his new group, Bolton and Benger wanted to end the isolation of the fundamental researchers and bring them directly into contact with all aspects of Du Pont's technology.

Regardless of how effective it had been, fundamental research had cushioned the impact of the Depression on the Chemical Department. Expenditures for fundamental research had remained almost constant while the rest of the budget had declined by a third.[87] This had occurred because the Executive Committee had continued to set aside $25,000 a month for fundamental research until October 1929. By this time the fundamental research account contained a large reserve that was drawn upon for the next several years.

With the reserve expected to run out in the spring of 1933, Bolton went before the Executive Committee in September 1932 to request that the program be continued and funded at an annual rate of $200,000 for 1933. In a balanced appraisal of the program over the previous five years, Bolton explained that his fundamental researchers had developed new techniques and scientific understanding of such phenomena as polymerization that would serve as the basis for applied research. Interestingly, he did not attribute the discovery of neoprene to fundamental research. Bolton's proposal implied that the work had really just begun and that if continued, significant new developments would be forthcoming.[88] He presented a coherent and convincing argument about the efficacy of his fundamental research program; however, it was in translating these ideas into policies at the group and bench-chemist levels that confusion and misunderstanding had arisen.

Overall, half the original sixteen researchers had left the program by 1932. Two had taken jobs with other companies, three had returned to graduate school, one had accepted a college teaching position, one had transferred into an applied research group, and one had gone to Europe. The physical chemistry group had been disbanded in the fall of 1931 and its researchers transferred into other groups.[89] Lenher left the Chemical Department, joined the Technical Laboratory of the Organic Chemicals Department, and eventually became an Executive Committee member.[90] Twenty men remained in the three major fundamental groups, and another eight men were in other groups that did some fundamental research.[91] Of course, the mainstay of the program had been Carothers's research.

Carothers had established enough of a reputation for himself, both inside and outside Du Pont, that he could continue to work on his scientific studies. In spite of his concerns about what management expected from him, Carothers, following his theoretical interests in the mechanism of polymerization, moved his research away from linear fiber-forming superpolymers toward the study of cyclic compounds consisting of eight- to twenty-carbon-atom rings. These compounds had been exceedingly difficult to synthesize before Carothers discovered that they could be made by heating a linear polymer in the molecular still. This technique permitted him to determine the effects of molecular geometry on bonding and explain the paucity of naturally occurring compounds containing nine- to fifteen-member rings. One of these compounds turned out to have a musky odor, and Du Pont sold it for a brief period as a perfume ingredient.[92] But as with his earlier work on linear polymers, the lack of commercial value for cyclic compounds did not burden Carothers.

His work on large-ring compounds completed his classic researches on polymerization and marked the end of his major scientific studies. In 1933, Carothers began casting about for new research areas but seemed unsure about what he wanted to do. He even briefly considered leaving Du Pont. Upon hearing of James B. Conant's election to the presidency of Harvard, Carothers dashed off a note to Roger Adams asking him to inquire as to whether he might be considered for the position of professor of organic chemistry. Carothers shared his intellectual discontent with Adams:

> Problems in this period have fallen into an unsatisfactory, indefinable class, they are neither theoretical nor practical....I haven't any confidence about practical problems, but enough nice theoretical ones have turned up during the past two years to last a long time.

Ten days later, he wrote Adams asking him to forget this "brainstorm which blew over rather quickly." Besides, he had just bought a house so that his parents, who had been financially hurt by the Depression, could move from Iowa to Delaware. And he had too many loose ends to tie up, especially in getting things ready for publication.[93]

Bolton saw Carothers's vacillation over research topics as an opportunity to encourage him to renew work on synthetic fibers. After a period of sporadic activity, the fiber work had come to a halt in the middle of 1933. Carothers had stopped the work because the problem appeared to be inherently insolvable. He reasoned that the desired end-product properties, high melting point and low solubility, were the same ones that made the spinning of fibers impossible. There did not seem to be any way around this obstacle. Carothers hypothesized that "if there were some means of spinning and synthesizing [the polymer] at the same time, as perhaps a silkworm may use, then it might be possible to get around this difficulty. I hope that we can undertake some experiments along these lines sometime."[94] But these ideas did not spur him to action.

The development of a new synthetic fiber remained at the top of Bolton's list of research priorities. In his 1933 annual report to the Executive Committee, he wrote, "The tremendous advance in the artificial silk industry in recent years has emphasized the importance of developing an entirely new textile fiber, in our opinion one of the most important speculative problems facing the chemist today."[95] Although he thought that cellulose was the most promising material, he looked upon Carothers's work as another line of attack.

Bolton and his assistants, especially Benger, had been trying to get Carothers to put at least one man on the synthetic fiber problem. So early in 1934, Carothers began a new attack on it.[96] Perhaps both he and Bolton were alarmed by the fact that the Rayon Department's Pioneering Research Laboratory was considering a synthetic fibers program.[97] In any event, Carothers determined that the obstacles that blocked the pathway could be overcome. The two problems he faced were the intractability of the molecular still and the melting points of polyamides, which were apparently too high for them to be spun into fibers. To solve the first problem, Carothers thought that a superpolymer could be prepared without using the still if he used a carefully purified amino acid ester rather than using the acid itself. To lower the melting point, he considered using a long-chain starting compound.[98]

On March 23, 1934, Carothers suggested to one of his assistants, Donald D. Coffman, that he attempt to prepare a fiber from an aminononanoic ester. After spending five weeks preparing this compound, Coffman quickly polymerized it and was convinced that he had made a superpolymer because on cooling it had characteristically seized the walls of the flask and shattered them. The following day, May 24, 1934, Coffman drew a fiber from the four grams of polymer that he had made. He recorded in his notebook that he

> heated [it] in a bath at 200°C just above its melting point. By immersing a cold stirring rod into the molten mass upon withdrawal a fine fiber filament could be obtained. It seemed to be fairly tough, not at all brittle and could be cold drawn to give a lustrous filament.[99]

Another sample yielded a "fiber having very good strength." In his quarterly progress report, Coffman wrote that these new fibers "by reason of their chemical and physical properties more nearly resemble silk than any other synthetic material hitherto obtained."[100] These were the first nylon fibers, although the nylon that was eventually commercialized was a different polymer: The term "nylon" was later coined to designate a broad class of polymers – linear polyamides. Although the future of the product was not apparent at this moment, the high melting point of the new fiber led everyone to recognize that a practical synthetic fiber was at least technically feasible. The discovery of nylon overshadows the rest of the work in this period, but there was also another related study that would have a large impact on the development of polymer science.

On July 1, 1934, a young physical chemist from Ohio State University joined the Du Pont Company and was assigned to Carothers's group. In his four years at Du Pont, Paul Flory began lifelong studies of polymers for which he was awarded the Nobel Prize for Chemistry in 1974. While at Ohio State, Flory had completed his dissertation on the photolysis of nitric oxide under a well-known physical chemist, Herrick L. Johnson.[101] Before joining Du Pont, he had done no work on polymers but had obtained his master's degree in organic synthesis. Because of the numerous problems facing nylon development, Carothers put Flory to work on those in which a physical chemist would be most helpful. Flory worked on calculating the growth of the polymer molecules in the reactor as a function of time, and on the preparation and analysis of compounds from which nylon could be made.[102] In addition to these more practically oriented studies, Flory began more fundamental investigations. He later recalled that Carothers had told him that he believed that mathematics could be used extensively in the study of polymers. Soon, Flory approached Carothers with ideas about calculating the distribution of the sizes of polymer chains during the course of their formation by condensation reactions.[103] These investigations led to his first pioneering paper on the subject, published in 1936.[104] Although Flory received considerable inspiration and encouragement from Carothers, their collaboration proved to be short-lived.

Not long after the first polyamide fiber had been prepared in May 1934, Carothers went into an unusually severe depression, which prompted him to see a psychiatrist in Baltimore.[105] He recovered from this attack and tried to go back to work. Not knowing that Carothers was in the middle of a major project, the president of the University of Chicago invited him to become chairman of its chemistry department. At first, Carothers dismissed the offer because he was very busy with the nylon work, which had reached "an exciting stage," but he did consider the advantages that he would have in a university and that he no longer enjoyed in industry, namely, "complete freedom in the selection of problems and the aiming of the work directly toward scientific contributions." At Du Pont, he felt that the choice of problems had become limited since he now had to "regard scientific contributions as an occasional and accidental by-product...."[106] In spite of these misgivings, Carothers decided to stay at Du Pont.

In the next two years, his bouts of depression became more frequent and severe. They culminated in the summer of 1936 in a major breakdown from which he never recovered. Personal problems, including the sudden death of his beloved sister, compounded his difficulties. Finally, on April 29, 1937, three weeks after the basic nylon patent application had been filed, and two days after his forty-first birthday, Carothers committed suicide with cyanide in a Philadelphia hotel room.[107]

In the years just prior to his death, Carothers had become obsessed with the idea that he was a failure as a scientist.[108] It is true that by 1933 he had worked out most of the ramifications of his one big idea. Perhaps his inability to come up with another one exacerbated his problems. It is equally probable, though, that Carothers was despondent because his mental state had affected his scientific creativity.

Elected to the National Academy of Sciences in 1936 and a potential Nobel Prize candidate, Carothers stood with a select few, very near the pinnacle of his profession. Bolton stated that "Carothers read from the depths of organic chemistry such as I have never seen."[109] And Bolton had known many of the great ones, including Willstätter, Conant, and Adams. The last had described Carothers as "the best organic chemist in the country."[110]

Carothers's illness and the staff needs of nylon development gave Bolton additional opportunity to bring Stine's fundamental research division back into the fold of Du Pont's standard industrial research practice. Soon it was "reported, reviewed, supervised, and administered in much the same manner as other lines of work." Significantly, Du Pont no longer recruited personnel strictly for fundamental research. Scientists were shifted back and forth between applied and fundamental research subjects, with each research group in the Chemical Department doing some fundamental research. After 1936, there were no longer any specially designated groups. Carothers had taken a leave of absence, and Kraemer left the Du Pont Company in 1938 to take a position with the Franklin Institute's Biochemical Laboratory. Some of the original teams shifted their efforts to analytical chemistry, and others simply disbanded. Between 1935 and 1940, much of the work centered on "further exploring the field of condensation polymers" and "supplying information to support the nylon development itself."[111]

In 1941 Lammot du Pont, after retiring as president of the company and becoming chairman of the board, expressed concern about fundamental research at Du Pont. He wrote to Bolton,

> I have always regretted the small amount of money and men put on fundamental research. . . . There does not seem to have been a disposition, on the part of the Executive Committee, at any time to curtail the amounts of funds available. The usual reason for not going further into fundamental research is the lack of available talent to carry on the work; and yet aggressive efforts to secure proper individuals never seem to be in great evidence. There seems to be a natural trend of development. What is undertaken as fundamental research develops into applied research as soon as it is successful. The tendency then is for men employed on the project to transfer their activities into the field of applied research, through simply continuing with that project.[112]

In responding to Lammot, Bolton felt obliged to defend his management of fundamental research.

Bolton's arguments highlight the changes that had occurred in the program since its inception.[113] First, he explained why fundamental research had grown so slowly: Four groups had been disbanded because of poor leadership or because the work "held little prospect of leading to knowledge that would serve as the basis for new lines of applied research"; Carothers's illness had disrupted the work of the large organic chemistry group; there had been shortages of qualified personnel; and many of the fundamental researchers had stayed with the development of nylon. In spite of these drawbacks, however, Bolton maintained that his department had done a large amount of fundamental research for the industrial departments, which was not included in this category because of the accounting classifications. Most of the Chemical Department's work was, he argued, "long range in character aimed at searching for new information on which it may be possible later to undertake the development of new processes and new products. . . ."

Significantly, Bolton replied to the unstated criticism that his fundamental research topics did not appear to be very fundamental. He less than convincingly explained that "[I]f the impression has been gained that the work which we have classified as fundamental does not belong in this category, it is due to our inability to portray properly the character of the work in the title of the project or in the brief reports that are submitted to the Executive Committee." He followed this with his modified definition of fundamental research: "In our judgment, we are carrying out a type of fundamental work not so abstract in character that doubt would be raised as to the future utility or value, but of the kind that has the possibility of providing information which would serve as a basis for applied research."

Because each research group in the Chemical Department now did some of this fundamental research, Bolton had essentially eliminated the radical program that Stine had set up in 1927. With the exception of Carothers's group, the fundamental research program had failed to incorporate into Du Pont university-style research led by high-caliber scientists who exercised a great deal of independence in their work.[114]

The discovery of neoprene and nylon has preserved a place in history for Du Pont's fundamental research program; otherwise, it might have been a failed and forgotten experiment in industrial research. But Stine's program "succeeded" because the company had hired Carothers. This new institutional arrangement played a historical role by providing an acceptable place for Carothers in the Du Pont Company. As this chapter has shown, however, the events surrounding the evolution of fundamental research at Du Pont, the work of Carothers, and the discovery of neoprene and nylon are complex. Like so many other turning points in history, this one seemed to have been the result of a confluence of unique events. Although a variety of internal and external events shaped the outcome, the critical factors were that Stine put together a program that was attractive to Carothers and encouraged him to work on the promising field of polymerization. Then Bolton arrived at the proper moment to reorient the work toward an important technical objective. Had Carothers been left entirely on his own, as Stine had envisioned, nylon would probably not have been discovered and developed. Bolton, the chemist with an industrial mindset, played a critical role in the nylon innovation by focusing the research on synthetic fibers. Clearly, tension existed between the pure-science idealist Carothers and the pragmatic Bolton, but nylon emerged from this tension. Ironically, Carothers agreed to work for Du Pont only after repeated assurances that he would not be expected to produce commercial results. However, Stine's promotion, the Great Depression, and the early commercially promising discoveries combined to divert Carothers from the purely scientific career he so desired. As will be shown in the following chapter, the importance of nylon later would be magnified because the timing of its arrival was perfect with respect to both the Du Pont Company and the U.S. economy. Nylon was an unprecedented and as yet unrepeated success for Du Pont.

13

The "D" of R&D: The Development of Neoprene and Nylon

By the late 1920s, Du Pont's research directors had begun to use the words "research and development" as if they were a single concept.[1] Later, "research and development" would be shortened to just "R&D." The merging of these two activities into one term suggests that it is very difficult to differentiate one activity from the other. Research is usually seen as literally searching for something, and successful research culminates in an invention which appears in incomplete form, existing more as a promise than a reality. Development consists of adjusting, altering, and adapting this idealized concept into a product that can compete successfully in the outside technological and commercial environment.[2]

Generally, most innovations spend a considerable amount of time in a state that is both research and development. Neoprene, after the initial discovery by Arnold Collins in 1930, spent nearly a decade undergoing simultaneous research and development as the product was constantly redefined and new production methods were explored. With nylon, if one considers the breakthrough as Julian Hill's discovery of the first synthetic fiber in 1930, then it too spent five years in a similar no-man's land. In early 1936, when he tried to prepare a history of nylon, Wallace Carothers concluded that ". . . many of these events had no clearly defined dates: they were simply ideas first grasped as possibilities, which, by slow growth became firm convictions."[3] Such is the nature of research and development.

That neither neoprene nor nylon materialized full-blown with concomitant cries of eureka suggests that the contextual setting of R&D plays a critical role in both the invention and development phases. Both of the initial discoveries by Collins and Hill contained an element of serendipity. Chemists frequently uncover remarkable, unexpected phenomena when breaking new scientific ground. What is unusual about neoprene and nylon is that the early discoveries were quickly perceived to have potential technological and commercial importance. Elmer Bolton had begun research on acetylene chemistry with the hope of connecting it to synthetic rubber and was probably elated that his earlier hunch had proven correct. The transformation of Collins's sticky solid into a successful synthetic rubber took its first important step when, within weeks of the initial discovery, samples of the new material were examined at Orchem's Rubber Laboratory. This laboratory's quick, confidential, and positive evaluation and continued experimentation proved critical not only for the development of neoprene but also for its definition as a rubberlike material.

Similarly, the polymer studies of Carothers and Hill did not lead Du Pont directly into the exploration of new kinds of plastics. From the day that Hill pulled the first polyester fiber, Du Pont focused its energies on creating a synthetic fiber. The Rayon Department, which had seen its rayon profits virtually disappear because of the Depression and increased competition, provided Du Pont with a strong incentive for developing synthetic fibers. Had the company not been in the fibers business, the polymer research might have followed a markedly different course than it did. Just as it is difficult to draw a sharp line between research and development, discoveries also cannot be understood in isolation from the institutional context in which they emerge. It seems doubtful that Carothers would have "discovered" neoprene and nylon if he had done his research at Harvard.

These inventions were first-rate achievements because the new substances were the first ones with properties that excelled their natural analogs to any significant extent. Neoprene resisted degradation by oxygen, oil, and gasoline, and nylon was stronger and more abrasion-resistant than silk. The outstanding physical properties of the new polymers led the Chemical Department's management to believe that neoprene and nylon had the potential to become outstanding products. However, the tasks of development and commercialization were formidable. From the preparation of the intermediate chemicals to the processing of the polymer into useful products, Du Pont had very few technological precedents to follow. At the heart of both production processes was the reaction of the intermediates to form the solid polymers. In the mid-1930s, there were no commercially produced synthetics that required the extent of control over the polymerization reaction that neoprene and nylon demanded. Therefore, Du Pont had to develop most of this technology itself. No other chemical company in the United States had the capability to develop neoprene and nylon in the 1930s. Du Pont had to draw upon all its deep and broad technological skills to achieve success.

At the same time that the company's researchers were developing processes to make these new products, others were investigating strategies for commercializing them. Both neoprene and nylon had to fit into existing fabrication networks. The former was sold unprocessed to rubber fabricators and the latter in the form of filaments to textile companies. Du Pont had to do the spinning step with nylon because the silk-throwers were incapable of adapting to the new technology. As Du Pont had done with cellophane, the company's technical staff worked closely with fabricators to improve the processing of the products. Du Pont retained control of neoprene and nylon because the fabricators depended on Du Pont for raw materials, technical assistance, new product development, and advertising. These activities reflected the skills in development and commercialization that Du Pont had developed in the 1920s. Without these components of the innovation process, neither neoprene nor nylon would be viewed as a paradigm for industrial research. They were exceptional discoveries, but the development and commercialization of both were equally exceptional.

Neoprene

Although rubber was not mentioned in Carothers's memorandum to Bolton concerning the discovery of neoprene, it soon became the target for the development of the new substance. A few weeks after the discovery, test-tube-size samples of the polymer were sent to Du Pont's Rubber Chemicals Laboratory at the Dye Works. Established in 1922, the laboratory developed and tested chemicals for use in the rubber-processing industry.[4] To staff this laboratory, Du Pont hired several experienced rubber technologists. Two of them, Oliver M. Hayden and Ernest R. Bridgwater, played critical roles in the development of neoprene.

When Hayden, who was head of the Rubber Laboratory, first saw a sample of neoprene he compared it to a tough, vulcanized rubber that could not be satisfactorily processed. Experienced in the art of rubber compounding, Hayden tried his recipes on neoprene but made only poor rubber.[5] For neoprene to have any future in the rubber industry, it was imperative that a soft plastic form, resembling unvulcanized rubber, be developed. Some means then had to be found to stiffen and toughen the substance in a manner analogous to vulcanization.

Research at the Experimental Station and Orchem's Jackson Laboratory in the summer of 1930 centered on making a soft plastic form of neoprene. The Jackson Laboratory won this contest when Ira Williams produced a plastic polymer by drowning the reacting chloroprene with ethanol at the proper moment. Williams also discovered that upon sitting or heating, the plastic polymer would toughen just as natural rubber vulcanizes with the addition of sulfur.[6] Because sulfur is not needed to cure neoprene, the chemistry involved is different from rubber vulcanization. Nevertheless, Williams's modification made the analogy between neoprene and rubber more exact and permitted it to be processed by the rubber industry.

Tests at the Rubber Laboratory showed that the new material had another potentially serious flaw. On exposure to air, or more specifically oxygen, neoprene rapidly deteriorated by emitting hydrochloric acid. Within a few months, the laboratory solved the problem by adding a common rubber-compounding ingredient, zinc oxide, to neoprene during processing.[7] Over the years, neoprene's outstanding characteristic has been its resistance to oxidation and ozone, which makes it very durable.

Du Pont's management soon began thinking about possible uses for neoprene. In October 1930 Bridgwater, sales manager of the Rubber Chemicals Division with ten years' experience as a rubber chemist, prepared a memorandum in which he discussed the commercial possibilities of the new substance.[8] He concluded that for the foreseeable future neoprene could not compete head-on with rubber. Throughout the thirties, he argued, rubber prices would be low because high prices in the mid-twenties had encouraged overplanting of trees from which rubber could be obtained cheaply with plantation labor. Instead of competing with an abundance of rubber, Bridgwater suggested finding uses for neoprene where rubber was not used or where it performed unsatisfactorily. He hoped that this strategy would lead to premium-price uses for neoprene.

With regard to the properties of the new material, Bridgwater stated that "we must avoid the mistake of thinking of [it] as synthetic rubber." Neoprene was a new material with new properties; markets should be developed by emphasizing its unique qualities, not by emphasizing its similarity to rubber. Because neoprene penetrated porous substances better than rubber latex, Bridgwater suggested that it might be used for impregnation of leather, paper, wood, and textiles. In a liquid suspension, neoprene could be used as a coating compound, paint, or bonding material. Impervious to oil, it could be used for numerous automotive applications. Other potential uses included inner tubes, golf ball centers, electric wire insulation, and balloon fabric coating. In his summary, Bridgwater observed that in most cases neoprene would have to supplant materials other than rubber, because he did not think that it was superior to rubber for many uses such as boots, shoe soles, and tires.

Bridgwater's memorandum was widely circulated and received favorable comments from the company's top management. About one year later he was made supervisor of the neoprene project, including research, manufacture, and sales development. He was told to devote as much of his time as was necessary to the project, even if that meant all his time.[9] Thus in the thirties, Bridgwater was the principal architect of neoprene's commercialization strategy.

Du Pont publicly disclosed neoprene a year and a half after its discovery, at a meeting of the Akron group of the Rubber Division of the American Chemical Society. The Publicity Department sent an announcement directly to 500 daily papers and indirectly to 1,300 more through the Associated Press. The press responded by printing over 400 editorials on neoprene, and the *New York Times* put it on the front page. The company news release called "DuPrene," the name used until 1936, "one of the outstanding chemical achievements of the century," because it was the first laboratory substance that resembled rubber both in properties and chemical structure.[10] Because Du Pont was uncertain about the commercial future of neoprene, the papers delivered at Akron down played its industrial potential.[11] Du Pont's small production facility produced so little product that samples were not even available. Bridgwater told his rubber chemicals salesmen not to waste their time discussing it with customers.[12]

For neoprene to become a successful product, Du Pont engineers had to learn to make a consistently good product in large quantities. When Du Pont announced neoprene, it did not have any to sell. In the following year, 1932, only about 8,000 pounds was made because of problems with the experimental pilot plant. Production jumped to 52,000 pounds in 1933 and doubled every year for the next five years.[13] Although sales were sometimes limited by a lack of supply, Du Pont held back rapid expansion of its production capability. This is not surprising because making neoprene was a difficult and dangerous job.

Neoprene was discovered because chloroprene liquid forms and polymerizes spontaneously. Because these reactions occur so readily, they are exceedingly difficult to control. Small amounts of impurities, including air, act as powerful catalysts that cause unwanted side reactions or even violent explosions. To rationalize the process, Du Pont engineers decided to break it up into three steps: reaction of acetylene to form MVA, addition of hydrochloric acid to MVA to form chloroprene (the easiest step), and polymerization of chloroprene to form neoprene.[14]

The first step, making MVA from acetylene, is a particularly difficult one. The principal difficulty was the formation of the highly unstable and explosive DVA, which also wasted acetylene.[15] In spite of all efforts to eliminate it, DVA persisted as an unwanted by-product. Over the years acetylene, MVA, and DVA have been safety hazards. In January 1938 a DVA tank exploded, killing three workers and causing extensive damage to the plant at the Dye Works. From 1938 to 1942 there were three more explosions, but these caused little damage because the MVA production area had been surrounded by massive steel-reinforced concrete barriers.[16]

To make neoprene on a large scale, Du Pont engineers had to develop new methods of polymerization. In the early years, the production process was little more than a scaled-up version of Collins's test tube method. Neoprene was produced by pouring liquid chloroprene into open pans and later into five-gallon wide-mouth bottles. It was allowed to sit until it had polymerized to the desired thickness. The reaction was stopped by drowning the viscous mass in ethanol. This exceedingly slow and uncontrollable process, called bulk polymerization, caused a lack of uniformity between batches and numerous by-products, one of which caused the product to have a terrible odor.[17]

Orchem's Howard Starkweather and a few engineers began to experiment with a new kind of process, emulsion polymerization, in which the liquid chloroprene was dispersed in a water emulsion. When put into operation in 1935, the new process increased reaction speed, raised yields by 50 percent, permitted much finer control of the process, eliminated the odor-causing compounds, and produced a more stable product. The new process also cut production costs in half.[18] Emulsion polymerization technology had been developed in Germany by I. G. Farben, so Du Pont had to work out patent licensing agreements with the German company.[19] At the same time, intensive engineering development activities significantly improved the performance of the entire neoprene production process. By the late thirties,

Du Pont had solved most of the production problems and had a satisfactory process for making neoprene.

While the engineers were learning to make neoprene, the marketing people were creating a demand for it. Along with the problems that are inherent in selling new synthetic substances, Bridgwater had to overcome difficulties resulting from the structure of the rubber industry. Rubber manufacturing was carried out by a few large and many small companies that sold their products to either middlemen or large consumers, such as the automobile companies. Following company policy, Du Pont automatically decided to sell an unprocessed product, not manufactured goods.

To make this strategy successful, Du Pont needed to work closely with rubber companies. Throughout the thirties, Du Pont technologists worked on improving neoprene using both rubber company facilities and its own test equipment. The technical service that Du Pont provided for users was an essential part of neoprene's successful commercialization. The company also benefited since information flowed in both directions. For example, wire and cable manufacturers discovered neoprene's excellent weather resistance.[20]

The first commercially successful type of neoprene, introduced in 1937, closely approximated the performance of rubber in standard rubber machinery.[21] The viscosity of rubber can be lowered in a milling machine by the shearing action of two closely spaced cylinders rotating at different speeds. This process, which works by breaking rubber molecule chains, failed with neoprene. However, using some earlier work of Carothers, Du Pont chemists substituted a chemical process for this physical one. Weak chemical links of sulphur were incorporated into the neoprene polymer chains. These weak links could be broken by the addition of another chemical, a thiuram disulfide. The amount of this chain-cleaving agent added to the polymer determines the number of chain breakages and, consequently, the polymer viscosity. This chemical process transformed the traditional rubber mill from a device for physically breaking down rubber molecules into a device for mixing neoprene with its additives. This modification of neoprene made it fully compatible with existing rubber-processing machinery.

Realizing that Du Pont could not rely on the rubber companies to create widespread demand for neoprene products, Bridgwater instituted an "indirect selling" effort aimed at middlemen and consumers.[22] In 1934, he hired Victor A. Cosler of the B. F. Goodrich Company to head a sales promotion group. Cosler and his three assistants established contacts with middlemen who solicited specialty business and represented a number of rubber manufacturers. The purchasing power of these jobbers enabled them to force their suppliers to make small-volume neoprene products that the manufacturers would not otherwise have produced. Because these jobbers profited from selling high-priced goods made from neoprene, they were generally successful in promoting its use.

Du Pont also educated consumers about the properties and uses of neoprene so they would put pressure on their suppliers to make neoprene goods. Some of these consumers, such as the manufacturers of automobiles, electrical equipment, and machinery, were so large that Du Pont salesmen called on them.

Yet for every large consumer there were hundreds too small to contact directly. To reach this group, Du Pont relied on publicity from trade journals; technical papers delivered at professional society meetings; and more general advertisements in radio, magazines, and newspapers. In 1938, Du Pont began the publication of the "Neoprene Notebook: Facts About Neoprene for the Engineer" to present "engineering information and laboratory data."[23] Although partly a technical publication, considerable space in each issue was devoted to describing new uses for neoprene. It was important for Du Pont to reach engineers because they usually decided what materials would be used in the equipment they designed. One 1939 technical journal advertisement, entitled "The Story of the Distraught Designer," showed how neoprene solved a difficult problem.[24] In these same journals, the company also advertised particular neoprene products, such as insulated electric cables and various kinds of hoses. Du Pont did not manufacture any of these products, but this well-orchestrated sales campaign aimed at fabricators, engineers, and consumers "indirectly" created demand for neoprene. Overall, this commercialization strategy allowed the company to keep control of its product without having to engage in a wide range of manufacturing operations.

The name change from "DuPrene" to neoprene in part reflected an all-encompassing concern for the product. Du Pont abandoned its "DuPrene" trademark in 1936 because it could not control the use of it. Bridgwater required that the trademark be applied only to the unprocessed material sold by Du Pont and not to any end products. He feared that unskilled or unscrupulous fabricators would use the trademark to sell inferior goods, thereby giving the substance a bad reputation.[25] Neoprene, a generic name invented by Du Pont, conveyed the idea that it was an ingredient, not a final product.

Throughout the thirties, neoprene did not compete with natural rubber on the basis of cost. In June 1932, Du Pont offered neoprene for sale at 75 cents a pound when natural rubber sold for 5 cents a pound. Production difficulties forced them to raise the price to $1.05 a pound a few months later. During the decade, rubber prices rose while the price of neoprene slowly fell. Still, in 1939 when neoprene sold for 65 cents a pound, rubber went for 18 cents a pound.[26]

High costs did not prevent Du Pont from developing significant markets for neoprene. So-called premium price applications capitalized on its physical properties. Telephone wire insulation proved to be the first significant neoprene market. Rubber is the better insulator, but neoprene is more weatherproof. Its principal advantage over rubber, resistance to degradation by oils and gasoline, led to many automotive and industrial uses. In fact, hoses and molded goods accounted for the bulk of sales in the first decade. In 1938, nearly two-thirds of the neoprene output went into these uses. Its offensive odor precluded its use in consumer goods until an odorless type was introduced in 1937. Afterward, sales of neoprene gloves, shoe soles, and heels grew rapidly.[27] In keeping with Bridgwater's strategy of not competing directly with rubber, Du Pont never placed a high priority on developing neoprene tires. Two companies, the Dayton Tire and Rubber Company and I. G. Farben, showed that they were feasible but had some serious technical drawbacks.[28] Whereas rubber was considered a general-purpose material, the properties of neoprene were tailored to each specific use. By altering the composition or structure of the polymer and changing the dozen or so chemicals added during fabrication, Du Pont produced hundreds of neoprene varieties for different specific applications.

In 1939, after nearly a decade of development, neoprene began to make a profit. A financial summary of the entire project, prepared in that year, showed that Du Pont had lost about $1.3 million on its total investment of $4.5 million. Neoprene profits for 1939 amounted to more than $300,000.[29] Later in the year, the Du Pont management approved a plant expansion that would double its production capacity to 5,000 tons a year.[30] By 1939, the future of neoprene looked very bright.

Just when Du Pont's strategy of slow and cautious development of neoprene was beginning to generate profits, World War II changed the situation completely. The war established a secure market for neoprene by increasing its production dramatically which cut its price from 65 to 30 cents a pound. Wartime rubber shortages led to many new uses, including direct military applications.[31] By 1943, neoprene production reached 60,000 tons a year, ten times that of 1941. After the war, sales of neoprene declined by a third but demand soon began to grow and production passed the wartime peak in 1950.[32]

In retrospect, what is most remarkable about neoprene's development was the fact that it was undertaken at all. From the beginning, Du Pont faced numerous technical and market obstacles that stood in the way of successful commercialization. The production technology necessary to make products of this type did not exist, and it soon became apparent that neoprene could not compete with rubber on the basis of price. Du Pont realized that neoprene products would have to be relatively high-priced specialty ones requiring considerable development and technical support for its customers. Nevertheless, Du Pont's management accepted this challenge.

There were several factors aside from profits that helped neoprene survive its first decade. In the 1930s, despite the Great Depression, Du Pont remained a profitable, confident, and aggressive company. When compared to the company's total resources, the $6 million it sank into neoprene was not a large expenditure.[33] Also, Du Pont received considerable favorable publicity for its discovery of a synthetic rubber that might free the United

States from being at the mercy of foreign manipulation of rubber supplies and prices. Another factor in neoprene's favor was its "product champions." These were people who had a personal commitment to the product that went beyond sales and profits. Neoprene brought Bolton credit for having started the project and for having acquired Nieuwland's catalyst for Du Pont. Charles Stine could also take some credit for neoprene because it was discovered by one of the groups in his fundamental research program. Subsequent to neoprene's discovery, both Stine and Bolton were promoted, Stine to the Executive Committee as vice president and advisor on research and Bolton as Stine's successor.[34] Stine and Bolton probably wielded enough power to defend neoprene from corporate skeptics.

Neoprene did not become a successful product solely because it was rubberlike or had unique properties. Du Pont succeeded with neoprene because the company had the technological capability to develop the new product and employed a coherent commercialization strategy. Du Pont could pursue a patient and cohesive strategy for commercializing neoprene because it was a proprietary product. Competition might have forced Du Pont to expand production while the technology was rapidly changing or to enter markets without adequate product testing. Neoprene was an important scientific discovery, but it took nearly a decade of intensive and creative work by chemists, engineers, salesmen, and particularly Bridgwater for the new product to become a commercial success.

Nylon

In contrast to the patient development of neoprene, a crash program brought nylon out of the laboratory into the marketplace in less than five years. Although it is impossible to determine how much the nylon project would have cost had it been done more slowly and cautiously, it does not appear that the time pressure led to wasteful spending. There are two principal reasons why nylon was developed so effectively. One was the early decision that full-fashioned silk hosiery would be the first large market for the new material. Preliminary experiments showed that nylon was the first synthetic substance that could be processed into all kinds of filaments, yarns, coatings, films, and plastics. However, Du Pont's management exercised considerable restraint by not yielding to the enthusiasm of researchers who saw nylon replacing, among other things, cellophane, photographic film, leather, and wool. Only silk stockings were picked for concentrated attack. As one writer stated in the *Atlantic Monthly*, "The silk stocking has become for virtually everyone, rich or poor, young or old, the symbol of liberty, democracy, and undisputed self-respect."[35] Each year about $70 million worth of silk went into stockings, which were knitted into eight pair per American woman per year.[36] By focusing directly on this one market, Du Pont avoided having conflicting demands made on the research personnel who were trying to develop a production process and on sales development people who were working with textile manufacturers to evaluate nylon's performance.

The second way in which Du Pont kept the development of nylon moving was by focusing on one process for each production step.[37] The research managers constantly put all their eggs in one basket. Of course, this strategy can lead to disaster if a particular approach proves unworkable. Fortunately for Du Pont, its managers exercised skillful judgment in making decisions and had enough perseverance when things were going badly that no major lines of work had to be abandoned. This does not imply that all the original processes were by any means elegant or straightforward. Expediency ruled. Some of the initial equipment, according to Crawford H. Greenewalt, who oversaw much of the work, accomplished its tasks through "brute force and awkwardness."[38] Still, the processes worked and produced nylon at a cost less than that of silk.

This get-a-workable-process approach to development depended heavily on Du Pont's impregnable patent position. Because nylon was unquestionably a Du Pont invention – no one else even had been close to it – the company did not have to worry about being undercut by competitors. To make money it was not necessary to have the best possible process, just one that worked. As long as nylon could be made at a reasonable cost, improvements could wait. Overall, the company's strong patent position, an intelligent development strategy, and a single, clearly defined market combined to make nylon a profitable product from the beginning.

Du Pont's quick and effective development of nylon is remarkable because an entirely new technology had to be put into place. Nylon had very few precedents to follow, but among the highly diversified product lines of the company were two that had particular relevance to it. The Ammonia Department, which in sales ranked tenth out of Du Pont's eleven major business areas while having the sixth-largest investment, had developed expertise in high-pressure catalytic reactions. This technology proved essential to the manufacture of nylon intermediates. The Rayon Department, having the biggest investment and ranking third in sales, gave Du Pont an entry into the textile fibers business.[39] But nylon required more than just a combination of existing techniques.

Entering into the completely new field of synthetic fibers, Du Pont had to go beyond the state of the art in several areas. Stine's fundamental research program had given the company a head start in fields critical to nylon development. Most important was Carothers's explanation of the nature of condensation polymerization. His theories gave the developers the conceptual tools they needed to produce these polymers commercially. Fundamental research had also been done on catalysis and general chemical engineering; so the company scientists were up to date on both of these crucial subjects. Du Pont brought to the development of nylon a wide variety of skills and expertise. In retrospect, the fit between nylon and Du Pont appears uncanny. But this does not mean that nylon development was easy or uneventful; nor did the outcome seem certain in May 1934.

What the new fiber might be good for could not be determined from the small samples that were made in the laboratory. Soon, Carothers had collected a lot of data on the fibers but did not know how the data correlated with "ultimate practical behavior."[40] Shortly before nylon's discovery, researchers in the Chemical and Rayon departments had begun to try to evaluate textile fibers on a more scientific basis.[41] At the Experimental Station, physicist John B. Miles, Jr., had attempted to define fiber characteristics, such as elasticity, by specific laboratory tests. His approach was much more fundamental than that of the Pioneering Laboratory in Buffalo. Its director, Hale Charch, believed that the only way to know whether nylon would have any useful properties would be to make fabric samples, and that tests on the fibers alone would prove inconclusive. When informed of some of Miles's results, Charch pointed out the limitations of his approach:

> I have felt that there may be a tendency to be too arbitrary about saying what is or is not a good textile fiber, or what is or is not needed. At best those questions are only partially answered, even in terms of rayon yarns with which we are supposed to be thoroughly familiar today. Certainly such questions are far less clearly answered in the case of a brand new textile fiber which has a set of properties which are unique. ...In other words...I do not believe we know, a priori with even a fair certainty what is or is not a commercial thread, and if we have a new thread...that does not coincide with properties with the threads we have been used to from our classical knowledge, this need not befog our thinking....
>
>   In the case of these polyamide fibers, they seem to me to have two very outstanding properties, i.e., high wet strength and potentially at least, a very high true elasticity. We know, I believe, a priori that we want both of these properties.[42]

Charch proved to be right; the science of fibers was in its infancy. Du Pont would not really know that it had an excellent fiber until sample garments had been prepared and worn.

In the summer of 1934, the fiber project became the major focus of activity in Carothers's group. Several of his assistants began preparing polyamides from virtually every combination of dibasic acid and diamine with between two- and ten-carbon-atom chains. Of the eighty-one possible compounds, only 2-10, 10-6, 5-6, 5-10, and 6-6 looked promising. (The numerical designation for the various types of nylon comes from the number of carbon atoms in the diamine and the dibasic acid, respectively.) Eventually 6-6, first prepared by Gerard J. Berchet on February 28, 1935, would become Du Pont's nylon.[43]

Initially, Carothers concentrated his efforts on 5-10. Enough polymer was prepared and spun that some knitted fabric samples were made and sent to the Rayon Department for testing. The quarterly research report (written by newcomer and future Nobel laureate Paul J. Flory) stated that

> tests indicated remarkable potentialities for polyamides as synthetic textile fibers, their outstanding properties being a high elasticity and tenacity unaffected by water, and an unusual fatigue resistance. At the same time it became apparent that the 5-10 polymer melted so low (190° C) that it could not withstand practical ironing temperatures.[44]

The principal advantages of 5-10 polymer were in processing: It could be polymerized and spun rather easily. The other possible alternative, nylon 6-6, which melted at very high temperatures (over 250°C), yielded a better product but the processing difficulties looked formidable if not insurmountable.

Bolton, however, insisted that the high cost of basic raw materials for 5-10 and its relatively low melting point overrode any other advantages that it might have.[45] He favored 6-6 polymer, which could be made from a cheaper starting compound, benzene. With Bolton's decision to push the development of 6-6 polymer, work on the other types soon came to a halt.[46]

The early assessments of nylon showed that major problems would have to be solved. Only one of the two raw materials, adipic acid, was produced on a fairly large scale, and that was in Germany. The other one, hexamethylene diamine, was a laboratory curiosity. To make a high-molecular-weight polymer from these two materials, they had to be combined in precisely equivalent molecular quantities; if either one was present in an excess of as little as 0.1 percent, the properties of the polymer were compromised. Instead of trying to achieve such precision by weighing, the neat solution was to form a salt of the acid and the amine, which naturally combined them in a 1:1 ratio. The salt was crystallized from the solution and used in the polymerization. However, this precise matching of the components led to polymers of too high a molecular weight to be useful, and methods of controlling the polymer chain growth had to be developed. Once a satisfactory polymer had been made, it had to be converted into fiber.

Du Pont's fiber-spinning technology had been developed for rayon and acetate, which did not melt and had to be spun from solutions. However, use of this kind of technology for nylon did not appeal to the Chemical Department management, and they decided to try a potentially simpler, faster, and cheaper process – melt spinning. This process entailed melting the solid polymer to a honeylike liquid that would be driven under pressure through a number of very small holes in a metal plate. The extruded filaments would form solid fibers upon cooling.

Until they had a better idea how the product was going to be used, the developers did not give too much thought to the problems that would occur after the very fine filaments had been twisted together (as is done with silk) in bundles of twenty or thirty to make a textile fiber. Ultimately, nylon had to be tested on standard textile machinery and put through such commercial finishing processes as washing and dyeing.[47]

After the major process steps had been conceptualized, teams of chemists and engineers could be assigned to work on each one. As new problems were recognized, the work was further subdivided. In retrospect, the development of nylon appears to be the solution of thousands of small problems; but this kind of engineering could begin only after the big decisions were made about how nylon was to be manufactured. These decisions were made very early and were not questioned when the work encountered apparent roadblocks. Generally, the development of nylon proceeded in a systematic and orderly manner.

The Du Pont Executive Committee left the job largely to the Chemical and Rayon departments. It does not appear that it actively participated in the major decisions. Because it did have to authorize all large expenditures, it kept up to date on the progress of the project. The committee also probably made suggestions to the principals involved but did not force major changes in the approach taken by the two cooperating departments. For the most part, the Executive Committee did a lot of cheerleading from the sidelines. Some of those who participated remember the committee "cracking the whip" over them to keep nylon moving along toward the earliest possible commercialization.[48]

On the organization charts, Elmer K. Bolton, director of the Chemical Department, and Leonard A. Yerkes, general manager of the Rayon Department, were responsible for the development of nylon. Yerkes, who had headed Du Pont's rayon business since its inception in the early twenties, left the management of the nylon project to his technical division, which was headed by Maurice du Pont Lee.[49] It was Lee's assistant, however, Ernest K. Gladding, who actively managed the nylon project. For his chief liaison with the Chemical Department, Gladding chose George Preston Hoff, a thirty-seven-year-old PhD chemist from Ohio State. Hoff had eight years' experience in rayon-process research.[50]

On the Chemical Department side, Bolton assigned his assistant director, Ernest B. Benger, a former Rayon Department research director, to keep close tabs on the nylon project. Bolton also relied on the remainder of his management staff to help manage the nylon project. Crawford Greenewalt, who was one of three research supervisors, played a particularly important role because of his chemical engineering background and his "take-charge" personality. (In 1948, Greenewalt would become president of the company.)

Although the potential for serious conflict over the development of nylon clearly existed, it does not seem to have occurred. The Rayon Department management concluded that expensive nylon would not compete with the much cheaper rayon for many years. And rayon did not make good full-fashioned hosiery anyway. Enthusiastic about nylon's prospects, the Rayon and Ammonia departments began to pay for the project in 1936.[51] After this date, even though the Chemical Department essentially did contract work for these departments, it did not turn over the project to them. Because the Chemical Department had made the invention, it could argue strongly that it should have considerable say about nylon's future. Also, the Rayon Department did not have the chemical and engineering skills that were required to make nylon yarn. The three departments divided the work, with the Ammonia Department making the intermediate chemicals, the Chemical Department handling the polymerization and melt spinning, and the Rayon Department concentrating on the textile end. This approach worked. But first, Du Pont's research management had to prove to itself and the company's executives that it indeed had a promising new material.

The Three Phases of Development

For the purpose of exposition, the nylon project can be split into three periods, each of which was characterized by a particular set of problems and goals. In the year following Bolton's decision in July 1935 to develop nylon 6-6, work centered on determining whether commercial success of the new fiber was *feasible*. After possible production processes had been shown to be workable at least in principle and the physical properties of the polymer had been firmly established, Du Pont decided that nylon did show promise as a new kind of textile fiber. This initiated the second phase of development, which lasted roughly from the summer of 1936 until the end of 1937. In this phase, nylon had to be shown to be *practicable*, not just feasible. Also, the critically important decision was made to concentrate on producing high-quality yarn for full-fashioned hosiery. This gave the developers a more precisely defined goal than just trying to get repeatable and predictable results from their apparatus. The specifications for each process then were determined by the requirements for hosiery yarn. The only way Du Pont could know if a yarn would make a durable and attractive stocking was to knit some. Therefore, to get answers to process questions, Du Pont had to wait until stockings were tested. By late 1937 Du Pont's small-scale equipment produced yarns that were knitted into nylon hosiery that compared favorably to silk stockings. After learning that a satisfactory or maybe superior product could be made, Du Pont turned its activities toward making a *reproducible* yarn on a larger scale. With bigger samples of yarn to knit, the textile companies could run nylon under standard commercial conditions.

In the feasibility stage of development, the most immediate, if not the most important, problem was to work out a scheme for making the intermediate chemicals, especially hexamethylene diamine (HDA).[52] HDA proved very difficult to manufacture, requiring a multi-step synthesis. The conversion of adipic acid to adiponitrile proved to be the critical one in the process. Before the decision to commercialize nylon 6-6 had been made,

William A. Lazier had suggested trying a vapor phase catalytic reaction, which posed two difficulties because adipic acid was very unstable at the temperatures required to vaporize it and the 35 percent yield of adiponitrile was too low for an economical process. To solve the first problem, engineers designed a rotating disc system to throw a thin film of adipic acid onto a heated surface. Therefore, the liquid would be exposed to high temperatures for a minimum amount of time. Yields improved to 85 percent when Lazier and his associates developed new catalysts.[53] In all this work, Du Pont benefited greatly from its expertise in the arcane subject of catalysis and its accumulated experience in chemical engineering design. After small-scale apparatus had proven that these processes would work, the design of larger equipment was turned over to the Ammonia Department, which knew that field quite well. The original intermediates processes proved adequate to launch nylon.

Once several-pound batches of intermediates became available, experiments on polymerization started. The major goal, then, became to find methods of producing polymer that would make uniform fibers. This meant stopping the reaction at a precise moment to control the polymer's molecular weight. After considerable experimentation, Wesley R. Peterson discovered that the addition of small amounts of acetic acid would regulate the extent of polymerization. This was another "simple" solution that required considerable time and effort to be discovered.[54]

Besides the HDA process and standardization of the polymer, the other major problem Du Pont faced in the early part of the development was that of spinning the polymer into fibers. At first, both melt and solution spinning were tried. In the latter process, the nylon polymer was dissolved in hot phenol or formamide, and the hot syrupy solution was pumped through a spinneret – a metal plate perforated with minute, precisely drilled holes.[55] As filaments emerged from the spinneret, the solvent evaporated and solid fibers were formed. Solvent spinning looked unpromising because of the hazards and expense of handling and recovering the solvents that could be used with nylon. Melt spinning had the appeal of simplicity, but it required developing a new technology for precisely metering a molasseslike fluid to the spinneret at a temperature of about 260 degrees centigrade. Also, at its melting temperature, some nylon polymer decomposed, releasing gaseous products in the melting chamber. Although the amount of decomposing polymer was not significant, the extruding filament broke whenever a gas bubble went through a spinneret hole. A practical continuous spinning process required filaments be spun in nearly infinite lengths without breaks. By the middle of 1935, Du Pont chemists had made only about one mile of yarn by pushing molten polymer through a hypodermic needle.[56] By early 1936, work on solution spinning was discontinued, even though melt spinning was still far from being a workable process.[57] Intensive work continued on it because Du Pont felt that the properties of the new fiber showed that it had considerable potential.

The properties of nylon fibers generated so much enthusiasm among the research management that any doubts about the feasibility of the manufacturing process were overshadowed. At the end of 1935, in his annual report to the Executive Committee, Bolton wrote, "[Nylon] excels all the commercial textile fibers in strength and furthermore is unique in possessing elastic recovery under varied conditions of humidity."[58] Although silk is not specifically mentioned in this report, Bolton's statements clearly indicate that he was thinking of nylon as a substitute for silk's major use, full-fashioned hosiery. Even though at this point nylon looked as if it might become a serious competitor for silk, Bolton also wanted to see if it might replace another natural polyamide – wool.

The most tempting diversion from the main goal of nylon full-fashioned hosiery was a wool-like version called Fiber W. Bolton, whose researchers had already conquered rubber and soon would replace silk, felt that synthetic wool "offered the keenest challenge to the chemist, but all [his] attempts in the past had failed. . . . " However, the discovery of synthetic polyamides made synthetic wool a possibility. A Chemical Department study of the form and properties of wool showed that the crimp in wool fibers gave them many of their desirable characteristics. So Bolton's chemists found ways to crimp nylon fibers. By late 1936 some small samples of fabric had been prepared which were, according to Bolton, "wool-like in appearance and feel, possess good crease retention, and resist wrinkling both wet and dry."[59] Nevertheless, he decided to carry Fiber W forward only to the extent that it did not interfere with the stocking fiber program. Although the consumption of wool greatly exceeded that of silk, it was not nearly as attractive a market for nylon. Because wool sold for less than half the price of silk, Du Pont doubted that nylon could compete with the cheaper fiber.[60]

From the development point of view, a wool-like fiber had an important disadvantage. Synthetic wool would be used in woven fabrics, which required very large quantities of yarn for testing. Conversely, a knit stocking contained ten grams of nylon. To enter the woolen goods business, Du Pont would have had to build a large plant to make enough fiber to determine whether the product had any potential. For these reasons, Du Pont wisely put this project on the back burner. The research managers did not get carried away with the scientifically and technologically interesting wool fiber that would have been costly to develop and difficult to sell. Synthetic wool would have been another scientific triumph to go alongside rubber and silk. But Fiber W never did make it out of the laboratory, because it lacked the resilience of wool.[61]

By the summer of 1936, Du Pont was ready to move nylon into a bigger scale of development. The quarterly progress report stated that the Rayon Department considered the new fiber to be "a high quality yarn superior to natural silk" that would have a large market at $2 a pound, roughly the price of silk. Preliminary estimates showed that nylon yarn could be produced for 80 cents a pound in a plant making 8 million pounds a year. Even at one-eighth of this production level, nylon would cost only $1.10 a pound.[62] These figures indicated to Du Pont that it did not need significant economies of scale to make nylon profitable. Even a very small plant could make money. On the basis of these optimistic forecasts, the research managers decided to expand the company's nylon manufacturing capacity from 2 to 100 pounds a day in order to improve the process and provide material for extensive testing.[63] Nylon had entered its second phase of development. It looked good; now it was time to prove that it was so.

To determine whether nylon could be a practicable fiber in terms of both production process and product properties, Du Pont needed to manufacture fibers in considerable quantities. The resulting material had to be tested on commercial knitting machinery. The overall goal of this development phase was to produce a fiber that would consistently make satisfactory full-fashioned hosiery. Because the textile end of the project belonged to the Rayon Department, the Chemical Department brought it on board in the fall of 1936.

The Rayon Department became a full partner in the development when Preston Hoff made his first official visit from the rayon plant in Buffalo to the nylon laboratory in Wilmington. Assistant director Benger, who was spending half his time on nylon, escorted Hoff through the laboratory. He wanted Hoff to stay very close to the work because "every week or two we are forced to make a decision or two which may have far reaching consequences on future developments." Also, he reminded Hoff that "a huge amount of money is being spent in this development – and all of it comes from your department."[64] In general, Hoff found Wilmington in a state of excitement that he felt was unwarranted. He reported to his superiors that there "has been too much wishful thinking in connection with [nylon] and the stage of advancement of the problem is exaggerated in the minds of the Executive Committee and perhaps others."[65] He conservatively estimated an annual production rate of 1 million pounds in five years,[66] thereby underestimating the ability of the Executive Committee to keep "the whip cracking" on the development. Five years hence, in 1941, Du Pont produced 7.2 million pounds of nylon.[67] Despite Hoff's reservations, the Rayon Department cooperated wholeheartedly on the project. And it did not take them long to realize that the Chemical Department was having difficulties melt spinning nylon fibers.

By mid-1936, there were some second thoughts about the decision to work only on melt spinning, and Bolton wrote that he was not sure that melt spinning would make it.[68] The big problem concerned continuous spinning, which would be necessary in a commercial plant. Spinning runs were frequently interrupted by broken threads and by clogged orifices in the spinneret.[69] In December 1936, Gladding witnessed an unsuccessful spinning trial and afterward tried to convince the Chemical Department managers – especially Greenewalt – to reconsider solution spinning by doing some experiments with this technique. But Benger "instructed [him] not to let himself be stampeded."[70] Melt spinning continued to be the focus of the work.

Hoff and the viscose research director, William Henry Bradshaw, had been in Wilmington the month before and suggested that a glass spinning assembly be constructed so that direct observation of the melted polymer would be possible. The Chemical Department acted on this suggestion. Experiments with the glass cell clearly showed that decomposing polymer gave off gas bubbles that broke the fiber upon passing through a spinneret hole.[71] Coffman, who had hand-pulled the first nylon fiber, and George D. Graves, another principal researcher on melt spinning, soon concluded that if the polymer were kept under pressure, the bubbles would dissolve harmlessly into the molten mass. This idea worked and removed the major obstacle to the commercialization of melt spinning.[72] By May 1937, continuous spinning times had been increased from 10 to 82 hours.[73]

By then, Du Pont's development team had made significant strides toward its goal of producing a standard and uniform product, but no yarn had been knitted into stockings. Although they were optimistic about the prospects for nylon, they really could not be sure that it would make acceptable stockings. The first test came in February 1937, when Everett Vernon Lewis, a Rayon Department research chemist, took a few carefully measured skeins of yarn for a knitting test at the Union Manufacturing Company in Frederick, Maryland. Lewis later recalled that the security precautions that his management insisted upon were more stringent than those he encountered later in the Manhattan project. On the train, he slept with the skeins, and after the test was over he gathered all the scraps and weighed them to make sure that no fiber was missing. The Frederick hosiery manufacturer experienced difficulties with the new fiber in nearly every one of the stocking production processes. It did not come off of the spools properly; it snagged on the knitting machines; and after dyeing it looked like a wrinkled mess that had "a not too pleasant gray color roughly approximating gun metal." Undaunted, Lewis attributed these difficulties to inexperience with a new material.[74]

Du Pont soon learned that quality requirements were very high for full-fashioned hosiery yarn. Further testing was done at the Van Raalte Mill in Boonton, New Jersey, and the first experimental stockings were made in April.[75] By July 1937, Van Raalte had knitted enough material to give Du Pont some definite feedback on nylon. G. J. Groh of the Rayon Department's Sales Service Section wrote that "the yarn performed quite well in all operations, but...the quality of the stockings produced was quite unsatisfactory in many respects." The outstanding defect was the tendency of the stockings to wrinkle during dyeing and the other finishing operations. These wrinkles "completely destroyed the uniform appearance of the stocking."[76] A few months later, it was discovered that these wrinkles could be eliminated by steam treating the stocking before dyeing.[77]

Thanksgiving and perhaps Christmas came early for Du Pont in 1937.

The Van Raalte mills had started turning out "full-fashioned hosiery [that were] excellent in appearance and free from defects."[78] These stockings were virtually indistinguishable from their silk counterparts. At this time the Du Pont management had in hand the results of a statistically unconvincing but nevertheless informative report on the reaction of women to nylon. A total of fifty-six hosiery and lingerie garments were distributed to the wives of the men working on the nylon project. The comments on the hosiery indicated that the experimental stockings, which the majority of the women called rayon not silk, were very durable. On the negative side, the women thought that the stockings wrinkled easily and were too lustrous and slippery.[79] By now, the earlier skeptic, Hoff, felt that "as the data accumulate, they continue to support our belief that in Fiber 66 we have a product that surpasses rather than approaches the natural one."[80] From the production standpoint, he believed that "we are not out of the woods but think we can see our way clear," and he thought that many of the problems would be solved in six months.[81]

But before a commercial plant could be built, Du Pont's management felt that a middle-sized pilot plant was necessary. The Executive Committee's authorization of a pilot plant on January 12, 1938, signaled the end of the second phase of development.[82] Nylon had been shown to be practicable. Now it had to be proven on a commercial scale, which meant making large quantities of uniform yarn suitable for full-fashioned hosiery.

Whereas earlier efforts had centered on making one good stocking, the focus of attention moved toward the production of millions of pairs. To accomplish this goal, an experimental unit about one-tenth the size of the projected full-scale unit was designed to produce 250 pounds of nylon yarn a day.[83]

The pilot plant had numerous objectives, some of which conflicted with each other. First, Hoff asserted, it would be used to prove the viability of the various process elements. Second, the uniformity of the product would be determined and improved if necessary. In particular, yarn would be spun from ten spinneret nozzles to see what kind of uniformity could be expected. Third, the accumulated data would be used by the Engineering Department to design the equipment for the commercial plant. Fourth, the pilot plant had to make "standard" yarn for knitting, finishing, and wear tests. Fifth, the yarn would be used to do research on the product and process. These last two goals, especially, came into conflict. The Sales Service Section wanted thousands of pounds of yarn for knitting tests whereas the researchers wanted to do experiments that usually produced an off-specification product. Hoff eventually ruled that research had a higher priority than sales.[84]

The research management expected that the pilot plant would take six months to build and another six months to provide sufficient data to begin construction of a plant. These predictions proved to be accurate. When the pilot plant started up on July 11, 1938, the Chemical Department turned it over to the newly formed nylon division of the Rayon Department. Gladding became manager of the division, and Hoff became its technical director.[85]

When the pilot plant was authorized, one problem, the sizing of the yarn, began to look much more formidable than it had previously. Silk filaments have a natural coating, sericin, that protects the fibers during textile processing. After the knitting is finished, the size is removed with boiling water. Of course, nylon had no natural size. Du Pont needed to find a material that would form a protective film, be removable in hot water, not discolor the yarn, apply conveniently, and not accumulate on knitting needles.[86]

The size problem took many months of trial-and-error work to solve. The Rayon Department retained a German textile expert, H. H. "Papa" Freund, to assist them on problems such as this. But Freund's bag of tricks did not contain a suitable size for a synthetic fiber.[87] To try a different approach, the Rayon Department authorized the Chemical Department to evaluate new and less obvious sizing materials. Working frantically, researchers in a number of departments contributed to the formulation of a four-component size for nylon. This type of industrial research, although not glamorous in any way, proved to be necessary for the successful development of nylon. The elimination of the nagging size problem occurred just when Du Pont's new nylon plant was beginning production.

Du Pont knew that it was going to build the plant before it decided on a location. As early as 1933, Du Pont's Executive Committee had wanted the Rayon Department to build a plant in southern Delaware.[88] In a joint evaluation, the Rayon and Engineering departments considered Buffalo, New York; Radford, Virginia; Clinton, Tennessee; and Seaford, Delaware. On October 5, 1938, they submitted to the Executive Committee a request for $7.25 million to build the plant at Clinton. This was tabled, and three weeks later the committee allocated $8.51 million for a 4-million-pound-per-year plant at Seaford. The facility was to be big enough to accommodate capacity increases of up to 12 million pounds per year. A week later, the committee okayed a $2.5 million expenditure for a nylon intermediates plant to be built at the Belle, West Virginia, works.[89] The Seaford plant began operation fifteen months after its authorization, in January 1940.[90] But from the start it could not make enough nylon to satisfy the large demand that had been generated since the company's public announcement of its new product.

Before it could introduce its new fiber, Du Pont had to come up with a name for it. It had started as Rayon 66, but that was quickly dropped because no one wanted it to be associated with such a low-status fiber.[91] Until 1938, it was usually called Fiber 66, but this was not the catchy name that the company sought. Several years earlier, Hale Charch had suggested the acronym Duparooh, which stood for Du Pont Pulls a Rabbit Out of Hat, but it never caught on.[92]

To come up with a name for the fiber, Du Pont set up a committee that consisted of Gladding, Yerkes, and his assistant, Benjamin M. May. An appeal for help brought nearly four hundred prospective names, but the list did not include nylon. Company president Lammot du Pont liked Delawear or neosheen. Gladding threw in Wacara, a play on Carothers's name. Yerkes pushed for nuray. None of these or any of the 395 other names appealed to everyone, so they started again. Gladding thought of norun, which would have caused problems because nylon stockings did run. He then turned it around to nuron but thought that sounded like a nerve tonic. So he changed the r to an l, making it nulon. This apparently was very similar to an existing trademark, and Gladding realized that many advertisements would refer to new nulon, a redundant-sounding phrase. Next, he changed the u to an i and got nilon, which unfortunately has three pronunciations: nillon, neelon, or nylon. The latter one was chosen, and Fiber 66 was given a name.[93]

Instead of registering nylon as a trademark, Du Pont made it a generic word that anyone would be free to use. The company's negative attitude toward trademarks had been engendered by the loss of its cellophane one in late 1937. The courts had ruled that Du Pont had used its trademark as a descriptive word for its product and therefore it had become common usage.[94] That hosiery became known as nylons probably would have cost them their trademark anyway.

Although Du Pont had tried to keep nylon a secret, word had spread through the textile industry, and several reporters had already guessed pretty closely what Du Pont was up to without knowing the chemical composition of the fiber.[95] Also, the Du Pont Plastics Department had been marketing nylon bristles, under the trademark Exton, in Dr. West's toothbrushes.

Because the technical specifications for a bristle were not nearly as exacting as those for a stocking fiber, the former offered an attractive entering wedge in the marketplace for nylon. Imperfect polymer produced in the pilot plant could be sold for toothbrush fibers. In marketing its bristles, Du Pont did not tell the public the chemical nature of its Exton bristles.[96]

The need to announce nylon arose because patents were beginning to issue. If Du Pont did not announce it, the press would continue to make all kinds of guesses about the prospects for and properties of the new material. At the time, Du Pont was still over a year and a half away from having anything to sell. Company officials worried about the impact of a public disclosure on Du Pont's ability to obtain more patents. When nylon became widely known, others might do some work and apply for patents on process and product modifications, or on new uses. This concern about protecting its proprietary position had an impact on the way in which Du Pont chose to announce its product.

Bolton suggested that Du Pont take the usual route for announcing important chemical discoveries, the presentation of a scientific paper at an American Chemical Society meeting. One was coming up in Milwaukee in early September, when some important U.S. patents would be issued. Yerkes vetoed this because a reputable scientific paper would have to include considerable detail. He did not want any data released beyond that given in the patents. In fact, Yerkes wanted to delay all publicity because Du Pont had not had a reasonable sales test, the pilot plant was unproven, and Du Pont was working with only one knitting company, a strategy which might prove impossible to continue after the announcement.[97] Yerkes's concerns, however, delayed the announcement by less than two months.

As a Du Pont vice president, a noted authority on research, and the founder of the fundamental research program, Charles Stine ultimately had the privilege of announcing nylon – not to a scientific society but to three thousand women's club members. Stine made the public announcement on October 27, 1938, at the New York World's Fair site as part of the *New York Herald Tribune*'s Eighth Annual Forum on Current Problems. He spoke in a session entitled "We Enter the World of Tomorrow," which was keyed to the theme of the fair, the World of Tomorrow. The first session dealt with the impending world's fair, whereas the second part was entitled "What Laboratories of Industry Are Doing for the World of Tomorrow."[98] Stine was preceded on the program by Floyd Carlisle, chairman of the board of the Consolidated Edison Company. Painting a picture of the electrical utopia of the future, Carlisle prophesied,

> The future New Yorker may walk on a street at night as bright as daylight flooded with changing colors to the accompaniment of symphonic music synthetically produced by blending of electric waves of varying frequency.[99]

This was not the kind of fantasizing that the pragmatic, down-to-earth Du Pont Company indulged in, however. Stine began his talk in predictable fashion by proclaiming that the "scale of industrial research makes important new developments inevitable." Then he proceeded to run quickly through Du Pont's newer and more interesting product lines. In the middle of his talk, Stine announced nylon:

> To this audience..., I am making the first announcement of a brand new chemical textile fiber. This textile fiber is the first man-made organic textile fiber prepared wholly from new materials from the mineral kingdom. I refer to the fiber produced from nylon.... Though wholly fabricated from such common raw materials as coal, water, and air, nylon can be fashioned into filaments as strong as steel, as fine as a spider's web, yet more elastic than any of the common natural fibers.[100]

Thinking that "strong as steel" meant indestructible stockings, the women at the forum burst into applause.[101] These women were not the only ones to have this misconception.

The next day's *New York Times* ran two articles on nylon, on pages 24 and 34. The *Times* did not put the story on the front page as it had done earlier with neoprene. The first article was entitled, "New Hosiery Strong as Steel," and the second one in the business section began, "Coal, air and water were revealed today. . . ." The idea that supposedly indestructible stockings could be made from these ingredients seemed to many a modern miracle. The phrase "coal, air, and water" became associated with nylon and the transforming magic of science. It was the new alchemy. Over the next few years, hundreds of cartoons featured nylon and many of them played off the coal, air, and water theme.[102] On Saturday, October 29, the day that Orson Wells's broadcast of the "War of the Worlds" sent the nation into a panic, the *New York Times* ran an editorial entitled "Time Defying Hosiery" which speculated whether women would be happy with stockings that lasted forever.[103] Although Du Pont intentionally made very guarded statements about nylon – the sales-promotion manager became known as the sales-demotion manager – public interest remained at a high level in the eighteen months that elapsed between the announcement and the first nationwide public sales.[104] Only a few women were lucky enough to get nylons during this period.

While work continued on the plant and process, sample stockings became available. In March 1939, more than five thousand pairs were sold to Du Pont's Wilmington office employees. Comments on the stocking were generally favorable.[105] As more and more data came in, the outstanding feature of nylons appeared to be their durability. Plus they *looked* like silk. (Several hucksters sold silk stockings as nylon at the time.[106]) The fact that nylon stockings felt cold and clammy did not dampen enthusiasm for them. Practicality and good looks seems to have outweighed comfort in women's fashions. Nylons went on sale in a Wilmington store in 1939, and the demand was overwhelming.

The clamor caused by nylon forced the company to abandon its original marketing structure. As it had done with other products, Du Pont worried about maintaining control over the marketing of its product. To keep shoddy or price-cutting manufacturers from putting inferior nylons on the market, Du Pont initially licensed particular manufacturers to knit nylons. This agreement also stipulated the minimum price at which nylon hose could be sold by the textile firms. By May 1, 1940, two weeks before nylon stockings would go on sale, only 10 percent of the U.S. knitting companies had been licensed. Obviously, the other 90 percent were upset by this situation. Concern over its standing in the textile industry and recent Supreme Court rulings against price fixing in license agreements led the Du Pont management to throw the business open to everyone. This announcement came two days before the national debut of nylon.[107]

Before dropping the minimum price scheme, Du Pont had given considerable thought to the question of what to charge for nylon stockings. In doing this, the company was going beyond its direct concern, selling yarn to knitters. The cost of the yarn accounted for less than a fifth of the total selling price of a pair of stockings. Since the new fibers had such good properties, Du Pont decided that nylon stockings should sell at the top end of the silk price schedule. Convinced that nylon would prove superior to silk, Du Pont priced nylon accordingly and initially set its price 10 percent higher than that of silk.[108]

When nylon became available on May 15, 1940, sales were brisk. For the remainder of 1940, Du Pont produced 2.6 million pounds of nylon, which sold for about $9 million. Profits on these sales probably amounted to about $3 million or enough to pay off the R&D expense that had been charged to the Rayon Department.[109] In the following year, Du Pont sold over $25 million worth of nylon yarn, which brought in $7 million in profits and a return on its investment of one-third.[110] In less than two years, Du Pont captured over 30 percent of the full-fashioned hosiery market. The United States's entry into World War II in December 1941 prevented the shipment of silk to this country and led to the diversion of all Du Pont's nylon into military uses.

During the war, Du Pont increased its nylon production threefold to over 25 million pounds a year. The biggest war-related uses of nylon were for parachutes, airplane tire cords, and glider tow ropes.[111] Overall, the war had little impact on the commercial development of nylon. In fact, the 1945 production level was precisely that predicted by Yerkes six months before the attack on Pearl Harbor.[112] This coincidence can be explained by the fact that the limits to the expansion of nylon were technological. Some of the initial "brute force and awkwardness" technology, especially the HDA process, created new problems as the scale of operations grew. As early as 1943, Du Pont began to think about what would happen after the war ended and women began to demand nylons.

The nylon division management attempted to determine just how big the market for nylon stockings would be after the war. At wartime prices, it figured that 30 million pounds could be sold for stockings in spite of the fact that nylons lasted roughly twice as long as silk. This durability factor combined with the prewar consumption of silk stockings led to a projected market of about 15 million pounds. Du Pont, however, felt that the earlier silk-stocking market could be doubled through astute merchandising. In particular, the sales manager wanted to push cool, sheer, and lightweight summer stockings to combat the bare leg craze. Division manager Gladding agreed that women "will be lured into buying sheerer hose as they did in silk when it became cheaper."[113] But it turned out that women did not have to be lured into buying nylons.

During the first two years after the war, the demand for nylons greatly exceeded the supply. This shortage led to several riots by impatient women who had stood in lines for hours waiting for the opportunity to buy stockings. Newspapers around the country ran feature stories with headlines such as "Women Risk Life and Limb in Bitter Battle over Nylons."[114] Soon, however, Du Pont had ample capacity to supply the hosiery market, which proved to be surprisingly stable. Between 1937 and 1949, per capita consumption of full-fashioned hosiery increased very little.[115] In the postwar era, most of the growth of nylon came in areas other than hosiery.

The huge amount of free publicity that nylon received from the postwar stocking frenzy stimulated textile manufacturers to capitalize on its good will. They attempted to make virtually everything out of nylon. Some applications, such as men's shirts and suits, did not work out, but others, especially knit lingerie, proved very successful. This market accounted for much of the growth of nylon until the mid-fifties; then tire cord and carpet fiber carried the load for the following decade. Nylon became far and away the biggest money-maker in the history of the Du Pont Company.[116]

Conclusion: A Tale of Two Products

The technological aspects of the development of neoprene and nylon were remarkably similar. Both were made from obscure and difficult-to-produce chemicals, were manufactured through polymerization reactions that had to be controlled to an unprecedented degree, and were processed with novel techniques. Both took about the same time, nine years, to go from initial discovery to full commercialization. R&D costs were $2.5 million and $4.3 million for neoprene and nylon respectively, which together represented only a small fraction of Du Pont's available resources. Financially, there was little risk involved in these projects.[117] Both products had just become established in the marketplace when World War II began in Europe. The war's impact on neoprene was spectacular. Du Pont produced a record 3.8 million pounds in 1939 but saw production jump to over 118 million pounds by 1944, a thirtyfold increase. Nylon, conversely, reached a production plateau at about 25 million pounds per year during the war, approximately the capacity that the company had predicted before the outbreak of hostilities. Rapid growth of nylon production began in 1946 and continued into the mid-1950s. Neoprene kept up with nylon's growth in this era, both products reaching the 200-million-pound-per-year level in the late 1950s.[118] The major differences between the two products were in dollars, not pounds.

Both products have been consistent money-makers for Du Pont for over forty years, but the total earnings generated by nylon are nearly an order of magnitude higher than those of neoprene.[119] Du Pont found large volume and relatively high-price uses for nylon. Neoprene, however, found markets in numerous small applications, where price determined what material would be used. Simply stated, nylon had a bigger advantage over other textile fibers than neoprene did over competitive products. Because of these market differences, neoprene has not received nearly the attention and acclaim that nylon has, although they had common research origins and followed parallel development paths. In the end, the market proved to be the critical factor.

Of course, on the eve of World War II, all of this lay in the future. But the Du Pont Company's managers were optimistic that these remarkable new substances would become large and profitable products and that further investment in high-caliber scientific research would lead to additional discoveries that Du Pont's legions of chemists, engineers, and salesmen could develop into successful products. This became known as the "nylon model" of innovation, which dominated Du Pont's research strategy for decades to come.

14

Developing a Discipline: Chemical Engineering Research at Du Pont

In the development of neoprene and nylon, Du Pont relied heavily on a body of chemical engineering principles that had only recently been articulated. Earlier chemical plants had been designed by experience with similar operations, but in the case of the new polymers there was no experience to draw upon. Instead, the company's engineers employed more general, almost theoretical, concepts that Du Pont chemical engineers in one of Charles Stine's fundamental research groups had played a major role in developing. By beginning early and hiring some outstanding people, notably Allan Colburn, Du Pont made major contributions to the development of chemical engineering in a manner similar to Carothers's contributions to polymer science.

As a young researcher at the Eastern Laboratory, Stine had become aware of the lack of guiding principles for chemical engineering. He spent much of his time scaling up processes for making chemicals such as TNT.[1] In Du Pont's subsequent efforts to become a dyestuffs producer, Stine became painfully aware that chemical plants could not be just larger versions of laboratory equipment. The company's lack of chemical engineers with conceptual tools for scaling up processes greatly hampered Du Pont's dyestuffs venture.[2] At this time, chemical engineering as a profession was a hybrid of chemistry and mechanical engineering that could not adequately address the problems of the United States's rapidly expanding chemical industry.

Although chemical engineers in the United States founded an organization, the American Institute of Chemical Engineers (AIChE), in 1908, the emergence of the *discipline* of chemical engineering is rightly linked to Arthur D. Little's espousal of the concept of "unit operations," which he stated explicitly for the first time in 1915. Little believed that his contemporary chemical engineers took a "natural history" approach to their discipline; that is, they learned everything there was to know about sulfuric acid manufacture or the production of paint pigments. What they did not realize, Little pointed out, was that all chemical processes consisted of different combinations of a relatively small number of operations such as distilling, cooling, heating, crystallizing, and drying. By studying these unit operations, a chemical engineer could apply his knowledge to the manufacture of any chemical, not just to the particular ones with which he was familiar.[3] Importantly, plants to make new compounds could be laid out by arranging a sequence of operations in pieces of equipment, each designed to perform one particular function. At this time, the limitation of Little's scheme was that for any given process, the unit operations had to be performed on substances at various temperatures, pressures, and other conditions, and chemical engineers had to approach these problems empirically.

The next important step in the development of the discipline occurred in the early 1920s, when Warren K. Lewis, a young professor of chemical engineering at the Massachusetts Institute of Technology, began to investigate the scientific principles of unit operations. His goal was to provide chemical engineers with mathematically sophisticated theoretical tools to predict the performance of chemical processing equipment from data such as the physical properties of the substances involved. These ideas provided the basis for chemical engineering research over the next three decades.[4] By the late 1920s, enough progress had been made so that a chemical engineer thought of himself as more than a hybrid of existing disciplines or someone who talked chemistry to engineers and engineering to chemists.

Needless to say, Du Pont benefited greatly from the expertise of this new generation of chemical engineers — one of them, Crawford H. Greenewalt, would become president of the company in 1948 — whose analytical skills and fundamental approach to engineering proved to be indispensable for the development of new chemical technologies. In the high-pressure field, particularly, new plants could not be designed by the extension of data from existing plants. Not surprisingly, much of the early chemical engineering research at Du Pont was done by the Chemical Department in connection with the development of high-pressure processes to produce ammonia and nitric acid in the mid-1920s. With success in those areas, the company would soon initiate more general chemical engineering studies.

In the mid-1920s, the Chemical Department developed the Du Pont nitric acid process, which would become the dominant one in the chemical industry. Forty years later, in 1964, plants using the Du Pont process produced 90 percent of the nation's output of nitric acid.[5]

A new method for making nitric acid had emerged in the years before World War I. For centuries, nitric acid had been made by the distillation of a mixture of potassium or sodium nitrate and sulfuric acid. The production of nitric acid remained small until the development of nitrocellulose, nitroglycerine, and nitrocotton (smokeless powder) in the nineteenth century created a large demand for it. Nevertheless, the traditional technology proved adequate to supply Du Pont with enormous quantities of nitric acid during World War I. At the same time, the Germans commercialized the Haber-Bosch process for the synthesis of ammonia, and following some earlier work of Wilhelm Ostwald, converted the ammonia to nitric acid by burning the ammonia and absorbing the resulting nitrogen dioxide in water.[6]

In the years following the war, it became apparent to Fin Sparre and others in the Du Pont Company that the development of a synthetic ammonia industry in the United States would make nitric acid manufactured from ammonia cheaper than that made from Chilean nitrates by the traditional process. Sparre, though, could not get the Chemical Department to begin research on this subject because Chemical Director Charles Reese maintained that acid made by the new process would be too expensive, and he was right in 1922.[7] Within a few years, however, the declining price of ammonia would change the relative economics of the two processes.

In 1924, the Chemical Department began nitric acid research. Guy Baker Taylor, who had earned a PhD in physical chemistry from Princeton University in 1913, led this effort. Before completing his graduate training, he had worked at the Eastern Laboratory in 1910 and 1911. After Princeton, Taylor was employed by the U.S. Bureau of Mines for six years. He rejoined Du Pont in 1919 and stayed with the company until his retirement in 1953.[8] On the nitric acid project, Taylor was assisted by Frederick C. Zeisberg and Thomas H. Chilton. Zip Zeisberg had been a "special student" in chemistry at the University of Virginia before joining the Mathieson Alkali Works at age nineteen in 1907. Two years later, Zeisberg took a position as a research chemist at Du Pont's Eastern Laboratory and in 1912 became the Chemical Department's specialist in acid manufacture.[9] Chilton had joined Du Pont in 1925 after earning a chemical engineering degree from Columbia University and working as a research chemist in New York City for three years. Chilton later would direct Du Pont's chemical engineering research for thirty years. His work on the ammonia oxidation nitric acid process introduced him to industrial chemical engineering.[10]

Starting work in the spring of 1924, Taylor's group set as their first goal the duplication of what had been achieved in Germany and to some extent by the U.S. government at Muscle Shoals during World War I. The nitric acid process consisted of three operations: the oxidation of ammonia to nitric oxide (NO) and water at high temperature over a platinum gauze catalyst; further oxidation of the NO to nitrogen dioxide (NO_2); and absorption of NO_2 gas into water to produce nitric acid. The first step was straightforward, and Du Pont designed converters similar to those that had been used at Muscle Shoals. The oxidation of NO to NO_2 was problematical because it was so slow. Finally, the absorption process was complicated by the peculiar chemistry of the nitrogen oxides. For every two molecules of NO_2 converted into nitric acid, one molecule reverted back to NO, which then had to react with oxygen to produce NO_2. The cycle then repeated itself. To produce the highest possible acid concentration and to recover the maximum fraction of nitric oxides, the absorption process was done in a vertical tower with a number of horizontal plates that divided it into discrete sections. Each plate had holes in it to permit the nitrogen oxides to flow up the tower and the nitric acid to flow down. The reaction between NO_2 and water occurred on each plate, and the NO formed was oxidized in the space between the plates. A large space had to be allocated for this latter slow reaction; otherwise, a considerable amount of the nitrogen oxides would go out the stack.[11]

Providing a large volume for oxidation of NO would not have been a problem except that the Du Pont engineers decided to construct the plant from high-chromium stainless steel because of the corrosive nature of nitric acid. The cost of this metal, which had just become commercially available, combined with the enormous volume needed for the oxidation and reoxidation of NO, yielded an expensive, if long-lasting, plant. By January 1925, Du Pont had a semiworks plant operating at Repauno and two years later a large-scale plant at the same facility. Up to this point, the Du Pont engineers had closely followed the processes developed in Germany and elsewhere.[12]

In the summer of 1925, Zeisberg visited Europe to investigate the nitric acid plants of the United Alkali Company in Great Britain and several plants in France. While overseas, Zeisberg learned that the Norwegian firm Norsk Hydro had been working on a more efficient absorption process that employed pressures much higher than Du Pont used in its towers.[13] The advantage of operating at higher pressure resulted from the physical-chemical properties of nitrogen oxides, which had been determined primarily in Germany in the 1910s. Studies of the reaction of NO with oxygen showed that its rate was proportional to the cube of the pressure. Translated into practice, this meant that an absorption tower at 10 atmospheres pressure would need for the oxidation reaction only 1/1,000 as much volume as one at atmospheric pressure. Consequently, at higher pressures much smaller towers could be used, and the product would contain 60 percent nitric acid, 10 percent more than that made by the atmospheric-pressure process. Because most of the acid used by Du Pont in its manufacturing operations had to be highly concentrated, less water had to be removed from the pressure-process product. In spite of these advantages, higher-pressure absorption towers had not been built previously because there had been no material that could withstand the combination of high pressure and extremely corrosive substances. High-chromium stainless steel made the pressure process feasible.[14]

By the end of 1926, Du Pont had constructed a 750-pound-per-day nitric acid semiworks that operated at 100 pounds per square inch or about 7 atmospheres pressure. Next, the engineers began to put together a pilot plant that was fifteen times bigger than the semiworks. By the fall of 1928, Du Pont had several commercial-scale pressure plants in operation and began to license the technology to other chemical companies.[15] Although the two processes, atmospheric and high pressure, produced nitric acid at about the same cost in the 1920s, the latter required only a third as much investment. Thus, at equivalent profit margins, the pressure process generated a return on investment three times that of the other one.[16] Eventually, the Du Pont pressure process would supplant its atmospheric pressure rival.[17] The outstanding success of this project certainly gave considerable credibility to chemical engineering research and development in the Chemical Department.

The nitric acid project was not the only one on which the chemical engineers in the department had worked. They also made important contributions to the development of high-pressure technology for the production of ammonia, methanol, and other compounds. By 1926 there were ten chemical engineers (or about 15 percent of the technically trained staff) in the Chemical Department. More than half of them had graduated from MIT.[18] They were scattered throughout the department, however, because no formal chemical engineering research group existed until Stine organized one in his fundamental research program.

In preparing his detailed memorandum on fundamental research to the Executive Committee in 1927, Stine asked twenty-five-year-old Crawford H. Greenewalt about possible areas for research in high-pressure technology and chemical engineering. Greenewalt had graduated in 1922 from MIT with a bachelor's degree in chemical engineering. A few months later, at age twenty, he joined the Du Pont Company and served as a control chemist at the Philadelphia plant until two years later, when he transferred to the Experimental Station. He had just been promoted to group leader when he received Stine's request.[19]

In his report to the Executive Committee, Stine drew heavily upon Greenewalt's suggestions.[20] Stine, who had earlier experienced the shortcomings of contemporary chemical engineering, maintained that

> One of the most important and indispensable portions of a fundamental research program is that dealing with physics. The du Pont Company has frequently neglected this field but cannot continue to do so. This kind of chemical engineering research is, for the most part, not carried on at colleges and universities, the Massachusetts Institute of Technology being a notable exception.[21]

From Stine's point of view, physics was the scientific foundation of chemical engineering. However, the unit operations concept offered another approach to the subject. There were many unit operations, Stine claimed, that could be explored in a fundamental manner: absorption of gases in liquids, evaporation, crushing and grinding of solids, flow of fluids, and agitation and mixing. Greenewalt agreed that "knowledge in these fields is at the present time largely empirical. . . ." He pointed to some earlier distillation studies at Du Pont as an example of the kind of work that might be done.[22]

As a corollary to this work, Greenewalt proposed and Stine accepted a program to determine the physical properties of substances, particularly at high temperature and pressure. Stine argued that Du Pont needed these kinds of data, which usually could not be found in handbooks, "to design plants intelligently." As in the other subjects that Stine had picked for his fundamental research program, the goal of chemical engineering research would be to put the discipline on a sound scientific footing. Still, it would be several years before he organized a chemical engineering group. By October 1928, the only work done along the lines Greenewalt had suggested was the construction of equipment to measure the densities and viscosities of vapors and liquids at high temperature and pressure.[23]

The fundamental chemical engineering research group was organized on July 1, 1929, with Chilton as its head and Raymond Genereaux, who had just joined Du Pont after receiving a chemical engineering degree from Columbia University, as his assistant.[24] In October, Chilton wrote a memorandum to Stine to outline the aims of his group. He began with a quotation from a paper by MIT's William H. McAdams, that he had heard presented at a recent American Chemical Society meeting. McAdams stated that "the ultimate problem of engineering design is the development of methods of computation sufficiently fundamental and dependable so that from the physical and chemical properties of the chemicals involved one can predict the behavior of new types of equipment with precision and assurance." Chilton pointed out that McAdams admitted that in many fields, realization of this ideal would be far in the future; nevertheless, Chilton believed that Du Pont could make some important contributions toward this end. As a consultant to Du Pont, McAdams tried to steer its research in the proper direction.[25]

Following the organizational structure outlined by Arthur D. Little in 1915, Chilton divided his research fields into chemical engineering unit operations, such as fluid flow, heat transfer, distillation, filtration, and crushing and grinding. He realized that not all unit operations were of equal importance to the Du Pont Company or offered "the same opportunity for the development of fundamental and useful relations."[26] Setting out to explore the scientific basis of the unit operations, Chilton followed the path laid out by McAdams. Because fluid flow, heat transfer, and mass transfer operations such as absorption and distillation could be analyzed by quantitative methods and by employing theoretical models, these areas became the subject of intensive chemical engineering research. Such other areas as agitation, mixing, filtration, crushing, and grinding, although not completely ignored, were less amenable to this type of analysis and consequently received much less attention.

Chilton's researchers conducted fundamental studies of all these unit processes, published numerous and important papers, and acted as internal consultants on chemical engineering problems. Besides its fundamental studies and work on practical problems, Chilton's group helped design equipment for use at the Experimental Station and served as a central clearinghouse for engineering data and reports. Chilton outlined his approach at the 1930 Du Pont chemical directors' meeting:

> While the mention that I have just made of fundamental problems sounds somewhat academic or somewhat like pure research, I believe that a summary of some of the investigations we have been making during the past year will throw a different light on our activities. While we desire to have this program of fundamental investigations always underway in order that we be accumulating information and may be

ahead of the game by having it on hand, . . . problems have been arising which we tackle for immediate solutions in order to obtain practical results.[27]

By the end of 1929, Chilton had a staff of five men in his group. Over the next several years, his staff remained at this level, and he had a budget of between thirty and forty thousand dollars a year.[28] The group occupied a small part of Purity Hall. One hot summer day, Genereaux recalled, the entire group fell asleep at their desks, to be awakened by the sound of Chilton laughing at them. He managed his staff in an informal manner. Genereaux remembered him as "an extremely thoughtful and extremely gentle person" who was "demanding but not pressuring" and combined technical expertise with an ability to work with people.[29] In spite of the relatively small size of Chilton's group, it played an important role by providing chemical engineering expertise for the Du Pont Company and contributed significantly through its publications to the development of chemical engineering.

Although many outstanding chemical engineers, including Chilton, worked for Du Pont in the 1930s, one in particular, Allan P. Colburn, made important contributions to chemical engineering. Colburn obtained a PhD in chemical engineering from the University of Wisconsin in 1929, only the third to receive such a doctorate from the university. One of the other two was his dissertation advisor, Olaf A. Hougen, who ranked as one of the leaders of the chemical engineering profession because of his long career in scholarship and teaching. When Colburn transferred from Marquette University as a junior in 1924, the chemical engineering faculty at Wisconsin had three members. After receiving his bachelor's degree, Colburn elected to continue his studies. For a thesis topic, Hougen assigned him the study of the condensation of water vapor from saturated air streams in tubular condensers.[30] This was an important problem in chemical engineering practice and one that centered on phenomena of general interest.

From an analytical point of view, rigorous mathematical solutions to problems of this type did not exist. Physicists had earlier abandoned them for this reason; however, following the example of Osborne Reynolds in England, German engineers, particularly Ernst Nusselt in the 1910s, had worked out semiempirical correlations that were applicable to a wide variety of conditions.[31] Although these correlations did not give much additional insight into the fundamental phenomena under investigation, they proved useful for understanding the relative importance of competing forces and for the design of chemical processing equipment. Hougen recalled that in the 1920s, any such scientifically oriented engineering research in America was in "a primitive stage" and that all five important books published on heat transfer in that decade were in German. For his dissertation, Colburn had to draw upon his high school German to learn the state of the art in his field.[32]

According to Hougen, Colburn's struggle with German foreshadowed his later method of attacking engineering problems. "The extraction of complex theoretical principles from lengthy German dissertations," Hougen recalled, "required exceptional capacity for intensive concentration. Allen studied [them] to the point of pain and fatigue. Colburn had an extraordinary capacity for intensive concentration and a mind unusually well organized for retention and retrieval."[33] Following the German model in his research, Colburn not only wanted to determine the characteristics of his particular condenser but also to develop a correlation that would apply to any similar piece of equipment. He pursued this general goal for much of his career.

Colburn joined Du Pont in September 1929 after finishing his dissertation at Wisconsin. It is not clear why he chose an industrial career. According to one of his friends, Colburn, an avid sportsman, later claimed that he was attracted to the Du Pont Experimental Station because it was adjacent to a golf course where employees regularly played six holes during their long lunch break.[34] As the holder of one of the twenty PhD degrees in chemical engineering awarded by American universities in 1929, Colburn had come to Chilton's attention because of his work in heat transfer, and Chilton assigned the new staff member that topic for his research.[35]

Over the next nine years, Colburn and Chilton published twenty-six papers either separately or together. At Du Pont Colburn was never satisfied with the application of his results to immediate problems but felt impelled to generalize upon the collected data. Then, Chilton noted, he could bring "theory into the service of the design engineer."[36] Another eminent colleague maintained that Colburn would take a very complex physical phenomenon, state the general mathematical equations governing it, and then solve these complex equations by recognizing the essential parts and developing a logical way to an approximate solution.[37] This approach to chemical engineering not only simplified the calculations that equipment designers needed to do, but through the process of simplification, Colburn also contributed to the fundamental understanding of seemingly complex phenomena by focusing attention on the controlling variables.

In this type of work, unlike that of Carothers, there was no conflict between "pure" and "applied" research, primarily because it proved impossible to distinguish one from the other. As historian Leonard Reich has pointed out in his study of engineers at General Electric and AT&T, the work that they did can be described as determining the science of technological devices.[38] Even though engineers used sophisticated scientific tools to analyze these devices, the insights they gained yielded practical benefits. Such is the nature of process- and equipment-oriented engineering research.

Colburn's most important contributions were to the development of chemical engineering science, that is, to a more generalized, conceptual, and mathematical approach to the discipline. Colburn showed that some of the central chemical engineering operations, such as momentum fluid flow, heat transfer, and distillation, could be understood as analogous phenomena. As early as 1910, Ludwig Prandl in Germany had used the methods worked out earlier by Reynolds for fluid flow to develop an analogous relationship for heat transfer. For fluid flowing in a pipe, for example, Reynolds found that over a wide range of conditions he could correlate a "dimensionless" number calculated from the physical properties of a given system with the pressure drop in a given pipe. Once established, this empirically determined relationship then could be used to predict pressure drops over a wide range of flow conditions. Prandl and Nusselt then showed that heat transfer could be handled in a similar fashion, but neither made the analogy exact. By modifying and simplifying some of these earlier correlations, Colburn formulated a more exact analogy between heat transfer and fluid flow in pipes.[39] Enthusiastic about his conceptual breakthrough, Colburn had come over to Chilton's house one evening to show him the results. This work won Colburn the AIChE's first William H. Walker award for an outstanding contribution to chemical engineering literature.[40]

Again following the work of Prandl, Colburn next set out to show that mass transfer – that is, operations such as distillation – could be understood analogously to the other two phenomena that he had linked together. This work produced the famous Chilton-Colburn analogy, which Chilton credited Colburn for originating.[41] These analogies, although empirically derived, provided part of the basis for a major development in chemical engineering in the following decades.[42] Colburn subsequently made many other contributions to chemical engineering during his career – but not as an industrial researcher.

In 1938, Colburn left Du Pont to become head of the chemical engineering department at the University of Delaware.[43] His poor health – he had contracted tuberculosis and had taken a two-year leave of absence beginning in the fall of 1935 – more than any other factor seems to have led to this change. When Delaware's president, Walter Hullihen, asked Chilton about Du Pont engineers who might be interested in the job, Chilton suggested Colburn, thinking that a slower-paced university life might be better for him in the long run.[44] Colburn accepted Hullihen's offer after consulting with Chilton. Colburn's $5,000 salary was the highest of any professor at Delaware, but $3,500 of it came from H. Fletcher Brown, a retired Du Pont executive for whom the university's new chemistry building would be named.[45]

Although ostensibly moving into a less demanding position, Colburn went at his new job with extraordinary energy. He soon abandoned his plans for a daily afternoon nap. He even continued to spend a half-day each week consulting for Du Pont.[46] One year after Colburn had assumed his post at the university, the dean of engineering wrote that the new professor had more than fulfilled his expectations. Colburn, he wrote, is "an exacting, inspiring, and effective teacher."[47] In his nine years as head of the department, Colburn continued to make important contributions to chemical engineering through his research, and he built a highly respected program at Delaware.[48]

Besides the work of Chilton and Colburn, another Du Pont chemical engineer, John Howard Perry, made an important contribution to the discipline in the 1930s by putting together the first edition of the *Chemical Engineers' Handbook* for the McGraw-Hill Publishing Company.[49] Perry earned a PhD in chemical engineering from MIT in 1922 and joined Du Pont in 1925. The handbook project originated in 1925 when Howard C. Parmalee, editor of *Chemical and Metallurgical Engineering*, organized an advisory board of prominent academic and industrial chemical engineers to suggest topics for a series of chemical engineering textbooks. Among the dozen planned works was a handbook. The committee wanted Du Pont's Zeisberg, who was then chairman of the literature committee of the AIChE, to head this undertaking, but when he declined, they asked Perry, who accepted.[50] William Calcott, head of the Jackson Laboratory, became assistant editor. Over the next seven years, Perry worked on the project both on the company's and his own time. He cajoled many of his associates at Du Pont to write sections for him. When finally published in 1934, the *Chemical Engineers' Handbook* consisted of 2,610 pages, about a quarter of which had been contributed by Du Pont engineers.[51] In the next twenty years, McGraw-Hill sold more than 150,000 copies of the handbook worldwide. Perry edited subsequent editions of the handbook, and he remained at Du Pont until his death in 1953.[52]

Throughout the pre–World War II era, chemical engineering research at Du Pont was done by a small group of outstanding engineers, each of whom specialized in a particular field. There were some organizational changes, however. In 1931, the Engineering Department established a unit parallel to the one in the Chemical Department, consisting of a director, two metallurgists, and two chemical engineers. Generally, the work of this group focused on different subjects than those of Chilton's researchers. The new group studied the properties of materials with specific emphasis on their application in chemical plants and physical processes such as crushing, grinding, and mixing.[53] In 1935 the Du Pont Company's management merged the two groups into one in the Engineering Department under Henry Belin du Pont, who like many other du Ponts, held an engineering degree from MIT and who had managed that department's earlier program. The new combined group consisted of twenty engineers and had an annual budget of $100,000. In mid-1938, Belin left the Experimental Station and went downtown; soon, he became a member of the Executive Committee. Chilton succeeded him as head of engineering research.[54]

After World War II, the expansion of university chemical engineering departments opened up many good positions, some of which were filled by members of Chilton's group. In the five years after 1945, six members of Chilton's group left Du Pont to take academic positions. Two of them,

James O. Maloney and Robert L. Pigford, became chairmen of the chemical engineering departments at the universities of Kansas and Delaware, respectively. Pigford replaced Colburn, who had been promoted to assistant to the president of the university. Over the next two decades, Pigford finished the job Colburn had started, that of establishing a first-rate chemical engineering program at Delaware.[55] The loss of these outstanding men must have handicapped Du Pont's research programs, but Chilton seems not to have stood in the way of his employees leaving to accept good academic positions. In most cases, Du Pont retained these experts as consultants in their respective specialties and no doubt followed the work of and recruited their best students.

The transfer of these men into universities perhaps reflected a parting of the ways for Du Pont and academic chemical engineering research. With their discipline firmly established, academic chemical engineers began to work on research problems based on increasingly sophisticated mathematical theories. Much of this research had little or no relevance to the problems faced by engineers in industry.[56]

In the postwar era, the company's engineering research programs expanded significantly in the traditional fields of chemical and metallurgical engineering and also into new fields such as applied and radiation physics.[57] Chemical engineering research began to shift its focus in this era. By the mid-1950s, Chilton abandoned the unit operations approach to chemical engineering research. Instead of having individuals who specialized in a particular unit operation, groups worked on more general problems such as reactor design or the economical attainment of high temperatures.[58]

It is difficult to assess precisely the impact of chemical engineering research on the Du Pont Company. Before he retired in 1958, Chilton stated the three overall research objectives that he had pursued throughout his career.[59] First, engineering research had to provide the technology for the manufacture of products that could not be made by existing techniques. This goal was particularly important in an era when the chemical industry had been rapidly expanding into new kinds of products and processes. Second, engineering research had to give Du Pont the knowledge it needed to scale up the manufacture of new products with a minimum lapse of time on process development and plant design, and with a minimum outlay of capital. Third, Chilton's chemical engineering research had to lay the basis for "re-examination and rationalization of processes and equipment for established lines of business." In achieving these goals, engineering research contributed to the growth and prosperity of the Du Pont Company. And through numerous publications, especially those of Colburn, Du Pont played a major role in the development of the discipline of chemical engineering. Throughout his tenure at Du Pont, Chilton and his staff made important contributions to the development of Du Pont's technological base and to the discipline of chemical engineering. Chilton and his associates shared the mutual respect of industry and academia.[60]

15

The Conduct of Research

Fundamentally, Du Pont's objectives for its R&D programs in the interwar period had changed little since the establishment of the Eastern Laboratory in 1902 and the Experimental Station in 1903; neither had many of the basic problems in managing R&D. But the scale of Du Pont's efforts in, say, 1941 and the nature of the diversified, decentralized corporation made research a far more sophisticated undertaking than it had been earlier. Industry had become more closely tied to academia. Recruiting had become more problematic. Managing researchers had become more complex. The routine of research had become more formalized. Coordinating research had become more challenging, and certainly the job of accounting for research had grown more intricate. Du Pont's executives had always expected much from research, but on the eve of World War II, they had come to regard research as the major avenue by which to increase the company's fortunes.

The conduct of research at Du Pont entailed a whole complex of tasks involving the bench chemist up to the Executive Committee advisor on research. After the decentralization of 1921 and with the continued diversification of the company, tension always existed in the company's R&D affairs. On the one hand, there was a perceived need for central control over the corporation's R&D functions; on the other, the decentralized structure demanded more localized governance. This tension between centralization and decentralization was probably greater in R&D than in any area of the company, largely because scientists have invariably sought autonomy in their work. Trying to harness scientists' objectives with often unclear or conflicting corporate objectives made the conduct of research at Du Pont ever problematic.

The Growth of Du Pont R&D, 1921–1941

Available statistics suggest the increasing scale of research at Du Pont. (See Tables 15.1a and 15.1b.) As noted earlier, Du Pont's research and development expenditures ballooned during and immediately after World War I, but with the recession of 1920 and 1921, Du Pont's Executive Committee scaled back its research budget dramatically. Not until 1928–29 did the company spend, in historical dollars, at the level it had a decade earlier.

Despite a cutback of about 20 percent in 1932 and 1933 – the depths of the Great Depression – Du Pont greatly increased its research expenditures during the late 1920s and throughout the 1930s. Between 1930 and 1940, R&D spending doubled. This growth is also reflected in the increase in the number of researchers at Du Pont. From a low of 133 in 1922, Du Pont increased its ranks of "research specialists" (i.e., research chemists and research managers) to almost 1,300 in 1940 and 1,500 in 1942. (See Table 15.2 for other research staff data.) As Du Pont's research expenditures and staff grew during these two decades, so did the complexity of conducting research, from the recruiting of a research force to executive decisionmaking about R&D strategy.

Recruiting a Research Force

From the outset of its corporate R&D program, Du Pont had faced problems in hiring a skilled research work force. Because of his prior work at Johns Hopkins University, Charles L. Reese had been able to recruit a number of its Chemistry Department's graduates, including Charles F. Lindsay, Charles M. A. Stine, Hamilton Bradshaw, and A. P. Tanberg. Indeed, there was a distinct "Hopkins mafia" in the management of Du Pont's research during the Reese era. But as Reese learned quickly, even Hopkins graduates sometimes left Du Pont. Nevertheless, he succeeded in recruiting a remarkable group of chemists, many of whom became research directors. By the 1910s, however, Reese faced greater competition in recruiting researchers, and he found that he could not simply rely upon his contacts with the faculty at Johns Hopkins University to fill positions.

Competition for graduate chemists grew for two related reasons. First, more and more corporations in the 1910s and 1920s founded their own research programs and thus competed for scientists. Second, some of these corporations, as well as those without their own research divisions, began to support the industrial fellowship programs pioneered by Robert Kennedy Duncan and widely copied by others. A charismatic salesman of research, Duncan succeeded in rapidly expanding his program, first at the University of Kansas and then at the University of Pittsburgh. Supported by the wealthy Mellon brothers, who had been captivated by his *The Chemistry of Commerce*, Duncan built the Industrial Fellowship program at Pittsburgh into the Mellon Institute of Industrial Research and School of Specific Industries. As enthusiasm for the program grew, more and more corporations supported research at the Mellon Institute; more and more universities established similar programs to support their students and faculty. By funding Industrial Fellowships, corporations gained greater access to science departments for the recruitment of their researchers.[1]

Table 15.1a. *Du Pont R&D Expenditures, 1922–29 (in thousands of dollars)*

	1922[a]	1923[a]	1924[a]	1925[a]	1926[a]	1927[b]	1928[b]	1929[c]
Total	1,185	1,441	1,700	1,994	2,243	2,200	2,612	3,645
Chemical Dept.	265[d]	296	361	452	562	654	818	934
Dyestuffs	421	390	452	496	433	502	490	694
Explosives	161	199	294	323	336	315	257	303
Plastics	104	114	125	123	143	51	29	152
Paint, Lacquer, and Chemicals	221[e]	317[e]	370	455	610	616	682	441
Du Pont Rayon Co.	—	n.a.	n.a.	n.a.	n.a.	203	385	371
Du Pont Cellophane Co.	—	—	n.a.	n.a.	n.a.	26	44	77
Du Pont Ammonia Co.	—	—	—	n.a.	n.a.	163	223	432
Grasselli Chemical Co.	—	—	—	—	—	—	—	381
Krebs Pigment and Chemical Co.	—	—	—	—	—	—	—	79
Other	—	—	—	—	—	46	117	116

Note: n.a. = not available. — = not applicable. Total figures do not correlate exactly with the sums of the departmental R&D expenditures. For 1927–29 data, Chemical Department figures include work done for industrial departments, which is also included in the individual departmental statistics. For these years, the sum of each column is greater than the total.

[a]C. M. A. Stine to Treasurer, Aug. 10, 1927, CRDD Files.

[b]"Expenditures for Chemical Research," Acc. 1813, Box 5.

[c]"Chemical Research – 1929," Acc. 1813, Box 5.

[d]Charles L. Reese to the Executive Committee, Mar. 27, 1924, Acc. 1784.

[e]Figures represent combined totals of the Paint and Cellulose Products Departments. The two were merged in 1924.

Table 15.1b. *Du Pont R&D Expenditures, 1930–41 (in thousands of dollars)*

	1930	1931	1932	1933	1934	1935	1936	1937	1938	1939	1940	1941
Total	5,412	5,506	4,560	4,690	5,745	6,555	7,652	9,538	9,776	10,454	11,000	12,401
Chemical Dept.[a]	1,182	1,002	751	741	876	873	1,120	1,282	1,129	1,099	1,333	1,446
Ammonia	802	457	428	338	383	455	542	694	720	790	928	1,063
Explosives	417	303	232	251	321	360	371	409	405	467	406	471
Fabrics and Finishes	731	922	576	627	687	807	938	1,133	1,093	1,088	1,143	1,234
Grasselli	537	545	393	426	523	513	617	714	611	605	600	588
Organic Chemicals	815	961	858	832	1,055	1,286	1,512	1,759	1,621	1,812	2,132	2,509
Pigments	336	349	287	300	385	427	464	588	636	737	738	867
Plastics	253	218	176	206	212	261	327	448	510	422	585	664
Rayon	411	828	776	919	1,134	1,307	1,647	2,468	2,648	3,016	2,781	3,006
Other	18	26	29	33	93	121	137	149	214	330	367	469

[a] Chemical Department figures include work done for industrial departments, which is also included in the individual departmental statistics. For this research, the sum of each column is greater than the total figure.

Sources: Except for Chemical Department, all data are from "Annual Research Expenditures Categories B, C, D, E. Years: 1930 to 1950 Inclusive," Apr. 30, 1946, Acc. 1814, Box 5. Chemical Department Statistics for 1930 to 1939 are in "Development of the Chemical Department" [ca. 1940], Acc. 1784.

Table 15.2. Du Pont R&D Personnel, 1921–41

	1921	1922	1923	1924	1925	1926	1927	1928	1929
Total company	135[a]	133[a]	151[a]	165[a]	215[a]	241[a]	279[a]	299[a]	572
Chemical Dept.	21[b]	21[b]	28[b]	38[b]	42[b]	60[b]	70[b]	79[b]	99
Engineering Dept.	—	—	—	—	—	—	—	—	—
Ammonia Dept.	—	—	—	4[c]	7[c]	13[c]	n.a.	n.a.	50
Electrochemicals Dept.	—	—	—	—	—	—	—	—	—
Explosives Dept.	n.a.	n.a.	n.a.	n.a.	n.a.	n.a.	n.a.	n.a.	39
Fabrics & Finishes Dept.	n.a.	n.a.	n.a.	n.a.	n.a.	n.a.	n.a.	n.a.	119
Grasselli Chemical Dept.	—	—	—	—	—	—	—	—	38
Organic Chemicals Dept.	n.a.	n.a.	n.a.	n.a.	n.a.	n.a.	n.a.	n.a.	71
Photo Products Dept.	n.a.	n.a.	n.a.	n.a.	n.a.	n.a.	n.a.	n.a.	9
Pigments Dept.	—	—	—	—	—	—	—	—	—
Plastics Dept.	n.a.	n.a.	n.a.	n.a.	n.a.	n.a.	n.a.	n.a.	19
Rayon Dept.	2[d]	2[d]	2[d]	4[d]	n.a.	n.a.	n.a.	48[d]	73
Haskell Laboratory	—	—	—	—	—	—	—	—	—

Charles Reese realized that support of graduate fellowships yielded advantages in recruiting. In 1918, he convinced Pierre and Irénée du Pont and the Executive Committee to support the company's own fellowship program. He argued that by providing fellowship funds to leading schools, Du Pont would be able to "secur[e] the services of their better" students.[2] The Executive Committee initially appropriated $25,000 to the Chemical Department, and at Reese's discretion Du Pont began to distribute money annually in parcels of $500 per fellowship.[3] Because Du Pont was in the chemicals business, these fellowships were given primarily to chemistry and chemical engineering departments at leading universities and colleges.[4]

From the outset of the Du Pont fellowships program, the company exercised little if any control over the fellowships, although the Chemical Department occasionally considered tightening its reins on the program. Typically, Du Pont annually gave a department one or more industrial fellowships, and the recipient department rotated the Du Pont fellowships among its professors, who in turn granted them to their students.[5] By 1927, however, Du Pont had grown concerned that, as Elmer Bolton expressed it, "in many cases the fellowship has been assigned to a Professor who is not particularly qualified for carrying out a high order of research work or is not working on a subject that might be of some interest to the Company." To rectify this problem, Bolton suggested that Du Pont assign its fellowships to particular professors, thereby raising the "possibility that the men working on these industrial fellowships are most likely to be employed by the donor of the fellowship."[6]

Records are too sketchy to conclude precisely how Bolton's proposal was handled, but there is no doubt that Du Pont's fellowship program became

1930	1931	1932	1933	1934	1935	1936	1937	1938	1939	1940	1941
687	755	672	725	785	847	912	1,051	979	1,034	1,261	1,341
123	127	117	116	119	116	125	137	140	141	155	169
—	6	9	12	9	21	23	23	23	23	26	29
88	73	56	50	53	62	84	104	112	123	138	150
n.a.	n.a.	n.a.	n.a.	n.a.	90	94	99	85	82	122	153
39	31	29	27	28	33	34	41	36	36	38	41
101	92	83	80	76	83	104	118	106	96	109	126
39	40	51	55	67	58	59	66	64	62	59	63
75	98	102	91	100	104	123	121	120	124	132	146
10	10	11	13	12	13	12	16	17	18	19	25
—	25	25	30	35	34	35	46	51	54	61	65
25	26	24	25	26	27	29	34	35	35	40	50
85	93	98	122	130	151	160	173	166	196	286[e]	319[e]
—	—	—	—	—	9	11	17	16	12	13	12

Note: n.a. = not available. — - not applicable.

[a]Number of "research specialists," as enumerated by Ira T. Ellis to C. H. Greenewalt, Feb. 14, 1955, Acc. 1814, Box 34.

[b]"Technical Employees" as enumerated in "Development of the Chemical Department," Acc. 1784.

[c]From Edward P. Bartlett, *The Chemical Division at the Du Pont Ammonia Department, 1924–1935* (n.p.: n.p., 1949), II, 2, Box 91.

[d]From Ferdinand Schulze, revised and enlarged from a manuscript prepared by Roy Soukup, *The Technical Division of the Rayon Department, 1920–1951* (Wilmington, Del.: Du Pont, 1952), pp. 61–75.

[e]This number is suspect because it conflicts strongly with personnel data presented in *The Technical Division of the Rayon Department* and because it does not correlate with research expenditures for the Rayon Department. For 1940, this number could have been about 190 and for 1941, 205.

Source: All data from 1929 to 1941 derived from "Research Study – Interim Report [to the Executive Committee]," July 7, 1948, in Official Annual Research and Development Statistics, Central Research and Development Department, Du Pont, Wilmington, Del. The sums for the departmental personnel figures do not correspond exactly with total company personnel figures.

more formalized in the late 1920s. The company established a Fellowship Committee chaired by the Executive Committee member who advised on research. The committee began to "maintain . . . a complete scholastic record of the individuals to whom these awards are assigned by the colleges, details of the research work performed and other data pertaining to the subject." Willis Harrington, who headed the committee until mid-1930, wrote president Lammot du Pont that "the fellowships, in general, are . . . unrestricted in scope, but we do have a few which are earmarked to certain professors

who are on our part-time retainership [i.e., consultants]."[7] Data from 1931–
32 suggest that the latter was true only in the instance of the University of
Notre Dame, where Julius Nieuwland (the Jesuit priest who had provided
Du Pont with a catalyst to polymerize acetylene) taught. Despite not having
as much control as it perhaps would have liked, the committee believed
that the Du Pont Fellowship Program benefited the company's recruiting
efforts. As the secretary of the committee explained in 1931,

> The purpose of these fellowships is to promote the advancement of
> science and the scientific training of young men, and to form a broad
> and favorable contact between the DuPont Company and the high grade
> colleges of the country. The reaction of the colleges to this plan is one
> of appreciation and cooperation, and the goodwill thus established has
> been of value to the DuPont Company, not only from an advertising
> standpoint but also from the favorable consideration accorded it in the
> problem of recruiting outstanding college men during years of keen
> competition.[8]

When Du Pont offered its fellowships, colleges and universities soon began
asking the company "for suggestions for research." The Chemical Department reported in 1920 that it had suggested about forty research topics and
that many of these had been undertaken by the fellowship recipients. Reports
from these fellows had yielded "interesting and valuable data."[9] In 1927,
Charles Stine requested that industrial department research directors continue to submit to him suggestions for research projects for Du Pont fellows,
and he urged that they read and criticize the fellows' reports. He stressed
that "only by taking an active interest in the work of the...fellows, can
we hope to get something like a proper return from the expenditures of this
money by the Company."[10] Evidently, this reporting system grew up as a
custom on the part of the recipient institutions rather than as a requirement
by Du Pont. Du Pont clearly did not expect the fellows to carry out critical
research for the company. Rather, the company suggested topics as a means
of evaluating fellows for potential employment.

From 1918 until 1934, Du Pont annually granted graduate fellowships
to about twenty-five institutions. In 1934, the company added another wrinkle in its relations with academia when the Executive Committee approved
a grant of five $2,000 postdoctoral fellowships to young organic chemists
at Harvard, Cornell, Ohio State, and the University of Illinois. In addition,
the committee appropriated $2,000 (total) for expenditures on equipment
for its postdoctoral fellows.[11] As Bolton explained to his friend and fellow
chemist James B. Conant, the objective of these fellowships was "to make
a small contribution to raising the level of organic research in this country
and to increase the number of men who have had post-doctorate work in
organic chemistry so as to make them available either for teaching or for
industry."[12] By industry, Bolton presumably meant Du Pont. The fellowships were assigned to particular young professors, who were then allowed
to select "competent [postdoctoral] fellows" to work under their direction.

At Illinois, Du Pont chose Reynold C. Fuson to administer this postdoctoral fellowship[13] rather than selecting two other professors who served as consultants to the company, Carl S. Marvel and Roger Adams, chairman of the Chemistry Department. Du Pont's rationale is not clear, but it probably wanted to cover all its bases in organic chemistry at Illinois. It would be impossible to measure how effective Du Pont's strategy with Fuson was, but certainly its relations with Marvel and Adams helped the company achieve remarkable recruiting success. On the occasion of the twenty-fifth anniversary of Marvel's and Adams's first consultations with Du Pont in 1928, their Du Pont–employed students wrote and performed a skit that bears witness to this fact.[14] The skit opened with a U.S. attorney, I. Trust Buster, arguing before the "22.4th short circuit court of Hawaii" that Du Pont was guilty of enslaving the chemistry department at Illinois:

> The Justice Department will show how the Du Pont Company has dominated, subjugated, intimidated, prostituted, and just plain raised hell with the University of Illinois Chemistry Department. We shall introduce evidence that will demonstrate how this was achieved by a well integrated plan of scholarships, assistantships and consultantships.

In defense of the company, Du Pont's attorney, C. P. Ureeah, replied,

> While it is true that we have had many contacts with the University of Illinois and that many of their graduates find employment within the confines of my Company, all of the dealings have been on an equitable, freedom of choice basis. The individuals have always been free to decide whether to work for us or starve. And my Company is proud to say that not many chose to starve.

Of course, not all Du Pont's chemists came from Illinois, and Du Pont's "well integrated plan of scholarships, assistantships and consultantships" did not solve all its recruiting problems. Part of the problem stemmed from Du Pont's decentralized organizational structure, which left each department's research organization fending for itself. By 1927, the disadvantages of this approach had become apparent. Because each department and subsidiary did its own head-hunting, potential research employees were often recruited by several different Du Pont Company representatives. The directors of the chemical divisions of each department finally concluded that "this makes a very bad impression, in those cases where it occurs, both upon the prospective employee and the faculty of the school where it occurs." Addressing this problem, the chemical directors suggested that Du Pont's Service Department develop a form to be "kept on file, giving complete and detailed data regarding men available each year from the different universities and colleges." The directors thought that the Service Department could "call together a committee from the different laboratories to try to make some kind of an equitable division of these men among the different laboratories, on the basis of assigning the men to the places they would best fit into."[15]

Although sound in theory, such a procedure did not work in practice largely because several of Du Pont's departments, believing firmly in the principle of departmental autonomy, failed to follow it. Du Pont's recently formed Personnel Division assumed the role of a coordinating organization, but in late 1928 and again in 1930, the division complained to the chemical directors that prospective employees were still being recruited by several departments. This was not only confusing the recruits but also making colleges "resentful" of such a practice. Moreover, each department was free to offer a salary to its own liking, and therefore the Personnel Division found a "great lack of uniformity" in hiring practices. As F. S. Johnson, head of the division, told the chemical directors, "Such wide variations are hard to explain to a ... man seeking detailed information on the opportunities the Company has to offer in its various departments and subsidiaries."[16]

Compliance with the Personnel Division's procedures was by no means a simple matter because it was impossible, given the competitive nature of Du Pont's research units, to achieve equity in recruiting. There was definitely a pecking order among research units at Du Pont, and consequently intense competition near the top for the prime position. Because of this competition, the strongest research units were the worst recruiting offenders. Two, in fact, never fully complied with the procedures during this era because they sought to build the best research organization at whatever cost. These were the Organic Chemicals and Chemical departments.

Little evidence remains about how Orchem recruited its research force, but the Chemical Department developed recruitment to a fine art. In fact, under Arthur P. Tanberg's direction of the Experimental Station, the Chemical Department was the last holdout in not complying with Personnel's hiring procedures. Only after Tanberg retired in 1947 did the department go through Personnel for its chemists. The skit quoted above makes clear how those in the Chemical Department viewed this change and the other departmental research organizations. While Tanberg was on the witness stand, the government attorney said, "I understand that you did the [Chemical Department's] hiring and firing." To this, Tanberg replied, "Yes, actually we never outright fired anyone. We just transferred 'em to Rayon or Grasselli, which amounts to the same thing." "But you hired your men, not the Personnel Division?" queried the attorney. "That's right," replied Tanberg, "it worked out best that way. I'm sorry to see that Dr. Brubaker hasn't continued this process. He gave in to the downtown office, ... so now the Chemical Department has to compete (sigh) with the other departments."[17]

These words perfectly capture the Chemical Department's and Tanberg's approach to recruitment. From 1921, when he was named director of the Experimental Station, until 1947, Tanberg was the Chemical Department's recruiter. With Stine's promotion to chemical director in 1924, the department placed greater emphasis on securing the best possible chemists. Stine paid particular attention to this, and it was during his administration that he and Tanberg worked out a "well integrated plan" to recruit the best possible chemists for the department.[18]

Tanberg's approach was to bring the "old boy" network to new heights of perfection. In 1925, Tanberg outlined the basis of his network. He listed the institutions that present members of the Chemical Department had attended and the levels of contact they had maintained with these schools. He used this network to secure information on students at each of the major graduate schools. As Tanberg explained, "the matter of getting a reliable opinion about a prospect is very largely a personal matter, and not one which can be reduced to a formula."[19] Tanberg was a master at recruiting researchers for the Chemical Department. He brought into play whatever resources were necessary to raise the research personnel level of his department. As competition within the industry increased, Tanberg's methods grew smoother, including preparation of slick brochures and summer employment of graduate students.

For certain industrial departments, such as Organic Chemicals, research positions provided a means for Du Pont to recruit PhD chemists whom it intended to shuttle out of research and into plant management, sales, and higher administration. Recruiting researchers, therefore, was one means of recruiting future executives. The research laboratory became a kind of half-way house between academic chemistry and the industrial world. The Jackson Laboratory was well-known for its high rate of moving young PhD chemists out of research – a fact that Bolton, like Hamilton Barksdale twenty-five years earlier, accepted as ultimately healthy for the department but not for the laboratory.[20]

The Chemical Department's hiring practices during the Tanberg era were flawed in one important respect: A strong strain of anti-Semitism and sexism prevailed in the department. Upon leaving the Chemical Department in 1929 to become director of the Société française du Lysol, Victor Cofman wrote a memorandum to Stine, Bradshaw, and Tanberg arguing that the Curies, Steinmetz, and Einstein would have been unwelcome at the Experimental Station because the Chemical Department excluded "whole groups." He thought that the department relied on " 'Blanket' rules which ... exclude exceptional individuals because of sex, or political or religious views."[21]

There is little evidence regarding sexism in the Chemical Department and throughout Du Pont's research program in the interwar period. Historian Daniel Kevles has maintained that women scientists were largely excluded from employment in American academia, except in women's colleges. The same appears to have been true in industry. There were a few exceptions in Du Pont, however. Hale Charch hired a number of women researchers for his Pioneering Research Laboratory in the Rayon Department. But the Chemical Department was almost exclusively a man's world – a white, Anglo-Saxon, Protestant man's world.

Although Kevles has argued that the "industrial laboratory was darkened by the anti-Semitism of the large corporations,"[22] anti-Semitism was not a policy of the Du Pont Company. In fact, other departments in the company employed large numbers of Jewish chemists. Orchem's Jackson Laboratory, especially after the acquisition of the Newport Chemical Company, had a significant number of Jewish researchers on its staff. Du Pont's Executive Committee had actually urged the Chemical Department to recruit "one or two highly competent and experienced [Jewish chemists] for specialized work" when Hitler began forcing Jews to resign their positions in German universities.[23] But the Chemical Department, probably because of the views of a few leaders in the department, did not attempt to recruit the German Jewish chemists. Rather than blithely ignore the committee, the Chemical Department urged that the company help the German chemists obtain academic appointments in the United States and then hire them as consultants.[24] This is precisely what the company did in the case of Herman Mark.

A major contributor to polymer chemistry, Mark had been a research chemist first for the I. G. Farben–supported Fiber Research Institute in Berlin-Dahlem and then, between 1927 and 1932, at the IG laboratories in Ludwigshafen. The political situation in Germany led Mark's research manager, who knew he was half Jewish, to suggest that Mark should seek an academic post outside Germany. No doubt with IG's help, Mark landed a job at the University of Vienna, where he concentrated his IG-supported research on polymerization reaction mechanisms. The German occupation of Austria in early 1938 forced Mark to leave Vienna; he accepted an offer from the Canadian International Paper Company to modernize its cellulose research lab. For two years Mark worked in Canada, and because Du Pont was a large consumer of the Canadian firm's cellulose, Mark and many of Du Pont's chemists came into direct contact with each other. Finally, in 1940 Du Pont offered Mark a job, not in its own laboratories but as an adjunct professor at Brooklyn Polytechnic Institute and as a Du Pont consultant. Supported by Du Pont's consulting payments for as many as fifteen days a month, Mark carved out a niche at Brooklyn.[25] By 1946, he had become a genuine academic entrepreneur and had founded the Institute of Polymer Research, at which a host of polymer chemists were trained (many of whom entered Du Pont's employ).[26] Du Pont probably could have hired Mark as early as 1933, when the Chemical Department was advised that he would be an excellent organic chemist to recruit for its fundamental research program. But the department's anti-Semitic bias militated against this.

In 1941, the new research director of the Rayon Department, Ernest B. Benger, asked his assistant directors how Du Pont's consulting arrangement with Mark (executed by the Rayon Department in 1940) was working out. W. W. Heckert's response was indicative of how many research managers felt: "Mark has greatly facilitated our men in acquiring a polymer background. I believe we can keep up with [the] literature (which will become more voluminous) most cheaply thru Mark. This can go on indefinitely. I feel that something of importance is certain to result from Mark's contacts."[27] Heckert's colleagues argued that Mark was providing the necessary and hitherto missing "link" between the various sections of Rayon's technical division.[28] Hence, as a consultant, Mark was perhaps more valuable to the Rayon Department than if he were in its own research organization or the Chemical Department. Once Mark got his program established at Brooklyn Polytechnic Institute, his value to Du Pont grew because of the company's increased recruiting power. These were some of the real benefits that Charles Stine envisioned when he formalized the Chemical Department's consultants program in the 1920s.

Consultants

Du Pont employed consultants almost as soon as the Experimental Station was established. But it did not formalize its consultants program to any extent until 1927, when Charles Stine succeeded in convincing Du Pont's industrial department research directors that the Chemical Department should serve as the central coordinating agency for the company's consultants. At this time the company retained only eight consultants. These consultants were generally from nearby institutions, and they usually visited Du Pont's laboratories every week or two. Under Stine's plan, departments and subsidiaries were free to use consultants whenever they wished, but because the Chemical Department paid the consultants, the departments and subsidiaries using them for "any appreciable amount of time" were billed for their services by the Chemical Department.[29]

Stine sought not only control but also expansion. To enlarge and improve Du Pont's roster, Stine invited Roger Adams to become a consultant. He envisioned that Adams would visit the Experimental Station once a month and then spend a month or so in Wilmington during summers. To entice him to make the long journey from Urbana to Wilmington, Stine offered Adams an annual salary of $5,000, well over half of his university salary. Stine also asked Adams to relinquish his consultantship with Abbott Laboratories and work with Du Pont on an exclusive basis.[30] Adams turned down Stine's offer but as requested made a counterproposal, which Stine accepted. He convinced Stine to allow him and Carl S. Marvel to alternate visits to Wilmington, so that Du Pont would see one or the other of them at least monthly. He also insisted that he be allowed to continue as a consultant to Abbott and other companies as well. For compensation, Adams accepted an annual salary of $3,000 plus travel expenses. On top of this, Adams accepted a salary of $750 for each summer month he worked at the Station.[31]

Although Stine recognized that Adams and Marvel would increase his department's recruiting power, he desired far more from these consultants.[32] According to Marvel, Stine initially expected the two academics to submit a monthly report "telling them about new things we saw in the literature that we felt they might be interested in." But this practice soon fell by the wayside; Adams and Marvel were more useful simply talking to Du Pont's research managers and research chemists. Adams and Marvel not only dispensed information on recent work but, probably far more important, served as counselors to both managers and researchers.[33] When one of them was due to be in Wilmington, the Chemical Department posted a schedule and allowed researchers to sign up to talk privately with the consultant. (This signing-up procedure was also designed to allow research managers to gauge the effectiveness of their consultants; if few or no research chemists wanted to meet with a consultant, managers knew that the consultant had not proven helpful to their staff.[34]) Often researchers not only reviewed their work and problems connected to it for the consultants but also bared their troubles with the way research was being managed in the laboratory. In the case of Adams at least, his close friendship with Bolton and his having served as a dissertation advisor to many of Du Pont's chemists greatly increased his worth as a counselor. As Theodore Cairns remembered, "if a research chemist brought up a problem, you knew that Bolton heard about it that night at dinner. That was the link with top management.... [There] were a lot of changes that I'm sure [could be] traced directly to Adams."[35] He – and Marvel – helped to shape Du Pont's research policies.

No doubt Adams gave Du Pont a great deal of assistance. Yet he, too, benefited from the arrangement far more than drawing a good extra salary and keeping Du Pont fellowship money flowing to the University of Illinois. As Adams explained to his friend James B. Conant (who in 1929 had been invited to consult with the Chemical Department), "I feel that I get quite as much out of the contact from the chemical standpoint as they do." Adams actively consulted with Du Pont until the 1950s, when he greatly curtailed his consulting schedule. Marvel was still regularly consulting with Du Pont in 1980 in spite of being almost ninety. Out of Marvel's 176 PhD's, forty-six joined Du Pont's research ranks.[36]

Adams and Marvel were two of Du Pont's most effective consultants. Both maintained a genuine intellectual interest in industrial chemistry while remaining within the academy. In the case of Marvel, his relationship with Du Pont actually shaped the direction of his research and led him into the study of polymer chemistry. Wallace H. Carothers opened Marvel's eyes to polymers after Carothers joined Stine's fundamental research program. As Marvel said in 1983, "I learned most of my polymer chemistry here [at Du Pont] from Carothers."[37] A later Du Pont consultant and Nobel Prize winner, Paul J. Flory, said something similar. As noted in Chapter 12, Flory was a member of Carothers's group and got his start in polymer chemistry from Carothers even though Carothers's mental health was rapidly deteriorating. Flory left Du Pont following Carothers's death in 1937, but after he joined Cornell University's faculty in 1948, he began a consulting arrangement with Du Pont that lasted until his death in 1985.[38]

Some Du Pont consultants, including Conant, took a dim and often condescending view of industrial research. Although Elmer Bolton was an old friend of his, Conant was suspicious of Du Pont and industrial research; he saw such research as a cut or two below academic science. When Du Pont established its fundamental research program, Bolton asked Conant to recommend chemists to fill the position of group leader in organic chemistry. Conant replied by recommending his student Louis Fieser, who was teaching at Bryn Mawr, as "the best bet among the younger organic chemists." Acknowledging that he would "hate to see [Fieser] leave the academic" world, Conant suggested "a much less able man" who "would accomplish more in an industrial position than . . . in academic work" because he was "an excellent experimentalist."[39] Only after Du Pont successfully recruited his own department member, Wallace Carothers, was Conant willing to consider a consultant's position. Conant found, as he admitted to Fieser, that "the crowd at duPont's were the first people I met who seemed to have read my papers intelligently."[40] Still, Conant remained a Du Pont consultant for only a year or two. His view of research in a corporation such as Du Pont was reflected in the words of his student Fieser: "The industrialists [i.e., research chemists at DuPont] are really a keen lot, though I don't think that they compare with us academics. . . . They impress me particularly as lacking in the fine critical judgement of the best teachers, and I wonder whether this is the cause or effect of their industrial relations."[41]

Conant had fretted a good deal over the Du Pont employee agreement form that he was asked to sign, which granted to Du Pont exclusive rights to inventions and proprietary knowledge that Conant might generate as a Du Pont consultant. He wrote his friend Adams about whether he should sign the form because he sensed that he was signing away his soul to the devil.[42] Adams had no such concerns. He advised Conant not to worry about the literal wording of the contract; Du Pont used such an agreement only "to protect themselves." Adams emphasized that "the DuPonts have bent over backwards to be square with their employees," and the company would be fair with Conant.[43] Nonetheless, the Harvard professor seems also to have troubled over Bolton's request that he consult exclusively with Du Pont. Except in rare instances, such as with Adams and with Arthur C. Cope of the Massachusetts Institute of Technology, Du Pont required an exclusive retainer during this period. Bolton had insisted on exclusive consulting because he correctly foresaw that Du Pont's competitors would soon rely as heavily on consultants as Du Pont. But by the early 1950s, Du Pont had to abandon its requirement of exclusivity because it could not retain the best scientists under such conditions.

For all its benefits of increased recruiting power, access to the best academic science, and counseling of both researcher and research manager, Du Pont's consultants program also entailed certain risks and liabilities. Consultants could serve as a catalyst within one's research organization; they could do the same in a competitor's laboratory. Information picked up at Du Pont might precipitate a major development in another company. Though Du Pont tried very hard to avoid such occurrences, they happened nonetheless. A reading of Frank M. McMillan's account of the invention and development of polypropylene and the actions of Herman Mark and Paul Flory suggest the nature of the problem for both Du Pont and its consultants.[44] This is not to suggest that Mark or Flory acted with any impropriety. Rather, it points up the difficulty that consultants faced in "compartmentalizing" information. Mark in particular could take a tiny glimmer of an idea and run with it wherever he was. As one Du Pont research director noted, Mark had an uncanny gift of "foreknowledge" – an ability to anticipate where an idea would lead and to put it into a larger framework.[45] For this reason, the Chemical Department, even though it was vitally interested in polymer chemistry, did not actively use Mark as a consultant. Mark consulted for the Rayon Department and a few other industrial departments – research units with narrower research needs and shorter time horizons than the Chemical Department.

No research director at Du Pont ever argued that the costs and risks of the consultants program outweighed the benefits. The critical factor was knowing what a particular research organization wanted from its consultants. Sometimes, as with Adams and Marvel, the company had very broad objectives; in other instances, it chose consultants to help solve well-defined problems or for their expertise in a narrow field of research. Whatever the objective, no one ever questioned that Du Pont furthered its own research objectives by retaining a group of outstanding university professors as consultants.[46]

Managing Researchers

Du Pont's research managers adhered to the concept of corporate culture. That is, they believed there was a "right" (i.e., Du Pont) way to conduct research. Accordingly, they followed a policy of building the company's research force from university graduate programs. The supple minds of fresh graduates provided managers with the best clay to mold Du Pont research.[47] Indeed, because they wanted to ensure that research was done the Du Pont way, the company's research managers had explicitly adopted a policy forbidding the recruitment or hiring of researchers from Du Pont's competitors, a policy "quite rigidly and generally adhered to." They had done so because they believed they had "more to lose in the near future from such a practice than to gain."[48] By about 1930, Du Pont, at least in its major research organizations, had developed a set of precepts that governed its management of research.

When a scientist or engineer joined Du Pont, one item was non-negotiable: The employee had to sign an agreement acknowledging that "inventions, improvements, or useful processes" made by the employee while working for Du Pont were the "sole and exclusive property" of the company. This agreement also stipulated that the employee would, as requested by Du Pont, "sign and verify all applications, papers, and specifications necessary to apply for and perfect patent letters of the United States and other countries" for their inventions or improvements.[49] Du Pont's researchers also agreed not to disclose or divulge confidential information or trade secrets.[50] This last requirement had very important policy implications for publication. Du Pont did not have an explicit publication policy during this era. If there had been a policy, it would have simply stated that Du Pont did not wish to disclose any proprietary information through the scientific and technical publications of its research staff.[51] The real question was what constituted proprietary information, and this boiled down to the subjective judgment of the individual research director.

As we have seen, when Stine sought to create and then staff his fundamental research program, he envisioned that the success of this program would hinge on a liberal publication policy. Publication would give Du Pont's research prestige, improve the morale of its research staff, make recruiting first-class scientists easier, and serve as a bargaining tool for acquiring research information from other institutions. Stine and Tanberg actively recruited scientists for the program by holding out the carrot that "the work of these [fundamental researchers] shall be published almost without restriction" and that these publications were expected to be "on a par with . . . university work."[52] Before Stine's promotion to director of the Chemical Department, Du Pont had been very conservative in allowing its researchers to publish their work.

In many respects, the publication plank in Stine's fundamental research platform was an attempt to counter what was perhaps a widespread view that Du Pont would not allow the publication of its research findings.[53] His strategy largely succeeded. With some notable exceptions, members of the Chemical Department's fundamental research program were allowed to publish their work. Some researchers, most notably Wallace Carothers, Elmer O. Kraemer, and Allan P. Colburn, were prolific, particularly during the "academic era" of the fundamental research program. Stine's vision of Du Pont research culminated in 1937 in the publication of the first volume of *Contributions to the Scientific Literature from the Experimental Station of the Chemical Department of E. I. du Pont de Nemours & Company*, which contained reprints of more than 150 articles written by Chemical Department researchers between 1924 and 1935. Most of these papers, A. P. Tanberg noted in his introduction to the volume, "describe research which was part of our program of fundamental research." Tanberg stressed that these publications had unquestionably helped Du Pont achieve the objectives Stine had set for his program.[54] Even within the fundamental research program, however, Du Pont had sometimes barred or delayed publications. As noted in Chapter 12, Ernest Benger had forced Carothers to delay publication of his synthetic fiber research findings, and all ultracentrifuge work on pigments was barred from publication for a period of years. Benger believed that publication should be permitted only in those instances in which publication posed no threat to the company's proprietary position.

In the late 1930s, the Chemical Department's liberal, though unwritten, publication policy on fundamental research experienced a major reversal, largely in response to the damage done to Du Pont's proprietary position on nylon by one of Carothers's early papers. Carothers had published in 1931 a paper in which he stated categorically that caprolactam could not be polymerized either with or without a catalyst.[55] In the spring of 1937, while negotiating on another matter, Du Pont (believing its patent position impregnable) informed I. G. Farben that it had succeeded with a major development of a polyamide fiber – what would soon be named nylon 66.[56] Once informed about nylon, I. G. Farben's researchers went over every inch of Du Pont research looking for a place to drive a wedge in the U.S. company's patent position. They shrewdly found Carothers's statement on caprolactam and by January 1938 had succeeded in polymerizing it into nylon 6.[57] To Du Pont's research managers, who thought they had built a perfect patent position, IG's nylon 6 was a low blow. A witch-hunt must have followed; the Chemical Department's liberal publication policy was quickly identified as the culprit. For a period of years after 1938, managers in the Chemical Department severely restricted publication of research results. (See Table 15.3 for data on the Chemical Department's publications, 1924–80.) This policy did not change until some of the department's brightest young researchers, greatly upset by not being able to publish their work, bent Roger Adams's ear and Adams in turn convinced Bolton that his policy was ultimately destructive of what had been achieved by the Chemical Department since 1927.[58]

Even after Adams prevailed upon Bolton to rescind his restrictions, the company implemented a rigid internal review process before a paper could be published. Hence it took longer for research findings to make their way into print, which ran counter to the urgent need for timeliness in the scientific world.[59]

In the industrial departments, researchers could expect a far tighter, though still unwritten, publication policy. Because research work in the industrial departments was usually of a much shorter range and hence more likely to have an immediate effect on the commercial position of the department, publication was more problematic and more apt to be prohibited. Each department maintained veto power over publication of work done by another department if a paper were perceived as relating to that department's business. Therefore, departments with more liberal publication policies were often stymied by more conservative departments. When papers were published out of these latter departments, they usually took the form of promotional or news pieces rather than research findings. In any case, nowhere in the decentralized Du Pont Company could a new researcher go and expect

Table 15.3. *Publications Appearing in* Contributions to the Scientific Literature from the Experimental Station of the Chemical Department of E. I. du Pont de Nemours & Co.

	1924–28	1929–33	1934–38	1939–43	1944–48	1949–53	1954–58	1959–63	1964–68	1969–73	1974–78
Number of papers published	7	114	42	13	42	82	134	314	425	543	496
Papers per researcher[a]	0.12	1.2	0.44	0.12	0.29	0.53	0.86	1.8	2.1	2.7	2.5

[a]Five-year averaged figures for numbers of researchers.

to find a clear and consistent written policy regarding publication. Nor could he find a similar statement regarding how research would be assigned to him and how free he was to conduct his own work.

Nevertheless, there was — at least in the strongest Du Pont research organizations — something of a consensus among research managers about how a new researcher should be handled and in what structure research work should be done. A new research employee could generally count on being assigned to a group — the basic unit of research in most departments, including the Chemical Department. Each group was headed by a group leader, who in turn reported to a research supervisor. Although practice varied from department to department and group leader to group leader, a new chemist was usually given a series of specific pieces of research, each designed to last a month or less so the group leader and superior managers could size up the capabilities of the new employee. As Ernest B. Benger noted, "the young man must be carefully supervised by an older man for a number of months. . . . He must not only be trained in the elements of the processes with which he is concerned, but he must be imbued with the spirit of the organization . . . and by slow steps brought to the point where he can accept some responsibility for himself."[60] The new researcher also learned that almost all investigations at Du Pont were done on a project basis, with specific objectives in mind. As noted, during the "academic era" of the fundamental research program, this was not the case. But after 1932 or 1933, the project system became the norm even for this program.[61]

How closely a researcher was supervised after being "checked out" varied widely within the company. Among the departmental research directors, opinion varied from the extreme of "close" supervision to one of "general" supervision. Research directors agreed, however, "that, in so far as possible, the policy of making a man responsible for his work should be followed, because this develops initiative, decision, and executive ability." The critics of close supervision were quite vocal in arguing that with first-class researchers, close supervision hampered "originality, initiative, and ingenuity."[62] As with other areas, the proper management of R&D calls for a delicate balance of control and detachment.

Although most research at Du Pont was done on a project basis during this era, several of Du Pont's research organizations allowed "bootleg" research to be done on a limited scale. Bootleg research was individual research done by researchers but not part of a project. This practice varied from department to department; in 1935, research directors in three departments acknowledged that they allowed "a certain degree of freedom among research personnel to develop new ideas without being too cramped by the rigidity of the project system." One organization permitted its chemists "to spend not over $100 in any one month, nor more than 10% of his forecasted appropriation" on bootleg research. The other two departments handled their bootlegging differently, but it still hovered around the 10 percent mark.[63] Even within a given department, policies on bootlegging varied widely. In Rayon, Hale Charch wanted his best Pioneering researchers following their own ideas at least 25 percent of the time; Lester Sinness of the viscose rayon research section did not believe in bootlegging. At the very least, freedom to bootleg kept researchers happy. In many cases, it actually led to major developments.

As was the case throughout the Du Pont Company, research directors were vitally interested in keeping their research staff happy. From the moment research directors began to recruit researchers, they kept incentives to perform and advance conspicuously in front of their staff. These incentives ranged from salary increases to bonuses to advancement up the research ranks and beyond. In the decentralized company, research managers were free to determine starting and subsequent salaries of their staff. Salaries varied widely from department to department, as did practices for salary advancement. In part, the market set limits on how widely such practices could vary, but nevertheless, Du Pont's research directors recruited new PhD chemists with offers that differed as much as 20 percent. Starting salaries at Du Pont were, on average, substantially above those offered by colleges and universities and competitive with or above those of other chemical companies.[64]

Bonuses also provided incentives. As early as 1908, the Executive Committee had given bonuses of Du Pont stock to researchers for outstanding contributions to the company. In 1911, the Executive Committee adopted a two-class bonus system that has prevailed (in periodically modified form) to the present. The "A" Bonus Award called for a gift of stock "for inventive or other conspicuous service," whereas the "B" Bonus Award, also a gift of stock, was "in the nature of profit sharing with employees who contributed most to the company's success."[65] As these criteria have been applied and modified over the years, the "A" bonus generally became, with some important exceptions, an award for "heroic" work and the "B" bonus an award for outstanding service to the company. In the period 1921–41, important "A" bonuses included those for Duco automotive finish (to E. C. Pitman, F. M. Flaherty, and J. D. Shiels), moistureproof cellophane (Hale Charch), neoprene (Wallace Carothers and others), and nylon (Carothers and numerous others), with values for individuals ranging from $10,000 to $220,000. The Executive Committee awarded numerous other, though smaller, "A" bonuses to research personnel. Literally hundreds of researchers received "B" bonuses ranging from a few shares to as many as twenty-five or thirty. Some researchers consistently received "B" bonuses.[66]

Since its inception, the "A" bonus system has been the focus of numerous debates. When the Executive Committee established the system, it sought to arrive at a procedure for making awards that was the least subjective possible. Strict criteria were laid out to identify candidates, and complex formulas were developed to calculate the size of awards. Yet because the system depended on the judgments of people from the group leader to research director and on up to the "A" bonus committee, the system was subjective and therefore subject to human error and criticism. From the vantage point of the researcher at the bench, the "A" bonus award has often been viewed satirically as "a very complicated system to award a pittance to the wrong person," yet it has nonetheless served as an important incentive for researchers.[67] A. P. Tanberg explicitly included a discussion of the bonus system in his brochures about the Experimental Station used by the Chemical Department to recruit topflight research chemists.[68]

Advancement up the research ranks also provided incentive. For research chemists, the next and perhaps most critical step up the ladder was to group leader (some departments, such as Orchem, called it division leader). Elmer Bolton regarded the group leader as "one of the key men" in research and stressed that he should be well compensated. Bolton explicitly drew a parallel between the group leader and the major chemistry professor in the university. Both the group leader and the professor excelled when they had five to eight research chemists working under them. As Bolton argued from personal experience, "When Emil Fischer was most productive, he had only eight to ten chemists working at any one time. When Willstätter was carrying out his work on chlorophyll and plant pigments, he complained because he had thirteen chemists, although he was devoting his time exclusively to research work and was not burdened by any outside duties." The group leader was critical, Bolton maintained, because "to him is entrusted the training of the new material and upon him rests the responsibility for the research ability of his men"; he was the key to research efficiency. Bolton sought to keep group leaders in their position as long as possible by keeping them happy.[69] A staff member who excelled here could also move further up the research ranks to become a research supervisor, an assistant or associate laboratory director, and thence to director. From here, he could become an assistant director of a departmental research division and then its director. Of course, the names and numbers of rungs up the research management ladder varied from department to department.

Bolton and his peers recognized, just at Reese and Arthur Comey had much earlier, that the company's manufacturing and sales divisions offered much greater economic incentives than were typically available in research. They often witnessed their best researchers leaving the laboratory in pursuit of these incentives. As Ernest Benger noted, there is "a strong feeling on the part of the research men that they must eventually get out of research into production or sales." He acknowledged that some researchers would make excellent executives in these other areas, but he also suggested that "innumerable good research chemists have been made into mediocre executives." Benger pleaded for changes in the reward system for research personnel, one which would "make it possible for research men to spend all their lives in research without a feeling that they are missing the rewards which come from advancement in title and position."[70]

Despite concern by Benger, Bolton, and others, this remained an unsolved problem at Du Pont. Only in 1946 with the creation of Du Pont's first research associates program in the Rayon Department (under the research direction of Benger, incidentally) was it even partially addressed. (This plan is discussed in Chapter 17.)

The sword of researchers' movement into sales or manufacturing was double-edged, however. It could just as easily be used by managers to weed out weak research chemists. Benger recognized this fact as well as anyone. He argued that misfits should be moved out of research: "No matter how carefully men are selected for research, a research organization generally consists of some men who are better qualified for manufacturing or sales positions."[71] The research director, Benger maintained, should not hesitate to encourage such men to move out of research as soon as possible by dumping them into sales or manufacturing rather than firing them.

Along with incentives offered explicitly and implicitly, research managers also made demands, both explicitly and implicitly. A. P. Tanberg succinctly stated the duties expected of a "first-class" research chemist in the Chemical Department: (1) "prosecution of work on a particular subject with a specific goal"; (2) "keep[ing] up-to-date on the published information touching on his problem"; (3) "keep[ing] the directors informed as to the progress of his work, not only through the medium of our report system, but also more frequently through verbal discussion."[72] Other departments made basically the same demands on their researchers as the Chemical Department, although in the decentralized company, details varied from department to department.

In the area of actual reporting, procedures differed greatly among departments. Moreover, from the decentralization of 1921 until the 1950s, the company maintained no central index or access system to all the company's research reports. Some departmental research divisions wrote few reports while others barred their circulation to other industrial departments. L. G. Wise, head of the Chemical Department's intelligence division, sought unsuccessfully in the mid-1930s to create a central indexing and filing system at Du Pont. He pointed out that it was difficult if not impossible to be sure that all research information generated in the company could be recovered, and he stressed that "if research is worth doing, the results should be worth keeping." In 1935, Wise argued, research was more or less "being thrown away" because of the way reports were being handled. He cautioned that "as time goes on and more and more data are collected, the difficulty in making such data available and useful will be greater and greater. The difficulty in correlating and codifying such a mass of information will also be greater and greater and after a time may become impossible."[73] Though a great advocate of research efficiency through complete literature searches, Bolton failed to push Wise's proposal successfully through. Chemical Department researchers and research managers who were active in the 1930s and 1940s have argued that industrial department autonomy precluded the creation of any report indexing system. Industrial department research divisions often did not want their counterparts in other departments to know what research they were doing.[74]

Other practices and policies varied greatly from one departmental research division to another. These included patent applications, sponsorship of seminars for researchers, travel to professional society meetings, and presentation of papers at those meetings. Like publication matters, presentations were always problematic, and one department could often veto a presentation to be given by another department's chemist. When Bolton clamped down on publication at the Station in the late 1930s and early 1940s, he also scotched presentation of papers because this too constituted disclosure. For example, in 1941 Herman Mark tried to line up a session of papers on condensation polymerization for the prestigious Gibson Island Conference for 1942. Because he was a consultant for the Rayon Department, which at this time was in charge of nylon research, Mark solicited papers from chemists in the nylon research division. But Bolton exercised his veto and prohibited presentations "because of the great activity along this line by the Chemical Department and the potential importance of their work to the company."[75]

The actual management of research across the decentralized company also differed among Du Pont's research divisions. Under Bolton's leadership, the Chemical Department developed probably the most complex system of management, embodied in what was called the Steering Committee. Chaired by Bolton, the Steering Committee initially included Bolton's associate and assistant managers, the director of the Experimental Station, the assistant director of the Experimental Station, and his assistant. Soon the Steering Committee would include the research supervisors. The committee initially met weekly, and attendance was all but mandatory; members who needed to travel were expected to organize their itinerary around the committee's meetings. One important function of the group was the research review, a practice of hearing researchers and group leaders present their work. Typically, a bench chemist appeared before the Steering Committee at least yearly and more often than not twice yearly. The work of the committee grew so much that in 1935 the committee began devoting an extra half-day a week to conducting research reviews.[76]

In the early days of the Steering Committee, the research review process was almost a meeting of peers talking over common problems, engaging in constructive debate, and arriving at a consensus about the best course of future action – whether to initiate, continue, modify, or drop a project. But as the decade of the 1930s proceeded, the Steering Committee's review process grew more formal even though that was not the conscious desire of Bolton. More and more, group leaders and their members played to the committee and told them what they thought the committee wanted to hear. Chemists were coached on their presentations. For instance, chemists fresh out of graduate school in the late 1930s, whose heads were full of the concept of "free radicals," were told not to mention the term in front of Bolton, who had learned his organic chemistry from an earlier generation of professors. The research review became something of an ordeal for many chemists, and some actually became physically ill when they went before the committee.[77]

Those members who sat on the Steering Committee during Bolton's long tenure as chemical director maintained that the committee was a democratic organization and that Bolton never overtly overrode the committee's decisions. Some of those men acknowledged, however, that Bolton's vote seemed to be larger than those of other members. Moreover, Bolton often controlled the tenor of the meetings. During many a research review, Bolton said, "This is very interesting chemistry, but somehow I don't hear the tinkle of the cash register," or "tell me again just what it is you're going to put into the barrel."[78] Without question, the Steering Committee did precisely what it was called; it steered the Chemical Department's research. No project could be initiated or long continued without approval by the Steering Committee. During Bolton's tenure the committee worked smoothly, and members generally came to know what positions their colleagues would take on a given issue.

To guide research across the company as a whole, Du Pont possessed nothing comparable to the Chemical Department's Steering Committee. With decentralization in 1921 and the subsequent growth of research divisions in each of the industrial departments, the coordination of research became a major issue, particularly as developments in chemistry led to the blurring — and in some cases, overlapping — of lines of research pursued in the departments. Du Pont struggled with this problem throughout the period and was successful in solving it only for a brief period in the 1930s. Part of the problem was inherent in the decentralized structure of the company, but after 1940 the rapid development of polymer chemistry also contributed to the situation.

Coordinating Research

The rebuilding of the Chemical Department under Stine's direction and Stine's subsequent election to the Executive Committee greatly facilitated the coordination of research among the industrial departments. By 1930, the Chemical Department had assumed "the responsibility of acting as a coordinating department so that overlapping of the research programs of the different manufacturing departments may be avoided as completely as possible."[79] Because Stine was a strong partisan of the Chemical Department, he reinforced this role for the department during his tenure on the Executive Committee and encouraged Bolton to assume greater responsibility for the coordination of research across the whole company. Records make clear that as chemical director, Bolton sought to be knowledgeable about and to coordinate as much as possible research being done in other departments.[80] Paradoxically, the chemical director could often be more effective in coordinating research than the Executive Committee advisor for research. The chemical director called and chaired the meetings of the departmental research directors – the chemical directors' meetings, as they were known – and he managed much research supported by the industrial departments. In contrast, the Executive Committee advisor on research was just that – an advisor who had to honor the autonomy of the departmental general manager. The research director in an industrial department worked for his general manager, not for the Executive Committee research advisor.

As chemical director, Stine had used meetings of the research directors to promote the coordination of research (by his own department).[81] He was also aided by president Lammot du Pont, who in 1929 asked the Executive Committee's research advisor, H. Fletcher Brown, to improve an "unfortunate" situation in which "the departments and subsidiary companies do not seek co-operation with the central Chemical Department."[82] Stine's and Brown's efforts yielded little real success until 1930, when several factors combined to make coordination of research across the Du Pont Company possible.

In addition to the almost sacred concept of industrial department autonomy, perhaps the greatest stumbling block to the proper coordination of research at Du Pont was the complete lack of standardization in research accounting within the company. This problem was not addressed until 1930, nine years after the decentralization of research and development at Du Pont. At a meeting of general managers in January, F. A. Wardenberg of the Du Pont Ammonia Corporation (soon to be turned into a department) asked his colleagues to discuss how they determined how much to spend on research. The great variety of responses from the general managers must have been appalling to some of those in attendance at the meeting – especially Stine.[83]

The general managers of the industrial departments shared their practices and thinking about research expenditures at their meeting. John W. McCoy of Explosives, who had been one of the pioneer chemists at the Eastern Laboratory, said his department did not even budget specifically for research but rather spent what it needed to from year to year. When asked how much he spent on average, McCoy replied his department's research expenditures "figured approximately 00.8%" of sales. Both E. G. Robinson of Dyestuffs and Wardenberg of Ammonia replied that their research units could spend almost endless sums of money on research but had to be constrained by a budget fixed at 3 percent of sales in Dyestuffs and 5 percent in Ammonia. Leonard Yerkes of Rayon and Cellophane figured research not as a percentage of gross sales but rather on a cost per pound of product sold. Viscoloid spent about 1.1 percent of its sales on research and chemical control; Fabrics and Finishes estimated its research and development at 2 percent of sales. As discussion continued, Stine pointed out that there was no clear understanding or agreement about "whether research expenditures meant pure research work on new products or the modification and development of present products." He urged that the company arrive at a clearer definition of control, process, development, and research work. The general managers agreed that this would be desirable and consented to let the Treasurer's Department develop a classification of expenditures, which would allow "a comparison to be made between departments, disregarding methods of accounting."[84]

The treasurer's office soon developed a proposal to classify research expenditures in three categories: (a) chemical control, (b) improvements in existing processes and products, and (c) new developments (including new processes and products). By dividing research expenditures in this way, the treasurer's office would be able to show how departments spent research monies as percentages of sales, earnings, and total capital investment. Such analysis would improve the company's ability to evaluate the performance of research work in the departments and across the company.[85] The general managers reviewed the treasurer's office proposal, and Stine obviously made some changes that both the general managers and the treasurer's office accepted. He divided the (c)-classification into two new categories: (c) "development of additions to established lines of product" (i.e., research work for developing new products or new processes within an existing line of business) and (d) development of new products or processes in entirely new fields. Stine also added an important fifth category – (e) fundamental research.

After his election to the Executive Committee in mid-1930, Stine also succeeded in modifying the report such that it recommended that research in categories (c), (d), and (e) be budgeted annually and that industrial department research budgets be reviewed by the Executive Committee. Moreover, in instances in which a department was to undertake a research project costing in excess of $5,000, the report called for specific approval by the Executive Committee. The Executive Committee received the final version of the treasurer's office report in late September 1930 and considered it in early October. The committee was reticent to adopt the report's recommendations without first reviewing the matter with some of the key departments. Eventually, on November 19, 1930, the committee adopted the report as policy after making several amendments to it. One of the important amendments was restricting the requirement for the Executive Committee's authorization for projects in excess of $5,000 only to categories (c), (d), and (e). Thus departments were free to spend as much as they wished on research projects for the control and improvement of existing products and processes without explicit committee approval.[86]

The events that led to the adoption of the treasurer's report brought significant improvement in the coordination of research at Du Pont. Specifically, it led Stine to call a meeting of the general managers on the day before the Executive Committee adopted the final report to discuss "research coordination." The general managers unanimously agreed to submit to Chemical Director Bolton a list of research projects – in categories (c), (d), and (e) – to be undertaken in 1931 and subsequent years by each of the departmental research organizations, complete with a short description of each project. Bolton's Chemical Department was to compile and distribute this list, known as the topical index of research subjects. This list was to be updated monthly. In their discussion, the general managers expressed their belief that the topical list was an "important step toward closer coordination" of Du Pont research, but Stine argued that it was "only the preliminary step" in the process. Subtly, Stine brought many of the general managers around to his point of view: "that on account of the Central Chemical Department's greater familiarity with the general program of work of the departments and subsidiaries, the Central Chemical Department be instructed to direct attention to certain lines of research work in which different departments may be interested."[87] Hence Bolton was given a license to be more aggressive in coordinating research within the entire Du Pont Company, and he definitely assumed this role during the 1930s.

Both Stine and Bolton continued to use the semiannual chemical directors' meetings to improve the coordination of research and to raise the standards of research throughout the company. These one- and sometimes two-day meetings usually featured presentations by various departmental research directors and division managers on the research work being done in their departments, as well as addresses by executives and administrators from downtown. More than once Vice President Stine delivered talks urging a more widespread adoption of his philosophy of research and the use of more critical judgment in the selection of research problems.[88]

Throughout this period – and, indeed, throughout Du Pont's entire history of formal R&D programs – problems of coordinating research were compounded by the different geographical locations of research facilities. The Chemical Department carried out projects for the industrial departments, but it had to deal with Rayon's research in Buffalo, New York; Plastic's research in Arlington, New Jersey; Fabrics and Finishes' in Parlin, New Jersey; Explosives' in Gibbstown, New Jersey; Orchem's at Deepwater, New Jersey; Paint's in Philadelphia (after 1927); and so on. During this period, only the Ammonia Department's research organization and part of Grasselli's, among industrial departments, were located on the grounds of the Experimental Station.[89] The Ammonia Department's research unit and the Chemical Department enjoyed particularly good relations. In the post–World War II expansion of research at Du Pont, executives sought to rectify these geographically induced coordination problems by relocating several departmental research organizations to the Experimental Station. But despite this effort and the measures Stine and Bolton took in the prewar era, problems of research coordination became acute after the war.

The Scale of Research

Once the Executive Committee adopted standard accounting procedures for research expenditures and once Stine joined the Executive Committee, the committee began to explore more deliberately and intensely the question of how much Du Pont should spend on research. Was 3 percent of sales an ideal figure? Or should it be more? Of this money, how much should be divided among the five research categories and, particularly, how much should go to research intended to create new industries and to fundamental research? Should there be a correlation between plant construction expenditures and money invested in research?

Du Pont's executives never established specific formulas to provide answers to these questions. Yet the fact that these questions were raised is indicative of the new attention being devoted to the basic problems of making R&D pay. The context of these questions is also important to bear in mind; the nation was in the midst of the Great Depression, when unemployment had grown from 3.2 percent in 1929 to 25 percent in 1933 and had shrunk only to 17 percent in 1936.[90] The Great Depression forced the Executive Committee to set at least a general policy regarding research expenditures. Sales dropped nearly 50 percent from their 1929 peak before they began to rise again in 1933.[91] As early as August 1930 Lammot du Pont had begun to urge not *retrenchment* of research because of the Depression but *refinement* of research capability through the "elimination of the weaker employees."[92] Bolton took the president's advice seriously and carried it out during the next two years. He reported in late 1932 that "we have taken advantage of these times to raise the standard of our research organization by the release of a relatively small number of men who have not measured up in the past to the standards that we have set for our various organizations."[93]

Reduction in such personnel naturally led to reductions in research expenditures. But in mid-1932 when it began to review departmental budgets for 1933, the Executive Committee, led by Stine, grew concerned that the industrial departments were cutting back their research budgets too much in order to bolster profit showings. As a consequence of discussions held during two of its meetings, the Executive Committee resolved to issue a statement to departments to reconsider their proposed research budgets. The committee's resolution stressed that research was instrumental in the company's commercial success and to be most effective it had to be carried out on a continuous basis. A short-term policy was, the Executive Committee's resolution argued, a nearsighted strategy that would undermine the longer-term goals of the company. Moreover, the resolution repeated the Development Department's recent conclusion that Du Pont's phase of major acquisitions was over and that "our Company must to an increasing degree, look to its own developments for profitable expansion." Finally, the resolution called for Stine "to confer with the heads of the industrial departments and wholly-owned subsidiaries in order to ensure that they have a clear understanding of the sense of this resolution."[94] Bolton called the Executive Committee's action "a far-sighted policy regarding research. . . . It has not been the policy of our Executive Committee to have research work follow the curve of profits as it is a demonstrated fact that progress in the expansion of an industry can not be accomplished by intermittent efforts in research that is curtailed at the first sign of reduced profits."[95]

The Executive Committee's actions in the face of the Depression soon led Walter Carpenter, Jr., to enunciate a major policy that prevailed at Du Pont until the mid-1960s. At a meeting of the chemical directors in late 1934, Carpenter stated that the ratio of research expenditures to sales that the company had been using since 1930 did "not make sense." He said what was important was the "ratio [of research expenditures] to the value of the research results." Carpenter argued that research's essential raw material was cash and the company had plenty of it "available for worth-while research." He then stated categorically that any "well conceived" R&D project that "we are prepared and willing to undertake . . . with perseverance, enthusiasm and ability" would be funded. Good research – research that led to "commercially exploitable processes and products" – was a "unique [product] in that there is no possible overproduction." With the Executive Committee's resolution and Carpenter's assurance that management was "committed and enthusiastic for research and development," research expenditures moved back up after 1932, and at an impressive rate. Research directors were to worry about hiring good researchers and running good projects; research expenditures would be determined by quality considerations rather than by a simple formula.[96]

Du Pont and Industrial Research in the United States

The growth of Du Pont's research programs between 1921 and 1941 was not without parallel either in U.S. industry in general or the chemical industry in particular. Indeed, between these years, the number of industrial research laboratories, as defined and counted by the National Research Council, grew from about 300 to more than 2,200. Research personnel in these laboratories grew from 9,300 to more than 70,000.[97] The national pattern of growth in R&D followed closely that of Du Pont's, reflecting especially rapid growth after 1932. "Research" had become a national watchword by 1941; it was hailed by the National Resources Committee, chaired by Secretary of the Interior Harold L. Ickes, as a "national resource." As part of the work of the National Resources Committee, the National Research Council prepared in 1940 a comprehensive survey of industrial research, which focused principally on the United States. Part of this survey included a history of the development of industrial research in the United

States, written by MIT historian Howard R. Bartlett. Bartlett documented the "prehistory" of organized industrial research in America and then described the founding of such large, well-known laboratories as the General Electric Research Laboratory, Bell Telephone Laboratories, George Eastman's Kodak Park, Du Pont's Eastern Laboratory and Experimental Station, and the General Motors Research Laboratory. But Bartlett also included historical sketches of some fifty other industrial research laboratories in chemistry, communications, petroleum, iron and steel, rubber, pharmaceuticals, and other industries.[98] In total, U.S. industry spent about $300 million for research in 1940. Yet of the more than 2,200 industrial firms supporting research laboratories, there was remarkable concentration of industrial research: A relatively small number of large firms accounted for the majority of funds allocated for research and research personnel employed. Du Pont was among those few firms, spending as much or perhaps more than any other U.S. company on research. The other pioneering firms in corporate R&D were also among the leaders in R&D expenditures.[99]

That Du Pont was among an elite group of corporations in terms of R&D programs is reflected not only by statistics but, perhaps more importantly, by the presence of its R&D leaders in a small, elite, and subtly powerful group known as the Directors of Industrial Research (DIR). The brainchild of none other than Charles L. Reese, DIR was formed in 1923 as an outgrowth of a conference organized by the Executive Committee of the Research Information Service, National Research Council (of which Reese was a member). The conference brought together a group of twelve corporate research directors to discuss informally the "existence of undesirable waste" in industrial research "because of failure of laboratories to publish or otherwise make known results which are rather incidental to their main interest and quest."[100] The informality of the meeting and the obvious value of exchanging views and ideas on common problems of research management led the group to suggest subsequent meetings, and soon, in the words of a later visitor, "you could not shake them apart now, if you should try."[101] The group elected Reese as its chairman and within a few meetings had established strict membership rules, including a limit of twenty-five, and had freed itself from any association with the National Research Council. Among the founding members of DIR were Reese, C. E. K. Mees of Kodak, Willis R. Whitney of GE, E. R. Weidlein of the Mellon Institute, Frank B. Jewett and E. B. Craft of Bell Telephone Laboratories, H. D. Batchelor of Union Carbide and Carbon Company, and Charles E. Skinner of Westinghouse. At their monthly lunch meetings, usually held in New York, members discussed a wide range of common problems and experiences such as salaries paid to researchers, publication policy, bonus systems, patenting costs and procedures, recruiting and managing researchers, relations with university research, and "winning the purse-string holders." The group also heard guest speakers, who discussed similar topics as well as such issues as bills pending before the U.S. Congress that affected industrial research. Occasionally, DIR took positions on such bills. In the late 1930s, members of DIR openly opposed Maurice Holland's (of the National Research Council) attempt to form an organization called the National Association of Research Laboratories because they saw no need for such an organization and believed it would unnecessarily duplicate or even undermine DIR.[102]

In 1924, members of DIR began to invite their colleagues to tour their companies' research facilities. For instance, Du Pont twice sponsored DIR meetings during the 1920s. Such tours were often very elaborate. In 1927, Charles Stine convinced president Lammot du Pont to host a lunch for his colleagues in DIR and used the occasion to give them a history of Du Pont and the development of its diversified business.[103] GE's Whitney and W. D. Coolidge, Kodak's C. E. K. Mees, and Bell's Jewett, Craft, and O. E. Buckley, among many others, also hosted DIR several times.[104] Stine's DIR-related tours of GE's and Bell Telephone's research facilities and his discussions with their research directors were instrumental in his plan to initiate a fundamental research program at Du Pont. In general, participation in the DIR by Reese, Stine, and Bolton appears to have been an important element in their management of the firm's research. They gained information and ideas from the DIR meetings while benefiting from their comradeship with a handful of men who steered the research helms of other major U.S. corporations.

Du Pont Research on the Eve of World War II

On the eve of World War II, Du Pont's research and development programs were without parallel in the U.S. chemical industry. The organization of R&D at Du Pont had gone through tremendous changes during the two decades between 1921 and 1941, beginning with the decentralization and retrenchment of research, which left the Chemical Department "dismembered," and ending with a rapidly growing research staff in which the central Chemical Department served as the paragon of chemical industry research and development.

Research at Du Pont had become a mature enterprise. With a top management committed by tradition to R&D, the company's most important research managers, particularly Stine and Bolton, had achieved many if not most of their objectives. The quality of Du Pont's research staff had been raised significantly thanks to Du Pont's graduate fellowship program, its relations with several key academicians who served as consultants, a poor academic job market in the 1930s, and the increased recruiting power gained by Stine's fundamental research program. The company had secured a considerable amount of control over research expenditures when the Executive Committee adopted a standard method of accounting for research among the industrial departments. Coordination of research had been achieved to some extent by the increasing power accorded Bolton and the great partisanship of the executive Stine. Led by Fin Sparre, Du Pont's program of diversification through acquisition was remarkably complete, and the Development Department had begun to look toward internal development rather than acquisition to bring about further diversification. This diversification had provided an important base upon which Stine's fundamental research program was predicated. Du Pont's R&D capabilities were further reinforced by its Patents and Processes Agreement with Imperial Chemical Industries. And finally, the company had an enormous winner on its hands with nylon, a pure product of Du Pont R&D, a paradigmatic invention for Du Pont in the postwar era.

The enormous success of nylon gave Du Pont's executives further resolve to expand the company's research efforts, and on a grand scale. But in many respects, the war delayed the implementation of Du Pont's research agenda. Having recently gone through the "Merchants of Death" or Nye Committee hearings, Du Pont was very reluctant to engage in any war-related work. Consequently, it hoped to fulfill its patriotic obligations while keeping its attention focused on the preparation for the postwar expansion of research.

Lammot du Pont, president of the Du Pont Company, 1926–40.

Charles M. A. Stine, chemical director, 1924–30, vice president
for research, 1930–45.

The Experimental Station, 1925. This is how the Station appeared when Charles Stine took control of the Chemical Department.

Wallace H. Carothers, leader of Stine's fundamental research program in polymer chemistry, c. 1930.

The Experimental Station, 1929. This photograph shows the new laboratory built to house Stine's fundamental research program—Purity Hall (center). The Chemical Department's extensive work for the Paint Department is also evident; note the numerous paint sample test boards to the left and behind Purity Hall as well as on the top of one of the older laboratories.

Chemical Department Steering Committee, c. 1935. Front (left to right), Ernest B. Benger, Arthur P. Tanberg, Elmer K. Bolton, Cole Coolidge, Crawford H. Greenewalt, Hamilton Bradshaw. Back (left to right). Merlin Brubaker, Paul Salzberg.

Elmer K. Bolton, chemical director, 1930–1951.

Exhibiting nylon stockings at the New York World's Fair, 1939. As part of its response to the Merchants of Death charges, Du Pont invested substantial sums for an exhibit, The Wonder World of Chemistry, at the New York World's Fair in 1939. The fair proved to be an excellent forum in which to introduce nylon, which was to go into commercial production the following year.

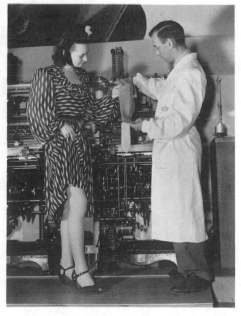

Roger Adams (left), one of Du Pont's major consultants between 1927 and 1960 and dissertation advisor to many Du Pont chemists, on a consulting visit at the Experimental Station.

The Du Pont Company's Presidents. Taken in 1949, this photograph shows the company's twentieth century leaders. Left to right, Walter S. Carpenter, Jr., Pierre S. du Pont, Crawford H. Greenewalt, Irénée du Pont, Lammot du Pont. Behind the presidents are portaits of the firm's earlier leaders, including the founder Eleuthere Irénée du Pont (center) and T. Coleman du Pont (lower right).

The Experimental Station, 1945. By the time this photograph was made, Building 262 (above and right of center)—no longer known as Purity Hall—had been significantly enlarged and the Nylon Research Laboratory (upper right)—soon to be renamed in honor of Wallace H. Carothers—had been constructed.

Chairman Walter S. Carpenter, Jr., (left) and President Crawford H. Greenewalt (right) examine the architect's model of the proposed expansion to the Experimental Station, c. 1948.

The expanded Experimental Station, 1950.

The Chestnut Run Site, c. 1955. To complement the fundamental and pioneering research done at the nearby Experimental Station, the company built this product development and end-use research center in 1954.

The Experimental Station, 1957. Du Pont continued to build new research laboratories at the Station during the 1950s following the major expansion of 1950.

W. Hale Charch, director of Pioneering Research, Textile Fibers Department, c. 1955.

The Nylon Rope Trick. Performed by Paul W. Morgan, c. 1960, this experiment provides a dramatic demonstration of one of the low temperature polymerization techniques developed by Pioneering Research in the 1950s.

Du Pont Leadership, 1940s–1970s. Left to right, Charles B. McCoy (president, 1967–74), Lammot du Pont Copeland (president, 1962–67), Walter S. Carpenter, Jr., (president, 1940–48), Crawford H. Greenewalt (president, 1948–62).

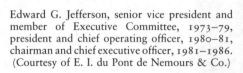

Edward G. Jefferson, senior vice president and member of Executive Committee, 1973–79, president and chief operating officer, 1980–81, chairman and chief executive officer, 1981–1986. (Courtesy of E. I. du Pont de Nemours & Co.)

The Experimental Station, 1987. This photograph shows the Greenewalt Laboratory devoted to life sciences research at the lower right of the Station campus. (Courtesy of E. I. du Pont de Nemours & Co.)

PART IV

Chemistry Enshrined

World War II ushered in a new, highly competitive era in the chemical industry that prompted Du Pont and other companies to invest heavily in research. During the war the U.S. government financed the commercialization of numerous polymers to replace scarce natural materials or to perform critical functions in new technologies. This led to the widespread dissemination of polymer technology, a field in which Du Pont previously held a wide margin of leadership in the United States. Other companies were catching up with Du Pont while it was preoccupied with designing and building the Hanford plutonium works for the Manhattan Project. This enormous effort yielded little of commercial value to Du Pont. Seeing the firm as a chemical company, Du Pont's leaders chose to get out of the nuclear arena as soon as the war ended rather than pursuing the uncertain development of commercial nuclear power. Parallel to the rapid growth of polymers was the Justice Department's campaign to make the chemical industry more competitive by terminating international agreements, such as the one between Du Pont and Imperial Chemical Industries of Britain, and vigorously enforcing the antitrust statutes, particularly against acquisitions.

Seeing these changes occurring, Du Pont's Executive Committee began as early as 1942 to develop strategies for the postwar era. The happy experience of neoprene and nylon in the 1930s suggested a way in which Du Pont could stay ahead of the competition, continue to grow, and avoid antitrust litigation. By expanding its fundamental research effort dramatically, not only in the Chemical Department but also in the industrial departments, the Executive Committee expected to reap a harvest of new nylons. (See Tables IV.1 and IV.2 for statistics on Du Pont's financial performance and R&D program, 1941–61.) Chapter 16 explores Du Pont's wartime activities, the development of the new strategy, and the major postwar expansion of research.

Chapter 17 traces the evolution of Du Pont's fundamental research and looks at its impact on the company and the larger chemical community. As the chemical industry increased its research capability, corporate scientists increasingly outnumbered their academic counterparts and took greater responsibility for advancing the chemical sciences through publication and other professional activities. At Du Pont, the work of the Chemical Department (renamed the Central Research Department in 1957) drifted to-

Table IV.1. *Financial Summary of the Du Pont Company, 1941–61*
(in millions of dollars)

	1941	1946	1951	1956	1961
Sales	480.1	648.7	1,531.1	1,888.4	2,191.0
Operating income	57.5	84.0	139.4	254.8	258.0
Average operating investment	628.4	891.8	1,553.2	2,251.7	3,120.6
Average number of employees	60,029	72,002	86,878	89,449	87,057

Source: Du Pont Company annual reports.

Table IV.2. *Research and Development Statistics for the Du Pont Company, 1941–61 (in millions of dollars)*

	1941	1946	1951	1956	1961
Total expenditures	12.4	26.0	71.9	140.3	160.8
Expenditures as percentage of sales	2.6	4.0	4.7	7.5	7.3
Expenditures as percentage of earnings (expenditures/income)	21.6	31.0	51.6	55.1	62.3
Expenditures as percentage of earnings (expenditures/ expenditures + income)	17.7	23.6	34.0	35.5	38.4
R&D professional staff	1,341	1,800	3,376	4,582	3,787

Source: Expenditures and staff data are from Official R&D Statistics, Central Research and Development Department.

ward academic-style science. The department had been assigned the difficult task of diversification through research. Therefore, it did fundamental research on a wide variety of subjects to discover leads that could be developed into new products. The Chemical Department became accomplished at research but virtually abandoned its development activities. Because the other departments were busy developing their own new products, they had little interest in picking up research that the Chemical Department had initiated.

The busiest department in the company was Textile Fibers, which commercialized two major fibers, Orlon and Dacron, while also expanding the nylon business dramatically. Chapter 18 details how Du Pont led the way in the synthetic fiber revolution of the 1950s and 1960s. To accomplish its goals, Textile Fibers relied heavily on its Pioneering Research Laboratory directed by R&D entrepreneur W. Hale Charch, who pushed hard to develop Orlon and Dacron for specific market opportunities. After the big

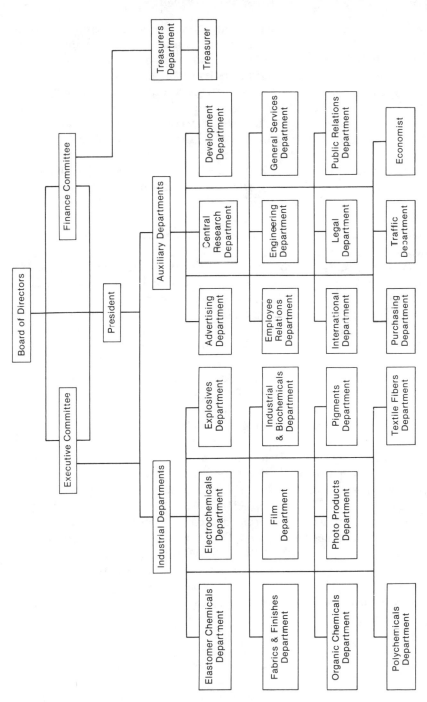

Figure IV.1. Organization of the Du Pont Company, 1961. Source: Adapted from Du Pont Company Annual Report for 1961.

three synthetic fibers had been turned over to product divisions, Charch believed that there was little market opportunity for another major fiber. Therefore he shifted his laboratory's research strategy.

After 1960 Textile Fibers concentrated on commercializing specialty fibers aimed at particular market needs and at new products based on extensions of Du Pont's technology. Chapter 19 examines the second stage of Textile Fibers's R&D. The results of these efforts were mixed. Lycra spandex was extremely successful, but Qiana, a silk-like nylon, was not. The department pioneered in spun-bonded products, hybrids of paper and fabric. All these projects required massive R&D efforts, which were supported by the profits from nylon, Orlon, and Dacron. To maintain the profitability of these products in spite of increased competition, Textile Fibers developed improved processes that lowered costs significantly. In the postwar era, textile fibers was the company's dominant business, although Du Pont also made significant strides in other areas.

Chapters 20 and 21 follow the growth of two other product lines, biological chemicals and plastics, respectively. Beginning from a small base in the old Grasselli organization, in the 1950s Du Pont built a strong agricultural chemicals business based on organic herbicides and fungicides. Less aggressive in the companion field of human pharmaceuticals, Du Pont management hesitated to make a large commitment to this complex and unfamiliar business.

Like agricultural chemicals, plastics was a small business at Du Pont before the war. World War II initiated a frantic rush to develop new plastics and expand markets for older ones. In this business, Du Pont preferred not to manufacture highly competitive commodity plastics but to deal in more sophisticated ones that could command premium prices. Following this strategy, the Polychemicals Department, formalizing a merger of the Plastics and Ammonia departments in 1949, concentrated on Teflon fluoropolymers, Delrin polyacetal resins, and linear polyethylene in the 1950s. When Polychemicals failed to maintain proprietary positions in the two latter products, the departmental management decided to concentrate on even more complex products for highly specific markets. The skyrocketing expense of developing these new products and the uncertain future that they faced in the marketplace led many Du Pont executives, by 1960, to ponder whether the company needed new approaches to compete in what many analysts were calling a "mature industry." (See Figure IV.1 for a view of the company's organization in the early 1960s.)

16

The War Years and Postwar Expansion of Research

World War II and its aftermath stand as the second great watershed in the history of the Du Pont Company's research and development program. Not as pronounced as that of the earlier world war, this latter watershed was nonetheless equally important. Responding to both internal and external events, Du Pont's managers reached decisions that shaped the company's history for the next quarter-century. In the previous decade, Du Pont had performed extremely well given that the U.S. economy was languishing in the worst depression in its history. The company had consolidated its many acquisitions and was rightly deemed a highly successful diversified chemicals manufacturer. Du Pont's Patents and Processes Agreement with ICI was providing the company with additional R&D capability while protecting it from competition with ICI in particular world markets. Technologies acquired by the company in a variety of ways had been developed into highly profitable ventures such as titanium dioxide pigments, tetraethyllead antiknock gasoline additive, Freon refrigerants, and moistureproof cellophane. Neoprene and nylon, both products of Carothers's fundamental research group, had become successful. Moreover, Du Pont's organizational and managerial structure was strong and stable, a picture far different from the 1910s.

Yet suddenly the world was turned upside down; many of the assumptions upon which the company's executives had founded their developmental strategy became either politically unacceptable or simply no longer true. The winds of change in the world were both strong and swift. Another wave of anti-big business sentiment emerged and soon led to the prosecution of corporations for violations of the antitrust statutes. The war itself yielded momentous scientific and technological developments. Spurred by the war, competition emerged rapidly in the American chemical industry after 1945. These factors combined to shake the house of Du Pont and force its executives to chart a new course for the corporation in the next generation.

Intensive research and development efforts based upon internally generated ideas and technology emerged as the principal means by which Du Pont's executives sought to maintain in the decade ahead the earnings and the rate of growth enjoyed by the company's stockholders in the previous decade. Executives came to believe that research – particularly fundamental research – would be the salvation of the company. This "faith," as one executive called it at the time, became unshakable by the end of the 1940s when Du Pont had completed its massive expansion of the Experimental Station, now devoted in large measure to longer-range, often fundamental, research conducted not only by the Chemical Department but also by all the industrial departments. The decade, therefore, was one of planning for and carrying out the expansion of research in the midst of war and cold war, extensive antitrust litigation, and increasing competition.

Although Du Pont's executives concluded readily that antitrust litigation or its threat meant the end of the era of acquisitions and the beginning of a new era of the internal generation of novel technology, they nevertheless faced tough decisions about how to proceed. The War Department's request during World War II that Du Pont manage the design, construction, and operation of the Hanford, Washington, plutonium production plant and Du Pont's success with this project, among other wartime undertakings, opened up the question of whether the company should become, in today's parlance, a major defense contractor. Furthermore, the virtually unique experience Du Pont gained at Hanford with nuclear reactor design and construction also presented Du Pont with the option of becoming the leading firm in the development of civilian nuclear power technology. Because the wartime emergency served as a great leveler – exposing other companies to truly large-scale projects and manufacturing operations while forcing Du Pont to yield much of its proprietary knowledge – Du Pont's executives foresaw that firms such as Allied, Union Carbide, Monsanto, and Dow would become far more competitive after the war. This competition would be manifested not only in the marketplace but also in the laboratory. It would mean that Du Pont would face new problems in the recruitment of research personnel and in maintaining a lead in areas the company considered its province. The course that Du Pont should take in the postwar era was thus a treacherous one for executives to chart. Certainly, the decade was not one of "business as usual."

The War

Du Pont's executives hardly welcomed World War II. In fact, they viewed it as a threat to the company. This attitude derived from two principal factors. First – and perhaps most important – they feared that any involvement with the war effort would lead to the company being branded once again a merchant of death and war profiteer, as it had been during the proceedings of the U.S. Senate munitions investigating committee (1934–36), chaired by Gerald P. Nye of North Dakota. Walter S. Carpenter, Jr., now president of Du Pont, and Lammot du Pont, now chairman of Du Pont's board of directors, had both sat through three days of Nye Committee hearings during which they and others from Du Pont had been grilled about the company's profits earned during World War I and its alleged continued influence in the international munitions industry.[1] Newspaper headlines pegged Du Pont as a merchant of death and doer of evil international deeds.[2] Although most careful observers agreed with *Fortune* that the company "came away with a clean bill of health," the Nye Committee investigations nevertheless left Du Pont's executives wary of any extensive involvement with war preparations.[3] Second, war promised to interrupt the rapid development of Du Pont's new businesses, especially the nylon venture. In response to nylon's instant commercial success and the rapidly developing field of polymers, Du Pont's executives had already authorized Elmer Bolton to hire a large number of additional research chemists for the Chemical Department.[4] Simply put, Du Pont did not need to increase its smokeless powder business to make the corporation grow or earn profits. Building more explosives capacity would be a step backward and away from the objectives the company's executives had been working toward for a generation.

But the war came. Well before the Japanese bombed Pearl Harbor on December 7, 1941, Du Pont's executives realized that the company would be drawn unavoidably into war work. Following Hitler's invasion of Poland on September 1, 1939, the U.S. Congress rewrote the Neutrality Act of 1937, which as a result of the Nye Committee's hearings had prohibited powder and other munitions from being exported to belligerent powers. The new Neutrality Act of 1939 lifted the munitions embargo. Du Pont's executives, however, chose not to expand the company's manufacturing capacity for military propellants. Nevertheless, Du Pont soon found itself building and operating new powder plants for both the British and U.S. governments on a cost plus fixed fee (4%) basis. By the end of the war, Du Pont had assumed responsibility for building and operating 65 percent of total U.S. Ordnance Department powder production and had manufactured more smokeless powder than in World War I. The U.S. government called upon Du Pont to manufacture or at least provide "know-how" for many other products under similar cost-plus-fixed-fee arrangements. Moreover, as U.S. involvement in the war drew nearer and the United States actually entered the war, the government asked Du Pont to engage in projects that drew heavily upon Du Pont's research and development organization in addition to its engineering design and construction labor force.[5]

Throughout the immediate prewar and wartime period, Du Pont's executives took the position that the company would cooperate fully with the government as requested but that they wished to keep the company on its highly successful track of commercial development as much as possible. They wanted the company to meet its patriotic responsibilities but not at the cost of being viewed again as a merchant of death. Soon after President Franklin D. Roosevelt created the National Defense Research Committee (NDRC), its chairman, Vannevar Bush, president of the Carnegie Institution and former Massachusetts Institute of Technology professor, called upon Du Pont to aid the NDRC's work. The Executive Committee reviewed this request in consultation with Elmer Bolton and Fin Sparre and resolved "to comply with all reasonable requests of the National Defense Research Committee to furnish it with data, technical and manufacturing information, and materials, and to perform experimental and research investigations in connection with the production of materials... without charge...." The committee's resolution called for Bolton, as chemical director, to coordinate all Du Pont's work for the NDRC. Following the creation of the Bush-headed Office of Scientific Research and Development (OSRD) and the bombing of Pearl Harbor, the committee modified its earlier resolution by specifying that all department heads comply with and "when practicable to give preference to all reasonable requests" of OSRD, NDRC, and other government agencies.[6]

Long before Pearl Harbor, however, the impending U.S. involvement in the war posed important tactical and strategic questions for Du Pont. On the tactical side, the Executive Committee responded to the excess-profits-tax statutes imposed by Congress between 1940 and 1943 by increasing its expenditures for research, which were counted as a fully deductible expense. Given the level of Du Pont's excess tax liability in 1940, the committee concluded that increased research would cost the company only $0.38 for each $1.00 expended. Although the committee sought to maintain "judicious spending," it nevertheless encouraged departments to take advantage of the excess-profits-tax picture to build for the future. In particular, the committee urged a "substantial" expansion of engineering research designed to lead to "the development of entirely new or improved machinery and chemical equipment" and "some" expansion in fundamental research "with a view to the long-time future development of the Company."[7] (See Table 16.1 for data on Du Pont's R&D staff, 1942–60.)

Strategically, Walter Carpenter and Executive Committee member Angus B. Echols posed the big questions on how Du Pont should proceed given the impending war. A long-standing member of the Executive Committee (since 1920), Carpenter had succeeded Lammot du Pont as president and chairman of the Executive Committee in 1940 and would preside over Du Pont during most of the decade. His analytical abilities had always been recognized in the company, and they played a critical role in this period.[8] In a memorandum to Sparre written eleven months before Pearl Harbor, Carpenter considered Du Pont's growing involvement with defense work and both short- and long-term problems posed by the war. Recognizing that large numbers of Du Pont employees were being transferred into defense work and that others would be drafted for the war, he asked Sparre to give thought to "ways and means" of handling their return to Du Pont's commercial operations after the war. Carpenter urged Sparre to consider establishing a group in the Development Department to give "constant thought" to how Du Pont and other industries would readjust in the postwar period. He envisioned this group laying the "ground work for policies to be adopted to facilitate our handling this big problem after the war." Finally, Carpenter

Table 16.1. *Du Pont R&D Staff, 1942–60*

Year	Research specialists	A research[a]	Other[b]	Total
1942	1,434			1,434
1943	1,500			1,500
1944	1,627			1,627
1945	1,774			1,774
1946	2,159			2,159
1947		1,442	1,160	2,602
1948		1,421	1,307	2,728
1949		1,440	1,438	2,878
1950		1,464	1,754	3,218
1951		1,586	1,790	3,376
1952		1,748	1,906	3,654
1953		1,932	2,000	3,932
1954		1,982	2,138	4,120
1955		2,040	2,223	4,263
1956		2,172	2,410	4,582
1957		2,169	2,462	4,631
1958		2,395	2,353	4,748
1959		2,323	2,191	4,514
1960		2,251	2,160	4,411

[a]Includes fundamental research, research on existing processes and products, research on new processes and products.
[b]Includes technical assistance to production and technical assistance to sales.
Source: Data from 1942 to 1946 come from Ira T. Ellis to C. H. Greenewalt, Feb. 14, 1955. Data from 1947 to 1960 come from Official R&D Statistics, Central Research and Development Department, 1947–60.

enumerated a long list of what proved to be the critical questions that this group should address:

> Should we endeavor to curtail to the very minimum all construction in connection with our commercial operations, with the idea that these could be undertaken after the war when there would be a surplus of men and materials, whereas at the present time we may encounter a scarcity of both?
> Should we hold from commercial exploitation until after the war some of our current developments? An important example would be the case of nylon. Are we correct on proceeding with the construction of enormous plants for the exploitation of this material at this time, or would we and the country be better served by a postponement of this?
> Should we during this period attempt to formulate a plan for the development of a new industry after the war, for example, the pharmaceutical industry for which we would make plans at this time and

perhaps actually set aside funds now to employ personnel to conduct a survey and research in connection with the development of that industry along new lines after the war? . . .

We should watch carefully the developments in our own and collateral lines in connection with the National Defense Program in order that we may not be expanding into industries for which there will be an excess of capacity after the war.

What should be our attitude with respect to priorities as they may apply to non-defense industries? Do we feel that our interests and the country's interests are best served by encouraging priorities for such purposes or are they injured by such a policy?[9]

Echols strongly advocated Carpenter's suggestion that a special task force be established in the Development Department to deal with the wartime and postwar commercial planning "recognizing of course," as he put it, "that the Defense Program must come first." Nevertheless, Echols placed greater emphasis on planning "in anticipation of peace." Arguing that postwar business in the United States would "be one of the greatest competition ever found in this country," Echols urged that Du Pont "make plans today and proceed with them promptly" when the war effort was over. He called again for expanding research. He also placed emphasis on finding new uses for existing products and developing more efficient processes. Research would prepare the company for assaults by competitors and the government alike.[10]

Three months before Pearl Harbor, Echols drafted a provocative report, "The Du Pont Company's Future Policy with Respect to Its Expansion in the Chemical Industry," which served in one way or another to stimulate Executive Committee discussion for much of the remainder of the decade.[11] Echols analyzed Du Pont's development after 1902 through a four-stage model. In stage I, Du Pont was solely an explosives manufacturer but moved to stage II through the acquisition of mechanical processing businesses. These included all Du Pont's businesses that converted cellulose into products (Pyralin plastics, Fabrikoid artificial leather, rayon, and cellophane) and Remington Arms, purchased by Du Pont in 1933. In stage III, the company acquired patents and know-how and further developed them through purely "chemical manufacture." With stage IV, Du Pont came into its own as a result of "Original Chemical Development Work." Expanded research had inaugurated this new era. After examining the profit picture in these stages, Echols concluded that Du Pont should "resolve, in the future, to avoid the 'Remingtons,' the 'Arlingtons,' and the 'Fabrikoids.' " It should "clean house" and abandon such businesses. Stage IV should be broadened by greatly expanding research. The wartime conditions made this all the more urgent. Echols saw the federal government "going into business in a big way" and the wartime emergency pushing many other companies into new areas. He urged that Du Pont plan its postwar future immediately.[12]

Several of Echols's peers on the Executive Committee took issue with his arguments, as did others in the company to whom Echols sent his memorandum for criticism.[13] The substance of their arguments need not concern us. What is important is that no one disagreed with Echols's proposition that Du Pont expand its research and development programs liberally. Thus even before the United States had officially entered the war, a consensus had emerged that Du Pont should intensify its research and development efforts. Yet the great press of Du Pont's war effort in the immediate aftermath of Pearl Harbor delayed detailed planning for the postwar expansion of Du Pont's research and development.

The United States's entry into the war rapidly altered Du Pont research. As Elmer Bolton wrote in his annual report for 1942, "research in the Chemical Department has undergone a rapid transition to a war basis." Throughout the war, approximately 25 percent of the Chemical Department's research staff was engaged in contract R&D work for the Office of Scientific Research and Development, the National Defense Research Council, and the War Department, and Du Pont did much war-related research on its own account. As a result, Bolton stressed, "fundamental research . . . has been curtailed and continuing work in this category is devoted exclusively to war objectives." The work done by the Chemical Department for the industrial departments was also affected by the war. Bolton stressed that "practically all general investigations and projects for industrial departments are in direct war or essential civilian categories, with emphasis on new products for war purposes and for replacement of critical materials."[14]

Some of the projects undertaken by the Chemical Department for war agencies included development of protection against war gases (uniforms, masks, antidotes, and decontaminants), synthesis of new war gases, development of new insecticides and antimalarial drugs, studies of anti-icing materials for airplane propellers, and the invention of self-sealing fuel cells for airplanes. Yet most of the Chemical Department's — and the industrial departments' — R&D efforts were directed at adapting and improving existing Du Pont products for wartime applications. Nylon provides perhaps the best illustration of this trend. With silk supplies cut off from the United States, nylon became a very important strategic material. Both the Rayon Department and the Chemical Department continued to do intensive research on nylon but with a focus on wartime applications rather than immediate commercial markets. Through experimentation with hot rather than cold drawing, Du Pont developed in 1942 a nylon yarn that was 25 percent stronger than the already strong nylon, and this yarn was immediately used in parachute shroud lines, cordage, and cords of bomber tires. The Rayon Department's support of fundamental viscose research in the Chemical Department led to a greatly improved Cordura rayon tire cord. Moreover, this research also allowed Cordura to be made on conventional rayon equipment rather than special machinery, thus bolstering critically short output when cotton proved to be an unacceptable cord for tires made from synthetic rubber. This development alone markedly improved the performance of rayon, even in the face of growing competition from nylon.[15]

The war also propelled development of two exotic materials that otherwise might have lain dormant or evolved more naturally: polyethylene and polytetrafluoroethylene. The history of the development of these two materials, which found use in radar equipment and the Manhattan Project, is treated in Chapter 21.

Unquestionably, emphasis on the short-range research and development of products for wartime applications forced a significant reduction in the amount of fundamental research conducted by the Chemical Department on both its own and the industrial departments' accounts throughout the war, just as Bolton had reported in 1942. "Many attractive problems," he noted in 1945, "have been set aside because they could not be pointed to specific war objectives."[16] Officially, the company adhered to the position taken by Vannevar Bush on war and basic research.[17] As the section on research in Walter Carpenter's report to the stockholders, *Du Pont's Part in the National Security Program*, concluded, "Although war stimulates applied research and accelerates the utilization of previously determined scientific facts, it brings fundamental research to a virtual standstill. Du Pont was able to carry out its wartime assignments largely because of the research carried out in time of peace in the various Company laboratories."[18] Certainly this kind of thinking lay behind much of the planning for the expansion of the Experimental Station in the postwar era. Other factors operated as well, including Du Pont's experience in the Manhattan Project in which it helped to translate a piece of exotic research in nuclear physics into one of the most awesome technologies of all ages.

The Manhattan Project and the Road Not Taken

Among the many projects the company undertook for the United States government immediately before and during the war, Du Pont's work on the Manhattan Project was the most dramatic and one that offered opportunities for the company in the postwar period. Deriving its code name from the Army Corps of Engineers, which officially managed it, the Manhattan Project was the multi-component program to develop the atomic bomb.

Du Pont's participation in the Manhattan Project grew like Topsy.[19] In the early fall of 1942, the government asked Du Pont to serve as a subcontractor to aid Stone & Webster in designing and constructing a plutonium separation plant. But within days of his assuming duties as director of the Manhattan Project, General Groves envisioned Du Pont playing a much more central role in the plutonium project, which was being coordinated by physicist Arthur Compton at the University of Chicago. Groves was familiar with Du Pont's outstanding engineering capability and wanted to use it to relieve the already overburdened Stone & Webster. Through almost four months of negotiations with Du Pont's executives and chief engineering and research personnel, Groves convinced Du Pont to assume much greater tasks for the project. In December 1942, Du Pont signed an agreement calling for the company to design and construct a pilot plant-sized pile (or reactor) and separation works and to design, construct, and operate the full-scale plutonium production and separation facilities to be located in a remote area of the United States. This area turned out to be in the desert of eastern Washington, and the plant became known as the Hanford Engineer Works.

Du Pont undertook this project only after receiving assurances from President Franklin D. Roosevelt, Secretary of War Stimson, and General George C. Marshall that the company's participation was vital to the nation's security. Not wanting again to be labeled a merchant of death, Du Pont committed itself to carry out this work at cost and, for legal reasons, for a fixed fee of one dollar. The company also insisted that the government eliminate its standard legal language providing contractors with rights to patents emerging from their work for the government. Du Pont would thus have absolutely no pecuniary or vested interest in the Manhattan Project. The company would, however, devote some of its best scientific and technical talent to this war effort.[20]

Despite its enormous scale (at the peak of construction, the Hanford Works would employ some 40,000 workers ranging from common laborers and skilled workers to engineers, chemists, and physicists), Du Pont was able to fit the project into its existing organizational framework. The Executive Committee created a new division – TNX – within the Explosives Department and placed it under the direction of Roger Williams, who was named assistant general manager of the department. Williams brought with him from the Ammonia Department engineer R. Monte Evans, who was responsible for the eventual operation (in Du Pont organizational parlance, the "manufacturing" operations) of the Hanford Works. For direction of the R&D unit of the TNX division, the Executive Committee tapped Crawford H. Greenewalt, who like Williams had participated in discussions leading up to Du Pont's acceptance of the project. Greenewalt was to serve as the liaison between researchers at Chicago's Metallurgical Laboratory and Du Pont's Wilmington operations, including the Engineering Department, which would manage the design and construction of Hanford.[21]

Du Pont's role in the Manhattan Project was to transform a piece of exotic research conducted by physicists at Chicago into a full-scale plant producing plutonium that would be used in the atomic bombs exploded at Alamogordo, New Mexico, on July 16 and over Nagasaki, Japan, on August 9, 1945. (The bomb dropped on Hiroshima on August 6 used enriched uranium made in Oak Ridge, Tennessee, rather than plutonium.) Crawford Greenewalt had his hands full with the scientists at Chicago, many of whom resented Du Pont's being brought into the project and feared losing control of their own creation.[22] Believing that the Chicago physicists could not adequately keep their research focused on the ultimate objective, Groves wanted Greenewalt to be named the "boss" of the physicists, but the pragmatic Greenewalt recognized this would be impossible. Only a distinguished physicist like Compton could serve that role.[23] Greenewalt assured Compton and his associates that he would play only a liaison role, and that Du Pont aimed "to do a job," not to "pick their brains" and "make a barrel of money out of atomic energy."[24]

Over the next three years, Greenewalt worked hard to earn the good will of the physicists and to keep the project moving toward completion. The physicists, Greenewalt reported, possessed "peculiar ideas as to the difference between 'scientific' and 'industrial' research."[25] Having managed the technical development of nylon, Greenewalt held up this project as a model of how Du Pont translated a piece of pure research into full-scale production; most of the physicists were impressed by what they heard and saw. Greenewalt also succeeded in convincing Compton to reorganize the management of the Metallurgical Laboratory along the lines of the Chemical Department's own Steering Committee (of which Greenewalt had been a member).[26] Other Greenewalt recommendations followed, including devising an improved reporting system and adopting a project system, both modeled on Du Pont's Chemical Department procedures.[27] By the spring of 1943, Greenewalt had established a remarkably good rapport with Compton, Norman Hilberry, and Chicago's most prestigious physicist, Enrico Fermi. But he had not lessened the fear and animosity of all the physicists. Eugene Wigner in particular caused much grief for Greenewalt and Du Pont and at one point voiced his discontent as broadly as the White House.[28]

Despite continued friction from some of the Chicago physicists, Du Pont successfully carried out the job it had contracted to do. Less than ten months after signing the contract, the company completed the pilot-scale reactor at the Clinton Engineer Works near Oak Ridge, Tennessee. By December 1943, the pile had produced enough plutonium to supply the completed separation semiworks, and by the following spring Clinton was shipping desperately needed samples of plutonium to the Los Alamos Laboratory, where the bomb was being designed and manufactured. Altogether, the Clinton operation was deemed – even by the Chicago physicists who operated it – an excellent nuclear physics research facility.[29]

For the full-scale plutonium production plant, Du Pont aided the Army in selecting a desert site in Washington and then began an all-out effort to acquire materials and ready the site for construction once plans had been approved. For Williams, Greenewalt, and Du Pont, major decisions about reactor design had to be made, and as early as possible. The key to successfully completing the project on time was to "freeze" on the major design questions and then pursue further design and development on the basis of those frozen design elements. Here was a major source of conflict. Greenewalt encountered continual trouble from the physicists in settling the major issues and then pursuing the research necessary to complete the design.

Although he appreciated the propensities of some scientists to follow interesting research questions, Greenewalt needed data for Du Pont's design engineers that could only be obtained by directing the work of the Chicago physicists. Physicists such as Wigner failed to appreciate the extent of the engineering problems in the project and generally underestimated their importance. Here was a classic case of "science" versus "engineering." Some Chicago physicists complained of excessive red tape and charged that Du Pont was too preoccupied with safety and margins of error rather than with speed in doing the job. A workable arrangement was not achieved until Greenewalt succeeded in getting Compton to have the Chicago team review with Du Pont's designers all blueprints for the Hanford works and sign off on them. Once this process began, some of the Chicago people began to appreciate the magnitude of the engineering involved.[30]

Du Pont maintained the Hanford project on schedule. Within hours of starting up the first full-scale reactor (Sept. 27, 1944), the wisdom of Du Pont's safety and margin-of-error cautiousness was dramatically demonstrated through the observation of a new phenomenon whereby the pile's reactivity rate began dropping as the pile, loaded according to the calculations of Chicago's physicists, approached full power. Essentially, the pile turned itself off. Had Du Pont designed the reactor as desired by Wigner and his recalcitrant colleagues with no space for additional uranium slugs, it would have proven to be an expensive, sophisticated heap of junk. But Du Pont's design anticipated differences between theory and practice and allowed for a quick correction that prevented an automatic shutdown.[31] Although myriad problems confronted Du Pont at Hanford, the company was able to furnish Los Alamos with enough plutonium to assemble both the bomb tested at Alamogordo and the one detonated over Nagasaki.

Du Pont's work was a triumph of advanced engineering in which the company's technical staff helped turn a piece of exotic theoretical and experimental physics into a massive commercial plant within a relatively short period. Clearly, the Manhattan Project – and Du Pont's involvement with it – affected the world. But how did it affect the Du Pont Company?

In a word, Du Pont's efforts at Clinton and Hanford offered an enormous but uncertain *opportunity* in the postwar era. Almost from the outset of the project, Du Pont's executives pondered this opportunity. In mid-February 1942, Elmer Bolton first raised the question of what kind of research Du Pont should presently be doing in order to be in a position to exploit nuclear physics commercially in the postwar era. Greenewalt, Williams, and Bolton discussed this matter and concluded that power generation would have to "carry the venture and that any use of radioactive materials would be a by-product." As to how Du Pont could position itself, the trio concluded that the "best way to educate [Du Pont] men now was to insert them into the Chicago program for training."[32] Subsequently, Bolton released to Williams and Greenewalt as many Chemical Department men as he thought he could spare in order to position his department for the postwar nuclear era.[33] Greenewalt continued to ponder the question and on more than one occasion explored it with Fermi and other scientists.[34]

Although Greenewalt was initially keen on the idea, by the end of 1942 he had begun to have second thoughts about Du Pont's role in any postwar nuclear program. He told Bolton that it "seem[ed] unlikely that commercial development will emerge for several years, hence research in this field is a large gamble, to be justified perhaps by advertising thru publications, service to other research jobs, etc.," and he doubted "that Du Pont research could be well justified even if government control would permit."[35] Nonetheless, as early as January 1944, he and Roger Williams began to urge Compton to initiate research at Chicago on military nonexplosive uses for reactors, including the generation of power.[36]

The question of whether Du Pont should pursue nuclear physics research in the postwar era came to a head in late July 1944 when Greenewalt wrote Williams an extensive memorandum on the pros and cons of Du Pont undertaking fundamental research in nuclear physics. He based his memorandum on the assumption – admittedly quite open to question – that the government would allow Du Pont to engage in such research and provide the company access to uranium, heavy water, design data, and "general know how." On the plus side, he argued that the field was one of great scientific importance and one in which Du Pont had acquired "some specialized knowledge." Echoing Charles Stine's words of 1926, Greenewalt suggested that Du Pont could gain prestige and improve its university relations through publications in nuclear physics. Du Pont's chemistry also stood to gain through such research because radioactive isotopes would aid "organic research on pharmaceuticals, insecticides, polymerization, and dyestuffs." Against these pros, Greenewalt enumerated the cons. Foremost was that "suitable physics personnel will be difficult if not impossible to get."[37] This was a problem that he was all too familiar with even under wartime emergency situations. For the previous six months, Greenewalt had sought to recruit first-class Chicago physicists to enter the employ of Du Pont on a temporary basis to serve as experts at Hanford. His invitations had been sternly rebuffed.[38] The physicists were very much opposed to industrial research.[39] Greenewalt believed that of all the renowned Chicago physicists, only Enrico Fermi was even a remote possibility for Du Pont's employ after the war.[40] Without nuclear physicists, Du Pont could not pursue fundamental research in the field.

Greenewalt articulated four other reasons against undertaking nuclear physics research. Money could be spent in other areas "with better chance[s] of return." Excepting power, no commercial applications could be clearly seen. If patents could be obtained, the time between research and commercialization might be too long to benefit from them. Finally, it would be unlikely that Du Pont would ever recover the money it spent on nuclear physics research.[41]

Despite Greenewalt's grave doubts about the wisdom of Du Pont entering nuclear physics, Charles Stine recommended to his colleagues on the Executive Committee in December 1944 that the research activities of the Chemical Department be broadened to include physics and nuclear physics.[42] The committee accepted Stine's proposal. Two months later – and approximately at the time of the first successful full-scale separation of plutonium at the Hanford works – Stine prepared a full-fledged position paper for the Executive Committee on Du Pont's future in atomic energy.[43] This paper raised most of the major issues confronting Du Pont and its nuclear work in the immediate postwar period. It also led Stine to temper his earlier enthusiasm for Du Pont's undertaking its own nuclear research program.

Stine noted that if Du Pont were to conduct nuclear research by and for itself, nuclear power (as opposed to atomic weaponry) was the prime target for commercialization. Nuclear physics might be developed for other commercial areas, as noted by Greenewalt, but Stine argued that none of this would be justified without a commitment to using or selling power given off in nuclear reactions. Nuclear research was vastly more expensive than chemical research. Stine concluded that the company could not justify independent research in nuclear physics. Yet he believed that if Du Pont could bide its time, important commercial applications would eventually emerge. "It would be most advantageous," he suggested, "if a way could be found to retain and utilize the Company's present knowledge of the field so that prompt advantage could be taken of developments of possible commercial interest when they occur."[44]

Stine saw both advantages and disadvantages in Du Pont's continued involvement with the U.S. government's nuclear program. He stressed that the company was "in an ideal position to undertake the necessary applied research and development work." Unlike some research projects, the objectives in the postwar period were clearly defined, much of the basic work had been done, and, though at times difficult, the relationship between Du Pont and the University of Chicago had been fruitful. Stine predicted that the government would seek to enlist Du Pont's aid after the war. If Du Pont agreed, it could potentially benefit through carrying out a patriotic duty, through keeping abreast of developments in nuclear physics that might allow the company to be first in a field of commercial importance, through using expertise gained from research on radioactive tracers in the company's ordinary research programs, and through employing as general consultants scientists engaged in government-supported nuclear research. Such an arrangement also posed disadvantages, however. These included "the necessity for immobilizing a considerable group of men on an effort of doubtful commercial interest to the Du Pont Company, the difficulty of carrying out highly secret research under close Government supervision, [and] possible political reverberations."[45]

Because of the urgency of the matter, Stine asked his colleagues on the Executive Committee to explore these issues as soon as possible because the "post-Hanford" era would begin by July 1, 1945. Already, members of

Du Pont's nuclear team were returning to Du Pont's normal lines of duty. In conclusion, he recommended against Du Pont doing any significant nuclear physics research on its own account but urged the immediate prosecution of discussions with the government regarding its plans for future research and development in nuclear physics.[46]

Du Pont's Executive Committee faced the issue of whether to continue in nuclear physics research on the government's account even sooner than Stine expected. Within days of Stine's report, Roger Williams reported orally to the committee that General Groves's assistant, Colonel Kenneth Nichols, had explored the question of whether Du Pont would be willing to assume the operation of the Clinton semiworks, thus taking Du Pont one step closer to the basic research in nuclear physics being done by the University of Chicago. The committee discussed this question at length, no doubt in light of Stine's position paper. Both immediate and long-term considerations entered their deliberations. Giving equal weight to the long-term picture, the committee voted to instruct Williams to decline Nichols's proposal on the quite legitimate grounds that the company was already stretched beyond its limits.[47] This was but the first step Du Pont took in withdrawing from nuclear physics research and defense contracting. Additional steps came quickly after the Japanese surrender.

Following his election to the Executive Committee in June 1945 in place of the retiring Charles Stine, the commercially minded Roger Williams enunciated a broad position on Du Pont's conducting research for the government: "I am for limiting Du Pont research contracts with all branches of the Government as much as possible inasmuch as we have more technical work to carry out for our own purposes than we have staff to carry it out."[48] Du Pont's executives had already charted a dramatic expansion in research, and they wanted to achieve this free of government involvement.

Du Pont informed Groves of its intent to withdraw when the contract expired in May 1946.[49] The general vigorously protested. During discussions with Walter Carpenter, Groves succeeded in convincing him to extend Du Pont's withdrawal date until October 31, 1946, ostensibly because the U.S. Congress had not yet established a nuclear energy policy. Groves nonetheless wrote Carpenter that Du Pont's decision was a blow and that Du Pont was "the outstanding company in America to carry on further work in this field."[50]

Although Groves seems to have been reconciled to Du Pont's decision, Secretary of War Robert P. Patterson was not. Upon hearing of Du Pont's withdrawal, he wrote Carpenter trying "to prevail upon you to reconsider."[51] Faced with a strongly worded letter, Carpenter agreed to meet in Washington with Patterson, General Dwight D. Eisenhower, and General Groves. Roger Williams accompanied him. Carpenter explained Du Pont's reasons for withdrawing from Hanford. Although Patterson and the two generals were unable to alter Carpenter's and Williams's stance, they succeeded in postponing Du Pont's withdrawal until December 31, 1946, or within sixty days of the passage of legislation establishing U.S. atomic energy policy, whichever came first.[52]

Du Pont had already urged Groves to recruit General Electric to run the Hanford plant. Groves had indeed contacted GE, which was reluctant to undertake the project in the absence of a national atomic energy policy. Carpenter and Williams strongly recommended that Groves go back to GE. Even if GE were unwilling to take over Hanford until Congress acted, Groves should nonetheless "urge upon them to undertake research and development work, particularly upon new piles in anticipation of their subsequently taking over the Hanford development." Du Pont agreed to cooperate with Groves and GE in this program.[53] Hence Du Pont got out of the nuclear energy field, and General Electric moved into it.

Du Pont helped GE immediately after it took over the management of Hanford and later in 1948. When the government sought a massive expansion of the Hanford works, GE asked Du Pont for additional aid. The company loaned GE some thirty of its former Hanford project employees to serve as pedagogues to their GE counterparts. As now-president Greenewalt wrote to Chairman of the Board Carpenter, "the alternative of our having to take the whole job over seems too horrible to contemplate."[54]

Yet less than a year later, the Atomic Energy Commission was knocking at the door again, asking Du Pont to undertake a survey for the commission "of all chemical activities bearing on the manufacture of plutonium" by a new generation of nuclear technology. Skeptical of further Du Pont involvement, Greenewalt laid this matter before the board of directors, which resolved to accept the AEC request "at its [i.e., Du Pont's] own expense as a public service" but with no further commitment implied.[55] Du Pont completed the survey in late March 1949. Greenewalt well knew that the survey would not be the end of it. As he wrote Carpenter, "I am very fearful that we will not be able to resist the Government completely and that there will be some task in connection with the over-all development that we will have to assume."[56] The following year, the crisis in Korea propelled the company back into the nuclear field when the Atomic Energy Commission and President Harry S Truman asked Du Pont to assume responsibility for design, construction, and operation of a plant for an entirely new generation of atomic materials, to be situated in South Carolina on the Savannah River. Amid the environment of the cold war and the Korean crisis, Du Pont found it impossible to turn down the government's request even though its executives knew that the Savannah River undertaking would siphon off from its commercial sphere talented research and engineering personnel, just as the Manhattan Project had commanded many of Du Pont's best and brightest.[57]

Du Pont received — and resisted — several other government requests to become a prime defense contractor in the postwar era, including assuming responsibility for the army's Redstone Arsenal guided-missile program in Huntsville, Alabama.[58] In declining this and many other offers, Du Pont's executives sought to keep the company on the commercial road where it had excelled. Still, they knew that this road would not be without hazard. Competition in the chemical industry lay ahead not just in terms of products but in the recruitment and retention of research personnel. The war had spurred many other firms to establish or expand research laboratories, and soon Du Pont would no longer be the only chemical company betting high stakes on the rewards offered by first-class research.[59] Antitrust activity against Du Pont also signaled a new era of competition, even with the company's old ally ICI. Furthermore, many opportunities, such as pharmaceuticals, demanded the company's consideration. These matters were very much in Du Pont executives' minds during the war and in the immediate postwar period as they set about to determine precisely where and how Du Pont should be headed in the future.

Big Business under Attack

All of Du Pont's planning for the postwar era was done under a growing storm cloud of anti-big-business sentiment and a revival of antitrust activity by the Justice Department. The collapse of the New Deal's recovery program in late 1937 led to the emergence of a previously minor strain of thought in Roosevelt's administration that the Depression stemmed from the misuse of power by big business. Stated succinctly, such proponents held the view the the Depression was nothing but a "strike of capital." Such thinking was manifested in the creation and work of the Temporary National Economic Committee (TNEC), the charge of which was to investigate the "monopoly problem" and to make recommendations on curbing it. More important, the Roosevelt administration beefed up the antitrust division of the Justice Department under Thurman W. Arnold, who was also a member of TNEC. Appropriations to Arnold's division grew by more than 500 percent between 1938 and 1942, and his staff quadrupled. Arnold and his lieutenants launched some 180 antitrust cases, a staggering number considering that it was about half of all the cases initiated between 1890 and 1938. Arnold was bent upon ending what he perceived as abuses by big business, which he believed were destroying the U.S. economy. As historian Ellis Hawley wrote, "Never had there been a similar effort to make [antitrust enforcement] a major tool of macroeconomic management." Arnold's strategy was to regulate "business conduct through consent decrees."[60] Despite the war, Arnold's strong influence continued as his division took on the role of preventing abuses of war-production regulations and ending production bottlenecks. Also, Arnold continued his attack on technologically based big businesses through his testimony before the Senate Committee on Patents in 1942, arguing that such "cartels" had found refuge under the patent laws. He cited the generation of defensive patents – a common pursuit in corporate R&D laboratories – as a typical abuse of power. "If patents become an instrument of business policy," Arnold argued, "things like that [cartelization and monopolization] will happen."[61]

The Supreme Court also moved to reinforce the Arnold-led assault on big business. For two decades the "rule of reason" had been a fundamental guiding principle for antitrust action, but the Supreme Court threw out this rule in favor of a new doctrine defining the existence of monopoly when "power exists to raise prices or to exclude competition when it is desired to do so."[62] This dramatic shift in interpretation of the Sherman Act greatly affected Du Pont's business and its strategy for growth. Moreover, the Justice Department's assault on cartels meant that it would interpret the Du Pont-ICI Patents and Processes Agreement as cartelization and use the Sherman Act to end the agreement. The Supreme Court's ruling on the Aluminum Company of America case, which resulted in what became known as "the Aluminum Doctrine," also signaled to Du Pont that its "monopoly" on nylon would come under fire. As early as 1941, A. B. Echols began arguing that Du Pont should license nylon, even though the company had only introduced the product in 1939.[63] Continuing to feel pressure from the Justice Department, Du Pont eventually licensed nylon to Chemstrand in 1951. Du Pont's ability to maintain price leadership in cellophane and titanium dioxide also meant that the Justice Department would bring cases against the company in these businesses.[64] Finally, that Du Pont held roughly 25 percent of General Motors' stock rankled Arnold and his successors, who believed that free trade was thereby restrained to the detriment of the U.S. consumer. In 1949, the Justice Department brought a case against Du Pont, General Motors, and related du Pont family interests seeking to demonstrate violations of both the Sherman and Clayton antitrust acts. Justice Department work both prior and subsequent to the General Motors case was particularly important because the department was seeking stronger antimerger interpretations of existing antitrust statutes.[65] These efforts did not go unnoticed by Du Pont's executives. Increasingly, they grew in the conviction that growth by acquisition was out of the question.[66]

Reorientation of the Development Department

Du Pont's decision to discontinue in the nuclear energy field and to decline becoming a major defense contractor in rocketry emerged in the context of anti-big-business sentiment. After the immediate shock of the rapid conversion of Du Pont to wartime conditions was over, Fin Sparre submitted a Development Department report on postwar problems such as competition, sagging businesses, rapidly changing technologies, and new products that potentially threatened Du Pont's established products.[67] The Executive Committee deliberated long and hard over this report and finally issued a resolution stating that all departments of the company had to look to the postwar period. Each department, the committee said, bore the primary burden for planning its own future, and in cases where more than one department was affected, interdepartmental committees should be established to address the issues. The committee's resolution also called for the inclusion of a "post-war" section in all quarterly reports of the departments, and in response many of the departments established postwar planning organizations.[68]

The Executive Committee's resolution on postwar planning could be interpreted as a retreat from its responsibility for long-term strategic planning for the Du Pont Company. But Fin Sparre certainly would not have viewed it that way. Spurred by Walter Carpenter, Sparre had considered postwar planning to be important, and he continued to look at long-term strategic opportunities for the Du Pont Company. In August 1944, however, Sparre turned sixty-five, Du Pont's mandatory retirement age. He hoped that the company would make an exception to the rule, but it did not. With Sparre's retirement, Du Pont lost its greatest advocate for centralized long-range strategic planning. The Executive Committee's earlier resolution charging the industrial departments with responsibility for long-range planning gained new meaning.

From the time Sparre left the directorship of the Experimental Station to work "temporarily" for the Development Department, he had served the critical role – both unprecedented and afterward unparalleled – of charting the corporation's strategy of diversification and growth. In many respects, he was not replaceable. Times, political conditions, and the state of the company had changed since 1916, however. Sparre's retirement coincided with the Justice Department's first salvos against Du Pont in the 1940s and the company's executives' conclusion that the era of acquisitions was over. But the extraordinary success of nylon provided them with a new model for Du Pont's growth. These factors combined to alter dramatically the function of the Development Department in the post-Sparre era. Sparre's successor, Ernest K. Gladding, was brought in from outside the department much against the wishes of Sparre himself, who had recommended his assistant for the position. Gladding had been the first director of the Rayon Department's nylon division and before that the head of the department's technical division. It was Gladding, the conservative research director, who had strictly forbidden W. Hale Charch's Pioneering Laboratory to work on synthetic polymers for applications in films and fibers. Less informed and far less a visionary than Sparre, Gladding ran an altogether different show in the Development Department. Moreover, Gladding lacked Sparre's commanding authority, which had come from his years of experience in running the department and from his membership on Du Pont's board of directors.[69]

Gladding spent ten months in the Development Department before he presented a new departmental charter for the Executive Committee's approval. In a draft of this charter, he stated explicitly that the function of the Development Department had shifted "for two main reasons: First the Company's growth has made it vulnerable to Governmental restrictions as exemplified by recent interpretations of the Anti-Trust and Restraint of Trade Laws, and the tenor of bills now before Congress; second, the weighty effect of our own research." He concluded that "the first of these effects forces, and the second enables us to depend for solid growth on our own research efforts." Given these facts and that Wendell Swint, director of the Foreign Relations Department, had assumed all the international negotiation work that Sparre had carried out, Gladding saw new functions for his department. He advocated what he called "correlative work" – becoming an intermediary between departments as they "expand into new and more diversified fields [where] there is created an increasing area of common interest both as to processes and products." The Development Department should be aimed at "minimizing overlapping expenditures of effort and dollars" and settling disputes between departments.[70]

Gladding also proposed that the Development Department be responsible for periodic reviews of all departments of the company. He believed that such reviews would be "purely objective" and hence constructive for departmental managers. These reviews, Gladding suggested, would include "an attempt . . . to appraise the durability of existing profits, to examine the broad objectives of departmental research from the point of view of determining whether they appear adequate to support a healthy growth, [and] to review departmental performance against outside competition and in comparison with the performance of other departments having generally similar activities." Finally, Gladding proposed that his department continue to monitor the activities of Du Pont's principal competitors by collecting data from published sources and issued patents, attending technical meetings, and having close contact with departmental sales divisions.[71]

The Executive Committee approved Gladding's recommendations for the functions of the Development Department. Hence, more than a year after Sparre's retirement, the Development Department was rechartered with a much narrower mission than in Sparre's era.[72] Now the Development Department's role would be essentially passive compared to the aggressive manner in which Sparre had helped to diversify the company and to bring it into new areas of research, development, and manufacture. Perhaps taking his cues from the Executive Committee – although President Walter S. Carpenter was a man of great vision – Gladding had formulated a charter that reflected a growing sense of completeness or wholeness at Du Pont and even greater departmental autonomy and authority. Nowhere in Gladding's charter was there room for the Development Department, in the words of a later critic, "to develop fields for research and investment apart from and ahead of present interests of the Company and to obtain support for such efforts independent of the Industrial Departments."[73] Clearly, Gladding and the Executive Committee believed that the long-term growth of the Du Pont Company should be managed by the industrial departments. There was no need for any type of organization within Du Pont, save the Chemical Department, to be responsible principally for charting the future independence of the industrial departments. Under Gladding, the Development Department increasingly became a staff support group for the Executive Committee rather than the strategically centered department it had been since Sparre had joined it.[74] Among many other studies and projects done by the Development Department for the Executive Committee, handling the large expansion of the company's research facilities was perhaps its most important.

The Expansion of Research Facilities

The expansion of Du Pont's research facilities in the late 1940s was a critical part of the company's postwar strategy. By 1950 the company had spent well over $50 million on new laboratories, and this figure would grow much higher in the next five years. Earlier, however, executives had had to decide whether to expand Du Pont's research facilities, where such labs would be built, and what kind of research would be carried out in them. Ideas changed over time, particularly as Du Pont's overall strategy unfolded.

The need for corporatewide planning for expansion of research facilities arose in late 1943 when Elmer Bolton asked the Executive Committee to approve an expansion of the Chemical Department by fifty chemists to carry out fundamental research as soon as the war ended. Such an increase in staff meant an equal growth in facilities at the Experimental Station. The Rayon Department had already asked the committee for funds to move the Pioneering Research Laboratory to an unspecified site in Wilmington, and apparently at least one other department had made a similar request. Bolton had shown his proposal to certain members of the committee before formally submitting it. Jasper E. Crane called the proposal "entirely premature." He explained to Bolton that his request failed to consider what the industrial departments wanted to do, whether research personnel would be available after the war, and the implications of expanded research for the company's physical plant. Crane staunchly supported the expansion of research by both the Chemical Department and the industrial departments, but he wanted more careful consideration about how and where laboratories would be built. Above all, he sought to avoid duplication of facilities such as libraries and shops.[75] Crane apparently convinced his colleagues on the committee to turn down Bolton's proposal without taking any formal action. Instead, the committee asked the departments to state their goals for laboratory expansion.

Bolton's proposal reflected his mindset that all fundamental research at Du Pont should be done by the Chemical Department, either on its own account or for the industrial departments. Bolton's views had been shaped by past events. The industrial departments had indeed been supporting long-range research work in the Chemical Department on an increasing basis. Bolton believed that this trend would continue and that his department must be adequately staffed to handle growing industrial department demands for its services.[76] But Charles Stine's decade-long efforts to raise the scientific quality of industrial department research, the success of nylon, and the developing executive consensus that the company's growth would come through internally generated technology combined to create a new order in Du Pont's research establishment. Crane's response to Bolton's proposal hinted at the new order that would emerge: The industrial departments would be undertaking fundamental and long-range research on their own.

When the Executive Committee learned that Rayon, Grasselli, and Electrochemicals all wanted to locate laboratories for long-range research in Wilmington, preferably in close proximity to the Experimental Station, it asked the Development Department to make a study of the expansion of all company research facilities. This study was to recommend location, type, and cost of such facilities. The committee specifically asked the Development Department to consider whether all the long-range research activities of the industrial departments should be located "on a common site in the close proximity to the research activities of the Central Chemical Department." Should these facilities be consolidated or should each department have its own building? Given how crowded the Experimental Station was, the committee asked the Development Department to recommend how much expansion could occur there. Finally, the committee suggested that the study consider whether the Du Pont Golf Course adjacent to the Station might not be taken over as the site for all contemplated laboratory expansions.[77]

Aided by the Engineering Department, the Development Department spent seven months gathering data and drafting its study for the Executive Committee. Submitted in December 1944, the report called for locating Du Pont's long-range research at a central facility in or near Wilmington and favored the Du Pont Country Club golf course as the site. Accepting it as a "progress report," the Executive Committee concurred in the two major recommendations, yet it asked the Development Department to explore other site options.[78]

While the Development Department continued its work, Vice President Charles Stine made one of his last attempts to shape the course of Du Pont research. Although he was the creator of Du Pont's fundamental research program and the major force behind the improvement of industrial department research, Stine was not convinced that the industrial departments should undertake their own fundamental research. Seeing that Crawford Greenewalt's responsibilities on the Manhattan Project were at an end, Stine seized him and created a unique position for him as administrative assistant to the vice president for research. Greenewalt stayed in this position for only a month before he became assistant director of the Development Department, but Stine's intentions for Greenewalt are clear. During his brief tenure under Stine, Greenewalt prepared two position papers on Du Pont research, one entitled "Fundamental Research: Definition and Justification" and the other "The Place of Physics and Physical Chemistry in Du Pont

Research." Though Greenewalt may have viewed these papers as mere academic exercises, Stine thought otherwise. For him, they were an opportunity to shape the thinking of the future chief executive of the company about research.

Two days after assuming his duties, Greenewalt presented Stine with an outline of his study of fundamental research at Du Pont. Under "organization," Greenewalt posed a number of questions he hoped to address in his study, including two basic ones: "Should fundamental research be under the auspices of a single department or should it be spread among the industrial departments in accordance with their particular field of interest?" and "What is the most reasonable ultimate expenditure in manpower and dollars in this field and on what time schedule can this expenditure be approached?"[79] Stine responded both in writing and orally to Greenewalt's outline and expressed his philosophy of industrial research. In his written response, Stine enunciated two basic principles, one ultimately rejected by Greenewalt and the Executive Committee and the other fully concurred in by both.

In a manner reminiscent of his earlier ideas of an elite fundamental research organization, Stine opposed the industrial departments doing fundamental research. As he wrote, "Considering the nature of the problems of the individual industrial departments, and the conditions under which the technical personnel of the industrial departments carry on their work, i.e., the continual necessity for consideration of sales, service, current processes, new products, improvement of present products, etc., it seems to me unlikely that the assignment of personnel to fundamental research work under the direction of the individual industrial departments would, in the long run, be as fruitful of results as if carried on in a central research organization."[80] Stine's viewpoint was clearly in the minority on the Executive Committee, and his retirement from the committee in June — five days after the committee approved in principle the Development Department's master plan for the expansion of research at the Station — meant that such a position would not be forcefully held within the committee.[81] In fact, Greenewalt's final report avoided entirely the issue of whether fundamental research should be done by the industrial departments.[82] The door was now fully open for industrial departments to do fundamental research by and for themselves.

In regard to a formula for the correct amount of money to spend on fundamental research, Stine's views prevailed, perhaps because they were consonant with those expressed much earlier by Walter S. Carpenter. Stine argued that although there must be "some limit" to how much a company could spend on fundamental research, the "nature and scope of the work" proposed and the "personnel available" were the determining factors in putting together a research budget.[83] In effect, Stine reiterated Carpenter's earlier policy that any good research project would be funded by the Executive Committee. Du Pont would not establish its research budgets by rigid adherence to formulas such as percentages of sales, earnings, and construction expenditures. Greenewalt adhered to this position in 1945 and through the remainder of his career at Du Pont.[84]

Following the completion of his two special reports for Stine, Greenewalt became assistant director of the Development Department. His task was to handle the department's work on the expansion of research facilities.[85] Greenewalt had to resolve two major questions about the project. The Executive Committee had already approved the idea of a central location and had resigned itself to encroaching on the golf course, but it was not clear how this site would be managed and whether the new research facilities would be housed in a single structure or in separate buildings spread over the grounds of the expanded Experimental Station. Greenewalt promptly tackled these issues. At the same time, he tried to persuade more industrial departments – especially the very independent Organic Chemicals Department – to locate at the Station. The first problem was easily dealt with when the Chemical Department agreed to manage the expanded Experimental Station site. In effect, it would be the landlord for the other departments. Moreover, as site manager, it would be responsible for all nontechnical personnel and all services at the Station and would bill the industrial departments for these services.[86]

Addressing the second question took more time. To explore alternatives, Greenewalt and others in Development spent considerable time at the relatively new Bell Telephone Laboratories facility in Murray Hill, New Jersey, which in the words of Jeremy Bernstein is "essentially one gigantic building."[87] Greenewalt concluded that this approach was not best for Du Pont. Rather, he envisioned the expanded Experimental Station being "something like a university campus," a phrase often used to describe the approach to the project.[88]

Once the decisions had been reached to construct separate laboratory buildings for each department and to have the Chemical Department serve as landlord for the Station complex, Du Pont made two innovative decisions about the construction of individual laboratories. First, all but a few special-purpose laboratories would be essentially identical, thus lowering construction costs and facilitating maintenance and safety practices. Second, the laboratory design would be based on the ideas of chemists rather than those of architects. A mockup of a single laboratory, based on the architects' ideas, was constructed at the Station, and groups of chemists from each resident department walked through it and made comments. The final laboratory design was derived from a distillation of these chemists' comments and became a model for many other industrial laboratories in the United States.

Planning moved quickly. On June 13, 1945, Gladding, Greenewalt, and J. H. Perry from the Development Department, Elmer Bolton, E. G. Ackart (chief engineer), and representatives of an architectural firm met with the Executive Committee to present the fully developed plan for the expansion along with a model of the project, which showed how it would cut into the golf course. The committee approved the plan in principle, although the plan did not specify the exact size of the new Du Pont Research Center, as it was becoming known.[89]

Elmer Bolton gave more attention to the nature and implications of the Research Center as the Development Department further refined its plan. Out of his thoughts and subsequent discussions with Walter Carpenter emerged a new charter for Du Pont research at the Research Center. In September 1945, Bolton wrote a statement outlining his thoughts on the new facility. Perhaps concerned about how the industrial departments were viewing the Station expansion, Bolton developed the thesis that all work at the Research Center should be limited to "fundamental and pioneering research." The implication was clear. Bolton saw that some members of the Executive Committee and perhaps the general managers of the industrial departments were viewing the expansion of the facilities at the Experimental Station as mainly the relocation of existing laboratories. For Bolton, such thinking was inadequate. If work at the Research Center were limited to fundamental and pioneering research, Du Pont's total research budget would necessarily be significantly increased. The Research Center would supplement, not supplant, existing research facilities and operating expenditures.[90]

President Walter Carpenter received a copy of Bolton's statement, and his response to Bolton made clear his understanding of Bolton's logic. Carpenter called Bolton's plan to limit research at the new Center to fundamental and pioneering work "impressive" and accepted it as "conclusive." In regard to the expenditure of money for the Center, Carpenter also realized that it would entail more than the capital for construction and equipment. Carpenter was comfortable with a larger research budget because, he said, "there is going to be more and more competition in the industrial world in the future than henceforth, which will, in turn, require more and more research for new and improved processes and products." But, he cautioned, "If research is done extravagantly, certainly less research can be afforded. Whereas what we want is more research – not less." In a way typical of his quest for clarity of purpose, Carpenter reminded Bolton of the need to know why Du Pont was expanding its research:

> Some men have pointed out the advantages of having this Research Center as a great monument to a great chemical industry. Others have pointed out the advantages from a public relations standpoint. Still others have mentioned that by affording comfortable and congenial surroundings, we can more easily attract new technical employees to our Company. Each of these points, and many others, may be desirable or incidental collateral advantages of pursuing one course or another; but it does seem to me that we should keep in mind, in connection with every move we make regarding this or any alternative program, the fundamental question – where are we going, and why, and how?

Carpenter asked Bolton to "put down, not in fifty pages, but perhaps a hundred words, a statement indicating where we are going, why we are going there, and how we can best get there." If Bolton could do this, Carpenter said, it would be much easier for the Executive Committee to reach decisions on both the large and small issues surrounding the proposed Research Center.[91]

Bolton's reply — some ten times longer than Carpenter had suggested — charted the future policy of the Du Pont Company's research program and indeed its strategy for future growth. The war had created a void in fundamental research. Academic science had "practically dried up," and industrial research organizations had had their research restricted. But, Bolton argued, "the country is about to enter a period of unparalleled scientific activity." Universities were expanding educational and research facilities; industry was poised to "undertake a very substantial expansion of personnel and of research facilities." (A Development Department study of 1945 had demonstrated the construction of fifty-four "comparatively new research laboratories" in the United States.[92]) Even small companies were planning to engage in research. The federal government had determined to continue military-related research in its army and navy laboratories, and it seemed certain that the government research foundation prescribed by Vannevar Bush would be established to support research "on an enormous scale."[93]

Du Pont's situation was clear, Bolton argued. Three things were necessary: Du Pont had to strengthen its research organizations and house them in modern research facilities; the company's existing processes had to be improved and new processes and products developed; and "fundamental research, which will serve as a background for new advances in applied chemistry, should be expanded not only in the Chemical Department but should [also] be increased in our industrial research laboratories and the Engineering Department." Bolton stressed that it was no longer "possible to rely to the same extent as in the past upon university research to supply this background so that in future years it will be necessary for the Company to provide this knowledge to a far greater extent through its own efforts." To "retain its leadership" Du Pont had "to undertake on a much broader scale fundamental research in order to provide more knowledge to serve as a basis for applied research." To do this, Du Pont had "to have a research center where environment, facilities, and associations are conducive to the best kind of creative work." Bolton concluded, "This is the only plan that will enable Du Pont to retain its strength and to insure future growth."[94]

Bolton's reply to Carpenter became something of a master plan for the Du Pont Company's growth strategy. Du Pont would seek its fortune through long-range research carried out principally at the greatly expanded Experimental Station. The Executive Committee bought Bolton's arguments in principle as well as the plans prepared by the Development Department. But it quarreled with some of the specifics of the plan, such as the dimensions of the standard laboratory units and the architecture and landscaping of the facility. Not until February 1946 did Gladding submit a plan he regarded as final. Seeing the estimated $24 million price tag, however, the committee began to chip away at cost reduction. One way was to design the expansion only to handle projected growth to January 1, 1950, rather than through 1952. The committee also eliminated facilities for Explosives and Electrochemicals. By mid-1946, the Research Center had been scaled back to $17 million. The committee approved the plan and authorized the expenditure.[95]

Curiously, soon after the committee appropriated the funds, Elmer Bolton wrote the committee and asked that the name "Du Pont Research Center" be dropped and the name "Experimental Station of E. I. du Pont de Nemours & Company" be retained. Bolton argued that the facility had been known for over forty years as the Experimental Station; hence its name was well established both in academic and industrial circles. The Chemical Department's publications had long been known as *Contributions to the Scientific Literature from the Experimental Station*. Moreover, the use of "Research Center" implied that all Du Pont research would be done there, when in fact Organic Chemicals, Electrochemicals, Photo Products, Explosives, and Fabrics and Finishes would be absent. Bolton estimated that only a third of all the company's research personnel would be stationed at the Center by January 1, 1950. He suggested that departments not represented at the Research Center might have difficulty recruiting personnel if the new name were adopted because graduates would "gain the impression that all important research" was carried out at the Center.[96] The Executive Committee concurred in Bolton's recommendation, and after July 3, 1946, the use of the name Du Pont Research Center was permanently dropped.[97]

Shortly thereafter the committee voted to put the entire project on hold. This action in no way signaled a retreat from its strategy of growth through research. Alarmed by skyrocketing construction costs in all areas of Du Pont's capital expansion program, the committee did not single out research facilities as a means of saving money. Rather, it hoped that delay would allow time for inflationary pressures to ease. Recruiting for researchers continued unabated, and to house the expanding research enterprise, the company crowded researchers into existing laboratories, put up temporary buildings, and converted nearby factory buildings into temporary research facilities. Research budgets grew far faster than had been forecast in 1946.[98]

By January 1948, Bolton believed the situation was getting out of hand and pressed hard for authorization to undertake the remainder of the Experimental Station expansion. With design work almost 90 percent complete, the two additions to the Chemical Department's buildings 75 percent finished, and relocation of the county's road by the Station more than half finished, Bolton believed the full project should go forward. He asked for a new authorization of $21 million and noted that these plans did not contain space for the growth of research personnel beyond the estimated completion date of the site in 1950. The proposal, he implied, was the bare bones, absolute minimum. He buttressed his case for the expansion by detailing the current inadequacies in research space, department by department, and summed up the situation by arguing that the current facilities "result[ed] in inefficient conduct of research." Moreover, much' research was being done under "hazardous conditions" because of lack of hood space.[99]

The Executive Committee carefully considered Bolton's request, and after hearing from each of the concerned industrial departments, its members approved the scope of the Station project but deferred final authorization until a firm estimate of construction costs was submitted.[100] This action was consistent with the recommendation of the company's economist who maintained that "all capital expenditures should, when reasonably possible, be postponed until construction costs are again back to more normal levels."[101] The new president of the company, Crawford Greenewalt, worried about such a large expenditure. But when he reflected that the company had not built any research facilities in ten years and that the company spent $35 million a year on research "without batting an eye," he gave his strong support to the project. Greenewalt thought that Du Pont would be "pennywise and pound-foolish" if it "took any chances whatever with our research position for the future."[102]

Even before the final estimate of the expansion projects had been finished, the Executive Committee approved the construction of two laboratories that were part of the project, a $3.5 million building for the Ammonia Department and a $1 million Pioneering Research Laboratory for the Rayon Department. Soon, the committee asked the Finance Committee to appropriate funds for the entire project. The Finance Committee agreed, asking only that the laboratory expansion program stay within the committee's forecast $340 million capital expenditure budget approved in late 1946 for 1947, 1948, and 1949. Indeed, the Finance Committee authorized $50 million for construction of R&D facilities, including the Experimental Station expansion.[103] With this authorization, departments not locating on the Station grounds built new research facilities or expanded existing ones. Some departments, including Rayon and Grasselli, expanded their research facilities both at the Station and elsewhere. Moreover, within four or five years of the dedication of the Experimental Station (May 10, 1951), both the Electrochemicals and Pigments departments had built new laboratories there for long-range research.

Led by the Rayon (soon to be renamed Textile Fibers) Department, Du Pont also established sales and technical support facilities in Wilmington approximately two miles from the Experimental Station. These facilities – called the Chestnut Run Site – were laid out like the Experimental Station and planned to complement the long-range research work being done at the Station. They focused on product development and end-use research.[104]

By expanding its research facilities so significantly – and, along with them, the company's R&D budget – Du Pont had clearly staked its future on the rewards of research. This strategy was one of the hallmarks of the presidency of Crawford H. Greenewalt, whose earlier career had exemplified the achievements possible through corporate R&D.

The Greenewalt Presidency

In the twentieth century history of the Du Pont Company, there was perhaps never a more perfect fit between corporate objectives and the career, style, and philosophy of the company's president than during the presidency of Crawford H. Greenewalt. When he succeeded Walter Carpenter in January 1948, Greenewalt was still fundamentally a research manager, although those in more senior positions sought to provide him with broader experience as quickly as possible following his tour of duty on the Manhattan Project.

Greenewalt's career was the embodiment of Du Pont's new strategy of growth. His work as supervisor of semiworks development for nylon earned him Bolton's accolades: "The successful conclusion of our [i.e., the Chemical Department's] phase of the work was in no small measure due to the contribution made by Greenewalt." Bolton said Greenewalt possessed "to an unusual degree a combination of research and executive ability."[105] Nylon's development clearly demonstrated how he could make critical technical decisions based on commercial criteria.

Greenewalt probably would have been content to stay in the Chemical Department for the remainder of his career. But he was called to assume other responsibilities. This call came entirely from members of the du Pont family – Pierre, Irénée, and Lammot du Pont – who were vitally concerned with keeping the company as a family-owned and -managed business. Greenewalt was family. His aunt had married a brother of the three du Pont presidents, and his familial ties grew stronger when in 1926 he married Margaretta, a daughter of the company's president, Irénée du Pont. Irénée and his brothers, as well as R. R. M. and Walter Carpenter (who were also considered "family"), carefully watched Greenewalt's career during the 1930s with the idea of executive succession in mind. Greenewalt's contentment with his situation in the Chemical Department no doubt worried the du Pont elders.[106]

But in 1942, they broke him loose from the department when the Executive Committee leaned on the Grasselli Chemicals Department to revamp its long-neglected research program. Greenewalt was given this difficult task as director of Grasselli's chemical division. In retrospect, he was perhaps lucky that the Manhattan Project pulled him away from the morass of the Grasselli organization, for it was with this project that Greenewalt came into his own as a translator of research into practice and as someone who could, as Harry Truman said, "take the heat."

Greenewalt's role as technical liaison between Chicago's Metallurgical Laboratory and Du Pont has already been discussed, but it is important to note the speed and extent with which Greenewalt grasped the nuclear physics that underlay the Hanford Works. Starting from virtually no knowledge of fission in October 1942, he rapidly acquired a deep knowledge of reactor physics — deep enough to keep a check on Chicago physicists and not to be cowed by them. One example of Greenewalt's scientific abilities will suffice: When in 1944 the reactivity of the first Hanford production pile dropped after the pile had been loaded with uranium and was approaching full power, Greenewalt offered two hypotheses to account for this phenomenon. Working quickly through one of them, he demonstrated that the pile reaction was creating a highly neutron-absorbent gas (Xenon-135) that lowered the reactivity rate of the pile. He informed both John Wheeler and Enrico Fermi of his calculations, and they, approaching the problem in different ways, confirmed his hypothesis.[107] Greenewalt so impressed Fermi and Compton that both offered him positions in their postwar research enterprises. Not clear about his future at Du Pont, Greenewalt seriously considered these offers but ultimately chose to remain with Du Pont.[108]

The Manhattan Project's success and the elder du Ponts' continued concerns about family management of the company quickly propelled Greenewalt to the top.[109] Following his work on the Manhattan Project, he was given a whirlwind tour through the company, serving in a sixteen-month period as Charles Stine's assistant, assistant director of the Development Department, and assistant general manager of the Pigments Department. In June 1946, he was named a vice president and member of the Executive Committee, and soon he was serving a short apprenticeship as vice chairman of the Executive Committee under Walter Carpenter. Although still relatively young, Carpenter stepped down as president in January 1948, and Greenewalt, at age 45, was named president by the board of directors of which he had been a member for six years.[110]

The Greenewalt presidency was marked by two major characteristics that are central to understanding the company's history. On the one hand, Du Pont had built up an extreme technological confidence through such successes as nylon and the Manhattan Project. On the other hand, the company faced great political and economic uncertainty as various branches of the federal government both courted and condemned Du Pont for its past achievements and present capabilities.[111] Facing these circumstances, Greenewalt ultimately followed his instincts — instincts that had been bred in the R&D laboratory.

Not long after assuming the presidency, Greenewalt articulated what he believed to be the Du Pont Company's two fundamental principles of growth and development that had served in the past and would continue to govern in the future. Writing in his first annual report as president, Greenewalt noted, "The first of these has been to seek diversification in any chemical field to which it can make a substantial technical contribution." Such a principle meant that "research results have been applied over a wide commercial area." But Du Pont had not done research and development in just any area of the chemical industry. Rather, as Greenewalt stressed, "the second principle has been to direct the Company's research and manufacturing efforts primarily to the large and difficult tasks which inherently require great resources in technical ability and finances."[112] Greenewalt's second principle was a corollary to the one laid down some forty years earlier by Pierre du Pont, who said that the company should always have a few really big, high-risk research projects going because the company stood to benefit both from potentially large payoffs and from keeping an expert force of researchers continually engaged by the company. Greenewalt, the chemical engineer turned executive, envisioned the company developing and managing large, integrated, continuous-process chemical plants that would be the embodiment of his principles.[113] In the future, Du Pont would marshal its resources to do what most other companies could not. From these efforts, "new nylons" would emerge.

New Nylons and Du Pont's Future

The rapid and strong impact that nylon's success had on the Du Pont Company's strategy of growth and its concomitant R&D policies is perhaps best expressed in the phrase "new nylons." By 1945, these two words had become shorthand for the whole paradigmatic shift in Du Pont's research program whereby all the industrial departments, not just the Chemical Department, would undertake fundamental research at the expanded Experimental Station. From a policy level, Crawford Greenewalt's widely circulated report, "Fundamental Research: Definition and Justification," stated the matter succinctly: "We are interested primarily in fundamental research studies which are likely to produce new nylons."[114] Greenewalt had included this statement in the final draft of his report despite the concerns of Elmer Bolton, who had cautioned him not to place "too great an emphasis on nylon as a model." Bolton argued that "a development of this importance can be expected only rarely and perhaps once in a generation and that it would be asking for too much of any fundamental research program to expect developments of this magnitude at frequent intervals." Greenewalt conceded that Bolton had "a good point" but argued that "some attempt should be made to put the possibilities on more of a statistical basis to indicate that the general level and importance of the attainments of a fundamental research investigation will be higher than if fundamental research did not exist."[115] His views were perfectly consistent with those expressed by Stine almost two decades earlier when Stine first sold the fundamental research program to the Executive Committee. Subsequently, especially during his tenure as president of the company (1948–62), Greenewalt often pondered the statistical basis of research and concluded that it was but a form of gambling where the odds were greatly improved through the conduct of fundamental research within a widely diversified company such as Du Pont.[116]

Following Greenewalt's logic, the Executive Committee proceeded to expand research and move it increasingly in the direction of fundamental research. This shift after 1945 opened up several issues and concerns, the two most important of which were what role the Chemical Department should assume now that the industrial departments would do fundamental research and whether the growth of Du Pont's research budget was out of control by the late 1940s given the state of the chemical industry and the U.S. economy.

The question about the role of the Chemical Department emerged from the creation in 1946 of the high polymer committee, made up of representatives from the Rayon, Plastics, and Ammonia departments, to coordinate the exploitation of nylon. In recommending the establishment of this committee to the Executive Committee, the general manager of the Ammonia Department (which was responsible for nylon intermediates) wrote that "responsibility for working toward new nylons or nylon substitutes we believe should continue to rest primarily in the Chemical Department with the several industrial departments cooperating in the evaluation of the products as well as in the supply of experimental raw materials."[117]

Responding to this statement, Bolton pointed up the ambiguity of the expression "new nylons." He told Roger Williams, executive advisor for research, that he interpreted the statement as meaning "the primary function of the Chemical Department was to carry out fundamental work that would lead to new classes of organic materials such as 'new nylons,' as contrasted with detailed exploration of all possibilities in a class that we discover and the evaluation of the products." Thus, the Chemical Department was "to open up new areas of chemistry which would provide new materials that might have the possibility of commercial utility." Reflecting the new thinking at Du Pont, Bolton maintained that his department "should not take and actually cannot take the sole responsibility for opening up new areas of chemistry but should share this responsibility with the chemical divisions of the industrial departments."[118]

Bolton sought to delineate the responsibilities of his department from those of the industrial departments. He argued that when the Chemical Department discovered a new class of chemicals, it should not be obliged to make a "detailed exploration" of this class. Rather, such work should be done by the industrial departments, thus allowing the Chemical Department to turn its "attention to new lines of fundamental research." The company ran risks with this approach because the Chemical Department could only establish a good (as opposed to excellent) patent position through the prosecution of broad patents, leaving the necessary support of such patents through narrower but more enforceable patents to the industrial departments. Bolton maintained that the company faced much higher risks of losing out on entirely new fields if the Chemical Department were not free to move its research along. As he explained to Williams, "This plan of action is offensive rather than defensive."[119] No doubt Bolton sought to avoid another situation like the development of nylon, in which the Chemical Department was forced to skew its research program significantly toward process development and exploitation of the polyamides. Bolton had long been concerned that nylon had led to an imbalanced research program in the Chemical Department.[120] Now that the industrial departments had greatly strengthened their research programs, Bolton was convinced that this situation could be avoided by quickly passing new discoveries along to the appropriate department.

Williams's response to Bolton's position paper, unfortunately, does not survive, but over the next year discussion continued on the role of the Chemical Department in the company, particularly as it related to the industrial departments. By mid-1947, Bolton had obtained a consensus within the Executive Committee supporting his position. The department's primary responsibility function was "to carry out a long-range type of research which may be expected to contribute to the future expansion of the company, particularly in new lines of business."[121] At the same time, the committee gave the departments its formal go-ahead to develop their own fundamental research programs.

Staking Du Pont's future on research, the Executive Committee began in the late 1940s to give more attention to numerical analyses of trends in research expenditures compared to other financial trends in the company as a whole, including sales, earnings, construction expenditures, and investment. Perhaps this change reflected the thinking of the new president Greenewalt, who as an engineer had long been accustomed to correlating data in order to understand phenomena.[122]

At the end of 1947, the Executive Committee asked the Development Department to undertake a study of Du Pont research as a means of "developing better ways of conducting research and utilizing its results."[123] The Development Department's report fell short of this goal, but it did provide a longer-range statistical perspective on Du Pont research than had been available before. The report's author drew some interesting conclusions from these data about long-term trends in Du Pont research. Placing great emphasis on the significance of research costs as a percentage of investment, the author demonstrated that this figure had moved from a stable level of about 2 percent in the period 1929 to 1944 to above 3 percent after the war. But by preparing data on "research effort vs. investment" (as measured by the number of research personnel per $1 million investment), the report showed a remarkable constancy in Du Pont research over the entire period 1929 to 1948. Over the period, the ratio had been 2.2, plus or minus 10 percent. As the author wrote: "Although the Company's total research expense increased over fivefold from 1929 to 1947, and the number of research personnel increased slightly over threefold in the same period, the actual volume of research, as measured by the number of personnel engaged in it, appears to have just about kept pace with the investment growth of the Company."[124]

The underlying reason for this flat curve was the rise in the cost of supporting research personnel. In 1929, this figure was $7,000 per researcher; in 1947, $15,800. This trend was likely to continue given growing competition for research personnel, and it pointed to "a continuing high research bill" just to stay even with the past in terms of research effort. Moreover, these figures looked even worse to the report's author, who argued that in reality, Du Pont's research effort was greater in the prewar era because the statistics did not reflect the research equivalent of the know-how and capital gained through acquisition of companies, patents, and processes, a route to innovation seen as no longer open to Du Pont.[125] The implication of these arguments was clear. To increase Du Pont's overall research effort, the company would have to spend even more for research than had been previously anticipated. Soon it appeared to many executives that research expenses were increasing too rapidly.

In 1950, with the company experiencing marked decline in sales leading to layoffs in some of its plants, executives carefully weighed current conditions against long-term research expenditure trends. In late September 1949, the committee sent word to the department heads that it wanted research managers to hold the line on their next year's budgets. But when research budget proposals came to the committee, all managers but one asked for more money. They also asked for a 10 percent increase in research personnel. The committee took a strong stand against these increases. It resolved to revise downward all research budgets to the 1949 level and to forewarn that 1951 budgets would not be allowed to exceed those for 1950. As part of its resolution, the committee explained its actions, reflecting its recently acquired knowledge of long-term research trends: Research personnel had increased at the rate of 8 percent per year since 1934 and at a much higher rate since 1945 (compared with the 5 percent rate of growth in investment since 1945); research costs had doubled; technical assistance to production had risen 50 percent, as had technical assistance to sales; and patent costs had increased by more than 25 percent. Although the committee accepted that research budgets would rise, it was alarmed at the recent trends. It stated the principle – clearly growing out of the recent analyses by the Development Department – that "the long-term trend of research costs should be nearly in line with the trend of total investment." As it was, the slope of the curve on research costs was far greater than that on permanent investments. Projected far enough into the future, research costs would equal total investment – a frightening prospect.[126]

Thus as the Du Pont Company prepared to enter the new half-century, its executives were seeking the right formula for success. In the face of growing hostility from the Antitrust Division of the Justice Department, they had concluded that further growth through acquisition was impossible.

Nylon's success gave them a ready solution to their dilemma: Du Pont would grow through its own R&D efforts. All the industrial departments would engage in long-range and fundamental research while the Chemical Department would devote itself almost exclusively to fundamental research aimed at leading the company into entirely new fields. After some delay, the Executive Committee reconciled itself to a major expansion of research facilities and a concomitant growth in R&D personnel. But at the same time, executives looking for the first time at long-term trends in research expenditures tempered their enthusiasm for "new nylons" with concern over how fast Du Pont's research budget was rising relative to other trends. Perhaps uneasy about how much money to put down, the executives nonetheless had chosen, in Crawford Greenewalt's words, to gamble at the table of research. For the next eight years, they stayed at this table, each year laying down high stakes and hoping for big payoffs in "new nylons."

17

The Pursuit of Science
at Du Pont

World War II created a new chemical community in which the distinctions between academic or pure science and industrial or applied science became increasingly blurred. This rapprochement had begun in the 1930s when the discoveries of neoprene and nylon showed how investment in pure science could yield enormous returns. But it was the great wartime cooperative programs – such as the Manhattan Project and the creation of the synthetic rubber industry – that generated mutual respect between pure and applied scientists. After the war, Du Pont and other chemical companies put increasing emphasis on doing their own science. In other words, they integrated backward in research. The pace of research in areas of interest to corporations had quickened, and universities did not have the resources to keep up. To redress this imbalance, companies gave more money to support academic research and postgraduate education. But companies relied on internal scientific research for future profits.

This additional activity made the already difficult job of research director even more challenging. The postwar PhDs came to industry armed with a sophisticated body of scientific knowledge, advanced research skills, and an expectation that they could enjoy professional status.[1] Not surprisingly, the 1950s witnessed the rapid growth of the field of research management, the goal of which, in part, was to lessen the strains between science and industry. Sociologists portrayed scientists as professionals who subscribed to a rigorous code of ethics and demanded that their efforts contribute to the larger corpus of knowledge, not just to company profits. These studies generally legitimized the individual scientist's need for some degree of autonomy, even in large corporations.[2]

Yet, in spite of the sociologists' efforts, industrial research actually had changed much less than the prophets had forecast. A Booz, Allen, and Hamilton survey in 1957 indicated that only 4 percent of industrial chemical researchers claimed to be working in basic science.[3] This fact contradicted what many young PhDs expected to find in industrial laboratories, and companies experienced considerable difficulty reconciling their scientists' expectations with the realities of industrial research. In the 1950s, managers had to work out compromises to keep their scientists happy and to keep their research productive.

In the postwar era, fundamental research at Du Pont continued to fall roughly into the two categories, one delineated by Charles Stine and one by Elmer Bolton in the 1920s and 1930s.[4] As Stine had pointed out in his proposals to the Executive Committee, he expected fundamental research to put a scientific foundation beneath Du Pont's technology. The study of catalysts represents perhaps the best example of this approach. They were enormously important to the production of almost all chemicals, but no one really understood how they worked. Consequently, companies invested large sums of money and much staff effort into finding the right catalyst to make a particular product. A general theory of catalytic action or even some empirically derived principles, Stine maintained, could save millions of dollars in R&D and production costs.

In contrast to this philosophy, the Bolton approach to fundamental research derived from the nylon model, in which scientists move into uncharted fields to be pioneers, scouting out the territory and laying claim to its riches before others appear on the scene. Bolton realized that this was only a first step and that any scientific finding would have to be coupled with a market opportunity to lead to a new product. By focusing the Chemical Department's programs on polymers, he believed those connections would be assured because of the importance of polymers to most of Du Pont's businesses and his own extensive knowledge of the field. In the postwar era, Du Pont's R&D organizations would pursue both types of fundamental research, with the industrial departments generally, though not exclusively, employing the Stine approach and the Chemical Department pursuing that of Bolton.

Du Pont and the Chemistry Community

As the leader of the U.S. chemical industry, Du Pont realized that it had a responsibility for the health of its supporting disciplines. In 1958, Du Pont employed approximately 4 percent of American industrial chemists, and the company's total number of PhDs in chemistry equaled about 30 percent of the U.S. chemists in academia.[5] Du Pont not only depended heavily on the advance of chemical sciences but also employed a significant fraction of the nation's resources in that area. In spite of strong challenges from other companies, Du Pont maintained its position of leadership by devoting to fundamental research about a fifth of its research budget, twice the average of its competitors.[6]

In terms of resources, academic chemistry paled in comparison to the prosperous corporations. The production of PhD chemists did not increase in the 1950s, when industry was booming, in part because of insufficient funds.[7] Universities increasingly looked to corporations for financial support and reoriented research objectives toward applied science. As early as 1948, Du Pont president Greenewalt became alarmed at this state of affairs and wrote to the Executive Committee research advisor, Roger Williams:

In recent years there seems to me to have been a most unfortunate trend away from fundamental research on the part of the universities and toward supported work in more nearly applied fields, which has had the effect of converting some of our universities into little more than academic A. D. Littles.[8]

Greenewalt maintained that his alma mater, the Massachusetts Institute of Technology, had been one of the worst offenders in this respect, but that its president Karl Compton had argued that his institution needed money and this was the only way to get it.

Under Greenewalt's leadership, the Executive Committee in 1948 voted to begin funding fundamental research in universities.[9] The issue had first come up in 1946, when the University of Chicago sought funds for its Institute of Nuclear Studies. Du Pont's management did not want to deal with requests for funds on a case-by-case basis, preferring instead to have a general policy.[10] The Executive Committee adopted such a policy after the University of Chicago again asked for funds for its Institute of Nuclear Studies, Metals, and Radiobiology and Biophysics. Du Pont decided to give $100,000 over five years for metals research at Chicago because this work was of interest to Du Pont. At the same time, the company appropriated funds for ten $10,000 grants-in-aid for fundamental research in universities. Up to this time, Du Pont's aid to education had consisted entirely of graduate and a few postdoctoral fellowships. In 1946 this program cost the company over $200,000.[11] Soon other companies set up similar fellowship programs, and it appeared that funding of graduate students might be nearing saturation. For the first time, in 1952, two students rejected Du Pont aid to accept other fellowships.[12]

In the 1950s, colleges and universities intensified their appeals for business support. Their efforts received a boost in 1951, when Alfred P. Sloan published an article, "Big Business Must Help Our Colleges," in *Colliers*, and two years later when a New Jersey court upheld the legality of corporate contributions to education. In this test case, one company's stockholders had sued, claiming that the practice was a misuse of corporate profits; the plaintiffs preferred larger dividend checks. When the threat of stockholder suits subsided, corporations significantly increased their contributions to education.[13]

To maintain its "corporate citizenship" or "industrial statesmanship," Du Pont explored new ways to aid scientific education within its larger policy. Du Pont did not give money to institutions for general use but attempted to target its assistance to specific needs. For example, because salaries of young professors were very low and many were leaving academia for better-paying jobs in industry, Du Pont provided summer research grants for young faculty members. The company also provided postgraduate teaching assistant awards because the best students usually got research fellowships and did not have to teach. Du Pont used these awards to keep some of the better students in the classroom, training the next generation of chemists. Other forms of aid included support of undergraduate science instruction in private liberal arts colleges and summer programs for retraining high school science teachers. Generally, Du Pont gave money to promote teaching and research in science and engineering. It did not give general, unrestricted funds or support other disciplines.[14]

Continuing its program of targeted giving, Du Pont discouraged institutions from constantly requesting money for projects; Du Pont had a policy and stuck to it. The only shortcoming of the company's approach was that its total support for education in absolute terms and as a percentage of earnings fell below that of other large corporations.[15] This worried some Du Pont executives, but Julian Hill, chairman of the company's Committee on Educational Aid from its founding in 1951 to 1964, maintained that "public relations, in the popular sense, is very low in our roster of motivations, if it can be said to be there at all" and that "trying to do the right thing well results in the best public relations."[16] Du Pont's level of overall support was considerably higher than the reported total because it did not take into account industrial department funds committed to support research outside the corporation. The departments funded work in universities and research institutes that had relevance to their commercial interests.

Du Pont's scientists and engineers served in professional organizations and government advisory agencies, although probably not to any greater extent than their corporate or academic colleagues. The public service career of Theodore L. Cairns, a research manager in Central Research, was extraordinary and serves to illustrate how much outside work an industrial scientist at Du Pont could take on if he so desired. As will be discussed later in this chapter, Cairns was one of Du Pont's outstanding chemists in the 1950s and 1960s and was elected to the National Academy of Sciences in 1966. Over the years, Cairns held numerous positions in the American Chemical Society and was a member of the editorial board of three chemical journals. In 1964 he became a member of the Committee for the Survey of Chemistry appointed by the National Academy of Sciences to assess the status of chemistry in the United States. Cairns also served on President Nixon's Science Policy Task Force and the President's Science Advisory Committee between 1969 and 1973. By the time Cairns became the director of Central Research in 1971, he had established himself as a major figure in the U.S. scientific community, primarily for his original work in chemistry and his service to the profession.[17] All his efforts benefited Du Pont's image in academia by showing that company employees could become full-fledged members of the larger scientific community.

Du Pont made its most direct contributions to science through the publications of its researchers. So did other companies. By the end of the 1950s, corporate chemists were writing a third of the articles that appeared in the top six chemical journals. Over the five-year period 1957-62, Du Pont scientists accounted for 8 percent of corporate contributions, followed by American Cyanamid, Monsanto, and Dow with 5, 4, and 3 percent re

Table 17.1. *Relative Intensities of Publishing for the Five Largest U.S. Chemical Companies, 1960–62 (in percent)*

	Sales	Publications
Du Pont	36.1	33.5
Union Carbide	25.4	13.8
Monsanto	15.4	15.3
Dow	13.3	12.9
American Cyanamid	9.8	24.5
Total	100.0	100.0

Source: Melville H. Hodge, Jr., "Rate Your Company's Research Productivity," *Harvard Business Review* 41 (Nov. 1963), p, 121.

spectively.[18] A comparison of the five largest U.S. chemical companies showed that the publications from three of them, Du Pont, Monsanto, and Dow, correlated closely with the relative sizes of their companies. Of the other two, American Cyanamid published more and Union Carbide less than expected (see Table 17.1). These data suggest that Du Pont did at least its "fair share" of publishing.

Publications presented a real dilemma for Du Pont's research directors. They always worried about the disclosure of information that would either give away company secrets or lead other researchers to make important discoveries. After Carothers's publications led I. G. Farben to discover nylon-6 and ultimately prompted Whinfield and Dickson to study polyesters, most of Du Pont's research managers supported the view that the risks of publication outweighed the benefits and therefore implemented a much more highly restrictive publication policy. De facto, it was a moratorium. (See Chapters 15 and 18 for additional discussion of the fallout from Carothers's publication.)

In response to requests to publish a paper, Du Pont research managers frequently asserted that the award of a patent should fulfill a chemist's desire for recognition for his contributions to the field. The problem with this argument, from the viewpoint of the chemist, was that academic chemists did not follow the patent literature. In addition, the names that appeared on a patent reflected lawyers' decisions based on patent law rather than the scientists who had contributed most to the work.[19]

This restrictive publication policy hurt the company's prestige. In 1944, in a letter to his boss, Hale Charch put forth his position:

> To my mind the most important thing we have to do ... is to re-establish our position in the *scientific world* and to regain what I believe is a lost prestige among scientists and Ph.D. students. We lost an enormous amount when work of the type Carothers was publishing stopped. I have had professors in high positions in certain universities pooh-pooh the du Pont Company as no longer doing fundamental research and

some of these men freely state that they feel we are not putting back into the chemical literature the kind of contributions we ought to for the advancement of science. Yet on the other hand, we are drawing on the chemical literature in connection with feeding our researches.[20]

Du Pont employees heard similar criticism at the Gibson Island conferences, which had been established in 1937 by Neil E. Gordon to provide a forum for discussion of important topics in chemical research. The week-long conferences were held on a secluded resort island in the Chesapeake Bay twenty miles south of Baltimore and mixed recreation with science. In such pleasant surroundings, one attendee maintained that "scientists from universities and colleges mingled and argued with those from industrial laboratories to the advantage of both groups, and scientists from competing industrial laboratories forgot their rivalries in their enthusiasm for the scientific chase."[21] In 1945, Du Pont scientists attended the conference without giving papers and heard remarks that Du Pont sent a lot of people to these meetings only to absorb information. The following year, Du Pont researchers began to appear on the program.[22] However, Du Pont remained very cautious about publication.

Each department worked out its own publication policy, but that of the Pioneering Research Laboratory in the Rayon Department is probably representative. As noted above, its director, Charch, generally favored publication. For a paper to be cleared for publication, however, it had to be approved not only by the research director but also by the department's patent division and other interested departments. In the late 1940s, the Rayon Department's patent division maintained a hard line against publication in spite of Charch's efforts. For example, researcher Lawrence Beste wrote a paper based on mathematical calculations of the distribution of components in condensation interpolymers. When the patent division said to put it on the shelf for two years, Charch replied, "It is stretching my imagination beyond its limits to see how this publication at this time, or any other time, is going to damage the company's interests. . . . " Four years later, this paper still had not been cleared for publication.[23]

A second example points to one danger of not publishing in timely fashion: losing priority for the work because other researchers publish first. In 1949, the Chemical Department held up a Pioneering Research paper on the crystal structure of Teflon, only to have outside researchers publish first.[24] This problem of establishing priority was becoming more difficult because university research institutes had in a sense integrated forward into doing the kind of work previously left to industry. In 1947, Pioneering Research Laboratory representatives visited MIT's textile laboratory and were impressed by the similarity of its work to their own. Charch recommended that "if we are going to get credit in the public eye for our pioneering work in this field, it is very evident that we cannot delay in bringing out our publications."[25] Not only did the company's image suffer from losing priority, but it also hurt the morale of the researchers who had done the work for Du Pont.

In 1948 Church appointed a three-man committee to investigate the reasons for his laboratory's low rate of publication. The committee concluded that the reason was "the lack of incentive for the authors themselves"; Pioneering researchers needed to be encouraged to prepare more papers. Church then set up a publications committee that reviewed all submitted papers (as well as potentially publishable work) and set priorities for publication. However, the cleared papers soon began to accumulate in the office of the patent division, which was busy gathering material for the cellophane antitrust suit.[26] After this crisis had passed, Church's researchers began to publish more papers, and so did other Du Pont researchers.

Although complete statistics for Du Pont publications in the 1950s and 1960s do not exist, there are enough data to establish some general trends. Between 1954 and 1958, the number of papers proposed for publication more than doubled. In this period, Textile Fibers's proposals increased from 13 to 82 per year, and the more scientifically oriented Central Research Department's (formerly Chemical Department) proposals increased from 17 to 53.[27] More comprehensive data for the Central Research Department show its production of scientific papers increasing dramatically in the 1960s. The department's researchers published three times as many papers in the mid-1960s as they did in the mid-1950s (see Table 15.3, p. 303). These data show that Central Research Department scientists in this era were actively participating members of the scientific community.

At Du Pont, as in science generally, a few researchers did a large proportion of the publishing. A 1958 company survey of scientists in Central Research and four industrial departments revealed that 70 percent had published one paper, but that only 5 percent had more than ten publications. If these data are extrapolated to include all 2,400 technical college graduates (1,600 of whom had PhDs) in Du Pont research, then about 120 company scientists had ten or more papers to their credit.[28] Although some outstanding researchers did not publish and neither did many research managers, this number provides a reasonable estimate of Du Pont's scientific elite. Keeping this group contented at Du Pont became a challenging job for research managers in the postwar era.

The increase in the number of researchers who had outstanding scientific reputations or who became specialists in particular fields created a problem for management: to provide them with jobs that carried income and status equal to their scientific standing. Du Pont research managers worried that key researchers might leave the company. In 1946, one chemistry professor informed Du Pont that "[t]he discouragements which come to a number of excellent men in your organization have led to the comment which is widespread today that the Du Pont Company has too many alumni in other organizations."[29]

To cope with this problem, the technical division of the Rayon Department instituted in 1946 a research associates program for accomplished scientists. The idea had originated in discussions between George Graves, assistant director of research in the Plastics Department, and Hale Charch.[30] Du Pont announced the new positions in *Science* and sent copies to prominent academics around the country. Research associates, the news release stated, were chosen from "men of long service, distinguished scientific attainments and high creative potential, with capabilities for originating, organizing, and conducting their own research programs," and they "will have substantial freedom in the selection of work" and "will be encouraged to attend any scientific meetings in which they are professionally interested, to contact other laboratories and workers... inside and outside the company, and to publish scientific papers." Generally, the academic community applauded Du Pont's program, and one chemistry professor stated that it was the "type of constructive leadership which the chemical industry owes to the Du Pont Company."[31]

Soon other Du Pont organizations initiated research associates programs, the success of which varied considerably across departments. In general, though, these new positions gave research managers a new degree of flexibility in handling their personnel. Research associates, because of their specialized knowledge or creative abilities, could enjoy a high degree of professional independence as long as they used their skills to solve the company's problems. Maintaining the appropriate balance between the pursuit of science and service to Du Pont would be a major challenge for Du Pont's research directors in the postwar era.

Fundamental Research in the Industrial Departments

Although the Executive Committee expected all the industrial departments to do some fundamental research, the amounts and types they did varied widely. In the 1950s, the general managers of the industrial departments were an aggressive, competitive, and independent group, many of whom were vying for a coveted spot on the Executive Committee. Because the performance of these general managers was judged on the respective returns on investment of their departments, they had strong incentives to favor short-term over long-term goals. When business conditions were bad, general managers cut costs, and fundamental research was an easy target. Frequently, fundamental researchers were seen as luxuries and were believed not to be pulling their weight. This is one reason why fundamental research is usually undertaken in a central research laboratory, because there it can be insulated more easily from short-term pressures and organizational conflicts. In spite of these limitations, fundamental research did flourish in some departments over a considerable time span.

Science thrived in departments when it could be closely integrated with the overall research program and when it was undertaken by individual scientists who had established outstanding reputations for doing important work. Research directors who could make this happen usually had no trouble maintaining fundamental research programs. But when fundamental researchers became separate from the rest of the organization, as Stine had done in Purity Hall, they were more visible and susceptible to criticism. The Polychemicals Department established a separate pure science group that fell into this trap. By contrast, Orchem's Jackson Laboratory and Textile Fibers's Pioneering Research Laboratory avoided this pitfall and maintained outstanding fundamental research programs over a long period of time.

Jackson Laboratory contested the claim of Central Research to be the premier scientific research organization in the Du Pont Company. Under the leadership of John M. Tinker, the laboratory was a leading center for organic chemical studies in the 1950s. Most of the chemists used science to create new dyes, but some did more theoretical work.[32] A notable example was Rudolph Pariser's study of the electronic spectra and structures of simple and complex unsaturated molecules, work that contributed to the basic understanding of color in dyes.[33]

In 1960 another Orchem researcher, Charles J. Pedersen, started on a path of research that led to his winning a Nobel Prize twenty-seven years later. Pedersen joined Du Pont after completing an MS from MIT in 1927 and spent the next forty-two years working in Jackson Laboratory. At age fifty-six he began his work on synthesizing macrocyclic polyethers. These compounds exhibited unique complexing properties toward metal ions. His work was recognized as a tour de force of organic synthesis and led others to elaborate on his discoveries. His original "crown" ethers were doughnut shaped, but other chemists have made a variety of complex shapes from footballs to vases standing on pedestals. This work brought no tangible benefits to Du Pont but by the 1980s these compounds were being developed to mimic enzymes, the efficient but fragile catalysts of biological reactions. In 1987, the Nobel Prize committee honored Pedersen for having opened up this exciting and useful new field of chemistry.[34] Although they have not won any Nobel Prizes to date, the chemists in Textile Fibers's Pioneering Research Laboratory also made important contributions to science.

In 1957, Hale Charch defended his record of supporting the Stine approach to fundamental research in a letter to his boss, who had remarked to him that the company did not do much work of this type.[35] Charch replied that he had "always been tremendously fascinated" by fundamental research and believed that it was "the very essence of the . . . work Pioneering ought to do." He briefly described twenty projects in his laboratory that had increased the scientific understanding of fibers. The difficulties sustaining this research, Charch conceded, had been numerous. There were only a small number of researchers who were capable of doing it right. When publication of the results was denied or delayed, the researchers became discouraged. Generally, the scientists believed that those who were in "more spectacular industrial problem-solving" received more recognition for their achievements than did those engaged in longer-range scientific studies. Charch admitted that he had been guilty of cutting back on fundamental research when he needed personnel to work on more urgent problems and that this would probably always be the case. There were also times when the need to do fundamental research was "severely questioned and has required considerable fortitude to defend. . . . " But Charch was committed to doing it:

> [T]his kind of basic study *is* part and parcel of our technological activities. . . . I think we do a long-term service to the technical and scientific foundations on which our business rests by trying to keep such work on a high level and rewarded on as nearly an equal basis as possible with both industrial problem solving and administrative positions.

Fundamental research had made some important contributions to the Textile Fibers Department. At the end of World War II (as discussed in Chapter 18), the Pioneering Research Laboratory faced an enormous challenge to evaluate the thousands of condensation polymers that potentially had fiber applications. In the mid-1940s, Robert M. Hoffman and several others began to study fiber resilience and within a few years had developed a set of criteria that could be used to predict the properties of a fabric from a set of fiber characteristics.[36] Soon, Charch called for a broadening of this approach to eliminate the empiricism, guess work, and hunches used to evaluate polymers. These older methods, he maintained, had to give way to "the scientific law and order" that characterized the most advanced branches of organic and physical chemistry.

Charch wanted to be able to relate the chemical structure and architecture of specific polymers to their fiber properties, hoping to save millions of dollars and years of research effort. In the 1950s, Pioneering Research did a considerable amount of work on the characterization of polymers.[37] This research proved to be important to the laboratory's development of interfacial polymerization, which became a general and highly effective procedure for the rapid preparation of many polymers on a small scale.[38] Importantly, it permitted polymers to be made that are thermally unstable or unmeltable, and literally thousands of new polymers could be made using this technique. This discovery was a major scientific one, but it also gave Du Pont an important advantage over its competitors in the preparation of novel polymeric compounds. Charch agreed that the work was "so complete and extensive that a whole monograph could be written about it without apologizing for its excellence and its contribution to polymer science."[39] Because of commercial considerations, he had to delay publication for about six years. The scientists involved, Paul W. Morgan and Emerson Wittbecker, accepted the delay, although it took away some of their scientific acclaim because by the time Du Pont published, other companies had been using the method for some time.[40] To Morgan, publication was "icing on the cake"; he did science because it interested him and he got his rewards by solving problems. Publication, patents, or company bonuses were secondary motivations, not the primary one, which was science itself.[41] This was not true with all Du Pont researchers.

Fundamental research in the Polychemicals Department initially followed a course similar to that in Textile Fibers. After arriving from the Chemical Department in 1950 to be assistant director of the department's research division, Frank C. McGrew realized that although the science of polymers had made great strides since the 1930s, there were still large gaps in knowledge, particularly in correlating the properties of polymers with their molecular architecture. This information would be important commercially because it would provide an explanation of how synthesis conditions affect the properties of the product. In 1950, trial and error predominated. For example, in the case of polyethylene, McGrew stated, "we should seek to explain transparency, tear strength, drawability, etc. as functions of average molecular weight, linearity, *and* other such molecular characteristics, and then to find the correlation between these molecular characteristics and synthesis variables."[42] McGrew set some of his researchers to work on polyethylene, and the result was a series of five papers that were published in the *Journal of the American Chemical Society* in 1953.[43]

Encouraged by this example, McGrew began hiring young physicists and physical chemists to staff what was informally called the "Polymer Science Institute." He wanted them to do polymer characterization, a subject that university researchers continued to neglect. One academic told a Polychemicals representative that he could not get good students to work on plastics because of the attraction of more "glamorous fields" such as transistors, solid-state physics, nuclear physics, and even metals. The professor maintained that because he had broadened his own studies to include metals as well as plastics, he had become "respectable." Another professor stated that at Cornell not even the presence of Nobel Prize winner Peter Debye and future Nobel Prize winner Paul Flory could generate enough interest in plastics to get good students to work in the field.[44] Facing this academic indifference to polymers, McGrew decided that Du Pont would have to do its own science.

In the mid-1950s, McGrew's Polymer Science Institute went to work on the characterization of polymers. Much of this work was published, some of it in an internally published book entitled *The Physical Nature of Synthetic High Polymers*. In the abundance of the 1950s, McGrew could justify this research by pointing out that it was necessary for the development of the newer, more complicated polymers such as Delrin polyacetal and Teflon polytetrafluoroethylene resins. Over time, however, resentment built up among the other researchers in the department because, they charged, a few members of the Polymer Science Institute were putting their scientific careers ahead of solving problems for their co-workers. When, under extreme competitive pressure in 1960, the department decided to cut back its research budget, McGrew's "Institute" was a prime candidate for elimination. Soon the work of these scientists was redirected toward the immediate needs of the department. This change caused many of the more academically oriented researchers to leave Du Pont. Not all did, however; one of them, William Simeral, eventually became an Executive Committee member.[45] Unlike Charch, McGrew was unable to maintain the confidence of management and the support of his research staff in his fundamental research group. Even though some of its members had contributed to the solution of their co-workers' problems, the "Institute" did not become an integral part of the research team.

Stine had anticipated these problems in the 1920s when he argued that fundamental research should be conducted in a central research laboratory insulated from short-term concerns and pressure. In the 1950s, Du Pont's Central Research Department would devote itself almost entirely to fundamental research. However, after Elmer Bolton retired, there was no one to ensure that the research would be directed toward areas of potential importance to Du Pont's business fields.

The Central Research Department (1950–1970)

In 1950 there was no question that the Chemical Department was an industrial research laboratory, but by the mid-1960s, the renamed Central Research Department (CRD) was the premier scientific organization in the Du Pont Company and one of the outstanding industrial basic science laboratories in the United States. This change had occurred gradually and was partly a response by the management of Central Research to the lack of a well-defined role for a central research unit in a radically decentralized corporation. The move toward academic-style science appeared to be the solution to many of the department's problems, but once the drift had begun it proved nearly impossible to contain or control. Du Pont's top management tolerated and even encouraged this type of research because, as one research administrator put it, they had an almost "mystical belief" that a "new nylon" would be discovered.[46] And Central Research's managers very much wanted to produce another "nylon." However, as Carothers had pointed out two decades earlier, the path from pure science to new technology is not straightforward and requires a rare combination of talents in a researcher or organization.

With the growth in size and competence of the research divisions of the industrial departments and with their new charter to do fundamental research, the role of the Chemical Department became much less clear than it had been previously. It enjoyed considerable freedom to do whatever it pleased. Conversely, the expectations of Central Research varied among the Executive Committee members and the managements of the industrial departments. The department could perform three different functions for the company. Most important was the goal that Bolton had set for it, opening up new fields of chemistry that would lay the foundation for large new businesses for Du Pont. A second approach was the one that Stine originally sought for his fundamental research program, that is, the scientific investigation of Du Pont's technology. The third mission was another that Stine had envisioned, to be a showplace of scientific research. Keeping these three different activities in equilibrium and satisfying the rest of the company's expectations of the department required a very delicate balancing act by the director of Central Research.

In 1949, Board Chairman Walter S. Carpenter and Executive Committee advisor on research Roger Williams debated the future role of the Chemical Department. Carpenter complained to Williams that he thought the department was spending too much effort on developing new polymers for films and fibers. Obviously, Carpenter believed the Chemical Department should be exploring other areas of chemistry. Bolton had emphasized the synthesis of new polymers because many of Du Pont's products were either made from polymers or were threatened by competition from them. By concentrating on this field, the Chemical Department acted as a central research laboratory working on the company's core technologies. The Chemical Department's polymer findings were often applicable in many departments other than Film and Fibers. In his reply to Carpenter, Williams pointed out the importance of polymers to most of Du Pont's businesses.[47] He admitted that the Chemical Department was doing considerable work in this area "but no more than is reasonable in view of the importance and opportunity in the field, the apparent large future dependence of our profits upon it, and the extent to which we shall soon have more active competition in it." Williams shared Carpenter's worries about Du Pont focusing its efforts on polymers but conceded that this field seemed to have the best opportunities for the future. Within a few years, however, when the industrial departments had begun to do their own fundamental research in polymers, the Chemical Department substantially reduced its efforts in this field. By this time, Williams had become converted to Carpenter's point of view.[48]

Soon after the retirement of Bolton in 1951, Williams met with the new director of the Chemical Department, Bolton's long-time assistant, Cole Coolidge, and his assistant, Paul L. Salzberg.[49] Williams said that he was generally satisfied with the programs of the Chemical Department and that its objectives should be to get the company into really new businesses. With the exception of new fibers, he noted, Du Pont had not had many new developments recently. Thus, Williams gave the Chemical Department the mission of diversification through research. Central Research would struggle to achieve this goal with mixed success over the next several decades.

The job of managing the Chemical Department soon fell upon Salzberg because Coolidge died of complications from surgery in 1953. Like Coolidge, Salzberg had spent his entire career in the Chemical Department, having joined Du Pont in 1928 after receiving his PhD in organic chemistry from the University of Illinois. After just one year at the bench, Salzberg became a group leader and moved up the Chemical Department's administrative ladder to become Coolidge's assistant in 1951. After succeeding Coolidge, Salzberg served as director until his retirement in 1967.[50] During these years, the department's researchers moved away from polymer science into fields that were new to Du Pont.

The Chemical Department – renamed Central Research in 1957 – failed to produce another nylon, although it made some scientific breakthroughs that ultimately had commercial significance. The late 1940s and early 1950s was an especially productive period in the department. Research on polymerization reactions initiated by light opened the field of photopolymerization, which later provided the basis for several important new products. Exploratory work on chemical reactions in supercritical water led to the preparation of very pure chromium dioxide, which had magnetic properties that suggested uses in magnetic tapes. Other discoveries having major commercial significance included urea and uracil herbicides, which propelled Du Pont into the agricultural chemicals business, a subject discussed in Chapter 20.[51]

In the 1950s, the Central Research Department carried out a broad-based research program.[52] The synthesis of new organic and inorganic compounds accounted for about a third and a sixth of the total research, respectively. A quarter of the effort centered on physical research, which included new physical techniques, chemical structure and reaction mechanism studies, and solid-state physics. The remaining quarter was divided between polymer and biological research.[53] Evaluating the results of such diverse programs generally proved to be difficult for the management of Central Research and the Du Pont Company. Much of this work had no immediate relevance to the businesses of the industrial departments, so they could offer little constructive input to CRD's programs. CRD managers, most of whom were organic chemists, faced a new challenge in managing its diverse programs.

The preparation of new organic compounds remained a major activity in the department. CRD considered itself to have one of the best organic synthesis groups in the world, and new organic compounds could be claimed for Du Pont through composition of matter patents. Some of these new compounds, everyone hoped, would exhibit properties that suggested practical uses. And the preparation of a novel compound could always be turned into a publication. In the late 1940s, chemists in CRD discovered that tetrafluorethylene would react with a wide variety of compounds to give four-membered rings. This reaction made it much easier to prepare a host of organic fluorine compounds.[54]

Another outstanding CRD accomplishment in organic synthesis was the preparation of cyanocarbons – compounds containing only cyano groups attached to the carbons – which were virtually unknown. Theodore L. Cairns, who would later direct Central Research in the 1970s, spearheaded the effort to prepare and evaluate these compounds, which were unusually reactive and could be used to make many other compounds. Cairns's group published a series of twelve papers in the *Journal of the American Chemical Society* in 1958 that stimulated researchers elsewhere to investigate these new compounds. Prospective applications included dyes, pharmaceuticals, pesticides, and incorporation in new types of polymers. Ultimately, however, no commercial uses resulted from this extensive research effort. Yet the cyanocarbons provided chemists with a new set of tools for understanding and building organic compounds. Partly for this work, Cairns was awarded medals for creative work in synthetic organic chemistry by the American Chemical Society and the Synthetic Organic Chemicals Manufacturers Association.[55]

CRD became an important center for research in physical organic chemistry when it hired Howard E. Simmons, Jr., in 1954. A recent PhD from MIT, Simmons had worked under John D. Roberts, a leading figure in the field. In CRD, Simmons did pioneering research on the formation of small strained rings, which led to a general new class of reactions, the Simmons-Smith reaction. At roughly the same time that Orchem's Pedersen synthesized macrocyclic polyethers, Simmons, in collaboration with Chung Ho Park, synthesized the first macrobicyclic amines, which are large rings that have hydrocarbon cavities in them. Later, concepts of macrobicyclic amines and macrocyclic polyethers were put together and laid the foundation for a new class of macrocyclic structures with potential uses as synthetic enzymes and catalysts. For his research, Simmons was elected to the National Academy of Sciences.[56]

In the late 1940s, CRD broadened its activities in physics and physical chemistry primarily as an adjunct to its work on synthetic organic chemicals. Physical research centered on characterizing chemical compounds with the new analytical techniques such as nuclear magnetic resonance (NMR), for which CRD acquired an early machine. William D. Phillips did pioneering work in the application of NMR to chemical structure analyses and later extended it to biological molecules. Physical research in CRD also focused on the elaboration of the mechanisms of organic reactions. In 1953, CRD hired an MIT-trained physical chemist, Richard E. Merrifield, who began investigations of semiconductors.[57]

By 1960, CRD had eighteen men working in the fields of physics and physical chemistry, which represented about 20 percent of its fundamental research effort. CRD's strategy by 1960 had evolved to one of exploring new physical phenomena that could form a starting point for new products, particularly in the electronics and semiconductor fields in which Du Pont had no commercial position. In the late 1950s and early 1960s, research competition in these areas was vigorous; in terms of physics publications by industry, Du Pont ranked about thirteenth with 2 percent of total, far below the leaders Bell Laboratories and General Electric, which together accounted for one-third of corporate physics publications. To evaluate its work, CRD relied heavily on the advice of outside consultants. In 1960, CRD reported to the Executive Committee that its consultants had been impressed with Du Pont's work in the field, that it had made some real discoveries, and that it should prosecute them vigorously.[58] However, the scientists in CRD were not interested in developing commercial products and neither were the industrial departments, which had their hands full with their existing businesses and which possessed no expertise to develop them. Thus the principal accomplishments of CRD's physical research were publications, not products.

CRD also diversified into inorganic and organo-inorganic chemistry. Much of CRD's efforts in these fields originated from Earl L. Muetterties, who was hired in 1952 after completing his PhD at Harvard on the chemistry of boron-nitrogen compounds. In the mid-1950s he discovered polyhedral borane anions that displayed a substitution chemistry similar to that of aromatic hydrocarbons. As one of Muetterties's associates stated, "It was like rediscovering benzene in the richness of its chemistry."[59] To explore this field, CRD put six to eight men on a task force that had the goal of obtaining broad patent coverage for Du Pont. At the time there were rumors that the Russians were using these compounds as rocket fuels, and the Redstone Arsenal was also working in the field. In the long run, however, nothing of commercial importance resulted from this work. Muetterties moved into other research areas (such as the coordination chemistry of surfaces) and made contributions to virtually every field of inorganic chemistry. CRD also established a first-class group in organometallic compounds, which benefited greatly from the contributions of George W. Parshall. Both Parshall and Muetterties were elected to the National Academy of Sciences.[60]

Perhaps the most promising area for diversification of CRD's program was biochemistry. Charles Stine had promoted biochemistry as a field of research for Du Pont when he was the Executive Committee advisor on research. In the early 1950s, CRD began a program to investigate chemicals for biological applications, and Charles W. Todd prepared substituted ureas as potential antibacterial agents, which when screened by Grasselli proved to be effective herbicides. Within a few years, CRD's program included agricultural and veterinary chemicals and bacteriological and microbiological studies.[61]

In the mid-1950s, CRD began work on the chemistry of nitrogen fixation in plants, a study that would develop into a major effort over the next decade. This work received an important boost in 1963 when Ralph W. F. Hardy, a University of Wisconsin biochemist, joined the company. Hardy brought Du Pont's nitrogen fixation research to international prominence. He published more than a hundred papers on the subject, was an invited speaker at more than a hundred national and international symposia, edited a multivolume treatise on nitrogen fixation, and coauthored a monograph on the subject. *Chemical Week* recently referred to him as a "Scientist Superstar" who was "one of the nation's top achievers in the dual role of scientist and scientific manager." By the late 1960s, Du Pont had invested between thirty-five and forty staff-years in nitrogen fixation research and had attained impressive scientific results but no new products.[62] This did not deter the chemists, though, because they expected a payoff only in the very long term.

After 1960, CRD came under increasing pressure to produce practical results in a shorter time frame. When it appeared that the company's growth was slowing, the Executive Committee requested that the entire company accelerate the development of new products. Thus was initiated the "new venture" era, which had a major impact on Du Pont's research programs and is the subject of Chapter 22. Salzberg took some steps to make CRD more industrially oriented by getting permission from the Executive Committee to carry developments further toward commercialization; he established a materials division in 1963 to evaluate new substances from CRD research for commercial use. Yet the bulk of CRD's work continued to drift toward academic science. CRD's managers still hoped that "another nylon" would be uncovered at the frontiers of science, but their work became increasingly unconnected with Du Pont's businesses or any business (see Chapter 25). One research manager recalls that all the projects were identified with some business objective, but frequently it was either weak or a "masterpiece of the imagination." The direction of many programs was left to the scientists themselves, many of whom had been recruited with an understanding that they were expected to do fundamental research and could generate their own programs. In general, they believed that management should leave them alone, and they resented or ignored attempts to focus their research on more specific objectives.[63]

As the external pressure for change intensified in the 1960s, following a general trend in industry away from basic science, Salzberg had to reorient some of his programs to more "relevant" ones. The solid-state physics research was transformed into another assault on catalysts. In a CRD annual report, he asserted that "the science of catalysis is still undeveloped, and selection of effective catalysts for a given reaction is largely empirical," a statement nearly identical to the one Stine had made in his fundamental research proposal forty years earlier. Salzberg also decided to restore polymer research to a level "commensurate with the company's stake in the field" and increased the number of scientists working on polymers from ten to thirty. Of the earlier diversification fields, only biology was singled out for increased emphasis and would continue to be CRD's main attempt to research the company into new businesses.[64]

In spite of these pressures, CRD continued to resemble in many respects an academic research laboratory. The number of publications coming out of the department hit new highs during this period. Every year, a few researchers from the department would take a leave of absence for university study and teaching. In the late 1960s, CRD began to employ postdoctoral research fellows, who would spend two years at Du Pont before moving on to careers in academia or with another company.[65] The motive behind this program was to raise the level of science at Du Pont above that of its competitors to the point at which breakthroughs of major scientific and commercial importance would be made in the company's laboratories. It also allowed Du Pont to keep up with the latest academic developments.

There were also external reasons for making industrial research similar to academic research. Du Pont was encountering growing problems in hiring and keeping good personnel. In 1967, consultant Roger Adams maintained that since the late 1950s the best PhD students had increasingly come to look down upon industrial positions. Adams suggested that Du Pont send chemists such as Howard Simmons to universities to give lectures on their work in industry to show students that pioneering and challenging work was being done at Du Pont.[66] Salzberg followed Adams's advice. As director of Central Research, Salzberg had allowed this kind of science to flourish.

When Salzberg retired in 1967, his former CRD colleague, retired president and current chairman of the board Crawford Greenewalt, wrote him, "It seems to me there is very little that the company does that is more important than the basic research of the Central Research Department and its sound stewardship is a matter of greatest importance to the company's future."[67] But Salzberg's "stewardship" had become a major issue as the company management in the 1960s increasingly emphasized development instead of fundamental research.

The problems of guiding Central Research fell squarely on the shoulders of Salzberg's successor, David M. McQueen, a physical chemist from the University of Wisconsin who had risen through the ranks of Central Research since he joined it in 1934. His own research on photochemistry and photography earned him thirty-five patents, although he published few papers.[68] As director of Central Research, McQueen vigorously defended the scientific tradition that Salzberg had established. His strategy, he argued, was "to reduce applied and commercial objectives to a scientific problem and then explore the more fundamental aspects of the problem to see if a fresh approach can be devised." McQueen saw in novel chemistry endless opportunities for Du Pont, so his department focused its research on new materials, structures, phenomena, and understanding. He wanted his researchers to make quantum leaps into new fields, not to cover an entire field or follow popular trends in research, as academics often did.[69]

Disagreeing with his critics in Du Pont, he emphatically rejected the Stine approach to fundamental research: "I do not favor the tremendous task of maintaining expertise in the many sections of science and engineering that back up the important areas of the company's technology, and I am particularly opposed to the popular concept of a central research organization as a stable of experts."[70] This backup work, he believed, should be left to the departments. McQueen was under considerable pressure from top management in the late 1960s to reorient the programs of his department closer to the existing business and technology of the company. During his four years as director, McQueen tried hard to maintain previous levels of basic science. Upon his retirement he wrote his successor, Cairns, that "according to my personal classification the company has at most twenty-some men engaged in science-oriented work. I hope it will be possible always to maintain an effort of this sort that cannot be pigeonholed in specific business classes."[71] And in the 1970s, Cairns upheld the tradition of doing high-quality science in Central Research.

In a company that had many traditions, basic scientific research, which had blossomed briefly with the work of Carothers in the 1930s, became an integral part of Du Pont R&D after World War II. This type of work raised morale, assisted recruiting, and generally promoted the image of the Du Pont Company as a first-class research organization and the leader in its industry. But the major reason that Du Pont's executives invested considerable sums on fundamental research was to lead to the discovery of "new nylons" – and when this did not occur in the twenty-five years following World War II, many in the company believed that it was time to reevaluate the role of science in the corporation. Chapter 25 will examine this reassessment of research in the 1970s.

18

Making a Revolution: Du Pont and Synthetic Fibers

In little more than a quarter-century, Du Pont R&D effected a revolution in textiles reminiscent of those sweeping changes in weaving and spinning techniques associated with the Industrial Revolution in eighteenth-century England. But this was a revolution in fibers – in the creation of wholly synthetic fibers to supplement and sometimes even supplant the natural ones that had been used throughout human history. Like the earlier revolution, the synthetic fibers revolution entailed the rapid development of novel production machinery, and it wrought changes in backward linkages, such as raw materials and intermediates, and in forward linkages, such as dyeing, finishing, and fabrication of apparel, carpeting, and entirely new structures that could not be made with natural fibers. The earlier textile-technology revolution centered on new production techniques for natural fibers the characteristics of which had been known at least in gross terms for centuries. But the synthetic-fibers revolution demanded the rapid acquisition of knowledge about and means to control the characteristics of the new fibers. It also required a fundamental understanding of the natural fibers targeted for displacement by the new synthetics.

On the eve of World War II, Du Pont was well poised to effect the synthetic fibers revolution. The firm had been manufacturing rayon and acetate fibers ("man-made" fibers based on natural cellulose) since the 1920s and had gained a keen appreciation for the textile fibers business. The importance of Du Pont's manufacture of cellulosic fibers to its growth in synthetics cannot be gainsaid. Yet rayon and acetate would never have brought about radical change in the industry; that remained for the wholly synthetic fibers such as nylon, acrylic, and polyester. In 1940, one year after Du Pont opened its first commercial nylon plant, approximately 500 million pounds of rayon and acetate were consumed in the United States compared to 4.5 billion pounds of natural fibers. Within the next twenty-five years, however, consumption of truly synthetic fibers outstripped cellulosic fiber consumption and totaled more than a third of natural fiber consumption. A decade later, synthetic production matched natural fiber production, and by 1980 more than twice as much synthetic fiber was consumed as natural fiber.[1] That year, Americans bought on a per capita basis thirty-one pounds of synthetics for every eleven pounds of cotton and wool.[2] (See Figures 18.1 and 18.2

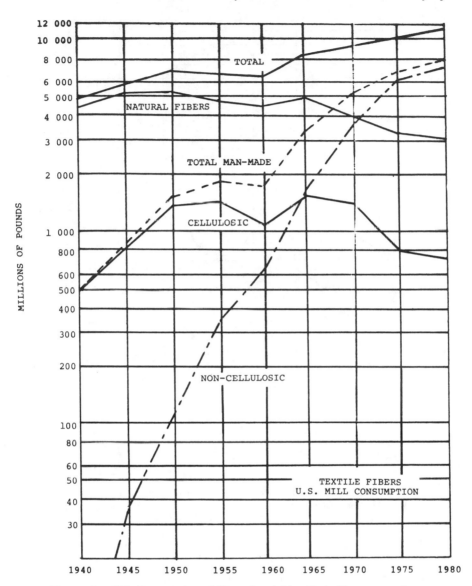

Figure 18.1. U.S. Consumption of Natural and Man-Made Fibers, 1940–80.
Source: Adapted from *Textile Organon* 502 (March 1981), p. 38.

for data on total consumption of natural and man-made fibers, 1940–80, and Du Pont fiber shipments, 1940–80.)

Of course, the critical step in Du Pont's rise as a giant in synthetic fibers manufacture was the commercialization of the first truly synthetic fiber, nylon, in 1939. Because of nylon's instant success, by 1941 Du Pont had

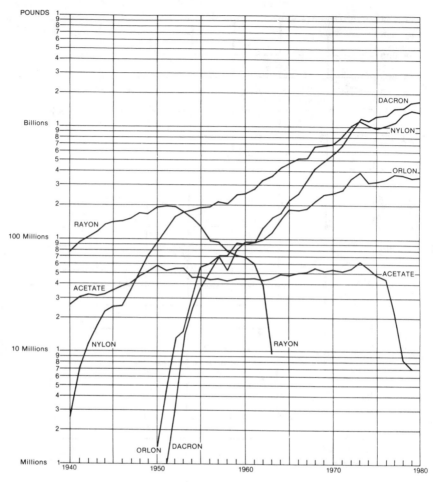

Figure 18.2. Du Pont World Fiber Shipments, 1940–80, Rayon, Acetate, Nylon, Orlon, Dacron. Source: Data (five-year intervals) from Textile Fibers Department, E. I. du Pont de Nemours & Co.

doubled the capacity of its first commercial nylon plant at Seaford, Delaware, had started up a second plant at Martinsville, Virginia, and had announced yet another expansion of nylon capacity.

The discovery of nylon led Du Pont and several other companies to begin a systematic search for other synthetic fibers. I. G. Farben polymerized caprolactam and spun it into a nylon-6 fiber, which had characteristics (except for a lower melting point) similar to those of Du Pont's nylon. In 1939, American Viscose and Carbide and Carbon Company commercialized Vinyon, fibers made from vinyl chloride copolymers, and Firestone Plastics Company followed in 1941 with its Saran fiber spun from polyvinylidene chloride.[3] But the great leap forward came in the early 1950s when Du Pont commercialized Orlon acrylic fiber and Dacron polyester fiber.

The discoveries of Orlon and Dacron were by no means as elegant scientifically as Carothers's discovery of nylon. Similarly, the development of each fiber was far messier and far more expensive than that of nylon. Nylon's silklike appearance and its properties of high tenacity and excellent abrasion resistance allowed Du Pont to chart a comparatively simple development strategy of replacing silk with nylon in women's hosiery. Orlon's and Dacron's initial markets were not that clear-cut. Each possessed unique properties that suggested logical market targets, but these markets fell through when tried. A less apparent property ultimately proved to be critical. This property was resilience – the ability of a fiber to recover from deformation. Under the direction of W. Hale Charch, the Pioneering Research Laboratory brought out the resilient properties of Orlon and Dacron. When produced in a dyeable, lofted staple form, Orlon soon penetrated the sock and sweater market. Charch wanted Dacron to replace wool and therefore encouraged his researchers to find ways to spin polyester fibers that were as resilient as wool. This strategy worked, but not exactly in the way Charch envisioned. Dacron polyester did penetrate the wool market for suiting material (mostly as a blend), but its important early market was in cotton-blended "wash and wear" shirts and blouses. Charch did not anticipate this market, but the resilience his laboratory developed in Dacron polyester and its inherent resistance to water proved to be decisive in its rise as the most important fiber in the United States.

With the development of Orlon and Dacron, Du Pont now had a family of man-made fibers, and it had to learn quickly what distinguished one fiber from another, how to sell each on this basis, and how to have them all prosper and grow. But two of Du Pont's fiber family members – rayon and acetate – were victims of sibling rivalry. There has probably never been a clearer case of the Schumpeterian principle of technological innovation bringing about the destruction of capital than with nylon's, Orlon's, and Dacron's impact on rayon and acetate. In 1941, rayon and acetate plants represented Du Pont's largest investments. From 1954 to 1963, Du Pont progressively closed down its rayon plants, and the company made no new major investments in its acetate business after 1950. While painfully aware of this massive destruction of capital, Du Pont's executives could appreciate that they, not their competitors, could fully exploit the inevitable product cycle.

This chapter focuses on Du Pont's execution of the synthetic fibers revolution. In particular, it concentrates on the research and development that lay behind the introduction of Orlon and Dacron. Unlike many other chapters in the history of Du Pont after World War II, these innovations strongly supported the wisdom of the overall corporate strategy of growth through internal research and development. By looking at development as well as research, the chapter articulates one of the company's greatest problems in the postwar period, which in a few words was the growing scale problem in the development of new industrial products. With nylon targeted for women's hosiery, development costs were contained because Du Pont needed comparatively small amounts of intermediates and polymer to see if it had a good product (a pair of stockings weighs only ten grams). But with less well-defined markets, Orlon's and Dacron's development costs greatly exceeded those of nylon because the company had to put a lot of fiber into the market for testing before it really knew whether it had a product or not. Making a million pounds of Dacron for market testing posed real problems in intermediates procurement, polymerization equipment, and spinning machinery. Here is where scale became expensive, and this problem would grow even larger as Du Pont elaborated the synthetic fibers revolution beyond Orlon and Dacron.

Organization of Fibers Research and Development

Before 1952, fibers research at Du Pont was housed in what was called the technical division of the Rayon Department. This division had responsibility for research on both fibers and cellophane until 1950, when the cellophane division was split off from Rayon and reorganized as the Film Department. In 1952, Du Pont changed the name of the Rayon Department to the Textile Fibers Department. Subsequently, the organization of the department changed, but the technical division (sometimes called the research division in the 1950s) remained the principal seat for fibers research. Development responsibilities shifted significantly with the organizational changes in the mid-1950s, a problem that will be discussed more thoroughly in this chapter.[4]

Throughout much of the period under discussion, the technical division was divided into sections corresponding to the businesses of the department – viscose rayon, acetate, nylon, and so on. There were also other sections, including pioneering research, development, and patent service. The technical division was headquartered in Wilmington, as were the directors of each of the sections, but the division's research was carried out at several locations, which changed over time (as indicated in Figures 18.3a and 18.3b).

The development of nylon at the Experimental Station in Wilmington initiated a profound change in the technical division in Textile Fibers. As discussed in Chapter 8, most of the research work done by the division in the late 1920s and 1930s was devoted to process work on rayon, acetate, and cellophane. Hale Charch, the head of the Pioneering Research Laboratory, had tried unsuccessfully to obtain permission to diversify the department's research into noncellulose polymer work.[5] The discovery and early promise of nylon vindicated Charch's view that other materials might compete with cellulose. Ironically, Charch did not have an opportunity to initiate exploration of noncellulose polymers until 1938, when his boss, E. K. Gladding, left the technical division to head the nylon division. Even then, his laboratory lacked the expertise in polymer chemistry necessary to

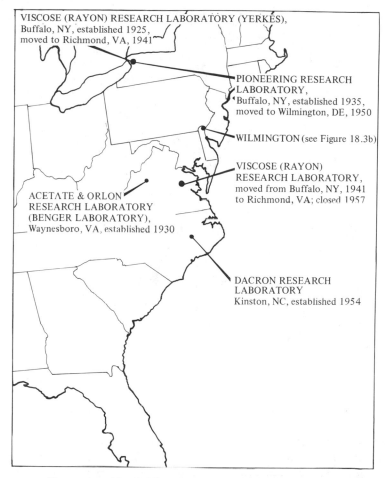

VISCOSE (RAYON) RESEARCH LABORATORY (YERKES),
Buffalo, NY, established 1925,
moved to Richmond, VA, 1941

PIONEERING RESEARCH
LABORATORY,
Buffalo, NY, established 1935,
moved to Wilmington, DE, 1950

WILMINGTON (see Figure 18.3b)

VISCOSE (RAYON)
RESEARCH LABORATORY,
moved from Buffalo, NY, 1941
to Richmond, VA; closed 1957

ACETATE & ORLON
RESEARCH LABORATORY
(BENGER LABORATORY),
Waynesboro, VA, established 1930

DACRON RESEARCH
LABORATORY
Kinston, NC, established 1954

Figure 18.3a. Textile Fibers Department Laboratory Locations.

do work comparable to that done in the Chemical Department, which had pursued exploratory work on fiber synthesis beyond nylon 6-6. For example, by 1938, that department's chemists had synthesized more than a thousand linear polymers and evaluated many of them as potential fibers.[6]

Looking at the results of the Chemical Department's high-quality scientific research on polymers, "a considerable number of people in the DuPont Company" determined that the Textile Fibers Department should have a greater research capability than heretofore. Accordingly, in 1939 Ernest B. Benger was brought back from the Chemical Department to direct research in the technical division under the figurehead manager, Maurice du Pont Lee. Leonard Yerkes, general manager of the Textile Fibers Department, gave Benger a mandate: The "Technical Division is to be strengthened and built up to perform its research and experimental duties in a more thorough,

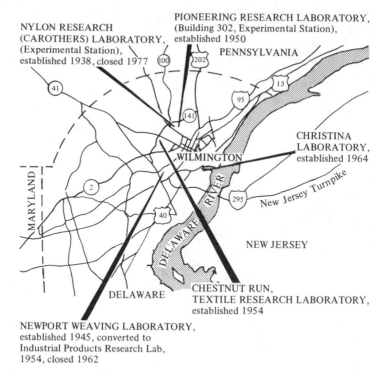

NYLON RESEARCH
(CAROTHERS) LABORATORY,
(Experimental Station),
established 1938, closed 1977

PIONEERING RESEARCH LABORATORY,
(Building 302, Experimental Station),
established 1950

PENNSYLVANIA

CHRISTINA
LABORATORY,
established 1964

WILMINGTON

MARYLAND

New Jersey Turnpike

NEW JERSEY

DELAWARE

CHESTNUT RUN,
TEXTILE RESEARCH LABORATORY,
established 1954

NEWPORT WEAVING LABORATORY,
established 1945, converted to
Industrial Products Research Lab,
1954, closed 1962

Figure 18.3b. Textile Fibers Department's Laboratories in the Wilmington Area.

systemmatic [*sic*] and broader manner than has ever been possible in the past."[7]

Benger swiftly effected major changes in the technical division with a goal of "having the Technical Division operate as a unit and...present[ing] a united front and unanimity of opinion to the Management."[8] Seeking better research personnel, Benger maintained that the division should "hire good men whether we ha[ve] a place for them or not."[9] He envisioned moving less competent research men out of the technical division to make room for higher-caliber researchers.

Recognizing that polymer chemistry was taught at very few universities in the United States, Benger took a major step to educate his research staff in 1940 when he brought Herman Mark to the United States to serve as a consultant to the Textile Fibers Department.[10] Mark's contribution to raising the level of knowledge among technical division research personnel became quickly apparent. As Lester S. Sinness, then assistant director of viscose research, recently said of Mark, "What he did was to educate us on high polymers, and on that basis, we could engineer an honest-to-God basic [research] program."[11]

Benger initiated important changes in the management of the technical division, many of them based on his experience in the Chemical Department.

For example, he instituted regular reviews whereby the divisions, from the director down to the bench chemist, reported formally on their research programs.[12] To build team spirit among his directors and to improve co-ordination, Benger started holding weekly (later biweekly) staff meetings, similar to the Chemical Department's steering committee meetings. In addition to dealing with the immediate problems of research management, the directors' meetings became – particularly after Andrew E. Buchanan was named Benger's assistant – a forum for discussing broad issues in the management of research. Out of such often freewheeling discussions emerged the research associate plan.[13]

Benger also enhanced the communication of research results and created a healthy sort of competition among his research divisions when he promoted an annual meeting of the entire technical division in Wilmington. He had several goals for the annual meeting. At the very least, he wanted to dazzle higher management in the company. Elaborate exhibits were staged by each of the research divisions to show results of research.[14] But the annual meeting also provided an opportunity to bring all research managers, research supervisors, and research associates together to discuss common problems. Benger's meetings helped him build a high level of camaraderie and an esprit de corps in the division, which are readily apparent in surviving records.[15]

The Pioneering Spirit

Nowhere was the spirit of R&D higher than in the Pioneering Research Laboratory when it was under the direction of Hale Charch in the 1940s and 1950s. Once Charch received permission in 1939 to pursue noncellulose research, he moved Pioneering swiftly into new areas of synthetic polymers. By the time of Charch's untimely death in 1958, Pioneering had been the seedbed of such successful products as Orlon acrylic, Dacron polyester, and soon-to-be-named Lycra spandex fibers. Pioneering Research's name perfectly fit its mission and achievements. Charch was in part responsible for this success. He possessed a keen appreciation for commercial objectives and clear entrepreneurial instincts.

In 1941, when the Textile Fibers Department was riding high with nylon, Charch cautioned against thinking that nylon was the first and last synthetic fiber. He argued that it would be "a gross mistake... to overlook the possibility of a competitive fiber from some other base than a polyamide." With increasing numbers of new polymers being synthesized, "it can be stated with almost complete certainty," Charch maintained, "that polyamide polymers are not the last super-polymers which the world is going to see in the form of threads and fibers."[16] The real problem lay in attacking the seemingly unlimited opportunities presented by the explosion in polymers.

Charch proposed that both Pioneering and the Chemical Department synthesize new polymers and evaluate them as fiber candidates. He intended this evaluation to be done within the context of commercial market opportunities. Specifically, Charch had begun (as early as 1936) to target wool for displacement by man-made fibers. He had initiated a long-term project to engineer a fiber to "show . . . any one or a combination of the properties of wool fibers, such as crimp, curl, [and] irregularity in denier."[17] Although his enthusiasm for wool-like fibers met with little interest in the department, Charch continued to ponder the matter. He identified a critical barrier to penetrating the wool fiber business: lack of a fundamental understanding of wool's properties and the nature of the wool textile business. By mid-1937 he had established a group of chemists who, as he wrote, "are thinking wool week in and week out."[18]

To many, Charch's actions might have seemed at best as duplicating work already being done in both the acetate and viscose research sections. These sections were working on wool-like acetate and rayon fibers, and the Chemical Department was trying to develop a crimped, wool-like nylon fiber based on its study of the form and properties of wool.[19] But Charch believed these efforts fell far short of the mark; he was in search of "radically new fiber products of woolly character" based on a "radical departure."[20]

Charch's thinking about these matters went through several stages before Pioneering ultimately hit upon the successful approach to the problem. The complexity of wool itself created the problem. Examination of wool under a microscope shows that it is not simply a crimped filament but rather has a scalelike structure. For many, trying to duplicate wool meant duplicating not only the material basis of wool but also its physical structure. Charch abandoned this notion, however. The reports of the viscose rayon division's sales section provided the key. Several of these stressed that broader penetration of fiber markets by rayon staple would not occur without increasing the resilience of Du Pont's fibers. Charch's thinking, therefore, began to focus on resilience as a critical fiber characteristic. Fully abstracted, wool is simply a resilient fiber. If Pioneering could develop a resilient synthetic fiber, such a fiber might be a candidate for the wool fiber market.

In the early 1940s, Charch launched a multipronged research program designed to obtain a more resilient fiber. One approach, which he pursued both in his own laboratory and in the Chemical Department, was aimed at building resilience into rayon by cross-linking cellulose molecules with synthetic polymers.[21] The Chemical Department investigated cross-linking mechanisms on a fundamental level while Pioneering worked more empirically at cross-linking rayon. Pioneering's efforts soon led to the development of Orlon, which is discussed below. But these efforts probably would have been unsuccessful had Charch not run two other projects as part of his overall resilience program. Both of these projects were of a fundamental character.

Charch organized a project aimed at correlating chemical structure with physical properties as a first step in building resilient fibers. Charch explained proudly, "This is a very fundamental line of activity and might best be compared to some of Carothers's early investigation[s] leading to the discovery of the first synthetic linear polymers. This line of activity reflects our repeated insistence that before true resilience is built into our fibers we have to develop some new basic chemical knowledge upon which to build more practical commercial applications."[22] Pioneering would continue its structure-property studies throughout the decade, and these would eventually allow the laboratory to design polymers for specific fiber applications.

Ironically, the resilience project Charch considered the least important eventually allowed him to recognize the significance of both acrylic and polyester fibers and to steer their development in ultimately successful directions. In many respects, this project was the most fundamental of the resilience program, for it was aimed at developing a comprehensive understanding of what resilience actually is in a fiber. Charch initially believed this chore was so simple that he established it as a part-time project.[23] But more than five years went by before Pioneering's researchers had gotten a firm grip on the elusive concept of resilience. The war interrupted these studies, but even after they were resumed in 1944, the solution to the problem of resilience proved more difficult than Charch had envisioned.[24] Nevertheless, throughout this period Charch believed that his main goal of "synthesizing specifically for resilience" would be stymied until his laboratory understood the concept of resilience.[25]

A group of physical chemists led by Robert M. Hoffman took up Charch's call. Hoffman joined Pioneering from Acetate Research in Waynesboro, Virginia, in August 1945. Although this group had made some progress on resilience, Hoffman's arrival proved to be critical. The group had been groping with the concept without great success; Hoffman furnished the key by introducing the time element in determining fiber behavior.[26] He and L. F. Beste developed three-dimensional "resilience maps," which provided a logical classification of fiber properties. Beste gave the study the rigorous mathematical analysis necessary to bring order out of chaos. Others contributed to the effort by devising a comprehensive set of new fabric tests, by reinterpreting older literature in light of new developments, and by correlating molecular fiber structure with mechanical fiber properties using X-ray diffraction techniques. This latter work gave Pioneering the capability to identify approximate structures for wool-like fibers.[27] By 1946, Pioneering's researchers had gained sufficient understanding of resilience to recognize it in, if not engineer it into, a new synthetic fiber.

Charch soon began to see even greater possibilities for his laboratory's fiber characterization work after receiving an enthusiastic response from Lester Sinness, director of viscose rayon research and a fellow physical chemist by training. Sinness had pointed out, "You may have a means here [in your research on resilience] of establishing correlation between fiber properties and fabric properties."[28] Charch became increasingly optimistic that this research would provide him with a new and powerful tool – a means of predicting properties of fabrics from the characteristics of a single fiber.[29]

By the end of 1946, Pioneering's resilience studies had yielded enormous results. With a quantitative understanding of the characteristics required for a wool-like fiber, Charch could cast aside the notion that the way to make a synthetic wool was to fabricate a synthetic fiber having wool's unique physical structure (i.e., its chemical composition, scaliness, nonuniform denier, and crimp). Now he could ignore wool's structure and simply find a fiber that had wool-like properties. As Charch wrote, "We don't need a Chinese copy of [wool] for a synthetic wool-like fiber."[30] With the ability to predict fabric properties from fiber characteristics, Pioneering could also now achieve major savings in time and money in the identification and development of commercially viable synthetic fibers.[31] Charch and his staff appreciated this benefit, for they were in the midst of developing an acrylic fiber later to be named Orlon and were well along on their development of polyester fiber, eventually known as Dacron. The success of the resiliency study in 1946 became apparent in the laboratory's work on polyester, leading Charch to advocate further refinement of resiliency criteria, which in turn greatly reinforced the development of Orlon and Dacron.[32] More important, Pioneering's resiliency study reinforced Charch's conviction that Orlon and Dacron were fibers of the future.

The Development of Orlon

In 1967, a quarter-century after its discovery and seventeen years after its commercialization, Orlon acrylic fiber ranked as the third-largest all-time earner among hundreds of products commercialized by Du Pont after 1930, right behind neoprene synthetic rubber and well behind nylon. The development of Orlon proved to be fraught with major hurdles, the largest of which was the new fiber's being so resistant to water (hydrophobic) that it could not be dyed with existing dyes and dyeing techniques. The Textile Fibers Department stumbled seriously along the way, largely because its managers became so enamored with Orlon's then-unique properties of extreme resistance to degradation by sunlight and bacterial action that they failed to grasp Charch's belief that Orlon was the wool-like synthetic he had been seeking for ten years. Not until the development of Orlon fell flat on its face, when the initial filament yarn plant failed to generate any business, did managers see fully the wisdom of Charch's views. Based on data derived from Pioneering's resiliency studies, Charch had maintained from 1946 onward that Orlon should be developed as a wool substitute by manufacturing it in staple form rather than as filament yarn. (See Figure 18.4 for a schematic explanation of fiber forms.) The Pioneering Research Laboratory had to reenter the Orlon staple development program in a significant way after it had formally turned over the development to the acetate research

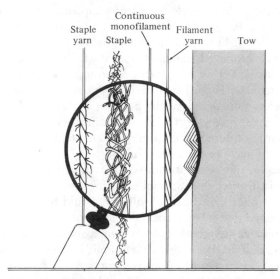

Figure 18.4. Forms of Fibers Made by Du Pont (see Figure 18.5 for a diagram of spinning methods). Source: Adapted from *Man-Made Fiber Fact Book* (Washington, D.C.: Man-Made Fiber Producers Association, Inc., 1978), p. 10.

division. Orlon staple proved to be an astounding success in knitwear once the dyeing problems were overcome.

Orlon's success rested on the intense efforts of many researchers in Pioneering, acetate research, and in the dye research laboratories of the Organic Chemicals Department. Outside processors also contributed to Orlon's success. Orlon's greatest champion, however, was Hale Charch.

Orlon emerged from Ray C. Houtz's discovery in 1941 of how to spin polyacrylonitrile into a fiber possessing a high melting point and good chemical stability. Houtz's discovery came while he was working on a project to improve the wet strength and resilience of rayon by cross-linking cellulose molecules with a vinyl polymer. Charch urged this approach after he observed the outstanding tensile properties of partially oriented polyvinyl alcohol films. Scanning the field of known vinyl polymers, researchers focused on polyacrylonitrile because of potential low-cost intermediates and its heat resistance. The Chemical Department devoted much attention to the polymerization of acrylonitrile, but Charch also asked its chemists "to react acrylonitrile with . . . regenerated cellulose in a manner so as to yield a fibrous, partially reacted product . . . as a basis for a crushproofed fiber or a fiber of lower water-sensitivity."[33] In Pioneering, Houtz tried to polymerize acrylonitrile in situ in rayon fibers but soon became convinced that polyacrylonitrile itself might make an excellent fiber.[34]

Houtz was by no means the first chemist to polymerize acrylonitrile. Herman Mark had described polyacrylonitrile in a patent issued to I. G. Farben in 1929.[35] The challenge of making a fiber out of the polymer lay in its intractability. Unlike nylon, polyacrylonitrile cannot be melt-spun because the polymer decomposes instead of melting. Houtz, therefore, began to look for a solvent. From the literature, he knew that common organic solvents, such as acetone, ethanol, and aromatic hydrocarbons, had no effect on polyacrylonitrile, yet he also learned through two patents of Herbert Rein assigned to I. G. Farben that highly concentrated solutions of some inorganic aqueous salts dissolved the polymer.[36] Rein's polymer solutions, however, yielded only very brittle fibers or films and were thus ruled out. Research therefore centered on obtaining an understanding of the structure of the polymer to account for its insolubility.

Two theories on this issue prevailed. One argued that polyacrylonitrile was a cross-linked, three-dimensional structure, thus explaining its insolubility. Making a fiber from such a polymer would have been impossible. The other suggested that it was a regular linear polymer "whose insolubility arose from secondary interchain forces of which one type would be hydrogen bonding."[37] Guided by the work of Du Pont's veteran consultant, Carl "Speed" Marvel, Houtz pursued an organic solvent for polyacrylonitrile using the latter theory.[38] At Illinois, Marvel had been studying the relationship between hydrogen bonding and the solubility of small molecules, and his approach was suggestive for Houtz.

Consequently, Houtz and his group tested several thousand polar organic compounds as potential solvents and found that many were indeed effective.[39] Marvel suggested that he try dimethylacetamide (DMAC), which he did without success. Houtz then tried dimethylformamide (DMF), and this compound worked well.[40] Only later did Pioneering discover that the DMAC sample tried by Houtz was an azeotrope of 90 percent DMAC and 10 percent water and that pure DMAC would work.[41] Houtz also later learned that the Chemical Department's G. H. Latham had demonstrated that the polymer could be dissolved in dimethylformamide. Houtz found that he could spin an interesting fiber from viscous DMF solutions of polyacrylonitrile with techniques similar to those used in either cellulose acetate manufacture ("dry spinning," which involves evaporation of the solvent from the spun fiber) or in viscose rayon production ("wet spinning," in which the filament is coagulated in a liquid after it emerges from the spinneret).[42] (See Figure 18.5 for a representation of fiber spinning methods.) Houtz's discovery was code-named Fiber A, and its path toward commercialization as Orlon was begun. But the journey proved to be far more arduous and expensive than Charch or anyone else in the technical division imagined, and more than once top management of the department bade the acrylic wayfarers to turn back.

Houtz soon produced polyacrylonitrile fibers with wool-like properties (achieved when the spun fibers were left undrawn or drawn only slightly) and also fibers that looked and felt like silk (after they had been drawn in a way similar to nylon). Determining what kind of fiber would be most attractive in the marketplace would be a critical factor in the success or

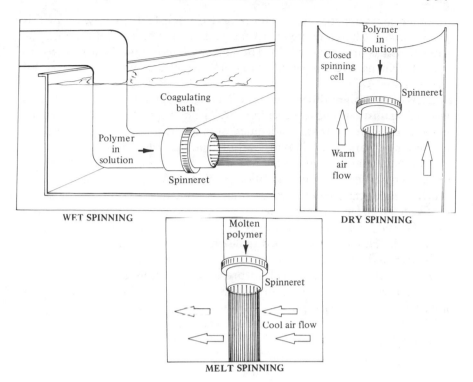

Figure 18.5. Spinning Methods Used in Man-Made Fiber Production. Source: Adapted from *Man Made Fiber Fact Book* (New York: Man-Made Fiber Producers Association, Inc., 1970), p. 6.

failure of Orlon. But in 1942, both the wool-like and silklike aspects of the new fiber seemed secondary after Pioneering observed that it possessed excellent resistance to light, chemicals, and bacteria.[43] Pioneering's researchers stepped up their development efforts in spite of the concerns of the department's general manager, Leonard A. Yerkes, that Fiber A was "highly inflammable."[44]

Pioneering soon encountered a fundamental problem in fiber development that had not existed with nylon: production of enough fiber to make meaningful evaluations of the fiber's commercial potential. Targeting markets required the immediate production of much more fiber for end-use evaluation than had been required for nylon, and Pioneering did not have the funds to scale up its operations. The laboratory nonetheless managed to produce enough fiber of both silklike and wool-like forms for the development section of the technical division to perform high-spot evaluations for end uses.[45]

In September 1942, Development issued its first report on Fiber A, which pointed up what would become the major problem: dyeing.[46] Without good dyeing, no apparel fiber could succeed commercially no matter how good its other characteristics were. Houtz and Charch had been aware of this problem, and Charch had gone to the Jackson Laboratory of the Organic Chemicals Department for help. The Jackson Laboratory soon reported to Charch that no dye among all Du Pont's dye classes was satisfactory for dyeing Fiber A.[47]

Lack of dyeability threatened to kill Fiber A.[48] Three other factors also worked against pushing its development. The first was World War II, which made it difficult to procure adequate supplies for scaling up the process beyond the laboratory.[49] Second, Carbide and Carbon Company introduced Vinyon N, a modification of its Vinyon, which contained 50 percent acrylonitrile and 50 percent vinyl chloride. To Yerkes, Vinyon N appeared to be much cheaper than Fiber A could ever be, and therefore he saw little incentive to go ahead with the project.[50] Finally, Du Pont's Haskell Laboratory of Industrial Toxicology revised its 1938 data on the safety of dimethylformamide. Haskell now warned that atmospheric concentrations must be kept low and that all skin contact with the solvent should be strictly avoided.[51] These problems had all presented themselves by mid-1944; in spite of Yerkes's general pessimism, the technical division pushed the new fiber by addressing each problem as directly as possible.

The dye problems and the war-induced procurement difficulties combined to shape the development of Fiber A. Although Benger succeeded in convincing Orchem to appoint representatives from its Jackson Laboratory and its Technical Laboratory to a Fiber A dye committee, he and his higher management chose a principal development strategy that did not depend entirely on Fiber A's dyeability.[52] The strategy keyed on Fiber A's extreme resistance to sunlight, chemicals, and bacteria. The development section soon sold the military on the critical importance of Fiber A for applications in jungles where U.S. servicemen had seen their cotton tents and shoelaces rot before their eyes. Though possessing a poor, off-white natural color and lacking dyeability, Fiber A might find excellent markets in tents, tarpaulins, and awnings. Such a strategy both appeased Yerkes and provided Du Pont the means to obtain a higher classification for materials procurement.[53]

Charch addressed the perceived threat of Vinyon N while arguing for Fiber A's development as a wool substitute. He assured Benger and Yerkes that Vinyon N posed no danger to Fiber A because the 50/50 polymer not only melted well below the thermal decomposition temperature of polyacrylonitrile but also made it far less resistant to common solvents.[54] Charch noted with alarm that his repeated urging to develop Fiber A as a wool-like staple "has been slow to soak into people's heads, I think largely because our idea of 'staple' is a 25¢ per pound product of the viscose rayon type. We have overlooked the unique properties of Fiber A as a curly staple which would bring it into the very high price wool field such as vicuna, cashmere, and a lot of fancy wools selling for upwards of $5.00 per pound and some even higher."[55]

Haskell's bad news about DMF's toxicity meant that process development would have to be done more carefully to ensure against exposure of re-searchers and operators to the solvent. Greater care meant greater expend-itures. But overall, the dry spinning process used for acetate was highly amenable to Fiber A production because the fiber could be spun in closed cells and the solvent recovered comparatively easily.

By the end of 1944, the Fiber A project, though behind schedule, was nevertheless alive and expanding. The technical division planned to double its daily production of polyacrylonitrile to almost seventy pounds.[56] Only with this scale of production could the development division fully explore and develop market opportunities for Fiber A.

A year later, however, continued delays in reaching goals for the scale-up of dry spinning operations at Waynesboro and failure to make any real progress on the dye problem led top management of Fibers to call for a complete review of the program. The technical division had been able to deliver only 3,255 pounds of usable Fiber A yarn, whereas the target had been 10,000–20,000 pounds.[57] Despite regular meetings of the Fiber A dye committee, no one had developed any great new leads to solving the problem of dyeing this hydrophobic fiber. The department had spent roughly $1 million on Fiber A; Pioneering's share represented $400,000 of the total.[58]

Before the review, Benger's assistant, Andrew Buchanan, informed Charch that management would be justified in suspending all work on Fiber A on the basis of the dyeing problem alone. He argued that Pioneering had been using a "shot-gun approach" to solving the dye problem while making only incremental improvements to Fiber A's other problems, such as its poor color and its high spinning costs. Buchanan urged Charch to concentrate on a "more fundamental approach to the general problem of dyeing hy-drophobic fibers."[59] Reading Buchanan clearly, Charch agreed to reduce Pioneering's 1946 expenditures on Fiber A by more than 60 percent and to shift the remaining 40 percent to more fundamental research on dyeing all hydrophobic fibers. At the same time, Charch concurred that acetate re-search should take formal responsibility for Fiber A's development.[60]

The management review, held in late November 1945, laid on the table the overriding concerns of Yerkes and his successor, Benjamin M. May, and also led to narrowing the scope of Fiber A's development. Benger stressed that most of Fiber A's major problems had been overcome and "we have an acceptable product and workable process now." Here, Benger was clearly alluding to filament yarn aimed at outdoor applications rather than Charch's much desired wool-like staple. May wanted to know only one thing: Would Fiber A compete with nylon and rayon? The head of the development sec-tion, R. M. Horsey, said emphatically that the new fiber would "not take business away from nylon or viscose rayon." Rather, it would penetrate the cotton market. Fiber A was a very good fiber, argued Horsey, but it would not be like nylon in that it had no obvious market like women's hosiery. The fiber would find markets in a "wide variety of applications where its unique combination of properties qualifies it above all other fibers." Once assured of the nonthreat of Fiber A to rayon and nylon, May and his assistants sought to contain the costs of developing the new fiber rather than to kill it. These managers wanted to target "a few of the best prospective applications and concentrate the pilot-production there instead of spreading samples more widely." This meant that Fiber A's development would be focused on markets where resistance to sunlight, solvents, and bacteria were primary desiderata. With this stricture, May allowed the development of Fiber A to proceed, and the group determined that they would make a definitive decision on whether to commercialize the new fiber by March 15, 1946.[61]

When informed of the outcome of this meeting, Church argued that May's stricture on market development was unwise. He strongly advocated developing markets for filament yarns where silklike qualities were sought, for staple where Fiber A could replace wool, and for fiber blending where Fiber A could enhance wool's utility in fabrics and knitwear. No doubt Church realized that his advocacy of staple fiber would remain hollow until the dye problem was solved. He therefore promised to "rejuvenate" the dye program with "a much more vigorous attack than we had ever given this subject before."[62] This included not only trying to synthesize dyes for Fiber A but also copolymerizing acrylonitrile with other monomers to make it more receptive to standard dyes. But Orchem was still not convinced to launch an all-out effort to solve Fiber A's dye problem.

The technical division fell short of its goal to bring the general manager to a decision on commercialization by March 15, 1946. Many of the reasons for this failure lay in the management of the acetate research section. Seeking to overcome delays, Benger and Buchanan removed acetate research's director Fenton H. Swezey from direct responsibility for Fiber A in February 1946 and appointed G. Preston Hoff, director of nylon research and the man who had so successfully directed the development of nylon, as special coordinator of Fiber A development. Later, in January 1947, Hoff was named director of acetate research, and Swezey became a research associate.

Hoff moved swiftly to arrive at decisions about a plant and the processes it would employ. The technical division's engineering research section had put together a study with cost estimates for plants of two different sizes – a 6-million-pound-per-year filament plant to satisfy the market projections of the development division and a smaller 2-million-pound-per-year filament plant to appease the more skeptical general management. Hoff dismissed the smaller plant out of hand and directed his division's efforts toward solving process problems and cutting estimated plant costs from $15 million to $9 million or below.[63]

Hoff's swift action won a strong vote of confidence in the Fiber A program by general management, and he received permission to continue it. Soon, Hoff reached several important decisions on its development, almost all of which were based on expediting rather than optimizing commercialization.

The most critical of these was to abandon development of a continuous process (from polymerization all the way through spinning, solvent extraction, drawing, and final packaging) for Fiber A production – something that Hale Charch had been advocating. As Hoff explained to Buchanan, this process would impede development. "The important thing," he said, "is to define the necessary minimum satisfactory elements of the process and establish their sequence." Hoff determined that "we should proceed on the basis of building demonstration equipment only, for the elements of the preferred process. An affirmative decision to commercialize the product could then carry with it a decision to scale up the preferred process equipment and operate it as a pilot plant."[64]

Fiber A moved steadily forward under Hoff's leadership. The development section continued to find new uses for filament yarn and to receive enthusiastic responses from the textile industry.[65] The Executive Committee authorized funds for construction of a dedicated Fiber A research building at Waynesboro, which was occupied in October 1946, and in May 1946 the committee authorized the Fibers Department to carry out the initial design of a commercial plant.[66]

This design work took one year to complete, but during this period the technical division and the general management had to make some tough decisions before commercialization could proceed. Tension existed between the needs of the acetate research section and those of the development section over operation of the semiworks. Continued problems with Fiber A processes interfered with output of fibers that the development section needed in building market opportunities for the new fiber. By the end of 1946, the semiworks had delivered only 17,000 pounds of Fiber A to the textile industry for evaluation, an amount that the development section considered far below what was necessary. Therefore the department's managers decided to construct a pilot plant at Waynesboro to produce 10,000 pounds a month and to put at least 120,000 pounds of Fiber A into Du Pont customers' hands by the time the commercial plant began producing fiber. The pilot plant would both produce fiber for trade evaluation and serve as the testing and training ground for the commercial process.[67]

The magnitude of the remaining process problems can best be measured by the fact that the pilot plant did not begin operation until June 1, 1949 – three months after construction began on what became known as the May Plant, the first commercial plant for Fiber A, now trademarked Orlon.[68] Moreover, the product made by the pilot plant was entirely different than that initially manufactured at the May Plant. This major change resulted not from factors growing out of scale-up but from problems associated with dyeing Orlon fibers.

The Orlon dye problem had become acute. But it had now become a generic problem for all hydrophobic fibers. Expansion of nylon beyond women's hosiery demanded better dyes and dyeing techniques.[69] Pioneering's work on polyester fiber, which began in 1944 and is discussed below, heightened the dyeing problem. Here were three synthetic fibers, each with unique properties unrivaled by natural fibers, which could not be satisfactorily dyed. Commercial exploitation and the growth of these hydrophobic fibers depended in large measure on solving the dye problems.

The efforts of the Fiber A dye committee had come to naught by mid-1946. For the next three years, Fibers and Orchem research units exchanged insults more than anything else. Fibers charged that Orchem was not interested in solving the problem of dyeing hydrophobic fibers. Orchem argued that the potential market for dyes for hydrophobic fibers did not justify expenditure of its precious research dollars when better opportunities existed elsewhere. Gradually Orchem devoted more effort to this problem after arguments reached the general manager level. Not until Fibers agreed to fund much of Orchem's research did Orchem's efforts fully satisfy Fibers.[70]

Charch was unquestionably the most outspoken critic of Orchem's research efforts.[71] Although he actively encouraged his management to prod Orchem into doing more research for Fibers, he basically decided that the technical division of Fibers would have to solve the problem by itself. To this end, Charch assigned a growing number of his own researchers to Fiber A dyeing. He also commissioned the Chemical Department to undertake fundamental research on dyeing hydrophobic fibers, began to follow closely ICI's fundamental research on dyestuffs, and initiated long-term fundamental dye research programs at the Textile Research Institute (Princeton University) and at the University of Illinois. But more important, Charch recruited Chiles E. Sparks, a group leader in the azo colors research division at the Jackson Laboratory, to work for Pioneering. With Sparks at Pioneering, Charch believed his laboratory had a good chance of solving the hydrophobic fibers dyeing problem because "the solution of the problem can conceivably come out of a knowledge of fiber technology as readily as it can come out of dyestuffs technology." Pioneering could pursue an integrated approach to the problem, an approach he argued that "has yet to be fully applied."[72] Sparks organized a broad-based dye research program on hydrophobic fibers.[73] Soon Pioneering began to meet with success through chemical modification of Fiber A.

Early in Fiber A's development, Pioneering researchers attempted to increase dyeability of the fiber through chemical modification. These efforts initially centered on copolymerizing acrylonitrile with a small percentage of methacrylic acid. Not satisfied, they tried styrene as a comonomer but then tried 2-vinylpyridine. A copolymer of 95 percent acrylonitrile and 5 percent 2-vinylpyridine, labeled A-3, yielded excellent dyeing results. Pioneering determined that Orlon A-3 had eliminated the Fiber A dye problem.[74]

Although impressed by the dramatic improvement in dyeability of Orlon A-3, the development section fretted about some of the practical problems posed by this approach.[75] The acquisition of enough 2-vinylpyridine presented the greatest drawback. The compound was not commercially available on a large scale, and Du Pont's supplier could make it only in low yields and at high costs. Du Pont's Explosives Department, which was anxious to manufacture intermediates for Textile Fibers, had little hope of making the compound. Instead, it urged substituting the more readily available 5-ethyl-2-vinylpyridine.[76]

Over the next year, however, Sparks and others in the technical division grew more sanguine about the 2-vinylpyridine copolymer. In fact, Sparks declared it "a practical dyeing yarn."[77] The Organic Chemicals Department conducted a concerted campaign to synthesize new dyes for Orlon A-3 to fill in the gaps of colors not available. Orchem's Technical Laboratory and Textile's newly equipped Newport Laboratory also worked on new dyeing processes with success, although few of these techniques had been fully tried in commercial equipment. The Explosives Department still urged the substitution of 5-ethyl-2-vinylpyridine. Sparks reported that fibers made from this copolymer showed inferior dyeing results but agreed to explore its feasibility on an even larger scale because the prospects for obtaining large quantities of 2-vinylpyridine had not improved during the previous year.[78] Hence at the end of 1948, Orlon's dye problem had really not been solved.

Du Pont's response to this situation is interesting. At the top level, the Executive and Finance committees approved the department's appropriation request for a 6.5-million-pound commercial filament yarn plant to be erected in Camden, South Carolina (dedicated on July 3, 1950, as the May Plant).[79] In a presentation to the Executive Committee, the technical division's W. W. Heckert drew a persuasive analogy between Orlon's dyeing problem and the lack of a sizing process for nylon when the Seaford plant was authorized. Du Pont research had found the solution to the size problem just in time for the Seaford plant to open on schedule. Would not Du Pont research on Orlon dyeing result in a similar triumph?[80] At the department level, managers determined that the pilot plant would produce both pure polyacrylonitrile fiber and Orlon A-3 (despite the improbability of procuring commercial quantities of 2-vinylpyridine monomer).[81] Trade evaluation of Orlon A-3 proved to be highly favorable, especially as progress was made on dyeing processes. But the development section's marketing work on unmodified Orlon for awnings and tarpaulins suggested that Du Pont could sell it despite lack of dyeability.

Nine months before the dedication of the May Plant, the department had still not decided which fiber to produce, modified or unmodified Orlon. But by early 1950, only a few months before the start-up, Du Pont's customers, anxious not to be left out on a new wonder fiber as some had been with nylon, had already contracted for the initial production of the May Plant's filament yarn, whether it was dyeable or not. This success in selling settled the matter. The plant would initially produce unmodified yarn. The development section continued to believe that Orlon's unique characteristics of sunlight and solvent resistance would make it "a commercial certainty."[82] With excellent initial sales, the department charted in January 1951 a filament yarn expansion program, which called for an output of 40 million pounds by 1955.[83] But by year's end, optimism had turned to grave doubts about the future of Orlon filament yarn.

As Du Pont learned more and more about the Orlon yarn process and its economics, the more discouraged its managers became. Process difficulties were not ironed out as had been expected, and studies indicated that no significant mill cost reductions could be expected in a plant of less than 15 million pounds annual output.[84] Within six months of the May Plant's opening, Du Pont found that it could not sell its total output despite significantly lowering prices. By August 1951, the handwriting was on the wall. All plans for expansion of filament yarn capacity were scotched, and research was reoriented to reflect changed conditions.[85] Orlon filament yarn never became a successful product.

The department's Orlon staple program took on new importance.[86] Charch had long been preaching that Orlon's significance lay in its wool-like properties. Interest in Orlon staple grew rapidly in the technical division after Pioneering developed modified A-3 Orlon. Although the principal problem with the staple centered on dyeing, commercialization of the product also involved other aspects of fiber development. Orlon staple was not simply continuous filament yarn cut into staple-length pieces. Rather, staple required the development of differently drawn filaments with different cross sections. Here is where Pioneering's fundamental research on fiber characterization and resiliency became of paramount importance. Moreover, the parallel development of Dacron polyester fiber had provided increased understanding of how to build resilience into a fiber. Dacron had demonstrated great responsiveness to physical as opposed to chemical changes in its molecular structure and had led Pioneering researchers to see orientation and crystallinity − determined by the degree to which fibers were drawn − as controlling factors in resiliency. This increased knowledge of Dacron's nature was fed back to Orlon's development, and wool-like Orlon fibers were engineered to be even more woolly than had been obtained previously.[87]

From the summer of 1948, Waynesboro's staple development was based on Orlon A-3.[88] The development section built a market evaluation and development program around this modified Orlon fiber. Subsequent events essentially undermined the development section's work.

Continued concern over the ability to secure enough 2-vinylpyridine led managers in February 1950 to decide to manufacture Orlon staple from a different copolymer than Orlon A-3. They made this decision less than two months after the Executive Committee had authorized $40 million for the construction of a 30-million-pound-per-year staple facility to be built at the May Plant site. The new staple was now to be spun from Orlon A-4 − a copolymer of acrylonitrile and 2-methyl-5-vinylpyridine. Pioneering and Orchem had only preliminarily evaluated A-4 as being more readily dyeable than A-3 with approximately the same dye fastness, and the Explosives Department had assured Fibers executives that it could produce enough of the new modifier.[89] With the decision to use Orlon A-4, the design for the commercial staple plant was frozen, and all subsequent development work was done on this basis.

These plans were shelved within a year, however. In late 1950, the Carbide and Carbon Company announced that using cuprous ions in the dye bath would dramatically increase polyacrylonitrile's receptivity to acid dyes. It now appeared that the dye problem had been solved and that no expensive modifier would be necessary.[90] The Fibers Department immediately initiated research at Pioneering, Waynesboro, the Jackson Laboratory, and Orchem's Technical Laboratory to determine if cuprous ions were indeed the solution to the long-unsolved dye problem.

With steel about to be erected for the May staple plant, a decision was necessary on which type of Orlon would be spun. Laboratory research suggested that copper dyeing was promising, but there were problems, especially in control of the dyeing and disposal of wastes. The trade-offs were clear: By choosing to go back to pure polyacrylonitrile, the department would be abandoning a known and increasingly satisfactory dyeing situation for a promising but unproven one; it would be gaining a higher thermal stability and a lower-cost polymer; and it would be scrapping for the second time strides made in developing markets, which would mean starting over again from designing new fabrics to building customer acceptance. Managers decided to take the risk in the hope that "an adequate dyeing technology could be built up using the newly discovered cuprous ion technique with acid dyes."[91] The commercial staple plant would manufacture straight polyacrylonitrile, to be known as Type 41 Orlon.

Fifteen months separated the date of this decision and the planned start-up of the staple plant. Only a limited amount of the new Type 41 staple would be available from the pilot plant at Waynesboro – nothing close to what the development section considered necessary to build markets for the 30-million-pound output of the May staple plant. Nevertheless, the development section implemented a strategy to build market acceptance for the new staple: Choose a few key areas for product development, prove them out as well as possible, and hope that "the trade at large would enter into a broad development program" once more staple became available.[92]

This strategy failed. Although Du Pont found that demand for Type 41 staple evaluations exceeded the supply available from the pilot plant, once commercial start-up began in May 1952, Type 41 met a rapid death in the marketplace. On the basis of their trust in Du Pont alone, customers bought some 14 million pounds of Orlon staple, largely as a pig in a poke. "The faith of our customers," noted a postmortem report, "was not justified by the performance of the commercial Type 41 product."[93] The failure of Type 41 staple was attributed to poor textile processing caused by static electricity, extreme nonuniformity of staple, and the development of odors in wool blends. Above all, the cuprous ion method of dyeing was declared a "complete failure."[94]

With Orlon filament yarn failing to grow and Type 41 staple yarn dead, the Textile Fibers Department found itself in a bind. Du Pont had invested almost $50 million in commercial plant and about $7 million in R&D.[95] The solution to Du Pont's problems with its acrylic fiber came from the rapid development of another modified polymer, Orlon A-6 (a copolymer of 94 percent acrylonitrile and 6 percent methyl acrylate) known as Type 42 Orlon. Even here, however, success was not certain, and Textile Fibers was lucky that its acetate research section had not totally abandoned polymer modification as a solution to the dye problem in favor of the cuprous ion approach.[96]

When Type 41 Orlon staple was declared dead, it was not obvious that the new Type 42 copolymer would save the day. In fact, some R&D managers argued against it. Returning to a modified Orlon entailed drawbacks, including a lower temperature resistance. This had been a major weakness with earlier Orlon copolymers and, when compared with Du Pont's other new fiber, Dacron, even unmodified Orlon's decomposition temperature seemed low.[97] But in switching to Orlon Type 42 staple, Du Pont would be making a highly unorthodox move in that not a single test of the Type 42 staple had been carried out in a customer's mill. For Du Pont, this was a drastic move.[98] But the department was in a position that demanded such action.

Du Pont's problems were exacerbated by the problems experienced by its competitor Chemstrand with Acrilan acrylic fiber. Like Orlon, Acrilan had been introduced with much fanfare, but once in customers' mills it performed poorly. The problems were so bad that Chemstrand had to close its plant to fix the fiber at the very same time Du Pont had announced the end of Type 41 Orlon. Customers were confused and rapidly grew suspicious of acrylic fibers. Almost all of them had suffered losses with acrylics.[99] Moreover, the introduction of Du Pont's Dacron and other synthetics by competitors added to the confusion. Even within Du Pont there was grave concern over competition between Dacron and Orlon not only for markets but also for research dollars.[100]

With the changeover from Type 41 to Type 42 Orlon, Du Pont found itself with a 30-million-pound-per-year plant turning out a product that was "to all intents and purposes . . . untried and untested, and which the trade is willing to buy only in pilot quantity." Managers in the Fibers Department realized that they had to launch an all-out fabric development program because it had already been demonstrated that "straight substitution of Type 42 for Type 41 was not satisfactory." They believed that there was "no magic button" to push to restore confidence in Orlon and that "the way back [would] be long and hard." Above all, they wanted to ensure that no additional radical changes would be made in Orlon staple, even though researchers might come up with something big and important. Research at the Jackson Laboratory on the mechanism of dyeing Type 42 Orlon suggested that a further modification would improve the dyeability of acrylic fibers. They found that Orlon could be dyed with basic dyes, a class very little used in textiles. This work soon led to the development of an Orlon with a styrenesulfonic acid copolymer, which was not introduced until 1957.[101]

Fortunately for Du Pont, Orlon staple – even the banished Type 41 – was enthusiastically received in the knitwear field. Fashion trends were moving consumers into bulky sweaters, for which Orlon proved to be ideal. The development section and the sales development force working on Orlon had failed to anticipate this market. In January 1951, when the sales force developed its first Orlon market forecast through 1955, sweaters figured as only 2 percent of the total market for Orlon staple.[102] Yet sweaters helped Du Pont dig itself out of the deep hole in which it found itself in 1953. Type 42 production started in March, and sales fell as low as 550,000 pounds in June and July. But soon everything turned around. With great help from the outside development of the turbo-processor, which produced high-bulk yarn – and Du Pont's purchase and dedication of turbo-processing patents – Type 42 Orlon took off. By the end of 1954, the May staple plant was sold to capacity. Sales continued to show strength, and in 1956 Du Pont doubled the capacity of the staple plant and announced the construction of a 40-million-pound-per-year staple plant at Waynesboro. The sweater market proved to be so strong that Fibers managers became concerned about being too dependent on it and therefore devoted considerable effort to woven fabric design, which had been the intended market for staple all along. By 1957, these efforts had begun to pay off when it sold 22 million pounds of Orlon (or roughly a third of total output) for woven fabrics, particularly worsted blends. Orlon sales had reached almost 100 million pounds a year by the end of the 1950s, and Orlon was a brilliant commercial success.[103]

The lessons of Orlon were important to the Textile Fibers Department. Orlon yarn's properties appeared to be so important and unique as to guarantee success, but these proved insufficient. The development of Orlon staple left a lasting impression on the department's managers. Du Pont could not afford to repeat the Orlon staple experience, in which continual changes in the experimental product undermined market development efforts. Du Pont could not pursue a strategy of developing only a few markets or applications for a fiber and then hoping converters would develop more. The company would have to devote considerably more effort – and therefore more money – to applications and market development.[104] The Orlon experience helped lead the department into a dramatically expanded end-use development program, which meant that in the future, the development of a product would be far more expensive than that of Orlon had been.

The Development of Dacron

The discovery and development of Orlon acrylic fiber dramatically confirmed Hale Charch's 1941 thesis that nylon polyamides would not be "the last super-polymers which the world is going to see in the form of threads and fibers." But the successful synthesis and spinning of polyester fibers in 1945 brought an embarrassment of riches to Du Pont and posed major issues regarding its development, especially because it appeared to possess properties that would make it competitive with both nylon and Orlon, not to mention rayon and acetate. Ultimately, polyester would become the most important synthetic fiber in the U.S. market, but its success as an innovation was by no means apparent in the early days of its development. Dacron's development uncannily paralleled Orlon's.

Pioneering's first fibers from polyethylene terephthalate (polyester) had the important properties of high tenacity and wet strength and excellent blending characteristics. Resiliency studies also indicated that this new fiber probably could be made into the most wool-like of any Du Pont fiber made to date. Charch wanted polyester's development to go this way. But keying on the high tenacity of the new fiber, striving to find a large and easily developed market, and wishing to avoid broad competition with nylon and Orlon, the department's managers decided that polyester's prime initial development would be as a tire cord. After a year of work, the project failed miserably, and the managers opened up the development of polyester in other areas.

Armed with even better resiliency data, Charch continued to advocate developing polyester as a wool substitute. His laboratory rapidly pushed the development of wool-like polyester fibers and fabrics and eventually demonstrated the potential of this approach. Wool-like fiber eventually became an important market for polyester, but the development of cotton/polyester blended fabrics − "wash-and-wear" or "permanently pressed" goods − by outside processors provided the great impetus to polyester's success. Polyester fiberfill also built capacity. Both these developments were based on the resilience of polyester, which the Pioneering Laboratory recognized and sought to maximize.

Charch's sense of proprietorship about Dacron polyester fiber ran very deep, even though legally Dacron was Du Pont's trademark for the polyethylene terephthalate fiber developed by Imperial Chemical Industries as Terylene. In 1946, at Charch's recommendation Du Pont purchased ICI's U.S. patent application on polyethylene terephthalate fibers. Over time, however, Charch came to regard Dacron as a Du Pont creation that bore little relation to Terylene.[105] Although the history of ICI's Terylene has been well documented, how Pioneering came upon polyethylene terephthalate has not been adequately told.

The origins of both Terylene and Dacron are rooted in the work Wallace H. Carothers carried out in the Chemical Department's Purity Hall in the late 1920s and early 1930s. As part of his research on polymers, Carothers published a paper in the *Journal of the American Chemical Society* (1929) describing the preparation of several aliphatic polyesters.[106] Carothers noted that all these polyesters had low melting points and were hygroscopic (i.e., they absorbed moisture or were easily hydrolyzed). In a subsequent paper, Carothers discussed the polymerization of what was called an "omega super polyester," which, with a molecular weight as high as 12,000, was both spinnable and drawable as fiber.[107] But these polyester fibers, like the earlier ones, melted at low temperatures, were easily hydrolyzed, and therefore did not appear to be commercially attractive. Subsequently, other researchers in the Chemical Department prepared many more polyesters, and in fact one chemist in Carothers's group, Edgar Spanagel, prepared polyethylene terephthalate in October 1934.[108] But follow-up work was not pursued primarily for two reasons. First, work on the extremely promising polyamides (i.e., nylon) had begun to command the Chemical Department's attention. But more important, there was no point in such follow-up because researchers had developed a mindset that polyesters were inherently low-softening and easily hydrolyzed.

This mindset went well beyond the Chemical Department, but certainly it originated there. In 1942 for example, at a routine consulting session with chemists in the nylon research section, Herman Mark suggested that polyesters might make higher-tenacity yarns than nylon because they could be handled more easily at very long chain lengths. Led by Vernal R. Hardy, a former member of the Chemical Department, nylon researchers informed Mark that "their water solubility and low softening point make the polyesters uninteresting."[109]

Chemists in the Pioneering Research Laboratory also operated within this conventional wisdom, but as they became more sophisticated in their knowledge of polymer chemistry they began to think that they could get around the problem of hydrolysis through some clever tricks.[110] Church later noted that there was "an ever-stronger urge to reinvestigate polyesters" in the early 1940s, but the outbreak of the war prevented him from establishing the necessary program to explore the polyesters.[111] Specifically, Church maintained that his best polymer chemists were young men whose draft deferments were contingent upon being assigned to work of immediate relevance to the war effort. Thus they were precluded from undertaking any exploratory research. In mid-1944, however, changes in draft deferment regulations eased the tight restrictions on military-related research, and Church quickly took advantage of the changes by launching a broad exploratory program under the title "New Condensation Polymers," which was run by Emmette F. Izard, one of Pioneering's best chemists.[112]

By this time, however, Pioneering's work on polyesters had been stimulated by both rumors and news about Terylene, which had been discovered in 1941 and, because of war-time security measures, had been kept out of Du Pont's purview by the British government. Izard's supervisor, W. W. Watkins, first learned of the British development while attending the Gibson Island research conference during the last week of June 1944. There, Herman Mark told Watkins about the English development of a new fiber that might be polyacrylonitrile and arranged a meeting with a representative from the Boston consulting firm of Arthur D. Little, Inc., which was studying the polymer for the U.S. Quartermaster's Office. From a conversation with this representative, Watkins quickly concluded that the British had not developed a polyacrylonitrile fiber because the new fiber was a melt-spun polymer.[113] But the representative's statement that the British fiber was much like nylon in its properties proved disconcerting. Two weeks later at the Gibson Island conference, Preston Hoff learned even more about the British fiber. Again Mark was the source. As Hoff wrote to Benger's assistant, "Dr. Mark mentioned that a Major Hobson of the Quartermaster Corps had brought back from England a sample of a fiber called 'Terrylite' and ... Dr. Mark thought it might be a polyurethane or similar condensation product. It was not obtained through the I.C.I."[114] Mark had not gotten the chemical identity, but Du Pont was well on its way to determining the mystery fiber's composition because the A. D. Little representative told Mark that "it was easy to guess from the name."[115] Thus the news from the Gibson Island meetings served as an important reminder that nylon and Fiber A would not be the last polymers to make good fibers.

Evidence suggests that by the time Izard began his polyester work (October 20, 1944), he had learned the actual composition of Terylene but that he and others in Pioneering were skeptical about the polymer. As he described his thinking at the time, "While ethylene glycol esters were not specifically mentioned in the project write-up it was intended that such esters would be studied and the ones actually mentioned in the project were our ideas of means by which we could produce other higher melting polymers or more stable polymers since we were still laboring under the delusion that even if [poly]ethylene terephthalate was as good as reported it would be too low melting or not stable enough, basing our opinions of course on the aliphatic derivatives produced in the past."[116]

Not until February 1945 did Izard seriously consider a polyester of ethylene terephthalate. His thinking on this polymer had not changed until he observed that a related terephthalate melted at a much higher temperature than he had assumed. Izard then concluded that indeed ethylene terephthalate might make a good polymer. He subsequently prepared a high-melting polymer of dihydroxyethyl terephthalate[117] using an ester exchange reaction, similar to that described by Carothers in 1930. With this and other successes in ester exchange techniques, Izard produced polyethylene terephthalate by reacting an excess of ethylene glycol with dimethyl terephthalate. The results were outstanding. With a high intrinsic viscosity and high melting point, polyethylene terephthalate proved to be easily melt-spun into a drawable fiber with excellent properties.[118] The rumors about Terylene had indeed proven to be true in spite of all the disbelief among Du Pont's researchers.

Within days of Pioneering's first preparation of fibers from polyethylene terephthalate, representatives from ICI met with Du Pont officials in Wilmington to convey information on Terylene. ICI had requested its New York office to inform Du Pont about the new fiber on February 19, 1945 (the same day Izard obtained a good polymer) and to set up a meeting of its England-based patent expert, R. R. Melhuish, with Du Pont. Charch had learned about this meeting, scheduled for March 15, and asked to be included.[119] No doubt he also pushed his researchers to learn as much as possible about Izard's polymer and the resulting fibers before the meeting with Melhuish so that Du Pont's position would be more firm.

At the meeting, Melhuish spent the morning briefing Du Pont on the history of Terylene.[120] ICI had not invented it. That honor belonged to two researchers from Calico Printers Association, Ltd., of Lancashire, J. R. Whinfield and J. T. Dickson, who based their work on the classic publications of Carothers. In 1940, Whinfield and Dickson substituted terephthalic acid for the aliphatic acids used by Carothers and achieved a stable fiber-forming polymer, polyethylene terephthalate.[121] They applied for two patents on their work, which they assigned to Calico Printers Association. Through the British Ministry of Supply, Calico Printers and ICI came together in late 1943 to discuss the development of this new polymer named Terylene. ICI had learned enough about Terylene to know that it did not want to miss out on its development.[122] It quickly negotiated a contract with Calico Printers giving ICI an exclusive, worldwide twenty-year license on Terylene. Du Pont's British ally now had its own "nylon."

Melhuish gave the Du Pont officials a sample of the polyester fiber, copies of the two patent applications, copies of ICI's most comprehensive technical report on Terylene, and a copy of a recent cable from England containing more up-to-date data on the fiber's properties. The meeting produced a consensus that Carothers's basic patents dominated the Terylene patents but that this did "not prevent [Whinfield and Dickson from] getting valid patents for Terylene."[123]

Charch was fully prepared to report on the substantial progress made by the Pioneering Laboratory. In the afternoon, he demonstrated that his laboratory had produced a polyester with higher intrinsic viscosity and stiffer fibers with higher tenacity than ICI's samples. Charch and others in the department told Melhuish that because the fiber looked so good, Du Pont planned for the "very rigorous prosecution of further studies."[124] Although Charch privately told Ernest Benger that "it was very interesting to note that both the English and our own people have apparently arrived very closely at the same point quite independently," he recommended that Du Pont negotiate to obtain the U.S. rights to Terylene because it was "one of the most important developments that has come to our attention for a long time."[125] Du Pont moved more aggressively with polyester than did ICI, largely because it possessed greater expertise in developing a fiber. Although the two firms shared information on polyester from 1946 to 1948, the rate and manner of development differed substantially. This difference grew even larger after Du Pont and ICI canceled their Patents and Processes Agreement in 1948.

Du Pont's Executive Committee must have been troubled to learn of the development of polyethylene terephthalate fiber – now code-named Fiber V

– especially in the way Charch discussed it. With his usual optimism, Charch argued that Fiber V's properties closely paralleled those of nylon but that its most attractive feature was "its extremely low cost."[126] Benger's assistant, A. E. Buchanan, tempered Charch's enthusiasm for the new fiber in his report to the Executive Committee by pointing out that Fiber V's excellent resistance to hydrolysis might make it impossible to dye. As Pioneering learned more about Fiber V's properties, Charch grew in his enthusiasm and continued to see it as a fiber that would be cheaper to make than nylon. Regarding the potential nondyeability of Fiber V, Charch believed Buchanan's statement to the Executive Committee to be "somewhat ultra-conservative."[127]

Despite any concerns about Fiber V destroying the company's recent extensive capital expenditures on nylon, the technical division received the full support of the Du Pont Company for the rapid development of the fiber.[128] With the Orlon experience still fresh in his mind, Charch wanted the development of Fiber V to follow an ideal process for innovation within the department. That is, he believed his laboratory's proper role was to pioneer products and processes, not to perfect them in a commercial sense. The Pioneering Laboratory should bring new products and processes to a point at which no major basic questions remained. Subsequent scale-up and development should be undertaken by a product division laboratory.[129]

Pioneering's work on Fiber V moved along rapidly but not entirely free of conflict with the development section of the technical division. Early in 1946, the development section proposed that initial primary development efforts be directed toward tire cord by establishing an extensive tire cord program. Charch objected strenuously. He argued that a special trade evaluation program would "interfere with the program on the fiber as a whole."[130] Fiber V was still in the early pioneering stage, he maintained, and trade evaluations should not be initiated until it became the province of an industrial research section. Yet three days later – perhaps after learning that he was in the minority on the tire cord program – Charch recommended to Benger that responsibility for Fiber V's development be transferred to the Nylon Research Laboratory. He chose this laboratory because the new polymer could be melt-spun in existing nylon equipment. With "no bugs or mysteries connected with any point in the process any longer," Charch maintained that problems hereafter would stem from scale-up and the preparation of large quantities of yarn for development section tests.[131]

Benger and his assistant Buchanan accepted Charch's recommendation, which meant that G. Preston Hoff, head of the nylon research division, would be responsible for Fiber V's development.[132] Nylon research would immediately relieve V. R. Hardy of his nylon work and assign him exclusively to Fiber V and also put two other men on Fiber V. Charch could expect that personnel from Pioneering would be transferred to the Nylon Research Laboratory, which would begin scale-up work immediately.

These decisions had several implications. First, by giving Hoff responsibility for Fiber V, the technical division hoped to achieve good coordination between the development of Fiber V and that of Orlon, for which Hoff had assumed responsibility three months earlier. Research priorities were being shifted to "problems that bear directly on rapid reduction to practice." Pioneering Research's Fiber V program would be at least partially governed by Hoff, but Buchanan assured Charch that he could carry out "some longer range studies bearing on the ultimate commercial process of Fiber V." Buchanan reiterated that Fiber V's initial development would be in tire cord. He and Benger were so convinced that Fiber V had all the right properties to be a great tire cord that they ordered all research on nylon tire cord to be shifted to Fiber V as soon as possible.[133]

This development strategy soon proved to be premature. In early September 1946, the technical division made its first disclosure of Fiber V to four major tire companies, giving each 1.5-pound samples of the cord and promising subsequent delivery to each company of 30 pounds of cord by October 1 and another 200 pounds by January 1, 1947.[134] All four companies were anxious to evaluate Fiber V, and they quickly built tires with the cord provided by Du Pont. The results were disappointing. In late November, both Goodyear and Goodrich reported that Fiber V tires suffered ply separation and fatigue failures at mileages significantly lower than control tires of rayon and nylon.[135] Although these initial failures did not spell an immediate end to the division's strategy, subsequent failures during the next few months brought a radical change. These failures convinced technical division management that a successful polyester tire cord would not be easy and that much more time would be required to develop an adequate adhesive for the new hydrophobic fiber. Therefore in early March 1947, they determined to abandon the single-market strategy and to develop Fiber V as a textile yarn, a move that would potentially bring Fiber V into competition with nylon and Orlon.[136] It would take another fifteen years before the industry solved the problems of using polyester as a tire cord, but once it did polyester became the predominant fiber for automotive tires.[137]

Fortunately for Fiber V's future, the earlier strategy of tire cord development had not affected the Pioneering Research Laboratory. Pioneering had been allowed to pursue its basic studies on the characterization of Fiber V polymer and to pursue the spinning of higher intrinsic viscosity Fiber V. Pioneering had also continued its work on fiber drawing (trying to correlate fiber properties with various drawing, heating, and relaxing treatments) and its fundamental studies of fiber-to-fabric properties. Only in the area of developing a continuous polymerization process was Pioneering's major Fiber V program directed toward immediate commercial ends. Pioneering's freedom to pursue Fiber V's development in the direction Charch wanted to go – making a wool-like fiber – proved to be critical.[138]

Early in 1946, Pioneering researchers had observed that Fiber V drawn at low ratios (e.g., four times) had an X-ray diffraction pattern very similar to that of wool.[139] This finding fit neatly with other physical property and fiber characterization data on Fiber V. R. M. Hoffman and his associates had gathered and begun to interpret an increasingly large body of data on fiber characteristics, and Fiber V data greatly expanded their understanding. Pioneering researchers learned that they could manipulate Fiber V's characteristics by varying the degree of crystallization. By the time the Fiber V development program had been fully turned over to Nylon Research, Pioneering had concluded that "we have not yet begun to scratch the surface of making yarn properties to ordered specifications. The possibilities seem limitless."[140] The issuance of Hoffman's report, "A Generalized Concept of Resilience," produced the framework by which Pioneering developed Fiber V as its best candidate for a synthetic wool. By knowing what the "wool-like" properties of wool were and keenly appreciating Fiber V's "extreme responsiveness to physical rather than chemical changes in its molecular structure," Pioneering was able to engineer a fiber that closely approximated the resiliency of wool.[141]

This knowledge came into play when managers decided to open up the development to include textile applications. After reviewing Pioneering's work, the development section enthusiastically endorsed Charch's approach to the fiber.[142] Pioneering soon won a license to assume a greater role in the Fiber V development program.

Pioneering aggressively pursued developing wool-like Fiber V. All its Fiber V work was concentrated on staple rather than continuous filament yarns. Pioneering's Fiber V research included work on polymerization, spinning, drawing, dyeing, and fabric development.[143] The laboratory produced a small amount of highly promising wool-like fiber. Researchers there wanted to initiate larger fabric tests with this fiber than their own spinning equipment allowed, so in the summer of 1947 they secured from Nylon Research twenty-five pounds of Fiber V spun to their specifications. Pioneering researchers employed their newly devised drawing and finishing techniques to create their favored wool-like candidate. In the late summer of 1946, they took this fiber to the Lowell Textile Institute to see how it performed on commercial staple-processing equipment.[144]

That Pioneering employed Lowell Textile Institute to help determine how its wool-like Fiber V handled on commercial textile machinery pointed up a severe problem in the Textile Fibers Department. The department's facilities for evaluating new fibers and developing fabrics from them seriously lagged behind its ability to produce new fibers.[145] Not until 1945 did it have its own weaving facilities, but this facility, the Newport Weaving Laboratory, lacked commercial machinery to carry out preweaving operations for woolens and worsteds. Gradually, the Newport operation added more textile processing machinery but at a pace far slower than Charch desired. The department finally took aggressive action to meet its needs for textile processing, end-use research, and fabric development in 1952 when it resolved to build an entirely new facility on a large site roughly two miles from the recently expanded Experimental Station. Seeing other departments with similar end-use research problems, the Executive Committee used the Fibers project as a vehicle to induce as many departments as it could persuade into locating their end-use research facilities on the same site. With the Fibers Department leading the way, the Chestnut Run campus emerged when the new, fully equipped Textile Research Laboratory opened its doors in January 1954.[146]

The Chestnut Run facility was a far cry from the hand spinner and weaver Pioneering researchers had found in Buffalo to convert their experimental staple into woven fabrics. When they had exhausted the possibilities offered by this artisan in 1947, they went to Lowell to obtain that institution's expertise with woolen textile processing. The Pioneering–Lowell relationship lasted for almost two years and provided Pioneering with the critical know-how it needed to keep the Fiber V project in a commercial context while ensuring its independence to pursue its own Fiber V program.[147]

In late February 1948, Pioneering's H. J. Kolb and a counterpart from the development section took two 200-pound samples of differently drawn and finished Fiber V tow along with a wool control to the worsted division of Pacific Mills in Lawrence, Massachusetts. A highly innovative firm, Pacific Mills would play an important role in the successful adoption of synthetics by woolen and worsted producers. Pacific converted the samples of Fiber V tow into staple on its Pacific Converter and processed the staple into sliver. The sliver was then taken to another New England firm and spun into 24-count worsted yarn. In turn, the yarn was woven into a gabardine at the Newport Laboratory and finished by a commercial dyeing firm in Philadelphia. The outcome of these long-drawn-out efforts proved highly encouraging. The development section pronounced the wool-like Fiber V fabric "the most resilient... we have seen to date." The fabric possessed a "liveliness and springiness similar to wool" and exhibited "excellent resistance to wrinkling and good recovery from wrinkling."[148] Thus Pioneering's resiliency studies, when pursued in the context of Fiber V's development, had begun to pay off.

Charch soon raised a major issue connected with the development of wool-like synthetic fibers. Although he had avoided pursuing artificial wool by exactly duplicating the physical and chemical structure of wool, he maintained that wool's crimp was critical to the fiber's performance in fabrics. Therefore, he became alarmed when he learned from Kolb that the operations on Fiber V at Pacific Mills had tended to remove much of the crimp put mechanically into the staple at Nylon Research. He told Kolb that he could not overemphasize the importance of imparting a permanent crimp.[149] Kolb, Hoffman, and other researchers in Pioneering quickly moved to incorporate the study of crimp into their fiber-to-fabric characterization work.[150] Generally, Pioneering's researchers followed Charch's leadership regarding the importance of built-in, as opposed to mechanically imposed, crimp in Fiber V staple. Yet the matter of crimp became a major issue within the technical division. Based on earlier unsuccessful attempts to build crimp into nylon, the head of Nylon Research and the management of the technical division opposed Charch's efforts to produce crimp spontaneously in Fiber V.[151] Although Pioneering discovered a promising means to achieve such crimp and strongly advocated its development, Fiber V staple was commercialized with conventional mechanical crimping techniques.

Pioneering Research was involved in other controversies concerning Fiber V's development. The major issue centered on the staple manufacturing process. When Buchanan, now head of the technical division following Benger's retirement, determined to call off heavy betting on tire cord and redirect the Fiber V development program toward staple, he gave Pioneering responsibility for developing a high-speed direct spin-draw process that would feed drawn fiber immediately into a cutter, thus producing a cut staple at the spinning machine. He also charged Pioneering with developing an alternative high-speed spinning process coupled with a separate high-speed drawing and cutting operation. Nylon Research was given the task of building a "conventional" process of making Fiber V tow and staple, much in the way nylon tow and staple were produced.[152] Keen competition, and even enmity, developed over these alternative processes. Charch strongly backed the direct spin-draw process, but its full development would have delayed the start-up of the commercial staple plant.[153] Therefore Du Pont relied upon its existing staple technology.

By mid-1948, the technical division had spent about $1.5 million on Fiber V. Buchanan believed that the time had come to evaluate the entire program, to assess weaknesses in the advancing research and development front, and to redefine overall objectives of the program if necessary.[154] The paramount research problem with Fiber V was its lack of dyeability. Unlike Orlon, the dyeability of which by this time had been significantly improved through copolymerization, Fiber V had remained undyeable despite a similar approach. But as with Orlon, Fiber V's immediate future development depended in large part on scaling-up to produce enough fiber for the development section's marketing research and development program. These scale-up problems entailed not only such things as polymerization (which everyone thought should be done by a continuous process), spinning, and drawing, but also securing adequate supplies of intermediates. Ethylene glycol posed no problems, but obtaining sufficient quantities of DMT with good color and high purity placed demands on the Explosives Department, which was pursuing the Fiber V intermediates business.[155]

One other issue that had been lingering since Pioneering had first spun Fiber V began to rear its ugly head. This was the issue of interfiber competition, and it had become a major concern of the Executive Committee. The committee had already committed itself to scaling up the Orlon process and was being primed to approve the commercial plant. Moreover, it had made substantial commitments to nylon plant expansion, especially for textile yarns and staples. In late August 1948, Textile Fibers submitted a report it hoped would assuage the committee's growing fears that Fiber V and Orlon would undermine the company's rapidly rising investment in nylon. Apparently, the committee was not persuaded by the report or the oral arguments of Fibers's managers because it asked for another study squarely addressing the issue of competition among Du Pont's synthetic fibers. In particular, the committee wanted an "amplification" of data on Fiber V's potential markets and comparative costs. From subsequent action by the committee's members, it is clear that the committee was not questioning Fiber V's development but rather sought to learn quickly and with the least expenditure how good Fiber V would be in both properties and cost. Therefore, the committee asked the Fibers Department to explore other routes to commercialization than the one the department normally would take, which was to build a pilot plant before the commercial unit.[156]

The Executive Committee's action resulted in greater attention being paid within the technical division to questions of interfiber competition. The threat of interfiber competition in turn moved the division to a more careful differentiation of properties and applications among the three synthetic fibers. Also, the committee's request for exploring a quicker route to commercialization led to a plan that no doubt saved time and expense in scaling up for critical market development and proving out commercial processes: The department would use a portion of its Seaford, Delaware, commercial nylon plant as a pilot plant for Fiber V.[157]

Fortunately for Du Pont, Fiber V could be polymerized, spun, and drawn with modified nylon technology. The Nylon Research Laboratory had produced Fiber V in semiworks quantities, and it therefore made sense to scale up in a pilot plant at the Seaford works. Thus the nylon approach significantly reduced the time and expense required to manufacture the quantities of Fiber V necessary for market testing and development.

But nylon technology also had its limitations, which the technical division grasped in short order. All the company's nylon was being made with a batch polymerization process. But a batch process for polyethylene terephthalate posed greater problems with water removal and decomposition when the polymer was remelted before spinning. A continuous process would eliminate these problems and reduce investment. Only recently, Nylon Research had developed a continuous polymerization process for nylon, and the first commercial unit had been installed. This process, however, would not work for Polymer V because its melt viscosity is some ten times that of nylon at a given temperature and a vacuum is required to control molecular weight.

Developing a continuous polymerization process posed enormous problems for the technical division, and it tested the nerves of executives who had approved the construction of the first commercial Fiber V plant. At the time construction began on this plant – located at Kinston, North Carolina

– the Nylon Research Laboratory had not succeeded in polymerizing ethylene terephthalate continuously, yet the plant was predicated on this approach.[158]

Through some intense and creative research and development work in Nylon Research and elsewhere in the technical division, a successful continuous polymerizing unit was designed and operated at Carothers Research Laboratory. This in turn was rapidly scaled up and installed at Seaford just in time to allow the operating division to gain experience with it before six such units were installed at Kinston. By the time of start-up – March 1953 – most of the process problems had been worked out. The decision to go with continuous polymerization had been the biggest gamble of the project and had paid off.[159] Moreover, new dyeing techniques and dyestuffs had significantly improved the Fiber V dyeing situation, and Nylon Research had worked out the bugs in the conventional staple process.[160]

By the time of the Kinston start-up in March 1953, the department had gained substantial experience with Dacron staple. The Seaford pilot plant produced by the end of 1951 about 2 million pounds of Dacron, which was sold to the trade for evaluation. In 1952 it manufactured 2.4 million pounds of staple and tow and 700,000 pounds of filament yarn.[161]

With this amount of fiber in the trade, problems began to emerge, some expected, some completely unanticipated. Static charge was a not wholly unanticipated problem, both in the working of the fiber and in fabrics. The division spent considerable time and money trying to eliminate or reduce static. Hole-melting from cigarette embers also showed up as a potential problem. But pilling – the development of little snarled balls of staple on the surface of some woven fabrics – took the department by surprise in the spring of 1950. The technical division responded aggressively to the pilling problem by launching a four-pronged approach: (1) developing a laboratory test to assess a fabric's tendency to pill, (2) finding the mechanism of pilling, (3) correlating fiber characteristics with the tendency of fabrics to pill, and (4) seeing if different fabric construction and finishing techniques would reduce pilling.[162]

Researchers in the Textile Research Laboratory quickly built machines that would simulate fabric wear and raise pills on certain fabrics. They also observed the mechanism of pill formation. Understanding pill formation was one thing; preventing it was another. Two approaches seemed workable. One was to adjust fiber properties, fabric construction, and fabric finishing to hinder raising a nap on the fabric, which was the first step toward pilling. The second was to change the fiber configuration so that if a nap were raised, pills would not form. This latter approach seemed the best route to take.[163] In the late 1940s, Joseph Rivers in Pioneering had explored different cross sections of Fiber V in an effort to affect resiliency. Among other shapes, he had spun cruciform fibers, which now showed a reduced tendency to pill. But the handle or feel of fabrics made from cruciform fibers was inferior.[164] Consequently, researchers experimented with a variety of cross sections hoping to find one that reduced or eliminated pilling while not sacrificing fabric handle. Fiber morphology became an important discipline in the department. Researchers thought they had found the perfect solution to the problem by the end of 1951: fibers with a ribbon cross section, which showed no pilling after fifty wearings in slacks. Soon after the Kinston plant opened, part of the operation was converted from round to ribbon cross-section fibers. But when these ribbon fibers went into the trade, another flaw emerged. Fabrics made from them and dyed in dark shades tended to glitter in the sunlight. Other fiber cross sections were tried in an attempt to solve the problem.[165] Eventually the Dacron Research Laboratory, established in 1954, developed a lower molecular weight fiber, which does not pill. This new fiber cost more than ordinary Dacron polyester, so not all Du Pont's customers adopted it.

Early sales of Dacron from the Kinston plant ran frighteningly parallel to those of Orlon from the May plant. Sales of Dacron from the Seaford pilot plant had been excellent, and the response of the market seemed excellent. But after the Kinston plant began producing staple in March (25-million-pound capacity) and filament yarn in July (12-million-pound capacity), the market seemed to vanish because of a widespread weakening of the textile industry.[166] Sales were so weak that the Kinston plant never ran all its polymerizers at once.[167] Markets deteriorated further and inventory mounted. With experience gained on the commercial equipment, total annual staple capacity was upgraded to 35 million pounds – little comfort in 1954 when Du Pont could sell only 10 million pounds of staple even though it dropped prices from $1.80 to $1.59 per pound. Additional price cuts, much experimentation to bring pilling under control, and important fabric developments from some of Du Pont's best customers led gradually to increased demand for Dacron staple. Blending Dacron staple with rayon, wool, and cotton – developments made largely by Du Pont's customers – created an important, enduring market for Dacron staple.[168] In 1956, Du Pont sold 25 million pounds of staple and tow, and the following year it marketed 47 million pounds of staple, tow, and fiberfill (synthetic down). Three years later, it sold 57 million pounds.[169]

Although not "another nylon" in terms of almost instantaneous market success and earnings and as a driving force in the growth of the Du Pont Company, Dacron proved to be a highly successful product. Du Pont – and an increasing number of competitors that entered the polyester business in the 1960s – dramatically expanded production in the next decade. With growing competition, Du Pont lost market position, seeing a drop from about 95 percent in 1960 (when its patents began to expire) to less than 58 percent in 1965 and 37 percent in 1971.[170] During the late 1960s and early 1970s, fashion trends – the craze for double-knit polyester fabrics in particular – brought about a significant shift in Du Pont's Dacron business. Although Dacron staple sales continued to grow, Dacron filament yarn business boomed, but once double-knits went out of fashion, the yarn business severely contracted. Nevertheless, during the double-knit boom, total Dacron earnings surpassed those of nylon – a milestone in the company's history.[171]

Interfiber Competition

The development and commercialization of Orlon and Dacron were major achievements. Du Pont moved aggressively with these fibers even though Executive Committee members worried that they would undermine the company's investment in nylon.[172] In retrospect, the problem of interfiber competition does not appear to have been all that serious, especially because Du Pont succeeded with both Orlon and Dacron while continuing to expand its nylon capacity dramatically. But the problem was real, and had Du Pont not managed it correctly, the history of its three fibers might have been different.

Concern over interfiber competition made it imperative for the technical division to define fiber characteristics precisely and to delineate respective market areas for each of Du Pont's fibers. This approach further reinforced a generally perceived need in the department to increase greatly the amount of assistance given to the company's fiber customers – assistance in the form of fabric development, processing and finishing specifications, and sales development. The Chestnut Run facility, opened in 1954, provided this kind of R&D.[173]

Such end-use research would have been undermined had the Textile Fibers Department not taken bold steps in reorganizing the way it sold fibers. Until 1952, Du Pont's fiber sales were conducted along the department's divisional lines: each fiber division possessed its own sales section. This organizational scheme resulted in what one manager called "a parochial, undesirably competitive attitude" among salesmen from the various divisions.[174] It was not uncommon for a fiber customer – a mill owner – to be visited by five different Du Pont fibers salesmen, each selling a different fiber, each claiming superiority for their particular fiber, and each belittling the other divisions' products. As Lester Sinness noted, such a customer, "understandably, was confused."[175]

The Textile Fibers Department solved this problem when in 1952 it adopted a functional organizational structure in the place of the product division scheme it had employed since the 1930s. Now a manager would preside over all departmental sales, and other managers would supervise manufacturing and research. A single sales-service organization handled service work for all fibers as well as all fabric and sales development. Under the new arrangement, a customer could get answers to questions about all Du Pont's fibers from a single individual.[176]

With these organizational changes and aggressive marketing programs, Du Pont contained as best as possible the problem of competition among its own fibers. The technical division's extensive knowledge of fiber properties and fabric characteristics provided a critical element in the department's efforts to target particular fibers for particular markets. And of course this knowledge greatly helped Du Pont in its pursuit of natural fibers markets. But at the same time this knowledge had made it clear – almost from the outset of Orlon and Dacron – that rayon and acetate would succumb to the new synthetics in most markets. It was only a matter of time.

Because of their keen appreciation for fiber properties, the technical division's managers were the first to appreciate fully the fate of Du Pont's cellulose fibers business. Competition within the rayon business itself had already made it difficult for the technical division to justify its rayon research budget, but the promise of both acrylic and polyester fibers greatly amplified the problem. In mid-1947, the research directors of the technical division had their first full discussion of this problem in one of their biweekly staff meetings. The question was one of what director Ernest Benger and then rayon research director Sinness called "the philosophy of research for the Viscose Rayon business." Both had reached the conclusion that "it is difficult, if not impossible, to invest money at this time in the Viscose Rayon business and obtain the return required by the Executive Committee rules." Those in the technical division favored systematic withdrawal from the rayon business and even more aggressive investment in new products, but as they recognized in 1947, "this opinion is not shared by all concerned," especially by those in the general management of the department.[177] Anticipating the fate of rayon, Sinness, director of viscose rayon research up to 1950, "progressively whittled down the size" of his section's activities. As a consequence, he was criticized – once "rather vociferously" – for being disloyal to his product area. But Sinness rejected such accusations, saying that product loyalty had nothing to do with the matter; the simple fact was that on a property basis, rayon "was outclassed."[178] Church vigorously supported Sinness's position, and by 1948 Pioneering refused to do any work on viscose and acetate fibers. They were a thing of the past, not of the future.[179]

Still, there were rayon diehards – mostly managers above those in the technical division who possessed a deep sense of responsibility for the $100 million investment Du Pont maintained in rayon and the 9,000 workers it employed in the business. Although Du Pont's rayon business was at its peak in 1950 on a poundage basis (at some 200 million annual pounds), the department had reached a serious impasse when it learned that lowering prices no longer resulted in increased rayon sales. Once this point was reached, managers knew that the fiber was in trouble. Keenly aware that in the past rayon had been "responsive to technology," some of them looked toward research to find a magic bullet with which to "blow the top off" the rayon market. Their search was one of desperation.[180]

As the fortunes of nylon, Orlon, and Dacron rose, those of rayon and acetate fell. In December 1957, the technical division closed its Viscose

Rayon Research Laboratory – more than a decade after it had wished. Du Pont remained in the rayon business only long enough to maintain its employees until nylon and Dacron expansions would be installed at its rayon sites.[181] Du Pont's acetate fiber business suffered a similar fate.[182]

Orlon and Dacron provided the Executive Committee with firm evidence that its strategy of growth through research and development had been successful and would continue to work. But research managers in the Textile Fibers Department knew that with nylon, Orlon, and Dacron, it was unlikely that another fiber would be as successful in terms of market size and earnings. The department would devote most of its research budget to expanding the synthetic fibers revolution through additional research on nylon, acrylic, and polyester fibers and their applications. The pioneering portion of the budget, however, would be directed increasingly toward "specialty" fibers that could be sold in much smaller quantities but at premium prices. This strategy called for new directions in fibers R&D.

19

New Directions in Fibers R&D

In 1948, not long after they had concluded that Du Pont should withdraw from cellulosic fibers manufacture, the managers of the technical division devoted considerable time to an examination of the future of synthetic fibers. Looking beyond nylon's, Orlon's, and Dacron's potential – and soon to be realized – large-volume sales, they saw the future in terms of specialty fibers. Managers envisioned developing fibers that would remain stable at very high temperatures, fibers that would provide good electrical properties, high-strength fibers, and elastomeric fibers, among others. Led by Hale Charch, the Pioneering Research Laboratory aggressively pursued these goals. Work toward a good elastomeric fiber resulted in the development of Lycra spandex, introduced in late 1959 and one of the greatest success stories in the Textile Fibers Department's history. Pioneering also developed other specialty fibers, such as Teflon fluorocarbon fibers and Nomex high temperature fibers. (See Figure 19.1 for data on Du Pont's specialty fiber shipments.)

Just as some of these specialty fibers began to emerge from the laboratory, however, department managers became increasingly concerned that the company's paramount position in synthetic fibers would not last much longer. Competition had begun to encroach upon Du Pont's profits, the company's basic patent position on its big fibers had begun to weaken significantly, and the company had begun to feel pressure from foreign competition.

Faced with this prospect, the department launched the most ambitious diversification program of any of Du Pont's industrial departments. Rather than confine itself to the development of new fibers, the department determined to pursue products that would take it at least one step closer to the consumer. During the previous decade the department's laboratories – particularly the Pioneering Research Laboratory – had made discoveries the full development of which required forward integration. Soon the department launched ventures in nonwoven or spunbonded sheet structures, synthetic paper, high-absorbency materials, and microfoam products. This diversification program commanded the innovative talents of many of the department's R&D personnel and absorbed an immense amount of capital. The department did not commercialize all the products it developed, and the growth of those it did commercialize proved to be far slower than expected. The combination of growing competition in the major fibers busi-

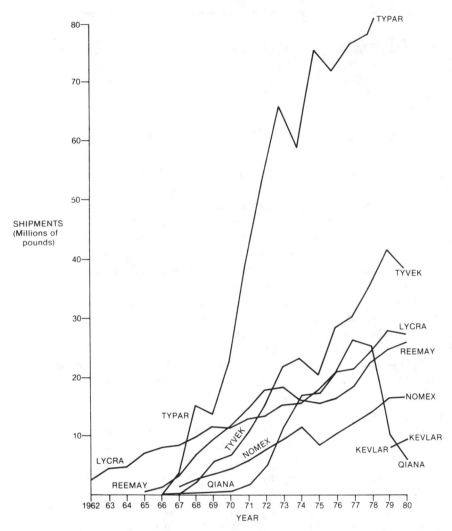

Figure 19.1. Du Pont World Fiber Shipments of Specialty Fibers and Spunbonded Sheet Structures, 1962–80 (excludes Sontara and Teflon). Source: Data from Textile Fibers Department, E. I. du Pont de Nemours & Co.

ness and losses in these new areas suggested by 1965 that Du Pont would experience major erosion in the profitability of the department. The recession in the U.S. economy in 1966 and 1967 dramatically confirmed this thesis. Textile Fibers's earnings – and hence Du Pont's earnings – dropped significantly. After the economy rebounded, Fibers's earnings lagged, in part because of the continued drain of the newer products. Yet the nation's double-knit polyester binge and strong demand for Du Pont's nylon carpet fibers eventually led to a new peak in earnings in 1973.

The department's earnings remained surprisingly consistent as a percentage of total Du Pont earnings after 1965, bringing in between 30 and 40 percent of total company profits. These figures were significantly below the 50–60 percent contributions of the early 1950s when nylon was growing at an extraordinary rate. But they suggest that despite the maturing of the fibers business, the department performed as well or better than the company during the 1960s and early 1970s. The company had worked hard during the 1960s to lessen its dependence on Fibers, but this goal had not been achieved owing in part to the department's success in remaining competitive. Process and product research in existing businesses had been particularly fruitful.

Pioneering the Future

Hale Charch led the technical division's 1948 study of the future. He believed that Du Pont was at the beginning of a "synthetic textile revolution" and that with greater fundamental knowledge of fibers and fiber properties, it could dramatically expand the revolution. "As our basic knowledge of fiber properties is enlarged," stressed Charch, "we are truly approaching the time when we can deliver fibers to predetermined specifications. This can only mean greater and greater diversification in the uses for synthetics which, in turn, means ever broader market opportunities."[1] Soon he established an agenda for the Pioneering Research Laboratory centered firmly on market considerations but based increasingly on a theoretical foundation.[2]

The pursuit of Charch's agenda was delayed by Pioneering Research's being brought back into the development of Orlon to a degree unexpected by Charch, by its continued work on Dacron, and by the significant disruption attending Pioneering's move from Buffalo to the Experimental Station in Wilmington in 1950.[3] Once settled in the new Experimental Station laboratory, however, Pioneering researchers initiated a series of programs that resulted in a wave of innovations that would long occupy the creative energies of much of the entire Textile Fibers Department. Many of these innovations stemmed from the discovery of an important new process for making polymers, which became known as low-temperature or interfacial polymerization. This discovery opened up a whole new world of polymers to researchers, and it greatly served the needs of those seeking to understand the molecular structure–polymer property relationships that Charch believed were keys to expanding the synthetic fibers revolution.

One of Pioneering's two research associates, Emerson L. Wittbecker, discovered interfacial polymerization while engaged in broad scouting work on new polymer structures. The immediate focus of his work was polyurethanes, which Du Pont had pursued off and on since the late 1930s. Charch had grown interested in polyurethanes because of reports he received about German work during World War II.[4] Pioneering briefly explored polyurethanes in 1946 but was unable to obtain a polymer with a higher melting point than the German Perlon U, which had far too low a melting point to be useful as a textile fiber.

Two years later, however, Wittbecker took up Charch's call for more theoretically directed research on new condensation polymers and returned to the polyurethanes. This time he succeeded in synthesizing a polyurethane with a melting point well above that achieved by the Germans. Wittbecker had predicted that if he made a polyurethane with a structure analogous to that of polyethylene terephthalate (Dacron), he could obtain a higher-melting polyurethane.[5]

Postwar reports from Germany had included an account of one laboratory that had reacted diamines with bis(chloroformates) in a two-phase oil-in-water emulsion system to yield polymers.[6] Throughout Du Pont and elsewhere, chemists were aware of this report and were highly skeptical that the reaction really worked because they knew that acid chlorides hydrolyze easily in water. Wittbecker nevertheless tried to follow it using the diamine piperazine he had worked with earlier. His attempts failed after considerable experimentation.

Yet the idea of carrying out a polymerization reaction at the interface of an emulsion system greatly intrigued Wittbecker. The critical factor, he reasoned, was controlling or eliminating hydrolysis, which terminated chain growth and thus yielded low-molecular-weight polymer. He therefore took a different tack and developed an oil-in-water technique that led to the rapid formation of polymer with a high molecular weight at the interface of the two phases.[7] This reaction occurred at room temperature. Refining the technique further, Wittbecker began to explore factors governing the polymerization reaction and was able to produce high-molecular-weight, high-melting polyurethanes that could be spun into fibers.

The importance of Wittbecker's work lay not with the polyurethane he produced but with the polymerization procedure he employed. Other Pioneering researchers were quick to observe that the two-phase system he used might work for reactions of acid chlorides with any compounds containing active hydrogen atoms. In late 1950, the Pioneering Research Laboratory was in a virtual uproar over Wittbecker's discovery. This new low-temperature technique – later to be dubbed interfacial polymerization – gave Pioneering the means easily to prepare thousands of new polymers at room temperature. Moreover, the technique offered the possibility of rapidly carrying out commercial polymerization processes at room temperature, thus saving time and energy.

Hale Charch was ecstatic over the discovery and implications of interfacial polymerization. He immediately assigned his entire first string of organic chemists "to explore the implications of this discovery," and they soon found that interfacial polymerization could be used to prepare polyamides, polysulfonamides, certain polyesters, polyurethanes, and polyureas.[8] Charch's laboratory director, Maurice L. Ernsberger, who had recently joined Pioneering from the Chemical Department, suggested that Pioneering's other research associate, Paul W. Morgan, study interfacial polymerization in a fundamental way.[9] Morgan carried through on this request and soon helped to provide a basic understanding of interfacial polymerization.[10]

Early, Morgan and his coworker, Stephanie L. Kwolek, explored Wittbecker's reaction without vigorous stirring by pouring a diamine solution onto a diacid chloride solution. They observed two distinct layers of liquids. The important action occurred at the interface where the layers met. A film formed here, and when Morgan reached into the beaker with a stirrer and pulled out the film, he observed the continuous formation of film at the interface. As he continued to pull the film from the beaker, it collapsed into something like a rope. As the rope was pulled, it grew in length as polymerization continued at the interface. Morgan called this "instant nylon," and later the reaction was renamed the "nylon rope trick."[11]

Initially, the nylon rope trick suggested that nylon might be commercially polymerized using interfacial or two-phase methods. But the nylons prepared this way possessed too wide a molecular weight distribution for commercial use. Interfacial polymerization was later used commercially to shrinkproof wool, to encapsulate insecticides, and to make polycarbonates, among other applications, but not by Du Pont.[12] Thus nothing of significant commercial importance emerged immediately from Wittbecker's discovery. Yet to say the discovery was not commercially significant is to miss the mark, for that overlooks the intellectual development that occurred in Pioneering around low-temperature methods for making condensation polymers. The foment in Pioneering surrounding Wittbecker's discovery soon yielded other approaches to low-temperature polymerization, which led to modified interfacial polymerization, solution polymerization, and modified solution polymerization.[13] These new methods – all low-temperature polycondensations – resulted directly in significant commercial products.

Paul Morgan's work, among that of several other researchers, was critical in developing processes for low-temperature polycondensations. Morgan wondered whether two phases were really needed to carry out low-temperature polycondensation or whether the reaction could be carried out in a single solvent. He reasoned how this reaction might be carried out, and in September 1953 Morgan demonstrated that polycondensations could be carried out in a single solution (the polymer precipitates out of the solution).[14]

Solution polymerization – or "S-polymerization," as it was called – appeared to Morgan and others as the most promising way to achieve wholly aromatic polyamides, which for some time had been an objective of Pioneering Research. Increasing knowledge of molecular structure had led Pioneering chemists to predict that a wholly aromatic polyamide would be stable at very high temperatures and would thus be likely to fill the bill of a highly temperature-resistant specialty fiber.[15]

Morgan led a program to prepare a wholly aromatic polyamide through S-polymerization. Eventually he and Kwolek succeeded in making such a polymer but not without modifying their two basic approaches to low-temperature polycondensation. As predicted, the wholly aromatic polyamides were indeed stable, but the polymerization was extremely difficult. Pioneering then entered a lengthy period of exploring a large number of wholly aromatic polyamides to find one with the best set of properties. By 1958, they had selected one for commercial development, which was eventually trademarked Nomex.[16] After a long period of development, Nomex fiber was commercialized in 1967.

This organic chemical work on temperature-resistant polymers was coupled with a "mechanical" discovery made by Morgan in 1952. Working with nylon 6-6 made by the interfacial polymerization process, Morgan shredded the polymer in a Waring Blendor and obtained a fibrous mass, which when soaked in water resembled paper pulp. He therefore laid this nylon mass onto a filter (roughly the way paper pulp is laid on a screen) and found that he had made a strong nylon paper.[17] This discovery of "fibrids," as they became known, opened up a major program in Pioneering to develop synthetic paper, which is discussed below. Fibrid technology was combined with the preparation of wholly aromatic polyamides to produce a temperature-resistant synthetic paper used in industrial applications. Based on the same polymer as the fiber, Nomex paper was commercialized in 1967, nine years after leaving Pioneering Research.

Like other fiber products for industrial applications, Nomex has been slow to become a commercial success in either fiber or paper form. At the time it was commercialized, Nomex was Du Pont's most expensive product in terms of precommercial research and development costs and the company's total cash commitment to the product.[18] Sales growth proved to be much slower than predicted, and Nomex became something of a thorn in the side of the department during much of the 1970s. By 1980, however, it had begun to generate significant earnings.[19]

Wittbecker's discovery of low-temperature polycondensation and Pioneering's aggressive follow-up led to other developments. Two are especially important: Lycra spandex fiber and Kevlar aramid fibers. The former emerged not long after Wittbecker's discovery, but the latter was not discovered until 1965. On a return-on-investment basis, Lycra stands out as one of the greatest Du Pont innovations, whereas on a property basis, Kevlar is truly a miracle fiber.

Commercialized in 1962, Lycra spandex fiber capped two decades of research to produce a good synthetic elastomeric fiber. The goal was to replace cotton-wrapped rubber. Pioneering began research on an elastic yarn in 1942 following a discovery by the Chemical Department that nitrogen-substituted nylon exhibited rubberlike properties.[20] Pioneering researchers demonstrated that this N-substituted nylon, dubbed Type 8, could be spun and drawn into rubberlike yarns. Type 8 nylon gave way to more interesting substituted nylons. Gradually, by the late 1940s, the technical division had improved the properties of substituted nylon enough to warrant extensive trade evaluation. The fiber looked very good in all critical properties save one: stress decay. When loaded or stressed over an extended period (a day's wearing of a girdle, for example), substituted nylon lost its ability to recover or retract. Because of this, the fiber could not be used in the foundation garment industry, which was then the principal market for elastic fiber.[21] Subsequently, Pioneering researchers explored elastomeric polyester fibers made using melt-blending and copolymerization techniques. These fibers looked promising at first, but continued study of them revealed deficiencies in stress decay.[22]

Charch continued his call for an elastic fiber. Pioneering's fiber property experts began to study systematically the properties necessary for a synthetic elastomeric fiber in much the way they had with wool.[23] This knowledge proved highly useful when the discovery of low-temperature polycondensation gave Pioneering's elastic fibers program a shot in the arm. Following a critical reexamination of Pioneering's work on elastic fibers, Joseph C. Shivers and Frank B. Moody made the first of a class of elastomeric polymers using a long-chain glycol as the component to impart elasticity. They carried out this work in the context of a growing consensus in Pioneering that a good elastic fiber would be a block copolymer consisting of "hard" and "soft" segments. The soft segments, researchers believed, would impart elasticity to the fiber whereas the hard segments – such as those in nylon or polyester – would provide chain tie points and a high melting point. The fiber prepared by Shivers and Moody confirmed this theory by showing elastic properties and a good melting point. However, the elastic properties were not great and the copolymer easily hydrolyzed. Nevertheless, their work reinforced the concept of segmented block copolymers as the route to a good elastomer.[24]

In early 1953, Shivers's group combined the idea of a segmented structure with low-temperature polycondensation techniques and made a polyurethane elastomer. This fiber appeared so promising that Pioneering's engineering group was brought in to evaluate it in September 1953. Walter E. Jordan, a physicist who had worked on the Manhattan Project, was manager of the engineering group and had been active in evaluating almost all the elastomeric fiber candidates in the technical division since the late 1940s. Unlike others in Pioneering, Jordan was skeptical of the hard–soft segment theory and urged Pioneering's organic group to consider a different approach. He got no satisfaction. Consequently, Jordan invited John H. Verbanc of Orchem to lecture to his group on the chemistry and properties of Orchem's new polyurethane elastomer (later named Adiprene) in the hope of stimulating some different thinking about elastomeric fibers. Verbanc lectured on Adiprene in Pioneering on December 18, 1953, and in less than a month Pioneering was well on the way to Lycra.[25]

Adiprene polyether urethane elastomer emerged from a clever polymerization carried out in 1950 by Orchem's Frederick B. Hill. Hill's first polymer was water-sensitive, but he and his colleagues soon substituted a related monomer and arrived at a most promising elastomer.[26] Verbanc's presentation on Adiprene gave Pioneering researchers the chemistry they needed to make a good synthetic elastomeric fiber. As it turned out, Adiprene could be interpreted in the framework of hard and soft segments.

Pioneering researchers responded to Verbanc's talk in three ways. First, one chemist in the organic group was assigned to spin some Adiprene Type N elastomer obtained from Orchem and first carried out this operation on December 22, 1953. The results looked promising. Second, on January 6, 1954, another researcher prepared the prepolymer for Adiprene and extruded it through a spinneret directly into a solution of diamines, which resulted in an elastic fiber superior to any previously prepared in Pioneering, including Adiprene N. Third, another chemist combined the basic chemistry of Adiprene with Pioneering's work on low-temperature polycondensation and arrived at a poly(ether-urea-urethane) elastomeric fiber with even better properties and a process that appeared to be easily commercialized using Orlon spinning technology.[27]

This Adiprene-inspired work on elastomeric fibers required additional research and development before commercialization was conceivable. Researchers explored different formulations that offered better properties, including strength and stress decay factors as well as resistance to degradation by light, solvents, and gases. Although Charch was enthusiastic about the new poly(ether-urea-urethane) elastomeric fibers, he tried to keep attention focused on polyester elastomers because he believed the lower cost of intermediates for polyesters justified additional work on them.[28]

Pioneering continued to work on polyester elastomers, but the outstanding properties of the segmented poly(ether-urea-urethane)s became increasingly clear. The department's managers soon realized that the properties of the best poly(ether-urea-urethane) formulation – now called Type 80 – were so good that if two deficiencies could be overcome, Du Pont would be able to command a high price. Early customer reactions to Type 80 were enthusiastic; some customers said they would pay as much as $9.00 per pound if it could be made resistant to yellowing and to degradation by ultraviolet light. Du Pont's estimators figured that the company could earn a 25 percent return on investment at a price of $4.00 per pound.[29]

By September 1955, there was sufficient technical and market evidence to suggest that Pioneering's elastomeric fiber could be commercialized. Development of this fiber worked far more smoothly than that of either Orlon or Dacron; indeed, the Lycra venture appeared to progress as smoothly as had nylon two decades earlier. The commercialization of Lycra depended on several factors. The inherent weaknesses of the product – ultraviolet light sensitivity and yellowing – first had to be overcome. Pioneering Research quickly found that the addition of titanium dioxide and a compound known as Daktose B eased the discoloration problem by substituting a graying comparable to that of rubber for the yellowing of the unmodified fiber. This was but a stopgap measure, and research into the discoloration problem continued throughout the next decade, resulting in the use of different chain extenders and different types of Lycra. A similar approach also reduced the ultraviolet light problem.[30]

Process scale-up presented the usual problems. As with Orlon and Dacron, there were the conflicting needs of the technical division to perfect the process through pilot plant studies and of the marketing division to get as much fiber as possible into customers' hands. Because Lycra was amenable to dry spinning using polyacrylonitrile solvents and techniques, scale-up was done in Waynesboro by the Orlon Research Laboratory. But until Orlon Research was able to construct a semiworks and then a pilot plant, Pioneering Research was called upon to produce its maximum of 150 pounds a month of the spandex fiber for trade evaluation. In addition, Pioneering worked on the early stages of a continuous-polymerization process for Lycra.[31]

While these technical problems were being addressed, marketing experts carried out more extensive evaluation and market development for both monofilament and staple Lycra. The market for Lycra continued to look good. By late 1959, Fibers management was convinced that Lycra could capture about 4 million pounds of the 14-million-pound U.S. market for covered elastic fibers by 1963. Therefore, management asked for authorization to construct a 4-million-pound continuous filament plant at Waynesboro. Managers predicted it would take five years to recover the initial plant operating losses and R&D and precommercialization expenses, which they projected would reach almost $28 million by start-up.[32]

To some this estimate seemed wildly optimistic, but it turned out to be rather conservative. In the first year of commercial operation, Lycra lost almost $4.5 million; the following year it almost broke even. By 1964, two years after commercialization, Lycra earned $6.3 million, and by 1969 this figure exceeded $30 million.[33] Two years later, Lycra had become one of the most profitable of all Du Pont products with a return on investment greater than 30 percent (after taxes).[34] Still later in 1976 – a poor year for Fibers profits – Lycra contributed 20 percent of the department's earnings on less than 1 percent of its shipments (on a poundage basis).[35] Lycra therefore became the archetype for the development of specialty fibers at Du Pont.

Lycra's success contrasts sharply with that of Kevlar aramid fibers, Du Pont's most recently commercialized fiber, which in 1980 *Fortune* magazine called "a miracle in search of a market."[36] Pound for pound, Kevlar is some four to five times stronger than steel, and it does not rust or corrode. Among many other applications, it is now used for underwater cables and to make lightweight bulletproof vests, and it has begun to replace asbestos for brake linings. Kevlar's most important application, however, is in the growing area of high performance composite materials. Like Nomex and Lycra, the invention of Kevlar flowed out of the discovery and subsequent elaboration of low-temperature polycondensation by Pioneering researchers in the 1950s and early 1960s. Indeed, Kevlar stemmed immediately from Nomex chemistry. In 1964, Paul Morgan and his associates decided to scout out para-linked as opposed to the meta-linked (as in Nomex) aromatic polymers. Morgan fully expected Nomex-type properties from such a polymer. He selected several approaches to achieve a para-linked aromatic polymer and assigned Stephanie Kwolek to try to synthesize poly(1,4-benzamide).

Within eight months, Kwolek had achieved this synthesis. She observed that the polymer was opalescent in solution, which suggested that it was highly crystalline. Moreover, when she spun the polymer into a fiber, she found that it was already highly oriented and had very high tensile strength and a modulus (a measure of stiffness) several times higher than Dacron polyester. She almost doubled its modulus by subjecting the fiber to a heat treatment. Kwolek had made the first liquid crystal polymer and provided the basis for the Kevlar fiber venture.[37]

Almost fifteen years passed before Kevlar was fully commercialized. The development of the fiber proved to be difficult and was set back when the Haskell Laboratory discovered that the solvent used in the Kevlar polymerization process was a carcinogen.[38] The substitution of a new solvent delayed commercialization of the product and drove up the costs. By 1982, the company had spent about $500 million on the fiber's development and commercialization without assurance that any single market would sustain the venture.[39] Du Pont had hoped that tire cord would provide such a market, but this has not materialized.[40] Therefore, Kevlar's success was left to the development of many applications rather than a single one like tire cord. By the mid-1980s, sales from these applications have added up to enough business to make Kevlar profitable. The task of finding markets was enormous because Kevlar's unprecedented precommercialization expenses meant that the department would have to sell much more of it than its other specialty fibers just to break even.

Critics of the Textile Fibers Department charged that its management had increasingly devoted its R&D efforts to ventures that required sales break-even points as high as $100 million and more. In addition to Nomex and Kevlar, these critics also focused on the department's simultaneous development and commercialization of three nonwoven – or what Du Pont calls spunbonded – products, Reemay, Typar, and Tyvek, which together totaled more than $100 million in precommercial R&D expenses by the late 1960s.[41]

The Textile Fibers Department's commercialization of spunbonded products stemmed in part from two related programs in Pioneering Research, one to develop a good nonwoven fabric based on Du Pont's synthetics and the other to develop a commercially viable synthetic paper. As early as 1944, Charch had initiated a project on nonwoven fabrics.[42] This work was not highly original because many manufacturers, from felt companies to other fiber companies, were engaged in efforts to use new synthetic bonding agents to hold fibers (both natural and man-made) together in a mat. Nevertheless, Charch continued to support the work, which was carried out principally under the direction of John Piccard. Eventually, Piccard broadened his work to include synthetic leather, and by 1950 he had combined a nonwoven polyethylene-polyester substrate with various coatings to produce what became the precursor to Corfam leather substitute, discussed in Chapter 22.[43]

Piccard's work in creating the nonwoven substrate followed existing practice. He employed the two principal methods of laying filaments onto a mat – the pneumatic technique used by the felt industry and the hydraulic technique used by the paper industry. In both cases, bonding agents were required to hold the synthetic fibers together, resulting in final products that did not have what is called good "drape." Nonwoven fabrics were usually stiff and also possessed poor "handle." Moreover, the requirement for bonding agents meant that synthetics offered few if any advantages over other fibers, and those advantages clearly did not outweigh the significant extra cost of the synthetic fiber.

The same held true in trying to use synthetics in paper. In the late 1940s, Charch had run a small program with the papermakers Crane and Company to explore the use of very fine denier, undrawn nylon monofilaments in paper.[44] But these efforts went nowhere. Unlike cotton rag or cellulose pulp, synthetic fibers – especially Du Pont's hydrophobic nylon, Orlon, and Dacron – could not be "beaten" into a pulp that would cohere and make a good paper.

Paul Morgan's discovery of fibrids in 1952 opened up the possibility of dispensing with bonding agents and achieving synthetic paper and nonwoven fabrics with good handle and drape. By shear-precipitating or "beating" nylon prepared by interfacial polymerization in a Waring Blendor, Morgan produced a "swollen fibrous pulp" that could be laid into paper. This pulp consisted of fibrids – short-to-medium-length fibers that were self-bonding. Although Morgan wrote that "this self-bonding character of interfacially prepared films and fibers should be very useful in making paper from these materials or in blends with other fibers," Pioneering did little with the fibrid discovery for almost two years.[45]

In June 1954, Esperanza Guandique observed the formation of these fibrids while wet-spinning one of the precursors of Lycra and soon demonstrated the commercial potential of fibrids. She produced what became known as Textryl "S," a suedelike sheet made from elastomeric fibrids.[46] Although this product was never of commercial importance, it nevertheless changed Pioneering's thinking about nonwovens. As Charch's protégé Norton Higgins noted, "More than anything else, this discovery gave us conviction that a drapeable, non-woven fabric could be made which looked like a fabric. It is important to bear in mind that until Textryl 'S' was made, non-woven fabrics looked rather more like a mat of fibers than a fabric."[47] Guandique's work quickly led Pioneering to focus on fibrids as a major research and development area.

Because papermaking techniques offered the quickest means to use fibrids, Pioneering secured funds to buy a used 30-inch Fourdrinier paper machine. Fibrids could be made into a variety of products from soft nonwoven fabrics to hard papers with this machine.[48] Pioneering's work generated considerable debate in the department about how best to exploit the fibrid discovery. Some favored Du Pont's entering the synthetic paper and nonwoven fabric businesses, whereas others opposed this as a departure from Du Pont's traditional role as a producer of primary goods.

Synthetic paper provides an excellent example of this debate. The Fibers Department carried out a study of the paper industry to determine whether Du Pont should enter the industry with synthetics. Managers were struck by the size of the potential market. General Manager Andrew Buchanan saw it as *"the most attractive new use area* vulnerable in large volume to present and future synthetic fibers." But paper manufacture was a high-investment, low-return business requiring high turnover and extensive merchandising capabilities. Therefore, Buchanan decided that Du Pont should restrict its synthetic paper work to the development of processes and products that could be adopted by existing papermakers, thereby making Du Pont "the supplier of raw materials rather than the converter." As Buchanan wrote, "By electing this policy, we can contemplate the entire paper industry as a user of our fibers and fibrids, a vastly greater market than we could contemplate if we tried to do the converting on a few (necessarily) of the thousands of specialized paper products that can develop out of this technology."[49] Therefore, Du Pont followed its usual path of working with paper manufacturers to interest them in using Du Pont fibrids for synthetic or partially synthetic papers. Buchanan believed so firmly in this approach and in the size of the potential market that he authorized major research and development expenditures involving twenty-five first-line researchers.[50] By 1959, the development effort appeared sufficiently promising for the department to establish a pilot plant to manufacture fibrids at its Spruance Plant in Richmond, Virginia. However, the market for fibrids for the paper industry failed to develop, largely because the price of fibrids was too high. Du Pont terminated its fibrid venture, but it did use fibrid technology to make Nomex papers at the Spruance Plant.[51] By this time, the department was in hot pursuit of an entirely different approach to the fabrication of sheet structures, which became known as spunbonded products.

The development of spunbonded products was an outgrowth of Pioneering's long search for ways to produce synthetic sheet structures. But some serendipity also played a role. In 1955, James R. White secured a sample of a new type of polyethylene from the Polychemicals Department. He noticed that the sample consisted of a nearly continuous bundle of filaments.

Intrigued by the sample, he learned that Polychem had separated the polyethylene from the solvent by quickly releasing pressure from the polymer solution at a temperature well above the atmospheric boiling point of the solvent. When this pressure release was made through a small opening – like a spinneret – "flash spinning" occurred. The result was an oriented polymer with a highly fibrillar structure, and White recognized that flash-spun polyethylene might make good "paper, nonwoven fabrics, [and] yarns." He tried to replicate the material he had received from Polychem but failed before he was transferred to a different project.[52]

Another Pioneering researcher, Herbert Blades, picked up on White's attempts. By using a different solvent and a larger spinneret hole, Blades succeeded in obtaining a continuous, strong, uniform flash-spun polyethylene. Blade's flash-spinning technique produced a web of very fine interconnected filaments. When spread out flat, these filaments could be self-bonded by putting the web through a calender. Subsequent treatments of the bonded structures yielded strong sheets that were either hard and paperlike or soft and fabriclike. Moreover, they could be printed, coated, laminated to other materials, or embossed. Thus, spunbonded polyethylene appeared to have commercial promise. By 1958, the Industrial Products Research Laboratory was carrying out a study of applications in which the new product, trademarked Tyvek, could be used. Following the creation of the new products division, Tyvek's development was taken out of Pioneering, and by 1959 the division had started up a batch process semiworks in Richmond, Virginia, to produce 150 pounds a day.[53]

By 1961, however, Tyvek's commercialization was clouded by the invention of two other spunbonded structures produced in a different way. George A. Kinney of the Carothers Research Laboratory (formerly the Nylon Research Laboratory) invented a new method of producing spunbonded sheet structures in 1958. His invention stemmed from his attempt to use electrostatic charging to attract very short nylon floc (1/8–1/4-inch fibers) to molten filaments as they emerged from a spinneret. Kinney succeeded in charging the filaments, and he soon discovered that they could be laid on an electrically grounded surface to form a "coherent web of well-separated, individual filaments that were uniformly and randomly dispersed." From this he posited that if they were laid on a grounded conveyor belt, continuous sheet structures would result. Here was an important discovery, for it meant that a nonwoven sheet could be created immediately below a melt-spinner and that the structure should have higher tear strength than staple-derived structures because it was made from continuous filaments.[54]

In December 1958, Kinney's supervisor called Norton Higgins, the Pioneering Laboratory's director, and told him that Kinney had found an alternative route to sheet structures that offered superior tear strength. As Higgins noted a year later, "Once I had seen Kinney's products, it was obvious that Pioneering should explore this technique as applied to 'Dacron.'

Work was started immediately. . . ."[55] Pioneering's investigation of electropneumatic spinning resulted in the development of spunbonded polyester (later called Reemay) and spunbonded polypropylene (later called Typar).[56]

Although much research and development work was required for each spunbonded product, by the end of 1959 Du Pont had three attractive sheet structures made from continuous filaments in addition to earlier ones made from fibrid technology. Moreover, both Kinney's work on electropneumatic spinning and Blades's work on flash spinning allowed Du Pont to obtain an important proprietary position in the nonwoven field. The critical question lay in which product to develop further and to commercialize. Because each sheet structure was made from a different polymer, each possessed different properties. End-use research suggested that Du Pont could find distinct markets for each spunbonded product without adverse interproduct competition.

A more serious problem emerged, however. This revolved around the question of forward integration. Some members of the marketing division feared a backlash from Du Pont's fiber customers if the company manufactured and sold nonwoven sheet structures.[57] This concern eased as the department actually committed itself to the commercialization of all three spunbonded products.[58]

That all three spunbondeds were developed simultaneously[59] and at precommercial research and development costs in excess of $100 million provides evidence about the size and power of the Textile Fibers Department in the 1960s. Du Pont had grown with the expansion of nylon and the development of Orlon, Dacron, and Lycra. The department had been successful with most of its major undertakings, and it was consistently generating a third or more of the company's earnings – earnings that had made Du Pont stock some of the very best to own during the 1950s.[60]

Reemay spunbonded polyester, Typar spunbonded polypropylene, and Tyvek spunbonded polyethylene have had mixed success in the marketplace. Reemay was perhaps the most disappointing of the three. The department began developing markets in apparel interlinings and footwear linings for Reemay made in a 72-inch wide semiworks, which was started up in 1962 at Old Hickory, Tennessee. The 144-inch wide commercial plant experienced construction delays and initial operating problems but began manufacturing Reemay for sale in 1965. Ten years later, the product was still losing money and did not break even until 1979. Typar faired better. Scale-up began in 1962 at Old Hickory, and market development was aimed primarily at replacing jute in tufted carpet backing. The commercial plant, also 144 inches wide, opened in 1966 and was initially plagued with problems in the bonding step. Typar operated in the red until the late 1970s when sales approached $100 million. The market for Typar carpet backing never solidified in the United States, but in Europe the product has performed well. Tyvek has become the most successful of the spunbonded products, although it too had a rough start. The Spruance Works in Richmond, Virginia, began manufacturing 60-inch-wide sheets in 1961 and started up the 144-inch-wide commercial plant in 1967. Major operating difficulties burdened the product, which by 1975 had sustained cumulative operating losses of over $110 million. Yet markets in packaging materials, protective clothing, and areas unanticipated by Du Pont had begun to develop in a big way, and a second Tyvek line was installed at the plant in 1975. By the late 1970s, Tyvek was earning a good profit, and the picture improved greatly in the 1980s.[61]

The department's decision to commercialize simultaneously three spunbonded products reflected its managers' thinking about the department's future. Competition – both domestic and foreign – had begun to affect Du Pont's fiber business. When Pioneering judged polypropylene an inferior fiber in 1958, the company's managers concluded that another high-volume, wide-use fiber such as nylon, Orlon, and Dacron was no longer a significant possibility. Du Pont would continue to invest in the expansion of these fibers, but if the department were to remain a pioneer in the field of synthetic fibers, it would have to find new ways to broaden business significantly. One way would be to integrate forward into the manufacture of nonwoven textile materials.

Textile Fibers' technical directors had long thought about diversifying its product lines. But until the late 1950s, diversification had not been a paramount goal. Paradoxically, however, changes in the department's R&D organization in the mid-1950s militated against its being able to carry out any significant diversification effort.

The reorganization of Fibers R&D did not stem from any single event but rather from a series of them. Following the advice of a member of the Executive Committee, the department created a technical section within the manufacturing division; responsibility for process development, which had always been shared between the manufacturing and technical divisions, was moved toward manufacturing by the appointment of a manager responsible for all process development work in manufacturing. Slightly later, the general management brought in George Graves from the Fabrics and Finishes Department to head the technical division in the place of W. W. Heckert.[62] As a matter of convenience, Heckert was then moved to the marketing division to head a new product unit at Chestnut Run; responsibility for new product work previously done by the technical division was now shared with the marketing division. These changes resulted in the technical division being renamed the research division, a move that fit the tenor of the companywide emphasis on basic, long-term research. Under Graves's leadership, the research division focused almost exclusively on "research" and did not venture into "development."[63] With process R&D managed by the manufacturing division and new-product R&D shared with the marketing division, serious fragmentation in the overall R&D function occurred. As Howard Swank said of this reorganization, "You never saw such a confused operation, because there was nobody [directly] responsible for carrying the product through its entire development."[64] This organizational structure seriously undermined the department's ability to bring out new products; some considered the successful development of Lycra during these years miraculous given the organizational hurdles.[65]

With Graves's retirement in 1959, the three-part R&D organization was abandoned. Swank became general director of the technical division, and the research divisions from the manufacturing and marketing divisions were reintegrated. Responsibility for new product and process development was now crystal clear.[66] As one observer said, "A miracle happened! Almost overnight, the climate changed, the bickering stopped, the committee system disappeared, people and facilities were made available, decisions came promptly, [and] markedly less time was spent on coordinating with other groups. What's most significant is that the [Fibers Department's diversification] program went from an unproductive, pessimistic status to a highly productive, optimistic status."[67]

Under Swank's leadership, the technical division pushed its diversification efforts. The three spunbonded ventures, Nomex high-temperature fibers and papers, and a host of other projects not eventually commercialized rapidly emerged. Ideas and projects included house-building materials; polymeric pipe for residential, chemical, and oil-field applications; absorbent materials for medical, disposable diaper, and feminine sanitary products; microfoams for packaging and cushioning applications; and entirely new techniques for manufacturing carpets.

Despite major efforts at diversification, the department did not abandon its pursuit of new fibers, even though many were skeptical that another such fiber could be commercialized. The nylon research division's discovery of an exotic superpolyamide, however, offered some members of the department hope that Du Pont had indeed hit upon another money-making fiber, much like Lycra. Trademarked Qiana and commercialized in 1968, this new fiber offered the aesthetics of silk (some experts could not tell the difference) and the functionality of polyester (wrinkle resistance, wash-and-wear, brilliant and fast coloration). The high cost of the intermediates, dodecanedioic acid and bis(p-aminocyclohexyl)methane, meant that the fiber would have to be marketed on a small, specialty basis (not unlike Lycra); it would have to command a price of $5 to $8 per pound. Although Qiana's precommercial R&D costs had amounted to $61 million by 1968, managers believed Qiana would move swiftly along twin economies-of-scale and learning curves, thus lowering intermediates and spinning costs and quickly earning a return on investment. But unlike Lycra, Qiana sales did not grow at the rate hoped for, nor did intermediates costs drop.

The department's managers therefore changed their strategy in the early 1970s. Believing that Qiana's necessary high price restricted sales even in the small premium-priced silk apparel market, they decided – though not without much internal conflict – to increase production dramatically, thereby driving down costs and increasing demand beyond the specialty market.[68] Plant expansion grew from an initial $41 million to $120 million in 1976. Sales did increase to a high of $79 million in 1977, the only year Qiana almost broke even.[69] By this time, other producers, including the Japanese, had introduced functionally and aesthetically comparable fibers made from cheaper polyesters.[70] Moreover, fashion trends had changed substantially away from "dressy" to "casual." Sales of Qiana dropped off sharply, and by the early 1980s, when it terminated the product, Du Pont had sustained cumulative operative losses well in excess of $200 million plus the high precommercial R&D costs.[71]

The products developed by the department in the late 1950s and early 1960s as part of its diversification effort were clearly expensive, and not all of them succeeded. Nevertheless, without these products, the earnings of the Textile Fibers Department in the 1980s would be far different. For example, in 1986 – a good year for Textile Fibers – they provided almost a third of the department's earnings.[72]

The same competitive pressures that led the department into its wide-ranging diversification program and that drove its Qiana venture also produced other responses from the technical division. These included greatly increasing the productivity of fiber manufacturing operations and significantly modifying existing fiber properties to maintain old and capture new markets. Though not as glamorous and newsworthy as the development of a new product or the discovery of a new fiber, this kind of work represented a large share of Fibers's R&D budget and contributed significantly to the department's earnings even in the face of increased competition.

The Competitive Environment

Until Du Pont granted a license for nylon 6-6 to the Chemstrand Corporation in 1951, the company had a monopoly on this fiber. It enjoyed a similar position in the United States on polyester fibers until the late 1950s, and Du Pont's rapid commercialization of Orlon gave the company a large share of the acrylic fibers market. Indeed, Du Pont's leadership in the synthetic fibers business was outstanding. Under severe antitrust pressure from the Justice Department, Du Pont's president Crawford H. Greenewalt determined in the late 1940s that Du Pont had to license nylon. Its expansion of nylon plants could not keep pace with increased demand for the fiber, and Du Pont wanted to avoid being stuck with idle plants should that demand drop. Greenewalt therefore found a licensee who was willing to pay some $110 million for Du Pont to set it up with a 50-million-pound-per-year nylon plant.[73] From that day forward, managers in the Textile Fibers Department knew that competition would rapidly mount.

In response, the Fibers Department moved boldly to improve processes and products through research and development. The "ETF" program perhaps best exemplifies the department's response to competition. "ETF" stood for the joint undertakings by the Engineering and Textile Fibers Departments to create the "optimum nylon plant." Conceived and sponsored by Andrew E. Buchanan, general manager of Fibers, and Granville M. (Slim) Read, Du Pont's chief engineer, ETF began in 1955 as an idea to improve the quality of nylon yarn while reducing investment by 50 percent and labor by 75 percent. ETF would allow Du Pont to maintain its profitability in the nylon business despite the growth of competition. Buchanan and Read appointed a special task force for "Blue Sky Nylon Technology," headed by Edward R. Kane (who at this time was director of the Dacron Research Laboratory and who eventually became president of the company). The ETF team included scientists and engineers from the Textile Fibers Department, the Engineering Development Laboratory, and the Engineering Research Laboratory.[74]

After four months of study, the ETF Task Force outlined for Buchanan and Read an optimum nylon plant. It would differ radically from Du Pont's existing plants. With the exception of the company's tire yarn, all nylon fibers were made from batch-produced, remelted nylon flake. All the plants used separate spinning and drawing processes. In the blue sky nylon plant, polymerization would be continuous and the polymer would be fed directly into coupled spin-draw machines, which would deliver the yarn onto customer packages. This idea of coupled spin-draw machinery had long been around, but at current rates of drawing, twisting, and winding, coupled processes offered no great advantages.[75] The ETF project could meet its productivity goals only if these processes were greatly speeded up.

The technological implications of such a speedup were considerable. Du Pont's existing continuous polymerization process for nylon would have to be improved to minimize yarn breaks and to achieve uniformity in the final product. But the greatest problem would be with the windup process. The speed of the drawing operations could be sustained only if some means were found to wind up the drawn filaments at this very high speed. Even if windup could be achieved, project engineers knew that they needed to find an alternative means to impart the typical half-twist per inch that customers needed to handle the yarn in their mills. Conventional downtwisters would not work because of the high speed of the projected process. The ETF task force argued that these requirements, though formidable, could be achieved and the new generation of nylon technology implemented by 1960. Buchanan and Read promptly organized the ETF steering committee to develop the optimum plant. Because Fibers was footing the bill, Kane took overall charge, but he worked closely with J. R. Brand from the Engineering Development Laboratory, who coordinated Engineering's work. By November 1956, Buchanan decided to extend the ETF undertaking to Dacron, and a separate Dacron ETF committee was organized under the direction of L. K. McCune, director of the Carothers Research Laboratory. The ETF efforts mounted through 1957. By late in the year, Fibers had assigned fifty-three full-time technical personnel to the nylon and Dacron ETF projects and Engineering had forty-one.[76]

The task force solved the problems inherent in ETF's goals. A high-speed windup was designed, and the Engineering Department's Mechanical Development Laboratory found an elegant means to achieve the necessary fiber coherence previously attained by imparting a small twist in the yarn. The solution used air jets to "interlace" or intermingle the filaments in the yarn, thus substituting for twisted yarn. Interlacing was readily incorporated into the process, and the Bunting and Nelson patent covering interlaced yarn later proved to be a valuable licensing asset.[77]

ETF achieved most of its goals. Time targets were hit almost precisely. The ETF task force installed a prototype ETF process at the Seaford nylon plant in 1957 and worked out most of the problems by 1959. With this success, the department substituted the ETF process for the old split processes in a new nylon tire yarn plant where the first spinning unit had already been started up. A similar change was made for the new Dacron installation at the department's Old Hickory, Tennessee, plant. By 1962, all the original Kinston Dacron processes had been changed to ETF. Subsequently, new installations and expansions were ETF, and many other plants were converted to the new processes. Only with specialty textile yarns did Du Pont continue to employ the old split spinning and drawing processes. Because the ETF process reduced fiber handling, yarn quality increased significantly. ETF also drove down labor costs, though not by the 75 percent established as a goal. Initially, capital costs proved to be the most disappointing, but later productivity increases drove down investment costs. The ETF development allowed Du Pont to remain highly competitive in nylon and to prepare for growing competition in polyester.[78]

The ETF undertaking coupled neatly with another important nylon development known as Bulked Continuous Filament, or BCF, which allowed Du Pont to capture a significant share of the tufted carpet market. BCF grew out of efforts in Pioneering in the late 1940s and early 1950s to alter yarn morphologies by subjecting yarns to steam, hot air, and various other fluids after spinning and drawing.[79] In 1951, Alvin L. Breen and others employed hot fluid jets, and their work yielded crimped yarns with a bulk that exceeded those of other "textured" filament yarns. Breen continued to pursue this approach, but serendipity changed his course. While experimenting with texturing, he unthinkingly activated his compressed air supply to the jet without turning on the heater. To his surprise, he observed that the resulting yarn possessed unusual texture, which could be imparted to nylon, Dacron, and Orlon, as well as rayon. Breen's discovery led promptly to a major departure from his earlier approach, and it resulted in the development and licensing of Taslan textured yarn in 1954.[80]

Later, in 1957, researchers in the Textile Research Laboratory were engaged in an attempt to produce a random-crimped bulky yarn. Fiber experts at Du Pont had demonstrated that such random crimped-yarns were necessary for best results in the rapidly growing tufted carpet business. Vance Senecal and Carl E. Hallden produced precisely such an engineered yarn by running nylon yarn through a steam jet, thus essentially duplicating the results achieved – and abandoned – earlier by Breen and his colleagues.[81]

Immediately, the Fibers Department launched a large task force to develop the yarn produced by Senecal and Hallden, now called BCF nylon. Du Pont introduced this new product to the carpet trade in mid-1958 as Type 501 nylon. A pilot plant was put in at the Seaford Plant using existing nylon technology; a bulking step was added to the separate spinning and drawing processes. Such a three-step process meant poor quality and high labor costs. At this point, technical managers determined that the fate of the BCF venture would rest on the development of the ETF process, then in final stages of development at Seaford. Howard Swank maintained that such a decision was a large gamble but one that would pay handsomely.[82] The question was whether a bulking operation could be achieved at ETF speeds and integrated with the ETF process. The stakes in the burgeoning tufted carpet market were high and growing. The perfection of the BCF product and process required some three hundred first-line technical personnel from Fibers and Engineering between 1957 and the mid-1960s.[83] BCF nylon generated handsome earnings. In 1972, the Development Department ranked it as the tenth most important earner for Du Pont in the 1960s, even though BCF was not produced on a large commercial scale until 1964. Du Pont enjoyed almost 45 percent of the carpet market compared to the 16 percent of its nearest competitor.[84]

The BCF venture and the ETF project provide excellent examples of large-scale research and development programs in which true partnerships between the Textile Fibers and Engineering departments produced important new processes and products. More important, the ETF and BCF developments illustrate how Du Pont managed to extend nylon's profitability even in the face of the rapidly mounting competition that followed the expiration of the basic nylon patents.

The nature of the apparel fibers market forced Du Pont always to offer something new or improved, which meant that new types of nylon, Dacron, and Orlon fibers had to be developed. Du Pont had to be responsive to the ever-changing fashions in fibers. Developing new fiber types on a regular basis drove up unit costs and placed a high R&D burden on a fiber. Eventually, in the highly competitive era of the late 1960s and 1970s, these factors made the apparel fibers business increasingly less profitable and placed great strain on the R&D organizations that supported the apparel line.

Apparel fibers were also subject to foreign competition. As early as 1960, Andrew Buchanan voiced a major concern about "the growing threat of imports." Fiber producers were particularly vulnerable, he argued, because even if they managed to get tariff protection for fibers, "we could be outflanked by heavy importation of fabric and garments."[85] In the quarter-century since Buchanan raised this concern, foreign competition became a major problem for U.S. fibers producers.

Faced with growing competition, synthetic fibers producers found themselves in a dilemma about whether to invest any more in the fibers business – including research and development. Those that saw the industry as nearing maturity, if not fully mature, generally chose not to sink additional funds in the business but rather to run their firms on a cash generation basis. Cash cow management became common after the great polyester bubble burst following the wave of enthusiasm for double-knit polyester fabrics. During the height of the polyester craze, many new producers had entered the business thinking that consumers would buy such fabrics forever. After double-knits went out of fashion, these new producers, such as Rohm and Haas, absorbed severe financial losses while older producers tried to maintain a positive cash flow as they watched their businesses slowly decline.[86]

Du Pont, among a few others, chose a different path. Sensing no clear leadership from the Executive Committee, the management of the Textile Fibers Department determined to stay the course.[87] That is, the department continued to pursue its diversification program, and it also kept pushing industrial fibers. Moreover, the department continued to invest in product and process improvements.

During the recession that followed its record earnings of 1965, there was pressure on managers to reduce the R&D budget. They achieved this principally by shifting R&D costs to the several new products that had been commercialized rather than cutting personnel. When earnings returned in 1968 to somewhere near their 1965 level, managers held the R&D budget constant until 1971, when Kevlar's development needs, as well as continued needs from some of the earlier new ventures, began to push the Fibers R&D budget and staff to new highs.[88] During this period, the department remained committed to supporting R&D work throughout most of its businesses. But the Arab oil embargo of 1974 and other events beyond Du Pont's control began to have a severe impact on the department's R&D programs. In 1974, when earnings were cut in half from the previous year's new record, the technical division initiated staff reductions. After 1975, when the Executive Committee began to look more closely at the department's affairs, even deeper cuts were made. Executives and departmental managers also began to target particular areas that should be managed on a cash generation basis.[89] Since 1976, the Executive Committee has forced the cutback of significant numbers of researchers in Textile Fibers (by more than 25 percent). Once almost twice as big as the largest other departments, Fibers's research was exceeded in size by Photo Products and Biochemicals research after 1980.[90] Some would argue that these cuts in Fibers R&D were made a decade too late, while others would say they should not have been made at all.

Despite these changes, however, until Du Pont purchased Conoco in 1981 it remained dependent upon the Textile Fibers Department for a large share of its earnings. Such dependence made the company highly vulnerable to textile trade cycles, a fact that worried many of Du Pont's executives as well as its stockholders. Beginning in the early 1960s, executives tried many ways to reduce Du Pont's heavy reliance upon fibers earnings, but these were largely unsuccessful owing in part to the continued aggressiveness of the Textile Fibers Department's R&D program, an aggressiveness that had made Du Pont the principal actor in the synthetic fibers revolution. Had Du Pont been as aggressive in the area of biological chemicals – pharmaceuticals and agricultural chemicals – it might have lessened its dependence on Textile Fibers.

20

Biological Chemicals

In 1980, the Du Pont Company signaled to the business world that it would stake much of its future welfare on research and development in the biosciences. As the company's chairman Irving S. Shapiro told *Business Week*, "We're placing a large bet on life sciences in the future." Shapiro's heir-apparent and former research chemist, Edward G. Jefferson, was viewed by analysts as the executive who had convinced his colleagues to make such a move and who would lead the company's life sciences research campaign.[1] Clearly, Du Pont's life sciences venture represents a major part of the corporation's post-1980 strategy – a strategy that will be discussed more fully in Chapter 25. Yet it may also be seen as the culmination of some forty years of effort by many in the corporation to move Du Pont away from its traditional lines of business.

As early as 1916, Du Pont's executives had included pharmaceuticals in their major diversification program, but the severe problems they faced in making their new dye business profitable led them quickly to abandon any idea of initiating a pharmaceuticals venture. Du Pont's recruitment of German dye chemists in 1920 to help straighten out the dye business resulted in getting Du Pont into a tiny agricultural seed disinfectant business. The company also acquired a larger inorganic insecticide and fungicide business when it purchased the Grasselli Chemical Company in 1928 and several related products when it bought the R&H Chemical Company in 1930. Thus Du Pont had the basis on which to build an agricultural chemicals business. But executives did not move aggressively in this direction until the late 1940s when the Grasselli Chemicals Department was given sole responsibility for agricultural chemicals. Once the company committed sufficient resources to agricultural chemicals research, Du Pont soon realized a growing, high-return business. Even then, however, the department chose to take more money out of the business than perhaps it should have, given that the field was rapidly growing and that research opportunities were abundant.

Executives continued to toy with the idea of venturing into pharmaceuticals for three more decades before finally deciding to enter veterinary pharmaceuticals in hopes of eventually moving to the human field. Owing largely to the growing antitrust climate, executives chose the route of internal generation rather than acquisition. Du Pont's move into pharmaceuticals proved to be difficult. With great patience, but perhaps even greater naïveté, the company tried unsuccessfully to research its way into the business. Finally, in the late 1960s, its executives concluded that acquisition was the only means by which Du Pont could become successful in pharmaceuticals. By this time, buying a pharmaceuticals firm was difficult because the industry had become one of the most profitable and fastest growing areas of U.S. business. Du Pont purchased Endo Laboratories, which proved to be too small for Du Pont to achieve its growth objectives. Nevertheless, the acquisition bolstered Du Pont's commitment to becoming a player in pharmaceuticals and helped set the stage for the company's major commitment to biosciences in the 1980s.

Early Strategy in Biological Chemicals

When Du Pont's executives determined in the late 1940s to consolidate the company's scattered businesses in agricultural chemicals, they chose to base the effort in the Grasselli Chemicals Department. They had already given Grasselli responsibility for veterinary pharmaceuticals. Seventeen years had elapsed from the time William Richter, general manager of Du Pont's Fabrics and Finishes Department and a member of Grasselli's board of directors, first urged the Executive Committee to consolidate all Du Pont's agricultural chemicals efforts in Grasselli.[2]

Richter's suggestion came on the heels of a decision by Vice President Charles M. A. Stine and Chemical Director Elmer Bolton to limit Grasselli's research to inorganic chemistry. An earlier decision to create the Pigments Department had resulted in Grasselli's losing its large pigments research program. Richter believed that Grasselli had the basis for establishing a solid agricultural chemicals business because it had long manufactured and sold such inorganic agricultural products as lead arsenate (insecticide), calcium arsenate (insecticide), Bordeaux powder (a fungicide made from copper sulfate and lime), and two organic insecticides, nicotine sulfate and *para*-dichlorobenzene. Moreover, Grasselli had developed contacts with several state agricultural experiment stations, which tested new formulations for the company. Richter believed that Grasselli was the logical department in which to consolidate the smaller programs of the Organic Chemicals Department and the recently acquired R&H Chemical Company.[3]

Even without such consolidation, however, Stine's and Bolton's decision to limit Grasselli research to inorganic chemistry seriously undermined Grasselli's ability to strengthen its agricultural business because inorganic compounds, especially the arsenicals, were coming under increasingly heavy attack for damaging plants and harming livestock and humans.[4] Grasselli's research managers were well aware of this problem and had initiated organic pesticide research.[5] But Stine's and Bolton's decision temporarily ended these efforts.

Du Pont pursued no coordinated agricultural chemicals research program until 1933, when a multidepartmental steering committee for insecticides and other agricultural chemicals was established. The head of Grasselli's pest control division chaired this committee.[6] In 1934, Orchem allowed Grasselli to transfer W. H. Tisdale, one of its two principal biologists, onto the Grasselli payroll. This move must also have signaled a change in Stine's and Bolton's policy barring Grasselli from research in organic chemistry. Later, Orchem's agricultural chemicals formulation specialist also transferred to Grasselli. Initially, Tisdale worked at Grasselli's main research laboratory in Cleveland, but in 1936 the pest control section (i.e., agricultural chemicals) was moved to the Experimental Station. In 1943, Grasselli took over the pesticide research operations of the former Bayer-Semesan Company, a Du Pont–Bayer joint venture that had been dissolved because of the war with Germany.[7] These included several biologists and a twelve-acre testing facility known as the Minquadale Laboratory. Orchem continued to be responsible for the manufacturing operations of the former Bayer-Semesan Company. Finally, in 1950, Du Pont consolidated its remaining non-Grasselli agricultural products, businesses, and research in the Grasselli Chemicals Department.

Du Pont's decision to pursue agricultural chemicals more aggressively stemmed largely from the work of Executive Committee member and research liaison Roger Williams. Late in 1949, Williams called his colleagues' attention to the size and growth of the agricultural chemicals business in the United States. He also pointed out that Du Pont's efforts in this field were spread over several departments, thus "obscuring" its importance. Williams called for a Development Department study on agricultural chemicals, which was subsequently made by his protégé Chaplin Tyler. Tyler's report resulted in the consolidation of agricultural chemicals in the Grasselli organization.[8]

The Executive Committee had already charged Grasselli with the responsibility for developing a business in veterinary pharmaceuticals, a tack taken in 1943–4 when they decided not to pursue a human pharmaceuticals venture. A complex set of circumstances lay behind this strategy.

Fin Sparre, the head of the Development Department, pushed the company's executives hard to venture into the pharmaceuticals business. Sparre had charted Du Pont's entry into pharmaceuticals in his 1916 plan for the diversification of the company away from explosives. During the Great Depression, he proposed to the Executive Committee that Du Pont buy Abbott Laboratories; instead, the company signed an agreement whereby Abbott would screen any new compound submitted by Du Pont for potential pharmacological applications.[9] In practice, this agreement never led to anything because departments submitted only the compounds in which they had absolutely no interest, and Abbott was less interested in Du Pont's compounds than its own.[10] In 1942, Sparre came back to the committee asking for authorization to negotiate the purchase of Abbott. Following a discussion with him, the committee resolved that although pharmaceuticals was a logical industry for Du Pont, under the present wartime conditions the company should not enter the field.[11]

Imperial Chemical Industries's decision to enter pharmaceuticals as a long-term strategic venture forced Du Pont's executives to reconsider perhaps sooner than they wished this important question of further diversification. Du Pont had known since 1941 that ICI was actively engaged in research on penicillin in collaboration with Howard Walter Florey and Robert Robinson at Oxford University. Wartime conditions in Britain led to the formation of the Therapeutic Research Corporation of Great Britain, a government inspired collaborative group charged with developing and manufacturing desperately needed pharmaceuticals, including penicillin. ICI soon was drawn into an agreement, signed in late 1942, with the Therapeutic Research Corporation. Although ICI believed that this agreement in no way affected its Patents and Processes Agreement with Du Pont, Du Pont's executives saw the matter differently. ICI maintained that it would continue to share its pharmaceutical research with Du Pont, except for information obtained through its agreement with the Therapeutic Research Corporation. Similarly, ICI assured Du Pont that research results from Wilmington would be kept confidential.

ICI recognized that problems of information flow could best be avoided if Du Pont would conclude an agreement with the Therapeutic Research Corporation similar to ICI's. The situation was complicated, however, because both Merck and Squibb in the United States had signed technical information exchange agreements with the British consortium on the specific subject of penicillin. Moreover, the National Research Council's chemotherapy research committee was actively engaged in effecting close cooperation on penicillin among all major U.S. pharmaceutical firms. Thus, Du Pont's signing an agreement with the Therapeutic Research Corporation would mean sharing research on a much wider basis than Du Pont had ever contemplated and also running risks of being viewed as party to a domestic cartel.[12]

Two of ICI's representatives came to Wilmington in April 1943 to discuss Du Pont's options in pharmaceuticals and to brief the company fully on ICI's venture. The ICI men told a group from the Chemical, Development, and Foreign Relations departments that their company's pharmaceuticals venture, although only launched in 1938, had already become profitable and that ICI had "made sufficient profits to write off all research work."[13] Elmer Bolton spoke for the Du Pont group and pointed out that presently Du Pont would not enter pharmaceuticals but hoped to "at a later date."[14] Following this meeting, Du Pont's managers prepared a written response to ICI's formal invitation.

Signed by the head of the Foreign Relations Department, Wendell R. Swint, Du Pont's reply stated that discussions with ICI had confirmed "that it is practicable to consider research [in pharmaceuticals] only if undertaken on a large scale." The company expressed doubt that it could find or divert a sufficient number of researchers or that it "could make any special contribution to the progress already achieved" in penicillin's development. Du Pont sought to keep its options open, especially on the synthesis of antibiotics as opposed to their manufacture through fermentation (as penicillin was made).[15] ICI, however, was not satisfied with Du Pont's position and soon brought the matter up again in October 1943.[16] This time the issue received the attention of Du Pont's Executive Committee because ICI suggested that it was nearing a major agreement on pharmaceuticals with the U.S. firm Squibb.[17]

The Executive Committee met to consider ICI's new proposal and the whole subject of a venture into pharmaceuticals by Du Pont. Swint, representatives of the Development Department, and Bolton participated in the discussion that followed Swint's reading of both the letter from ICI and his proposed reply. The committee devoted most of the day to this issue and resolved finally to reply along the lines proposed by Swint with some minor modifications. ICI must have been surprised by Du Pont's response, for it called the entire Du Pont–ICI Patents and Processes Agreement into question.

Du Pont's reply to ICI made four basic points: (1) Du Pont was interested in pharmaceuticals; (2) the company was already making a few pharmaceutical products and selling them to pharmaceutical companies; (3) Du Pont had seriously considered pursuing pharmaceuticals either through internal generation or acquisition, but it had "concluded to postpone further consideration of the matter for the duration of the war;" (4) Du Pont considered its agreement with ICI to cover the field of pharmaceuticals without any amendment to the agreement. ICI could not, therefore, enter into an agreement with Squibb without breaking the terms of the 1929 Patents and Processes Agreement. Eliminating pharmaceuticals would consequently involve too large an area of the organic chemistry industry, hence calling the entire association into question.[18]

Following its resolution regarding Du Pont's response to ICI, the committee made one further resolution that set the stage for the company's future policy on pharmaceuticals. The committee members requested that the Development Department continue to follow the pharmaceutical industry, pursuant to their resolution of September 2, 1942, but with one important modification. Charles Stine recommended – and his colleagues unanimously concurred – that veterinary pharmaceuticals also be considered in the Development Department's study.[19] This resolution soon led the Executive Committee to abandon any serious consideration of a human pharmaceuticals venture in favor of a business in veterinary pharmaceuticals, which in turn led to Du Pont's full-fledged efforts to become a major manufacturer of agricultural chemicals.

Stine alone was perhaps responsible for shifting Du Pont's interest in pharmaceuticals toward veterinary medicine. Here, Stine's great personal interests intersected with those of the Du Pont Company, and when combined with his superior ability to sell research, Stine carried the day. For a number of years, Stine had operated an experimental dairy farm located near Newark, Delaware, said to be "one of the most scientifically controlled dairy farms in the United States."[20] Managing a herd of dairy cattle led Stine to consider such destructive cattle diseases as chronic mastitis and Bang's disease. As a member of the University of Delaware's board of trustees and its agriculture committee, he had promoted research there on these diseases, and now he pressed Du Pont to enter the field of veterinary pharmaceuticals.[21] Within six months, the Development Department had completed its initial report on the field, and the Grasselli Chemicals Department, because of its already extensive contacts with the state university agricultural experiment stations, had been targeted as the likely industrial department to sponsor such a venture.[22] Soon – well before the end of the war – Du Pont had committed itself to the venture and had hired an experienced research supervisor to establish a research program in the Grasselli organization.[23] Located originally in a Quonset hut rented from the University of Delaware's School of Agriculture, Du Pont's veterinary pharmaceuticals research was soon moved nearby to a new and expansive site south of Newark, Delaware, in 1951. Reflecting the man who inspired them, these facilities were dedicated as the Stine Laboratory.[24]

Thus, by 1950 Du Pont had charted its course in the biological chemicals area. The Grasselli Chemicals Department would be charged with responsibility for building a business in biological chemicals, including agricultural chemicals and veterinary pharmaceuticals. The company had rejected ICI's proposal to enter the field of human pharmaceuticals through joint research efforts. By 1950, executives had also ruled out buying into the pharmaceuticals business because Du Pont had been indicted in six antitrust cases and no one believed that acquisition was a tenable strategy given the political climate in the United States.

Building a competent biological chemicals research unit in the Grasselli organization proved to be difficult given the mind-set of the department's managers, who were accustomed to doing business in commodity chemicals. In 1941, Crawford H. Greenewalt had been named director of research in Grasselli, but within months of his appointment, he was drawn into Manhattan Project work. Grasselli's managers chose Greenewalt's assistant, John Woodhouse, who had recently been recruited from the Ammonia Department.

Woodhouse has characterized Grasselli's top managers as being hostile to research and particularly to the development of new products, which had been one of the hallmarks of the Ammonia Department.[25] Woodhouse was thus caught in the middle between a management antagonistic to research and the Executive Committee, which wanted Grasselli to move aggressively into biological chemicals research and development. Fortunately for Woodhouse, the committee's research liaison after the war was Roger Williams, who had been Woodhouse's mentor in the Ammonia Department. Together Woodhouse and Williams successfully schemed to get new research facilities for Grasselli without the full support of the department's general management. Williams also encouraged Woodhouse to recruit talented researchers for the biological chemicals field. Woodhouse made headway in this endeavor, but his work was cut short in 1950 when he was transferred to the company's new Savannah River nuclear project. His successor, Max T. Goebel, proved far more conservative than Woodhouse. Grasselli's experience with research and development in agricultural chemicals and veterinary and, eventually, human pharmaceuticals varied greatly over the next two decades.

Agricultural Chemicals

Research during and immediately following World War II led to a profound change in the use of chemicals in agriculture. Some have even used the word "revolution" to describe this change, particularly in the areas of weed and insect control. In weed control, for example, the total market for herbicides in 1940 was estimated to be about $2 million. By the early 1960s, U.S. farmers spent more than $270 million to control weeds on 70 million acres of land.[26] Sales of insecticides grew from $9.2 million in 1939 to more than $170 million in 1954.[27] After the war, *Barron's* identified agricultural chemicals as one of the most profitable growth areas in the already highly touted chemicals industry.[28] The wartime development of the herbicide 2,4-D[29] and the insecticide DDT[30] clearly served as major driving forces in the growth of the agricultural chemicals business. Not surprisingly, Du Pont had a stake in both the 2,4-D and DDT businesses.

Du Pont's Chemical Department obtained a patent in June 1943 claiming the use of 2,4-D as a plant growth regulant. This patent grew out of research initiated in 1937 on the new and hot topic of plant growth stimulants.[31] In 1920, plant physiologists isolated growth hormones responsible for making a plant bend toward a light source.[32] By 1934, three such hormones had been identified. More important, scientists in the Netherlands and in California synthesized one of these compounds and demonstrated that it produced responses in plants identical to its natural counterpart. With this discovery, research on synthetic growth hormones took off.

In March 1941, 2,4-D was synthesized in the Chemical Department, and Grasselli's biologists demonstrated that the compound was definitely a plant growth regulant. In June, an article appeared in the *Journal of the American Chemical Society* describing the synthesis of 2,4-D and a related compound, 2,4,5-T. The Chemical Department's John F. Lontz applied for a patent on 2,4-D as a "Plant Regulant Composition" in February 1942, and he received it in June 1943.[33] Strangely, although scientists at many locations, including those at Grasselli, were experimenting with 2,4-D as a growth regulant, none observed its herbicidal action until late 1942. By this time, the war had put a cloak around scientific publications, and experimentation with 2,4-D was taken over by the War Research Service, which under the direction of George W. Merck assumed responsibility for biological warfare research and development.[34] Work on 2,4-D was carried out at Camp Detrick as well as at the Department of Agriculture's facility at Beltsville, Maryland.

By 1944, the compound had been demonstrated to be an excellent herbicide. Publications by the principal researchers from the War Research Service began to appear in 1944, and these revealed for the first time in print that 2,4-D was herbicidal.[35] One article in particular suggested that the compound might be an important selective weed killer.[36] Not until these publications were issued did Grasselli undertake any extensive research on 2,4-D as a herbicide. By March 1946, the department had begun commercial production of the compound, but because so many others had entered the business as well, Grasselli closed down its operations in early 1950.

The development of 2,4-D during and immediately after the war initiated a profound change in thinking about agricultural chemicals. Specifically, it led to the creation of "weed science" in schools of agriculture and at agricultural experiment stations.[37] The new compound opened up the possibilities of formulating herbicides that could be used as soil sterilants; herbicides that could control broad-leaved plants after they appeared; and, more promising once explored, preemergent herbicides for agricultural crops.

For Du Pont, 2,4-D no doubt yielded many lessons. Although the Chemical Department could be proud of its early synthesizing of the compound and of obtaining a patent on 2,4-D as a plant growth regulant, no one in the company could have been pleased that it had missed 2,4-D's value as an herbicide. The 2,4-D experience pointed up critical deficiencies in the screening tests used by the Grasselli pest control research organization to evaluate the action of chemicals on plants and insects. Although the company might have one of the best capabilities in organic synthesis, without good screens to identify biological activity in its many forms, Du Pont could not expect to make much headway in the agricultural chemicals business.

Until perhaps recently, screening has been the critical first step in the successful development of an agricultural chemical. The process begins with the primary screen, which was typically done by Grasselli's biologists with only one plant (tomatoes) to detect herbicidal activity and with one type of insect (fruit flies) to detect insecticidal activity. Biologists sprayed a dilute solution of a newly synthesized compound on the plant or insect and then waited for the results. If the tomato plant died in a week or less, the compound was judged to be herbicidal. So also with the fruit fly. Depending on the level of activity, biologists and chemists then determined whether to follow up the primary screen with more refined screening (on different plant or insect species) or with primary screening of analogs (or related compounds). Often a related compound proved to be more biologically active than the original one. With luck in synthesizing and screening the lead compound and skill in follow-up screening and synthesizing analogs, the laboratory could develop a promising herbicide or insecticide. Candidates would then have to go through tests at the Haskell Laboratory of Industrial Toxicology to determine their safety. If Haskell's initial tests indicated a safe compound, larger plot and small field tests were then typically performed.

In many respects, bringing out a new herbicide or insecticide is comparable to bringing out a new dye. Synthesis of a new compound is important, but the screening process itself, be it for a dye or a herbicide, is where critical judgments have to be made on how to pursue a compound. This process is labor intensive and expensive. As with dyestuffs, there are only a limited number of classes of herbicides, insecticides, and fungicides, so an ability to synthesize analog compounds based on primary screening results is also critical.

Over time, Du Pont's primary screens have grown in their sophistication. Now the company screens new compounds in all areas where there is an important market for agricultural chemicals. For herbicides, this involves cereals, corn, rice, sugar beets, sugarcane, citrus, and other crops under a variety of soil, climate, and planting conditions. Had Du Pont developed such thorough primary screens in the late 1930s and early 1940s, it would have become the unquestioned leader in the field of agricultural chemicals. It certainly would not have missed the herbicidal activity of 2,4-D.

The development of the powerful insecticide DDT stemmed from wartime efforts of the U.S. Department of Agriculture, which, in response to requests from the War Department, established a major research facility for its division of insects affecting man and animal and expanded the operations of its division of insecticide investigations. Both these divisions investigated samples of the J. R. Geigy Company's new Gerasol Dust Insecticide, which they determined to be DDT and which they found to be an outstanding louse powder, larvicide, and insecticide.[38] The wartime need for such a powerful chemical led to the rapid procurement by the federal government of manufacturing capacity under license from Geigy. Du Pont was among the first fourteen companies in the United States making DDT during the war after the Cincinnati Chemical Works (a Geigy subsidiary) began production in 1943.[39]

Du Pont's manufacture of DDT never led to any profits. By 1954, Du Pont lost three cents on every pound of DDT it manufactured, so it ceased production.[40] However, Du Pont's experience with DDT led to its development of Marlate methoxychlor insecticide, which proved to be a profitable product in spite of its inability to compete in price with DDT.[41] In 1942, the Chemical Department had prepared a sample of methoxychlor in research aimed at finding pest control chemicals.[42] Yet, not until chemists heard about the activity of DDT a year later did they adequately screen and thereby observe the good insecticidal action of methoxychlor, which is chemically related to DDT. As with the herbicide 2,4-D, Du Pont's screens had proved to be highly inadequate. Nevertheless, Du Pont was able to obtain a composition of matter patent on methoxychlor, and Grasselli began commercial production early in 1950.

Du Pont overcame many of its weaknesses in agricultural-chemicals research through the recruitment of personnel with training in agronomy, weed and insect control, and plant and animal metabolism. Bricks-and-mortar expansion also helped, including the occupation of Grasselli's new research laboratory at the Experimental Station in 1950, the move of the screening operations from Minquadale to bigger and better facilities north of Wilmington the same year, and the use of larger test facilities offered by the new Stine Laboratory site.

Du Pont's discovery and development of the substituted urea herbicides offers an excellent instance of the strengths and weaknesses of Grasselli's research in agricultural chemicals at the time. The substituted ureas are an important class of herbicides not only because of the large number of commercial products they yielded, but also because they opened up the idea of selective weed control agriculture.[43]

The discovery of the substituted urea herbicides stemmed from research initiated in 1947 by the Chemical Department on chemicals for biological applications.[44] This work was supported by Grasselli and was focused primarily on veterinary pharmaceuticals. Initial work centered on already-known biologically active compounds, some of which exhibited herbicidal activity. Almost a year later, Charles W. Todd of the Chemical Department synthesized a derivative of diethylurea[45] as part of his program to develop drugs to treat parasite-induced diseases in chickens.

When Grasselli ran this new compound through its primary screens, a discerning biologist, Harry C. Bucha, noted unusual herbicidal activity. One week after Bucha sprayed a 1 percent solution of Todd's compound on a tomato plant, he observed that the plant was not dead. Normally, he would have destroyed it and declared the compound worthless as a herbicide. But Bucha noted that the plant showed considerable yellowing in the veins of the leaves and decided to continue the test. He speculated that the compound was blocking some basic mechanism of the plant's growth. After two weeks, the treated tomato plant died. Bucha's observation and speculation led to a follow-up program of more careful screening and synthesis of other substituted ureas. Chemists chose which analogs they would first synthesize on the basis of which intermediates Du Pont made. The first of these[46] demonstrated significantly greater herbicidal activity than Todd's compound when screened in July 1949. Wider screening revealed activity on many grasses and annual weeds. Grasselli's research managers knew they had a compound (generically known as monuron) with potential commercial importance.

Originally, researchers viewed the substituted ureas as industrial herbicides — as soil sterilants when applied at rates of twenty to forty pounds per acre. But the arrival of Dale E. Wolf in Grasselli changed the department's thinking about the commercialization of its new discovery. Wolf was the nation's first holder of a doctorate in weed science and coauthor of the first textbook in the field.[47] With much effort, Woodhouse had recruited him from Rutgers University, where he was running a growing pioneering research program in weed control.[48] Wolf had published the first paper on using 2,4-D as a preemergent herbicide on corn and was developing concepts of selectivity in weed control.[49] At Du Pont, he quickly oriented Grasselli's screens to reflect market opportunities. With the substituted ureas applied at low concentrations, he could realize the potential of selective weed control. Wolf pushed Goebel to make several hundred pounds of monuron and another analog, diuron, and to distribute these compounds to select agricultural colleges and universities where they would be screened for many more applications than Du Pont could handle at the time.[50] Wolf would eventually become the group vice president (i.e., general manager) of Du Pont's Agricultural Chemicals Department.

On the basis of monuron's soil sterilant properties alone, Grasselli's managers determined early in 1950 to proceed toward its commercialization as an industrial weed killer for such applications as railroad rights-of-way, tank farms, and billboard frontage. Therefore, the department commissioned Du Pont's Haskell Laboratory of Industrial Toxicology to carry out comprehensive research on the safety of monuron and related compounds. At the same time, Grasselli began work on scaling-up the process for making monuron on a commercial basis.

Up to this point, Grasselli had spent slightly over $100,000 on the substituted ureas. But early in 1951, research managers determined to step up the pace of development. With a basic patent application filed and others submitted around it, Du Pont decided to inform the scientific community about the new biologically active compounds by publishing an article in *Science* and offering the compound for testing by government and university scientists.[51] Such an announcement carried a commitment for Grasselli to make the compound on a pilot plant scale – on the order of 10,000 pounds. Some two hundred researchers accepted Du Pont's offer. With additional information derived from these researchers and a favorable toxicological report from the Haskell Lab, Grasselli in 1952 began to offer monuron commercially as an industrial weed and brush killer under the trade name Telvar. By this time, precommercial R&D expenses had exceeded $500,000.

Much work remained to make the substituted ureas important agricultural herbicides. In early 1951, Grasselli's chemists synthesized diuron,[52] which proved to be highly selective and helped make Du Pont a pioneer in developing chemicals for selective weed control. Two of its first important commercial applications were on sugarcane and pineapple. As with any agricultural chemical, Grasselli had to devote considerable resources to make sure its products met the government's safety standards before it could be registered for commercial use in particular applications.

The initial assumption of using the substituted ureas, especially monuron, as soil sterilants raised questions about how safe lower applications would be when applied to the same fields over a period of years. Would the compound build up to a sterilant level after a few years, rendering valuable agricultural land worthless? A large number of researchers who had obtained samples of monuron and diuron raised this concern. Grasselli's research managers recognized very early that without addressing this question, Du Pont would not be able to proceed very far in the use of the substituted ureas in agriculture.

Early in 1953, they established a five-member task force to determine the fate of the urea herbicides following application. This study focused on questions of volatilization, leaching, chemical decomposition, and biological degradation. Led by Gideon D. Hill, the group published the results of their two-year study in the *Agronomy Journal*.[53] Hill and his colleagues argued that both monuron and diuron were broken down in agricultural soils "in an orderly and predictable manner" and that soil buildup would not occur if the products were applied as directed.[54]

Residue studies in plants and soil greatly challenged Grasselli researchers. Both areas of research led to the development of new techniques of analysis, some of which became standard outside the Grasselli organization. Understanding the fate of the urea herbicides had been particularly challenging but critical to the commercial success of the venture.

Despite the company's widespread enthusiasm for fundamental research, Grasselli's research managers did not organize a formal project aimed at a fundamental understanding of the mode of herbicidal action of substituted ureas. Nevertheless, because of the work of an astute microbiologist employed in Grasselli's pharmaceutical division, the mechanism of action of the new herbicide class was articulated. This understanding proved to be of major importance in Du Pont's efforts to gain broad patent coverage.

Conrad E. Hoffmann joined Grasselli's veterinary medicine research program in 1952 after completing his PhD at Western Reserve University. Prior to entering the doctoral program, Hoffmann had been employed by the pharmaceutical house of Lederle. There he had worked with an organism known as *Euglena*, which was sometimes classed among the protozoa and sometimes among the algae. Although Hoffmann was assigned to a formal research project, his supervisor gave him the opportunity to spend 10 percent of his time on his own work. Because of his familiarity with *Euglena*, Hoffmann chose to work with it as his bootleg project. In a conversation with some of his colleagues, Hoffmann learned that a Grasselli biologist had observed that in low concentrations monuron inhibits the motility of certain algae, including *Euglena*. Hoffmann knew that *Euglena* is a photosynthetic organism. In the presence of light, it can grow in media containing no carbon source of energy other than carbon dioxide from the air. But in the dark, it can only grow if it is supplied carbon-based energy such as ethanol. He decided to see if he could detect herbicidal activity in the ureas being studied in Agchem using *Euglena*.[55] He soon found that monuron readily killed *Euglena* but was comparatively inactive toward other protozoa, which do not contain chlorophyll. Keying on the importance of chlorophyll in the herbicidal mechanism, Hoffmann then determined that *Euglena* continued to grow in the presence of monuron if cultured in the absence of light. With this finding, Hoffmann deduced that the action of monuron was limited to the light phase of growth in plants, and he demonstrated that the other ureas synthesized by Agchem worked in the same way.

Hoffmann pursued the study of the mechanism of herbicidal action of the ureas. He determined that monuron did not interfere with the synthesis of chlorophyll nor did it deactivate or combine with the chlorophyll. He conjectured that the mechanism of action must occur at an earlier stage of photosynthesis. Biologists were familiar with the first step in photosynthesis, known as the Hill Reaction. Studying this reaction in material treated with monuron, Hoffmann observed that the photolysis of water – the critical part of the Hill Reaction – was completely inhibited. He suggested that the herbicide served as an inhibitor of the enzymes that made the Hill Reaction go. Hence, in his bootleg research Hoffmann explained the basic mechanism of the substituted urea herbicides. Hoffmann's work yielded more than a fundamental understanding of why the ureas kill certain plants. It provided a useful correlation of data on the growing number of analogs that Agchem's synthesis group was turning out and that were being screened.

Max Goebel and his staff had been plagued by the problem of how to obtain broad patent protection on substituted ureas. The trick was to include as many substituted ureas with known herbicidal activity as possible in the broad patent and not to leave any holes. Because of the demands of fully screening compounds included in the patent application, Goebel and his staff had felt uneasy about including some of the compounds that they knew or suspected were herbicidal but had not been fully tested. They knew that if they included a single compound that turned out not to be herbicidal as claimed by the patent, the entire patent could be invalidated. Hoffmann's results came at a critical moment when Grasselli was trying to pack as much as possible into the patent application without unduly delaying it or including too many conjectural claims. When Hoffmann delivered a handwritten report to Goebel on the correlation of traditional Agchem screening data with his *Euglena*-based findings, Goebel saw at once the value of his work. Goebel concluded that Du Pont's application was as good as possible and that Du Pont should not attempt to obtain additional coverage in the basic patent through the refiling procedure.[56]

After Goebel took this step, he effectively closed down the work of the synthesis group that had been preparing new substituted ureas. The group had made some eight hundred such compounds by this time. Other factors also contributed to Goebel's decision. At the height of the urea synthesis program, Grasselli had only four of its own chemists and four chemists in the Chemical Department at work on substituted ureas. When the veterinary pharmaceuticals division of Grasselli research discovered a promising lead to a bactericide, most of Agchem's chemists were assigned to follow up this discovery. Only two synthesis chemists were left to work on agricultural chemicals, and following Goebel's decision, they were ordered not to make any more substituted ureas. The Patent Office also contributed to Goebel's decision because an examiner decided that new substituted ureas did not constitute a new invention. He ruled that it was "no longer unobvious to make a substituted urea as a herbicide."[57] Later, the ban on substituted urea synthesis was lifted after some personnel changes in Grasselli's research management and after one of the chemists synthesized some promising ureas on a bootleg basis. Du Pont pursued patents on these compounds and won an appeal against the patent examiner's position on the patentability of new substituted ureas.

The substituted ureas were Du Pont's first major discovery in agricultural chemicals. Grasselli's old line of herbicides provided the company approximately 8 percent of the growing U.S. herbicide market. With the introduction of Telvar monuron and Karmex diuron, Du Pont gained market share, particularly after Grasselli developed these compounds into highly selective agricultural herbicides. Karmex became especially important after Grasselli formulated it for weed protection of cotton. By 1960, Du Pont had captured 20 percent of the U.S. herbicide market.[58]

Despite Du Pont's early lead in the substituted ureas and its good patent position, the company quickly saw competitors in the field. Geigy, BASF, and Hoechst each responded quickly to Du Pont's disclosures and soon developed competitive products. Grasselli's comparatively small synthesis team following Todd's lead, and its decision not to continue synthesis work on ureas after 1953, no doubt especially hurt Du Pont's position. Hoechst synthesized linuron, which proved excellent for soybean protection. Du Pont was forced to license this compound to market its own version of linuron, trademarked Lorox.[59] Geigy patented fluometuron (trademarked Cotoran), which Goebel had not protected because he had learned about the compound from a Dutch scientist and thus believed it in the public domain.[60] Cotoran proved to be a direct competitor of Karmex in cotton applications and actually offered advantages. Other competitors also developed urea herbicides.

Along with competition in the substituted ureas, Du Pont suffered from being unable to find a good herbicide for corn, which constitutes one of the largest markets for herbicides in the United States. In the late 1950s, Geigy had opened up a new class of herbicides – the triazines – that were effective on corn. Grasselli's chemists synthesized numerous triazines, but the department did not find a good one that it could make without infringing on patents or losing money. Thus Du Pont lost herbicide market share in the 1960s and 1970s.

Despite Grasselli's inability to keep competitors out of the field of substituted ureas, Du Pont earned a high rate of return on its investment. Total R&D costs amounted to less than $2 million; commercial production of the herbicides required no inordinate capital expenditures; and the products sustained no initial operative losses. The urea herbicides made Grasselli's agricultural chemicals business grow and allowed the department to enter European markets in the early 1960s.

Grasselli's experience with the substituted ureas also led to significant new concepts in weed control and improvements in screening. The substituted ureas provided the means for Grasselli's research organization to develop nascent ideas about selectivity in weed control and to demonstrate the advantages of preemergence treatment.[61] Moreover, this new class of herbicides demanded that the Grasselli organization develop expertise in such areas as metabolism and residue determination. Finally, growing sophistication in the synthesis area after the ban on synthesizing new substituted ureas was lifted helped lead to the next major class of herbicides developed by the company, the uracils.

Following up a suggestion by one of Grasselli's consultants, Raymond Luckenbaugh prepared for the first time a cyclic, five-membered, ring-substituted urea, which showed herbicidal activity. Additional research by Harvey Loux of Grasselli and Linus Ellis of Central Research led to Loux's synthesis of the first member of the uracil class of herbicides. This resulted eventually in the commercialization of bromacil, terbacil, and lenacil.[62]

Du Pont's less-than-ideal experience in protecting and fully exploring the substituted ureas influenced the manner in which the uracils were handled. Once the lead compound showed promise, Grasselli's research managers pursued follow-up work far more aggressively than with the ureas. More chemists synthesized analogs around the initial compound, and far greater attention was paid to securing an impenetrable patent position. Even while work on the uracil patent application was in progress, the substituted ureas continued to be instructive. For example, Gideon Hill attended a conference on herbicides where he heard Hercules Chemical Company announce a new herbicide made from a polycyclic substituted urea. Hill immediately called Wilmington about Hercules's product and to inquire if the uracil application included polycyclic substitutions. It did not. This approach was immediately included in the broad application. As a result of this care, Du Pont succeeded in securing excellent protection on the uracils.[63] Eventually, Du Pont got three commercial products out of the substituted uracils and also formulated bromacil and diuron into another product sold to control weeds in citrus orchards.

Uracil herbicides have not been extraordinarily large on a poundage basis, but they have yielded a high rate of return on investment.[64] Despite these handsome returns, Du Pont's share of the herbicidal market continued to shrink after its high point in the late 1950s, owing almost exclusively to its continued lack of a herbicide for corn.

In 1959 Grasselli was reorganized into the Industrial and Biochemicals

Department.[65] The reorganization itself had little effect on the department's program of R&D in Agchem. But the failure of the bactericide program led management to place increasing emphasis on agricultural chemicals research during the 1960s, including work on the uracils and new synthesis and follow-up programs. (The bactericide failure is discussed later in this chapter.) Research in the 1960s led to the two most successful products in the department's history up to the development of the sulfonylurea herbicides in the late 1970s and early 1980s, Lannate methomyl insecticide and Benlate benomyl fungicide.

Lannate grew out of James B. Buchanan's formulation in January 1962 of a research program that led to a new class of chemicals, the carbamylhydroxamates, which he thought would be biologically active.[66] In his project proposal, Buchanan specifically listed the compound that became the active ingredient in Lannate – methomyl.[67] He began to synthesize compounds in the class in February and by November had prepared an analog of methomyl. When this compound went through the routine screens as INC-1335 – one of about 5,000 compounds screened in 1962 – it showed only minor insecticidal activity. The compound could certainly have been dropped given these results.

Indeed, INC-1335 was dropped until September 1963, when another senior research chemist, John K. Scroggin, decided for reasons that are unclear to run INC-1335 through a finer insecticidal screen, one to evaluate activity on boll weevils. Because of the problem of keeping boll weevils, the department did not routinely screen all compounds on them. INC-1335 demonstrated outstanding results on boll weevils; managers quickly declared this class of compounds a major insecticidal lead.

Once synthesized, methomyl showed vastly improved insecticidal properties and was effective against chewing insects on cotton, tobacco, and vegetables. In spite of increasing government scrutiny in the registration process, Lannate methomyl cleared relatively quickly for an insecticide primarily because of its properties of quickly killing insects and then rapidly breaking down, thus constituting what specialists call a "low-residual" insecticide.

Lannate's properties and the growing concern over DDT and other organochlorine insecticides gave Du Pont its first significant insecticide. Although Marlate methoxychlor was a good earner, it had given Du Pont less than 1 percent of the market. Lannate changed this situation while yielding a handsome return on investment.[68]

Although the development of Benlate benomyl fungicide occurred in the second half of the 1960s, its origins go back to the early 1950s, when Grasselli's synthesis group was working actively on the substituted ureas.[69] Some eight months after diuron was synthesized and shown to be an excellent herbicide, a benzothiazoleurea was prepared and demonstrated herbicidal activity. Harry J. Gerjovich, one of the few synthesis chemists remaining in agricultural chemicals, subsequently conceived the idea that alkyl-2-benzothiazolecarbamates would be biologically active and began synthesizing such compounds in 1954. One of the early compounds submitted showed excellent fungicidal activity.[70] Most important, it proved to operate systemically rather than topically, hence being the first really promising systemic fungicide, an achievement that everyone knew would open large market opportunities. But additional tests and fieldwork demonstrated that the compound acted inconsistently in adverse weather. It was good enough, however, to warrant synthesis and screening of related compounds. Gerjovich pursued some of this work until mid-1956, when he was put on another project. During that time, Gerjovich had conceived of but not synthesized a large number of benzoheterocyclic carbamates. Among several approaches to this class, Gerjovich had included the benzimidazolecarbamates but had never attempted to synthesize them because he believed they were the most difficult of his proposed classes.

Hein L. Klopping, familiar with Gerjovich's work, began to synthesize the benzimidazolecarbamates early in 1957. He prepared a new compound known as MBC[71] soon after initiating his program, and it showed fungicidal activity in the primary screen. Using MBC as an intermediate, by August he had synthesized methyl 1-methoxycarbonyl-2-benzimidazolecarbamate. When submitted to both primary and then secondary screening as INU-811, it showed excellent systemic fungicidal properties on powdery mildew and apple scab. Research managers concluded that they had a potentially great product, and they encouraged further synthesis. Because of its promise, the lead compound, INU-811, was submitted for preliminary toxicological testing in mid-November, and in February 1958, Grasselli requested Haskell Lab to carry out more extensive toxicity tests on the compound.[72]

Haskell's results looked bad; they reported that the compound markedly depressed the production of sperm in rats.[73] Not pleased by these results, Max Goebel requested that a similar study be carried out by his own scientists at the Stine Laboratory. Stine confirmed Haskell's findings with rats.[74] These results suggested that the consumption of plants treated with the compound could lead to sterility in animals and humans. Goebel immediately shut down all work on this class of compounds.[75] Probably with Goebel's special permission, Klopping continued to prepare several different types of benzimidazoles, hoping to find a safer compound. He synthesized the first member of the benomyl family in July 1959.[76]

Du Pont's research managers did not want to give up on INU-811. If it were potentially unsafe as a fungicide, perhaps it could serve as an effective male sterilant. In 1960, the department submitted the compound along with four others to the Wildlife Research Laboratory of the Department of Interior's Fish and Wildlife Service as a chemical that could potentially control deer mouse population. In July 1961, biologists at the Wildlife Research Laboratory reported that INU-811 showed no effect on deer mice at the level of dosage suggested by Du Pont.[77]

These negative results led research managers to question the earlier findings about the safety of INU-811. They determined to put the chemical through another round of tests using not only rats but dogs and monkeys as well. Rather than having Haskell carry out these tests, they chose to do them in the department's Stine Laboratory. In April 1964, Stine summarized its work. At large dosages administered both orally and by injection, all three species showed marked reduction in the weight of male testes and prostates. From these data, Stine's scientists concluded that INU-811 "may be useful not only for its anti-testicular effect but may have even greater commercial importance in cases of prostatic hypertrophy, both benign and malignant."[78]

With these results, research managers sought to interest physicians at Albany Medical College in INU-811 both as a male sterilant and for treatment of prostate disorders, areas that the college was pursuing. Max Goebel and several members of his staff went to Albany to give a review on INU-811 to two researchers. Upon examining the data, one of these researchers told Goebel and his cohorts that INU-811 not only was *not* a good sterilant, but that it would probably be entirely safe if consumed in much smaller doses. He said that the test dosages had been far too high to make an accurate judgment about the compound's safety as a fungicide.[79]

With these views and subsequent discussion in Wilmington, the cautious Goebel determined to reactivate the INU-811 fungicide program. Early in 1965, he ordered ninety-day feeding studies at low-dosage levels to be carried out by the Haskell Laboratory and a renewed synthesis and screening program on INU-811 analogs.[80] One obvious path to pursue was to follow up Klopping's work of 1959 on the benomyl family. Harvey Loux soon synthesized the butyl analog, which was both stable and active. This compound became Benlate benomyl fungicide.

Results of the first ninety-day low-dosage feeding study demonstrated the verity of the Albany Medical College researcher's thesis about the safety of INU-811 at lower intakes. Even at the highest dietary level, rat testes showed no pathological changes.[81] Also, no doubt at Goebel's request, the Stine Laboratory had carried out a new, carefully designed series of higher-dosage tests on monkeys and dogs, which suggested that the earlier observation of reduced generation of sperm was limited to rodents.[82]

Research managers determined in early 1966 to find the benzimidazole with the best index of high fungicidal activity and low toxicity. They would then choose the two best candidates for the very expensive two-year toxicity studies. Seven compounds were tested in 1966 for both activity and toxicity. Benomyl showed the best activity/toxicity index and was thus viewed as the prime candidate. Although more toxic, INU-811 was the best systemic fungicide, so it was also chosen for the two-year study.[83] Ultimately, benomyl was chosen for commercialization.

By 1968 the department was ready to build a commercial plant. Construction began in 1969 at the Belle plant, and the process came on stream in mid-1970. Even before the commercial plant opened, benomyl cleared government registration,[84] and the department began marketing Benlate benomyl produced in its semiworks at the Experimental Station. The product – the first systemic fungicide sold commercially – was an instant success. It earned profits on semiworks quantities. After 1972, Benlate became the most profitable agricultural chemical produced by Du Pont.[85]

Benlate's history was markedly different from that of other agricultural products developed by the department. Its commercialization had taken almost twenty years from the time the first good lead compound was synthesized until the product cleared federal registration. Normally, an agricultural chemical took five or six years to develop.[86] The company's concern for safety, especially as manifested in the cautious Max Goebel, had led to the abandonment of the benzimidazoles for a long time. Better toxicological studies and the company's contact with specialists at Albany Medical College provided the means for Du Pont to salvage the promising lead it had obtained in the 1950s. The long delay, although serving to satisfy fully Goebel's and others' legitimate concerns over the safety of the product, resulted in a substantial reduction in the length of time Du Pont could maintain a proprietary position on benomyl. The basic patent on the product dated from Klopping's 1959 work, and Du Pont was unsuccessful in its request to the Patent Office that the patent be extended because of the unusual circumstances surrounding the product's development.

The virtually instant success of Benlate and Lannate, the continued excellent earnings from the uracils and the licensed linuron, and solid earnings from other products not discussed made Du Pont's agricultural chemicals business one of its best on a return-on-investment basis in the early 1970s. The philosophy of the general management had been extremely conservative during the previous two decades. The department had not dramatically expanded its research effort in agricultural chemicals but rather had allowed it to grow gradually with the growth in sales.[87]

On a market-share basis, Du Pont's agricultural chemicals business looked much weaker than its earnings data would suggest. Du Pont lacked a herbicide that could be used on corn. Not until the late 1970s and early 1980s did Du Pont develop herbicides for cereals.[88] With insecticides, until the development of Lannate, Du Pont had little position in spite of its methoxychlor. The long delay in getting Benlate to market led to a reduction in its fungicide market share, which had been Du Pont's forte.[89]

Max Goebel and his successors were conservative research managers. Goebel's actions of cutting back on the synthesis of new substituted ureas in the mid-1950s and shutting down work on the benzimidazoles in 1958 illustrate this point. They were also conservative in methodology. The principal approach taken during Goebel's era was the synthesis and screening of new compounds and subsequent follow-up analog synthesis and secondary screening if biological activity was observed. Goebel's staff did not pursue any directed, systematic fundamental research on biological mechanisms as they might relate to herbicides, insecticides, and fungicides.

In the 1970s, as personalities and sentiments changed on the Executive Committee, Du Pont's agricultural chemicals business came under increasing scrutiny. U.S. and worldwide consumption of agricultural chemicals was expanding dramatically, and some members of the Executive Committee believed that the managers of Du Pont's Agchem business were taking too much money out of the business rather than putting it back into research and were following policies that would eventually leave Du Pont without a business once competition began to impinge upon Benlate and Lannate.[90] George Levitt's discovery of the important sulfonylurea herbicides in 1975 did not really assuage these executives. With the movement toward more centralized management of research and development and better overall control of corporate strategy resulting from the creation of the Corporate Plans Department (discussed in Chapter 25), executives targeted research in agricultural chemicals for dramatic expansion. Along with this expansion, they also envisioned the implementation of a more fundamental approach to agricultural chemicals research and the exploration of the new recombinant DNA and genetic-engineering techniques that had burst upon the scene. Although the company's executives were perhaps justified in their view that Du Pont had not moved aggressively enough in agricultural chemicals, this business was and had always been significantly better than Du Pont's pharmaceuticals. The history of Du Pont's pharmaceutical research contrasts quite sharply with that of agricultural chemicals.

Pharmaceuticals Research and Development

Du Pont's late wartime and early postwar strategy of not entering the human pharmaceuticals business but researching its way into veterinary pharmaceuticals remained virtually intact until 1957. More than once, company president Crawford H. Greenewalt had to respond to inquiries from stockholders about why Du Pont was not pursuing the exciting pharmaceuticals field. Invariably, he explained that the marketing problem was the primary factor, but he also admitted that the entire field "would be not only new but quite difficult." Nonetheless, Greenewalt believed that Du Pont's "quite ambitious program" in veterinary pharmaceuticals was likely to lead to "developments of interest for human medication as well."[91] Despite the Executive Committee's hopes that Du Pont's veterinary pharmaceuticals research might result in new human drugs, researchers hired to staff this division of Grasselli's research were carefully instructed never to mention that Du Pont had any intentions in human pharmaceuticals. Publicly, Du Pont was strictly in the veterinary medicine field.[92] By 1957, however, this position had changed.

In the early days of veterinary pharmaceuticals research, there was a lot of stumbling around by researchers trying to come up with something of commercial interest. The work of a young organic chemist named Walter A.

Gregory in the early 1950s gave the division its first important lead. Following the publication of the structure of one of the newer antibiotics, Parke-Davis's Chloromycetin (chloramphenicol), Gregory determined to synthesize analogs of this natural compound in an attempt to improve it. He had first thought of this approach in 1949 and had entered an idea for what later became Tevenel in his idea notebook. But almost two years elapsed before he returned to his idea. Pursuing what seemed to him to be the easiest synthesis to carry out, Gregory prepared a compound dubbed SMP-1,[93] which showed good antibiotic activity in certain bacterial spectra. With this lead, the synthesis work of the division picked up. Goebel pulled synthesis chemists off work on the substituted ureas to do follow-up work on SMP-1.[94] Gregory synthesized two additional important compounds, one of which was called AMP.[95] It became the prime subject of the division's research and development. With SMP-1, Du Pont ran into a three-way patent interference with two large drug firms, which resulted in a cross-licensing agreement whereby any of the three could sell the compound commercially; but none did. Du Pont licensed Smith, Kline, and French to make Gregory's second derivative, but the firm never followed up on it commercially. Du Pont's research managers, however, chose to develop the synthetic antibiotic AMP as aggressively as they knew how – and for human applications.

The veterinary pharmaceuticals division carried AMP all the way through clinical trials before abandoning it. This development included the usual toxicological, registration, and formulation work and scale-up of the process to a commercial level. During this period, however, from roughly 1952 to 1957, there was increasing concern that chloramphenicol caused aplastic anemia. No mechanism had been established for the development of this disease nor had any model been worked out to account for it. Given AMP's relationship to chloramphenicol, some members of the department feared pushing the drug beyond the clinical phase even though Du Pont had announced the drug as Tevenel and built a plant. AMP's inventor, Gregory, maintains firmly that Grasselli did not abandon Tevenel because of the possibility of its causing aplastic anemia. Neither tests conducted by Du Pont nor the clinical trials (involving about 1,000 patients) showed any evidence of this problem.[96] Rather, asserts Gregory, Grasselli determined to drop Tevenel because of the continued dominance of Grasselli's old-line salesmen, who feared that some of the big drug firms such as Merck, who were big Grasselli customers, would take revenge and find another supplier of sulfuric acid.[97] Even if Tevenel had been pushed to market, the department would still have faced a problem in selling the drug, for it had no pharmaceutical detail men. This same problem would emerge a few years later with a new antiviral drug.

Stopping the Tevenel project left a major vacuum in the pharmaceutical research program of the department. Nothing important stood in its place. Grasselli's general manager therefore asked the Executive Committee for permission to explore acquisition opportunities in the pharmaceuticals field.[98] The committee waited until the Development Department could prepare a report on this matter and then ruled that Du Pont could not take any action toward acquiring a pharmaceutical company until the outcome of the General Motors antitrust case was clear.[99]

The Development Department's report to the Executive Committee did produce a major change in official policy on the pharmaceutical area of Grasselli research. The study pointed up the committee's naïveté about veterinary pharmaceuticals. Examining the sources of contributions to animal health, the Development Department found that they were made by firms engaged primarily in human, rather than exclusively veterinary, drug development. The size of the market dictated this. Veterinary pharmaceuticals constituted only about a twentieth of the market for human pharmaceuticals. Moreover, the Development Department estimated that about 70 percent of the Stine Laboratory's research program was applicable to human pharmaceuticals.[100] As a consequence of this weighty evidence, Grasselli's managers and the Executive Committee agreed — not by any formal declaration — that Grasselli should make human pharmaceuticals its prime research target, an agreement that confirmed the drift that had been silently occurring at Stine for some time.[101]

Three basic assumptions on the part of corporate and departmental executives lay behind this decision for Du Pont to venture into the ethical (i.e., prescription) drug field. All three stemmed from the extraordinary hubris that prevailed in Du Pont in the 1950s. The executives believed that the company could be successful in the drug venture because Du Pont possessed an enormous reservoir of organic compounds that were potentially proprietary. Indeed, they claimed that the company owned the "world's largest store" of new compounds. In addition, the executives argued that Du Pont had an advantage over U.S. pharmaceutical companies because it maintained the best staff of organic chemists in the United States. Therefore, once leads were turned up in screening the thousands of new compounds synthesized by Du Pont, these organic chemists could easily follow up with analog work. Finally, executives believed that Du Pont's venture into the ethical drug field would succeed because of the company's reputation for quality in all its products. They especially thought that Du Pont was "well-known and respected by the medical profession."[102]

These assumptions notwithstanding, however, Du Pont faced a very difficult challenge in this venture, particularly because neither the Executive Committee nor departmental general managers were willing to spend the kind of money necessary to realize their hopes. For example, up through 1963, Du Pont spent only a total of $14.8 million on human pharmaceuticals research ($0.8 million of which was funded from the Central Research budget), and the budget for 1964 was only $3.6 million ($0.6 million of which was Central Research).[103] Spending on pharmaceuticals research represented only about a fourth of the total R&D budget of the Industrial and

Biochemicals Department. With such small expenditures, it was impossible for pharmaceutical research managers to recruit the personnel they needed and to set up the screening programs that were the key to developing a new drug.

Du Pont's human pharmaceuticals screening program was particularly weak well into the 1970s. At the time of the decision to move openly into this area and away from an exclusively veterinary program, the department really had only two routine screens in place. One was an antiparasite screen established in 1956, which was aimed at finding activity against parasite-induced diseases in chickens. The other was an antiviral screen, established in 1955. Until 1963, this antiviral screen was the "sole high-capacity, systematic" screen at the Stine Laboratory.[104] As noted earlier, antibacterial screening had been done, but there was no high-volume, systematic screen in place until after 1964. Screens for central nervous system activity were not established until 1963, and screens for cardiovascular and renal systems and metabolic drugs were not developed until 1964. Du Pont's Central Research Department began a synthesis program to build new steroid hormones for birth control drugs in 1962, but screening of its compounds was contracted out until Stine established an endocrinological screen in 1964.[105] Thus, lack of adequate screening largely vitiated the advantages that Du Pont's executives had envisaged for its human pharmaceuticals venture.

Some Du Pont research managers believed that the traditional, empirical approach to drug development — screening a vast number of compounds and then following up on compounds showing positive activity — was antiquated and that Du Pont needed a more deductive approach. They felt that compounds should be synthesized on the basis of a fundamental understanding of human physiology, disease processes, and the pharmacological actions of various chemical functional groups. Hence a fundamental approach would provide Du Pont with a competitive advantage.[106] Yet even with this approach, if valid, Du Pont fell well short. Central Research's work was of this ilk, but it represented only a tiny fraction of Du Pont's total pharmaceuticals research effort. The medicinal chemistry section of I&B research, organized in January 1963, also pursued this approach, but only eleven researchers worked in the section in 1964 out of a total of some forty in pharmaceuticals R&D.[107]

Failure to proceed with the Tevenel development, the lack of other major leads in either human or veterinary pharmaceuticals, and the absence of any really strong financial commitment to pursue the pharmaceuticals venture aggressively raised the possibility in the research managers' minds in the late 1950s and early 1960s that Du Pont might easily terminate the entire venture. To buy time and to gain critically needed experience in certain areas of pharmaceuticals, Goebel orchestrated a development that was highly unusual for Du Pont: a government research contract. Late in 1961, Goebel convinced his management and the Executive Committee to approve a three-year, $3.5 million contract with the U.S. Army to develop "new incapacitating and/or lethal agents."[108] As part of the agreement, there was an understanding that the contract could be renewed for another three years. Other than a small nerve gas research program conducted by the Organic Chemicals Department during World War II, Du Pont had not engaged in such research. Indeed, Du Pont's executives had developed a strong aversion to carrying out research for the federal government, as noted in Chapter 16. This contract and its renewal represented the largest R&D contracts Du Pont ever signed with the U.S. government, with the exception of the Manhattan Project and the Savannah River endeavor, which Du Pont did not undertake until requested personally by the president of the United States.[109] And these latter two projects were really not contracts for research and development but rather for construction and operation.

The army R&D contract did indeed provide the security Goebel sought for the pharmaceuticals research effort. Among the fifty-two average technical staff years devoted to pharmaceuticals (including Central Research) in 1964, sixteen were supported by the army contract. This percentage shrank over the next few years until the contract expired in 1968, largely because by 1964 the division had made a research hit, a compound that promised to be the first drug to treat upper respiratory viral infections.[110] The development and marketing of this drug, trademarked Symmetrel, would finally convince the company's executives that Du Pont needed to pursue a different strategy if it were truly interested in becoming a player in the pharmaceuticals business.

Symmetrel antiviral drug showed the strengths and weaknesses of Du Pont's pharmaceuticals venture. Given that the antiviral screen was the initial first-rate screen developed by the Stine Laboratory, it is not surprising that an antiviral drug first emerged from the post-1957 research efforts. The development of this drug, amantadine hydrochloride, also demonstrated the belief by many that screening the thousands of compounds synthesized by Du Pont would lead to commercial drugs. In this case, the Explosives Department had submitted a sample to I&B's agricultural and pharmaceutical screens. The compound[111] showed activity in the primary antiviral screen (a tissue culture screen), and researchers decided to do follow-up screening in animals. The compound showed activity against the influenza virus, so a group of chemists at Stine and in Central Research immediately began to synthesize around the compound. After a major analog synthesis campaign, an old compound, amantadine hydrochloride, turned out to have the most activity against influenza. Du Pont's patent position was therefore limited to a use patent. With such a relatively weak position, some believed Du Pont would see competition in the area by early 1966.[112]

From the initial screening in 1961, Du Pont moved rapidly with the development of Symmetrel. By early 1964, it had taken the drug through clinical trials on some 2,000 patients and expected Food and Drug Administration approval by November 1964. The department expected to begin marketing Symmetrel by January 1, 1965, just in time for the major flu season. To prepare for expected demand, Du Pont manufactured 15,000 pounds of the drug in bulk and then contracted for its processing into capsules and syrup well before FDA approval. Once the FDA approved the drug, Du Pont would then put the capsules and syrup into final packages. The department expected initial sales of $5 million in 1965, increasing to $15 million in 1969 and generating $8.6 million in operative earnings.[113]

Du Pont faced two major problems with this drug and indeed with its entire pharmaceuticals venture. First, the company lacked any pharmaceutical marketing capability. Du Pont had never sold a drug before; it had no sales force. The department established a pharmaceutical marketing section in early 1964 and hired a manager in February. He in turn planned to hire about a dozen people "to effect distribution" of the drug.[114] The department's strategy was to rely almost exclusively on direct mail promotion and trade journal advertising rather than employing the large staff of detail men conventionally used by the industry. Detail men called on physicians, giving them a strong sales pitch in hopes of getting them to write prescriptions for the corporation's products. Managers viewed Symmetrel as a "unique product not requiring conventional selling methods."[115] A Development Department analyst pointed out, however, that once competitors began to introduce their own versions of antiviral drugs, they would be employing their 600- to 1,000-person detail forces to sell their products.[116] Clearly the Du Pont hubris about the uniqueness of the drug and the reputation of the name Du Pont shaped the department's strategy for entering the business. On top of this, there was a great deal of naïveté that Du Pont could penetrate the industry with a single drug – a drug that turned out initially to be only a seasonal one at that.

Du Pont's second great problem was its lack of experience in dealing with the Food and Drug Administration.[117] In this case, Du Pont needed to secure FDA's approval on Symmetrel as quickly as possible and for the specific therapeutic and prophylactic uses for which the company had developed the drug. Owing to Du Pont's ignorance in such matters, its Symmetrel marketing effort was further hamstrung.

The FDA did not approve Symmetrel until October 1966 and then only as a prophylactic agent against A_2 or Asian influenza. Du Pont had claimed that the drug was both an effective therapeutic agent and a prophylactic against all A-type strains of influenza, but it lacked the critical skills to convince the FDA that this was the case. Only much later did the Center for Disease Control in Atlanta help Du Pont secure the approvals it originally sought. By this time, Symmetrel had been severely crippled. Because of delays in the FDA approval process, the department did not believe that its initial marketing of Symmetrel after October gave it an opportunity to demonstrate the potential of the drug. But managers looked to the 1967–68 influenza season as the critical test of Du Pont's strategy.

The results were more than disappointing. Symmetrel sales reached only $250,000 despite the existence of a "mild epidemic" of Asian influenza that season. Physicians in the United States regarded Symmetrel as not being a "serious" drug,[118] and Du Pont blamed the Public Health Department's physicians because of their strong emphasis on vaccines rather than on prophylactics or on antiviral therapeutic agents, which the department continued to believe was Symmetrel's real strength (even though it could not market the drug as such). The department's general management promptly called for a rethinking of the entire venture strategy and immediately disbanded the small, fourteen-person marketing force.[119]

By mid-1969, the department had spent a total of $13.5 million on Symmetrel, including R&D, selling, and operating expenses.[120] Du Pont was several years away from winning the FDA's approval for Symmetrel as an antiviral therapeutic drug; as a prophylactic it promised to have only a limited seasonal market. Yet Symmetrel survived because researchers outside Du Pont discovered that it was effective against some of the symptoms of Parkinson's disease. FDA approval for this therapy provided Du Pont the needed sales to keep Symmetrel on the market. Even so, the managers expected the drug to be marginally profitable at best.

Having spent some $44 million on human and veterinary pharmaceuticals up through 1969 ($26 million on human pharmaceuticals since 1962), plus several millions in Central Research,[121] the department could have ended the entire pharmaceuticals venture and declared the company's attempt to "crash the drug industry" (as one skeptic in the Development Department put it) a mistake.[122] Some forty researchers in I&B would have to be cut and a smaller number in Central Research redeployed. Quitting would also have meant abandoning the promising agreements that the department had made in 1966 with J. R. Geigy and Syntex Corporation to exchange research in the respective areas of anti-inflammatory agents and endocrinology for Du Pont's research in the antiviral field.[123]

Du Pont could have pursued other options. These included a far more aggressive licensing program to obtain drugs that the company could market under its own name or expanding its R&D efforts dramatically in the hope of making one or more major discoveries. Both these options meant that Du Pont would still have to solve its problem of not having any drug-marketing capability. Another option explored was the possibility of arranging some kind of joint venture with a pharmaceutical company to provide marketing capability and to obtain business guidance for Du Pont's research, which some managers still believed was superior to that of the average pharmaceutical firm. The department explored this option with seven European companies, but none was willing to enter into such an arrangement.[124]

That left one alternative: acquisition. From the time Symmetrel had been discovered until it was first marketed, managers had ruled out this strategy despite the strongly expressed views of the Development Department that Du Pont could not successfully market Symmetrel without the help of a "real" drug company.[125] Not long after assuming leadership of the Industrial and Biochemicals Department in 1967, Edward R. Kane, a veteran physical chemist from the Textile Fibers Department and eventual president of the company, took a firm position that Du Pont had to acquire a drug firm. He had evaluated Du Pont's entire pharmaceuticals venture, its Symmetrel program, its agreements with Geigy and Syntex, and its research leads coming out of I&B and Central Research. From this survey he concluded that acquisition – still a forbidden word in many quarters of the company at the time – had to be pursued. In late December 1967, prior to receiving results on Symmetrel in the first full influenza session, he discussed this situation with the Executive Committee. After the extraordinarily low sales of Symmetrel, he came back to the committee with a strong recommendation that Du Pont buy its way into the business. Kane's views prevailed. By the fall of 1968, he had convinced the committee to allow his department to pursue the acquisition strategy.[126]

Finding a pharmaceutical company was not easy. A widely held company was out of the question, and there were few closely held or privately owned companies that Du Pont could afford and that would serve Du Pont's purposes. Moreover, unlike most of Du Pont's acquisitions of the late 1920s and early 1930s, acquiring a drug company would probably involve a greater percentage of cash than shares of stock.[127] Finally, the old rule of thumb that Walter Carpenter had used to figure a company's worth – ten times average annual earnings – simply would not hold.

After a wide search for acquirable companies, the department settled on Endo Laboratories and received the Executive Committee's authorization to buy the company in September 1969.[128] Endo's sales in 1968 were about $20 million and earnings $3 million. Since 1959, the company had grown at a rate of almost 9 percent per year compared to the industry's average of 7.7 percent. Endo's principal product was an anticoagulant named Coumadin, which had captured 85 percent of the U.S. market. In addition, the company sold two narcotic analgesics that held about 14 percent of the market, narcotic cough syrups claiming 9 percent of the market, an antispasmodic drug with 6 percent, and a few other drugs occupying lesser percentages of the U.S. market.[129]

Kane had already been elected to the Executive Committee at the time of Endo's acquisition. He maintained in 1978, while president of Du Pont, that "Endo has been very good for us." The acquisition, he claimed, "has been a success." Although new research had not brought products along as fast as he had hoped, the acquisition, he argued quite correctly, served the purpose of committing Du Pont to the pharmaceuticals business. As he said, it took "us off what was then an on-again, off-again, should we be in pharmaceuticals or shouldn't we" vacillation.[130]

Even after the acquisition cleared the Federal Trade Commission, many worried about how well Du Pont would perform in the business. As one member of the Executive Committee wrote the company's president soon after the acquisition, "While we are eager to capitalize on our investment [in Endo], we must continue in the immediate future not to be too quick to 'DuPontize' Endo."[131] From the other side, some Endo researchers believed that Du Pont's executives and managers had little idea of the commitment necessary to bring a drug into being from research to marketing. They felt that Du Pont actually retarded their work.[132]

Some members of the Du Pont Company believed that Endo was too small an acquisition to achieve the objective of making Du Pont a major player in the pharmaceuticals industry.[133] Du Pont perhaps looked too hard for a bargain company rather than for a firm of major substance.[134] In the 1970s, Du Pont continued in vain to seek other acquisitions to enhance its pharmaceuticals business.[135] These criticisms notwithstanding, the Endo acquisition definitely gave Du Pont a small but substantial product line and a marketing organization, both of which it had lacked. On the research side, Du Pont probably got less than it had hoped for. Only after the acquisition had been made did Du Pont learn that the various research groups in Endo squabbled among themselves and were often very secretive.[136]

The Endo acquisition and growth in the agricultural chemicals business brought about a reorganization in Du Pont departments in 1972. The biological chemicals end of the Industrial and Biochemicals Department had developed sufficiently to warrant the creation of a separate Biochemicals Department with two main divisions, agricultural and pharmaceutical chemicals. The turbulent economy of this era, coupled with the lack of any effective mechanism within the corporation to articulate and implement a major new strategy, made it difficult for the new department to pursue research and development as aggressively as some members of the Executive Committee wished.[137]

Nevertheless, by the early 1970s, Du Pont had become a player in the pharmaceuticals industry after a long, frustrating, and unsuccessful effort going back at least to 1957. The irony is that Du Pont became a player only after making an acquisition, a strategy executives had rejected since at least 1933. Despite having produced only one relatively unimportant drug on its own – Symmetrel – Du Pont had made some headway. Its work on virology, done in both I&B and more especially in Central Research, was widely recognized, and it had actually led to Symmetrel.[138] After Du Pont placed similar efforts in other parts of the business and after the purchase of Endo, departmental managers hoped that other products would soon follow.

The human pharmaceuticals industry was a far tougher business to develop than agricultural chemicals. Unlike in agricultural chemicals, Du Pont's researchers did not make a major strike comparable to the substituted ureas, the uracils, or the sulfonylureas. Even if they had, Du Pont would still have lacked marketing capability, a capability that Du Pont had gained, at least in rudimentary form, in agricultural chemicals with its acquisition of Grasselli in 1928.

Perhaps because they were under the same general management, the research divisions of both Du Pont's agricultural chemicals business and its pharmaceuticals business failed to exercise leadership in the developing areas of recombinant DNA work and genetic engineering in the 1970s. Nevertheless, the mere fact that Du Pont did have a large, ongoing effort in both agricultural chemicals and pharmaceuticals made it easier for the Executive Committee to commit a very substantial sum of money to moving the company into the new life sciences research areas and to greatly expanding traditional research approaches. The chances of earning a return on this investment were thus far greater for these executives than for those in the 1950s who laid bets on the company's succeeding in pharmaceuticals in the absence of any marketing expertise.

21

Keeping Ahead of the Competition: Du Pont Plastics

World War II revolutionized the chemical industry by greatly accelerating the rate and extent of the displacement of natural substances by synthetic polymers. In the succeeding decades, these new petrochemically based substances would become the major growth area in the chemical industry. Polymers found uses as synthetic fibers, synthetic rubbers, plastics, films, coatings, adhesives, and other applications. To capitalize on these opportunities, oil companies integrated forward, plastics users integrated backward, and other companies diversified into the field. The race to exploit polymer technology generated intense competition in the industry. Chemists in laboratories around the world spent the 1950s synthesizing thousands of new polymers looking for candidates for commercialization. The economics of any new polymer depended on the cost of the necessary intermediate chemicals. For example, Du Pont's enormous production capacity for making nylon and Dacron intermediates prompted researchers to use these materials to make other products such as plastics and films. Additional economies of scale could be attained by building larger polymerization reactors. With every new polymer, development groups had to match plant capacity with the expected market. Driven by economies of scale, companies frequently built larger plants than existing markets could support. Polyethylene proved to be a classic example when numerous companies entered the business by building large plants in the late 1950s only to find insufficient outlets for the product.

Even in "commodity" plastics, competitive advantages could be gained because polymers are infinitely variable. Minor and inexpensive modifications of manufacturing processes can alter the polymer's properties significantly. Companies competed by offering processors a product that was specifically tailored to the customer's needs. To stay ahead in this game required efficient communication between the salespeople in the field and the researchers in the laboratory. This sometimes proved to be difficult for Du Pont because its departments were functionally organized with separate manufacturing, sales, and research divisions.

Du Pont was neither organizationally nor strategically oriented toward slugging it out in commodity-plastics markets. The company expected to develop profitable new products that had superior properties to the commodities. The source of these innovations would be, of course, Du Pont's broad and deep knowledge of polymers that had led to nylon. In the 1950s, Du Pont would develop Teflon, Delrin, and new polyethylene resins which fit the above criteria. Only one of these products, Teflon, was as successful as Du Pont had hoped. With the other two, proprietary positions proved impossible to attain, and competitors quickly entered these businesses, taking much of the profit out of them. Reacting to this situation, by the early 1960s Du Pont managers were directing their researchers to look for polymers of a new, higher level of sophistication to avoid highly competitive businesses. This new round of innovation uncovered many polymers with outstanding properties, but most of these specialty products to date found limited markets, in part because of high costs.

The Plastics Department and World War II

Because of Du Pont's intensive research in the field of polymers that began with Carothers's work, the company found itself in a good position to take advantage of the wartime boom and continued growth of polymer technology in the postwar era. In the decade following 1939, the production of plastics increased 600 percent, largely as the result of wartime necessity.[1] Du Pont benefited from this overall expansion but also witnessed the rise of competition from Union Carbide, Dow, and even oil companies. Organizationally, however, Du Pont was not so well prepared to meet the challenges of a new era. The Plastics Department specialized in celluloid plastics, already seventy years old by 1940, and had emphasized marketing much more than research.

The Executive Committee asked Plastics general manager Arnold Pitcher in 1937 to try to strengthen his research organization.[2] He increased his spending on research over the next four years, but the Executive Committee was still not satisfied. In 1941, in a rare instance of interference in the internal affairs of an industrial department, the committee passed a resolution calling "for a more ambitious and aggressive managerial and research policy in the plastic material industry." Stating the charge more explicitly, the committee maintained that "it is recognized that constant research and incessant effort to originate and perfect new and better plastic materials will be necessary to maintain and if possible improve the company's competitive position in this industry."[3]

The first thing that Pitcher did was to acquire a new research director, John Arthur Almquist, who was assistant chemical director of the Ammonia Department under Roger Williams. Two years later, Almquist became assistant general manager of the department and was replaced by John L. Brill, a Massachusetts Institute of Technology-trained chemical engineer and another longtime associate of Williams. These transfers brought people with a strong background in research and engineering into a department that lacked expertise in both areas. The department next started to put together an organization that could meet the challenge of the rapidly growing and expanding plastics field.[4]

On the eve of the United States's entry into World War II, Du Pont was investigating a number of interesting polymers. Through a complicated set of agreements with Union Carbide and the Shawinigan Corporation, Du Pont became a major producer of polyvinylbutyral resins, which became the interlayer for automotive safety glass in the late 1930s.[5] The Ammonia Department had discovered a new clear polymer of methyl methacrylate in 1931 while investigating uses for some of the compounds from its high-pressure research. Although Rohm and Haas discovered the same polymer earlier than Du Pont, and Imperial Chemical Industries held patents on the best process for making the monomer, Du Pont secured rights to participate in this business and began to sell its Lucite resins in 1937.[6] Researchers in the Chemical Department were working to develop nylon plastic, Teflon, and polyethylene and had prepared the first polyurethanes. The war would cause Du Pont to emphasize some of these products and ignore others.

On March 16, 1941, Edward R. Stettinius, Jr., who had been chairman of the board of U.S. Steel Corporation and who had recently been appointed by Franklin D. Roosevelt to be chairman of the priorities board of the Office of Production Management, stated that wherever possible plastics should be substituted for aluminum, brass, and other strategic materials.[7] The plastics industry had already begun to grow rapidly in the late 1930s, but World War II increased its rate of growth and, more important, led to the large-scale production of many new kinds of plastics. Most of these new materials had been produced before the war, but uncertainty about markets and unavailability of important intermediate compounds hindered their growth. For example, to produce nylon Du Pont had to make its own intermediates because they were not available commercially. Only a wealthy corporation such as Du Pont could risk putting money into the large-scale manufacture of new materials that the market might reject. Wartime contracts, however, assured plastics manufacturers of markets for their products, and the rapid development of petrochemical technology provided cheap raw materials. The war transformed some of the existing resins, such as polyvinyl chloride and polystyrene, from specialties into commodities. Du Pont left these products to other companies.[8]

Some Du Pont plastics benefited from the war. Du Pont's methyl methacrylate polymers found a large market in glazing in bombers and fighter planes. Throughout this period, Du Pont's output was approximately half that of Rohm and Haas, the other U. S. manufacturer.[9] Besides increasing the production of many plastics, World War II led to the commercialization of "exotic" plastics such as Teflon and polyethylene, which would become important products for Du Pont in the postwar era.

The Polychemicals Department

By 1945, Du Pont's managers realized that polymer-based technology was changing the structure of the chemical industry. The departmental organization that Du Pont had implemented in the 1920s, which had performed so well in the 1930s, appeared to be inadequate to meet the challenges of the late 1940s. The wide variety of skills and technical expertise needed to produce polymeric products made it increasingly difficult for Du Pont to achieve the major goal of the 1921 reorganization, to give each general manager complete responsibility for his business.

Lucite plastic provides one example of how polymer technology had diffused responsibility. The Ammonia Department had developed Lucite in the 1930s because it was originally derived from high-pressure processes that were the core of the department's technology. However, the Ammonia Department knew nothing about marketing plastics to the numerous small fabricators that dominated the industry. Ammonia sold bulk chemicals, whereas Plastics sold specialty products. For this reason, the Executive Committee decided that Lucite should be marketed by Plastics because it knew the industry. Between the manufacture of the monomer and the selling of plastic resin or sheet, however, was the polymerization process. In this case, the Executive Committee ruled that because polymerization had a critical impact on the properties of the final product, Plastics should also take over this part of the operation.[10] In effect, Ammonia "sold" methyl methacrylate monomer to Plastics at an internally determined transfer price. Thus, the general manager of Plastics had full responsibility for the profitability of Du Pont's Lucite products but did not have control over the process of making or the cost of his intermediates. Nylon provides a more dramatic example of this same phenomenon.

After struggling for fifteen years with complex and expensive technology and low prices for its commodity chemicals, the Ammonia Department discovered a gold mine in supplying nylon intermediates to the Rayon Department. Because these chemicals were not available commercially outside Du Pont, a transfer price was determined within the company. Generally, the Ammonia Department management succeeded in negotiating prices that yielded a handsome return on its investment. In 1948, nylon intermediates accounted for over half the department's earnings and a third of its sales.[11]

To create a department with strong research, manufacturing, and sales, President Greenewalt merged the Ammonia and Plastics departments. This was a controversial move and one that had a major impact on Du Pont's ability to keep pace in the rapidly expanding plastics business. In merging these two departments, Greenewalt was following the organizational principles laid down by the previous generation of Du Pont executives. He wanted to create a strong department in the field of plastics and to place the entire responsibility for success on one management. The Ammonia Department had strengths in research and manufacturing; the Plastics Department knew the marketing side of the business.[12]

Interestingly, Walter Carpenter, chairman of the board, opposed the merger for several reasons. First, he argued that with the shifting foundation of the chemical industry, it was impossible to concentrate Du Pont's polymer-based technology in one department. He pointed out that the new department would manufacture polyethylene, which would probably find its major outlets in packaging film, the territory of the newly created Film Department.[13] A more glaring defect in the proposal was that the new department's most profitable and fastest growing business would be supplying the Rayon Department with nylon intermediates. This was the type of business the Ammonia Department's management preferred, not selling hundreds of different products to an even greater number of customers. Carpenter pointed out that the difference in management philosophies of the two departments could cause problems, particularly because the "merger" really would be a takeover by the Ammonia Department, the management of which was not comfortable with and knowledgeable about the plastics business. (As discussed later in the chapter, the Ammonia Department's management philosophy led to one major fiasco after the merger.)

Carpenter's biggest concern was that the plastics field was too big for any one department to handle. He believed that if Du Pont maintained the separate Plastics Department, it would encourage all the other departments of the company to continue research on plastics. Carpenter argued that "we should expect to get as many, if not more, promising polymers for the Plastics field out of all the other departments of the company, than we could secure through one Ammonia Department." Finally, he pointed out that the Ammonia Department had a large business in high-pressure products that had nothing to do with polymers, and that the merger would lead to the neglect of these products. On the whole, Carpenter thought the disadvantages of the merger outweighed its advantages.[14]

Greenewalt rejected Carpenter's idea of the Plastics Department as the sales agent for all the plastics developed by other departments in favor of continuing the established policy of a decentralized organizational structure in which each department sold the products that it made. In this era when the general managers of the various departments were known as barons who ruled their respective domains with near total authority, most new products probably would have been developed by the department that made the initial discovery, instead of turning them over to the Plastics Department. The Executive Committee acknowledged that polymer-based technology was becoming increasingly central to the chemical industry but felt that the company's structure after the merger would be adequate to exploit the field successfully.

Greenewalt went ahead with the merger of the two departments, which was essentially a takeover of the Plastics Department by the much larger Ammonia Department because its key personnel assumed the major managerial positions in the new department.[15] The consolidation occurred on Oct. 1, 1949, the day that Plastics general manager Arnold E. Pitcher, who had joined the old Arlington Company as a salesman in 1910, retired. Appropriately, he was replaced by Emil D. Ries, an MIT PhD chemical engineer who had joined the Ammonia Department in 1930 and had become its general manager in 1948.[16]

The Polychemicals Department manufactured and sold three very different product groups: chemicals made by high-pressure technology (including ammonia, methanol, and ethylene glycol antifreeze), nylon intermediates, and plastics. At the time of consolidation, the first group accounted for half of the new department's sales with the remainder divided between the other two. During the 1950s, the Polychemicals research organization made important contributions in the fields of nylon intermediates and plastics while providing essential technical service and market-oriented research for the older products. A decade after the merger, the department's investment was evenly divided among the three product groups, but the chemicals group provided only 23 percent of sales and 15 percent of earnings. Although the department's plastics sales and earnings tripled in the 1950s, transfers of nylon intermediates to the Textile Fibers Department generated about two-thirds of total earnings for the period. Therefore, the merger of Ammonia and Plastics did not create a department entirely focused on plastics.[17]

The split personality of the department had an impact on its research programs and strategies for innovation. Research to improve the yield or efficiency of the processes for making nylon intermediates generated large returns because any technical improvements would be instantly translated into cost savings. The only risks in this kind of research were those associated with accomplishing the technical goals; competitive products and market factors did not have to be considered. In plastics R&D, however, not only did difficult production problems have to be overcome, but of equal or perhaps greater concern was whether Du Pont could establish a proprietary position for the product, how much competition the new product would receive from existing plastics, and in what markets the new product could be used. These complicating factors made innovation in plastics much more difficult than in nylon intermediates, and it seems reasonable that this situation may have caused the department's management to take a cautious approach to the rapidly expanding plastics business in contrast to more aggressive competitors.

Ries's job was indeed a challenging one after he assumed the leadership of the Polychemicals Department. One of his most important tasks was to put together an effective R&D organization. The research division of the Polychemicals Department was directed by the team of John S. Beekley and Frank C. McGrew for most of the 1950s. Beekley, a pioneer in Du Pont's ammonia venture, joined the company in 1924 after receiving his PhD from

Princeton University and spent the next several years developing Du Pont's innovative process for converting methane to hydrogen. He succeeded Roger Williams as research director in 1942 and at the time of the merger became the head of the new Polychemicals research division. Beekley's gentle, fatherly style of management contrasted with the intense, intellectual demeanor of his new assistant, McGrew, who joined the Polychemicals Department in 1950. The former Adams student at the University of Illinois had been a member of the Chemical Department since 1937. As discussed in Chapter 17, McGrew brought to Polychemicals a strong emphasis on scientific understanding as a key component of industrial research.[18]

At this time, Du Pont's plastics business represented more of a promise than a reality. Plastics accounted for only $38 million of the company's nearly $1 billion annual sales.[19] The department had a group of relatively new plastics, nylon resins, methacrylates, polyethylene, and Teflon, from which it expected to prosper in the coming years. Sales of Zytel polyamide resins (nylon plastics) grew rapidly after Du Pont installed enough intermediates production capacity to satisfy the textile fiber market, leaping from $2.6 million in 1949 to $24.5 million in 1951, but additional growth came slowly.[20] The high cost of nylon resin, primarily the result of its expensive intermediates and Du Pont's pricing policy, limited its use. One of the first "engineering" or high-performance plastics, nylon replaced metals in many applications in the textile, automotive, and appliance fields.[21]

In methacrylates, Du Pont's Lucite encountered stiff competition from Rohm and Haas's Plexiglas in the postwar period. During the wartime boom, Rohm and Haas had invested so much capital in acrylic polymers that its future depended on its ability to find new markets in a peacetime economy. For example, the Philadelphia firm developed acrylic polymers for multi-viscosity motor oils. With its large plant running near capacity, Rohm and Haas produced acrylic monomer and polymers at much lower cost than Du Pont could achieve. Rohm and Haas set prices low enough that Du Pont could not make any money at all. Throughout the 1950s, Lucite did not generate any significant earnings for Du Pont.[22] For the Polychemicals Department, Lucite was just one plastic among many. It tried to convince other departments to develop new acrylic products, but these departments had their own research agendas.

Polyethylene

This first 1-billion-pound-per-year plastic in the late 1950s was not produced commercially in the United States until 1942. Du Pont had the inside track with polyethylene yet by the end of the war had yielded its position of leadership to Union Carbide. The polymer had been discovered by ICI in 1933, but the lack of a viable production process and any particular markets delayed its commercialization until 1940. ICI had first informed Du Pont about polyethylene in 1935, but Du Pont did little work on it because the British chemists had not devised a process for making it on a large scale. The biggest obstacles were the high pressure needed to polymerize the ethylene and an inability to control the reaction. Du Pont's Chemical Department began a systematic study of high-pressure reactions in 1936 and by 1940 had developed an improved process for making polyethylene. By this latter date the British had determined that polyethylene was an excellent insulation material for the high-frequency electrical cables used in radar.[23] The Ammonia Department then picked up the project and built a small semiworks the following year.[24] After a conference with officials of the army and navy in February 1942, Du Pont began to build a 50-ton-per-year pilot plant and to design a 500-ton-per-year commercial plant. The Ammonia Department completed the pilot plant in December 1942 and started up the larger plant in March 1943.[25]

Union Carbide approached Du Pont in October 1942 about sublicenses of the ICI patents. Du Pont was willing to offer a license only for the duration of the war, but Carbide would not agree to this time limitation. While Carbide was negotiating this issue, it signed a contract with the navy to manufacture polyethylene and began construction of a 500-ton-per-year plant. Ignoring the patents, Carbide started selling a product that had several advantages over that produced by Du Pont.[26] By the end of the war, Du Pont's production had risen to 750 tons per year, whereas Carbide had increased its capacity to nearly six times that of Du Pont.[27]

The new Polychemicals Department faced the challenge of keeping pace with Union Carbide in the rapidly expanding polyethylene business. This versatile material was finding increasing use in all segments of the plastics market, including film, coated paper, molded and extruded articles, insulated wire and cable, blown bottles, and pipe. Between 1948 and 1953, the two U.S. producers increased their production by nearly 50 percent a year. In the next few years, seven new producers entered the field after Judge Sylvester J. Ryan ordered Du Pont and ICI to license their shared polyethylene patents to all comers on a reasonable basis. Ryan's decree was part of the final decision in the Du Pont-ICI antitrust case. For the remainder of the decade, polyethylene production continued to grow at 40 percent a year, with Union Carbide and Du Pont maintaining approximately a third and a fifth of the market, respectively. The highly competitive nature of this business, however, kept profits low for even the largest producers.[28]

Like most polymeric materials, polyethylene was not one product but many, because varying the synthesis conditions altered the molecular structure and properties of resulting polymer. Thus, each manufacturer sold many different types of polyethylene for different uses. One of the major shortcomings of Du Pont's process, which relied on a tubular reactor, was that it was difficult to convert from making one kind of polyethylene to another. The company had built two large tubular reactors scaled up from a wartime semicommercial unit. In 1951, the Polychemicals Department planned a major expansion of its polyethylene capacity but was not satisfied with the high-cost and low-quality resins produced in the tubular reactors. Du Pont knew that the autoclave-type reactors used by ICI produced a cheaper and more uniform product but had the serious disadvantage of exploding at frequent intervals. Researchers in the Polychemicals Department were thus given the jobs of building a much larger reactor than ICI had ever built and of eliminating the hazard of explosions. This task they accomplished successfully. The new reactor allowed Du Pont to produce better grades of polyethylene than it previously had made.[29]

In late 1953, the department management decided that it had one grade of resin that was so good it could displace all others. Accordingly, Ries decided to withdraw the numerous Du Pont polyethylenes from the market and offer only one superior type. The top management of the department was still dominated by Ammonia Department men who were accustomed to the manufacture and sale of large-volume chemicals, not whole families of resins. Unfortunately for Du Pont, plastics consumers refused to go along with this new approach. Because this new resin behaved differently than standard ones in processing and failed to demonstrate superior qualities in all uses, Du Pont lost business rapidly. This decision had to be reversed after five months, and Du Pont again began to sell an entire line of resins.[30]

In 1956, the new general manager of Polychemicals, Robert L. Hershey (Ries had retired), summarized the company's position in this important field. He stated that primarily through the development of high quality resins, Du Pont was recognized as one of the leaders in polyethylene, which had such a broad range of properties that it "had opened market outlets more diverse and of greater potential than any other plastic." Although Du Pont preferred not to manufacture high-volume and usually low-price plastics – all the other polyethylene producers also made other commodity plastics – Hershey argued that polyethylene provided an entrée for Du Pont into all kinds of more lucrative specialty markets for polyethylene and other plastics. In this highly competitive but expanding business, he contended that Du Pont should have the moderate goal of getting a fair share of the profits to be made.[31]

Teflon

Whereas polyethylene symbolized the new competitive era in the plastics business, Teflon polytetrafluoroethylene (PTFE) fits more closely with the prewar examples of neoprene and nylon. Roy Plunkett had discovered Teflon at the Jackson Laboratory in 1938, but for the next three years Du Pont did very little with the new and unusual material because no satisfactory processes existed for the preparation of tetrafluoroethylene monomer or its polymerization. When sufficient monomer became available, Robert M. Joyce, a young Illinois PhD in the Chemical Department, began experiments that led to the effective control of the rapid and explosive polymerization of tetrafluoroethylene gas to solid polymer. An early test sample performed successfully as a gasket in a nitric acid plant. Soon, the Arlington semiworks was making large quantities for use as nose cones on artillery-shell proximity fuses, but the major impetus for the further development of Teflon came from the Manhattan Project.[32] To produce uranium-235 by the gaseous diffusion method, the scientists and engineers at Oak Ridge needed materials that could withstand extremely corrosive environments. As had been done with other critical problems, such as the development of synthetic rubber, the government authorized a cooperative research program in fluorine chemistry, which had prompted Du Pont to intensify its efforts with Teflon and other related compounds.[33] By 1944, the company was selling Teflon to the military. In 1949, Du Pont authorized a 1-million-pound-per-year plant, but because of continuing difficulties in the production and fabrication of the unusual material, the commercial growth of Teflon proceeded slowly until the mid-1950s.[34]

Teflon was as novel a substance in the 1950s as synthetic rubber and fibers had been in the 1930s. As with these earlier innovations, Du Pont had secured a strong proprietary position, so the company could develop and commercialize Teflon without paying much attention to competitors' activities. An unusual polymer, Teflon posed many challenges and presented many opportunities for the Polychemicals research division. The monomer, which was manufactured by the Organic Chemicals Department from one of their Freon compounds, was expensive to make because of the process employed and the fact that the product by weight was three-quarters fluorine, a relatively expensive element. By 1950, several methods of polymerization had been developed from earlier studies in the Chemical Department, but the properties of the polymer produced varied significantly from batch to batch.[35]

Polychem researchers studied the intractable Teflon molecules. The same properties that made Teflon attractive also made it very difficult to study scientifically or to fabricate into useful objects. It has outstanding thermal stability and could be used at much higher temperatures than other plastics of the 1950s. However, Teflon, even at very high temperatures, does not melt so it cannot be molded like other plastics. It is unaffected by most acids, bases, and solvents, so products cannot be formed by dissolving the polymer and then evaporating the solvent. Finally, Teflon is one of the slipperiest substances known, making it very difficult to bond to any other surface. Only Teflon's outstanding properties as an electrical insulating material did not present an accompanying processing difficulty.[36]

Because of its unusual properties and its high cost, Teflon would remain a relatively low-volume polymer for Du Pont. By 1960, production was still less than 10 million pounds per year, and sales were $28 million. But Teflon has been a very profitable product for Du Pont. In the quarter-century following the end of World War II, Teflon earned for Du Pont the same amount of money that the much-higher-volume polyethylene did and yielded a 23 percent pretax ROI, over three times that of polyethylene.[37] Certainly, Du Pont's proprietary position accounted for some of the success of Teflon; it gave the company the incentive to invest the considerable resources necessary to transform this chemical curiosity into a useful product.

In the 1940s, researchers in the Chemical and Plastics departments worked out the basic technologies for polymerizing and fabricating Teflon. The Chemical Department had invented a polymerization process that produced a white fluffy powder called granular polymer that could be fabricated using the techniques of powder metallurgy such as pressing followed by sintering. At the Plastics Department's Arlington works, researchers learned how to apply these techniques to the preparation of shapes such as sheets, rods, and tubes. Such fabrication methods involved compressing Teflon powder into the desired shape and sintering the product at very high temperatures to fuse the particles together into a solid. This work had proceeded on a primarily empirical level.[38] In 1954, the manager of the research division handling Teflon began a meeting by saying, "I must admit that any one of you could ask an embarrassingly long list of questions about the why's of Teflon's performance which we cannot answer completely."[39]

If Du Pont, with its well-equipped and -staffed laboratories, was having trouble coping with Teflon, one can imagine the kinds of problems encountered by small fabricators. In the fall of 1953, a manager from the sales division addressed the Teflon research group on the subject of the problems that customers were having using Teflon. He stated that fabricators had no guidelines to follow for determining the suitability of Teflon for various applications and ended with a plea for intensive activity to establish better product specifications and better means of communicating research results to customers. The research division responded by sending some of its research staff to visit a few of Du Pont's larger customers, a radical departure from standard practice. At the same time, representatives from research, manufacturing, and sales divisions began to meet informally to coordinate their activities. Later this effort would become more formal.[40]

Although Teflon gave the manufacturing and sales divisions numerous headaches, the research division remained optimistic about its commercial potential. Among many other Du Pont researchers, Wilbert L. Gore held an unshakable faith in Teflon's future. In 1953, Gore, then a research supervisor, was already displaying the confidence and optimism that later would make him a successful entrepreneur. In a memorandum to his supervisor, Gore proposed an intensive crash program to solve the fabrication problems with Teflon. He argued that it "may be the most profitable product our department can exploit" and that "its uniqueness makes the penetration of Teflon into large markets surprisingly independent of price...."[41] Gore believed that his proposal could lead to a market of 80 million pounds at the existing price level. At this time, Du Pont was selling less than 2 million pounds per year. Gore did not get his task force, probably because the

Research Division had just established a fifty-man task force to develop another new polymer.

Gore soon became intimately involved in this other project but continued to experiment with Teflon at home in a small basement workshop. His work centered on extruding Teflon paste around a wire, until one day his son Robert, a junior chemical engineering major at the University of Delaware, suggested making a ribbon cable by putting the wire between two films of Teflon, pressing the films together, and then sintering to solidify the bond between the films. After giving his son all the theoretical reasons why this would not work, Gore tried it anyway and it worked. When Gore presented his invention to Beekley, the research director replied that some of Du Pont's customers might be interested in it but not Du Pont because the company had determined not to integrate forward where it would bring Du Pont into competition with its customers. With the approval of Du Pont, Gore resigned in 1958 to exploit his invention. He probably knew more about Teflon fabrication than any of the other processors. His intimate familiarity with this unique material allowed him to create a profitable business in insulated wire and cable which found increasing use in the electronics and aircraft industries.[42] Gore's growing business consumed considerable quantities of Teflon but not enough to increase the total demand significantly.

In the early to mid-1950s, the Teflon enthusiasts in the research division could not understand why a product with such tremendous potential was having so much trouble finding markets. To answer this question, the department hired McKinsey & Company to assess the situation as well as that of Polychem's other plastics. The conclusion of the study was that Du Pont's plastics salesmen were doing a poor job selling Teflon because it was so different from the other lines they sold. It could not be fabricated with the molding equipment their customers had, and many of its prospective users were not plastics fabricators. To solve these problems, the consultants recommended setting up a separate Teflon marketing organization with a strong technical component. The salesmen would then be able to bring their customers' problems back to Du Pont, where prompt action could be taken.[43] After Du Pont acted on these recommendations, sales of Teflon trebled between 1954 and 1960.[44] Sales continued to grow in the 1960s, helped by introduction of Teflon-coated cookware in 1961.

Although Teflon has many important electrical and chemical uses, it is best known to the general public as the nonstick coating on cookware. Du Pont commercialized its Teflon dispersions for coatings in 1951 but did not sell its product for cookware for another decade, even though it had done successful experiments with waffle irons. Du Pont did not go ahead because Teflon, when heated to very high temperatures (600° to 700° F), gives off noxious fumes that cause temporary flu-like symptoms. Du Pont's management was generally reluctant to sell products to consumers, especially if their misuse of that product might lead to injuries and lawsuits brought against the company. Polychem's management accepted this po-

sition until Teflon-coated omelet pans imported from France were enthusiastically received in the United States. After doing some studies of its own
to back up French studies and watching the development of markets in
Europe, Du Pont decided in 1961 to allow its resin to be used for cooking
ware. Teflon-coated cookware became a market success, and the anticipated
problems with fumes never occurred in household use.[45]

It took Du Pont fifteen years to turn Plunkett's fortuitous discovery into
a successful commercial product. Teflon was neither easy nor cheap to make
or use. With its outstanding scientific and technical capabilities, the Polychemicals Research Division eventually learned how to tame this unique
substance. The entirely new fabrication techniques required that Du Pont
have unusually close coordination between research, manufacturing, and
sales. In the case of Teflon, special arrangements were made to ensure that
there were no organizational or bureaucratic obstacles standing in the way.
In many respects, this decentralization of the management of Teflon mir-
rored the earlier decentralization of the Du Pont Company in 1921. As the
product lines of the company became more complex, several departments
divided their businesses into product divisions (or profit centers), hoping to
concentrate responsibility for success or failure as well as to focus energies
on the particular problems of a given business.

At the same time that it was developing Teflon, Polychemicals research
also investigated other fluorocarbon polymers. In the early 1940s, chemists
in the Chemical Department had prepared many different copolymers of
tetrafluoroethylene (TFE) and other compounds. The goals of these studies
were to uncover novel materials and, perhaps more important, to discover
a copolymer that could be processed like any other plastic while retaining
the excellent properties of Teflon. Du Pont eventually commercialized many
of these copolymers and developed several more in the 1960s and 1970s.[46]
Teflon opened up the whole field of fluorocarbon polymers for Du Pont.

Delrin

By 1956, *Fortune* magazine noted, the plastics trade was "puzzled by Polychem's failure to produce important news during its first seven years of
activity."[47] Soon, however, Du Pont would explain the reason for the long
silence: Since late 1952, the Polychemicals research division had been concentrating its energies on the development of a new plastic, a formaldehyde
polymer that the company named Delrin acetal resin. Called "synthetic
stone" by Frank McGrew, this new material was a tough, rigid solid that
Du Pont hoped would displace nonferrous metals, such as brass and aluminum, in many applications.[48] Although not having any single outstanding
property, Delrin had a combination of properties that made it appear suitable for a wide range of uses, and it was made from a cheap raw material.

Polyformaldehyde first came to the attention of Polychem's management in early 1950 when it asked the Chemical Department about new polymers that were candidates to become plastics. Formaldehyde polymers were the last item on the list, even though the Chemical Department had done some work with them.[49] They had been made by many researchers including polymer science pioneer Hermann Staudinger as part of his 1920s studies of polymer structure. These polymers were useless, however, because at relatively low temperatures they would revert to formaldehyde. In 1948, the Chemical Department initiated research to prepare very pure formaldehyde, a difficult task because it is so reactive; it forms compounds with water or even itself. During this study, the chemist involved discovered that the purified monomer would spontaneously polymerize to solids with good strength, resilience, and better thermal stability than those prepared by earlier researchers. Still, these new polymers were too brittle and thermally unstable for commercial use. Having pursued all the existing leads on the subject, the Chemical Department halted the project in the spring of 1949, only to start it up again after Polychem approved and funded a new project.[50]

The Chemical Department assigned Robert N. McDonald, a thirty-three-year-old Yale University PhD, to the project. Over the next year or two, his work would lead Polychem to decide that the new polymer, in spite of its deficiencies, had considerable commercial potential. McDonald's polymers had properties similar to nylon plastics and were the most thermally stable formaldehyde ones yet produced. Encouraged by these results, Polychem assigned four chemists to investigate polyformaldehyde.[51] At this point, however, Du Pont was far away from having either a commercial process or product.

According to the account later given to *Fortune*, Executive Committee member Roger Williams intervened in 1952 on behalf of Delrin. As advisor on research, Williams periodically reviewed the research programs under way at Du Pont. At one such meeting with Polychem, after hearing a summary of the half-dozen new polymers being investigated by the research division, Williams suggested that it "quit monkeying around with a lot of things" and concentrate on Delrin for six months with the goal of achieving a technical breakthrough. If these efforts failed, then the project would be dropped in favor of another candidate.[52] In this era, Executive Committee members did not give orders to the industrial departments, but because Williams was an old Ammonia man the Polychem management probably attached more weight to his counsel than others'. Following his suggestion, a task force was immediately formed.

In September 1952, Polychem increased its R & D staff on the Delrin program from six to fifty. The Task Force attacked all the phases of the development simultaneously. Groups went to work to characterize both the product and process for making it, while members of the sales division began to formulate plans for marketing the new product.[53] Before any of these groups could make any real progress, however, one critical problem remained to be solved: Delrin was still too thermally unstable to be molded in commercial equipment.

Three months into the task force campaign, its leader Francis B. Vaughan, a forty-one-year-old MIT chemical engineering graduate who had worked in the Ammonia Department and on the Manhattan Project, wrote to Research Director Beekley that without a stable polymer, "we can make no claim as to being on schedule."[54] However, the researchers had discovered that the internal bonds of the polymer were stable and that decomposition began at the ends of chains. These results prompted the researchers to try attaching a different kind of molecule or "cap" on the ends of the polymer chains to stop the initiation of decomposition. Three months after Vaughan's report, McGrew informed Beekley that capped polymer showed a marked increase in stability so that the polymer-processing and product studies could begin to move forward.[55]

Now the task force shifted into high gear. Chemists and physicists began to study the polymer to produce the scientific information needed to set standards at every point in the production process. Other chemists worked on methods of preparing purer formaldehyde monomer. They explored two routes, the original one that McDonald had employed and a new one developed in Polychem. Next, the details of the polymerization and capping operations had to be worked out. Even before the final process elements had been decided upon, engineers began studies to design the commercial plant. At the same time, work began on a semiworks at the Belle plant primarily for the purpose of providing polymer for product development. And finally, the task force had to determine what kind of plastic Delrin would be and what markets it could serve.[56] This latter problem proved to be critical for deciding the pace and extent of the entire development effort.

Early in the task force's history, Parke Woodworth of the new product development section tried to characterize Delrin. He saw its primary strengths as low cost, stiffness, and toughness. In order to find uses rapidly, he believed that emphasis should be placed on replacing existing plastics, which would be faster and easier than supplanting other materials. Unfortunately for Du Pont, the principal plastic Delrin appeared to compete with seemed to be Zytel nylon resins.[57] Expected to be a low-price, high-volume plastic, Delrin became known as the "poor man's nylon."[58]

Within a year, however, the task force was forced to redefine the product. Primarily because of the high cost of purifying formaldehyde, Delrin would be more expensive than previously believed. To bring the price down to a reasonable level, a large plant producing about 30 million pounds a year would have to be built. To achieve this volume of sales quickly and avoid a long period of high-cost manufacture, Delrin would have to grow at a higher rate than any other plastic in history. With these problems in mind, the task force arrived at a new conception of the product. Delrin would be "a premium-priced plastic product aimed at markets that cannot be served by plastics other than nylon and hopefully not even that."[59] This proved to be a remarkably accurate description of Delrin because it eventually did find markets primarily as a replacement for metals and did not affect the growth of nylon plastics. Although the task force had made the right assessment, it did not gain much credence.

Worried about the ability of a higher-cost polymer to find markets and about potential competition from other new plastics, Vaughan observed that "the worth of the enterprise was . . . severely questioned." Accordingly, the sales division requested in August 1954 that the decision for commercialization be delayed for at least nine months while it conducted market surveys. This relaxation of the timetable was welcomed by Clement Hamblet, a process engineering expert who replaced Vaughan as the task force leader because of the extremely difficult process problems encountered with Delrin. Besides this important work, the delay also allowed Hamblet to test another potentially fatal concern about the process, that it could not be operated on a large scale. He wanted to see if the 50,000-pound-per-year semiworks could produce Delrin of consistently good quality.[60]

While the Belle operators were struggling to solve the demanding analytical and control problems of the semiworks, the chemists at the Experimental Station made two important improvements to the process. One was a simpler method of preparing very pure formaldehyde; the other was an easier method for capping the polymer chains. But the cost of Delrin still appeared to be so high that commercialization would be risky. As one observer put it: "If the cost is low enough, a very general picture of uses is sufficient; and likewise if the knowledge of usefulness of the product is sufficiently detailed to show a good potential in price insensitive uses, then one does not need the ultimate in processing economy to make a start."[61] Because significant cost reductions were not forthcoming, Du Pont had to rely on this latter approach.

Gore, at that time still a senior supervisor in the staff section of the Polychem research division (a group that did engineering studies and cost estimates for new or competitive plastics), developed a novel technique for determining the market potential for Delrin. Assisted by Robert E. Gee and for one summer a whole group of college students, Gore studied a large number of specific applications for Delrin, primarily in nonferrous metal areas. For each use, he estimated the cost to manufacture the existing product and compared that to the cost of a Delrin equivalent. As long as the Delrin part was cheaper, then manufacturers would have an incentive to switch. The first forty-four items that Gore and Gee studied showed that at sixty cents per pound, then considered a relatively high price, Delrin could find markets of nearly 40 million pounds per year just in this number of applications. A more complete study raised the total to 143 million pounds, with automobile parts accounting for a third of this volume, and estimated a total use potential of approximately 1 billion pounds a year. They concluded that their study, "though not complete, has uncovered enough high value applications for Delrin so that (together with the cost estimates in hand) a commercial undertaking of large magnitude can now be prepared." Although this study did not serve as an accurate market forecast, its optimistic conclusion encouraged Polychem's management to go ahead with the Delrin program.[62]

Earliest possible commercialization now became the major focus of the task force, which was placed under the direction of William Henry Linton, an MIT PhD chemical engineer. No longer would the team look for new process steps but instead would polish the ones that showed the most promise. The major issue then became how much capacity Du Pont would install. In late 1955, Polychem asked the Engineering Department to calculate investment and operating costs for plants with a capacity of 2, 20, and 40 million pounds.[63] Soon, Linton abandoned the idea of building a 2-million-pound semicommercial plant because it would be expensive to build, would quickly be obsolete, and was probably unnecessary. The sophisticated analytical techniques used in the laboratory and projected for use in the plant made surprises in larger-scale equipment less likely and therefore obviated the need for a pilot plant. (The smaller Belle semiworks did not consist of the same process elements that would be used in the commercial plant and was used mainly to provide material for market evaluation.[64]) After considerable agonizing, Polychem decided to build a 20-million-pound-per-year plant that could be expanded to 40 million pounds per year.

The Polychem management worried about the Executive Committee's response to an appropriation request for such a risky venture. The size and cost of the initial plant were abnormally large, the product had no "outstandingly unique characteristics," and an unprecedented rate of sales growth was required to make the venture profitable in a reasonable amount of time. But in this era the Executive Committee rarely said no to general managers. On November 2, 1956, a few days after the basic Delrin patent was issued, the Executive Committee authorized Polychem to begin designing the plant. A year later, the committee authorized construction of the plant, which went into commercial operation in January 1960.[65]

Delrin had been commercialized in only seven years, but because of the intensity of its development the price had been high. It had been the most expensive R&D effort in the company's history; the total cost was $50 million, 60 percent for R&D and 40 percent for the plant. Included in these figures were $4 million for sales development work and $5 million for the start-up of the plant.[66] It is not possible to separate any inefficiencies caused by the task force approach from the costs resulting from the inherent difficulties in producing Delrin. It appears that the task force, because it frequently pursued several parallel lines of development, spent considerably more money than if a slower and smaller development effort had been mounted. No one would have worried about Delrin's high development cost, however, had it begun to generate profits immediately.

The year 1960 was a bad one for Du Pont's plastics business in general and for Delrin in particular. The new plastic lost $8.8 million because with the large plant running at 15 percent of capacity, Du Pont's cost was about $4.00 per pound while the selling price was set at $0.85 per pound. The following year saw sales increase to 6.8 million pounds sold at $0.65 per pound, resulting in another $8 million loss.[67] But with production increasing rapidly, Du Pont expected Delrin to be solidly in the black within a few years. These expectations were doused when a competitor announced its formaldehyde polymer.

Upon learning that Celanese planned to produce a product similar to Delrin, Du Pont filed suit in April 1961 charging that Celanese was infringing on its 1956 McDonald patent. Celanese countered that its product, Celcon, did not fall under the claims of the McDonald patent because it was made from trioxane, a cyclic compound made from three molecules of formaldehyde and had a small percentage of a second ingredient making it a copolymer. Countering these arguments, Du Pont maintained that its patent covered all formaldehyde-based polymers with certain characteristics, particularly thermal stability, independent of the monomer used or incorporation of a small amount of another compound. Celanese vowed to fight Du Pont and continued to develop Celcon.[68]

Soon Du Pont learned that not only did it have a competitor, but that Celcon was easier to process than Delrin and had better thermal stability. To make matters even worse, an outside patent firm hired to present the case in court concluded that Du Pont's patent was flawed.[69] In 1963, after receiving this discouraging news, Du Pont dropped the suit against Celanese and had to share the rapidly growing market with its competitor.[70]

In the 1960s, the market for acetal resins grew at the rate of 25 percent a year, while Delrin grew at a lower rate of 20 percent. The difference in the two growth rates reflected Celcon's increasing market share. Eventually, it captured about half the market.[71] These sales, which were lost to Du Pont, had a large impact on the financial fortunes of Delrin. Without Celcon, Du Pont could have paid off much more rapidly its R&D and early operating debts and begun to generate profits. Polychem had based all its plans on having a strong proprietary position, but in an era of intense competition in the chemical industry, this proved impossible to achieve. Delrin was a magnificent technical achievement and eventually became a commercial success, but the early emergence of competition prevented it from being a highly profitable product.

Linear Polyethylene and Polypropylene

Even though Delrin represented the largest R&D program of the Polychemicals Department in the mid-1950s, another line of research led to results that had far-reaching scientific, technological, and commercial importance.

The discovery of organo-metallic catalysts that produced a new type of polyethylene consisting of essentially linear chains and high-molecular-weight polymers of propylene, which had heretofore been unattainable, won a Nobel Prize and created important new synthetic polymers.[72] Remarkably, this discovery occurred almost simultaneously in several laboratories in the United States and Europe. In the ensuing struggle for scientific acclaim and commercial markets, Du Pont was not as successful as some of its competitors.

At the beginning of 1954, the exploratory research section, a group of about ten men, began to investigate polymers that would be stiffer than polyethylene. As its name suggests, this small group did scouting work looking for new polymers that might have some commercial potential. The chemist in charge of the group, W. Frank Gresham, was a legendary research director at Du Pont, who in his thirty-six years with the company held 136 patents alone or jointly. After receiving his PhD from Harvard University in 1936, Gresham joined the Ammonia Department and became manager of exploratory research after the merger in 1950.[73] Although a soft-spoken Alabama gentleman, Gresham earned the reputation as a demanding boss and a brilliant chemist. In 1953, Arthur W. Anderson, an Illinois PhD who had joined the old Plastics Department in 1941, transferred into Gresham's group. Anderson was known as a brash, outspoken, and confident chemist. He and Gresham made an effective team, even though Anderson recalls that they often fought like cats and dogs over chemistry.[74] It would not take very long until this collaboration led to some exciting new chemistry.

Addressing the stiffness issue, Anderson suggested that limp polyethylene might be stiffened by copolymerizing it with a large molecule that would create bulky pendants on the polymer chain, thus decreasing its flexibility. The chemist assigned to the task, Nicholas G. Merckling, did the standard literature search and noted a German patent assigned to BASF on the basis of experiments made in 1943. The German chemist, Max Fischer, had modified a well-known catalyst for polymerizing ethylene to low-molecular-weight liquids and produced a mixture of liquid and solid. The fact that the catalyst, a mixture of titanium tetrachloride, aluminum chloride, and aluminum powder, had given some solid led Merckling to try it. After several experiments, Merckling (at the suggestion of his supervisor, Ivan Maxwell Robinson) did an experiment with ethylene only and obtained a sample of a different type of polyethylene.[75] This was a particularly exciting discovery because Du Pont had already made this "linear polyethylene" by another method.

In the late 1940s, while studying the effects of extremely high pressure on polymerization reactions, two researchers in the Chemical Department prepared a new kind of polyethylene that was different enough from the normal type that it could be considered an entirely new material because of its increased stiffness, toughness, and strength. Research on this new polymer showed that unlike the highly branched chains that resulted from the commercial process, these polymers showed little branching and were essentially linear. The difference in properties resulted from the ability of the linear chains to fold and pack more tightly together than the highly branched chains. Although these results were interesting, Du Pont did nothing with the new material because the pressure needed to make it greatly exceeded the limits of commercial feasibility.[76] Several years later, however, when Merckling produced a stiff polymer, his superiors recognized that he had made linear polyethylene by a relatively low-pressure process.

About a week after Merckling's initial discovery, Anderson and Robinson met with Gresham to plan further experiments. Anderson correctly believed that the catalyst system was a novel one and that the active compounds were reduced forms of titanium chloride. They all recognized that this catalyst might allow them to make altogether new polymers and decided to initiate a broad program to investigate a wide series of olefin polymers and copolymers. Gresham reported to his boss that "we are on the brink of a tremendously interesting field of polymer chemistry."[77] The pace of the research accelerated. With six technicians working two shifts, twenty small-scale polymerizations could be done in one day.[78] Guided by Anderson's hypothesis, the researchers varied the catalyst composition to yield improved products and by late April prepared a very small sample of a new polymer, high-molecular-weight polypropylene. On May 21, 1954, an experimental run with propylene HPL 4427-86 yielded about half a gram of "a solid, coarse, free flowing powdery material" that was converted into a film by heat and pressure. An infrared analysis of the sample showed that it was indeed polypropylene.[79] Now, Du Pont had two new materials, linear polyethylene and polypropylene, to evaluate for commercial potential.

Of course, a critical element in any commercialization program would be the degree of patent protection that Du Pont could obtain for these three basic discoveries, the catalyst system, linear polyethylene, and polypropylene. Du Pont soon realized that there would be several contenders for each of these inventions. In September 1954, Du Pont learned that Karl Ziegler, director of the Max Planck Institute for Coal Research in Mülheim, West Germany, had discovered catalysts similar to those Du Pont was using and was offering to discuss his linear polyethylene process for $50,000 in advance. Several U.S. companies had already accepted his offer.[80] Two months later, Du Pont sent a delegation to initiate discussions with Ziegler. Upon seeing Ziegler's patent applications, General Manager Ries reported to the Executive Committee that "his work has been remarkably parallel to our own. We have little to learn from him that our researchers had not already uncovered, and conversely we have very little information that is not covered in his disclosures. His dates are generally earlier than ours; in fact, his earliest application in Germany was filed approximately three months before we made our first discovery...." Ries concluded that Du Pont's application would probably end up in interference with Ziegler's in the Patent Office and that he doubted "very much that there is any probability of obtaining a dominating patent position over Ziegler."[81] On the basis of this report, Du Pont paid Ziegler $50,000 to get a look at his process, which consisted of little more than laboratory results.[82]

Even at this early date, it was apparent to Ries that the linear polyethylene business was going to be competitive. Ziegler continued to license his technology to all comers, which in the United States included Goodrich-Gulf, Hercules, and Exxon.[83] The Ziegler process, however, turned out not to be the only way to make linear polyethylene. In 1954, Phillips Petroleum and Standard Oil Company of Indiana discovered two other catalyst systems that produced linear polyethylene during research programs originally aimed toward synthesis of hydrocarbons. Although the Ziegler licensees, Phillips, and Standard of Indiana had their own processes, Du Pont had been the first to make linear polyethylene and hoped to receive a composition-of-matter patent that would give it a stronger position in the field.[84]

Before the discoveries of 1954, Du Pont had been unable to convince the Patent Office that linear polyethylene was indeed a patentable invention. But the widespread publicity given the discoveries changed the mind of the patent examiner, and Du Pont received a patent on linear polyethylene in late 1957.[85] Even though outside attorneys attested to the validity of the patent's claim, they advised Du Pont that the outcome of patent suits was subject to considerable uncertainty, especially when the case involved complex chemistry that judges had difficulty comprehending.[86] Following this cautionary advice, Du Pont preferred to offer reasonable licenses on its patent rather than use it to prevent others from making the product. Because the Ziegler licensees could deduct a certain proportion of their royalties paid to Ziegler if they were forced to license others' patents, these manufacturers signed up with Du Pont because it did not cost them any more money. Independent producers, Phillips in particular, balked. Though Du Pont brought suit against Phillips, it eventually settled for an exchange of options and patent rights.[87] Generally, aggressive action in the marketplace, not patent monopolies, would be the critical factor in determining leadership in the industry.

In early 1955, Polychem's general manager Ries informed the Executive Committee that to stay in the polyethylene business, Du Pont would have to manufacture linear polyethylene, and even though there would be considerable competition, "prompt and proper action" could give Du Pont "a solid advantage in the field." At this point, Ries correctly realized that the real value of the new product was its properties. Others had touted the fact that polyethylene could now be made much more cheaply at lower pressures. Ries, however, had been informed by his research division that the complexities of the new process would make the linear product cost about the same as the old polyethylene. He estimated that at equal prices the new material might displace between half and three-quarters of the existing product and concluded that Du Pont had a "real opportunity to capture a leading position" in linear polyethylene.[88] One year later, his successor, Robert Hershey, was not so sanguine about Du Pont's prospects.

By early 1956, Hershey told the Executive Committee that eight companies had announced they were building plants with a combined capacity of 380 million pounds to manufacture linear polyethylene. Phillips was building a 110-million-pound-per-year plant that was expected to start up (at a lower capacity) in late 1956. Most of the other companies expected to be selling linear polyethylene by at least mid-1958. Hershey hoped that Du Pont would make a decision on commercialization in early 1957. To reach that point, Polychem needed to operate successfully its recently constructed small-scale plant, improve both its process and product, and begin a market development program. The decision to commercialize was spurred by the discovery that a major product improvement could be achieved by incorporating a higher 1-olefin monomer in the polymerization of ethylene.[89] Hershey concluded that Du Pont could profitably sell linear polyethylene, which he believed would be a large-volume plastic that would open new markets and expand existing ones. Yet for a company that was used to investing in high-profit proprietary products such as nylon, linear polyethylene was not really a very attractive venture. Conversely, Hershey and the Executive Committee realized that Du Pont needed to add this product in order to continue to be a broad-based manufacturer of plastics.[90]

Faced with considerable uncertainty about its product and process, the size of the market, the extent of the competitive activity, and the competing demands of Delrin for R&D staff and resources, Du Pont did not begin to manufacture linear polyethylene until 1960 and would capture only about 10 percent of the market. By 1970, the product was still $20 million in the red.[91]

The reason for this disappointing performance was competition. The numerous manufacturers kept bringing new capacity on stream well ahead of anticipated demand. From its beginning, the industry suffered from overcapacity and cost-cutting. Other companies had joined in the plastics gold rush only to find many others working the same veins.[92] A major concern of Du Pont from the beginning was that competitors would not be primarily motivated by profit considerations but would be moving into the business for strategic reasons. For example, W. R. Grace, a shipping company used to low profit margins and hoping to diversify into chemicals, might find acceptable a rate of return far below what was satisfactory for Du Pont. Of greater concern for Du Pont, however, was forward integration into chemical manufacture by oil companies, something it had long feared. Phillips in the 1950s set out to become the leader in petrochemicals. With a corporate commitment to raising its petrochemicals business to parity with its oil and gas business, Phillips moved aggressively into plastics.[93] Several oil companies joined in the battle royal that raged around linear polyethylene's chemical cousin, polypropylene.

The thirty-year war over polypropylene has been waged both in the courts and in the marketplace. Du Pont, though a pioneer in the field and one of the five contestants for the patent rights, eventually elected not to manufacture and sell it because the business was too competitive.[94] Within months of the experimental run with propylene HPL 4427-86, spurred on by rumors of similar work elsewhere, Du Pont quickly put together a patent application on polypropylene and filed it in August 1954.[95] Soon it learned that there were four other contenders. Phillips and Standard Oil of Indiana separately maintained that they had discovered polypropylene during their catalyst research, which had also produced linear polyethylene. Hercules and the Italian chemical company Montecatini also each claimed to be the first inventor. The research of these latter two companies derived from that of Ziegler, who never established a position for himself on polypropylene.[96]

Because of the complexity of a five-party interference on the patent applications, things moved slowly in the Patent Office. It was not until 1958 that the "count" or exact statement of the invention was agreed upon. Throughout the 1960s, the parties involved amassed evidence in the form of more than one hundred witnesses, 18,000 pages of evidence, and 1,000 exhibits to support their claims. Not until 1971 did the Patent Office decide that Montecatini was the senior party in the interference proceedings, which placed the burden on the others to show why Montecatini should not be granted the patent. Du Pont finished second in this round but had not missed the first ranking by much.[97]

Although there was no way of knowing it at the time, had the Polychem researchers immediately X-rayed the polypropylene sample prepared on May 21, 1954, Du Pont might have won the senior party status and eventually received a basic patent. The X-ray diffraction pattern was seen as the critical measurement that determined whether a new structure had been prepared. Without it, the patent examiner could maintain that Du Pont did not know what it had. Between the time the polypropylene sample was prepared and the X-ray was taken, Montecatini filed patent applications in Italy, which became the earliest date that it could claim for U.S. patent purposes.[98] (Domestic inventors can use laboratory notebooks or other records to establish a date for an invention, but foreign applicants are limited to actual filing dates.) Du Pont, then, probably missed out on winning the senior party status by about one month. The field of polymer research had become so competitive that even the slightest delays could be very costly, and so pressure to produce results quickly was added to the other demands placed on Polychem's scientists. The research game was getting harder to play.

Largely independent of the patent question – Du Pont did not expect to get a dominating patent position in polypropylene or really expect that anyone else would either – the Polychemicals Department management had to decide what course of action to take with the new polymer.[99] Polypropylene never engendered the kind of enthusiasm that

Delrin or even linear polyethylene had at Du Pont. Several years elapsed before Polychem had a clear idea of the nature of the product.[100] By 1958, the year in which the first commercial sales were made, Du Pont jumped on the bandwagon and decided to build a semiworks to test fully the elements of its process.[101]

Two researchers studied the situation and concluded that there would be plenty of room in the plastics field for material with polypropylene's properties in applications such as film, moldings, bottles, monofilaments, fibers, and pipe.[102] These were essentially the same uses that polyethylene had found. By 1960, considerable capacity had come on stream, but demand had developed slowly. Most producers had counted heavily on polypropylene becoming an important textile fiber, but no one apparently did the necessary development and marketing work.[103] Faced with this discouraging outlook, the Executive Committee decided to postpone building a plant until the internal demand for polypropylene was sufficient to justify the investment. The Film Department had begun to realize that polypropylene posed a serious threat to its principal product cellophane, and in 1962 it started selling polypropylene film. Textile Fibers was developing a spun-bonded polypropylene.[104] But these products grew slowly, and Du Pont never did enter the polypropylene manufacturing business. From the legal side, Du Pont remained a contestant until 1981, when Phillips won the patent battle after the courts had decided that Montecatini had committed fraud during the proceedings.[105]

The independent, simultaneous discovery of Ziegler-Natta (what Du Pont called "coordination") catalysts by Ziegler and chemists in Du Pont's Polychemicals Department in late 1953 and early 1954 proved to be a major scientific, technological, and commercial breakthrough. Ziegler and his institute became very wealthy from the royalties paid on his polyethylene process, even though the Phillips process came to be the dominant one in the industry. The problems with the Ziegler process led Frank McMillan, who was very familiar with this field and the author of a book about it, to state that Ziegler made more money than any of his licensees.[106] Du Pont's chemists had a right to feel disappointed if not somewhat bitter, because they had made the same discovery that earned someone else fame and fortune. The legal and commercial aspects of these inventions prevented the industrial scientists at Du Pont and in the other companies from publishing their results and receiving credit for their scientific achievements. Perhaps in this particular case, immediate publication by the Du Pont chemists might have given the company a better legal position because not all the publicity would have gone to Ziegler and Natta, who shared a Nobel Prize in 1963.[107] In any event, the Polychem scientists led by Gresham, Anderson, and Robinson had made outstanding contributions of Nobel Prize caliber, but the extremely competitive nature of polymer R&D prevented them or Du Pont from receiving widespread recognition or monetary rewards for this work.

Reorientation of Research

In the 1950s, the Polychemicals Department had invested about $150 million in research, its annual research budget having tripled from the beginning to the end of the decade. But soon the department's managers began to look at its research budget much more critically. In 1960, Polychem commercialized three of its major research achievements — Delrin, linear polyethylene, and a melt-processable Teflon resin. First-year losses for these products added up to $14.7 million in a year when another major product, regular polyethylene, suffered from overcapacity and low prices. The combined effect of these factors led to a dramatic decline in the department's plastics earnings from $37.5 million in 1959 to $16.2 million in 1960. This was a major problem for Polychem's new general manager Walter Salzenberg, a chemical engineer who had spent his entire career in the Grasselli organization until he became assistant general manager of Polychem in 1957. He soon decided that his department needed to cut costs to fight increasing competition.[108]

Salzenberg's plans called for tightening the reins on the department's research programs. Earlier, the department had subscribed to the general company philosophy that all research proposals that were *technically* sound would receive funding. Now Salzenberg wanted his research director, McGrew, who had succeeded Beekley in 1958, "to exercise greater discrimination in the selection of objectives and in the prompt termination of effort when the odds against success became clear." Whereas the research unit had previously developed a product and then tried to find uses for it, Salzenberg now wanted it to work from a market back to a product, something that was very difficult to do with polymers. He assigned McGrew to find a candidate "where we *know* that the market will be large, and where the stakes justify, even at long odds, a long-term commitment of appropriate size to the purpose." As an example, Salzenberg suggested developing a cheap, fire-resistant thermoplastic that would be used as a material for building construction, and discovering a mechanism for directly converting heat to electricity.[109] The general message that Salzenberg sent to his research directors was that the department did not need and could not afford any major new products.

Although the research directors of this era frequently complained about a lack of direction from their general management, the other side of the coin was that research directors had considerable autonomy over their programs. An R&D entrepreneur, McGrew had operated under the latter conditions for his entire career and did not respond favorably to Salzenberg's suggestion.

In 1964, the general manager instituted a more radical restructuring of research by decentralizing the research division, leaving McGrew in charge of only the general section. That the product divisions of the department had gained control over their research programs became apparent to

McGrew when he called a meeting of the new divisional research heads and no one showed up.[110] The powerful research organization that he helped to build in the 1950s had been broken up by management trying to cope with the dynamic and volatile plastics business in the 1960s.

Because the Plastics Department management had soured on large-scale projects, the department's researchers shifted toward technically sophisticated specialty polymers such as extremely durable Vespel polyimide resins and a new fluorocarbon resin, Nafion, that has had a major impact in the chlor-alkali industry. Neither product has yet become a big money-maker.[111] Du Pont's plastics researchers have committed themselves to developing polymers such as Vespel and Nafion, believing that numerous high technology applications will be found over time. Perhaps one of them will turn out to be another neoprene.

The Polymer Revolution at Du Pont

Two other polymer-based product lines, films and elastomers, followed the same general pattern that Plastics had set. Despite the growth of polyethylene film in the 1950s, cellophane continued to be what one company official would later call "a money-making machine."[112] The production of cellophane in the United States peaked in 1960 at over 400 million pounds a year. Du Pont had roughly 60 percent of this business, which generated about $160 million in sales and yielded a 20 percent before-tax return on investment.[113] During the 1960s, the Film Department management watched its premier product being replaced by polyethylene and polypropylene film, which were both highly competitive businesses. To keep its position in the packaging field, the Film Department produced these new films but never made any money on them. Du Pont in the 1970s would relinquish its market share in packaging by getting out of the commodity film business, preferring to concentrate on higher-price specialty films such as its Surlyn ionomer films.[114] Du Pont managed to make an orderly retreat from the cellophane business until the rise in energy prices in 1974 gave polypropylene a significant cost advantage. Then cellophane sales collapsed.[115]

Fortunately for the Film Department, packaging films were not the only ones that it produced. Mylar, an extraordinarily strong polyester film that had originated in the development of Dacron, created many new opportunities for the Film Department. In the late 1950s and 1960s, Mylar and cellophane generated nearly two-thirds of the sales of the Film Department and nearly all of its earnings. With its unusual strength, heat resistance, and excellent insulating properties, Mylar opened up many new markets for Du Pont film, including a base for magnetic tape, capacitor dielectrics, and numerous other applications. In the 1970s, Mylar became the department's major product.[116]

The Elastomer Chemicals Department had been split out of the Organic

Chemicals Department in 1957 so that Orchem's business would be simplified. Also, the Executive Committee wanted to focus top-level management attention on the neoprene and rubber chemicals business. Neoprene had been the first special-purpose rubber, but in the 1950s and 1960s Du Pont researchers developed a number of elastomers that served very specific markets. The most successful product was Viton fluoroelastomer, which had outstanding thermal stability and found uses primarily in the aerospace industry.[117]

None of the new products challenged the value and earnings supremacy of neoprene in Elaschem during its first decade. Neoprene had a nice balance of properties and cost so that it found a market niche between the high-priced specialties that Elaschem had developed and the low-cost general-purpose rubbers that were used in tires. This latter market was by far the largest for elastomers and was viewed by some as the major growth opportunity for Elaschem.[118]

By the early 1960s, Elaschem began to search for another broad-based product to supplement neoprene, which was beginning to experience competition from other producers and materials. Elaschem's general manager, Charles J. Harrington, decided that a polyolefin terpolymer, trademarked Nordel, that was under development in his department might make a good, low-cost tire material. He was not alone in this belief, because other companies were developing similar materials using Ziegler-Natta catalysts with the hope of penetrating the very large tire market. Harrington pushed the tire program very hard until it became apparent that Nordel was not the material that tire manufacturers wanted.[119] After this failure, Elaschem, like the Plastics and Film departments, devoted its innovative energies to developing technically sophisticated specialty products.[120]

Conclusion: Technological Push in Specialty Products

In the 1950s, the polymers business expanded at a great rate, creating opportunities for significant growth. Du Pont shied away from the fastest growing and most competitive products, instead developing more specialized products such as nylon, Teflon, and Delrin resins. Sales of these products never reached the level of polyvinyl chloride, polystyrene, or polypropylene, but they did become major businesses for Du Pont. By 1960, however, opportunities for investment in projects of this magnitude appeared to be limited and risky because other companies had also begun to develop higher-performance polymers such as ABS plastics and polycarbonates. Looking for a competitive advantage, Du Pont managers raised the ante one more time and assigned their research divisions to develop products of an unprecedented degree of technical complexity for special high-priced uses. Du Pont continued to see its technological capability as its major advantage over the competition.

The switch to a specialty products strategy signaled a decline in major growth opportunities in polymers. The battle would shift to fighting for particular niches. In other words, the polymer bonanza was over. For significant growth in the future, Du Pont would have to look for new, rapidly developing fields. Aware that the company's growth was slowing, the Executive Committee in the 1960s called for its research organizations to rededicate themselves to developing major new products.

PART V

Challenge and Response

The 1950s were a halcyon age for the entire U.S. chemical industry. By leading the way in the synthetic fibers revolution, the Du Pont Company saw its sales double during the decade and maintained its return on investment at above 10 percent. Du Pont operated like a well-oiled machine; its structure and administrative procedures had withstood the challenges of depression, war, and expansion. But while the industrial departments were busy taking advantage of the opportunities in the chemical industry, the Executive Committee began to ponder what changes the 1960s might bring. (See Tables V.1 and V.2 for statistics on the company's growth and R&D programs, 1961–80.)

In the late 1950s, some Executive Committee members saw trends that worried them. Du Pont was growing increasingly dependent on textile fibers, a business that had to become competitive as more companies entered the field. As Hale Charch and others had observed, there would probably not be another major new fiber. The company's established products, such as neoprene, dynamite, paint, and cellophane, were experiencing intense competition from established chemical companies and many newcomers to the industry. Perhaps the most disturbing trend, however, was Du Pont's failure in the 1950s to generate many proprietary and fast-growing new products. Over the next few years, these concerns grew until President Greenewalt decided that it was time to act.

To forestall the pending maturity of the company's businesses, Greenewalt in 1961 called upon each department to devote more resources to developing products for markets that were new to Du Pont. He in essence called for an internal regeneration of each department's product line and a concomitant shift in markets served. Since the 1920s, Du Pont had defined its territory as that of a manufacturer of sophisticated chemical products, eschewing entering the production of bulk commodity chemicals and finished goods. Hoping to move the company into fast-growing businesses, Greenewalt removed these constraints. Now Du Pont would move into any field in which the company's organization and skills could be applied. This philosophy was the same one that the Executive Committee had espoused in 1916 when it realized that the company's future lay not in the wartime smokeless powder plants but in the organizational capabilities the company had developed for the war effort. Just as it had under Sparre, a revitalized

Table V.1. *Financial Summary of the Du Pont Company, 1961–80*
(in millions of dollars)

	1961	1965	1970	1975	1980
Sales	2,191.0	2,999.3	3,618.4	7,221.5	13,652
Operating income (net)	258.0	384.9	328.7	271.8	716
Average operating investment	3,120.6	4,267.0	6,585.0	11,418	17,448
Average number of employees	87,057	106,013	115,126	132,235	135,900

Source: All data from Du Pont Company annual reports.

Table V.2. *Research and Development Statistics for the Du Pont*
Company, 1961–80 (in millions of dollars)

	1961	1965	1970	1975	1980
Total expenditure	160.8[a]	238.3[a]	270.3[a]	336[a]	484[a]
Expenditures as percentage of sales	7.3	8.0	7.5	4.7	3.6
Expenditures as percentage of earnings (expenditures/income)	62.3	61.9	82.2	123.6	67.6
Expenditures as percentage of earnings (expenditures/ expenditures + income)	38.4	38.2	45.1	55.3	40.3
R&D professional staff	3,787[a]	4,295[a]	4,362[a]	4,593[a]	4,050[b]

[a]Official R&D Statistics, CRDD.
[b]Corporate R&D Planning Division to R. C. Forney, Mar., 1983, EC Files.

Development Department was expected to play a key role in the new diversification program. Greenewalt hoped to be as successful with this strategy as the Du Pont brothers had been in the 1920s.

Researchers in the industrial departments brought forth an unprecedented number of new products in the 1960s, but the goal of internal renewal and diversification was not attained. The task of moving the company in new directions proved to be too large for the industrial departments, which were already overburdened fighting off competitive advances against existing product lines. The efforts of the Development Department also fell short. Most of the new products that Du Pont introduced were extensions of existing businesses rather than bold moves into new fields. In addition, these new products were expensive to develop, faced extended periods of unprofitable operation, and encountered competition very quickly. By 1969, the Executive Committee considered the entire effort a failure. The history of the new venture era is explored in Chapter 22.

In marked contrast to the rest of the company, the long-lagging Photo Products Department successfully diversified into the fast-growing medical technology and electronics businesses. This small department did not have large businesses to run and had not shared in the postwar affluence. Rather than initiate massive development projects centered on new materials, Photo Products found important market niches for existing company technology. Photo Products' ventures began with small, inexpensive research projects that became profitable soon after commercialization. Critical to these successes was a departmental management committed to innovation and an entrepreneurial research organization. Chapter 23 examines the transformation of the Photo Products Department from headache to hero.

Although the Executive Committee had foreseen very clearly the changes that would occur in the chemical industry in the 1960s, no one could have predicted the violent swings that would mark the 1970s. At the beginning of the decade, Du Pont found itself exhausted by the intense new product push of the 1960s. While attempting to get control of the continuing high expenditures on these new products, Du Pont's management had to cope with recession, competitive inroads against its fibers businesses, new environmental legislation that required hundreds of millions of dollars of investment in pollution control equipment, environmentalists' attacks against some of its best-earning products such as tetraethyllead and Freon, and new concerns about the toxic effects of chemicals on workers and consumers. Then, in 1973 and 1974 came the Arab oil embargo, which rapidly drove feedstock prices sky high and eventually changed the economic structure of the chemical industry. In response to these external onslaughts, the Du Pont Company moved into a defensive posture in the 1970s and tried to ride out the storm. Much of the company's research in this era was geared toward meeting these externally induced problems; work on toxicology was central here.

With the passage of federal legislation in the 1970s, toxicological research became a necessary part of the innovation process. Unlike some other companies, Du Pont could more easily comply with the new regulations because of its long tradition of doing extensive toxicological studies. Du Pont became a pioneer in the United States in this field when the company established the Haskell Laboratory in 1935. Chapter 24 examines Du Pont's experience from the perspective of the growing awareness of the dangers of chemicals in the twentieth century.

A major lesson of the 1960s was that Du Pont's organizational structure, which had served the company well for nearly a half-century, needed overhauling. To align its resources with existing opportunities, Du Pont reorganized its industrial departments in the 1970s. These departments were instructed to keep their research programs confined to logical extensions of their respective business fields. By the end of the decade, an Executive Committee member, Edward G. Jefferson, would be given responsibility for overseeing all of Du Pont's research, especially diversification research. In

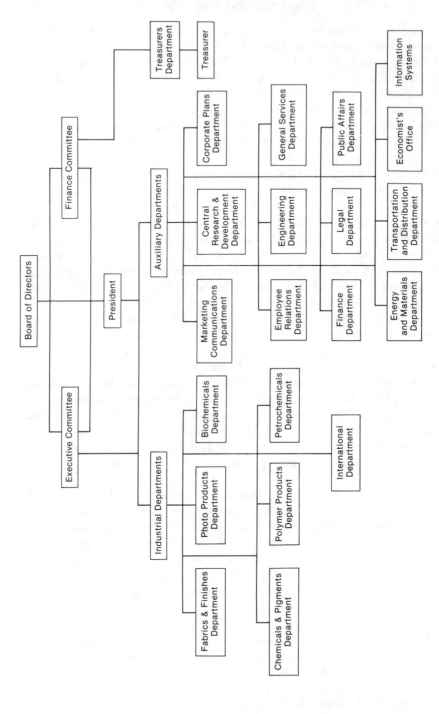

Figure V.1. Organization of the Du Pont Company, 1980. Source: Adapted from Du Pont Company Annual Report for 1980.

1979, Jefferson initiated a new corporate research effort in the life sciences, which included agricultural chemicals, pharmaceuticals, and molecular biology. It was to these fields – and electronics – that the company looked for growth in the 1990s and beyond. When he became head of the company in 1981, Jefferson accelerated the transformation of Du Pont through the purchase of Conoco and other organizational and administrative changes. The reworking of Du Pont's strategy and structure is the subject of Chapter 25. (See Figure V.1 for a view of the company's organization in 1980.) The 1960s and 1970s were turbulent decades that called into question Du Pont's time-honored traditions and brought dramatic changes.

22

The New Venture Era

Although the company's balance sheet for 1959 showed that Du Pont was in excellent financial health, some of its executives had become increasingly concerned about its ability to grow in the future as it had in the past. The chemical industry, particularly plastics and fibers, had become increasingly competitive, so President Greenewalt decided that it was time to break out of some earlier constraints and reemphasize the importance of new products to the company's health. Greenewalt maintained that "times had changed since the 30's and 40's when we turned our back on numerous opportunities beyond industrial chemistry because money and manpower were efficiently employed" and that "the policies and procedures of that era are not necessarily those of today." In a meeting with the general managers, he proclaimed that Du Pont would go into any business, no matter how large or small, if it could make a contribution. The primary assets of Du Pont were people and their skills, so there was no reason why the company could not move beyond chemistry. He informed those attending the meeting that he had committed Du Pont to a companywide program of diversification "beyond existing fields of interest and beyond chemistry." When asked about the always touchy issue of integrating forward and thereby competing with its customers, Greenewalt replied that the rest of the world felt "it was good, clean fun to play in our yard" and he had no objection to Du Pont's playing in theirs. When asked if small ventures were really all right, he responded by saying that the committee had permitted the Engineering Department to go into the manufacture of diamond knives, the proceeds of which could not be seen under the finest electron microscope. Finally, Greenewalt announced that history was repeating itself because he was revitalizing the Development Department to play a role similar to the one it had played in the diversification program of the 1920s. Its major new function would be to develop new ventures that went beyond the spheres of interest of the industrial departments.[1] With these initiatives, Greenewalt intended to renew Du Pont's former vigor.

In the late 1950s, Du Pont appeared to be in the doldrums. One report to the Executive Committee noted that "there is a noticeable shortage of vigor and vitality and enthusiasm that should be evident and contagious in a company that has the wealth of skills, and talents, and resources as Du Pont."[2] A general manager stated that he was tired of hearing members of the Executive Committee and others complain that "we'll never have another nylon."[3] Du Pont's managers did have reasons for being pessimistic about the future. Corporate earnings had peaked in 1955 and in the recession of 1958 fell 27 percent below the record level. The prices that Du Pont could charge for its products were falling while costs were rising. In particular, R&D costs had increased more than three times in the previous decade, and since the mid-1950s Du Pont's enormous technical effort had not produced any fast-growing and highly profitable new products.[4] When Du Pont had put a new product into the marketplace, competitors had usually countered with similar goods or different products to serve the same function. In response to the 1958 business downturn, President Greenewalt called for a corporate austerity program that further reinforced many employees' feelings that a new era had begun at Du Pont and perhaps even in the chemical industry.

Many analysts believed that the chemical industry had begun to mature. World War II had greatly accelerated this process of maturation by diffusing know-how throughout the industry. One Du Pont analyst stated that since the war, in spite of Du Pont's intensified research efforts, competitors had made equal if not greater strides and, as a consequence, the company no longer occupied "its former unique position in a generalized technological sense."[5] Although the industry was growing when measured by the volume of production, price erosion had slowed the rate of sales growth to only slightly above that for all manufacturing. Only a few years earlier, *Fortune* had been touting the twentieth century as the "chemical century" in a salute to what had become the United States's premier growth industry. This rhetoric had helped to attract many invaders into chemicals, including petroleum refiners, a plumbing supply company, a flour mill, a farm implement manufacturer, and a steamship line.[6] Turn-key plants, designed and constructed by engineering firms, made it easy for these companies to acquire chemical technology. In the face of this increasing competition, Du Pont had to evaluate its position and develop strategies for the future.

One Executive Committee member, David H. Dawson, noted with some alarm that if the problem was one of maturation, then Du Pont was maturing faster than the others.[7] In most major performance categories, Du Pont was still the leader, but Celanese, Hercules, Dow, Monsanto, and Union Carbide were closing in fast. It was these comparative statistics that led the Du Pont management to conclude that the source of the company's problems was not just the maturation of the chemical industry but that Du Pont was not doing as good a job as it could.

Dawson began to worry about the long-range future of the company soon after he was elected to the Executive Committee in 1955.[8] Many in Du Pont speculated that either he or Samuel Lenher, who also joined the committee in 1955, would succeed Greenewalt.[9] The other committee members were too close to retirement to be considered serious candidates. Although neither would become president, both Dawson and Lenher played critical roles in formulating and directing the new venture programs of the 1960s.

In November 1957, Dawson presented his scenario of the company's future to an informal group of development managers from the industrial departments. The ideas that he presented would gain credence with the Executive Committee over the next several years and lead to the new venture program.[10] He urged the development managers not "to grow complacent and accept as inevitable the conclusion that we must accept lower rates of growth, lower returns, or both" because of the impending maturity of the chemical industry. He challenged them to think about the world in 1970 and warned them that the company's most important markets by that time might not be fibers, films, and plastics. In essence, Du Pont researchers should be solving not contemporary problems, but those of the future.

Dawson outlined a number of ways in which Du Pont could stave off maturity and maintain its postwar rate of growth and earnings. Du Pont, he asserted, should put "greater emphasis on entry into the more dynamic phases of the economy, that is, pharmaceuticals and electronics. The company already had Teflon and silicon, which were important products in the latter area. Du Pont in this era could enter these businesses only on a product-by-product basis because the Executive Committee completely ruled out the possibility of significant acquisitions until the General Motors antitrust suit was settled.[11] Dawson also suggested that Du Pont consider integrating both backward and forward from its middle ground as a manufacturer of complex chemical products. He realized that investments in chemicals such as acrylonitrile or ammonia were prosaic but they offered a guaranteed market and avoided the long period of unprofitable operation that new products frequently encountered. In the other direction, Dawson recommended integrating forward especially with Du Pont–patented materials such as Teflon and Delrin. If this were done with a new product, Du Pont could avoid the pitfall of having to compete with its customers.

In addition, Dawson believed that new products should be exploited more aggressively in Europe, where Du Pont had been building plants to produce its older products. For much of his presidency in the 1950s, Greenewalt had lobbied the Executive Committee to authorize building foreign plants, especially in Europe. He encountered such stiff opposition, however, that he could do nothing until certain members retired. Encouraged by the formation of the European Common Market, Greenewalt reorganized the International Department in 1958 and began to plan for Du Pont's expansion overseas.[12]

Most important for the future, however, Dawson asserted that Du Pont had to make patentable discoveries that could be quickly turned into new products. He explained that a recent study had concluded that products that Du Pont either invented or pioneered in the market earned a 50 percent higher return on investment than products that Du Pont developed either simultaneously with or later than competitors.

Even though the Executive Committee considered all these alternatives, it agreed with Dawson that the principal source of the company's growth and profitability would continue to be new proprietary products that originated in Du Pont's laboratories. The sheer size of the company required that more new products would have to be introduced each year to ensure growth. One Development Department report stated that "it would be trite to say we need another nylon; actually our sales are about six times what they were when nylon was introduced, and we would need several nylons to even approach the earlier effect on our business."[13] To meet its growth objectives, Du Pont had to add $830 million in sales from new products in the 1960s. This meant introducing about sixteen major new products, each of which would generate sales of $50 million per year. In the 1950s, Du Pont had introduced only three products of this magnitude, Orlon and Dacron fibers and Mylar film.[14] Clearly, Du Pont research faced unprecedented challenges in the 1960s.

The Executive Committee believed that it had the financial resources to commercialize these desired new products. The company had no debt because it financed all its construction out of earnings and still had three-quarters of its profits left to pay out as dividends. In 1959, the Treasurer estimated that Du Pont would have about $300 million dollars to invest in new products in the 1960s.[15] The challenge was to find attractive investments for this cash.

Du Pont's executives maintained their confidence that the company's organizational structure and administrative policies were basically sound and that some fine-tuning was all that was necessary.[16] Vice President Samuel Lenher, advisor on research, attempted to do this in 1959. First, he tried to get the departments to cooperate more fully with each other by routinely sharing research results. Lenher succeeded in persuading each department at least to circulate lists of its latest research reports. Departments considered research results to be proprietary and frequently would not allow other company employees to read them. In many ways, Du Pont had operated like a dozen separate companies, which had the effect of fragmenting its overall research effort. Du Pont did much more research than any other U.S. chemical company but lost its economies of scale when departments would not cooperate with each other. Also, Lenher encouraged Central Research to carry its developments further toward commercialization. He and others on the Executive Committee felt that Central Research had interpreted its charter to do fundamental and long-range research too strictly and needed to do some development work to make its discoveries attractive for an industrial department to pick up and carry forward.[17]

Responding to this assessment of Du Pont research, Central Research director Paul Salzberg analyzed the company's lack of big new products in a manner similar to that of Dawson. Salzberg believed Du Pont had abandoned the nylon model for what he called imitative research: "We have most likely lost the venturesome creative spirit in our research organizations as the result of imitative work and trying to keep up with the competition." According to Salzberg, Du Pont was wasting much of its research effort trying to make competitive businesses more profitable. Part of this was attributable to Du Pont's hubris of technological superiority, which Salzberg considered to be pure myth. He recalled how he "was first disillusioned with respect to the impotence and stupidity of our competitors in connection with the methyl methacrylate business. It was predicted that by virtue of superior technology, engineering and resources, [Du Pont] would shortly put Rohm and Haas out of the ... business. . . . It [now] looks like they licked the pants off us." In highly competitive businesses, Du Pont had inherent disadvantages because of its higher wages and overhead and the fact that it spent much more on research than did its competitors.[18]

Salzberg believed that there had not been a lack of potential new ventures in Du Pont; it was just that the highly conservative general managers of the departments devoted the overwhelming majority of their research dollars to keeping their older businesses healthy instead of investing in new ones. "The emotional impetus of saving a big business," he argued, "is most difficult to resist but I am forced to conclude that it is in part the cause of the 'unproductivity of our research.' "

To set things right, Salzberg wanted a rededication of Du Pont research to pioneering science that would lead to proprietary products. He believed that science was inexhaustible and that there was room for all who did real research. To understand what kind of research the departments were doing, the Executive Committee needed to separate research done to support existing businesses and that done to generate new proprietary products. These two basic types of research were so different, Salzberg maintained, "that they must be controlled and supported differently, judged by different standards, and carried out by different organizations under different philosophies."

Following Salzberg, Greenewalt soon steered through the Executive Committee new budget rules that dropped the older concepts of fundamental research and the other classifications in favor of "Supporting" and "Pioneering," which pertained to old and new products respectively. The Pioneering definition also contained the charge that all the departments of the company were "to undertake aggressive research and development programs aimed at the commercialization of new patented products. . . . "[19] Salzberg soon met with all the research directors to point out that the new accounting rules challenged each of them to put increased emphasis on new products.[20]

There was a general feeling in Du Pont that the company had made many important discoveries since World War II but that efforts to translate these discoveries into commercial products had fallen short. Lenher quoted to the Executive Committee an address by Robert Robinson, the English Nobel–Prize winning chemist, who had stated that "the flood of research and development is still rising while large-scale exploitation of discoveries lags behind."[21] In 1960, Du Pont's research managers, seeking to lift their company to new heights, began an intensive search for leads that could be turned into new products. Soon, Du Pont's industrial departments would be commercializing new products in unprecedented numbers.

Some members of the Executive Committee believed that these actions would not remedy the company's problems. Early in 1960, Dawson wrote to Lenher that the industrial departments had done a good job of doing research in support of their existing businesses, which he considered to be the most important factor in maintaining the profitability of the company, and in developing new products related to their established lines of business. However, he stated, "With some pleasing exceptions . . . these products have shown a decreasing ability to grow rapidly into large, high earning developments, and too frequently have been characterized by heavy capital development costs, the need for immediate large capital expenditures to produce competitive selling prices, and protracted periods of loss and delay in recouping development costs." He continued, "Much of this may be thought of as inevitable in maturing fields where each new product must compete with older large volume products, Delrin with nylon, Mylar with cellophane, Dacron with nylon, etc." Dawson concluded that "inevitable or not, [this interproduct competition] decreases, *relatively*, the attractiveness of research directed toward such objectives, and may safely be forecast to represent an increasingly severe problem."[22]

To accomplish this critically important task of diversification more effectively, Dawson suggested establishing a new department. Because diversification was a corporate function, he believed that it should be administered at the corporate level instead of allowing each department to pursue its own independent program. With their hands full exploiting their existing businesses, the industrial departments did not need this additional responsibility.[23] Moving cautiously, Dawson tried to get the Executive Committee to play a stronger role in charting the company's future direction.

Soon, Executive Committee members Dawson, Lenher, and George Holbrook would constitute a subcommittee on planning. Until this time the Executive Committee had not done any formal planning. The Executive Committee had been just, as one member put it, "a group of men on the rear platform of an observation car [of a train], busy looking at where they had been."[24] The only real control it had exercised over the direction of the company was through the approval or disapproval of departmental requests for funds for major expenditures. Because the company had excess cash that it wanted to invest, the Executive Committee usually granted departmental funding requests if the technical objectives of the proposal appeared attainable.[25]

The subcommittee on planning decided that a revitalized Development Department would be the proper agency in the company to sponsor projects that represented significant diversification for Du Pont. After considerable discussion, the Executive Committee passed a resolution on August 3, 1960, that charged the Development Department "with responsibility for seeking attractive commercial investment opportunities in fields not adequately covered by current endeavors in the Company's industrial departments."[26] The resolution suggested some courses of action that should be considered to implement this program. The Development Department might sponsor research and development within Du Pont or in outside organizations; conduct market analyses, surveys, or special studies; assist and advise Central Research and the Engineering Department on new product ventures not sponsored by the industrial departments; act as the principal agency for planning and programming commercialization of these ventures; and propose acquisitions of technology or companies. This resolution did not represent a radical departure from Du Pont's approach to diversification – the major responsibility would still be on the industrial departments – but it was the company's first major change in the postwar era.

The Development Department staff immediately began to ponder how to put this resolution into action. Chaplin Tyler, who had been a member of the department since the Sparre era, argued that the "demand for results is sure to be insistent, if for no other reason than the Subcommittee's consciousness of its own heavy responsibility." In view of these circumstances, he believed that "an atmosphere of urgency is likely to prevail" so that the Development Department needed to launch a multifaceted program that was going to require a lot of money, staff, and sustained intensive effort.[27] The first thing the department needed was to find an individual to head its new division.

Edwin A. Gee and Diversification in the 1950s

The Executive Committee selected Edwin A. Gee, a forty-year-old chemical engineer who was assistant director of sales in the Pigments Department, for the job. Dawson had hired Gee from the U.S. Bureau of Mines in 1948 and probably recommended him for the new position. That he had worked for another organization, unlike most Du Pont employees, was another factor in Gee's favor. He had also earned the reputation for being a tough, blunt iconoclast – just the type of person that the committee wanted.[28] In the fall of 1960, he assumed the responsibility for moving the Du Pont Company into new business areas. Over the next two decades as assistant director and director of the Development Department and later as an Executive Committee member, Gee was the most outspoken and persistent critic of Du Pont's traditions of managing R&D.

Gee had been intimately involved in two unsuccessful diversification programs of the Pigments Department in the 1950s. As a metallurgist in the Bureau of Mines, Gee had worked with Wilhelm Kroll, who had developed a process for the manufacture of titanium metal. During World War II, the military became interested in lightweight titanium metal. The Pigments Department, one of the major manufacturers of titanium dioxide pigments, had developed a process for making titanium tetrachloride, the key intermediate in new methods of making pigment and titanium metal. In late 1947, in conjunction with the construction of a large plant to make pigment by the new process, Pigments decided to build a 100-pound-per-day titanium metal production unit. Encouraged in this endeavor by the government, which was the only consumer of titanium, Du Pont improved its process and built a larger plant. Du Pont thus became the first volume producer of titanium metal.[29]

Military interest in titanium as an airframe material led the government to stockpile the metal and sign contracts to install additional capacity both at Du Pont and several other companies. Consequently, Du Pont's sales of titanium grew rapidly in the early 1950s, reaching $25 million in 1956, making it the third-biggest volume product introduced by Du Pont since the end of World War II. But military interest in titanium began to wane, and the government stopped stockpiling the metal. The market for titanium collapsed. In 1958, Du Pont sold only $3 million of the metal. It soon became apparent that the only way to salvage this business was to integrate forward into the manufacture of products from titanium. Du Pont's principal competitor, the Titanium Metals Corporation of America, did this successfully and captured half the remaining market. Du Pont placed its bets on a new type of titanium powder that could be shaped into products more easily than the competitor's product. When Pigments discovered a major technical deficiency in its titanium powder, Du Pont ceased to be a factor in the business.

At the same time that it was manufacturing titanium, the Pigments Department was also producing high-purity silicon for the rapidly growing electronics industry. In 1941, researchers in the Pigments Department looked at silicon as a potential competitor for titanium dioxide. This work went nowhere, but soon Du Pont was asked by one of its consultants, Frederick Seitz of the University of Pennsylvania, if the company could produce very pure silicon for diodes in radar equipment. Over the next three years, Pigments sold about 300 pounds of silicon to the government for this purpose. With the cessation of government contracts after the war, interest in silicon lagged until Du Pont received an order from Bell Labs for 300 pounds in 1952. Bell Labs needed silicon for use in transistors. In filling this order, Du Pont became the first commercial manufacturer of semiconductor-grade silicon.[30] Du Pont's interest in silicon increased two years later when Texas Instruments announced that it had successfully made a silicon transistor. Du Pont saw itself in the position of being a raw materials supplier to what promised to be a large new industry, and in 1957 the Executive Committee authorized the construction of a plant to produce 50,000 pounds per year of semiconductor-grade silicon.[31] However, Texas Instruments, the major producer of silicon transistors, integrated backward into the manufacture of its own silicon, and an improved process was developed by other companies.[32] Du Pont's position as a nonintegrated silicon producer deteriorated rapidly in the late 1950s, and the company soon withdrew from the business. Du Pont's experience with titanium and silicon had demonstrated to Gee and the Executive Committee that it was very difficult to diversify into new businesses and that Du Pont had to avoid repeating the mistakes of the 1950s.

The Development Department and Diversification

After receiving his new commission directly from President Greenewalt, Gee went back to his office and began to ponder what he should do. Gee and his boss, Henry E. Ford, who wanted nothing to do with this whole business,[33] met with each member of the subcommittee on planning separately and discovered that two of its members disagreed on virtually everything. Lenher warned Gee that the entire committee might not be in agreement with the August 1960 resolution and that a selling approach was needed.[34] After these meetings, Gee concluded, "Unfortunately, there was little indication that the required policy guidance would be forthcoming. We apparently must fire blindly and hope to avoid the recoil."[35] Gee had been charged by the Executive Committee to run a major program of corporate diversification, but he was not sure that he would be supported by the Executive Committee or by the general managers of Du Pont's departments.

Gee interviewed the Executive Committee members, general managers, and research directors but found little consensus concerning the lack of profitable diversification or what should be done. Paul Salzberg and Merlin Brubaker of Central Research, upon whom Gee depended for research leads, again pointed to imitative research as the culprit. Uniqueness was what counted in a new product. But, they argued, some people in Du Pont had lost faith in basic research as the key to important discoveries.[36] Several departments, such as Textile Fibers, told Gee that they had their hands full running their own businesses and that Gee could do whatever he liked as long as he left them alone.[37]

Making his own analysis of the situation, Gee soon decided that Du Pont had a "diversification gap" caused by complete reliance on internal research for new business opportunities. Historically, he argued, the products coming out of Du Pont research had accounted for only about half of the company's growth; the other half came from acquisitions of technology or companies. Gee saw his job as closing that gap through diversification, that is, by developing new products for markets that were new to Du Pont. Since the retirement of Fin Sparre, Gee argued, diversification had been "everyone's job but no one's real effort." To solve this problem of locating responsibility for diversification, he agreed with Dawson that Du Pont needed a central diversification department. Soon, he proposed that Du Pont establish a corporate diversification department with responsibility for moving the company into new businesses and having a director with stature equal to the departmental general managers.[38]

When in early 1961 Gee made his first pitch to the subcommittee on planning to establish a Diversification Department, he cautioned that the

matter was a difficult and controversial one. "It strikes at the very heart
and fabric of the entire corporate structure," he noted. But, Gee stressed,
"immediate and bold moves are required to inject into this company once
again a spirit of drive and confidence." The resolution of August 1960 had
been a step in the right direction, yet it did not go far enough. What the
company needed, Gee contended, was a statement of long-term objectives
by the Executive Committee and the establishment of a Diversification Department to help move the company in the direction that the committee
had selected. The new organization would assume primary responsibility
for corporate planning and diversification and would be formed from Gee's
section of the Development Department combined with Central Research
and the Engineering Department's R&D group.[39]

Both the Executive Committee and the general managers had expected
Central Research to create new business opportunities for Du Pont from its
extensive fundamental research programs. In the 1950s, the department's
scientists had made some interesting discoveries in fields outside Du Pont's
expertise but had been unable to develop them for commercial evaluation
or to sell them to an industrial department. Gee believed that Central Research "had become expert at discovering cures for unknown diseases,"
because it had become isolated from the commercial world and "excessively
scientific." To provide a development and commercial component to Central
Research's fundamental research, Gee wanted to include it in his new
department.[40]

Gee also had misgivings about the new-product program initiated early
in 1960 by the Engineering Department at Greenewalt's suggestion. The
department's new-products group evaluated proposals such as using
Du Pont's Adiprene urethane rubber in lightweight horseshoes for racing
horses, tire chains, and molded golf balls. Although nothing was done with
the horseshoe idea, the department did develop the other two products.
When the first tire chains had become available for testing in July, the
department sent an engineer to Tierra del Fuego. Although they worked
well in the cold, deep snow of Tierra del Fuego, they later failed by slipping
on the wheels in Wilmington's slushy wet snow. Engineering dropped its
golf ball effort when the Elastomer Chemicals Department complained that
Du Pont would be competing with its customers.[41] Gee maintained that the
Engineering Department's ideas were usually far from Du Pont's areas of
expertise and that "commercial guidance" was needed in its program. This
could be achieved by putting much of the Engineering Department's R&D
organization into his Diversification Department. The scientific and technical abilities of the Central Research and Engineering departments, Gee
concluded, were among the best in the world, but he had "little confidence
in their ability to develop new business ventures without the aid of experienced, commercially-oriented management." After listening to Gee's presentation, the subcommittee rejected his proposal.[42] Even if they had
approved it, Greenewalt, who had spent twenty years in Central Research,

probably thought this move was too drastic and would interfere with the fundamental research he believed was critical to the company's future.[43]

Shortly after this decision, however, Greenewalt gave Gee a new responsibility. Greenewalt thought that the general managers had become too independent and believed that the good of the entire company needed to be reasserted. The president explained to the general managers that the Development Department would be appraising each department's diversification activities in order to detect inadequacies in technology, markets, and organization. Any discovered weakness would be discussed with the general manager, and if the conclusions of the Development Department were not accepted, the matter would be brought to the Executive Committee's attention. Thus Gee was given the power to interfere in the internal affairs of the industrial departments.[44]

After reviewing the available data on the diversification programs under way in the departments, Gee was not optimistic about the ability of the departments to commercialize them successfully. He shared Dawson's concern that the industrial departments were developing major new products for already crowded markets. Overall, Gee believed the ventures should be viewed as a portfolio, weighing risks against opportunities and ranking all new venture activities on a companywide basis. Because each department handled its ventures in its own way, Gee could not even compile comparable statistics for them. Instead of a comprehensive review, Gee's staff was forced to focus on auditing individual ventures. Generally, Gee saw his department doing for capital investment policy what the Employee Relations Department did for employees.[45] Under the circumstances, however, the best that he could do might be to stop marginal new ventures that were being kept alive just because each general manager thought he should have one, and Gee could make sure the have-not departments received the resources they needed to move into new businesses.

While assessing the ventures of the other departments, Gee began to formulate his own plan of action. Earlier he had suggested to the Executive Committee a number of other possible programs. These included increasing the study of acquisition opportunities; investing in embryonic companies; analyzing opportunities for consumer-need-oriented research; and doing more government research. To his surprise, the Executive Committee told him to explore all of them.[46]

Probably the quickest means of getting into a new business was through the acquisition of existing companies. In 1960, Du Pont's Legal Department held that the use of its stock in an acquisition could be problematical until *U.S. vs. General Motors, Du Pont, et al.* was finally settled. On March 21, 1961, the Supreme Court ruled that Du Pont had to divest its extensive holdings of GM stock.[47] Then Du Pont considered purchasing oil, pharmaceutical, and aircraft companies. In 1962, however, Gee reported to the Executive Committee that he was continuing to look for major acquisition opportunities but had found none that justified "the economic expenditures involved, not to mention collateral labor, public relations, and legal problems."[48] At this time the general antitrust climate against mergers was growing stronger.[49] These difficulties soon led Gee to abandon this strategy of diversification.

Gee explored another possible avenue for broadening Du Pont's R&D: to do government-funded research. In 1959, government research money accounted for nearly 30 percent of the total R&D budget of the chemical and allied products industry.[50] From the end of World War II until 1957, Du Pont had done almost no R&D for the government, and it proceeded very cautiously when it began to accept small contracts, usually by the Explosives Department.[51] Du Pont's representative in Washington, Homer H. Ewing, argued that by eschewing government research Du Pont was being denied access to important research findings that were available to government contractors and that the government allowed cooperation between companies on projects, something that the antitrust laws otherwise prohibited.[52] Apparently some members of the Executive Committee worried so much about losing proprietary rights to inventions or information through participation in the government research network that they shied away from government research. Clearly they thought Du Pont stood to lose more than it gained.

Having had experience in government research, Gee saw it as an opportunity for Du Pont to broaden its technological base. He received some support from Greenewalt, who hoped that Du Pont might gain new technologies as a by-product of government research. Gee tried to get Du Pont involved in National Aeronautics and Space Administration (NASA) programs; the company went as far as making an unsolicited proposal to study the physical chemistry of comets.[53] But the Executive Committee ultimately rejected the idea of vigorously soliciting government contract research. Gee reported that its position had "further crystallized and we expect only limited diversification opportunity in this area over the next five years." The Executive Committee determined to stay the course; Du Pont would continue to do in the future what it had in the past, and that was to fund and control its own R&D.

Embryonic Ventures

With both government-sponsored R&D and major acquisitions out of the question, Gee promoted another approach for Du Pont to gain access to new technology being developed outside the company. He believed that a "sizable fraction of today's pioneering technology is developing in small, highly technical companies where a few talented individuals of high dedication are attempting to exploit a concept." Du Pont could gain a "window on this technology," Gee argued, by making minority investments in these companies. These investments would also be a source of good ideas, people, and even some profit. But above all Gee hoped to find a few small firms that Du Pont could eventually acquire as the basis for major new ventures.[54] This type of investment was a relatively recent phenomenon but was becoming increasingly popular. Even if faced with competition in this field, Du Pont could have significant advantages in choosing and assisting embryonic ventures because of "its tremendous resources of skilled people, broad technology, marketing know-how, and management. . . . "[55] Because developing companies operated so differently than Du Pont, Gee wanted his embryonic ventures to be incorporated as a subsidiary company to insulate the entrepreneurs from attempts to "Du Pontize" them.

Gee met with Lenher on this subject and was told that Greenewalt had expressed concern that this was the first specific proposal submitted by Gee and wondered if this meant that this was the most important one. In a memorandum written to the file, Gee recorded that "I am not sure that it isn't" and that the committee was looking on these investments in terms of earnings, which was a complete misunderstanding of the concept. Gee stressed to the committee that no short-term earnings could be realized from investing in embryonic companies and that some moderate capital losses were a virtual certainty.[56] If he could get his subsidiary approach approved, Gee hoped that he could avoid having each investment proposal come under the intense scrutiny of the committee members who were used to dealing with hard numbers in making investment decisions.

Gee failed to convince the Executive Committee that his embryonic venture group should operate in a semiautonomous fashion. Because of the need to deal promptly and directly with entrepreneurs, Chaplin Tyler, who prepared the reports to the committee, argued that if the subsidiary idea could not be accepted, then "the venture should be seriously questioned."[57] But when the Executive Committee position became apparent, Tyler backed off somewhat. He concluded that the subsidiary proposal could be dropped, so long as the department were given the authority to make small investments on the order of $300,000 without Executive Committee approval. Nevertheless, Tyler worried that good opportunities would be lost due to the slow-moving nature of decision making at Du Pont and because investments in embryonic companies were of the type that were sure "to induce debate, diversity of viewpoint, and delay."[58] Unconvinced by these arguments, the Executive Committee delegated none of its responsibility to the Development Department for investing in embryonic companies. But the committee did determine to try Gee's ideas, at least on a limited basis.

Over the next few years, Du Pont invested in and made loans to three embryonic companies. Two of them prospered. One was Block Engineering, which had "an impressive number of novel and proprietary ideas in the field of optics, spectroscopy, and interferometry," and the other was Dana Laboratories, Incorporated, which had "good management and excellent sales talent in the field of precision instrumentation." The third company, Cryogenic Technology, Incorporated, encountered financial difficulty and eventually declared bankruptcy.[59]

The difficulties with this third company prompted a reevaluation of the entire program in an effort to reassure the Executive Committee. A failure of this type had been predicted. But when it happened the committee was upset. The manager of the program, Daniel D. Friel, maintained that other investment companies had reported a 50 percent failure rate and argued that Du Pont needed to invest in about fifteen companies and wait for ten years before the program uncovered a new Polaroid, Xerox, or Perkin-Elmer.[60]

The committee permitted the program to continue, but it became increasingly difficult to get investments approved. Gee recalls that the committee put pressure on these small companies to establish accounting, human resources, and management policies similar to those used by Du Pont. With little authority to act independently, Gee constantly had to act as a buffer between the individual entrepreneurs and the Executive Committee. This frustrated him to the extent that he stopped putting much effort into the program.[61] The company eventually sold its holdings in the embryonic companies and made a small profit.[62] Officially the embryonic venture was a failure because it did not open new technological and business opportunities for Du Pont. However, the Executive Committee's unwillingness to give the program sufficient time to develop and to delegate some authority for dealing with entrepreneurs contributed to the lack of success.

Instrument Products Venture

The second program that Gee initiated was the development of marketable products from the large number of analytical and process instruments that Du Pont manufactured for its own use. This project turned out to be a very successful one when several years later it led the company into the medical field. In 1960, a companywide survey of potential candidates for commercialization produced a list of 150 instruments.[63] Only two years earlier, Du Pont had let one important one get away.

In the mid-1950s, Steve Dal Nogare, a chemist in the Polychemicals Department, made a significant improvement in gas chromatography, a chemical separation method that came into prominence after 1953. His temperature programming technique, however, did not interest the company, which did not even patent it. But an entrepreneurial glassblower in the department, Frank Martinez, received permission to manufacture these instruments on his own. After placing a single small advertisement in *Analytical Chemistry*, he was swamped with orders and soon resigned from Du Pont in 1958 to pursue his new business. Within a few years, Martinez had a multi-million-dollar-per-year business.[64] It was this type of opportunity that Du Pont wanted to take advantage of in the future.

Although not enthusiastic about an instruments venture, the Executive Committee allowed Gee to proceed and gave him $1.8 million to spend. A review of the list of Du Pont instruments by Gee's staff showed that many were obsolete, some were too specialized, and others were too proprietary to be sold commercially. Soon the list had been reduced to two instruments, a photometric process analyzer and a differential thermal analyzer. The former instrument had been developed in the Engineering Department and over one hundred of them were already in use in Du Pont's plants. Over the next ten years, Du Pont sold over one thousand of these instruments, many of which were used to measure stack emissions.[65] The differential thermal analyzer originated in the Plastics Department, which used the technique to characterize polymers. Starting from the work of earlier researchers, Jen Chiu made numerous important improvements to the apparatus and extended its applications. Over a thousand of these units were also sold in its first decade. By late 1963, Du Pont had instrument sales of about $1 million a year from these two instruments.[66]

This growth rate might have been satisfactory for an entrepreneurial company, but for Du Pont, which was looking to establish new $50-million-per-year businesses in the 1960s, the instrument venture as originally conceived turned out to be only a small opportunity. Nevertheless, venture manager John C. Metzger, Jr., was convinced that the instrument business was a growing one and was a good field for diversification. In late 1963, the instruments group in the Development Department initiated its own R&D program.[67]

The research group in the instruments venture developed a concept for automated analyses for routine medical tests, which became the basis for the highly successful Automatic Clinical Analyzer (ACA). In 1963, Du Pont entered into a consulting agreement with Walter J. Blaedel, professor of analytical chemistry at the University of Wisconsin, in the field of automated wet analytical chemistry. Using Blaedel's concepts, the Du Pont researchers started to perform continuous analyses using flow streams with pumps and plastic tubing. The general usefulness of this approach had already been demonstrated, and some equipment was already available on the market. Du Pont soon learned that many of the options in this type of system had been eliminated by others' patents and that the flow system had shortcomings. In August 1964, research supervisor Donald R. Johnson and his associates arrived at the concept of using small, discrete packets made of optically clear Surlyn film that would be the reagent container and reaction vessel. The "reading" of the results by a spectrometer could also be done in the packet. Starting from this concept, by 1967 the researchers had developed a satisfactory prototype and shipped it to the University of Wisconsin Clinical Laboratory for testing. When the results looked promising, Du Pont went ahead with the commercialization of the ACA. The first ones were sold in 1971. Under the leadership of Robert A. Piper, sales grew rapidly, and by 1980 Du Pont had sold about $200 million worth of ACAs and packets used in them. The ACA saved the instrument venture – the other products grew in volume but yielded little profit – and was the major success of the Development Department's entire new venture program.[68]

Building Products Venture

The third major project undertaken by the Development Department evolved out of what was labeled "need-oriented" research. Almost all Du Pont's research efforts began with discovering new materials that might be useful in some way. What Gee wanted to do was to turn this process around by starting with a market need and then looking for technologies to fill it, the assumption being that much of the needed technology would be found in the company.[69] This program soon came to focus on house construction.

The Development Department initiated a research and development program to develop products from Du Pont materials for the building industry. Since the mid-1950s, the Pioneering Research Laboratory in the Textile Fibers Department and the Engineering Department had been investigating ways in which Du Pont could manufacture such products.[70] Russell W. Peterson, who had pushed this idea and transferred from the Textile Fibers Department to the Development Department to head the venture, believed the building industry would have to abandon its traditional and inefficient practices to provide housing for the maturing baby-boom generation. What he expected was the long-awaited application of mass production to housing construction. Peterson predicted that a few nationwide corporate builders would emerge, and Du Pont, based on its broad experience with materials, could be one of them. The company would never go this far, but it attempted to develop a line of products suited to a new housing industry.[71]

In early 1961, Peterson suggested to his boss, Howard W. Swank, that Du Pont should "decide promptly and with firm resolve to enter the home-building industry as a major supplier of materials, components, and possibly prepackaged homes." The Textile Fibers Department was not interested in such a radical diversification; it had plenty of fiber-related opportunities, so Peterson sent his proposal to the Executive Committee and the general managers.[72] After nearly two years of trying to generate support for this venture in the company, Peterson finally found a home for it in the Development Department.

In his proposal to the Executive Committee, Peterson argued that Du Pont had the necessary skills to capitalize on the predicted revolution in housing construction. Du Pont probably had more knowledge and experience with polymeric products than any other company, and Peterson saw their use increasing dramatically in homes. His research group would concentrate on making shapes out of Du Pont materials, and these products could be marketed effectively to a small number of corporate builders that he expected to emerge in the coming years. The first material selected for evaluation was caprolactam, which was the intermediate for nylon 6, a competitor of Du Pont's nylon 6-6. The Explosives Department, after years of on-and-off research and controversy with the Textile Fibers Department, decided to build a plant to manufacture caprolactam. The Plastics Department had done some work on casting liquid caprolactam into molds, where it was polymerized to solid shapes, but because of the department's enormous investment in intermediates for nylon 6-6, caprolactam was a pariah. Peterson hoped to make shutters, windowsills, and bi-fold doors for closets from it. He estimated that it was not unreasonable that Du Pont's building products business might reach $300 million by 1975. The Executive Committee approved the program, which began in April 1963.[73]

After about two years, the Building Products Venture had articulated an overall business strategy of developing a low-maintenance house exterior, including roofing, siding, shutters, trim, windows, and doors, and supplementing this with a line of interior products. Peterson expected to sell between $500 and $2,000 worth of these products per house. The low-maintenance house exterior was based on Tedlar polyvinyl fluoride film and Polymer W, an ethylene copolymer filled with cement. Polyvinyl fluoride film had been prepared in the 1940s and showed outstanding outdoor stability, but technical problems remained to be solved and there were no large markets for it. Work on this polymer continued intermittently until 1960, when the Film Department decided to build a plant to make Tedlar film for lamination to other materials for use as house siding. Polymer W had been developed by the Plastics Department as a replacement for asphalt in shingles and as a substrate for Tedlar laminates. Another major product line was cast nylon 6 shutters and bi-fold doors. For interior use, Du Pont developed Corian polymethyl methacrylate "synthetic marble" for countertops and other uses. The Building Products Venture research group worked up prototypes of these products for testing and made estimates of large-scale production costs.[74]

By late 1967, the Polymer W–Tedlar siding composition and Polymer W roofing material had been dropped from the program because of their high costs and marginal advantages over other materials. This left a large hole in the venture because these products were targeted toward large-volume applications. The other two projects were moving toward commercialization, but there were still unanswered questions about them. For example, Corian turned out to be a good product that was attractive and easy to work with. One application, an integral countertop and sink bowl unit for bathrooms, had been enthusiastically received. But Corian products were being manufactured by an uneconomical batch process. In a report to a skeptical Executive Committee, Peterson maintained that "we are confident we have a product; it is less certain that we have a business." Defending the building products venture, he conceded that they had made some mistakes, resulting not from technological miscalculations but from a lack of understanding of the construction business. This was an acceptable shortcoming for a Du Pont R&D project; an admission of failure to meet technological goals would have led to prompt termination of the venture.[75]

The Executive Committee allowed the venture to continue for several more years. The cast nylon 6 business was dealt a severe blow when cheap stamped metal doors captured the bi-fold market. The remaining opportunity in window shutters did not justify a venture, and the Explosives Department shut down its caprolactam plant in 1967. The venture needed a new product with a much larger volume, and its staff made a second survey of company technology but came up with nothing that might save the enterprise. Therefore, in 1971 the project was terminated after about $50 million had been spent. Only Corian survived, and it has not generated significant earnings for Du Pont.[76]

Gee's successor as head of the Development Department summed up the Building Products Venture by stating that the anticipated revolution in housing construction had not occurred and that "mass production, industrialization, and centralization have as yet contributed little toward providing lower cost housing and creating needs for new functional materials in volume." In addition, Du Pont had encountered difficulty selling moderately priced, high-quality goods in an industry where the emphasis was on lower cost regardless of quality or performance. Finally, Du Pont's expected "stream of proprietary building materials . . . ha[d] in fact been more like a trickle."[77]

Chromium Dioxide

In the mid-1960s, while still managing the major ventures discussed above, the Development Department took over two related projects that had originated in the Central Research Department. These involved applications for chromium dioxide, which the department's chemists had prepared and had learned possessed unusual magnetic properties. In late 1963, the Development Department joined Central Research to determine the commercial value of chromium dioxide magnetic tape. Six months later, Gee's department took over the venture and ran it for two years before turning it over to the Photo Products Department. Eventually, it would become a moderately successful product for that department.[78]

Gee hoped to tap a much larger market with a chromium dioxide photocopier. In 1964, Central Research discovered that the magnetic properties of chromium dioxide could be used to fix images. With help from the Engineering Department over the next three years, Central Research developed a prototype machine. Because Du Pont lacked skills in the marketing end of the copier business, Central Research turned to the Development

Department for help in finding a business partner. In 1968 the office copier became a new venture in the Development Department, which promptly brought in an outside firm to help design a commercial machine and hired consultants to help appraise the venture. Nearly everyone soon reached the conclusion that Du Pont would have a difficult time challenging Xerox, which had 60 percent of the market. The business partner selected, Pitney Bowes, concluded that Du Pont's technology was not superior to Xerography in any important ways. Finally, at a time when the company had become short of cash, there was no low-cost way to get into the business. The Development Department estimated that the negative cash flow in this venture would quickly hit $100 million. Following this assessment, the venture was terminated.[79] The office copier was the last of the Development Department ventures because the large number of expensive ventures continuing throughout the company had consumed the firm's cash and exhausted the patience of the Executive Committee.

The Development Department and the New Venture Programs

From a strictly financial point of view, the Development Department's new venture programs of the 1960s were not successful. At its peak in 1967, the department had a budget of $13 million and over five hundred employees.[80] The total precommercial expense for the new ventures amounted to $100 million, and by 1980 cumulative earnings for the commercialized ventures probably had not equaled this figure.[81] The ACA has been an important product, though, which established a position for Du Pont in the rapidly developing biomedical field. All the other projects were in a sense castoffs from the industrial departments. Given Du Pont's decision that new products were needed quickly, few really new programs could have been developed within the comparatively short life span of Du Pont's new venture program.

Parallel to the new venture program in the Development Department, the industrial departments accelerated their efforts to move new products rapidly through the development and commercialization phases. Table 22.1 lists the products commercialized by Du Pont in the 1960s. As stated earlier, there was no overall coordination of this effort, and each new product was judged by the Executive Committee on its individual merits when a department made a request for funds large enough to require committee approval. By this time, a project usually had considerable momentum. Ever since he had been in research himself, President Greenewalt had recognized that stopping an R&D program was exceedingly difficult. Gee attempted to gather enough data so that the Executive Committee could make independent assessments of the departmental projects. To reduce dependence on usually optimistic departmental sales and earnings projections, Robert E. Gee developed independent forecasts based on sophisticated computer

Table 22.1. *New Products Commercialized, 1960–69*

Product	First Commercial Year
1. Vexar plastic netting	1960
2. Teflon FEP resin	1960
3. Teflon FEP film	1960
4. Alathon HDPE resin	1960
5. Delrin acetal resin	1960
6. Pyre-M.L. wire enamel	1961
7. Budium can coating	1961
8. Tedlar PVF film	1961
9. Vazo catalysts	1962
10. Uracil herbicides	1962
11. Linuron herbicides	1962
12. Plastic pipe products	1962
13. Lycra spandex fiber	1962
14. Elvax vinyl resin	1963
15. Zepel durable repellents	1963
16. Dycril printing plates	1963
17. Dymetrol strapping	1963
18. Nordel hydrocarbon elastomer	1964
19. Corfam poromeric products	1964
20. Clysar polyolefin film	1964
21. Detaclad metal cladding	1965
22. Pigmentary potassium titanate	1965
23. Surlyn A ionomer resin	1965
24. Reemay spunbonded polyester	1965
25. DuLite coil coatings	1966
26. Kapton polyimide film	1966
27. Krytox fluorinated oils	1966
28. Typar spunbonded polypropylene	1966
29. Crolux photopolymer ERPF	1966
30. Skamex metallurgical additive	1967
31. Symmetrel antiviral drug	1967
32. Nomex HT fiber	1967
33. Tyvek spunbonded olefin	1967
34. Metallized mylar	1968
35. Vespel polyimide products	1968
36. Instrument products	1969
37. Nylon shutters / bi-fold doors	1969
38. Vydax fluorocarbon telomers	1969
39. Immersion freezing of foods	1969
40. Riston photoresists	1969
41. Crofon fiber optics	1969

Source: "Supplement to 'Exhibit A' – NVD Report, Item 3 – New Ventures Commercialized (41)," Acc. 1850.

models of new ventures. This analysis was provided to departments as a service; the Executive Committee did not require it.[82] To keep better informed on these ventures and on the company's R&D programs in general, the committee passed a new set of R&D rules in 1964.

Reclassifying R&D

The 1960 rules, which classified all research as either "supporting" or "pioneering," failed to give the committee an accurate picture of Du Pont's R&D program because they divided new venture expenses into the two categories. (A technical problem was that the rules restricted "pioneering" research to ventures of a proprietary nature, something that was difficult to assess early in a project.) Committee member Robert Hershey, who had succeeded Lenher as advisor on research in 1963, argued that "in recent years there has been an increasing feeling in the Executive Committee that the information it receives about major new developments in the industrial departments should be provided more frequently and comprehensively so that the committee can accumulate a substantial background of knowledge to prepare it to deal with appropriation requests."[83]

To accomplish this goal, Hershey suggested dividing R&D into three classifications, Exploratory, Improvement of Existing Businesses, and New Venture Developments. He defined exploratory research as lacking an essential element in "the outline of a new business venture." When departmental management felt that a project had reached a well-defined state and that most of the remaining work would be development and commercialization, it could declare it a New Venture, a phase that lasted until the investment went into the books of a department. But, more importantly, New Venture expenditures were to be reported below the department's bottom line; that is, costs were not assigned to existing products and investments. Because the general managers believed that they were judged primarily on the return-on-investment of their department, these new rules allowed them to spend freely on new ventures without hurting their reported profits.[84] Declaring a New Venture, however, had its drawbacks. The Executive Committee expected quarterly and annual reports on them, and this meant that the committee could more easily meddle in what the general managers had considered their exclusive domain. This stipulation did not deter most general managers from declaring their major R&D projects new ventures.

Top Management and New Ventures

Although the new R&D budget rules of 1964 gave the Executive Committee the option of exercising a stronger role in directing Du Pont's R&D programs, it seemed to be unable to guide the company in any given direction even though the general managers and the committee members themselves began to feel that the company had serious problems that were not being addressed adequately. Part of the problem concerned leadership. Greenewalt had retired and relinquished the presidency to Lammot du Pont Copeland in August 1962. The fifty-seven-year-old Copeland was the son of Louisa d'Andelot du Pont, an older sister of Pierre, Irénée, and Lammot. When Greenewalt brought Copeland down from the Finance Committee in 1959 to serve also on the Executive Committee, it must have surprised many company personnel. Copeland had not been the heir apparent. The most qualified candidate for the job was Dawson, who had been a major architect of the new venture program and had demonstrated his ability as a skillful analyst and strategic thinker. He also wanted the Executive Committee to play a stronger role in charting the company's future course. But in 1962, the board of directors, which was dominated by family members, selected one of their own and the company's largest stockholder, Copeland, to head the company. He would not turn out to be a propitious choice.

Copeland had been involved in the financial side of the business but had no experience running a large, technically complex business. He graduated from Harvard with a BS in industrial chemistry in 1928 and joined the company in the laboratory of the Fairfield, Connecticut, plant of the Fabrics and Finishes Department. During the next decade Copeland specialized in field technical service and marketing studies. Generally, he received good marks on the report cards that were kept on young family members in the company. During World War II, Copeland served as a member of the post-war planning group in the Development Department and became a member of the board of directors in 1942, replacing his father, who had retired. A year later he became a member of the Finance Committee, which usually consisted of major stockholders. In 1954 he became chairman of the Finance Committee.[85]

As president, Copeland relied heavily on the counsel of the other committee members, many of whom had been general managers of industrial departments. Under these circumstances, decision making by committee became more difficult, and the staunch opposition to a proposal by one member was almost always certain to prevent its passage.[86] Generally, Copeland held fast to the traditions of Du Pont management and did not believe that major changes were needed in policy, organization, or strategy. Other committee members were not so sanguine about the company and its future.

By 1964, some Executive Committee members expressed doubt that the new venture program was solving the company's problems. The committee's radical faction asserted that Du Pont was pouring enormous sums of money into products aimed at highly competitive or nonexistent markets. In essence, nothing had changed since 1960. Discontent focused primarily on the leadership and planning roles of the Executive Committee and the disappointing productivity of Du Pont's R&D. One of the more outspoken critics was Lester Sinness, who had joined the committee from the Textile Fibers Department in 1963. He pointed to the company's failure to increase earnings and maintained that "the financial fraternity is becoming accurately aware of our current situation and future prospects." Sinness recalled Du Pont's earlier round of self-examination in 1961 when most of the proposals for changes "became submerged in a welter of conflicting opinion in the Executive Committee." Sinness singled out low research productivity as the major cause of Du Pont's deteriorating earnings:

> Speaking as a man who spent over sixteen years in the research area of the Company, I consider the research output of the Company as a whole to be disgracefully and inexcusably low in proportion to the calibre of men we employ, the facilities we give them, and the amount of money we allow them to spend....
>
> During the last twenty years our research establishment has become overfed, complacent and diffuse, while lecturing the world on the sacred character of fundamental research. In the meantime, our competition is passing us by.[87]

The second major problem of the company, Sinness argued, resulted from the "malfunctioning" of the Executive Committee:

> [T]hrough a distorted preoccupation with the concept of Departmental autonomy...the Executive Committee loses sight of its own responsibilities. [It] appears to sit only as a judicial body reviewing the past performance of the Departments and weighing whatever projects and proposals on policy or procedures may emanate from either the Industrial or Staff Departments. The Executive Committee seldom discusses or initiates anything of and by itself.

Through its "ritualized schedule of charts and reports," the committee, according to Sinness, had no time to examine and discuss periodically the future of the company and determine if company policies, organization, and procedures needed altering. Finally, he concluded that very little leadership emanated from the committee.

Although Sinness presented probably the most radical critique of the company and the Executive Committee, other members expressed similar opinions. Dawson stated that Du Pont needed to adopt an open-minded and even experimental approach to management and organizational problems because even with its long record of success, changes were needed. Characteristically, he wanted the Executive Committee to take a more active role in originating and implementing programs to ensure the future health of the company. Showing considerable foresight, he recommended realigning the industrial departments and restricting them to specific business areas, moves that would be made in the mid-1970s.[88] Other committee members, however, such as Charles B. McCoy, sided with Copeland and took a more traditional stance. McCoy did not think that new procedures would change things very much because "as long as, by and large, one deals with the same group of people, the possibilities are limited to boosting their creative output and the quality and timing of their decisions."[89] This round of discussion, like the earlier one, led to no major changes even though the data that Gee was accumulating showed some disturbing trends.

For years, Du Pont executives had been fond of telling the press that R&D was a form of gambling with the odds heavily weighted against success.[90] In the 1960s these words came back to haunt Du Pont. By 1964, it had become apparent to the committee that the new products that Greenewalt had called for a few years earlier were costing a tremendous amount of money and, contrary to expectations, were taking much longer to commercialize. Some of the products introduced between 1960 and 1964, such as Delrin resins, Tedlar film, Nordel elastomer, and Corfam leather replacement, continued to consume large amounts of money. To find out what was going on, the committee commissioned the Development Department to do some historical analyses of Du Pont's research projects.

The Development Department compiled an enormous amount of data on over one hundred new products introduced by Du Pont since 1930.[91] This represented the company's first attempt to characterize empirically and statistically the innovation process. These data would establish historical norms for new products and reveal changes that had occurred over the decades. The norms would be used to evaluate the predicted performance of Du Pont's current new products because there was increasing suspicion that many of the departmental forecasts were wildly optimistic. The other goal was to verify what everyone already knew; that beginning in the 1950s, the development and commercialization phases of new ventures had become very expensive. This trend was disconcerting but could have been tolerated if the new products, once introduced, grew rapidly and generated significant earnings. This had not been the case, however, because initial operative losses were also growing rapidly.

The Development Department reports showed how this situation had evolved and that things were continually getting worse (see Figure 22.1). These historical studies of Du Pont's new products yielded dramatic, but not unexpected, results. A brief statement of the conclusions was that "with few exceptions, the effectiveness of diversification research over the past fifteen years has been exceedingly poor relative to traditional expectations of commercial [i.e., Du Pont] performance." Venture bigness and risk had increased significantly, but profits had not been adequate to justify the risks. Although research-phase costs of new products had remained constant at about $700,000 and lasted a little over three years, development costs had increased between three- and ten-fold and the time required between two- and four-fold. The enormous projects of the Textile Fibers Department, the spunbonded fabrics and Nomex, were the worst in these aspects.

Statistical analyses showed that a venture incurring heavy precommercialization costs and taking over six years to develop would have difficulty breaking even ten years after commercialization. To compare ventures,

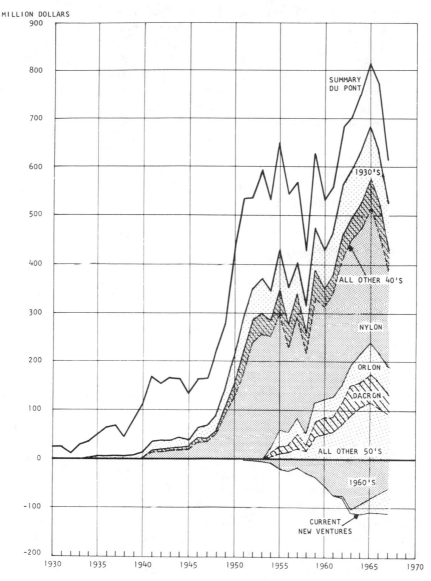

Figure 22.1. New Products Commercialized, 1930–67, Annual Operative Earnings. Source: R. M. Busche to E. B. Yelton, "Development and Commercialization of New Products," July 22, 1968, Development Department Files.

Du Pont calculated the "venture worth" at the time of commercialization by discounting profits for the first ten years by a set interest rate, which was also charged against the precommercial expenses. At an interest rate of 10 percent, which was roughly Du Pont's return on investment in the 1950s, only three products introduced between 1952 and 1967 had a positive venture worth, Viton fluoroelastomer, urea herbicides, and Quinacridone pigments. By this measure, such important products as Mylar film and Lycra spandex fibers had a negative venture worth. Included in this analysis were five commodity investments, and all these placed in the top ten out of thirty-two ventures analyzed. As Dawson had pointed out in 1957, commodity ventures, although not highly profitable, at least did not lose money. The author of the report concluded that these data were an "indictment" of Du Pont's research program rather than an indication that the company should invest more heavily in commodity chemicals.[92]

Development costs and initial commercial losses were taking an increasingly large bite out of Du Pont's earnings. In 1955 these two costs accounted for only 4 percent of earnings but had risen to about 14 percent in the early 1960s and reached 25 percent in 1967.[93] By this latter year, the new products introduced in the 1960s were over $400 million in the red. No other group of products had ever reached that level of indebtedness. The most recent products were setting new records for absorbing money.[94] These products threatened to swallow all of Du Pont's available capital, and prospects for some return on that money seemed to be far in the future.

Du Pont was clearly in a predicament, and although the reports graphically detailed the symptoms, they offered little in the way of diagnosis or cure. One prescription called for a renewal of entrepreneurial and creative spirit – which is what Greenewalt had asked for in 1960 – and more extensive use of venture-analysis techniques to avoid costly mistakes.[95] These reports shied away in their conclusions from what the Executive Committee soon would have to acknowledge: In a rapidly maturing industry, Du Pont's traditional innovation strategy was no longer viable.

In 1966, a year in which Du Pont spent a record $531 million on new construction, the fibers market faltered.[96] Realizing that the economic boom of 1961 to 1965 had covered up the growing competitiveness of the chemical industry and Du Pont's declining growth and profitability relative to other chemical companies, Wall Street soured on Du Pont and its stock fell from 250 to 150 during 1966, lowering the paper value of the company by $4.6 billion.[97] When these negative trends continued into 1967, the Executive Committee reported to the Finance Committee on what had gone wrong and what the prospects were for the future.[98] The decline in fibers earnings was in the committee's estimation inevitable and unavoidable, although some mistakes had been made that had exacerbated the situation (such as the heavy losses incurred in attempting to commercialize three spunbonded fabrics at once). In addition to the decline in fibers earnings, Du Pont's European investment of $230 million was not generating any earnings, and the committee was not sanguine about its prospects in the near term.

Looking at the performance of the industrial departments, the committee saw a direct correlation between low departmental earnings and large poor investments for new ventures. Of the recent $638 million in major capital investments, the committee estimated that about 30 percent "have *to date* had an adverse effect on our earnings, and although some may eventually be reasonable contributors to earnings, they will for the most part be written off or at best limp along as problem children." The future of some of its products looked reasonably bright, but the committee expected that except for fibers, Du Pont's performance would be about the same as some of its better-performing competitors. Executives believed that Du Pont could stabilize the situation and hold its position but saw "little basis for expecting that we can exceed importantly the earnings performance of other large, able chemical companies. To do so would require the addition of large volume, high return, rapid growth products [and] there are not too many of these on the horizon at this time." The other chemical companies had been relentlessly pursuing Du Pont ever since World War II and probably caught up by the late 1950s. Du Pont had made one last attempt to regain supremacy through the new ventures program, but by the late 1960s it appeared that it had not accomplished what the company had hoped.

At the end of 1967, Copeland retired and passed the reins to Charles B. McCoy, who inherited the job of bringing Du Pont's new venture expenses under control. The board of directors looked to a trusted member to set the company on a more prosperous path. McCoy was a second-generation Du Pont employee; his father John W. McCoy had been a charter staff member of the Eastern Laboratory after receiving a degree in chemistry from the University of Delaware. The senior McCoy rose through the ranks of the Explosives Department, Du Pont's traditional breeding ground for executives, and served on the Executive Committee from 1935 to 1947.[99] Charles B. followed in his father's footsteps after earning an MS in chemical engineering from the Massachusetts Institute of Technology in 1932. During the 1930s, McCoy held a number of jobs, including a four-year stint in the Foreign Relations Department's London office. In 1940, he joined the Explosives Department and became director of sales three years later. McCoy next served as assistant general manager of the Electrochemicals Department from 1950 to 1958 and general manager of the Elastomer Chemicals and the Explosives departments before being elected to the Executive Committee in 1961.[100]

A judicious man, McCoy proceeded cautiously, allowing the existing ventures to go forward but carefully scrutinizing requests for funds for new ones. He was hoping that the situation would improve soon. As he told *Forbes*, "We have an identifiable two dozen fairly important new products that we are bringing along right now; ... we've got this unusually big lump moving through the snake and it hasn't come out yet."[101] Most of these products would be in the black in five years, he predicted. According to *Fortune*, Chairman of the Board Greenewalt remarked "with feigned seriousness that he is shocked by the company's aggregate outlays on them and hopes they will be commercial soon."[102] The message that the Du Pont management sent to the business press was that although the company had been through some rough times, there was no reason to panic and that drastic changes were not needed. Generally Du Pont followed a course that was consistent with that evaluation.

In the 1960s, of the sixty new ventures under way at Du Pont, two-thirds were commercialized. The terminated ventures accounted for only 10 percent of the R&D expenditures on new ventures. In 1967, Du Pont had a number of ventures that had consumed over $60 million each, including two of the spunbonded fabrics, Nomex, caprolactam (which was terminated in 1967), and Corfam leather replacement.[103] This last product, one of the most ballyhooed in Du Pont history, increasingly became a "problem child" in the late 1960s. It soon became the company's most highly publicized failure.

Corfam

Beginning in the 1910s, Du Pont researchers had from time to time attempted to develop a substitute for shoe leather. Most of these efforts centered on coating fabrics with nitrocellulose or polyvinyl chloride (vinyl), which created nonporous, unleatherlike materials. In 1949, a researcher in the Pioneering Research Laboratory of the Textile Fibers Department discovered a new approach based on porous nonwoven fabrics. Between 1950 and 1955 three departments, Textile Fibers, Film, and Fabrics and Finishes (F&F), did seventy-five man-years of research and spent over $2 million trying to develop nylon-based compositions. In 1955 the Executive Committee ruled that F&F should carry the development forward even though the other two departments had extensive experience in the manufacture and processing of filmlike materials. The committee chose F&F because it had been in the coated fabrics business since it had acquired Fabrikoid in the 1924 merger of the Paint and Cellulose Products departments. Nevertheless, finishes, not films, were the department's major product line. Over the next several years, its researchers worked out a new composition for the product based on a nonwoven Dacron substrate with a porous polyurethane binder and a porous outer coating. By 1958, F&F had all the major components of a product, began the development of a process to make it, and initiated market analyses.[104]

Leather appeared to be a material vulnerable to substitution. Shortages were predicted in the future, and besides leather had some weaknesses, such as nonuniformity of properties, irregularly shaped hides, stiffening after being wetted and then dried, and high maintenance requirements through frequent polishing. A market research task force was soon assembled and a sophisticated venture analysis program developed. The conclusion of this study was that "a satisfactory product, which could be sold at leather equivalent prices to the shoemaker, would find an adequate market."[105] In 1962, F&F distributed 15,000 pairs of shoes for testing, and the results showed that 8 percent of the Corfam wearers complained of some discomfort compared to 3 and 24 percent respectively for leather and vinyl.[106] These results were encouraging enough to push Corfam's development forward.

Because F&F developed an overly complicated mechanical process to manufacture Corfam, its price had to be set at about that of finer grades of shoe leather. This, in part, led to F&F's decision to market Corfam in top-quality shoes. Also, this strategy avoided the problem of having Corfam lumped together with cheap and inferior materials such as vinyl. Du Pont thought it had a product that was actually superior to leather and believed that it could win the confidence of shoe manufacturers, retailers, and customers.[107]

In the fall of 1963, thirty high-quality shoe manufacturers that Du Pont had selected exhibited Corfam shoes at the National Shoe Fair, and the following summer Du Pont's plant opened.[108] The introduction of Corfam was heralded in a *Fortune* article by Lawrence Lessing entitled "Synthetics Ride Hell-Bent for Leather," which contained statements such as "in scale and significance it may well be another nylon" and "behind it stands a market development program of such size and savvy that it may well stand as a model of how to introduce a new product."[109] In tests, reported Lessing, Corfam had proven itself to be the equal of fine leather. In some ways the new material was better than leather because Corfam was unaffected by moisture, weighed a third less, kept its luster, and did not have to be broken in. With considerable fanfare, Corfam was introduced in 1964.

Over the next five years, shoe retailers sold 75 million pairs of Corfam shoes. But the new product failed to generate a profit in any year, and venture losses piled up until they reached about $70 million.[110] These losses were much larger than what the venture analysts had predicted because technical and marketing expenses turned out to be twice what had been assumed.[111] F&F's process was cumbersome and a constant source of headaches for those trying to operate it. Corfam encountered more retailer and consumer resistance than had been expected. This latter problem centered on foot comfort – about 15 percent of Corfam shoe wearers complained of having hot feet. Du Pont researchers could prove scientifically that Corfam breathed better than leather under laboratory conditions, but this did not persuade skeptical consumers. Some at Du Pont linked the problem to bad fitting by retail shoe clerks. Corfam shoes did not stretch, so proper fit was essential, which usually meant buying a larger size shoe than usual, something that many consumers refused to do. By 1969, a substantial fraction of both retailers and consumers had turned against Corfam.[112]

This happened at a time when the U.S. shoe business was changing dramatically. In the second half of the 1960s, stylish foreign-made shoes began to take a significant share of the market for men's and women's casual and dress shoes. Between 1965 and 1969, imports grew from 9 to 26 percent of the U.S. market. Consequently, Corfam and high-priced U.S. leather shoes lost out in the expensive shoe market. European shoes became popular, in part because they were made from many different styles of leather. Du Pont had difficulty producing its one variety of Corfam and with its inflexible process could not constantly change the product to keep up with the latest fashions. To make matters worse, the leather industry promoted glovelike leathers that Corfam could not duplicate. But it was the imports that pushed Corfam out of expensive shoes into cheaper ones where it had to compete with vinyl, which had unexpectedly captured 20 percent of the shoe market. Corfam was a much better product than vinyl but could not find a market niche at a price that would yield Du Pont a profit. Du Pont saw little hope for lowering the cost of Corfam significantly because of the mechanical nature of the manufacturing process; it was not as easy to scale up as a purely chemical plant would have been. When it lost the high-priced shoe market, Corfam had no chance of becoming profitable.[113] Du Pont stuck with Corfam for several more years and developed a cheaper product but finally sold the plant and process to Poland in 1971, where it has operated successfully ever since. Corfam became known as Du Pont's Edsel and became a symbol to its executives of the shortcomings of the new venture program.[114]

Conclusion: The Need for Change

A survey of seventy Du Pont executives in 1969 showed that most of them considered the entire new product push of the 1960s a failure. The program had been initiated in part to lessen Du Pont's dependence on Textile Fibers. But at the end of the decade the position of fibers in the company's business had changed very little, still accounting for about a third of sales and over 40 percent of company earnings.[115] Only one new product, Lycra spandex fibers, had made it to the goal of $50-million-per-year sales, and total sales from new products were roughly half of what had been needed to maintain Du Pont's earlier rate of growth.[116]

Rather than moving the company into new directions, the new ventures program of the 1960s had been an intensified version of the traditional Du Pont innovation strategy. In the 1960s Du Pont commercialized forty-one new products and abandoned twenty other new ventures. Because each department initiated its own programs, there was no overall trend in the new products and no strategy of moving into new businesses such as pharmaceuticals and electronics or integrating forward or backward. Of the commercialized ventures, over half were polymer products and only a few of these required forward integration. Another six ventures were textile fibers, and all of them were among the ten largest in terms of expense.[117] If Du Pont was hoping to lessen its dependence on textile fibers, allowing that department to carry out such large new ventures was not the way to do it. However, the Executive Committee upheld the tradition of autonomous departments and permitted the Textile Fibers Department to pursue its destiny independently. The Instrument Products Venture, which led to the development of the Automatic Clinical Analyzer, represented the most successful diversification. Of all the new products introduced, only one was a pharmaceutical, Symmetrel, an antiviral drug that found only limited markets. Most of the new products, however, were introduced into the company's traditional markets.

In an industry in which Du Pont had numerous and competent competitors, it became increasingly difficult for the company to find promising proprietary products that would find large markets. Nevertheless, Du Pont maintained a steadfast belief in its technological superiority and attempted to differentiate itself from its competitors by developing products that raised chemical technology to a new level of complexity. Delrin, Corfam, and the spunbonded fabrics were all magnificent technological achievements, but the price for these feats was very high. Other companies developed less sophisticated products to serve many of the same markets. Du Pont had concentrated on technical virtuosity, developing products that had superior properties but at a price that customers were not willing to pay.

R&D had become very costly for Du Pont; it spent about five times what it had predicted at the beginning of the decade. In the 1960s the company spent over $1.6 billion on new products. In 1969, these products were on balance contributing nothing to Du Pont's earnings, although over half of them were generating some profits.[118] A decade later, the picture looked a little brighter, although cumulative earnings probably fell short of the total development cost. In 1979, the new products of the 1960s accounted for 15 percent of total sales and 28 percent of Du Pont's profits.[119] Remarkably, Corfam and caprolactam were the only major products that had been terminated, although some of the others were still struggling. Six products, including three fibers, had surpassed $100-million-per-year sales, and a similar number had made important contributions to earnings.[120]

Du Pont survived its new venture program of the 1960s and eventually gained considerable benefits from it, but from a strategic and financial point of view it was a failure. It did not move the company in new directions. Considered as an investment, Du Pont's new product venture has not paid an adequate return. The program also limited Du Pont's future options because it consumed the company's cash reserves.

In the 1960s, Du Pont paid out 70 percent of its earnings as dividends and financed its new products from internal sources. Du Pont did not borrow money. The most obvious thing to do with excess cash being generated by a maturing business is to acquire a company in a newer, faster-growing business with some connection to the present company. Of course, pharmaceuticals was the most profitable industry in the 1960s and a logical diversification for Du Pont. However, pharmaceuticals did not appeal to many Du Pont executives because it was a business that was very different from chemicals, especially in marketing; despite what Greenewalt might have said in the late 1950s, Du Pont continued to see itself as a chemical company. In addition, the antitrust situation muddled the issue.

Another logical acquisition would have been an oil company. Both the Plastics and Explosives departments wanted to build plants to supply their own raw materials, but the Executive Committee was wary of moving into such a competitive and unfamiliar business. Internal analyses showed that chemicals represented only 6 percent of oil company revenues and that the industry was basically fuel-oriented. To manufacture its own petrochemicals, Du Pont would also have to get into the fuel business to such an extent that it would become at least the twentieth largest oil company in the United States. Oil company profits were generated from the production of oil, so exploration, a risky business, was essential to ensure future profits. The characteristics of this industry were so foreign to Du Pont's experience of turning low-priced chemicals into sophisticated, higher-priced products that the Executive Committee shied away from petrochemicals. In addition, the industry was not as profitable as chemicals, which was why the oil companies were integrating forward into chemicals. To obtain adequate supplies of needed raw materials at reasonable prices, Du Pont could always play one supplier off against another.[121]

Even without the large increase in oil prices in 1974, investment in an oil company would have provided a moderately profitable outlet for Du Pont cash and increased the company's R&D on intermediates from petrochemicals, an area in which Du Pont was lagging. But an investment in an oil company was too conservative for Du Pont; it would have been seen as a sign of defeat, that Du Pont's R&D could no longer generate enough opportunities for investment. Anticommodity sentiment in Du Pont ran very strong. In the 1960s, Du Pont had integrated backward in a few areas and had made money doing so, but it was not a major strategy.

By 1970, Du Pont's executives had concluded that its traditional high-risk, high-investment, high-reward innovation strategy no longer worked. Clearly, the Du Pont Company would have to change its strategy to maintain growth. These changes would be very difficult for such a proud and tradition-bound organization to make. Setting the tone for the 1970s, one Du Pont executive asked,

> Is Du Pont destined to be a chemical company forever? Or are we a collection of high quality resources that can be put to work wherever prospects for profits are? The Executive Committee led us out of the wilderness of a single product business between 1910 and 1920 into broad participation in one of the great growth industries of the time. Why can't their successors take on a similar task now that the bloom is off the rose in the chemical industry?[122]

The prescriptions for leading Du Pont in new directions invariably required that the Executive Committee assume much more leadership in the strategic management of the company, which also invariably meant exercising more control over the industrial departments. In the 1970s, with a good deal of hesitation, the Executive Committee took on these tasks.

23

Successful Diversification: The Photo Products Department

In the 1950s, rumors frequently circulated through Du Pont's Photo Products Department that the company's management was tired of trying to keep up with Eastman Kodak and was considering getting out of the business. When this did not happen, departmental employees liked to joke that their jobs had been saved only because company president Crawford Greenewalt had a strong interest in photography as a hobby.[1] Although this was said in jest, the department's researchers knew they were in the company's smallest department, that their turf was dominated by Kodak, and that their future lay largely in their own hands. However, the Executive Committee did have reasons for continuing Du Pont's photographic products business. The overall market for image-forming technology was growing at a healthy rate, and Kodak showed signs of some vulnerability despite its long, successful past. Although still a formidable competitor, it had become large and tradition-bound, with an enormous investment in existing technologies. As a much smaller organization, Photo Products had the opportunity to jump quickly into developing market niches, capture a major fraction of the new business, and achieve significant growth for the department. This is largely what Photo Products did in the late 1950s and 1960s. So successful was the department in this strategy that the Executive Committee began to give it responsibility for diversification into related technologies such as instruments and electronics. In the two decades after 1960, Photo Products grew at twice the rate of the entire company, and its contribution to company earnings increased from 2.5 percent in 1959 to 19 percent in 1979.[2] By extending the company's technology into new and fast growing markets, Photo Products transformed itself from a headache for top management into one of the company's star performers.

Development of Du Pont's Film Business

Du Pont's involvement with photographic films began in 1912 when H. Fletcher Brown, head of the Smokeless Powder Operating Department, wrote to the Development Department suggesting that the company consider making film base as an outlet for nitrocellulose.[3] During the next decade, Du Pont spent over $500,000 trying to develop a film base and emulsion coatings.[4] However, rather than go it alone, in 1924 Du Pont formed a joint venture with the Pathé Cinema Société Anonyme of Paris, France. For 49 percent of the stock in the new Du Pont–Pathé Film Manufacturing Corporation, Du Pont gained access to Pathé's technology. The new company first produced 35-mm positive movie film, which had a large market because hundreds of prints were made from one master negative.[5] Over the next decade, the film company captured 20 percent of the positive film business and 40 percent of the much smaller negative film business but did not challenge Eastman Kodak in its primary stronghold, amateur roll film.[6] By the late 1920s, Du Pont sold about $4 million worth of film a year, and the business returned a healthy profit even though Du Pont had less than 5 percent of the total photographic film market.[7]

The fortunes of the Du Pont film company improved when it introduced an X-ray film in 1932. After World War I, the use of X rays increased dramatically and reached 35 million exposures a year in the early 1930s. Applications varied. As Fortune reported in 1932, "Yale requires freshmen to be X-rayed as part of their physical examination, and the state of Tennessee requires the X-ray examination of boilers." In the next few decades, the use of X rays continued to grow, doubling every five years. Soon X-ray film accounted for half the film company's profits with sales of $10 million a year by the late 1940s, capturing about a fourth of the market.[8]

In the 1940s, Du Pont bought out the minority interest in the Du Pont–Pathé Film Company and purchased two additional companies to add to its new Photo Products Department. The Patterson Screen Company manufactured X-ray and fluoroscopic screens and provided an adjunct to Du Pont's X-ray film business. Du Pont also acquired the Defender Company, a manufacturer of sensitized paper and portrait film, which had been a large consumer of Du Pont film base. Department general manager George A. Scanlan justified the acquisition on the basis that Du Pont's photographic products were all mature, his department needed some fast growing products, and sensitized paper was one such product.[9] With the addition of Defender, total sales of the Photo Products Department reached $20 million a year, or about 2 percent of the company's total. It was still Du Pont's smallest department and held only a small share of the market compared to Eastman Kodak.[10]

In the 1950s, Kodak stepped up its competition with Du Pont, and the Photo Products Department suffered. Seeking in 1952 to explain the reasons for its decline in profits, general manager Sam G. Baker attributed the department's inability to increase production efficiency to "a failure to do the right kind of research, to include process work as a subject for research, and to supply adequate technical talent for support of production." Until Baker took over the department in 1950, it did not have a plant process group or research programs focused on increasing the efficiency of its plants. Baker complained that the department's new research laboratory at the plant in Parlin, New Jersey, was "constructed almost entirely without facilities for engineering and process research and provide[d] facilities mainly for bench work on emulsion chemistry, synthetic organic chemistry, and sensitometry." He also believed that the department's research was too theoretical and deficient in pursing commercial objectives, the result being that Du Pont had "been consistently behind and ha[s] persisted in the role of a follower, not a leader."[11]

Emphasis on Innovation

To upgrade his research division, Baker acquired Frank Signaigo, a veteran Textile Fibers Department research director, and expanded its activities dramatically.[12] During his tenure as general manager, between 1950 and 1955, Baker increased spending on process improvement from $0.4 to $2.5 million per year. At the same time, however, he did not shortchange new product research, which grew from $1.0 to $2.4 million per year.[13] Even with these changes, however, Baker did not expect to see any significant improvements occurring for three or four years, and he was right. Yet Baker failed to anticipate from what direction the improvement would come. Instead of relying on process improvements or trying to beat Kodak in amateur photography, Photo Products eventually outflanked its larger adversary through the introduction of new products. Nevertheless, the department's management had to learn the hard way that challenging Kodak's core business was a risky strategy.

Rather than continuing to yield to Kodak in amateur photography, Photo Products attempted to enter the color film business in the 1950s. Color film had been an objective of Du Pont research since Technicolor (for motion pictures) and Kodachrome (for still photography) had been introduced in the mid-1930s. The Chemical Department spent over $500,000 on new types of color film between 1937 and 1953.[14] In the mid-1950s, Photo Products was desperate for new products. So it picked up this project. By the end of the decade, researchers had developed an amateur color film that the Photo Products Department believed produced pictures that were superior to prints made from Kodak's Kodachrome. Because of this promising development, Du Pont entered into a partnership with Bell & Howell to commercialize the new product.[15]

To counter this attack on one of its major business lines, Kodak soon introduced Kodachrome II, which was superior to Du Pont's new film. As one Photo Products researcher later realized, Kodak had done much more research on color film than Du Pont and could quickly match any competitor's improvements.[16] When it announced Kodachrome II, Kodak also issued the warning, "Experimentally we have finer materials..., but it will be a while before we have them commercially."[17] Within a few years, Du Pont matched the technical quality of Kodachrome II in the laboratory but did not have an adequate large-scale manufacturing process. Also, a very large advertising budget would have been necessary to establish Du Pont in the market. Faced with this discouraging situation, the Photo Products Department terminated the venture in 1965 after spending about $10 million, which was not a large sum of money compared to other corporate ventures of the day. But it was large for a small department.[18] Photo Products was more successful with other ventures that did not directly challenge Kodak.

Photo Products' first major successful innovation started with the usual goal: to make the company's movie film competitive with that of Kodak, which enjoyed a proprietary position with its preferred cellulose triacetate film base. Photo Products had been seeking a new film base since the late 1930s, but it was not until 1947 that an attractive candidate appeared. In that year, Francis P. Alles, a research supervisor, learned that the Rayon Department had prepared polyester films that possessed outstanding clarity and excellent tensile and tear strength.[19] Films made by Rayon's process, however, could not be used for photographic film because its specifications for clarity and uniformity were much higher than for general-purpose film. Starting from different concepts, Photo Products researchers developed a new process for a pilot plant producing ten-inch-wide film. Evaluation of polyester film base from this machine showed that it had properties superior to triacetate except that it could not be spliced easily, a requirement for movie film.

While researchers tried to find a simple method for splicing polyester film, a large 45-inch-wide commercial production machine was built. But when this machine was finished, it would not produce a satisfactory product. Polyester films become strong through stretching in both directions. To make an optically clear film, this stretching has to be carefully balanced, and this proved difficult to achieve in a 45-inch-wide film. At this point, Photo Products launched a task force to study the fundamentals of the stretching process in the laboratory. Team leader Abraham B. Cohen, a young Cornell PhD who would later play a critical role in the development of other products, put his researchers on a three-shift-per-day, seven-day-per-week schedule to learn about film stretching. Within six months the problems had been solved, and the plant start-up began under the direction of Ivan Lundgaard. But splicing still stood in the way of making it a successful movie film.[20] By this time, however, movie film no longer looked like a major growth market.

The outstanding dimensional stability of polyester film suggested its use as graphic arts film, which was dominated by heavy and cumbersome glass plates. Dimensional stability was particularly critical in color printing to ensure proper alignment of the images because color reproductions were made by printing one color at a time. After the introduction of Du Pont's polyester-based graphic arts films in 1955, sales quickly increased fivefold to $10 million per year and reached nearly $50 million by 1970.[21] Graphic arts films, along with polyester-based X-ray film, eventually resuscitated the department.

The X-ray film market had been targeted early by George Loving, who would become general manager of the department in 1963 but died tragically in a plane crash later that year.[22] Researchers concentrated on movie film until 1957, when Kodak introduced the first automatic processing machine for X-ray film. By selling a whole system, Kodak increased its market share significantly. As a result, Du Pont's once-profitable X-ray film business began to suffer, sending the Photo Products Department into red ink. Ironically, this dark cloud turned out to have a silver lining. The new processors chewed up Kodak's acetate film and Du Pont discovered that its stronger polyester film worked beautifully in them. With its superior film base, Photo Products regained its position in X-ray films by 1959.[23] Kodak also made polyester base because in 1955 it had obtained a license from Du Pont to manufacture everything but movie film, which at the time was the market that Du Pont had in mind for its film. That Du Pont had a substantial lead in polyester film technology offset somewhat this strategic error. Kodak moved more slowly into polyester film because it already had a large investment in triacetate production facilities.[24] For once, Photo Products had gotten a jump on Kodak and attempted to maintain an advantage in the marketplace. To support its X-ray film business, Photo Products put increased emphasis on the work of Robert Upson, whose group was developing improved photographic emulsions. It also began providing extensive customer service. Soon the company's X-ray film sales took off, growing at 15 percent a year, and reaching $100 million a year, or 40 percent of the market, by 1970.[25]

A third major research program of the 1950s developed printing plates using a new type of image-forming technology, photopolymerization. For reasons that will be discussed below, Dycril printing plates never lived up to Du Pont's expectations but did lay the groundwork for a second generation of highly successful products. Photopolymerization work at Du Pont had its origins in the Chemical Department in the late 1930s. Its researchers had studied the initiation of polymerization reactions with light, and in 1948 the department started a program to use this phenomenon to create images. Up to this time, all photography was based on the transformation of silver halides to silver crystals upon exposure to light. In Du Pont's Chemical Department, researcher Louis Plambeck discovered that he could spread a syrupy liquid methyl methacrylate polymer solution on a plate, expose the plate to ultraviolet light through a negative, and solid would form in the exposed areas. After the liquid had been washed away, a relief image remained (see Figure 23.1). Another researcher suggested that this technology could be used to make relief printing plates, and it could. However, the syrupy liquid proved difficult to use.[26]

Research then shifted toward making a solid photopolymer composition

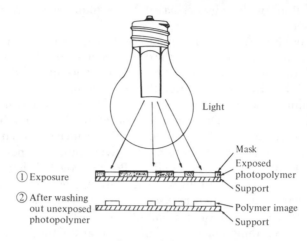

Figure 23.1. Production of Photopolymer Images.

that would change in some property such as solubility or melting point upon exposure. Plambeck and his associates soon worked out a solid composition that became insoluble on exposure to light, so the unexposed material could be dissolved away. In the mid-1950s, Photo Products developed a process to make photopolymer plates, and the commercial plant started up in 1961.[27] The Dycril trademarked plates, though, were hampered with an expensive process that limited their application to the relatively small, premium end of the market. Hercules introduced a successful automated liquid system that was used in the large newspaper printing business; Du Pont had abandoned liquid photopolymers because it had not considered selling entire systems.[28] Because of its higher cost, Dycril did not find adequate markets to generate profits. Yet it provided the technical basis for other more successful products.

Successful New Products

A related photopolymer development, Riston resists, was the company's most outstanding new product during the 1970s, generating pretax earnings of over $150 million and yielding a high return on investment.[29] The Riston project began in 1961, when Photo Products chemist David H. Woodward asserted that Du Pont's solid photopolymer compositions might be used to make printed circuits for incorporation in all kinds of electrical devices. At that time, a Kodak system employing a liquid photoresist had been used for several years. Before this technology became available, coarse printed circuits had been prepared by printing chemically resistant patterns on copper and etching away the unprotected metal. In the Kodak process, which was basically similar to the one that Du Pont developed (see Figure 23.2),

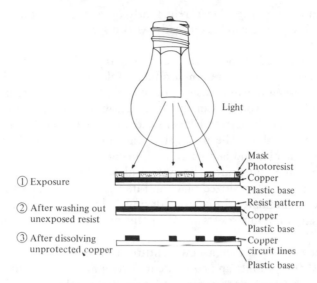

Figure 23.2. Production of Photocircuits.

a liquid photoresist was coated over a copper and plastic laminate. After the liquid dried, a template or negative of the circuit was laid over the composite and exposed to ultraviolet light, which initiated chemical reactions that made the photopolymer in the circuit areas insoluble. Next, a solvent was used to wash out the unexposed polymer, leaving a circuit pattern defined by the resist. Finally, the unprotected area was etched away and the photoresist removed, leaving a copper printed circuit. As had been the case with Dycril printing plates, Woodward believed that a solid film would be easier to use than the existing liquid system.[30]

Although this concept appeared to be a good one to several people in the Photo Products research division, they could not engender much enthusiasm for it either in the marketing division, which in this era exerted considerable influence on the department's research programs, or in higher management, which had the final say in these matters.[31] Generally, it appeared that Du Pont would again be challenging Kodak in a field where it dominated, as had been the case with color film. The market for printed circuits also did not appear to be large or rapidly growing. Subsequent developments would prove these assumptions false.

The Riston program accelerated in early 1966, when Monroe Sadler, who had been director of Central Research's applications research, was transferred into Photo Products to head its new venture activities. He was very impressed with the potential for Du Pont's photoresist plates and decided to increase the intensity of the development effort. In a conversation with veteran researcher Cohen, who was not involved with Riston, Sadler asked for an opinion about the progress of the program. Cohen said that he thought it should be done differently, and Sadler asked him if he wanted to be put in charge of it. Cohen reluctantly agreed to take on the job and soon convinced the researchers already working on it of the validity of his approach.[32]

Cohen had looked at the product critically from the customer's point of view and decided that a superior product could be made if Du Pont built its own developing machine instead of making films that were compatible with Kodak's processor. In Cohen's conception, the Riston system would consist of a photopolymerizable layer sandwiched between Mylar polyester and polyethylene films. The processing machine automatically peeled off the polyethylene film and laminated the photopolymer-Mylar combination to a copper-plastic substrate. The system also included equipment for the exposure of the now-sensitized plate and its development into a resist. The Riston process eliminated the coating, drying, baking, edging, and inspecting steps necessary for liquid resists and cut panel preparation time from minutes to seconds.[33]

Cohen next put together a new venture team with groups working simultaneously on product and equipment development, manufacturing, and marketing. Because of space limitations at the Parlin Laboratory, two trailers were purchased and turned into development laboratories. Building equipment was a relatively new activity for the department, and Cohen stated that "some of the procedures we used in the early stages not only were unorthodox but built character."[34] Within six months of the organization of the venture team, Cohen was ready for a commercial test of his system.

The first commercial test was for a manufacturer who was producing a very high percentage of imperfect panels. Cohen and Robert Heiart had designed a portable unit for testing and took it to the plant. After showing how the system operated, about forty-eight test panels were made, and the plant management decided to process them into finished units. When the panels came out beautifully, Du Pont had its first potential customer. Cohen, however, dampened their enthusiasm by telling them that Du Pont was anywhere from six months to a year away from having anything to sell. Having heard of the successful test, assistant general manager Phillip Wingate jumped on a plane and came to see the results firsthand. When the potential customer's top management asked him if they could buy the product, Wingate said, "Yes." Stunned but excited by his success, Cohen went home and set up a small production unit while continuing to improve the process and product. The following spring, Cohen made a presentation to IBM, which was also won over to Riston. Du Pont's photopolymer system fit IBM's needs for sophisticated printed circuits. After the IBM success, Du Pont had people beating down the door to get the product, and for a considerable period thereafter sales were limited by supply.[35] Under these circumstances, Riston made money right from the start, and precommercial R&D expenses were only $1.6 million. By 1977, it had reached Edwin Gee's successful new product target of a $50-million-per-year business with a net return on investment of 20 percent.[36]

The Riston story stands in stark contrast with most of Du Pont's developments of the 1960s. It was done quickly, inexpensively, and immediately found a profitable and growing market niche. Although Photo Products had conceived of the product in the early 1960s, it required management backing, an accelerated development program, and the astute judgment of Cohen to make Riston into a highly successful innovation.

With Riston well on its way, Photo Products picked another project to organize as a new venture and push toward commercialization: the Cromalin color proofing system. The research division had been working for some time on a proofing system for high quality color reproductions. Color graphics in magazines and other printed material are made by printing four separate images, each a different color. The photographic films used to make these images are black and white but have been sensitized for a particular color – red, yellow, blue, or white. The only method to determine what the final photograph would look like was to prepare printing plates from the photographic films and run a test picture. High-quality reproductions, which most advertisers and many magazines demanded, usually required several iterations of the process in order to balance the colors properly so that, for instance, a model's hair did not have a green tint. Each time the original photographs were touched up, a new set of plates had to be made and tested. Overall, the proofing process was time-consuming and expensive. In the early 1960s, 3M introduced its Color Key system employing four separate single color films. The film would be exposed and processed to provide single-color images which could then be overlaid to produce a color picture.[37]

In 1964, Cohen and co-worker Marion Burg invented a process for quick, dry-process color proofing. Their process was based on a photopolymer composition that was transformed from tacky to hard upon exposure to ultraviolet light. In color proofing, a positive transparency of the red image, for example, would be used as a mask for the photopolymer film, while the unexposed portions, which represent the image, remained tacky. Next, a red toner was applied to the plate and formed the red image by sticking to the tacky areas. In the original conception of the system, this image would then be transferred to another surface simply by turning it over and pressing it to transfer the toner particles, which would be set by heating. Researchers in Photo Products worked on developing this system for a number of years, but potential customer response was not enthusiastic, especially because the accurate transfer of the image required considerable skill.[38]

In 1970, Wingate, now general manager, asked Cohen if he would take over the Cromalin color proofing system and organize a new venture around it. Cohen replied that he would take on the job but was not happy with the Cromalin system. Instead he proposed switching to an alternative that had been examined earlier and was similar to the Riston approach; the photopolymer layer would be sandwiched between Cronar photographic film base and a protective film cover. In use, the protective cover would be removed and the film base laminated to printing paper. The first color positive would be used to expose the plate, and the toner applied. Then the next color would be developed by placing another layer of Cromalin film on the first one, thus building up the full color image. Cohen remembers that initially this concept did not receive much support, especially from the sales division, which had done a sophisticated, computer-aided study showing that it had less than no value for the customer. But Wingate gave him unqualified support. In showing the system to potential customers, Cohen found the production people very enthusiastic about it even though the technical people expressed only mild interest. Encouraged by this favorable response, Cohen moved the development of Cromalin ahead expeditiously; it could even be manufactured with the same equipment used for Riston.[39]

The first major test for Cromalin came at the Drupa trade show in Germany, and the product was a sensation. Originally, no one believed that Cromalin proofs would be accepted as final and that printing would still be the ultimate test. However, Cromalin proofs proved to be very accurate and were accepted in lieu of actual printing plate reproductions.[40] Like Riston, Cromalin was developed rapidly at relatively low cost and generated profits immediately. Although it has not grown as fast as Riston, by 1980 Cromalin represented an approximately $50-million-per-year business that had an unusually high rate of return.[41]

Even with Riston and Cromalin apparently headed for successful commercialization, in the early 1970s the Executive Committee still worried about the future of the department, which was heavily dependent on silver-halide-based photographic products. Edwin Gee, who had served as general manager of Photo Products for two years until being promoted to the Executive Committee in 1970, was concerned about the department's low rate of return but conceded that he "found no clear answer while I was there, since our ability to compete with Kodak requires a very high product technical expense."[42] Generally, Kodak continued to lead in process technology, but Du Pont had overcome some of Kodak's advantage by introducing new products and by having an aggressive marketing organization.[43] As one observer put it, Photo Products "had been stretched almost to the breaking point . . . by trying to keep pace with Kodak in its primary markets."[44]

Photo Products put its hopes for the future on research, but in the 1970s the continuity of the department's program depended upon its ability to increase earnings. General Manager Wingate recalled that a one-month downturn in earnings would prompt questions from some Executive Committee members. If earnings decreased for three months or longer, there was pressure to cut costs, and the research budget was always a prime candidate for pruning. To provide a stable business base upon which to build, Photo Products worked hard to reduce manufacturing costs and improve the quality of its products. In X-ray film, especially, product consistency was critical; doctors would not tolerate extraneous marks on X rays caused by film imperfections. Not only did Photo Products make improved film in this era but also had an excellent sales force to sell it.[45] The sales division also spearheaded Photo Products' drive to expand into foreign markets.

Photo Products began first to market and then to manufacture its products around the world in the 1960s. Previously the department had negligible sales outside the United States, but by 1975, 40 percent of its sales were in foreign markets. Expansion overseas began when General Manager John M. Clark directed the purchase of the Adox Company in Germany in 1962.[46] The Adox line of products was not very important and had been almost totally abandoned before the subsidiary became profitable. Despite the Executive Committee's contention in 1967 that the Adox acquisition was a "clear-cut mistake," it gave Photo Products a foothold in an important market.[47] And in the 1970s, Du Pont's investment in Adox would begin to pay dividends under the leadership of William M. Stanton as Photo Products European sales grew rapidly. Stanton, a former laboratory director, had been transferred to sales because general management believed that successful sales in photo products required a superior technical understanding of the products and markets involved.[48] While Photo Products was expanding overseas, the Executive Committee began to concentrate the company's major diversification efforts in this department.

Diversification

In the early 1970s, Photo Products moved aggressively into instruments and electronics as a result of internal departmental realignments, acquisitions, and the continuing efforts of research. After becoming general manager, Gee successfully lobbied the Executive Committee into transferring the instruments business from the Development Department to his new province.[49] He argued that Photo Products was already in the mechanical equipment business and that the department's X-ray film sales force could effectively market the Automatic Chemical Analyzer (ACA). The mechanical equipment that Gee referred to was a line of automatic film processors, which Photo Products had tried to develop in response to Kodak's pioneering efforts in this field. More and more customers were buying entire systems. Although film sales were not dependent on the availability of Du Pont equipment, as one report stated, "the sales growth opportunity is significantly increased when [our] equipment is being used...." In 1968, Photo Products started selling processors, consisting of rollers, tanks, and driers assembled primarily from purchased components.[50] Once established in Photo Products, the new Instrument Division broadened its product line through the purchase of Bell & Howell Company's analytical instrument business and Ivan Sorvall, Incorporated, which made mass spectrometers and high-speed centrifuges, respectively. Not even these products gave Du Pont the breadth that it needed to be a profitable analytical instrument manufacturer. Through 1980, Photo Products had not earned any money from its analytical and process instruments, but the ACA had become a very successful product.[51]

Another successful diversification was Photo Products's move into electronics, which began with Riston and was strengthened by the addition of the electronic materials business of the Electrochemicals Department and the acquisition of Berg Electronics. On January 1, 1972, Du Pont instituted a major reorganization that transferred Electrochemicals' product line, consisting of dispersions of precious metal and glass powders used to produce electronic microcircuits and capacitors, to Photo Products. Electronics manufacturers printed these pastes on alumina ceramic wafers to form circuits for various functions. At the time it was relocated in Photo Products, the electronic products division was about a $15 million a year business. By the end of the decade, Du Pont's sales had grown to over $100 million a year and the product line had over 500 different compositions. In addition to being a rapidly growing business, the electronic materials line also was very profitable.[52]

Berg Electronics proved to be another big winner for Photo Products. Du Pont was able to buy Berg in 1972 because antitrust constraints had been relaxed in the late 1960s. The company had been formed by inventor-entrepreneur Quentin Berg, who had worked for the dominant firm in connectors, AMP, Incorporated, before resigning in 1947 to start his own company. Although his business had been growing at the rate of 25 percent a year for a decade and had reached $17 million in sales, Berg was, by the early 1970s, looking for a way to free himself to pursue other interests.[53] Berg knew Edward Boelter, manager of Photo Products' electronic pastes business, and made an offer to him to sell out to Du Pont. Berg had singled out Du Pont because he thought his organization could prosper in such a technically competent company and in one that had a reputation for being a good place to work.[54] In 1972 he accepted an offer of $24.3 million worth of Du Pont stock for his company, which manufactured electrical connectors that are basic materials for building circuits and electronic hardware. Although Berg had only 3 percent of the domestic market – AMP had over 50 percent – Berg enjoyed, according to a Du Pont report, "an excellent reputation for engineering innovation and competence with the major electronics companies."[55] Not surprisingly, its largest customer was IBM, which accounted for nearly a quarter of Berg's sales. In Berg, Photo Products saw the nucleus for a major new business that was closely related to several others it was developing. A year after the acquisition, general manager Wingate reported that sales were up 50 percent from 1972, that a detailed examination of the company showed it to be a sound and growing one, and that the "product line is well-engineered and directed at the fastest growing segments of the electronics market."[56] Realizing the growth potential of the connector business, particularly in Europe where Berg had only a small facility, Photo Products expanded the operation as rapidly as it could, increasing investment nearly tenfold in eight years. In the 1970s,

Berg grew at a rate of 34 percent a year and doubled its domestic market share, making it second only to AMP. By 1979 Berg had become a $170 million business that had a net return on investment of 20 percent.[57] Thus Berg turned out to be exactly the type of business opportunity that Du Pont had tried to generate internally through research in the 1960s.

Conclusion: A New Du Pont Formula?

The Photo Products Department existed for a long time in the shadow of Du Pont's larger departments and the Eastman Kodak Company. The complacency and hubris that affected other departments did not affect Photo Products. In the mid-1950s, it desperately needed new products, and the Executive Committee was willing to support an expanded research program. Throughout the 1950s and 1960s, Photo Products research expenditures averaged 11.5 percent of sales and consumed 36 percent of the department's earnings. Comparative companywide statistics were 7.0 percent and 21 percent, respectively.[58] Instead of spending this money on fundamental research, Photo Products pursued a diversified innovation strategy aimed at creating market niches for new products in rapidly growing markets.

This strategy was not the result of a brilliant top management decision. It evolved over a number of years through experience with various new products. Color film and Dycril photopolymer plates were commercial failures but did not impose a heavy financial burden on the department because these ventures were relatively small in scale. Unlike the Textile Fibers or Plastics departments, Photo Products could not risk $100 million on a new venture; its top bet was only about $10 million. Although the development of Cronar films taxed the department's resources in the late 1950s, this one new product saved Photo Products's business. Riston and Cromalin were remarkable because each cost less that $3 million to develop. Generally, Photo Products succeeded in its new venture program where many other departments failed.

Photo Products's achievements in innovation resulted from several factors. First, the department's top management was not preoccupied with running a large established business. Photo Products had to improve its technical capabilities; its general managers recognized this fact and gave research and development appropriate attention and resources. However, top management did not stifle its researchers. After Cohen had proven that he had the ability to link emerging technology to a developing market, general manager Wingate gave him considerable freedom to run his own programs. In some of the larger, more bureaucratized departments, it is doubtful that a venture manager could have gained the support of top management that Cohen did in Photo Products.

A chronic problem in Du Pont was that individual achievement was rewarded by promotion up the line in the research, manufacturing, or marketing divisions of a department. Ambitious younger employees did not want to leave their place on the ladder for a venture management job that had uncertain status and promised no predictable future position. In the 1960s, many departments experimented with the venture system; that is, bringing together all the elements needed for a successful innovation together under one manager, instead of having the research division carry a development to a certain stage and then transfer the project to the operating divisions. A major deficiency of the new venture system at Du Pont was identifying individuals capable of running them and then giving them enough autonomy to do their job effectively. A standard approach was to have venture managers report directly to an assistant general manager, whose confidence had to be won. Not many accomplished this goal. Photo Products's Cohen was very much the exception rather than the rule.[59]

The new ventures of Photo Products, more than those of any other department, created new businesses for Du Pont outside the company's traditional chemically based industries. The success of Cronar polyester film base, Riston photoresists, and the Cromalin color proofing system showed that Du Pont could innovate into new, expanding markets without making heavy up-front investment in research and development. It was this type of innovation that the company's management would encourage in the future. Along with new product-oriented research, Du Pont in the 1970s had to increase significantly its resources committed to ensuring that the company's products were not harmful toxicologically or environmentally.

24

Toxicological and Environmental Research

The enormous increase in the number and quantity of chemicals manufactured in the twentieth century has resulted in a concomitant need for information on the effects of these chemicals on workers, consumers, and the environment. Until recently, the generation and tabulation of such data in the United States has been carried out in an unsystematic fashion by several federal and state government agencies, industry, and the medical profession. Although widespread concern over the toxicity of chemicals was sometimes stimulated by dramatic incidents, such as the "loony gas" episode with tetraethyllead or the adulteration of food with poisonous compounds, most Americans attributed these and similar problems to the unusual toxicity of a chemical or to criminal behavior by unscrupulous businessmen. Generally, chemicals were considered to be harmless unless proven otherwise. It was not until the 1960s that Americans began to believe that systematic investigation and regulation of the toxicological and environmental impact of chemicals was necessary.[1] By this time, however, Du Pont had been doing research on the toxic effects of chemicals for thirty years at its Haskell Laboratory for Toxicology and Industrial Medicine.

Origins of Toxicology

Toxicological studies began in Europe in the late nineteenth century and were part of a larger effort to improve the life of the industrial worker. Much of the early work centered on the elimination of poisons such as lead, the dangers of which had been recognized for two thousand years. Some of the European studies were devoted to determining the hazards associated with the handling of new chemicals. Modern toxicological science had its origins in the work of K. B. Lehmann, director of the Institute of Hygiene at the University of Würzburg. In 1884, Lehmann began studies of the effects of gases and vapors on cats. By 1900, German medical journals were full of articles on the toxic effects of chemicals, whereas in the United States the literature was sparse.[2]

Although the United States lagged behind the European nations in the recognition and amelioration of occupational illnesses,[3] these issues became part of the campaign for reform that historians have called the Progressive

Era. Alice Hamilton, a young MD, pioneered in occupational health and safety reform, which she chronicled in her autobiography, *Exploring the Dangerous Trades*. Few American doctors prior to Hamilton had taken industrial diseases seriously. Her work began with a survey of working conditions in Illinois factories in 1910. In the United States at this time there was little in the way of legislation requiring factory safety inspections or compensation of workmen for injuries sustained from occupational accidents or diseases. Hamilton recalled that "the employers could, if they wished, shut their eyes to the dangers their workmen faced, for nobody held them responsible, while workers accepted the risks with fatalistic submissiveness as part of the price that one must pay for being poor."[4] Because no statistics were kept on the incidence of occupational illnesses, many employers flatly denied their existence and attributed worker diseases to other causes, most notably alcohol. When confronted with European statistics, employers dismissed the results as being peculiar to European workmen, who were less healthy and poorer than American ones. To Hamilton, who lived in a settlement house in an immigrant, working-class section of Chicago, it seemed impossible that European living conditions could be much worse than those in her neighborhood. Proceeding cautiously, Hamilton carefully documented cases of occupational illness in various trades, but especially in those using lead, and convinced many employers to clean up their operations. Because she had no legal authority, Hamilton had to rely on the good will of employers for access to factories.[5]

The efforts of reformers such as Hamilton led to increased governmental attention to dangers in the workplace. After its founding in 1913, the U.S. Department of Labor investigated occupational diseases, and its Bureau of Labor Statistics collected data on working conditions. Two years later, the Public Health Service organized its section of industrial hygiene and sanitation. Beginning in 1911, many states passed workman's compensation laws that provided income for workers disabled by accidents. Generally, this legislation did not include occupational diseases because the connection between the workplace and any particular disease was considered to be tenuous.[6]

Du Pont encountered its first toxicological problems when it began to manufacture dynamite in the 1880s. Nitric acid fumes destroyed lung tissue and caused numerous fatalities; nitroglycerin absorbed through the skin caused headaches. Concern for the health of its work force led Du Pont to hire physician Walter G. Hudson in 1904. While organizing a medical division, including plant physicians, Hudson spent his spare time investigating poisonous gases that were generated by the use of explosives in mines. In this period, Du Pont began to make new chemicals for use in explosives, and the toxicity of these compounds was not known. Because of Hudson's efforts, Du Pont avoided some of the health problems that other manufacturers experienced making explosives during World War I.[7]

Conservation and the efficient use of resources, which had been keynotes of the Progressive platform, became a national priority during World War I. Concern for occupational health and safety increased as the supply of workers decreased. In addition, many of the available employees were women and blacks who had no prior experience in factory work. As Du Pont's medical director, Hudson had responsibility for ensuring healthful working conditions in the company's plants. Because of Du Pont's experience with many hazardous chemicals, Hudson also served as chairman of the subcommittee on industrial diseases and poisons of the Council of National Defense. During the war, Hudson sponsored animal studies in New York laboratories to determine the toxicity of a large number of compounds. Apparently exhausted by his wartime efforts, Hudson died in 1920 at the age of fifty.[8]

With the "Return to Normalcy" in the 1920s, public and governmental interest in occupational safety and diseases subsided, although the manufacture of new chemicals accelerated and health problems continued to occur. The war had led to the recovery of a wide range of coal tar chemicals, many of which Du Pont used in its new businesses. One of these chemicals, benzene, caused immediate problems for Du Pont. Because it was a cheap and effective solvent for rubber, Du Pont used benzene to make coated fabrics at its Newburgh plant. In the spring of 1920, two workers in the plant died from benzene poisoning, prompting an investigation by the company's safety division. Dr. A. K. Smith discovered that all the workers had cotton plugs in their noses to stop chronic nose bleeds caused by benzene fumes. At this time, the proportion of benzene in the solvent was cut from 60 to 45 percent and the ventilation improved. Two years later, however, another worker died, and Du Pont abandoned the use of benzene.[9]

Because other manufacturers were experiencing similar problems, the National Safety Council Congress in Boston in 1921 held a session on benzene poisoning. Dr. Lothar E. Weber of the Boston India Rubber Laboratory stated that benzene "has been criticized as very dangerous [and] very injurious... and, personally, I feel an injustice has been done to this particular substance." Weber maintained that the British used solvent naphtha, a mixture of benzene, toluene, and xylene, and did not have problems with poisoning, and he concluded that because the latter two substances should be as toxic as the former, the extent of benzene's toxicity was unclear. In response, C. F. Horan of the Hood Rubber Company replied that inhalation experiments with benzene, toluene, and xylene on guinea pigs and rabbits showed acute toxicity of benzene compared to the other two compounds. Not persuaded, Weber rejoined that he was not going to change his opinion altogether on the basis of a few guinea pig experiments.[10] Thus from early on, correlation of animal experiments with human exposure has been a controversial aspect of toxicology.

Not long after the benzene crisis, Du Pont experienced the tetraethyllead (TEL) poisonings. The symptoms of lead poisoning had long been known, but this new organic form, which could be absorbed through the skin, acted differently. The episode received nationwide attention, not so much because of concern for the health of chemical workers but because of the wild behavior of the victims and fear that the public might also succumb. The surgeon-general of the Public Health Service intervened to make sure that TEL in gasoline posed no hazard and gave it a clean bill of health. Although not required to by any regulatory or legislative body, Du Pont designed and installed a completely closed process to protect the lives of its employees. The TEL incident, according to Henry Field Smyth, a pioneer in industrial toxicology, "called attention to the fact . . . that when manufacturing exists which is constantly producing new poisonous substances, we have no machinery for evaluating their dangers until much harm may have already been done."[11] A few years later, the medical director of the Du Pont Company would reach a similar conclusion.

In the 1920s, Du Pont's need for toxicological data increased, in part to ensure that the company's products posed no risks for consumers.[12] Before introducing moistureproof cellophane for food packaging, in 1927, Du Pont commissioned Henry Field Smyth to carry out guinea pig feeding studies in his private laboratory in Philadelphia. (He was also professor of industrial hygiene at the University of Pennsylvania.) Smyth concluded that the cellophane coating was "absolutely harmless."[13] However, a few years later, one of the principal ingredients, tricresyl phosphate (TCP), was implicated in a major public health disaster. Poisonous drinks concocted by bootleggers had been a serious problem throughout the Prohibition Era, but a drink called "ginger jake," which had been laced with TCP, caused thousands of cases of paralysis and numerous deaths in 1930 and 1931.[14] After learning that moistureproof cellophane contained TCP, the National Institute of Health undertook experiments with chickens and discovered that the birds developed symptoms of paralysis at a dosage of 10 milligrams of TCP per day. Although it was unlikely that humans could receive such a high dose from consuming foods wrapped in cellophane, Du Pont replaced TCP in the coating after learning of these results.[15] Still, had this episode been made public, it might have caused a serious setback for the company's fastest growing and most profitable product. These situations and others in the 1920s and early 1930s clearly indicated a need for toxicological data on chemicals, but Du Pont did not undertake such work in-house until a problem of unprecedented severity turned up in a company plant.

Disaster at the Dye Works

By 1932, Du Pont Company physicians had discovered that an alarming number of workers in a particular area of the Deepwater dye works had developed bladder tumors, some of which were cancerous. A few years earlier, company officials had become aware of the potential hazard involved in the manufacture of dyes. In 1928 Victor Cofman, a chemist in the Chemical Department who was working primarily on developing new chemotherapeutic agents, informed Chemical Director Charles M. A. Stine that Lesley J. Barley of Imperial Chemical Industries had told him that several cases of bladder tumors had occurred among British dye workers. Barley then consulted with I. G. Farben and Du Pont; the former informed him that it had experienced similar problems, but Elmer Bolton, then chemical director of the Dyestuffs Department, replied that no Du Pont workers had developed tumors.[16]

Apparently neither Barley or Bolton knew that an extensive literature on this problem had been developing in Germany since the first cases of "aniline tumors" were discovered by L. Rehn in 1895. Epidemiological evidence gathered about 1920 indicated that 177 cases had been identified. Although most industrial physicians and toxicologists in Germany recognized that these tumors were of occupational origin, there was no consensus about what chemicals were responsible. In German plants, dye workers were exposed to many chemicals so no single agent could be identified. Complicating the issue further was the fact that these tumors usually did not develop until the worker had been exposed for at least ten years. In addition, animal experiments with the suspected carcinogens had given inconclusive results. None of the chemicals caused bladder tumors in guinea pigs, rats, mice, or rabbits. But in the late 1920s, Du Pont officials, even the company doctors, were apparently unaware of this literature even though a good summary of it had been published in the *Journal of Industrial Hygiene*.[17]

About one year after Cofman's memorandum, a bladder tumor was diagnosed in an employee at the dye works. Two years elapsed before a second case emerged, but by the fall of 1932, Du Pont had twenty dyeworkers with bladder tumors.[18] Faced with this unprecedented toxicological problem, Du Pont decided to send its medical director, George H. Gehrmann, to Europe to solicit information and assistance. Gehrmann, a former plant physician and medical director since 1926, sailed for Europe on September 10, 1933, to visit German and Swiss dye plants. Upon his return, he reported that the Germans received him cordially, were very frank with him, and showed him "the intimate details of all the operations in which we were interested." Physicians employed by I. G. Farben informed Gehrmann that the German dye makers had begun to take preventive measures around 1915 and believed that closed manufacturing operations and strict plant hygiene would eliminate 90 percent of the cases. One plant had had no cases in employees who began work after a new process had been installed. Generally, Gehrmann was very impressed by the cleanliness and sophistication of the German operations. Although their safety measures had been effective, the Germans still had not been able to identify the chemicals that were causing the problem. But they strongly suspected one or all of aniline, alpha- and beta-naphthylamine, and benzidine.[19]

At Elberfeld, Gehrmann visited I. G. Farben's central toxicological laboratory under the leadership of a Dr. Gross, who studied the toxicity of chemicals, including their chronic effects and pathological changes resulting from exposure to them. Gross also collected statistics on bladder tumor cases. Data on eighty cases showed that seventy-four of the men had been exposed to beta-naphthylamine (beta), aniline, or both. After returning to the United States, Gehrmann attempted to put into practice what he had learned from I. G. Farben.[20]

He proposed a comprehensive plan to cope with what he called "the most serious occupational disease we have ever encountered." In the factory, a sealed processing system operated by the most physically fit and intelligent workmen would be required. The Medical Division would medically screen all applicants for work in the dangerous areas, conduct periodic physical examinations of the workers, and generally police operations through inspections. Rigorous personal and plant hygiene standards would have to be maintained, and every employee would be made fully aware of the potential consequences of the failure to follow them. Finally, Gehrmann recommended that Du Pont follow the lead of I. G. Farben and set up a laboratory for scientific medical research.[21]

The Haskell Laboratory

That Du Pont needed to do systematic and ongoing toxicological research had been argued in 1930 by Wilhelm Hueper, a young pathologist employed by a Philadelphia cancer research institute supported by Irénée du Pont. Hueper proposed that Du Pont establish a biological laboratory, and his boss Ellice McDonald passed the memorandum on to Irénée du Pont, who at this time was no longer a member of the Executive Committee but was vice chairman of the board. The proposed laboratory would serve a dual function of evaluating both the harmful and beneficial biological properties of all substances manufactured by the company.[22] Hueper made this recommendation after he and McDonald had visited the Dye Works and seen workers handling the chemicals that were suspected to cause bladder tumors.[23]

Hueper's proposal eventually made its way to Bolton, who had just become head of the Chemical Department. Bolton assured Stine, his research liaison on the Executive Committee, that a biological laboratory was not needed at Du Pont. Toxicology matters were being adequately handled by the various departments, he maintained, and the Dyestuffs Department had an arrangement with a pharmaceutical company to examine all new chemicals for beneficial physiological properties. Stine sent Bolton's memorandum to Irénée du Pont, who informed Hueper that business conditions were too bad to warrant starting such a venture.[24]

In spite of the ongoing Depression, in 1933 the Executive Committee had seriously to reconsider establishing a toxicological research laboratory. In November 1933, Gehrmann presented his ideas to the Executive Committee.

In general, he stated that the toxicity of most new and many old chemicals was unknown and that there had been "a tendency to believe that they are harmless until proven otherwise," a policy that "had been costly in terms of money, health, and life."[25] Here he alluded specifically to benzene and TEL. Even when toxicological information for such chemicals existed, it was for acute poisoning, not chronic exposure. In many Du Pont processes, he maintained, company employees were being exposed to low concentrations of chemicals that were very toxic in high concentrations. The effects of long-term exposure to such substances were unknown. In particular, Gehrmann pointed to the bladder tumor problem. By this time the Dye Works cases had reached thirty-five, eleven of which were malignant and one fatal. Gehrmann suspected that 1,000 men had been exposed to potentially carcinogenic substances, but he hoped that medical research at Du Pont could find an antidote for the offending chemical. To implement his proposal, he estimated that a new laboratory would cost $100,000 and require $50,000 a year to operate.[26] Although not passing any formal resolution on the subject, the Executive Committee permitted Gehrmann to begin looking for personnel to staff a toxicology laboratory.

Because toxicology research at Du Pont would not begin for about a year, Gehrmann and several local physicians who were assisting him went to Memorial Hospital in New York and presented papers in a symposium chaired by Russell S. Ferguson, a urologist on the hospital's staff. In his opening remarks, Ferguson stated that "the industry is to be congratulated upon accepting the scientific implications and responsibilities in presenting the results through the medium of this symposium."[27] Gehrmann made a full report on the situation at Du Pont and what he had learned in Germany, and the others discussed specific medical aspects of bladder tumors such as diagnosis and treatment.[28] These papers were published in the *Journal of Urology* in 1934. In the next two years, Gehrmann also published short articles in two major medical journals, *Surgery, Gynecology and Obstetrics* and the *Journal of the American Medical Association.*[29] His efforts alerted the medical profession to this occupational disease but contributed little to solving the problems connected with it.

In July 1934 the Executive Committee formally appropriated $130,000 to build and equip a medical research laboratory at the Experimental Station.[30] Gehrmann had already hired a director, Wolfgang F. von Oettingen, and sent him to Europe to confer with leading toxicologists. The forty-six-year-old Oettingen held a PhD in chemistry from the University of Göttingen (1913) and an MD from the University of Heidelberg (1916). From 1924 to 1934, he had taught pharmacology at Western Reserve University in Cleveland. To Du Pont, Oettingen brought one of his younger associates, William B. Deichmann, to be a junior pharmacologist. The original staff also included Frank Wiley, a biochemist, and Wilhelm Hueper, the pathologist who when working for McDonald in 1930 had suggested that Du Pont establish a medical research laboratory.[31] The fractious Hueper had been fired by McDonald and was working in a hospital in Uniontown, Pennsylvania, when Oettingen hired him.[32] The facility opened on January 22, 1935, with considerable fanfare and speeches by dignitaries such as Royd R. Sayers, medical officer in charge of the Office of Industrial Hygiene and Sanitation of U.S. Public Health Service. The laboratory was named in honor of Harry G. Haskell, a retired Du Pont executive who had established the company's medical division in 1915.[33]

Under Oettingen's leadership, the laboratory first sought to determine the mechanism of formation of bladder tumors. Gehrmann still hoped that some method could be discovered to treat the men who had been exposed to bring their bladders back to normal. By late 1935, Du Pont's roster of cases had grown to seventy, forty-nine of which were at the dye works, and twenty-one others had been diagnosed among the workers at the old Newport Chemical plant in Carrollville, Wisconsin, which Du Pont had acquired in 1931. Five workers had already died.[34] Researchers at Haskell designed experiments to determine which chemicals were causing the tumors. The evidence Du Pont had accumulated from worker exposure strongly implicated beta as the tumor-causing chemical. Contrary to some European studies, Du Pont found no tumors in workers exposed only to aniline for many years.[35] On the basis of these findings, Haskell researchers decided to do long-term tests with animals fed a diet that included beta.

In its early stages, a bladder tumor caused no symptoms, and diagnosis could be made only through visual inspection of the interior of the bladder by insertion of a cystoscope through the urethra. The unpleasantness of the procedure, which caused some workers to develop influenza-like symptoms, complicated the diagnosis and early treatment of bladder tumors. In Great Britain and Germany, most workers refused to undergo the examination. At Du Pont, worker resistance grew to Gehrmann's policy of requiring frequent examinations.[36]

The researchers chose female dogs for their experiments, in part because a children's cystoscope could be used to inspect their bladders. This was a fortunate choice because beta does not cause tumors in rats or mice. Fifteen dogs were fed beta for over three years, and the first tumors began to develop in the third year. Hueper, Wiley, and Humphrey D. Wolfe, a physician at the dye works, published these results.[37] Haskell also tested seven other chemicals including alpha-naphthylamine, benzidine, and aniline. After five years, none of the dogs fed these chemicals had developed bladder abnormalities.[38] In its first big project, Haskell had made an important contribution to the understanding of bladder tumors in dye workers by discovering a single agent responsible for them.

Although Haskell's experiments showed that exposure to beta caused bladder tumors in dogs, there was still no way to predict the level and duration of exposure that would generate tumors in humans. To lessen exposure of its employees, the dye works instituted new hygiene rules, moved most of the beta operations into one building, and greatly improved the ventilation in the building.[39] In the early 1940s, analysis of workers' urine showed that they still were absorbing considerable quantities of beta. To protect these employees, Du Pont relied on detecting what was considered to be reversible preliminary damage to the bladder. Through urine analysis, which largely replaced the unpopular cystoscopy, indexes were established "to determine the degree of exposure and the ability of each individual to handle that exposure."[40]

Gradually, over the next decade, the high carcinogenicity of beta became recognized as new cases of bladder tumors occurred in spite of increased safety measures.[41] In 1951, Du Pont constructed a new building with a completely closed process for the production of beta. However, Du Pont ceased beta operations in December 1955, after Michael H. C. Williams, a physician at ICI, convinced all the major dyestuff producers in the world to stop manufacturing the dangerous chemical, almost two decades after research at Haskell had shown it to be a powerful carcinogen.[42]

Ongoing Toxicological Research

In its first eighteen months of operation, Haskell undertook twenty-five projects for various departments. The results of many of these investigations were published in the *Journal of Industrial Hygiene and Toxicology*. But Haskell soon began to feel the effects of the companywide restriction on publication which followed the I. G. Farben disclosure of nylon-6.[43] By 1939, the original four-man professional staff had all left Du Pont.[44] The crackdown on publishing was not the only reason they left Du Pont, but it was a contributing factor. In the wake of these resignations, Gehrmann polled the general managers on their attitudes toward publication, and virtually all of them approved it in principle.[45] But future Haskell researchers would not publish the results of many specific studies. The laboratory was set up as a service division that had to solicit business from the other departments and that had little time or money for preparing manuscripts.

John H. Foulger succeeded Oettingen as director of Haskell in 1938. With a PhD in biochemistry and an MD, both from the University of Cincinnati, he had joined Haskell as a senior toxicologist in 1935 and was director until 1952. Throughout most of Foulger's tenure, the budget of Haskell was about $100,000 a year, approximately 70 percent of which came from specific departmentally funded projects. Haskell's total research budget was small, but Du Pont was under no constraint to spend even that amount. Few chemical companies spent any money on toxicology, except Dow and Union Carbide, which had set up laboratories in the same year that Haskell opened. The manufacture of toxic chemicals was unregulated in this era, and there were few laws governing their use.[46] The bladder tumor episode had prompted Du Pont to begin toxicology research, and the continuing need for information kept it going. But the Executive Committee had ensured that Haskell could not tell an industrial department general manager what chemicals he could or could not make. This situation troubled Foulger considerably.

Foulger's view of Haskell's function was much broader than the charter the Executive Committee had given the laboratory. The committee had authorized Haskell, in addition to studying the bladder tumors and the toxicity of a few specific compounds, "to study the toxicity of all proposed new products in order to give advice as to the proper type of building and equipment before manufacture is started" and to study any material at the request of a department.[47] Medical Director Gehrmann, however, in his speech at the laboratory's dedication and in a letter explaining the new facility to ICI, stated that Haskell had the responsibility to ensure the safe handling of all the chemicals manufactured and sold by Du Pont.[48] Gehrmann, Oettingen, and later Foulger were all physicians and saw themselves as professionals with an independent position analogous to the attorneys in the Legal Department. Because of its special expertise and its role in representing the company in legal disputes, the Legal Department could assert its autonomy and not be subservient to the industrial departments. Whereas the Legal Department, however, could claim that failure to heed its advice might cost the company millions of dollars, Haskell officials could not make the same argument as forcefully in light of the weak laws covering occupational disease and public safety. Still, this did not stop Foulger from trying.

Beginning in 1943 and continuing at regular intervals for the next fifteen years, Foulger and his successor complained to their superiors in the Service Department about the shortcomings of the project system. The crux of the issue was almost always money; the industrial departments did not want to spend money for something that at best would allow them to proceed with a development and at worst would squash it. From Haskell, no news was good news. Usually when money was forthcoming, it was late in the development, often when a full-scale plant was under construction. For example, during World War II, the Grasselli Chemicals Department had built a plant to manufacture DDT without sponsoring any toxicology studies at Haskell. When government information became available, considerable alterations had to be made to the plant. What worried Foulger was that "in planning post-war activity almost all departments are working with new materials about which little is known. We have reason to believe that many offer serious health hazards. Our attempts to obtain funds for investigation are almost invariably refused because the prospect of large-scale manufacture is not immediate."[49]

In spite of their reluctance to spend money on toxicological studies, the departments did support Haskell's research at a level of about $70,000 a year. Most of this money came from the Organic Chemicals, Textile Fibers, and Explosives departments. A few departments tried to capitalize on Haskell's scientific reputation without spending the money to have its products tested. In particular, Foulger pointed his finger at the sales division of Gras-selli, which "wishe[d] to use approval of Haskell Laboratory in its promotion of new (and toxic) insecticides but will not approve expenditure adequate for a study of these compounds in the lab."[50] All these problems, Gehrmann and Foulger believed, could be solved if only the Executive Committee would authorize an annual budget for Haskell and allocate the costs to the departments. The project system, Gehrmann concluded in 1945, "does not work to the advantage of the company, and we are not doing the kind of job that should be done."[51] Although it would not abandon the project system, thereby compromising the autonomy of the general manager, the Executive Committee and the departments in the late 1940s began to put more funds into toxicological studies.

Du Pont's need for toxicological information increased because the company was manufacturing many new chemicals every year, and the federal government was beginning to take a more active role. Earlier, the extent of testing that Haskell would do on any compound was determined by the judgment of the laboratory's staff and the amount of money that a department was willing to spend. By the late 1940s, Haskell had developed a sequence of tests for a compound starting with very short, intense exposure of a few animals and ending with several-year, low-exposure studies done on several species. These tests yielded information of three types: the required dosage to kill, the effects of longer-term lower-exposure levels, and carcinogenicity. The cheapest, quickest test determined the approximate lethal dose (ALD) by administering a series of dose levels to five or six rats. The lowest killing dose is the ALD. A more statistically reliable test for acute toxicity determined the "LD_{50}," or dose required to kill 50 percent of a group of animals. To determine if a compound had cumulative toxic effects, Haskell researchers gave a group of about ten rats one-fifth of the ALD for ten days, thereby giving the animals a total of twice the approximate lethal dose. For longer-range chronic exposure, experiments were run for thirty to ninety days. Finally, there were lifetime or two-year studies of rats. Haskell also had special tests to determine skin and eye irritation, tests with dogs to determine the maximum allowable concentrations of vapors, and tests with selected species designed to determine carcinogenicity.[52] In all, the cost of a test was proportional to the number of animals involved and the length of the experiment. In 1950, when Haskell's total budget was $200,000 a year, a two-year feeding test and a cancer study cost $20,000 and $100,000 respectively.[53]

In its first decade, Haskell had done few long-term studies because it had no authority to carry on an experiment after the project funding had run out. Soon, however, the federal Food and Drug Administration (FDA) would begin strongly to suggest lifetime studies for substances that came into contact with foodstuffs. Stiffer guidelines followed in the wake of the "elixir of sulfanilamide" disaster in which over one hundred people died after taking this new medicine. This episode aroused public concern over toxic substances and prompted Congress to pass the Food, Drug, and Cosmetics Act of 1938. In an important step for the future of toxicological testing, the FDA decided to do a comprehensive study of the glycol solvent suspected as the toxic agent in the elixir. When the lifetime study revealed bladder tumors that had not shown up in ninety-day tests, the FDA began to recommend these long-term studies.[54]

The need for long-term studies was dramatically demonstrated by the case of benzidine, which had long been implicated as causing bladder tumors, even though none had been induced in dogs after five years of feeding.[55] In 1948, Gehrmann, Foulger, and Fleming presented a paper at the Ninth International Congress of Industrial Medicine in London in which they argued that they would not be convinced of the carcinogenicity of benzidine until shown solid epidemiological evidence. This was lacking because most workers had been exposed to both beta and benzidine.[56] Two years later, however, outside researchers discovered that one dog out of seven fed benzidine for five years developed bladder tumors.[57] This was followed by a study of dye workers in a British plant which showed twenty-three cases of bladder tumors among 198 workers exposed only to benzidine.[58] Subsequent long-term tests confirmed that benzidine is a carcinogen, though a much weaker one than beta.[59] The increasing complexity of toxicological testing stretched Haskell's limited resources to the limit in the postwar years.

Haskell Expands

In 1950, Roger Williams convinced the other members of the Executive Committee that an expanded toxicological laboratory should be built outside of Newark, Delaware, on land the company owned adjacent to the Stine Laboratory. Haskell did not have space at the Experimental Station to do long-term tests, so it farmed out the business to Lloyd Hazelton's laboratory in Falls Church, Virginia, or to Harold C. Hodge at the University of Rochester. Because of construction material shortages due to the Korean war, the new, expanded Haskell Laboratory would not open until 1954. But Du Pont did not wait to expand its medical and toxicology research programs. In 1952, John A. Zapp, Jr., a forty-one-year-old biochemist, became the director of the laboratory, a position he would hold for the next twenty-four years. Williams informed Zapp that his job was to keep the company out of trouble by producing valid information on the toxicity of the company's chemicals. And, Williams added, "Don't expect to be popular."[60] As it was doing throughout the company, the Executive Committee gave Haskell more money for fundamental research. Between 1948 and 1954, Haskell's annual budget increased tenfold to over 1 million dollars a year, and the portion of Haskell's budget going into fundamental research increased from 20 to 40 percent.[61]

In the 1950s, Haskell broadened its charter to include the entire relationship between workers and their jobs, not just the toxicological aspects. Earlier Foulger, almost as a hobby, conducted experiments aimed at revealing early physiological changes, such as lowered blood pressure, caused by exposure to chemical compounds. He hoped that his work might lead to measurable indications of toxic effects before any major bodily damage had been done.[62] Foulger's interest in physiology led him to hire Lucien M. Brouha, a fifty-one-year-old physician and physiologist, who was an expert in the field of industrial fatigue. Brouha moved Haskell's research in new directions by investigating the workplace in a systematic fashion to determine the effects of environment and job design on worker fatigue. Haskell installed rooms in which temperature, humidity, and wind could be varied over wide ranges. These rooms were used to investigate fatigue, but the Textile Fibers Department also used them to study the basic factors in clothing comfort.[63]

Brouha's work received a big boost in 1953 when he observed the operation of the Lauru Platform in Paris. Lucien Lauru and Camille Soula had built a triangular platform upon which subjects could do all kinds of tasks. Piezoelectric crystals, which convert pressure into electricity, were placed below the platform so the amount of effort exerted could be accurately recorded. Soon, the Haskell Laboratory would have the world's second Lauru Platform. With it, Brouha hoped to redesign many jobs that Du Pont employees did in order to make them less fatiguing. For example, an engineer in a plant had stipulated that fifty-pound bags be stacked seven high in a storage area, but Brouha showed that the effort needed to lift the sixth and seventh bags was very high compared to each of the other five. With his "teeterboard," as his technicians called it, Brouha studied the energy expended by a secretary during a day at her desk or by plant workers performing routine tasks. More than fifty other corporations sent experts to Haskell to observe Brouha's operation. Lillian Gilbreth, who along with her husband Frank had been pioneers in the field of time and motion study, visited the facility and was enthusiastic about it. Back in the 1910s, she recalled, "we worked out techniques in the dark, [and] we never knew whether we were really right or not." Gilbreth concluded that "now, at last, we can confirm them on Dr. Brouha's platform."[64] Although the work might have been interesting from a scientific standpoint and did find some application in the company's plants, by the late 1950s it began to be criticized by other departments as being too far from Haskell's main responsibility. By this time fundamental research accounted for a half of the laboratory's budget.[65]

In 1958, at the suggestion of the Executive Committee advisor on research, Samuel Lenher, Zapp began an assessment of Haskell's role in the Du Pont Company. This was particularly timely in view of the passage by Congress of the Food Additives Amendment to the Food, Drug, and Cosmetics Act. The new law contained stricter guidelines for substances that were intentional or incidental food additives, and included the Delany clause, which banned from foods any chemical that caused cancer in animals or humans. Worries about chemicals in foods had reemerged in the early 1950s. In 1954 *Fortune* stated that "pure" food had recently become a "cause célèbre" and that this new concern was different from that expressed in the 1930s. The earlier problems generally involved unprincipled, criminal business elements that adulterated foods, but the new fear was "that the human race is slowly poisoning itself by the sheer number and variety of synthetic chemicals."[66]

In his resulting report, Zapp hammered at the same theme articulated by Foulger fifteen years before, that Haskell's perceived responsibilities were far greater than its ability to enforce its recommendations. In spite of Haskell's advice, Zapp argued, "the Departments can and do at times choose to assume a calculated risk. Consequently, not all investigations which Haskell recommends are carried out." Increasingly, however, the government was insisting on more tests on more chemicals. Zapp predicted that "toxicity investigations of the future are likely to increase in scope . . . , since by both law and custom fewer calculated risks will be tolerated." Both Dow and Union Carbide, he asserted, had independent toxicology laboratories which could "undertake their own projects and publish results without the okay of the [concerned] operating division."[67]

The Employee Relations Department requested that the Development Department make a study of the situation. Its representatives interviewed people in the industrial departments and at Haskell. Generally, they discovered that Zapp had followed Williams's advice to get the facts. The report noted that Haskell "has maintained its leadership in the field and has developed an enviable position with government, industry and the medical profession." Haskell was testing 250 compounds annually, which was ten times the number tested in its early days. The interviewees generally lauded Haskell for its high quality work and its high prestige, which had helped in some presentations to the FDA. But some accused the laboratory of being a "junior FDA" in backing up the government's position without adequately fighting for the company's point of view and of being too inflexible and arbitrary in its recommendations. The real issue with the departments, however, was the usual one – the high cost of Haskell's services. Because of the peculiarities of its financing and the extensive facilities and equipment maintained by Haskell, its tests cost about 50 percent more than those contracted to outside laboratories. Consequently the departments were having about a third of their work done outside, and a few departments sometimes did their own studies.[68]

The final Development Department report made several recommendations to solve these problems but clearly stated that it did not want to undermine the supremacy of the departmental general managers. Although admitting that "Haskell is rightfully disturbed over the somewhat cavalier approach to potential toxicity of chemicals taken by a few individuals," the report's author believed that problems of this sort could be overcome by intensified educational efforts by Haskell's staff. To improve relations with the departments and obtain more business for the laboratory, the Development Department suggested that the price for Haskell's services be reduced to that charged by other toxicology laboratories, the difference to be made up by a subsidy authorized by the Executive Committee.[69] The committee passed this recommendation as a formal resolution.[70]

In spite of not doing all the work that should have been done, Haskell's sixty-two-person staff handled all of the work it possibly could. With the increased number of studies required by the Food Additives Amendment, Haskell had either to expand its staff or cut back on its fundamental research program. The Development Department report suggested the latter approach and singled out the physiology work of Brouha and his associates. This type of research, it argued, was better suited for the National Institutes of Health, the armed forces, or the universities. Proper areas for research, the report argued, would be to develop techniques for reducing costs and improving the effectiveness of investigations.[71] Taking this advice and following the general company trend, Haskell began to cut back on its fundamental research programs.

Increasing Concerns about Chemicals

The impact of chemicals on human beings and the environment became a major public issue in the 1960s. In 1962, birth defects from the drug thalidomide and the publication of Rachel Carson's *Silent Spring*, which detailed the harmful effects of pesticides on humans and animals, created widespread concerns that chemicals and drugs were not being adequately tested. Exposure of workers to chemicals in the workplace, which did not pose a threat to the general public, received less attention.[72] In 1965, William W. Frye, professor of medicine at Louisiana State University, issued a report deploring the general weakness of laws regulating occupational health. There were no national job health standards, and only a few of the forty-two state occupational health agencies had strong powers of enforcement. The Frye Report also urged the U.S. Public Health Service to devote $50 million a year on occupational health instead of the approximately $8 million it was spending.[73] Eventually, worker health would become part of the larger "environmental" movement, but not until the 1970s.

The Haskell Laboratory's management recognized fully the growing concern about chemicals in the environment and expanded the lab's programs. Du Pont could no longer generate just enough data to satisfy Haskell and the departments that a particular chemical posed no serious risk; more frequently, the company had to satisfy the requirements of new laws and the growing demands of government agencies. The Federal Hazardous Substances Labeling Act and the Color Additives Amendment, both passed in

1960, led Du Pont to reevaluate the toxicity of many compounds it had been making and using for a long time.[74] And the FDA began to put pressure on companies to publish their toxicological findings. Haskell published some but not all of its data because of the time required to prepare papers and the difficulty of obtaining clearance from the various departments. In the future, argued an Employee Relations Department annual report, Du Pont's policy of giving each department with an interest in a particular chemical a veto over publication might have to be changed to satisfy the FDA.[75] Du Pont fully expected new regulations, but the Employee Relations Department annual report for 1968 concluded that "the information and professional competence in the fields of toxicology and industrial hygiene accumulated at Haskell over the years places the company in a good position to exert a constructive influence in the establishment of realistic safety and health standards in the future."[76]

Although those in Du Pont who followed developments in Washington knew of the rising tide of public sentiment about the safety of chemicals, none could have predicted the magnitude of the changes in public policy during the 1970s. Nor could they have fully anticipated the intensity of debate regarding issues of toxicity and carcinogenicity. The Occupational Health and Safety Act of 1970, which required employers to provide a safe place of employment, and the Toxic Substances Control Act of 1976, which was intended to fill in the gaps left by earlier legislation, gave government agencies power to regulate the chemical industry with regard to toxic chemicals.[77] Public interest grew as a result of widely publicized incidents such as the fifty deaths of Rohm and Haas employees who had been exposed to bis(chloromethyl) ether, the discovery of a rare form of liver cancer in three workers exposed to vinyl chloride, and the Kepone fiasco in which an insecticide plant contaminated not only its workers but the James River in Virginia as well.[78] Du Pont did not suffer any such disasters but was affected by the new regulations and the growing fears of chemically caused cancer.

Federal regulatory agencies continued to increase the number and complexity of tests recommended for any substance. To protect themselves from potential future lawsuits, chemical companies began to do full testing of chemicals even when there were indications that such comprehensive studies were not necessary. Du Pont routinely evaluated a prospective new chemical by testing it for oral and inhalation toxicity, skin and eye irritation, effects on aquatic life, and carcinogenicity. If the chemical reached the pilot plant or commercial stage, then long-term studies would be done. Complete testing for one chemical, following the 1978 EPA guidelines, required from 500 to 1,000 animals, lasted from three to five years, and cost over $500,000.[79] Not surprisingly, Haskell's expenditures soared in the 1970s.

The Haskell Laboratory budget increased from $2.3 million in 1970 to $13.3 million in 1979. Additional wings were added to the building complex at regular intervals.[80] The dramatic increase in the number of animals required for a given test, the length of time involved, and the procedures needed to evaluate the effects of the chemicals on animals taxed Du Pont's and the nation's resources in terms of laboratory space and animals, toxicologists, and pathologists.[81] The latter had to do the laborious task of evaluating thousands of animal organ tissue cross-sections for signs of abnormalities. All these data then had to be compiled and statistically analyzed.

To relieve individual corporate laboratories of some of this testing burden, in 1974 eleven major chemical companies, including Du Pont, formed the Chemical Industry Institute for Toxicology and built a $12 million laboratory to house it at Research Triangle Park in North Carolina. One of its first tasks was to undertake chronic inhalation tests on commodity chemicals and to do "megamouse" studies to determine the importance of population size and dosage in toxicological studies.[82]

The new regulatory environment for chemical manufacture, use, and disposal prompted the Du Pont Executive Committee to give Haskell the corporatewide responsibility that it had sought since its creation. Edwin Gee, Executive Committee advisor on research and "environmental" issues in the early 1970s, circulated a document stating that if Haskell had good reason to study a particular compound and could not get funding from the appropriate departments, then the laboratory could carry out the work with administrative funds.[83] Whereas Haskell representatives previously had to be invited into a plant, they began to conduct an increasing number of industrial hygiene surveys without having to secure permission from the concerned departments. With the increase in the scope and size of Haskell's programs, the Employee Relations Department began to look upon the laboratory as a cancerous growth in its organization. Therefore in 1973, Haskell was transferred into the Central Research Department, which was a far more congenial setting for a scientific research organization. In addition, Du Pont executives hoped that there would be synergism between the biologists in Central Research and the Haskell staff.[84]

Throughout the 1970s, fundamental research accounted for about 20 percent of Haskell's total budget.[85] Major efforts centered on finding shortcuts for screening chemicals similar to the Ames test developed in 1974 by Bruce Ames at the University of California. He devised a bacteria test to determine if a chemical is a mutagen and possibly a carcinogen. In spite of limitations, the Ames test has become a cheap and quick screening method for potential carcinogenicity.[86] Du Pont and other researchers have sought other non-animal-based tests. Besides the expense and time involved in animal studies, animal-rights groups have become politically powerful and have exerted pressure on federal agencies to reduce the number of animals used in studies and to sponsor research on alternative methods. Most toxicologists, however, believe that the interactions between chemicals and organisms are so complex that a reasonable correlation with human exposure can only be established by animal testing. Research continues on understanding the metabolic pathways of chemicals in animals so that in the future the toxic effects of at least some compounds might be predicted.[87]

But testing of compounds, not research, continued to be Haskell's principal mission.

In the 1970s, many times a promising new chemical has had to be abandoned for toxicological reasons.[88] Perhaps the most dramatic example was the case of hexamethylphosphoramide (HMPA), which Du Pont had selected as the solvent for its high-strength Kevlar fibers. HMPA was a common solvent, but no long-term chronic tests had ever been done on it. Tests at Haskell showed HMPA to be a powerful nasal carcinogen in rats. These results immediately led to a dramatic decrease in plant exposure levels and a search for a new solvent.[89] At a significant cost in both time and money, Du Pont altered its Kevlar process to use a different solvent.

Conclusion: A New Dimension of Innovation

Having pioneered in industrial toxicology in the United States, Du Pont through its Haskell Laboratory was far better equipped to cope with challenges of the 1970s than many companies. The major change within Du Pont was that Haskell's advice began to carry more weight in corporate decisions concerning the manufacture, use, and disposal of chemicals. For a long time, Du Pont had relied on the good faith of the general managers in matters of industrial hygiene and toxicology, but with the new laws and regulatory apparatus Du Pont could no longer afford to take some of the calculated risks it had assumed in the past. In the 1970s, toxicology became an integral part of innovation, adding new elements of uncertainty to what was already a risky process.

Redirecting R&D: The 1970s

The New Venture era had strengthened Du Pont's already deep research and development capability, increasing expenditures and personnel by 50 percent and 30 percent respectively. By the late 1960s, however, the high costs and risks and uncertain rewards of commercializing new products combined with a generally lower level of profitability to sour the Executive Committee on large new ventures.

A major question facing the company's management in the 1970s was how to employ effectively its 5,000-person R&D staff.[1] One answer was to reduce the level of effort, which Du Pont did. When adjusted for inflation, R&D expenditures remained constant throughout the decade, while R&D expenditures per dollar of sales decreased by 50 percent to 3.3 percent by 1979. Other U.S. chemical companies also cut back on research in a corresponding manner as the industry continued to mature. Consequently, Du Pont remained the R&D leader.[2] Under such circumstances, much of the industry's research shifted from offensive to defensive, to shore up the existing businesses against inroads by competition. Du Pont had neglected many older product lines in the rush to get out new products in the 1960s, so research in support of its existing businesses appealed to the Executive Committee.

This new research strategy prompted many of the industrial departments to decentralize into product-oriented profit centers. Selling products possessing no technical advantages, the company that responded most quickly to a customer's specific needs became the preferred supplier. In a profit center, research, production, and marketing were more closely integrated than they could be in a large, functionally organized department. Thus, profit centers could more rapidly transform information from the marketplace into improved products. Sometimes the departmental research organizations were decentralized into those profit centers, which resulted in further fragmentation of Du Pont's research program. Although this new research strategy was effective for defending the company's existing products, it threatened to make new-product and diversification research even more chaotic than it had been in the 1960s.

By degrees in the 1970s, the Executive Committee moved away from its long-standing laissez faire policy toward the management of the company's new-product R&D. Du Pont could no longer afford to allow the industrial departments to undertake the development and commercialization of all promising research leads. Priorities had to be established, and choices had to be made. The Executive Committee reluctantly and cautiously began to exercise more authority in what had historically been the domain of the general managers of the industrial departments. At the end of the decade, the Executive Committee appointed one of its members to play a much stronger role in managing R&D that might lead the company in new directions. And finally, the committee decided to focus its exploratory research in the 1980s on what the company called "Life Sciences." Overall, in response to the maturation of its major products and general economic turmoil, Du Pont altered its strategy and structure in the 1970s more than in any decade since the 1920s. These changes, however, were evolutionary, not revolutionary.

Challenging Tradition

On January 1, 1970, Edwin A. Gee, who had run the Development Department's New Venture program in the 1960s before becoming head of the Photo Products Department, was elected to the Executive Committee and became the new advisor on research.[3] A year earlier, President McCoy had asked committee members to play more active roles as advisors and to dig deeper into the affairs of the departments.[4] Gee's predecessor, George Holbrook, had initiated a series of discussions with Du Pont's research directors to find ways to focus more sharply the company's technical resources, which were dispersed among the departments.[5] Contributing to this dialog in a position paper, Gee called for nothing less than an entirely new research strategy. He struck at the heart of Du Pont's postwar research tradition by asserting that competitive research capability and other factors have made "unique proprietary positions of high profitability increasingly a thing of the past."[6]

Gee put forward four ways in which Du Pont could adjust its research programs to these changed conditions. Over the next decade, the Executive Committee would generally follow Gee's suggestions. First, he proposed to cut fundamental research and concentrate on areas in which Du Pont had an existing competitive advantage. Central Research's centers of excellence should follow, not precede, business success and corporate commitment. Second, Du Pont should be more wary of launching high-risk and high-investment ventures. After a major venture was initiated, the Executive Committee had to pay more attention to it, because it could become a significant drain on company earnings. Third, he believed that research and development expenditures should be cut on products that had fallen to commodity status. As he had done earlier, Gee called for more emphasis on the purchase and sale of technology. In addition, the health of Du Pont's existing products needed to be ensured by doing research aimed at lowering production costs. Fourth, Gee maintained that the Executive Committee had to play a larger role in allocating the company's research resources. For example, the Textile Fibers Department had the company's largest and most powerful research organization, but by 1970 opportunities for additional investment in fibers appeared limited. Gee wondered if Du Pont should put the Textile Fibers Pioneering Research Laboratory to work on nonfibers research. In addition to implementing these suggestions, he recommended reducing R&D spending by 10 to 15 percent over the next two years, which with inflation would lower the level of effort by 25 percent. The Executive Committee did not act immediately on Gee's organizational and strategic proposals but did cut back on research expenditures during the economic recession of 1969 and 1970.

Although many of Gee's proposals were new to Du Pont, they reflected a growing consensus among U.S. business managers that research needed to be managed more effectively to keep it in line with business objectives. In the chemical industry, this attitude probably reflected increasing management frustration at the inability of research to develop major proprietary products, a situation brought about by the highly competitive nature of chemical R&D and the maturation of traditional markets for new products. As early as 1965, a *Fortune* article entitled "Harnessing the R&D Monster" quoted Charles A. Thomas, head of Monsanto, as saying that "the nation's R&D is now stumbling in a plethora of projects, sinking in a sea of money, and is being built on a quicksand of changing objectives."[7] *Fortune* pointed out that management's concern about the productivity of R&D was widespread, and that there was an increasing number of conferences on the problems of R&D. In 1971, *Fortune* reporter Dan Cordtz wrote that companies were sharpening the focus of research, tying it more securely to corporate goals, looking for profits sooner, and doing less basic research. This latter type of work, which was not expected to pay off for five or ten years, Cordtz concluded, "has become a luxury few can afford."[8] Many executives at Du Pont were wondering how much exploratory research the company should do and how it should be evaluated.

When the Executive Committee decided that Du Pont should de-emphasize diversification and new products in general, the role of Central Research became even more problematical than it had been previously. A major "lesson" that the company had learned from the New Venture push of the 1960s was that it was very difficult to diversify through research alone. To many Du Pont managers, Central Research's programs in certain fields of electronics and life sciences were scientific forays into regions where Du Pont had no business experience. Others saw Central Research as a scientific research organization that had goals independent of those of the rest of the Du Pont Company.[9]

In December 1969, the Executive Committee appointed a four-man Central Research Department Study Committee to determine, as one member put it, "what [was] the best program for Central Research to make the best contribution to more dynamic growth for the Du Pont Company (in the next few years)."[10] The committee's final report, prepared by chairman Herman E. Schroeder of the Elastomer Chemicals Department, recommended to Central Research's director, David M. McQueen, that his department have substantially greater business orientation and specifically be more strongly influenced by business considerations early in the decision-making process. Specifically, Central Research's mission would be "to promote diversification through the establishment of new technology in support of a business strategy."[11]

McQueen countered these arguments in a series of memoranda to Gee in which he reemphasized the importance of scientific and technological novelty in Du Pont research. None of his department's major breakthroughs, he asserted, had originated from an attack on a specific market goal or from an industrial department pointing to an opportunity. McQueen maintained that Central Research had produced a long and continuous stream of novel research leads that were passed over by managers in the industrial departments, who favored incremental changes in technology and products similar to the ones they already produced. In his view, it was not Central Research's fault that the departments were too conservative to develop and commercialize really novel research leads.[12] McQueen vented some of his frustrations of being a research director in a difficult era:

> [T]he recent earnings situation of the Company has seen too much top management back-pedaling to place the blame on research. But what can research do of itself? Basically, it can only provide candidates for development, and management must accept the responsibility for decisions on which candidates to invest money and manpower in and which not. . . .
>
> The atmosphere today is such that anything really new is viewed with suspicion and only the extension of areas of past success is commended. But for the future health of the Company, *now* is the time to encourage imaginative, discovery-oriented research. There is no doubt in my mind that such research can be as effective today as it ever was.[13]

Three months after stating his case, McQueen reached the mandatory retirement age, having served Du Pont in the Central Research Department for thirty-seven years.

Gee and two other members of the Executive Committee wanted to appoint someone with industrial department experience as McQueen's successor. They believed that the department had become too inbred and independent of the rest of the company.[14] As one Executive Committee member put it, a more commercially oriented director of Central Research would lend "commercial reality" to its programs.[15] As a compromise, three other committee members favored bringing in an industrial department man as assistant director rather than as head. When the committee voted, Irving Shapiro and Edward R. Kane (who would become Du Pont's next management team in 1973) cast their ballots in favor of the compromise.[16] Thus, McQueen's assistant, Theodore L. Cairns, became the new director of Central Research, and the committee appointed William Simeral as his assistant. Simeral had begun his career in the Plastics Department's "Polymer Science Institute" and had moved through the ranks of that department's research organization to become head of its commercial resins division in 1968.[17] That the committee decided to promote Cairns, who had a research philosophy similar to McQueen's, probably reflected the importance placed by many in the company on maintaining Du Pont's high standing in the U.S. scientific community. Bringing in an "outsider" to head Central Research would have implied to professors and students that Du Pont was no longer going to offer careers in purely scientific research. Rather than take this dramatic step, the committee decided on a more moderate move and began to explore ways in which the industrial departments could exert more influence on Central Research's programs.

To evaluate the entire company's exploratory research efforts, the Executive Committee in 1971 appointed a committee on exploratory research consisting of Cairns, Simeral, the head of the Development Department, and two industrial department research directors.[18] This committee soon discovered that the official definition of exploratory research permitted wide latitude in interpretation, and this latitude was being fully exercised by the industrial departments. The research in this category was divided between the types of fundamental research delineated by Stine and Bolton decades earlier. About 80 percent of the work was directed at the evolutionary development of the existing business lines. The other 20 percent represented research in new fields such as pharmaceuticals, agrichemicals, and electronics. The merits of these lines of research, the committee concluded, would have to be determined on a subjective basis because major new earnings from exploratory research would not be realized for ten to twenty years. This was a position that McQueen and virtually every one of his predecessors had taken when attempts were made to evaluate the productivity of long-range research. The major conclusions of the committee were that the company's exploratory research programs were attacking too many separate objectives instead of concentrating on selected opportunities and that the fields and intensity of effort should be determined at the corporate, not departmental, level. After reviewing the company's exploratory research aimed at new fields, which was less than $10 million a year, the committee believed this work could not have a large impact on Du Pont's fortunes in the foreseeable future.[19]

The committee's findings disappointed Gee. After reading the final report, he wrote to Cairns, "It was my hope that we would develop insights and convictions or at least outline differing points of view about research."[20] But he found no such things in the report. He went on to express his concern about the future of the Du Pont Company and to reiterate his thesis that it needed a new research policy for the 1970s.

Reporting to his fellow committee members, Gee proposed a moderate approach to exploratory research. He argued that some randomness was necessary and expressed mixed feelings about greater corporate surveillance. Overall, Gee stated that no significant changes in organization or program were needed but made several suggestions concerning the coordination and direction of Du Pont research. To accomplish these goals, he proposed that an ongoing advisory committee be established to undertake specific studies such as whether it was time for Du Pont to pick a new area for research or whether the company should have a central polymer research organization.[21] As business conditions improved between 1971 and 1973, the Executive Committee allowed research budgets to increase a little and was content to let the departments carry out their own programs. By 1974, Gee had begun to worry about the dramatic decline in the number of new ventures under way at Du Pont and formed a committee of research directors to investigate whether there was major R&D work that should be started to put the company on an upward growth curve.[22]

Before any initiatives could be started, however, the company would be caught in a severe cost–price squeeze caused by the sharp increase in oil prices following the Arab oil embargo and Du Pont's inability to pass higher costs on to consumers by raising prices. Especially hard hit was Textile Fibers, upon which the company depended heavily. That department saw its profits shrink to nothing in 1975. Not surprisingly, under these conditions the research directors' subcommittee reported that there were no areas in which it recommended starting major research efforts.[23] It reached this conclusion, in part, because the company's financial position had deteriorated so much that Du Pont's executives were no longer looking for new investment opportunities.

In 1974 and 1975, Du Pont could not generate internally all the cash it needed to finance its ongoing new ventures, the modernization of facilities, and capacity expansions. The company's capital expenditures topped $1 billion in 1974, one-third higher than the previous year's record high. To finance this construction, Du Pont had to borrow $450 million. Although Du Pont's debt ratio was much lower than those of other U.S. chemical companies, incurring long-term debt was a new and upsetting experience for Du Pont's board of directors and management. This capital shortage led the Executive and Finance committees to look long and hard at all project requests. In early 1974, the Treasurer's Department estimated that the company could afford to fund only two-thirds of the over $4 billion that the departments wanted to put into plant investment. Because Du Pont expected to require only $400 million for new products, the Executive Committee decided to go ahead with most of them. Nevertheless, over 90 percent of new investment would go to keeping established products healthy.[24]

R&D in a Maturing Industry

A survey of Du Pont's businesses conducted by the Development Department in 1972 showed that the company had twenty-one major product lines, some three-quarters of which were over thirty years old[25] (see Table

Table 25.1. *Du Pont's Major Product Groups, 1961–70*

Product	Date commercialized	Cumulative operative earnings,[a] 1961–70, $millions
Nylon fibers	1939	1,656
Nylon intermediates	1939	658
Dacron polyester fibers	1953	560
Orlon acrylic fibers	1950	441
TEL gasoline additive	1924	420
Neoprene	1932	368
Titanium dioxide pigments	1931	330
Cellophane	1923	281
Mylar polyester film	1952	247
Freon fluorocarbons	1931	217
Polyester intermediates	1950	197
Teflon fluorocarbon resins	1944	167
Herbicides	1953	151
Auto refinishes	1924	141
X-ray products	1932	122
Auto finishes	1918	121
Lycra spandex fibers	1962	118
Nylon resins	1945	115
Butacite safety glass interlayers	1938	70
Polyolefins	1943	65
Graphic arts films	1939	64

[a]Operative earnings are before deducting overhead and taxes.
Source: David Brearley to Monroe S. Sadler, "Major Products," Apr. 13, 1972, Executive Committee Files.

lines, some three-quarters of which were over thirty years old[25] (see Table 25.1). These products accounted for 90 percent of Du Pont's earnings in the 1960s and were expected to contribute substantially to the profits of the 1970s. Yet some of these products were showing signs of age and others were showing signs of neglect. TEL antiknock and cellophane were in irreversible decline, and other formerly healthy products such as Mylar and Teflon were experiencing increasing competition. While Du Pont had been attempting to commercialize new high-profit products in the 1960s, other chemical companies had been working hard to improve their products in order to take market share away from Du Pont. And on a broad front they had been successful, in part because Du Pont management frequently saw increasing competition as a sign that a product had become a "commodity" and then refused to devote adequate resources to fight back.

In 1971, the Boston Consulting Group, which Gee had hired, criticized this strategy, describing it as "invent, skim the cream with high profit margins, lose market share, lose cost differential, abandon, [and] replace with new invention."[26] But the New Venture program of the 1960s had proven that Du Pont could not quickly bring out enough new products to replace maturing ones. The Boston Consulting Group recommended that Du Pont stick it out with its older products because eventually falling profit margins would force less efficient producers out of the business, leaving only a few survivors. The dominant producer then would have a profitable business that would be growing slowly enough to discourage potential competitors from entering the field. Although anticommodity sentiment ran strong at Du Pont, in the highly competitive business climate of the 1970s Du Pont management had little choice but to defend its existing businesses.

Developing lower-cost processes was one strategy Du Pont had employed to keep its products profitable. A dramatic example of this was the chloride process for the manufacture of titanium dioxide pigments. When Du Pont needed additional TiO_2 capacity in the late 1940s, the Pigments Department management decided to build a commercial-scale chloride process plant. This posed major challenges to the engineers who had to design and operate the new plant without the benefit of pilot plant experience. Not surprisingly, engineers encountered tremendous technical difficulties handling the hot corrosive gases used in the process. After the plant was constructed in 1951, for the next three years it was run as a pilot plant with many changes in equipment and process concepts. But when finally straightened out, the new process gave Du Pont both lower investment and operating costs. On the basis of this superior process, Du Pont increased its market share of this commodity from 25 to 39 percent between 1956 and 1976. In the 1960s, TiO_2 ranked seventh among Du Pont products in operative earnings.[27] In the critical fibers area, however, Du Pont was not doing as well. As polymerization and spinning became more efficient, the cost of intermediates became an increasingly important part of total fiber cost.

By 1970, Du Pont was committed to new intermediates processes for nylon and Dacron, which together accounted for 40 percent of the company's operative earnings in the previous decade. The principal Dacron intermediate, dimethyl terephthalate (DMT), had been made in the Explosives Department by the oxidation of *para*-xylene with nitric acid. By 1970, several competitors had introduced superior processes using air instead of nitric acid. This was just one more ironic twist in a long battle at Du Pont over intermediates processes. In the 1930s, the Ammonia Department had become the manufacturer of nylon intermediates by working out an adipic acid process based on the air oxidation of cyclohexanol. Explosives, which used nitric acid to make explosives, backed a nitric acid process and had lost. A decade later, however, the Ammonia Department began to use nitric acid in one of the two oxidation steps in the adipic acid process. At about the same time, the search for a DMT process was under way, and Explosives triumphed with nitric acid. When other companies developed air oxidation processes in the late 1960s, Du Pont was forced to license one for over $20 million in patent royalties.[28] This process at least prevented the company from falling behind the competition.

With nylon intermediates, Du Pont was more successful at maintaining technological and cost advantages. In part this was the result of the company's larger scale of production. Between 1950 and 1964, output of nylon intermediates increased from 150 million to 500 million pounds per year and the cost per pound decreased from $0.37 to $0.14.[29] During this period, Du Pont had made several important changes in technology, including an entirely new process for making hexamethylenediamine (HDA). The original process used the other nylon intermediate, adipic acid, as the starting material. When the wartime synthetic rubber program made butadiene available on a low-cost basis, Du Pont researchers investigated processes for adding two cyano groups to butadiene to yield adiponitrile, which would be hydrogenated to HDA. This direct approach seemed futile because it violated the normal pathway of organic chemical reactions, so chemists attempted to place chlorine atoms on the ends of the butadiene molecule and then replace them with cyano groups. In 1946, Gerald Whitman in the Chemical Department discovered how to carry out this reaction with high yields, and the Ammonia Department developed a full-scale process from it.[30] The new process was an improvement over the adipic acid one, but the HDA was still two to three times as expensive as adipic acid.[31]

The idea of directly adding cyano groups to the ends of butadiene was revived in 1962 by Frank McGrew, research director of the Plastics Department. He believed that coordination chemistry offered a new approach. Subsequently, McGrew contacted an expert in the field, Professor Daryle Busch at Ohio State University, about someone that Du Pont might hire to carry out such new research. Busch replied that the company already had the man it needed in William C. Drinkard, who was working for the Fabrics and Finishes Department. McGrew arranged to transfer Drinkard into the Plastics Department but assigned him to work in Central Research under Richard V. Lindsey, who also did research in the same area. In less than a year, Drinkard and Lindsey had discovered a zero-valent nickel complex that put the cyano groups on the ends of the butadiene molecule. This particular catalyst proved to be inadequate in terms of yield and efficiency, but continuing work in Central Research and in the Plastics Department led to the development of a commercial process. Six years after the initial breakthrough, Du Pont began production in a 150-million-pound-per-year plant.[32]

The introduction of the new adiponitrile process proved to be timely for maintaining the company's competitive position in nylon. Monsanto had developed a process based on the electrolytic coupling of acrylonitrile, which gave Du Pont's principal competitor a one- or two-cent-per-pound advantage. The direct cyanation process reversed this situation. In the early 1970s, Du Pont's nylon production topped 1 billion pounds a year, requiring nearly a half-pound of adiponitrile per pound of nylon. At a production rate of 500 million pounds per year, a one-cent-per-pound cost saving was worth $5 million.[33]

With the dramatic increase in petrochemical costs in 1973 and 1974, having a low-cost intermediates process became even more critical. The earlier Du Pont process had consumed about sixty pounds of chlorine per one hundred pounds of adiponitrile produced. Chlorine gas is produced by an electrolytic process that consumes large quantities of energy. Not having to use increasingly expensive chlorine was a major asset for Du Pont's process. Finally, the old process had created large quantities of by-product salt that had to be safely disposed of. In the 1970s, when Du Pont's executives were looking for examples of the kind of research that the company should be doing, they could find no better process example than the direct cyanation of butadiene.

Product improvement was another element of Du Pont's research strategy of the 1970s. Super-tough nylon resin (Zytel ST) offers a very successful example. In plastic molded parts, nylon had a long-recognized deficiency that when notched by poor mold design, surface scratches, or other physical damage, cracks propagated readily from the notch causing the part to fail. In 1973, Plastics Department research associate Bennett N. Epstein was assigned to scout methods of toughening nylon resins. A few months later, he discovered that by blending nylon with a significant fraction of other specific types of resins, the final product's toughness improved dramatically. He also proposed a theory of toughening, which Du Pont chemists applied to other resins.[34] Zytel ST was an immediate success because automotive companies were looking for improved resins to replace metal to reduce car weight. Apparently, Zytel ST caught the other nylon producers flat-footed, and Du Pont strengthened its claim to being the innovative leader in nylon resins. Within a few years of Epstein's discovery, Du Pont was selling over 10 million pounds per year of Zytel ST at a 10-cent-per-pound premium over standard nylon resins.[35] Thus, an inexpensive and short-lived research program quickly yielded a $1-million-per-year profit.

Throttling R&D

Product and process improvement research would come to dominate the company's strategy under Gee's successor as Executive Committee advisor on research, Richard E. Heckert, who joined the committee in September 1973 and was assigned the research portfolio the following August. Heckert had earned a PhD in organic chemistry from the University of Illinois in 1949 and had spent five years in the Chemical Department before moving into the Film Department. He later served as assistant general manager of the Film and Plastics departments before heading the Fabrics and Finishes Department in 1969.[36] Soon after becoming research advisor, Heckert formed an ad hoc R&D committee "to study alternatives for the future scope and nature of our R&D program." He noted that the Executive Committee considered it necessary to reduce the company's overall research effort. In July 1975, the R&D committee, which was chaired by Heckert and consisted of five research directors, issued its report. The committee concluded that "the company is supporting more new product and diversification programs than it can reasonably expect to commercialize" and that Du Pont should lower its overall research budget.[37]

Soon Heckert made a similar report to the Executive Committee. With profit margins eroding rapidly because of increasing competition and rising energy and raw material costs, Du Pont did not have enough excess capital to support expansions of existing businesses and had "little incentive for the generation of high-risk, capital intensive new ventures." Under these circumstances, Du Pont had no choice but to cut back on R&D and to redirect its R&D programs to support existing businesses. Specifically, Heckert recommended cutting R&D expense by 3 to 4 percent a year for several years, restricting industrial department research to the periphery of its established businesses, and requiring that Central Research receive up to half of its budget from projects supported by industrial departments. As late as the early 1950s, Central Research had gotten 50 percent of its budget from work for the industrial departments, but by the 1970s this amount had declined to 10 percent.[38] Of course, the purpose of this change was to bring the department's research programs closer to the immediate concerns of the company. Change in R&D comes slowly, however. Over the next several years Heckert, assisted by the other research directors, began to implement his proposals.[39]

To many people both inside and outside the company, it appeared that Du Pont had lost its faith in scientific research. Central Research Director Cairns reported to Heckert that Du Pont's research image had reached a low ebb in the universities.[40] Not even the company's board of directors was immune to worrying about the health of the company's research. In 1977, Heckert assured the board of directors that although Du Pont's R&D was in a period of transition, the company still spent much more than its competitors and research was still critical to the company's future. There had been a shift in focus, Heckert concluded, away from the development of entirely new products. He explained to the Board that "the many challenges and opportunities presented by a changing external environment – increasing government regulation, rising costs of energy and raw materials, growing strengths of competition – dictate focusing our efforts on areas where we are the strongest."[41] When these factors were combined with Du Pont's shortage of capital, the overall climate did not favor bold, venturesome research programs. In fact, in several cases Du Pont was attempting to salvage threatened businesses.

Of all the Du Pont industrial departments, the Organic Chemicals Department suffered the most from the new environment described by Heckert. None of Orchem's three major businesses – dyes, tetraethyllead gasoline antiknock compound, and Freon fluorocarbons – escaped the 1970s unscathed. The dye business did not even survive in spite of a major effort to save it.

Du Pont's dye profits peaked in the early 1950s and by the mid-1960s had fallen to unsatisfactory levels. A major cause of this decline was the return of German dyes made in new plants built after the war. By the late 1960s, Swiss dyemakers had installed a large modern plant at Toms River, New Jersey. The Chambers Works dye manufacturing facilities at Deepwater were state of the art for the mid-1930s and consisted of over 200 batch-operated sets of equipment, which produced 2,500 different products. To improve its competitive position in dyes, Orchem's managers decided to discontinue about 40 percent of its product line and to build an integrated manufacturing facility based upon modern processing technology and materials handling concepts.[42] In 1972 the Executive Committee authorized $65 million to construct a computerized, high-volume dye plant in Manati, Puerto Rico. The site was chosen primarily because the plant would be given a fifteen-year exemption from all taxes. Dye intermediates would continue to be made at the Chambers Works and would be shipped to Puerto Rico for the last few steps, which would be carried out in nine large, computer-controlled reactor systems.[43] Orchem experienced numerous difficulties in getting this new technology to work at the same time that increasing competition further eroded profits. By 1976, Du Pont dyes lost money, and in 1980 the company closed the Manati plant and got out of the dye business entirely.[44]

Another long-time contributor to Orchem's earnings was tetraethyllead (TEL), which after the major fibers was the most important contributor to Du Pont earnings in the 1960s. At its peak in the early 1970s, TEL sales were over $200 million a year and operative earnings over $50 million. With new production technology, Du Pont had actually increased its market share in spite of the entrance of new competitors into the business.[45] The growing national concern over air pollution, particularly smog caused by automotive emissions, led General Motors in 1970 to announce that it was equipping its cars with catalytic converters. Leaded gas could not be used in such cars because lead poisoned the platinum catalyst in the converters. At the same time, the newly founded Environmental Protection Agency began to attack the use of TEL in gasoline as posing a potential health hazard and to regulate the amount of TEL that could be added to gasoline.[46] Although TEL remained a very profitable product for Du Pont, sales began to drop after 1972.[47]

This was a gradual decline compared to what happened to the Freon fluorocarbons business. In June 1974, two University of California chemists published a paper in *Nature* claiming that chlorofluorocarbons used as propellants in aerosol products were depleting the ozone layer in the upper atmosphere, which shielded the earth from harmful ultraviolet radiation.[48] This publication occurred only one year after Du Pont had begun to consolidate its Freon manufacturing capacity in one large, backward-integrated unit at Corpus Christi, Texas, to obtain the lowest-cost position in an increasingly competitive business. The aerosol market began to shrink after the ozone theory was published. In 1976, Du Pont sold $260 million worth of Freon yet lost money. As expected, the Food and Drug Administration and the Environmental Protection Agency in 1978 banned all propellants that were fully halogenated (containing only fluorine and chlorine atoms on the carbons). Orchem looked for other compounds for aerosol propellants, but its most promising prospect failed the Ames test for mutagenicity. It was no understatement when an Orchem assistant general manager bemoaned, "In the last five years we have been impacted probably more than any single department by environmentalism, regulatory action, and toxicological problems."[49]

The new federal environmental and toxicological regulations had primarily an indirect impact on Du Pont's R&D programs. In 1977, Du Pont spent $40 million or about 10 percent of its total R&D budget on research related to government regulations. One company observer estimated that Du Pont would have done about three-quarters of this work anyway, leaving only about $10 million of expense that he considered unnecessary.[50] Where regulation really hurt Du Pont research was in pollution control equipment, which in the late 1970s was consuming 30 percent of the company's new investment.[51]

Reorganizing for R&D

The ongoing capital shortage at Du Pont required that the company develop a systematic procedure for ranking investment opportunities. To accomplish this task, the Executive Committee decided in late 1974 to establish a Corporate Plans Department from part of the Development Department, the remainder of which would be merged with Central Research to create a Central Research and Development Department.[52] These were moves that Gee had been advocating for a long time. In the 1960s, Gee contended, the Executive Committee had to accept what the general managers told them about projects. As an Executive Committee member several years later, he continued to argue for the formation of a Corporate Plans Department, directed by one of the corporation's outstanding younger department heads. The company had not had a man with such corporate presence in this type of function since Fin Sparre retired in 1944.[53] Eventually George J. Prendergast, Jr., who had been in the Treasurer's Department, was chosen to head the new department. The Executive Committee gave it broad responsibility for coordinating all strategic business planning activities in the company, specifically by analyzing Du Pont's portfolio of businesses. With such analysis, the committee could establish priorities for the allocation of resources. The staff of the new department consisted of 12 of the Development Department's 126 employees.[54]

Approximately thirty other Development Department employees moved into Central Research to form the Central Research and Development Department. Former director Monroe S. Sadler became Cairns's assistant. The others who accompanied Sadler had been a New Business Opportunities group that pursued ventures requiring little capital and making use of existing company resources. It was really a remnant of the New Venture activities of the 1960s. Other members of the department, such as the real estate group, were reassigned.[55] On paper, at least, Du Pont now provided Central Research with a development division. But it was only about a tenth the size of the research division, and Cairns continued to emphasize the scientific work of his department. The development division was confined for a number of years to looking for uses for materials that the research division had synthesized. Nothing of value to the corporation came from this work.[56]

The Corporate Plans Department under Prendergast had a more successful experience. In the late 1960s, when Du Pont's performance was considered unsatisfactory by top management, Executive Committee member Robert Hershey and Prendergast studied the evolution of the company's departments and looked closely at the strategy behind the decentralization of the company in 1921.[57] Both saw striking parallels between the company's problems in 1920 and those of the late 1960s. At the top of the list was the problem of managing increasingly large and complex businesses. This had led to the diffusion of responsibility for the success or failure of a particular business segment. One solution was to institute another round of decentralization, this time by creating product divisions within the departments. A profit center manager would be held accountable for the performance of his or her division. An added benefit would be the creation of a new job in which younger executives could be given broad managerial experience.

The creation of profit centers forced department managers to decide whether to decentralize research as well. In theory, if a division manager was to have full responsibility for a product line, then he or she should have control over research. But decentralization of research created personnel problems because most divisional units were rather small and offered little opportunity for advancement except by leaving research. In the eyes of many, the remaining central research unit would be the real research division. Also, having a number of small research units under divisional heads limited the flexibility of the work effort because reassigning chemists from one division to another proved difficult. The Du Pont departments in the 1960s and 1970s experimented with many forms of research organization but no general model emerged.[58] Each business had to tailor its research to suit its own needs. At the same time there was pressure to decentralize research, however, there was an increasing trend in Du Pont toward greater top-management involvement in research.

A major obstacle faced by the Corporate Plans Department and the Executive Committee was allocation of research effort. Each industrial department funded its own research programs, the extent of which depended on the department's size and profitability, not on the potential of research fields. In the early 1970s, Textile Fibers had about 1,000 research personnel, twice the number of any other department.[59] With profits sagging and opportunities for new fibers being limited, the Executive Committee played a direct role in formulating policies for dealing with the situation. In July 1976, the committee established a subcommittee on Textile Fibers chaired by Gee, the department's Executive Committee liaison. In cooperation with the general manager, the subcommittee charted a plan to make Du Pont fibers more competitive, which included significant reductions in research.[60] By 1979, Textile Fibers research personnel had been reduced by 40 percent from the peak level of a decade earlier. This reduction was accomplished largely through natural attrition. The Organic Chemicals, Industrial Chemicals, and Pigments departments also had their research budgets cut significantly after 1975, while the other industrial departments kept R&D spending constant.[61]

With limited resources to commit to research and limited capital to commercialize new ventures, Corporate Plans analyzed Du Pont's research programs to determine the fraction of the total that was spent on basic science, new products, diversification, and supporting the existing businesses. In 1975 the Executive Committee had amended the research rules so that an industrial department had to receive the committee's permission to start research programs that were not peripheral to its existing product lines or technology. Earlier, the committee had imposed stricter rules on New Venture programs.[62] Overall, these changes and the philosophy of Gee and Heckert had led departments to shift their research emphasis toward short-term support and extension of existing businesses. The company's long-range and diversification research became increasingly concentrated in the Central Research and Development Department. Prendergast and his committee liaison, Edward G. Jefferson, agreed that Central Research had a critical role to play in the company's future and that top management should be more actively involved in selecting research areas.[63] To accomplish this goal, the Executive Committee in December 1978 made its member who served as research liaison directly responsible for Central Research, with other research directors reporting to him on a dotted-line basis.[64]

The earlier relationship between the Executive Committee advisor on research and the director of Central Research had long been a source of frustration for both parties. For example, in 1951 Roger Williams met with Elmer Bolton's successor, Cole Coolidge, and argued that as head of the Chemical Department he was the only research director who had an overview of the company's R&D and suggested that Coolidge attempt to guide and influence the research programs of the industrial departments. He pointed out that earlier both Stine and Bolton had performed this role, not only because of their position as director of the Chemical Department but because of their reputations as research pioneers and elder statesmen in Du Pont. Even though Coolidge enjoyed no such status in the company,

Williams thought he also should attempt to play this role. If the research directors did not take Coolidge's advice, Williams suggested going over their heads to the departmental management. In an era when the general managers of the industrial departments only nominally submitted themselves to the authority of the Executive Committee, Williams's proposal must have shocked and astounded Coolidge. When asked by Coolidge why he did not do this job himself, Williams replied that as advisor on research, he did not have direct authority over the research organizations of the company. Neither did Coolidge, however, and Williams acknowledged that Coolidge's authority could be exercised only informally, not organizationally. Finally, as was commonplace in meetings between Executive Committee advisors and their advisees, Williams disclaimed all that he had asked Coolidge to do by saying that he was not giving orders, only expressing his point of view, which did not necessarily represent the consensus of the Executive Committee.[65] The liaison relationship continued to operate in this fashion until the change in 1979.

The committee assigned Jefferson to the new position. For many in Du Pont's research ranks, this appointment was the first good news they had heard from top management in a long time. Irving S. Shapiro, a lawyer, had become head of the company in 1973, and researchers interpreted the selection of a nontechnical person to run the Du Pont Company as a de facto de-emphasis of research. The modest cuts in the research budget in the mid-1970s and the increasing concern that management expressed about the productivity of Du Pont's research efforts had hurt morale in the ranks and even among research directors.[66] Research had continued, however, carried along by momentum rather than by encouragement from management. Besieged research directors looked forward to the day when the turmoil surrounding research would end and no more high-level investigative committees would be formed.

In Jefferson, who had a PhD in physical chemistry from Kings College, University of London, and had begun his career in research, Du Pont's research organizations found an enthusiastic supporter. In spite of the external difficulties in the 1970s, Jefferson continued to view research as the critical component in the technology-intensive Du Pont Company. With the increasing rate of product obsolescence, he believed, research might actually prove to be more important in the future.[67]

Jefferson faced his first major decision soon after assuming his new job in January 1979. The director of Central Research and Development, Cairns, was nearing retirement, so a replacement had to be chosen. Cairns had vigorously upheld the tradition of doing first-class science during a period when many in management considered it irrelevant to the company's strategy. Rather than punish the department for its independent stance, Jefferson backed the nomination of Howard E. Simmons, Jr., who had been director of research under Cairns. By supporting Simmons, who was an outstanding scientist and a member of the National Academy of Sciences, Jefferson calmed the nerves of Du Pont scientists who feared that research was no longer viewed as the mainspring of the company.[68]

Life Sciences Research

As the research executive, Jefferson began looking for areas in which Central Research could do basic science that would have a major impact on a number of the company's businesses in the future. A December 1978 article in the *Economist* on the emerging field of recombinant DNA caught Jefferson's eye. The new techniques, the author predicted, would lead to new drugs such as hormones, vaccines, antibiotics, and antiviral agents, superior plants that might fix their own nitrogen, new catalysts for the production of chemicals, and many other related uses.[69] This new field of biology emerged from university research directed toward incorporating DNA of one organism into the genetic code of another. Because DNA acts as the template for the production of chemicals in cells, recombinant DNA techniques could make feasible large-scale production of important human proteins that exist in the body only in very small quantities. For example, one major line of research involved attempts to incorporate the DNA segment coded to produce human insulin into bacteria that would then produce this chemical. Another target has been interferon, an antiviral agent produced by human cells in minute quantities.[70]

By the late 1970s, recombinant DNA was attracting a great deal of attention in the U.S. scientific and business communities. Funding from the National Institutes of Health increased from virtually nothing in 1975 to $100 million in 1979. A number of the top university scientists teamed up with venture capitalists to form companies to exploit the new techniques. Soon multinational pharmaceutical, chemical, and petrochemical companies began to invest in these small firms. By the end of 1978, corporations had invested over $30 million in four companies. The largest drug companies had also begun in-house research programs in genetic engineering, but Du Pont had not participated in any way in this burgeoning field of science and technology.[71]

Du Pont's Executive Committee expected that in the 1980s biologically related products would become a much larger component of the company's business portfolio. In 1979, agricultural chemicals and pharmaceuticals represented 5 percent of Du Pont's total sales and about 10 percent of earnings. Agricultural chemicals accounted for over 80 percent of this total.[72] Central Research had begun biochemical research in the late 1940s and by the mid-1960s was doing pharmaceutical research centered mainly in virology. By the early 1970s, biology and biochemistry was the single largest research area of Central Research, accounting for one-quarter of the total effort.

Although a Du Pont researcher had been the first to isolate human fibroblast interferon from cells, Central Research did not move into the field of recombinant DNA.[73]

One reason why Central Research hesitated was that Du Pont did not have the reputation as a company that did pioneering work in the biological sciences. Because of this, recruiting of first-rate scientists would have been difficult. To become a major center for biological work, Du Pont had to increase substantially its commitment to what it called "Life Sciences." This is exactly what Jefferson proposed to do and got the Executive Committee's permission in April 1979 to begin accelerated recruiting.[74]

If one were to look for a precedent for this decision, the case of Stine in 1927 getting permission to begin research in polymer science immediately comes to mind. Of course, this earlier research led to nylon and a host of other polymer products. If history is going to repeat itself in Life Sciences, Du Pont will probably need to hire several scientists of the caliber of Wallace Carothers. In 1927, there was little academic or industrial research on polymers, but in 1979 there were already 50 universities and 12 companies doing molecular biological research in the United States alone.[75] Jefferson and the other members of the Executive Committee recognized that the competition was intense but also believed that the field was broad enough for many to make important contributions. Even if Du Pont scientists do not make the pioneering breakthroughs, the company will have in place the expertise to make use of them.

By late 1980, Central Research and the Biochemicals Department submitted their plans to increase the number of Life Science researchers from 630 to 1,730 in four years. The work would be roughly divided between plant-related and human-health-related sciences. To accommodate these researchers, several laboratories needed to be expanded and a major new facility built at the Experimental Station.[76] When opened in 1984, the principal Life Sciences laboratory was named in honor of Crawford H. Greenewalt, who had begun his career as a researcher in 1921 and for more than sixty years had been an ardent supporter of the research tradition at Du Pont.[77]

Conclusion: Change But Also Continuity

The 1970s witnessed Du Pont beginning to make changes to adapt itself to new conditions. Clearly, by the 1960s there was considerable evidence that old strategies and structures were no longer adequate. The establishment of the Corporate Plans Department and the assignment of an Executive Committee member to be directly responsible for Central Research and indirectly for company diversification were significant departures from Du Pont's long tradition of decentralized management.

After becoming head of the company in May 1981, Jefferson continued the transformation of Du Pont. Most dramatic was Du Pont's acquisition of Conoco a few months later, which was the culmination of several decades of internal company debate about whether Du Pont should integrate backward into petrochemicals. The Conoco acquisition also solved another long-standing Du Pont concern by making the company less dependent on textile fibers for its earnings. Only through the addition of a business the size of Conoco could Du Pont significantly reduce the importance of its giant fibers business. Jefferson also instituted structural changes, which included assigning Executive Committee members direct responsibility for the industrial departments and giving the Finance Committee more say in strategic matters. The role of these two committees had been essentially unchanged for over sixty years. But Jefferson reasserted one critical aspect of Du Pont's traditional strategy by stressing research and development as the critical component of the company's strategy. Of course, all the other functions had to be done well, but it was research that gave Du Pont its competitive edge.[78]

Reprise: Science and Corporate Strategy at Du Pont

Eight decades have brought great changes in the nature, scale, scope, and quality of the Du Pont Company's research and development programs. The Eastern Laboratory, founded in 1902 and closed in 1972, is now just a memory for some; to others it provides quiet testimony of change in Du Pont R&D. The Experimental Station, begun a year after Eastern Laboratory opened, stands today as the most visible symbol of Du Pont's commitment to research and development. Established immediately downstream from the company's century-old black powder mills, the Experimental Station speaks of both the change and the continuity in Du Pont's R&D programs.

The Station's initial structures consisted of a small laboratory and experimental black powder and smokeless powder mills built on one of the Brandywine's banks. Over time, however, the company expanded the Station's facilities, gradually filling – and indeed overrunning – what Fin Sparre once described as an "almost unlimited" property. Moving further up the hill from the Brandywine, successive new laboratories reflected new corporate strategies. "Purity Hall," built in 1927 midway up the hill, housed Du Pont's first formal fundamental research program. The laboratories constructed in the major post-World War II expansion of research represented yet another level of development in Du Pont's corporate strategy. Most recently, the massive, imposing Greenewalt Laboratory was built far up the hill from the Brandywine to house life sciences research, thus embodying Du Pont's major research and development thrust of the 1980s.

Although construction at the Experimental Station provides abundant physical evidence of the changes in the company's R&D programs, the mission of the site remains basically the same as when it was founded. Pierre du Pont's position, articulated in 1907, that the Station should always be working on several big, expensive research projects in which the potential rewards justified the great risks, still governs much of the Station's work, just as it did in Pierre's day.

This continuity in Du Pont's willingness to wager for high stakes at the table of research has been paralleled by other elements in its R&D programs. Many of these aspects concern the management of research. Recruiting and retaining a high-caliber staff of researchers, determining how much money to spend on research and in what areas, balancing short-term needs with long-term strategies, and knowing when to abandon particular research projects are but some of the issues that Du Pont's research managers and executives have faced since the Eastern Laboratory and the Experimental Station were established. Within each of these issues, of course, lie whole subsets of other issues such as publication and patenting policies, relationships between research managers and executives, and the relationship of the firm to the larger scientific community.

By appreciating the elements of continuity in Du Pont's R&D programs, one is better able to understand the importance of the changes that have resulted from both internal and external factors. The corporation's strategy has changed over the course of this century. With each shift in strategy, R&D has been vitally affected.

When executives established the Eastern Laboratory, they hoped that by bringing science to bear directly on practice, processes and products in high explosives could be improved. This strategy succeeded beyond their wildest imagination. Under Charles Reese's firm leadership, the laboratory rationalized processes and improved products, yielding impressive returns on this modest investment in research. The circumstances of Eastern's founding were quite different from those of the other industrial research pioneers in the United States, General Electric, American Telephone and Telegraph, and Eastman Kodak. These firms turned to formal scientific research programs to protect their substantial investments from threatening competition. Du Pont had no such immediate pressures but rather was led by a group of executives bent upon consolidating and rationalizing the industry. Research provided them one important means of rationalization.

A year later, executives founded the Experimental Station with the goal of dealing more rationally with inventions and inventors outside the company. But even before the new facility could be built, external pressures wrought changes in the Station's charter. Like other American pioneers of industrial research, Du Pont was threatened by competition in one of its new product lines. The competitor was the U.S. military. Believing that the navy and army might build their own smokeless powder capacity, Du Pont's executives resolved to stay well out in front of the government through scientific research in smokeless powder and ballistics. This strategy worked. Du Pont's leadership in these areas provided the key to its being able to retain all of its smokeless powder assets when the Justice Department split up the Du Pont "powder trust" in 1913. The outbreak of World War I soon revealed the importance of this decision.

Several pieces of Progressive Era legislation also shaped the Station's research and development programs, but the antitrust sentiment had the greatest impact on the company. Threatened again after 1907 with the loss of their market for smokeless powder, Du Pont's executives determined to diversify the company to make it less dependent upon government business. The extraordinary expansion of smokeless powder capacity during World War I made diversification all the more imperative.

Diversification and R&D were closely coupled as early as 1908. Du Pont's research organizations provided executives with the technical resources to evaluate diversification opportunities. If research managers had been left to choose, they would have opted to research the company into new businesses. Executives did not initially follow that route; the company purchased its first two departures from explosives, the Fabrikoid (artificial leather) Company and the Arlington (celluloid plastics) Company. But when the circumstances of World War I essentially forced Du Pont into becoming a dyestuffs manufacturer, there was no possibility of acquisition. Du Pont's R&D organization had its first big opportunity to show how it could contribute to the company's diversification.

The dyestuffs venture proved to be a trial by fire. In many respects, the efforts of Du Pont's growing R&D staff were insufficient. Successful dyestuffs manufacture required tens of millions of dollars more than executives had been led to believe the venture would cost, the recruitment of a critical number of German dye chemists, and the erection by the United States of a protective tariff on dyestuffs. The venture taught executives that diversification based principally upon internal research and development was difficult. For the next two decades, Du Pont would diversify through the acquisition of new technologies and smaller companies. Research and development organizations would be built around these acquisitions, allowing the company to commercialize products by scaling-up and rationalizing processes and developing new markets, thus making such products part of the industrial scene.

Du Pont could build research organizations around its acquisitions because after 1921 the corporation was decentralized. Diversification had brought problems of effectively managing the company's increasingly varied business, so after much debate, its executives determined to set up each of Du Pont's businesses as an autonomous department, responsible for its own manufacturing, marketing, and research.

The decision to decentralize the entire corporation had engendered a renewed debate concerning the best way to organize research. Was a central research unit best, or should research be closely aligned with a business by being organized departmentally? This debate had first arisen in 1904, not long after proponents of the decentralized Eastern Laboratory concluded that the new, centralized Experimental Station threatened to absorb resources critical to Eastern's growth. This early debate had served to identify clearly the fundamental issues surrounding the two approaches to research management. These issues had changed little between 1904 and 1921. They have not changed much since then either. Unable to reach a "one best" solution to the problem of organizing research, the Executive Committee had voted to pursue both approaches. The centralization of research under Charles L. Reese in the 1910s – precisely at the time the company was diversifying its product lines – had created certain problems. The general managers of the new departments now wanted control of research in their own product areas. Although reluctant to split up the Chemical Department, the company's executives consented. But they did not completely abandon the idea of a central research unit. Instead, they placed a small group of researchers from the old research organization in a new central Chemical Department to conduct research for all the industrial departments.

With this organization, Du Pont pioneered in the management of modern industrial research, just as it had pioneered in overall modern corporate management. Each of the industrial departments would run its own research program, but research would also be conducted on a corporate basis in the Chemical Department. This scheme has endured at Du Pont. But it has also been fraught with inherent tensions – tensions stemming from the problem of coordinating the often longer-term, less-focused research of the central research organization with the more commercially oriented, shorter-term, more tightly focused research of the industrial departments. As the product lines of the industrial departments broadened, similar tensions would also build up within the industrial departments.

The small Chemical Department probably would have withered in the early 1920s had Du Pont not been a well-diversified company. Under the astute leadership of Charles Stine, the department gradually emerged as a major force in the company. Stine initially sought ways simply to keep his small research unit intact; then he found the key that allowed him to build his program. He convinced the Executive Committee that Du Pont's seemingly disparate businesses really possessed common scientific bases. If these common scientific bases were better understood, Du Pont's businesses would inevitably benefit. Stine identified several such areas for his department to explore. These included polymers, catalysis, high-pressure reactions, physico-chemical phenomena, and chemical engineering. In response, the committee granted Stine a larger budget for "general research" and in 1927 approved his "radical" plan for a high-caliber program of fundamental research.

Stine's program in Purity Hall soon led to dramatic changes in both the Chemical Department and in the entire strategy of the Du Pont Company. Fundamental research on polymers, headed by Wallace H. Carothers, yielded major understanding of their nature, which brought widespread attention to the growing scientific prowess of the company. Quite unexpectedly, this research also produced neoprene and nylon. Du Pont was successful in commercializing these important discoveries because it already had extensive commercial and technical capabilities in rubber chemicals, organic synthesis, high-pressure reactions, and fibers. The company's executives appreciated these capabilities, but nylon's unprecedented success proved to be so powerful that it soon brought them to derive a new formula for growth. By putting more money into fundamental research in both the Chemical Department and the industrial departments, Du Pont would discover and develop "new nylons" – that is, new proprietary products sold to industrial customers and having the growth potential of nylon.

Du Pont's Executive Committee articulated and applied this formula only after two major external developments had occurred. The first was World War II. Science was applied to an unprecedented degree and scale during the war; Du Pont itself had played a major part in the war effort when it assumed responsibility for building and operating the Manhattan Project's plutonium production and separation facility. This was large-scale technology based on the very latest basic science. The wartime emergency led many of Du Pont's competitors to engage in research and development projects and manufacturing operations that were extraordinary for them at the time but that would become commonplace after the war. The war was thus a great leveler in terms of scientific and technical talent in the chemical industry. To maintain its wide lead in the industry, Du Pont would have to strengthen its already strong research efforts.

The second external development was the vigorous attack on the company by the Thurman Arnold–led Antitrust Division of the Justice Department. Before the decade of the 1940s was over, Du Pont faced six antitrust indictments. Captivated by the emerging nylon model, Du Pont's executives concluded that its generation-old strategy of growth through acquisition was no longer politically feasible and that fundamental research would more than fill the void. This new strategy had been fully developed by 1946 and would remain unaltered for the next decade and a half. This model of fundamental science inducing corporate growth became the foundation of Du Pont's corporate culture. Science was now more firmly than ever at the center of its corporate strategy.

During this period, the industrial departments became more autonomous than before. Many of them carried out their own research programs on polymers, the area of chemistry that now formed Du Pont's core technology. Ironically, the Chemical Department – soon to be renamed the Central Research Department – was instructed to leave polymer research to the industrial departments, a move contrary to the central research philosophy that Stine had articulated when he won approval to found a fundamental research program. In developing a mentality of "new nylons," executives and research managers alike had forgotten why the company had so easily and swiftly developed nylon. The Chemical Department's pioneering work on polymers had fitted neatly into the company's existing businesses, technologies, and levels of expertise. With Central Research's programs being pushed away from the company's commercial interests, the nylon model became skewed.

The role of Central Research in the company became more problematic than ever by the 1950s. The department was urged simply to explore new areas rather than providing the fundamental knowledge base for Du Pont's technologies. The company's executives still believed, however, that Central Research would discover new nylons. As the department moved into physics and biology, it began to lose contact with many of the industrial departments and consequently took on the trappings of a high-quality scientific research establishment divorced from any commercial objectives. Soon, many in the company began to criticize Central Research for pursuing science that was out of step with corporate strategy. Given Central Research's directives from the Executive Committee, it is difficult to project a different scenario for the department in this period.

The executives' faith in the nylon model seemed to be borne out in the late 1940s and early 1950s with the development and commercialization of Orlon and Dacron and the continued spectacular growth of nylon. Du Pont had effected a revolution in textile fibers with these products, and the Textile Fibers Department's Pioneering Research Laboratory promised even more new products. A prolific research organization, Pioneering helped Textile Fibers become the dominant department in the company. The synthetic fibers revolution propelled the department's earnings skyward. During the 1950s, the department contributed at least half of the company's total earnings; its capital investment was by far the greatest; and its research staff was substantially larger than the nearest department's. In many respects, Du Pont was a fibers company that had some other businesses on the side.

Du Pont's executives had not planned this course of events. In fact, the company had hoped to dominate the burgeoning field of plastics, just as it had that of synthetic fibers. But this had proven impossible. World War II had produced a highly competitive climate in plastics. Du Pont's research turned up some excellent products, which the company developed in the 1950s and early 1960s, but competitors quickly outflanked Du Pont's major new thrusts. Consequently, the company turned to an even tighter strategy of developing high-performance, high-cost, proprietary plastics that would avoid the competitive situation that prevailed in the industry.

At the same time, Du Pont's other businesses were also seeing more competition. Its executives soon began to evaluate Du Pont's performance against its own past and against that of its competitors. The industry showed some signs of maturing, but rather than accept lower rates of growth and profitability, some executives focused on Du Pont's internal functioning. Soon a diagnosis emerged: Although the company's expenditures for research had grown dramatically since World War II, the productivity of research as measured by new products commercialized had not grown. To maintain the company's past rate of growth, it needed an increasing number of major new profitable products. A shortfall had occurred, the Executive Committee reasoned, because the company's research organizations had taken too seriously their mission to concentrate on basic research; development, the other half of R&D, had fallen through the cracks in Du Pont's organization.

Development was everybody's business but nobody's specific job. President Crawford Greenewalt and the Executive Committee soon concluded that Du Pont's research organizations were storehouses of potential new products, especially products that would lead the company into rapidly growing new businesses. All that was necessary was to issue a call for their development. In 1961, Greenewalt did precisely that. He and his colleagues on the Executive Committee launched a bold program of diversification, which they compared to Du Pont's first diversification efforts when the company successfully moved away from being purely an explosives manufacturer. Rather than relying on the acquisition of new technologies and small companies, however, the New Venture program would be based on Du Pont's own R&D.

Although the manager of the New Venture program called for the creation of a diversification department, the company's approach to R&D remained essentially unchanged. The Executive Committee believed that a renewed commitment to the principles that had been so successful in the past would provide the necessary growth; no structural or policy changes were necessary. The rate and direction of innovation would still reside with departmental businesses they already knew. Instead of moving the company in new directions, the New Ventures program of the 1960s resulted in a deepening of commitment to Du Pont's existing lines of business. Many of the largest and most expensive ventures were in fact in the Textile Fibers Department.

Without a program for reallocating corporate resources, Textile Fibers continued to dominate the company. Thus as a strategic move to lessen the company's dependence on textile fibers, the New Ventures program could not and did not succeed. By the end of the 1960s, the Executive Committee declared the entire program a failure; the company had spent $2 billion to develop over forty new products, many of which were facing extended periods of operating losses.

Du Pont's predicament called into question the company's entire postwar strategy. Large-scale projects had become so expensive and risky that the company could afford only a limited number of them. Nevertheless, the Executive Committee remained reluctant to play a stronger role in the direction of research and development programs until capital shortages in the mid-1970s forced it to select particular projects for development and commercialization. Gradually, the committee assumed a larger role in the management of Du Pont research.

For much of the 1970s, a decade marked by extreme economic turmoil outside the company and a gnawing sense of uncertainty over strategy inside the company, Du Pont employed its research organizations to keep its existing businesses healthy. But late in the decade a new strategy emerged entailing the consolidation of existing businesses and a corporatewide reallocation of research monies. The decision to embark upon an ambitious program of research in the life sciences and the acquisition of Conoco marked President Edward G. Jefferson's determination to reduce the company's dependence on textile fibers and to find new growth opportunities.

The debates over research policy within the Executive Committee in the 1970s no doubt had some of the same ring as those in 1904 and 1921. The company and the world were far more complex than earlier in the century, but many of the fundamental issues remained the same. One of these issues turned on the degree to which the company should organize and centrally control research. Others focused on questions of precisely who should be managing Du Pont's research programs and how the company could recruit the scientists it needed to realize its strategy. Other issues also remained the same, such as achieving the proper mix of short-term and long-term research. In fact, over the course of this century, research managers and executives have faced these issues and have had to resolve them not once and for all but for the time being, in the context of the state of science in the United States and Du Pont's own corporate strategy.

In addition to underscoring both change and continuity in R&D at Du Pont during the past eight decades, this study also highlights several other important themes. The first is simple. Du Pont was among a handful of pioneers in industrial R&D in the United States, and like those other pioneers Du Pont came to dominate its respective business. Science became a part of these corporations' strategies, and because of this the twentieth century has been fundamentally different than the preceding ones.

The embodiment of science in corporate strategy has produced a series of changes in the scientific community and in the education of scientists. Industrial research both offered new opportunities for and placed new demands on professional scientists. This subject has been discussed in a number of recent works, but the history of Du Pont's R&D programs suggests that no single thesis can explain the dynamic relationship between the corporation and the professional scientist throughout this century. Du Pont has both depended upon and contributed to the scientific community; to a certain extent, the relationship has been symbiotic but one never entirely free from tension.

This study suggests that public policy has definitely shaped Du Pont's strategy of research. This was particularly true of the founding period of Du Pont's R&D programs and in the World War II and immediate postwar periods. The late New Deal's antitrust attack on Du Pont unquestionably led to Du Pont's spending more on fundamental research. Although this policy was good for the scientific community, it was not necessarily the best allocation of Du Pont's resources. The company had grown impressively through a strategy of commercializing acquired technologies, and public policy essentially closed off this avenue to Du Pont from the late 1930s until recently. Environmental regulations since the 1960s have also affected Du Pont's R&D programs.

Although a book about science and corporate strategy, this has also been a study of people. Individuals have been important in shaping Du Pont's R&D. At the top managerial and executive levels, men such as Irénée du Pont, Charles Stine, Elmer Bolton, Hale Charch, and Crawford Greenewalt, among many others discussed, have molded Du Pont's research programs. Similarly, at the researcher level, individual scientists have not only contributed to the company and to the scientific community but through their work have also sometimes led the company in important new directions. Despite the institutionalization of research in the corporation, individuals have made a difference. Du Pont's research, just like the whole company, is not monolithic; it is a collection of people who share a common culture.

Finally, we must not forget that Du Pont's R&D programs have yielded a surprising number of products that have become household words in spite of the fact that Du Pont has never really sold its products directly to individual consumers. Duco, cellophane, nylon, Teflon, Orlon, Dacron, and Lycra are all familiar parts of our material world. Du Pont has also produced many remarkable specialty products used in hundreds of ways in industry. Often cheaper, better performing, and more versatile than natural materials, Du Pont's products have helped to transform our world. The majority of these products have stemmed from a remarkable and complex institution: modern industrial research and development. Understanding something about this institution is a key to comprehending the modern world.

Appendixes

Appendix I. *Financial History of the Du Pont Company, 1905–80*
(in millions of dollars)

	1905	1910	1915	1920	1925	1930	1935	1940
Sales	27.7	33.2	131.1	94.0	84.6	186.4	216.0	346.2
Total net income	5.1	6.3	57.8	15.1	20.6	56.0	62.1	86.9
Net operating income	—	—	—	—	11.5	19.5	34.8	55.7
Average operating investment	39.7^c	50.1^c	122.2^c	66.9^c	106.1	341.6	416.3	589.5
Average number of employees	n.a.	n.a.	n.a.	n.a.	15,037	37,026	42,648	53,253

1945	1950	1955	1960	1965[a]	1970[a]	1975	1980
611.3	1,298	1,909	2,143	3,399	4,118	7,222	13,652
77.5	308	432	381	428[b]	340[b]	276[b]	726[b]
46.7	187	292	249	419	334	272	716
832.8	1,408	2,112	2,933	4,267	7,167	11,408	17,448
63,939	79,986	87,453	88,514	106,013	124,558	134,600	135,900

Note: n.a. = not available. — = not applicable.
[a]1974 *Annual report.*
[b]Earnings before minority interests taken into account.
[c]Permanent investment in manufacture.
Source: Du Pont Company annual reports.

Appendix II. *Evolution of the Industrial Departments of the Du Pont Company*

Ammonia Department (1931–49)
    Name change from Du Pont Ammonia Corporation
    Became part of Polychemicals Department
Biochemicals Department (1972–80)
    Split off from Industrial and Biochemicals Department
Cellulose Products Department (1921–25)
    Became part of Paint, Lacquer, and Chemicals Department
Central Research Department (1957–75)
    Name change from Chemical Department
    Became Central Research and Development Department
Central Research and Development Department (1975–80)
    Formed by merger of Central Research Department and part of Development
        Department
Chemical Department (1911–57)
    Name changed to Central Research Department
Chemicals, Dyes, and Pigments Department (1977–80)
    Formed by merger of Organic Chemicals, Pigments, and Industrial Chemicals
        departments
    Named changed to Chemicals and Pigments Department
Chemicals and Pigments Department (1980)
    Name change from Chemicals, Dyes, and Pigments Department
Corporate Plans Department (1975–80)
    Formed from part of Development Department
Development Department (1902–75)
    Merged into Central Research and Development Department and Corporate
        Plans Department
Du Pont Ammonia Corporation (1929–31)
    Became Ammonia Department
Du Pont Cellophane Company (1923–36)
    Became part of Rayon Department
Du Pont Fibersilk Company (1920–24)
    Became Du Pont Rayon Company
Du Pont Film Manufacturing Corporation (1931–41)
    Name change from Du Pont–Pathé Film Manufacturing Corporation
    Became Photo Products Department
Du Pont–Pathé Film Manufacturing Corporation (1924–31)
    Became Du Pont Film Corporation
Du Pont Rayon Company (1925–36)
    Became Rayon Department
Du Pont Viscoloid Company (1925–36)
    Became Plastics Department
Dyestuffs Department (1921–31)
    Became Organic Chemicals Department
Elastomer Chemicals Department (1957–79)
    Split off from Organic Chemicals Department

Became part of Polymer Products Department
Electrochemicals Department (1942–72)
  Name change from R&H Chemicals Department
  Became part of Industrial Chemicals Department
Explosives Department (1921–71)
  Became part of Polymer Intermediates Department
Fabrics and Finishes Department (1929–80)
Film Department (1950–76)
  Split off from Rayon Department
  Became part of Plastics Products and Resins Department
Grasselli Chemical Company (1928–36)
  Became Grasselli Chemicals Department
Grasselli Chemicals Department (1936–59)
  Name change from Grasselli Chemical Company
  Became Industrial and Biochemicals Department
Industrial and Biochemicals Department (1959–72)
  Name change from Grasselli Chemicals Department
  Split into Industrial Chemicals Department and Biochemicals Department
Industrial Chemicals Department (1972–76)
  Split off from Industrial and Biochemicals Department
  Became part of Chemicals, Dyes, and Pigments Department
Krebs Pigment and Chemical Company (1929–35)
  Became Krebs Pigments Department
Krebs Pigment Department (1935–42)
  Name change from Krebs Pigment and Chemical Department
  Became Pigments Department
Lazote, Incorporated (1924–29)
  Became Du Pont Ammonia Corporation
Organic Chemicals Department (1931–77)
  Name change from Dyestuffs Department
  Became part of Chemicals, Dyes, and Pigments Department
Paint Department (1921–27)
  Became part of Paint, Lacquer, and Chemicals Department
Paint, Lacquer, and Chemicals Department (1927–29)
  Became Fabrics and Finishes Department
Petrochemicals Department (1977–80)
  Name change from Polymer Intermediates Department
Photo Products Department (1941–80)
  Name change from Du Pont Film Manufacturing Corporation
Pigments Department (1942–77)
  Name change from Krebs Pigments Department
  Became part of Chemicals, Dyes, and Pigments Department
Plastics Department (1936–49)
  Name change from Du Pont Viscoloid Company
  Became part of Polychemicals Department
Plastics Department (1962–76)
  Name change from Polychemicals Department
  Became part of Plastics Products and Resins Department
Plastic Products and Resins Department (1976–79)

Formed by merger of Plastics and Film departments
Became Polymer Products Department
Polychemicals Department (1949–62)
Formed by merger of Plastics and Ammonia departments
Became Plastics Department
Polymer Intermediates Department (1972–77)
Formed from Explosives Department
Became Petrochemicals Department
Polymer Products Department (1979–80)
Formed by merger of Plastics Products and Resins and Elastomer Chemicals
department
Pyralin Department (1921–25)
Became Du Pont Viscoloid Company
R&H Chemicals Department (1932–42)
Name change from Roessler and Hasslacher Chemical Company
Became Electrochemicals Department
Rayon Department (1936–51)
Name change from Du Pont Rayon Company
Became Textile Fibers Department
Roessler and Hasslacher Chemical Company (1930–32)
Became R&H Chemicals Department
Smokeless Powder Department (1922–35)
Formed from and absorbed back into Explosives Department
Textile Fibers Department (1951–80)
Name change after splitting Film Department off from Rayon Department

Appendix II. Evolution of the Industrial Departments of the Du Pont Company

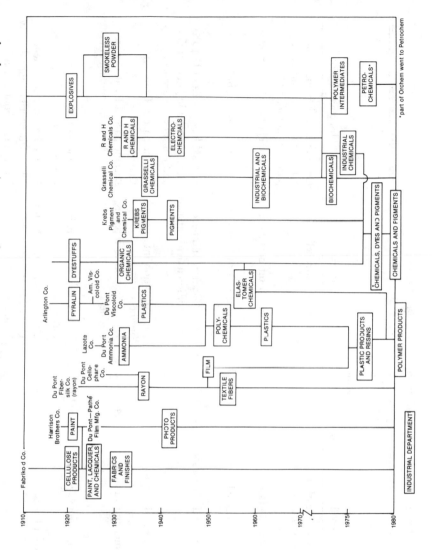

Appendix III. *Major Acquisitions of the Du Pont Company, 1910–33*

Year	Acquisition / joint[a] venture	Products[a]	Price $ million (% Du Pont ownership if less than 100%)	Rationale[b]	Subsequent history[c]
1910	Fabrikoid Co.	Artificial leather (nitrocellulose-coated fabrics)	1.2[d]	Outlet for nitrocellulose	Combined with paint business to form Fabrics and Finishes Department in mid-1920s
1915	Arlington Co.	Celluloid plastics	6.7[e]	Outlet for nitrocellulose	Became Plastics Department in 1921
1916	Fairfield Rubber Co.	Rubber-coated fabrics	0.6[e]	Complement to Fabrikoid	Combined with Fabrikoid
1917	Harrison Brothers and Co.	Paints and chemicals	7.7[e]	Diversification and need for additional acid capacity	Formed basis of Paint Department (1921) and later Fabrics and Finishes Department
	Becton Chemicals	Paints and varnishes	1.1[a]	Diversification into paint business	Became part of Paint Department
1918	Flint Varnish and Color Works	Paints and varnishes	1.4 (70%)[f]	Diversification into paint business	Became part of Paint Department. Minority holding bought in 1921
1920	Chicago Varnish Works	Paints and varnishes	1.0[f]	Diversification into paint business	Became part of Paint Department
	Du Pont Rayon Co. (joint venture)	Rayon fibers	4.0 (60%)[g]	Diversification into highly profitable and growing business	Became Rayon Department in 1936. Du Pont bought minority holding for about $62 million in 1929[h]

608

Year	Company	Product		Purpose	Outcome
1923	Du Pont Cellophane Co. (joint venture)	Cellophane films	1.0 (52.%)[i]	Diversification, technology similar to rayon's	Became part of Rayon Department in 1936. Minority holding acquired for $12 million in 1929[j]
1924	Lazote, Inc. (joint venture)	Synthetic ammonia	2.3 (63%)[k]	Manufacture of important raw material	Became Ammonia Department in 1929. Du Pont purchased minority holding in 1929
	Du Pont Pathé Film Co. (joint venture)	Photographic film	0.0 (51%)[l]	Diversification (Du Pont had struggled for years to get into business)	Became Photo Products Department after purchase of minority holding in 1941
1925	Viscoloid Co.	Celluloid plastics	2.0 (83%)[m]	Increase market share in celluloid plastics	Became part of Plastics Department. Minority interest acquired in 1928
1926	National Ammonia Co.	Ammonia marketing organization	6.2[n]	Secure marketing organization for Du Pont ammonia	Became part of Ammonia Department
1928	Cellulose Acetate Technology	Cellulose acetate fibers	25% of profits[o]	Diversification, establish position in new fiber	Incorporated into Rayon Department. Minority interest acquired in 1936
	Grasselli Chemical Co.	Acids and inorganic chemicals	64.0[p]	Increase market share in heavy chemicals	Became Grasselli Chemicals Department
1929	Krebs Pigment and Chemical Co.	Lithopone white pigment	5.9[q]	Increase market share in pigments	Formed part of Pigments Department
1930	Roessler and Hasslacher Chemical Co.	Electrochemicals	31.6[r]	Provide captive source of metallic sodium used to make other Du Pont products	Became Electrochemicals Department

Appendix III (*cont.*)

Year	Acquisition / joint[a] venture	Products[a]	Price $ million (% Du Pont ownership if less than 100%)	Rationale[b]	Subsequent history[c]
1931	Commercial Pigments Corporation (joint venture)	Titanium dioxide white pigments	0.0 (70%)[s]	Establish a position in important new pigment	Formed part of Pigments Department. Minority interest purchased in 1934
	Newport Chemical Co.	Dyestuffs	10.0[f]	Acquire important class of dyestuffs and fine technical organization	Incorporated into Organic Chemicals Department
1933	Remington Arms Co.	Arms, ammunition, and cutlery	3.1 (56%)[u]	Secure a market for sporting smokeless powder[v]	Became a wholly owned subsidiary in 1979[v]

Sources:

[a]For the dates and list of Du Pont acquisitions, see Willard Fritz Mueller, "Du Pont: A Study in Firm Growth" (PhD diss., Vanderbilt University, 1956), Table 7. Mueller gives the amounts paid for each acquisition but does not give his sources. On the purchase of technology, see Willard F. Mueller, "The Origins of the Basic Inventions underlying Du Pont's Major Product and Process Innovations, 1920 to 1950," in *The Rate and Direction of Inventive Activity: Economic and Social Factors* (Princeton, N.J.: Princeton University Press, 1962), pp. 323–46. See also "E. I. du Pont de Nemours & Company – Acquisitions," LMSS, Series A, File 418–26, Box 8.

[b]See appropriate chapters for the discussion of these acquisitions.

[c]See Appendix II. For dates of purchase of minority interest, see the company's annual reports.

[d]R. R. M. Carpenter to the Finance Committee, "History and Prospects of the Fabrikoid Industry," Nov. 4, 1921, GM Suit, PD, p. 1772.

[e]"The New Industries of E. I. du Pont de Nemours & Company," Oct. 24, 1921, GM Suit, PD, pp. 1667–76.

[f]William Zintl, *History of the Du Pont Paint Business* (n.p.: n.p., 1947), p. 20, Acc. 1850.

[g]EC Minutes, Apr. 12, 1920.

[h]Du Pont exchanged the minority holders' 400,000 shares of common stock in the Du Pont Rayon Company for 350,000 shares of Du

Pont common stock at $180 per share and exchanged nonvoting debenture stock on a one-to-one basis. The $62 million figure represents only the common stock. ("Minutes of the Special Meeting of the Stockholders of the Du Pont Rayon Company...," Mar. 29, 1929, II, 4, Box 92.)

*"DuPont–La Cellophane Agreement," June 23, 1923, United States v. E. I. du Pont de Nemours & Company, Civil Action No. 1216, Government Exhibit 1001.

*Du Pont acquired the 48,000 minority shares of cellophane company stock for 67,200 shares of Du Pont stock selling at $180 per share. ("Minutes of Special Meeting of the Stockholders of Du Pont Cellophane Co....," Mar. 29, 1929, II, 4, Box 18.)

*Lazote, Inc., Board of Directors Meeting #1, Aug. 4, 1924, Papers of the E. I. du Pont de Nemours & Co., Inc., II, 1, Box 1271. The 63 percent ownership figure is from *Du Pont Company Annual Report 1926.*

Du Pont Company Annual Report 1926.

*"Du Pont Viscoloid Company Board of Directors #1, Apr. 28, 1925, II, 4, Box 141.

*"National Ammonia Company, Inc., Board of Directors Meeting #1, May 28, 1926, II, 1, Box 1330.

*Walter S. Carpenter to the Executive Committee, Nov. 23, 1936, II, 2, Box 820. Du Pont also paid the Usines du Rhône Company $175,000 for the rights to make cellulose acetate plastics. ("Memorandum of Agreement entered into on the 31st day of December, 1927, by and between Usines du Rhone...," II, 2, Box 820.

Du Pont Company Annual Report 1928 stated that the company exchanged 149,392 shares of its common stock to purchase Grasselli. On the day of the agreement, Oct. 24, 1928, Du Pont's stock sold for $429 per share.

*"Fin Sparre to the Executive Committee, "Krebs Pigment and Chemical Co. – Report on Accomplishment of Objectives," Mar. 31, 1932, GM Suit, PD, pp. 4823–7.

Du Pont Company Annual Report 1930 stated that the company bought Roessler and Hasslacher for 241,130 shares of common stock. On the day of the agreement, Mar. 25, 1930, Du Pont common stock sold for $131 per share. Sparre, "Krebs Pigment and Chemical Company."

*Du Pont purchased Newport for 99,715 shares of 6 percent, nonvoting, debenture stock of a par value of $100 per share. James Kupperian to the Board of Directors, Newport Chemical Corporation, South Milwaukee, Wis., Aug. 24, 1931, II, 2, Box 350.

*"Development Department to the Executive Committee, "Remington Arms Company, Inc. – Accomplishment of Objectives," Sept. 3, 1937, United States v. Imperial Chemical Industries et al., District Court of the United States for the Southern District of New York, Civil No. 24–13, Defendants' Exhibit No. D-1810.

Du Pont Company Annual Report 1979.

Appendix IV. Research and Development Budgets of the Du Pont Company, 1921–80 (in millions of dollars)

	1921	1925	1930	1935	1940	1945	1950	1955	1960	1965	1970	1975	1980
Total company	1.73	1.99	5.5	6.6	11.0	19.6	57.5	123	169	238	270	336	484
Total industrial department expenditures (includes Du Pont subsidiaries)	n.a.	n.a.	4.2	5.4	9.3	16.2	48.6	107	145	210	234	300	409
Chemical Department (and successors, Central Research and Central Research and Development)	0.3	0.45	1.06	0.87	1.33	2.22	4.3	6.2	8.2	16.4	18.0	27.3	50.9
Engineering Department	—	—	—	0.15	0.15	0.66	4.4	8.9	14.6	3.7	6.1	8.7	24.1
Haskell Laboratory	—	—	—	0.06	0.10	0.12	0.3	1.1	1.2	1.6[a]	2.3[b]	3.8[c]	7.7[d]
Development Department	—	—	—	—	—	—	—	—	1.5[e]	8.3[f]	4.7[g]	—	—

Note: n.a. = not available. — = not applicable. All figures are in historical dollars.

Sources:

[a] Annual Report of the Public Relations Department, Feb. 10, 1966, Acc. 1615, Box. 14.

[b] Central Research Department to the Executive Committee, "Addition to Haskell Laboratory," Nov. 14, 1974, EC Files.

[c] Figure is for 1976; in that year the department also did $6.6 million work for other departments.

[d] Does not include $15.4 million work for other departments.

[e] Figure is from 1962, the first year corporate R&D statistics were reported (R&D Statistics, 1960–64, CRDD).

[f] Development Department to the Executive Committee, "Addition to Haskell Laboratory," Nov. 14, 1974, EC Files.

[g] Development Department to the Executive Committee, "Annual Report – 1970," Jan. 6, 1971, DD Files.

General Sources: 1921–25: C. M. A. Stine to Treasurer, Aug. 10, 1927, Acc. 1784. 1930–40: Neal Thurman to E. K. Gladding, "Research Study – Interim Report," July 9, 1948, CRDD, and "Annual Research Expenditures," Development Department Chart, Acc. 1814. 1950–60: R&D Statistics, 1947–60, CRDD. 1965–70: R&D Statistics, 1965–74, CRDD. 1975–80: R&D Statistics, 1975–80, CRDD.

Notes

Abbreviations used in Notes for Hagley Museum and
Library Accessions

Accession Number or Abbreviation	Collection Title
14	Miscellaneous Papers of General Henry du Pont
228	Papers of Irénée du Pont
372	Technical Section, Explosives Department, E. I. du Pont de Nemours & Co.
414	Report of Daniel C. Spruance on the Technical Development of Viscose, 1899
473	Papers of John Jacob Raskob
504	Papers of Francis Gurney du Pont
509	Papers of Hudson Maxim
640	Miscellany of F. W. Pickard
889	Edmund Nelson Carpenter and Donald F. Carpenter Miscellany
1005	Papers of J. Thompson Brown
1006	Du Pont Company Organization Charts
1034	Personal Papers of Irénée du Pont
1193	The Charles H. Rutledge Collection
1383	Papers of Edmund Nelson Carpenter
1345	Arthur La Motte Papers
1383	Edmund N. Carpenter Papers
1387	Chambers Works History
1404	Papers of Lammot du Pont Copeland
1410	Records of the E. I. du Pont de Nemours & Co., Public Affairs Department
1416	Casper E. Crane Personal Papers
1438	Du Pont Company Miscellany, 1905–16
1460	Records of E. I. du Pont de Nemours & Co., Secretary's Office and Miscellaneous Administrative Records
1465	E. I. du Pont de Nemours & Co., Photo Products Department Records
1517	Du Pont Family Papers
1599	Eugene du Pont (1873–1954) Papers
1615	Records of E. I. du Pont de Nemours & Co., Employee Relations Department and Predecessors
1662	Records of the E. I. du Pont de Nemours & Co., Administrative Papers of the Office of the President

1689 Oral History Interviews, Biographical Sketches, and Brief History of the Du Pont Company Used in Preparation for Book by Alfred D. Chandler and Stephen Salsbury, *Pierre S. du Pont and the Making of the Modern Corporation*

1706 Papers of Charles M. A. Stine

1771 Records of E. I. du Pont de Nemours & Co., Textile Fibers Department

1784 Records of E. I. du Pont de Nemours & Co., Central Research and Development Department

1813 Papers of Willis F. Harrington

1814 Papers of Crawford H. Greenewalt

1815 Papers of Charles B. McCoy

1842 Correspondence of John R. Johnson and Wallace H. Carothers

1850 Papers relating to the Du Pont R&D History Project

1851 Records of the Directors of Industrial Research

1889 Crawford Greenewalt's Manhattan Project Diary

1896 Wallace H. Carothers Correspondence

GM Suit, DTE United States v. E. I. du Pont de Nemours & Co., General Motors Corporation et al., Civil Action No. 49-C-1071, Defendents' Trial Exhibit, followed by source (Du Pont, General Motors, etc.) and document number

GM Suit, GTE United States v. E. I. du Pont de Nemours & Co., General Motors Corporation et al., Civil Action No. 49-C-1071, Government Trial Exhibit, followed by source (Du Pont, General Motors, etc.) and document number

GM Suit, PD United States v. E. I. du Pont de Nemours & Co., General Motors Corporation et al., Civil Action No. 49-C-1071, Printed Documents, followed by page number

GM Suit, PD, 2d Series United States v. E. I. du Pont de Nemours & Co., General Motors Corporation et al., Civil Action No. 49-C-1071, Printed Documents, 2d series, followed by page number

GM Suit, TR United States v. E. I. du Pont de Nemours & Co., General Motors Corporation et al., Civil Action No. 49-C-1071, Transcript, followed by page number

LMSS Longwood Manuscripts, Group 10, Pierre S. du Pont Papers

II, 1 Records of E. I. du Pont de Nemours & Co., Inc., Series II,

II, 2 Parts 1, 2, & 4. Cited as II, 1, II, 2, or II, 4, plus the

II, 4 appropriate box number

Interviews

Note: Unless otherwise noted, all interviews are in Acc. 1878, Hagley Museum and Library.

Anderson, Arthur W. Interview with John K. Smith, Apr. 17, 1985.

Berchet, Gerard. Interview with John K. Smith, Nov. 10, 1982.

Bolton, Elmer K. Interview with Alfred D. Chandler, Richmond D. Williams, and Norman B. Wilkinson, 1961, Acc. 1689.

Brubaker, Merlin. Interview with John K. Smith, Sept. 27, 1982.

Burdick, C. Lalor. Interview with David A. Hounshell and John K. Smith, Oct. 13, 1982.

Cairns, Theodore L. Interviews with David A. Hounshell and John K. Smith, Nov. 12, 1982, and by John K. Smith, Nov. 19, 1982.

Cohen, Abraham B. Interview with John K. Smith, Jan. 30, 1986.

Cooper, Edward B. Interview with John K. Smith, Apr. 22, 1985.

Elley, Harold W. Interview with David A. Hounshell and John K. Smith, Sept. 20, 22, 1982.

Ernsberger, Maurice L. Interview with David A. Hounshell, Jan. 15, 1986.

Franta, William A. Interviews with David A. Hounshell and John K. Smith, Apr. 4, 1983, and with John K. Smith, Mar. 18, 1985.

Gee, Edwin A. Interview with David A. Hounshell and John K. Smith, Nov. 11, 1985.

Genereaux, Raymond. Interview with John K. Smith, Oct. 28, 1982.

Gore, Wilbert L. Interview with John K. Smith, Apr. 9, 1985.

Graves, George D. Interview with John K. Smith, May 24, 1983.

Greenewalt, Crawford H. Interviews with David A. Hounshell and John K. Smith, Oct. 15, Nov. 8, and Dec. 15, 1982, Jan. 19, 1983.

Hamblet, Clement H. Interview with John K. Smith, Mar. 18, 1985.

Hanford, William E. Interview with John K. Smith, Oct. 29, 1985.

Heckert, W. W. Interview with David A. Hounshell and John K. Smith, June 29, 1983.

Hill, Gideon D. Interview with David A. Hounshell, July 16, 1986.

Hill, Julian. Interview with David A. Hounshell and John K. Smith, Dec. 1, 1982.

Hoffmann, Conrad E. Interview with David A. Hounshell, July 14, 1986.

Jefferson, Edward G. Interviews with David A. Hounshell and John K. Smith, July 24, 28, 31, and Aug. 1, 1986.

Lenher, Samuel. Interviews with David A. Hounshell and John K. Smith, Oct. 4, 1982, and Jan. 18, 1983.

Luckenbaugh, Raymond W. Interview with David A. Hounshell, July 8, 1986.

Marvel, Carl S. Interview with David A. Hounshell and John K. Smith, May 2, 1983.

McGrew, Frank C. Interview with David A. Hounshell, Aug. 2, 1983.

McQueen, David M. Interview with David A. Hounshell and John K. Smith, Sept. 20, 1982.

Morgan, Paul W. Interview with David A. Hounshell and John K. Smith, Oct. 16, 1985.

Plambeck, Louis. Interview with John K. Smith, Sept. 12, 1985.

Rivers, Joseph T. Interview with David A. Hounshell, Jan. 20, 1986.

Salzberg, Paul L. Interview with John K. Smith, Sept. 29, 1982.

Simmons, Howard E., Jr. Interview with David A. Hounshell and John K. Smith, Aug. 1, 1986.

Sinness, Lester S. Interview with David A. Hounshell and John K. Smith, Oct. 23, 1985.

Spanagel, Edgar. Interview with John K. Smith, Nov. 9, 1982.

Swank, Howard W. Interview with David A. Hounshell, Jan. 16, 1986.

Tyler, Chaplin. Interviews John K. Smith, Oct. 7, 20, 1982.

Wardenberg, Frederick M. Interview with Alfred D. Chandler, Richmond D. Williams, and Norman B. Wilkinson, June 21, 1961, Acc. 1689.

Williams, Roger. Notes on interview with Alfred D. Chandler, Richmond D. Williams, and Norman Wilkinson, June 20, 1962, Acc. 1689.

Wolf, Dale E. Interview with David A. Hounshell, Oct. 8, 1986.

Woodhouse, John C. Interviews with David A. Hounshell and John K. Smith, Oct. 11, 16, 1982, and with John K. Smith, Nov. 16, 1982.

Woodward, Harold. Interview with David A. Hounshell and John K. Smith, Aug. 5, 1983.

Zapp, John A., Jr. Interview with John K. Smith, Apr. 17, 1986.

E. I. du Pont de Nemours & Co. Records

Note: Unless otherwise noted, records are located in Wilmington, Delaware.

Agchem Files	History Files, Agricultural Chemicals Research and Development Division, Experimental Station
Cons. Proj. Files	Construction Projects Files, Records Management Center
CRDD Files	Central Research and Development Department Files, Du Pont Building
CRDD Notebooks	Central Research and Development Department, Technical Records Center, Experimental Station
DD Files	Development Department Files, Central Research and Development Department, Du Pont Building
EC Files	Executive Committee Files, Du Pont Building
EC Minutes	Minutes of the Executive Committee, Du Pont Building
Engrg. Hist.	Engineering Department History File, Part I, Engineering Department, Newark, Delaware
HL Hist. File	Haskell Laboratory Historical Files, Haskell Laboratory, Newark, Delaware
HL Reports	Haskell Laboratory Reports, Haskell Laboratory, Newark, Delaware
PPD Files	Polymer Products Department Files, Du Pont Building
PPD Research Files	Polymer Products Department, Experimental Station
PPD Pub. Aff. Files	Polymer Products Department, Public Affairs Group, Product Files, Du Pont Building
PRL Authors	Authors Files, Pioneering Research Laboratory Library, Textile Fibers Department, Experimental Station
PRL Hist. Files	Pioneering Research Laboratory Historical Files, Textile Fibers Department, Experimental Station
PR Records	Records of the Pioneering Research Division, Textile Fibers Department, Records Management Center
Special Compensation Files	Records of the Special Compensation and "A" Bonus Committees, Du Pont Building
TF Files	Textile Fibers Laboratory File Room, Chestnut Run

Introduction

1 The relationship between science and big business has been treated in a number of works, including David F. Noble, *America by Design: Science, Technology, and the Rise of Corporate Capitalism* (New York: Knopf, 1977); Alfred D. Chandler, Jr., *The Visible Hand: The Managerial Revolution in American Business* (Cambridge, Mass.: Harvard University Press, 1977); Reese V. Jenkins, *Images and Enterprise: Technology and the American Photographic In-*

dustry (Baltimore: Johns Hopkins University Press, 1975); George Wise, *Willis R. Whitney, General Electric, and the Origins of U.S. Industrial Research* (New York: Columbia University Press, 1985); and Leonard S. Reich, *The Making of American Industrial Research: Science and Business at GE and Bell, 1876–1926* (New York: Cambridge University Press, 1986).

2 Norman B. Wilkinson, *Lammot du Pont and the American Explosives Industry, 1850–1884* (Charlottesville: University Press of Virginia, 1984). The company's entry into dynamite was achieved through the purchase of a one-third interest in the new Repauno Chemical Company. Lammot du Pont personally acquired a one-third interest, and Du Pont's friendly competitor, Laflin & Rand Powder Company, bought the remaining interest.

3 Steven W. Usselman, "Running the Machine: The Management of Technological Innovation on American Railroads, 1860–1910" (PhD diss., University of Delaware, 1985), pp. 242–50, 266–73, 297–300. See also Howard R. Bartlett, "The Development of Industrial Research in the United States," in National Research Council, *Research: A National Resource* (Washington, D.C.: U.S. Government Printing Office, 1941), pp. 26–27.

4 Allan Nevins, *John D. Rockefeller: The Heroic Age of American Enterprise* (New York: Scribner, 1940), I, pp. 650–1. On Frasch, see his entry in the *Dictionary of American Biography*, vol. 6, pp. 602–3.

5 Andrew Carnegie, *The Autobiography of Andrew Carnegie* (Boston: Little, Brown, 1920), p. 182.

6 See Bartlett, "Development of Industrial Research," pp. 20–9; Kendall Birr, "Science in American Industry," in *Science and Society in the United States*, ed. David D. Van Tassel and Michael G. Hall (Homewood, Ill.: Dorsey, 1966), pp. 35–80, and Jeffrey L. Sturchio, "Chemists and Industry in Modern America" (PhD diss., University of Pennsylvania, 1981).

7 Quoted in Matthew Josephson, *Edison* (New York: McGraw-Hill, 1959), pp. 133–4.

8 David A. Hounshell, "Edison and the Pure Science Ideal in 19th Century America," *Science* 207 (1980): 612–17. The figure of forty employees comes from a personal communication from Paul Israel, a member of the Edison Papers editorial staff, to David A. Hounshell.

9 Robert Friedel and Paul Israel with Bernard S. Finn, *Edison's Electric Light* (New Brunswick, N.J.: Rutgers University Press, 1986).

10 See, e.g., Karl T. Compton, "Edison's Laboratory in War Time," *Science* 75 (1932): 70–1. The West Orange laboratory is now a national historic site, and a comprehensive history of the lab is now in preparation by W. Bernard Carlson and Andrew J. Millard.

11 Arthur D. Little, "Industrial Research in America," *Journal of Industrial and Engineering Chemistry* 5 (1913): 793.

12 John J. Beer, "Coal Tar Dye Manufacture and the Origins of the Modern Industrial Research Laboratory," *Isis* 49 (1958): 123–31. See also idem., *The Emergence of the German Dye Industry* (Urbana: University of Illinois Press, 1959).

13 "The Industrialization of Invention: A Case Study from the German Chemical Industry," *Isis* 73 (1982): 364.

14 Ibid., p. 370.

15 Ibid., p. 378. Meyer-Thurow offers the literal translation: "scientific mass work."

16   Ibid.

17   Beer, "Coal Tar Dye Manufacture," p. 130.

18   David C. Mowery, "The Relationship between Intrafirm and Contractual Forms of Industrial Research in American Manufacturing, 1900–1940," *Explorations in Economic History* 20 (1983): 351–74. On Arthur D. Little, Inc., see also E. J. Kahn, Jr., *The Problem Solvers: A History of Arthur D. Little, Inc.* (Boston: Little, Brown, 1986).

19   On Duncan, see Bartlett, "The Development of Industrial Research," pp. 71–2; Richard L. Lesher, "Independent Research Institutes and Industrial Application of Aerospace Research" (PhD diss., Indiana University, 1963), pp. 76–9; and Harold Vagtborg, *Research and American Industrial Development* (New York: Pergamon, 1976), pp. 124–9.

20   Little, "Industrial Research in America," pp. 799–800, discusses trade association research. The problems with antitrust legislation are noted in an editorial, "Research," *Journal of Industrial and Engineering Chemistry* 5 (1913): 967.

21   Robert Wiebe, *The Search for Order, 1877–1920* (New York: Hill and Wang, 1967).

22   Glenn Porter, *The Rise of Big Business, 1860–1910* (New York: Crowell, 1973), pp. 28, 55–7.

23   Ellis W. Hawley, "Antitrust," *Encyclopedia of American Economic History*, ed. Glenn Porter, vol. II, p. 774.

24   Reich, *Making of American Industrial Research*, pp. 40, 62–9, and Jenkins, *Images and Enterprise*, pp. 300–24.

25   George Wise, "A New Role for Professional Scientists in Industry: Industrial Research at General Electric, 1900–1916," *Technology and Culture* 21 (1980): 408–29.

26   This statement is widely attributed to Irving S. Shapiro, chairman of the board from 1973 to 1981, but it does not, to our knowledge, appear in print.

27   *Du Pont Annual Report, 1984*. These figures include Conoco.

Part I: The Experimental Era

1   Alfred D. Chandler, Jr., and Stephen Salsbury, *Pierre S. du Pont and the Making of the Modern Corporation* (New York: Harper & Row, 1971), pp. 118–19.

Chapter 1. Organizing for Research and Development, 1902–1911

1   T. Coleman du Pont to Francis I. du Pont et al., Feb. 4, 1903, II, 2, Box 806. See also Alfred D. Chandler, Jr., and Stephen Salsbury, *Pierre S. du Pont and the Making of the Modern Corporation* (New York: Harper & Row, 1971), pp. 47–76.

2   Arthur La Motte, "Diary of a Dynamiter," July 9, 1902, Acc. 1345.

3   Quoted in [E. I. du Pont de Nemours & Co.], *The Story of the Eastern Laboratory, 1902–1952*, p. 6, Pamphlet Collection, Hagley Museum and Library.

4   Norman B. Wilkinson, *Lammot du Pont and the American Explosives Industry, 1850–1884* (Charlottesville, Va.: University Press of Virginia, 1984); Jeffrey L. Sturchio, "Chemists and Industry in Modern America" (PhD diss., University

of Pennsylvania, 1981), pp. 106–11; and Arthur Pine Van Gelder and Hugo Schlatter, *History of the Explosives Industry in America* (New York: Columbia University Press, 1927), pp. 561–71.

5 Van Gelder and Schlatter, *Explosives Industry*, pp. 571–3; "Information received from Mr. A. La Motte on June 1, 1944," Acc. 1850; and "Diary of a Dynamiter."

6 Van Gelder and Schlatter, *Explosives Industry*, p. 581.

7 Ibid., pp. 363–64.

8 These chemists included George Eustis Potts (hired in 1893), Sidney S. Emery (hired ca. 1895), Arthur La Motte (hired in 1896), Arthur Pine Van Gelder (hired in 1898), Torstan Ivarson (hired in 1898), Ira Pierce (hired in 1900), and Charles A. Patterson (hired in 1900), LMSS, File 1095.

9 Charles L. Reese, "The Eastern Laboratory: Its Work and Development," paper given at High Explosives Operating Department Superintendents' Meeting, New York, Apr. 20–6, 1911, II, 2, Box 577, pp. 307–16.

10 Reese, "Eastern Laboratory," pp. 307–9.

11 See *National Cyclopaedia of American Biography*, s.v. "Reese, Charles Lee"; *Dictionary of American Biography*, s.v. "Reese, Charles Lee"; Arthur M. Comey, "Charles Lee Reese," *Industrial and Engineering Chemistry* 20 (1928): 224–6; Robert E. Curtin, "Charles Lee Reese, 1862–1940," *Journal of the American Chemical Society* 62 (1940): 1889–91; David H. Wilcox, Jr., "Charles L. Reese," in *American Chemists and Chemical Engineers*, ed. Wyndham D. Miles (Washington, D.C.: American Chemical Society, 1976), pp. 401–2. See also H. M. Pierce's account of Reese in his letter to P. S. du Pont, Feb. 28, 1941, Acc. 1034, File 203.

12 Comey, "Charles Lee Reese," p. 224. Reese's papers at the Historical Society of Delaware suggest that he was at Göttingen only briefly.

13 Ira Remsen, Testamental Letter, July 10, 1888, Reese Papers, Historical Society of Delaware, Box 1, File 7.

14 Walker Brown to Major Johnson M. Welch, July 2, 1896, Reese Papers, Box 1; Francis Reese to Charles L. Reese, May 8, 1899, Box 3; Ira Remsen to S. W. Chaplin, Apr. 21, 1899, Box 1.

15 Ira Remsen to George C. Stone, Dec. 18, 1899; Edward Renouf to George C. Stone, Dec. 13, 1899; H. M. Morse to George C. Stone, Dec. 18, 1899, Reese Papers, Box 1.

16 H. M. Barksdale to Reese, Mar. 25, 1902, Reese Papers, Box 6. On New Jersey Zinc's work on the contact process, see Charles L. Reese, "The Schroeder Contact Process of Sulphuric Acid Manufacture: Experimental Investigations and Observations," *Journal of the Society of Chemical Industry* 22 (1903): 351–4, and George C. Stone, "The Schroeder Contact Process of Sulphuric Acid Manufacture: Manufacturing," ibid., 350–1. On the planning of Eastern Laboratory prior to Reese's employment, see "Diary of a Dynamiter," May 10, 1901. La Motte's diary also notes Jackson's deteriorating mental health. See entries of Sept. 6, 1900; Jan. 4, 1901; and Jan. 11, 1901.

17 Barksdale to Reese, March 25, 1902.

18 Reese, "Eastern Laboratory," pp. 307–8, 310. For an example of Eastern Laboratory's reports, see "Distillation of Weak Nitric with Sulphuric: Resume of Results to Date," Aug. 23, 1902, in Acc. 1784.

19 Reese, "Eastern Laboratory," p. 310. On SE Compound, see also Charles L. Reese, "Twenty-five Years' Progress in Explosives," *Journal of the Franklin*

Institute 198 (1924): 748–9, and Van Gelder and Schlatter, *Explosives Industry*, p. 364.

20 "Diary of a Dynamiter," May 26, 1903.

21 Ibid., June 3, 1905. See also entries for 1903 and 1904.

22 Ibid., July 13, Sept. 20, 1905; May 21, 1907.

23 Reese, "Eastern Laboratory," p. 309.

24 Report of special committee to review the general question of laboratories, July 11, 1904, EC Minutes, July 12, 1904. The report was written by Barksdale.

25 EC Minutes, June 22, 1904.

26 Francis I. du Pont to Executive Committee, June 1, 1904, Acc. 1784. This document is obviously misdated and should be July 1, 1904, because the special committee was not established until June 22.

27 Report of special committee.

28 Francis had relinquished his role as head of the Smokeless Powder Operating Department to assume the directorship of the new General Experimental Laboratory.

29 Du Pont to Executive Committee, June 1, 1904.

30 Report of special committee.

31 Du Pont to Executive Committee, June 1, 1904.

32 Report of special committee.

33 Ibid.

34 Ibid.

35 Francis I. du Pont to Executive Committee, July 11, 1904, EC Minutes, July 12, 1904. Cf. Barksdale's account of the Station's founding in Report of special committee.

36 EC Minutes, March 7, 1903. See also T. Coleman du Pont to Francis I. du Pont et al., Feb. 4, 1903, II, 2, Box 806.

37 A. J. Moxham to T. C. du Pont, Feb. 7, 1903, II, 2, Box 806.

38 T. C. Du Pont to A. J. Moxham, Feb. 9, 1903, II, 2, Box 805.

39 See, e.g., EC Minutes, April 14, 1903.

40 Ibid.

41 Ibid.

42 Report of the committee on experimental laboratory, April 21, 1903, EC Minutes, May 12, 1903.

43 Report on the Committee on Government Smokeless Powder, July 20, 1903, in EC Minutes, July 21, 1903.

44 Helen E. Davis, "A History of the Relations of the Du Pont Company with the United States Government, 1802–1923," Acc. 372, p. 20. See also Van Gelder and Schlatter, *Explosives Industry*, pp. 875–80, and James J. Stokesberry, "The Development of Smokeless Gunpowder by the United States Navy, 1889–1900" (MA thesis, University of Delaware), 1965, pp. 21–45.

45 Captain Sidney E. Stuart, Report of Inspector of Powder, 1894, as quoted in Davis, "History of the Relations of the Du Pont Company with the United States Government," p. 23.

46 Ibid., pp. 36, 56, 65. *New York Times*, Dec. 19, 1903. The military was being drawn into the sweeping reform movement that has become known to historians as the Progressive Era when Francis du Pont wrote his report to the Executive Committee. Although the roots of the movement go back to 1887, when Congress established the Interstate Commerce Act to try to end rate

abuses by the railroads, and to 1890, when it passed the Sherman Antitrust Act, the full force of the movement did not develop until after Theodore Roosevelt took office following President McKinley's assassination. By 1902, Roosevelt had taken his stand on the issue of trusts and had determined to use the Sherman Antitrust Act to break up big businesses believed to be antithetical to the public good. Muckraking, begun in 1894 with Lloyd's *Wealth against Commonwealth*, grew to new heights with the serial publication of Ida Tarbell's *History of the Standard Oil Company* in *McClure's* in 1903.

47 Report of Committee on Government Smokeless Powder, July 20, 1902.
48 EC Minutes, July 21, 1903.
49 EC Minutes, July 29, 1903.
50 EC Minutes, Sept. 8, 1903.
51 Ibid.
52 Ibid.
53 On mine safety legislation, see William Graebner, *Coal-Mining Safety in the Progressive Period: The Political Economy of Reform* (Lexington: University Press of Kentucky, 1976).
54 EC Minutes, Sept. 8, 1903.
55 EC Minutes, Oct. 21, 1903.
56 Ibid.
57 EC Minutes, Nov. 18, 1903.
58 EC Minutes, Dec. 17, 1903. See also A. J. Moxham to T. C. du Pont, Nov. 24, 1903, and T. C. du Pont to A. J. Moxham, Nov. 25, 1903, II, 2, Box 806.
59 A. J. Moxham to P. S. du Pont, Nov. 18, 1903, II, 2, Box 812.
60 EC Minutes, Dec. 17, 1903.
61 Ibid.
62 EC Minutes, Mar. 17, 1914.
63 EC Minutes, Mar. 30, 1904.
64 Report from Experimental Laboratory, n.d., included in ibid.
65 Ibid.
66 *Dictionary of American Biography*, s.v. "Du Pont, Francis Irénée"; Henry Clay Reed, *Delaware: A History of the First State* (New York: Lewis Historical Publishing, 1947), pp. 545–6; and Van Gelder and Schlatter, *Explosives Industry*, pp. 175, 815, 848, 879, 880.
67 A. J. Moxham to Experimental Station, Sept. 19, 1907, II, 2, Box 205. On Francis I. du Pont and late reports, see the EC Minutes, Aug. 4, 1910, and October 6, 1910. See also A. J. Moxham and Irénée du Pont to the Executive Committee, Aug. 31, 1910, Acc. 1850, Box 6.
68 *National Cyclopaedia of American Biography*, s.v. "Sparre, Fin." Sparre's obituary appeared in *Wilmington Journal Every Evening*, Oct. 9, 1944. See also the Du Pont Company's biographical sketch of Sparre (Aug. 10, 1944) in Acc. 1410, Box 62, and the resolution of the board of directors, E. I. du Pont de Nemours & Co., made shortly after Sparre's death on Oct. 7, 1944, also in Acc. 1410, Box 62.
69 H. M. Pierce to P. S. du Pont, Feb. 28, 1941, Acc. 1034, File 203. On Du Pont's agreement with Wingett, see Alfred I. du Pont and Irénée du Pont to Executive Committee, Mar. 24, 1910, II, 2, Box 205.
70 Charles E. Arnold, Sr., *My Remembrances of the Du Pont Experimental Station* (n.p.: n.p., 1947), p. 12.
71 Maxim's monthly salary is given in EC Minutes, Mar. 17, 1904. Wingett's

monthly salary was $300. See EC Minutes, Apr. 26, 1905, and Jan. 15, 1908. See also Alfred I. du Pont and Irénée du Pont to Executive Committee, Mar. 24, 1910, II, 2, Box 205.

72 Hudson Maxim, "The Story of Smokeless Powder," *Cassier's Magazine* 16 (July 1899): 239–49; Francis I. du Pont, "Brief Account of the Beginning of the Smokeless Powder Business by the E. I. du Pont de Nemours & Co.," Acc. 1006, Box 6; *National Cyclopaedia of American Biography*, s.v. "Maxim, Hudson"; and Hudson Maxim and Clifton Johnson, *Hudson Maxim* (Garden City, N.Y.: Doubleday, Page, 1924). See the contract between Du Pont and Maxim, dated Oct. 17, 1898, in Acc. 509.

73 Contract between Maxim and Du Pont, Jan. 4, 1905, Acc. 509. See also EC Minutes, July 10, 1907, and "Estimate of Expenditures by Development Department and Experimental Station for Years 1907, 1908, and 1909," II, 2, Box 1006.

74 See, e.g., James E. Brittain, "The Introduction of the Loading Coil: George A. Campbell and Michael I. Pupin," *Technology and Culture* 11 (1970): 36–57.

75 See EC Minutes, Nov. 18, 1903; Mar. 17, Dec. 13, Dec. 28, 1904; Aug. 15, 1905; Davis, "History of the Relations of the Du Pont Company with the United States Government," pp. 47–50; and "The Manufacture of Stabillite: Summary Report Showing the Details of the Manufacture of Stabillite with Historical Data from the Beginning of the Study to Date," B22-2, Apr. 6, 1915, II, 2, Box 310.

76 Van Gelder and Schlatter, *Explosives Industry*, p. 884; "The Manufacture of Stabillite"; Hudson Maxim, "Advantages of Stabillite: Reasons Why It Has Come to Stay," June 1905, Acc. 1438. Trinitroanisole is the methyl ether of picric acid; its formula is $C_6H_2(NO_2)_3OCH_3$.

77 EC Minutes, Nov. 18, 1903.

78 "The Manufacture of Stabillite" and Arnold, *My Remembrances*, pp. 15–17.

79 EC Minutes, Dec. 13, Dec. 28, 1904; "The Manufacture of Stabillite."

80 EC Minutes, Aug. 15, 1905.

81 Parraga Brothers to Development Department, Apr. 1906, quoted in "The Manufacture of Stabillite."

82 Figures on expenditures for Stabillite's development are from EC Minutes, Jan. 4, Jan. 30, Apr. 10, July 10, Sept. 18, Oct. 16, Dec. 18, 1907, Jan. 15, July 15, 1908. On negotiating a contract with the government, see EC Minutes, Jan. 4, 1907. Government purchases are detailed in "The Manufacture of Stabillite." Subsequent development is discussed in EC Minutes, Aug. 28, 1907, Jan. 15, Apr. 1, July 1, 1908.

83 "The Manufacture of Stabillite."

84 EC Minutes, July 14, 1909.

85 Irénée du Pont to Executive Committee, Dec. 23, 1910, II, 2, Box 205.

86 On Stabillite's problems, see Van Gelder and Schlatter, *Explosives Industry*, p. 884; "The Manufacture of Stabillite"; "The Stability of Stabillite: Summary Report Obtained from the Beginning of Study to January 1, 1912, with Conclusions to August 1914, Inclusive," Apr. 6, 1915, B22-3; II, 2, Box 310.

87 "Annual Report on Stabillite for Year Ending December 31, 1907," Jan. 2, 190[8], Acc. 1438.

88 "The Manufacture of Stabillite."

89 "The Stability of Stabillite." On the introduction of diphenylamine, see Van

Gelder and Schlatter, *Explosives Industry*, pp. 820, 884; Davis, "History of the Relations of the Du Pont Company with the United States Government," pp. 42–43; Ralph Earle, "The Development of Our Navy's Smokeless Powder," *U.S. Naval Institute Proceedings* 40 (1914): 1055; Fin Sparre, "Investigation of Various Subjects in Europe, September-October-November, 1909: General Report on Places Visited and Subjects Investigated," Feb. 10, 1910, B73-1, II, 2, Box 326. On diphenylamine research at the Experimental Station, see the Research Reports, B42-1 through B42-19 in II, 2, Box 314 and Acc. 1784, Box 2.

90 Van Gelder and Schlatter, *Explosives Industry*, p. 882, citing a *Washington Post* article on testimony at the appropriation hearings; Earle, "Development of our Navy's Smokeless Powder," p. 1057.

91 Chandler and Salsbury, *Pierre S. du Pont*, pp. 23–4, 33–4.

92 Ibid., pp. 20–1. Marquis James, *Alfred I. du Pont, the Family Rebel* (Indianapolis: Bobbs-Merrill, 1941), p. 86.

93 EC Minutes, Apr. 6, 1903.

94 Alfred I. du Pont and Irénée du Pont to Executive Committee, Mar. 24, 1910, II, 2, Box 205. See also EC Minutes, Apr. 26, 1905.

95 EC Minutes, 1903–07, passim.

96 A. J. Moxham to Experimental Station, Sept. 19, 1907, II, 2, Box 205. C. M. Barton to A. P. Tanberg, Dec. 26, 1947, History files, CRDD Files.

97 [C. M. Barton] to A. J. Moxham, Sept. 20, 1907, II, 2, Box 205.

98 EC Minutes, Oct. 16, 1907.

99 EC Minutes, Oct. 29, 1907.

100 EC Minutes, Nov. 21, Dec. 6, 1907.

101 EC Minutes, Jan. 15, April 1, 1908.

102 T. C. du Pont to P. S. du Pont et al., Apr. 20, 1908, II, 2, Box 205.

103 EC Minutes, April 1, 1908.

104 EC Minutes, May 6, 1908.

105 A. I. du Pont to F. L. Connable, May 19, 1908, Acc. 1599, Box 1.

106 EC Minutes, May 20, July 15, 1908, Feb. 6, 1909. See also draft, P. S. du Pont to Executive Committee, May 14, 1908, II, 2, Box 205 and P. S. du Pont to C. M. Barton, Aug. 17, 1908.

107 Alfred I. du Pont and Irénée du Pont to Executive Committee, Mar. 24, 1910, II, 2, Box 205. See also Annual Report of Experimental Station for 1910, Jan. 27, 1911, II, 2, Box 167.

108 EC Minutes, Feb. 7, 1910.

109 Alfred I. du Pont and Irénée du Pont to Executive Committee, Mar. 24, 1910.

110 In other words, Francis du Pont was taken off the project. See Annual Report of the Experimental Station for 1910, Jan. 27, 1911, II, 2, Box 167; Irénée du Pont to Francis I. du Pont, Nov. 1, 1910, II, 2, Box 205.

111 Annual Report of the Experimental Station for 1911, Jan. 22, 1912, II, 2, Box 167.

112 Ibid.

113 Pierre S. du Pont to C. M. Barton, Aug. 17, 1908, II, 2, Box 205.

114 EC Minutes, Oct. 6, 1910.

115 Alfred I. du Pont to Frank L. Connable, Apr. 22, 1908, Acc. 1599, Box 1.

116 Ibid.

117 A. J. Moxham to C. M. Barton, Sept. 19, 1907, II, 2, Box 205.

118 *Du Pont Company Annual Report, 1907.*

119 Through Moxham, Du Pont initiated a project in 1902 to develop a pulp container to replace the steel kegs used for black and smokeless powder. Although one goal of the project was to lower the unit cost of the 6,000 kegs used each day by Du Pont, the other driving force for the project was the threat of federal legislation prohibiting railway shipment of powder in steel kegs because of safety problems. Du Pont believed that, if perfected, pulp kegs would be safer than steel containers. The pulp keg project ran from 1902 to 1912, when a large-scale but unsuccessful pulp keg mill burned down. Du Pont sank perhaps $500,000 into the project, which was abandoned because the Experimental Station was unable to make the pulp kegs moistureproof (an absolute necessity for storing the hygroscopic black powder) and because the threat from the federal government never materialized. The pulp keg project closely paralleled both in time and management the Stabillite and continuous black powder manufacturing projects.

120 On synthetic glycerin, see EC Minutes, Apr. 6, 1903. On glycerin as a by-product of fermentation, see EC Minutes, Aug. 31, 1904. See also Annual Report of the Experimental Station for the Year 1908, Jan. 20, 1909, II, 2, Box 166, and "Production of Glycerine or Glycerine Substitute," Research Reports (B1-1 to B1-45), Acc. 1784.

121 P. S. du Pont to C. M. Barton, Aug. 17, 1908.

122 Irénée du Pont, notation of June 13, 1911, on Charles L. Reese (per Wm. S. Weedon) to H. M. Barksdale, June 9, 1911, II, 2, Box 1015.

123 Irénée du Pont to Executive Committee, May 26, 1910, Acc. 1850. The development of a synthesis process for amyl acetate is covered in "Synthetical Production of Amyl Acetate" [Aug. 1911], B10-34 and Sept. 1, 1911, B10-35; Fin Sparre to Charles L. Reese, Oct. 3, 1911, II, 2, Box 1012; EC Minutes, Aug. 18, 1910, Jan. 18, Apr. 11, May 9, July 11, Nov. 14, 1911, Apr. 9, 1912.

124 This paragraph is based on annual reports of the Experimental Station, II, 2, Boxes 166–7, and Acc. 1784.

125 Edward H. Taylor, "Permissible Explosives," in *Report of Proceedings at the Fourth Convention of the Sales Department of E. I. du Pont de Nemours & Co.* (Wilmington: Du Pont, 1916), pp. 139–40.

126 Annual Report of the Experimental Station, Jan. 4, 1908, II, 2, Box 166.

127 C. M. Barton to A. P. Tanberg, Dec. 26, 1947.

128 Annual Report of the Experimental Station for the Year 1908, Jan. 20, 1909, II, 2, Box 166. See also EC Minutes, June 3 and 28, 1905, July 1 and 15, 1908. On the growing pressure to develop safer explosives, see Graebner, *Coal-Mining Safety.* See also Van Gelder and Schlatter, *Explosives Industry,* pp. 344–45, and Charles L. Reese, "Twenty-five Years' Progress in Explosives," and Reese, "Eastern Laboratory."

129 Annual Report of the Experimental Station for the Year 1908. See also C. M. Barton to William B. Dwinnell, Feb. 19, 1908, II, 2, Box 205.

130 EC Minutes, Dec. 8, 1910.

131 EC Minutes, Mar. 17, 1904.

132 Fin Sparre, "Experimental Station, 1908," II, 2, Box 205.

133 P. S. du Pont to Executive Committee, Oct. 21, 1908, Acc. 1850.

134 Comparative Statement of the Number of Men and Salaries of the Chemical Department, Dec. 31, 1911, and Dec. 31, 1912, Dec. 31, 1912, II, 2, Box 1003A. Figures from 1907 to 1911 are in annual reports of the Experimental Station. On quality of chemists at the Station, see, e.g., *American Men of Science* (4th ed., 1927), s.v. "Murrill, Paul I.," and "Hibbert, Harold."

135 Irénée du Pont to Executive Committee, Dec. 23, 1910, II, 2, Box 205.

136 Reese, "Eastern Laboratory," p. 316.

137 Ibid., pp. 310–12.

138 C. A. Woodbury, "The Investigation and Development of Explosives at the Eastern Laboratory," paper given at the High Explosives Operating Department Superintendents' Meeting, April 17–23, 1913, II, 2, Box 585, p. 321. See also Woodbury, U.S. Pat. No. 1,149,487.

139 Woodbury, "Investigation and Development of Explosives," pp. 320–1.

140 Ibid., p. 321.

141 "Dr. Charles M. A. Stine: A Biographical Sketch" (Mar. 31, 1939), Acc. 1706.

142 Reese, " Eastern Laboratory," p. 312.

143 *The Story of the Eastern Laboratory, 1902–1952,* p. 8. See also the testimony of Fin Sparre in U.S. Congress, Senate Special Committee Investigating the Munitions Industry, *Munitions Industry,* Part 5, Sept. 12, 13, 14, 1934, E. I. du Pont de Nemours & Co., 73rd Cong., 1934, pp. 1101–02.

144 See Reese, "Eastern Laboratory," pp. 314–15, and Woodbury, "Investigation and Development of Explosives," pp. 319–20.

145 *The Story of the Eastern Laboratory, 1902–1952,* p. 7.

146 George M. Atkins, Jr., "Arthur Messinger Comey," in *American Chemists and Chemical Engineers,* p. 89.

147 *Du Pont Dynam-Item,* Oct. 14, 1920.

148 See, e.g., Arthur M. Comey, "Certain Phases of Technical Chemical Research: Organization of Research of the du Pont Powder Co.," *Metallurgical and Chemical Engineering* 10 (1912): 141–42.

149 Ibid., pp. 142–3.

150 Report of special committee to review the general question of laboratories, July 11, 1904.

151 Reese, "Eastern Laboratory," p. 308.

152 Comey, "Certain Phases of Technical and Chemical Research," p. 143.

Chapter 2. Reorganization and Diversification

1 P. S. du Pont to the Officers and Employes of E. I. du Pont de Nemours & Co., Jan. 27, 1911, II, 2, Box 1003.

2 H. M. Barksdale to High Explosives Operating Department et al., May 6, 1911, II, 2, Box 131.

3 Alfred D. Chandler, Jr., and Stephen Salsbury, *Pierre S. du Pont and the Making of the Modern Corporation* (New York: Harper & Row, 1971), pp. 301–21.

4 Coleman's other major organizational change was the creation of eight standing committees subordinate to the Executive Committee: manufacturing and sales, purchasing, appropriations, development, legal, employees, reports, and accounting. EC Minutes, Jan. 18, 1911.

5   Irénée du Pont to Geo. H. Kerr, Oct. 4, 1937, Acc. 1034, File 240. See also Henry Clay Reed, *Delaware: A History of the First State* (New York: Lewis Historical Publishing, 1942), vol. 3, pp. 418–19; *Dictionary of American Biography, Supplement Seven*, s.v. "du Pont, Irénée"; and *New York Times*, Dec. 20, 1963.

6   Quoted from Helen E. Davis, "A History of the Relations of the Du Pont Company with the United States Government, 1902–1923," Acc. 372, pp. 65–6.

7   EC Minutes, Nov. 4, Dec. 16, 1908, Jan. 20, 1909.

8   P. S. du Pont to Officers..., Jan. 27, 1911. See also Irénée du Pont to C. M. Barton, Jan. 28, 1911, II, 2, Box 205.

9   Irénée du Pont to C. M. Barton, Feb. 10, 1911, II, 2, Box 205.

10   See, e.g., H. M. Barksdale to A. J. Moxham, May 16, 1912, II, 2, Box 1002.

11   The evidence for Irénée's role in the Chemical Department is abundant, especially in Acc. 228 and II, 2.

12   Comparative Statement of the Number of Men and Salaries of the Chemical Department, Dec. 31, 1911, and Dec. 31, 1912, II, 2, Box 1003A.

13   C. L. Reese to P. S. du Pont, et al., May 5, 1911, II, 2, Box 1003; C. L. Reese to the Heads of All Departments, II, 2, Box 1003A; C. L. Reese to P. S. du Pont, et al., Sept. 30, 1911, II, 2, Box 205.

14   C. L. Reese to P. S. du Pont, et al., Sept. 30, 1911.

15   Reese's handling of the Experimental Station's reports may be seen in the "B" Research Reports, contained in Acc. 1784 and in II, 2, Boxes 307–44.

16   EC Minutes, 1911–17, passim. See also A. J. Moxham to H. M. Barksdale, May 8; H. M. Barksdale to A. J. Moxham, May 16; A. J. Moxham to H. M. Barksdale, May 20; H. M. Barksdale to A. J. Moxham, May 22, 1912, II, 2, Box 1002, and EC Minutes, Oct. 8, 1912.

17   Charles L. Reese, Statement of the Chemical Department including the Eastern Laboratory and Experimental Station, May 29, 1913, Acc. 1784; Arthur D. Little, "Industrial Research in America," *Journal of Industrial and Engineering Chemistry* 5 (1913): 795.

18   Statement of the Chemical Department..., May 29, 1913.

19   Ibid., p. 19.

20   Ibid., pp. 19–20.

21   Quoted from Chandler and Salsbury, *Pierre S. du Pont*, p. 290. See also Davis, "A History of the Relations of the Du Pont Company with the United States Government, 1802–1923," pp. 59–62.

22   Fin Sparre, Statement of Work at the Experimental Station during the Years 1911 & 1912 with Respect to the Financial Profit Accruing from the Results of the Work, Acc. 1784.

23   C. A. Woodbury, "The Investigation and Development of Explosives at the Eastern Laboratory," paper given at the High Explosives Operating Department Superintendents' Meeting, Apr. 17–23, 1913, II, 2, Box 585.

24   Statement of Work at the Experimental Station....

25   C. M. Barton to C. L. Reese, July 20, 1911; H. F. Brown to C. L. Reese, Aug. 15, 1911, II, 2, Box 269.

26   Fin Sparre to C. L. Reese, Jan. 5, 1914, II, 2, Box 340.

27   Fin Sparre to Chemical Director, Oct. 24, 1914, II, 2, Box 340. The Station's reports are B139-1 through B139-5, Acc. 1784, Box 5, and II, 2, Box 340.

28   R. G. Woodbridge, Jr., to W. M. Whitten, Jr., May 6, 1920, Acc. 1784.

29 U.S. Congress, Senate Special Committee Investigating the Munitions Industry, *Munitions Industry*, Part 5, Sept. 12, 13, 14, 1934, E. I. du Pont de Nemours & Co., 73rd Cong., 1934, p. 1103.

30 Duties of the Development Department, Mar. 5, 1909, II, 2, Box 205.

31 EC Minutes, Apr. 21, 1909. See the Development Department's reports: W. W. Richards, Artificial Leather and Allied Products – Preliminary Report, Dec. 23, 1908, GM Suit, PD, pp. 3–25, and Irénée du Pont to T. C. du Pont et al., Apr. 27, 1908, GM Suit, PD, pp. 1–2.

32 Irénée du Pont, Addendum to Report of May 12th to the Executive Committee Relative to Artificial Leather, May 18, 1909, GM Suit, PD, pp. 26–7.

33 EC Minutes, May 19, 1909.

34 Fin Sparre to C. M. Barton, May 29, 1909, II, 2, Box 228. See also C. M. Barton to Irénée du Pont, Dec. 20, 1909, II, 2, Box 228.

35 C. M. Barton to Chas. L. Reese et al., June 10, 1909, II, 2, Box 228.

36 C. M. Barton to Irénée du Pont, June 10, 1909, II, 2, Box 228.

37 J. A. Haskell to C. M. Barton, June 14, 1909, II, 2, Box 228.

38 On the Nobel–Du Pont agreement, see Chandler and Salsbury, *Pierre S. du Pont*, pp. 170–3, 194–200, and William J. Reader, *Imperial Chemical Industries: A History* (London: Oxford University Press, 1970), vol. 1, pp. 194–205.

39 J. A. Haskell to C. M. Barton, June 25, 1909, II, 2, Box 228.

40 H. F. Brown to C. F. Burnside, July 16, 1909, II, 2, Box 228.

41 List of Subjects to Be Investigated by Dr. Sparre on His Trip Abroad during October and November 1909, II, 2, Box 244.

42 Investigation of Various Subjects in Europe, B73-1 through B73-21, II, 2, Box 326. See also his letters in II, 2, Box 244.

43 Fin Sparre to C. M. Barton, Oct. 15, 1909, II, 2, Box 244. See also his report on the Besançon factory, B73-20, in II, 2, Box 326.

44 Fin Sparre to C. M. Barton, Nov. 2, 1909, II, 2, Box 244.

45 Fin Sparre to C. M. Barton, Oct. 18, 26, 27, 1909, II, 2, Box 244.

46 C. M. Barton to Irénée du Pont, December 20, 1909, II, 2, Box 228.

47 Annual Report of the Development Department for the Year 1909, Feb. 9, 1910, in GM Suit, DTE DP72.

48 EC Minutes, Sept. 15, 1909.

49 Irénée du Pont to Executive Committee, Sept. 29, 1910, GM Suit, PD, pp. 30–1. Cf. Irénée's earlier report in GM Suit, DTE, DP72.

50 EC Minutes, July 7, 8, 19, 1910.

51 Fin Sparre to C. M. Barton, Aug. 30, 1910, II, 2, Box 253.

52 [Hamilton M. Barksdale(?)] to T. C. du Pont, May 29, 1912, II, 2, Box 1014. The "acetone oil" and "P_2" solvents were by-products of, respectively, acetone and formaldehyde manufacture; see Sparre to Barton, Aug. 30, 1910.

53 Return-on-investment figures appear in R. R. M. Carpenter to Finance Committee, Nov. 1921, GM Suit, PD, p. 1724.

54 Research Reports B95-1 through B95-89, Acc. 1784, Box 4. There are a number of other B-Reports series that cover nitrocellulose research contained in II, 2, Boxes 328–44 and Acc. 1784.

55 William Coyne to H. M. Barksdale, April 10, 1911, II, 2, Box 1014.

56 Irénée du Pont to the President, Fabrikoid Board [of Directors], Dec. 10, 1914, Acc. 228, ID-14P.

57 See H. F. Brown to Charles L. Reese, Jan. 13, 1913; C. L. Reese to Irénée

du Pont, Apr. 4, 1913, II, 2, Box 1013; and H. F. Brown to Irénée du Pont, Apr. 7, 1913, II, 2, Box 1013.

58 See, e.g., Irénée du Pont to H. F. Brown, Mar. 26, 1913, II, 2, Box 1013; Irénée du Pont to the President, Fabrikoid Board, Dec. 10, 1914, Irénée du Pont to C. L. Reese, Apr. 26, 1915, Pierre S. du Pont to Irénée du Pont, Apr. 22, 1915, Frank Kniffen to C. L. Reese, May 19, 1915, Acc. 228, ID-14P.

59 Irénée du Pont to C. L. Reese, May 3, 1915, Acc. 228, ID-14P.

60 Frank Kniffen to C. L. Reese, May 19, 1915.

61 [Charles E. Arnold], "New Types of Artificial Leather," June 22, 1915; C. L. Reese to Irénée du Pont, July 13, 1915, Acc. 228, AD-14P.

62 Irénée du Pont to C. L. Reese, July 14, 1915, Acc. 228, ID-14P.

63 See Research Reports B95-40 and B95-41, Fin Sparre to Chemical Director, Jan. 6, 1916, and Hamilton Bradshaw to Chemical Director, July 15, 1916, Acc. 1784.

64 Pierre S. du Pont to Experimental Station, Sept. 28, 1916, Acc. 1662, Box 16.

65 Wm. M. Whitten, Jr., to Wm. Coyne, Sept. 8, 1917, Acc. 228, ID-14P.

66 Charles E. Arnold to P. S. du Pont et al., Sept. 25, 1918, Acc. 1662, Box 69.

67 Carpenter to Finance Committee, Nov. 1921. After 1919, however, Du Pont experienced losses in the Fabrikoid business. In 1921, Du Pont cut back Fabrikoid research dramatically, and until vinyl-coated fabrics began to be made in the 1940s, Du Pont's Fabrikoid business remained essentially unchanged from the product and processes refined by the Experimental Station after the acquisition.

68 Annual Report of the Development Department for the Year 1909, Feb. 9, 1910, p. 2.

69 Fin Sparre to C. L. Reese, Dec. 8, 1911, enclosing Research Report B91-8, Acc. 1784.

70 C. L. Reese to Irénée du Pont, Dec. 16, 1911, II, 2, Box 1012.

71 Fin Sparre to C. L. Reese, May 1, 1913, enclosing Research Report B91-26, Acc. 1784.

72 Paul Mueller to R. R. M. Carpenter, July 4 and 18, 1913, Acc. 228, ID-30. This arrangement came after a long series of negotiations, which are well documented in Acc. 1662, Box 1; Acc. 228, ID-30; and the GM Suit, PD, pp. 69, 70, 72–3, 74.

73 Development Department to the Executive Committee, Feb. 16, 1914, GM Suit, PD, pp. 86–119.

74 EC Minutes, April 14 and 27, 1914; Irénée du Pont to Executive Committee, April 24, 1914, Acc. 228, ID-30.

75 Fin Sparre to Chemical Director, Jan. 19, 1914, Acc. 1784, and R. R. M. Carpenter to Irénée du Pont, June 4, 1914, Acc. 228, ID-30.

76 O. W. Pickering. R. R. M. Carpenter to Irénée du Pont, June 4, 1914.

77 Development Department to Executive Committee, Nov. 11, 1914, GM Suit, DTE DP73.

78 EC Minutes, Nov. 23, 1914.

79 R. R. M. Carpenter to Executive Committee, Dec. 11, 1914, GM Suit, PD, pp. 148–9. See also Walter S. Carpenter to R. R. M. Carpenter, Dec. 11, 1914, GM Suit, PD, pp. 149–55, and EC Minutes, Dec. 21, 1914.

80 R. R. M. Carpenter to Executive Committee, Dec. 22, 1914, GM Suit, PD, p. 157.

81 EC Minutes, Sept. 13, 1915. There is some uncertainty regarding the exact purchase price. The $8 million figure is cited from Willard F. Mueller, "Du Pont: A Study in Firm Growth" (PhD diss., Vanderbilt University, 1956), p. 445. Cf. Development Department to Executive Committee, Sept. 12, 1915, GM Suit, PD, pp. 200–15. The relative magnitude of the acquisition excludes Du Pont's heavy purchases of General Motors stock, which amounted to $48,758,000 between 1917 and 1919. Du Pont paid $8,753,000 for Harrison Brothers & Company (Paints) in 1917. Figures from Mueller, "Du Pont: A Study in Firm Growth," p. 445. The company later bought the Viscoloid Company in 1925 for $9.5 million.

82 Excerpt from Report of Executive Committee to Board of Directors…, Sept. 22, 1915, GM Suit, PD, pp. 222–4.

83 A. Felix du Pont to Irénée du Pont, July 21, 1921, Acc. 1662, Box 10.

84 C. L. Reese, Report of Expenditures and Accomplishments of the Chemical Department during the Years 1916, 1917, and 1918, Sept. 19, 1919, Acc. 1784; Organization Chart for the Chemical Department, Dec. 1, 1917, II, 2, Box 1003A; Chemical Director to Hamilton Bradshaw et al., Jan. 30, 1920; C. L. Reese to E. K. Bolton et al., May 24, 1920, II, 2, Box 291; C. L. Reese to W. P. Allen et al., Mar. 20, 1921, Acc. 1662, Box 16.

85 Anon. to Mr. Gudger, "Progress Report, Synthetic Camphor," Sept. 20, 1917; Agreement between Arlington Company and Roland L. Andreau, Aug. 22, 1916, Hamilton Bradshaw to Chemical Department, April 25, 1917, Acc. 1784; Summary Report of Work Done at the Experimental Station, June to December 1916, Acc. 228, ID-19; C. L. Reese to Marston T. Bogert, July 31, 1917, Acc. 228, ID-204; EC Minutes, May 15, 28, June 11, 1917, Sept. 16, 1918; Hamilton Bradshaw to Chemical Department, Feb. 19, 1920, Acc. 1784; Research Reports B153-1 to B153-4, B153-8, B153-11 to B153-18, Acc. 1784; and "Camphor in U.S.A.," *Du Pont Magazine* 35 (Mar. 1931): 9.

86 Chandler and Salsbury, *Pierre S. du Pont*, pp. 308–21.

87 Quoted from ibid., p. 320.

88 EC Minutes, Sept. 28, 1914. As presented to the board of directors, the reorganization plan had not specified how the Chemical and Engineering departments would be managed. At its Sept. 21, 1914, meeting, the new Executive Committee appointed a subcommittee chaired by Irénée du Pont to study the question.

89 [Irénée du Pont], Proposed Re-Organization: E. I. du Pont de Nemours Powder Company, Aug. 11, 1914, Acc. 1662, Box 60.

90 P. S. du Pont to J. A. Haskell et al., Oct. 31, 1917, Acc. 1662, Box 60. Pierre's views of Reese are also evident in LMSS, File 418.

Chapter 3. World War I and the Venture into Dyestuffs

1 Alfred D. Chandler, Jr., and Stephen Salsbury, *Pierre S. du Pont and the Making of the Modern Corporation* (New York: Harper & Row, 1971), p. 360. Sales and earnings data appear in Du Pont Company annual reports.

2 Executive Committee to P. S. du Pont, Jan. 26, 1916, GM Suit, DTE DP82.

3 Development Department to Executive Committee, Dec. 30, 1916, GM Suit, PD, pp. 329–48.

4 EC Minutes, Feb. 5, 1917.

5   C. L. Reese to Executive Committee, Mar. 31, 1915, GM Suit, DTE DP77. On Du Pont's R&D work on diphenylamine, see Summary Report of Work Done at the Experimental Station during the Year 1914, pp. 151–2, II, 2, Box 167; Research Report B150-1, "Organic Research: Production of Diphenylamine," June 26, 1915, II, 2, Box 212; and diphenylamine files in II, 2, Boxes 211 and 212.

6   J. B. Niles to Irénée du Pont, Sept. 3, 1914, Wm. M. Whitten, Jr., to H. F. Brown and H. G. Haskell, Dec. 18, 1914, Acc. 228, ID-18; Research Report B150-1.

7   Research Report B150-4, "Organic Research: Production of Diphenylamine," Oct. 25, 1916, II, 2, Box 212; Fin Sparre to Chemical Director, Apr. 12, 1915, II, 2, Box 211; EC Minutes, June 21, 1915.

8   C. L. Reese to Executive Committee, Mar. 31, 1915.

9   C. L. Reese, "Twenty-five Years' Progress in Explosives," *Journal of the Franklin Institute* 198 (1924): 761.

10 Ibid., 761–2.

11 C. L. Reese, "Industrial Benefits of Research," Reprint and Circular Series of the National Research Council, Nov. 18, Feb. 4, 1921. Both Reese and Sparre had observed the manufacture of tetryl when they toured Germany in 1908 and 1909. Fin Sparre to C. M. Barton, Oct. 27, 1909, II, 2, Box 244.

12 Reese, "Industrial Benefits of Research," p. 10.

13 A. E. Houlehan, "Memorandum on the Manufacture of Organic Compounds," May 3, 1915, II, 2, Box 292.

14 A. D. Chambers to R. R. M. Carpenter, July 26, 1915, GM Suit, DTE DP78.

15 On National Analine's recent formation, see Williams Haynes, ed., *American Chemical Industry* (New York: Van Nostrand, 1949), vol. 6, pp. 292–6.

16 EC Minutes, Dec. 29, 1915. On Poucher, see *National Cyclopaedia of American Biography*, s.v. "Poucher, Morris Richard," 33: 552–3.

17 W. S. Carpenter to Executive Committee, Dec. 29, 1915, GM Suit, DTE DP95.

18 Ibid.

19 Summary Report of Work Done at the Experimental Station, January to June 1916, Inclusive, Acc. 228, ID-19.

20 "Historical," Acc. 1410, Box 4.

21 R. R. M. Carpenter to C. L. Reese, Mar. 21, 1916, as quoted in ibid.; EC Minutes, Mar. 21, 1916.

22 R. R. M. Carpenter to E. N. Carpenter, Mar. 22, 1916, Acc. 889, Item 31.

23 Carpenter's and Chambers's activities in England are detailed in E. N. Carpenter's diary, a transcript of which is in Acc. 1383.

24 EC Minutes, June 14, 1916. See also EC Minutes, June 12, 1916.

25 EC Minutes, June 15, 1916. See also EC Minutes, March 27, June 26 and 30, 1916.

26 EC Minutes, June 26, 30, July 8, Aug. 2, 1916. See also William J. Reader, *Imperial Chemical Industries: A History* (London: Oxford University Press, 1970), vol. 1, pp. 276–7.

27 Development Department to Executive Committee, Progress Report – Excess Plant Utilization, Sept. 15, 1916, Acc. 1850.

28 P. S. du Pont to J. A. Haskell, Sept. 8, 1916.

29 EC Minutes, Dec. 12, 1916. See also Reader, *Imperial Chemical Industries*,

vol. 1, pp. 277–8; Anon., Notes on the Du Pont–Levinstein Patented Inventions and Secret Processes Agreement Made November 30, 1916, n.d., and Irénée du Pont, Memorandum of Du Pont–Levinstein Contract Concerning Patents and Secret Processes Relating to Dyestuffs, n.d., Acc. 1662, Box 25.

30 See, e.g., EC Minutes, Sept. 25, 1916, and [Fin Sparre(?)] to Chas. A. Meade, "General Discussion of Utilization of Plants from the Standpoint of New Industries," May 31, 1916, GM Suit, PD, pp. 257–62.

31 EC Minutes, Sept. 25, 1916.

32 Reese to Executive Committee, March 30, 1917, Acc. 1784. See also "Historical," p. 3. Work of the Chemical Department is reviewed in Hamilton Bradshaw to Chemical Director, Research Subjects of the Organic Department [of the Experimental Station], Aug. 5, 1916, and H. W. Elley to Chemical Department, Aug. 10, 1916, II, 2, Box 292.

33 C. Chester Ahlum, "Thirty-Nine Years with Du Pont," May 1, 1947, Acc. 1850.

34 For a fuller biography of Stine, see Chapter One and Chapter Five. Ahlum's "Thirty-Nine Years with Du Pont" provides information on his career. On Taylor, see *American Men of Science*, s.v. "Taylor, William Anthony," 6th ed., 1938. On Bolton, see Robert M. Joyce, "Elmer Keiser Bolton, 1886–1969," *Biographical Memoirs* 54 (Washington, D.C.: National Academy Press, 1983), pp. 50–72; Fin Sparre to Chemical Director, Dec. 8, 1915, Acc. 1784, and Elmer K. Bolton, Interview by Alfred D. Chandler, Jr., Norman Wilkinson, and Richmond Williams, 1961, Acc. 1689. On Bartleson, see the biographical file in Acc. 1850. On Lee, see Henry Clay Reed, *Delaware: A History of the First State* (New York: Lewis Historical Publishing, 1942), 3, p. 7. Little is known about Maguire other than he later headed the Engineering Department's dye plant and acid plant design division.

35 Ahlum, "Thirty-Nine Years at Du Pont."

36 C. M. Stine and C. C. Ahlum, Information Obtained from Levinstein Ltd., Manchester, England, December & January, 1916–1917; Intermediate Products and Azo Colors, Imprints Collection, Hagley Museum and Library; Bartleson's and Bolton's reports are in B155-1 to B155-12, Information Obtained from Levinstein Ltd., December and January 1916–17, Acc. 1784. See also Ahlum, "Thirty-Nine Years with Du Pont." Groups of Du Pont chemists returned to England in the winters of 1917–18 and 1918–19 to gather additional information from Levinstein. "Historical," p. 3.

37 Though diffuse, the evidence for this assessment is abundant and is distributed mainly throughout the EC Minutes between Dec. 1916 and Mar. 1922.

38 EC Minutes, Feb. 12, 1917.

39 EC Minutes, Mar. 5, 1917; P. S. du Pont to Executive Committee, Mar. 5, 1917, Acc. 1850.

40 EC Minutes, Apr. 2, 16, 1917.

41 EC Minutes, Apr. 23, 1917.

42 EC Minutes, Apr. 30, 1917.

43 EC Minutes, May 14, 1917.

44 EC Minutes, June 18, 26, 1917. The fee to Poucher was $100,000 (EC Minutes, Sept. 18, 1916, and Apr. 3, 1917).

45 EC Minutes, Aug. 17, 1917.

46 EC Minutes, Jan. 20, 1919. Cf. EC Minutes, Jan. 11, 1918.

47 C. L. Reese to W. W. Bacon et al., Feb. 1, 1917, Chemical Department Organization, Acc. 228, ID-361.

48 Ibid. Data on the Experimental Station's organic division are found in Summary Report of Work Done at the Experimental Station, June to Dec., 1916, Inclusive, Acc. 228, ID-19.

49 Ahlum, "Thirty-Nine Years at Du Pont."

50 EC Minutes, May 3, 14, 1917; *Chambers Works History*, vol. 3, chap. 6, p. 3, Acc. 1787.

51 On Holmes, see *American Men of Science*, 6th ed., 1938. On Houlehan, see the notice of his death, Mar. 11, 1924, in Acc. 1850.

52 EC Minutes, Nov. 12, 1917; Mar. 29, 1918; June 30, 1919.

53 EC Minutes, Feb. 22, May 24, July 29, Sept. 9, Dec. 30, 1918; Mar. 10, July 14, Aug. 25, 1919.

54 This figure is calculated on the basis of Executive Committee appropriations for laboratory and semiworks facilities at Deepwater, as recorded in EC Minutes.

55 *Chambers Works History*, vol. 3, chap. 6, p. 3.

56 EC Minutes, Jan. 20, 1919.

57 Raskob was a major critic of the dyestuffs venture.

58 EC Minutes, May 17, 1919.

59 EC Minutes, Aug. 4, 1919, quoting letter from Finance Committee to Executive Committee, July 31, 1919.

60 Ahlum, "Thirty-Nine Years with Du Pont." Figures from *Chambers Works History*, vol. 3, chap. 6, pp. 3–4.

61 R. E. Rose, "Foreign Dye Patents: Their Relation to the Development of the American Dye Industry," *Journal of Industrial and Engineering Chemistry* 11 (1919): 1074.

62 Ibid., p. 1073; E. F. Hitch and I. E. Knapp, "Some Problems in the Identification of Dyes," *Journal of Industrial and Engineering Chemistry* 11 (1919): 1077–9.

63 Rose, "Foreign Dye Patents," p. 1074.

64 Hitch and Knapp, "Some Problems," p. 1076. Cf. Harold E. Woodward, "Jackson Laboratory – Azo Division, 1917–1942," Acc. 1850.

65 Charles L. Reese, "Introductory Remarks," *Journal of Industrial and Engineering Chemistry* 11 (1919): 107.

66 Williams Haynes, *American Chemical Industry* (New York: Van Nostrand, 1942), vol. 3, pp. 240–76.

67 Du Pont was by no means unique in this regard. See Charles H. Herty, "American Progress in Dye Manufacture," *Journal of Industrial and Engineering Chemistry* 16 (1924): 1021. On Du Pont's problems, see Chas. A. Meade to Irénée du Pont, May 5, 1920, Acc. 1662, Box 50; Woodward, "Jackson Laboratory – Azo Division, 1917–1942"; W. S. Calcott, "[History of the Organic Chemicals Department]," July 17, 1945, Acc. 1850.

68 Fin Sparre to Chemical Department, June 28, Aug. 1, 1916, II, 2, Box 292.

69 Thomas H. Norton, *Artificial Dyestuffs Used in the United States* (Washington, D.C.: U.S. Government Printing Office, 1916); Haynes, *American Chemical Industry*, vol. 3, pp. 229–30; Thomas H. Norton, "A Census of the Artificial

Dyestuffs Used in the United States," *Journal of Industrial and Engineering Chemistry* 8 (1916): 1039–46.

70 Sparre to Chemical Department, Aug. 1, 1916.

71 EC Minutes, May 4, 1918; Haynes, *American Chemical Industry*, vol. 3, p. 244; "Historical," p. 3.

72 The following two paragraphs are based entirely on Lammot du Pont to Executive Committee, Nov. 29, 1918, Acc. 1460, Box 3. On the Alien Property Custodian, see Haynes, *American Chemical Industry*, vol. 3, pp. 258–62.

73 EC Minutes, Nov. 30, Dec. 2, 9, 1918.

74 Haynes, *American Chemical Industry*, vol. 3, p. 259.

75 Ibid., p. 260.

76 Ibid.

77 W. C. Spruance, "Acquisition of 'The Know How' in the Dyestuffs Business," July 22, 1921, Acc. 1662, Box 25.

78 Eysten Berg to Irénée du Pont, Oct. 25, 1920, Acc. 1662, Box 35.

79 EC Minutes, July 26, 28, 1920; see also Spruance, "Acquisition."

80 EC Minutes, July 26, 1920.

81 On Kunz's position as special assistant to Chambers, see the Aug. 1920 organization chart for the Miscellaneous Manufacturing Department, Imprints Department, Hagley Museum and Library. See also Haynes, *American Chemical Industry*, vol. 4, p. 301.

82 Eysten Berg to Irénée du Pont, Oct. 25, 1920; Berg to Irénée du Pont, Feb. 24, 1921, Acc. 1662, Box 35; Bolton interview.

83 Telegram, Berg to Du Pont, Feb. 24, 1921, Acc. 1662, Box 35; Spruance, "Acquisition." See also the notice in *Pharmazeutische Zeitung* (Feb. 26, 1921): 177.

84 Bolton interview.

85 Jordan did not reach Wilmington until July 1921 (he had been arrested in Feb.). D. H. Way, "History of the Azo Colors Area: Du Pont Chambers Works, Deepwater, N.J.," Sept. 1950, Acc. 1850.

86 Vol. 13 (Feb. 1921): 108.

87 See, e.g., Calvert W. Tazewell to W. M. Whitten, Jr., Mar. 31, 1921, and C. L. Reese to Irénée du Pont et al., Apr. 8, 1921, Acc. 1662, Box 16.

88 Irénée du Pont to Eysten Berg, Mar. 22, 1921, Acc. 1662, Box 35. Cf. Elmer K. Bolton to W. M. Whitten, May 7, 1920, Acc. 1784.

89 Irénée du Pont to C. L. Reese, Apr. 28, 1921, Acc. 1662, Box 16.

90 Ahlum, "Thirty-Nine Years with Du Pont." See the organization charts of the Dyestuffs Department for documentation on the Germans' positions, Imprints Department, Hagley Museum and Library.

91 Elley interview.

92 W. S. Calcott, "[History of the Organic Chemicals Department]," July 17, 1945. Cf. Harold Woodward, "Jackson Laboratory – Azo Division, 1917–1942" and D. H. Way, "History of the Azo Colors Area."

93 EC Minutes, Apr. 26, 1921.

94 Haynes, *American Chemical Industry*, vol. 3, pp. 257–76.

95 EC Minutes, Dec. 21, 1921, Jan. 4, 1922.

96 EC Minutes, Jan. 4, 1922.

97 EC Minutes, Mar. 1, 1922.

98 Irénée du Pont to Executive Committee, Feb. 25, 1922, as noted in EC Minutes, March 1, 1922.

99 Walter S. Carpenter, Jr., to Jasper Crane, n.d. [ca. 1935], II, 2, Box 1050. This is merely one of the dozens of documents written by Carpenter citing the $40 million figure.

Chapter 4. Decentralization

1 C. M. A. Stine to William Rintoul, Dec. 13, 1929, Acc. 1784.

2 Eastern Laboratory (1902), Gibbstown, N.J.; Experimental Station (1903), Wilmington, Del.; Jackson Laboratory (1917), Deepwater, N.J.; Delta Laboratory (1917), Arlington, N.J.; Redpath Laboratory (1920), Parlin, N.J.

3 Hamilton Bradshaw to Dr. [Ernest] Benger et al., Mar. 21, 1919, II, 2, Box 291. See also C. M. Stine to Hamilton Bradshaw et al., Mar. 25, 1919, II, 2, Box 291.

4 EC Minutes, Mar. 3, 10, Apr. 21, 1919. The program is in II, 2, Box 291.

5 On Reese's illness, see W. D. Schrack to Charles H. Herty, May 19, 1919, Papers of Charles H. Herty, Woodruff Library, Emory University, Atlanta.

6 Stine to Rintoul, Dec. 13, 1929.

7 Memorandum: Experimental and Technical Supervising Functions Affecting the Production Dept., Oct. 16, 1919, II, 2, Box 291.

8 Wm M. Whitten to C. L. Reese, Semi-Annual Report of the Chemical Department, Jan.–June 1920, Inclusive, Sept. 28, 1920, Acc. 1784.

9 Wm. M. Whitten, Jr., to C. C. Ahlum et al., Apr. 29, 1920, Acc. 1784.

10 All these responses are in Acc. 1784.

11 Fletcher B. Holmes to Wm. M. Whitten, Jr., May 7, 1920, Acc. 1784.

12 EC Minutes, Nov. 1, 9, 1920.

13 Alfred D. Chandler, Jr., *Strategy and Structure* (Cambridge, Mass.: MIT Press, 1962), pp. 96–110.

14 EC Minutes, Nov. 9, 1920.

15 [Charles L. Reese] to [Executive Committee], Nov. 8, 1920, Acc. 1850.

16 Charles A. Meade to Irénée du Pont, Dec. 31, 1920, Acc. 1662, Box 50.

17 Wm. M. Whitten, Jr., to C. L. Reese, Semi-Annual Report of the Chemical Department, July–Dec., 1920, Mar. 31, 1921. Acc. 1784.

18 Irénée du Pont to R. R. M. Carpenter, Jan. 31, 1921, Acc. 1034, File 222.

19 Irénée du Pont to Executive Committee, Apr. 27, 1921, Acc. 1850. See also EC Minutes, May 3, 1926.

20 EC Minutes, Sept. 7, 1921.

21 See, e.g., Irénée duPont to C. L. Reese, Aug. 24, 1923, Acc. 1662, Box 16.

22 Irénée du Pont to H. G. Haskell, Oct. 13, 1921, Acc. 1662, Box 60.

23 See, e.g., Hamilton Bradshaw, Memorandum for Dr. Reese, n.d. [Oct. 1921?], Acc. 1784.

24 C. A. Patterson, Chairman, Committee of General Managers to Executive Committee, Oct. 14, 1921, Acc. 1814, Box 5.

25 Ibid.

26 Ibid.

27 EC Minutes, Oct. 19, 1921.

28 Stine to Rintoul, Dec. 13, 1929.

29 EC Minutes, Dec. 7, 1921. See also EC Minutes, Nov. 16 and 30, 1921.

30 EC Minutes, Jan. 4, 1922.

31 F. W. Pickard, "The Du Pont Company in War and Peace," Paper read before the Business Science Club of Philadelphia, Feb. 6, 1920, Acc. 640.

32 Elmer K. Bolton, Interview with Alfred D. Chandler, Jr., Norman Wilkinson, and Richmond Williams, 1961, Acc. 1689.

Chapter 5. Rebuilding a Central Research Organization

1 Charles M. A. Stine to Jackson Laboratory, Eastern Laboratory et al., "Reports of Experimental Work," Oct. 10, 1919, II, 2, Box 291.

2 Charles M. A. Stine to William M. Whitten, May 7, 1920, Acc. 1784. See also Stine to Whitten, "Memorandum," May 3, 1920, Acc. 1784.

3 Irénée du Pont to Charles L. Reese, Aug. 24, 1923, Acc. 1662, Box 16.

4 EC Minutes, Nov. 16, 1921.

5 The expression was used by Roger Williams. See Notes on Interview by Alfred D. Chandler, Richmond D. Williams, and Norman B. Wilkinson, June 20, 1962, Acc. 1689.

6 EC Minutes, Nov. 30, Dec. 7, 1921, Jan. 4, 1922.

7 Alfred D. Chandler, Jr., and Stephen Salsbury, *Pierre S. du Pont and the Making of the Modern Corporation* (New York: Harper & Row, 1971), pp. 433–74. The quotation appears on p. 454.

8 Irénée du Pont to J. A. Haskell, Nov. 13, 1918, GM Suit, PD, 2d series, p. 495.

9 On Kettering, see Stuart W. Leslie, *Boss Kettering* (New York: Columbia University Press, 1983).

10 J. A. Haskell to Irénée du Pont, Nov. 15, 1918, GM Suit, PD, 2d series, pp. 497–9.

11 Charles M. A. Stine to W. C. Durant, Sept. 13, 1919, Acc. 1662, Box 29.

12 Eastern Laboratory to Charles M. A. Stine, Oct. 15, 1919, Acc. 1662, Box 16.

13 K. W. Zimmerschied to Charles M. A. Stine, Oct. 28, 1919, Acc. 1662, Box 29.

14 Charles L. Reese to J. A. Haskell, Nov. 4, 1919, Acc. 1662, Box 29.

15 F. O. Clements to Charles M. A. Stine, Nov. 24, 1919, GM Suit, PD, p. 1109.

16 Charles M. A. Stine, "Memorandum: Points to be Discussed with Mr. Kettering's Engineering Division...," Nov. 28, 1919, Acc. 1662, Box 36.

17 F. O. Clements to Charles M. A. Stine, Jan. 23, 1920, Acc. 1662, Box 36.

18 Charles M. A. Stine to Lammot du Pont, Jan. 26, 1920, GM Suit, PD, p. 1179.

19 John Marshall to Charles M. A. Stine, Jan. 30, 1920, Acc. 1662, Box 29.

20 Charles M. A. Stine to C. F. Kettering, Feb. 2, 1920, Acc. 1662, Box 29.

21 C. F. Kettering to Charles M. A. Stine, Apr. 12, 1920, Acc. 1662, Box 36.

22 Lammot du Pont to Executive Committee, "Chemical Work for General Motors," Apr. 22, 1920, GM Suit, PD, pp. 1429–31; Minutes of the meeting with GM, written by Stine, are attached to Charles L. Reese to Lammot du Pont, April 28, 1920, in EC Files. See also Lammot du Pont to C. L. Reese, May 4, 1920, EC Files, and EC Minutes, May 3, 1920.

23 Charles M. A. Stine to Lammot du Pont, May 1, 1920, GM Suit, DTE, DP95.

24 For Du Pont's concerns, see Charles L. Reese to C. F. Kettering, June 1, 1920,

GM Suit, PD, 2d series, pp. 773–6. For the proposed agreement, see Lammot du Pont to Executive Committee, June 15, 1920, EC Files.

25 Lammot du Pont to Charles M. A. Stine, May 7, 1920, GM Suit, PD, 2d series, p. 771.

26 Thomas Midgley to Charles M. A. Stine, Apr. 15, 1921, Acc. 1662, Box 16.

27 Ibid.

28 Exhibit A, N. P. Wescott to Fin Sparre, June 9, 1936, "Origins and Early History of Tetraethyl Lead Business," in GM Suit, PD, pp. 5853–5922. See also drafts of this agreement in EC Files; Charles L. Reese to Executive Committee, Nov. 3, 1921, EC Files; Midgley to Stine, Nov. 9, 1921, GM Suit, PD, 2d series, p. 943.

29 Lammot du Pont, "Memorandum for File," Nov. 6, 1922, EC Files. On Lammot's efforts, see Lammot du Pont to C. F. Kettering, Nov. 19, 1921, Mar. 27, Apr. 1 and 14, 1922, GM Suit, PD, 2d series, pp. 947, 999–1000, 1007–8, 1177–86; Kettering to Lammot du Pont, Mar. 29 and Apr. 3, 1922, GM Suit, PD, 2d series, pp. 1003, 1009–11; Kettering to du Pont, May 2, 1922, EC Files.

30 Stine detailed his strategy in a letter to William Rintoul, Dec. 13, 1929, Acc. 1784.

31 Charles L. Reese to the Executive Committee, Mar. 27, 1924, Acc. 1784.

32 Charles M. A. Stine to H. Fletcher Brown, "Chemical Vise and Audit," Oct. 31, 1924, Acc. 1784. See also Charles M. A. Stine to Charles L. Reese, Oct. 29, 1923, Acc. 1784.

33 Charles M. A. Stine to the Executive Committee, Feb. 12, 1925, Acc. 1784.

34 "Development of the Chemical Department," 1940, Acc. 1784.

35 Hamilton Bradshaw to the Executive Committee, "Chemical Department Budget Appropriation for 1929," Dec. 14, 1928, Acc. 1784.

36 Ibid.

37 See, e.g., Elmer K. Bolton, "Development of Research in the Du Pont Company," Dec. 20, 1932, II, 2, Box 1035.

38 Stine to Rintoul, Dec. 13, 1929.

Chapter 6. Research to the Rescue: Du Pont Finishes

1 Du Pont research expenditures peaked at $3.45 million in 1919. (William Coyne to Irénée du Pont, "Chemical Department 1921 Appropriation," Nov. 19, 1920, Acc. 1662, Box 16.) The company would not return to this level of research expenditure until 1929. ("Talk Given to the Du Pont Board of Directors, Dec. 17, 1934, by Dr. C. M. A. Stine," Acc. 1706.)

2 Hunter Grubb to Irénée du Pont, Nov. 4, 1921, Acc. 1662, Box 32.

3 "Comparison of Operating Control Data of Sherwin-Williams Co., and Paint, Lacquer, and Chemicals Department (Excluding Fabrikoid Products) For 12 Month Period Ending August 31st, 1918 to 1924," July 7, 1925, Acc. 1662, Box 32.

4 "185,000,000 Gallons of Paint," *Fortune* (Aug. 1935): 70–83.

5 William Zintl, *History of the Du Pont Paint Business* (n.p.: n.p., 1947), p. 103, Acc. 1850.

6 Irénée du Pont to Hunter Grubb, Jan. 2, 1924, Acc. 1662, Box 32. The first advertisement appeared in the *Saturday Evening Post* on Feb. 24, 1923.

7 EC Minutes, June 28 and Oct. 18, 1922.

8 Zintl, *History*, pp. 3–7. For the early history of Du Pont's film research, see Chapter 23.

9 "Improvement of Pyroxylin Finishes by the Development of High Solids Content Improved Working Qualities and Better Covering Power Which Has Made These Finishes Available For Use in a Much Wider Range of Industries," Mar. 16, 1925, Special Compensation Files.

10 John Marshall, "Two-Decades of Progress in Finishes," *Agricultural Newsletter* (Mar.–Apr. 1940): 34–5, Pamphlet Collection, Hagley Museum and Library, and Zintl, *History*, pp. 45–6. For extensive discussions of the prior art, see Briefs for Plaintiff and Defendant, E. I. du Pont de Nemours & Co. v. The Glidden Company, United States District Court for the Eastern District of New York. In Equity No. 5544, Sept. 1932. Cited hereafter as Glidden Suit.

11 Zintl, *History*, p. 46, and Flaherty, "Viscolac – A New Economical Lacquer," *Du Pont Magazine* 26 (Mar.–Apr. 1922): 5, 12.

12 Harry C. Mougey to G. R. Downs, Feb. 24, 1922, GM Suit, DTE DP200.

13 On GM and its paint problem, see Stuart Leslie, *Boss Kettering* (New York: Columbia University Press, 1983), pp. 191–4. On the GM paint committee, see F. O. Clements et al., "Report of Paint and Enamel Committee of General Motors Corporation," Aug. 22, 1923, GM Suit, DTE GM113.

14 M. J. Callahan, "The Development of Duco Type Lacquers," *Journal of the Chemical Industry* (Aug. 31, 1928): 232–9, and H. C. Mougey to F. O. Clements, "Du Pont Enamels," June 19, 1922, GM Suit, DTE GM267.

15 Zintl, *History*, p. 47.

16 Flaherty Testimony, GM Suit, TR7653-57.

17 On the panels for testing, see J. J. Moosman to H. C. Mougey, Mar. 14, 1922, GM Suit, DTE DP202, and F. O. Clements to Car Division Managers, "Minutes of Second Meeting of the Committee Appointed to Study Enameling and Varnish Drying Practices," Mar. 22, 1922, GM Suit, DTE DP202. For Flaherty's discussion with Kettering, see Flaherty Testimony, GM Suit, TR7692.

18 William P. Allen to the Executive Committee, "Relations with the General Motors Corporation," Feb. 12, 1923, GM Suit, PD, pp. 1953–4. On Hitt's improvement, see Glidden Suit Testimony, p. 47, and U.S. Patent number 1,710,453.

19 Allen, "Relations," p. 1954.

20 Herman L. Weckler Testimony, GM Suit, TR8004-53.

21 F. O. Clements to Car Division Managers, "Minutes of Meeting of the Committee Appointed to Study Enameling and Varnish Drying Practices," Jan. 29, 1923, GM Suit, PD, 2d Series, pp. 1224–31.

22 Allen, "Relations," pp. 1953–68.

23 H. H. Rice to F. O. Clements, Feb. 28, 1923, GM Suit, PD, p. 1994.

24 F. O. Clements to A. P. Sloan, June 20, 1923, GM Suit, PD, pp. 2046–8.

25 On the process of finishing automobiles, see W. L. Carver, "Labor Costs Halved by Use of Duco in Finishing Oakland Bodies," *Automotive Industries* (Sept. 13, 1913): 521–6. The comment on the weakest links in the system is in H. C. Mougey to Murphy Varnish & Co., Aug. 22, 1922, GM Suit, DTE DP203.

26 Callahan, "The Development of Duco Type Lacquers."

27 Clements to Sloan, June 20, 1923, and Clements, "Report of Paint and Enamel Committee."
28 F. O. Clements to A. P. Sloan, Nov. 29, 1923, GM Suit, PD, p. 2155.
29 H. C. Mougey to W. P. Allen, Nov. 26, 1923, GM Suit, PD, p. 2241.
30 A. P. Sloan to W. P. Allen, Feb. 4, 1924, GM Suit, PD, p. 2278.
31 Leslie, *Boss Kettering*, p. 193.
32 J. J. Moosman to E. M. Flaherty, "Fisher Body Corporation," June 6, 1924, Acc. 1850.
33 Sales statistics for Duco are from Glidden Suit, Plaintiff's Exhibit PE16. The profit figures and the 1928 sales volume are from "Reports to Board of Directors" in Acc. 1517, Box 20. Company statistics are from *Du Pont Company Annual Report 1928*.
34 Report to Board of Directors, Jan. 1924, Acc. 1517, Box 20.
35 N. P. Wescott to F. Sparre, "Proper Functions of Flint and Parlin Divisions with Respect to Viscolac and Duco Enamels," Oct. 30, 1922, Acc. 1662, Box 20.
36 Ibid.
37 Zintl, *History*, p. 81.
38 In 1923 the Paint Department requested that the central Chemical Department take over its chemical control work. (EC Minutes, Oct. 10, 1923.) Not until 1927 would the department establish the Central Technical Laboratory at its Philadelphia plant (Zintl, *History*, pp. 82–3).
39 Charles M. A. Stine to the Executive Committee, Jan. 27, 1926, and Jan. 20, 1927, Acc. 1784, and Zintl, *History*, pp. 84–7.
40 Williams Haynes, *American Chemical Industry: A History* (New York: Van Nostrand, 1945–54), vol. 4, pp. 358–9.
41 Stine, Jan. 20, 1927, and Charles M. A. Stine to the Executive Committee, Jan. 31, 1928, Acc. 1784.
42 Charles M. A. Stine to the Executive Committee, Jan. 15, 1930, Acc. 1784.
43 In 1941, Du Pont's Dulux finish would be used on 75 percent of refrigerators, 60 percent of kitchen cabinets, 35 percent of washing machines, and 90 percent of metal signs (Zintl, *History*, p. 94).
44 William P. Allen to Fin Sparre, "Paint Study," Dec. 13, 1926, Acc. 1662, Box 32. EC Minutes, April 2 and Aug. 27, 1930.
45 "185,000,000 Gallons of Paint," p. 70.
46 C. R. Mudge to "A" Bonus Committee, [Duco Patent], March 1, 1934, Special Compensation Files.
47 In the reissue, Du Pont removed the following statement from the patent: "My new solutions are also distinguished from pyroxylin solutions of the prior art by the presence of a derivative of a viscosity-reducer of the character above described, the viscosity-reducer itself having been changed or decomposed during the reduction period." (U.S. Patent number 1,629,999 and U.S. Patent Re. 16,803.) Although not part of the formal claims, the implication of this statement was that the patent only applied to low-viscosity lacquers made with a viscosity reducer. By this time, the preferred method did not use any viscosity-reducing chemicals, just heat and pressure.
48 Mudge, [Duco Patent].
49 Zintl, *History*, p. 52.
50 Brief for the Defendant, Glidden Suit, pp. 40–2.

51 Zintl, *History*, pp. 52–3. Du Pont's market share comes from "Approximate Percent of the United States Market Enjoyed By Du Pont Products," GM Suit, PD, p. 3879.

52 William Richter to W. S. Carpenter, Jr., "Duco Suit," June 22, 1932, Acc. 1813, Box 13; and Brief for the Defendant, Glidden Suit.

53 M. J. Callahan to E. M. Flaherty, "The Glidden–Duco Suit," July 1, 1932, Acc. 1813, Box 13; and Brief for the Plaintiff, Glidden Suit.

54 The quote from the official decision of the court was transcribed by James K. Hunt, who saw it in the *U.S. Patent Quarterly* 18 (July–Sept. 1933): 242–3, Acc. 1410, Box 5.

55 Opinion of the Court, U.S. Circuit Court of Appeals, 2nd Circuit, Glidden Suit.

56 Zintl, *History*, pp. 53–4.

57 "185,000,000 Gallons of Paint," p. 78.

58 Mudge, [Duco Patent].

59 Haynes estimated that Du Pont's Duco royalties ran between $1 million and $2 million per year. Haynes, *American Chemical Industry: A History*, vol. 5, p. 348. A 1934 Du Pont report predicted that they would be in the range of $400,000 a year (Mudge, [Duco Patent]).

60 The initial plant cost $2.5 million. Comparative figures for Dulux were $950,000 for R&D and $1.8 million for a plant (James K. Hunt, "Supplementary Statement on 'Dulux' Synthetic Resin Enamels," July 21, 1954, Acc. 1410, Box 5.)

61 George F. Baldwin, *History of the Du Pont Paint Business, 1947–1961* (n.p.:n.p., 1962), Acc. 1850.

62 "185,000,000 Gallons of Paint," p. 70.

63 Zintl, *History*, p. 103, and Baldwin, *History*.

Chapter 7. Research Efficiency: The Organic Chemicals Department

1 The name change is noted in *Du Pont Company Annual Report 1931*. The departmental sales figures for 1930 and 1931 are in Charles M. A. Stine to the Executive Committee, "Research Expenditures," July 12, 1932, Acc. 1784. Statistics on dye sales and profits are in Reports to the Board of Directors, Acc. 1517, Box 20.

2 "Approximate Percent of United States Market Enjoyed By Du Pont Products," GM Suit, PD, p. 3879.

3 Orchem also introduced a wide range of organic chemicals, including rubber-processing chemicals, synthetic camphor, alcohol sulfate detergents, petroleum chemicals, water repellants, perfumes, and vitamin D. George Albee, "Orchem," *Du Pont Magazine* 39 (Mar.–Apr. 1945): 4–8.

4 William S. Calcott, "History of the Organic Chemicals Department," July 17, 1945, Acc. 1850.

5 Ibid.

6 Dye research in the 1930s is discussed in four annual reports, "Review of Chemical Research – Organic Chemicals Department," 1931 (Acc. 1813, Box 14), 1932 (Box 17), 1933 (Box 19), 1934 (Box 21). About a third of the work centered on the control and improvement of existing lines and two-thirds went into the development of modifications of dyes.

7 For a short biography of Bolton, see "Elmer K. Bolton," Acc. 1410, Box 63. A longer one is Robert M. Joyce, "Elmer Keiser Bolton, 1886–1969." *Biographical Memoirs* 54 (Washington, D.C.: National Academy Press, 1983), pp. 50–72.

8 He did his dissertation under Charles Loring Jackson on some iodine derivatives of organic compounds. Joyce, "Biographical Memoir," p. 52.

9 Roger Adams to Lammot du Pont, Dec. 6, 1944, Acc. 1662, Box 17.

10 Richard Willstätter, *From My Life: The Memoirs of Richard Willstätter*, trans. Lilli S. Hornig (New York: Benjamin, 1965), p. 233.

11 Elmer K. Bolton, interview by Alfred D. Chandler, Richmond D. Williams, and Norman B. Wilkinson, 1961, Acc. 1689.

12 Elmer K. Bolton, "Fundamental Research in the Chemical Industry" [an address delivered on the occasion of the presentation to Dr. Bolton of the Willard Gibbs Medal of the American Chemical Society's Chicago Section, May 21, 1954], Acc. 1850.

13 Elmer K. Bolton, "Research Efficiency," July 16, 1920, Acc. 1784.

14 Bolton interview.

15 Willis F. Harrington, undated and untitled memorandum, Acc. 1813, Box 20.

16 Elmer K. Bolton to J. Warren Kinsman, Nov. 23, 1931, PPD Files.

17 Elmer K. Bolton, "Certain Phases of Research Work," Jan. 18, 1929, Acc. 1662, Box 17.

18 Julian W. Hill Interview.

19 Bolton, "Certain Phases."

20 Willis F. Harrington to Roger Adams, Oct. 14, 1941, Acc. 1813, Box 34.

21 Reports to Board of Directors, Acc. 1517, Box 20.

22 Pierre S. du Pont to Irénée du Pont, "Doping of Fuel," March 24, 1922, LMSS, Series A, File 624, Box 1.

23 Pierre S. du Pont, "Memorandum of Visit to Dayton with Mr. Irénée du Pont," July 6, 1922, LMSS, Series A, File 624, Box 1.

24 Kettering's visit is noted in N. P. Wescott to Fin Sparre, "Origins and Early History of the Tetraethyl Lead Business," June 9, 1936, Exhibit B, "Chronological Outline of Tetraethyl Lead Development," GM Suit GTE 773. His proposal that Du Pont manufacture 100 gallons per day is in Pierre S. du Pont, "Fuel Dope," July 12, 1922, LMSS, Series A, File 624, Box 1. The visit to Dayton is noted in William S. Calcott, "Tetraethyl Lead," n.d., Acc. 1850.

25 Calcott's obituary is in *Chambers Works News* 16 (Feb. 29, 1952), Acc. 1850. Bolton's comment is from the Bolton interview.

26 Calcott, "Tetraethyl Lead."

27 W. F. Harrington to C. F. Kettering, Sept. 12, 1922, GM Suit, DTE GM72. The decision to go ahead with the 100-gallon-per-day plant was made at a conference between Kettering, Midgley, and Harrington. "Informal Progress Report," Sept. 18, 1922, GM Suit, PD, pp. 1875–7.

28 Calcott, "Tetraethyl Lead." The death was noted in N. P. Wescott to Fin Sparre, "Origins and Early History of the Tetraethyl Lead Business," June 9, 1936. Exhibit "D," "Deaths from T.E.L. Poisoning – Number, Sequence, Location," GM Suit, GTE 774. On the pressure to start up the plant, see "Tetra Ethyl Lead Poisoning," Feb. 9, 1924, Acc. 1615, Box 11.

29 C. Chester Ahlum, "Thirty-Nine Years with Du Pont," May 1, 1947, Acc. 1850.

30 E. Krause to George Calingaert, Nov. 30, 1922, GM Suit, DTE GM254. The

assistant director of the MIT Research Laboratory of Applied Chemistry sent this letter to Midgley. (Walter G. Whitman to Thomas Midgley, Jr., Dec. 18, 1922, GM Suit, DTE GM253.)

31 Lynwood Bryant, "The Problem of Knock in Gasoline Engines," *Regional Economic History Center Working Papers* 3, no. 4 (1980): 43.

32 Wescott, "Origins."

33 Wescott, "Origins," Exhibit "D."

34 Alfred P. Sloan to Charles F. Kettering, June 23, 1924, GM Suit, DTE GM82. Irénée's letter is quoted in Wescott, "Origins." Du Pont nominated Dr. A. K. Smith to the committee. (Willis F. Harrington to Alfred P. Sloan, "Proposed Experts' Committee to Develop Additional Information Relative to Tetra Ethyl Lead," June 30, 1924, GM Suit, PD, 2d series, pp. 1541–42.)

35 On Standard's chlorine process, see Wescott, "Origins." On the use of ethylene dibromide in TEL, see Leslie, *Boss Kettering*, p. 168.

36 Alfred P. Sloan to Irénée du Pont, June 26, 1924, GM Suit, PD, 2d series, pp. 1527–8.

37 Pierre S. du Pont to Charles F. Kettering, June 24, 1924, GM Suit, PD, 2nd series, pp. 1533–4; and Pierre S. du Pont to Alfred P. Sloan, June 25, 1924, GM Suit, PD, 2d series, pp. 1535–6.

38 Wescott, "Origins."

39 Willis F. Harrington to the "A" Bonus Committee, [Tetraethyllead], March 26, 1927, Special Compensation Files.

40 Wescott, "Origins."

41 Ibid.

42 James McEvoy to Alfred P. Sloan, Oct. 31, 1924, GM Suit, PD, p. 2599.

43 Alfred P. Sloan to James McEvoy, Nov. 11, 1924, GM Suit, PD, pp. 2607–9.

44 Wescott, "Origins."

45 Calcott, "Tetraethyl Lead."

46 Alfred P. Sloan to Irénée du Pont, Dec. 12, 1924, GM Suit, PD, pp. 2621–3.

47 Charles K. Weston to H. G. Haskell, April 1, 1925, GM Suit, PD, 2d series, pp. 1664–8.

48 On the contract, see Irénée du Pont to Thomas Midgley, Jr., April 2, 1925, GM Suit, PD, p. 2757. The quoted passage is from Irénée du Pont to Thomas Midgley, Jr., April 9, 1925, GM Suit, PD, p. 2761.

49 Wescott, "Origins."

50 George A. Brooks, "Extract from Minutes of Meeting of the Executive Committee of General Motors Corporation Duly Held on the 21st Day of October, 1925," GM Suit, PD, pp. 2889–90.

51 Wescott, "Origins."

52 *Du Pont Company Annual Report 1948.*

53 W. D. Humphrey to Fin Sparre, "Du Pont Refrigerants – A Comparative Study of Our Activities in this Field and of the Progress of the Industry as a Whole," March 30, 1931, II, 2, Box 1036.

54 *New York Times*, May 16, 1929.

55 Humphrey, "Du Pont Refrigerants."

56 Leslie, *Boss Kettering*, pp. 217–24.

57 E. F. Johnson and E. R. Godfrey, "Report on Operations of Kinetic Chemicals, Inc. from 1930 through 1943," October 1944, GM Suit, PD, pp. 8585–617.

58 Johnson and Godfrey, "Report."

59　Ibid. Du Pont also conducted its own tests. H. L. Miner to Willis F. Harrington, "Comparative Tests to Determine Fire, Toxicity, and Irritant Characteristics of Well Known Refrigerants," Oct. 20, 1931, Acc. 1813, Box 9.

60　Johnson and Godfrey, "Report."

61　Refrigerator sales are given in *Statistical Abstract of the United States*, 1975, p. 695. Freon sales are in Johnson and Godfrey, "Report," Table 5.

62　"Monomers and the Man: The Origin of a Legend," *Journal of Teflon* 4, no. 3, (1964): 2–7. This article includes a reproduction of Plunkett's laboratory notebook page.

63　Elley interview.

64　D. W. Jayne to Fin Sparre, Sept. 20, 1930, Acc. 1813, Box 5.

65　Ibid. Sparre conveyed similar views directly to the Executive Committee in a letter of Sept. 19, 1930, Acc. 1813, Box 5.

66　Development Department to Executive Committee, Oct. 31, 1930, Acc. 1813, Box 5.

67　For biographical information on Gubelmann, see *American Men of Science*, 7th ed. (1944) and Willstätter, *From My Life*, p. 234. See also P. J. Wingate, *Colorful Du Pont Company* (Wilmington, Del.: Serendipity Press, 1982), pp. 89–91, and "U.S. Patents of Ivan Gubelmann," Imprints Collection, Hagley Museum and Library.

68　On Gubelmann's role with the camphor plant, see "Camphor in U.S.A.," *Du Pont Magazine* 35 (Mar. 1941): 8–11, 24.

69　Wingate, *Colorful Du Pont Company*, p. 90.

70　Du Pont Company Organization Charts, Imprints Collection, Hagley Museum and Library.

71　Wingate, *Colorful Du Pont Company*, pp. 90–1. Biographical information on Tinker is found in "J. M. Tinker Retires after Distinguished Lab Career," *Chambers Works News* 26 (Mar. 1, 1962), pp. 1–2, Acc. 1850.

72　Wingate, *Colorful Du Pont Company*, pp. 91, 93–5, 97. Biographical information on Stallman is found in "Well-Known Dye Scientist Retires at 65," *Chambers Works News* 23 (Feb. 1, 1961), Acc. 1850, and *American Men of Science*, 9th ed. (1955).

73　Herman Schroeder telephone interview with David A. Hounshell.

Chapter 8. New Fibers and Films for a New Era:
The Rayon Department

1　D. C. Coleman, *Courtaulds: An Economic and Social History*, vol. 2, *Rayon* (Oxford: Clarendon Press, 1969), pp. 4–22. On the uses of Chardonnet artificial silk, see pp. 61–2.

2　Fin Sparre to the Executive Committee, "Proposed Utilization of Excess Plant Capacities," Dec. 30, 1916, GM Suit, PD, p. 336.

3　Coleman, *Courtaulds*, vol. 2, pp. 105–8, 111–13. Courtaulds had wanted to have a plant in America because Congress was about to impose a 30 percent ad valorem tariff on rayon.

4　Fin Sparre to the Executive Committee, "Progress Report – Excess Plant Utilization," Sept. 15, 1916, Acc. 1850. See also Coleman, *Courtaulds*, vol. 2, pp. 146–7.

5 Fin Sparre to R. R. M. Carpenter, "Progress Report [on Excess Plant Utilization]," Apr. 20, 1918, GM Suit, PD, p. 659.
6 Ibid.
7 Ferdinand Schulze, revised and enlarged from a manuscript prepared by Roy Soukup, *The Technical Division of the Rayon Department, 1920–1951* (Wilmington, Del.: Du Pont, 1952), p. 3.
8 EC Minutes, Nov. 19, Dec. 23, 27, 1919, and Apr. 5, 12, 1920, and Schulze, *Technical Division*, p. 5.
9 On Yerkes, see Acc. 1410, Box 63. Yerkes's trip to Europe is noted in EC Minutes, Apr. 12, 1920.
10 Schulze, *Technical Division*, pp. 3, 127–8.
11 The spinning process description comes from Samuel Hollander, *The Sources of Efficiency* (Cambridge, Mass.: MIT Press, 1965), pp. 30–1. The finishing steps are outlined in Schulze, *Technical Division*, p. 132.
12 On sales volume and price, see Schulze, *Technical Division*, p. 5. For return on investment, see Stocking and Mueller, "The Cellophane Case and the New Competition," *American Economic Review* 45 (Mar. 1955): 62.
13 *Historical Statistics of the United States*, pp. 900–1.
14 On rayon and fashion in the 1920s, see C. H. Ward-Jackson, *A History of Courtaulds* (London: Curwen Press, 1941), pp. 133–45.
15 S. L. Johnston, "The Rise of Rayon," *Du Pont Magazine* 19 (Aug. 1925): 10.
16 Schulze, *Technical Division*, pp. 5, 129–31.
17 Hollander, *Sources of Efficiency*, pp. 185–8.
18 Schulze, *Technical Division*, p. 127.
19 On Rocker, see Acc. 1771, Box 6.
20 Schulze, *Technical Division*, pp. 61–2, 127, 131.
21 Ibid., pp. 61–75.
22 On Benger, see *American Men of Science*, 7th ed. (1944), p. 129; and Acc. 1771, Box 6.
23 On Gladding, see Acc. 1193, Box 6.
24 On Lee, see Acc. 1771, Box 6.
25 Development Department, "Annual Research Expenditures in Categories B, C, D, and E. Years: 1930 to 1950 Inclusive," Apr. 30, 1946, Acc. 1814, Box 5.
26 Schulze, *Technical Division*, p. 131.
27 Hollander, *Sources of Efficiency*, pp. 31, 174–5.
28 Schulze, *Technical Division*, p. 132.
29 Roy Soukup, *The Rayon Technical Division* (n.p.: n.p., 1947), p. 30, Acc. 1771, Box 6.
30 Hollander, *Sources of Efficiency*, pp. 189–207.
31 Schulze, *Technical Division*, pp. 135–38.
32 Joseph Leeming, *Rayon: The First Man-Made Fiber* (Brooklyn: Chemical Publishing, 1950), pp. 84–5.
33 Schulze, *Technical Division*, pp. 128–9.
34 Leeming, *Rayon*, pp. 86–8, and Jesse W. Markam, *Competition in the Rayon Industry* (Cambridge, Mass.: Harvard University Press, 1952), p. 33.
35 On uses for rayon, see *The Story of Rayon* (New York: The Viscose Company, 1929), pp. 37–8, and Alex Sommaripa, "Beauty ... Softness ... Economy," *Du Pont Magazine* 21 (Apr. 1927): 7. On rayon consumption, see Markam, *Competition*, p. 30. On rayon dresses, see Ann Mullany, "The Fashion Significance

of Rayon," in *Rayon and Synthetic Yarns* (Brooklyn: Brooklyn Museum, 1936), pp. 25–30.

36 Markam, *Competition*, pp. 178–80.

37 Ibid., pp. 21–2.

38 Walter S. Carpenter, Jr., to the Finance Committee, "The Rayon Industry," Sept. 15, 1933, II, 2, Box 818.

39 Coleman, *Courtaulds*, vol. 2, pp. 401–6.

40 L. A. Yerkes to W. S. Carpenter, Jr., July 10, 1936, II, 2, Box 819.

41 Schulze, *Technical Division*, p. 135.

42 W. H. Charch to E. B. Benger, July 26, 1926, II, 4, Box 97. The problem of low wet strength is detailed in A. E. Jury to L. A. Yerkes, ca. 1924, GM Suit, PD, 2d series, pp. 1447–8.

43 E. B. Benger to Hamilton Bradshaw, Feb. 21, 1928, Acc. 1784.

44 Schulze, *Technical Division*, p. 135.

45 E. K. Gladding to B. M. May, June 19, 1931, II, 2, Box 818.

46 W. H. Bradshaw to L. A. Yerkes, Nov. 24, 1933, GM Suit, PD, pp. 5143–4.

47 A. Hershberger to E. K. Gladding, Apr. 26, 1935, PR Records, 1935, File P-15.

48 H. H. Parker to G. P. Hoff, "Akron Conferences on Tire Cord with Goodyear, with Firestone, and with Goodrich Tire and Rubber Company," July 20, 1934, GM Suit, PD, p. 5298.

49 E. K. Gladding to H. J. White, Jan. 13, 1932, GM Suit, PD, pp. 4790–1.

50 F. M. Pralatowski to B. M. May, "Cordura Yarn," Apr. 22, 1935, PR Records, 1935, File P-15.

51 W. D. R. Straughn, "The Place of Rayon in Tires," speech delivered on January 9, 1946, before the American Association of Textile Technologists, Acc. 1193, Box 5.

52 "Annual Dollar Volume of Sales of Cellophane," United States v. E. I. du Pont de Nemours and Company, Civil Action No. 1216, DE 537. Cited hereafter as Cellophane Suit. Defendant Exhibits, Government Exhibits, and Transcript will be designated by DE, GE, and TR, respectively.

53 For cellophane's return on investment, see Stocking and Mueller, "Cellophane Case," p. 59. Company sales and profit figures were taken from the *Du Pont Company Annual Report 1938*.

54 S. L. Johnston, "Selling with Cellophane," *Du Pont Magazine* 18 (Dec. 1924): 10.

55 This expression is used in Du Pont Company, *Cellophane 25th Anniversary, 1924–1949* (Wilmington, Del.: Du Pont, 1949); Pamphlet Collection, Hagley Museum and Library.

56 The company's management had been aware of the new product as early as 1914, when it appeared that cellophane might be a competitor for celluloid plastics, which the company was considering manufacturing. Cellophane had just begun to be manufactured in France at this time. (Paul Mueller to R. R. M. Carpenter, Mar. 30, 1914, Acc. 228, File ID-30.)

57 On the early development of viscose films, see C. H. Ward-Jackson, *The Cellophane Story: Origins of a British Industrial Group* (Bridgwater, Eng.: British Cellophane, Ltd., 1977), pp. 9–21. According to legend, Brandenberger was disgusted with the filthy tablecloths he found in French cafes and wished to

make one that could be wiped clean between patrons. For the dirty linen legend, see "Just All About Cellophane," *Fortune* (Feb. 1932): 74.

58 W. W. Richards to F. Sparre, "Cellophane," Feb. 17, 1944, Cellophane Suit, GE 1.

59 Fin Sparre to the Executive Committee, "Cellophane," Apr. 14, 1923, Cellophane Suit, GE 392. On Spruance, see *Du Pont Company Annual Report 1934*, p. 29. Twenty-four years earlier, Spruance had accompanied Arthur D. Little to Europe to investigate the viscose process. ("Report to Daniel C. Spruance, Esq. on the Technical Development of Viscose on the Continent of Europe and Great Britain," Oct. 10, 1899, Acc. 414.)

60 "Howard J. White Notes," June 27, 1945, II, 2, Box 618.

61 Sparre, "Cellophane."

62 Henry Ernst Testimony, Cellophane Suit, TR 5357-62.

63 Howard White to F. Sparre, [1923], II, 2, Box 798.

64 Ward-Jackson, *Cellophane Story*, pp. 37–8 and Sparre, "Cellophane."

65 W. C. Spruance to F. Sparre, Jan. 26, 192[3], II, 2, Box 798.

66 Sparre, "Cellophane."

67 Ibid.

68 George Rocker to F. Sparre, "Our File 87-CR," Jan. 9, 1923, and William S. Pritchard to F. R. Squair, Jan. 22, 1923, II, 2, Box 798.

69 Sparre, "Cellophane."

70 "Du Pont–La Cellophane Agreement," June 23, 1923, Cellophane Suit, GE 1001.

71 Schulze, *Technical Division*, pp. 47–9.

72 Ernst Testimony, TR 5343-62.

73 "Extract from Report From Mr. L. A. Yerkes, President, to Board of Directors," Du Pont Cellophane Company, Inc., Feb. 23, 1924, II, 2, Box 505.

74 Ernest B. Benger Testimony, Cellophane Suit, TR 5426.

75 James Piani, "That New Wood Product – Cellophane," *Du Pont Magazine* 17 (Dec. 1923): 10. On Piani, see Ward-Jackson, *Cellophane Story*, pp. 37–9.

76 On Benz, see Ward-Jackson, *Cellophane Story*, p. 39.

77 L. A. Yerkes to Board of Directors, Du Pont Cellophane Company, "General Situation," May 27, 1924, II, 2, Box 505.

78 "Some Remarks Made at Meeting of Board of Directors, Du Pont Cellophane, Inc., Held on Thursday, November 20, 1924," Cellophane Suit, DE 444.

79 "Memorandum of Some Remarks Made at Meeting of Board of Directors, Du Pont Cellophane Company, Inc., Thursday Dec. 11, 1924," Cellophane Suit, DE 337.

80 L. A. Yerkes to Board of Directors, Du Pont Cellophane Company, Jan. 14, 1925, Cellophane Suit, GE 460.

81 L. A. Yerkes to Board of Directors, Du Pont Cellophane Company, Jan. 17, 1927, Cellophane Suit, GE 481.

82 L. A. Yerkes to W. S. Carpenter, Jr., "Cellophane Forecast," Dec. 18, 1928, II, 2, Box 818.

83 Richards, "Cellophane."

84 One economist calculated that after 1932, to achieve production costs competitive with Du Pont, a prospective entrant would have had to build a plant that would have increased domestic production capacity by 40 percent. Charles

Parrish Blitch, "Product Innovation and Price Discrimination: A Case Study of Cellophane" (PhD diss., University of North Carolina, 1966), pp. 86–94.

85 Sparre, "Cellophane."

86 C. F. Brown to J. F. Hatt, "Converter Policy," Apr. 28, 1941, Cellophane Suit, GE 5047.

87 "Just All about Cellophane," pp. 76, 101.

88 On lollypops, see E. B. Benger to O. F. Benz, "Sticking of Cellophane to Lollypops," Oct. 17, 1924, Cellophane Suit, DE 391A. On knives and cigars, see Schulze, *Technical Division*, p. 140. On the National Biscuit Company tests, see O. F. Benz to E. B. Benger, "Our File 1107 VCC," July 10, 1924, Cellophane Suit, DE 388A.

89 E. B. Benger to O. F. Benz, "National Biscuit Company – Your Letter July 10th," July 11, 1924, Cellophane Suit, DE 389A.

90 L. A. Yerkes to the Board of Directors, Du Pont Cellophane Company, Aug. 19, 1924, II, 2, Box 505.

91 Benger Testimony, Cellophane Suit, TR 5426-39.

92 E. B. Benger to M. Du Pont Lee, "Waterproof Cellophane," Sept. 25, 1924, Cellophane Suit, DE 393.

93 Herbert T. Pratt, "William Hale Charch," in Wyndham D. Miles, ed., *American Chemists and Chemical Engineers* (Washington: American Chemical Society, 1976), pp. 76–7. The story about the hiring of Charch is from Robert E. Ellsworth, "Personality: W. Hale Charch," *Modern Textiles Magazine* 34 (July 1953): 44.

94 R. E. Cullen to M. D. Lee, May 21, 1924, Cellophane Suit, DE 392.

95 Schulze, *Technical Division*, pp. 140–1.

96 As a reward for his success, Charch received one of the largest individual bonuses in the history of the Du Pont Company. "Moistureproof Cellophane – 1929 'A'-Bonus Recommendation," Feb. 10, 1930, Special Compensation Files.

97 "Moistureproof Cellophane – 1929 'A'-Bonus Recommendation."

98 Steven M. Spencer to J. K. Hunt, July 13, 1943, Cellophane Suit, GE 2467. The U.S. patent is number 1,737,187.

99 Richards, "Cellophane."

100 E. B. Benger to J. E. Brandenberger, June 4, 1928, Cellophane Suit, DE 395.

101 "Annual Dollar Volume of Sales of Cellophane."

102 The forecast is in B. M. May to W. S. Carpenter, Jr., Dec. 19, 1928, II, 2, Box 818. The actual sales figures are given in "Annual Dollar Volume of Sales of Cellophane."

103 Ernst Testimony, TR 5365-73.

104 Blitch, "Product Innovation," p. 160.

105 E. K. Bolton to L. A. Yerkes, "Conversation with Dr. J. G. Davidson, General Sales Manager, C + C Chemicals Corp.," Jan. 18, 1932, Cellophane Suit, GE 4181.

106 On the other patent applications see J. E. Hatt to W. S. Carpenter, Jr., "Summary Moistureproof Cellophane Patent Situation," Aug. 26, 1930, Cellophane Suit, GE 2469. Yerkes's report on defensive research is in L. A. Yerkes to Board of Directors, Du Pont Cellophane Company, Inc., Jan. 22, 1934, Cellophane Suit, GE 488.

107 J. E. Hatt to the Executive Committee, "Competitive Moistureproof Material," Feb. 18, 1931, Cellophane Suit, GE 2482; and L. A. Yerkes, "Cellophane Competitive Situation," July 13, 1931, Cellophane Suit, GE 2483.

108 W. S. Pritchard to B. M. May, "Sylvania Suit," Aug. 4, 1932, Cellophane Suit, GE 2811.

109 Stocking and Mueller, "The Cellophane Case," p. 43.

110 Blitch, "Product Innovation," p. 162.

111 Ibid., pp. 152–67.

112 Ralph C. Russell Testimony, Cellophane Suit, TR 6476–88.

113 On the engineering consulting service, see Russell Testimony, TR 6488. The packaging development service is mentioned in "Competitive Imports: 1927–1928–1929," [1930], Cellophane Suit, GE431.

114 Robert R. Smith obituary, *Wilmington News Journal*, June 1, 1982.

115 Robert R. Smith Testimony, Cellophane Suit, TR 5704-6.

116 Smith Testimony, TR 5676-88; and Du Pont Company, *Selling in Seconds* (Wilmington, Del.: Du Pont Company, 1938), Pamphlet Collection, Hagley Museum and Library.

117 C. B. Larrabee, "When, Why, and How to Package," in "The Importance of Visibility in Modern Packages," Brief Excerpts of the Speeches Delivered at the Recent Packaging Convention of the American Management Association, ca. 1933, II, 2, Box 81.

118 *Cellophane: 25th Anniversary, 1924–1949.*

119 Colby, "The Ten Most Beautiful Words," *Buffalo News*, July 11, 1940, in *Cellophane 25th Anniversary*, p. 7; Cole Porter, "You're the Top." Words and Music by Cole Porter. New York, Harm, Inc., 1974.

120 Yerkes made his recommendation to the board of directors on November 15, 1927. The minutes from that meeting were reprinted in Marian C. Lepper to Alma M. Cohn, "Pioneering Research on Rayon," April 17, 1930, PR Records, 1930, File P-100.

121 E. B. Benger to E. K. Gladding, Jan. 24, 1928, II, 4, Box 98; and E. B. Benger to H. Bradshaw, Feb. 21, 1928, Acc. 1784.

122 W. H. Charch to Russell M. Pickens, "The Technical Aspect of Pioneering Research on Rayon," Jan. 10, 1929, PR Records, 1929, File P-1.

123 W. H. Charch to Russell M. Pickens, "Pioneering Research on Synthetic Resins for Thread Forming," July 15, 1929, PR Records, 1929, File P-1.

124 G. P. Hoff to E. B. Benger, "Pioneering Research," July 17, 1929, PR Records, 1929, File P-1.

125 E. B. Benger to E. K. Gladding, "Synthetic Resins in Connection with Rayon and Cellophane," May 19, 1930, PR Records, 1930, File P-3.

126 E. B. Benger to H. Bradshaw, Jan. 28, 1930, Acc. 1784. Benger left the Rayon Company on July 6, 1930. See Benger chronology in Acc. 1771, Box 6.

127 Joseph F. Haskins to E. B. Benger, "The Study of Cellulose," Sept. 6, 1930, PR Records, 1930, File P-1.

128 Walter S. Carpenter, Jr., to L. A. Yerkes, Nov. 5, 1930, II, 2, Box 818.

129 W. H. Charch to E. K. Gladding, "Discussion of Basic Study for New Fibers, Fiber Materials, and Solutions," Sept. 21, 1933, PR Records, 1933, File P-9.

Chapter 9. From Nitrates to Nylon: The Ammonia Department

1   Du Pont invested about $30 million in ammonia and related technologies in about a decade. ("Permanent Investment – Eleven Largest Plants – Du Pont Company. As of August 31, 1937," Acc. 1813, Box 26.)

2   On the nitrogen problem, see Williams Haynes, *American Chemical Industry: A History* (New York: Van Nostrand, 1943–54), vol. 2, chaps. 6–12.

3   *Du Pont Annual Report 1918*, p. 8. Billion is 1,000 million.

4   "Nitrogen IV: We Hoped to Make Money," *Fortune* (Aug. 1932): 58.

5   On Du Pont's interest in the Haber-Bosch process, see F. C. Zeisberg, "The Haber Process of Synthesizing Ammonia," July 27, 1916, Acc. 1784.

6   On Williams, see Acc. 1410, Box 63, and "Roger Williams," Notes on interview by Alfred D. Chandler, Richmond D. Williams, and Norman B. Wilkinson, June 20, 1962, Acc. 1689.

7   Roger Williams to Hamilton Bradshaw, "Recent Developments Concerning the Haber Process," Nov. 21, 1919, Acc. 1784.

8   F. C. Zeisberg to Fin Sparre, "Ammonia Synthesis," Jan. 10, 1922, Acc. 1662, Box 16; and Fin Sparre to the Executive Committee, "Synthetic Ammonia – Claude Process," April 4, 1923, GM Suit, PD, pp. 1998–2004.

9   Sparre, "Synthetic Ammonia – Claude Process."

10   Roger Williams and F. C. Blake to Charles L. Reese, "Ammonia from Atmospheric Nitrogen," Acc. 1784, Box 5.

11   Fin Sparre to the Executive Committee, "Synthetic Ammonia," Feb. 14, 1924, GM Suit, PD, pp. 2296–316.

12   EC Minutes, July 9, 1924. On the details of the agreement, see Sparre, "Synthetic Ammonia."

13   Edward P. Bartlett, *The Chemical Division at the Du Pont Ammonia Department, 1924–1935* (n.p.: n.p., 1949), II, 2, Box 91. On Wardenberg, see Acc. 1410, Box 63.

14   On the recruitment of men from the Fixed Nitrogen Research Laboratory, see Tyler interview, Oct. 7, 1982, pp. 21–2. See also Bartlett, pp. 13, 15, 21, 23. For biographical details on Larson, Dodge, and Almquist, see *American Men of Science*, 6th ed. (1938).

15   Bartlett, *Chemical Division*, pp. 9–18, 28, 56.

16   Ibid., pp. 16, 29, 38, 56. By 1929, Du Pont had invested $15 million in the Belle plant (Bartlett, p. 45). In 1928, the Executive Committee appropriated $7 million for its expansion (Bartlett, p. 38). The difference between these figures places the 1928 investment at approximately $8 million.

17   The chemical reactions involved were: $CO + 3H_2 = CH_4 + H_2O$; $CO + 2H_2 = CH_3OH$. On the development of the Du Pont methanol process, see Bartlett, *Chemical Division*, pp. 18–20. On synthetic methanol, see Haynes, *American Chemical Industry*, vol. 4, chap. 11.

18   Bartlett, *Chemical Division*, pp. 18–19, 29–30.

19   Jasper E. Crane, "Development of the Synthetic Ammonia Industry in the United States," *Industrial and Engineering Chemistry* 22 (July 1930): 795–9.

20   "Nitrogen I: We Must Have It," *Fortune* (Aug. 1932): 48. The statistics are from Crane, "Development of Synthetic Ammonia," p. 796.

21   On Du Pont's plant capacity increases, see Bartlett, *Chemical Division*, pp. 29–30. For 1929 sales, see "Classification of Expenditures for Chemical Work –

Year 1930, Together with Total Expenditures for 1929," II, 2, Box 1035. The 1930 and 1931 sales and profit figures are from Charles M. A. Stine to the Executive Committee, "Research Expenditures," July 12, 1932, Acc. 1784.

22   Bartlett, *Chemical Division*, pp. 5–7.

23   "Classification of Expenditures." On personnel, see Bartlett, *Chemical Division*, p. 55, and Roger Williams to F. A. Wardenberg and Walter Dannenbaum, "Reduction in Chemical Division Expenditures," Sept. 9, 1931, II, 2, Box 1037.

24   Woodhouse interview, Oct. 11, 1982.

25   Report to Board of Directors, Acc. 1517, Box 20.

26   On the activities of the ammonia technical division, see J. A. Almquist et al., "Past, Present, and Projected Activities of the Chemical Department," Nov. 1930, Acc. 1784. On the sale of the contact hydrogen process to the Japanese, see Williams interview.

27   Williams interview and Almquist, "Past."

28   On Duus, see *American Men of Science*, 6th ed. (1938). For his development of methanol antifreeze, see Almquist, "Past," and Bartlett, *Chemical Division*, pp. 64–5.

29   For a survey of the products of the Ammonia Department, see J. F. T. Berliner, "A Story of Progress," *Du Pont Magazine* 31 (June 1937): 5–7, 24. On investment, see "Du Pont Investment in Largest Du Pont Plants," Nov. 7, 1940, Acc. 1813, Box 24.

Chapter 10. Du Pont R&D in the International Sphere

1   H. G. Haskell to Jasper E. Crane, July 10, 1923, United States v. Imperial Chemical Industries et al., Government Trial Exhibit 37. Government Trial Exhibits hereafter cited as GTE, followed by the exhibit number. Defendants' Trial Exhibits cited as DTE followed by the exhibit number.

2   Details about Du Pont's early international agreements are covered in Alfred D. Chandler, Jr., and Stephen Salsbury, *Pierre S. du Pont and the Making of the Modern Corporation* (New York: Harper & Row, 1971), pp. 169–200, 273, 299; W. J. Reader, *Imperial Chemical Industries* (London: Oxford University Press, 1970), vol. 1, pp. 159–61, 194–215; and Graham D. Taylor and Patricia E. Sudnik, *Du Pont and the International Chemical Industry* (Boston: Twayne, 1984), pp. 35–41.

3   The full agreement appears in GTE 3.

4   Jasper E. Crane, Memo of Conversation with Sir Harry McGowan, Sept. 19, 1923, GTE 43.

5   J. P. Laffey to H. G. Haskell, July 18, 1923, GTE 39. See also Minutes of Meeting Held at Nobel House, Apr. 29, 1924, GTE 48.

6   Note to the Executive Committee, Dec. 7, 1927, GTE 124.

7   Wendell R. Swint to Jasper E. Crane, Dec. 17, 1926, GTE 122; Reader, *Imperial Chemical Industries*, vol. 2, pp. 48–9.

8   Minutes of Foreign Relations Committee, Feb. 14, 1928, GTE 182.

9   J. K. Jenney to W. R. Swint, Mar. 23, 1928, GTE 188.

10   Minutes of Meeting..., Oct. 12, 1928, GTE 174.

11   Lammot du Pont to Sir Harry McGowan, Nov. 23, 1928, GTE 191; McGowan to du Pont, Jan. 4, 1929, GTE 192.

12 Meeting Held in Lammot du Pont's Office, Feb. 18, 1928, GTE 185.
13 See, e.g., the concerns of the Smokeless Powder Department in Agenda of Meeting..., GTE 184.
14 E. G. Robinson to Fin Sparre, Apr. 5, 1929, GTE 210.
15 Memorandum from Mr. Walker, Feb. 4, 1929, GTE 194.
16 Reader, *Imperial Chemical Industries*, vol. 2, p. 51.
17 Harry McGowan to Lammot du Pont, Apr. 29, 1929, GTE 163.
18 Reader, *Imperial Chemical Industries*, vol. 2, p. 51. We have found no such directive in Du Pont–related records.
19 See, e.g., G. W. White to Harry McGowan, Aug. 14, 1929, GTE 235.
20 Consolidated Minutes of Meetings of Subcommittee..., May 6, 7, 8, 10, 12, 13, and 14, 1929, GTE 219. For Fin Sparre's views, see Sparre, "Importance of ICI Relationship," presented at the chemical directors meeting, May 26–7, 1930, Acc. 1784.
21 First Meeting of Sub-Committee..., Mar. 4, 1929, GTE 205.
22 G. W. White to Harry McGowan, Aug. 14, 1929, GTE 235.
23 Ibid. The agreement was effective July 1, 1929.
24 Articles of Agreement,... Imperial Chemicals Industries... and E. I. du Pont de Nemours & Co., July 1, 1929. A copy is reprinted in Reader, *Imperial Chemical Industries*, vol. 2, pp. 506–13.
25 First Meeting of Sub-Committee..., Mar. 4, 1929, GTE 205.
26 Lord Melchett to the Management Board, June 20, 1929, GTE 641.
27 Articles of Agreement..., July 1, 1929.
28 G. P. Pollitt to the [ICI] Executive Committee, Nov. 2, 1929, GTE 567.
29 H. Greville Smith to G. P. Pollitt, Nov. 16, 1929, GTE 290. See also Smith to M. T. Sampson, Nov. 14, 1929, GTE 288.
30 C. M. A. Stine to W. R. Swint, Nov. 23, 1929, II, 2, Box 543; Confirmation of Outgoing Cable from H. Greville Smith, GTE 289.
31 H. Greville Smith to G. P. Pollitt, Nov. 16, 1929; Confirmation of Outgoing Cable, GTE 289.
32 Smith to Sampson, Nov. 14, 1929, GTE 288.
33 F. A. Freeth to ICI, Ltd. (N.Y.), Aug. 30, 1929, attached to H. G. Smith to C. M. A. Stine, Sept. 13, 1929, II, 2, Box 548.
34 C. M. A. Stine to A. P. Tanberg, Dec. 30, 1929, II, 2, Box 530.
35 C. M. A. Stine to F. A. Freeth, Jan. 10, 1930, II, 2, Box 530; C. M. A. Stine to R. L. Kramer, Jan. 7, 1930, II, 2, Box 548. See also C. M. A. Stine to G. B. Taylor, Jan. 8, 1930, II, 2, Box 548; C. M. A. Stine to Wm. Rintoul, Jan. 15, 1930, II, 2, Box 548; Minutes of General Managers' Meeting, Feb. 17, 1930, Acc. 1813, Box 3.
36 C. M. A. Stine to A. Michels, Feb. 19, 1930, II, 2, Box 548.
37 C. M. A. Stine to Executive Committee, Annual Report – 1929, Jan. 15, 1930, Acc. 1784.
38 J. K. Jenney, Rules re. Correspondence and Exchange of Technical data..., Jan. 3, 1930, attached to W. F. Harrington to Executive Committee, Feb. 13, 1930, Acc. 1813, Box 4; J. K. Jenney to T. E. Doramus, Jan. 3, 1930, II, 2, Box 534; Minutes of the Executive Committee, Feb. 19, 1930.
39 J. Stuart Groves to E. G. Robinson, Summary for the Year 1935, Jan. 10, 1936, II, 2, Box 539. The records of the Foreign Relations Department at Hagley

Museum and Library are replete with documents showing the difficulty of exchanging reports.

40 L. G. Wise to H. P. Corson, May 20, 1935, II, 2, Box 534.

41 J. K. Jenney, "Mechanisms of Exchange of Information with ICI," June 16, 1930, Acc. 1784.

42 Ibid.

43 Sparre, "Importance of ICI Relationship."

44 Jenney, "Mechanisms of Exchange...."

45 The Records of the Foreign Relations Department at Hagley Museum and Library amply document the exchange of technical information via technical delegations. The Ammonia Department stationed John L. Brill at ICI for an extended period in 1929 and 1930. See E. K. Bolton to W. F. Harrington, Feb. 26, 1930, Acc. 1813, Box 4.

46 Sparre, "Importance of ICI Relationship."

47 P. Chorley to Mr. Demuth, Nov. 19, 1942, Government Rebuttal Exhibit 1374.

48 J. K. Jenney to H. W. Elley, July 11, 1930, II, 2, Box 543.

49 Foreign Relations Committee to H. W. Elley, July 10, 1930, II, 2, Box 543.

50 E. G. Robinson to C. J. T. Cronshaw, Aug. 26, 1930, II, 2, Box 539.

51 Lammot du Pont to Harry McGowan, Oct. 13, 1931, II, 2, Box 543; also in GTE 654.

52 Lammot du Pont to H. J. Mitchell, Jan. 14, 1937, GTE 683. The Chemical Department eradicated all reference to nylon from its quarterly reports on fundamental research that were sent to ICI as well as from other reports. See also E. B. Benger to H. Bradshaw, Jan. 16, 1935, DTE 1117; H. C. Haskell to E. K. Bolton et al., Dec. 30, 1936, DTE 1131; L. A. Yerkes to E. K. Bolton et al., Dec. 31, 1936, DTE 1132; H. Bradshaw to E. K. Bolton, May 12, 1937, DTE 1136. ICI used the word "hide" in the Chairman to Mr. Cushion, n.d., GTE 626.

53 L. G. Wise, Memorandum for Group Leaders, June 27, 1939, DTE 2151.

54 See, e.g., G. W. White to Harry McGowan, Sept. 3, 1937, GTE 426.

55 P. C. Allen to W. F. Lutyens, June 18, 1942, GTE 669.

56 Lord Melchett to J. E. Crane, Mar. 16, 1939, GTE 668.

57 J. E. Crane to Lord Melchett, Apr. 4, 1939; Melchett to Crane, April 26, 1939, GTE 668; Allen to Lutyens, June 18, 1942; Fin Sparre, Du Pont–ICI Relations, Sept. 17, 1942, GTE 671; W. R. Swint to E. J. Barnsley, Sept. 24, 1942, GTE 673.

58 C. H. Greenewalt to Alkali Group, ICI, May 6, 1940, GTE 1419; Allen to Lutyens, June 18, 1942.

59 L. A. Yerkes to J. K. Jenney, Mar. 16, 1943, II, 2, Box 1043-A.

60 I. L. Clifford and J. Ferguson, "Polythene Patents – Du Pont Policy," April 21, 1945, GTE 682.

61 Leonard S. Reich, "Research, Patents, and the Struggle to Control Radio: A Study of Big Business and the Use of Industrial Research," *Business History Review* 51 (1977): 208–35.

62 Clifford and Ferguson, "Polythene Patents – Du Pont Policy."

63 Ibid.

64 P. C. Allen, *Diary*, quoted in Reader, *Imperial Chemical Industries*, vol. 2, p. 433.

65   Reader, *Imperial Chemical Industries*, vol. 2, p. 432.

66   On the ICI side, see ibid., pp. 50, 432–3.

67   G. W. White to H. McGowan, Nov. 27, 1929, GTE 570; Francis Walker to G. W. White, Feb. 7, 1930, DTE 1434; White to Walker, Feb. 18, 1930, GTE 572.

68   G. W. White to F. Walker, Apr. 4, 1930, GTE 573.

69   Ibid.

70   J. K. Jenney, Memorandum, Apr. 24, 1930, II, 2, Box 539. See also Walker to White, Feb. 7, 1930.

71   W. Sheldon, Critical Annotations of Du Pont's List..., Oct. 16, 1930, DTE 1448. See also List of Processes Offered by ICI to Du Pont..., DTE 1445.

72   Francis Walker to C. J. T. Cronshaw, June 19, 1930, GTE 594. See also Walker to Cronshaw, Sept. 17, 1930, GTE 576.

73   Quoted in Reader, *Imperial Chemical Industries*, vol. 2, p. 433.

74   Ibid.

75   See, e.g., the following material relating to the first evaluation: Tabulation of Patents and Processes Offered by E. I. du Pont de Nemours & Co. to ICI..., GTE 290; Minutes of Meeting of Committee Appointed for the Evaluation..., Oct. 21, 22, and 23, 1930, GTE 579, 580, and 581, respectively; Francis Walker to C. J. T. Cronshaw, Oct. 24, 1930, GTE 582; Fin Sparre, Memorandum for Mr. Francis Walker, Oct. 29, 1930, GTE 583; S. P. Stotter, Evaluation of Processes, Nov. 10, 1930, GTE 584.

76   Fin Sparre to Executive Committee, Nov. 24, 1930, GTE 586.

77   The differentials were as follows: $110,100 to Du Pont for 1929–34; $32,200 to Du Pont for 1934–9; $216,900 to ICI for 1939–44; and $187,300 to Du Pont for 1944–8. L. W. B. Smith and Fin Sparre to Lammot du Pont, Apr. 29, 1936, DTE 1493; [?] to Lord McGowan and W. S. Carpenter, Jr., Oct. 18, 1945, DTE 1513; Wendell R. Swint to Executive Committee, May 6, 1946, DTE 1529; Wendell R. Swint and S. P. Leigh to Lord McGowan and W. S. Carpenter, Jr., May 17, 1946, DTE 1533; Wendell R. Swint to Executive Committee, Dec. 7, 1948, DTE 1550; Compensation Received by Du Pont from ICI..., DTE 2219.

78   W. R. Swint to F. A. Wardenburg et al., Nov. 2, 1933, II, 2, Box 543.

79   E. M. Flaherty to Wm. Richter, Nov. 9, 1933, attached to Wm. Richter to W. R. Swint, Nov. 14, 1933, II, 2, Box 543. See Swint's rough tabulation of the survey in the same accession and box.

80   F. A. Wardenburg to W. R. Swint, Nov. 13, 1933, II, 2, Box 543. Cf. J. Stuart Groves to E. G. Robinson, Nov. 14, 1933, II, 2, Box 543.

81   See, e.g., C. Dill to W. R. Swint, Nov. 20, 1933, and E. B. Benger to W. R. Swint, Nov. 21, 1933, II, 2, Box 543. See also the earlier discussion of the value to negative research in Minutes of Meeting of Committee Appointed for Evaluation..., Oct. 20, 1930, DTE 1449.

82   On this complex set of agreements, see Sheldon Hochheiser, *Rohm and Haas* (Philadelphia: University of Pennsylvania Press, 1986), pp. 76–7.

83   On the importance of the phthalocyanines, see P. J. Wingate, *The Colorful Du Pont Company* (Wilmington, Del.: Serendipity Press, 1982), p. 103. On ICI's development of this class of dyes, see the assessment of J. E. Cole, head of the Jackson Laboratory's miscellaneous dyes division, in Summary for the Year 1938, Interchange of Information..., II, 2, Box 540.

84 Reader, *Imperial Chemical Industries*, vol. 2, pp. 432–34.

85 W. R. Swint to General Managers et al., June 21, 1948, DTE 625. See also the cancelation agreement, June 30, 1948, DTE 624.

86 Minutes, Rayon Department Technical Division Staff Meeting of July 23, 1948, July 27, 1948, in PR Records, Box 180187.

87 Wingate, *Colorful Du Pont Company*, p. 190.

88 Minutes of the Executive Committee, Jan. 24, 1923.

89 [Leonard Yerkes?], The Dye Industry in Germany, [1919], Acc. 1662, Box 59.

90 F. W. Pickard to Executive Committee, April 14, 1923, attached to F. W. Pickard to J. J. Raskob, Apr. 14, 1923, Acc. 473, File 690, Box 2.

91 Quoted in Taylor and Sudnik, *Du Pont and the International Chemical Industry*, p. 106, from "Du Pont–IG Relationship," Feb. 1943, Papers of Roy Prewitt, Box 13, Records of the Federal Trade Commission, R.G. 122, National Archives, Washington.

92 W. S. Carpenter, Jr., to Lammot du Pont et al., May 10, 1929, Acc. 228, Series, H, VC-5. Du Pont's thinking is revealed in Minutes of Foreign Relations Committee, Feb. 14, 1928, GTE 182. See also E. G. Robinson to Fin Sparre, Apr. 5, 1929, GTE 210.

93 Dr. Karuch to Fritz ter Meer, Feb. 28, 1934, translated and printed in Hearings before the Committee on Patents, U.S. Senate, Seventy-Seventh Congress on S.2303 and S.2491, Part 6, May 20–2, 1942, p. 2891. See also George W. Stocking and Myron W. Watkins, *Cartels in Action* (New York: Twentieth Century Fund, 1946), pp. 107–17.

94 W. S. Carpenter, Jr., Memorandum of Meeting with I.G. Officials, Oct. 23, 1935, attached to Carpenter to Executive Committee, Oct. 23, 1935, II, 2, Box 1038.

95 Ibid.

96 Lammot du Pont to General Managers and Presidents of Subsidiaries, June 18, 1936; C. L. Burdick to Fin Sparre, Investigation of Patent and Processes Situation Respecting Du Pont and I.G., June 16, 1936, II, 2, Box 1038.

97 E. K. Bolton to Jasper Crane, June 11, 1936, II, 2, Box 1038.

98 C. Lalor Burdick, interview with David A. Hounshell and John K. Smith, Oct. 13, 1982, Hagley Museum and Library.

99 These agreements are discussed in Taylor and Sudnik, *Du Pont and the International Chemical Industry*, pp. 137–41, and Stocking and Watkins, *Cartels in Action*, pp. 107–17. Du Pont and IG had signed many other, narrower licensing agreements, which are detailed in "Du Pont–I.G. Relationship" (see note 91).

100 Burdick interview. The precise nature of Carothers's statement is discussed in Chapter 15. On IG's development of nylon 6, see Basil G. Achilladelis, "A Study in Technological History: Part I. The Manufacture of 'Perlon' (nylon 6) and Caprolactam by I. G. Farbenindustrie," *Chemistry and Industry* (Dec. 5, 1970): 1549–54.

101 On the negotiations and agreements, see the following documents: Fritz ter Meer to J. E. Crane, Oct. 10, 1938; Fin Sparre to J. E. Crane, Oct. 26, 1938; Fin Sparre to W. H. Hutz, Jan. 1, 1939; Fin Sparre to Executive Committee, Feb. 1, 1939; Kleine and Mediger to Fin Sparre, May 26, 1939, II, 2, Box 1049. On the cancelation of the agreement, see J. E. Crane to Fritz ter Meer, Apr. 18, 1941, II, 2, Box 1038.

102 J. E. Crane, "One Way of Looking at Research," talk presented at the chemical directors' meeting, May 20, 1930, Acc. 1416, Box 7.
103 Ibid.
104 Ibid.
105 Bolton to Crane, June 11, 1936.

Chapter 11. Development Power: The Case of Titanium Dioxide Pigments

1 On the early history of lithopone, see Joseph H. Mattiello, ed., *Protective and Decorative Coatings* (New York: Wiley, 1942), vol. 2, pp. 377–8. For the 1914 production figures see Williams Haynes, *American Chemical Industry: A History* (New York: Van Nostrand, 1942), vol. 3, p. 449. For the 1928 statistics see William Richter to Willis F. Harrington, Feb. 18, 1930, Acc. 1813, Box 4.

2 For lithopone production and market-share statistics, see Richter to Harrington, Feb. 18, 1930. On the Grasselli acquisition, see Lammot du Pont to Colonel William Donovan, Oct. 5, 1928, Acc. 1662, Box 37.

3 E. W. Furst to W. F. Harrington, Apr. 23, 1930, Acc. 1813, Box 5.

4 Jelks Barksdale, *Titanium: Its Occurrence, Chemistry, and Technology* (New York: Ronald Press, 1949), pp. 355–64.

5 Ibid.

6 Fin Sparre to the Chemical Department, "Pigments," Dec. 9, 1916, Acc. 1784.

7 Charles A. Meade to Irénée du Pont, Mar. 22, 1921, Acc. 1662, Box 61.

8 On the early negotiations see William Richter to Lammot du Pont, Mar. 5, 1928, Acc. 1662, Box 32. On Commercial Solvents Corporation and butanol see Haynes, *American Chemical Industry*, vol. 4, pp. 188–91. On Du Pont's purchasing of butanol from the Commercial Pigments Corp., see William Richter to E. C. Thompson, Jan. 10, 1928, Acc. 1813, Box 1. For the relationship of CPC to the Commercial Solvents Corp. and details of the first proposed venture, see W. J. Beadle to the Executive Committee, "Commercial Pigments Corporation," Dec. 30, 1930, Exhibit N, United States of America v. National Lead Company, et al., In the District Court of the United States for the Southern District of New York, June 1943, No. C-114-455 (Criminal), Exhibit 177. Cited hereafter as Titanium Dioxide Suit.

9 On the price reduction see Zack Phelps to William Richter, Dec. 23, 1928, Acc. 1813, Box 1. The quotation is from Harry S. Colton, "Memorandum," Dec. 4, 1929, Acc. 1813, Box 1.

10 J. Eliot Booge to Z. Phelps, "Manufacture of Titanium Pigments," Dec. 4, 1929, Acc. 1813, Box 6. On Haupt, see Winfield Scott Downs, ed., *Who's Who in Engineering*, 3d ed. (New York: Lewis Historical Publishing, 1931), p. 569.

11 D. W. Jayne to Willis F. Harrington, et al., "Titanium Pigment Situation," Jan. 20, 1930, Acc. 1813, Box 6.

12 Fin Sparre to E. C. Thompson, "Titanium-Lithopone-Commercial Pigments License," Dec. 21, 1929, Acc. 1813, Box 6.

13 Zack Phelps to Willis F. Harrington, "Manufacture of Synthetic Titanox by

Krebs," Dec. 17, 1928, and Willis F. Harrington to Zack Phelps, "Manufacture of Synthetic Titanox by Krebs," Dec. 18, 1929, Acc. 1813, Box 6.

14 William Richter to Zack Phelps, Dec. 26, 1929, Acc. 1813, Box 6.

15 William Richter to E. C. Thompson, Feb. 10, 1930, Acc. 1813, Box 6.

16 Fin Sparre, "The Krebs Pigment and Chemical Company," Apr. 8, 1929, Titanium Dioxide Suit, Ex. 173.

17 "Operating – Research Conference - 'F' Process Lithopone," Feb. 13, 1930, Acc. 1813, Box 6.

18 J. E. Booge to E. C. Thompson, "Possibility of 180 Strength for 'F' Process Lithopone," Feb. 24, 1930, Acc. 1813, Box 6.

19 J. E. Booge to Zack Phelps, "Future of Lithopone Type Pigments," Jan. 6, 1930, Acc. 1813, Box 6.

20 William Richter to C. M. Stine and F. Sparre, "Titanium Pigments," January 18, 1930, Acc. 1813, Box 6. E. C. Thompson to William Richter, "Titanium Pigments," January 16, 1930, Acc. 1813, Box 6.

21 In this period, a large amount of correspondence passed between Booge, Phelps, Thompson, Richter, Stine, Sparre, and Harrington. See Acc. 1813, Box 6.

22 William Richter to Fin Sparre, Feb. 13, 1930, Acc. 1813, Box 6.

23 Fin Sparre to T. S. Grasselli et al., "Titanium Oxide and Titanium Pigments," Feb. 24, 1930, Acc. 1813, Box 6.

24 Fin Sparre to C. M. A. Stine, "Titanium Pigments," Feb. 19, 1930, Acc. 1813, Box 6.

25 Minutes of Meeting Held on 12th December 1929, ICI Research Department Report, File #Q.115/1/32, in Acc. 1813, Box 4.

26 C. M. A. Stine to Hamilton Bradshaw, Dec. 28, 1929, and C. M. A. Stine to T. S. Grasselli and A. S. Krebs, Dec. 28, 1929, Acc. 1813, Box 1. Keats did go to England in January to exchange information on TiO_2. See C. M. A. Stine to Wm. Rintoul, Jan. 15, 1930, II, 2, 548.

27 Sparre to Stine, "Titanium Pigments." Sparre may have based his views of ICI's work on a memorandum to him from Hamilton Bradshaw, Nov. 20, 1929, II, 2, 534. Richter to T. S. Grasselli, "Titanium," Feb. 19, 1930, Acc. 1813, Box 6.

28 C. M. A. Stine to the Executive Committee, Jan. 15, 1930, p. 11, Acc. 1784.

29 George A. Pierce, "Conference on Patent Situation," Feb. 18, 1930, Chemical Department Laboratory Notebook No. 1168, p. 36, CRDD Notebook.

30 Zack Phelps to Willis F. Harrington, "Titanium Research – Chemical Department," Mar. 24, 1930, Acc. 1813, Box 6.

31 C. H. Biesterfeld to Hamilton Bradshaw, Jan. 3, 1930, and Hamilton Bradshaw to Fin Sparre, Jan. 17, 1930, Acc. 1813, Box 2.

32 Hamilton Bradshaw to Fin Sparre, "Titanium Oxide – Semi Works Plant," Mar. 28, 1930, Acc. 1813, Box 6.

33 Hamilton Bradshaw to Fin Sparre, "Titanium Pigment Work," June 11, 1930, Acc. 1813, Box 6.

34 Hamilton Bradshaw to E. C. Thompson, July 25, 1930, Acc. 1813, Box 6. A third reason was to accumulate information on the behavior of Norwegian ore in the sulfuric acid process.

35 Hamilton Bradshaw to the Executive Committee, "Major Experimental Projects No. 1264-3 Titanium Pigments," Sept. 6, 1930, Acc. 1813, Box 6.

36   William Richter to R. R. M. Carpenter, "Lithopone Prices," Dec. 1, 1930, Acc. 1813, Box 6. The sales and profits figures are from Beadle, "Commercial Pigments Corporation," Exhibit P.

37   Beadle, "Commercial Pigments Corporation."

38   CSC held the U.S. rights to Weizmann's patents for the production of butanol by fermentation (Haynes, *American Chemical Industry*, vol. 5, p. 157).

39   Beadle, "Commercial Pigments Corporation."

40   On the Executive Committee authorization, see Fin Sparre to the Executive Committee, "Commercial Pigments Corporation," Apr. 18, 1931, Titanium Dioxide Suit, Ex. 182. On the plant inspection, see "Inspection of Commercial Pigments' Plant at Baltimore," June 24, 1931, Titanium Dioxide Suit, Ex. 196. On the patent situation, see Fin Sparre to Executive Committee and Board of Directors Grasselli Chemical Company, July 3, 1931, Titanium Dioxide Suit, Ex. 192.

41   On the formation of the new company, see Fin Sparre to the Executive Committee, "Krebs Pigment and Chemical Company: Report on Accomplishment of Objectives," Mar. 31, 1932, GM Suit, PD, p. 4823. On the assets of the new company, see Beadle, "Commercial Pigments Corporation."

42   William Richter to E. M. Furst, July 30, 1931, Acc. 1813, Box 10.

43   J. E. Booge to Hamilton Bradshaw, "Study of Titanium Dioxide – Pressure Hydrolysis," Aug. 17, 1931, Acc. 1813, Box 10.

44   [J. E. Booge], Memorandum, Jan. 11, 1932, Acc. 1813, Box 13.

45   W[illiam] R[ichter] to T. S. G[rasselli], Apr. 7, 1932, Acc. 1813, Box 13.

46   C. H. Rupprecht to William Richter, Apr. 28, 1932, Acc. 1813, Box 13.

47   E. J. Cornish to G. Jebson, Apr. 22, 1931, Titanium Dioxide Suit, Ex. 183.

48   Sparre, "Krebs Report on Accomplishment of Objectives."

49   W. S. Carpenter, Jr., to Willis F. Harrington, Feb. 20, 1934, Acc. 1813, Box 18.

50   C. H. Rupprecht to Board of Directors, Krebs Pigment & Color Corporation, "Appropriation Request AG-1, $4,983,500 – Purchase of Ground and Erection of New Titanium Pigment Plants," July 9, 1934, Acc. 1813, Box 18.

51   Elmer K. Bolton to the Executive Committee, "Annual Report – 1931," Jan. 20, 1932, Acc. 1784.

52   Elmer K. Bolton to the Executive Committee, "Annual Report – 1939," Jan. 11, 1940, Acc. 1784, and Barksdale, *Titanium*, pp. 364–5.

Chapter 12. The "Radical Departure": Charles Stine's Fundamental Research Program

1   Charles M. A. Stine to the Executive Committee, "Pure Science Work," Dec. 18, 1926, Acc. 1784, Box 16. Herbert Hoover, "The Vital Need for Greater Financial Support to Pure Science Research," *Mechanical Engineering* 48 (Jan. 1926): 6-8.

2   Stine, "Pure Science Work."

3   EC Minutes, Dec. 22, 1926.

4   C. E. K. Mees, "The Future of Scientific Research," *Industrial and Engineering Chemistry* 6 (Aug. 1914): 618–19, and Arthur D. Little, "Industrial Research in America," *Industrial and Engineering Chemistry* 5 (Oct. 1913): 793–801. Mees specifically used the term fundamental research in the bibliography of

his book (C. E. K. Mees, *The Organization of Industrial Scientific Research* [New York: McGraw-Hill, 1920], p. 156).

5 Elbert C. Lathrop to William M. Whitten, "Chemical Department Staff Meeting," May 5, 1920, and Ernest B. Benger to William M. Whitten, "Efficiency of Chemical Department," May 5, 1920, Acc. 1784.

6 Reid thought that Stine should send Du Pont research staff to his laboratory for a year at a time. Interestingly, among the topics that Reid suggested was the causes and mechanisms of polymerization. Whether Stine got the idea from Reid cannot be determined (E. Emmet Reid to Charles M. A. Stine, Dec. 23, 1926, Acc. 1784, Box 16). Stine and Bolton visited Bell Labs in Mar. 1927. (Charles M. A. Stine to Edward B. Craft, Mar. 24, 1927, Acc. 1784, Box 16). Stine wrote to Whitney about the National Electric Light Association (NELA) laboratory. (Charles M. A. Stine to Willis R. Whitney, Mar. 24, 1927, Acc. 1784, Box 16). Whitney wrote back that under the first director of NELA, the work was pure science, but more recently it had worked on "such problems as may lead to results of practical importance." He stated further that "since we are part of an industrial organization our investigations should be directed along those lines which are not only of scientific interest, but also promise to yield knowledge of importance to industry." (Willis R. Whitney to Charles M. A. Stine, Mar. 28, 1927, Acc. 1784, Box 16.)

7 Charles M. A. Stine to the Executive Committee, "Fundamental Research in the Du Pont Company," Mar. 31, 1927, Acc. 1784, Box 16.

8 From the salary ranges that Stine listed, $8,000 to $15,000 a year, he expected to hire some of the top men in the profession. At this time Du Pont was hiring PhDs for about $3,000 a year. ("Notes on Meeting of the Directors of the Chemical Sections of the E. I. du Pont de Nemours & Co. and Subsidiaries at Wilmington, Del., April 22, 1927," Acc. 1662, Box 17.) At this time Roger Adams, who was a full professor and chairman of the department, made $8,000 a year. (H. E. Cunningham to Roger Adams, July 3, 1928, Adams Papers, Box 9, University of Illinois Archives, Champaign-Urbana, Illinois.) It seems that Stine had men such as Adams in mind. Adams later claimed that Du Pont had offered him a full-time position in 1928, probably during his tenure as resident consultant that summer. (Roger Adams, Interview by John B. Mellecker, Nov. 20, 1964, Feb. 12, 1965, and Mar. 15, 1965, Tape 2, Side 2, Adams Papers, Box 9.)

9 EC Minutes, Apr. 6, 1927.

10 George L. Clark to Charles L. Reese, Apr. 23, 1925; Charles L. Reese to Charles M. A. Stine, Apr. 29, 1925; and Irénée du Pont to Charles M. A. Stine, May 1, 1925, Acc. 1662, Box 16.

11 Charles M. A. Stine to Lammot du Pont, Apr. 19, 1927, and Lammot du Pont to Charles M. A. Stine, Apr. 20, 1927, Acc. 1784, Box 16.

12 EC Minutes, Dec. 22, 1926.

13 *Du Pont Company Annual Report 1926.*

14 Charles M. A. Stine to the Executive Committee, "Expenditures for Fundamental Research during the Year 1927," Apr. 16, 1927, Acc. 1784. The funding plan is outlined in M. D. Fisher, "Fundamental Research," Advice of Action of the Finance Committee, May 3, 1927, Acc. 1784.

15 Stine, "Expenditures for Fundamental Research." The term "Purity Hall" appears in L. G. Wise and N. G. Fisher, "History, Activities, and Accomplish-

ments of Fundamental Research in the Chemical Department of the Du Pont Company, 1926–1939 Inclusive," Aug. 14, 1940, Acc. 1784.

16   Wise and Fisher, "History."

17   See Kraemer's biography in Acc. 1850.

18   Elmer O. Kraemer to Hamilton Bradshaw, May 17, 1927, Acc. 1784.

19   James Burton Nichols, "Biographical Sketch," Aug. 25, 1978, Acc. 1850.

20   On Svedberg, see Stig Claesson and Kal O. Pederson, "The (Theodor) Svedberg," in *Dictionary of Scientific Biography* (New York: Scribner, 1976), vol. 13, pp. 158–64.

21   Nichols, "Biography." His major project involved measuring the particle size and molecular weight of egg albumen.

22   For details of the construction of the ultracentrifuge, see Nichols correspondence with Svedberg in Acc. 1850.

23   Charles M. A. Stine to the Executive Committee, [Annual Report of the Chemical Department for 1927], Jan. 31, 1928, Acc. 1784. The growth of the group is discussed in Arthur P. Tanberg to Charles M. A. Stine, "Fundamental Research to Date," Oct. 24, 1928, Acc. 1784., Box 16.

24   Adams Interview.

25   Carl S. Marvel, notes of interview by Jeffrey L. Sturchio, Nov. 13, 1984, Center for the History of Chemistry, Philadelphia.

26   Louis F. Fieser to James B. Conant, Nov. 26, 1927, Conant Papers, Harvard University Archives, Cambridge, Mass.

27   Henry Gilman to Arthur P. Tanberg, Sept. 10, 1927, and Arthur P. Tanberg to Henry Gilman, Sept. 13, 1927, Acc. 1784, Box 16.

28   Arthur P. Tanberg to Reynold C. Fuson, Mar. 24, 1928, and Nov. 20, 1928, and Reynold C. Fuson to Arthur P. Tanberg, Dec. 5, 1928, Fuson Papers, Box 1, University of Illinois Archives.

29   For general biographies of Carothers, see Roger Adams, "Biographical Memoir of Wallace Hume Carothers," *National Academy of Sciences, Biographical Memoirs* 20, no. 12 (1939): 293–309; Julian W. Hill, "Wallace Hume Carothers," *Proceedings of the Robert A. Welch Foundation Conferences on Chemical Research* 20, *American Chemistry Bicentennial*, ed. W. O. Mulligan (Houston: Welch Foundation, 1977): 322–3.

30   Wallace H. Carothers to Pauline G. Beery, Apr. 4, 1932, Acc. 1784.

31   Carothers's tenure at the University of South Dakota is covered in Arthur M. Pardee to Roger Adams, Feb. 19, 1938, Adams Papers, Box 54. See also A. Truman Schwartz, "The Importance of Good Teaching: The Influence of Arthur Pardee on Wallace Carothers," *Journal of College Science Teaching* (Feb. 1981): 218-21. Johnson's comments on Carothers's early work are in John R. Johnson to Roger Adams, Nov. 3, 1938, Adams Papers, Box 54.

32   W. H. Carothers to W. G. Machetanz, Apr. 22, 1923, Acc. 1850.

33   W. H. Carothers to W. G. Machetanz, Jan. 15, 1928, Acc. 1850.

34   On Adams as a consultant, see C. M. A. Stine to Roger Adams, Sept. 13, 1927, Adams Papers, Box 9. The job offer was discussed in two exchanges of letters between Stine and Carothers, Sept. 20, 23, 26 and Oct. 9, 1927, Acc. 1784.

35   W. H. Carothers to A. P. Tanberg, Oct. 13, 1927, Acc. 1784. Concerning his difficulties in Cambridge, he wrote, "My mind has certainly been a perfect chaos for the last weeks – and indeed for most of the time since my stay here at Cambridge." W. H. Carothers to J. R. Johnson, Apr. 1, 1927, Acc. 1842.

Early in 1928, Carothers wrote to a friend that "the record of my tortuous wanderings during the past few years would make a rich case for the psychopathologists, but so far I have placed little of it in their hands." Carothers attributed his psychological problems to "a completely arrested development on one side." As a child he had been fearful of stern, aloof males such as his father and minister. Carothers had no desire to emulate these men and continued to see himself as a child at age thirty-one. Carothers to Machetanz, Jan. 15, 1928.

36 H. Bradshaw to W. H. Carothers, Nov. 4, 1927, Acc. 1896.

37 Carothers to Machetanz, Jan. 15, 1928.

38 The exact origin of Carothers's ideas is unclear. He later stated that he had begun thinking about polymers shortly before his first visit to Du Pont in Sept. 1927, and "in a rather vague way planned some experiments." (W. H. Carothers to A. P. Tanberg, "Early History of Polyamide Fibers," Feb. 19, 1936, Acc. 1784.) He made a similar statement four years earlier in W. H. Carothers, "Fundamental Research in Organic Chemistry at the Experimental Station – A Review," Aug. 5, 1932, Acc. 1784, Box 16. Stine later wrote to Roger Adams that Carothers's interest in polymerization was "one of the principal reasons why I wanted to employ [him]. He had been giving thought and study to polymerization and polymeric molecules." C. M. A. Stine to R. Adams, Dec. 2, 1938, Adams Papers, Box 54. Independent of the origin of his ideas, Carothers was strongly encouraged by Stine and Bradshaw to study polymerization. (A. P. Tanberg to W. H. Carothers, Nov. 16, 1927, Acc. 1784.)

39 W. H. Carothers to Hamilton Bradshaw, Nov. 9, 1927, Acc. 1784. For the history of this controversy over polymers, see Yasu Furukawa, "Staudinger, Carothers, and the Emergence of the Macromolecular Chemistry" (PhD diss., University of Oklahoma, 1983).

40 W. H. Carothers to John R. Johnson, Feb. 14, 1928, Acc. 1842.

41 These points have been made in interviews with many of Carothers's friends and associates.

42 For correspondence during this period, see Adams Papers, Box 7, and W. H. Carothers to J. R. Johnson, Oct. 8, 1928, Acc. 1842.

43 W. H. Carothers to A. P. Tanberg, July 12, 1929, Acc. 1784.

44 Carothers first wrote out his ideas in detail in W. H. Carothers to C. M. A. Stine, "Proposed Research on Condensed or Polymerized Substances," March 1, 1928, Acc. 1784.

45 Carothers, "Early History."

46 The quote is from Hill, "Carothers." Wallace H. Carothers, "Polymerization," *Chemical Reviews* 8 (1931): 353–426. Earlier he had published a similar paper; "An Introduction to the General Theory of Condensation Polymers," *Journal of the American Chemical Society* 51 (1929): 2548–59. Both of these papers are reprinted in H. Mark and G. S. Whitby, eds., *Collected Papers of Wallace Hume Carothers on High Polymeric Substances* (New York: Interscience, 1940).

47 C. M. A. Stine to the Executive Committee, "Annual Report – 1929," Jan. 15, 1930, Acc. 1784.

48 Chemical Department Organization Chart, November 13, 1929, Acc. 1784.

49 Charles M. A. Stine to the Executive Committee, "Annual Report – 1929," Jan. 15, 1930, Acc. 1784.

50 Julian Hill had come from MIT; John B. Miles, Jr., from Princeton; Howard

Starkweather from Harvard; Frank Van Natta from Michigan; George L. Dorough from Johns Hopkins; Herbert G. Tanner from Stanford; and Gerard Berchet from Colorado (*American Men of Science*, 6th ed. [1938]). On Lenher, see Lenher interview, Oct. 4, 1982.

51   Charles M. A. Stine to William Rintoul, Dec. 13, 1929, Acc. 1784.

52   Elmer K. Bolton to J. Warren Kinsman, Nov. 23, 1931, Acc. 1850.

53   The history of early synthetic rubber research is briefly summarized in G. S. Whitby and M. Katz, "Synthetic Rubber," *Industrial and Engineering Chemistry* 25, no. 11 (1933): 1204–11, and no. 12 (1933): 1338–48; and Harry L. Fisher, "The Origin and Development of Synthetic Rubbers," *Symposium on the Application of Synthetic Rubbers*, Cincinnati Spring Meeting, ASTM, March 2, 1944, pp. 3–16. The chemical structure of isoprene and butadiene are $H_2C = C(CH_3) - CH = CH_2$ and $H_2C = CH - CH = CH_2$, respectively. Chemists succeeded in polymerizing butadiene in 1910. Whitby and Katz, "Synthetic Rubber," pp. 1207–8.

54   Bolton to Kinsman, Nov. 23, 1931. The patent issued for the process was U.S. Patent 1,777,600. It does not discuss how the butadiene was to be converted into synthetic rubber. In 1926, German investigators published an article that indicated that it was difficult to get good yields from this process. The article was Fritz Strauss and Leo Kollek, "Uber Diacetylen," *Berichte der Deutschen Chemischen Gesellschaft* 59 (1926): 1664–81.

55   Nieuwland's notes for this talk are in the Nieuwland papers, Box 9, University of Notre Dame Archives. On Nieuwland, see Theodore J. Crovello, "Nieuwland Address," *American Midland Naturalist* 100, no. 2 (Oct. 1978): 1–3; and W. S. Calcott, "Father Nieuwland, the Chemist," *Catalyzer* (Feb. 1937): 39–44.

56   Bolton to Kinsman, Nov. 23, 1931.

57   Hugh Clark, "Neoprene," June 15, 1942, pp. 47–9, Acc. 1850. Because Nieuwland held several key patents that Du Pont had prosecuted for him, Du Pont and Notre Dame concluded a royalty agreement in 1932. Nieuwland died in 1936, leaving the university as his sole heir. Notre Dame received more than $2 million over the life of Nieuwland's patents. (Anonymous memorandum, "Notre Dame Royalty," March 27, 1952, Acc. 1850.)

58   The chemical structures of MVA and DVA are $HC \equiv C - CH = CH_2$ and $CH_2 = CH - C \equiv C - CH = CH_2$.

59   W. S. Calcott to H. Elley, "Conception and Invention of DuPrene," Dec. 14, 1931, Acc. 1850. Also see Bolton to Kinsman, Nov. 23, 1931.

60   Arnold M. Collins, "The Discovery of Polychloroprene," Charles Goodyear Medal Address – 1973, *Rubber Chemistry and Technology* 46, no. 2 (June 1973): G48–G52. O. M. Hayden, "SDO New Corrosion-Resisting Coating," *Industrial and Engineering Chemistry* 24, no. 5 (1932): 563; Calcott, "Conception"; and U.S. Patent 1,812,544.

61   Wallace H. Carothers, Quarterly Report, March 31, 1930, Acc. 1784.

62   Wallace H. Carothers to E. K. Bolton, "History of Work on D.V.A., M.V.A., and C.D.," Nov. 19, 1931, Acc. 1850.

63   Carothers, "Quarterly Report," and Carothers, "History of Work."

64   Arnold M. Collins, entry in CRDD Notebook 1176, p. 86.

65   W. H. Carothers, "Memorandum for E. K. Bolton," Apr. 18, 1930, Acc. 1784. The chemical structure of chloroprene is $H_2C = C(Cl) - CH = CH_2$. It is similar to the chemical constituent of natural rubber, isoprene, which has a methyl

group (CH$_3$) where chloroprene has a chlorine atom. To form a polymer, chloroprene reacts with itself to form chains with the general formula:

$$—(CH_2 – C(Cl) = CH – CH_2)—$$

(repeating unit)

66 Collins, "Discovery": G47.
67 Two University of Chicago researchers made 1-chlorobutadiene, which polymerized to a hard, brittle substance. Irving E. Muskat and Herbert Northrup, "Preparation and Chlorination of Butadiene," *Journal of the American Chemical Society* 52 (1930): 4043–55. Several years later, Carothers and Gerard Berchet determined that 1-chlorobutadiene was also the product of the reaction of either butadiene or MVA with chlorine. It is Nieuwland's catalyst that causes the compound to rearrange to 2-chlorobutadiene. W. H. Carothers and G. J. Berchet, "XV. Halogen-4-butadienes-1,2. The Mechanism of 1,4 Addition and of alpha, gamma-Rearrangement," *Journal of the American Chemical Society* 55 (1933): 2807–13.
68 Carothers, "Fundamental Research."
69 Carothers, "Early History."
70 Ibid. See also W. H. Carothers and J. W. Hill, "Artificial Fibers from Synthetic Linear Condensation Superpolymers," *Journal of the American Chemical Society* 54 (1930): 1579–87.
71 On Stine's promotion see EC Minutes, June 18, 1930. On the makeup of the Executive Committee, see the company's annual reports for 1928, 1929, and 1930.
72 Elmer K. Bolton, "Certain Phases of Research Work," Jan. 18, 1929, Acc. 1662, Box 17.
73 Charles Stine pointed out Bolton's opposition because Adams's draft of Carothers's biographical memoir read as if Bolton had initiated fundamental research at Du Pont. C. M. A. Stine to R. Adams, Dec. 2, 1938.
74 On the synthetic rubber work, see D. H. Powers, "Synthetic Rubber – Report on the Work Carried Out on Synthetic Rubber from March 1926 to March 1928 and from June 1928 to December 1928," Jan. 2, 1929, Acc. 1850.
75 E. K. Bolton to the Executive Committee, "Annual Report – 1930," Jan. 14, 1931, Acc. 1784.
76 Ernest B. Benger to E. K. Bolton, "Fundamental Research Policy," Nov. 7, 1930, Acc. 1784, Box 16.
77 U.S. Patent 2,071,250.
78 W. H. Charch to W. H. Carothers, Jan. 17, 1931, PR Records, 1931, File P-5.
79 Carothers, "Early History."
80 Ibid.
81 Wise and Fisher, "History."
82 E. K. Bolton to the Executive Committee, "Annual Report – 1932," Jan. 6, 1933, Acc. 1784. The changes are also noted in Wise and Fisher, "History."
83 Carothers, "Fundamental Research."
84 Elmer O. Kraemer, "Fundamental Research in an Industrial Laboratory," Topics for Discussion at Conference, July 30, 1931, Acc. 1784, Box 16.
85 Kraemer noted on his agenda that Benger, Coolidge, Cameron, Carothers, Chilton, Kenney, and Kraemer attended. Because Benger was the ranking official at the meeting, he probably gave these opening remarks. Kraemer recorded them under the title of "New Ideas After Arrival" as part of "Survey of Activities

of Colloid Group Since Its Inception with Reference to Technical Applications," Acc. 1850.

86 Charles M. A. Stine to Hamilton Bradshaw, May 3, 1920, Acc. 1784.

87 "Development of Chemical Department," ca. 1940, Acc. 1784.

88 Elmer K. Bolton to the Executive Committee, Sept. 28, 1932, Acc. 1784.

89 Wise and Fisher, "History."

90 Lenher interview.

91 The statistics concerning the fundamental research personnel were obtained from the Chemical Department organization charts in Acc. 1784 and biographical entries in *American Men of Science*, 4th, 6th, and 7th eds. The number of men doing fundamental research at Du Pont in the fall of 1932 was calculated from organization charts and the five-year summary reports submitted to Tanberg in August 1932 (Acc. 1784, Box 16).

92 For details of the large-ring work, see Hill, "Carothers," pp. 243–5 and several papers on the topic reprinted in the Mark, ed., *Collected Papers*.

93 W. H. Carothers to R. Adams, May 10 and 21, 1933, Adams Papers, Box 7.

94 W. H. Carothers to W. H. Charch, Sept. 18, 1933, PR Records, 1933, File P-9.

95 E. K. Bolton to the Executive Committee, "Annual Report – 1933," Jan. 2, 1934, Acc. 1784.

96 The reasons why Carothers went back to work on fibers cannot be determined from the existing records. In a 1936 review Carothers wrote, ". . . in early 1934 I decided it was worth one more effort. . . ." (Carothers, "Early History.") Vice President Stine prepared a statement on Bolton's contribution to nylon in which he said, "In January or February 1934 Dr. Bolton told Dr. Carothers that he wanted Dr. Carothers to think again about synthetic fibers. . . ." C. M. A. Stine, " 'A' Bonus Memorandum," May 8, 1941, Special Compensation Files. In a similar document, Bolton asserted, "In 1934, Carothers was encouraged to reattack the problem of developing a synthetic fiber based on superpolymers." E. K. Bolton to L. A. Yerkes, June 27, 1941, Special Compensation Files. Twenty years later, Bolton, in an oral history interview, claimed to have continually prodded Carothers to take another look at fibers. Then, Bolton stated, "he came in one day and said, 'I think that I have got some new ideas.' " Elmer K. Bolton interview by Alfred D. Chandler, Richmond D. Williams, and Norman B. Wilkinson, 1961, Acc. 1689.

97 W. H. Charch to W. H. Carothers, Sept. 27, 1933, Acc. 1784.

98 Carothers, "Early History."

99 Coffman recorded Carothers's initial instructions in a laboratory notebook. CRDD Notebook 1293, p. 39. The experiments are recorded in CRDD Notebook 2150, pp. 140–6.

100 Donald D. Coffman, "Polyamides as a Source of Synthetic Fibers," Chemical Department Report ESP-34-81, June 25, 1934, Technical Records Center, Central Research and Development Department, Experimental Station, Du Pont Company.

101 On Flory, see Paul Flory, Interview by Charles Overberger, Feb. 14, 1982, American Chemical Society, Educational Activities Department; Paul Flory, Interview by David W. Ridgway, ed. by Robert C. Brasted and Peter Farago, *Journal of Chemical Education* 54 (June 1977): 341–4; Harold A. Sheraga,

"Paul J. Flory on His 70th Birthday," *Macromolecules* 13 (May–June 1980): 8A–10A; and Walter H. Stockmeyer, "The 1974 Nobel Prize for Chemistry," *Science* 186 (Nov. 22, 1974): 724–6.

102 Flory's activities in this period can be traced in "Summary of Work Done at the E.S. on Fiber 66, July 1935 through July 1938," Acc. 1784, Box 16.

103 Flory Interview by Overberger, pp. 12–13.

104 Flory's first internal report on the subject was "Distribution of Molecular Size in Linear Condensations of the Polyamides Type I," March 28, 1935, Acc. 1784, Box 16. He published these and other results in Paul J. Flory, "Molecular Size Distribution in Linear Condensation Polymers," *Journal of the American Chemical Society* 58 (1936): 1877–85.

105 Wallace H. Carothers to Roger Adams, July 22, 1934, Adams Papers, Box 7.

106 Wallace H. Carothers to Robert M. Hutchins, Nov. 4, 1934, Presidential Papers, University of Chicago, Box 101, Folder 3. (Cited hereafter as Presidential Papers.)

107 In June 1936, he suffered a major breakdown and spent five weeks at the Philadelphia Institute. (Carothers to Johnson, July 9, 1936, Acc. 1842.) Then he went to Europe, where he met Roger Adams, and they hiked in the Alps. Adams's concerns about Carothers are in D. Stanley and Ann Tracey Tarbell, *Roger Adams: Scientist and Statesman* (Washington: American Chemical Society, 1981), pp. 118–21. The death of his sister, Isabel Carothers Berolzheimer, on Jan. 7, 1937, dealt him a severe blow from which he never recovered. Adams, "Biographical Memoir." The date of her death is erroneously listed as 1936. Her obituary was in the *New York Times* on Jan. 9, 1937. His obituary was in the *Wilmington Journal Every Evening* on Apr. 30, 1937.

108 Carothers's obsession that he was a failure has been noted by many of his friends and associates. The psychiatrist in Philadelphia concurred in this assessment. Ira H. Carothers to Roger Adams, Dec. 2, 1937, Adams Papers, Box 54.

109 Bolton interview.

110 Roger Adams to Frederick Woodward, Nov. 8, 1934, Presidential Papers.

111 Wise and Fisher "History." On Kraemer, see *American Men of Science* 6th ed. (1938).

112 Lammot du Pont to Elmer K. Bolton, [Apr. 16, 1941], Acc. 1662, Box 22.

113 Elmer K. Bolton to Lammot du Pont, Apr. 16, 1941, Acc. 1662, Box 22.

114 The question remains as to how much influence Stine exerted on Du Pont's research programs as Executive Committee advisor on research during the 1930s while Bolton was reorienting the programs of the Chemical Department. In general, in this era, the committee members focused on matters of broad policy and let the departmental managers run their organizations. Yet Stine certainly read the annual reports of the Chemical Department. Did he disapprove of Bolton's management of the fundamental research program? From the surviving documentation, it is not possible to answer this question definitively; there are some indications, however, that Stine became more and more removed from Du Pont research as it was practiced in the 1930s. Following in the footsteps of his father, Stine became a prolific lecturer and author. For Stine's speeches, see Acc. 1706.

Chapter 13. The "D" of R&D: The Development of
Neoprene and Nylon

1 The words were apparently first conceptually connected in the early 1920s. The first citation in the Oxford English Dictionary dates from 1923 (R. W. Burchfield, ed., *A Supplement to the Oxford English Dictionary* [Oxford: Clarendon Press, 1982], p. 1204).

2 On development, see Thomas P. Hughes, "The Development Phase of Technological Change," and Lynwood Bryant, "The Development of the Diesel Engine," *Technology and Culture* 17 (1976): 423–47.

3 Wallace H. Carothers to Arthur P. Tanberg, "Early History of Polyamide Fibers," Feb. 19, 1936, Acc. 1784.

4 "Rubber Laboratory," sketch for pamphlet printed for a Rubber Laboratory Open House held in 1953, Acc. 1850.

5 G. J. Groh to J. B. Quig, "Sales Service Test RS-1," July 12, 1938, II, 2, Box 951.

6 W. S. Calcott to H. Elley, "Conception and Invention of DuPrene," Dec. 14, 1931, Acc. 1850. See also U.S. Patent 1,950,436.

7 Calcott, "Conception," and O. M. Hayden, "Reflections on the Early Development of Neoprene," text of speech delivered at Rubber Division of the American Chemical Society in Montreal on May 1, 1978, Acc. 1850.

8 E. R. Bridgwater to J. Warren Kinsman, "Commercialization of C. D.," Oct. 20, 1930, Acc. 1813, Box 7.

9 E. G. Robinson, "DuPrene-(C.D. Polymer)," Sept. 24, 1931, Acc. 1813, Box 7.

10 "Du Pont Announces a New Synthetic Rubber at Akron Group Meeting," *The Rubber Age* 30 (Nov. 10, 1931): 115–16, discusses the secrecy before the meeting. Charles F. Weston, "News Publication, Tuesday, November 3, 1931," Acc. 1850, is Du Pont's press release. Charles K. Weston to E. G. Robinson, Dec. 4, 1931, Acc. 1850, details the publicity campaign.

11 The papers that announced the discovery are J. A. Nieuwland, W. S. Calcott, F. B. Downing, and A. S. Carter, "The Controlled Polymerization of Acetylene," *Journal of the American Chemical Society* 53 (1931): 4197–202 and W. H. Carothers, I. Williams, A. M. Collins, and J. E. Kirby, "A New Synthetic Rubber: Chloroprene and Its Polymers," ibid.: 4203–25. The final paragraph of the latter paper briefly mentions that the differences between neoprene and natural rubber are sufficient to suggest some potential uses for the new substance.

12 E. R. Bridgwater, "Sales Bulletin RC-168," Acc. 1850.

13 O. M. Hayden, "Neoprene Chronology," Acc. 1850. This chronology was kept by Hayden until 1958. He wrote the first seven pages in 1938.

14 P. R. Johnson, "Polychloroprene," *Rubber Chemistry and Technology* 49, no. 3 (1976): 657–8. The problems of neoprene manufacture are discussed in V. A. Cosler, "A Gigantic Test Tube," *India Rubber World* 93, no. 2 (Nov. 1, 1935): 31–3.

15 U.S. Patent 2,048,838; Calcott, "Conception"; and Johnson, "Polychloroprene," p. 653.

16 Hayden, "Chronology," and Donald C. Thompson, "Polychloroprene," Mar. 18, 1944, Acc. 1850.

17 Herbert W. Walker, *The Chemistry and Technology of Neoprene* (n.p.:n.p.,

1954). The conversion of chloroprene to neoprene was 25 to 35 percent in 35 to 45 hours. Higher conversions yielded a stiff and unworkable polymer.

18 F. B. Holmes to W. S. Calcott, " 'A'-1936-Neoprene-Emulsion Polymerization," Dec. 31, 1936, Acc. 1850. The cost reduction is in L. S. Munson to E. G. Robinson, "1939 'A' Bonus Recommendations," Jan. 31, 1940, Acc. 1850.

19 Hugh Clark, "Neoprene," June 15, 1942, Acc. 1850, pp. 18–20.

20 George S. Albee, "I Remember Rubber," *Du Pont Magazine*, Dec. 1956–Jan. 1957, p. 4.

21 O. M. Hayden, "A Brief History of Neoprene" (1958), Acc. 1850; Thompson, "Polychloroprene"; and U.S. Patent 1,950,439.

22 E. R. Bridgwater to Cesare Protto, "DuPrene Development and Sales Promotion," June 22, 1936, Acc. 1850.

23 *Neoprene Notebook* 1 (Jan. 1938): 1.

24 This advertisement appeared in *National Petroleum News, Oil and Gas Journal, Motor Age, Inland Printer, Machine Design*, and other publications. *Neoprene Notebook* 12 (Feb. 1934): 48.

25 E. R. Bridgwater, "DuPrene – Protection of Our Trademark Rights," May 22, 1934; and E. R. Bridgwater, "Proper Use of Our Trademark 'DuPrene'," Sept. 13, 1935, Acc. 1850. See also Clark, "Neoprene," p. 7.

26 A. B. Echols to Lammot du Pont, "Financial Picture of Neoprene, 1928–1939," Sept. 7, 1939, Acc. 1662, Box 19.

27 Albee, "I Remember Rubber," discusses early neoprene products. Echols, "Financial Picture," gives sales by product. "Effect of an Odorless Neoprene Polymer on the Growth of Markets for Neoprene," May 12, 1947, Acc. 1850, shows how sales of neoprene heels, soles, and gloves increased after the odorless type was introduced.

28 Between 1934 and 1936, the Dayton Tire and Rubber Company and I. G. Farben made neoprene tires for experimental purposes. The tires were unsatisfactory, mainly because neoprene is less elastic than natural rubber and generates enough internal heat to cause blowouts. "DuPrene Tires," June 22, 1934, Acc. 1850. On I. G. Farben, see O. M. Hayden, "Trip to Europe, Jan. 3–Mar. 14, 1936," Acc. 1850.

29 Echols, "Financial Picture."

30 Hayden, "Chronology."

31 Ibid. Wartime use of neoprene is discussed in *Neoprene* (Washington, D.C.: U.S. Department of Labor, Division of Labor Standards, 1944).

32 Government uncertainty about the disposal of wartime plants and Du Pont's uncertainty about the continued demand for neoprene delayed the repurchase of the plant until 1949. During the Korean war, Du Pont's neoprene output hit new highs, and no postwar slump occurred. Neoprene in World War II is discussed in Clark, "Neoprene," pp. 34–6; Hayden, "Chronology"; and Thompson, "Polychloroprene."

33 Echols, "Financial Picture."

34 "Organization Changes," June 19, 1930, Acc. 1662, Box 19.

35 Margaret Dana, "Silk Stockings and How to Know Them," *Atlantic Monthly* 161 (April 1938): 519–22.

36 *Statistical Abstract of the United States* (Washington: U.S. Government Printing Office, 1939), p. 812.

37 Greenewalt interview, Nov. 8, 1982.

38 Ibid.

39 *Du Pont Company Annual Report 1935.*

40 W. H. Carothers to A. Stuart Hunter, Oct. 10, 1934, PR Records, 1934, File P-9.

41 A. S. Hunter, "The Basic Study of Textile Fibers," May 4, 1934, PR Records, 1934, File P-9.

42 Miles discussed his approach to fiber testing in J. B. Miles to E. O. Kraemer, April 13, 1934, PR Records, 1934, File P-9, and Miles to Kraemer, Oct. 11, 1934, PR Records, 1934, File P-26. Charch expressed his point of view in W. H. Charch to J. B. Miles, Jr., "Properties and Testing of Synthetic Fibers," Nov. 23, 1934, PR Records, 1934, File P-9.

43 Carothers, "Early History."

44 Wallace H. Carothers and George D. Graves, "Polyamide Fibers – Summary Report, July 1 to September 30, 1935," Acc. 1784, Box 16.

45 The 5-10 polymer was made from pentamethylene diamine and sebacic acid. This latter compound could be derived from castor oil, a natural product available in limited quantities.

46 "Excerpts from Research Steering Committee Minutes Concerning Polyamide Projects," Mar. 24, 1966, CRDD Files.

47 On the problems encountered in the development of nylon see Crawford H. Greenewalt, "Nylon Yarn – 'A' Bonus," June 11, 1941, Special Compensation Files.

48 Greenewalt interview, Nov. 8, 1982.

49 For information on the organization and personnel of the Rayon Department, see Ferdinand Schulze, revised and enlarged from a manuscript prepared by Roy Soukup, *The Technical Division of the Rayon Department, 1920–1951* (Wilmington, Del.: Du Pont, 1952).

50 On Gladding, see Acc. 1193, Box 6. On Hoff, see *American Men of Science*, 7th ed. (1944).

51 E. K. Bolton to the Executive Committee, "Annual Report – 1935," Jan. 2, 1936, Acc. 1784.

52 Carothers's group and outside consultants had held a brainstorming session on this issue in July 1934, long before nylon 6-6 had been chosen as the particular one to be developed. Because of its wide availability and low cost, phenol, a benzene derivative found in coal tar, was chosen as the starting chemical. (Carothers, "Early History.") He recorded the suggestions for making the intermediate compounds on July 12, 1934, in CRDD Notebook 2198, pp. 13–17.

53 Greenewalt, "Nylon Yarn – 'A' Bonus."

54 Ibid.

55 Carothers and Graves, "Polyamide Fibers – Summary Report, July 1 to September 20, 1935," Acc. 1784, Box 16.

56 Graves interview.

57 W. H. Carothers and G. D. Graves, "Polyamide Fibers – Summary Report, January 1 to March 31, 1936," Acc. 1784, Box 16.

58 Bolton, "Annual Report – 1935."

59 E. K. Bolton to Executive Committee, "Annual Report – 1936," Jan. 14, 1937, Acc. 1784.

60 E. K. Bolton to Executive Committee, "Annual Report – 1937," Jan. 13, 1938, Acc. 1784. On the relative economics of silk and wool, see George D. Graves, "Fiber W – Discussion with V. R. Hardy and J. B. Miles," June 9, 1938, II, 2, Box 1049.

61 For problems with Fiber W, see C. H. Greenewalt to E. K. Bolton, Jan. 20, 1939, II, 2, Box 965.

62 W. H. Carothers and G. D. Graves, "Polyamide Fibers – Summary Report, April 1 to June 30, 1936," Acc. 1784, Box 16.

63 Ibid.

64 G. P. Hoff, "Visit to Experimental Station, October 28–29," Nov. 12, 1936, II, 2, Box 958.

65 G. P. Hoff to W. H. Bradshaw, Dec. 23, 1936, II, 2, Box 963.

66 G. P. Hoff, Memorandum, Sept. 2, 1936, II, 2, Box 963.

67 D. F. Holmes, *History of the Du Pont Company's Textile Fibers Department* (n.p.: n.p., 1980), part I, p. 8.

68 E. K. Bolton, "Annual Report – 1936."

69 Greenewalt, "Nylon – 'A' Bonus." G. D. Graves to F. M. Pralatowski, "Sand Filter," Jan. 30, 1941, II, 2, Box 974, gives a summary of the melt-spinning project.

70 G. P. Hoff, "Memorandum," Dec. 14, 1936, II, 2, Box 963.

71 W. H. Bradshaw, "Wilmington Visit – November 19–20 – Rayon 66," Nov. 23, 1936, II, 2, Box 958. The experiments with the glass cell are detailed in George D. Graves, "Summary of the Work Done at the Experimental Station on Polyamides during December 1936 and January 1937," Acc. 1784, Box 16.

72 Greenewalt, "Nylon Yarn – 'A' Bonus."

73 G. D. Graves, "Summary of the Work Done at the Experimental Station on Polyamides during April and May 1937," Acc. 1784, Box 16.

74 Lewis recalled his trip in a letter, E. Vernon Lewis to Charles H. Rutledge, July 6, 1966, Acc. 1193, Box 4. His report on the trip is E. V. Lewis, "Hosiery Test," Feb. 22, 1937, II, 2, Box 951.

75 G. P. Hoff "Memorandum," May 7, 1937, II, 2, Box 951.

76 G. J. Groh to J. B. Quig, "Sales Service Test RS-1," July 12, 1937, II, 2, Box 951.

77 G. D. Graves, "Summary of the Work Done at the Experimental Station on Polyamides during August and September, 1937," Acc. 1784, Box 16.

78 G. P. Hoff to Dr. Parker, "Fiber 66 and Fiber W," Nov. 9, 1937, II, 2, Box 963.

79 W. R. Tyson to G. D. Graves, "Fiber 66 Service Test," Oct. 27, 1937, II, 2, Box 970.

80 G. P. Hoff to E. K. Gladding, "Status of Fiber 66," Nov. 10, 1937, II, 2, Box 963.

81 G. P. Hoff, [Pilot Plant Note], Nov. 29, 1937, II, 2, Box 955.

82 EC Minutes, Jan. 12, 1938.

83 Bolton, "Annual Report – 1937."

84 G. P. Hoff to E. K. Gladding, "Objectives of Plant 66," July 21, 1938, II, 2, Box 963.

85 Bolton, "Annual Report – 1937." On the new division, see Schulze, *Technical Division*, p. 37.

86   On the size development program, see E. W. Spanagel to C. C. Rainey, Jan. 8, 1940, II, 2, Box 975. The specifications for a size are give in "Copied from Dr. Hoff's original notes – Nov., 1937," II, 2, Box 959.

87   Schulze, *Technical Division*, pp. 168–9; and Spanagel interview.

88   EC Minutes, November 15, 1933.

89   EC Minutes, July 20, Oct. 5, 12, 26, Nov. 2, 1938.

90   Schulze, *Technical Division*, p. 37.

91   Assistant General Manager Benjamin May wrote to Yerkes that he did not think that it was wise to call the new fiber rayon, especially because it is "so distinctly different and superior that to call it something else might be better." B. M. May to L. A. Yerkes, Jan. 15, 1936, II, 2, Box 819.

92   W. H. Charch to A. P. Tanberg, "Designation of Rayon 66," Mar. 31, 1936, II, 2, Box 958.

93   Charles H. Rutledge, "The Name Nylon and Some of Its Adventures," June 20, 1966, Acc. 1193, Box 2.

94   J. P. Kranz to C. H. Rutledge, "Cellophane and Nylon Hosiery," June 16, 1966, II, 2, Box 958.

95   Two articles hinted of nylon's existence; the later one being very specific: "Silk Is Done," *American Textile Reporter* 51 (July 8, 1937): 1–2, and Stephen S. Marks, "Entirely New Synthetic Yarn for Women's Hose Developed," *Daily News Record*, July 18, 1938.

96   Like silk, hog bristles came from the Far East. At Du Pont, Paul Austin led the bristle research and development program in the central Chemical Department. Du Pont estimated the total market for bristles to be 4 million pounds a year. Bolton, "Annual Report – 1936," and L. L. Leach to G. P. Hoff, "Monofils," Aug. 6, 1937, II, 2, Box 954. On the Dr. West toothbrushes, see E. K. Bolton, "Annual Report – 1938," and E. B. Benger to G. P. Hoff, "Synthetic Bristle," Aug. 10, 1937, II, 2, Box 954. The development of toothbrush bristles is also covered in P. R. Austin, "Paul Tales II: Three Decades with Du Pont, 1933–1966," unpublished autobiography.

97   E. K. Bolton to L. A. Yerkes, E. K. Gladding, et al., May 26, 1938, and L. A. Yerkes, "Fiber 66," June 6, 1938, II, 2, Box 1049. Yerkes won Bolton over to his point of view; E. K. Bolton to J. W. McCoy, June 7, 1938, II, 2, Box 1049.

98   "Tentative Program, *New York Herald-Tribune*, Eighth Annual Forum on Current Problems," Oct. 27, 1938, Acc. 1193, Box 2.

99   *New York Times*, Oct. 28, 1938, p. 24.

100 Charles M. A. Stine, "What the Laboratories of Industry Are Doing for the World of Tomorrow," Oct. 27, 1938, II, 2, Box 598.

101 *New York Times*, Oct. 28, 1938, p. 34.

102 Six nylon cartoons were published by the *New York World-Telegram*, May 16, 1940, II, 2, Box 598.

103 *New York Times*, Oct. 29, 1938, p. 18.

104 "Nylon," *Fortune* (July 1940): 114.

105 Kenneth F. Mayer to R. A. Ramsdell, "Hosiery Sale," Mar. 22, 1939, II, 2, Box 951.

106 *New York Times*, May 2, 1940, p. 42.

107 "Nylon," *Fortune*, pp. 114, 116.

108 *New York Times*, May 14, 1940, p. 34. Nylon sales manager Robert A.

Ramsdell is credited with having suggested that Du Pont sell nylon at a price 10 percent higher than that of silk. E. K. Gladding to E. B. Benger, Jan. 15, 1941, Special Compensation Files.

109 The production figure for 1940 comes from Holmes, *Textile Fibers History*, part I, p. 8. The total sales and profits were estimated from 1941 data, "Nylon Investment," Acc. 1813, Box 10. The total R&D cost was $4.3 million, but only $3.2 million of that was charged to the Rayon Department. (A. B. King to W. S. Carpenter, Jr., A. B. Echols, et al., "Out of Pocket Cost of Nylon Development to Du Pont Company [to January 1, 1940]," Acc. 1813, Box 33.)

110 "Nylon Investment."

111 R. A. Ramsdell to E. K. Gladding, "Postwar Sales Report No. 3," Aug. 30, 1944, II, 2, Box 971.

112 L. A. Yerkes to the Executive Committee, May 16, 1941, Acc. 1813, Box 9.

113 E. K. Gladding to L. A. Yerkes, "Nylon's Plans for the Immediate Post-War Period," Apr. 5, 1943, II, 2, Box 971.

114 The quoted headline appeared in the Augusta, Georgia, *Chronicle*. ("The Lighter Side of Nylon," [ca. 1964] II, 2, Box 608.)

115 In this era, consumption of full-fashioned hosiery remained at about 7.5 pairs per woman per year. The hosiery figures were obtained from the *Statistical Abstract of the United States*, 1939 and 1950 editions.

116 On nylon in the 1950s, see Holmes, *Textile Fibers History*, part II, chap. 4.

117 Neoprene and nylon research costs are from Echols, "Financial Picture," and King, "Out-of-Pocket Cost," respectively.

118 Hayden, "Neoprene Chronology," and Holmes, *Textile Fibers History*.

119 "Exhibit A – Performance of New Products Commercialized from 1930 to 1967," Acc. 1850.

Chapter 14. Developing a Discipline: Chemical Engineering Research at Du Pont

1 James K. Hunt, "Dr. Charles M. A. Stine – A Biographical Sketch," March 31, 1939, Acc. 1706, and Charles M. A. Stine to Hamilton Bradshaw, "Memorandum," May 3, 1920, Acc. 1784.

2 Stine, "Memorandum."

3 On the American Institute of Chemical Engineers and the emergence of chemical engineering as a discipline, see Terry S. Reynolds, *75 Years of Progress – A History of the American Institute of Chemical Engineers, 1908–1983* (New York: American Institute of Chemical Engineers, 1983). On the importance of the concept of unit operations to the development of chemical engineering, see Jean-Claude Guédon, "Conceptual and Institutional Obstacles to the Emergence of Unit Operations in Europe," in William F. Furter, ed., *History of Chemical Engineering*, Advances in Chemistry Series (Washington: American Chemical Society, 1980), vol. 190, pp. 45–75.

4 On Warren K. Lewis, see Glenn C. Williams and J. Edward Vivan, "Pioneers in Chemical Engineering at M.I.T.," and H. C. Lewis, "W. K. Lewis, Teacher," in Furter, *History of Chemical Engineering*, pp. 129–40. On Lewis's use of mathematics for chemical engineering and the conflicts it caused with his senior colleague William H. Walker, see "Reminiscences of William H. Walker,

'Father of Chemical Engineering'," *Chemical Engineering*, July 1952: 158–59, 178.

5   Thomas H. Chilton, *Strong Water: Nitric Acid, Its Sources, Methods of Manufacture and Uses* (Cambridge, Mass.: MIT Press, 1968), p. 98.

6   Ibid., pp. 60–6.

7   Fin Sparre to the Chemical Department, Aug. 8, 1919, Acc. 1784. Reese stated his position on the subject in a discussion following the presentation of a paper at an AIChE meeting. The comments were printed along with the paper (Guy B. Taylor, "Some Economic Aspects of Ammonia Oxidation," *Transactions of the American Institute of Chemical Engineers* 14 [1921–22]: 59–66).

8   Thomas H. Chilton, "Guy Baker Taylor," in Wyndham D. Miles, *American Chemists and Chemical Engineers* (Washington: American Chemical Society, 1976), p. 470.

9   On Zeisberg, see Thomas H. Chilton and Herbert T. Pratt, "Frederick Clemens Zeisberg," in Miles, *American Chemists and Chemical Engineers*, pp. 530–1, and Acc. 1410, Box 62.

10   For biographical details on Chilton, see *Who Was Who* (Chicago: Marquis, 1973), vol. 5, pp. 129–30. See also "Man of the Month – Thomas H. Chilton," *Chemical Engineering* (Jan. 1951): 233.

11   Chilton, *Strong Water*, pp. 60–6.

12   Clifford A. Woodbury, "Recent Advances in the Manufacture of Nitric Acid," paper presented at meeting of the chemical directors, May 26–7, 1930, Acc. 1784. On the chemistry of the process, see Guy B. Taylor, Thomas H. Chilton, and Stanley L. Handforth, "Manufacture of Nitric Acid by the Oxidation of Ammonia," *Industrial and Engineering Chemistry* 23 (1931): 860–5.

13   Fred Zeisberg to Hamilton Bradshaw, Aug. 16, 1925, Acc. 1784.

14   Chilton, *Strong Water*, pp. 88–96.

15   Woodbury, "Recent Advances."

16   H. G. Chickering to F. Sparre, "Comparative Costs of Nitric Acid Manufacture, Repauno Works – Year 1929, Atmospheric vs. Pressure Process," Feb. 14, 1930; H. G. Chickering to F. Sparre, "Addenda to Office Report of February 14, 1930, Comparative Cost of Nitric Acid Manufacture, Atmospheric vs. Pressure Process," Mar. 12, 1930; and F. Sparre to W. F. Harrington, "Nitric Acid," Mar. 12, 1930, Acc. 1813, Box 2.

17   Chilton, *Strong Water*, p. 98.

18   The annual reports of the Chemical Department detail the chemical-engineering-related studies during these years (Acc. 1784). The statistics on the number and percentage of chemical engineers in the Chemical Department were calculated from Chemical Department organization charts in Acc. 1784 and biographical entries in *American Men of Science*, 5th ed. (1933).

19   On Greenewalt, see Acc. 1410, Box 63, and "Crawford H. Greenewalt – Positions Held in the Du Pont Company, 1922 to date," GM Suit, DTE DP465.

20   Crawford H. Greenewalt to C. M. A. Stine, "Fundamental Problems in High Pressure Research," Mar. 30, 1927, and "Fundamental Research on Chemical Engineering Problems," Acc. 1784, Box 16.

21   Charles M. A. Stine to the Executive Committee, "Fundamental Research in the Du Pont Company," Mar. 31, 1927, Acc. 1784, Box 16.

22   William A. Peters, an expert in the field of distillation, had joined Du Pont in

1915. His research focused on the performance of distillation towers containing glass rings of various sizes instead of the columns that contained metal plates. (William A. Peters, "Distillation – Efficiency Capacity of Fractionating Columns," Report B197-2, Acc. 1784, Box 11.) On Peters, see *The National Cyclopedia of American Biography*, vol. 39, pp. 426–7.

23 Arthur P. Tanberg to C. M. A. Stine, "Summary of Fundamental Research to Date," Oct. 24, 1928, Acc. 1784, Box 16.

24 On the organization and personnel of the chemical engineering group, see Donald F. Boucher, *History of the Engineering Technology Laboratory, Part I: The First 25 Years, 1929–1953* (Wilmington, Del.: Du Pont, Engineering Department, Engineering R&D Division, 1980), pp. 15–23. On Genereaux, see *American Men of Science*, 9th ed. (1955).

25 Thomas H. Chilton to C. M. A. Stine, "Chemical Engineering Research," Oct. 21, 1929, Acc. 1813, Box 1. Beginning in 1929, McAdams spent about two days a month at Du Pont (Boucher, *History*, p. 22).

26 Chilton, "Chemical Engineering Research."

27 Thomas H. Chilton, "Plans for Chemical Engineering Work at the Experimental Station," paper presented at meeting of chemical directors, May 26–7, 1930, Acc. 1784.

28 For statistics on chemical engineering research, see "Talk Given to Board of Directors, Dec. 17, 1934, by Dr. C. M. A. Stine," Acc. 1706.

29 Genereaux interview.

30 Olaf A. Hougen, "Allan P. Colburn," *Chemical Engineering Education* 3 (Fall 1969): 168–71, 193.

31 See *Dictionary of Scientific Biography*, s.v. "Reynolds, Osborne," and s.v. "Nusselt, Ernst Kraft Wilhelm." On semiempirical correlations, see Hougen, "Colburn," p. 171.

32 Hougen, "Colburn," p. 171.

33 Ibid.

34 Conversation with John Munroe, Dec. 1984. Colburn's fondness for sports is noted in Hougen, "Colburn," p. 171. On playing golf at lunch, see Genereaux interview.

35 For the number of PhDs awarded in chemical engineering, see James O. Maloney, "Doctoral Thesis Work in Chemical Engineering in the United States from the beginning to 1960," in William F. Furter, ed., *A Century of Chemical Engineering* (New York: Plenum, 1982), pp. 211–24. On Chilton's interest in Colburn, see Thomas H. Chilton, "Allan Philip Colburn – The Years with Du Pont," *International Journal of Heat and Mass Transfer* 7 (1964): 1347–51.

36 For the papers that Colburn and Chilton published, see Boucher, *History*, exhibit R. The quote is from Chilton, "Colburn," p. 1348.

37 Robert L. Pigford, "Allan Philip Colburn – The Years in Education," *International Journal of Heat and Mass Transfer* 7 (1964): 1356.

38 Leonard S. Reich, "Irving Langmuir and the Pursuit of Science and Technology in the Corporate Environment," *Technology and Culture* 24 (1983): 199–221.

39 Hougen, "Colburn," pp. 170–1, and Robert L. Pigford, "Chemical Technology: The Past 100 Years," *Chemical and Engineering News* (Apr. 6, 1976): 197–8.

40 Chilton, "Colburn," pp. 1348–9. The award-winning paper was Allan P. Col-

burn, "A Method of Correlating Forced Convection Heat-Transfer Data and a Comparison with Fluid Friction," *Transactions of the American Institute of Chemical Engineers* 29 (1938): 174–210.

41 Chilton, "Colburn," pp. 1349–50.

42 In 1960, three professors at the University of Wisconsin published a landmark textbook that treats momentum, heat, and mass transfer analogously and analyzes them in a fundamental fashion using sophisticated mathematical techniques. R. Byron Bird, Warren E. Stewart, and Edwin N. Lightfoot, *Transport Phenomena* (New York: Wiley, 1960).

43 Up to this time, Delaware's chemical engineering program had been an adjunct of the chemistry department. The faculty consisted of one man, Edward M. Schoenborn, who had received an MS degree in chemical engineering from Ohio State University in 1935. Delaware's curriculum was not accredited by the Engineer's Council for Professional Development. Walter Hullihen, "President's Report," Dec. 11, 1937, Hullihen Papers, University of Delaware Archives, Newark, Delaware. On Schoenbron, see *American Men of Science*, 9th ed.

44 Chilton, "Colburn," p. 1350. The dates of his absence from Du Pont are in Boucher, *History*, Exhibit B.

45 Robert L. Spencer to Walter Hullihen, Mar. 23, 1938, Hullihen papers. On his salary, see Walter Hullihen to J. P. Cann (p. 615), 1938, Hullihen papers and "University of Delaware Faculty Salary List" (p. 908), 1938, Hullihen papers.

46 His plans to take a daily nap were noted by Pigford, "Colburn," p. 1353. Colburn's consulting is mentioned in Boucher, *History*, p. 22.

47 Robert L. Spencer to G. E. Dutton, Mar. 9, 1939, Hullihen papers.

48 Later, he served as assistant to the president of the university from 1947 to 1950 and as provost of the university from 1950 until his death in 1955. Hougen, "Colburn," p. 173.

49 John H. Perry, ed., *Chemical Engineers' Handbook* (New York: McGraw-Hill, 1934).

50 Sidney D. Kirkpatrick, "John Howard Perry," in Miles, *American Chemists and Chemical Engineers*, pp. 387–8.

51 Ibid.

52 Sidney D. Kirkpatrick, "Building the Literature of Chemical Engineering," *Chemical Engineering* (July 1952): 173.

53 On the Engineering Department's technical division, see Boucher, *History*, pp. 18, 33–8.

54 On Henry Belin du Pont, see Acc. 1410, Box 62. On the number of personnel in the new group, see Boucher, *History*, pp. 17–18. The expenditure figures are from "Annual Research Expenditures – Categories B, C, D, E. Years: 1930–1950 Inclusive," Apr. 30, 1946, Acc. 1814, Box 5.

55 For the list of chemical engineers who left Du Pont, see Boucher, *History*, exhibit Q. On Maloney and Pigford, see *American Men and Women of Science*, 14th ed. (1979), Physical and Biological Sciences Section.

56 On the criticism of academic chemical engineering, see Robert L. Pigford, "Chemical Technology: The Past 100 Years," *Chemical and Engineering News* (Apr. 6, 1976): 200–2; and Olaf A. Hougen, "Seven Decades of Chemical

Engineering," *Chemical Engineering Progress* 1973 (Jan. 1977): 102–4. W. Robert Marshall voiced similar criticisms of his colleagues in academia in 1964. W. Robert Marshall, Jr., "Science Ain't Everything," *Chemical Engineering Progress* 60 (Jan. 1964): 17.

57 Thomas H. Chilton, "Advances in Technology Through Engineering Research, a Five Year Report of Engineering Accomplishments," Sept. 1958, Engrg. Hist. Files.

58 Ibid.

59 Ibid.

60 After retiring from Du Pont in 1959, Chilton spent the next ten years traveling the world, spending a year each at various universities. He died in 1973. (See Chilton entry in *Who Was Who*, vol. 5.)

Chapter 15. The Conduct of Research

1 Howard R. Bartlett, "The Development of Industrial Research in the United States," in National Resources Planning Board, *Research: A National Resource* (Washington, D.C.: U.S. Government Printing Office, 1941), II, pp. 71–2; Richard L. Lesher, "Independent Research Institutes and Industrial Applications of Aerospace Research" (PhD diss., Indiana University, 1963), pp. 76–9; Harold Vagtborg, *Research and American Industrial Development* (New York: Pergamon, 1976), pp. 124–9.

2 Charles L. Reese to Pierre S. du Pont, Apr. 24, 1918, Acc. 1662, Box 16.

3 EC Minutes, May 17, 1918. In 1932, Bolton reported that the average annual expenditure for Du Pont Fellowships was "about $22,500." By this time, awards were for $750, and the company had sponsored 329 fellowships since 1918. (Elmer K. Bolton, "Development of Research in the Du Pont Company," Dec. 20, 1932, II, 2, Box 1035.) By 1952, Du Pont had awarded 1,037 graduate fellowships and was spending about $275,000 annually. (Cole Coolidge, "Organization of Du Pont Research," June 23, 1952, Acc. 1850.)

4 F. S. Johnson to H. R. Carveth, Apr. 10, 1931, Acc. 1813, Box 8.

5 Willis F. Harrington to Lammot du Pont, Jan. 2, 1930, Acc. 1813, Box 2; E. K. Bolton to E. M. Flaherty, Jan. 15, 1930 (attached to W. F. Harrington to J. E. Crane, Jan. 13, 1930), Acc. 1813, Box 2.

6 E. K. Bolton to J. B. Conant, Dec. 10, 1927, James B. Conant Papers, Harvard University Archives, Cambridge, Mass., Box 5.

7 Harrington to du Pont, Jan. 2, 1930.

8 Johnson to Carveth, Apr. 20, 1931. Bolton reiterated this point in 1932 in "Development of Research in the Du Pont Company."

9 "Semi-Annual Report of the Chemical Department, January–June, 1920," Sept. 28, 1920, p. 69, Acc. 1784.

10 Notes on Meeting of the Directors of the Chemical Sections of E. I. du Pont de Nemours & Co...., Apr. 22, 1927, Acc. 1662, Box 17.

11 EC Minutes, Oct. 3, 1934. See also EC Minutes, Sept. 28, 1934.

12 E. K. Bolton to J. B. Conant, Dec. 31, 1936, Acc. 1850.

13 E. K. Bolton to R. C. Fuson, Oct. 31, 1940, Papers of Reynold C. Fuson, University of Illinois Archives, Box 1.

14 A copy is in the Papers of Roger Adams, University of Illinois Archives, Box 6.

15 Notes on Meeting of the Directors..., Apr. 22, 1927.

16 "The Aim and Problems of the Personnel Division," presented at the chemical directors' meeting, May 26–7, 1930, Acc. 1784. The complaints in 1928 were issued in F. C. Evans, "Scouting for Chemists in Our Colleges," Oct. 27, 1928, Acc. 1784.

17 Skit, Adams Papers.

18 On Tanberg, see his obituary, *Wilmington Morning News*, July 15, 1963.

19 A. P. Tanberg to C. M. A. Stine, June 9, 1925, Acc. 1784.

20 Elmer K. Bolton, "Certain Phases of Research Work," Oct. 27, 1928, Acc. 1662, Box 17.

21 Victor Cofman to C. M. A. Stine et al., May 9, 1929, Acc. 1784.

22 Daniel J. Kevles, *The Physicists: The History of a Scientific Community in Modern America* (New York: Knopf, 1978), p. 211.

23 F. W. Pickard to E. K. Bolton, Apr. 25, 1933, Acc. 1662, Box 17.

24 E. K. Bolton to J. E. Crane, Sept. 29, 1933, II, 2, Box 1035.

25 Abundant information on Mark's consulting with the Rayon Department is contained in PR Records.

26 Biographical information on Mark has been based principally on Herman Mark, "Polymer Chemistry in Europe and America – How It All Began," *Journal of Chemical Education* 58 (1981): 527–34. Du Pont managed to secure Mark a position at Brooklyn Polytechnic Institute through William F. Zimmerli, who had first called Mark to Du Pont's attention in 1933. (See Hamilton Bradshaw, Memorandum for File, June 2, 1933, Acc. 1784.) Zimmerli, who had a PhD from Heidelberg (1912), had been Du Pont's European technical representative during much of the 1930s and was a member of Sparre's Development Department until 1942 when he left Du Pont to become a vice president of General Aniline and Film Corporation. Spurred by Ernest Benger, who had been impressed with Mark and wanted to retain him as a consultant to the Rayon Department, Zimmerli used his influence as a member of Brooklyn Poly's board of directors to convince Brooklyn's president, H. S. Rogers, and dean, E. R. Kirk, to offer Mark an adjunct professorship. Zimmerli assured Rogers that Du Pont had retained Mark as a consultant and was providing him "adequate support." At this time, Brooklyn Poly operated a national testing laboratory for shellac (the Shellac Bureau), and Mark was initially assigned to this operation. On Zimmerli's and Benger's efforts, see the interview with Mark in the American Chemical Society's Eminent Chemists Videotape Series, Oct. 31, 1981. See also G. Allan Stahl, "Herman F. Mark: The Geheimrat," in *Polymer Science Overview: A Tribute to Herman F. Mark*, ed. G. Allan Stahl (Washington: American Chemical Society, 1981), pp. 81–83. On Zimmerli, see *American Men of Science*, 7th ed. (1944).

27 Heckert's comments are penciled on G. P. Hoff's copy of Ernest B. Benger to V. L. Bohnson et al., Feb. 21, 1941, II, 2, Box 963.

28 See, for example, D. F. B[abcock(?)] to W.W.H[eckert], Feb. 24, 1941, and W. H. Charch to E. B. Benger, Sept. 22, 1941, II, 2, Box 963.

29 Notes on Meeting of the Directors..., Apr. 22, 1927. The consultants were: J. A. Nieuwland (Notre Dame), Morris Kharasch (Maryland), A. H. Pfund (Johns Hopkins), E. E. Reid (Johns Hopkins), H. S. Taylor (Princeton), E. C. Bingham (Lafayette), and E. O. Kraemer (Wisconsin).

30 C. M. A. Stine to Roger Adams, Sept. 13, 1927, Adams Papers, Box 9. As of Sept. 1, 1928, Adams's salary at Illinois was $8,000 a year (H. E. Cunningham to Roger Adams, July 3, 1928, Adams Papers, Box 9).

31 Adams's terms are apparent in C. M. A. Stine to Roger Adams, Apr. 16, 1928, Adams Papers, Box 9. See also Marvel interview.

32 Stine to Adams, Sept. 13, 1927.

33 Marvel interview. Exactly when Adams and Marvel stopped writing reports is unclear. In late 1929, however, they were still submitting quarterly literature surveys. See Elmer K. Bolton to James B. Conant, Dec. 23, 1929, Conant Papers, Box 5.

34 Cairns interview, Nov. 12, 1982.

35 Ibid.

36 On Marvel, see Marvel interview; "Carl Shipp Marvel: 'Speed at 90,' " *Macromolecules* 17 (1984): 1641–3; and J. E. Mulvaney, "Interview with Carl S. Marvel," *Impact* 53 (1976): 609–13.

37 Marvel interview.

38 On Flory and Carothers's influence, see Harold A. Scheraga, "Paul J. Flory on His 70th Birthday," *Macromolecules* 13 (May–June 1980): 8A–10A; Walter H. Stockmayer, "The 1974 Nobel Prize for Chemistry," *Science* 186 (1974): 724–6; and the interview with Flory in the American Chemical Society's Eminent Chemists Videotape Series, Feb. 14, 1982.

39 James B. Conant to Elmer K. Bolton, May 2, 1927, Conant Papers, Box 3.

40 James B. Conant to L. R. Fieser, Apr. 9, 1929, Conant Papers, Box 3.

41 L. R. Fieser to James B. Conant, Apr. 6, 1929, Conant Papers, Box 5.

42 See, for example, Conant's letters to Elmer K. Bolton, June 6 and 18, July 12 and 15, 1929, Conant Papers, Box 3.

43 Roger Adams to James B. Conant, July 11, 1929, Conant Papers, Box 8. See also Adams to Conant, June 1, 1929, Conant Papers, Box 5.

44 Frank M. McMillan, *The Chain Straighteners* (London: Macmillan, 1979). Mark's cachet, "Geheimrat" (or "Privy Councillor"), did not grow out of thin air. As McMillan wrote, Mark "constituted a one-man Early Warning System on new developments in polymers for a number of research laboratories for whom he consulted" (pp. 40–1). See also pp. 113–16.

45 Herman Schroeder, unrecorded interview with David A. Hounshell, Feb. 8, 1984.

46 The above section has been informed by our interviews with Julian Hill, Merlin Brubaker, David McQueen, Carl S. Marvel, Samuel Lenher, Chaplin Tyler, Raymond Genereaux, J. Burton Nichols, and Theodore Cairns.

47 Research managers, including Charles Stine, Elmer Bolton, and Merlin Brubaker, emphasized this point. See especially Brubaker interview.

48 Notes on Discussion at Chemical Directors' Meeting Held at Wilmington, May 24, 1935, Pioneering Research Laboratory Technical Correspondence, 1935, File P-31, PR Records.

49 Throughout this period, the employee agreement on proprietary information was known as Form G-166. Similar forms had been used from as early as 1903.

50 This policy, which was implemented in 1908, was periodically updated and appeared in the company's "Manual of Standard Practice." See also EC Minutes, Nov. 20, 1929.

51 Norton A. Higgins has argued that Du Pont's patent policy established its publication policy, de facto. Higgins, telephone conversation with John K. Smith, Apr. 1, 1985.

52 A. P. Tanberg to R. C. Fuson, March 24, 1928, Fuson Papers, Box 1.

53 These perceptions were based on fact. In several important instances, researchers had been barred from publishing their work, and this news circulated in the chemical community. See, e.g., the case of publication on nitric acid manufacture, documented in Acc. 1662, Box 16.

54 A. P. Tanberg, "Introduction," June 30, 1938, *Contributions to the Scientific Literature from the Experimental Station....* (Wilmington, Del.: Du Pont, 1938). Du Pont was by no means a pioneer with the *Contributions*. At Kodak's Research Laboratory, C. E. Kenneth Mees initiated in 1913 a numbered series of publications in leading professional and scientific journals. Kodak annually abridged and bound these publications and issued them under the title *Abridged Scientific Publications*. In 1915, Kodak also began to abstract all photographic literature and publish these abstracts as *Kodak Abstract Bulletin*. At American Telephone and Telegraph, the *Bell System Technical Journal* was published beginning in 1922, and with the incorporation of Bell Telephone Laboratories in the mid-1920s, the *Bell Laboratories Record* began publication in 1925. General Electric also began publishing the *General Electric Review* in 1903. See also the wide variety of research laboratory publications listed in *Industrial Research Laboratories of the United States* (7th ed., 1944), pp. 315–16.

55 Wallace H. Carothers and G. J. Berchet, "Amides from ε-Aminocaproic Acid," *Journal of the American Chemical Society* 52 (1930): 5289–91.

56 EC Minutes, May 12, 1938. See also Fin Sparre to Fritz Ter Meer, May 3, 1938, *U.S. v. I.C.I., et al.*, D.T.E. 1145.

57 B. Achilladelis, "A Study in Technological History. Part I. The Manufacture of 'Perlon' (nylon 6) and Caprolactam by I. G. Farbenindustrie," *Chemistry and Industry* (1970): 1549–52.

58 Cairns interview, Nov. 12, 1982.

59 The Chemical Department established a publications committee in the mid-1940s to review manuscripts and Du Pont's proprietary position prior to releasing them for publication. Ibid.

60 Ernest B. Benger, "Organization of Industrial Research," *Industrial and Engineering Chemistry* 22 (1930): 572–3. Elmer Bolton expressed similar views in his "Certain Phases of Research Work," Oct. 27, 1928, Acc. 1662, Box 17. It should be noted that the nomenclature for "research group" and "group leader" varied from department to department and over time, but the basic organizational structure remained constant.

61 On the project system, see A. P. Tanberg to J. A. Burckel, Sept. 20, 1938, Acc. 1784.

62 Notes on Meeting the Directors..., Apr. 22, 1927. See also Notes on Discussion at Chemical Directors' Meeting..., May 24, 1935.

63 Notes on Discussion at Chemical Directors' Meeting..., May 24, 1935.

64 Differences in salary practices are detailed in Notes of Meeting of the Directors..., Apr. 22, 1927. Du Pont followed national trends in salary scales for industrial research through the Directors of Industrial Research. See, e.g., the minutes of their meeting of Dec. 20, 1935, Acc. 1851, Box 1.

65 EC Minutes, Jan. 26, 1911. Subsequent modifications to the bonus system are

indexed in "Special Compensation Policy Changes," Special Compensation Files.

66 Special Compensation Files. See especially C. L. Burdick to J. E. Crane, Sept. 25, 1942, for a comprehensive analysis of "A" bonus awards (and data on "B" bonus awards). In 1941, there were 133 "A" bonus awards and 2,400 "B" bonus awards.

67 Our advisors, Robert M. Joyce and Herman E. Schroeder, conveyed this jewel of Du Pont culture to us at a meeting on Oct. 18, 1982.

68 *The Central Chemical Department and Its Laboratory: The Experimental Station, Wilmington, Delaware* (Wilmington, Del.: Du Pont, 1928), pp. 28–9.

69 Bolton, "Certain Phases of Research Work."

70 Benger, "Organization of Industrial Research," p. 575.

71 Ibid., p. 573.

72 A. P. Tanberg [to C. M. A. Stine], Dec. 1, 1926, and C. M. A. Stine to J. B. Jessup, Dec. 3, 1926, Acc. 1784.

73 L. G. Wise, "A Central Filing System," Apr. 29, 1935, attached to Wise to Ernest Benger, Apr. 29, 1935, Acc. 1784.

74 This state of affairs was reported to us by Charles H. Arrington, Herman E. Schroeder, and Robert M. Joyce, on the occasion of our R&D history project advisory committee meeting, Mar. 26, 1985, Hagley Museum and Library. For later evidence, see J. M. Clark, "Discourse re Plastics Department Electrochemicals Department Hassle," Nov. 2, 1965, Acc. 1404, Box 9.

75 G. P. Hoff to Herman Mark, Oct. 13, 1941, II, 2, Box 963.

76 Information on the steering committee has been gathered from Ruth Phelps, "Chemical Department Steering Committee: A Brief History," June 10, 1930, Acc. 1814, Box 5; Early Minutes of the Steering Committee, Acc. 1784; A. P. Tanberg to J. A. Burckel, Sept. 20, 1938, Acc. 1784.

77 The shift toward increasing formality in the steering committee has been noted by a number of former members of the Chemical Department in interviews with the authors. See especially McGrew interview and Cairns interview, Nov. 12, 1982.

78 Julian Hill interview.

79 A. P. Tanberg to Burckel, Sept. 20, 1938, Acc. 1784.

80 See, e.g., Elmer K. Bolton, "Development of Research in the Du Pont Company." In *Industrial Research Laboratories of the United States* (7th ed., 1940), Bolton was listed as the "executive officer in charge of research."

81 See, e.g., "Notes on Meeting of the Directors of the Chemical Sections," April 22, 1927. See also E. B. Benger to J. Weir, June 14, 1935, II, 2, Box 530.

82 Lammot du Pont to H. F. Brown, July 17, 1929, Acc. 1662, Box 17.

83 General Managers' Meeting, Jan. 20, 1930, Acc. 1813, Box 3.

84 Ibid.

85 Maxwell Moore to E. G. Ackart et al., Apr. 2, 1930, Acc. 1813, Box 5.

86 EC Minutes, Oct. 29 and Nov. 19, 1930.

87 Charles Stine to E. G. Ackart et al., "Research Coordination," Nov. 18, 1930, Acc. 1662, Box 17.

88 During Bolton's administration, there were no official minutes kept of the chemical directors' meetings. However, agendas were circulated, and occasionally those directors in attendance reported on the meeting to their general managers. For an example of such a meeting at which Stine spoke, see W. H.

Charch to E. K. Gladding, Nov. 16, 1937, "Chemical Directors' Meeting, Wilmington, November 12, 1937," PR Records. On the policy of no minutes, see Benger to Weir, June 14, 1935.

89   Grasselli's main research laboratories were in Cleveland.

90   For figures on unemployment, see Series D 85–86, *Historical Statistics of the United States, Colonial Times to 1970*, Part 1 (Washington: U.S. Bureau of the Census, 1975).

91   Annual Reports, Du Pont, 1929–33.

92   Ernest B. Benger to A. P. Tanberg, Aug. 29, 1930, Acc. 1784.

93   Elmer K. Bolton, "Development of Research in the Du Pont Company." See also A. P. Tanberg to E. B. Benger, Sept. 26, 1930, Acc. 1784, and A. P. Tanberg to E. K. Bolton, Oct. 29, 1930, Acc. 1662, Box 17.

94   EC Minutes, July 13, 20, 1932.

95   Bolton, "Development of Research in the Du Pont Company."

96   Walter S. Carpenter, Jr., "Outline of Talk . . . at Chemical Directors' Luncheon," Dec. 7, 1934, attached to Ernest B. Benger to E. R. Allen et al., Dec. 24, 1934, II, 2, Box 1035.

97   Bartlett, "Development of Industrial Research in the United States," p. 37.

98   Ibid., pp. 19–77.

99   See data in George Perazich and Philip M. Field, *Industrial Research and Changing Technology* (Philadelphia: U.S. Works Projects Administration, 1940).

100 Robert M. Yerkes to F. B. Jewett, Jan. 22, 1923, quoted in Alfred D. Flinn, "Directors of Industrial Research: Brief History," June 1934, in Directors of Industrial Research Minutes, 1923–42 (bound volume), Acc. 1851, Box 1.

101 Ellwood Hendrick, quoted in ibid.

102 DIR Minutes, 1923–42, Acc. 1851, Box 1.

103 DIR Minutes, May 17, 1927, Acc. 1851, Box 1.

104 These tours are noted in the DIR minutes.

Chapter 16. The War Years and Postwar Expansion of Research

1   U.S. Congress, Senate Special Committee Investigating the Munitions Industry, *Munitions Industry*, Part 5, Sept. 12, 13, 14, 1934, 73d Cong., 1934, E. I. du Pont de Nemours & Co.

2   See the large newspaper clipping file, "Merchants of Death," in Acc. 1410, Box 36. See also Acc. 1410, Box 52, and "The Du Pont Company and Munitions," Report to Stockholders and Employees of E. I. du Pont de Nemours & Company (Wilmington, Del.: Du Pont, [1934]).

3   "Du Pont II: A Management and Its Philosophy," *Fortune*, Dec. 1934: 88.

4   Elmer K. Bolton to Executive Committee, Oct. 27, 1939, in L. G. Wise and N. G. Fisher, "History, Activities, and Accomplishments of Fundamental Research in the Chemical Department of the Du Pont Company, 1926–1939 Inclusive," Aug. 14, 1940, Acc. 1784; EC Minutes, Nov. 1, 1939.

5   For a brief summary of Du Pont's wartime activities, see Walter S. Carpenter to the Stockholders of E. I. du Pont de Nemours & Co., Wilmington, Del., March 7, 1946, *Du Pont's Part in the National Security Program*, Pamphlet Collection, Hagley Museum and Library. For more detailed, documented histories of each Du Pont wartime project, see Acc. 1410, Boxes 28–31.

6   EC Minutes, Sept. 25, 1940, Jan. 2, Feb. 19, 1942.

7   A. B. Echols to Executive Committee, Oct. 29, 1940, Acc. 1813, Box 31. For information on excess profits taxes, see *Dictionary of American History*, vol. 2, s.v. "Excess Profits Tax."

8   On Carpenter, see *National Cyclopedia of American Biography*, vol. 62, s.v. "Carpenter, Walter Samuel, Jr."

9   W. S. Carpenter, Jr., to Fin Sparre, Jan. 7, 1941, II, 2, Box 832.

10   A. B. Echols, "Memorandum," Feb. 3, 1941, attached to A. B. Echols to W. S. Carpenter, Jr., et al., Feb. 3, 1941, Acc. 1813, Box 34.

11   Aug. 29, 1941, Acc. 1813, Box 36.

12   See especially A. B. Echols to W. S. Carpenter, Jr., Sept. 5, 1941, Acc. 1813, Box 36.

13   See Acc. 1813, Box 36, for these responses.

14   E. K. Bolton to Executive Committee, "Chemical Department Annual Report 1942," Jan. 15, 1943, Acc. 1784.

15   The Chemical Department's wartime work is covered in its reports to the Executive Committee for 1942, 1943, for the period from January 1, 1944, to March 31, 1945, and for the period from April 1, 1945, to March 31, 1946, as well as in "Outline of the Activities of the Chemical Department, E. I. du Pont de Nemours & Company, in Connection with the War Effort," Oct. 4, 1946, Acc. 1784. The Cordura development is covered in the above-cited documents and in *Du Pont's Part in the National Security Program*, pp. 47–8.

16   E. K. Bolton to Executive Committee, "Report of the Work of the Chemical Department from January 1, 1944 to March 31, 1945," Apr. 6, 1945, Acc. 1784.

17   Bush maintained that the war, although a great boon to applied research, had prohibited basic research from being done, and therefore a severe shortage of scientific capital had arisen. See Vannevar Bush, *Science the Endless Frontier: A Report to the President* (Washington: U.S. Government Printing Office, 1945). See especially pp. 4, 12–17.

18   Pp. 22–3.

19   Du Pont's role in the Manhattan Project has been treated by Richard G. Hewlett and Oscar E. Anderson, Jr., *A History of the United States Atomic Energy Commission*, vol. 1, *The New World* (Washington: U.S. Atomic Energy Commission, 1972); Leslie R. Groves, *Now It Can Be Told* (New York: Harper & Row, 1962); and Vincent C. Jones, *Manhattan: The Army and the Bomb* (Washington: Center for Military History, U.S. Army, 1985).

20   EC Minutes, Dec. 9, 11, 14, 16, 1942. Du Pont's board of directors ratified the Executive Committee's action on Dec. 21, 1942 (Greenewalt Diary, Acc. 1889, Dec. 21, 1942). On the company's commitment of its best technical personnel to the Manhattan Project, see Greenewalt Diary, Nov. 11, 1942.

21   Greenewalt Diary, Acc. 1889, Dec. 16, 17, 18, 1942.

22   Hewlett and Anderson, *New World*, p. 191.

23   Greenewalt Diary, Acc. 1889, Dec. 18, 19, 22, 1942.

24   Ibid., Dec. 28, 1942. See also Greenewalt interview, Dec. 15, 1982.

25   Greenewalt Diary, Acc. 1889, Dec. 28, 1942.

26   Ibid., Dec. 28, 1942, Jan. 13, Feb. 3, 1943.

27   Ibid., Mar. 12, Apr. 24, July 29, 1943.

28   Ibid., Jan. 4, 5, 6, Mar. 20, 25, Apr. 7, May 20, July 30, 31, Aug. 3, 5, 12,

13, 16, 19, 21, Sept. 16, Oct. 18, 28, 1943, Apr. 10, 22, 1944. Both Arthur H. Compton, *Atomic Quest: A Personal Narrative* (New York: Oxford University Press, 1956), and Hewlett and Anderson, *New World*, discuss the discontent of the Chicago physicists.

29 Hewlett and Anderson, *New World*, pp. 210–12.

30 Both the Greenewalt Diary and Greenewalt interview are replete with discussions of getting major design questions frozen and the animosity this induced at Chicago. See also Hewlett and Anderson, *New World*; Richard G. Hewlett, "Beginnings of Development in Nuclear Technology," *Technology and Culture* 17 (1976): 474–5; Crawford H. Greenewalt, "Reminiscences," in *The Nuclear Chain Reaction – Forty Years Later*, Robert G. Sachs, ed. (Chicago: University of Chicago Press, 1984), pp. 277–80; and Samuel K. Allison, unpub. address before the trustees of the University of Chicago, Jan. 14, 1960, in Acc. 1814, Box 31.

31 Hewlett and Anderson, *New World*, pp. 305–8; Greenewalt Diary, Acc. 1889, Sept. 27, 28, 29, 30, 1944.

32 Greenewalt Diary, Acc. 1889, Feb. 15, 1943.

33 Ibid., Mar. 2, 1943.

34 Ibid., Mar. 9, July 27, Dec. 2, 1943.

35 Ibid., Dec. 8, 1943.

36 Ibid., Jan. 15, Mar. 28, 1944.

37 Ibid., July 27, 1944.

38 Ibid., Feb. 17, Mar. 4, 13, 15, 21, June 22, 1944.

39 See, e.g., Samuel K. Allison to Roger Williams, Mar. 13, 1944, in ibid., Mar. 13, 1944.

40 Greenewalt Diary, Acc. 1889, July 27, 1944.

41 Ibid.

42 EC Minutes, Dec. 13, 1944.

43 Charles M. A. Stine to Executive Committee, Feb. 12, 1945; II, 2, Box 830.

44 Ibid.

45 Ibid.

46 Ibid. The postwar history of nuclear energy is treated in Hewlett and Anderson, *New World*, and in Richard G. Hewlett and Francis Duncan, *A History of the United States Atomic Energy Commission*, vol. 2, *Atomic Shield* (Washington: U.S. Atomic Energy Commission, 1972) and idem., *Nuclear Navy, 1946–62* (Chicago: University of Chicago Press, 1974).

47 EC Minutes, Feb. 22, 1945.

48 Roger Williams to W. S. Carpenter, Jr., Aug. 28, 1945, II, 2, Box 832.

49 Hewlett and Anderson, *New World*, pp. 425, 629.

50 L. R. Groves to W. S. Carpenter, Jr., Feb. 27, 1946, II, 2, Box 830.

51 Robert P. Patterson to W. S. Carpenter, Jr., Mar. 15, 1946, II, 2, Box 830.

52 [W. S. Carpenter, Jr.], "Memorandum," Apr. 11, 1946, II, 2, Box 830.

53 Ibid.

54 C. H. Greenewalt to W. S. Carpenter, Jr., Feb. 16, 1948, II, 2, Box 843.

55 Minutes of the Board of Directors' Meeting, Dec. 20, 1948, E. I. du Pont de Nemours & Co., Wilmington, Del.

56 C. H. Greenewalt to W. S. Carpenter, Jr., Feb. 22, 1949, II, 2, Box 843.

57 EC Minutes, Aug. 17, 24, 1950.

58 EC Minutes, Mar. 23, 1949. See also EC Minutes, Sept. 27, 1945.

59 Du Pont had already begun to feel the effects of increased competition in recruitment of high-caliber PhD chemists. See E. K. Bolton to Lammot du Pont, April 16, 1941, Acc. 1662, Box 22. Carpenter had keenly appreciated that there would be increased research competition following the war. See his letter to E. K. Bolton, Oct. 9, 1945, II, 2, Box 832.

60 Ellis W. Hawley, "Antitrust," in *Encyclopedia of American Economic History*, ed. Glenn Porter (New York: Scribners, 1980), vol. 2., p. 780. This section's interpretation of changing antitrust interpretations during this period is based mainly on Hawley's work. See also the important article by John McDonald, "Businessmen and the Sherman Act," *Fortune*, Jan. 1950, pp. 104–8, 110–12, 114.

61 Statement of Thurman W. Arnold in U.S. Congress, Senate Committee on Patents, Hearings on S. 2303, 77th Cong., 2d Sess., Apr. 13–17, 1942, pp. 630–1.

62 Justice Harold Burton in the *American Tobacco* case of 1946, as quoted in McDonald, "Businessmen and the Sherman Act," p. 105.

63 "The Du Pont Company's Future Policy with Respect to Its Expansion in the Chemical Industry," Aug. 29, 1941, Acc. 1813, Box 36. See also the Development Department's views in N. P. Wescott to A. B. Echols, "Future Expansion Policy," Oct. 14, 1941, in Acc. 1813, Box 36.

64 Du Pont's interpretation of the "Aluminum Doctrine" led it to set up a new competitor in the cellophane business, Olin Industries. C. H. Greenewalt to W. S. Carpenter, Jr., May 27, 1947, II, 2, Box 829, and Jan. 18, Mar. 11, 1949, II, 2, Box 843.

65 Hawley, "Antitrust," p. 783.

66 See, e.g., Development Department to Executive Committee, "Future Activities of Du Pont Company," Aug. 5, 1949, LMSS, Series A, File 418-26-80. Du Pont's annual reports detail the antitrust cases brought against the company. A good summary of cases appears in Acc. 1410, Box 6. See also Greenewalt interview, Jan. 19, 1983.

67 Fin Sparre to Executive Committee, "Post War Problem – 1942," Feb. 5, 1943, II, 2, Box 1032.

68 EC Minutes, Mar. 17, 1943.

69 On Sparre's recommendation of a successor, see Walter S. Carpenter's memorandum of a meeting with Sparre, Feb. 20, 1944, II, 2, Box 832. Gladding had long been a Rayon Department research manager and had most recently headed the department's nylon division. (*Who Was Who in America*, [Chicago: Marquis, 1960], vol. 3, s.v. "Gladding, Ernest Knight.") Sparre had been a member of the board since 1930. See the board's statement on the occasion of his death in Acc. 1410, Box 63.

70 [E. K. Gladding], "Development Department Functions," Acc. 1814, Box 5. A slightly edited version of Gladding's draft went to the Executive Committee under the same title, Oct. 25, 1945, a copy of which survives as an appendix to E. A. Gee to the Executive Committee, "Development Department Functions," Oct. 31, 1963, DD Files.

71 Ibid.

72 EC Minutes, Oct. 31, 1945. It appears that Walter Carpenter, at least, had not

envisioned the Development Department having a different function when he appointed Gladding. See W. S. Carpenter, Jr., to E. K. Gladding, Aug. 28, 1944, II, 2, Box 832.

73 D. H. Dawson to G. H. Greenewalt, Jan. 9, 1956, Acc. 1814, Box 5.

74 R. E. DeRight to E. A. Gee and J. N. Tilley, "Scope and Program of the Development Department," Apr. 9, 1964, DD Files.

75 Jasper E. Crane to E. K. Bolton, Nov. 13, 1943, II, 2, Box 1035.

76 E. K. Bolton to Executive Committee, Oct. 27, 1939, in Wise and Fisher, "History, Activities, and Accomplishments of Fundamental Research in the Chemical Department of the Du Pont Company, 1926–1939 Inclusive," Acc. 1784. See also Bolton to Lammot du Pont, Apr. 16, 1941, Acc. 1662, Box 22.

77 EC Minutes, May 17, 1944.

78 Ibid., Dec. 20, 1944.

79 C. H. Greenewalt to C. M. A. Stine, Feb. 7, 1945, Acc. 1814, Box 37.

80 [C. M. A. Stine] to C. H. Greenewalt, February 8, 1944, Acc. 1814, Box 37.

81 Stine retired on June 18, 1945, and the Executive Committee adapted the Development Department's report on June 13, 1945. EC Minutes, June 13, 1945.

82 C. H. Greenewalt, "Fundamental Research: Definition and Justification," [Feb. 1945], II, 2, Box 837.

83 [Stine] to Greenewalt, Feb. 8, 1944.

84 See Chapter 15 for a discussion of Carpenter's philosophy. Greenewalt's philosophy is stated in a letter to Karl T. Compton, Nov. 6, 1950, Acc. 1814, Box 39.

85 Greenewalt interview, Jan. 19, 1983.

86 EC Minutes, June 13, 1945; Cole Coolidge to E. K. Gladding, Sept. 24, 1945, CRDD Files; and W. S. Carpenter, Jr., to E. K. Bolton, Oct. 9, 1945, II, 2, Box 832.

87 *Three Degrees above Zero* (New York: Scribner, 1984), p. viii.

88 Greenewalt interview, Jan. 19, 1983.

89 EC Minutes, June 13, 1945.

90 W. S. Carpenter, Jr., to E. K. Bolton, Oct. 9, 1945, II, 2, Box 832.

91 Ibid.

92 J. H. Perry to S. W. Sawin, Feb. 19, 1945, PR Records, Box 180181.

93 E. K. Bolton to W. S. Carpenter, Jr., Oct. 10, 1945, II, 2, Box 832.

94 Ibid.

95 EC Minutes, June 12, 1946. See also W. S. Carpenter, Jr., to E. K. Gladding, June 10, 1946, II, 2, Box 832. The "Appropriation Request for the Expansion of the Chemical, Engineering, and Industrial Departments," Project 283-11, Jan. 30, 1948, Cons. Proj. Files, contains additional material on the expansion.

96 E. K. Bolton to Executive Committee, June 27, 1946, CRDD Files.

97 EC Minutes, July 3, 1946.

98 "Appropriation Request." On research budgets, see the Development Department's report, "Research Study – Interim Report," July 9, 1948, in official Annual Research and Development Statistics, Central Research and Development Department, Wilmington, Del.

99 "Appropriation Request."

100 EC Minutes, Feb. 11, 1948.

101 E. F. Lincoln to E. K. Bolton, Feb. 5, 1948, attached to "Appropriation Request."

102 C. H. Greenewalt to W. S. Carpenter, Jr., Mar. 5, 1948, II, 2, Box 843. See also Greenewalt to Carpenter, Feb. 16, 1948, II, 2, Box 843.

103 Greenewalt to Carpenter, Mar. 5, 1948. See also Minutes of the Finance Committee, Mar. 5, 1948, and EC Minutes, Mar. 10, 1948.

104 Information on the construction of laboratories by the industrial departments is contained in the EC Minutes, passim.

105 E. K. Bolton, "Crawford H. Greenewalt," Sept. 12, 1938, LMSS, Series A, File 418-14. See also Bolton's letter on Greenewalt for 1939 in the same file.

106 R. R. M. Carpenter to Lammot du Pont, Oct. 12, 1937, LMSS, Series A, File 418-14. Especially see du Pont's notations.

107 Greenewalt Diary, Acc. 1889, Sept. 28, 29, 1944. See also Compton, *Atomic Quest*, and Crawford H. Greenewalt to Arthur H. Compton, Sept. 15, 1955, Acc. 1814, Box 30.

108 Greenewalt Diary, Acc. 1889, Dec. 3, 1943 (Compton offer) and Greenewalt interview, Dec. 15, 1982 (Fermi offer).

109 Concerns about family management are revealed in Greenewalt Diary, Acc. 1889, May 15, July 7, 1944. That Walter Carpenter was vitally concerned about owner management is abundantly clear in his letter to R. R. M. Carpenter, Jan. 30, 1942, II, 2, Box 825.

110 "Crawford H. Greenewalt: Positions Held in Du Pont Company 1922 to Date," GM Suit, DTE DP465. See also Greenewalt interview, Jan. 19, 1983, and Ruth Miller's interview of Greenewalt, June 2, 1950, Acc. 1850.

111 Greenewalt once said to a congressional committee, "There was a curious question at that time [ca. 1944–48] whether the Army and Navy E's [i.e., achievement awards] that we got would or would not eventually outnumber the antitrust actions, and I am glad to tell you that the E's eventually won out." "Du Pont: The Top Level," *Fortune*, Oct. 1950, p. 93.

112 *Du Pont Company Annual Report 1949*, p. 13.

113 Greenewalt interview, Jan. 19, 1983.

114 Greenewalt, "Fundamental Research."

115 C. H. Greenewalt, "Discussion with Dr. Bolton on Definitions and Justification for Fundamental Research," Feb. 22, 1945, Acc. 1814, Box 37.

116 Particularly see Greenewalt's discussion of fundamental research in his interview with *Fortune* reporter Ruth Moore (see note 110).

117 Quoted in E. K. Bolton to Roger Williams, June 17, 1946, Acc. 1814, Box 37.

118 Ibid.

119 Ibid.

120 See, e.g., E. K. Bolton to Executive Committee, Oct. 27, 1939, in Wise and Fisher, "History, Activities, and Accomplishments of Fundamental Research in the Chemical Department of the Du Pont Company, 1926–1939 Inclusive," Acc. 1784.

121 E. K. Bolton, "The Functions of the Chemical Department," July 14, 1947, CRDD Files. See also EC Minutes, July 16, 1947.

122 See, e.g., C. H. Greenewalt to W. S. Carpenter, Jr., May 27, 1947, II, 2, Box 829, and "Tables Showing Du Pont Labs, Construction and Research Expenditures...," July 4, 1946, Acc. 1814, Box 13.

123 Roger Williams to E. K. Gladding, Dec. 29, 1947, Acc. 1814, Box 37.

124 Neal Thurman to E. K. Gladding, "Research Study – Interim Report," July 9, 1948, CRDD Files.
125 Ibid. See also Cole Coolidge to W. S. Carpenter, Jr., Dec. 21, 1944, II, 2, Box 832, and Roger Williams to W. S. Carpenter, Jr., June 7, 1946, Acc. 1814, Box 37.
126 EC Minutes, Nov. 10, 1948, Jan. 19, Sept. 21, Nov. 30, 1949. See also Development Department to Executive Committee, "Future Activities of Du Pont Company," Aug. 5, 1949, LMSS, Series A, 418-26-8.

Chapter 17. The Pursuit of Science at Du Pont

1 "Why Industry Lures Pure Scientists,"*Business Week* (Jan. 12, 1952): 40–4; and "The New World of Research," *Business Week* (May 28, 1955): 104–32.
2 "The New World of Research," and Francis Bello, "Industrial Research: Geniuses Now Welcome," *Fortune* (Jan. 1956): 96–9, 142–50. On research management generally, see Simon Marcson, *The Scientist in American Industry* (New York: Harper, 1960) and William Kornhauser, *Scientists in Industry* (Berkeley: University of California Press, 1962).
3 "Company Research Staffs Clamor for More Rapport with Management," *Business Week* (Nov. 2, 1957): 120.
4 See Chapter 12.
5 The Du Pont statistics were calculated from data in W. R. G. Bender, *The Scientist as a Person* (Wilmington, Del.: Du Pont, 1958), Pamphlet Collection, Hagley Museum and Library. The comparative industry statistics are from Arnold Thackray, Jeffrey L. Sturchio, P. Thomas Carroll, and Robert Bud, *Chemistry in America, 1876–1976* (Dordrecht, Holland: Reidel, 1985), Tables 5.5 and 5.18.
6 Du Pont fundamental research statistics were compiled from company research statistics in Acc. 1850. The chemical industry figure is from William C. Lillieholm, "For Research a Mighty Challenge," *Chemical Week*, Aug. 14, 1965, pp. 49–72.
7 For the production of PhD chemists, see Thackray et al., *Chemistry in America*, Table 3.3.
8 C. H. Greenewalt to Roger Williams, Apr. 27, 1948, Acc. 1814, Box 30.
9 EC Minutes, Oct. 6, 1948.
10 Robert M. Hutchins to W. S. Carpenter, Jr., Jan. 26, 1946; W. S. Carpenter, Jr., to Robert M. Hutchins, Feb. 15, 1946; and Spencer Brownell, Jr., to W. S. Carpenter, Jr., Feb. 3, 1946, Acc. 1814, Box 30.
11 For a short history of Du Pont's aid to education, see Julian W. Hill to P. L. Salzberg et al., "Du Pont Aid to Education – Supplement to Minutes of April 7, 1964 Meeting," Apr. 16, 1964, Acc. 1850.
12 Julian W. Hill to Executive Committee, "Du Pont Company Aid to Scientific Education for the Academic Year 1953–1954," Nov. 20, 1952, Acc. 1615, Box 14.
13 Julian W. Hill to P. L. Salzberg et al., "Committee on Educational Aid, Background Information for Meeting on August 13, 1963," Aug. 5, 1963, Acc. 1850.
14 Hill, "Du Pont Aid to Education," Apr. 16, 1964.

15 For example, in 1958 Du Pont gave $1.3 million to education, which represented 0.34 percent of the company's earnings. The leaders were RCA (1.12 percent), American Cyanimid (0.98 percent), and Dow Chemical Co. (0.86 percent). (Julian W. Hill to P. L. Salzberg and E. F. DuPont, "Du Pont Aid to Education in 1970–1971," Feb. 16, 1960, Acc. 1850.)

16 Hill, "Du Pont Aid to Education," Apr. 16, 1964.

17 On Cairns, see his company biography in Acc. 1850. See also David M. Kiefer, "Theodore Cairns Wins Perkin Medal for 1973," *Chemical and Engineering News* (Nov. 20, 1972): 7–8.

18 Melville H. Hodge, Jr., "Rate Your Company's Research Productivity," *Harvard Business Review* 41 (Nov. 1963): 109–22.

19 This point was made by many chemists who worked at Du Pont in this era.

20 W. H. Charch to W. W. Smith, "Publicity," June 5, 1944, PR Records, Box 180177.

21 On the history of the Gibson Island conferences, see F. R. Moulton, "The AAAS–Gibson Island Research Conferences," [1946], Acc. 1850.

22 W. E. Roseveare, "Gibson Island Meeting on Textiles," July 30, 1945, PR Records, Box 180180. J. Burton Nichols of the Chemical Department presented a paper at the 1946 conference. (Acc. 1850.)

23 W. H. Charch to W. W. Smith, "Publication of L. F. Beste – Distribution of Components in Copolymers," Nov. 20, 1946, PR Records, Box 180183. This paper was still on Charch's priority list four years later (Carl E. Black, "Pioneering Publications Committee, Minutes of the Meeting – March 3, 1950," Mar. 8, 1950, PR Records, Box 180194).

24 C. E. Black to W. H. Charch, "Publication of the Crystal Structure of Teflon," Nov. 3, 1949, PR Records, Box 180193.

25 W. H. Charch to A. E. Buchanan, "Textile Laboratory – M.I.T. – E. R. Schwarz," Mar. 27, 1947, PR Records, Box 180185.

26 E. F. Izard, R. A. A. Hentschel, and C. E. Black to R. M. Hoffman, "Proposed Plans for a Publication Committee," Dec. 1, 1949, PR Records, Box 180191; W. H. Charch to C. E. Black, "Clearance of Technical Division Publications through Patent Service," Feb. 17, 1950, PR Records, Box 180194.

27 H. J. Barrett to H. E. Ford, "Du Pont Publication Program," May 1, 1959, DD Files.

28 Bender, *The Scientist as a Person.*

29 H. W. Rinehart, [untitled memorandum], Jan. 30, 1946, II, 2, Box 831.

30 On the origins of the research associates plan, see Ferdinand Schulze, revised and enlarged from a manuscript prepared by Roy Soukup, *The Technical Division of the Rayon Department* (Wilmington, Del.: Du Pont, 1952), p. 67. See also "Technical Division Bi-Weekly Staff Meeting," Mar. 30, June 22, July 6, Aug. 23, 1945. PR Records, Box 180180.

31 The announcement appeared in *Science* (Feb. 1, 1946): 141. The response from academics is in Rinehart, Jan. 30, 1946. On the development of research associate programs in other companies, see "Climbing the Research Ladder," *Chemical and Engineering News* (Dec. 3, 1956): 5920–3.

32 P. J. Wingate, *The Colorful Du Pont Company* (Wilmington, Del.: Serendipity Press, 1982), pp. 91–122.

33 Pariser's papers appeared in the *Journal of Chemical Physics* 23 (1955): 711–25 and 24 (1956): 250–68.

34 On Pedersen and the Nobel Prize, see the *New York Times*, Oct. 15, 1987.

35 W. H. Charch to G. D. Graves, "Basic Research," Mar. 22, 1957, PR Records, Box 191130.

36 On fiber resilience studies, see Chapter 18.

37 W. H. Charch, [untitled address], Mar. 11, 1948, PRL Authors.

38 For more on interfacial polymerization, see Chapter 19.

39 Charch, "Basic Research."

40 J. R. Schaefgen, "Gordon Research Conference on Polymers, June 30–July 4, 1958," July 14, 1958, PR Records, Box 191133.

41 Morgan interview.

42 McGrew quotes from an April 1951 memorandum in F. C. McGrew to C. H. Hamblet, et al., May 16, 1955, PPD Research Files.

43 "The Molecular Structure of Polyethylene," *Journal of the American Chemical Society* 75 (1953): 6110–30.

44 W. F. Busse to D. E. Strain, "Getting Good Students to Do Thesis Research on Plastics in Universities," Mar. 27, 1957, PPD Research Files.

45 Franta interview. The eventual Executive Committee member, William G. Simeral, was a physicist who had joined the Polychemicals Department in 1953. He advanced through a number of research and management positions until he was elected a member of the Executive Committee in 1981. On Simeral, see *American Men and Women of Science*, 15th ed. (1982).

46 C. H. Arrington, "Research Policy – Central Research, 1945–1980," [1985], Acc. 1850.

47 Roger Williams to W. S. Carpenter, Jr., Nov. 30, 1949, Acc. 1814, Box 37.

48 Cole Coolidge, "Chemical Department – Statistical Data on Research and Other Technical Activities 1952–1953," Oct. 31, 1952, Acc. 1784.

49 P. L. Salzberg, "Memorandum for File," July 23, 1951, DD Files.

50 On Coolidge, see E. K. Bolton, "Cole Coolidge: 1897–1953," *Science* 119 (Feb. 5, 1954): 175–6. On Salzberg, see his company biography in Acc. 1850.

51 For short summaries of this work, see "Review of Selected CR&D Developments," Aug. 1978, CRDD Files.

52 On Central Research in the 1950s and 1960s, see "Research: Where Du Pont Bets on the Future," *Business Week* (Nov. 2, 1965): 84–8.

53 These figures were calculated from "Chemical Department – Statistical Data in Research and Other Technical Activities," for the 1950s, Acc. 1784.

54 On this work, see D. D. Coffman, P. L. Barrick, R. D. Cramer, and M. S. Raasch, "Synthesis of Tetrafluorocyclobutanes in Cycloalkylation," *Journal of the American Chemical Society* 71 (1949): 480–96. For a review of subsequent work, see the series of papers published in the *Journal of the American Chemical Society* 81 (1959): 2723–8, 4904–8, 4269–72, 4908–11.

55 This series of papers was published in the *Journal of the American Chemical Society* 80 (1958): 2775–847. See also Keifer, "Theodore Cairns."

56 Simmons biography, Acc. 1850, and Simmons interview.

57 On the growth of Du Pont's program in physics and physical chemistry, see David M. McQueen to the Executive Committee, "Physical Research," March 11, 1960, DD Files. On the NMR work of Phillips, see G. F. Biehn to M. M. Brubaker, "Major Published Scientific Accomplishments of the Du Pont Company, 1949–1960," Sept. 12, 1961, DD Files. On the work of Merrifield, see "Research: Where Du Pont Bets the Future."

58 McQueen, "Physical Research." The publishing statistics are from Hodge, "Rate Your Company's Research Productivity."

59 R. G. Bergman, G. W. Parshall, and K. N. Raymond, "Earl Leonard Muetterties, 1927–1984," *Organometallics* 4 (1958): 1–4.

60 On Parshall, see *American Men and Women of Science*, 15th ed. (1982).

61 "Statistical Data on Research and Other Technical Activities," Acc. 1784.

62 On Hardy, see his company biography in Acc. 1850 and "Scientist Superstar in a New Role," *Chemical Week* (Dec. 12, 1984): 12–16. Hardy, who had been director of research for life sciences at Du Pont, took early retirement from Du Pont in 1984 and became president of BioTechnica International. The estimate of man-years invested in nitrogen fixation work is from "Research: Where Du Pont Bets the Future."

63 Arrington, "Research Policy – Central Research."

64 P. L. Salzberg to the Executive Committee, "Annual Report for 1966 and Budgets for 1967," Jan. 25, 1967, Acc. 1784.

65 See the Central Research Department annual reports, Acc. 1784; Cairns interviews, Nov. 12, 19, 1982.

66 Roger Adams to T. L. Cairns, Sept. 20, 1967, Rogers Adams Papers, Box 33, University of Illinois Archives, University of Illinois, Urbana, Illinois.

67 C. H. Greenewalt to P. L. Salzberg, July 13, 1967, Acc. 1814, Box 5.

68 On McQueen, see his company biography in Acc. 1850 and McQueen interview.

69 David M. McQueen to P. L. Salzberg, "Enduring Themes of Central Research Department," Jan. 5, 1965, CRDD Files.

70 David M. McQueen, "Selection of Research Programs," July 22, 1966, CRDD Files.

71 David M. McQueen to T. L. Cairns, "Exploratory Research," July 8, 1971, Acc. 1784.

Chapter 18. Making a Revolution: Du Pont and Synthetic Fibers

1 Data from *Textile Organon* 52 (Mar. 1981).

2 U.S. Bureau of the Census, *Statistical Abstract of the United States 1985* (Washington: U.S. Government Printing Office, 1984), p. 767.

3 For a brief history of synthetic textile fibers, see *Chemistry in the Economy* (Washington: American Chemical Society, 1973), pp. 87–115.

4 For the sake of clarity and consistency in this chapter, we will use the name Textile Fibers Department to refer to the Rayon Department before it officially adopted the new name. Similarly, we will use the name technical division to refer to the research unit of the department.

5 See Chapter Eight, section titled "Pioneering Research."

6 E. K. Bolton to the Executive Committee, "Annual Report – 1938," Jan. 12, 1939, Acc. 1784.

7 Maurice du Pont Lee to G. P. Hoff, July 7, 1939, II, 2, Box 963.

8 R. M. Horsey to H. R. Fry et al., Nov. 10, 1939, II, 2, Box 963. See also Minutes of the Technical Division Weekly Staff Meeting, July 23, 1941, PR Records, Box 110195; Ernest B. Benger to W. H. Bradshaw et al., Nov. 14, 1939, and Benger to W. H. Charch et al., Aug. 28, 1940, II, 2, Box 963.

9 Minutes of Technical Division Weekly Staff Meeting, Oct. 17, 1941, PR Records, Box 110195.

10 For details on Mark's coming to the United States and Benger's role in it, see Chapter 15, section titled "Recruiting a Research Force."

11 Sinness interview. See also marginal notes of W. W. Heckert on Ernest Benger to V. L. Bohnson et al., Feb. 21, 1941, II, 2, Box 963. See also J. B. Miles to W. W. H[eckert], Feb. 24, 1941, and Hale Charch to Ernest B. Benger, Sept. 22, 1941, II, 2, Box 963.

12 On the evolution of research reviews and their intention, see discussion led by Lester S. Sinness noted in the Minutes of the Technical Division Bi-Weekly Staff Meeting, Jan. 5, 1945, PR Records, Box 180180.

13 Minutes for most of the technical division staff meetings in the Benger era survive in the PR Records. The research associates plan is discussed in Chapter 17.

14 In 1950, W. W. Heckert, assistant manager of the technical division, wrote that "the only reason for having an exhibit is to do an internal selling job, particularly to those on the 9th Floor [i.e., the Executive and Finance committees]." W. W. Heckert to W. L. Hyden, March 13, 1950, PR Records, Box 180193.

15 This is not to say that there were no differences of opinion among research directors in the technical division, for there certainly were, as will be noted later in this chapter. For more information on the annual meetings of the technical division, see PR Records, MR-46-3, MR-48-8, and miscellaneous documents.

16 W. H. Charch to G. P. Hoff, Aug. 7, 1941, PR Records, Box 110195, also excerpted in a note from L[eonard] A. Y[erkes] to W[alter] S. C[arpenter], Jr., n.d., II, 2, Box 831.

17 W. H. Charch to E. K. Gladding, March 23, 1936, PR Records, Box 72486.

18 W. H. Charch to J. S. Denham, June 24, 1937, PR Records, Box 72489.

19 For information on the Chemical Department's efforts to develop a wool-like nylon, see Chapter 13.

20 The first quoted expression appears in Charch to Denham, June 24, 1937, whereas the latter quotation appears in W. H. Charch to Maurice du Pont Lee, "Annual Report for 1937 – Pioneering Research," Nov. 26, 1937, PR Records, Box 72488.

21 W. H. Charch to E. B. Benger, Sept. 30, 1941, PR Records, Box 110195.

22 W. H. Charch to G. W. Filson, Aug. 14, 1941, PR Records, Box 110195.

23 Ibid.

24 W. H. Charch to L. S. Sinness and F. H. Coker, July 12, 1944, PR Records, Box 180177.

25 W. H. Charch, "For File PD-1," Mar. 1944, PR Records, Box 180177.

26 R. M. Hoffman, "Resilience," Oct. 18, 1945, PR Records, Box 180181.

27 W. W. Heckert, "Textile Fiber Resilience Criteria," Special Compensation Files.

28 Lester S. Sinness to W. H. Charch, Aug. 18, 1944, PR Records, Box 180179.

29 R. M. Hoffman to W. H. Charch, Feb. 20, 1946, PR Records, Box 180184.

30 Marginal notation on H. J. Kolb, "Resilience Program," Nov. 13, 1946, PR Records, Box 180184.

31 Heckert makes this point in "Textile Fiber Resilience Criteria."

32 See Charch's comments on p. 24 of *History of Fiber V in Pioneering Research,*

compiled by R. M. Hoffman and edited by W. H. Charch, ca. 1953, typescript in PRL Hist. Files.

33 W. H. Charch to P. L. Salzberg, Dec. 3, 1941, PR Records, Box 110195.

34 E. A. Tippetts, "Fiber-Forming Polyacrylonitrile 'Orlon,' " Special Compensation Files.

35 German Patent 580,351, July 26, 1929.

36 U.S. Patent 2,117,210, May 10, 1938, and U.S. Patent 2,140,921, Dec. 20, 1938.

37 Ray C. Houtz, " 'Orlon' Acrylic Fiber: Chemistry and Properties," Address Presented at the Conference on Textiles, Gordon Research Conferences, Colby Junior College, July 18, 1949, PRL Authors.

38 Ibid. On Pioneering's use of Marvel as a consultant, see W. H. Charch to A. P. Tanberg, Sept. 23, 1941, PR Records, Box 110195.

39 Houtz, " 'Orlon' Acrylic Fiber."

40 Tippetts, "Fiber-Forming Polyacrylonitrile 'Orlon.' "

41 Chemstrand introduced its Acrylan in 1949, which was wet-spun from DMAC.

42 Houtz, " 'Orlon' Acrylic Fiber" and Tippetts, "Fiber-Forming Polyacrylonitrile 'Orlon.' "

43 Tippetts, "Fiber-Forming Polyacrylonitrile 'Orlon.' "

44 G. W. Filson to W. H. Charch, Dec. 30, 1942, Acc. 1850.

45 L. P. Haner to R. C. Houtz, "On 'Orlon' History," Feb. 3, 1949, PR Records, Box 180192.

46 Ibid.

47 C. E. Sparks, "Dyestuffs for Fiber A," JLR-43-458, No. 1, Aug. 6, 1943, filed as MR 1636, PR Records, Box 150137.

48 E. B. Benger to W. H. Charch, Jan. 4, 1944, PR Records, Box 180179.

49 A. E. Buchanan, "Minutes of Fiber A Meeting," Nov. 21, 1944, PR Records, Box 180181.

50 W. H. Charch to E. B. Benger, July 6, 1944, PR Records, Box 180179.

51 Medical Research Project Report, MR-121, Mar. 9, 1944. The earlier report was MR-1603, July 28, 1938. The reports are summarized in C. M. Smith, "Visit to Buffalo, May 31–June 8, Fiber A," June 20, 1944, PR Records, Box 180179.

52 E. B. Benger to J. W. Kinsman, Jan. 14, 1944; Kinsman to Benger, Jan. 17, 1944; Benger to W. H. Charch, Jan. 4, 1944, PR Records, Box 180179.

53 J. B. Quig to C. R. Humphreys, Apr. 5, 1944, PR Records, Box 180179; R. M. Horsey to L. Yerkes et al., "Fiber 'A' Program," June 7, 1944, PR Records, Box 180179; R. M. Horsey to J. B. Quig, Feb. 22, 1945, PR Records, Box 180181.

54 W. H. Charch to E. B. Benger, July 6, 1944, PR Records, Box 180179.

55 W. H. Charch to R. M. Horsey, May 24, 1944, PR Records, Box 180179.

56 JTW, "Monomer and Polymer Consumption," Nov. 14, 1944, PR Records, Box 180179. See also A. E. Buchanan, "Minutes of Fiber A Meeting," Nov. 21, 1945, PR Records, Box 180181.

57 Buchanan, "Minutes of Fiber A Meeting."

58 A. E. Buchanan to W. H. Charch, Oct. 17, 1945, PR Records, Box 180181.

59 Ibid.

60 W. H. Charch to A. E. Buchanan, Oct. 29, 1945, PR Records, Box 180181.

61 A. E. Buchanan, "Minutes of Fiber A Meeting."

62 W. H. Charch to A. E. Buchanan, Nov. 29, 1945, PR Records, Box 180181.

63 W. T. Anderson to G. M. Karns and W. C. Eberlin, "Fiber A Plant Study," April 9, 1946; W. E. Larsen, "Minutes of Meeting on Fiber A Held at Wilmington on April 15–16, 1946," PR Records, Box 180183.

64 G. P. Hoff to A. E. Buchanan, May 22, 1946, PR Records, Box 180183.

65 G. P. Hoff to A. E. Buchanan, June 20, 1946, PR Records, Box 180183.

66 EC Minutes, July 31, 1946, May 7, 1947.

67 J. H. Ellett, "Pilot Plant Operation," in *The Story of "Orlon" Acrylic Fiber*, Oct. 13, 1949, in II, 2, Box 608.

68 The Orlon trademark was officially announced on Aug. 23, 1948.

69 W. H. Charch to W. W. Watkins, March 13, 1944, PR Records, Box 180180. Hosiery nylon had been dyed satisfactorily with acetate dyes, but expansion of nylon beyond stockings required deeper and faster dyestuffs, which simply did not exist for nylon in 1944.

70 A full record of the Textile Fiber – Orchem dyeing effort is in PR Records.

71 See, e.g., W. H. Charch to E. B. Benger, July 5, 1946, PR Records, Box 180184.

72 W. H. Charch to E. B. Benger, June 19, 1946, PR Records, Box 180184.

73 C. E. Sparks to A. E. Buchanan, Aug. 12, 1948, PR Records, Box 180189.

74 L. G. Ray to R. A. Scheiderbauer, Sept. 20, 1948, PR Records, Box 180189, provides an excellent summary of Pioneering's work on Fibers A-1 (methacrylic copolymer), A-2 (styrene copolymer), and A-3. On the early work with methacrylic acid modifiers, see A. K. Schneider to J. W. Hill, "Conference on Nylon and Fiber A Dyeing," June 26, 1944, PR Records, Box 180179.

75 These problems included lack of a full range of colors, the necessity of dyeing "at the boil" (which most commercial dyers could not do with their existing equipment), and the failure of the fiber to dye properly when blended with wool.

76 C. E. Sparks to D. F. Holmes, Nov. 11, 1948, PR Records, Box 180189.

77 C. E. Sparks, "Annual Report: Dyeing of Synthetic Fibers," Oct. 5, 1948, PR Records, Box 180190.

78 Ibid.

79 EC Minutes, Oct. 6, 1948. The Finance Committee authorized the plant on Oct. 15, 1948.

80 W. W. Heckert, "Status of Fiber A Research," n.d. [ca. 1948 – recopied March 18, 1949], in Acc. 1193, Box 5.

81 Ellett, "Pilot Plant Operation."

82 D. L. Holmes to W. L. Hyden, Nov. 30, 1948, PR Records, Box 180189.

83 The figure on expansion is from D. F. Holmes, *History of the Du Pont Company's Textile Fibers Department* (Wilmington, Del.: Textile Fibers Department, Du Pont, 1983), p. 69.

84 Ibid.

85 W. W. Heckert to W. H. Charch et al., Aug. 8, 1951, PR Records, Box 184995.

86 Ibid.

87 Hale Charch's comments in *History of Fiber V in Pioneering Research*, p. 24.

88 Acetate research devoted an increasing amount of its R&D work to Orlon staple. By October 1949, half its Orlon research staff was working on staple. W. E. Eberlin, "Research Plans – Process," in *The Story of "Orlon" Acrylic Fiber*.

89 J. H. Trepagnier to H. A. Lubs, "Status of the Dyeing of Hydrophobic Fibers – January 1950," Feb. 16, 1950, PR Records, Box 180195. See also "Report of 'Orlon' Product Committee Study of 'Orlon' Acrylic Staple – July, 1953," July 30, 1953, II, 2, Box 609.

90 "Research Items Used in the Rayon Department Monthly Report to the Executive Committee, December, 1950," Jan. 29, 1951, PR Records, Box 180193.

91 "Report of 'Orlon' Product Committee Study of 'Orlon' Staple – July, 1953."

92 Ibid.

93 Ibid.

94 Ibid.

95 Control Division, "History: Textile Fibers Plants, Permanent Investment," July 24, 1958, Acc. 1850; R. M. Busche to E. B. Yelton, "1969 Status: Development and Commercialization of New Products," July 31, 1969, DD Files.

96 Some research managers had wanted to end all work on modified Orlon. E. A. Tippetts, "Dyeability of Type 42 'Orlon' Acrylic Staple," Feb. 28, 1955, Special Compensation Files.

97 J. B. Quig stressed the hazards of a lower softening point in his comments in "A Survey of Present Research Problems: 'Orlon' Acrylic Fiber," II, 2, Box 608.

98 Both Holmes, *History of the Du Pont Company's Textile Fibers Department*, and "Report of 'Orlon' Product Committee Study of 'Orlon' Acrylic Staple – July, 1953," stress this point.

99 Ibid. See also "The Chips Are Down," *Chemical Week* (Aug. 8, 1953): 67.

100 Hoffman and Quig make this point repeatedly in the "Survey of Present Research Problems: 'Orlon' Acrylic Fiber."

101 "Report of 'Orlon' Product Committee Study of 'Orlon' Acrylic Staple – July, 1953."

102 Holmes, *History of the Du Pont Company's Textile Fibers Department*, p. 70.

103 Ibid., pp. 70, 76.

104 The paradox was, however, that at least initially, Orlon's success rested on a single market – knitted wear.

105 Charch's views about Dacron are expressed in his comments in *History of Fiber V in Pioneering Research*.

106 W. H. Carothers and G. A. Arvin, "Polyesters," *Journal of the American Chemical Society* 51 (1929): 2560–70.

107 W. H. Carothers and J. W. Hill, "Linear Superpolyesters," *Journal of the American Chemical Society*, 54 (1932): 1559–66.

108 Experimental Station Notebook 2260, p. 21, CRDD Notebooks. In this entry, Spanagel described the reaction of ethylene glycol with dimethyl terephthalate at 200° C, followed by a vacuum cycle at 240° C to produce a polymer. He also produced other polyesters in 1934, including some based on aromatic acids.

109 J. M. Swanson, "Meeting with Dr. Mark – 10/26/42," Nov. 9, 1942, II, 2, Box 963.

110 Specifically, they thought that by using hindered acids, they could produce a hydrolytically stable polyester. On Aug. 17, 1942, Stanley B. Speck of Pioneering first suggested the hindered acid approach to overcome the hydrolytic instability of polyesters. *History of Fiber V in Pioneering Research*, p. 9.

111   Ibid.

112   Ibid., p. 7.

113   Emmette F. Izard to W. W. Smith, Mar. 29, 1946, PR Records, Box 180184.

114   Quoted in *History of Fiber V in Pioneering Research*, p. 11.

115   Ibid., p. 12.

116   Izard to Smith, Mar. 29, 1946. Izard wrote: "Later in 1944 during one of Dr. Mark's visits to Pioneering he told us of a rumored new polymer that I.C.I. were working on which he called Tery and reported to be polyethylene terephthalate." Managers in the Chemical Department also must have heard about ICI's work. On October 3, 1944, H. B. Dykstra, one of the department's patent experts, wrote M. M. Brubaker a memorandum entitled, "Fiber-Forming Polymer from Terephthalic Acid and Ethylene Glycol," which discusses his search for a disclosure on such a polymer and argues that Carothers's basic patent on superpolymers (U.S. 2,071,250) would dominate the new polymer. A copy of Dykstra's memorandum is in PR Records, Box 180181.

117   The correct chemical name for this compound is bis (2-hydroxyethyl) terephthalate.

118   Izard to W. W. Smith, Mar. 29, 1946.

119   W. H. Charch to R. M. Horsey, Mar. 2, 1945, PR Records, Box 180181.

120   The following account of the meeting derives principally from W. H. Charch, " 'Terylene' Fibers – ICI – Calico Printers Assn.," Mar. 21, 1945, PR Records, Box 180181.

121   J. R. Whinfield, "Textile Fibers: Variations on Some Familiar Themes," Jubilee Memorial Lecture, *Chemistry & Industry* (March 14, 1953): 226–9. A transcript of this lecture, as published, is in PR Records, Box 191115. See also J. R. Whinfield, "The Development of Terylene," *Textile Research Journal* 23 (May 1953): 289–93.

122   W. J. Reader, *Imperial Chemical Industries: A History* (London: Oxford University Press, 1975), II, pp. 381–5.

123   Charch, " 'Terylene' Fibers," Mar. 21, 1945.

124   Ibid.

125   W. H. Charch to E. B. Benger, Mar. 21, 1945, PR Records, Box 180181.

126   W. H. Charch to A. E. Buchanan, "Material for Annual Report to Executive Committee," Mar. 21, 1945, PR Records, Box 180180.

127   W. H. Charch to W. R. Haefele, May 16, 1945, PR Records, Box 180181.

128   A. E. Buchanan to W. H. Charch, Apr. 24, 1946, PR Records, Box 180184.

129   Charch implicitly expressed this philosophy in W. H. Charch to E. B. Benger, Feb. 1, 1946, PR Records, Box 180184.

130   W. H. Charch to R. M. Horsey, Jan. 29, 1946, PR Records, Box 180184.

131   Charch to Benger, Feb. 1, 1946. Cf. W. F. Underwood to E. B. Benger, Feb. 7, 1946, PR Records, Box 180184.

132   Buchanan to Charch, Apr. 24, 1946.

133   Ibid. On the tire cord program, see also W. W. Heckert to E. B. Benger, Mar. 20, 1946, PR Records, Box 180184.

134   Donald F. Holmes, "Disclosure of Fiber V to the Tire Companies," Sept. 9, 1946, PR Records, Box 180184.

135   D. M. Thornton, "Report of Interview, Fiber V Tire Cord," Nov. 22, 1946, PR Records, Box 180184.

136 D. M. Thornton, "Program: Initial Characterization of Fiber V...," n.d. [received in Pioneering Research Mar. 8, 1947]. See also "Minutes of the Fiber V Coordination Meeting of April 29, 1947," May 6, 1947, PR Records, Box 180185.

137 Unfortunately, space considerations prevent a discussion of Du Pont's efforts to develop polyester for industrial uses, including tire cord. This is an important part of Dacron's history.

138 After the decision to devote all research effort on Fiber V to tire cord, Pioneering Research reclassified much of its work on Fiber V toward the more fundamental aspects of fiber development, but Charch did not significantly alter the substance of this research.

139 Carl E. Black made this discovery, which was reported in a bimonthly memorandum dated Feb. 4, 1946. *History of Fiber V in Pioneering Research*, pp. 31–2.

140 Ibid., p. 33.

141 Ibid., p. 25.

142 J. B. Quig to R. M. Hoffman, July 23, 1947, PR Records, Box 180185. See also *History of Fiber V in Pioneering Research*, pp. 41–2.

143 W. H. Charch to A. E. Buchanan, Aug. 13, 1947, PR Records, Box 180185.

144 H. J. Kolb to V. R. Hardy, May 15, 1947, and J. T. Rivers to R. M. Hoffman, Sept. 10, 1947, PR Records, Box 180185.

145 Charch found this condition unacceptable. See W. H. Charch to H. C. Freeling, Nov. 3, 1948, PR Records, Box 180188.

146 On Chestnut Run's history and operations, see Textile Fibers Department, "Chestnut Run: History and General Information," June 15, 1962, TF Files and Holmes, *History of the Du Pont Company's Textile Fibers Department*, p. 20.

147 See PR Records, Boxes 180185 and 180188, for records on the work at Lowell.

148 H. J. Kolb, "Memorandum: Fiber V Test at Pacific Mills," Feb. 20, 1948, and E. H. Largen to F. H. Thompson, "Finishing of Spun Fiber V Fabric," July 1, 1948, PR Records, Box 180188.

149 W. H. Charch to H. J. Kolb, Mar. 2, 1948, PR Records, Box 180188. See also Charch to F. K. Signaigo, May 12, 1948, PR Records, Box 180188.

150 See, e.g., R. M. Hoffman to F. K. Signaigo, "Crimp in Fiber V," Oct. 1, 1948, PR Records, Box 180188.

151 V. R. Hardy to H. J. Kolb, July 12, 1948; F. K. Signaigo to V. R. Hardy, July 16, 1948; F. K. Signaigo to W. H. Charch, Aug. 26, 1948, PR Records, Box 180188.

152 W. H. Charch to A. E. Buchanan, Aug. 13, 1947.

153 The history of Pioneering's draw-spin process in well treated in *History of Fiber V in Pioneering Research*, pp. 50–69. See also W. H. Charch to F. K. Signaigo, Sept. 1, 1948, PR Records, Box 180188.

154 H. C. Froehling to A. E. Buchanan, et al., "Coordination Meeting – Polymer V," July 9, 1948, PR Records, Box 180187.

155 The department's immediate goal was to begin producing 1,000 pounds per month of "wool-like" staple beginning Jan. 1, 1949, and to prepare markets for pilot plant production of 1.8 million pounds per year. See H. C. Froehling, "Coordination Meeting – Fiber V Staple," Oct. 11, 1948, and Froehling to W. L. Hyden, "Fiber 'V' Program," Oct. 24, 1948, PR Records, Box 180188.

156 EC Minutes, Sept. 8, 1948.

157 Froehling to Hyden, Oct. 25, 1948. See also Froehling to A. E. Buchanan, Nov. 4, 1948, PR Records, Box 180188.

158 Swank interview.

159 Ibid. See also C. E. Sparks, "Polyethylene Terephthalate – Continuous Polymerization," Special Compensation Files.

160 On the history of Fiber V dyeing, see C. E. Sparks to L. F. Salisbury, "History of Fiber V. Dyeing," Nov. 24, 1950, in PRL Hist. Files, and J. H. Trepagnier, "History of Dyeing 'Dacron' Polyester Fiber – 11/15/50 to 8/1/53," II, 2, Box 595.

161 Holmes, *History of the Du Pont Company's Textile Fibers Department*, pp. 79, 80.

162 Quig, "History of 'Dacron' Polyester Fiber," p. 11, Acc. 1850.

163 Ibid., pp. 11–12.

164 Rivers's work is well documented in PR Records. See also Rivers interview.

165 Quig, "History of 'Dacron' Polyester Fiber," p. 13.

166 Holmes, *History of the Du Pont Company's Textile Fibers Department*, pp. 80–1.

167 Swank interview.

168 Hart, Schaffner & Marx introduced the Dacron and worsted wool-blended suit, and Brooks Brothers initiated the permanently pressed shirt of 60 percent Dacron and 40 percent cotton in January 1953. Some members of the technical division, including Charch and Quig, had advocated developing polyester-blended fabrics.

169 Holmes, *History of the Du Pont Company's Textile Fibers Department*, pp. 80–3.

170 Ibid., p. 132.

171 In 1971, Dacron generated $156 million in earnings compared to nylon's $105 million. This figure for Dacron was, however, significantly below nylon's record earnings of $220 million in 1965. W. R. Beacham to H. W. Swank et al., "Historical Data," Feb. 1, 1973, Acc. 1850. Dacron's profits for 1973 exceeded those for 1971. Edwin A. Gee to Executive Committee, "Textile Fibers Department," July 3, 1976, EC Files.

172 Roger Williams to E. K. Bolton et al., Nov. 3, 1949, PR Records, Box 180192.

173 Sinness interview and Holmes's *History of the Du Pont Company's Textile Fibers Department*.

174 Holmes, *History of the Du Pont Company's Textile Fibers Department*, p. 25.

175 Sinness interview. See also W. H. Charch's annotation on L. S. Sinness to W. H. Charch, June 4, 1951, PR Records, Box 184993.

176 Sinness interview. See also the chapter on Du Pont in E. Raymond Corey and Steven H. Star, *Organization Strategy: A Marketing Approach* (Boston: Harvard University Graduate School of Business Administration, 1971), pp. 187–200.

177 Minutes of the Technical Division Staff Meeting, June 27, 1947, PR Records, Box 180185.

178 Sinness interview.

179 W. H. Charch, notes of presentation to Pioneering Research Staff, Jan. 1948, PRL Authors File.

180 J. B. Quig to J. L. Martin, Nov. 10, 1952, II, 2, Box 618.

181 Holmes, *History of the Du Pont Company's Textile Fibers Department*, pp. 46–9.
182 Ibid., pp. 49–51, 91.

Chapter 19. New Directions in Fibers R&D

1 W. H. Charch to W. W. Heckert, Oct. 27, 1948, PR Records, Box 180187. See also Charch to A. E. Buchanan et al., "Research and the Future," Jan. 14, 1948, PRL Authors, and Minutes of Special Staff Meeting, Jan. 16, 1948, PR Records, Box 180187.

2 W. H. Charch, notes of presentation to Pioneering Research Staff, Jan. 1948, and idem. [remarks at Pioneering Research Review], Mar. 11, 1948, PRL Authors.

3 Charch noted these delays in several of his presentations to his staff. See also R. M. Hoffman to W. H. Charch, Sept. 19, 1949, PR Records, Box 180190, which notes that Pioneering had "most of our high caliber organic chemists" at work on the dye problem for Orlon and Dacron.

4 W. H. Charch, handwritten annotation on Paul R. Austin to W. H. Charch, Oct. 12, 1945, PR, Box 180181; W. H. Charch to E. B. Benger, "Polyurethanes – New German Mission," Oct. 12, 1945, PR, Box 180180.

5 R. C. Houtz to R. E. Burk, "Polyurethanes," Nov. 26, 1948, PR Records, Box 180188 and W. H. Charch, Draft of "A" Bonus Recommendation, "Interfacial Polymerizations and Their Applications," Oct. 30, 1953, PRL Hist. Files.

6 This work is discussed in L. H. Smith, *Synthetic Fiber Developments in Germany* (New York: Textile Research Institute, 1946), pp. 700–10.

7 Wittbecker designed experiments to circumvent hydrolysis by cutting the reaction time for polymerization to a minimum. Starting with a solution of diamine, caustic, and an emulsifying agent in cold water, he added a second solution of acid chloride prepared in an anhydrous organic solvent while rapidly stirring the diamine mixture. Charch, Draft of "A" Bonus Recommendation.

8 "Research Items Used in the Rayon Department Monthly Report to the Executive Committee, January, 1951," Feb. 23, 1951, PR Records, Box 184993; Pioneering Research Division, Quarterly Report, Nov. 16, 1950, to Feb. 15, 1951, PR Records, Box 184993. Work on polyamides was done by Eugene Magat in the Nylon Research Laboratory, which by this time had been dedicated as the Carothers Laboratory.

9 M. L. Ernsberger to R. C. Houtz, Jan. 22, 1951, PR Records, Box 184993.

10 See, e.g., Emerson L. Wittbecker and Paul W. Morgan, "Interfacial Polycondensation. I.," *Journal of Polymer Science* 40 (1959): 289–97; Paul W. Morgan, "Interfacial Polycondensation: A Versatile Method of Polymer Preparation," *Society of Plastics Engineers Journal* 15 (1959): 485–95; Paul W. Morgan and Stephanie L. Kwolek, "Interfacial Polycondensation. II. Fundamentals of Polymer Formation at Liquid Interfaces," *Journal of Polymer Science* 40 (1959): 299–327; Paul W. Morgan, *Condensation Polymers by Interfacial and Solution Methods* (New York: Interscience, 1965); and Paul W. Morgan, "Comments on the Status and Future of Interfacial Polycondensation," *Journal of Macromolecular Science and Chemistry* 5 (1981): 683–99.

11 Morgan interview.

12 Commercial applications of interfacial polymerization are reviewed in Morgan, "Comments on the Status and Future of Interfacial Polycondensation," pp. 685–6.

13 Morgan interview.

14 Ibid.

15 G. F. Lanzl, " 'Nomex' Process and Product," Special Compensation Files.

16 The history of Nomex is covered in ibid.; Morgan interview; "Nomex History" and "History of HT-1," PRL Hist. Files; and D. F. Holmes, *History of the Du Pont Company's Textile Fibers Department* (Wilmington, Del.: Textile Fibers Department, Du Pont, 1983), pp. 91, 149, 151, 152, 195, 196, 260, 261, 267.

17 Lanzl, " 'Nomex' Process and Product." Morgan submitted a patent proposal on Nov. 24, 1953, which when issued with its ninety-two claims as U.S. Patent 2,999,788 dominated synthetic-paper products made with fibrids.

18 R. M. Busche to E. B. Yelton, "1969 Status: Development and Commercialization of New Products," July 31, 1969, DD Files. Precommercial R&D costs totaled $52 million, whereas maximum net cash commitment was estimated at $90 million (figures are on a historical-dollar basis).

19 Edwin A. Gee to Executive Committee, "Textile Fibers Department," July 8, 1976, EC Files; Edwin Gee, "Specific Businesses," June 15, 1976, "New Products Commercialized between 1958–1977," 1979 data, Acc. 1850.

20 Elmer K. Bolton to Executive Committee, "Annual Report – 1942," Jan. 15, 1943, Acc. 1784.

21 Du Pont's work on elastic fibers is covered in D. F. Holmes to G. P. Hoff, "Fiber O-5," Jan. 20, 1949, PR Records, Box 180192; R. C. Houtz, "Economic and Property Goals in New Fiber Research," Nov. 30, 1951, PR Records, Box 184993; and Holmes, *History of the Du Pont Company's Textile Fibers Department*, p. 88.

22 Houtz, "Economic and Property Goals in New Fiber Research," and R. L. Hallett to H. J. Kolb, "Evaluation of Elastomers," Mar. 30, 1953, PR Records, Box 191115.

23 Pioneering's critical reexamination of elastomeric fibers is indicated in John R. Schaefgen, "Requiescat in Pace," Aug. 9, 1951, PR Records, Box 184993.

24 Shivers and Moody's work is covered in Walter E. Jordan, " 'Lycra' Spandex Fiber Development," Apr. 24, 1962, PRL Hist. Files. R. C. Houtz provides an interesting historical perspective on segmented copolymers in a letter to H. W. Gray, Apr. 20, 1954, PRL Hist. Files.

25 Jordan, " 'Lycra' Spandex Fiber Development."

26 Herman E. Schroeder, "Facets of Innovation," *Rubber Chemistry and Technology* 57 (1984): G88–G93.

27 Jordan, " 'Lycra' Spandex Fiber Development." Richard N. Blomberg spun Adiprene N obtained from Orchem; Walter Steuben spun Adiprene prepolymer into a diamine solution; August H. Frazer combined the Adiprene chemistry with the new polymerization techniques.

28 W. H. Charch, "Pioneering Elastic Fiber Memorandum," Dec. 28, 1954, PR Records, Box 191121. See also W. H. Charch to D. M. McQueen, Aug. 29, 1952, PR Records, Box 191112, and Charch to N. A. Higgins, Oct. 25, 1955, PR Records, Box 191124.

29 E. T. Houvouras to Wm. Kirk, Jr., Apr. 25, 1956; R. E. Seaman, "Filament

Elastomer Program and Textile Research," Apr. 26, 1952; and W. L. Hyden to H. C. Froehling, Sept. 20, 1956, PR Records, Box 191127.

30 Plans for the scale-up and commercialization of Lycra and details of research needs for this process are detailed in W. H. Charch to G. D. Graves, June 28, 1956; D. G. O'Dell to E. A. Tippetts, and Hyden to Froehling, Sept. 20, 1956, PR Records, Box 191127.

31 Ibid. The department initially hoped to use the Orlon solvent dimethylformamide (DMF) but found dimethylacetamide (DMAC) better for Lycra spinning.

32 Appropriations Request, " 'Lycra' (Formerly Fiber K) Elastomer Production Facilities – 4 MM Pounds per Year," Project No. 3442-2, Jan. 20, 1961, EC Files. See also Holmes, *History of the Du Pont Company's Textile Fibers Department*, pp. 88–9, 140–1. Projections on the potential of staple never panned out because of the development of "core spinning," by which conventional staple fibers (cotton, polyester, etc.) were wrapped around a fine-denier Lycra monofilament, thus yielding the same results as incorporation of Lycra staple into yarns while protecting the Lycra filament from light. This core spinning could be done on conventional cotton equipment. See Holmes, *History of the Du Pont Company's Textile Fibers Department*, p. 141, and W. H. Charch to E. A. Tippetts, May 28, 1957, PR Records, Box 191130.

33 W. R. Beacham to H. W. Swank et al., "Historical Data," Feb. 1, 1973, Acc. 1850. These are worldwide earnings figures.

34 Development Department to Executive Committee, "Du Pont's Major Products," April 14, 1972, DD Files.

35 Edwin Gee, "Specific Businesses," June 15, 1976.

36 Lee Smith, "A Miracle in Search of a Market," *Fortune* (Dec. 1, 1980), pp. 92–5.

37 The history of Kevlar is covered in G. F. Lanzl, "Basic Chemical Discoveries Leading to Kevlar Aramid Fibers," Special Compensation Files; Morgan interview; Stephanie L. Kwolek, "Liquid Crystalline Polyamides," *Chemist* 57, no. 11 (1980): 9–12; J. R. Schaefgen, "Aromatic Polyamides – Solution Properties and Fiber Applications," paper presented at the American Chemical Society, Cellulose, Paper, and Textile Division meeting, Honolulu, Apr. 6, 1979; and Paul W. Morgan, "Brief History of Fibers from Synthetic Polymers," *Journal of Macromolecular Science. Part A. Chemistry* 15 (1981): 1113–31.

38 John A. Zapp, Jr., "HMPA: A Possible Carcinogen," letter to the editor, *Science* 190 (1975): 422.

39 The $500 million figure derives from data supplied by Textile Fibers Department to David A. Hounshell.

40 Smith, "A Miracle in Search of a Market," p. 92. On market development, see D. K. Barnes to Executive Committee, May 4, 1979, EC Files, and Gee interview. Kevlar is used in tires, but the growth in this market has been slow.

41 For criticism of the department's strategy, see Edwin A. Gee to R. C. Forney, April 9, 1975, Acc. 1850. Gee totaled operative losses from these spunbonded products as well as Nomex and Qiana (to be discussed below) from 1960 to 1973 and pegged them at $440 million with an investment of $320 million. Precommercial R&D costs for the spunbondeds appear in Busche to Yelton, "1969 Status: Development and Commercialization of New Products."

42   See, e.g., W. H. Charch to G. W. Filson, "Fabric without Weaving," Aug. 3, 1944, PR Records, Box 180177.

43   Piccard's work in Pioneering on nonwoven structures is thoroughly documented in PR Records. See particularly the Quarterly Reports and the PM-1 files.

44   See the "Confidential – to Dr. R. M. Hoffman Only" file in PR Records, Box 72480.

45   Quoted in J. M. McCartney to N. A. Higgins, "Fibrid History," July 12, 1960, PRL Hist. Files. Slightly later, McCartney also prepared fibrids through turbulent mixing techniques.

46   Ibid.

47   N. A. Higgins to Otis Shealy, "History of the Development of Textryl 'S' and EP Structures," Dec. 18, 1959, PR Records, Box 184997.

48   For more information on Pioneering's fibrid work, see R. A. A. Hentschel, "Fibers for the Paper Industry History 1954–1959," PRL Hist. Files.

49   A. E. Buchanan, Jr. to E. S. Nickerson, "Fibrids," June 19, 1957, Acc. 1814, Box 27.

50   Ibid.

51   The history of Du Pont's synthetic papermaking efforts may be followed in the Papers and Textryls files of PR Records.

52   O. L. Shealy, "Invention of Flash Spun Nonwoven Products and Process – Tyvek Spunbonded Olefin," Special Compensation Files.

53   The new products division based its initial scale-up work on the same solvent used by Blades (methylene chloride), but in 1960 R. Dean Anderson explored on a bootleg basis alternative solvent systems. By the end of the year, he demonstrated that Freon-11 yielded an equally good product while avoiding some of the drawbacks to methylene chloride. Anderson's work led to a major change in the development and provided the basis for the commercial process eventually adopted. Ibid.; Holmes, *History of the Du Pont Company's Textile Fibers Department*, pp. 152–3.

54   J. C. Shivers, "Invention of Continuous Filament Nonwoven Products and Process – Typar Spunbonded Polypropylene," Special Compensation Files.

55   N. A. Higgins to Otis Shealy, Dec. 18, 1959, PR Records, Box 184997.

56   Pioneering's efforts with polypropylene are discussed in A. F. Smith to F. R. Millhiser, "Discussion with Pioneering Research," Dec. 14, 1959, PR Records, Box 184997. See also H. C. Arvidson, Jr., and W. E. Jordan to G. F. Lanzl, "Pioneering Research Division," Mar. 20, 1961, PR Records, Box 44359.

57   The concerns raised by the sales division about forward integration were pointed out to us in private communications by Norton A. Higgins and the late George F. Lanzl.

58   On expected markets for spunbonded products, see R. C. Weigel to Executive Committee and Finance Committee, "Progress Reports: Nomex, Teflon Fiber, and Spunbonded Ventures," Dec. 1, 1966, EC Files. See also the earlier assessment in W. W. Heckert to H. W. Swank, "Opportunities for Diversification," Nov. 18, 1959, PR Records, Box 184997.

59   The department also commercialized "Sontara," a sheet structure that resulted from the invention of spunlacing or hydraulic needling, but space considerations prevent its discussion. On the history of Sontara, see Holmes, *History of the Du Pont Company's Textile Fibers Department*, pp. 155–6.

60 Fibers earnings data are found in Beacham to Swank et al., "Historical Data," Feb. 1, 1973; E. A. Gee to C. B. McCoy, "Research and Development," Nov. 2, 1972, and E. A. Gee to Executive Committee, "Textile Fibers Department," July 8, 1976, Acc. 1850.

61 Data for this paragraph came from Holmes, *History of the Du Pont Company's Textile Fibers Department*, pp. 152–5; Weigel to Executive and Finance Committees, Dec. 1, 1966; Beacham to Swank, "Historical Data," Feb. 1, 1973; Gee to Executive Committee, "Textile Fibers Department," July 8, 1976; "New Products Commercialized between 1958–1977," DD Files; Kelso Files, Misc. Data, Acc. 1850.

62 Graves had been a principal in the development of nylon while a member of the Chemical Department and then, beginning in 1938, had served as assistant to G. Preston Hoff in the newly created nylon research division but left the department to assist Crawford H. Greenewalt on Du Pont's Manhattan Project. On Graves, see his biography in Acc. 1410 and *American Men of Science*, 8th ed. (1949).

63 Graves's correspondence with W. H. Charch throughout this period, now preserved in PR Records, makes this point most clearly. See also Swank interview.

64 Swank interview.

65 A quick but highly instructive example of how the organizational structure worked against development of new products is found in R. W. Peterson to T. N. Broaddus et al., "Departmental Development Plan: Paper Binder Fibers," Mar. 23, 1959, PR Records, Box 184999. To implement this plan, seven signatures from the sales, manufacturing, and research divisions were required, and each signer possessed a veto on the program.

66 Swank interview.

67 Edwin A. Gee, paraphrasing Russell Peterson, to Lester S. Sinness, "Thoughts on Planning for Diversified Growth," Jan. 18, 1963, DD Files.

68 Even Holmes, *History of the Du Pont Company's Textile Fibers Department*, p. 145, acknowledges the controversial nature of Qiana marketing strategy.

69 Kelso Files, Acc. 1850.

70 Qiana's opponents within the Textile Fibers Department had argued in favor of Qiana-like polyesters. In fact, Du Pont itself moved ahead with Dacron types that competed with Qiana. See Gee, "Specific Businesses," June 15, 1976, Acc. 1850.

71 Gee to Executive Committee, July 8, 1976, Acc. 1850.

72 Information supplied by Textile Fibers Department to David A. Hounshell.

73 Greenewalt interview, Oct. 15, 1982; *Du Pont Company Annual Report 1951*, p. 10; "Agreement between E. I. du Pont de Nemours & Co. and The Chemstrand Corporation," June 2, 1951, Acc. 1850.

74 This history of the ETF project is based on C. E. Sparks, "Coupled Spin-Draw (ETF) Machines – Nylon and 'Dacron' Yarns," Special Compensation Files; J. R. Brand, *The EDL Story, 1944–1979* (Wilmington, Del.: Engineering Development Laboratory, Engineering Department, Du Pont, 1979), pp. 14–16; Development Engineering Division, Engineering Department, Du Pont, *Fifteen Years of Research and Development at the Mechanical Development Laboratory*, Engrg. Hist. Files, pp. 14–16; D. F. Boucher, *History of Engineering Technology Laboratory, Part II: Years of Change* (Wilmington, Del.: Engi

neering R&D Division, Engineering Department, Du Pont, 1980), pp. 8, 44–5, 51–2, 57; Holmes, *History of the Du Pont Company's Textile Fibers Department*, pp. 58–61; and Swank interview.

75 It will be recalled that Pioneering worked on a coupled process for Dacron polyester in 1948.

76 Engineering assigned 26 researchers on nylon and 15 on Dacron, whereas Fibers had 40 on nylon and 13 on Dacron.

77 William W. Bunting, Jr., and Thomas L. Nelson to E. I. du Pont de Nemours & Co., U.S. Patent 2,985,995.

78 Swank interview.

79 In the late 1940s, researchers from Pioneering went to Owens-Corning to experiment with Dacron spinning on that company's fiberglass-making machine, which contained an air blast chamber immediately below the spinneret that modified the fiber morphology. Subsequently, Pioneering paid increasing attention to modification of fibers by air and other fluids below the spinneret.

80 C. E. Sparks, "Producer Bulked Filaments (BCF) Yarns by Jet Crimping – Nylon and 'Dacron,'" Special Compensation Files, and Holmes, *History of the Du Pont Company's Textile Fibers Department*, pp. 61–2, 66. Du Pont licensed converters to use the Du Pont–developed texturing process to create Taslan nylon yarns rather than selling Taslan itself.

81 Sparks, "Producer Bulked Filament (BCF) Yarns."

82 Swank interview. See Holmes, *History of the Du Pont Company's Textile Fibers Department*, p. 66, for information on the introduction of Type 501 nylon.

83 Holmes, *History of the Du Pont Company's Textile Fibers Department*, p. 66.

84 Development Department to Executive Committee, "Du Pont's Major Products," Apr. 14, 1972, EC Files.

85 Andrew Buchanan, Speech before the Annual Meeting of the American Cotton Manufacturers Institute, Apr. 8, 1960, Acc. 1850.

86 On Rohm and Haas's venture in synthetic fibers, especially its shift from nylon to polyester, see Sheldon Hochheiser, *Rohm and Haas: History of a Chemical Company* (Philadelphia: University of Pennsylvania Press, 1986), pp. 153–65.

87 Swank interview.

88 "Research and Development Statistics," July 1975; Swank interview. The effects of inflation on budgets during these years must also be factored in to account for increased spending after 1968.

89 Edwin A. Gee to R. C. Forney, Apr. 9, 1975, Acc. 1850.

90 Data from David S. Weir to R. C. Forney, Mar. 1983, EC Files.

Chapter 20. Biological Chemicals

1 "Du Pont: Seeking a Future in Biosciences," *Business Week*, Nov. 24, 1980, p. 86.

2 Wm. Richter to W. F. Harrington, June 25, 1931, Acc. 1813, Box 8. Until 1936, Du Pont retained Grasselli as a wholly owned subsidiary of E. I. du Pont de Nemours & Co., complete with its own Board of Directors.

3 Orchem had initiated research on and screening of organic chemical insecticides, fungicides, and herbicides by this time. See the Annual Reports of the Organic Chemicals Department for 1931–1934, Acc. 1813, Boxes 14, 17, 19, and 21.

Most of Orchem's agchem business had been conducted through the Bayer-Semesan Company. See Records of the Bayer-Semesan Company, in II, 1, Boxes 301–3.

4   James Wharton, *Before Silent Spring: Pesticides and Public Health in Pre-DDT America* (Princeton, N.J.: Princeton University Press, 1974).

5   See, e.g., E. A. Taylor, "Recent Advances in Inorganic Chemistry," Acc. 1784.

6   "Memorandum of Conference," Aug. 2, 1933, Acc. 1813, Box 16.

7   R. W. Varner to R. W. Luckenbaugh, "History of Agricultural Chemicals Research in Du Pont," Jan. 9, 1984, Agchem Files.

8   EC Minutes, Oct. 26, 1949. Tyler's report was issued on June 23, 1950.

9   EC Minutes, Feb. 8, 21, 1933.

10 Robert M. Joyce to David A. Hounshell, Oct. 3, 1986.

11 EC Minutes, Sept. 2, 1942. The Development Department's report, dated Aug. 24, 1942, is summarized in Exhibit B, "Executive Committee Communications Regarding Acquisition of a Pharmaceutical Company," appended to R. C. Bergman to E. A. Gee, May 5, 1964, DD Files.

12 W. Sheldon to J. K. Jenney, Dec. 11, 1941, and P. Chorley to J. S. Groves, Mar. 4, 1943, II, 2, Box 543.

13 J. K. Jenney, Memorandum of Meeting of April 8, 1943, Apr. 12, 1943, II, 2, Box 543.

14 Ibid. See also the minutes prepared by J. E. Kirby, Apr. 16, 1943, and W. Sheldon to J. K. Jenney, Apr. 17, 1943, II, 2, Box 543.

15 Wendell R. Swint to M. G. Tate, Apr. 30, 1943, II, 2, Box 543.

16 E. J. Barnsley to W. R. Swint, Oct. 12, 1943, II, 2, Box 543. A more candid history of ICI's pharmaceuticals venture, written by a Mr. Willcox of ICI, appears in W. R. Swint to E. K. Bolton et al., July 20, 1943, II, 2, Box 543.

17 Swint to J. E. Crane et al., Oct. 19, 1943, II, 2, Box 543.

18 EC Minutes, Nov. 4, 1943. Du Pont's concern about ICI's pharmaceuticals venture conflicting with the Patents and Processes Agreement grew as the decade progressed. See especially R. E. De Right, "Memorandum: Pharmaceuticals," May 25, 1945. United States v. Imperial Chemical Industries, et al., District Court of the United States for the Southern District of New York, Civil No. 24-13, Defendant's Exhibit D-1653.

19 EC Minutes, Nov. 4, 1943.

20 "Biographical Sketch, Dr. C. M. A. Stine," Acc. 1410, Box 63.

21 "Dr. Charles M. A. Stine: A Biographical Sketch," attached to J. K. Hunt to Lincoln T. Work, Mar. 31, 1939, Acc. 1706.

22 EC Minutes, Apr. 26, 1944.

23 De Right, "Memorandum: Pharmaceuticals."

24 EC Minutes, Apr. 26, 1950. Grasselli also operated shorter-lived research facilities: the Livestock Parasite Laboratory in Kansas City (Aug. 1947 – Nov. 1948) and the Texas Parasite Laboratory and Field Station near San Antonio (1949–54). Varner to Luckenbaugh, Jan. 9, 1984.

25 Woodhouse interview, Nov. 16, 1982.

26 Gale E. Peterson, "The Discovery of 2,4-D," *Agricultural History* 41 (1967): 243.

27 John H. Perkins, *Insects, Experts, and the Insecticide Crisis: The Quest for New Pest Management Strategies* (New York: Plenum, 1982), p. 13.

28 S. B. Self, "Chemists' Goal," *Barron's*, Jan. 7, 1946, p. 9.

29 2,4-dichlorophenoxyacetic acid.

30 dichlorodiphenyltrichloroethane.

31 Chemical Department Annual Reports for 1937 and 1938, Acc. 1784.

32 The following account of 2,4-D's development is based on Peterson, "The Discovery of 2,4-D."

33 U.S. Patent 2,322,761, June 29, 1943.

34 In fact, after the war researchers learned that British scientists had discovered the herbicidal activity of 2,4-D earlier than the Americans. See E. John Russell, *A History of Agricultural Science in Great Britain, 1620–1954* (London: Allen & Unwin, 1966), pp. 441–3.

35 C. L. Hamner and H. B. Tukey, "The Herbicidal Action of 2,4 Dichlorophenoxyacetic and 2,4,5 Trichlorophenoxyacetic Acid on Bindweed," *Science* 100 (Aug. 18, 1944): 154.

36 P. C. Marth and J. W. Mitchell, "2,4-Dichlorophenoxyacetic Acid as a Differential Herbicide," *Botanical Gazette* 106 (1944): 224. See also the earlier article, J. W. Mitchell and C. L. Hamner, "Polyethylene Glycols as Carriers for Growth-Regulating Substances," *Botanical Gazette* 105 (1944): 482, among other articles published on selective weed control.

37 See, e.g., Gilbert H. Ahlgren, Glenn C. Klingman, and Dale E. Wolf, *Principles of Weed Control* (New York: Wiley, 1951).

38 Geigy's Paul Herman Mueller had first synthesized DDT in September 1939 and had observed its great insecticidal activity as part of an ongoing research program in insecticides.

39 The development of DDT is well treated in Perkins, *Insects, Experts, and the Insecticide Crisis*. See also Thomas R. Dunlap, *DDT: Scientists, Citizens, and Public Policy* (Princeton, N.J.: Princeton University Press, 1981).

40 Raymond W. Luckenbaugh, "Du Pont Agricultural Chemicals: A History," Agchem Files.

41 Dunlap, *DDT*, p. 81, argues that methoxychlor, which was considerably less toxic (and therefore much safer) than DDT, cost four times as much as DDT.

42 "Review of Selected CR&D Developments," Aug. 1978, CRDD Files. See also the account of Du Pont and DDT in Woodhouse interview, Oct. 16, 1982.

43 The carbamate herbicides, particularly the chloroforms first made in the late forties, offered selective control of grassy weeds, but the substituted ureas possessed far greater potential for selectivity.

44 The following account of Du Pont's development of the substituted urea herbicides is based on M. T. Goebel, "A Case History in Research," paper presented at the 1955 Educators Conference, Du Pont Co., June 21, 1955, Pamphlet Collection, Hagley Museum and Library; C. W. Davis, "Biologically Active Substituted Ureas," Feb. 22, 1960, Special Compensation Files; G. D. Hill, "History and Development of the Phenylurea Herbicides," paper presented at the Beltwide Cotton Production Conference, Jan. 7, 1980; Luckenbaugh, "Du Pont Agricultural Chemicals"; Luckenbaugh interview; Gideon Hill interview; Wolf interview; "Review of Selected CR&D Developments."

45 3-(p-chlorophenyl)-1, 1-diethylurea.

46 3-(p-chlorophenyl)-1,1-dimethylurea (monuron).

47 Ahlgren et al., *Principles of Weed Control*.

48 Woodhouse interview, Oct. 16, 1982.

49 J. C. Anderson and D. E. Wolf, "Pre-emergency Control of Weeds in Corn with 2,4-D," *Agronomy Journal* 39 (1947): 341–2; 40 (1948): 453–8.

50 Wolf interview.

51 H. C. Bucha and C. W. Todd, "3-(p-chlorophenyl)-1,1-dimethylurea – A New Herbicide," *Science* 114 (1951): 493–4.

52 3-(3,4-dichlorophenyl)-1,1-dimethylurea.

53 G. D. Hill et al., "The Fate of Substituted Urea Herbicides in Agricultural Soils," *Agronomy Journal* 47 (1955): 93–104.

54 G. D. Hill, "History and Development of the Phenylurea Herbicides," paper presented at the Beltwide Cotton Production Conference, Jan. 7, 1980. Subsequent research has confirmed these conclusions. See R. L. Dalton et al., "Disappearance of Diuron from Cotton Field Soils," *Weeds* 14 (1966): 31–3, and G. D. Hill, "Characteristics of Herbicides by Chemical Groups, I. Substituted Ureas," *23rd Annual California Weed Conference Proceedings* (1966): pp. 158–70.

55 Hoffmann interview. For more information on Hoffmann, see *American Men and Women of Science*, 14th ed. (1979).

56 Goebel asked Hoffmann to write up his research for publication. Hoffmann promptly followed up on Goebel's request, but he soon learned that Goebel had developed cold feet. As Grasselli's general manager wrote in 1955, "We have been forced to reserve publication until the possible practical implications of his work...have been thoroughly evaluated" (C. W. Davis to "A" Bonus Committee, Feb. 28, 1955, Special Compensation Files). Indeed, Hoffmann was not allowed to publish his work until someone from the U.S. Department of Agriculture published an article on the mode of action of the substituted ureas. The above account of Hoffmann's work is based on the Hoffmann interview and C. W. Davis, "A Fundamental Contribution to the Biochemistry of Photosynthesis," Feb. 28, 1955, Special Compensation Files.

57 Quoted in Luckenbaugh interview.

58 Market share is from C. E. Davis, "Biologically Active Substituted Ureas."

59 Linuron is 3-(3,4-dichlorophenyl)-1-methoxy-1-methylurea. Despite having to license this compound, Du Pont has made consistently excellent profits on Lorox.

60 Luckenbaugh interview.

61 Ibid. See also G. D. Hill and Wolf interviews.

62 Luckenbaugh interview. R. E. Drexel, " 'Hyvar' X Bromacil Weed Killer," Feb. 20, 1970, Special Compensation Files.

63 Luckenbaugh interview. See also G. D. Hill interview.

64 Kelso files, Acc. 1850.

65 The ammonia and organic chemicals manufacturing operations of the Belle, West Virginia, plant were transferred to Grasselli from the Polychemicals Department (except for the highly profitable nylon intermediates business), thus making up the Industrial and Biochemicals Department.

66 The following account of Lannate's development derives mainly from R. E. Drexel, " 'Lannate' Methomyl Insecticide," Feb. 24, 1972, Special Compensation Files; Luckenbaugh, "Du Pont Agricultural Chemicals"; Luckenbaugh interview; W. A. Bours to the Executive Committee, "Whither 'Lannate,' " Feb. 6, 1975, EC Files; and G. D. Hill interview.

67   S-methyl N-[(methylcarbamoyl)oxy]thioacetimidate.

68   Union Carbide developed a product directly competitive with Lannate, Temik aldicarb, but in the last several years, this compound has come under increasing attack because it does not break down. See Eliot Marshall, "The Rise and Decline of Temik," *Science* 229 (1985): 1369–71.

69   The following account of Benlate benomyl's development is based on R. E. Drexel, " 'Benlate' Benomyl Fungicide," Feb. 24, 1972, Special Compensation Files; Luckenbaugh, "Du Pont Agricultural Chemicals"; and Gary B. Levin, "History of the Technical Development of Benomyl," June 3, 1982, Agchem Files.

70   Methyl 2-benzothiazolecarbamate.

71   Methyl 2-benzimidazolecarbamate.

72   W. K. Lowen to J. W. Williams, Nov. 12, 1957, and Feb. 3, 1958, Agchem Files. Specifically, Grasselli asked for Haskell's ten-dose, subacute oral test.

73   Haskell Laboratory Report 11-58 (Preliminary), Mar. 25, 1958, Agchem Files.

74   H. R. Rosenberg to R. S. Johnson, Apr. 29, 1958, Agchem Files.

75   Raymond Luckenbaugh has said that Goebel ordered all samples of benzimidazole compounds locked up and that most researchers in the department never knew why. Telephone interview with David A. Hounshell, Sept. 12, 1986.

76   Drexel, " 'Benlate' Benomyl Fungicide."

77   Donald A. Spencer to Richard S. Kittila, July 28, 1961, Agchem Files.

78   W. F. Strauss to R. W. Luckenbaugh, Apr. 6, 1964, Agchem Files.

79   Raymond W. Luckenbaugh, telephone interview with David A. Hounshell, Sept. 12, 1986. See also Rayner S. Johnson, "Addendum," May 8, 1969, Agchem Files.

80   R. W. Luckenbaugh to J. W. Clayton, Jr., Jan. 21, 1965. H. J. Gerjovich to W. K. Lowen, "U-811-Analog Syntheses," Jan. 28, 1965, Agchem Files.

81   Agricultural Chemicals Research, "Fungicide 811," April 7, 1965, Agchem Files.

82   W. F. Strauss to R. S. Johnson, Feb. 15, 1965, Agchem Files.

83   R. W. Luckenbaugh to J. W. Clayton, Jr., Nov. 8, 1966, Agchem Files.

84   Du Pont had continued its toxicological studies not only to meet the demands of registration clearance with the Department of Agriculture (and later the Environmental Protection Agency), but also to satisfy itself about the safety of benomyl. Even after the completion of the two-year feeding studies, which showed benomyl to be safe, there were questions about the metabolites of benomyl, especially MBC. Later in 1969 the new development of liquid chromatography proved to be of critical importance in learning about the fate of benomyl metabolites in animals. This technique greatly helped Du Pont's case for the safety of benomyl.

85   Kelso Files, Acc. 1850.

86   Warren K. Lowen, "The Search for New Agrichemicals," Development Managers Meeting, June 11, 1974, DD Files.

87   Jefferson interview, Aug. 1, 1986.

88   These products were based on the sulfonylureas, discovered by George Levitt in the mid-1970s.

89   Partial data on Du Pont's market share in herbicides, fungicides, and insecticides

is in R. E. Drexel to Executive Committee, Industrial and Biochemicals Department Annual Report for 1971, Dec. 30, 1971, EC Files.

90   Jefferson interview, Aug. 1, 1986.

91   C. H. Greenewalt to Ben May, Aug. 9, 1951, Acc. 1814, Box 10.

92   Hoffmann interview.

93   SMP-1 stood for N-dichloroacetyl-1-*p*-methylsulfonyl)-2-amino-1,3-propane-diol.

94   Luckenbaugh, "Du Pont Agricultural Chemicals."

95   AMP was a *p*-aminosulfonylphenyl derivative.

96   SMP-1 was later manufactured and marketed by European drug firms under the generic name thiamphenicol. The most recent data suggest that after more than 50 million patients were treated with the drug, there are no documented cases of aplastic anemia. See Fred E. Hahn, ed., *Modes and Mechanisms of Microbial Growth Inhibitors*, vol. 6, *Antibiotics* (Berlin: Springer-Verlag 1983), p. 43.

97   Walter A. Gregory, telephone interview with David A. Hounshell, Sept. 17, 1986. Cf. R. E. Drexel to Executive Committee, Proposal to Acquire Endo Laboratories, Inc., Sept. 25, 1969, EC Files.

98   EC Minutes, Feb. 21, 1957.

99   EC Minutes, May 31, Dec. 6, 1957.

100 R. C. Bergman to E. A. Gee, "Pharmaceuticals Venture," May 5, 1964, DD Files.

101 The most decisive step can be measured by the creation in 1962 of the Industrial and Biomedical Department's pharmaceutical research division.

102 Bergman to Gee, May 5, 1964.

103 Ibid.

104 Ibid. See also Hoffmann interview.

105 Bergman to Gee, May 5, 1964.

106 This view is discussed in ibid.

107 Ibid.

108 EC Minutes, Nov. 1, 1961.

109 E. G. Y[elton], "R&D Contracts with the Federal Government," Aug. 22, 1975, CRDD Files. See also Bergman to Gee, May 5, 1964, and Hoffmann interview.

110 W. E. Gordon to Executive Committee, "Departmental Review – Tuesday, October 27, 1964," Oct. 19, 1964, EC Files.

111 Octochloroadamantane.

112 Bergman to Gee, May 5, 1964.

113 Gordon to Executive Committee, Oct. 19, 1964.

114 Bergman to Gee, May 5, 1964.

115 Ibid.

116 Ibid.

117 Robert M. Joyce to David A. Hounshell, Oct. 3, 1986.

118 Ibid. Cf. the harsher analysis of David M. McQueen to Edwin A. Gee, July 28, 1970, Acc. 1850.

119 E. R. Kane to Executive Committee, Aug. 1, 1968, and R. E. Drexel to Executive Committee, Sept. 25, 1969, EC Files.

120 Drexel to Executive Committee, Sept. 25, 1969.

121 Ibid.

122 D. Brearley to E. A. Gee and J. N. Tilley, "Pharmaceuticals," June 21, 1963, Acc. 1404, Box 8.

123 Du Pont was pleased with these agreements, as evidenced in Drexel to Executive Committee, Sept. 25, 1969.

124 Ibid. See also E. R. Kane to Executive Committee, Aug. 1, 1968.

125 Bergman to Gee, May 5, 1964. Cf. Gordon to Executive Committee, Oct. 19, 1964, and Drexel to Executive Committee, Sept. 25, 1969.

126 Kane to Executive Committee, Aug. 1, 1968. See also Kane's "From the President's Desk," talk given at Development Managers' Meeting, Dec. 12, 1978, CRDD Files.

127 Treasurer to Executive Committee, "Financial Implications of Acquiring a Drug Company," Jan. 1, 1968, CRDD Files.

128 EC Minutes, Sept. 30, 1969.

129 Drexel to Executive Committee, Sept. 25, 1969.

130 Kane, "From the President's Desk."

131 J. A. Dallas to C. B. McCoy, Jan. 28, 1970, Acc. 1815, Box 32. Indeed, Du Pont did not fully consolidate Endo until 1981 by relocating Endo's administrative, marketing, and research activities to Wilmington. See M. B. Burton to Executive Committee, Nov. 21, 1980, EC Files. Geographical factors worked against assimilating Endo with Du Pont, as did Du Pont's long-time maintenance of Endo as a wholly owned subsidiary. Endo's laboratories and the Stine Laboratory also overlapped, and competition rather than cooperation resulted. Robert M. Joyce to David A. Hounshell, Oct. 3, 1986.

132 Hoffmann interview. Alan Rubin, telephone conversation with David A. Hounshell.

133 Jefferson interview, July 24, 1986.

134 Hoffmann interview.

135 Joyce to Hounshell, Oct. 3, 1986; Hoffmann interview; Industrial and Biochemicals Department to Executive Committee, Apr. 21, 1971, EC Files.

136 Hoffmann interview.

137 Jefferson interview, Aug. 1, 1986.

138 McQueen to Gee, July 28, 1970, Acc. 1850. See also Hoffmann interview.

Chapter 21. Keeping Ahead of the Competition: Du Pont Plastics

1 "A 1950 Guide to the Plastics," *Fortune* (May 1950): 109.

2 EC Minutes, Sept. 1, 1937.

3 EC Minutes, June 11, 1941. See also copy of resolution in Acc. 1813, Box 34.

4 On Almquist and Brill, see *American Men of Science*, 9th ed. (1955).

5 On Du Pont safety glass, see correspondence in II, 2, Box 1048; and A. F. Randolph, "Evolution of Safety Glass," *Modern Plastics* 18 (June 1941): 31–8.

6 Edward P. Bartlett, *The Chemical Division of the Ammonia Department, 1924–1935* (n.p.: n.p., 1949), II, 2, Box 91. See also Woodhouse interview, Oct. 14, 1982.

7 DuBois, *Plastics History U.S.A.*, p. 197. On Stettinius, see *The National Cyclopedia of American Biography*, vol. 38, s.v. "Stettinius, Edward R., Jr."

8   Neal Thurman to C. H. Greenewalt, Aug. 2, 1949, Acc. 1814, Box 5.

9   "Lucite Cast Sheeting," Acc. 1410, Box 30.

10 EC Minutes, Oct. 13, 1943.

11 Chaplin Tyler to Henry E. Ford, "Question of Realignment of Polychemicals Department's Chemicals Business," Apr. 26, 1959, CRDD Files.

12 Crawford H. Greenewalt to W. S. Carpenter, Jr., Mar. 5, 1948, II, 2, Box 843. Four years earlier, Carpenter had commissioned a Development Department study on this subject. (W. S. Carpenter, Jr. to E. K. Gladding, Aug. 28, 1944, II, 2, Box 832.)

13 To prevent Du Pont's cellophane film business from becoming just a small part of the Rayon Department, the company split off a separate Film Department in 1950 to manage this business in an era when cellophane expected strong challenges from synthetic films such as polyethylene.

14 W. S. Carpenter, Jr., "Proposed Consolidation of Ammonia and Plastics Departments – Development Department Report on Subject," July 27, 1949, Acc. 1814, Box 17.

15 EC Minutes, July 20, 1949.

16 On Pitcher's retirement see "History of Du Pont's Plastics Department," Nov. 28, 1965, Pamphlet Collection, Hagley Museum and Library. On Pitcher see "Transcription of Arnold E. Pitcher's Recollections of the Plastics Industry, 1910–1949," Recorded for the Plastics Pioneers Association, May 23, 1955, Acc. 1850. On Ries, see *American Men of Science*, 9th ed. (1955).

17 Tyler, "Question of Realignment."

18 On the team of Beekley and McGrew, see Gore interview. For biographical details, see *American Men of Science*, 9th ed. (1955). On McGrew's accepting the Polychemicals job, see McGrew interview.

19 Tyler, "Question of Realignment."

20 "Kelso Files," Acc. 1850. Du Pont also sold nylon bristles under the tradename Tynex.

21 Walter S. Fedor, "Thermoplastics: Progress Amid Problems," *Chemical and Engineering News* 39 (May 29, 1961): 107–9.

22 John H. Fahs, "Methacrylates," Aug. 14, 1959, CRDD Files; and W. H. Salzenberg to Executive Committee, "Whither Methacrylates," July 15, 1965, EC Files.

23 P. C. Allen to W. F. Luytens, "Exchange of Information of Polythene with Du Pont's," June 18, 1942, United States v. Imperial Chemical Industries, et al., Government Trial Exhibit 669.

24 Polychemicals Department to "A" Bonus Committee, "Polyethylene-Aqueous System Process," Feb. 3, 1955, Special Compensation Files.

25 "Polythene," Acc. 1410, Box 30.

26 For the licensing negotiations, see W. F. Glassock, "Polythene," Feb. 14, 1945, ICI Case, Government Rebuttal Exhibit 1365. On Union Carbide and polyethylene, see "The Polyethylene Gamble," *Fortune* (Feb. 1954): 136.

27 "Polythene."

28 On polyethylene in the 1950s and 1960s, see "The Polyethylene Gamble"; Jules Bachman, *The Economics of the Chemical Industry* (Washington: Manufacturing Chemists Association, 1970): 115–18; and Fedor, "Thermoplastics."

29 On the tubular process, see Polychemicals Department, "Polyethylene-

Aqueous System Process," Feb. 3, 1955, Special Compensation Files. On the autoclave process, see Polychemicals Department to "A" Bonus Committee, "Polyethylene-Autoclave Process," Jan. 11, 1960, Special Compensation Files.

30 Robert L. Hershey to the Executive Committee, "Polyethylenes – Opportunities for Du Pont," Mar. 22, 1956, PPD Research Files.

31 Ibid.

32 On Teflon process development, see Polychemicals and Organic Chemicals Departments to the Executive Committee, "Granular Teflon Development," Feb. 6, 1956, Special Compensation Files. On the first use of Teflon, see Robert M. Joyce, "Teflon," Feb. 18, 1981, Acc. 1850.

33 On fluorocarbon research in World War II, see Charles Slesser, ed., *Preparation, Properties and Technology of Fluorine and Organic Fluoro Compounds* (New York: McGraw-Hill, 1951).

34 "Research Is Always Beginning, Even after 25 Years," *Journal of Teflon* 4, no. 3 (1964): 4–5.

35 Carleton A. Sperati, "A Review of Product Studies on Teflon-TFE-Fluorocarbon Resins," Dec. 15, 1958, PPD Research Files.

36 Ibid.

37 On Teflon sales and earnings, see "Kelso Files" and "Exhibit A: Development and Commercialization of New Products," Acc. 1850.

38 Polychemicals and Organic Chemicals Departments to the "A" Bonus Committee, "Granular Teflon Development," Feb. 6, 1956, Special Compensation Files.

39 J. W. Haught, "Introduction," in C. A. Sperati to J. V. E. Hardy, "Review of Teflon Tetrafluoroethylene Resin," July 22, 1954, PPD Research Files.

40 Sperati, "Review."

41 W. L. Gore to E. B. Cooper, "Potential Rewards from Teflon Fabrication Research," July 31, 1953, PPD Research Files.

42 Still later, he developed porous PTFE products that became a household word – Gore-Tex. Gore interview.

43 Franta interview.

44 "Kelso Files."

45 Franta interview; George F. Baldwin, *History of the Du Pont Paint Business, 1947–1961* (n.p.: n.p., 1962), Appendix A, "Selected Finishes Research Developments," p. 3, Acc. 1850, and John A. Zapp, Jr., *The Anatomy of a Rumor* (Wilmington: Du Pont, 1961), Pamphlet Collection, Hagley Museum and Library.

46 C. A. Sperati, "Fluoroplastics," in *Modern Plastics Encyclopedia, 1986–1987*, pp. 22–5.

47 Herbert Solow, "Delrin: du Pont's Challenge to Metals," *Fortune* (Aug. 1959): 164.

48 McGrew interview.

49 Ibid. For an overview of the Delrin project, see Francis B. Vaughan, "Delrin Acetal Resin Research and Development: A Case History," Feb. 5, 1960, CRDD Files.

50 "History of Delrin Development to Plant Commercialization," Jan. 1960, PPD Files.

51 Ibid. The number of chemists was determined from organization charts in PPD Author Files. On McDonald, see *American Men and Women of Science*, 14th ed. (1979).

52 Solow, "Delrin," and Vaughan, "Delrin History."

53 Ibid. See also "History of Delrin Development."

54 F. B. Vaughan to J. S. Beekley, "Polymer F – Status of Development," Dec. 30, 1952, PPD Research Files. On Vaughan, see *American Men of Science*, 11th ed.

55 On end-capping, see F. C. McGrew to J. S. Beekley, "Polymer F," Mar. 3, 1953, PPD Research Files. See also Plastics Department to "A" Bonus Committee, "Development of Delrin Acetal Resin," Mar. 31, 1967, Special Compensation Files.

56 "History of Delrin Development" and quarterly progress reports in PPD Research Files.

57 Parke Woodworth to R. R. Warner, et al., "Polymer F," Oct. 21, 1952, PPD Research Files.

58 This phrase was used in Francis Bello, "The New Breed of Plastics," *Fortune* (November 1957): 223. Solow's article a year and a half later refers to it as "poor man's metal," reflecting a shift in Du Pont's thinking about the new material (Solow, "Delrin").

59 D. L. Dennison to W. F. Leach, "Delrin Evaluation Program," Dec. 1, 1953, PPD Research Files.

60 C. H. Hamblet to J. S. Beekley, "Delrin Acetal Resin – Programs in Manufacturing and Research Division," Sept. 2, 1954, PPD Research Files.

61 On the process developments, see "History of Delrin Development." The quote is from E. A. Smith, "Delrin Acetal Resin for Staff Meeting of July 25," July 22, 1955, PPD Research Files.

62 On hiring college students for the summer, see Cooper interview. On the development of this technique, see Gore interview. The preliminary evaluation was Robert E. Gee to R. R. Warner, "The Value of Delrin in Specific Applications," Sept. 6, 1955, PPD Research Files. The later report is R. E. Gee and W. L. Gore, "Utility Analysis for Delrin Resin," Dec. 30, 1955, PPD Research Files.

63 "History of Delrin Development." On Linton, see *American Men and Women of Science*, 14th ed. (1979).

64 On the Belle semiworks, see E. H. Berg to T. C. Hill and J. B. Tepe, "PE-100240 – Washington Works – Delrin Pilot Plant Process – Trip Report – Belle Works – February 4, 1957," Feb. 8, 1957, PPD Research Files.

65 "History of Delrin Development."

66 E. A. Smith to F. C. McGrew, "Delrin Acetal Resin – Initial Plant Size," Feb. 27, 1962, PPD Research Files.

67 Ibid.

68 On Celanese and Celcon, see Fedor, "Thermoplastics"; Lawrence Lessing, "How Du Pont Keeps Out in Front," *Fortune* (Dec. 1962): 207; and "Du Pont Drops Celcon Suit against Celanese," *Chemical and Engineering News* 41 (May 13, 1963): 21.

69 In the patent, Du Pont apparently made claims that the weight of the evidence in the laboratory notebooks did not support (McGrew interview).

70 "Du Pont Drops Celcon Suit."

71 R. L. Schuyler to Executive Committee, "Delrin Expansion Program – U.S. and Europe," July 9, 1970, EC Files.

72 For a general account of these developments, see Frank M. McMillan, *Chain Straighteners* (London: MacMillan, 1979).

73 On Gresham, see his obituary in the *Wilmington News Journal,* May 3, 1983, and Roger Morris, "Gresham Wins 1st Annual IRI Achievement Award," *Du Pont Innovation* 5 (Fall 1973): 18–20.

74 Anderson interview.

75 Plastics Department to the "A" Bonus Committee, "Coordination Catalysts," Feb. 1, 1967, Special Compensation Files. See also I. M. Robinson to W. F. Gresham, "Acid-Catalyzed Polymerizations," Feb. 17, 1954, PPD Research Files.

76 Polychemicals Department to "A" Bonus Committee, "Discovery of Linear Polyethylene," Feb. 23, 1962, Special Compensation Files.

77 W. F. Gresham, "New Catalyst System for Polymerization and Copolymerization of Olefinic Compounds," Mar. 26, 1954, PPD Research Files.

78 I. M. Robinson to W. F. Gresham, "New Polymerization Catalysts for Olefinic Materials," Apr. 21, 1954, PPD Research Files.

79 For an account of Du Pont's polypropylene discovery, see "Opening Brief on Behalf of Plaintiff Du Pont," Consolidated Civil Action No. 4319, United States District Court for the District of Delaware.

80 J. H. Balthus to R. E. Foster, "Ethylene Polymerizable Catalysts," Sept. 24, 1954, PPD Research Files.

81 E. D. Ries to the Executive Committee, "Proposed Agreements with Prof. Dr. Karl Ziegler, Max-Planck-Institut Für Kohlenforschung, Mülheim/Ruhr, Germany, Relating to Polyethylene," Apr. 5, 1955, EC Files.

82 R. L. Schuyler to Executive Committee, "Proposed Agreement with Professor Karl Ziegler," May 3, 1967, EC Files.

83 W. H. Ditmar to D. R. Darnell, "Linear Polyethylene," June 7, 1957, PPD Research Files.

84 On Phillips and Standard of Indiana, see McMillan, *Chain Straighteners,* pp. 68–72.

85 Polychemicals Department to Executive Committee, "Proposed Licensing under, and Enforcement of, the Expected United States Patent of Larcher and Pease Re Linear Polyethylene," Nov. 5, 1957, EC Files.

86 Beale and Jones to Allan R. Plumley, Oct. 25, 1957, letter attached to Polychemicals Department "Proposed Licensing."

87 On the Ziegler licensees, see Executive Committee to Finance Committee, "Revision of Licensing Program under, and Enforcement of, U.S. Patent #2,816,883 of Du Pont Regarding Linear Polyethylene," Apr. 2, 1958, EC Files. On Phillips, see Polychemicals Department to Executive Committee, July 17, 1961, EC Files.

88 E. D. Ries, "Proposed Agreements with Prof. Dr. Karl Ziegler."

89 A product application was filed in March 1956; it matured to a patent many years later (1978). U.S. Patent 4,076,698, Arthur W. Anderson and Gelu S. Stamatoff.

90 Hershey, "Polyethylenes – Opportunities for Du Pont."

91 For Du Pont's market share, see Bachman, *Economics,* p. 116. On the financial

status of linear polyethylene, see "Supplement to Exhibit A – NVD Report. Item 3 – New Ventures Commercialized (41)," Acc. 1850.

92 On the competitiveness of the polyethylene business, see Fedor, "Thermoplastics," and Bachman, *Economics*. For 1964 market share figures, see "U.S. Polyethylene Capacity – Estimated as of 1964 Year End," Acc. 1404, Box 17.

93 Ditmar, "Linear Polyethylene."

94 "Who Owns Polypropylene? A Court May Soon Decide," *Chemical Week* (Apr. 15, 1984): 44–8.

95 "Opening Brief," p. 80.

96 McMillan, *Chain Straighteners*, pp. 92–140.

97 "Who Owns Polypropylene?"

98 "Opening Brief," pp. 41–68.

99 R. C. Doban to D. E. Strain, "Polymers and Copolymers from Propylene," Nov. 7, 1955, PPD Research Files.

100 The first catalysts that Du Pont's chemists used created two kinds of polypropylene, an amorphous and a crystalline polymer, which had radically different properties. The former was soft and pliable, resembling "vinyl" plastics, whereas the latter was a stiffer and much higher-temperature-melting version of linear polyethylene. (R. C. Doban, "Synthesis and Characterization of Highly Amorphous Polypropylene," June 25, 1956, PPD Research Files.)

101 Doban, "Synthesis," and A. H. Nicholas, "Crystalline Polypropylene Plant – Basic Design Data Report," Jan. 16, 1961, PPD Research Files.

102 S. P. Foster and J. C. Gebhard to J. S. Beekley, "The Effect of Crystalline Polypropylene on the Sales of Polyethylene," July 17, 1958, PPD Research Files.

103 Fedor, "Thermoplastics."

104 A. J. Vaughan to J. M. Nelson, "Polypropylene – Meeting with Textile Fibers and Film Departments," Oct. 30, 1967, PPD Research Files.

105 "Who Owns Polypropylene?" and "Phillips Finally Wins Its Patent," *Chemical Week* (Mar. 23, 1983): 13–14.

106 McMillan, *Chain Straighteners*, p. 171.

107 Anderson interview.

108 For the growth of Polychem's research budget, see company research statistics in Acc. 1850. On the analysis of the department in 1961, see Walter H. Salzenberg "Performance Analysis – Polychemicals Department," Jan. 25, 1961, EC Files. On Salzenberg, see his company biography in Acc. 1410, Box 62.

109 Salzenberg, "Performance Analysis."

110 On the decentralization of Plastics R&D, see Franta interview.

111 Franta interview. On Nafion membranes, see Stephen C. Stinson, "Electrolytic Cell Membrane Development Surges," *Chemical and Engineering News* (Mar. 15, 1982): 22–6.

112 J. W. C., untitled address, May 11, 1978, PPD Files.

113 F. C. Clarke, "Cellophane Sales History," Mar. 25, 1968, PPD Files.

114 C. D. Bell to the Executive Committee, "Whither – Polyolefin Films," Nov. 4, 1971, EC Files.

115 "Cellophane: Down But Not Out," *Modern Packaging* (May 1978): 51–3.

116 On Mylar, see Du Pont Company Press Release, Jan. 22, 1958, Acc. 1410, Box 8. Earnings and Return on Investment statistics are in "Film Department," Mar. 1, 1963, Acc. 1404, Box 10.

117 On the formation of the department, see William C. Kay to C. B. McCoy, "Reorganization of Organic Chemicals Department," Oct. 29, 1969, Acc. 1815, Box 33. On Viton, see Herman E. Schroeder, "Facets of Innovation," Remarks at the Presentation of the Charles Goodyear Medal, Indianapolis, Indiana, May 9, 1984, *Rubber Chemistry and Technology* 57 (July–Aug. 1984): G82–G106.

118 C. J. Harrington, "Past, Present, and Glorious Future of the Elastomer Chemicals Department," July 11, 1973, Talk to Development Managers' Meeting, CRDD Files.

119 On Nordel, see Schroeder, "Facets," and Charles J. Harrington to the Executive Committee, "Nordel Hydrocarbon Rubber," Aug. 3, 1967, EC Files. On the general development of EPDM rubbers, see *Chemistry in the Economy* (Washington: American Chemical Society, 1973): 134–6.

120 Schroeder, "Facets."

Chapter 22. The New Venture Era

1 E. A. Gee to H. E. Ford and J. N. Tilley, "Planning for the Diversified Growth of the Du Pont Company, Meeting of July 26, 1961," July 27, 1961, DD Files.

2 E. A. Gee and J. C. Metzger to the Subcommittee on Planning, "Diversification in the Du Pont Company," Apr. 6, 1961, EC Files.

3 D. H. Dawson to C. H. Greenewalt, L. duP. Copeland, et al., "Discussions with General Managers of Company Performance and Organization (Apr.–July, 1961)," July 16, 1961, Acc. 1814, Box 3.

4 The earnings figures are from company annual reports, and the research statistics are from S. Lenher to C. B. McCoy, "Technical Activities Expense," Dec. 23, 1959, Acc. 1814, Box 37.

5 On the maturation of the chemical industry, see Perrin Stryker, "Chemicals: The Ball is Over," *Fortune*, Oct. 1961, pp. 125–7, 207–18. The quotation is from C. S. Tyler to W. S. Carpenter, Jr., "The Outlook for the Du Pont Company – Statistical and Product Trends," Aug. 9, 1957, Acc. 1850.

6 "The Chemical Century," *Fortune*, Mar. 1950, pp. 69–76, 114–22. The listing of invaders is from Tyler, "Outlook."

7 D. H. Dawson to C. H. Greenewalt, Jan. 3, 1961, Acc. 1404, Box 9.

8 On Dawson, see company biography in Acc. 1850.

9 Greenewalt interview, Jan. 19, 1983.

10 D. H. Dawson, "Development Managers' Meeting," Nov. 19, 1957, DD Files.

11 Du Pont acquisitions were usually handled through an exchange of stock, but until the GM suit was resolved, the value of that stock would be difficult to determine. (R. R. Pippin to the Subcommittee on Planning, Dec. 5, 1960, DD Files.)

12 On Du Pont's overseas business, see Greenewalt interview, Jan. 19, 1983; and Graham D. Taylor and Patricia E. Sudnik, *Du Pont and the International Chemical Industry* (Boston: Twayne, 1984), pp. 187–95.

13 N. E. Krase, "What We Need from Research," Talk Prepared for Meeting of Research Directors on Jan. 27, 1959, Acc. 1850.

14 R. E. Gee, "Updating Points in E. A. G. Speech to Subcommittee (Feb. 23, 1963) 'Diversification'," Mar. 20, 1963, Acc. 1850.

15 D. Brearley to H. E. Ford and J. N. Tilley, "Forward Integration," Feb. 4, 1959, Acc. 1814, Box 5.

16 The Olympian posture of the Executive Committee was noted by a *Business Week* reporter who stated, "If you ask...where the company is going and how it is changing, you get the idea that such questions are in bad taste." ("A Giant Gets in Quick Step," *Business Week*, Nov. 9, 1963.)

17 On improving communication of research results, see S. Lenher to C. H. Greenewalt, "Communication in Research," Oct. 20, 1960, Acc. 1814, Box 5. On the problems of Du Pont research, see S. Lenher, "Research and Development," A Resume of the Important Points in Mr. Lenher's Talk to the Development Managers, Mar. 10, 1959, compiled by M. Fields and F. F. Benti, Jr., Mar. 12, 1959, DD Files. On the broadening of the charter of Central Research, see EC Minutes, Mar. 11, 1959.

18 P. L. Salzberg, "Du Pont Research," Jan. 22, 1960, DD Files.

19 EC Minutes, May 11, 1960.

20 P. L. Salzberg to S. Lenher, "Pioneering Research in the Industrial Departments," Aug. 1, 1960, Acc. 1814, Box 5.

21 S. Lenher to C. H. Greenewalt, J. F. Daley, et al., "Research, Development, and Commercialization," Jan. 21, 1959, Acc. 1814, Box 5.

22 D. H. Dawson to S. Lenher, "Research Policies," Feb. 26, 1960, Acc. 1814, Box 5.

23 Between 1958 and 1963, only 9 percent of Du Pont's total construction expenditures went into new products for new markets. E. A. Gee, "Diversification," Speech to Subcommittee on Planning, Feb. 25, 1963, DD Files.

24 On the role of the Executive Committee, see Dawson, "Discussions." The quotation is from H. B. du Pont to C. H. Greenewalt, L. duP. Copeland, et al., Mar. 14, 1961, Acc. 1814, Box 2.

25 On the Executive Committee in the 1950s, see Greenewalt interview, Jan. 19, 1983.

26 EC Minutes, Aug. 3, 1960. For an overview of the Development Department's programs, see Norman Fast, "The Evolution of Corporate New Venture Divisions" (PhD diss., Harvard University, 1977).

27 C. Tyler to H. E. Ford and J. N. Tilley, "Planning for the Diversified Growth of the Du Pont Company," Aug. 19, 1960, DD Files.

28 Gee interview.

29 On Du Pont and titanium metal, see Gee interview; F. H. Weismuller to the Executive Committee, "Titanium Metal," Feb. 13, 1957, Special Compensation Records; and J. Schroeder to the Executive Committee, "Metals Program – Titanium," Feb. 22, 1962, EC Files.

30 F. H. Weismuller to the Executive Committee, "High Purity Silicon," Feb. 23, 1955, Special Compensation Records.

31 EC Minutes, Jan. 30, 1957.

32 F. H. Weismuller to the Executive Committee, "Electronic Grade Silicon," Apr. 14, 1961, EC Files.

33 Gee interview.

34 E. A. Gee, "Diversification, Meeting Notes – S. Lenher, H. E. Ford, 10/4/60," Oct. 5, 1960, DD Files.

35 E. A. Gee, "Planning for Diversified Growth, Meeting Notes – S. Lenher, H. E. Ford," Nov. 9, 1960, DD Files.

36 E. A. Gee, "Diversification, Meeting Notes – P. L. Salzberg, M. M. Brubaker, Central Research Department, H. E. Ford, 10/3/60," Oct. 7, 1960, DD Files.

37 Gee interview.

38 Gee mentioned the phrase "diversification gap" in a draft of a talk to be given to the subcommittee. (E. A. Gee, "Functions of the Development Department," Sept. 1, 1960, DD Files). Gee soon submitted a report that contained these proposals. (E. A. Gee to H. E. Ford, "Planning for the Diversified Growth of the Du Pont Company," Nov. 10, 1960, DD Files.)

39 Gee and Metzger, "Diversification in the Du Pont Company."

40 Gee to Ford, "Planning for the Diversified Growth of the Du Pont Company," Nov. 10, 1960, DD Files.

41 J. R. Brand, *The EDL Story, 1944–1979* (Wilmington, Del.: Du Pont Engineering Department, 1980), pp. 26–8; and V. W. Haedrich to the Executive Committee, "Progress Report – Engineering Department New Venture Studies," Apr. 4, 1961, EC Files.

42 Gee and Metzger, "Diversification in the Du Pont Company." The subcommittee's rejection of the proposals is in the Subcommittee on Planning to the Executive Committee, "Diversification in the Du Pont Company," Apr. 14, 1961, EC Files.

43 In 1963, two years after his first proposal, Gee revived his plan for the Diversification Department. E. A. Gee to L. S. Sinness, "Thoughts on Planning for Diversified Growth," Jan. 18, 1963, DD Files.

44 E. A. Gee, "Executive Committee Meeting – New Ventures, June 22, 1961," June 23, 1961, DD Files.

45 E. A. Gee to the Executive Committee, "Development Department Functions," Oct. 31, 1963, EC Files.

46 Gee, "Planning for the Diversified Growth of the Du Pont Company," Nov. 10, 1960; and Gee interview.

47 Arthur Lloyd Welsh, "The Du Pont–General Motors Case" (PhD diss., University of Illinois, 1963).

48 E. A. Gee, "Remarks by Edwin A. Gee – Special Meeting of the Executive Committee," Oct. 10, 1962, DD Files.

49 On antitrust policy in the 1960s, see Sylvestro Petro, "The Growing Threat of Antitrust," *Fortune*, Nov. 1962, pp. 128–31, and Ellis W. Hawley, "Anti-Trust," in Glenn Porter, ed., *Encyclopedia of American Economic History* (New York: Scribners, 1980), vol. 2, p. 780.

50 *Funds for Research and Development in Industry, 1959* (Washington: National Science Foundation, 1962), p. 16.

51 Edmond G. Young, "R&D Contracts with the Federal Government," Aug. 22, 1975, DD Files.

52 H. H. Ewing to H. E. Ford, "Research in the Government, Part I," Aug. 10, 1959, DD Files.

53 Greenewalt's position is stated in E. A. Gee, "Planning for Diversified

Growth," July 27, 1961. Gee's attempts to get Du Pont involved in government research are evident in quarterly reports to the Executive Committee (H. E. Ford to the Executive Committee, "Quarterly Report – Second Quarter 1961," June 30, 1961, and "Quarterly Report – Third Quarter 1961," Sept. 30, 1961, EC Files).

54 Gee, "Planning for the Diversified Growth of the Du Pont Company," Nov. 10, 1960.

55 Congress enacted the Small Business Investment Act of 1958 that permitted companies to get loans from the Small Business Administration for the purpose of investing in small companies. This act had led to the formation of over one hundred venture capital companies. (C. Tyler to the Subcommittee on Planning, "Diversification through Investment in Embryonic Ventures," Mar. 21, 1961, DD Files.)

56 E. A. Gee, "Memorandum to File," Apr. 21, 1961, DD Files.

57 C. Tyler to the Executive Committee, "Diversification through Investment in Embryonic Ventures," July 6, 1961, DD Files.

58 C. Tyler to E. A. Gee, "Diversification through Embryonic Ventures," Aug. 30, 1961, DD Files.

59 D. D. Friel to the Executive Committee, "Embryonic Investment Activity," Aug. 26, 1964, DD Files.

60 Ibid.

61 Gee interview.

62 D. Brearley to G. J. Prendergast, Jr., "Development Department Diversification Program of the 1960s," July 21, 1976, Acc. 1850.

63 D. R. Johnson, "Anatomy of a Winner: Instrument Products," May 18, 1973, Acc. 1850.

64 J. Mitchell, Jr., "The Role of Analysis in an Industrial Department," Oct. 1979, Report No. PM 447, PPD Research Files.

65 Gee interview and Johnson, "Anatomy."

66 Mitchell, "Role," pp. 264–81, and Johnson, "Anatomy."

67 J. C. Metzger to the Executive Committee, "Instrument Venture," Jan. 2, 1964, DD Files.

68 On the development of the Automatic Clinical Analyzer, see Johnson, "Anatomy"; William G. Simeral, "The Evolution of Research and Development Policy in a Corporation: A Case Study," in *Partners in the Research Enterprise: A National Conference on University–Corporate Relations in Science and Technology* (Philadelphia: University of Pennsylvania Press, 1983); and P. J. Wingate to the Executive Committee, "Automatic Clinical Analyzer," Mar. 9, 1977, Special Compensation Records.

69 Gee, "Planning for the Diversified Growth of the Du Pont Company," Nov. 10, 1960.

70 W. H. Charch to P. R. Austin, J. S. Beekley, et al., "Du Pont and the Building Materials Industry," Aug. 3, 1955, PR Records, Box 191121.

71 R. W. Peterson to the Advisor on Research, "The Building Products Venture," Feb. 27, 1963, DD Files.

72 R. W. Peterson to H. W. Swank, "Proposal to Enter the Home Building Industry," Apr. 28, 1961, DD Files.

73 Peterson, "Building Products Venture." On caprolactam, see J. L. Fahs, "Cap-

rolactam Research and Development: A Case Study," Feb. 1, 1960, DD Files. The Executive Committee approved the venture on Mar. 27, 1963, EC Minutes.

74 E. A. Gee to the Executive Committee, "Building Products Venture – Status Report," Nov. 30, 1967, DD Files.

75 Ibid. The quotation is from E. A. Gee to the Executive Committee, "Building Products Venture – Status Report," Dec. 14, 1967, DD Files.

76 M. S. Sadler to the Executive Committee, "Building Products Venture," Aug. 12, 1971, DD Files.

77 Ibid.

78 "Magnetic Chromium Dioxide for Recording Tape (Crolyn)," in "Review of Selected CR&D Developments," Aug. 1978, CRDD Files.

79 Bruce F. Day, "The Office Copier Venture – The Anatomy of a Loser," May 18, 1975, Acc. 1850; and E. B. Yelton to the Executive Committee, "Annual Report – 1969," Dec. 31, 1969, DD Files.

80 M. S. Sadler to the Executive Committee, "Annual Report – 1974," Appendix A, Nov. 27, 1974, DD Files.

81 Brearley, "Development Department Diversification Program of the 1960s."

82 E. A. Gee to the Subcommittee on Planning, "Industrial Department Diversification," Nov. 23, 1962, DD Files.

83 R. L. Hershey to the Executive Committee, "R&D Rules," May 27, 1964, EC Files.

84 Ibid.

85 "Lammot du Pont Copeland," biography in Acc. 1404, Box 17. His report cards are in LMSS, Group 10, Series A, File 418-14.

86 Gee interview.

87 L. S. Sinness to L. duP. Copeland, "Major Problems of the Company," Aug. 21, 1964, Acc. 1404, Box 9. In his statement, Sinness went on to account for this situation in research:

> The most significant causes for low research productivity appear to be: (1) the concept of fundamental and basic research ("interesting chemistry") as an end in itself, with inadequate attention to evaluation and reduction to commercial practice, (2) inadequate use of market research and of market-oriented research objectives, (3) the helter-skelter fragmentation of new venture scouting throughout the Company, . . . and (4) a persistent series of unfortunate appointments to the Departmental Research Director level of men whose only qualification was scientific facility but who possessed no experience or innate appreciation of the commercial side of the business.

88 D. H. Dawson to L. du P. Copeland, "Whither the Du Pont Company," Aug. 26, 1964, Acc. 1404, Box 9.

89 C. B. McCoy to L. duP. Copeland, "Planning, Etc.," Aug. 24, 1964, Acc. 1404, Box 9.

90 *Fortune* quoted Greenewalt in 1950: "Industrial research involves the finding of ways to deal with an inherently bad statistical situation. The odds are very bad indeed." (Lawrence Lessing, "How to Win at Research," *Fortune*, Oct. 1950, pp. 116–17.)

91 R. M. Busche to E. B. Yelton, "Development and Commercialization of New Products," July 22, 1968, DD Files.

92 R. M. Busche to W. A. Franta, "Research Effectiveness – Selected Ventures Commercialized, 1952–1967," Jan. 11, 1968, DD Files.

93 W. A. Franta and G. Prendergast to the Executive Committee, "Development and Commercialization of New Products," July 18, 1968, DD Files.

94 Busche, "Development and Commercialization of New Products."

95 Ibid.

96 *Du Pont Company Annual Report 1966.*

97 Gilbert Burck, "Du Pont under Pressure," *Fortune*, Nov. 1967, pp. 136–41, 177–82.

98 EC Minutes, Mar. 1, 1967.

99 On J. W. McCoy, see Acc. 1410, Box 62.

100 On C. B. McCoy, see his biography in Acc. 1850.

101 "Du Pont," *Forbes*, Dec. 15, 1969, p. 22.

102 Burck, "Du Pont under Pressure," p. 180.

103 M. S. Sadler to the Executive Committee, "New Venture Development," Oct. 15, 1970, Exhibit A, DD Files; and T. R. Priebe to M. S. Sadler, "New Venture Development – Supplemental Information to 'Exhibit A'," Oct. 12, 1970, Acc. 1850.

104 W. F. H. Mattlage to the Executive Committee, "Definition of the Corfam Product," Mar. 29, 1967, Special Compensation Records. The Executive Committee decision was recorded in EC Minutes, Oct. 26, 1955.

105 W. D. Lawson, "History and Analysis of Corfam," 1972, Pamphlet Collection, Hagley Museum and Library.

106 "The $100-Million Object Lesson," *Fortune*, Jan. 1971, p. 109.

107 R. E. Heckert to the Executive Committee, "Whither Corfam," Nov. 20, 1969, EC Files.

108 "The $100-Million Object Lesson."

109 Lawrence Lessing, "Synthetics Ride Hell-Bent for Leather," *Fortune*, Nov. 1964, pp. 172–86.

110 The sales figure is from Heckert, "Whither Corfam," and the losses are from Priebe and Sadler, "New Venture Development."

111 Lawson, "History."

112 Heckert, "Whither Corfam."

113 Ibid.

114 On the sale of Corfam technology to Poland, see Maurice Barnfather, "Polish Joke," *Forbes*, Mar. 2, 1981, p. 46. See also Leonard Sloane, "Du Pont's $100-Million Edsel," *New York Times*, Apr. 11, 1971.

115 J. T. Axon, "New Venture Development in Du Pont: An Analysis of the New Venture Development Program, 1960–1969," Draft No. 10, Sept. 21, 1970, Acc. 1850.

116 Sales figures are from "Kelso Files," Acc. 1850.

117 "Supplement to 'Exhibit A' – NVD Report: Item 3 – New Ventures Commercialized (41)."

118 Priebe and Sadler, "New Venture Development." See also "New Venture Development in Du Pont," July 29, 1970, Exhibit A, Acc. 1850. Of this total $1.6 billion, $1 billion represented R&D costs and $600 million went into investment in new plants.

119 "New Products Commercialized Between 1958–1977," Acc. 1850.

120 Ibid.

121 On Du Pont and petrochemicals, see E. A. Gee to the Executive Committee,

April 1, 1965, DD Files, and E. A. Gee to the Executive Committee, "The Petroleum Industry," Feb. 24, 1966, DD Files.

122 Axon, "New Venture Development."

Chapter 23. Successful Diversification: The Photo Products Department

1 The authors have been told this anecdote by several employees of the Photo Products Department in this era. For one example, see the comment by David W. Woodward in Woodward interview.

2 Sales and earnings figures for 1960 were calculated from Du Pont R&D statistics in Acc. 1850. Those for 1979 are from John G. Metzger to the Executive Committee, "Photo Products Department – Annual Report," Dec. 5, 1979, EC Files.

3 H. F. Brown to R. R. M. Carpenter, Sept. 13, 1912, Acc. 1465.

4 EC Minutes, Apr. 26, May 3, 1920.

5 V. B. Sease, "Brief History of Du Pont Film Plant at Parlin, N.J.," Aug. 4, 1944, Acc. 1410, Box 42.

6 "Du Pont II: An Industrial Empire," *Fortune*, Dec. 1934, p. 167.

7 The sales figures for 1929 is from "Chemical Research Expenditures – 1929," Apr. 8, 1930, Acc. 1813, Box 5. Du Pont's share of the market was calculated from earnings data from "Du Pont Film Manufacturing Corporation – Net Operating Profit of Principal Products as a Percentage of Total Net Operating Profit," July 1, 1941, Acc. 1813, Box 9, and "Sunlight and Shadow," *Fortune*, May 1932, pp. 50–55, 108–14.

8 On Du Pont's entry into X-ray film, see Sease, "Brief History." The quotation is from "Sunlight and Shadow," *Fortune*, May 1932, p. 53. For a history of Du Pont's X-ray film business, see M. S. Sadler to the Executive Committee, "Du Pont's Major Products," Apr. 14, 1972, EC Files.

9 On the Patterson Screen Company, see "Patterson Screen Company Joins Forces with Du Pont," *Du Pont X-Ray Notes* 1, no. 1 (1943): 1–2, Acc. 1410, Box 62. On Defender, see G. A. Scanlan to W. S. Carpenter, Jr., "Reasons for Acquisition of Defender," Apr. 12, 1945, II, 2, Box 836.

10 Sales statistics for the various departments were calculated from Du Pont R&D statistics for this period, Acc. 1850.

11 S. G. Baker to C. H. Greenewalt, "State of the Business," Oct. 15, 1952, Acc. 1814, Box 17.

12 On Signaigo, see his biography in Acc. 1850.

13 See Du Pont R&D Statistics in Acc. 1850.

14 On the history of color photography, see *Color*, Life Library of Photography (New York: Time-Life Books, 1970). On Du Pont's research on color film, see the annual reports of the Chemical Department in Acc. 1784. In the late 1940s, color was the largest research effort under way in the Chemical Department. See Cole Coolidge, "Statistical Data on Research and Other Technical Activities, Years 1951–1952," Oct. 31, 1951, Acc. 1784.

15 On the development of color print film in Photo Products, see H. L. Graham, "Special Meeting with the Executive Committee," Oct. 1, 1964, and H. L.

Graham to the Executive Committee, "Color Photographic Products," June 22, 1965, EC Files.

16 Cohen interview.

17 Robert Sheehan, "The Kodak Picture – Sunshine and Shadow," *Fortune*, May 1965, p. 158.

18 Graham, "Color Photographic Products," and Cohen interview. The $10 million figure comes from T. R. Priebe to M. S. Sadler, "New Venture Development, Supplemental Information to 'Exhibit A'," Oct. 12, 1970, Acc. 1850.

19 G. H. Loving to the "A" Bonus Committee, "Development of 'Cronar' Polyester Photographic Film Base," Feb. 27, 1963, Special Compensation Files.

20 Loving, "Development," and Cohen interview.

21 Sadler, "Du Pont's Major Products."

22 Cohen and Woodward interviews.

23 Cohen interview and Sadler, "Du Pont's Major Products."

24 Public Affairs Department News Release, Oct. 6, 1955, Acc. 1410, Box 3.

25 Sadler, "Du Pont's Major Products."

26 On photopolymerization research, see Plambeck and McQueen interviews. See also "Dycril Photopolymer Printing Plates" in "Review of Selected CR&D Developments," Aug. 1978, CRDD Files; and Henry Davidson, "Retired Du Ponter Found Printing Plate Method," in the "Brandywine Crossroads Supplement" to the *Wilmington News Journal*, May 17, 1983.

27 On Dycril, see "Du Pont 'Dycril' Photopolymer Printing Plates – Background Memorandum," Acc. 1410, Box 42; and H. L. Graham to the Executive Committee, "Dycril Photopolymer Printing Plates," May 5, 1966, EC Files.

28 Cohen interview.

29 Riston earnings were calculated from the annual reports of the Photo Products Department, EC Files.

30 On Riston, see Monroe S. Sadler, David W. Woodward, and A. B. Cohen, "Role of R&D in Developing New Products and Product Areas," in Victor J. Danilov, ed., *Research Decision-Making in New Product Development* (Beverly Shores, Ind.: Industrial Research, 1968), pp. 33–55; and P. J. Wingate to the "A" Bonus Committee, "Riston Photopolymer Resist Film," Feb. 4, 1970, Special Compensation Files.

31 Cohen interview.

32 Ibid.

33 M. S. Sadler et al., "Role of R&D."

34 Cohen interview.

35 Ibid.

36 The precommercial R&D expenses are from R. M. Busche to E. B. Yelton, "Development and Commercialization of New Products," July 22, 1968, Appendix A-6, DD Files. The sales and earnings statistics are from the Photo Products Annual Report for 1977, EC Files.

37 On Cromalin, see P. J. Wingate to the "A" Bonus Committee, "Cromalin Color Proofing System," Jan. 3, 1973, Special Compensation Files; and P. J. Wingate to the Executive Committee, "New Venture Development Request," June 18, 1970, EC Files.

38 Wingate, "Cromalin," and Cohen interview.

39 Cohen interview.

40 Ibid.

41 J. C. Metzger to the Executive Committee, "Annual Report – 1976," December 5, 1976, EC Files.

42 E. A. Gee to C. B. McCoy, "Photo Products Annual Report," Dec. 27, 1971, Acc. 1815, Box 34.

43 E. A. Gee to C. B. McCoy, "Annual Report, Photo Products Department," Dec. 23, 1970, Acc. 1815, Box 34.

44 M. S. Sadler to E. A. Gee, "Photo Products Department Annual Report," Dec. 17, 1971, Acc. 1815, Box 34.

45 Phillip Wingate, letter to authors, May 1986.

46 Ibid. See also Graham, "Special Meeting."

47 EC Minutes, Mar. 1, 1967.

48 Phillip Wingate, letter to authors, May 1986.

49 Gee interview.

50 The quotation is from P. J. Wingate to the Executive Committee, "Equipment Business, Photo Products Department," Aug. 29, 1974, EC Files. On the development of equipment systems, see E. A. Gee to the Executive Committee, "Systems Development – Hazeltine Corporation," Mar. 6, 1969, EC Files. On the transfer of instrument products to the Photo Products Department, see E. A. Gee and M. S. Sadler to the Executive Committee, "Instrument Products Profit Center," July 16, 1969, EC Files.

51 On the purchase of additional instrument lines, see P. J. Wingate to the Executive Committee, "Purchase of Bell & Howell Company's Analytical Instruments Business," July 13, 1970, and "Proposal for Acquisition of Ivan Sorvall, Inc., Newton, Connecticut," Oct. 17, 1972, EC Files. On the evolution of the instrument business, see the 1979 Annual Report of the department, EC Files.

52 On the growth of the electronic materials business, see the annual reports of the Photo Products Department and J. C. Metzger to the Executive Committee, "Electronic Materials Division, Facilities Expansion – Niagara Falls," Apr. 6, 1968, EC Files. On the use of the electronic materials, see "Before the Name Goes On," *Du Pont Magazine* 71 (Sept.–Oct. 1977): 25–7.

53 P. J. Wingate to the Executive Committee, "Proposal for Acquisition of Berg Electronics, Incorporated, New Cumberland, Pennsylvania," Mar. 9, 1972, EC Files.

54 Phillip Wingate, letter to authors, May 1986.

55 P. J. Wingate to the Executive Committee, "Expansion of Berg Electronics," July 24, 1973, EC Files.

56 Ibid.

57 J. C. Metzger to the Executive Committee, "Berg Electronics, Worldwide Facilities, Expansion Program," Dec. 7, 1979, EC Files.

58 Du Pont R&D Statistics, Acc. 1850.

59 On new venture management at Du Pont, see Russell W. Peterson, "New Venture Management in a Large Company," *Harvard Business Review* 45 (May–June 1967): 68–76. For a critical analysis of Du Pont's new venture system, see M. S. Sadler to the Executive Committee, "New Venture Development," Oct. 15, 1970, EC Files.

Chapter 24. Toxicological and Environmental Research

1 There has been little scholarship on the history of toxicology. Some useful sources are John A. Zapp, Jr., "Industrial Toxicology: Retrospect and Prospect," in George D. Clayton and Florence Clayton, eds., *Patty's Industrial Hygiene and Toxicology*, vol. 2A, *Toxicology* (New York: Wiley, 1981): 1467–91; Henry F. Smyth, Jr., "Toxicology of Industrial Chemicals," *Archives of Environmental Health* (Mar. 1964): 384–92; Horace W. Gerarde, "Occupational Medicine Research: Industrial Toxicology," *Journal of Occupational Medicine* 8 (Apr. 1966): 167–71; Ludwig Teleky, *History of Factory and Mine Hygiene* (New York: Columbia University Press, 1948); Peter S. Barth, with H. Allen Hunt, *Worker's Compensation and Work Related Illness and Diseases* (Cambridge, Mass.: MIT Press, 1980); David Rosner and Gerald Markowitz, "Research or Advocacy: Federal Occupational Safety and Health Policies during the New Deal," *Journal of Social History* 18 (1984–85): 365–81; and James Wharton, *Before "Silent Spring": Pesticides and Public Health in Pre-DDT America* (Princeton N.J.: Princeton University Press, 1974).

2 Teleky, *History*, pp. 180–1, and Alice Hamilton, *Exploring the Dangerous Trades: The Autobiography of Alice Hamilton, M.D.* (Boston: Little, Brown, 1943), pp. 3–11, 113–26.

3 When she began to read the literature on occupational disease, Alice Hamilton found very little of it was in English (Hamilton, *Exploring*, p. 115). The early classic work on occupational disease was Thomas Oliver, ed., *Dangerous Trades* (London: John Murray, 1902). On early legislation in Europe, see Teleky, *History*, pp. 22–74.

4 Hamilton, *Exploring*, p. 4.

5 Ibid., pp. 5–11.

6 On the history of workman's compensation, see Roy Lubove, *The Struggle for Social Security* (Cambridge, Mass.: Harvard University Press, 1968), pp. 45–65.

7 Walter G. Hudson, *Explosives – Industry Poisons* (New York: William Wood and Co., 1917), reprinted from the *Medical Record*, Jan. 20, 1917, Pamphlet Collection, Hagley Museum and Library. On Hudson, see his obituary in the *Du Pont Magazine* 14 (Jan. 1921): 12.

8 Hudson obituary.

9 On the toxicity of benzene, see Frank P. Underhill and Benedict R. Harris, "The Influence of Benzol upon Certain Aspects of the Organism," *Journal of Industrial Hygiene* 3 (1921–22): 491–3. On the benzene problems at Du Pont, see L. A. De Blois, "Notes on Frank Cassidy – Fatality Newburgh, Chronic Benzene Poisoning – Personal Injury #495," May 19, 1922, Acc. 1615, Box 11.

10 L. A. De Blois, "Benzol Poisoning," May 13, 1922, Acc. 1615, Box 11.

11 Henry Field Smyth, "Recent Developments in Industrial Hygiene," *American Journal of Public Health* 16 (Feb. 1926): 127.

12 G. H. Gehrmann to Wm. B. Foster, W. F. Harrington, F. C. Evans, "Proposal for Scientific Medical Research," Nov. 28, 1933, Acc. 1813, Box 16.

13 Henry Field Smyth, "Report on the Toxicity of the Moistureproof Coating on Cellophane," Dec. 15, 1927, PRL Hist. Files. On Smyth, see *American Men of Science* (7th ed.), 1944.

14 The development of the "ginger jake" problem can be followed from the entries

in the *New York Times Index for 1930* under the heading of Alcoholic Poisoning.

15 C. R. Mudge to W. F. Harrington, Aug. 10, 1931, and M. I. Smith, "Memorandum," July 27, 1931, Acc. 1813, Box 11. See also Gehrmann, "Proposal" and Zapp interview.

16 Victor Cofman to C. [M.] A. Stine, "Cancer Produced by Chemical Irritants, Discussion of March 20, 1928," Acc. 1034, File 288.

17 Alice Hamilton, "A Discussion of the Etiology of So-Called Aniline Tumors of the Bladder," *Journal of Industrial Hygiene* 3 (1921–22): 16–28. A later and more extensive review of the literature on bladder tumors is W. C. Hueper, " 'Aniline Tumors' of the Bladder," *Archives of Pathology* 25 (June 1938): 856–99.

18 Victor D. Washburn, "The Treatment of Anilin Tumors of the Urinary Bladder," *Journal of Urology* 38 (1937): 232–41.

19 George H. Gehrmann, "Report of a Visit to European Dye Plants to Investigate Means of Preventing Tumors of the Bladder in Dye Workers," [1933], Acc. 1813, Box 16. On Gehrmann, see *National Cyclopedia of American Biography* 48: 242–3.

20 Gehrmann, "Report."

21 Gehrmann, "Proposal."

22 W. C. Hueper to Ellice McDonald, July 28, 1930, Acc. 1034, File 288.

23 Wilhelm C. Hueper, "Adventures of a Physician in Occupational Cancer: A Medical Cassandra's Tale" (1976), National Library of Medicine, Bethesda, Maryland, pp. 139–40.

24 E. K. Bolton to C. M. A. Stine, August 7, 1930, Acc. 1034, File 288. Hueper noted his discussion with Irénée in Hueper, "Adventures," p. 141.

25 Gehrmann, "Proposal."

26 Text of Gehrmann presentation to the Executive Committee, [1933], HL Hist. Files.

27 R. S. Ferguson, "Introduction to Symposium on Anilin Tumors of the Bladder," *Journal of Urology* 31 (1934): 121.

28 G. H. Gehrmann, "The Carcinogenetic Agent – Chemistry and Industrial Aspects," *Journal of Urology* 31 (1934): 126–37.

29 G. H. Gehrmann, "Papilloma and Carcinoma of the Bladder Among Dye Workers," *Surgery, Gynecology and Obstetrics* 60 (1935): 555–6, and "Papilloma and Carcinoma of the Bladder in Dye Workers," *Journal of the American Medical Association* 107 (1936): 1436–7.

30 EC Minutes, July 3, 1934.

31 On the staff at Haskell, see William Chambless, *Fifty Years of Research and Service: Haskell Laboratory for Toxicology and Industrial Medicine* (Wilmington, Del.: Du Pont, 1985). On Oettingen's trip to Europe, see W. F. von Oettingen to G. H. Gehrmann, July 17, 1934, HL Hist. Files.

32 Hueper, "Adventures," pp. 142–9.

33 Copies of the speeches are in Acc. 1410, Box 39.

34 For statistics on the cases, see G. H. Gehrmann to J. E. Crane, Sept. 24, 1935, II, 2, Box 1046; and Washburn, "Treatment."

35 Gehrmann, "The Carcinogenic Agent."

36 On worker resistance to cystoscopic exams, see Gehrmann to Crane, Sept. 24, 1935, and Gehrmann, "Report."

37 Wilhelm C. Hueper, Frank Wiley, and Humphrey D. Wolfe, "Experimental Production of Bladder Tumors in Dogs by Administration of Beta-Naphthylamine," *Journal of Industrial Hygiene and Toxicology* 20 (Jan. 1938): 46–84.

38 John H. Foulger, "Medical Research Project No. MR-14, Aniline Tumors of the Bladder, Studies of Urinary Bladder Tumors," Progress Report – February, 1945," HL-2-45, HL Reports.

39 *Chambers Works History*, vol. V (n.p.: n.p., n.d.), Chapter VI, "Naphthalene Intermediates," Acc. 1387.

40 J. H. Foulger, "Urinary Excretion of Beta-Naphthylamine Base and Derivatives," HL-2-43, HL Reports.

41 T. S. Scott, "The Incidence of Bladder Tumors in a Dyestuffs Factory," *British Journal of Industrial Medicine* 9 (1952): 127–32.

42 On Du Pont's new building for making beta, see *Chambers Works History*. On the closed process and on Williams's crusade against beta, see Zapp interview. In 1975, the *New York Times* reported that Paul Humanick, plant manager at the Chambers Works, said that Du Pont had paid compensation for 330 cases of bladder cancer, which had caused 138 fatalities (*New York Times*, Jan. 2, 1975).

43 The number of projects undertaken is mentioned in G. H. Gehrmann, "The Haskell Laboratory of Industrial Toxicology," May 18, 1936, HL Hist. Files. In 1936 Haskell researchers published five articles in *The Journal of Industrial Hygiene and Toxicology*. The abrupt end to publishing is noted in Hueper, "Adventures," p. 150.

44 Chambless, *Fifty Years*, pp. 15–21. After leaving Du Pont, Hueper became an outspoken and controversial critic of U.S. industry's and government's lack of interest in occupational cancer. Hueper's bitterness toward Du Pont is evident in the dedication of his first book on occupational cancer: "This book is dedicated to the memory of those of our fellow men who have died from occupational diseases contracted while making better things for an improved living for others" (W. C. Hueper, *Occupational Tumors and Allied Diseases* [Springfield, Ill.: Charles Thomas, 1942]). This was an intentional paraphrase of Du Pont's slogan (Hueper, "Adventures," p. 163).

45 G. H. Gehrmann to W. F. Harrington, May 29, 1940, Acc. 1813, Box 32.

46 On Foulger, see Chambless, *Fifty Years*, p. 26. Historical statistics on Haskell's expenditures are in Employee Relations Department to the Executive Committee, "Annual Report – 1960," Feb. 10, 1961, Acc. 1615, Box 14. On toxicological research in this era, see "Making Synthetics Safe," *Fortune* (Oct. 1954): 138–42.

47 EC Minutes, July 3, 1934.

48 G. H. Gehrmann, [Text of Speech], Jan. 22, 1935, Acc. 1410, Box 39; and G. H. Gehrmann to J. K. Jenney, Apr. 5, 1935, II, 2, Box 538.

49 J. H. Foulger, "The Haskell Laboratory Budget," Dec. 20, 1943, HL Hist. Files.

50 Ibid.

51 G. H. Gehrmann to E. F. du Pont, "Haskell Laboratory Budget," July 16, 1945, HL Hist. Files.

52 John A. Zapp, "Evaluation Procedures in Use at the Haskell Laboratory of Industrial Toxicology," Nov. 19, 1951, Miscellaneous Report MR-51-11, PR Records.

53 "Making Synthetics Safe," p. 140.

54 On the "elixir of sulfanilamide" disaster, see Wharton, *Before Silent Spring*, pp. 237–38. On longer tests and the FDA, see Zapp interview and Zapp, "Industrial Toxicology."

55 Foulger, "Medical Research Project No. MR-14."

56 G. H. Gehrmann, J. H. Foulger, and A. J. Fleming, "Occupational Carcinoma of the Bladder," *Proceedings 9th International Congress of Industrial Medicine* (London, 1948), pp. 472–5.

57 S. Spitz, W. H. Magerigan, and K. Debriner, "The Carcinogenic Action of Benzidine," *Cancer* 3 (Sept. 1950): 789–804.

58 Scott, "Incidence of Bladder Tumors."

59 Michael H. C. Williams, "Occupational Tumors of the Bladder," in Raven, ed., *Cancer* (London: Butterworth, 1948), vol. 3, pp. 341–2.

60 On Roger Williams and the expansion of the Haskell Laboratory, see Zapp interview. On the farming out of long-term testing, see "Making Synthetics Safe," p. 139.

61 Employee Relations Department, "Annual Report – 1960."

62 On Foulger's interest in physiology studies, see Zapp interview; J. H. Foulger, "Survey of Special Medical Examinations of Rayon and Cellophane Workers," HL-3-40, HL Reports; and John A. Zapp, Jr., "Statistical Approaches to Some Problems of Industrial Preventive Medicine," *Human Biology* 19 (May 1947): 27–52.

63 Bill Davidson, "Stoop or Bend?," *Collier's*, May 27, 1955, pp. 30–3. On the all-weather rooms, see Du Pont Company News Release, Mar. 5, 1952, Acc. 1410, Box 39.

64 Davidson, "Stoop or Bend?"

65 Employee Relations Department, "Annual Report – 1960."

66 "Making Synthetics Safe," p. 142.

67 John A. Zapp, Jr., to A. J. Fleming, "The Haskell Laboratory," Mar. 24, 1958, HL Hist. Files.

68 F. E. French, Jr., to H. E. Ford, "Haskell Laboratory Review," July 23, 1959, DD Files.

69 Ibid.

70 EC Minutes, Sept. 9, 1959.

71 French, "Haskell Laboratory."

72 The significance of these two events is noted in Employee Relations Department, "Annual Report – 1962," Feb. 10, 1963, Acc. 1615, Box 14.

73 The Frye Report is discussed in "Industry Doctors Try New Approach," *Business Week*, May 13, 1967, pp. 80–6.

74 Employee Relations Department, "Annual Report – 1962."

75 Employee Relations Department, "Annual Report – 1961," Feb. 9, 1962, Acc. 1615, Box 14.

76 Employee Relations Department, "Annual Report – June 30, 1968," July 3, 1968, Acc. 1615, Box 14.

77 On legislation, see Chambless, *Fifty Years*, pp. 40–1.

78 On Rohm and Haas, see Sheldon Hochheiser, *Rohm and Haas: History of a Chemical Company* (Philadelphia: University of Pennsylvania Press, 1986), chap. 12; and Willard S. Randall and Stephen D. Solomon, *Building 6: The*

Tragedy at Bridesburg (Boston: Little, Brown, 1977). On Kepone and vinyl chloride, see Barth, *Worker's Compensation*, pp. 4–5.

79 Zapp, "Industrial Toxicology."

80 On the growth of Haskell's budget, see Central Research Department, "Addition to Haskell Laboratory," Appropriation Request, Nov. 14, 1974, and the Central Research Department annual reports in EC Files. On the physical growth of the Haskell Laboratory, see Chambless, *Fifty Years*, pp. 27–8.

81 See for example, "Will There Be Enough Toxicologists?," *Chemical Week* 119 (Nov. 17, 1976): 38–9, and "Wanted 1000 Toxicologists," *Chemical Week* 121 (Sept. 21, 1977): 51–2.

82 On the Chemical Industry Institute of Toxicology, see "Companies Step Up Toxic Substances Testing Pace," *Chemical Week* 117 (July 23, 1975): 33, and William Rettig, "Industry's Preemptive Strike against Cancer," *Fortune*, Feb. 13, 1978, pp. 116–19.

83 On Gee as environmental advisor, see Gee interview. On the policy change regarding Haskell, see Zapp interview.

84 Zapp interview.

85 On Haskell's research in the 1970s, see the Central Research Department annual reports in EC Files.

86 On the Ames test, see Rettig, "Industry's Preemptive Strike."

87 Zapp interview, and Charles F. Reinhardt, "Industrial Methods of Detecting Environmental Cancer Hazards," *Journal of the Medical Society of New Jersey* 75 (Oct. 1978): 756–8.

88 Leon Goldberg, "Preface," in Chambless, *Fifty Years*.

89 John A. Zapp, Jr., "HMPA: A Possible Carcinogen," letter to the editor, *Science* 190 (1975): 422. Similar articles were published in *Chemical and Engineering News* 54 (Feb. 3, 1976): 3, and *Nature* 247 (1975): 735.

Chapter 25. Redirecting R&D: The 1970s

1 E. A. Gee to C. B. McCoy, "Research and Development," Nov. 2, 1970, Acc. 1850.

2 D. S. Weir to R. C. Forney, "Corporate Research and Development Report – 1983," Mar. 1983, EC Files.

3 Gee interview. See also Gee's company biography in Acc. 1850.

4 This change was noted in "Du Pont," *Forbes*, Dec. 15, 1969, p. 33.

5 George E. Holbrook to D. M. McQueen et al., Aug. 8, 1969, Acc. 1850.

6 Gee to McCoy, "Research and Development."

7 Herbert Kay, "Harnessing the R&D Monster," *Fortune*, Jan. 1965, pp. 160–3, 196–8.

8 Dan Cordtz, "Bringing the Laboratory Down to Earth," *Fortune*, Jan. 1971, pp. 106–8, 119–22.

9 See, e.g., Monroe S. Sadler to E. A. Gee, May 5, 1961, Acc. 1850.

10 Ivar A. Lundgaard, "Notes for December 16, 1969 Meeting," Acc. 1850.

11 Central Research Department Study Committee to David M. McQueen, Jan. 14, 1970, Acc. 1850.

12 David M. McQueen to Edwin A. Gee, Sept. 25, Oct. 26, 1970, Acc. 1850.

13 David M. McQueen to Edwin A. Gee, Mar. 17, 1971, Acc. 1850.

14 Edwin A. Gee to Charles B. McCoy, Feb. 12, 1971, Acc. 1850.

15 Lester S. Sinness to Charles B. McCoy, May 28, 1971, Acc. 1814, Box 9.

16 David H. Dawson to Charles B. McCoy, May 27, 1971, Acc. 1814, Box 9.

17 On Cairns, see Chapter 17. On Simeral, see *Chemical Week*, Oct. 12, 1977, p. 58.

18 Committee on Exploratory Research to the Executive Committee, Apr. 20, 1972, Acc. 1850.

19 Ibid.

20 Edwin A. Gee to T. L. Cairns, Nov. 2, 1972, DD Files.

21 Edwin A. Gee to the Executive Committee, "Exploratory Research Study," June 11, 1973, DD Files.

22 Research spending statistics are in Weir, "Corporate Research and Development." Gee's concerns were noted in Research Director Subcommittee to Research Directors, Jan. 8, 1975, DD Files.

23 Edwin A. Gee to the Executive Committee, "Textile Fibers Department," July 8, 1976, Acc. 1850. On the conclusions of the subcommittee, see R. G. Bennett et al. to C. H. Arrington et al., Feb. 26, 1975, DD Files.

24 Norman Copeland, "New Product Development in Times of Limited Resources," Talk given at Development Managers Meeting, Feb. 12, 1974, DD Files.

25 David Brearley to Monroe S. Sadler, "Major Products," Apr. 13, 1972, EC Files.

26 Boston Consulting Group, "Du Pont Future Potential," 1971, Acc. 1850.

27 On the new TiO_2 process, see Pigments Department to the "A" Bonus Committee, " 'Z' (Chloride) Process Titanium Dioxide Pigment," Feb. 11, 1953, Special Compensation Files. On the success of the business, see Brearley, "Major Products."

28 On Dacron intermediates, see A. I. Mendolia to the Executive Committee, "Polyester Intermediates Expansion Program," Apr. 23, 1970, EC Files. On air versus nitric acid oxidation, see Anderson interview.

29 Walter H. Salzenberg, "Whither 66 Nylon Intermediates," Feb. 4, 1965, EC Files.

30 Emil D. Ries to the "A" Bonus Committee, "Butadiene Process for Adiponitrile," Feb. 24, 1953, Special Compensation Files.

31 Everett B. Yelton to Committee on Special Compensation, "Improved Adiponitrile Process," Feb. 22, 1974, Special Compensation Files.

32 Ibid.

33 Everett B. Yelton to the Executive Committee, "Polymer Intermediates Department – Annual Report," Jan. 27, 1975, EC Files.

34 Ivar A. Lundgaard to the Committee on Special Compensation, "Super-Tough Zytel Nylon Resin," May 16, 1980, Special Compensation Files.

35 William G. Simeral, "Remarks to Development Managers," Nov. 11, 1980, CRDD Files.

36 On Heckert, see "He's Still Wearing Corfam Shoes," *Chemical Week*, Nov. 7, 1973, p. 84.

37 Richard E. Heckert et al. to the Executive Committee, "Report of the Ad Hoc R&D Committee," July 10, 1975, CRDD Files.

38 For statistics on the budget of Central Research, see Acc. 1850.

39 Central Research over the next several years increased its level of support from the industrial departments to about 20 percent. See the department's annual reports in EC Files.

40 Theodore L. Cairns to Richard E. Heckert, Apr. 29, 1976, CRDD Files.

41 R. E. Heckert, "Research and Development," Remarks to the Board of Directors, June 20, 1977, EC Files.

42 William C. Kay to the Executive Committee, "Plans for the Organic Chemicals Department's Dyes Business, 1969–1977," June 18, 1969, EC Files.

43 Organic Chemicals Department, "New Facility to Manufacture Dyes," Appropriation Request, June 8, 1971, EC Files.

44 On the problems with the new plant, see John D. Cullen, "Whither Orchem," Talk to the Development Managers Group, Mar. 8, 1977, DD Files. On the closing of the Manati plant, see Executive Committee to the Finance Committee, "Liquidation of Du Pont Puerto Rico, Inc. Assets and Adjustment of Permanent Investment at Manati Plant," May 2, 1980, EC Files. On Du Pont's decision to get out of the dye business, see *Du Pont Company Annual Report 1980*.

45 Brearley, "Major Products."

46 Joseph C. Robert, *Ethyl: A History of a Corporation and the People Who Made It* (Charlottesville: University Press of Virginia, 1983), pp. 290–310.

47 Cullen, "Whither Orchem."

48 "Why Aerosols are under Attack," *Business Week*, Feb. 17, 1975, pp. 50–1.

49 Cullen, "Whither Orchem." On the FDA and EPA ban, see "Phase Out Set for Fluorocarbon Aerosols," *Chemical and Engineering News* 55 (May 16, 1977): 4. Concern over chlorofluorocarbons mounted in the 1980s as scientific evidence about the ozone layer's depletion accumulated. In 1988, Du Pont publicly committed itself to phasing out its production of chlorofluorocarbons.

50 "The Effect of Federal Legislation on Research and Development at Du Pont," Apr. 22, 1977, CRDD Files.

51 Heckert, "Research and Development."

52 George J. Prendergast to the Executive Committee, "Corporate Plans Department – Proposed Budget 1975," Feb. 13, 1975, EC Files.

53 Edwin A. Gee to Charles B. McCoy, "Executive Committee Staff Assistance," Aug. 11, 1967, Acc. 1404, Box 8. In the early 1970s, Gee wrote a number of position papers in support of a corporate planning group. (E. A. Gee, "Discussion Paper on the Development Department and Corporate Planning," Part I, Oct. 12, 1971; Part II, Feb. 16, 1972; and Part III, Mar. 14, 1972, Acc. 1850. See also E. A. Gee to I. S. Shapiro and E. R. Kane, "Corporate Planning," July 17, 1974, Acc. 1850.)

54 Prendergast, "Corporate Plans Department."

55 On the personnel and activities of the Development Department at the time that it was split up, see Monroe S. Sadler to the Executive Committee, "Development Department Annual Report for 1974," Nov. 27, 1974, DD Files. On the New Business Opportunity group, see Norman Fast, "The Evolution of Corporate New Ventures Divisions" (PhD diss., Harvard Business School, 1977), chap. 5. On Sadler, see his company biography in Acc. 1850.

56 On the work of the development division, see the Central Research and Development Department annual reports for the late 1970s in EC Files.

57 Robert L. Hershey to the Executive Committee, Dec. 22, 1966, Acc. 1404, Box

10, and G. I. Prendergast and D. W. Smith, "Possible Steps to Improve Du Pont Performance," Nov. 30, 1967, Acc. 1404, Box 8.

58 This discussion is based upon comments made by many current and retired Du Pont research directors.

59 Weir, "Corporate Research and Development."

60 EC Minutes, July 21, 1976. See also Edwin A. Gee to the Executive Committee, "Textile Fibers Department," July 8, 1976, Acc. 1850.

61 Weir, "Corporate Research and Development."

62 A general manager still retained the option not to declare a major development a New Venture and carry it along without the committee's permission. On the research and development policies, see W. E. Buxbaum to Control and A&BA Managers, "Research and Development Rules and Applicable Administrative Procedure," July 18, 1975, EC Files.

63 Jefferson interview, July 28, 1986.

64 Irving S. Shapiro to Heads of Industrial Departments, Chief Engineer, and Director, Central Research and Development Department, "Research and Development," Sept. 27, 1978, EC Files.

65 P. L. Salzberg, "Memorandum for File," July 23, 1951, DD Files.

66 On Shapiro, see Peter Vanderwicken, "Irving Shapiro Takes Charge at Du Pont," *Fortune*, Jan. 1974, pp. 79–81, 152–6; and "Managing No. 1 Chemical Company is a Two-Man Job," *Chemical Week*, Aug. 29, 1973, pp. 27–8. On the morale of the Du Pont research organizations, see Jefferson interview, July 28, 1986.

67 On Jefferson, see "Du Pont's Jefferson," *Chemical Week*, Jan. 30, 1980, pp. 36–7. On Jefferson's attitudes toward research, see Jefferson interviews.

68 Jefferson interview, July 28, 1986. On Simmons, see Chapter 17 and his company biography in Acc. 1850.

69 Jefferson interview, July 31, 1986. The article was "Industry Starts to Do Biology with Its Eyes Open," *Economist*, Dec. 2, 1978, pp. 95–102.

70 For the history of recombinant DNA research, see Susan Wright, "Recombinant DNA Technology and Its Social Transformation, 1972–1982," *Osiris*, 2d Series, 2 (1986): 303–60.

71 Ibid.

72 Dale E. Wolf to the Executive Committee, "Biochemicals Department Annual Report – 1979," EC Files.

73 On the biological research in Central Research, see the department's annual reports in EC Files. The interferon work was published. (Ernest Knight, Jr., "Interferon: Purification and Initial Characterization from Human Diploid Cells," *Proceedings of the National Academy of Sciences* 73 [1971]: 520–3.)

74 Jefferson interview, July 31, 1986.

75 Cynthia G. Loew, "Public Policy Issues in Molecular Genetics," June 1979, Acc. 1850.

76 H. E. Simmons and M. B. Burton to the Executive Committee, "Life Sciences Research Facilities," Nov. 26, 1980, EC Files.

77 Stuart Diamond, "Testing the Formula for a New Du Pont," *New York Times*, Oct. 7, 1984.

78 Jefferson interview, July 31, 1986. On Du Pont R&D in the 1980s, see David Webber, "Du Pont Bets Its Future on Massive R&D Expansion," *Chemical and Engineering News*, Feb. 6, 1984, pp. 7–12; and "How Du Pont Spends Its $1.1 Billion Budget," *Chemical Week*, July 31, 1985, pp. 20–3.

Essay on Sources

The basis for this study is the surviving records of E. I. du Pont de Nemours & Co., which are either in the company's possession or preserved at the Hagley Museum and Library in Wilmington, Delaware. The latter has extensive though not comprehensive records for the pre–World War II period. Because of the company's records-retention policy, instituted in 1966, most of Du Pont's existing records postdate 1960. The company still retains the formal minutes of its Executive Committee, Finance Committee, and board of directors for the entire period after 1902. We relied heavily upon the Executive Committee minutes, particularly for the period before 1915 when reports and discussions were included in the minutes. The current report files of the same committee served as a prime source for the 1960–80 era. The histories of particular developments or discoveries were often written up as part of the "A" Bonus awards, the records for which are preserved in the Du Pont Company's Special Compensation Committee files. These histories were highly valuable, but we have assiduously tried to verify their conclusions with information obtained from other sources before we relied on them.

Because Du Pont is a decentralized company and has undergone many reorganizations in the past fifteen years, the quality of departmental records varies widely. Some departments have been more conscious of the historical value of their records than others. In general, departmental records for the post–World War II history of the Du Pont company are far from complete. The departments keep their laboratory notebooks and technical reports indefinitely, and in several instances these resources provided invaluable information. We also supplemented the often thin written record with interviews, which are now preserved as oral histories at the Hagley Museum and Library.

Some departments have prepared histories of their operations. Among the several we consulted, we found the *History of the Du Pont Company's Textile Fibers Department*, written by Donald Holmes and updated by E. M. Hicks, Jr. (1983), the earlier *The Technical Division of the Rayon Department, 1920–1951* by Ferdinand Schulze and Roy Soukup (1952), Edward P. Bartlett's *The Chemical Division of the Du Pont Ammonia Department, 1924–1935* (n.d.), and William M. Zintl's *History of the Du Pont Paint Business* (1947) to be the most reliable.

At Hagley, we drew heavily on Du Pont Company records in Series II, a large and diverse collection of the company's twentieth-century records. Unfortunately, the files of key research figures such as Reese, Stine, and Bolton do not survive. We also relied on the presidential papers in Accession 1662, which include the executive papers of Pierre, Irénée, and Lammot du Pont. Other presidents' papers are in Series II, Part 2 (Walter S. Carpenter, Jr.), Accession 1814 (Crawford H. Greenewalt), Accession 1404 (Lammot du Pont Copeland), and Accession 1815 (Charles B. McCoy). The papers of Vice President Willis F. Harrington (Accession 1813) proved to be of major importance. In addition to these papers, we drew from some thirty other manuscript accessions at Hagley, which are enumerated above at the beginning of the Notes.

Fortunately for historians, antitrust cases against Du Pont brought about the liberal use of the discovery provision, which resulted in the preservation of thousands of documents that might otherwise have perished. We relied heavily upon such records. These include the GM case, the cellophane case, the ICI case, and the titanium dioxide (National Lead) case. The complete records of these cases are preserved at the Hagley Museum and Library.

During the course of our research, we gathered a miscellany of Du Pont–related records from various individuals we interviewed. These materials are now preserved in a separate accession (1850) at the Hagley Museum and Library.

We supplemented research in Du Pont Company records with other manuscript collections. These included the Papers of Julius Nieuwland at the University of Notre Dame, the Papers of Roger Adams and the Papers of Reynold C. Fuson at the University of Illinois, the Papers of James B. Conant at Harvard University, the Papers of Robert Maynard Hutchins at the University of Chicago, the Papers of Walter Hullihen at the University of Delaware, the Papers of Charles H. Herty at Emory University, and the Papers of Charles L. Reese at the Historical Society of Delaware.

Although much has been written about the du Pont family and the Du Pont Company, only a handful of works have real scholarly merit. Alfred D. Chandler's chapter on Du Pont in his *Strategy and Structure: Chapters in the History of the American Industrial Enterprise* (1962) proved highly valuable to our discussion of the company's diversification of the 1910s and the reorganization of 1921. Chandler and Stephen Salsbury's *Pierre S. du Pont and the Making of the Modern Corporation* (1971) contains information from documents that unfortunately no longer survive and served as an important guide to research in Hagley's collections and to the interpretation of those research materials. *Du Pont and the International Chemical Industry* (1984), by Graham Taylor and Patricia Sudnik, is an ambitious book the utility of which was more limited because its authors relied on inaccurate sources for general company history. William J. Reader's *Imperial Chemical Industries: A History* (2 vols., 1970 and 1975) provided us with a well-documented and -reasoned administrative history of the Du Pont–

ICI relationship written from the ICI perspective. We found Willard F. Mueller's PhD dissertation, "Du Pont: A Study in Firm Growth" (Vanderbilt University, 1956) still valuable for its information on the acquisitions and new products of the company. The nineteenth-century background to the company's twentieth-century R&D programs is treated in Norman Wilkinson's *Lammot du Pont and the American Explosives Industry, 1850–1884* (1984) and Jeffrey L. Sturchio's PhD dissertation, "Chemists and Industry in Modern America: Studies in the Historical Application of Science Indicators" (University of Pennsylvania, 1981).

Historical scholarship on industrial research and development in the United States has flourished in the last decade. John J. Beer's *The Emergence of the German Dye Industry* (1959) continues to provide the basis for this new scholarship. George Wise's award-winning article, "A New Role for Professional Scientists in Industry: Industrial Research at General Electric, 1900–1916," *Technology and Culture* 21 (1980): 408–29, gave us a fresh look at the creation of industrial research laboratories at the turn of the century, and his *Willis R. Whitney, General Electric, and the Origins of U.S. Industrial Research* (1985) offers an important history of both Whitney and General Electric. Leonard Reich contrasts the history of R&D at General Electric with that of American Telephone and Telegraph in *The Making of American Industrial Research: Science and Business at GE and Bell, 1876–1926* (1986). Reese V. Jenkins looks at the early history of R&D at Eastman Kodak in *Images and Enterprises: Technology and the American Photographic Industry 1839–1925* (1975). Our study of Du Pont has benefited from these works and especially from the papers presented by George Wise (on GE) and Jeffrey Sturchio (on Kodak) at "The R&D Pioneers: A Critical Look at General Electric, Du Pont, AT&T Bell Laboratories, and Eastman Kodak, 1900–1985," a Hagley Museum and Library conference sponsored in 1985 by our R&D history project (with financial support from the Du Pont Company).

Throughout this book, we relied on the standard secondary literature and contemporary journal articles, all of which are fully cited in the Notes.

Index